...And the Resources You Nee[...]

Write your Business Plan with the World's B[...]lanning Software—**Business Plan Pro**

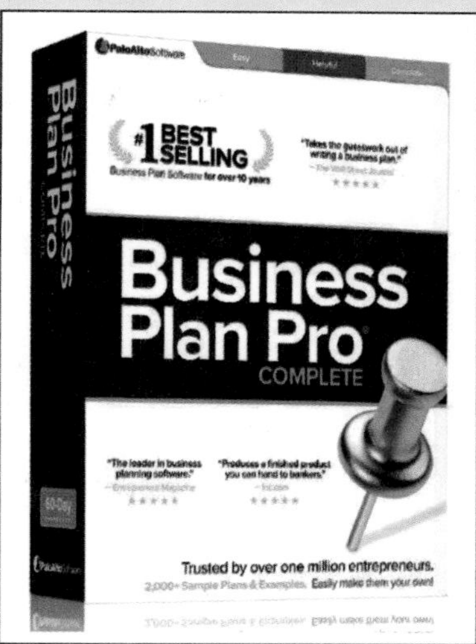

Business Plan Pro fully supports students with the creation of a professional business plan. Its wizard-based environment helps students step-by-step, and provides guidance with its integrated financials, and real-world forecasting tools.

With 68 sample plans, grading sheets, built-in research data, and use of an SBA-approved document format, this software is a great option for instructors who incorporate a quarter/semester-long business plan project into their course.

Why use Business Plan Pro with *Entrepreneurial Small Business*?

- ✔ Easy step-by-step process
- ✔ Sixty-eight sample plans
- ✔ Complete, integrated financials
- ✔ Real-world forecasting tools
- ✔ Substantial savings over the national academic price of the identical software.

Order *Entrepreneurial Small Business* with Business Plan Pro using ISBN: 9780077713195

Entrepreneurial Small Business

4e

Jerome A. Katz
Saint Louis University

Richard P. Green II
Texas A&M University–San Antonio

McGraw-Hill Irwin

ENTREPRENEURIAL SMALL BUSINESS, FOURTH EDITION

Published by McGraw-Hill/Irwin, a business unit of The McGraw-Hill Companies, Inc., 1221 Avenue of the Americas, New York, NY 10020. Copyright © 2014 by The McGraw-Hill Companies, Inc. All rights reserved. Printed in the United States of America. Previous editions © 2011, 2009 and 2007. No part of this publication may be reproduced or distributed in any form or by any means, or stored in a database or retrieval system, without the prior written consent of The McGraw-Hill Companies, Inc., including, but not limited to, in any network or other electronic storage or transmission, or broadcast for distance learning.

Some ancillaries, including electronic and print components, may not be available to customers outside the United States.

This book is printed on acid-free paper.

4 5 6 7 8 9 0 DOW/DOW 1 0 9 8 7 6 5

ISBN 978-0-07-802942-4
MHID 0-07-802942-2

Senior Vice President, Products & Markets: *Kurt L. Strand*
Vice President, General Manager: *Brent Gordon*
Vice President, Content Production & Technology Services: *Kimberly Meriwether David*
Managing Director: *Paul Ducham*
Executive Brand Manager: *Anke Weekes*
Marketing Manager: *Michael Gedatus*
Development Editor II: *Kelly I. Pekelder*
Director, Content Production: *Terri Schiesl*
Project Manager: *Melissa M. Leick*
Cover Designer: *Jana Singer*
Buyer: *Jennifer Pickel*
Media Project Manager: *Prashanthi Nadipalli*
Compositor: *MPS Limited*
Typeface: *10/12 Times*
Printer: *R. R. Donnelley*

All credits appearing on page or at the end of the book are considered to be an extension of the copyright page.

Library of Congress Cataloging-in-Publication Data

Katz, Jerome A.
Entrepreneurial small business / Jerome A. Katz, Saint Louis University, Richard P. Green II, Texas A&M University/San Antonio.—Fourth Edition.
pages cm.—(Entrepreneurial small business)
Includes bibliographical references and indexes.
ISBN 978-0-07-802942-4 (alk. paper)—ISBN 0-07-802942-2 (alk. paper) 1. Small business—Management. 2. New business enterprises—Management. 3. Entrepreneurship. I. Green, Richard P. II. Title.
HD62.7.K385 2013
658.02'2—dc23

2012043794

To our parents, who gave us inspiration.

To our children, who gave us motivation.

To our spouses, who gave us dedication.

ABOUT THE AUTHORS

Jerome A. Katz

Jerome (Jerry) Katz is the Coleman Foundation Professor Chair in Entrepreneurship at the John Cook School of Business, Saint Louis University. He is also the founder and director of Saint Louis University's Billiken Angels Network. Previously he held the Mary Louise Murray Endowed Professorship in Management at the Cook School, and prior to his coming to Saint Louis University he was an Assistant Professor of Management at the Wharton School, University of Pennsylvania. Jerry holds a PhD in organizational psychology from the University of Michigan, and other graduate degrees from Harvard and the University of Memphis.

Throughout the years he has worked in or advised his family's businesses including stints working in the family's discount department store, sporting goods wholesaling, pharmacies, auto parts jobbing, and secondary market wholesaling of frozen food. As a professor he has served as adviser to over 400 business plans developed by students at Saint Louis University, whose Entrepreneurship Program (which Jerry leads) has been nationally ranked every year since 1994. Earlier in his career he served as Associate Director for the Missouri State Small Business Development Centers. He has taught, trained or consulted on entrepreneurship education and business development services in Sweden, Switzerland, the United Kingdom, Brazil, Singapore, Israel, Croatia, and the West Bank. His consulting firm, J. A. Katz & Associates, has a client list including the Soros, GE, Kauffman and Coleman Foundations as well as the Jerusalem Institute for Israel Studies, Sweden's Entrepreneurship and Small Business Research Institute, the International Labor Organization (ILO), RISEbusiness, the National Federation of Independent Business, the National Science Foundation, and the Committee of 200.

Twice *Inc.* magazine identified him as one of the world's top small business researchers. He has done research and theorizing on career models of entrepreneurship and entrepreneurship/small business education, as well as collaborating with others on topics as diverse as opportunity recognition (with Connie Marie Gaglio), the properties of emerging organizations (with William Gartner), Internet-based businesses (with Scott Safranski), and international entrepreneurship (with Sumit Kundu).

Jerry edits two book series, *Advances in Entrepreneurship, Firm Emergence and Growth* (with Tom Lumpkin, published by Emerald) and *Entrepreneurship and the Management of Growing Enterprises* (published by Sage) and has edited over a dozen special issues on small business, entrepreneurship, and entrepreneurship education for journals such as *Entrepreneurship: Theory & Practice,* Academy of Management *Learning & Education, Entrepreneurship & Regional Development,* and *Simulation & Gaming.* He has been a member of the founding editorial boards of *Entrepreneurship: Theory & Practice, Entrepreneurship & Regional Development,* Academy of Management *Learning & Education, International Journal of Entrepreneurship and Small Business,* and the *International Journal of Technoentrepreneurship.* He has also served on the editorial boards of the *Journal of Business Venturing, Journal of Small Business Management,* and the Academy of Management *Executive.*

Following his parents' tradition of civic entrepreneurship, Jerry has served the profession working his way up to become Senior Vice President for Research and Publications of the International Council for Small Business and eventually Chair of the Entrepreneurship Division of the Academy of Management. He was also one of only a handful of small business or entrepreneurship faculty to be elected to Academy-wide office, serving as a Governor of the Academy of Management from 2000–2003. He developed eWeb, one of the first websites dedicated to entrepreneurship education, and he was a winner of top-tier ratings from Anbar, Argus, LookSmart, and Studyweb. Other innovations in small business education in which he was involved included co-developing the *Gateways to Entrepreneurship Research Conference,* as well as the first adjunct teacher's guide and first center director consortia in the field.

For these efforts, he has been a recipient of more than a dozen major professional awards including Babson's Appel Prize for Entrepreneurship Education, the Family Firm Institute's LeVan Award for Interdisciplinary Contributions to Family Business, the Outstanding Lifetime Achievement

Award given by the Academy of Management's Entrepreneurship Division, as well as Mentorship Awards from the Entrepreneurship Division of the Academy of Management, and from Saint Louis University's Graduate Student Association. In 2004 he was elected the fiftieth fellow of the U.S. Association for Small Business and Entrepreneurship, and in 2005 he received Saint Louis University's John Cook School of Business Alumni Award for Outstanding Educator. Today his papers can be found in seven different compendia of seminal works in entrepreneurship and small business.

Richard P. Green

Richard Green is a successful serial entrepreneur who has started, built, and sold several businesses across an extraordinarily wide range of industries. His first business was an electrical sign repair company, which he began while an undergraduate student. Since then, Richard has started two other sign companies, a structural steel business, a manufacturer of stainless steel products, a real estate brokerage, a tax return preparation service, and a bed-and-breakfast. During the "go-go banking" years, he held controlling interest in a state-chartered bank. More recently, Richard, with his long-time associate Richard Carter, conducted the start-up of Lineas Aereas Azteca (Azteca Airlines), served as co-owner with his spouse of a San Antonio bed-and-breakfast, the Adams House, and served as chief financial officer for a high-tech start-up, Celldyne Biopharma LLC. As a corporate entrepreneur, Richard has worked on expansion plans for companies as diverse as the Mexican airline Aerolineas Internationales, Minneapolis based Land O'Lakes, Inc., and the Venezuelan dairy, Criozuca, S.A.

Richard brings a similarly diverse set of skills to *ESB,* ranging from a pilot's license (he was a professional pilot, instructor, and check airman for TWA) to a CPA. A late-life Ph.D. (from Saint Louis University), he has been an assistant and associate professor of accounting at the University of the Incarnate Word and Webster University, and is currently coordinator of the accounting program at Texas A&M University—San Antonio. His academic achievements are similarly impressive, with papers in the proceedings of NACRA, American Accounting Association Midwest, the American Association for Accounting and Finance, and the International Council for Small Business, as well as journals such as the *Atlantic Economic Journal* and *Simulation & Gaming.* Richard also authored more than three dozen articles in popular magazines on topics ranging from personal computers to financial decision making. Richard is co-developer (with Jerry) of the measures for financial sophistication in the Panel Study of Entrepreneurial Dynamics, and is senior author of *Investigating Entrepreneurial Opportunities: A Practical Guide for Due Diligence* (Sage). He has received research grants from Pharmacia Corporation and the Kauffman Foundation.

Always active in professional and civic roles, Richard's contributions have ranged from serving as chair of the Airline Pilots Association's grievance committee to serving on the City of San Antonio's Air Transportation Advisory Committee. He is a member of the American Accounting Association, Academy of Management, United States Association for Small Business and Entrepreneurship, North American Case Writers Association, and the World Association for Case Method Research and Application.

PREFACE

This book got its start with a simple question from my mother, "What is the difference between what you teach and what your father did for a living?"

We were sitting *shiva* (which is the ancient Jewish tradition of mourning), in this case after the death of my father, a Polish immigrant to the United States who had been a small business owner for almost 50 years at the time of his death in 2003. When sitting *shiva* the immediate family mostly sits and reflects and prays for a week, so my mother, sister, and I had plenty of time to talk. And talking as we did, the question came up.

I gathered my thoughts for a minute. First off, I realized that throughout his life my father had picked up on my comments about the very rare high-growth, high-tech businesses that came through my class. Somehow he thought that was who I had as my run-of-the-mill student. That was funny to me, because in teaching entrepreneurship for nearly 20 years, fewer than a dozen of the several hundred business plans I worked on involved high-growth, high-tech firms.

But thinking about what my father heard, I realized that I talk about two sets of rules, one for when I have a potentially high-growth business and another for the more conventional businesses that most of my students start and that my own father had mastered three times in his life. The answer to my mother came out this way:

Conventional Small Businesses	**High-Growth Ventures**
Imitation	Novelty
Autonomy	Involve key others
Control as goal	Growth as goal
Financial independence	Wealth
Fund with your own money	Fund with other peoples' money
Cash flow as key	Profits as key
Cash crunch? Tighten belt	Cash crunch? Sell more

The list goes on, and you will have a chance to see it in Chapter 1, and you will discover that the list exemplifies the prevention vs. promotion focus discussed in Chapter 2, but this list gives you an idea of the difference. I told my mother that when I am teaching to students who have really big dreams, I try to get them to create businesses that would be innovative, using new technologies or markets. These would be businesses that could grow to be big businesses, creating major wealth for their founders. The founders are in it for the wealth. They expect to go after others' investment in the business and they expect to give away some of their autonomy along with their stock. My father's businesses were imitative, businesses like those already existing. He did the businesses to have a comfortable income and wanted to limit his growth to what he could comfortably control personally. No investors, no one second guessing him. When times got tough, my father would cut his expenses; in a high-growth business that's when it needs to sell more. My father's business was built on his personal reputation, while high-growth firms try to maximize the reputation of the firm or its products.

I kept talking, but as I listened to myself, I realized that I had never seen a book that talked about small business the way I described it. I have students who have started such businesses—in fact the vast majority of my students have started businesses in their own ways much like my father's three firms. I continue to help those alums out with advice, just as I did my father and his business. But in the end, what was important was that they *were* a different kind of business, and I felt that no book really addressed it that way anymore.

That was why I decided to write *this* book, and get Richard to join me in the effort. Why Richard? Because I knew a person with a story like his would make a great co-author for a book like this. His story goes like this:

"When Jerry first asked me if I would be interested in co-authoring a new small business management text, I was a bit reluctant. Where would I create time for such a daunting task?" I asked myself. "But when he described his vision—a text about starting and managing the type of small businesses that we patronize every day—restaurants, beauty salons, plumbing companies, lawn care firms—I became enthusiastic. Yes, I definitely wanted to be part of a project that would deal with the 98 percent of businesses that start small and stay that way, not the 2 percent that become CNNs, Oracles, and Dells.

"In many ways, I exemplify the type of entrepreneur for whom we wrote this book: people who start and operate the many ordinary enterprises with which you do business every day.

"I come, unlike Jerry, from a family of employees. Neither of my grandfathers and none of my many uncles and aunts were ever business owners. My father began working as an employee while he was still in high school, and he continued as an employee until his retirement. I, on the other hand, started my first entrepreneurial enterprise the summer I was 12. I began my first "real" business the summer I was 18. In the years since, I have started several businesses and purchased three. In between businesses I have been, as my father and his father, an employee.

"Not a single business that I have owned has ever been high tech, high growth, or even high innovation. I started every one either because I needed a source of income right then or because I expected to lose my current job very soon and didn't want to live on unemployment. I have been an owner-manager in the electrical sign business, structural steel erection, light manufacturing, consumer electronics retailing, real estate brokerage, construction, farming, and lodging.

"Why so many businesses, you may ask. My mother probably would say that I have a short attention span. However, the real answer is that each time I started a business I took the first opportunity available, not necessarily the best opportunity. And what was the result? Some, such as the Grandview Sign Service Co., went broke (but not before it paid for flying lessons). Signgraphics, Inc. was sold. Paul's Sound Shop was a victim of recession. Real estate brokerage was financially very successful, but I hated the business. When my top producing salesman finally passed his broker's exam, I eagerly made a deal for him to buy the company. I am still actively engaged in construction and in the lodging industry.

"My interest in entrepreneurship as a field of study stems from this varied experience. I asked myself many questions, including, Why did I just make a living in the sign business, while Ted Turner made himself a billionaire from the same beginnings? Why is it that Paul's Sound Shop didn't become a retail behemoth as Best Buy did, although both started about the same time? And am I a success because I made money in several different businesses, or a failure because none became big businesses? This book is largely the result of my search for answers to these questions."

Together, Richard and I crafted our approach for *Entrepreneurial Small Business,* and as we will point up in the business planning chapter, all plans start with a vision.

The ESB Vision

In *Entrepreneurial Small Business,* you will not find a lot on venture capital, and very little on strategic concepts like "first to market." What you *will* find is a lot of coverage of the kinds of businesses most people (and especially most undergraduate and lifelong learning students) really *do* start—small businesses in traditional industries and markets. These businesses are vitally important—we will tell you why we think so in a moment—and helping them survive has long been an art. Today like never before, that art is supplemented by science, and that is where your class—and this book—can help. In *ESB* we try to build a book that can combine the art of small business survival and the science of small business. If you can get the benefit of both *before* you get into your business, you are likely to do better than someone who has to get by with the advice they can catch on the fly as they get started.

ESB takes its information from the nearly 150 journals in entrepreneurship generating new understanding of what it takes to be successful, from national studies like the Panel Study of Income Dynamics (PSED) at **http://projects.isr.umich.edu/psed/** the Kauffman Firm Study, and the surveys of the National Federation of Independent Business, global studies like the Global Entrepreneurship Monitor (GEM) at **www.gemconsortium.org** and the best of modern wisdom from experts in entrepreneurship from government, business, and the Internet. The point of *ESB* is to get that knowledge and make it available to you, the small business owner of today or tomorrow. You and your business deserve every break you can get, and our economy and society *need* you to survive and succeed.

Why is that so important? It turns out that small business is essential for big business, and it is essential for high-technology, high-growth business, and it is essential to our communities. In a world of relentless cost cutting and global competition, big businesses outsource everything but their most critical tasks. Often the best expertise, the best service, or sometimes even the best price exists in small businesses. Whether it is janitorial services or new product development, big businesses increasingly depend on small businesses to get their jobs done.

Small business is essential to our communities in much the same way. If you come from a small town or a neighborhood that gets passed-by by the big chains, you know how important small businesses can be. Without small businesses, there might be *no* places to buy products or needed services. Big business and small communities depend on small business to get the job done.

For high-tech businesses, the same argument can be made, but there is also another issue—that small business *defines* the community in important ways. If you work in IT, biotech, nanotech, medicine, media, or the like, when you finish your day in the lab or cubicle, where do you want to be? In a soulless, interchangeable town or a vibrant and diverse locale? These members of the "creative class," as Richard Florida calls them, are demanding customers. They make their livings from their minds, and those minds crave stimulation, whether at work or at play. A big part of stimulation comes from being diverse, different, *special,* and that is where small businesses come into play. You can go to a dozen different small coffeebars, and each is distinctive. Go to a dozen Starbucks, and they are all pretty much the same. There are times we all crave the expected, but the creative class also often craves the unexpected, and that is much more likely in small businesses than chains and large firms. No high-tech center can survive as a place to live without the excitement and variety a population of small businesses can provide.

The fact is that *every* small business is important, for two reasons: first, because we can never be sure which ones are unimportant (if you can believe there could be such a thing), and second, it takes a lot of small businesses to support and enable one billion dollar business.

For us, one of the lessons of the Panel Study of Income Dynamics (PSED) was that while high tech might be the ship folks hope will come in, for it to work that ship needs to be supported by an ocean of small businesses. Billion dollar high-tech companies are rare. Less than one in 100,000 start-ups achieves that billion-dollar level. The irony is that *nobody* knows which of the next 100,000 start-ups is going to be that next billion dollar business. All we can do is try and start as many as possible, knowing the more that get started, the greater the chance of that one breakthrough success.

And the fact is that nearly every big business got its start as a small business. HP really *did* start in a garage, and Walmart started small in rural Arkansas. They are giants today, but some part of their culture got defined in those early days when they were small businesses. When they started, none of their founders *knew* they were going to become billionaires, and neither did their investors, bankers, lawyers, or friends. You start your business, you take your chances, and the rest of us hope you make it.

In the meantime, however, those hundreds of thousands of starts literally help support big business and high-tech businesses. They do this by providing jobs and wages to half the country so people can buy things. They do this by providing products and services to big and high-tech businesses, and they do this by training and preparing the next generation of workers and owners. Small businesses for the past 25 years have been the major source of new jobs created in the United States. While the Fortune 500 have cut their payrolls by millions, the slack created has been filled by small businesses and especially those small businesses that grow to multiple sites or multiple shifts.

When you start on the path to creating your own small business, you make life better for us all. *Entrepreneurial Small Business* is dedicated to giving you the specific help you need to get started and be successful.

The Fourth Edition of ESB

In each edition of *Entrepreneurial Small Business,* we try to follow a theme. For this fourth edition of *ESB* we have focused on more about making do in tough times. We have added to our coverage of the ways to use the Internet to help do more with less. We have added examples and vignettes about entrepreneurs managing their ways out of difficult situations. And we have added material on mindsets and techniques designed to help you get your business started for less—things like lean start-ups, effectuation methods, bricolage, and bootstrapping. We have done major revisions of our chapters on entrepreneurs (now moved to Chapter 2), strategy (Chapter 7), and promotion (Chapter 10), as well as updating throughout the book.

As you will see in the Acknowledgments, we get feedback from many professors, instructors, and students as well. We work hard to use these insights to improve the coverage, flow, and usefulness of the text for students and faculty alike. This involves a few major changes among many small changes, like these:

Chapter 1: In addition to providing the latest statistics on small business starts and closures, this chapter starts with a new opening vignette about Paul Scheiter of Hedgehog Leatherworks. This student-started business will appear throughout the text, along with Tim Hayden (whose vignette opens Chapter 3) so you can see how a small business handles different types of challenges. This chapter also provides an overview of the critical success factors for people starting a small business, to help orient readers to best practices. It also adds a section on entrepreneurial occupations, as well as bringing the discussion of the types of small business owner orientations from Chapter 20 to the start of the text, replacing the dynamic capitalism model.

Chapter 2: In prior editions of *ESB* this was the third chapter, but many faculty asked us to move it earlier because so many courses start with an exploration of the entrepreneur. In this revised chapter, we have a new section on "The Personalities of Entrepreneurs," which translates the latest research on entrepreneurial cognition and behavior into behaviors students can learn—like passion, perseverance, planning style, professionalization, and a promotion/prevention balance—that can make them think, act, and look more like successful entrepreneurs. We also added Skill Module 2.1 that lets students get a sense of the ideas behind the personality factors. This chapter also has new material on using social networks in business.

Chapter 3: This chapter received a major revision for the Third Edition, and has largely had an updating of its vignettes, statistics, and website addresses for this edition, although we couldn't help beefing up consideration of social networking sites in discussing how to build legitimacy.

Chapter 4: The growth of the Internet as a social and data resource has remade searching for and testing ideas, and this chapter has added new material on how to find business and product ideas on the web as well as how to test them out. This includes new material in the text, like a section on "The Source of Business Ideas," a new Small Business Insight on Scott Wilson's use of KickStarter.com to test out his idea for TikTok Watchbands (replacing our original introduction to Paul Scheiter in prior editions), as well as a new Skill Module 4.1 on "Checking Ideas on the Web." We also revised material on how to evaluate feasibility based on a reviewer's suggestion and screening ideas to work with a broader range of businesses. Borrowing from the creativity literature, we added how to apply the SCAMPER model using a mindmap.

Chapter 5: The statistics quoted in this chapter have been replaced with the most current available from the Kauffman Foundation, the PSED, and the SBA. The discussion of home-based business has been expanded. Specific examples of successful part-time businesses have been included.

Chapter 6: The opening vignette has been replaced with the story of a builder who has had to reinvent his business because of the effects of the recent recession. There is a new section on lean start-ups and lean management. A new sidebar tells the story of a start-up that was just the opposite of lean: a "fat" start-up that went bust. We also include a new account of the amazing recovery from failure pulled off by Harlan Sanders at an age when most folks take to their rockers. We know that this is an old story, but we also have discovered that our students have no idea that Sanders was a real person who overcame real difficulties.

Chapter 7: The goal for this chapter for this edition was to simplify what for many was one of the most complex chapters in *ESB*. To do this, we started with Skill Module 7.1, which helps students identify the one number many of them find is crucial to their thinking—how much do they feel they need to make for self-employment to make sense. We call this the "Magic Number" and show how to find it. To help make firm-offered benefits more real, we added a Skill Module 7.4 on Perceptual Mapping. We also reorganized the section on Strategy Selection to make it easier to understand, including retiring the SWOT analysis (although you can still find it on the Online Learning Center). The Post-Start-Up section also received a makeover, with a refined focus on the key strategies and tactics small businesses (again thanks to reviewer input) are most likely to use, which we found was more concrete and action-oriented than the prior focus on resources. We also added a new end-of-chapter mini-case.

Chapter 8: The biggest change is our use of a new business plan in the appendix for this chapter. MyLibros.com will move over to the OLC, and in its place is the plan for Red Jett Sweets, a cupcake truck in Fort Worth, Texas. This plan is exceptionally detailed. The text has the plan's narrative and financials. The extensive appendices, showing virtually all the computations underlying the development of the business (e.g., product production costs, scheduling, etc.), are available on the OLC. The plan is used in Chapters 13 and 14 to help students apply their understanding of the financial and accounting aspects of the business. This chapter also has new material on leveraging feedback and the strategies behind the use of business plans in starting businesses.

Chapter 9: This chapter also received a major revision. The pricing section was completely revamped with new explanations of elasticity, markup pricing, and the roles of supply and demand and perceived value in determining prices. The former Price Setting section was revamped and is now called "The Pricing Toolbox" to reflect its role. We've added a section called "Pricing in Practice" based on reviewer suggestions, which shows the specifics of how to price a product and a package of services to help students negotiate this often obscure but crucial process. Those looking for the section on product and service life cycles will find the material moved to the discussion of life cycles in the business in Chapter 20.

Chapter 10: This chapter also received a significant updating to better reflect the impact of the Internet on promotion. We added the marketing funnel to the text to help students understand how difficult it can be to find one customer, and we reorganized the chapter to better use the funnel as an organizing principle. Given how the major market data companies now make their basic information on customer segments available by zip code, we added new material and a Skill Module on how to find and use this data on what we call predetermined market segments. Material on all forms of advertising, including press and public relations, have been pulled together, as has all information on customer retention. The "Conveying Your Message" section helps students more directly compare traditional and Internet-based advertising approaches and understand how each can contribute to their promotion efforts. We also included a new mini-case on Orabrush, which became an example of an Internet phenomenon leveraging years of conventional promotional efforts.

Chapter 11: Among updates for this chapter were a revamped Skill Module 11.2 focusing on using free commercial websites that offer a broad range of demographic data by zip codes, improving upon the prior offerings from the Census Bureau. We also include an update to the AuctionDrop end-of-chapter case connecting students to online videos of its founder. This chapter also has new material from reviewer suggestions on negotiating with catalogs for inclusion, working with "daily deal" sites, leveraging the Internet's ever-improving location-based services and subleasing.

Chapter 12: To help build on students' prior work, the examples in this chapter build on the day care center introduced in Chapter 10. A revamp is evident in the appendix to the chapter, where the PizzMO offering is updated to combine up-and-coming technology, merging RedBox and pizza delivery. This chapter also received a refresh of its factual information, updated statistics, URLs, and vignettes.

Chapter 13: In this chapter we try to show students the common sense basis of accounting and we stress its importance in management. We included suggestions from both professors and students to simplify and make the explanation of accounting easier to understand. The opening vignette has been changed to the story of a brick and mortar store, the Curious Sofa, that experienced very high growth and wide publicity. However, because of the lack of good information to make decisions, the firm ran into severe problems with the 2008 recession. It survives today because the owner reinvented the business. We also include a precautionary tale of a San Antonio builder who ended up in prison primarily because of commingling of funds. Key software for small business accounting is specifically listed. Students will be challenged by an ethics case that presents a side-by-side example of how the timing of recognizing revenues can change the stated profitability and financial position of the firm. As in the earlier editions, we do break away from the student business plan in Chapter 8 to illustrate the functions of creating a complete master budget for the firm.

Chapter 14: This chapter retains its clear focus on cash management. The opening vignette has been changed to the story of a successful turnaround of a firm that nearly failed because of lack of cash, even though it had accounting profits. We have simplified and "cleaned up" the examples of cash budgeting.

Chapter 15: This chapter has been extensively rewritten to keep it current with the rapidly changing finance sector. There is a new discussion of direct public offerings, with an emphasis on the promise of the Jumpstart Our Business Startup Act. There is an entirely new section on bootstrapping as a management technique, which includes specific examples and current statistics on the use of bootstrapping. Crowdfunding is explicitly discussed in a new section. We also have a new discussion of angel investors as source of start-up funds.

Chapter 16: We have included the story of the turnaround accomplished by Cabot Mills in Vermont, illustrating how effective operational management can provide a path to new markets. We also include a new section on outsourcing, which includes a chart of specific business functions and activities that may be outsourced. There is a new cautionary tale of a bio firm that lost a significant sum through an ill-advised outsourcing decision. A new Skill Module challenges students to explore the challenge of international outsourcing.

Chapter 17: This chapter has an updated account of the effects of the Americans with Disabilities Act, building from the recently settled lawsuit against Clint Eastwood. We also include a new ethics case based on an actual firm, Celldyne Biopharma LLC, which was driven out of business by the cost of defending against a lawsuit. Students will be challenged by the ethical issues raised in this sad tale. The section on risks to buildings and land has been updated to include the 2011 Joplin tornado. There is also the story of the amazing turnaround from destruction to active business by a pharmacy whose building was blown away in the Joplin storm but was back in business in less than a week.

Chapter 18: This chapter has seen some of the state-specific examples removed to help one of the longer chapters in the book move along a bit faster. In addition, we've added material on LLC operating agreements (thanks to a suggestion from one of our reviewers). We have heard how hard it can be for students to wrap their heads around all the different forms of intellectual property protection. To help remedy that, we introduce a new Table 18.8, which lists the many elements of intellectual property that you typically find or create when starting a new business, and the table then offers suggestions on what IP methods apply. The full descriptions of the techniques remain in the chapter, but we think the table will help simplify how to think about this key topic. You'll also notice that the cover sheet from Apple's original iPod patent has been replaced with one from a small business—Paul Scheiter's patent for a retractable clasp for his knife sheaths. We thank one of our reviewers for helping us build our vignettes through the text.

Chapter 19: Many of the changes in this chapter come from the joys and problems the Internet offers around human resource issues. An example of a way the Internet helps is making it possible to create drafts of employee handbooks, and we show students where to do this. But we also take some time to caution entrepreneurs on the potential legal problems of checking out candidates using social media sites. Based on reviewer feedback we've added material explaining the key difference between wage and salaried positions and beefed up our discussion of illegal interview questions.

Chapter 20: This chapter benefitted from a bookwide reorganization. We now have all the book's discussions about life cycles in one place, to help students see the longer and shorter cycles of a business at the same time. To do this we moved the product and service life cycle materials from Chapter 9 here. Similarly, we move the discussion of firm-level growth strategies to Chapter 1 to dovetail with the other directional thoughts entrepreneurs have when establishing their firms. Otherwise, like all of *ESB*'s chapters, we have updated the facts, figures, vignettes, and website addresses to be current.

End-of-Book Cases: We included new end-of-book cases based on the surprising competition in the man candle industry (Case 7), on the changing methods of distribution in the music industry

(Case 11), and on legal conflicts over idea ownership between student inventors and their universities (Case 18).

When we look at the detailed list above, we recognize that about half of the ideas come from our own experience and discussions with our friends and colleagues at work. But it is important to recognize that the other half of the ideas, improvements, corrections, and revamps come from the suggestions of readers just like you—faculty and students who are using *Entrepreneurial Small Business* to help them pursue their dreams of business ownership.

You are our target customer. Your satisfaction or dissatisfaction is central to our making this text work. Do you have a better idea about how to talk about something? Did we get something wrong? Is there something we're missing that could help others in their entrepreneurial quests? Tell us. Richard's email is **rgreen@tamusa.tamus.edu** and Jerome's is **kataja@slu.edu**. We try to respond to all emails, and as you can see, we do try to improve the book based on your feedback.

The ESB Package

Professors reading this are probably wondering how all this translates into helping them teach their courses. One way we hope to help is through providing "imitation with a twist," which you will learn more about in Chapter 7. There are many other small business texts out there, and from an author's perspective, they can be intimidating because so many of them *are* so good. So how can *ESB* expect to get your attention? As you will find as you look through the book, all the major topics you expect to see are present—that's the imitation that is basic to all mature industries (like small business education).

Fostering Entrepreneurial Education Together

What adds value are those aspects of the book that are distinctive—our "twists." We give the specifics on how to sell, how to negotiate, how to ask for help, and how to handle a crisis, building from the best of research and professional practice. You will see it in small touches in the chapters, such as our discussion of issues such as when you get or use gifts as a way to fund start-ups, or why an LLC should be your default legal form of organization. We tried hard to give students the easiest introduction possible to the potentially frightening issues of accounting and financial reports. *ESB* is also the first book we know of that has devoted a chapter to the special needs and problems of part-time businesses. It is the first book to embrace not just business plans, but the increasingly popular external projects, such as those sponsored by Students in Free Enterprise (SIFE) or the Small Business Institute (SBI). See the website for these resources. We include real-life, high-quality *student written* examples of the reports we expect students to work up as they start their business. And all the while we tried to keep the *ESB* vision in the forefront—asking ourselves what the absolutely critical things are for our students to know in order to start their small businesses and succeed in them despite a lot of competition. We have tried whenever possible to focus on providing just what is needed, and what would be relevant for the traditional small businesses our students most often start.

The ESB Role/Goal/Celebration

This book started with a wife and mother's simple question about the difference between the traditional small businesses her husband started and the high-growth ventures she heard about in her son's stories. Today there is a groundswell of converging ideas in business, economic development, job creation, and government showing us that the revitalization of those traditional small businesses is a key component of reviving our economies and communities.

Our students know this. The Kauffman Foundation–sponsored surveys of youth attitudes report the highest rates ever recorded for young people planning to be self-employed. Adults in our neighborhoods know this. Every day over 2,700 new businesses start in the United States, and about 2,695 of them are small businesses. New forms of small business, such as eBay selling, are further swelling the numbers of small businesses in ways that government record keeping does not yet record. Like those students and adults, *Entrepreneurial Small Business* also knows this revitalization is taking place, and we want *ESB* to help.

For students, we want *Entrepreneurial Small Business* to be your handbook, lightning rod, and motivator. When you read this book, mark it up! If something is important to the way you plan to run your business, dog-ear the page or highlight the material. Write how something applies to your proposed or existing business. If you have not started a journal for business ideas, start using the margins or end pages of this book to hold them. We know from experience there is a simple way to see if a book is really valuable. In college, the *really* valuable book is the one students do not sell at the end of the semester, because they actually see themselves using that book. If you are serious about becoming an entrepreneur and we did *our* job right, then success is measured in books kept and marked up. If you are serious and the book did not do the job for you, let *us* know what we need to do better. We got this far on the wisdom of a network of a lot of students and faculty, and as you go through this semester, you become part of the network, too.

For faculty, our job as educators is not just to know about this small business groundswell, and not just to help make this work, but to *celebrate* this. Academics have the power to legitimize through their acceptance and support, and they have the power to propagate through their contacts with hundreds of students and businesses a year. But most of all, we have the power to excite and to energize, most often through our own energy and support and occasionally even by the new opportunities and vistas we open for our students. You and all of us collectively have an important contribution to make to the revitalization of small business as a key component of the economy, just doing what you do every day.

We want to be a part of that effort with you—providing the examples to celebrate, the realities that help prepare our students for what they will face, and most of all the skills, knowledge, and resources that will prove to them that most critical of concepts in life and in small business success—"help helps."

We are the authors behind *Entrepreneurial Small Business.* We want to help. Let us know how we could do so better in the future. Welcome!

Jerome A. Katz
Saint Louis University
katzja@slu.edu

Richard P. Green II
Texas A&M University—San Antonio
rgreen@tamusa.tamus.edu

ENTREPRENEURIAL SMALL BUSINESS:

Entrepreneurial Small Business provides students with a clear vision of small business as it really is today. It focuses on small businesses that students might actually start versus high-growth firms dependent on venture capital. It presents the *realities* small business owners face every day and strategies for those starting or maintaining a small business.

There are several chapters that emphasize the distinct focus of this book.

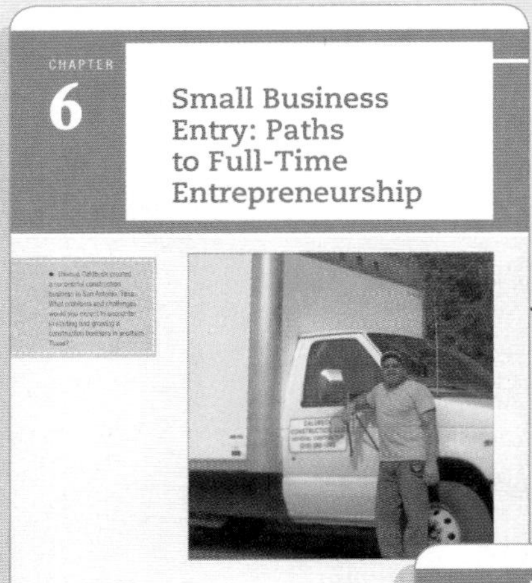

Chapter 6: Small Business Entry: Paths to Full-Time Entrepreneurship

Most small businesses go into established lines of business. This text emphasizes the benefits of this strategy.

SMALL BUSINESS REALITY: Almost two-thirds of people starting business today plan to use imitation as their approach.

CHAPTER 3 Small Business Environment: Managing External Relations

Chapter 3: Small Business Environment: Managing External Relations

Part-time businesses are tremendously important as they are a major portion of all current entrepreneurship, and it's the way most people enter into self-employment. This chapter discusses the benefits—and challenges—of part-time entrepreneurship.

SMALL BUSINESS REALITY: 75 percent of those starting a business already work full time for someone else and are pursuing their new business part time.

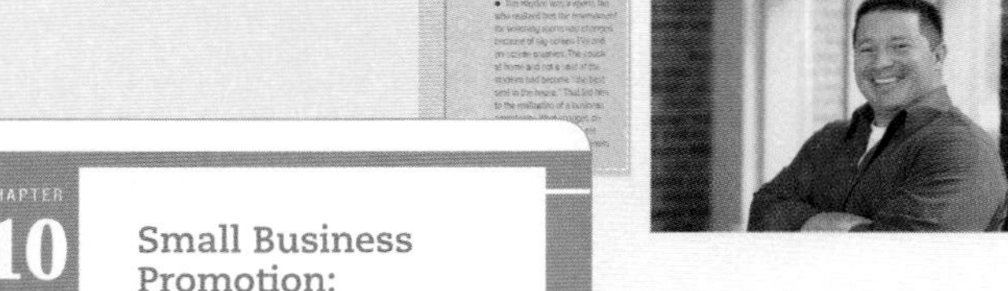

Chapter 10: Small Business Promotion: Capturing the Eyes of Your Market

All small businesses must understand how to manage the business's cash flow. This chapter focuses on the basics of cash, budgets, shortages, and strategies to deal with cash flow problems.

SMALL BUSINESS REALITY: About 55 percent of small businesses that fail do so because of cash flow problems.

Finally. . . a book about the kinds of businesses your students are most likely to start!

Business Plans

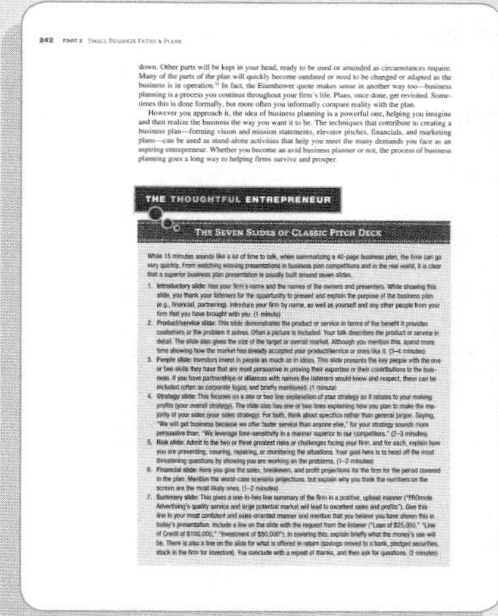

242 PART 2 SMALL BUSINESS PATHS & PLANS

down. Other parts will be kept in your head, ready to be used or amended as circumstances require. Many of the parts of the plan will quickly become outdated or need to be changed or adapted as the business is in operation.[31] In fact, the Eisenhower quote makes sense in another way too—business planning is a process you continue throughout your firm's life. Plans, once done, get revisited. Sometimes this is done formally, but more often you informally compare reality with the plan.

However you approach it, the idea of business planning is a powerful one, helping you imagine and then realize the business the way you want it to be. The techniques that contribute to creating a business plan—forming vision and mission statements, elevator pitches, financials, and marketing plans—can be used as stand-alone activities that help you meet the many demands you face as an aspiring entrepreneur. Whether you become an avid business planner or not, the process of business planning goes a long way to helping firms survive and prosper.

THE THOUGHTFUL ENTREPRENEUR

THE SEVEN SLIDES OF CLASSIC PITCH DECK

While 15 minutes sounds like a lot of time to talk, when summarizing a 40-page business plan, the time can go very quickly. From watching winning presentations in business plan competitions and in the real world, it is clear that a superior business plan presentation is usually built around seven slides.

1. **Introductory slide:** Has your firm's name and the names of the owners and presenters. While showing this slide, you thank your listeners for the opportunity to present and explain the purpose of the business plan (e.g., financial, partnering). Introduce your firm by name, as well as yourself and any other people from your firm that you have brought with you. (1 minute)
2. **Product/service slide:** This slide demonstrates the product or service in terms of the benefit it provides customers or the problem it solves. Often a picture is included. Your talk describes the product or service in detail. The slide also gives the size of the target or overall market. Although you mention this, spend more time showing how the market has already accepted your product/service or ones like it. (3–4 minutes)
3. **People slide:** Investors invest in people as much as in ideas. This slide presents the key people with the one or two skills they have that are most persuasive in proving their expertise or their contributions to the business. If you have partnerships or alliances with names the listeners would know and respect, these can be included (often as corporate logos) and briefly mentioned. (1 minute)
4. **Strategy slide:** This focuses on a one or two line explanation of your strategy as it relates to your making profits (your overall strategy). The slide also has one or two lines explaining how you plan to make the majority of your sales (your sales strategy). For both, think about specifics rather than general jargon. Saying, "We will get business because we offer faster service than anyone else," for your strategy sounds more persuasive than, "We leverage time-sensitivity in a manner superior to our competitors." (2–3 minutes)
5. **Risk slide:** Admit to the two or three greatest risks or challenges facing your firm, and for each, explain how you are preventing, insuring, repairing, or monitoring the situations. Your goal here is to head off the most threatening questions by showing you are working on the problems. (1–2 minutes)
6. **Financial slide:** Here you give the sales, breakeven, and profit projections for the firm for the period covered in the plan. Mention the worst-case scenario projections, but explain why you think the numbers on the screen are the most likely ones. (1–2 minutes)
7. **Summary slide:** This gives a one-to-two line summary of the firm in a positive, upbeat manner ("PROmote Advertising's quality service and large potential market will lead to excellent sales and profits"). Give this line in your most confident and sales-oriented manner and mention that you believe you have shown this in today's presentation. Include a line on the slide with the request from the listener ("Loan of $25,000," "Line of Credit of $100,000," "Investment of $50,000"). In covering this, explain briefly what the money's use will be. There is also a line on the slide for what is offered in return (savings moved to a bank, pledged securities, stock in the firm for investors). You conclude with a repeat of thanks, and then ask for questions. (2 minutes)

Business plans are a part of every small business course. A business plan may not be necessary to start your business, but it is critical to plan and understand your business in any circumstance.

Chapter 8 includes practical information helpful to any small business owner, such as:

- The elevator pitch—how to quickly get people interested in your business.
- A single-page approach to organizing your business plan.
- How to write your executive summary—a key component of the business plan.
- Seven types of business plans and what components they should include.
- Tips on presenting your plan, such as the seven slides of a business plan presentation.

Chapter appendixes contain samples of important business plan components:

Feasibility Plan (after Chapter 4)
Industry Analysis (after Chapter 7)
Cover Letter and Résumé (after Chapter 8)
Full Business Plan (after Chapter 8)
Marketing Plan (after Chapter 12)

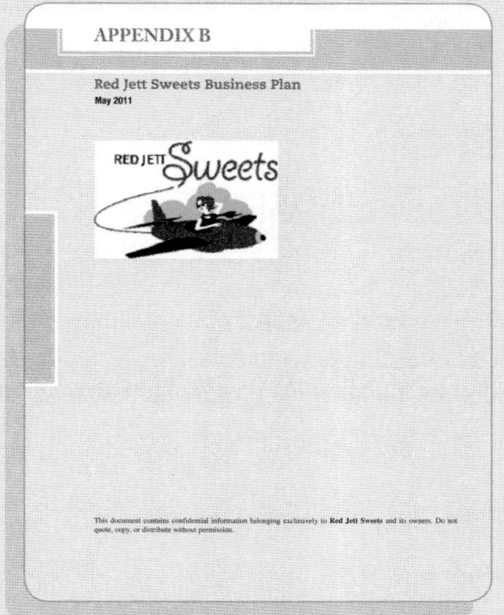

APPENDIX B

Red Jett Sweets Business Plan
May 2011

This document contains confidential information belonging exclusively to **Red Jett Sweets** and its owners. Do not quote, copy, or distribute without permission.

Additional business plan supports include online examples of feasibility plans and business plans on the website. One online feasibility study and business plan focus on the same company, allowing you to see how the business developed.

ESB Features

To help students learn more about the benefits of small business ownership, as well as the challenges many small business owners face, ESB is full of practical advice and examples from true small businesses in a variety of industries. Its focus is to give students the tools and knowledge they need to go out and start their small business.

220 PART 2 SMALL BUSINESS PATHS & PLANS

Going up? Each year, Wake Forest University's Babcock Graduate School of Management holds its annual elevator pitch contest. Teams must progress through a rigorous weeding-out process to advance to the semi-finalist stage, where they get the chance to present their pitch to real venture capitalists and experts on a two-minute elevator ride. To read more about this year's contest, visit http://business.wfu.edu/elevator/

close asking for money from seed investors. This is about 115 words and would take about half a minute to say. Note that a lot of it sounds like a sales pitch, and that is intentional. Listeners might be customers or investors, but either way, the goal is to sell them on the idea and their need for it. With this background, Skill Module 8.1 explains how to craft an elevator pitch.

SKILL MODULE 8.1 How to Write Your Elevator Pitch

Elevator pitches have four success factors: the hook, the purpose, the what and where, and the delivery.

First, find a hook—something about your product or service that people would remember and take to heart. "We tutor kids others call too difficult." "When government or industry wants to find the newest businesses, they come to us." "We are one of the nation's biggest suppliers of parts for old Corvettes."

Stan Mandel supervises Wake Forest University's Elevator Pitch Competition, so he knows pitches. He suggests using analogies. If you're planning a large, discount pen store, you might say "We will be a Walmart for pens." For CellTunes, it might be "We'll be the Home Shopping Network for music." It helps people quickly understand your firm. Great pitches or concepts aim to get the listener to ask questions or take some other form of "next step." Stan suggests different pitches for different sorts of audiences—investors, customers, suppliers, and so forth.

Second, focus on the purpose your product or service serves for the customer. Do not talk skills ("I am a graphic designer."); talk about how you make customers happy ("I produce designs that sell books!").

Third, tell the listener the business's situation: where the business "is at"—if it's a start-up, state what the business is seeking (funding, partners, distributors, etc.). If it is operating, tell the listener where he or she can buy the product or service.

Once your elevator pitch is written, you need to become conversationally perfect in your delivery. You want to be able to give the pitch or concept dozens, even hundreds, of times. Yet it is important that the pitch does not sound memorized. It needs to sound like regular conversation, preferably a conversation whose topic excites you. To achieve this, you must master the material, and then keep working on it so that it becomes a natural part of what you say to others. Have family and friends listen to it. Consider using a video camera to see how natural you seem when making the pitch. Remember, the elevator pitch is often the first real insight people have about your business, so it is essential to have a pitch that flows and sells for you.

Skill Modules

Skill Modules are a key component of this text. They are included in every chapter to help students understand and practice critical competencies for small business owners. These are resources that students can use in the course and that they can continue to use as they plan or grow their small business.

Examples include:

- Competency Self-Assessment
- Checklist for Maximizing Success on eBay
- Sweet and Short Industry Analysis
- The Art of Closing
- Finding SBIR Grants

See the inside front cover for a full listing of Skill Modules.

Focus on Small Business

Each chapter opens with a vignette that highlights an entrepreneur and an aspect of a small business that relates to the chapter concepts. Discussion questions are included for students to consider as they read the chapter.

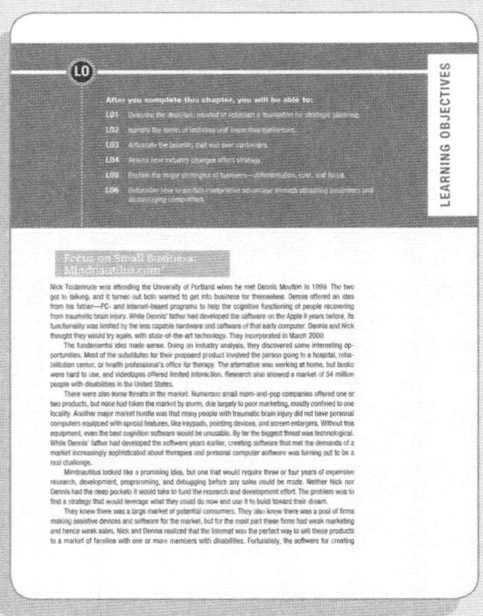

LO LEARNING OBJECTIVES

After you complete this chapter, you will be able to:

Focus on Small Business: Mindnautilus.com

Nick Tostenrude was attending the University of Portland when he met Dennis Moulton in 1999. The two got to talking, and it turned out both wanted to get into business for themselves. Dennis offered an idea from his father—PC- and internet-based programs to help the cognitive functioning of people recovering from traumatic brain injury. While Dennis' father had developed the software on the Apple II years before, its functionality was limited by the less capable hardware and software of that early computer. Dennis and Nick thought they would try again, with state-of-the-art technology. They incorporated in March 2000.

The fundamental idea made sense. Doing an industry analysis, they discovered some interesting opportunities. Most of the substitutes for their proposed product involved the person going to a hospital, rehabilitation center, or health professional's office for therapy. The alternative was working at home, but books were hard to use, and videotapes offered limited interaction. Research also showed a market of 54 million people with disabilities in the United States.

There were also some threats in the market. Numerous small mom-and-pop companies offered one or two products, but none had taken the market by storm, due largely to poor marketing, mostly confined to one locality. Another major market hurdle was that many people with traumatic brain injury did not have personal computers equipped with special features, like keypads, pointing devices, and screen enlargers. Without this equipment, even the best cognition software would be unusable. By far the biggest threat was technological. While Dennis' father had developed the software years earlier, creating software that met the demands of a market increasingly sophisticated about therapies and personal computer software was turning out to be a real challenge.

Mindnautilus looked like a promising idea, but one that would require three or four years of expensive research, development, programming, and debugging before any sales could be made. Neither Nick nor Dennis had the deep pockets it would take to fund the research and development effort. The problem was to find a strategy that would leverage what they could do now and use it to build toward their dream.

They knew there was a large market of potential consumers. They also knew there was a pool of firms making assistive devices and software for the market, but for the most part these firms had weak marketing and hence weak sales. Nick and Dennis realized that the Internet was the perfect way to sell these products to a market of families with one or more members with disabilities. Fortunately, the software for creating

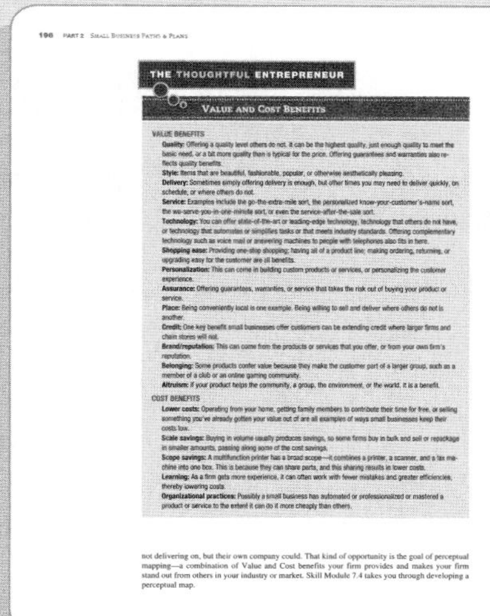
THE THOUGHTFUL ENTREPRENEUR

VALUE AND COST BENEFITS

Thoughtful Entrepreneur Boxes

These boxes illustrate topics for students who want to explore the more complex issues and practices small businesses encounter.

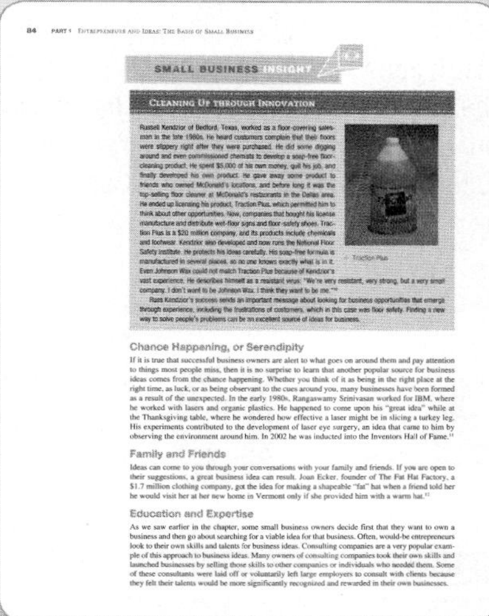
SMALL BUSINESS INSIGHT

CLEANING UP THROUGH INNOVATION

Chance Happening, or Serendipity

Family and Friends

Education and Expertise

Small Business Insight Boxes

These boxes include "under the radar" advice from real small business owners and helpful statistics from small businesses around the country.

End-of-Chapter Materials

End-of-chapter materials include:

CHAPTER SUMMARY

An end-of-chapter summary is included, bulleted by chapter objectives, to help students review the chapter material and study for tests.

DISCUSSION QUESTIONS

Discussion questions are included in each chapter that can be given as assignments or that can be used for in-class discussion. Suggested answers are included in the Instructor's Manual.

EXPERIENTIAL EXERCISES

The experiential exercises include brief activities students can complete to get more information on the chapter topic, to look for additional resources, and to help build their competencies in a certain aspect of small business ownership. An icon indicates which exercises involve use of the Internet. www

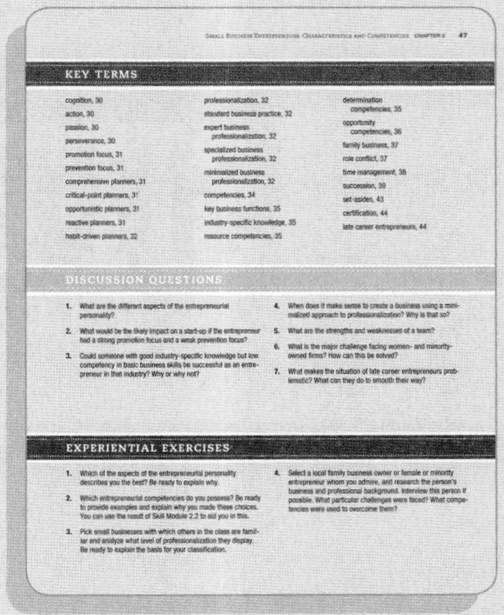
KEY TERMS

DISCUSSION QUESTIONS

EXPERIENTIAL EXERCISES

MINI-CASE

A mini-case for each chapter is included as an additional opportunity for the student to apply the lessons of the chapter.

SUGGESTED CASES & VIDEOS

A listing of full-length end-of-book cases as well as suggested video segments appears at the end of each chapter.

Additional Resources

Cases & Video Cases

A case for each chapter (20 total) is included at the end of the text and 15 video cases are included online. These cases offer additional opportunities for students to analyze situations in a carefully crafted case drawn from real-world small businesses, along with discussion questions that can be used in class or as an assignment. The Instructor's Manual provides suggestions on how to use and discuss each of these cases. Videos are available on the instructor DVD. In addition, longer cases (most with instructors' notes) are identified. All of these longer cases are available from McGraw-Hill's Create (www.mcgrawhillcreate.com). These types of relevant cases are brought together in a new "Suggested Cases" listing at the end of each chapter.

SHORT VIDEOS

Entrepreneurial Small Business Fourth Edition offers an unprecedented selection of short online video clips (most two to three minutes) for use in the class or as supplements. Each chapter identifies multiple videos from ItsYourBiz.com, the Web's foremost online channel for small business news and help. Many chapters also include videos from Stanford Technology Ventures Educators' Corner. The Business Plan and Financing chapters include Elevator Pitches from MSNBC's *Your Business*. All of these videos come with instructors' notes in the Video Guide, and all are available for free online at the respective websites.

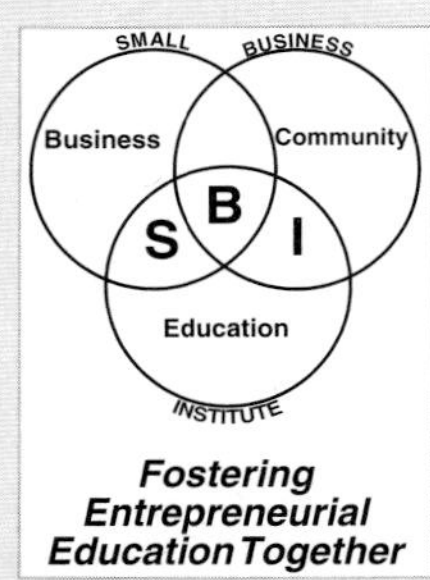

Website Appendixes

CONSULTING TO SMALL BUSINESS—SBI AND BEYOND

Some courses give students the opportunity to work on consulting projects, or "live" cases. The appendix includes key guidelines and information about how to carry out effective fieldwork. Information is included such as meeting with the client, setting objectives, preparing the final report, ethical considerations, and ongoing communication with the client.

SIFE (STUDENTS IN FREE ENTERPRISE)

Increasingly popular external projects, like the ones sponsored by Students in Free Enterprise, are included on the website. The appendix introduces SIFE and illustrates the process for developing and completing an SIFE project.

Supplements for Students and Instructors

Instructor's Manual

The Instructor's Manual includes lecture outlines, chapter summaries, descriptions of the text features, answers to end-of-chapter materials, additional activities, and references to relevant articles.

Test Bank

The Test Bank includes multiple-choice, true–false, and short-answer questions, along with the correct answer and a rationale for the answer. The Test Bank is also available in a computerized version that allows you to add and edit questions.

PowerPoints

PowerPoint presentations for each chapter are available to instructors and students on the Online Learning Center. Included are figures from the text, lecture outline material, figures that expand concepts in the books, and questions that can be used in class.

Small Business and Entrepreneurship DVD, volume 2

Fifteen videos are included, and each of the videos brings important concepts to life by taking viewers on fieldtrips to real-life companies, to hear directly from entrepreneurs as well as presenting news features on small business and entrepreneurial topics. Video cases and notes are included for professors in the Instructor's Manual. A wealth of shorter video clips are available on the OLC as well. Additional clips online include footage from SBTV.com and Stanford's Technology Venture Program.

Online Learning Center (OLC)

www.mhhe.com/katz4e
The text-specific website includes a wealth of information for both students and professors. Professors can access downloadable supplements as well as all of the student material. The Student Edition includes professional resources, interactive exercises, sample business plans, financial worksheets, video clips, key term review, additional chapter quizzes, and links for every chapter. Look for the OLC icon in the textbook!

Additional Readings

The Instructors' Guide provides a chapter-by-chapter mapping of readings from McGraw-Hill's *Annual Editions: Entrepreneurship*.

Student Study Guide

The Study Guide contains various ways to review—learning objectives from the chapter, key term exercises, assessment/concept checks, critical thinking exercises, and practice tests (and answers). This guide is now available as part of the website for student use.

Business Plan Pro

Business Plan Pro is the industry-leading business planning software program used by professionals to develop effective business plans. It has all you need to create a complete and accurate business plan:

- 500+ sample business plans
- Step-by-step guidance
- Lender-ready documents
- Sales forecasts
- Financing tools
- Industry research data
- Ability to print and publish your plan

Online Courses

If you are interested in educating students online, McGraw-Hill/Irwin offers *Entrepreneurial Small Business* content for complete online courses. We have joined forces with the most popular delivery platforms available, such as WebCT and Blackboard. These platforms have been designed for instructors who want complete control over course content and how it is presented to their students. You can customize the *ESB* Online Learning Center content or author your own course materials—it's entirely up to you. The content of *ESB* is flexible enough to use with any platform currently available (and, it's free). If your department or school is already using a platform, we can certainly help.

ACKNOWLEDGMENTS

This section is the one sure to get longer as a textbook goes into revisions. We don't mind fighting for the space, because a text like *Entrepreneurial Small Business* could not be made without the contributions of a lot of people. Recognizing them here is a small recompense, but one we've valued in their works. It is also a lesson to you fledgling entrepreneurs out there—*all* ventures (and believe us, a textbook is a venture) require the support and advice of many other people to be successful. Here are the ones to whom we remain beholden.

Let's start with our mentors, professors who, through their academic lives, have served as inspiration to us all about the enduring importance of small business: Frank Hoy (Worcester Polytechnic Institute), Charles Matthews (University of Cincinnati), George Solomon (George Washington University), as well as three pioneering Coleman Chairs, Gerry Hills (Bradley University), Bob Brockhaus (retired from Saint Louis University), and Gerry Gunderson (Beloit College).

There is also a group of faculty who were essential to *ESB* as it was developed and revised. Some of these started as doctoral students or protégés and are now long-established professionals and professors in their own right while others started as colleagues and remain friends long years later—Kathy Lund Dean (The Board of Trustees Distinguished Chair in Leadership and Ethics at Gustavus Adolphus College), Lisa Gundry (DePaul University), Janice Jackson, Gregory Konz, (U.S. Jesuit Conference), Laurel Boone JD (Saint Louis University), Scott Safranksi (Saint Louis University) and Susan Peters, the Forrest S. William Professor of Entrepreneurship at Francis Marion University in Florence, South Carolina, and who is the lead author for *ESB's* instructors' manual and student guides. These people contributed much of the specialized expertise on which the text is built. Of course, the errors we have introduced over the years are our fault, not theirs.

At Saint Louis University, we use *ESB* in many of our classes, and the feedback SLU's Entrepreneurship Teaching Team provides us is invaluable. Over the past three years, that team has included Professors Jintong Tang and Vince Volpe, and adjuncts Tim Hayden (VividSky, FanzLive and now Saint Louis University), Trey Goede (Affinity Wind), Don Dent (Carbolytic Materials Corp.), Marian Nunn (Nunn Advisory Services), Steve Wideman (Wideman Management Group), Jennifer Ehlen (Thompson Street Capital), attorney Jim Rittenbaum, Jim O'Donnell (O'Donnell Capital), Steve Epner (BSW Consulting), Laura Burkemper (The Catalyst Group), Paul Scheiter (Hedgehog Leatherworks), and Ron Roy (FanzLive). We also benefit from a group of entrepreneurship-minded Saint Louis University faculty from across our campus called Coleman Fellows sponsored by the Coleman Foundation: Alesia Slocum, David Barnett, Huliyar Mallikarjuna, Martin Brief, Mildred Mattfeldt-Beman, Sridhar Condoor, Steve Wernet, and Steve Jenkins. Professor Jim Fisher of Saint Louis University's Emerson Center for Business Ethics deserves special thanks for contributing the videos used in Chapter 3.

We also want to thank a remarkable group of students, who agreed to share their work with you. Every business plan, industry analysis, marketing plan, and feasibility study you see in this book or on our website was authored by a student. This gives you a very realistic idea of what students *can* do using the ideas and approaches in *ESB*. Our thanks go out to our students and alums of the Entrepreneurship Program at Saint Louis University (in alphabetical order): Katie Anich, Kevin Antes, Tiffani Cage, Brittany Crittenden, Julia Dalton, Rebecca Ellis, Beatrice Emmanuel, Collin Fischer, Natalie Gamez, Tim Geldmacher, Alon Ginzburg, Gary Hartmann, Tim Hayden, Patrick Hughes, Caroline Jack, Nicole Johnson, James P. Keating, Scott Kettner, Jordan Koene, Angela Lawrence, Eric McMahon, Plamen Radev, Theresa Resnik, Todd Robben, Melanie Salzman, Kristin Scully, Jonathan Taulbee, Denis Thein, Tim Tobben, Chris Wallace, Dan Watkins, and Michael Zimmer. As you would expect with our network of colleagues, there is also a host of students at other schools who contributed to the materials *you* see in *ESB*. These include Shannon Sheehee (California Polytechnic University–Pomona), Yong Xu (California Polytechnic University–Pomona), Mingkit "Jerry" Lai (California Polytechnic University–Pomona), and Laurel Ofstein (DePaul). In particular we want to thank Katie Anich, Nicole Johnson, Melanie Salzman and especially Natalie Gamez for their contribution of the Red Jett Sweets business plan that you will see in Chapter 8.

One of the unpredictable benefits of starting a project like *ESB* is that you make new collegial relationships along the way. *ESB* gave us the chance to get to know and appreciate the talents of people like Rick Koza of Chadron State College, who did the initial draft of the first SIFE module ever included in a small business text, as well as David Tooch of the University of New Hampshire, who worked on most of the cases at the end of the text. Robert Ledman of Morehouse College also contributed the Saunders case at the book's end. Ed Rogoff of City University of New York and Allison Lehr of CUNY's Field Center for Entrepreneurship contributed business plans that their students had done according to the model used in *ESB.*

ESB also builds from an ongoing series of books and special issues edited or co-edited by Jerome Katz over the years, which includes the research series *Advances in Entrepreneurship, Firm Emergence and Growth* (published by Emerald), the text-supplement series *Entrepreneurship and the Management of Growing Enterprises* (published by Sage), and special issues of journals such as *Entrepreneurship: Theory & Practice, Entrepreneurship & Regional Development,* Academy of Management *Learning & Education,* and *Simulation & Gaming.* To the dozens of contributors, reviewers and co-editors who made those publications possible and that information available, a collective thanks does not do justice, but is all that is possible. Andrew Corbett (Babson), Theresa Welbourne (Nebraska), Ron Mitchell (Texas A&M), Tom Lumpkin (Syracuse University), and Connie Marie Gaglio (San Francisco State) deserve special mention for their unique and repeated contributions to the informational underpinnings of *ESB.* One name that deserves special mention, however, is Dean Shepherd (Indiana) whose work as an author and later as a co-editor of the Emerald series shaped many of the key ideas of *ESB.*

Evaluation is central to the professional approach, whether in small business or in publishing. One of McGraw-Hill's strengths is its unwavering professionalism in the pursuit of publishing. At first, it is frankly daunting. It seems that *every* detail of *every* aspect of a textbook is subject to review—and that perception turns out to be accurate. Yet it serves a purpose. When McGraw-Hill releases a textbook, it has been reviewed, rewritten, and refined until it is a truly first-class product. It is a time-consuming, painstaking, and often underappreciated effort, but it produces textbooks that you have to admire.

At the core of this effort are faculty. These faculty contributed feedback about chapters within the text, the text organization as a whole, and some reviewed the entire manuscript to help us develop the best product available for your small business course. For a text as complex and far ranging as *ESB,* a large, diverse, and committed set of faculty offering opinions and reviews is needed, and we were fortunate to have more than three dozen dedicated colleagues willing to take time to help make this edition of *ESB* better. They have our thanks, and should have yours too, because without them, opening a book like *ESB* would be a game of chance. These faculty include:

James Bell
Texas State University

Heather Dixon-Fowler
Appalachian State University

David Hensley
The University of Iowa

Chandler Atkins
SUNY Adirondack

Bill Zannini
Northern Essex Community College

Todd Finkle
Gonzaga University

Sharon Kerrick
University of Louisville

Connie Marie Gaglio
San Francisco State University

Don Lewis
Texas A&M University

John Wuebben
Miracosta College

McGraw-Hill went to extraordinary lengths to get feedback for the first, second and third editions, and the more than 150 faculty who contributed reviews and insights were central to the creation of a text which was useful from the start. It is on their contributions that this fourth edition is built. Those reviewers in whose debt we remain include David Aiken, Mark Andreason, Dave Arseneau, Jay Azriel, Calvin Bacon, Barrett Baebler, Kunal Banerji, Kevin Banning, Mike Bark, Kenneth Becker, Verona K. Beguin, James Bell, Jim Benton, Phil Bessler, George Blanc, Kay Blasingame-Boike, David Borst, Susan Bosco, Don Bradley, Steven Bradley, Harvey Bronstein, Mark Brostoff,

Ingvild Brown, Russell Brown, Rochelle Brunson, Bob Bryant, Robert J. Calvin, Teresa Campbell, Sheri Carder, Kevin Carlson, Martha Carney, Shawn Carraher, Carol Carter, Ed Cerny, Robert Chelle, Jewel B. Cherry, Felipe Chia, John Christesen, Rod Christian, Michael Cicero, William Clark, Ed Cole, J. Robert Collins, Roy Cook, Dan Creed, Wayne Michael Dejnak, Christine DeLaTorre, Cory L. Dobbs, Michael Dougherty, Mike Drafke, Glenda Eckert, Micki Eisenman, Robert Ericksen, Michael Fathi, Mark Fenton, Gil Feiertag, Brian Fink, Dana Fladhammer, Rusty Freed, Leatrice Freer, Janice Gates, David Gay, Richard Gentry, Jim Giordano, Vada Grantham, Clark Hallpike, David Hansen, Donald Hardwick, Joe Hartnett, Gene Hastings, Brad D. Hays, Linda Hefferin, David Hensley, Diane Henslow, Kirk Heriot, Abel Hernandez, Anne Hernandez, Dorothy Hetmer-Hinds, Bob Hill, Mark Hoelsher, Edward Huff, Fred Hughes, Samira Hussein, Ralph Jagodka, Ken Jones, Lou Jourdan, Rusty Juban, Linda Kice, Kelly Kilcrease, Jack Kirby, Larry Klatt, Mary Beth Klinger, Vicky Koonce, Scott Kunkel, William Laing, Ed Langlois, John Leaptrott, Les Ledger, Art Lekacos, Richard Lester, Paul James Londrigan, Terry Lowe, Luigi Lucaccini, Leyland Lucas, Shawna Mahaffey, Tim March, Greg McCann, Joseph McDonnell, Pam McElligott, Norman McElvany, Clarence McMaster, Todd Mick, Angela Mitchell, Douglas Moesel, Greg Moore, Mehdi Moutahir, John Mullane, Terry Noel, Don A. Okhomina Sr., Glenda Orosco, Eric Palmer, Gerald Perry, Fred Pragasm, Mark Pruett, Jude Rathburn, Deana Ray, William Rech, Levi Richard, Darlington Richards, Kenneth C. Robinson, Benjamin Rockmore, Mary Ellen Rosetti, Matt Rutherford, John Sagi, Martin St. John, Tammy Schakett, Duane Schecter, Jim Schroeder, Gregory Schultz, Gerald Segal, Tom Severance, Owen Sevier, Jack Sheeks, Cynthia Singer, Bernard Skown, Rick Smith, Bill Snider, Robert Sosna, Stuart Spero, William Steiden, Deborah Streeter, John Striebich, Ram Subramanian, James Swenson, Yvette Swint-Blakely, Vanessa Thomas, Kathleen Voelker, Ken Walker, Frank Weidmann, Charles Wellens, Rebecca White, Jim Whitlock, Dennis Williams, Ira Wilsker, MaryLou Wilson, John Withey, Betty Wong, and Robert Zahrowski.

Penultimately, there is the team at McGraw-Hill. We had both written books before and thought we had some appreciation of the process of book publishing. However, publishing a *textbook* is a far cry from publishing text supplements or research tomes. In those cases, it is usually just words, with an occasional figure. For a textbook, it is figures, pictures, tables, key terms, URLs, cases of all different lengths, examples, discussion questions, experiential exercises, skill-building exercises, footnotes, business plans, manuals, website components, *and* words. And like a car assembled at one point where dozens of items miraculously come together, the assembly of a modern textbook is a similar experience.

We were fortunate to have Kelly Pekelder serve as our developmental editor—the person who has to check all the elements and bring them together at the end. She took on an awesome amount of responsibility for ESB late in the project, and made sure we were able to get this book to you on time and up to the usual high standards of McGraw-Hill. The job of a sponsoring editor in a revision is that of the corporate entrepreneur or product champion, assembling the resources to make it happen, and motivating everyone to keep his or her eyes on the timeline, budget, book outline, and, oh, yes, the market. For *ESB4* that role was ably held by Anke Weeks, who quietly went about keeping it all on track. Michael Gedatus, who has progressed through several roles with *ESB* is now our marketing manager and the person responsible for the selling effort that got *ESB* into your hands. As such, he comes onboard late in the process, but at the critical time for the book's commercial success. In addition, there are people such as Paul Ducham, our Managing Director, Jana Singer, our designer, Melissa Leick, our project manager, Prashanthi Nadipalli, our media producer, Allison Grimes, our photo research coordinator, and Jennifer Pickel, our buyer, who made all this possible. To each and every one of these fine publishing professionals, we offer our deepest appreciation. One other McGraw-Hill professional, Ryan Blankenship, continues to have a special place in our hearts. He was the person who recognized the value of *ESB* and sold McGraw-Hill on our idea, and sold us on McGraw-Hill. We remain in his debt.

Keeping with this networking idea, you will see that this book makes extensive use of several strategic partnerships. These include the Global Student Entrepreneur Awards program (www.gsea.org), which celebrates collegiate entrepreneurs, and the Panel Study of Entrepreneurial Dynamics. I know this is a lot of cut material, but given it is at the end of the section, it shouldn't be a problem. Our strategic partners for videos continue to include SBTV.com (the Web's premier online channel for small business news and help), The Stanford Technology Ventures Program, and MSNBC's Your Business. We are grateful for their continuing support of *ESB*. From examples such as these, we hope you will see the practical value of strategic partnerships, which we talk about in Chapters 3 and 7. The fact is that we can show you more about the world of small business *because* of our partnerships, and that makes the book, and your experience, better.

Finally, *Entrepreneurial Small Business* will enter its tenth year of existence during this edition, and the thinking and talking about it stretches back almost 20 years, in classrooms, at meals, at social get-togethers, and over many, many phone calls, e-mails, presentations, and papers. What started as a labor of learning among professors and protégés became a labor of love among colleagues. Often this labor was possible because of time contributed by (or stolen from) families and significant others. The number of meals missed, calls taking over the family phone, late nights spent over the computer, or weekends spent at work over the past 20 years are innumerable. What those family members and significant others saw was the passion for discovery and the excitement of finding and telling others about a better way of doing things in small businesses or explaining small business. For all of the network, and especially the authors, that support was the critical enduring ingredient in making *Entrepreneurial Small Business* a reality. For that reason, we want to recognize the enormous emotional and motivational contributions made by Dave Peters, James F. Amrhein, Nora L. Peterson, Josh Katz, Lauren Katz, and Cheryl Nietfeldt.

BRIEF CONTENTS

CONTENTS

1

PART ONE

Entrepreneurs and Ideas: The Basis of Small Business

CHAPTER

1

Small Business: Its Opportunities and Rewards

● Paul Scheiter of Hedgehog Leatherworks in the woods. How did he use his passion for the outdoors to help him find his business idea?

LEARNING OBJECTIVES

After you complete this chapter, you will be able to:

LO1 Understand the scope of small business in the United States.

LO2 Learn the differences between small businesses and high-growth ventures.

LO3 Discover the rewards entrepreneurs can achieve through their businesses.

LO4 Be able to dispel key myths about small businesses.

LO5 Identify actions key to becoming a small business owner.

LO6 Understand how small businesses are important to our economy and your community.

LO7 Recognize the seven key strategies of the entrepreneurial way.

Focus on Small Business: Paul Scheiter, Hedgehog Leatherworks[1]

From a young age, Paul Scheiter had an insatiable passion for the outdoors. As a child he spent his free time exploring, hiking, and camping. As he grew older, Paul began to hone his skills as a minimalist, taking with him only the bare essentials necessary to live in the woods. He quickly learned that the most important tool for survival is a well-made, reliable, sharp knife. This single tool in the hands of a skilled person could be used to provide shelter, water, fire, and food—everything one needed to remain comfortable in the wild.

In 2005, Paul made his first significant investment in a knife. It was a $300 state-of-the-art tool that would handle just about any survival task under the sun. Upon purchasing the tool, he was shocked to discover this expensive knife came with a cheap plastic case (called a "sheath"). The knife rattled inside the sheath, which made noise, dulled the sharp edge, and was uncomfortable to carry. Ultimately the sheath broke while Paul was hiking, and he lost the knife.

After this bad experience, Paul determined to make a better product. He sought the guidance of a former St. Louis County police officer, Bill Shoemake, who had become a master leathersmith in his retirement. Bill helped Paul design a leather sheath that was far superior in fit, finish, strength, and comfort. After benefiting from Bill's mentorship through the early stages of learning his craft, Paul was inspired to share his product with the world.

Paul launched his business, Hedgehog Leatherworks, from his dorm room at Saint Louis University (SLU), while simultaneously declaring his major in entrepreneurship. He connected with the faculty and with the university's network of entrepreneurs to absorb as much business knowledge as possible. By finding great mentors, Paul built and implemented a plan for growing his business, refining it along the way through various business plan competitions. Eventually, Paul won second place in the Global Student Entrepreneurship Awards, a worldwide competition for full-time college students who run full-time businesses.

Today Hedgehog Leatherworks is the world's leader in producing high-end knife sheaths. Paul's products are the top choice of many elite military operatives, are in wide use by expert survival instructors, and are the prized possessions of many people who appreciate "plain old" American craftsmanship. Paul keeps his finger on his community through social media and develops new concepts through the direct input of his consumer base. You can learn more about Paul and his company at **www.hedgehogleatherworks.com.**

Following the motto Paul learned at SLU to "Do well. Do good," he continues to give back, teaching and mentoring students at Saint Louis University, working with the outdoor community, and guiding young entrepreneurs around the country.

Since 1998, the Global Student Entrepreneur Awards, a program founded at the John Cook School of Business at Saint Louis University, has honored outstanding undergraduates who juggle a course load as a student and run their own businesses at the same time. Visit **www.gsea.org** for more details on this year's application process, information on past winners, and access to entrepreneurial resources.

DISCUSSION QUESTIONS

1. Do you think Paul was originally thinking about starting a business when he made his first sheath?
2. What drove Paul to start a business of his own?
3. How important were contacts and connections to the growth of Paul's business?
4. Do you think Paul would credit his planned approach with the success of his business? What is your own opinion?

Starting an Entrepreneurial Small Business: Four Key Ideas

small business
Involves 1–50 people and has its owner managing the business on a day-to-day basis.

self-efficacy
A person's belief in his or her ability to achieve a goal.

Paul's story makes a simple point—you can start a **small business**, and there are ways to help you be a success at it. Consider the four key things that Paul did right:

1. **Believe that you can do this:** Paul's belief in himself and what needed to be done to make a better sheath powered his efforts. That belief in yourself is called **self-efficacy**, and learning how to start a business in this class and from this book will help you build it for yourself.[2] Those who have belief in themselves and in the passion of their beliefs are more likely to keep at it until they succeed.
2. **Planning + Action = Success:** A plan without action is futile. Actions without plans are usually wasted. Success comes from having the right sort of plan to get you to the right actions as quickly as possible. Like Paul, those who plan and act are the ones who most often succeed.[3]
3. **Help Helps:** Successful entrepreneurs learn—from other entrepreneurs, from experts in their chosen field, from potential customers, or even from their professors![4] Skill Module 1.1 will help you find some of the best sources of help on the Web. Remember, those who get help succeed bigger and more often.
4. **Do well. Do Good:** In the long run, you will depend on partners, investors, employees, customers, and neighbors. If you always remember, as Paul has, to do good for others as you try to do well in your business, you'll feel better about your business and life, and those around you will too.[5]

entrepreneur
A person who owns or starts an organization, such as a business.

Entrepreneurial Small Business believes in the power of those four ideas, and we'll help you understand each of them and how to use them to make your entrepreneurial dreams come true. There are literally millions of those entrepreneurial dreams out there because there are so many ways to become an **entrepreneur**.

SKILL MODULE 1.1

The Small Business Online Scavenger Hunt

It can be mind-boggling to discover how much material is on the Web ready to help aspiring entrepreneurs. To help you get a feel for what is out there, we have put together a Web Scavenger Hunt focusing on key information. In a few cases like NFIB.org you may have to register, but all registrations for Web sites listed here are free. Along the way you will get to peruse some of the "best of the best" entrepreneurship information on the Web.

1. Which two entrepreneurship magazines have a section dedicated to franchising right on the home page? Your choices: **www.inc.com**, **www.fastcompany.com**, **www.businessweek.com/small-business**, **www.entrepreneur.com**.
2. If you wanted to find stories about business in Albuquerque (or run the name of a business from there to see what they have done), which site would give you the biggest selection of local stories? **www.bizjournals.com**, **www.usatoday.com/money/smallbusiness**, **www.wsj.com** (*The Wall Street Journal*).

3. Several sources have information categorized by industry, but if you want to stay compliant with the laws and regulations for an industry, which is your best online bet? **www.bizjournals.com**, **www.business.gov**, **www.sba.gov**.
4. Which of the following offer a free business planner link on their home page? **business.usa.gov**, **www.sba.gov**, **www.entrepreneur.com**, **www.startupbusinessschool.com**.
5. Which of the following offer free downloadable business forms clickable from the More section of their home page? **www.usatoday.com/money/smallbusiness**, **www.entrepreneur.com**, **www.sba.gov**.
6. Which site has relevant small business information organized by zipcode? **www.nfib.org**, **www.sba.gov**, **www.inc.com**.
7. Who offers online videos about small business topics? **www.inc.com**, **www.itsyourbiz.com**, **www.usatoday.com/money/smallbusiness**, **www.sba.gov**.
8. Which of the following sites would connect you to answers from the nation's largest surveys of current business owners? **www.sba.com**, **www.bizstats.com**, **www.411sbfacts.com**.
9. You can search for patents for free at **www.google.com/patents** or **www.uspto.gov**. Which will also let you search for trademarks?
10. If you want to find out what the profit margins are for businesses in the restaurant industry, which site would give you the answer? **www.sba.gov**, **www.entrepreneur.com**, **www.bizstats.com**.

By the time you have checked out these sites, you will be up to speed on some of the largest and most credible sets of free, high-quality small business information available today.

Entrepreneurs Are Everywhere

In addition to Paul, the United States had 14.7 million other entrepreneurs in 2010 according to the last count made by the U.S. **Small Business Administration** (SBA).[6] What were they doing? Just about everything! Entrepreneurs could be found in just about every type of work there is, literally in hundreds of **occupations**. In fact, there are occupations composed mostly of entrepreneurs. Table 1.1 shows the 10 occupations with the largest numbers of entrepreneurs as well as the 10 occupations with the highest percentages of entrepreneurs.

LO1 Understand the scope of small business in the United States.

Small Business Administration
A part of the U.S. government, which provides support and advocacy for small businesses.

occupation
The type of activity a person does regularly for pay.

TABLE 1.1 The Top 10 Occupations For Entrepreneurs[7]

Top 10 Occupations with the Highest Numbers of Entrepreneurs		Top 10 Occupations with the Highest Percentage of Entrepreneurs (percent)	
Owner-managers	1,613,811	Animal breeders	100
Farmers	920,920	Funeral service managers	90.7
Retailers	752,138	Farmers and ranchers	85.4
Carpenters	487,809	Chiropractors	80.3
Child care workers	395,271	Podiatrists	78.4
Construction workers	693,894	Model and pattern makers	70.2
Wholesalers	377,337	Optometrists	66.9
Hairstylists	360,050	Medical practitioners	65.9
Real estate agents	333,583	Dentists	63.9
Drivers	322,512	Entertainers and athletes	60.6

Source: U.S. Census Bureau, Current Population Survey, March 2012, custom computation using DataFerret by Jerome Katz.

Entrepreneurs can be found in nearly every line of work there is. Into what occupation would your business put you?

goods or services
The tangible things (goods) or intangible commodities (services) created for sale.

firm
An organization that sells to or trades with others.

Notice that while there are entrepreneur-rich occupations that require college and even graduate school, there are also occupations popular with entrepreneurs with very basic entry requirements. What is most important here is finding something you want to do. When you decide on what your business is going to be, you are choosing your occupation. As the entrepreneur, you may be the owner of the business, but your occupation will depend on what type of **goods or services** you and your **firm** are producing. So the owner of an online store is a retailer, while the owner of a construction firm will be a construction manager. Paul is a leather manufacturer because Hedgehog Leatherworks makes the leather sheaths he sells online. Whatever you want to do, there is probably a way to do it as an entrepreneur.

Michael Dell is well known now as the CEO of Dell Computer, a major industry leader in PC production. Before his success, though, Dell spearheaded at least three other much smaller businesses. What factors do you think led to Dell's decision to expand his earlier ventures and eventually to his successful capturing of the PC market?

novelty
Characterized by being different or new.

imitative
Characterized by being like or copying something that already exists.

self-employed
Working for yourself.

founders
People who create or start new businesses.

franchise
A prepackaged business bought, rented, or leased from a company called a *franchisor.*

buyers
People who purchase an existing business.

heir
A person who becomes an owner through inheriting or being given a stake in a family business.

small and medium enterprise
The international term for small businesses.

independent small businesses
A business owned by an individual or small group.

owner-managed firms
A business run by the individual who owns it.

Truly entrepreneurial businesses are characterized by **novelty**, in their products, services, or business models. Small businesses, on the other hand, are **imitative** in nature, with most small firms doing what other firms do, with only slight variations. But when we think about the people who start firms for the first time, the situations they face are situations of novelty. So whether they start the successor to Amazon.com or the pizzeria on the corner, the person who starts a business is living the life of the entrepreneur. We recognize this distinction and address the challenges facing entrepreneurs, while focusing on the small businesses they plan to create or enter.

In *Entrepreneurial Small Business* we use the popular broad definition of *entrepreneur*[8]—anyone who owns a business is an entrepreneur. This, of course, means anyone who is a small business owner is an entrepreneur.[9] It also means that the **self-employed**, anyone who works for himself or herself instead of for others, is also an entrepreneur. According to the Census Bureau, there were about 14.7 million self-employed people in 2010. Within the population of entrepreneurs, it is sometimes useful to split out certain groups. One of these is **founders**, the people who start a business, whether it is one of their own devising, or a **franchise**, which is a prepackaged business you buy or lease from a franchisor. Other groups consist of **buyers**, those who purchase an existing business, or of **heirs**, those who inherit or are given a stake in the family business. These roles deal with the entry stage of the business from the perspective of the entrepreneur. After entry, another role emerges, that of the owner-manager, the role in which most entrepreneurs spend their working lives. Throughout this text the terms *small business owner, entrepreneur*, and *self-employed* are used interchangeably. When founders or buyers or postentry owner-managers are discussed, we specify which one is the focus.

The Many Types of Entrepreneurial Small Businesses

LO2 Differentiate between small businesses and high-growth ventures.

You might be surprised to know that even with 14.7 million entrepreneurs out there, the number of firms is even greater—27.3 million in 2010![10] These firms are called many different things, such as **small and medium enterprise** (SME), **independent small businesses**, or **owner-managed firms**. However they are labeled, there are more firms than entrepreneurs because many

serial entrepreneurs
People who open multiple businesses throughout their career.

entrepreneurs become **serial entrepreneurs**,[11] by starting additional businesses after their first one. As we will see a bit further into the chapter, this enormous population of small businesses is one of the major forces in the U.S. economy. But for now, just realize that you can pursue many dreams as an entrepreneur. No one is limiting you to just one. And after your first business, there is no telling how far you can go. Consider a 9-year-old in Texan named Michael.

Michael started selling collectible stamps through the mail.[12] He typed his catalog one key at a time since he had never learned to type, and he made $2,000. His next business was selling newspaper subscriptions by phone from home; he made $18,000 on this venture. His third business was reselling IBM PCs from his dorm room at the University of Texas at a time when IBM was trying to limit sales to official IBM dealers like Sears and IBM's own personal computer stores.[13] It was Michael's fourth business, selling PCs, that we know today as Dell Computer. The 9-year-old was Michael Dell.

Michael Dell's four businesses point up the difference between small businesses and high-growth ventures. Both may be small when they start. However, small businesses are usually intended to remain small, generally a size that the owner feels comfortable controlling personally. For Michael Dell, his stamp, newspaper, and IBM PC resale businesses were designed to be small-scale operations that he could handle alone. He did everything himself, and he worked when he wanted to. The businesses were fairly conventional, with dozens or even hundreds of competitors all imitating one another.

High-growth ventures start small but are intended to grow rapidly, often requiring a team of partners or managers to handle the growth. When Dell got serious about the upgraded PC business, he created a company and started hiring others to help out. He moved from his dorm room to a commercial location, kept open regular hours, and started thinking about putting together a much bigger operation. That much bigger operation is the Dell Computer known worldwide today. While the computer business as a whole was established, Dell's approach to assembly from highly standardized (and therefore low-cost) parts was fairly revolutionary, as was his use of mail-order and later telephone and Web-based ordering. In his fourth business, Dell led the industry because of his **innovativeness**, and others imitated him.

innovativeness
Refers to how important a role new ideas, products, services, processes, or markets play in an organization.

The differences between small businesses and high-growth ventures aren't just semantic. They're fundamental. Table 1.2 shows the differences between small businesses and high-growth ventures.

TABLE 1.2 Difference between Small Business and High-Growth Ventures

	Small Businesses	High-Growth Ventures
Preferred funding source	Owner's own money	Other people's money
When the firm's in trouble	Cut costs	Sell more
What's more important	Sales	Marketing
Personal control preference	Retain autonomy	Involve key others
Focus	Efficiency	Effectiveness
Metastrategy	Imitation	Novelty
External control preference	Control firm	Control market
Grow	When necessary	When possible
Human resources	Personalize	Professionalize
Acceptance	Personal validation	External legitimacy
What limits growth	Loss of control	Market response
Delegation orientation	Delegation is difficult	Delegation is essential

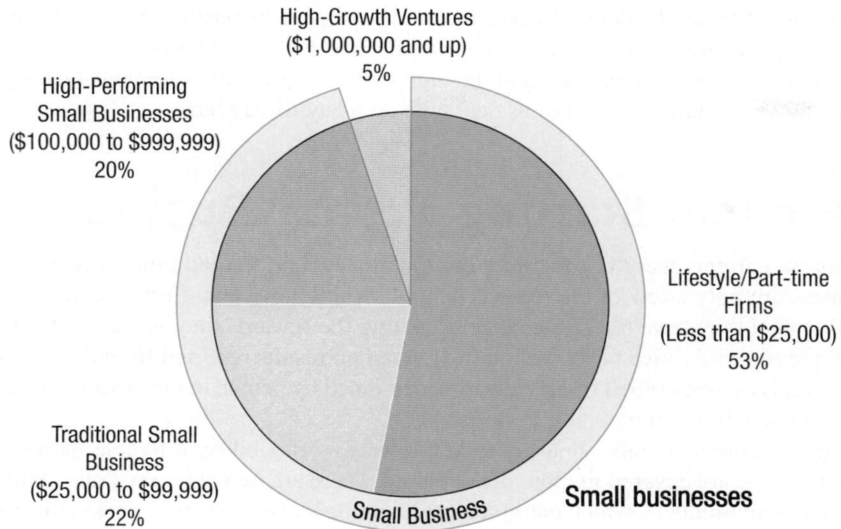

FIGURE 1.1

Types of Firms

Entrepreneurs and Firm Growth Strategies

When creating his stamp business as a child and Dell Computer as a young adult, Michael Dell had different goals and ambitions for each of these firms. As you can imagine, that kind of broad approach, called the **overall growth strategy**, represents another driver of the variety of entrepreneurship. The overall growth strategy describes the kind of business the owner (or owners) would like to have, from the perspective of how fast and to what level they would like the firm to grow. There are four generic growth strategies that account for nearly all businesses. They are:

- **Lifestyle or part-time firms**: These typically have sales of $25,000 a year or less, which provides enough profit or salary to supplement an income but usually not enough on which to live. These businesses start and stay very small, often operating seasonally or when the owner wants to work in the business. Growth in these firms tends to quickly level off after the owners operate long enough to learn the basics of making money in their industry and setting. About 53-percent of all small businesses fall into this category including Michael Dell's first three businesses. (See Figure 1.1.)
- **Traditional small businesses**: These are the smallest full-time businesses, with schedules defined by customer, not owner, needs. Most often, these are one-site businesses with sales of between $25,000 and $100,000. Growth levels off after operations settle into a consistent, money-making pattern, generating enough income to provide a living for the owner and family. Around 22 percent of small businesses fall into this category including Paul Scheiter's when he started out.
- **High-performing small businesses**: These tend to level off after success defined by sales of between $100,000 and $1,000,000, depending on the industry. These firms grow at rates more like 5 to 15 percent a year, adding employees, and often growing through multiple locations and higher levels of professionalization, in order to maximize their profitability over a long term, while reaching a plateau that lets them remain manageably small. About 20 percent of businesses fall into this category, including Paul Scheiter's business.
- **High-growth ventures**: These aim to achieve growth rates of 25 percent or more a year, with sales of more than $1 million. These firms aim to become big businesses and pursue high levels of professionalization and external funding. Such firms represent about 5 percent of all businesses.

overall growth strategy
One of four general ways to position a business based on the rate and level of growth entrepreneurs anticipate for their firm.

lifestyle or part-time firm
A small business primarily intended to provide partial or subsistence financial support for the existing lifestyle of the owner, most often through operations that fit the owner's schedule and way of working.

traditional small business
A firm intended to provide a living income to the owner, and operating in a manner and on a schedule consistent with other firms in the industry and market.

high-performing small business
A firm intended to provide the owner with a high income through sales or profits superior to those of the traditional small business.

high-growth venture
A firm started with the intent of eventually going public, following the pattern of growth and operations of a big business.

main street businesses
A popular term for small businesses reflecting the idea that these are the kinds of firms you would expect to find on the main street of a typical American city, and are the opposite of big businesses or "Wall Street" businesses.

Entrepreneurial Small Business focuses on the 95 percent of businesses outside of the high-growth sector. These are what are often called **main street businesses** and include the lifestyle firms, the traditional small businesses, and the high-performing small businesses that represent the businesses most of us start and most of us deal with on a day-to-day basis.

Rewards for Starting a Small Business

LO3 Discover the rewards entrepreneurs can achieve through their businesses.

Why become an entrepreneur? If you said, "For the money," or, "To do things my way," you'd be right, but these are only a few of the reasons behind owning your own firm. We know that people go where they feel they have the best chance of getting the rewards they value most. The kinds of rewards people report are also fairly well known based on results reported from the Panel Study of Entrepreneurial Dynamics (PSED). The rewards mentioned by people in the process of starting their own firms are listed in Figure 1.2.

Nearly all entrepreneurs talk about three key rewards—flexibility, a livable income, and personal growth. These are covered in more detail below. There are two other rewards—building great wealth and creating products, which entrepreneurs mention more often than working people in general. There are also rewards that entrepreneurs mention *less often* than working people in general. These are social rewards, like the respect or admiration of others, or power over others, and family rewards, like continuing a family tradition in business. Those items are marked with an asterisk (*) in Figure 1.2. These "go it alone" tendencies are probably a good thing, because they help entrepreneurs keep some distance from others and pursue what they think is right.

growth rewards
What people get from facing and beating challenges.

The three most popular types of rewards for small business owners are growth, flexibility, and income. **Growth rewards** are what people get from facing and beating or learning from challenges. Self-professed computer nerd Marc Fleury's first venture went under with the dot-com bust.[15] His second business, The JBoss Group, was built around the challenges of going it alone financially while outperforming and outlasting his first venture. JBoss, which sells programming and support

FIGURE 1.2

Rewards New Entrepreneurs Seek through Small Business[14]

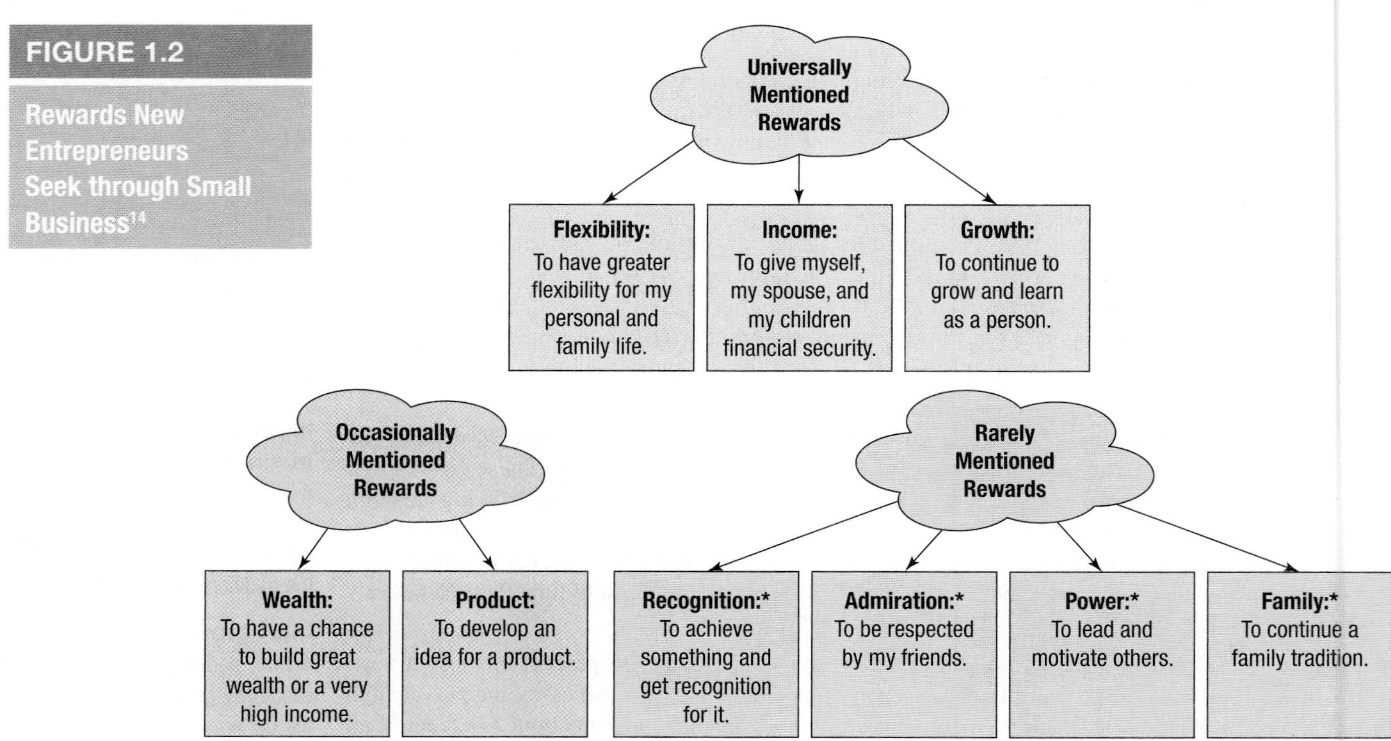

* *Items entrepreneurs mention much less often than people in general.*

services, was successful from day one, and was eventually sold to Red Hat. Until then it was entirely self-funded.

Income rewards refer to the money made from owning your own business. For more than three-quarters of entrepreneurs, this means seeking to match or slightly better the income you had before you started your own business. Only one entrepreneur in four says that she or he is seeking high income through her or his business. But entrepreneurs are looking in the right place. More than 75 percent of the millionaires in the United States are entrepreneurs.[16] Two-thirds of the millionaires are business owners, and one-third are self-employed professionals like doctors, lawyers, or therapists.

income rewards
The money made by owning one's own business.

Flexibility rewards are perhaps the most rapidly growing type of reward. They refer to the ability of business owners to structure their lives in the way that best suits their needs. When Cyndi Crews was laid off from her work as an Information Technology resources manager of a large corporation, she bought a franchise of Schooley Mitchell Telecom Consultants. Today she advises companies on how to get the most from their telephone systems. She runs the business from her home in Lumberton, Texas, where she is able to set her own work schedule. This ensures her the flexibility she needs to take time off to be with her young son and husband.[17] Another variant of this is pursuing spiritual or religious goals through business. For example, Noah's Ark, a Kosher deli with branches in Teaneck, New Jersey and New York City closes from 4 P.M. on Friday until 6:30 P.M. or so on Saturday night in observance of the Jewish Sabbath.

flexibility rewards
The ability of business owners to structure life in the way that suits their needs best.

Myths about Small Businesses

LO4 Dispel key myths about small businesses.

Here is a sobering truth, while 56 percent of U.S. youth 15–25 years old polled in 2010 expressed an interest in becoming entrepreneurs, only 10 percent were doing anything to actually get a business started.[18] The challenges of small business scare off or derail people. For years potential entrepreneurs have mentioned problems like these:

- Not enough financing.
- You can't start businesses during a recession.
- To make profits, you need to make something.
- If you fail, you can never try again.
- Students don't have the skills to start a business.

Over the past 10 years small business experts in academia and government have studied small business and potential entrepreneurs and learned that a lot of the challenges scaring people away from small business are the stuff of urban legends. Let's look at these five problems with the latest information.

1. **Not enough financing:** A May 2012 survey of entrepreneurs found getting financing or credit was eighth on a list of 10 possible worries, with only 3 percent expressing that concern.[19] The SBA reports that bank financing is up from its low in early 2009, and the same is true for funding from family, friends, and angels.[20] New sources of financing like **crowdfunding** sites Kickstarter.com and Rockethub.com are providing funding, while **bootstrapping**[21] techniques like making your local coffee shop into your virtual office are being discovered and recommended by entrepreneurs to one another as often as phone apps.
2. **You can't start businesses during a recession:** Businesses started in recessions start lean—no fancy offices, no bonuses. That means they learn from the start how to do more with less, which makes them better able to handle future times of scarcity and trouble. According to a 2009 *BusinessWeek* report, seven of the ten largest companies in the 2009 Fortune 500 were started in recessions. Among famous businesses that started in recessions are GE (1876), Allstate (1931), Krispy Kreme (1937), Trader Joe's (1957), Southwest Airlines (1967), FedEx (1973), CNN (1980), and Wynn Resorts (2002). In 2002, in the wake of the world dramatic drop in airline traffic following 9/11, worldwide 21 airlines were started and 16 were still going in mid-2009.[22]
3. **To make profits, you need to make something:** Again in 2011, amid a recession, Sageworks reported that of the 10 most profitable industries for small businesses, 9 were services

crowdfunding
Funding a business online through the collective involvement of others who provide donations, loans, or investments.

bootstrapping
Using low-cost or free techniques to minimize your cost of doing business.

like dentists, tax preparers, mining support services, credit counselors, insurance brokers, and legal and health practitioners. Whereas getting a DDS or MD degree takes years and tens of thousands of dollars, bookkeeping and credit counseling require little specialized training.[23]

4. **If you fail, you can never try again:** If you close a business and pay off your debts, you did not fail. If you learned how to do better next time, then you can honestly say you have paid (in dollars and hours) for another piece of your education. A large number of today's successful entrepreneurs had failures along the way. Today vegetarians who frequent restaurants are thankful for Paul Wenner's Gardenburgers, but few realize that Paul learned the food business by owning a restaurant that eventually went out of business. Other famous failures include Ray Kroc (famous for McDonald's, failed at real estate), Henry Ford (two failed auto companies before making Ford), and the founders of California Pizza Kitchens, Rick Rosenfield and Larry Flax, who previously failed at screenwriting, a regular Italian restaurant, and a mobile skateboard park.[24]
5. **Students (or moms or some other group) don't have the skills to start a business:**[25] It would be hard for an undergraduate to open a medical practice (watch *Doogie Howser, MD*, on Hulu.com if you want to see what that this might have been like), but lots of students have useful business skills. If you are a student, you probably have a good idea what other students want to buy or have. That is the start of a retail business with a student market. If you have negotiating skills, the sky is the limit in retail and wholesaling, especially for products you already understand (T-shirts, energy drinks, backpacks, MP3 players, textbooks, etc.). In fact, you may have high-level but undocumented skills in developing Web sites or programming (like the founders of Facebook or Yahoo!). Competitions like the Global Student Entrepreneur Awards (www.gsea.org) or the NFIB Young Entrepreneurs Awards (www.nfib.com/YoungEntrepreneurFoundation.aspx) showcase dozens of highly successful students who started and grew their businesses. Any mompreneur has managed a household, negotiated for family purchases, and solved thousands of problems ranging from broken equipment to angry family members. It was more than enough to get Mary Kay's Mary Kay Ash, Body Shop's Anita Roddick, or Baby Einstein's Julie Aigner Clark started in small businesses that grew to be big ones. The same is true for any group—second career entrepreneurs include Josie Natori (investment banking to Natori lingerie), Jim Koch (consulting to brewing Samuel Adams beer), or George Foreman (boxer to entrepreneur).

George Foreman: boxer to entrepreneur.

6. **Ninety percent of all new businesses fail within two years:** This statement is wrong in two major ways. First, the percentage is wrong. Studies show that 69 percent of businesses are still going after two years, 51 percent are still going at 5 years, 34 percent make it past 10 years and 25 percent survive 15 years. Second, looking at the businesses that close, the vast majority close but don't fail. Only one firm in three that closes was considered financially unsuccessful by its owner.[26]

Myths like these hold back many potential entrepreneurs. Knowing the truth is a powerful way to keep up your motivation for the undeniably tough work of starting your own business. When you encounter doomsayers, check out the facts at reputable sites like www.sba.gov or www.411sbfacts.com or in entrepreneur-focused magazines like *Inc., Fast Company, BusinessWeek/SmallBiz,* or *Entrepreneur.* There you will find the facts you need, and the support and advice that underlies the idea that help helps.

Getting Started Now: Entry Competencies

LO5 Identify actions key to becoming a small business owner.

There are a million things you *could* do to start a business, but which ones are best? Sometimes the answer will come to you in the form of an opportunity or offer, and sometimes you'll need to take the first steps yourself. In order to start a business, you need four elements to come

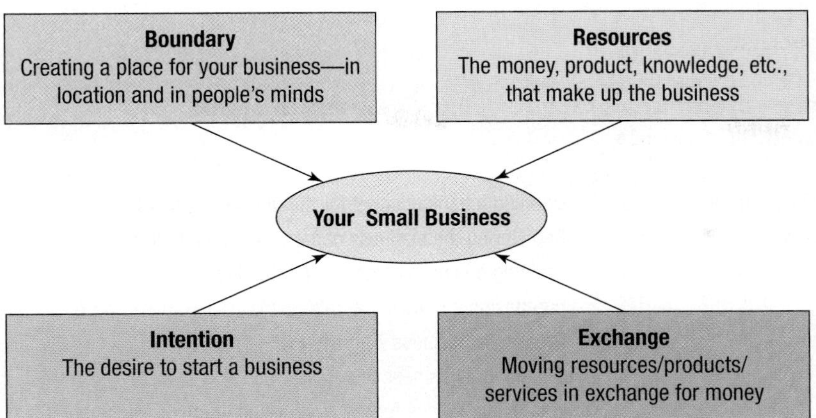

FIGURE 1.3

Four Elements Needed to Get Your Business Started (BRIE)

together—boundary, resources, intention, and exchange.[27] This is referred to as the BRIE model, as shown in Figure 1.3.

A business needs the benefits of a *boundary*—something that sets it up as a firm, and sets it off from the buying or selling or bartering we all do occasionally. A boundary can be something as simple as a business name or government registration, a phone or e-mail address dedicated to the business, or a specific location for the firm in a home, commercial space, or even on the Internet. Having a boundary gives you a place to locate and protect the resources you've gathered for the business. *Resources* include the product or service to be offered, informational resources on markets and running a business, financial resources, and human resources such as your own time to devote to the business, or that of others working with you or for you.

Intention is the desire to start a business and is the most frequently occurring element of the BRIE model. Those 56 percent of young Americans who think about starting their own business are expressing their intentions. *Exchange* is also needed. This refers to moving resources, goods, or service to others, in exchange for money or other resources. If the firm doesn't exchange with its environment, there is no "business" taking place.

BRIE Self-Assessment

SKILL MODULE 1.2

The BRIE (boundary-resources-intention-exchange) model is a proven[28] and handy way to think about the activities necessary to get a business started. It also is a model that will come up again in later chapters of the book. At this point in the course, how many of the items have you done so far to get your business started the right way?

The complete list of BRIE activities is given in the following table. Look at the BRIE list and check off actions you've taken already. Next to each item are parentheses which tell you in which chapter that topic is covered, in case you want to skip ahead to see how we suggest you do it. This exercise can help you think through which chapters are **most** important to your preparing your business.

The list can also be scored as a checklist. Go through the list and check off which items you have already done in starting a business. Then write in the first column how many of each BRIE category you've done so far. Once you are done, you can see how to score the BRIE checklist at the end of the Skill Module.

(Continued)

BRIE Checklist

Boundary—creating a place for your business in space and in people's minds		
Number of boundary actions done	☐	Opening a bank account for the business (Ch. 14)
	☐	Registering the business name with the state (Ch. 18)
	☐	Creating business cards and/or stationery (Ch. 10)
	☐	Purchasing a domain name (Ch. 11)
	☐	Creating a business Web site (Ch. 11)
	☐	Obtaining a business telephone line
	☐	Identifying a place for the business at home or elsewhere (Ch. 11)
Resources—the things that make up the business, like money, products, knowledge, etc.		
Number of resource actions done	☐	Organizing a start-up team (Ch. 19)
	☐	Obtaining copyright, patents, trademarks (Ch. 18)
	☐	Purchasing raw materials, inventory, supplies (Ch. 16)
	☐	Acquiring major items (equipment, facilities, property) (Ch. 16)
	☐	Hiring employees and managers (who do not share ownership) (Ch. 19)
	☐	Participating in classes or workshops on starting a business (If you are taking a small business course, you can check this item.)
	☐	Participating in programs that help new businesses get established like SIFE, CEO or SBIDA (on Web site)
Intention—demonstrating a determination to get the business going and for it to be successful		
Number of intention actions taken	☐	Thinking about the business (Ch. 4, 5 & 6)
	☐	Undertaking marketing and promotional efforts (Ch. 7 & 10)
	☐	Developing your product or service (Ch. 4 & 9)
	☐	Beginning your full-time commitment to the business (> 35 hrs/wk)
	☐	Preparing a business plan (Ch. 8)
	☐	Defining market opportunities (Ch. 4 & 12)
	☐	Developing projected financial statements (Ch. 7, 13 & 14)
Exchange—making investments in and sales from the business		
Number of exchange actions done	☐	Generating sales revenue (Ch. 10)
	☐	Arranging child care to work on business
	☐	Establishing credit with a supplier (Ch. 15)
	☐	Saving money to invest in the business (Ch. 13 & 15)
	☐	Investing money in the business (Ch. 15)
	☐	Seeking funds from financial institutions or others (Ch. 15)
	☐	Seeking funds from spouse or household partner (Ch. 15)
	☐	Seeking funds from current employer (Ch. 15)

The scoring is straightforward. At a minimum you need to have taken at least one action in each of the BRIE categories[29] to successfully start and grow a business. Business survival rates increase with the number of items checked across the different categories.[30] So people who can check three or four items in each BRIE category are more likely to have surviving and growing firms than those who check only one item per category. Having a BRIE category with nothing checked indicates that it is likely that something major is being overlooked, so the business is likely to fail. It is also important to balance BRIE activities. For example, having lots of boundary activities done and only a few exchange ones is likely to lead to an unbalanced approach to business and a lesser chance of survival.

The BRIE model factors outline the activities that need to take place to get a firm going. Skill Module 1.2 is a self-assessment that can help you recognize what important steps you have taken to start your business, and what remains to be done.

The BRIE model can help you deal with one of the biggest hurdles to starting a business. According to the experts, the biggest problem is simply inaction as mentioned earlier. Stanford management professors Gerry Salancik and Bob Sutton[31] say that even when people know taking action would be in their own best interests, most people tend to procrastinate, sticking with inaction or doing familiar things that have not worked. Salancik and Sutton recommend taking small steps toward a goal as an easy way to start. The BRIE checklist gives you the kind of small steps that can make all the difference. Consider coming back to this checklist periodically to help assess your preparations for business and determine what you still need to do. Taking lots of small steps is a sure way to achieve your goals.

Small Business and the Economy

LO6 Recognize how small businesses are important to our economy and your community.

We've talked about why small business is important for the individuals for whom income, growth, and flexibility were among the most important rewards of ownership. But you also need to know that small business is vitally important to your community and even to our economy. Part of this comes from the new things small businesses contribute to the economy, particularly new jobs and innovations, as well as the basics that small businesses provide for all of us—jobs, taxes, and products or services.

New Jobs

Since the 1970s big business has cut tens of millions of jobs. In the meantime, small business has added tens of millions of jobs. In the latest statistics, small businesses created 65 percent of the new jobs created since 1994.[32] When the Census Bureau looked more closely at the figures, it concluded that small business start-ups in the first two years of operation accounted for virtually all the net new jobs in America.[33] Small business *is* the engine of job generation, but it is important for existing jobs, too. Small businesses employ more than half of all Americans, providing wages, salaries, and the taxes those working people pay the government.[34]

One reason small businesses are a key employer is because they are more willing than most large businesses to offer jobs to people with atypical work histories or needs, like people new to the workforce, people with uneven employment histories, and people looking for part-time work. These employment issues are at the core of what makes small business attractive to local and state governments.

Innovations

Small business is a key element of every nation's economy because it offers a very special environment in which the new can come into being. Austrian economist Joseph Schumpeter labeled this process **creative destruction**.[35] It refers to the way that newly created goods, services, or firms can hurt existing goods, services, or firms. For example, when a new restaurant opens in your neighborhood, people flock to it to find out what it's like. This helps the new restaurant, but it also causes the other restaurants in the area to lose business, at least temporarily. One of the most

creative destruction
The way that newly created goods, services, or firms can hurt existing goods, services, or firms.

Before starting Apple Computer, HP employee Steve Wozniak and his friend Steve Jobs offered their personal computer design to Steve's employer, but HP turned it down. If you came up with an idea while working for someone else, why might you offer it to your boss first?

famous examples of creative destruction is the personal computer, which started as a hobby that big business spurned.

Apple founders Steve Jobs and Steve Wozniak offered the first Apple personal computer to Wozniak's employers at 36 Hewlett-Packard (HP) firms.[36] They rejected the offer, saying that personal computers would never be a success, but they gave Wozniak permission to go ahead on his own. Apple made the personal computer popular and paved the way for IBM PCs and the personal computer explosion. That explosion redrew the lines of the entire computer industry, but it also created tremendous new wealth, utility, and innovation. Big business often has trouble with innovations that would eat away at existing business, but small businesses are more likely to see new revenues in innovations.

Why do so many innovations come from small business? Remember that most people going into small business mention flexibility as a key reward, such as the flexibility to do the work they think is important. Small business owners are more free of the judgments and social constraints of workers elsewhere.[37] To give you an idea how much more powerful innovation is in small business, the U.S. Small Business Administration reports that among firms that hold one or more patents, small businesses generate 16.5 times the number of patents per employee than do big businesses. And the patents produced in those small businesses are twice as likely to be among the top 1 percent of all patents cited by others.[38] That citation is a measure of the importance of the invention.

In the end, the freedom small business gives owners to pursue and perfect their dream creates the innovations from which we all benefit—not just major inventions like the personal computer, but whole classes of products such as snowboards (21-year-old Dimitrije Milovich in 1969),[39] earmuffs (15-year-old Chester Greenwood in 1858)[40], computer-controlled telephone systems (Krisztina Holly in 1992),[41] date rape drug testing coasters (Brian Glover, 35, and Francisco Guerra, 34, in 2002),[42] and Kitty Litter (Ed Lowe, 27 in 1947)[43] that were developed by innovative small business owners.

Think of the innovative contributions of small businesses in general and student-started small businesses in particular. Each group has made a tremendous difference in our industries, our economies, and our lives. Table 1.3 shows examples from both groups in seven different situations.

New Opportunities

People who own their own business are presented with tremendous opportunities—not only to improve their life and wealth, but also to help them move into and upward in the economy and society of the United States. The opportunities small business offers for getting into the economic mainstream of American life makes it attractive to people who foresee problems fitting into existing businesses—not only people with innovative ideas, but immigrants; people facing unusual schedules,

TABLE 1.3 Major Inventions from Small Businesses and Student-Started Businesses[44]

Where Innovation Is Used	Innovations from Small Businesses	Innovations from Student-Started Small Businesses
Medicine	Heart valves (Demetre Nicoloff)	Video laryngoscope (Aircraft Medical)
Business Processes	Assembly lines (Olds)	JIT PC assembly (Dell)
Computing Hardware	Supercomputers (Cray)	Home computers (Apple)
Computing Software	Relational databases (Oracle)	Social networking (Friendster, Facebook)
Everyday Technology	Photocopiers (Chester Carlson)	Google
Leisure	Outboard engines (Cameron Waterman)	Snowboards (Dimitrije Milovich)
Fashion	Gore-Tex (W. L. Gore)	Extreme custom nail polish (Dineh Mohajer)

demands, or limitations on their lives; and even people who need a second chance.[45] For many such people, small business *is* the best business opportunity.

Small businesses offer communities another type of opportunity—the opportunity to enjoy goods and services. Imagine a neighborhood or town without a grocery store or a pharmacy. In important ways, the town would not seem like a real community. A small grocery, drugstore, hardware store, or gas station might be able to use its low overhead and capacity to adapt to local needs (e.g., a grocery store stocking a lot of fishing supplies to appeal to visiting fishing enthusiasts) to make a profit where larger chain stores could not.[46] For a small town or a neighborhood to be able to stand on its own, it needs a variety of businesses.[47]

Small businesses provide unexpected opportunities to large businesses and entrepreneurial high-growth firms. High-growth ventures and big businesses are like a giant boat, and where the boat sails, the economy sails along too. But for the boat to work, it has to be supported by deep water. The ocean supporting the boat consists of the tens of millions of small businesses. Without small businesses offering supporting services or offering to subcontract at low cost to the high-growth ventures and big businesses or creating the kinds of communities where creative and entrepreneurial people like to live,[48] those economic boats would lose their buoyancy or profitability and sink like stones. For example, industry giant Procter & Gamble outsourced the making of Ivory and other bar soaps to a small Canadian company, Trillium Health Care Products,[49] saving millions of dollars a year. In addition, big business depends on small business as a source of key ideas for new products. You might think this means high-tech inventions, but there is a lot of money to be made from everyday inventions. Consider the Buffalo hot wings in the Small Business Insight box below.

SMALL BUSINESS INSIGHT

SUCCESS: MOTHER TERESSA AND BUFFALO HOT WINGS[50]

The Anchor Bar looks like a pretty run of the mill neighborhood bar and grill outside downtown Buffalo, New York, but this unassuming place is the home of a major food invention—the Buffalo hot wing. Back in 1964, the owners of the Anchor, Teressa and Frank Bellisimo, started splitting wings in half, broiling (and later frying) them, then covering them in a Tabasco-like sauce (Frank's, but no relation to Frank Bellisimo), and serving them with celery and blue cheese dressing for dipping. These came to be called "Buffalo hot wings" and became a local staple. And Teressa, who came up with the recipe, got the local name "Mother Teressa."

(Continued)

Home page of the Anchor Bar, which is the birthplace of a now widely known and wildly popular food item, the Buffalo Hot Wing. Anchor Bar & Restaurant.

As Buffalonians emigrated to warmer places, they reported missing the hot wings they grew up with, and so hot wings began to appear in other parts of the country. It was only a matter of time until franchised restaurants grew up around the concept, and today there are chains such as Buffalo Wild Wings, Wing Zone, Wingstop, and Winger's selling thousands of Buffalo hot wings and their variants. Even big business got into the act with the world's largest pizza chain, Domino's, selling its own version of Buffalo hot wings starting in 1992. Other big businesses benefiting from the innovation included big food companies like French's (which owns the Frank's Red Hot Sauce brand), making wing sauce, cooking kits, and recipe books. By 1995 Domino's was selling 10 million wings a week, and Pizza Hut valued the wing business nationally at an estimated $400 million. So it is easy to see how small business innovations can become an important source of opportunity for big business growth.

Two Aspects of Global Entrepreneurship

As important as entrepreneurship is in the United States, it is more important elsewhere. While in any given year about 10 percent of the workforce in the United States is self-employed or contemplating starting their own business, the rates in other parts of the world can be 50 percent or even 100 percent higher than in the United States. There is a pattern (see Figure 1.4) to which countries are likely to have high rates of entrepreneurship, and which will have lower rates.[51]

factor-driven economy
A nation where the major forces for jobs, revenues, and taxes come from farming or extractive industries like forestry, mining, or oil production.

efficiency-driven economy
A nation where industrialization is becoming the major force providing jobs, revenues, and taxes, and where minimizing costs while maximizing productivity (i.e. efficiency) is a major goal.

- In nations where there is little manufacturing, most industry relates to farming and extracting raw materials, such as mining and forestry. In these **factor-driven economies** such as Pakistan, Jamaica, and Venezuela, entrepreneurship is essential to helping build personal wealth and breaking the cycle of low-wage jobs, and entrepreneurship levels are very high.
- As economies develop and go beyond basic manufacturing to a more industrialized economy as is seen in countries such as Russia, Brazil, and China, it is called an **efficiency-driven economy**. In these nations, entrepreneurship becomes a key way to build the middle class, and a growing retail and wholesale sector grows alongside businesses serving the needs of large industrial concerns. Entrepreneurship levels in such economies are in the middle range.

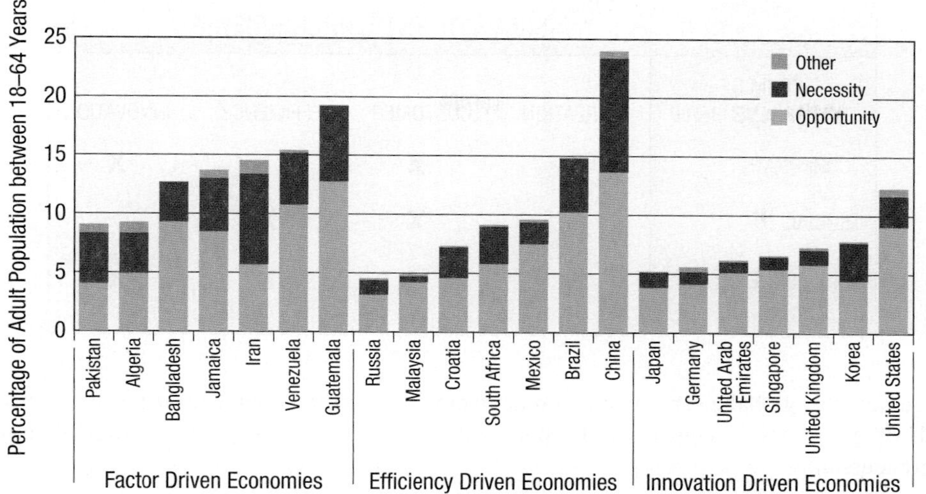

FIGURE 1.4

Early-Stage Entrepreneurial Activity for 21 Nations in 2011, by Phase of Economic Development

Source: Custom tabulation of 2011 GEM Adult Population Survey by Yana Litovsky

- **Innovation-driven economies** are focused on high-value-added manufacturing but is marked by a very large service sector, providing high-end services to not only the resident population, but also for export. Examples of such countries include Germany, the Republic of Korea, and the United States. Entrepreneurship levels in these countries average the lowest of the three types of economies.

innovation-driven economy
A nation where the major forces for jobs, revenues, and taxes come from high-value added production based on new ideas and technologies and from professional services based on higher education.

One other important difference across countries in Figure 1.4 is the amounts of two types of entrepreneurship. One type is based on entrepreneurs who are going into business to improve themselves financially, or to launch an improved product or service into the market. This is called **opportunity-driven entrepreneurship**. The other type is where the person becomes an entrepreneur because they do not see any workable prospects for getting employed by someone else. This is called **necessity-driven entrepreneurship**. As economies move from a factor-driven basis to an innovation-driven basis, the proportion of opportunity-driven entrepreneurship generally increases.[52]

opportunity-driven entrepreneurship
Creating a firm to improve one's income or a product or service.

necessity-driven entrepreneurship
Creating a firm as an alternative to unemployment.

The lesson here is that entrepreneurship is happening around the globe in virtually all types of economies, and as global trade (both face-to-face and Web-based) increases, the impact of global entrepreneurship will be increasingly faced by entrepreneurs and their firms everywhere.

The other aspect of global business relates to exporting. Originally, small business was synonymous with local business. The vast majority of firms sold in their home communities, and it was a very rare firm that sold nationally. Up through the beginning of the 20th century, it was rare for small businesses to sell in any other country.

That is no longer true today. Small businesses account for 33.7 percent of the value of all goods and services exported from the United States, and represent 98 percent of all exporting firms. According to the U.S. government there were 286,661 small business exporters in 2010, and the average amount each firm exported was $1,337,468.[53] Generally most of these firms export on the basis of personal ties. An entrepreneur trades with the country of his birth, ancestors, or prior experience. The key for such exporters are the personal ties which make exporting predictable and safe.[54]

Another approach that has grown dramatically in the past 15 years is using **ecommerce**, particularly auction sites like eBay, to handle global trade. The formal title for this is **virtual instant global entrepreneurship** (VIGE).[55] VIGE depends on using Web sites like eBay (for products) or eLance (for services) to quickly establish a global presence. Many of these VIGE sites offer procedures, services, and Web page templates which incorporate best practices for global trading. For example, eBay leads new sellers through the creation of seller and product descriptions found to be the most effective. eBay and eLance also organize the seller's accounts to handle international payments, shipping, insurance, and basic customer service issues. The VIGE site provides the assurance of honesty on the part of buyers and sellers, using rules, warrantees, and most of all, mutual ratings of buyers and sellers.

ecommerce
The general term for conducting business on the Internet.

virtual instant global entrepreneurship
A process that uses the Internet to quickly create businesses with a worldwide reach.

FIGURE 1.5

The Form and Focus of Entrepreneurship

FORM OF ENTREPRENEURSHIP	FOCUS OF ENTREPRENEURSHIP			
	CREATION	CUSTOMER	EFFICIENCY	INNOVATION
CORPORATE		X		X
SOCIAL	X	X	X	
INDEPENDENT	X	X	X	X

CSI entrepreneurship Acronym for the three forms of entrepreneurship, corporate, social and independent.

forms of entrepreneurship The settings in which the entrepreneurial effort takes place.

creation The entrepreneurial focus which looks at the making of new entities.

customer-focus The entrepreneurial focus which refers to being in tune with one's market.

efficiency The entrepreneurial focus which refers to doing the most work with the fewest resources.

innovation The entrepreneurial focus which looks at a new thing or a new way of doing things.

independent entrepreneurship The form of entrepreneurship in which a person or group own their own for-profit business.

corporate entrepreneurship The form of entrepreneurship which takes place in existing businesses around new products, services, or markets.

social entrepreneurship The form of entrepreneurship involving the creation of self-sustaining charitable and civic organizations, or for-profit organizations which invest significant profits in charitable activities.

Together, the global push for entrepreneurship in countries, and within those countries the growth of global trade, helped by the potential of ecommerce, is another powerful impact of entrepreneurship.

Beyond Small Business: CSI Entrepreneurship

The primary focus of *Entrepreneurial Small Business* is on people who plan to start a business of their own. These people are independent entrepreneurs, but they aren't the only type. Founders of social ventures are called social entrepreneurs, while entrepreneurs employed by others in existing companies are often called corporate entrepreneurs. Together, the three represent what might be called **CSI entrepreneurship** or the three **forms of entrepreneurship**.[56]

The three forms differ in which aspect of entrepreneurship they focus:[57] **creation** which looks at the making of new entities, **customer-focus** which refers to being in-tune with your market, **efficiency** which refers to doing the most work with the fewest resources, and **innovation** which looks at a new thing or a new way of doing things. In **independent entrepreneurship** (what we have discussed as small business), all four elements are essential, and that is what makes small business so important as the role model for the other forms. The relation of the three forms of entrepreneurship to the different focuses are shown in Figure 1.5.

In **corporate entrepreneurship**, the focus is typically on customer-focus and innovation, bringing new products or services to market, or opening up new markets to your firm. Famous examples of corporate entrepreneurship include the creation of new brands like Apple's iPod or GM's green energy services. **Social entrepreneurship** on the other hand involves creating new charitable and civic organizations which are financially self-sufficient like Bangladesh's Grameen Bank (which won the 2006 Nobel Peace Prize), or for-profit companies that use much of their profit to fund charities, like Ben & Jerry's. In social entrepreneurship, the key elements involve creation, efficiency, and customer-focus, since few social ventures have a lot of funding. Independent entrepreneurship involves all four elements since creating a new business around a product, service, or market requires creation as well as innovation, and since few start-ups are well funded, efficiency is at a premium, while customer focus is essential to getting new sales and cash into the firm.

You might notice that profit or wealth is not mentioned as a focus. That is because the goal of any type of entrepreneurship is to achieve some sort of gain, and those gains are not always measured entirely using money. For example, innovation-driven entrepreneurs are often as interested in having their idea used or known—called **mindshare**—as making money. Customer-focused entrepreneurs often will accept lower profits if it means keeping customers happy. Often creation-driven entrepreneurs will sacrifice profits by reinvesting them to keep the creation going. So while achievement of some kind of outcome is essential to an entrepreneur, it is often balanced against one or more of the four **focuses of entrepreneurship**.

Entrepreneurial skill is always in demand so it is typical for entrepreneurs to move among independent, corporate, and social sectors. Think of the United Kingdom's Sir Paul McCartney.[58] Originally he was a member of and partner in a four-person Liverpool garage band called the Quarrymen, which later became another small business called The Beatles. Like many, Paul started out as an independent entrepreneur. But The Beatles became a high-growth venture, eventually creating Apple Corps Ltd., a major corporation marketing The Beatles music and themed goods. Paul had become

Paul McCartney has demonstrated CSI Entrepreneurship, starting out as a partner in a local band called The Beatles. They became hugely popular (and profitable) and morphed into Apple Records, in which Paul was a manager and corporate entrepreneur, finding new bands to sign onto the label. In later life, when Paul's first wife died of cancer, Paul became a social entrepreneur promoting breast cancer research and treatment as well as promoting British music.

a corporate entrepreneur. When Paul's first wife Linda died of breast cancer (Paul's mother died of the same disease), he became an advocate for breast cancer research and treatment, eventually helping create the Linda McCartney Cancer Center in Liverpool. Meanwhile, he was a prolific behind-the-scenes supporter of British music. In both of these roles he was a social entrepreneur.

mindshare
The degree of attention your target market pays to your idea or organization.

focuses of entrepreneurship
The key directions the organization intends to pursue.

Challenge and the Entrepreneurial Way

Entrepreneurs' stories usually tell us about challenges faced and overcome. What is fascinating if you hear enough stories is that there are some strategies that are used again and again. Knowing these strategies can help you achieve your own entrepreneurial dreams. What are the strategies? Some of them you have heard all your life; others might be new:

LO7 Recognize the seven key strategies of the entrepreneurial way.

- **If you don't succeed the first time, try, try again:** This is called the strategy of **perseverance**, and has famous examples like Thomas Edison's testing of more than 8,000 different materials to find one that would work correctly for his lightbulb. Like Edison, it only works if you try different people, products, or pitches.
- **Scale back:** Maybe you have an idea but can't get the resources to get it started. Try scaling it back to the level of resources you currently have available. If you can't afford to open a restaurant, consider starting with a food truck or a catering service, or make yourself into a rent-a-chef service.
- **Bird in the hand:** Instead of planning a firm and then looking for resources, why not start with the resources you already have (knowledge, contacts, money, etc.) and think about what is the best use you can make of them? This is one of the strategies of the technique of **effectuation**.[59]
- **Pivot:** Go ahead and start the business in any way you can and look for better opportunities as you go along. It happens all the time. William Wrigley Jr. started out selling soap and baking powder and, to get people's attention, he gave away gum as a promotional item. Wrigley switched to selling gum when he realized how popular a product his Juicy Fruit gum was.[60] This approach is also called the corridor principle because until you start going down the corridor (or in your case doing your business) you can't tell what opportunities you might find.

perseverance
The behavior of continued effort to achieve a goal.

effectuation
An approach used to create alternatives in uncertain environments.

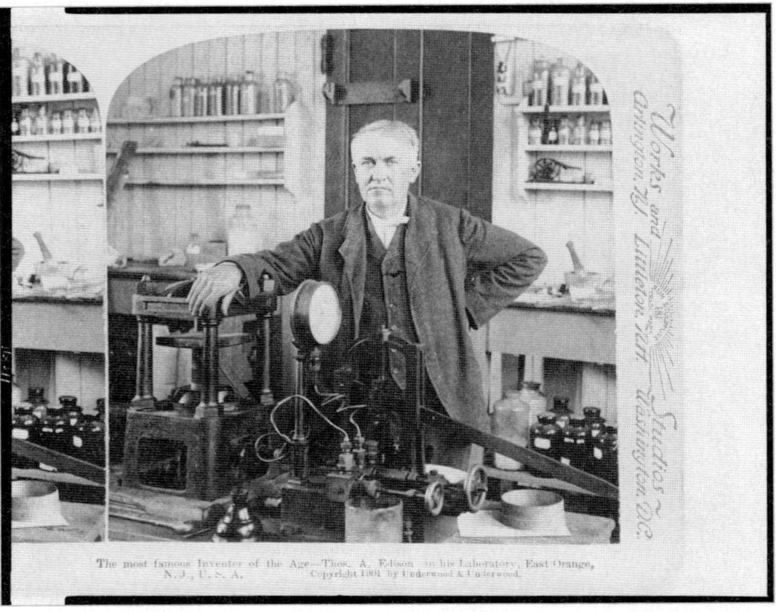

Works and Studios
The most famous Inventor of the Age—Thos. A. Edison in his Laboratory, East Orange, N.J., U.S.A.
Copyright 1901 by Underwood & Underwood.

● Edison's testing 8,000 materials to find one for his lightbulb shows his perseverance. What is your best example of sticking with something tough?

- **Take it on the road:** Sometimes the place you live isn't the best market for your product or service. Trying another market (in person or via the Internet) might help you find the traction you need to succeed.
- **Ask for help:** Today everyone can harness the wisdom of crowds, whether it is asking your personal and group connections on Facebook or LinkedIn for ideas, advice, opinions, or donations, or going to the many specialized Web sites out there for **crowdsourcing** such as Kickstarter.com or Rockethub.com for funding or Coolbusinessideas.com or Quirky.com for finding or testing product ideas.
- **Plan to earn:** Think through your capabilities, prospects, and passions to find the best idea for you, and then plan for action to make it happen.

crowdsourcing
Techniques often based on Internet-based services to get opinions or ideas through the collective involvement of others.

In this chapter we have considered some of the key ideas and myths about small business. We have seen the work of founders of small businesses that stayed small and those that started small and grew larger. Either way, when small businesses are created, nearly every part of our society benefits—through new jobs, new ideas, and the new opportunities created for individuals, communities, and the economy. The key element in getting small businesses started is helping people who have the intention to start a business take the steps to get it done, and that is the goal of this text. If we can help you follow in the model of Paul Scheiter, you are certain to do well. He did.

CHAPTER SUMMARY

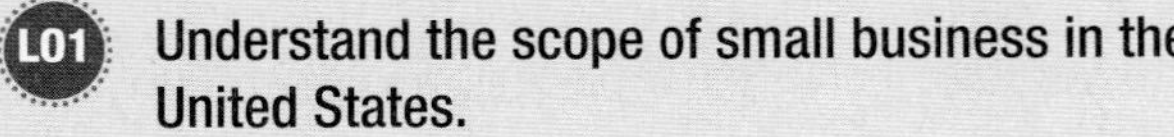

LO1 Understand the scope of small business in the United States.

- There were 27.3 million small businesses in the United States in 2010.
- About 56 percent of Americans aged 15–25 have thought about self-employment.
- Start-up success comes from combining planning and action, as well as believing in yourself.
- Getting help helps your chances of business survival.
- Successful entrepreneurs not only do well, they do good for others.
- The focus in this text is on owner-managed businesses with 1 to 50 people.
- An entrepreneur (alias *self-employed* or owner or owner-manager or founder) is someone who owns a business.
- An entrepreneur can create a new business or buy an existing business or a franchise.

LO2 Differentiate between small businesses and high-growth ventures.

- Small businesses form the economic core and largest segment of the economy.
- Small businesses range from low to moderate in innovativeness and growth rate.
- Small businesses are usually intended to remain small, generally a size that the owner feels comfortable controlling personally.
- High-growth ventures have high innovativeness and growth rates.
- Every owner has a chance to decide on his or her firm's approach to growth.
- Lifestyle/part-time firms start and remain small and centered on the owner's needs.
- Traditional small businesses are more customer-driven, but remain small and simple, providing an income for the owner.
- High-profit businesses add employees and locations in order to provide a substantial income to the owner.
- High-potential ventures attempt to grow enough to become a big business.

LO3 Discover the rewards entrepreneurs can achieve through their businesses.

- Nearly all people starting small businesses have flexibility, income, and growth as reasons for starting those businesses.
- While providing a good income is important to three-quarters of entrepreneurs, only one in four says generating great wealth is important.
- Small business owners are less motivated by social reasons (recognition, admiration, power, or family) than the general public.

LO4 Dispel key myths about small businesses.

- Dispelling the myths is important to supporting one's motivation to become an entrepreneur.
- *Myth 1:* There's not enough financing to start businesses. While we all would like more money, the vast majority of people starting small businesses report finding funding is not a problem.
- *Myth 2:* You can't start businesses during a recession. Seven of the top ten largest Fortune 500 companies started as small businesses in recessions. Businesses started in recessions tend to be "lean and mean" and able to cope with bad times as well as good.
- *Myth 3:* To make profits, you need to make something. Today the most profitable small businesses are typically in the service sector.
- *Myth 4:* If you fail, you can never try again. Lots of successful entrepreneurs have one or more failures in their background. If you pay off your debts and learn from the experience, you are positioned to try again.
- *Myth 5:* Students (or moms or some other group) don't have the skills to start a business. Facebook's Mark Zuckeberg was a student, May Kay's Mary Kay Ash a mother, and Samuel Adams' Jim Koch a consultant when they started their businesses. You could too.
- *Myth 6:* Ninety percent of new businesses fail within two years. In reality, 69 percent of new businesses are still going after two years.

LO5 Identify actions key to becoming a small business owner.

- The BRIE (boundary, resources, intention, exchange) model describes the actions that need to take place for the business to be created in the earliest stage.
- The more BRIE activities that were pursued, the greater the likelihood of the new business surviving.
- The BRIE checklist gives easy-to-perform actions to help move prospective entrepreneurs from inaction to action.
- The BRIE actions also identify the competencies you need to master to get your business started.

LO6 Recognize how small businesses are important to our economy and your community.

- Small businesses are important because they are the major source of new jobs in our economy.
- Small businesses are also the major source of innovations in society.
- Small businesses offer many benefits to localities including employment, taxes, new revenue inflow, support for other businesses, and visibility.
- Small business is also the major source for new opportunities, such as moving up in the economy and society, the opportunity for customers and businesses large and small to obtain needed goods and services.
- The CSI model describes how entrepreneurship plays out throughout our society though, Corporate, Social, and Independent Entrepreneurship (which includes small business).
- Exporting through VIGE and traditional approaches is a major economic force for small businesses worldwide.

LO7 Recognize the seven key strategies of the entrepreneurial way.

- **Persevere:** When you don't succeed the first time, try, try again.
- **Scale back:** Start smaller and build up.
- **Bird in the hand:** Do the best you can with what you already have.
- **Pivot:** Start up and keep your eyes open for better opportunities along the way, then pivot into them.
- **Take it on the road:** Go where there is a receptive market.
- **Ask for help:** From friends, from crowds, getting help helps.
- **Plan to earn:** Plan now to map your actions.

KEY TERMS

small business, 4
self-efficacy, 4
entrepreneur, 4
Small Business Administration, 5
occupation, 5
goods or services, 6
firm, 6
novelty, 7
imitative, 7
self-employed, 7
founders, 7
franchise, 7
buyers, 7
heir, 7
small and medium enterprise, 7
independent small business, 7
owner-managed firms, 7
serial entrepreneur, 8
innovativeness, 8
overall growth strategy, 9
lifestyle or part-time firm, 9
traditional small business, 9
high-performing small business, 9
high-growth venture, 9
main street businesses, 10
growth rewards, 10
income rewards, 11
flexibility rewards, 11
crowdfunding, 11
bootstrapping, 11
creative destruction, 15
factor-driven economy, 18
efficiency-driven economy, 18
innovation-driven economy, 19
opportunity-driven entrepreneurship, 19
necessity-driven entrepreneurship, 19
ecommerce, 19
virtual instant global entrepreneurship, 19
CSI entrepreneurship, 20
forms of entrepreneurship, 20
creation, 20
customer-focus, 20
efficiency, 20
innovation, 20
independent entrepreneurship, 20
corporate entrepreneurship, 20
social entrepreneurship, 20
mindshare, 21
focuses of entrepreneurship, 21
perseverance, 21
effectuation, 21
crowdsourcing, 22

DISCUSSION QUESTIONS

1. Describe the population of small businesses in America. How many firms are there and how many new firms are started each year?
2. Why do you think 56 percent of 15–25 year olds say they would *like* to start a small business, but only about ten percent who express an interest actually do anything?
3. What are the differences between small businesses and high-growth ventures?
4. What kind of reward do you think might be the one most often mentioned by Independent entrepreneurs? Corporate entrepreneurs? Social entrepreneurs?

5. Describe the BRIE model and how it applies to creating a firm.
6. Why are small businesses better at innovation than large businesses?
7. Why is the presence of small businesses important for large businesses?
8. Take 10 businesses that operate in your community and categorize them in the appropriate type of overall growth strategy. Why did you put them there?
9. Many people think of the United States as one of the most entrepreneurial countries in the world. Are there other countries with higher levels of entrepreneurship? Name two and explain why their levels of entrepreneurship might be higher than that of the United States.
10. How does the story of Sir Paul McCartney reflect the key ethical idea of this chapter, "Do well. Do good"?

EXPERIENTIAL EXERCISES

1. Go through the list of reasons people give for going into self-employment, and identify which of the reasons seem to fit you. Explain why you identify with each reason.
2. Think about the list of reasons people give for becoming self-employed. If you can, interview local entrepreneurs about their reasons and see how your real-life examples fit with the national survey results.
3. Check your state and locality's Web site(s) for information on programs that support economic development through small business creation and job creation. You can get a start at USA .gov's State and Territory Business Resources page: **business .usa.gov/stateandlocal.** Pick a state and make a list of programs that might be worth looking into as you develop your business idea.
4. Look at the local newspaper's Web site, or the **bizjournals .com** Web site for the paper in your region. Use the terms "entrepreneur" and "small business owner" to find articles about local entrepreneurs. From this, compile a list of prospective "local small business heroes and heroines" to serve as role models and prospectors for local sources of help.
5. For students in your class thinking about (or in the process of) starting their own businesses, find out which of the items on the BRIE checklist they have completed. Ask them which items they expect they will complete or get help on by taking this class.

www

MINI-CASE

SUCHIN PRAPAISILP AND GLOBAL FOODS—"YOU WORK HARD, YOU CAN MAKE IT."[61]

Small business to the rescue! It had to be a heady day when Suchin Prapaisilp signed an agreement with the city of Kirkwood, Missouri, to open a Global Foods supermarket in 1998. The store had become available again. A&P supermarkets couldn't make it there by the 1970s. National Supermarkets couldn't make it there by the 1990s. And a team of local grocery managers couldn't make it there by 1998, but Chin (as he's known locally) was sure he could. And he was so sure that he convinced Kirkwood's city council to grant him a favorable package to make it happen. The deal was that the store would offer half traditional American foods for the local community and half international foods for the regional community.

As satisfying as that moment in the public and industry spotlight was, it was a long road getting there. When he came to America in 1974, 22-year-old Chin's day stretched from 4 A.M. to midnight. He worked for others making donuts, then doing a factory shift. He closed the day as a kitchen helper. In his off hours he taught dance and even delivered phone books. But his philosophy is, "You work hard, you can make it." Chin and his newly arrived brother Chatchai opened a small grocery store in St. Louis in 1975, and in 1986 opened a bigger grocery that became the anchor for a miniboom of Asian businesses in the neighborhood. This kind of steady growth gave Chin the experience and capital to aim for an opportunity like Global, which would take $2.15 million for the building and improvements. But even with experience and capital, as one of Chin's American employees at Global volunteered, "They took a big gamble opening the store."

The store got a tremendous response, but not exactly as expected. It became the favorite source for exotic ingredients for recipes in the local newspapers, and international customers were regularly coming from as far as 100 miles away to shop Global's well-stocked aisles. But the American products weren't selling as well as expected, and they were taking up space that could be more profitably used for international foods. In the spring of 2000, Chin and Global were doing all right, but Chin knew he could make it better still.

CASE DISCUSSION QUESTIONS

1. What can Suchin do to resolve the problem?
2. Why would Suchin acting on his own to change the grocery be a problem?
3. Was Suchin an entrepreneur? If he was an entrepreneur, what role or roles was he playing—founder, buyer, or owner-manager—at the time he opened Global Foods?

SUGGESTED CASES AND ARTICLES

- Brothers Going Separate Ways or Not?, C-1

Available on McGraw-Hill Create™

- St. Louis: Inner City Economic Development
- Cameron Auto Parts (A)—Revised
- Early-Stage Business Vignettes
- Organizing from Scratch: The Learning Lab Denmark Experience
- Quixotico: The Fat Thursday Venture

SUGGESTED VIDEOS

www.mhhe.com/katz4e

Video Case:

- For a written video case and corresponding clip, visit the OLC at www.mhhe.com/katz4e and select "Chapter 1".
- Do-Gooders Who Spread the Dough

SBTV.com Videos:

- Ten Start-Up Mistakes
- NFIB Entrepreneur in the Classroom
- From Female Motorcyclist to Global Entrepreneur
- A Pioneer in Social Entrepreneurship: Equal Exchange

STVP Videos:

- The Biggest Successes are Often Bred from Failures—Randy Komisar
- Start-Ups: How to Avoid Being Squashed by Big Companies?
- Being Small Inside of Big
- Entrepreneurship Is Social Entrepreneurship
- Examples of Social Entrepreneurs

CHAPTER

2

Small Business Entrepreneurs: Characteristics and Competencies

● New advances in technology and communications are helping entrepreneurs like Laura Tidwell fulfill their career goals while also balancing their family life priorities. In addition to learning how to take advantage of these resources, what other entrepreneurial skills and qualities enabled Laura to grow her business into what it is today?

LEARNING OBJECTIVES

After you complete this chapter, you will be able to:

LO1 Recognize the key aspects of the entrepreneurial personality.

LO2 Assess the operational competencies of the successful entrepreneur.

LO3 Describe the challenges of family business owners.

LO4 Recognize the special nature of entrepreneurial teams.

LO5 Identify the challenges women and minority business owners face.

LO6 Describe the situation of people who become business owners later in life.

Focus on Small Business: Internet Entrepreneur Laura Tidwell[1]

The two things people could always say about Laura Tidwell was that she had tremendous drive and a winning personality. In 1990 at the age of 16 she parlayed both, entering Brigham Young University as a communications major specializing in advertising. But her life became complex, and at 18, she found herself divorced, broke, and the single mother of a toddler. Yet Laura was determined to have a career in advertising—one that would allow her to stay at home, earn a decent living, and raise her daughter. Laura remained convinced that the key for her lay in advertising. She only needed to find the right type of work in advertising.

While socializing at a club in 1994, one of her dance partners told Laura that he wrote Web pages for a living. Never having heard of such a job, she asked, "Web, as in spiders?" Although he initially laughed at her response, he did take the time to explain his job. She suddenly realized that the Web was the answer to her dream. That night she decided to become the owner of a home-based Internet advertising company.

Laura lacked expertise and funding, but she had a goal and the determination and self-confidence to make it a reality. Laura learned the business every way she could using Web-related sources, but she focused on developing contacts at Internet trade shows and through industry associations. She realized she needed even more expertise and started working for people in the industry, at first for free and then in a paying job with an Internet start-up company. By 1996 the then 22-year-old Laura thought she had learned enough, knew enough people in the industry, and saved enough money to step out on her own. She quit her job and started her own Internet advertising business, Advantage Advertising.

Operating out of the one-bedroom apartment she shared with her daughter in Troy, Alabama, Laura began with only one small business client. Seeking big name clients that would prove her firm's credibility, she bravely made an offer to representatives of Encyclopedia Britannica and of The Thomas Register whom she met at a trade show. She would handle their online advertising purchases, such as banner ads, free of charge for a period of time. In return they would become her clients if they were satisfied with the quality of her service. Intrigued, they gave her a chance, and she quickly proved her worth, making these large companies her first major clients.

This gave Laura the visibility and credibility she needed to attract additional clients, and she has enjoyed a thriving, profitable, growing business ever since. Today you can find her firm at **www.theadfirm.com**. Specialists in advertising construction products, her clients include Rheem Water Heaters and Tendura Flooring. Her advice to future entrepreneurs? "Accept challenges. Don't be afraid to think outside the box." It worked for her.

DISCUSSION QUESTIONS

1. Why did Laura Tidwell decide to become an entrepreneur?
2. What skills did she develop to become a successful entrepreneur?
3. What opportunities did Laura find and pursue?

LO1 Recognize the key aspects of the entrepreneurial personality.

The Psychology of Entrepreneurs

In the opening vignette above, Laura Tidwell displayed three of the key characteristics of successful entrepreneurs introduced in Chapter 1: she believed in herself and her ability to create a business that would let her work and take care of her daughter, she sought out help from others to learn her business, and she persevered over several years until she achieved her goal. These are aspects of Laura's behavior, her way of looking at and thinking about herself and her world, which is called **cognition**, and her visible **actions**. Is Laura's pattern of entrepreneurial behavior the only type there is?

cognition
A person's way of perceiving and thinking about his or her experience.

action
The visible behavior a person takes.

The answer is that there is no one pattern of entrepreneurial behavior or entrepreneurial type. In Chapter 1 we broke up the entrepreneurs around the world into opportunity-driven and necessity-driven types. We talked about entrepreneurs in corporate, social, and independent settings and how their focuses differed. We even discussed the four kinds of overall growth strategies entrepreneurs typically design their businesses around. There are literally hundreds of ways to think about entrepreneurial personalities. That is good because it means there can be more than one personality type that can lead to success, and it increases the likelihood that there is an approach to entrepreneurship that will fit with your interests and style.

Successful entrepreneurial behavior leads to the creation of a new firm that meets the goals of the entrepreneur. Some parts of entrepreneurial behavior can be done in very different ways, while some elements tend to be more consistent across people. In this chapter we will consider the ways people are different, the ways they are the same, and close with a look at the patterns leading to successful entrepreneurial behavior for several distinct groups of entrepreneurs.

The Five Ps of Entrepreneurial Behavior

There are five aspects of behavior that most successful entrepreneurs display. These are not the only possible behaviors that you could consider, but they are behaviors that have been shown in the research to relate to success among entrepreneurs. The five behaviors include the following:

passion
An intense positive feeling an entrepreneur has toward the business or the idea behind the business.

1. **Passion:** Passion is an intense positive feeling the entrepreneur has toward the business or even the idea behind the business. It comes from being actively involved in moving the business forward. Passion has multiple benefits, such as increasing your commitment to the business (which relates to perseverance), and inspiring key stakeholders like potential investors, employees, or subcontractors. Passion is displayed in three ways: (1) by looking at the challenges of the business in a creative way, (2) by being persistently focused on the business, and (3) by being absorbed by the tasks and concerns of the business.[2] When we talk about entrepreneurs who "live for the business," we're talking about passion. When you see entrepreneurs get excited as they describe something about their business, we see and respond to their passion.

perseverance
The ability to stick with some activity even when it take a long time and its outcome is not immediately known.

2. **Perseverance:** Perseverance is best thought of as a type of learned optimism,[3] the ability to stick with some activity even when it takes a long time, and when a successful or unsuccessful outcome is not immediately known. It is one of the most powerful contributors to entrepreneurial success like that of J. J. Rosen who literally taught himself programming to make his business work (see Small Business Insight box on page 32).[4] In Chapter 1, we talked about

Passion is an intense positive feeling about what you do, and this entrepreneur clearly has it. How do you display passion when you feel it?

the strategy of perseverance with the old expression "If you don't succeed the first time, try, try again." Trying again is the behavior behind perseverance, but requires thinking about what went wrong and what went right, and adjusting your next try to achieve a better result. Behind this thinking and behavior is the attitude of *learned optimism,* knowing that you can and will keep at this until you have mastered it.[5] The danger is to keep trying the same action repeatedly without learning. That is a problem behavior called *perseveration*.

3. **Promotion/Prevention Focus:** Most of us have some mix of two internal focuses (also called our regulatory focus), a **promotion focus** intent on maximizing gains, which gives us a bias toward pursuing opportunities likely to lead to those gains, and a **prevention focus** intent on minimizing losses, with a bias toward inaction or protective action.[6] Being a successful entrepreneur involves balancing the two focuses. In an established industry or a poor one, a prevention focus can work well, while a promotion focus can yield better results in richer, dynamic, uncertain environments or industries.[7] A reckless pursuit of opportunity may bankrupt your company, while a protection-at-all-costs focus may mean you will miss the opportunities necessary to keep cash flowing into your firm. Successful entrepreneurs deal with preventing problems by planning ahead of time and creating actions to avoid or deal with problems. For J. J. Rosen, keeping his day job until his software business took off was one way to protect his family and business. Those same successful entrepreneurs also plan where to find opportunities and how to pursue them. But planning is rarely perfect; you have to be ready to act when the situation demands it. Your own promotion/prevention balance is likely to come into play in those quick decision situations. Trust your plans, and where the plans don't have the answer, trust your "gut" or intuition. Entrepreneurs may have regrets about their choices, but they generally feel better having taken charge of the choice process.[8]
4. **Planning Style:** There is more than one way to plan. In fact, there are five ways.[9] **Comprehensive planners** take a long-term view, develop long-range plans for all aspects of the business, are comfortable with planning, and act based on the plans they've developed. **Critical-point planners** plan around the most important aspect of the business first, act on it, and then consider if additional plans are needed. It is not a very long-term approach to planning. **Opportunistic planners** generally start with a goal and look for opportunities to achieve it. Once they find a good opportunity, even if it isn't the one related to their original goal, they act on it, so it is very short term in orientation. **Reactive planners** are completely passive, waiting for cues from the environment to determine what actions to take. Their focus is entirely short term, and there is little in the way of goals driving their efforts. They can make the most of a

promotion focus
An entrepreneur's attention to maximizing gains and pursuing opportunities likely to lead to gains.

prevention focus
An entrepreneur's attention to minimizing losses, with a bias toward inaction or protective action to prevent loss.

comprehensive planners
Entrepreneurs who develop long-range plans for all aspects of the business.

critical-point planners
Entrepreneurs who develop plans focused on the most important aspect of the business first.

opportunistic planners
Entrepreneurs who start with a goal instead of a plan and look for opportunities to achieve it.

reactive planners
Entrepreneurs with a passive approach, who wait for cues from the environment to determine what actions to take.

SMALL BUSINESS INSIGHT

J. J. ROSEN AND ATIBA SOFTWARE AND CONSULTING[10]

After graduating from Vanderbilt University in 1992 as a psychology major, J. J. Rosen landed his first job as a child-support coordinator for the Tennessee District Attorney General Conference, an administrative branch of the state's court system. As he closely observed the work processes, he soon realized that much of the work performed by the state's child-support collection agencies could be done more efficiently and effectively if it were computerized. There were just two problems—many of these agencies had no computers, and no specialized computer software existed to handle the type of functions needed by the organizations. J. J. set out to resolve this problem, fulfill a need, and take advantage of this potential business opportunity.

Here J. J. faced his third problem—while he had an idea for software, he did not know how to write a computer program. Driven to make his idea a reality, J. J. taught himself this skill. A few months later he had mastered programming well enough to create child-support services software that could track child-support payments and collection efforts. With this product, the Atiba Software and Consulting Company was born as a part-time venture. Promoting his software as a better idea and offering very low prices to get an initial customer base, he sold the software statewide. Soon his business was growing through word-of-mouth advertising, and he landed his first major client, Andersen Consulting, within a year of starting. Only then did J. J. quit his job in the district attorney's office and embark on his own business full time. By 2012 Atiba had more than 500 clients. For J. J., the idea drove the business, carefully.

habit-driven planners Entrepreneurs who do not plan, preferring to let all actions be dictated by their routines.

professionalization The extent to which a firm meets or exceeds the standard business practices for its industry.

standard business practice A business action that has been widely adopted within an industry or occupation.

expert business professionalization A situation that occurs when all the major functions of a firm are conducted according to the standard business practices of its industry.

specialized business professionalization A situation that occurs when businesses have founders or owners who are passionate about one or two of the key business functions, such as sales, operations, accounting, finance, or human resources.

minimalized business professionalization A situation that occurs when the entrepreneur does nearly everything in the simplest way possible.

situation because there is no other plan competing for their attention. **Habit-based planners** do not really plan at all because their actions are dictated by their routines. They do today what they did yesterday. They don't plan, and they don't even tend to react to changes in their environments. Simply put, results from small business owners in countries around the world have shown that in terms of getting a start-up launched, keeping it going, and making a living from it, comprehensive planners do the best, followed by critical point planners, and opportunistic planning types.[11] Reactive and habit planners generally do very poorly in business, even if they manage to get their firms started.

5. **Professionalization:** One hallmark of successful entrepreneurs is that they usually do at least one thing much better than average. That average is called a **standard business practice** and every industry has them. Doing that level or better is what professionalization is all about. There are three levels of professionalization: **expert professionalization** when most aspects of the business meet or exceed the industry's standards, **specialized** when one or two aspects of the business are at this level, or **minimalized** when none of the business can achieve the industry standard. Consider the oldest professionalized firm in the world, the Zildjian Company. The company started in Turkey in 1623 with a formula for making an alloy ideal for cymbals. At this stage the company was specialized. In 1929, when Avedis Zildjian inherited the company, he moved it to America and applied his marketing, financial, and business knowledge to bring the firm up to the level of expert professionalization, where it remains today.[12]

Notice that these behaviors are relevant to more than starting a business. They are useful behaviors in business in general and even in life. If you are an employee, your bosses will want you to show passion (often called engagement) in the business, be persevering and strike a balance of promotion and prevention. The fact that these five ideas are behaviors means that you can learn how to display them, even if it is not the way you were behaving originally. That is what education, skill development, and practice are all about. Each of these types of behavior can be assessed formally using psychological questionnaires, but you can make a general assessment with items like those in Skill Module 2.1.

SKILL MODULE 2.1

Entrepreneurial Personality Overview[13]

The complete assessment of each of the five Ps would require more than 100 questions, but you can get a very general sense of how you lean by answering and scoring the questions below.

In the following questions, determine how strongly you agree with the statement from 1 (Strongly Disagree) to 5 (Strongly Agree). If you are not sure, make your best guess.

	Strongly Disagree				Strongly Agree
1. I am better than my peers at being able to solve problems.	1	2	3	4	5
2. I am better than my peers at making money.	1	2	3	4	5
3. I am better than my peers at being creative.	1	2	3	4	5
4. I am better than my peers at getting people to agree with me.	1	2	3	4	5
5. I am really excited to be establishing a new company.	1	2	3	4	5
6. I am really energized by owning my company.	1	2	3	4	5
7. I am really in love with creating a new firm.	1	2	3	4	5
8. I am really excited to create something out of nothing.	1	2	3	4	5
9. I really enjoy nurturing a new business through its emerging success.	1	2	3	4	5
10. My personal philosophy is to do "whatever it takes" to establish my own business.	1	2	3	4	5
11. I would rather own my own business than earn a higher salary employed by someone else.	1	2	3	4	5
12. Owning my own business is more important than spending time with my family.	1	2	3	4	5
13. There is no limit to how long I would give a maximum effort to establish my business.	1	2	3	4	5
14. Overall, I am more oriented toward achieving success than preventing failure.	1	2	3	4	5
15. I often think about the person I would ideally like to be in the future.	1	2	3	4	5
16. I frequently think about how I can prevent failures in my life.	1	2	3	4	5
17. I am anxious that I will fall short of my responsibilities and obligations.	1	2	3	4	5

For the next set of questions, rank them by putting a "1" by the statement that most closely fits your approach or belief, "2" by the next closest fit, and so on.

Rank (1–5)	
	A. I am most comfortable when I have planned for everything.
	B. If I've taken care of the biggest challenge, I feel my job is done.
	C. I am always looking for the next big thing, and when I find it I go for it.
	D. If someone offers me a good opportunity, I'll go for it.
	E. Whatever happens, I stick to what I have been doing all along.

For the next set of questions, rank them by putting a "1" by the statement that most closely fits your approach or belief, "2" by the next closest fit, and so on.

Rank (1–3)	
	F. I feel best when everything I do is done the best way possible.
	G. I think it is important to be known for doing one thing extremely well.
	H. I believe it is more important to get the job done than to try and make it perfect.

Scoring of the Entrepreneurial Personality Overview can be found in endnote 14 in the back of the text.[14]

LO2 Assess the operational competencies of the successful entrepreneur.

competencies
Forms of business-related expertise.

Entrepreneurial Operational Competencies

All the aspects of the entrepreneurial personality depend on hard work, but there are other specific types of business-related expertise—called **competencies**—that appear repeatedly in successful entrepreneurs around the world.[15] While there could be as many competencies as there are personality types, theories, like the BRIE (boundary/resources/intention/exchange) model introduced in Chapter 1, help us focus on those few competencies that are essential to successfully starting and running a business. After you have read about these entrepreneurial competencies, use Skill Module 2.2 to assess your competencies.

SKILL MODULE 2.2 Competency Self-Assessment

In this exercise, rank your skill or competency at different types of business activities. The goal is to see where you feel you have strengths and on which competencies you need to work. For each skill, think of a person or a company that does a really good job at that activity. Then compare your own performance to it using one of four levels of competency: *needs development* means that you still have to learn the skill; *needs refinement* means that you have the rudiments of the skill, but still need to practice it and carefully check your performance; *competent* means you can perform the activity consistently and without mistakes; *excellent* means you perform the activity as well as your role model, or nearly so. The categories of competencies are built from those listed in the text.

		Level of Competency			
Skill	Role Model	Needs Development	Needs Refinement	Competent	Excellent
Key Business Functions					
Sales					
Operations (production)					
Accounting					
Finance					
Human resources					
Industry Specific Knowledge					
Industry expertise					
Industry skill					
Market knowledge					
Ability to diagnose					
Ability to see opportunities					
Resource Competencies					
Business information					
Business financing					
Space for the business					
Raw materials					
Support people					

Determination Competencies					
Business as primary focus					
Ability to manage time					
Ability to find/get help					
Ability to sustain relationships					
Willingness to act					
Opportunity Competencies					
Found profitable idea					
Idea imitates with a twist or is new, but tested					
Idea is hard to copy					

Entrepreneurs often find it useful to copy this list and ask people who know them well to fill it in with them in mind. Good examples can include business consultants or bankers, people who have worked with you, or even family members. Comparing what others see to what you see in yourself can help you put in perspective which skills need further development or better demonstration to others. In big business, such an approach is called "360 degree feedback," but it can also be applied in small businesses.

The competency suggested by *boundary* relates to the organizational and business processes of a firm. This type of expertise can be called *basic business competency*.[16] There are certain fundamental activities that all businesses must perform, which are called the **key business functions**, and include sales, operations (also called *production*), accounting, finance, and human resources. Getting organized and registered—which creates the boundary—is an example of an operations activity.

key business functions
Activities common to all businesses such as sales, operations (also called *production*), accounting, finance, and human resources.

There is also **industry-specific knowledge**. A restaurant really is different from a mechanic's shop or a computer store or a portrait studio. Each requires you to understand a particular industry and market, and each requires a very particular kind of skill. This was a large part of the reason that Laura Tidwell, in the example at the start of this chapter, worked for others before going off on her own. Some of these skills focus on knowing your new business and its context (Chapters 5 and 6), having the kind of skills that fit the business, being able to diagnose your business's health (Chapters 8, 12, 13, 17, and 18), and being able to see future business opportunities while doing your everyday work (Chapters 4, 7, and 20).

industry-specific knowledge
Activities, knowledge, and skills specific to businesses in a particular industry.

Resources lead to specific **resource competencies**.[17] For even the smallest part-time business, the entrepreneur needs to find or gain access to resources such as time, information, financing, space for the business, raw materials, and a variety of people (advisers, suppliers, service providers, customers). For J. J. Rosen of Atiba Software, getting the computer programming knowledge was critical. Knowing the best place to get raw materials or set up your operation, finding better information than your competition on your market, or having enough financing to ride out downturns in sales are examples of resources that could give you an advantage. You'll learn more about gathering resources in Chapter 5 (Small Business Entry: Paths to Part-Time Entrepreneurship), Chapter 11 (Small Business Distribution and Location), Chapter 14 (Cash: Lifeblood of the Business), Chapter 15 (Small Business Finance: Using Equity, Debt, and Gifts), and Chapter 19 (Human Resource Management: Small Business Considerations).

resource competencies
The ability or skill of the entrepreneur at finding expendable components necessary to the operation of the business such as time, information, location, financing, raw materials, and expertise.

Intention reflects your determination to start your business and make it a success. These determination-driven skills can be called **determination competencies**[18] and are demonstrated by focusing on your business over other choices and being ready to find out about and do what it takes to pursue opportunities that will help get the business going. The entrepreneurs we have mentioned in this chapter—Tidwell and Rosen—displayed tremendous determination to do the work

determination competencies
Skills identified with the energy and focus needed to bring a business into existence.

Look carefully at this photo of a Common Dog vehicle. How do the descriptions of product services, contact information, and endorsement slogans all demonstrate Common Dog's grasp of opportunity competencies?

and stick with the business through thick and thin. Many of these determination competencies are essential to deciding if a business is feasible for you, a topic that is covered in Chapter 4 for the time before you start a business and in Chapter 20 for businesses already in operation. Time management competencies are covered in this chapter in the section on Family Businesses. The competencies related to getting help are seen in Skill Module 1.1 and in Chapter 3, where we will look at the social skills related to building and sustaining legitimacy and relationships.

opportunity competencies
Skills necessary to identify and exploit elements of the business environment that can lead to a profitable and sustainable business.

Exchange deals with the actual process of exploiting the opportunity for profit—which is a fancy way of saying "making sales." The competencies that make this work are called **opportunity competencies**,[19] which include identifying an opportunity, a product, or service idea that is likely to lead you to a profit and is ideally distinctive to your firm and, you hope, hard for others to copy. For Bill Gates and J. J. Rosen, the opportunity each found was for creating software that would make life and work easier. You'll learn more about the opportunity process and protecting opportunities through strategic planning in Chapter 4 and Chapter 7, where we will discuss the strategy of imitation with a twist.

Research suggests that people can learn what they need to know to have adequate levels of expertise in all five competency areas. In fact, students who go through formal training or classes often score higher on the expertise tests than people running businesses.[20] In addition to training or classes, you can get consulting assistance from public or private sources, or you can even buy expertise in package form by adopting industry standard techniques. You can use state-of-the-art services or you can franchise.

The presence and absence of certain skills makes a tremendous difference in distinguishing those who start businesses from those who don't. But for those businesses that do get started, the amount of expertise is what distinguishes the more successful from the less successful firms. The concern about expertise leads to thinking about the level of professionalization you choose to use in your firm.

The Sociology of Entrepreneurs

Entrepreneurs can be as strongly affected by their social or sociological characteristics as by their personality characteristics.[21] These sociological characteristics relate to the social groups to which they belong. Family, gender, race, nationality, religion, age, and other types of group memberships, such as being a member of a team or a veteran, are typical examples. Some of these memberships are important enough that they are protected from discrimination by federal laws, and government and companies dealing with the government make special efforts to support members of those groups.

Others lack such protections but are still powerful influences on the individual entrepreneur. The challenges members of these groups face share some similarities, as do the programs designed to support them. To get an idea of how this works, the section below considers entrepreneurs in family businesses and teams, women entrepreneurs, and second-career entrepreneurs. While there are lessons and advice given for each of the groups below, the lessons can apply to everyone, for example, the techniques of time management, which are discussed in the Family Business section, or the methods for managing idea ownership, discussed in the Teams section.

Family Businesses

LO3 Describe the challenges of family business owners.

We think that the U.S. economy is built on an array of very large, publicly held companies—General Motors, Boeing, IBM, Bank of America, Exxon, and others—but this is only part of the picture. Many of America's largest companies—Mars, Hallmark, Dell, Motorola, Nordstrom, Campbell Soup—fully one-third of the S&P 500 companies—are family owned and managed.[22] Small and large, they make up over half the businesses in the United States historically and were the creators of well over half the new jobs in the United States.[23] But our interests are in those small businesses that are also family businesses, and those represent 39 percent of American businesses, or about 10.8 million firms. Defined as firms with a majority family ownership and direct daily family involvement, **family business** is a major economic force, employing 58 percent of America's total workforce.[24]

family business
A firm in which one family owns a majority stake and is involved in the daily management of the business.

Small, family-owned businesses have many advantages. If the business is managed at the top by a group of tight-knit family members, communication-based integration can be more effective, and decision making can be easier and quicker.[25] A strong family bond can become a strong business culture, enabling members to make effective, coordinated decisions with little or no formal communication. Family members already have developed strong relationships and interact on a regular basis both in and outside the workplace. Families are a major source of funds and personnel for new small businesses,[26] providing a support network made up of people the entrepreneur knows and trusts. Family businesses are also a self-perpetuating source for future small businesses. Many new entrepreneurs have been raised in families in which one or both parents or other relatives owned a family business,[27] as you can see in the examples of the Ross and Enstrom families below. As children of family business owners, these individuals learned how business works by observing their family at work. They gained early experiences that helped them develop the skills, competencies, and self-confidence that contributed to later decisions to become entrepreneurs and to their ability to succeed.[28] In fact, most entrepreneurs come from families of entrepreneurs.

There are two challenges typical to family businesses—role conflict and succession.[29] **Role conflict** describes the kind of problem that arises when people have multiple responsibilities, such

role conflict
The kind of problem that arises when people have multiple responsibilities, such as parent and boss, and the different responsibilities make different demands on them.

SMALL BUSINESS INSIGHT

TWO ROUTES TO THE FAMILY BUSINESS[30]

Ross's Teal Lake Lodge and Teal Wing Golf Club is a family-owned business. Victoria Ross began helping wait tables at the Hayward, Wisconsin, resort when she was only 6 years old. By the time she was 18, she had moved into management positions. Having already earned her bachelor's degree in business administration, she is now working on her master's in global tourism. At 25, Ross is ready to take over the family business.

Jamee Enstrom Simons took a different track to management of her family's business, Enstrom's Almond Toffee. She began working in the company when still a child, hand dipping chocolates after school. Jamee eventually became a registered nurse, but when her parents expressed interest in selling the company, she and her husband bought it in 1993. Under her leadership, sales revenues for Enstrom's Almond Toffee reached $10 million in 2001.

Ross and Simons both gained the confidence and skills they needed to succeed as small business owners from their early experiences in the families' businesses.

as parent and boss, and each makes different demands on them.[31] As a boss, you might want your daughter to stay at the store and work, while as a parent you might want your daughter to take time off to be with her own children. Role conflict is at its worst when people fail to recognize it. Often, reminding yourself and others that you face multiple, conflicting roles helps them understand the types of choices that must be made and the kinds of decisions that are most important.[32] For family business, the most effective approach for avoiding role conflict is to keep family issues out of the family business, as you can see in the case of Boyd Coffee (see Small Business Insight box on page 39). Whenever possible, try and make decisions based on business necessities. When making a decision from a family perspective, broaden it to apply equally to nonfamily as well as family members. For example, if family members in the business can take off for their children's graduations, so should employees who are not part of the family.[33]

Role conflict breeds another unending problem—the shortage of time. Entrepreneurs are among the most rushed people in the workforce. Part of this comes from the responsibilities of ownership. Entrepreneurs are *always* working, even if it is just thinking about what to do next at work. Add family responsibilities, and schedule overload is almost a certainty. There are, however, a collection of techniques for **time management**, which can help meet the challenges of schedule overload. Consider these basic methods:

time management
The organizing process to help make the most efficient use of the day.

- **List**—Whether you use a pad of paper, a specialized form like a Franklin Planner, a PDA, or Microsoft Outlook's Task function, the key to staying on top of your responsibilities is to list them as soon as you get them. Then as you finish them, you can enjoy crossing them off the list.
- **123 Prioritize**—As you look at your list, prioritize your tasks based on their *importance* to your business and their *due date*. The most important tasks due soonest get a priority of 1. Tasks with lesser importance or a longer time to completion get ranked 2, and your "back burner" concerns get ranked 3. If there are tasks (of any level) that can be lumped together, so much the better. How do you decide importance? If the task will not help your business or family, it is probably not a priority 1 task.
- **Delegate**—Look at your task list and see which tasks you can get others to do for you (for free or at a price). When you're overloaded, getting more people on the job for you is a powerful way to get more done.
- **Repeat**—Take a few minutes every day to repeat the above steps. It will save you time later.

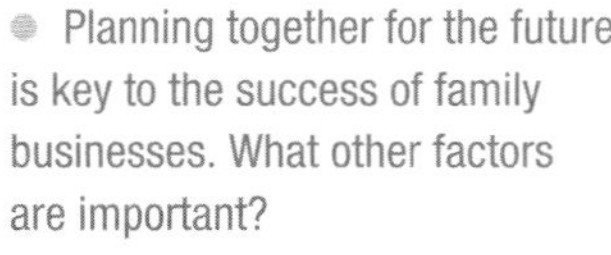

Planning together for the future is key to the success of family businesses. What other factors are important?

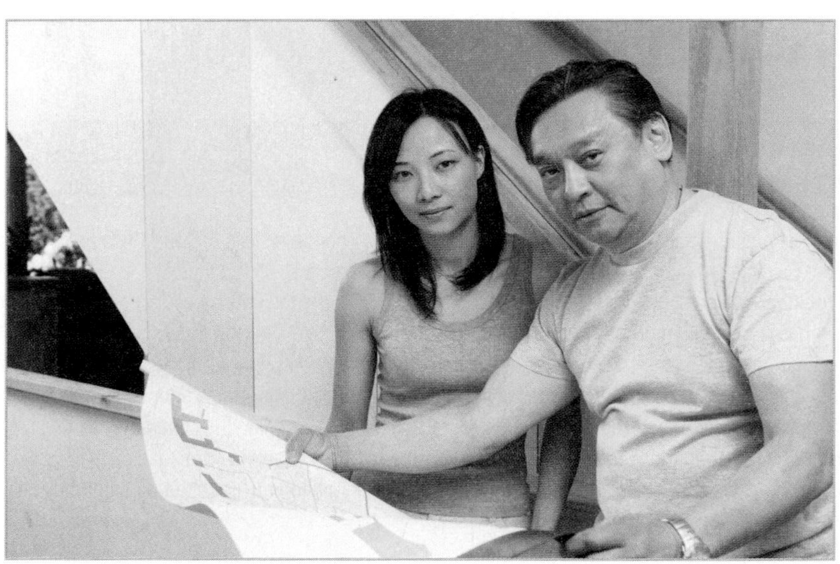

- **Strategize**—Once a week, take a few minutes to look at the things you *didn't* do this week and check if you are overlooking something which could be important to your business, family, or yourself, but is getting overlooked in the short run. Entrepreneurs are notorious for overlooking their health and cheating themselves and their businesses out of time to think about the big picture and their firm's future. Ten minutes a week spent this way can make a world of difference.[34]

Thirty-nine percent of U.S. family-owned businesses are expected to face the retirement or semi-retirement of their CEO within the next five years. This statistic grows in importance if you factor in the idea that only one-third of family-owned businesses survive beyond the first generation.[35] Part of the problem can be an entrepreneur, like Rudy Boyd, who has difficulty letting go. Problems can arise when the owner cannot come to grips with retirement or envision someone else running the company.[36] Owners often resist giving up control and undermine—consciously or unconsciously—potential successors.[37] This is a problem because top managers at family firms tend to stay in their positions much longer than those at nonfamily firms. One study found that CEOs of family firms had an average tenure of 17 years as opposed to just 8 years for CEOs in other businesses.[38]

When the current owners are ready to think about what follows them, we get into **succession**—the process of intergenerational transfer of a business. Often the lack of a clear succession plan is the death knell for those family firms facing their first intergenerational transition.[39] If the founder dies, becomes seriously ill, or is incapacitated before he or she can groom a successor, the new family leader may be suddenly thrust into the role before coming up to speed on vital company information and developing needed skills. Also, in the absence of a succession plan, private and public dissension among various factions of the family becomes more likely, negatively affecting operations within the firm, and may eventually cause the business to fail.[40]

succession
The process of intergenerational transfer of a business.

SMALL BUSINESS INSIGHT

BOYD COFFEE[41]

Boyd Coffee, started in 1900 in Portland, Oregon, had survived its first transition from founder P. D. Boyd to heir Rudy Boyd. Rudy's sons, David and Dick Boyd, grew up working in the family business. In 1975, Rudy officially retired, but he refused to leave the business. Even though David, the eldest son, became the CEO, Rudy stayed on as chairman of the board, and for many years he remained an active and influential presence around the company—often to the irritation of son David. A few years after Rudy's "retirement," the board of directors of Boyd Coffee—Rudy, his wife Ellen, David, and Dick, then president—voted 3–0 (with David abstaining) to remove David as CEO and name Dick the new CEO.

David and Dick believed the management change was based solely on members of the family taking sides in the David/Rudy conflict, rather than on sound business judgment. With the loss of the CEO position, David also wondered whether he had originally received the job because he had earned it through hard work and demonstrated ability or simply because of his name and family position as the eldest. Although after the awkward switch the brothers continued to work together for many years, their personal and professional relationships deteriorated to the point where they seldom communicated. The tension and lack of coordinated effort between the two inevitably led to the financial decline and instability of Boyd Coffee. Finally, in 1997, David threatened to dissolve the company. Only when faced with such a drastic possibility did the brothers begin the slow and difficult process of reconciliation.

With the assistance and guidance of outside advisers and consultants, the brothers have now made succession planning their top priority. They have established a family trust that allows younger family members the opportunity to leave home and develop their business skills and networks independently. The brothers also have encouraged their children to gain work experience outside the family business before deciding whether they want to return to work for the company, something the brothers never got to do.

As is true of so many things in a successful small business, the answer lies in taking a professional approach to the problem. In this case the professional approach involves crafting a succession plan like the one created by Boyd Coffee after Dick became president. Succession plans deal with the people who will take over, what roles they will fill, and what supports (such as training, outside assistance, voting power, resources control) they will receive.[42] Problems arise when there are no successors available within the family. One study found that only 5 percent of all entrepreneurs were able to rely on family members to take over.[43] Sometimes none of the children have an interest in the family business. The opposite problem arises in situations like that at Boyd Coffee when several family members believe they should take over the top spot and vie for the position to the detriment of both family and business. Problems like the Boyd Coffee competition remind us that it is important to plan how disputes will get resolved. Expect those disputes. The owners of a family business tend to be especially passionate about their enterprise, because they have a huge economic incentive to pay very close attention.[44]

One way to maximize communication in the succession process is to create a family council. A family council includes family members with immediate interests in the business (spouse, sisters and brothers, older children, etc.). The focus of council meetings is the business-family relationship. The meetings can also be a good forum for grappling with issues like role expectations, commitment, and personal responsibility.[45]

An advisory board, or a formal board of directors, can also contribute important skills and strategic direction. At Helzberg Diamonds, Barnett Helzberg Jr. set up a board to confront planning issues and to "help bring order (read *professionalization*) to the seat-of-the-pants decision making" at the firm. The board was critical to succession planning at Helzberg when trusted board members convinced Mr. Helzberg that he needed to step aside as president. He brought in someone else who had the skills to lead day-to-day operations while keeping the chairmanship himself.[46]

The key difference between a family council and a board of directors is that the function of the family council is to keep the family involved while the board is focused on running the business. The board includes significant nonfamily membership.[47] Careful use of a family council can also help by keeping family members involved in an appropriate way, allowing you more room to maintain a different balance with your board of directors.[48]

In addition, a good plan, like the one Boyd Coffee developed, also talks about the handling of the assets of the company in order to minimize the tax burden on the family and the firm and provide a suitable income for the former owner and his or her household. Because of the legal, tax, accounting, and leader development complexities, succession planning is best done with the advice of experts.[49] For family councils and boards of advisers, it is often helpful to get professional advice at the start, and then continue on your own. One organization that tracks experts in family business is the Family Firm Institute.

One special situation of the family business is the case of a married couple who jointly own and manage their business.[50] You only need to consider the divorce rate in general to realize that marriage and business can be a volatile mixture. The problems of a lack of agreement, difficulty keeping business and family issues separate, and how to handle endings[51] are very much in evidence in couples' businesses, and the solutions are very much the same—being clear about responsibilities, trying to maintain boundaries between work and home, having outside advisers to help sort out thorny issues, and planning for how the firm might end or change.[52]

Entrepreneurial Teams

LO4 Recognize the special nature of entrepreneurial teams

While the classic image of the entrepreneurial small business would involve the image of the solo entrepreneur, the modern reality is different. The majority of new businesses have a team of two or more co-owners, and the trend is toward even more businesses being developed by teams of entrepreneurs. Figure 2.1 shows you the latest breakdown from the Panel Study of Entrepreneurial Dynamics.

Most teams are family related. In fact 53 percent of teams are spouses or life partners working together. Another 18 percent of the teams have different arrangements of family members working together, while only 15 percent of teams are composed of unrelated business associates.[53]

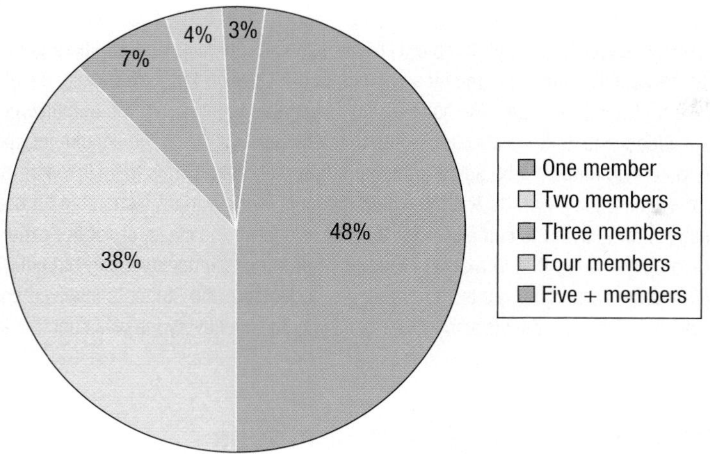

FIGURE 2.1

Number of Owners Involved in Start-Ups from the Panel Study of Entrepreneurial Dynamics

Adapted from Howard E. Aldrich, Nancy M. Carter, and Martin Ruef (2004). Teams, In Gartner, William B., Shaver, Kelly G., Carter, Nancy M., and Reynolds, Paul D., eds. *Handbook of Entrepreneurial Dynamics: the Process of Business Creation.* Thousand Oaks, CA: Sage, 2004, Table 27.1, page 307

That means about 520,000 new firms a year are started by teams, with about 442,000 started by family teams. [54]

Why so many teams? There are advantages to a team. When family members start a business, they start with already knowing and trusting each other. Teams are also likely to have more money, time, and expertise to put into a business. If the team members live together, they can save even more for the business.

When putting a team together it is important to work out key issues ahead of time. For example, team members might be putting different amounts of money or time into the business, but might be expecting identical returns, which creates an equity problem.[55] A team can also face conflict over idea ownership (see The Thoughtful Entrepreneur box below), shared goals and how to make decisions, especially when the team is evenly split on choices.[56] Legal solutions to setting up partnerships are discussed in Chapter 18, and the solutions mentioned above for couples—being clear about responsibilities, trying to maintain boundaries between work and home, having outside advisers to help sort out thorny issues, as well as planning for how the firm might end or change[57]—work just as well for teams composed of unrelated individuals as they do for couple-based teams.

THE THOUGHTFUL ENTREPRENEUR

MANAGING IDEA OWNERSHIP ON A TEAM

In one of my classes students were supposed to work on teams around an idea. Greg, a student in the class, had an idea for an iPad stand with embedded lights that would pulse in time to music. He did a quick look online and did not find any such products available yet. The professors approved the idea as a project possibility for the class.

Greg described the idea to the class, and two other students, Nancy and Jim, joined the team. They all worked on the project and did the presentation for a grade. After that, Greg said he wanted to concentrate on getting into law school and was planning to put the idea on hold. Nancy, however, wanted to go ahead with the idea and kept working on it. When Greg found out, he want ballistic. "She stole my idea!" he would tell anyone who would listen.

The disputing alums came back to the professor. The first question was what was said to Nancy and Jim about ownership rights when they joined the team. It turns out Greg had not specified anything. In his own mind, however, Greg thought it should be obvious that the idea was his and that Jim and Nancy were contributing their labor for a grade. In Nancy's mind, it was clear that she and Jim were Greg's partners in the business, contributing their time, ideas, and sweat equity. Now they had to negotiate after the fact.

Ownership problems like this happen all the time in teams. The best way to handle it is to come out right at the start and specify or negotiate who owns what. There is no one "right" answer; it depends on how the group and their larger organization (the school) handle it. Some schools maintain that all ideas generated for school projects belong to the school. Others say the idea belongs to the student, but in that case, which student?

Where there are no school rules defining "ownership," everything starts with the person who has the idea. If the person with the idea wants to keep absolute rights to the ownership, he or she should not take on other team members, or take on only members who agree (in writing) that the idea belongs to its inventor, even after noninventing students contribute their work to it. Why would students work without ownership? It can be for a grade or to save themselves from having to come up with their own idea for the class, or for the experience, or for the bragging rights of "I helped bring that to market." On the other hand, the noninventing but contributing students can try to negotiate some ownership rights. But whatever is decided, the students involved should make sure everyone has a copy of it. Emailing the agreement is a good way to show everyone was sent it at the same time.

Women and Minorities in Small Business

LO5 Identify the challenges women and minority business owners face.

Women-owned businesses are one of the fastest growing sectors of all U.S. businesses.[58] Between 1997 and 2012, the number of private businesses with at least 51 percent female ownership increased by 54 percent, while the rate for firms overall was 37 percent.[59] Around 29 percent of all businesses are majority owned by women, with another 17 percent equally owned by women and men.[60]

Although in 2012, there were 8.3 million businesses owned by women, women-owned firms accounted for only 4 percent of small business revenue nationally.[61] Why the smaller impact? Generally it is explained by the kinds of occupations and industries women choose when starting their businesses. For example, Table 2.1 shows that more women choose service industries that tend to have lower average sales levels, while there are more men in construction and financial industries, which have higher average sales levels. Men also report more high-tech firms, as well as firms where technology is central to the business. Both are associated with higher firm sales.[62]

The entrepreneurs' goals in starting the business might also play a role. For example men more often mention making money as a motivation, while women more often mention having flexibility for personal and family life. The overall growth strategies discussed in Chapter 1 also differ, with more women choosing single-person lifestyle firms over the small business forms that employ others. Along these strategy lines, women prefer less-risky firms, which also tend to be the firms with lower returns.[63] Another idea from Chapter 1 was whether the entrepreneur chooses to start a business to pursue opportunity or out of necessity, here however American women and men report similar trends, with about 70 percent of each group mentioning opportunity.[64]

TABLE 2.1 Percentage of Women Entrepreneurs in Different Industries, 2012[65]

Industries with More Women Than Average*	Percentage	Industries with Fewer Women Than Average*	Percentage
Health Care and Social Assistance (doctors, dentists, residential and child care)	52.9	Professional/Scientific/Technical Services (lawyers, CPAs, consulting)	29.1
Educational Services	45.2	Accommodation and Food Services	24.7
Personal Services (e.g., beauty salons, dry cleaners, auto repair, etc.)	40.3	Finance, Insurance, and Real Estate	21.3
Administrative Services	36.9	All other industries	18.6
Retail Trade	34.0	Construction	7.5
Arts, Entertainment, and Recreation	30.5		

*The average percentage of women across all industries was 29.2 percent.

Source: *The American Express OPEN State of Women-Owned Businesses Report—A Summary of Important Trends, 1997–2012.*

Women-and minority-owned businesses are rapidly increasing. Due to unprecedented educational and financial opportunities now available What are some of the challenges you perceive still facing minority and women entrepreneurs may be able to tap into which traditional entrepreneurs lack?

Representing approximately 22 percent of all U.S. businesses, the number of minority-owned firms has likewise grown explosively in recent years.[66] While the total number of U.S. self-employeds edged up by only 6 percent between 2000 and 2010, minority-owned businesses witnessed a remarkable 43 percent growth rate. During that same time period, the number of African American-owned businesses climbed by 13 percent, Hispanic-owned businesses by an incredible 86 percent, and Asian or Pacific Islander-owned businesses by 6 percent.[67]

What are the reasons for such phenomenal growth in the number of minority entrepreneurs? The establishment of both public and private funding and networking initiatives have helped to level the business playing field for minority entrepreneurs by offering information, advice, and funding access. Another explanation lies in the growth of racial and ethnic groups within the U.S. population, a trend that is expected to continue. The two fastest growing minority groups (Hispanics and Asian Americans) represent the largest segments of minority business owners. Hispanics represent 46 percent of all ethnic business owners, Asians 25 percent, and African Americans 24 percent.[68]

Despite the growth in the number of women and minority entrepreneurs, both groups still face the challenge of access. Access refers to the simplest form of discrimination—often women- or minority-owned firms are simply excluded from the opportunities offered to firms owned by white males. This can result from the way that networks built from interpersonal relations in business exclude women and minorities. When business relationships build from shared hobbies, sports, or even college ties, social situations that are all male or largely white outside of work can lead to unintegrated business networks.

Access problems for women- and minority-owned small businesses crop up most often as discrimination in financing.[69] This means that they may not be given the same access to funds[70] or contracting opportunities[71] that white male-owned firms are given. For example, a national survey of small business finances found that minority business loan applicants were denied at twice the rate of whites, even though application rates did not vary by race.[72] The same study found that Asian and Hispanic business owners pay higher interest rates on their loans. These differences in loan denial rates and in interest rates occurred even when all business-related differences were considered.

There are two solutions for access-based challenges. One solution is institutional, when minority- and women-owned small businesses pursue dedicated contracting funds, known as **set-asides**, among big companies and government agencies. The good news is that governments at all levels have special contracting opportunities for small businesses that are owned and operated by minorities or women. For example, the U.S. government allocated nearly $23.5 billion on set-aside based contracts in 2011.[73] Big companies and those with government contracts also have similar programs, typically with two to three times.as much money as the federal government allocates.[74] Qualification for set-asides requires certification as a business owned and operated by a woman or a minority (or both).[75] For corporations, certification is handled by organizations that are not affiliated with the government or big business, such as the National Minority Supply and Diversity Council

set-asides
Government contracting funds which are earmarked for particular kinds of firms, such as small businesses, minority-owned firms, women-owned firms, and the like.

certification
An examination based acknowledgement that the firm is owned and operated as specified.

or the Women's Business Enterprise National Council. **Certification** consists of proving that the business is truly owned and operated by a woman or minority. A similar process is used by the U.S. government, with the Small Business Administration certifying firms for the SBA's 8(a) Business Development Program, whose details are online at the SBA site. It is also good to know that the Commerce Department has the Minority Business Development Agency (www.mbda.gov/gov/) that can provide help, along with local SBA, SCORE, and Small Business Development Center offices.

Certification is not for every women- or minority-owned small business. For example, the SBA 8(a) and most corporate certification programs require a business to be in operation at least two years. As is true for any program involving government or big business, the small business needs to put more energy and resources into record keeping than it might otherwise do, especially businesses that opt for minimalized or specialized levels of professionalization. For those businesses that qualify, certification provides a ready means of access to opportunity and to networks of businesses and government agencies which can be leveraged to gain access to other sectors of business.

The second approach to solving problems of access is personal and involves making extra efforts to network. As discussed in Chapter 3, building a social network is central to business success. For minority-owned and women-owned businesses, networking is especially important because such firms need to network even more than other types of firms. While networking with other minority-owned or women-owned firms will feel comfortable, and lead to business within that group, the real gains in business require networking in more diverse and potentially less comfortable situations, such as industry and trade associations, chambers of commerce, and the like. Success comes from the number of different types of contacts one makes, and for a minority- or women-owned business, this requires having business contacts from other races, genders, ages, and sectors.

LO6 Describe the situation of people who become business owners later in life.

Second Career Entrepreneurs

late career entrepreneurs
(also known as *second career entrepreneurs*) People who begin their businesses after having retired or resigned from work in corporations at age 50 or later.

A special group of entrepreneurs are called second career or **late career entrepreneurs**—people who begin their businesses after having retired or resigned from work in corporations at age 50 or later. Whether these individuals start their business as part of a postretirement career plan or after early retirement has forced them to reevaluate their lives, a late career as a business owner has become a necessity for them.[76]

As increasing numbers of corporations merge, downsize, reorganize, and/or close altogether, many firms are offering attractive retirement packages to encourage employees to voluntarily leave the organization.[77] Workers are opting to accept generous offers to retire early (between ages 50 and 64). People's decisions of whether to return to work depend on their individual level of wealth (retirement income and savings), their health, and their work experience, as well as general economic conditions.[78]

Second career entrepreneurs face distinctive challenges such as maintaining self-confidence as they retrench themselves.

About a third of the retirees who return to work decide to become self-employed.[79] Those who do face three challenges—adjusting to the entrepreneurial life, reestablishing self-confidence, and keeping personal finances out of the business.

Working for others for most of their life, late career entrepreneurs are likely to have gotten used to having many of the daily chores of running a business done for them. Even for former managers, the mechanics of getting the location cleaned or the payroll checks written may have been things they could take for granted. As entrepreneurs, they have to do these things themselves or arrange to have them done. All entrepreneurs get used to a do-it-yourself approach, and this is a challenge for everyone, but it can be especially trying for late career entrepreneurs, who may have hoped that life would get easier rather than harder later in their careers.

The key for managing the demanding life of the entrepreneur is to get advice from people in your line of business, or from consultants (which can include the free consulting available through Small Business Development Centers or SCORE) about the basic activities of the small business. Make sure you have all the demanding aspects of running a business covered. Pick one or two that are particularly hard or onerous and consider subcontracting those out in order to keep the early stage of the business manageable.

The second challenge comes from a loss of confidence.[80] The stigma attached to older workers' departure from their former job can make a tremendous difference in their level of confidence.

Being given early retirement can be seen as a company's effort to replace expensive (if capable) older talent with junior people who work for less. But being laid off or downsized suggests that the person was expendable at best, deadwood at worst. The difference in labeling makes a difference in the late career entrepreneur's self-confidence.

When there are self-confidence issues, the first solution is to take some time to get over the shock to self-image. Counseling, whether job or psychological, can also help tremendously. When the person is ready, the solution often involves redefining one's life. The goal is to describe life in ways that help the individual take control over it. A layoff becomes an indication that it was time to move on. A downsizing becomes something that occurs to those best able to land on their feet. In taking control over the past, it can become easier to assert control over the present and future.

The second self-confidence solution comes from networking. Entrepreneurs as a group are an energetic and optimistic group. Just talking to people you know, as Donna Herrle did (see Small Business Insight box see below), or joining local entrepreneur organizations, such as the chamber of commerce or the local chapter of a trade or professional organization, can expose you to people full of energy and ideas. This is contagious, and as you hear the stories of perseverance and overcoming challenges that abound among entrepreneurs, the possibilities for a successful entrepreneurial life seem to become more realistic.

The third problem is keeping personal finances out of the business.[81] Often when individuals are laid off or given early retirement, they can receive lump-sum financial settlements. Frequently, people intending to become late career entrepreneurs plan to use a substantial portion of these funds to start the new business. Sometimes this happens because late career entrepreneurs see their personal funds as "easy money," funds that can be obtained quickly and without a lot of hassles. The problem is that many people who take the easy money are also taking the easy way out. They fail to carefully consider how they will invest the money in the business, and how it will be used. Taking the easy way out can often mean late career entrepreneurs underprepare for the rigors of business, and they are risking their retirement nest egg.

For late career entrepreneurs, the solution is to treat their own money as objectively as possible. Invest it only if you can make a strong case that the investment in the business is going to produce reasonable returns. Treat your own money as an outsider's investment. Do a business plan and

SMALL BUSINESS INSIGHT

DONNA HERRLE[82]

Imagine getting an invitation to a wine and cheese party for a new business, where the owner shows a "before" picture of herself in her corporate garb and an "after" picture of her in her home office, wearing pajamas and slippers, with the adage "change is good" over them both. That is what Donna Herrle, 51, sent to business acquaintances, friends, former co-workers, and family when she started her Pittsburgh graphic design business, Drawing Conclusions. A graphic designer and former sales manager of design and print services, she was out on her own after being laid off from corporate America in 2002. That layoff had set off alarm bells for Donna, who feared the loss of security a regular paycheck had brought her. At loose ends after the layoff, she also wondered what she should, or could, do.

Her turnaround and focus on starting Drawing Conclusions came about from talking to everyone she knew. She was surprised at how many others had been in or were facing the same situation, and the advice she got helped her make her own transition to self-employment. The advice she received again and again was to plan the business carefully and keep networking, and the work would come.

And the work came. One client brought a project to the wine and cheese party, based on Donna's graphically impressive invitation. Five more projects came in within 10 days of the party. Within a year she had over 50 clients and gross sales in six figures.

consider seeking outside funding from friends and family to help keep you honest about the chances for the business.

This chapter starts with the idea that while no single explanation can really cover all 14.7 million self-employed people in the United States, there *are* aspects of the entrepreneurial life that apply to many. Some of these are general ideas, such as the entrepreneurial career or the competencies needed to be successful in small business. There are also types of entrepreneurs that describe many, but not all, self-employed people. Whether we look at attitudinal or behavioral types like the classic entrepreneur or small business owner, or if we look at demographical groups such as women entrepreneurs, the more we know about people pursuing entrepreneurship, the better it is for identifying important issues in their business and personal lives. Every entrepreneur's story is uniquely his or her own, but across millions of entrepreneurs, there are some similarities, and these help make it easier to think about the entrepreneurial process and get the right kind of help to entrepreneurs.

CHAPTER SUMMARY

LO1 Recognize the key aspects of the entrepreneurial personality.

- In addition to self-efficacy from Chapter 1, there are five other key behaviors for entrepreneurial success.
- *Passion:* The intensely positive feeling entrepreneurs have for their business.
- *Perseverance:* The ability to stick to activities over long periods, even in the face of setbacks.
- *Promotion/Prevention Focus:* The behaviors related to pursuing gains and preventing losses.
- *Planning Style:* Ranging from comprehensive to habit-based, this reflects how much and about what you ordinarily plan.
- *Professionalization:* The extent to which a firm meets or exceeds the standard business practices for the industry.

LO2 Assess the operational competencies of the successful entrepreneur.

- Forms of business-related expertise are called *competencies.*
- To be successful, an entrepreneur needs competency in the key business functions (e.g., sales, operations, etc.), industry-specific knowledge, resource competencies, determination competencies, and opportunity competencies.

LO3 Describe the challenges of family business owners.

- Family businesses are one of the major forms of small business.
- The major challenges facing the family business are role conflict, time management, and succession.
- All three challenges can be met through careful planning.
- Married couples and nonfamily partnerships face many of the same problems and solutions.

LO4 Recognize the special nature of entrepreneurial teams.

- The majority of businesses are started by teams.
- Spouses or life partners are the most common form of team.
- Couple teams can benefit from trust and financial flexibility.
- Typical problems include lack of agreement, separating work and family issues, and handling endings.
- Similar problems also crop up in non-spouse teams.

LO5 Identify the challenges women and minority business owners face.

- Women-owned and minority-owned businesses are growing at rates faster than other types of businesses.
- The major challenge facing these businesses is gaining access to opportunity.
- Access is achieved through networking and set-asides.

LO6 Describe the situation of people who become business owners later in life.

- Late career entrepreneurship happens when a person is laid off, downsized, or given early retirement.
- The challenges facing late career entrepreneurs come from having to do everything themselves, loss of confidence, and using too much of their personal money too soon in the business.
- Having to do everything can be handled by identifying the tasks to be done ahead of time. Loss of confidence can be dealt with through taking time to heal and by networking with enthusiastic entrepreneurs. Late career entrepreneurs should use their own money only when it makes sense for the business, usually proven through a business plan.

KEY TERMS

cognition, 30
action, 30
passion, 30
perseverance, 30
promotion focus, 31
prevention focus, 31
comprehensive planners, 31
critical-point planners, 31
opportunistic planners, 31
reactive planners, 31
habit-driven planners, 32
professionalization, 32
standard business practice, 32
expert business professionalization, 32
specialized business professionalization, 32
minimalized business professionalization, 32
competencies, 34
key business functions, 35
industry-specific knowledge, 35
resource competencies, 35
determination competencies, 35
opportunity competencies, 36
family business, 37
role conflict, 37
time management, 38
succession, 39
set-asides, 43
certification, 44
late career entrepreneurs, 44

DISCUSSION QUESTIONS

1. What are the different aspects of the entrepreneurial personality?
2. What would be the likely impact on a start-up if the entrepreneur had a strong promotion focus and a weak prevention focus?
3. Could someone with good industry-specific knowledge but low competency in basic business skills be successful as an entrepreneur in that industry? Why or why not?
4. When does it make sense to create a business using a minimalized approach to professionalization? Why is that so?
5. What are the strengths and weaknesses of a team?
6. What is the major challenge facing women- and minority-owned firms? How can this be solved?
7. What makes the situation of late career entrepreneurs problematic? What can they do to smooth their way?

EXPERIENTIAL EXERCISES

1. Which of the aspects of the entrepreneurial personality describes you the best? Be ready to explain why.
2. Which entrepreneurial competencies do you possess? Be ready to provide examples and explain why you made these choices. You can use the result of Skill Module 2.2 to aid you in this.
3. Pick small businesses with which others in the class are familiar and analyze what level of professionalization they display. Be ready to explain the basis for your classification.
4. Select a local family business owner or female or minority entrepreneur whom you admire, and research the person's business and professional background. Interview this person if possible. What particular challenges were faced? What competencies were used to overcome them?

MINI-CASE

GEORGE WASHINGTON, DISTILLER AND SEVENTH-CAREER ENTREPRENEUR[83]

When he stepped off the podium in front of Federal Hall in New York City on March 4, 1797, George Washington was probably thinking not about the presidency he just handed over to John Adams, but about his audacious plan to start a new career to rescue his Virginia farm, Mount Vernon, from bankruptcy. For Washington, farmer, surveyor, soldier, commander, legislator, and president, this new role might be called his seventh career, but it was necessary.

Washington had owned a plantation for much of his adult life, and he tried to get back to it between stints as the nation's top general and as president. By the time he could retire to Mount Vernon, he discovered the business was in trouble. The number of people for whom he was responsible had grown from 10 when he inherited the farm to 300 as he left the presidency. Unfortunately his land-holding size and productivity had not kept pace. He was facing bankruptcy.

Knowing this even as he was preparing to end his term, Washington picked up on the idea of a distillery when James Anderson, a Scottish immigrant to Virginia, pitched the idea. Washington had shown himself supportive of inventions, having developed new ways of training mules and preparing wheat for market. He had even received America's third patent.

Anderson's idea made financial sense. Taxes on imported rum were high, and this was putting a crimp in the average American's drinking habits. Back in 1797, the average American was annually drinking 5 gallons of distilled spirits like rum and whiskey (today the average is 1.8 gallons). So there was a ready market.

So, working with Anderson, Washington started with two small stills in 1797 making a 110-proof rye whiskey. Production grew in 1799 to 11,000 gallons sold in two versions (50 cents/gallon for regular and $1/gallon for premium whiskey) and to $7,500 profit made, making Washington America's leading distiller. While Anderson could handle the role of running the distillery itself, the business side was in Washington's hands. Unfortunately, he failed to train a successor. Then Washington died in 1799. The distillery passed into several hands but began a seemingly unstoppable decline and was closed for good in 1814.

CASE DISCUSSION QUESTIONS

1. What advantages would George Washington bring to James Anderson's idea for a Virginia distillery?
2. Washington's farm was operating even as he got the distillery off the ground. What kind of problems could that raise for the ex-president?
3. At his death, Washington's distillery was the largest in the United States. Did this make Washington a high-growth entrepreneur or a small business owner? Why?

SUGGESTED CASES AND ARTICLES

- Real Estate Millionaires of Memphis, C-2

Available on McGraw-Hill Create™

- Bob's Home Repair
- Jilbert's Dairy
- Cecil Tire or That Dog Won't Hunt

SUGGESTED VIDEOS

www.mhhe.com/katz4e

Video Case:

- For a written video case and corresponding clip, visit the OLC at www.mhhe.com/katz4e and select "Chapter 2".
- Small Business Volunteering

SBTV.com Videos:

- Managing To Do Lists
- Senior Citizen Entrepreneur
- Minority Entrepreneurs Break through Barriers

STVP Video:

- Learning to Take Risks: A Personal Story

CHAPTER

3

Small Business Environment: Managing External Relations

● Tim Hayden was a sports fan who realized that the environment for watching sports had changed because of big-screen TVs and on-screen graphics. The couch at home and not a seat at the stadium had become "the best seat in the house." That led him to the realization of a business opportunity. What changes do you see in your environment that might lead to new business opportunities?

LEARNING OBJECTIVES

After you complete this chapter, you will be able to:

LO1 Describe the elements that make up the small business environment.

LO2 Demonstrate your ability to scan the small business environment.

LO3 Apply the techniques of building legitimacy for your organization.

LO4 Navigate the techniques of social networking.

LO5 Explain the basic skills for handling a crisis.

LO6 Recognize how small businesses can achieve sustainability.

LO7 Identify the major steps in making ethical decisions in small business.

Focus on Small Business: Tim Hayden and the Missed Home Run[1]

Tim Hayden had been an avowed "sports fanatic" all his life. Friends could set their clocks by Tim. He was always watching games in the stands or on TV. Of all sports, he loved baseball the most. Sitting in the bleachers at the home of the St. Louis Cardinals, Busch Stadium, what he was sensing there distressed him. It seemed that fewer people were in the stands than in earlier years. He wished he could do something about it.

The final push to action for Tim came in 1998 when Mark McGwire crushed his 70th home run on his way to a baseball record. Tim and his father were sitting in the stands that historic night. However, they missed seeing the home run because they were standing in line at the concession stand.

As McGwire rounded the bases, Tim's friends at home were watching numerous instant replays from every conceivable camera angle while listening to the commentators talk about inside stories. In addition, they could see the exact positions of each pitch location and the in-depth scouting report on McGwire's home runs.

But here he was in the stadium, where he had paid good money for the ticket. And yet the best seat in the stadium was at home in front of his big-screen TV.

At that moment he realized that others might be thinking the same way. He thought he finally knew one of the reasons why attendance was down. Sitting at home with a large-screen TV, the refrigerator nearby, the bathroom a few steps away, the seat comfortable and the room air-conditioned, how could the stadium compete? Television baseball had become so much more detailed and informative than the in-stadium variety, with last pitch graphics, hit location graphics, and detailed stats on all the players constantly shown on the big screen at home. The "best seat in the stadium" had indeed shifted to home, and the fans with it.

Tim sensed a business opportunity in that shift. Sports teams had to bring fans back to the stadiums, where teams make their most profit. He also realized that for a fan, there was an undeniable energy being among tens of thousands of fellow fans with the chance to see that once-in-a-lifetime play.

Being digitally savvy, he knew that combining a fan's personal cell phone or PDA with a Wi-Fi Web-based application, he could bring the at-home experience into the stadium. Fans sitting in the stands could see any instant replay from dozens of camera angles, as well as all the cool graphics that you see on TV, with the ability to order food and drink to their seat, and maybe connect with other fans in the stadium. And even better, it could all be on-demand.

From his own pain, the feelings of other baseball fans, and over the next four years a careful study of the trends in the various sports leagues and televised sports, Tim Hayden realized that the enhanced digital experiences (they weren't as prevalent in 2002) and new TV graphic techniques of sports broadcasters had fundamentally changed the environment for sports watching. It also opened up a business opportunity.

DISCUSSION QUESTIONS

1. What were the different types of data Tim used to figure out the problem of reduced attendance?
2. What kind of data do you think would have been most useful and why?
3. Do you think the change in fan behavior came about from changes in society (fan demographics) or in technology?
4. What do you think was key to Tim's making the jump from a problem to a business opportunity?

The Environment of Small Business

LO1 Describe the elements that make up the small business environment.

environment
The sum total of forces outside of the entrepreneur and the firm.

organizational identity
Part of the BRIE model; composed of the name, description, and distinctive elements of a firm, such as trademarks, uniforms, logos, characters, and stories.

bootstrapping
Using low-cost or free techniques to minimize your cost of doing business.

The moment Tim's frustration with missing the home run made him rethink what was happening around him, he became aware of the **environment**—all of the forces outside the firm or in this case the individual entrepreneur (or entrepreneur-to-be). In Tim's case, the environment was the source of his inspiration (if you recall the BRIE model from Chapter 1, this would fall under Intention), as well as the data from friends, family, co-workers, and the media giving him the background on the nature and scope of the problems with attending professional sporting events.

Following the BRIE model in starting a business, the entrepreneur creates a boundary within the environment, setting his firm apart from the rest of the environment. In doing this, the entrepreneur gives the firm an **organizational identity**. Organizational identity is not just the name of a firm, but its basic description—what it does and where it does this. It can include formal elements like a registration with the state, or a Web site or e-mail account with the firm's name on it, or a telephone number in the firm's name. But there are also important informal elements of identity. Often the firm and the entrepreneur are one and the same, but as the firm grows beyond the entrepreneur's direct personal control, for example, by adding a part-time employee or running an order-taking Web site 24/7, parts of the identity of the firm can grow beyond the entrepreneur alone.[2] And as the firm establishes a track record for performance, that performance, along with the goods or services it creates become key elements of the firm's and entrepreneur's identity. For example, it is hard to think of Famous Amos without thinking about his cookies.

In creating a firm using the BRIE model, the entrepreneur gathers resources from the environment. These can include information on how to do the business or who to sell to, funding to run the business, space for the business, and raw materials for the business to use to make goods or deliver services. If the environment is rich with resources as it is during economic boom times, it can be easy to gather what is needed. In tougher times, such as during economic recessions, gathering resources can be harder. As entrepreneurs face resource constraints, they often learn to get by with less, or substitute a more readily obtained resource, or ask to borrow, rent, or trade for the resource. These techniques are called **bootstrapping** (which is covered in detail in Chapter 5) and are part of the culture of most successful start-ups.

The environment is at the core of exchange in the BRIE model, since exchange is literally the firm or entrepreneur dealing with the environment—buying, selling, or trading across the boundary of the firm. In the end, entrepreneurs carve a firm out of the environment by gathering resources, setting them up inside a boundary and trading or exchanging them across the boundary. In short, almost everything a firm does involves the environment. This chapter will help you understand more about the environment and its components, and how you can organize yourself and your firm to manage its relations with the environment.

The Elements of the Small Business Environment

Environment is a difficult concept to consider because it is so big. It literally includes the entire world outside yourself and your business. As an entrepreneur, or entrepreneur-to-be, how do you go about understanding it, much less using it to help focus and operate your business? The key is to have a model of the environment in mind, which can help you focus on a part of the world at a time.

You may have seen a diagram of the environment like the one in Figure 3.1 in your introductory business or management text. It makes sense to revisit it here thinking about how these terms apply to small businesses. The **internal environment** of a firm consists of those people inside the boundary—the owner, any employees, and any other owners or board members of the firm. As every company matures, it adds to its **organizational culture** a set of shared beliefs or basic assumptions that demonstrate how things get done. Organizational culture also includes common, accepted ways of dealing with problems and challenges within a company.[3]

internal environment
The people and groups within the boundary of a firm, including the owners, managers, employees, and board members of the firm.

organizational culture
A set of shared beliefs, basic assumptions, or common, accepted ways of dealing with problems and challenges within a company that demonstrate how things get done.

For example, Brian and Lisa Jolles are the married co-owners of Jolles Insurance in Ellicott City, Maryland. They recognized that they needed to set an example of healthy living for their employees in order to promote wellness to their insurance customers. They did this by establishing exercise as part of the organization's culture. Employees are encouraged to walk during lunch to control stress and hunger. Wellness is so much a part of the culture that the Jolles run an adult exercise boot camp for employees, clients, neighbors, and friends three days a week, sponsor a Web site (www.wepromotehealth.com), and even sponsor a Health and Wellness Day at a local park, which initially drew 500 participants and since then has become a communitywide annual event.[4] Being a small business makes managing organizational culture easier than in larger businesses because, in a small business, there is a lot of flexibility in terms of roles and expected behaviors, especially when the business is first getting started.

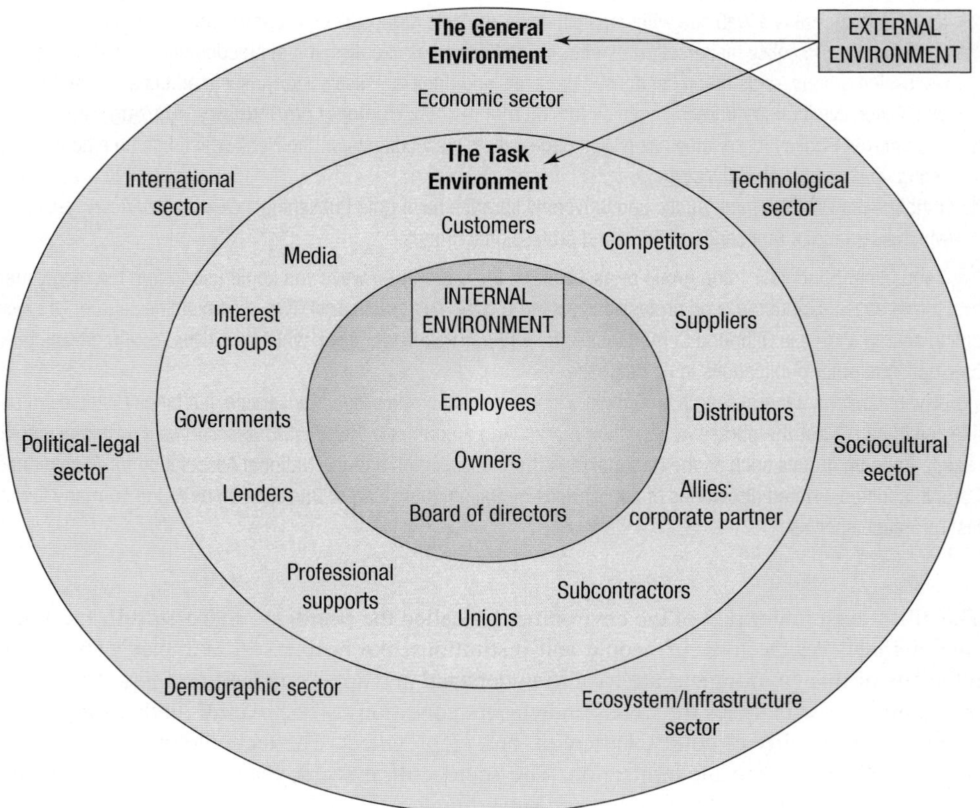

FIGURE 3.1

The Organization's Environment

Source: Adapted from Angelo Kinicki and Brian K. Williams, *Management: A Practical Introduction* (New York: McGraw-Hill, 2009), p. 73.

external environment
The forces, institutions and people (i.e., the rest of the world) outside the boundary of the firm.

task environment
A part of the external environment made up of those components that the firm deals with directly such as customers, suppliers, consultants, media, interest groups, and the like.

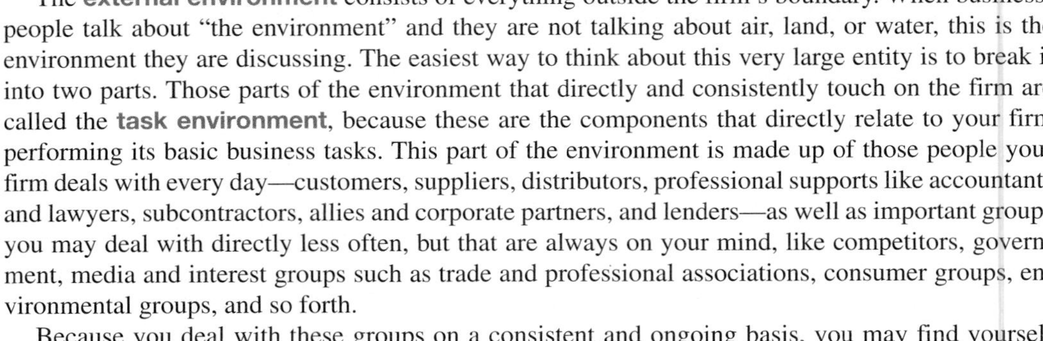

The **external environment** consists of everything outside the firm's boundary. When businesspeople talk about "the environment" and they are not talking about air, land, or water, this is the environment they are discussing. The easiest way to think about this very large entity is to break it into two parts. Those parts of the environment that directly and consistently touch on the firm are called the **task environment**, because these are the components that directly relate to your firm performing its basic business tasks. This part of the environment is made up of those people your firm deals with every day—customers, suppliers, distributors, professional supports like accountants and lawyers, subcontractors, allies and corporate partners, and lenders—as well as important groups you may deal with directly less often, but that are always on your mind, like competitors, government, media and interest groups such as trade and professional associations, consumer groups, environmental groups, and so forth.

Because you deal with these groups on a consistent and ongoing basis, you may find yourself having trouble recognizing new trends or changes among these members of your task environment. One simple way to do this is to take some time to reflect on whether and how business and relations have changed with each group over the past 6 months or 12 months. Another simple way is to look at the professional and trade publications for their industries. You can find these using the techniques given in Skill Module 3.1 and on the Online Learning Center. In particular, look for articles that talk about "trends" or "future" in the title.

SKILL MODULE 3.1 Finding Your Trade or Professional Association and Their Magazines

In this skill module we will start with finding your professional or trade organization, and with that information in hand, find that group's publications. There are four ways to find the organizations:

1. The American Society of Association Executives Gateway (**www.asaecenter.org/directories/association-search.cfm**) has a searchable online directory of nearly 7,000 trade and professional associations.
2. An industry portal is a Web site with capabilities for multiple groups like current members, potential members, media, and policy makers. Portals offer multiple services like disseminating documents, chat rooms, discussion groups, registration services, databases, and the like. Polson Enterprises maintains one of the most extensive industry portals pages on the Internet (**www.virtualpet.com/industry/mfg/mfg.htm**).
3. The Internet Public Library also has a Web page called "Associations on the Net," which has an extensive listing on **www.ipl.org/div/aon/**.
4. If that does not work, most public and university libraries have Gale Publishing's *Directory of Associations,* which lists tens of thousands of trade and professional groups.

trade magazines
The magazines that target specific industries and professions.

If you cannot find your trade group or association, there are three ways you could use to find the magazines that target specific industries and professions (called **trade magazines**). Two use an online search. The best online search source is Oxbridge Communications' **www.mediafinder.com**, which has over 75,000 newsletters, catalogs, and other publications in its database.

Or you can try a general search on Google. Enter the name of the product or service. If it takes multiple words, like "child care," put the phrase in quotation marks. Add a comma and the word *association.* For this example, Google turns up groups such as the National Child Care Association and the National Association for Family Child Care. In addition, printed directories of publications by Bacon Publishing or Burrelle can be found on many libraries' reference shelves.

general environment
A part of the external environment made up of sectors of major forces that shape the people and institutions of the task and internal environments, such as the economic sector or the demographic sector.

The other, even larger part of the environment is called the **general environment**. It represents the major forces on the lives of people and institutions like businesses, and even nations. Some components of this environment are easy to understand and apply to small business. For example, the economic sector includes the trends and current conditions of the overall market for goods and services, the availability of equity and credit, and employment. The technological sector includes innovation, invention, and modernization. The sociocultural sector includes cultures often based on things such as nationality or religion and subcultures which are based on groups formed around shared interests within a larger culture. For example, think of the contributions of the hip-hop subculture to modern music and lifestyle marketing.

The demographic sector includes trends in the mix of ages, races, and gender in society. For example, Jim Allsup had experience handling claims for Social Security, so he decided to start a business of his own using that experience. He did some research and discovered as the baby boom generation (born 1946–1964) aged, the disability services market would grow right along with the retiree services market. From his work experience, he already knew that the Social Security Disability Insurance program was nearly impossible for people to deal with on their own, which delayed disability payments. He felt he could provide a valuable service to people to help them qualify faster for these payments, and in 1984 created Allsup, Inc., to do just that. Today, Allsup, Inc., is the nation's largest and most successful SSDI claims-assistance company, with 580 employees.[5]

Hip-hop is a subculture that has made major impacts on fashion, design, language, and music. Part of the sociocultural sector, these subcultures shape new directions for entrepreneurship.

Part of the work Allsup, Inc., has done was to testify before congressional committees about needed reforms in the nation's disability insurance programs. This points to another arena in the general environment, the political-legal sector. This sector reflects the broad trends affecting law, government, and politics, including changes in political parties and players, new legal and policy initiatives, and intersections of government, politics, or law with the other forces in the general environment, such as when forces from the technological, economic, and international sectors led to a federally mandated changeover from analog to digital television in 2009.

Those pressures in the international sector that led to the American decision to adopt DTV included the push for a single global standard for DTV displays and broadcasts. However the United States adopted a different standard from the one the Japanese DTV industry and government recommended. These cross-national factors reflect the international sector of the general environment. Today small businesses in rural Nebraska can be competing with firms in China or eastern Europe for business in the next county. Inexpensive worldwide communication, shipping, and money transfers mean that small businesses compete globally for business, and need to be aware of global trends.

Finally, there is the ecosystem/infrastructure sector, which reflects the physical world in which we live. This sector includes the natural components, such as raw materials, weather, and ecological forces, as well as created components such as cities, roads, and other elements of the infrastructure. Changes here are sometimes unpredictable, like the highly destructive Hurricane Katrina of 2005, but sometimes more predictable, like the worldwide decrease in forested areas over the past 200 years.

For all of these factors of the general environment, it is important to note that every one of them depends on the specific social and institutional supports for the general environment sector you are considering. In a country like Peru, which has an extremely high percentage of people who want to become entrepreneurs, the lack of a financial and transportation infrastructure has made it difficult to get businesses started or get goods or services to markets. Other countries may have high levels of corruption which makes starting a business risky. So the general environment always needs to be considered in terms of its social supports and institutional (or government and business) supports. Now that you have a way to segment and focus on a sector of the environment, you are ready to learn how to analyze it.

Environmental Scanning for Small Businesses

LO2 Demonstrate your ability to scan the small business environment.

Big corporations have whole departments focused on scanning the environment and the firm's competitors. Almost no small business can afford to try that approach, but they can benefit tremendously from even a small amount of environmental scanning such as those shown in

Skill Module 3.2 and on the Online Learning Center. There are several low-cost and relatively fast ways to monitor the environment.[6] They include:

- Looking for trends and future-looking articles in the trade and professional press of your industry or those of members of your task environment (see Skill Module 3.1).
- Asking your customers, suppliers, banker, attorney, and accountants what they see on the horizon for business in general, for business in your community in general, or for your industry or line of business in particular.
- Keeping notes on the things that bother you about the way work is done now, or what bothers you about how something has changed (whether a product, service, or process you deal with), and periodically do some fast research (typically searching on the Web) on what causes it and how others feel about it. For opinion Web sites, try ePinions, Yelp, Amazon, Buzzillions, Mouthshut, TrustedReviews, ConsumerSearch, or CitySearch.
- Subscribing to a couple of magazines/newsletters (online or hard copy) or online newsfeeds or blogs outside your area of business. In the science/technology area, for example, look at *Discover, Wired, Scientific American,* or even *Popular Mechanics*. For online versions, you can subscribe to the RSS feed or a summary e-mail to several of the print magazines, or online sources like Gizmag. For all of these, tag or record interesting ideas so you can come back to them when you have time to think. By the way, you can find a list of online and print magazines organized by topic areas on Yahoo! Directory's News and Media section (**dir.yahoo.com/News_and_Media**).

SKILL MODULE 3.2 Finding Out How the Small Business Economy Is Doing

A key element in environmental scanning is assessing the overall environment and its trends. There are several ways to do this, from the simple to the complex. Simple approaches use a single or small set of numbers, like Network Solutions' Small Business Success Index (**www.networksolutions.com/smallbusiness**), the Kauffman Index of Entrepreneurial Activity (**www.kauffman.org/research-and-policy/kauffman-index-of-entrepreneurial-activity.aspx**), the Gazelle Index (**www.gazelleindex.com**), or the National Federation of Independent Business's *Small Business Economic Trends* (**www.nfib.com/research-foundation/surveys/small-business-economic-trends**), which offers its monthly Index of Small Business Optimism. For these, your greatest concern is the trend, and whether it is rising or falling. At the other extreme, the Small Business Administration's Office of Advocacy offers its Quarterly Indicators (**http://archive.sba.gov/advo/research/sbei.html**) with a compendium of measures and the SBA's own analysis of them. One other key source of data for your state is the Office of Advocacy's Small Business Profiles for the States and Territories (**http://archive.sba.gov/advo/research/profiles/**), but these report data from one or two years earlier. You can learn more about these different sources of information in our online skill modules.

Bill Gates is famous as a trend-spotter (although he has made some bad calls too), but one of the tricks he swears by is "Think Week," where he goes away by himself and spends time thinking and researching to help him focus on what is coming and what is important to his business. Most of us can't afford a week off, but putting aside three to four hours every three months to review what you have noticed and what notes you have made can do a lot to achieve the major benefits of environmental scanning, and still leave time to get your own work done.

Do not be afraid to make a bad decision. The trick with all forward-looking choices is to use a "real options" approach. To do this, you establish benchmarks to achieve, timetables for their achievement, and a formal review process to get you to make the tough "continue" or "stop" decisions. Microsoft initially dismissed the Internet, but they revisited their decision and changed course to make Internet Explorer the most used browser in the world.

So now you know what the environment is, what its different components are, and how and where you might keep an eye on the environment to help you prepare for the future. That leaves open how you deal with the environment on a daily basis as you begin or run your business. In the next section we look at the major techniques for managing your relations with the environment.

Five Skills for Managing Relations with the Environment

Having learned about the different types and sectors of the environment, and the way to scan and analyze them, it only makes sense to look at how to apply that knowledge to help launch and grow your own small business. In this section five approaches to managing relations with the environment, what is called **external relations**, will be introduced:

- Building legitimacy
- Developing a social network
- Handling a crisis
- Achieving sustainability
- Making ethical decisions

external relations
The general description for the processes and skills used in the management of a firm's interactions with people, organizations, and institutions outside of its boundary.

The goal of any small business owner is to manage external relations in order to create social capital. **Social capital** includes characteristics of a business, like trust, consistency, and networks, that help make business operations smooth and efficient. Small businesses high in social capital are more trusted, checked up on less, treated more fairly by regulators, and given the benefit of the doubt when problems occur.[7] This social capital is capital in the same sense that cash or land can be. You can accumulate it or spend it, and the more of it you have, the greater the value of your firm. Social capital is the major component of what accountants call "goodwill," and you can find it on a business's balance sheet. Let us look at the five techniques for managing external relations and building social capital.

social capital
Characteristics of a business, like trusts, consistency, and networks, that represent potential social obligations which are an asset of the firm or entrepreneur.

Building Legitimacy

Legitimacy means that a firm is worthy of consideration or doing business with because of the impressions or opinions of customers, suppliers, investors, or competitors.[8] Gaining legitimacy is one of the top challenges facing new small businesses, but it can be especially difficult for entrepreneurs seen as "different"—women, minorities, home-based businesses, businesses started by young people, entrepreneurs introducing a new technology, or people new to the area or industry. Achieving legitimacy is also a major goal of all new businesses or of existing businesses that have gone through a significant change, like getting new owners or changing their product lines. Achieving legitimacy means building trust among customers and other key groups.

LO3 Apply the techniques of building legitimacy for your organization.

legitimacy
The belief that a firm is worthy of consideration or doing business with because of the impressions or opinions of customers, suppliers, investors, or competitors.

There are three general forms of legitimacy that you can develop—based on your people, based on your product, and based on your organization.[9] Each is discussed below.

Remember that often the owner *is* the business in many peoples' minds. So, he or she is the most important element of social capital to customers and supporters of a business, such as bankers, lawyers, and suppliers. Having people in the organization—an owner, employees, or even media spokespeople—whom customers know and respect increases the firm's legitimacy. Making sure the people of your business always work in the best, friendliest, and most professional way also helps build the business. Some of the major examples of people-based legitimacy are given in Table 3.1.

Also, many small business owners think that the most important source of legitimacy comes from an understanding of the product or service offered.[10] If customers do not understand it, the company is unlikely to get any customer attention because customers may not trust it. Fortunately, most small businesses offer products or services with which customers are already familiar (what we will call an "imitative strategy" in Chapter 7). The goal then becomes making sure the customer knows about the details of the product, its high quality and environmental friendliness, its competitive advantage, how to use it, and has the assurance that it will be backed up by the firm. Table 3.2 describes many forms of product-based legitimacy.

If the customer understands the product, the final key legitimacy factor is promoting knowledge about the organization itself. This might focus on telling about the history or visibility the firm already enjoys. It might come from published information that makes sure your firm looks like a substantial and professional business. Whatever gives customers confidence in the quality and survivability of the firm helps the selling process and in turn increases the all-important trust factor. Table 3.3 gives the key factors for organizational legitimacy.

TABLE 3.1 People-Based Legitimacy Indicators

People	More Legitimate	Less Legitimate
Good will	Having well-known or well-regarded owners, employees, supporters, or spokespeople	Lacking well-known or well-regarded owners, employees, supporters, or spokespeople
Public recognition	Firm, owner, or employees receive awards (e.g., "Small Business of the Year") or make notable achievements outside the business (e.g., president of the PTA or BBB)	Little or no public recognition
Product/service name recognition	Selling brand name merchandise or services	Nonbrand name
Business network membership	Membership in trade (e.g., National Restaurant Association) and business (e.g., BBB, NFIB, Chamber of Commerce) organizations	No memberships
Organizational size	Having employees	Only yourself
Attire	Wearing uniforms or business attire	Casual attire

TABLE 3.2 Product-Based Legitimacy Indicators

Product	More Legitimate	Less Legitimate
Customer assurance	Publicly stated guarantees, bonding, try-before-you-buy policies, return policies, etc.	None stated or given
Experiential supports	Documentation, demonstration offered	None offered
Customer service	Providing customer service live or online	No customer service
Quality standards	Meets or exceeds industry standards for quality	Fails to meet industry standards for quality
Environmental friendliness	Uses recyclable materials, demonstrates green design, or has a low carbon footprint.	Shows no concern for the environment or natural resources
Certifications	**ISO**, **Baldrige Award**, minority or women-owned business, professional licensing	None or self-certified
Testimonials	Present testimonials from customers satisfied with the product	No information from users
Intellectual property	Has trademarks, service marks, patents or copyrights	None
Industry leadership	Setting technological or service standards adopted by competitors	Common technologies or services
Media product/ service visibility	Interviews, articles, placements, or columns in print or electronic media about the product	Little or no attention in print or electronic media about the product

ISO
Stands for the International Standards Organization, and refers to certification for having met a standard of quality that is consistently evaluated around the world (see www.iso.org).

Baldrige Award
The Malcolm Baldrige National Quality Award is given by the U.S. government to businesses and nonprofit organizations that have been judged outstanding in seven measures of quality leadership; strategic planning; customer and market focus; measurement, analysis, and knowledge management; human resource focus; process management; and results (see www.quality.nist.gov).

TABLE 3.3 Organization-Based Legitimacy Indicators

Product	More Legitimate	Less Legitimate
Media organization visibility	Interviews, articles, or columns in print or electronic media about the organization	Little or no attention in print or electronic media about the organization
History	In operation for a long time	New
Time commitment	Full time	Part time
Hours of operation	9–5, 9–9, 24/7	1–5, 6–9
Days of operations	M–F, 7 days a week	One day, weekends only
Phone line	Dedicated to business	Shared with home
Phone answering	Human answered	Answering machine, voice mail
Legal form	Corporation, partnership, or LLC	Sole proprietorship
Physical setting	Commercial site like a store, office building, or mall	Home-based business; a business with no physical location; a business run out of a post office mailbox
Public listings	Yellow Pages, Dun & Bradstreet Business Profile, business directories	White pages or none
Internet identity	Uses business name **katz@sb2020.com**	Uses generic name **katz@yahoo.com**
Graphic design (business cards, stationery, Web sites, etc.)	Professionally done	Personally done
Partnering	Partners with known businesses	Partners with unknown businesses or no partnering
Dealer network membership	Being an authorized dealer or agent	Unauthorized, gray, or black market dealer or agent
Code of Ethics	Adopting your industry's code of ethics, creating one of your own, displaying the code	None

Another approach to building organization-based legitimacy, which has grown in popularity since the original list was crafted, is the creation and display of a company code of ethics. In practice, good codes of ethics reflect the passions of the founder, the culture of the firm, and three classes of ethical standards found in research on existing codes of ethics.[11] These three classes are:

- Employees Should Be Dependable Organizational Citizens (e.g., finish your work, follow rules and orders, be on time, do not swear, dress appropriately, etc.)
- Do Not Do Anything That Will Harm the Organization (e.g., protect confidential information, do not take drugs, kickbacks, or company property, etc.)
- Be Good to Customers (e.g., be truthful, be helpful, listen attentively, etc.)

Across these three types of legitimacy indicators, there are 30 characteristics, and few small businesses incorporate all these elements. Most of the time the small business owner will pick two or three legitimacy-building features from each of the product, organizational, and people indicator listings and then work to implement them. Once implemented, they should be locked in. Part of legitimacy and building trust comes from the consistency of a firm's actions over time. Repeating one legitimacy characteristic daily does more to build your social capital than changing the legitimacy characteristics stressed by the firm in hopes of finding the perfect mix of characteristics.[12]

LO4 Navigate the techniques of social networking.

Developing a Social Network

social network
The entrepreneur's set of relationships and contacts with individuals and institutions.

Another basis for building social capital is through building a social network. A **social network** is the entrepreneur's relationships and contacts with others.[13] Social networking is a way to work trust, reciprocity, and long-term relationships into your day-to-day business operations. It's a way to build your company's expertise by convincing others to share their skills and knowledge with your firm. The most successful owners are those who recognize that others have the expertise needed and establish relationships that give them the benefits of that expertise. In many of the stories of small business owners in this book you will see how success hinges on getting others to help you. You might be new to your business, industry, or locality, but, with the right expertise, your business can improve its chances of succeeding. The key is building a network of people who trust you and are willing to help you,[14] and who can depend on you for help and advice in return. Through this mutuality, social networking helps build long-lasting relationships.

Reputation has a positive community impact; it increases trust and creates a culture that enables people to make good decisions. Social networking helps all those aspects of small business by building your reputation as giving the most expert business goods or services and as being an important community resource. Social networking can help your long-term reputation as a business owner by showing others who you are[15]—a consistently top-notch community player.

You probably already know many of the people who can help you build a social network. Figure 3.2 gives a list of the most popular places to look for network contacts.

FIGURE 3.2

Sources for Network Connections

Family: Start here, and ask your parents, grandparents, and extended family. Include in-laws.

Friends and neighbors: Include your friends, and friends of friends.

Kids: Think about the people you've met through your children at their school and in their extracurricular activities.

Bank: You probably have a bank account, possibly several. Get to know your bankers and ask them for introductions or referrals.

Customer contacts: You are a customer, patient, or client to doctors, dentists, insurance agents, lawyers, and small business owners of all sorts. They know you and because they're in business, they may have the kind of contacts you need.

School: Think about students, faculty, and support organizations where you or your family have gone to school. Many colleges have alumni offices and entrepreneurship or small business development centers, and these can put you in touch with helpful others.

Hobbies: Hobbies often bring together people with diverse backgrounds. That makes them a great place for finding different sorts of contacts.

Business associations: Most communities have some form of a chamber of commerce. Most industries and professions have associations. People join these in order to network. Ask the officers of the chamber of commerce or the association for referrals. Be willing to assist others who ask for your help.

Other organizations: Religious, civic, community, and political organizations often publish member lists. Go over these to see if you recall people who have the business ties or expertise you need.

Work: Consider co-workers, bosses, customers, suppliers, and people in other firms with whom you deal. Note that work contacts can be problematic. Check company rules or expectations first. Many firms consider such contacts a conflict of interest.

Small business support organizations: There are always organizations dedicated to small business such as the National Federation of Independent Business, National Small Business United, the National Association for the Self-Employed. You can get lists of these by searching Google's directory for "small business associations." Many of these organizations have local chapters, and all encourage members to contact and help one another.

Electronic networks: There are different kinds of electronic social networks: *business networks* like Ecademy.com or LinkedIn.com, or *interpersonal networks* like Classmates.com, Facebook.com, or MySpace.com. Once you belong, you can search for friends, family, and co-workers who already belong to start your network, and then add their contacts to yours, as well as finding new contacts with similar interests, and even potential customers.

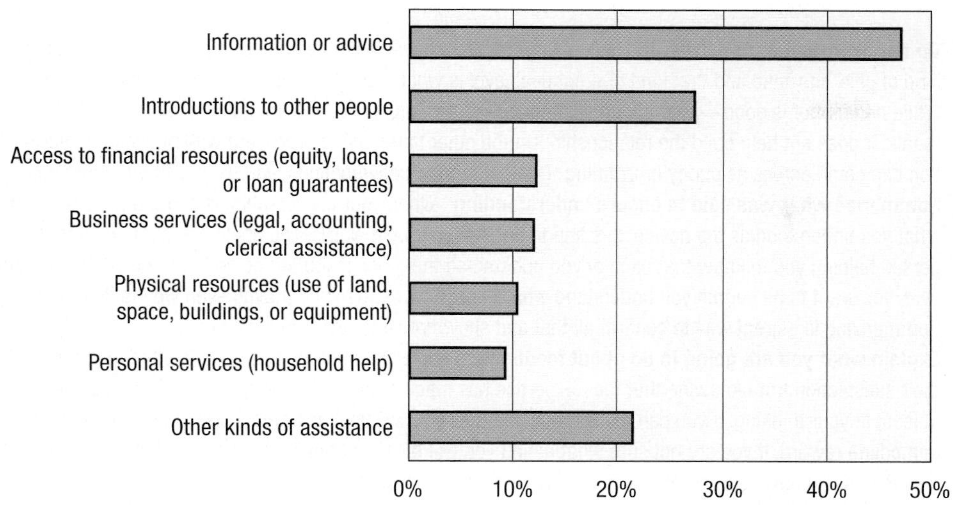

FIGURE 3.3

Types of Help Sought from the PSED

Source: Adapted from H. E. Aldrich and N. M. Carter (2004). Social Networks, In Gartner, William B., Shaver, Kelly G. Carter, Nancy M. and Reynolds, Paul D. (Eds.) (2004). *Handbook of Entrepreneurial Dynamics: The Process of Business Creation.* Thousand Oaks, CA: Sage, Table 29.1, page 331.

What kind of help do entrepreneurs seek from their social network? The Panel Study of Entrepreneurial Dynamics (PSED) provides some insight as to the type of help people starting their own business seek out and these results are shown in Figure 3.3. Information is the number one type of help, followed by introductions to others. In the PSED, most prospective and early stage entrepreneurs reported having one or two people in their helping network, and they typically reported around three contacts a month across their whole network of folks providing help.[16]

Knowing whom and what to ask is only part of the story. The other part involves building the relationships and encouraging others to help you. One of the key parts of social networking is actually seeking the help or advice of others. Asking for help well is a skill. A little advance thinking and preparation can dramatically produce positive results. Skill Module 3.3 gives you one of the most successful methods for asking others for help.

Asking for Help

SKILL MODULE 3.3

The best people to ask for help are often the people who are the busiest. Knowing this, some small business owners shy away from imposing. In reality, there is no substitute for expertise, and getting it from others is one of the most efficient and effective ways to do it. Building on the ideas of Paula Caproni,[17] here is an eight-step approach to asking others for help:

- **Request from people you trust:** Either ask people who already know you, or establish a relationship with the people you want to ask before seeking help from them. This can be as little as a few minutes of talk to find common ground or common friends at a chamber of commerce reception, but it is an important foundation for the relationship.
- **Ask for specific behavior:** Your request is more likely to fit someone's schedule if it is specific and something that has a definite end. So, asking, "How can I get an introduction to someone in purchasing at BigCorp?" is more likely to get a positive response than, "What can I do to sell more?"
- **Do not be defensive:** When explaining what you need, do not blame others for your needing help. And when asked questions by potential helpers, do not get upset or accusatory. Often they need to know what you have tried, how you did it, and how it worked out. They also often need to know what you are capable of doing, or what expertise you bring to the situation. Give concise answers and show your willingness to answer more. After all, they need the information to help you.

(*Continued*)

- **Do not overreact or underreact:** Think of your regular conversations with good customers or friends. That kind of give-and-take and that kind of emotional level is what a good asking-for-help exchange sounds like. While being brief is good—after all, time is money—if you sound like you are holding back or are unwilling to talk, it does not help build the relationship. On the other hand, going overboard with praise and information can come across as phony or irritating. Think of regular conversations, and try to emulate them here.
- **Summarize what was said to ensure understanding:** When your conversation is nearing the end, repeat what you understood as the advice. It is fine to put it in your own words. The goal here is for you and the person helping you to know that each of you understood the other. If you are going to try the advice on your own, you want to be certain you understand what to do, how to do it, and maybe even why to do it that way. Summarizing is a great way to confirm all that and show how attentive you have been.
- **Explain what you are going to do about feedback:** People you approach as experts often take part of their satisfaction from knowing that their expertise has made a difference—especially in your business, but at least in your thinking. If you can tell such people how you will use their help, it can provide them with an immediate reward. If you are not sure what action you will take, be honest about this, but also point to the new things you have learned or discovered from the help they offered.
- **Thank the person for the input:** This is in part providing an immediate payout to the person helping you, but also laying a foundation for future contact. Provide a simple thanks and mention how you hope to return the favor or help someday. A good handshake and a smile, and you are ready to get back to business.
- **Follow through:** It is always a good idea to inform any person who tried to help you about how your efforts came out. Tell them how you solved your business problem in general terms. If their help was used, mention this. Thank them for their help (whether you used it or not). Finish with a mention of your appreciation of their help and your willingness to help them in the future.

mutuality
The action of each person helping another.

Remember, social networking makes a difference in how you'll conduct business every day. It means asking for help when you need it, respecting the other person's time and expertise, and most importantly being willing to reciprocate if asked. **Mutuality** is the idea and action of each person helping the other. Part of building social capital with social networking comes from the help people in the network can provide one another. Why help? Reasons may be making a new friend or making a friendship stronger, creating a relationship that can lead to future business or friendship, having a chance to demonstrate expertise, incurring a debt for future repayment, or even just wanting to help others. Helping others means you understand the idea of positive community impact, trust, and relationships—critical success factors in building an ethical business.

networking
Interacting with others in order to build relationships useful to a business.

Building social capital through social networking involves giving information, letting people know they belong, and providing social support and approval. You have to take the time to build and keep up your relationships with others in your network. This is called **networking**, which means small business owners interacting with others in order to build relationships useful to the business. Key skills for effective small business networking are given in Skill Module 3.4.

SKILL MODULE 3.4 Networking Skills[18]

Networking is a skill like any other. In business you often know the kind of situation you are about to go into or are likely to face. Knowing this, you can take several steps to prepare yourself to socialize with others as a basis for establishing a business relationship. Here are the steps you can take to prepare:

- **Know who you are:** Craft a 30-second spot about yourself and your firm, and practice it until it sounds like a natural expression of your interests. This is often called an *elevator pitch,* and Chapter 8 (Business Plans) gives details on putting together a winning one.
- **Know whom you want and why:** Once you know who will be attending an event (from your buddy, looking at the materials for the event, or going through the member list of the sponsoring organization), start putting

together a list of names of people and organizations you want to make contact with. Make sure you keep track of why you are looking for particular people. When you are at the event, walk around the room to see who is there from the list, or ask the organizers of the event if the people you seek are around.

- **Buddy up:** When you know you are going to a particular event, check around to find a friend or business associate (a customer, supplier, lawyer, insurance agent, banker, etc.) who has attended a similar event before. Ask if you can go with him or her, and ask about the people and firms likely to be there.
- **Bone up on small talk:** What do you say after hello? A good place to start is to give your elevator pitch and close with why you were looking forward to meeting the person. If you think your business can help the other person's, talk about that. If the other person wants to limit the conversation to social topics, go with that. To help with chitchat in those situations, make sure you look at the local newspaper (sports section included) on the day of the event, and take a look at *The Wall Street Journal* or *USA Today* front page if you can.
- **Do not forget why you're there:** People tend to gather in groups of like-minded folks. This can mean that all the golf players are together talking strokes, but it can be deadly if it means that all the women entrepreneurs are gathered together and not networking with the male business owners. If you are at a networking event and you start feeling comfortable, check to make sure it is not because you have actually stopped networking.
- **Make the connection:** The key to making networking work is to make the personal connection. Business-people *expect* to be approached by others at events. Do not be shy. Just walk up and say hello. If necessary, ask a friend or an event organizer to make the introduction, but, however you do it, meet the people.
- **Follow up:** After you meet someone at a networking event, periodically keep up the contact through e-mails, phone, mail, or personal contact. If you can offer help or information, that is the best reason to stay in touch.

Most entrepreneurs who recognize the value of networking develop some means of keeping track of their contacts. Using paper-and-pencil contact managers such as those from Rolodex or Franklin Covey, computer software such as Microsoft Outlook (which is a part of MS Office), or specialized contact management software such as ACT! or Goldmine, or online services,[19] that you can quickly find using a Google search for "online contact management." The goal is to make sure you keep track of your social and business contacts. The best approaches help you identify whom you need to contact to keep relationships fresh. This is because networking is one of the key skills for *all* business owners, female and male, minority and majority, high tech and no tech. Because in the end, business is all about making the sale and the sale depends on making a connection with customers, and that connection is what networking is all about.

SMALL BUSINESS INSIGHT

ELECTRONIC EVOKE

Scott Bertelsmeyer, David Birkenmeier, and Jon Taulbee's feasibility study involved the creation of a new electronic version of Evoke, an award-winning children's game with modest sales. After studying the industry, the team realized that electronic Evoke's success would depend on using characters children recognize, like SpongeBob SquarePants, Harry Potter, X-Men, or Disney characters. But determining the licensing costs for brand-name characters was a problem. The big studios did not want to deal with smaller-scale projects like Evoke. The threesome sought help by looking for a licensing expert on LinkedIn. While none of them had one in their immediate network, they found several possibilities whom they might get to through someone they were already linked with (called an intermediary in LinkedIn). They e-mailed an intermediary for an introduction to Scott McMillan, then Senior Licensing Manager at Nelvana Ltd.—a producer, distributor, and consumer products licensor of animated shows such as *Babar, Franklin the Turtle,* and *The Berenstain Bears.* Scott, himself a student pursuing an MBA at the University of Toronto's Rotman School of Business, responded that day, providing Scott, David, and Jon with the information they needed to cost out using licensed characters. The entire process took less than one day, from the initial search to the final follow-up phone call. You can see the Evoke feasibility analysis on the *Entrepreneurial Small Business* Web site.

TABLE 3.4 Online Social Networking Sites

Site Name	Total Visitors (2011)	Strength of Site
Facebook.com	750,000,000	Largest site. Has a large core of personal sites.
Twitter.com	250,000,000	Designed for quick updates. Largest number of users connected via mobile phone users.
LinkedIn.com	110,000,000	Largest site focused on business users.
MySpace.com	70,500,000	Another personal site, but users spend more time on-site than Facebook.
Google+	65,000,000	Owned by Google. Tight integration with Google services.
DeviantArt.com	25,500,000	Focused on artists an art lovers.
LiveJournal.com	20,500,000	A blog-based social media site.

Sources: "Top 15 Most Popular Social Networking Sites I June 2012," Ebizmba.com, June 2012, www.ebizmba.com/articles/social-networking-websites.

Social networking across the nation and around the world has become a lot easier with the maturing of this type of Web site. In fact, today there are so many online social networking sites that it can be tough to decide which to choose to promote your business. Table 3.4 gives you a quick guide to the major social networking sites.[20]

A lot of entrepreneurs find starting on Facebook, LinkedIn, and Twitter to be the "Big 3" of social networking. Many businesses have a company or product page on Facebook and LinkedIn pages for the company, the owner, and even key employees. Because of the 140-character limit on Twitter, tweets are always the fastest way to get the word out. As a result, and because tweets can be linked to your LinkedIn and Facebook accounts, Twitter is becoming the most popular way to update what you or your company is doing.

Small businesses planning to rely primarily on online social networking as their means of prospecting for customers often use multiple sites, in order to get to potential customers in as many ways as possible. If you use this approach, consider also subscribing to a social network aggregating site like FriendFeed or Ping.fm, which can help you check up on or manage multiple sites through a single source. Regardless of the site or sites you use, there are four best practices which can help any online social networking effort become more successful (whether you are pursuing it online or in person):

- Make it easy for people to contact you (this often means giving one of your e-mail or social network addresses).
- Take the initiative to ask others on the network (including colleagues from school and work, and friends and family) to link with you and then help them out online.
- Find and link up with network mavens—people who like to gather and share their enormous networks—and help out whenever you can.[21]
- Keep at it—successful online networking requires consistent involvement. It can be weekly, but it needs to be every week.

Electronic social networks are usually fast and easy to develop, as well as often free. Face-to-face social networks often have membership costs, but offer the all-important personal touch as well as those all-important local connections. When either type of social network works, it can produce results from unexpected sources, as you can see in the example of Electronic Evoke. While the personal connection from face-to-face networking is always a great thing to have, if you cannot easily develop a large face-to-face network in your community, industry, or market, electronic social networking is the best way to go.

Handling a Crisis

LO5 Explain the basic skills for handling a crisis.

While some challenges come slowly and give the small business owner a chance to think about how to choose, all businesses sooner or later face some sort of crisis. A crisis is a situation that poses a major problem for the business or its people, in which the survival of the business is at stake, and immediate action is necessary.[22] For owners, knowing what to do during a crisis is a very specialized and very emotionally demanding form of decision making. Small business owners are optimists about their businesses, and it can be wrenching when something goes wrong. When the crisis is in full swing, knowing what to do is critical. The gold standard for crisis leadership comes from Norman Augustine,[23] former president of Lockheed Martin—a Fortune 500 company. Although originally given for large businesses, the six steps to follow can be readily adapted to small ones.[24] The steps are:

1. Admit you're in trouble—quickly. It is better to say, "If there is a problem, I will find it and fix it," than to delay an admission until fact-finding is done.
2. Get to the scene as soon as possible. Your job? Show caring and accountability.
3. Communicate facts you know (and those you don't) to employees, customers, and suppliers.
4. Have one person serve as the firm's spokesperson. It is best if it can be the owner, but an articulate employee, family member, or outside professional (e.g., lawyer) can stand in.
5. Separate crisis management from the everyday management of the firm. If you are doing both, try to take time to do each separately. Delegate as much as possible of the everyday management to employees or family while you concentrate on dealing with the crisis.
6. Deal with the crisis quickly. Take steps to solve the problem, and make the process of dealing with the problem as open as possible.

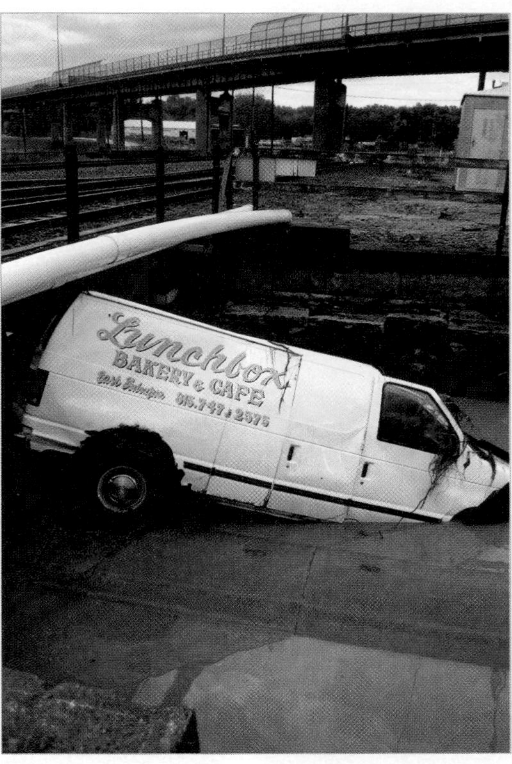

For a small business, an accident like this can become a crisis. Knowing what to do can help minimize its impact on your firm, customers and employees.

Managing crisis is a difficult but necessary skill. Obviously, anticipating problems and avoiding them or handling them before they become major is a better approach, but only one business in ten has a disaster or crisis plan.[25] To help small businesses with crisis planning the federal government has created a new Web site www.ready.gov to bring all these resources together in one location. They recommend a three-step process for preparing for disasters:

1. Plan to Stay in Business (using a disaster plan like the one called READYBusiness offered by Louisiana State University's EDEN—Extension Disaster Education Network [www.eden.lsu.edu/LearningOps/ReadyBusiness/default.aspx]).
2. Talk to Your People (plan with co-workers, practice your plans, and have a crisis communications approach in place).
3. Protect Your Investment (using insurance, backup procedures and supplies, etc.).

In the end the best way to manage a crisis is to plan ahead, but in the middle of a crisis, the key for a small business owner is to keep calm, take care of the people involved, and keep people informed.

LO6 Recognize how small businesses can achieve sustainability.

Achieving Sustainability

If you look at a management, entrepreneurship, or small business text from 10 years ago, you would be hard-pressed to see anything related to sustainability or green business. Those elements we called corporeal forces in the general environment were taken for granted. Today, however, some of the negative effects of industrialization on the earth and the living species inhabiting earth are becoming apparent. **Sustainable entrepreneurship** is an approach to the operation of the firm, the line of business of the firm, or both, which identifies or creates and then exploits opportunities to make a profit in a manner that minimizes the depletion of natural resources, maximizes the use of recycled material, improves the environment, or any combination of these outcomes. Positive outcomes along these lines are described as "greener," so the approach is also sometimes called **green entrepreneurship**.

sustainable entrepreneurship
An approach to operating a firm or a line of business which identifies, creates and exploits opportunities to make a profit in a way that can minimize the depletion of natural resources, maximize the use of a recycled material, or improve the environment.

green entrepreneurship
Another term for sustainable entrepreneurship taken from the popular belief that green is the color of a healthy environment, as in forests or fields.

As a nation, we have increased our greenness over the past 20 years through a variety of actions. We drive more fuel-efficient cars today because of government mandated fuel efficiency standards. Companies and individuals do more recycling of trash. The latest effort to replace regular light bulbs with compact fluorescent lights is another green effort.

Entrepreneurs can do quite a lot to manage their firm's impact on the environment. Recycling is one approach many businesses use. According to the NFIB poll, recycling among small businesses

TABLE 3.5 Recycling Rates

NFIB Poll Question: Does your business recycle the following?	
Paper	45% recycle
Cans	45% recycle
Plastics	35% recycle
Glass	27% recycle

Source: NFIB, Small Business Poll, *Waste and Hazardous Materials.* 7, no. 2 (2007).

varies, depending on what is being recycled. Recycling rates for the major types of trash are given in Table 3.5.

A great way to start thinking about minimizing waste and environmental degradation is to run your thoughts about your business through a "green audit" like the one developed by Friends of the Earth in Scotland, www.green-office.org.uk/audit.php?goingto=audit0, or another developed by the University of Oregon Campus Recycling Program, www.proprofs.com/quiz-school/story.php?title=green-office-audit. Minimizing paper use, using telecommuting and electronic communication, replacing paper copies with Web-based documents, buying products for the business made from recycled materials or products which can be recycled are all ways to create a more sustainable enterprise.

The business itself can focus on ways to enhance others' sustainability efforts, and make a profit doing it. Have you read about buildings in your area being LEED certified? It stands for "Leadership in Energy and Environmental Design" and is a certification standard from the U.S. Green Building Council for buildings that are more environmentally friendly, www.usgbc.org/leed. Construction companies have found this area to be a new source of sales and profits, as new buildings are designed to be more energy efficient and recyclable, and older buildings get retrofitted for energy savings and healthier internal environments. Similarly, green retailing, selling products that have a better environmental footprint, is a growing segment. Whether talking about greening your own business or making a profit from helping others get greener, sustainable entrepreneurship is another method for managing external relations with customers, governments, and the physical environment.

Making Ethical Decisions

LO7 identify the major steps in making ethical decisions in small business.

ethics
A system of values that people consider in determining whether actions are right or wrong.

ethical dilemma
A situation that occurs when a person's values are in conflict, making it unclear whether a particular decision is the right thing to do.

Ethics comprise a system of values people use to determine whether actions are right or wrong. We consider ethics in determining whether a decision we are about to make is good or bad. And, we make judgments about actions—something is good or bad; someone is right or wrong—based upon our own personal ethics. An **ethical dilemma** occurs when a person's values are in conflict, making it unclear whether a decision we're thinking about making is right or not.[26] An ethical dilemma also occurs when there are several different options for a decision we have to make and the best choice isn't clear. Of the five environment managing techniques discussed in this section, making ethical decisions is undoubtedly the hardest. Part of it is because the ethical problems that keep entrepreneurs up at night are ones where there is not a satisfying yes or no answer. Consider the case of Martin Tobin on the next page.

Making Sarski pay could have negative consequences, and Tobin paying could have negative consequences. While there is a set of standard practices in place, Sarski is asking for special consideration. Tobin knows he and Sarski have a long relationship and he expects them to work together for a long time to come. So what *should* he say to Sarski?

LaRue Hosmer was initially a professor of entrepreneurship who came from a family logging business. He later turned his eye toward the challenge of making ethical decisions in business. He came up with a model widely used today, but it is focused more on big business than small ones. Adapting his approach[27] to small business making ethical decisions involves three steps:

1. **Define:** Define the moral problem.
2. **Generate:** Generate alternatives that could meet the ethical, legal, and economic goals every business must balance.
3. **Implement:** Pick the best alternative you and your business can live with and implement it.

THE THOUGHTFUL ENTREPRENEUR

TOBIN REAL ESTATE AND DEVELOPMENT

As Martin Tobin hung up the phone, he felt a headache coming on. Martin and several family members owned Tobin Realty & Development, the community's largest real estate sales and development company. The phone call was from one of the builders Tobin used fairly regularly, and it wasn't good news. The builder, Bob Sarski, had hit a "soft spot" in the soil just before pouring a large new home's concrete foundation. Sandy places in the dirt meant unstable concrete and an unsteady foundation—definitely not what a homeowner wants! Digging out all the sand from a soft spot is an expensive process and delays the build.

During the phone call, Sarski told Tobin he couldn't pay for this "extra" work, costing thousands of dollars. Normally, builders pay for all digging costs, including soft-spot excavation. But, with the bad economy, Martin knew that Sarski's money was tight. Tobin needed this home built, but if he paid for this problem, what else would the builder ask for? How long would construction be delayed if Tobin didn't pay? Or worse, would Sarski walk off the job completely and find a new project that provided cash flow? Martin leaned back in his chair, rubbing his temples to try to relieve his headache.[28]

The model is given in Figure 3.4. As you might expect, although the steps sound easy, doing them well requires working through some complicated issues. Let us look at each step in turn.

Define the Moral Problem: To determine the moral dimension of a problem, you need to carefully think the problem through. For small businesses, there are typically four questions used to define the moral problem under consideration:

1. Who will be hurt (and how much)? Obviously more hurt is worse, but you also need to consider how likely recovery is and how long will it take to recover.
2. Who will benefit (and how much)? A tiny benefit for many is often of little use—think of those class action lawsuits that end up giving each of millions of claimants a few dollars off their next purchase. The overall size of the benefit needs to be weighed against the number who benefit, and balanced against the costs of the harm done to others by the solution.
3. What do you (or your firm) owe others? When you make a decision, it should reflect your real or presumed obligations to people and institutions in your firm and in its task environment. How you act under pressure is seen by many as the acid test of who you are and what your firm is about.
4. What do others owe you (or your firm)? Just as you and your firm make a commitment to others, they make commitments to you and your firm. Depending on the decision, there may be obligations from others or forms of support you can expect that help make doing the ethical thing easier on you or the other party involved.

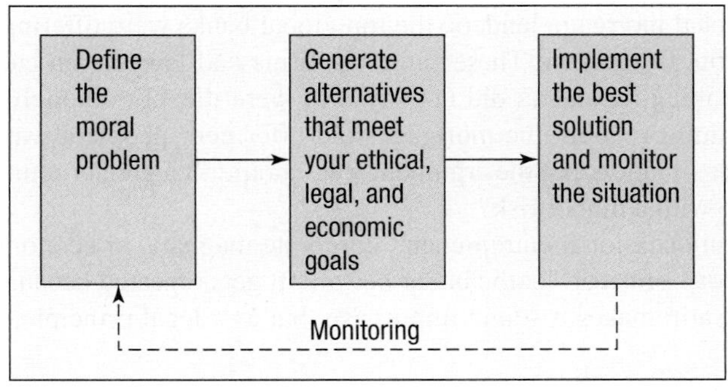

FIGURE 3.4

The Ethical Decision-Making Model for Small Business

Source: Adapted from LaRue T. Hosmer, *The Ethics of Management*, 6th ed. (Boston: McGraw-Hill/Irwin, 2008).

Generate alternatives that meet your ethical, legal, and economic goals: Once you have defined the moral problem you face, you need to generate a variety of alternatives to handle it. These alternatives need to be evaluated to find the best one. At this stage, it makes sense to compare the alternatives to the economic, legal, and ethical standards of your firm, industry, and community.

Start with economic standards. Often ethical dilemmas crop up in business because the answer sought by the other person would cost your business money. Sometimes the amount of money is more important symbolically than in reality. Have you seen a friend who will drive several miles to save a penny on a gallon of gas? Do the math. A typical gas tank size is 15 gallons and the average gas mileage of cars in the United States is 27.5 miles/gallon. If gas is $2.50 a gallon, then each mile costs 9 cents, and saving a penny a gallon only makes economic sense if the round-trip to the cheaper gas station is under 1.66 miles. Still, many people will pay more rather than feel they were taken advantage of.

That sense of being taken advantage of is a tough emotion to set aside, but in the end, part of being a professional in business, and part of being an honest decision maker requires that people do that. There is no easy way. It takes courage to do the right thing, and self-control to quash the emotional desire to lash out or get even.

Legal standards seem easy at first. If the answer is against the law, simply do not do it. But in reality, everyone's compliance with the law is less than perfect. Think about your classmates. How many occasionally drive above the speed limit? How many have a couple of pirated songs on their MP3 player or iPod? Could one of your classmates with a part-time business have claimed more business expenses on a tax return than could be documented? Realize that even generally law-abiding people have their lapses. If the stakes or emotions are high enough, or the risk of being caught or being prosecuted is relatively low, people you would consider law-abiding could make a decision to do something illegal.

There are times when doing what is legally supported may not be the optimal solution. Consider EntreQuest, a Baltimore training firm with a famous example. When starting out, the two co-founders, Joe Mechlinski and Jason Pappas, heard through their grapevine that their first, biggest, and at that time only client was going to break their contract with EntreQuest. If that happened, Joe and Jason could take the client to court—but it would cost money, and even if they won, how would the client (or prospective clients) feel about EntreQuest? Jason and Joe had the law on their side, but decided to be proactive and meet with the client to find a better solution. It worked, and the resulting new contract made EntreQuest even bigger profits than before.[29]

So, when thinking through the legal standards, recognize that having the law on your side may feel good, but may not be workable as a solution. You can find yourself in the legal "right" but still unable to make a viable business decision by pursuing legal recourse. Still, the simple advice that you should not break the law knowingly and willfully makes a lot of sense as a legal standard for making moral decisions.

That leaves the ethical standard. Most professions (e.g., social workers, MDs, pharmacists, lawyers, etc.) and many occupation-specific organizations (e.g., Realtors®, Society of Professional Journalists, Association for Computing Machinery, etc.) have codes of ethics to help clarify their standards to members and the public. But there are several areas in business that do not have explicit standards, or that have standards but cannot enforce them on all members of an occupation. Think about the mortgage banking industry and the subprime crisis in The Thoughtful Entrepreneur.

To be fair to the local mortgage lenders, the top global banks were offering subprime loans and reporting record profits from them. These same big firms had lawyers on call to keep everything legal. The federal banking regulators did not say they were illegal (although some state attorneys general were complaining). Subprime mortgages did offer poor people a way to own a home, although it was a riskier situation, but the argument was, shouldn't a greater return (owning a home or a bigger home) come with a higher risk?

caveat emptor
A Latin expression which means "let the buyer beware" which has been made into a philosophy sometimes used by businesses to put the burden for consumer protection onto the customer.

You can still see an occasional entrepreneur, corporate magnate, or economic pundit invoke the old Latin phrase **caveat emptor**, let the buyer beware. It gets repeated because it has popped up in legal cases, and the Latin makes it sound impressive, but as a legal principle, it has been routinely

THE THOUGHTFUL ENTREPRENEUR

Anatomy of a Subprime Loan[30]

A divorced mother of two has a house worth $250,000 and is making $20,000 a year working part time. Money is obviously tight. She had to declare bankruptcy two years earlier in the aftermath of a divorce. She hears about low mortgage rates on the radio and TV, and decides to try to lower her monthly payments.

The mortgage broker assures her this is possible. But because she has a low credit score and a bankruptcy to boot, she doesn't get the low, low rate she heard on radio and TV. They offer her 8.875 percent for a subprime loan (the national conventional mortgage rate is 5.7 percent). She goes for it. But the lender requires more collateral than her home (which has $60,000 in equity already). So she gets her parents to put up their nearby $400,000 home.

The final deal is a monthly payment of $1,700, with a variable rate loan starting at 8.875 percent. The bad news grows. In the second year, she is told the rate will go up to 10 percent (although using the federal APR reporting rules, they should have said 13 percent), and her payment will jump to $2,000 a month. Unable to meet the payments, she tries to sell her home, but that fails in a tough market and she defaults on her loan, moving her family to an apartment. Now she has to tell her parents they will need to pick up her loan payments or pay off her loan or give up their home too.

When companies like CountryWide, Ameriquest, Wells Fargo, and HSBC offered subprime mortgages, it seemed to legitimize it for thousands of small mostly local mortgage brokers. Until the middle of 2008, the practice did not violate any laws or regulations applied to the mortgage industry. It was even acceptable under the ethical code of the National Association of Mortgage Brokers. The lender knew the borrower had a poor track record in making financial decisions, and knew their precarious current financial condition, but made the loan anyway. Thousands of brokers did the same. Today, loans like this are called subprime loans, and they make up most of the nearly $3 trillion of toxic debt saddling the United States. It was legal, but was it ethical?

discredited.[31] Caveat emptor is often the first line of defense by rip-off artists, frauds, and producers of shoddy merchandise. Using it as a defense puts the entrepreneur who uses it, and, usually by association, the whole small business community, in a negative light. If you find a business using caveat emptor as a principle, avoid them. If you have to deal with them, get everything in writing and watch them like a hawk. If they ask you if you trust them, use another famous line, from former President Ronald Reagan, "Trust, but verify."

The 40th President of the United States, Ronald Reagan, popularized the translation of a Soviet-era proverb "Trust, but verify." He used it on USSR Premier Mikhail Gorbachev to get a workable deal banning intermediate range nuclear missiles. When looking for a workable deal of your own and getting hit with *caveat emptor* (let the buyer beware), hit back with Reagan's equally punchy "Trust, but verify," and follow your advice. Don't get caught unaware.

Assuming you realize the caveat emptor approach is not the way to go, you may still need to make a decision you believe is ethical. Here are four proven philosophies to try when you are thinking through alternatives to help you determine how ethical the choices are.

Golden Rule
An ethical model which suggests you treat others in the manner you wish to be treated.

utilitarianism
An ethical model that supports seeking the greatest good for the greatest number of people.

universalism
An ethical model that suggests that there is a code of right and wrong that everyone can see and follow.

billboard principle
An ethical model that asks whether someone would be comfortable having his or her decision and name advertised on a billboard for the public to see.

- **Am I treating others the way I would want to be treated?** You've probably heard of this one before. It's the **Golden Rule**, and almost every major religious tradition in the world has some version of it. Dumping toxic waste in someone's pond would be acceptable behavior if he or she could dump toxic waste in your pond. An unlikely example, but the point is that you need to think how you'd feel if someone took the same action *toward you* that you're thinking about taking. The Golden Rule can be one of the easiest ways to think about ethical dilemmas and potential solutions. It's a simple question: *Would I want to be treated in the way I am thinking about treating someone else?*
- **Is my solution the best thing for the most people over the long term?** You may have heard of an idea called **utilitarianism**. Basically, it means that the action resulting in the greatest good for the greatest number of people is the right action to take. This idea has a strong community focus. One of the most important aspects of it is that you have to consider how your actions will affect other people. It's not about what's fun or quick in the short term but asks you to think about peoples' best interests down the road. If your solution means that many people will benefit from your actions, with acceptable costs to you, it's probably a good solution.
- **What if everyone did what I want to do? What kind of world would it be?** Those questions in a nutshell are the idea of **universalism**, a code of right and wrong that everyone can see and follow. You may have read about universalism in philosophy class, since it's the brainchild of the German philosopher Immanuel Kant. You may have also heard it expanded by mothers everywhere. You get your ideas of right and wrong from your family, religion, education, and community.
- **What if my decision were advertised on a billboard?** If you have tried ways to think this through and still can't decide whether what you plan to do is ethical, try the **billboard principle**. As the name implies, this asks whether you'd be comfortable having your decision (with your name, of course) advertised on a billboard for everyone you know to see. Picture it in your mind! Would you be proud to see your potential course of action up there in giant letters? Would you be ashamed? Would others think worse of you if they knew what you had done to resolve your ethical dilemma? Those questions are the heart of the billboard principle.

Implement the Best Solution and Monitor the Situation: After running your list of alternative solutions through the four philosophies in the prior section, were you able to cross any off the list? You probably were. The four philosophies won't automatically give you the best solution to your dilemma, but they're where the rubber hits the road. If your potential solution can't pass and meet at least a couple of these philosophies, you need to rethink what you're about to do.

Occasionally you will be able to make a decision entirely on your own, with minimal emotional fallout, and make it stick for your firm. Saying "no" to a salesperson who suggests a kickback for extra discounts could be such a situation. Often though, you will need to work through a solution with someone else.

In such ethically charged situations, the best outcome is a situation where both sides feel satisfied about (or at least about the same with) the result. In presenting your solution,[32] it works best to focus on what the customer or other party wanted and why. You should then make sure they accept that basic review. Then add what you were seeking and take questions if the other party has any. Then introduce your solution along with why you think it would fill both parties' needs. If the other side rejects it, rather than asking for an explanation of why, ask instead what part needs to be adjusted, and how they would recommend adjusting your offer. Do not be afraid to ask how they reasoned out their suggestion, and be willing to suggest adjustments to their suggestion.

If you get a response that seems to reject the entire proposal, ask them if there is any point to start from so that you can build a better version. Bring up a point you took from their prior requests or suggestions, or one they seemed to approve of during your presentation. Starting from a small patch of common ground is not uncommon in negotiating sessions. If this does not work, be ready to talk about your **BATNA**, or Best Alternative to a Negotiated Settlement, and ask for theirs. Often, the alternative to negotiating together can be "lumping it" (suffering with what aggravated you or the other party, possibly with loud complaints to others) if the amounts are small, or undertaking legal action if the amounts warrant legal fees or the hassles of enforcing small claims court decisions. When compared to the BATNA's of both parties, finding a solution together often makes more sense.

BATNA
An acronym for "Best Alternative To a Negotiated Settlement" in which the second-best outcome is identified by the parties in a negotiation to help clarify the value of achieving a successful negotiation.

In cases like EntreQuest, the result is a win-win, with both sides happier for all the emotional trauma of the confrontation and discussions. But it is important to monitor the situation. Sometimes even when the customer seems pleased, he or she is not telling you the whole story, as we can see in the case of David and Veronica Sullivan of Starlit Dry Cleaners.

The idea of adding monitoring takes a page from decision-making theory, which usually includes a feedback loop to link the solution to the original problem. In the real world, often the first solution is not optimal, and you need to keep tracking it and revising it until it works well. In ethical decision making, the same thinking makes sense.

It is important to understand why acting in an ethical fashion is important. There are costs to firms for their illegal and even unethical behaviors. Research by Thomas, Schermerhorn, and Dienhart has shown that managers tend to focus on government fines and penalties, which have real but relatively small costs to the firm. What managers tend to underplay are results that are quieter, spread out over a longer term, and actually more damaging to the firm's reputation and finances, as seen in Figure 3.5. There is every reason to think that these results are as descriptive of small business owners as they are of managers in larger firms.

Before leaving the method for ethical decision making, it is worthwhile to look at one very special situation close to the heart of many small businesses—the problem of inventing a product or service too far ahead of its time. Small businesses are often the first to try something innovative.

SMALL BUSINESS INSIGHT

THE HORRORS OF THE UNSATISFIED CUSTOMER[33]

David and Veronica Sullivan live in a small southwestern U.S. community and have owned several Starlit Dry Cleaners stores for almost 10 years. When customers are unhappy with how their clothes turn out, David tries everything he can to satisfy the customer, including recleaning their clothes free of charge. Usually, customers are happy with this extra attention, but as David notes, not always: "Sometimes a customer won't go away satisfied, no matter what I do. And sometimes people blame Starlit for damaging clothes that they brought in already damaged! Then, it's my word against theirs."

David recalled a customer whose beautiful suede jacket had a spot right on the collar when she picked it up. Even though the counter worker had noted the spot on the cleaning ticket when the jacket was brought in, the customer insisted Starlit had ruined her jacket. The spot remained stubbornly in place, even after several attempts to remove it. David didn't want to send the customer away empty-handed, and agreed to pay for half the jacket's cost. He says, "I thought we had an agreement, and she seemed happy with our paying half the cost. After about a week, she started calling our house, complaining about how we had cheated her and ruined her clothes without fairly paying her! Veronica and I also heard she complained about us to anyone who would listen: in the grocery store, at the vet's, everywhere. Not about the business, but about Veronica and me personally. We still will get customers who bring us something suede and ask if we're sure we can clean it, because they heard about us ruining someone's jacket. It's unbelievable."

Today with Internet opinion sites like ePinions.com, and space for comments on Google and Yahoo! map pages showing your business, it can be hard to track all the ways and places people can be talking about you. For the Sullivans, putting up a big sign in their stores offering a satisfaction guarantee for qualifying suede articles could do a lot to stave off the previously heard problems. What other sorts of ways could you think of?

FIGURE 3.5

The Business Costs of Ethical Failures

Source: T. Thomas, J. Schermerhorn, Jr., and J. Dienhart, "Strategic Leadership of Ethical Behavior in Business," *Academy of Management Executive* (May 2004), p.58.

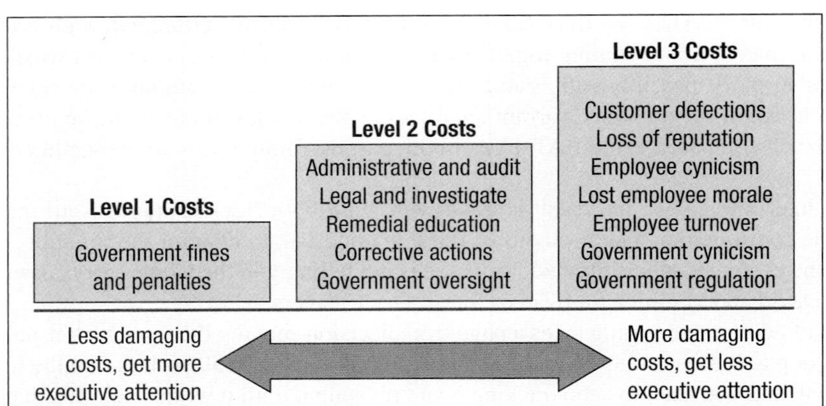

Innovation is the creation of something new or trying something for the first time. Innovation also suggests that you're not sure how a new idea is going to turn out. Taking advantage of an innovative idea is often the reason small business owners start their business in the first place.[34] Sometimes small businesses become very successful at doing new things better that anyone else—and may get into ethical hot water because of it.

It's important to remember that since small businesses often find a niche of customers that big business has forgotten, it's easy for that small business to become a target if it becomes successful. Big businesses have the resources to fight smaller upstart firms that threaten their profits and the ways they do business. Small business owners should be prepared for this and should think about where they stand on ethical issues, like Carl Moore did.

SMALL BUSINESS INSIGHT

THE BLEEDING EDGE OF INNOVATION

Carl Moore fought the battle of his professional life, and lost. In November 2003, the U.S. Justice Department shut down Moore's company, Rx Depot, which helped Americans buy prescription drugs from Canadian pharmacies for a lot less money than they cost in the United States. This practice is called *reimporting.* Rx Depot and its Canadian subsidiaries helped Americans, mostly seniors on fixed incomes, buy name-brand prescription drugs for up to 60 percent less than they would pay in U.S. pharmacies. American drug companies were furious and said that Rx Depot was breaking the law by reimporting Canadian drugs. The Justice Department went after Moore using another argument: that the safety of the Canadian drugs can't be assured and that Americans should use only U.S. pharmacies.

Rx Depot was on the cutting edge of online prescription services and risked everything by being an industry innovator. At the heart of the issue were seniors who say they can't afford their health-related medicines without using discounters like Rx Depot. They say seniors suffer most from high drug costs and that Rx Depot was, literally, a lifesaving business.

Moore said his service filled a need better than anyone else has been able to, a common reason why small businesses become very successful. Was Rx Depot a risky business? Was Moore putting senior citizens in danger? Moore believed the Canadian drugs were as safe as the drugs sold in the United States and that the fight was about huge lost profits for powerful U.S. drug firms. According to Moore, charging U.S. citizens much more money for the same, safe drugs is what he would consider to be unethical. Rx Depot's innovation had redefined a whole industry. Today buying drugs online from Canada and other countries is so common that the AARP provides guidelines to help customers be safe when ordering, but that came about because of Carl's innovative idea. Carl Moore's innovation put him at the forefront of a major ethical debate and cost him his company.[35]

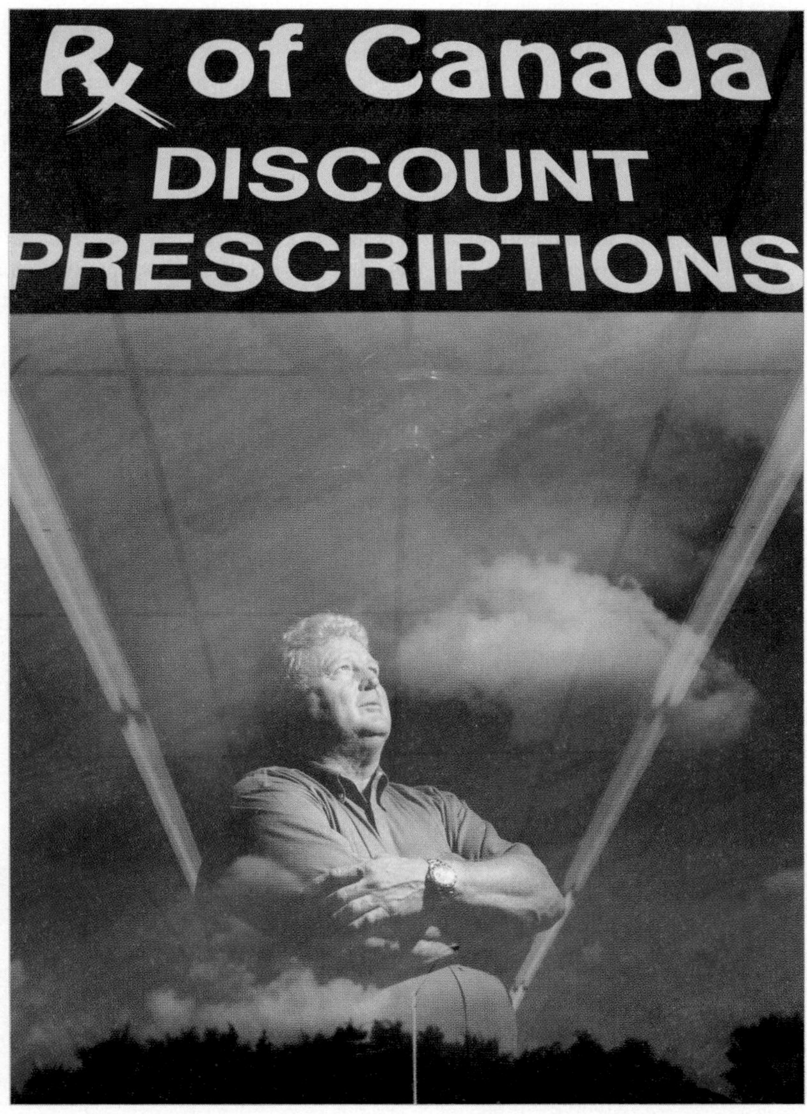

Rx Depot owner Carl Moore found himself on the losing end of the recent battle over reimporting prescription drugs to the States. What are some resources you can think of that would help small business owners like Moore to continue producing innovative products and services while managing questions of ethical practices?

Ethical decision making probably represents one of the most complex and difficult kinds of external relations management situations you will have to face. Often the stakes may be as high as your reputation or even your entire business. You may feel under a lot of pressure. The approach we've shown you is considered one of the best ways to manage the procedure for finding an ethical solution.

You can also minimize the need for high-pressure ethical decision-making situations by integrating the lessons of legitimacy, social networking, crisis management, sustainability, and ethical decision making into your everyday activities and into the structure of your business. How do you do this on an everyday basis? There are several approaches which can help:

1. Craft codes for legitimacy, social networking, sustainability, crisis management, and ethical decision making that reflect the personal values you can live with and live up to. Don't get bogged down in details of what to permit or prohibit. Think about the general explanation of what you consider important in positively managing your firm's external relations.
2. When hiring employees, subcontractors, or service providers, make sure you discuss with them your expectations about mutual responsibilities, ethics, and service levels.
3. When external relations lapses occur, if they are not so major that legal action or the demise of the firm is at stake, try to use them as learning experiences for the rest of the firm by talking openly about the issues. They make good opportunities to bring up your expectations again.

4. When counseling around external relations issues, try to use the following approach to help the learning occur:
   a. Do not get emotional. Talk the issues through calmly, even when it is hard.
   b. Be specific about what the problem is and why it violates the way things are supposed to be done in the firm. Have the other person reason out loud why his or her behavior was a lapse to make sure he or she understands.
   c. Once he or she understands, work on what future behavior should be (and why), as well as what needs to be done to make things right from the lapse.
   d. Be consistent. Make sure everyone who has a lapse faces this process, and where consequences need to happen, they should be appropriate to the severity of the problem, specific to the problem, and the same for everyone who had that level of lapse.
5. Remember, you are the role model for ethics, social networking, and legitimacy. Employees, subcontractors, and even customers look at your approach as the role model for the way your business will approach these issues of managing external relations.[36]

Our goal in this section of the chapter is to give you some tools you can use to examine your problem and come to decisions you can be proud of. To accomplish that we have looked at the environment in which business operates, what makes it up, and how to analyze it and manage your external relations with it. The environment is critical to business—every business depends on the environment and a workable set of environmental conditions to get started, and from then on, many of the challenges, crises, and opportunities a firm faces come from the environment. But the lesson of this chapter is that while no one can really control the environment, it is possible to become better able to understand it. And through efforts such as developing social capital and planning ahead of time, small business owners can give themselves and their firms an edge when dealing with external environment.

CHAPTER SUMMARY

LO1 Describe the elements that make up the small business environment.

- Everything outside the business is its environment.
- The internal environment consists of everyone within the firm.
- The task environment comprises those institutions the firm deals with directly.
- The general environment is the sectors shaping the larger world.
- Small businesses are constantly interacting with and being affected by the environment.

LO2 Demonstrate your ability to scan the small business environment.

- It is important for entrepreneurs to take time to scan the environment for trends and changes which could affect the business.
- Even simple environmental scanning approaches can achieve good results.

LO3 Apply the techniques of building legitimacy for your organization.

- Legitimacy is others' belief that your firm is worthy of their business.
- Legitimacy can come from the way your firm deals with people, from the products or services you sell, and from the way you run your firm.
- Legitimacy (like social networking, crisis management, sustainability, and ethical decision making) is a way to build social capital with your environment.

LO4 Navigate the techniques of social networking.

- Social networking involves building relationships via mutual contact and help.
- You can network in person and over the Internet.
- There are ways to optimize your inquiry for help.

LO5 Explain the basic skills for handling a crisis.

- Crises are problems that risk a business's existence and require immediate action.
- There is a six-step process for handling a crisis taken from big business.
- Being honest and open is a big part of handling crises.
- The three steps of disaster preparedness are planning, talking to your people, and protecting your investment.

LO6 Recognize how small businesses can achieve sustainability.

- Sustainable entrepreneurship seeks to run the business in a way which minimizes its impact on the environment.
- One way to minimize impact is through recycling.
- Another way is by creating green products or services.
- Using audits and certifications can help the firm be greener.

LO7 Identify the major steps in making ethical decisions in small business.

- Ethics is a system of values that people use to determine whether actions are right or wrong.
- The three steps of ethical decision making are: define the moral problem, generate alternatives, and implement the best solution.
- Workable solutions are those that meet your ethical, legal, and economic goals.
- The four philosophies you can use to check solutions are the Golden Rule, utilitarianism, universalism, and the billboard principle.
- Remember that innovations can lead to potentially risky ethical situations.

KEY TERMS

environment, 52
organizational identity, 52
bootstrapping, 52
internal environment, 53
organizational culture, 53
external environment, 54
task environment, 54
trade magazines, 54
general environment, 54
external relations, 57
social capital, 57
legitimacy, 57
ISO, 58
Baldrige Award, 58
social network, 60
mutuality, 62
networking, 62
sustainable entrepreneurship, 65
green entrepreneurship, 65
ethics, 66
ethical dilemma, 66
caveat emptor, 68
Golden Rule, 70
utilitarianism, 70
universalism, 70
billboard principal, 70
BATNA, 71

DISCUSSION QUESTIONS

1. What is the difference between the general environment and the task environment? Is it possible to say one is more important to a small business than the other?
2. In doing environmental scanning, the chapter mentions looking at the trade press and magazines outside your area of business, as well as asking customers, suppliers, your attorney, and your accountant for ideas about what is happening and what is coming next. If you have employees in your small business, should you ask them too? Why (or why not)?
3. What are the three general forms of legitimacy? Give two examples of ways to build legitimacy in each general form.
4. Why is a social network important for a small business?
5. Do you think that a small business could get by if it only did social networking using online sites like Facebook or LinkedIn? What would they miss by using this approach and do you think it is important?

6. What are the three keys to success in building your network using a social networking Web site?
7. What are the six steps of handling a crisis?
8. How do the six steps of handling a crisis compare to the U.S. government's three step approach to planning for disasters?
9. Why should small businesses make stronger efforts to achieve sustainability?
10. What are the three steps of ethical decision making?
11. What are the four philosophies you can use to evaluate alternatives you have generated to solve an ethical problem?

EXPERIENTIAL EXERCISES

1. Pick an existing business, or use one you own or are thinking about developing. For that business, identify at least two key players in at least two areas of its task environment (e.g., media and competitors). How did you determine which organizations fit? If you can, partner with another student to do the work on the same business and compare results.
2. Decide on three areas of the general environment you do not usually consider. Put together a profile of sources (online, print, or both) that you would use to do environmental scanning in those three areas, say every month during this class. One good source for each area is fine. Compare your general environment areas and sources to two others in the class. Arrange to compare findings after your first run-through of sources. In particular, what did you find that was "news" to you? What "news" did your classmates come up with for you?
3. Evaluate a franchise using the tables for the three forms of legitimacy. Go to the franchise's local operation to look around and check out the franchisor's Web site (e.g., **mcdonalds.com** for that chain). What forms of legitimacy are evident from your research? How positive a feeling does this give you about the firm?
4. Go to the Web sites of Facebook and LinkedIn. From what you can learn from the Web sites, how do these two social networking sites differ? Consider the market to which they are aiming, their relative sizes, and the kinds of methods they offer for online social networking. For a small business considering online social networking, which would you recommend first, and why?
5. Here are a set of challenging situations small business owners might find themselves facing. How would you handle them? Compare your solution to those of others in your class. When differences occur in the answers, what causes them?
   a. You own a dress shop specializing in prom dresses. A customer brings back a prom dress the week after her high school's prom. She swears she never wore the dress, but it seems to you that there were places where the dress shows wear or spots having been cleaned off. You have a "No Return" policy on the receipts and posted on the wall, but the customer says she will tell all her friends you were unfair if you do not refund her money.
   b. Last week one of your best employees asked to leave an hour early to take her spouse to the doctor. You said it was okay. Now another employee, who is an average but not great worker, is citing what happened last week and asking to be let go an hour early to go to "an appointment." The employee will not tell you what it is for.
   c. You need to buy office supplies. Do you go to Walmart with its visibly lower prices or the local office supply store, a small business like yours? Would it make a difference if the local office supply store bought from you?
6. When talking about codes of ethics, you were encouraged to do a Google search. One of the sites that may have turned up is the Center for the Study of Ethics in Professions at the Illinois Institute of Technology. Check out the site's collection of Codes of Ethics. Select one in an area that matches your small business interests (e.g., business, management, real estate, service, etc.) and look at one of the codes for that area. What do you need to do to prepare yourself to understand and follow that code when you enter your business?
7. You can complete and discuss the self-assessment below.

Is your behavior ethical?

For this exercise, you will be using the same set of statements twice. The first time you answer them, focus on your own behavior and the frequency with which you use it for each question. On the line before the question number, place number 1–4 that represents how often you did, do, or would do the behavior if you had the chance. These numbers will allow you to determine your level of ethics. You can be honest without fear of having to tell others in class of your score. *Sharing ethics scores is not part of the exercise.* The scale is:

Frequently 1 2 3 4 Never

The second time you use the same statements, focus on other people in an organization that you work for or have worked for. Place an O on the line after the number if you observed someone exhibiting this behavior. Also place an R on the line if you reported this behavior either within the organization or externally to some other person or organization.

1–4 O-R

College

____ 1. ____ Cheating on homework assignments.

____ 2. ____ Cheating on exams.

____ 3. ____ Turning in papers as your own work that were completed by someone else.

____ 4. ____ Helping someone do any of the above.

Job

____ 5. ____ Lying to others to get what you want or stay out of trouble.

____ 6. ____ Coming to work late and getting paid for it.

____ 7. ____ Leaving work early and getting paid for it.

____ 8. ____ Taking long breaks or lunches and getting paid for it.

____ 9. ____ Calling in sick to get a day off, when you are not sick.

____ 10. ____ Socializing rather than doing the work that should be done.

____ 11. ____ Doing personal work on company time.

____ 12. ____ Using the organization's phone to make personal calls.

____ 13. ____ Using the organization's computer and Internet access for personal use.

____ 14. ____ Using the company copier for personal use.

____ 15. ____ Using the company car for personal use.

____ 16. ____ Mailing personal things through the company mail.

____ 17. ____ Taking home company supplies and keeping them, or taking home company tools or equipment without permission for personal use and then returning them.

____ 18. ____ Giving company supplies or merchandise to friends or allowing them to take them without saying anything.

____ 19. ____ Putting in for reimbursement for meals and travel or other expenses that weren't actually eaten or taken.

____ 20. ____ Taking a spouse or friends out to eat and charging it to the company's expense account.

____ 21. ____ Taking a spouse or friend on business trips and charging the expense to the company.

____ 22. ____ Accepting gifts from customers or suppliers in exchange for giving them business.

____ 23. ____ Being pressured, or pressuring others, to sign documents containing false information.

____ 24. ____ Being pressured, or pressuring others, to sign documents you haven't read, knowing they may contain information or decisions that might be considered not in your or their best interest.

____ 25. ____ If you were to give this assessment to a person you work with whom you don't get along with very well, would she or he agree with your answers? Use a scale of 1–4 on the line before number 25.

Note to students: This self-assessment is not meant to be a precise measure of your ethical behavior. It is designed to get you thinking about ethics and your behavior and that of others from an ethical perspective. It is also designed to help you see situations in which you might have to think twice about your decision, because there is an ethical part to it. There is no right or wrong score. Another ethical issue of this exercise is your honesty when rating how often you might do these things—how honest were you?

Scoring: To determine your score, add the numbers 1–4. Your total will be between 25 and 100. Place the number here ______ and on the continuum below that represents your score. The lower your score, the more you need to be thinking about the types of behavior you are doing in your organization.

Needs some thought A role model
25——30——40——50——60——70——80——90——100

Discussion Questions:

1. For the college items 1–4, who is harmed and who benefits from these behaviors?
2. For job items 5–24, select the three (circle their numbers) that you consider the most severe unethical behavior. Who is harmed and who benefits from these behaviors? Would it matter if they were in a small business or a big company? Why?
3. If you observed unethical behavior but didn't report it, why not? If you did report it, why? What was the result? Was it worth it to you to report the behavior?
4. As a small business manager, you know unethical behavior can threaten the company's existence. If you know some of the employees are stealing from the company, would you tell the owner? Why or why not?
5. If you were a small business owner and you caught your employee, who is also your friend, doing any of the three behaviors you circled in Question 2 (most severe), what would you do?

Application:

1. What did I learn from this exercise?
2. How might I use this self-understanding in the future if I own my own or manage a small business?
3. As a small business owner, what can I do to prevent unethical behavior?

MINI-CASE

THE GIFT[37]

You have recently been hired as the purchasing manager at CDI Electronics, a small electronics research firm. You've been getting settled in your new position and becoming acquainted with the other 26 CDI employees. You've also started getting to know the vendors with whom CDI does business.

It's late November and the holidays are approaching. In your mail for the day is a small package containing an expensive watch from one of CDI's main vendors. Your first reaction is to send the watch back because accepting expensive gifts from vendors clearly violates all the company policies you've ever seen in larger companies you've worked in. It is a very fine watch with your name engraved on the back, along with the vendor's logo.

Before you get a chance to return the watch, Jim Fitzpatrick, an employee who's been with CDI since its beginning 12 years ago, approaches you about the situation. Apparently, everyone at CDI except for Joe Balsam, the founder and current CEO, received similar watches. According to Jim, this vendor sends some type of gift each holiday season, and CDI employees look forward to receiving the gift. He goes on to say that while everyone enjoys the gifts and is most appreciative, no preferential treatment is given to the vendor, nor is any expected.

Jim is concerned. He and the other CDI employees have noticed that your watch has just been sitting on your desk for the past two days. Employees are wondering why and what you may be thinking. They're concerned that if you make an issue of the gift, there will be trouble over gifts accepted in past years, because no one knows how Joe Balsam might react if he knew. Joe is apparently unaware of the annual gifts.

After Jim leaves your office, you sit and think about your options. The easiest solution would be to accept the gift as others have done in the past. Or you could go to Joe for guidance and cover yourself that way. There is a risk, though, that bringing it to Joe's attention would cause him to crack down on the practice if he doesn't like it. You haven't known Joe for very long, and you're really not sure if he'll go along with the gifts or not.

CASE DISCUSSION QUESTIONS

1. What is the important decision you're faced with, and why is it an ethical dilemma?
2. Is this a situation that matters in the short term or the long term? Why?
3. What do the four questions defining a moral problem (page 67) tell you?
4. The case tells you some of the obvious solutions or courses of action. What are some of the creative solutions you can come up with?
5. Using Figure 3.4, recommend your "best" ethical course of action, and see if it passes any or all of the four ethical tests. What do the four tests tell you about your possible decision?
6. Defend the course of action you've decided to take to a small group of your classmates.

WHOLE GROUP DISCUSSION QUESTIONS

1. How did your individual answers differ from your group's answers? Were your answers generally the ones the group decided to adopt? Why or why not?
2. Did your group members help you think about aspects of the decision you didn't think of yourself? How might you change your ethical decision-making process because of what your group said?

SUGGESTED CASES AND ARTICLES

- G&R Garden Center: Lawn Care Services Division, C-3

Available on McGraw-Hill Create™:

- It May Be Legal, But It's Just Wrong!
- Odwalla, Inc., and the E. Coli Outbreak (A)
- Heidi Roizen
- Environmental Entrepreneur
- Egghead.Com: Managing A Security Breach
- Walking the Walk: Putting Social Responsibility into Action at the White Dog Café

SUGGESTED VIDEOS

www.mhhe.com/katz4e

SBTV.com Videos:

- Proper Introductions in Business
- Preparing for Business Emergencies
- Social Networking Tricks for Your Business

STVP Videos:

- Why are Ethics Important?—Frank Levinson
- Establishing Credibility—Peter Seligman
- How Do You Hire Ethical People?—Frank Levinson
- Importance of Networking—Tina Selig
- Achieving Resource Sustainability
- Social Responsibility from the Ground Up

CHAPTER

4

Small Business Ideas: Creativity, Opportunity, and Feasibility

● Go Games is a recent expansion of the Magnetic Poetry line by Dave Kapell. Its company, Magnetic Poetry, was formed through several intriguing circumstances which were marked by creativity, opportunity, and feasibility. How did Dave's later business practices continue to promote creative, feasible opportunities?

LEARNING OBJECTIVES

After you complete this chapter, you will be able to:

LO1 Recognize the sources of opportunity entrepreneurs draw on to get business ideas.

LO2 Identify the way ideas are screened for business potential.

LO3 Understand how creativity methods can help business owners recognize new opportunities.

LO4 Understand the five pitfalls that hinder innovation.

LO5 Identify strategies for innovation in your business.

LO6 Describe how to conduct a comprehensive feasibility study for your business ideas.

LO7 Discuss the model for pilot testing Internet businesses.

LO8 Recognize the value of building a creative culture in your business.

Focus on Small Business: Dave Kapell: Poetry in Motion[1]

Dave Kapell was a guitarist and songwriter who played in funk and heavy metal bands in Minneapolis. His bands were popular locally, but he still worked at other jobs doing clerical work for nonprofits and driving a cab. Problem was, he often suffered from writer's block (an especially bad ailment for a lyricist!) and was constantly looking for things to inspire him so that he could write more songs. He happened to see a documentary on the life of David Bowie and learned that Bowie used a technique that Kapell found very intriguing. Following Bowie's suggestion, he began to cut up magazine stories, entries from journals, and even letters from family members and rearrange these small bits of paper to try to spark inspiration for songs. He would often have all these pieces laid out in a room, or across the front seat of his cab. There was just one problem.

Dave suffered from allergy attacks that caused him to sneeze, and when he sneezed, he would send the pieces of paper scattering all over the room or the seat of his car. He thought about gluing them to cardboard backing, but then he would have to put them away and take them out again whenever he wanted to use them. This is when opportunity met need.

One of Dave's roommates was an employee at a pizza restaurant, and the restaurant had a batch of refrigerator magnets it had intended to give to customers as advertising. But the magnets were misprinted and could not be used. Dave's friend brought these magnets home, and Dave came up with the idea of gluing the words to them. He then put the word magnets on a cookie sheet and kept them there so that he wouldn't have to put them away every day. It could have ended there. After all, Dave had solved the problem of the disrupted word collection. But one day someone in the house wanted to actually use the cookie sheets for what they were intended for—bake cookies! Now Dave had the problem of what to do with the magnets, so he casually put them on the refrigerator.

As Dave's roommates and friends came through the kitchen, Dave noticed that they all stopped by the fridge and played with the magnets—rearranging the words the magnets were holding to the fridge into phrases that were funny and bizarre. Dave would say that, while he never intended to start a business, this was a lightbulb experience. His friends started asking for sets of these words, and Dave saw an opportunity. He recalled, "I told everyone that I could make a kit for seven bucks, and I was earning seven dollars an hour in my job at the time and my student loans were coming due, so I made up a bunch of kits. I took 100 kits to my first craft show, and I figured that would be enough for the whole weekend. They sold out in three hours. I knew I was on to something."[2]

That was 1993, the year Dave's company, Magnetic Poetry, was born. As the idea took off, Dave realized he could no longer make the kits himself. He saved $5,000 from craft fairs and began visiting local screen-printing and die shops in Minneapolis. He paid for 1,000 prototype sets. But the road was not smooth yet. Dave knew next to nothing about distribution. He also learned that retailers are not interested in amateur packaging, and Dave's kit looked like a cardboard jewelry box. Pam Jones, a manager of a local art museum gift shop, gave Dave lots of tips on product presentation. In three weeks, he developed a clear plastic package that Jones thought would fit on her gift shop's shelves. By the end of that first day, she sold the 12 kits Dave gave her. The new packaging was attractive to retailers such as bookstores, gift shops in the Guggenheim and Whitney museums in New York City, and Signals catalogs. By 1994, Dave's kits were selling in the Museum Company in the eastern part of the United States, and at the San Francisco Museum of Modern Art on the West Coast.

As time went on, Dave decided to do his own manufacturing, since he felt he wasn't getting quick enough turnaround from his manufacturer. He went back to Murray Condon, who had helped him with his prototypes, and the two formed a separate company called Screen D'or Graphics, Inc. Kapell funded the company with the goal of a three-day order-to-delivery turnaround. He now had a number of employees in production, sales, administration, inventory control, and shipping and was looking for other opportunities for his kits, such as introducing them in foreign languages. Today, the Magnetic Poetry product line features over 100 products. Its word kits include everything from the Shakespearean, Artist, and Genius kits to the Dog Lover, Romance, and College kits. (The Original kit remains wildly popular, too.) Magnetic Poetry also has new products that go beyond the magnetic word tile genre, including a Poetry Beads kit, magnetic travel games, and Writer's Remedy, a cookie jar filled with words to help cure writer's block. The Web site (www.magneticpoetry.com) also offers more than a dozen kits for online play.

Polished versions of the hand-glued magnets that once decorated Dave's refrigerator door in his Minneapolis home now can be found on millions of such doors and metal surfaces across the country. Since Dave Kapell invented Magnetic Poetry in 1993, more than 3 million kits have been sold. Magnetic Poetry, a cultural phenomenon, has appeared in the movies *Conspiracy Theory, City of Angels,* and *Notting Hill,* as well as on Jerry Seinfeld's refrigerator on the TV show *Seinfeld.*[3]

DISCUSSION QUESTIONS

1. How did Dave Kapell discover that his idea would be a good business opportunity?
2. How did Dave evaluate whether or not his idea for Magnetic Poetry was successful?
3. What other opportunities might there be for Magnetic Poetry in the future?

opportunity recognition Searching and capturing new ideas that lead to business opportunities. This process often involves creative thinking that leads to discovery of new and useful ideas.

The Source of Business Ideas

LO1 Recognize the sources of opportunity entrepreneurs draw on to get business ideas.

entrepreneurial alertness A special set of observational and thinking skills that help entrepreneurs identify good opportunities; the ability to notice things that have been overlooked, without actually launching a formal search for opportunities, and the motivation to look for opportunities.

Do you recall seeing a new product or service in a store, or maybe hearing about an idea on radio or television, and thinking, "Now, why didn't I think of that?" In fact, most of the ideas that are turned into new businesses, or result in "new and improved" products and services, come from information and observations that we are surrounded by every day. Does it seem to you that successful business owners must possess unusual powers of observation or use top-secret strategies unknown to anybody else when seeking ideas for new businesses or innovations to their existing businesses? It's far more likely that these people have learned to pay attention to the cues that are around them and to ask many questions of things that most people take for granted, such as the way Dave Kapell did when making Magnetic Poetry. This search and capture of new ideas that lead to business opportunities is called **opportunity recognition**. Researchers in the field of entrepreneurship and small business believe that opportunity recognition behavior is the most basic and important entrepreneurial behavior.[4]

The exact reasons why entrepreneurs seem to be better able to find ideas that work are unclear. The notion of **entrepreneurial alertness** is one that has captured the attention of scholars in the field. This phrase means that entrepreneurs have a special set of observational and thinking skills that help them identify good opportunities. Some scholars have suggested that entrepreneurs are able to notice things that have been overlooked, without actually launching a formal search for opportunities.[5] Others suggest that we also consider the motivations of entrepreneurs to search for new ideas.[6] For example, if an owner of a fast-food restaurant notices that customers are asking for substitutions of healthier ingredients to the food items, she may be motivated to contact her suppliers to ask about obtaining new ingredients and to change the menu and increase the healthy offerings on the menu to keep customers satisfied, possibly bringing in more customers.

Ideas for new businesses come from a great variety of sources. A person who desires to start a business may begin searching for opportunities that exist in the marketplace, perhaps as a way to use skills and knowledge that he or she has acquired in college or in work experience. In the nationwide Panel Study of Entrepreneurial Dynamics,[7] a sample of 480 entrepreneurs were asked whether the business idea or the decision to start some kind of business came first:

TABLE 4.1 What Came First for New Businesses

Business idea	37%
Decision to start a business	42%
Idea and decision were simultaneous	21%

Source: Adapted from G. E. Hills and R. P. Singh, "Opportunity Recognition." In *Handbook of Entrepreneurial Dynamics: The Process of Business Creation*, ed. W. B. Gartner, K. G. Shaver, N. M. Carter, and P. D. Reynolds. Thousand Oaks, CA: Sage, 2004. Table 24.1, page 266.

But regardless of whether the idea came first or the decision to start a business came first, we now examine the factors that lead small business owners to their business idea.

Work Experience

Many successful business owners spent years working for a company and gained valuable experience about how things might be done differently. Sometimes the idea grows out of listening to customer complaints.

You can use your own work and personal experiences to think of ideas for doing things differently. Sometimes the best business ideas come from your own frustration or from not finding exactly what you are looking for as a consumer. Anita Roddick, founder of The Body Shop International PLC, whose 1,900 skin and body care retail stores are in 50 countries spanning 25 languages and 12 time zones,[8] got the idea for her business because she was very frustrated at having to spend a lot of money on moisturizer in fancy bottles from the big name cosmetics companies. Her idea was to give customers an inexpensive, good quality product made from natural ingredients in a recyclable bottle.

A Similar Business

Even if you don't have years of work experience in an industry or market, you might see a business in an area that intrigues you because you like certain products, or you learn that there is a growing market for this business and you think of a way to expand on the opportunity. The mini-case at the end of this chapter introduces Amy Nye Wolf, who founded AltiTUNES, a chain of airport music stores she eventually sold to Inmotion Entertainment. She got the idea for the business while traveling through Heathrow Airport in London while a college student.

Hobby or Personal Interest

Many people find a way to turn their hobbies into successful businesses. David and Tom Gardner, the founders of Motley Fool, didn't start out wanting to write an online investment advice newsletter and Web site. They were avid players of a dice baseball game in high school called Strat-O-Matic, and they had a league in their town outside Washington, DC, where they grew up. Tom recalled, "It was a numbers game, and we kept lots of stats. There were so many different variables, just like the stock market and just like businesses have. And it was also a people thing, which is a big part of running a business, because all the fun of it was making trades with your competitors."[9]

SMALL BUSINESS INSIGHT

CLEANING UP THROUGH INNOVATION

Traction Plus

Russell Kendzior of Bedford, Texas, worked as a floor-covering salesman in the late 1980s. He heard customers complain that their floors were slippery right after they were purchased. He did some digging around and even commissioned chemists to develop a soap-free floor-cleaning product. He spent $5,000 of his own money, quit his job, and finally developed his own product. He gave away some product to friends who owned McDonald's locations, and before long it was the top-selling floor cleaner at McDonald's restaurants in the Dallas area. He ended up licensing his product, Traction Plus, which permitted him to think about other opportunities. Now, companies that bought his license manufacture and distribute wet-floor signs and floor-safety shoes. Traction Plus is a $20 million company, and its products include chemicals and footwear. Kendzior also developed and now runs the National Floor Safety Institute. He protects his ideas carefully. His soap-free formula is manufactured in several places, so no one knows exactly what is in it. Even Johnson Wax could not match Traction Plus because of Kendzior's vast experience. He describes himself as a resistant virus: "We're very resistant, very strong, but a very small company. I don't want to be Johnson Wax. I think they want to be me."[10]

Russ Kendzior's success sends an important message about looking for business opportunities that emerge through experience, including the frustrations of customers, which in this case was floor safety. Finding a new way to solve people's problems can be an excellent source of ideas for business.

Chance Happening, or Serendipity

If it is true that successful business owners are alert to what goes on around them and pay attention to things most people miss, then it is no surprise to learn that another popular source for business ideas comes from the chance happening. Whether you think of it as being in the right place at the right time, as luck, or as being observant to the cues around you, many businesses have been formed as a result of the unexpected. In the early 1980s, Rangaswamy Srinivasan worked for IBM, where he worked with lasers and organic plastics. He happened to come upon his "great idea" while at the Thanksgiving table, where he wondered how effective a laser might be in slicing a turkey leg. His experiments contributed to the development of laser eye surgery, an idea that came to him by observing the environment around him. In 2002 he was inducted into the Inventors Hall of Fame.[11]

Family and Friends

Ideas can come to you through your conversations with your family and friends. If you are open to their suggestions, a great business idea can result. Joan Ecker, founder of The Fat Hat Factory, a $1.7 million clothing company, got the idea for making a shapeable "fat" hat when a friend told her he would visit her at her new home in Vermont only if she provided him with a warm hat.[12]

Education and Expertise

As we saw earlier in the chapter, some small business owners decide first that they want to own a business and then go about searching for a viable idea for that business. Often, would-be entrepreneurs look to their own skills and talents for business ideas. Consulting companies are a very popular example of this approach to business ideas. Many owners of consulting companies took their own skills and launched businesses by selling those skills to other companies or individuals who needed them. Some of these consultants were laid off or voluntarily left large employers to consult with clients because they felt their talents would be more significantly recognized and rewarded in their own businesses.

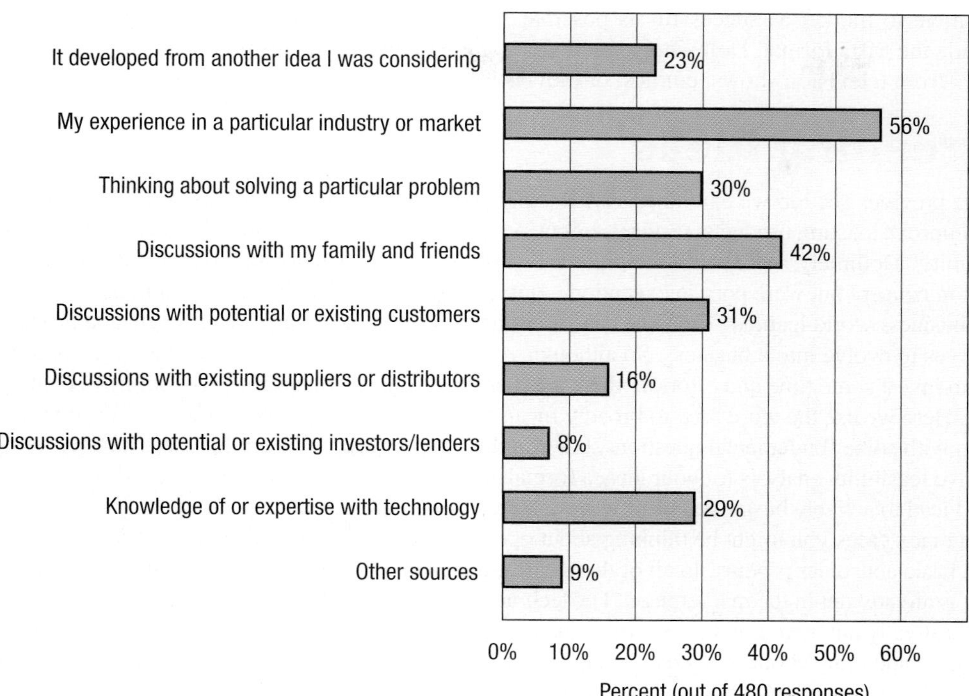

FIGURE 4.1

What Led to Your Business Idea?[13]

Source: Adapted from G. E. Hills and R. P. Singh, "Opportunity Recognition." In *Handbook of Entrepreneurial Dynamics: The Process of Business Creation*, ed. W. B. Gartner, K. G. Shaver, N. M. Carter, and P. D. Reynolds. Thousand Oaks, CA: Sage, 2004. Table 24.4, page 268.

In the Panel Study of Entrepreneurial Dynamics, 480 entrepreneurs were asked, "What led to your business idea?" Figure 4.1 presents the results of this question. Work experience in a particular industry or market was the most frequently mentioned source of ideas, followed by discussion with family and friends.

Idea Sites

Today you can find Web sites where people post ideas they have and products and services they would like to see. Examples include **www.halfbakery.com**, **www.ideabuyer.com**, **www.999ideas.com**, **www.newideatrade.com**, **www.marketlaunchers.com**, **www.inventionsforsale.com**, **marketplace.yet2.com**, and **www.coolbusinessideas.com**. Spending an hour or two surfing these ideas may give you ideas of your own or suggest an invention you need to get your business going. There are also crowdfunding sites like **www.kickstarter.com** and **www.rockethub.com**, where you can post your idea and see if people will actually fund your effort to get it going.

Technology Transfer and Licensing

One powerful but rarely used source of ideas are universities and government agencies. Both develop a tremendous range of new technologies or refinements of existing technologies, *but never do anything with them!* Major universities and government agencies, like NASA and the Departments of Agriculture and Defense, all offer technological inventions for free to small businesses to develop. There are even government programs to help fund such efforts. A good place to start are government technology commercialization sites such as NASA's (**www.nasa.gov/offices/oct/home/index.html**), the Department of Defense's site at (**www.acq.osd.mil/ott/techtransit/**), or the Byrd National Technology Transfer Center Web site at (**iridium.nttc.edu**). If you have a university nearby which has government funded research, you can contact their technology transfer office and find out about inventions available for commercialization in your own backyard, or check out the Web site of the Association of University Technology Managers at **www.autm.net**, or the multiuniversity iBridge Network at **www.ibridgenetwork.org/**.

What these organizations will offer you is an arrangement called licensing. A **license** is a legal agreement granting you rights to use a particular piece of intellectual property (for example, a technology). In return, you (the **licensee**) are required to pay the owner of the license (the **licensor**). These payments can consist of an upfront or annual flat licensing fee or a **royalty**, which is a payment per item sold. Often the licensor will provide access to the idea's creator to help make

license
A legal agreement granting you rights to use a particular piece of intellectual property.

licensee
The person or firm which is obtaining the rights to use a particular piece of intellectual property.

licensor
The person or organization which is offering the rights to use a particular piece of intellectual property.

royalty
A payment to a licensor based on the number or value of licensed items sold.

the move to market as successful as possible. Examples of licensed products you see every day include the MP3 format, Dolby noise reduction, or Gatorade, as well as products with famous characters from television shows, comics, or movies.

Screening Ideas

In the previous section we examined various ways you can search for your business idea or for ideas that improve existing products, services, or business processes. Is every good idea a viable business opportunity? Definitely not. The marketplace is replete with examples of bad business ideas that seemed great in concept but were poor in execution—witness the dot-com bubble that burst in the early 2000s. The business world learned—in some cases very harshly—that not every idea is evaluated properly or deserves to evolve into a business. So although you may feel strongly that an idea is the *right* idea for you to invest some time and effort in, there are many more steps you need to take before opening your door. Here we use the word *idea* to broadly mean a new or improved product, service, or process. We begin with some fundamental questions. Later in this chapter you will learn how to conduct a comprehensive feasibility analysis for your idea, a formal approach to assessing whether your idea is sound and could lead to a viable business. For now we offer a simple approach to help you quickly screen ideas.

LO2 Identify the ways ideas are screened for business potential.

In many cases you might be thinking about opening a service locally or starting a Web site or creating a basic consumer product. In all of these cases, it is likely that you can quickly and easily check out what is already out in the marketplace. The techniques are given in Skill Module 4.1. The fact that your idea is already out there is not necessarily a bad thing for you. You can check out what your competitors are doing and think about if you can do better. This can be by making a better product or service, or by doing a better job at marketing their product or service through some kind of contracting arrangement.

SKILL MODULE 4.1 Checking Ideas on the Web

When we think of a new idea, we generally assume that if it is new to us, it is new to the world. With the help of the Internet, we can now do a much better job of making sure that's true. Take the example of a book holder on an adjustable spring-loaded arm, like some types of desk lamps. It would let you read in bed at a comfortable angle, without tiring your arms. Because you have not seen one before, it seems like it could be a new product idea.

Start your browser, point it to **shopping.google.com** and type the product description, *book holder for bed,* right in:

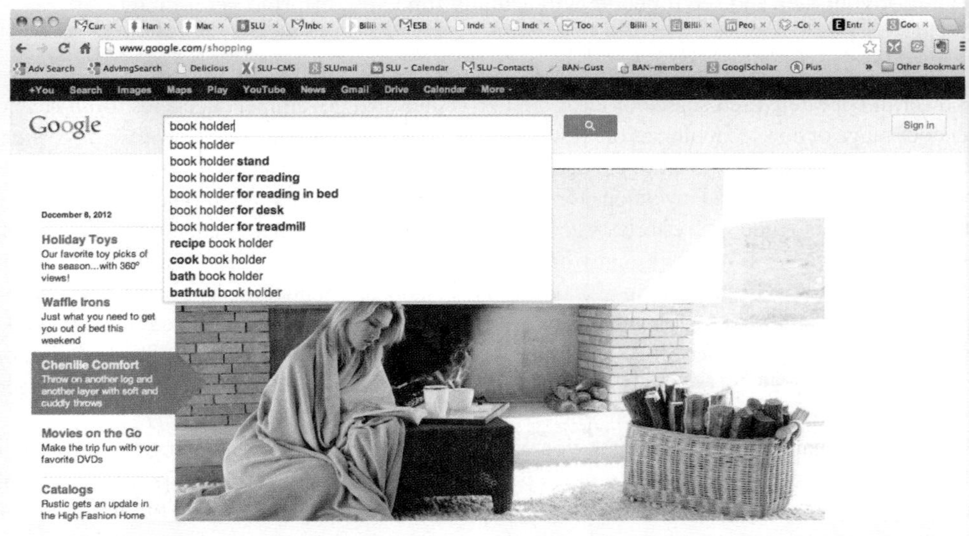

In this case, the idea is popular enough that before we could type-in "bed," Google pulled it up as one of the more popular product searches. Going to the page will give you an idea of what kinds of holders already exist. Note that you might have to try several different ways to describe your product. For example, if you tried "spring-loaded book holder" you could get a different mix of products. So try to think of different ways to describe the product.

If you find out your idea for a product already exists, you might be out of luck for getting a patented product, but your finding could help you get into business a great deal quicker. If the product of your dreams already exists, it means you can probably make a deal to start selling it tomorrow. The fact the product existed, and you—an interested potential customer—did not know about it means that the product probably has room for growth, adding new markets and means of distribution—including you!

If you are considering a service, like dog walking, the same basic approach applies. Bring up **maps.google.com** and put in the service and the zip code or locality where you would like to deliver the service. It should show you where potential competitors are located. Remember that many services are local, so if there is no one in your immediate vicinity, that may be enough space in which to get started.

A popular approach to organizing an opportunity screen comes from two collegiate idea competitions: the University of Texas—Austin's Idea To Product (I2P) and the NCIIA's Invention To Venture (I2V). A typical I2P analysis consists of a one-page response to seven questions—two about the product, four about the market, and one about intellectual property protection:

1. **What is your product or idea?** This is a nontechnical description of the concept simple enough for everyone to understand it.
2. **How is your product or idea better?** This is where you explain how your approach is *better* than other approaches. Reasons can include: it is simpler, more capable, more durable, cheaper, or more stylish. In Chapter 9 we talk about the features of products in detail.
3. **How would you define the best initial set of customers? (Who will buy it?)** This question looks at the specific individuals, groups, or organizations you would approach *first* to buy your product or service.
4. **Why will they buy it?** The question might better be phrased, "Why would they buy *yours*?" Ideally if there are competing products or services, you want to explain why the customer would buy your product or service instead of the competition's. If you cannot come up with a strong case on behalf of your own idea, it probably is not going to work. The only way to know for sure is to ask potential customers about their interest.
5. **Describe how you create value for your customers.** Good products or services meet the customer's basic need. Great products or services create additional value for customers, helping them get more out of work or life, or making life easier, or helping them meet other goals (e.g., saving money, living greener, helping others). For example, the value of a folding umbrella is greater than that of a large traditional umbrella because it is easier to carry and pack.
6. **What is the market and its size?** This looks like the simplest question but is actually the hardest one. "Everyone" does not work as an answer. While precise numbers are unlikely at this point, you need to have some idea if we are talking about a market of hundreds, thousands, or millions. Where there are competing products, you can get an idea of the market size. For new products or services, you have to look at the type of customer and then look for demographic, census, or marketing information which can give you a sense of the size of a market. The market needs to be big enough for you to make the kind of income you need to feel satisfied.
7. **Can you develop IP protection for your idea?** This question asks you to think of your strategy for protecting your idea from competitors. Examples include patents, trademarks, or trade secrets (see Chapter 18 for more information), licensing, and strategic partnerships or distribution agreements (see Chapter 11). IP protection is not essential, but an idea you can protect gets more attention than one anyone can copy.

You can see in Exhibit 4.1 how the questions might be answered. The process requires some research about the technology or method behind the idea, competition, and market as well as some imagining about how people would respond to the product. All in all an I2P style approach gives a good start to organizing your thoughts about the business potential of a new product or service.

EXHIBIT 4.1

An I2P Analysis: Cell Phone Frequency Blocker by Edin Rakovich, Saint Louis University

1. What is your product or idea?
The CFB (Cell Phone Frequency Blocker) is a one of a kind product. It is based on the wireless router technology. The CFB is a close proximity cell phone frequency scrambler. Once an individual would enter the proximity of the CFB, their cell phone signal would drop to zero and that individual would not be able to make or receive phone calls or text messages. The CFB would be simple enough for anyone to deploy it; however, it would be only available to registered institutions, such as schools, churches, and other community organizations.

2. Is your product or idea innovative? Describe.
Yes, it is something that is in need, but has not been thought of for use in these centers. Similar products are being used by the military and government agencies.

3. Who will buy it?
The initial customer group is wide and can range from elementary and middle to high schools. Places like churches and other religious centers are great candidates as well.

4. Why will they buy it?
The CFB appeals to all places of interest by eliminating the distractions that arise from cellular phones. During school hours students would focus more on the materials at hand, and during church services there would be no abrupt noise disruptions.

5. Describe how you create value for your customers.
The CFB provides the only legal approach to cell phone blocking, assuring users of their compliance with laws while providing a peaceful, call-free environment.

6. What is the market and its size?
To start, the product would be offered for free to a local education center and to a local church. Once the testing period is complete, the product could be offered to any institution. If the product was just available to schools, there are 98,706 schools in the United States. However, companies could acquire the CFB for special meetings of all types. The product would be available as long as these companies register the product.

7. How do you anticipate developing IP protection for your technology?
I would start by acquiring a patent either with the help of the program or on my own.

In addition to an I2P analysis, there are still three additional questions you should consider to complete an initial idea screening. They focus on people, resources, and profits:

8. **Who are the people behind the idea?** If a great idea with high market potential also has a person or team behind it that is a good fit, the idea is much more likely to be successful than it would be without that person or team. While your skills and talents might have led you to discover the idea, do you have all the skills necessary to turn this idea into a business?
9. **What resources are needed to take the idea and sell it to the customer?** Beyond the start-up dollars that will be needed to buy any raw materials to make the product or develop the service, what information, relationships, and degree of effort will be needed to turn the idea into reality?
10. **Can the idea generate sufficient profit?** Can the sales meet your profit expectation? One of the mistakes would-be entrepreneurs make is to assume that everyone will love the idea and that people will be standing in line to buy it once the business opens. Be conservative, factor in the value of your own time, and *then* estimate future profits. In addition, consider expanding your

offerings to increase profits (for example, selling supplies used with the product, or an extended warranty, or support services, etc.).

Few ideas initially prove outstanding in all ten areas. For example, businesses imitating a pioneer are not usually unique, although they may be innovative and offer customers a better product than the pioneering company. For example, Facebook learned from the mistakes of Friendster, the original social networking site, and far surpassed the pioneer in subscribers, revenues, and profits. What is important once you have collected the initial data for an opportunity screening is to look at the strengths. If the idea's strengths are attractive enough, the importance of spending some time thinking of ways to offset the weaknesses grows dramatically. The way to success in those cases often comes from creatively rethinking the idea in order to realize the attractive business opportunity inside it. The techniques for doing this are found in the next section.

From Ideas to Opportunities through Creativity

LO3 Understand how creativity methods can help business owners recognize new opportunities.

You might have a viable business idea, but is it the best one to pursue? Are you sure you have the right approach for making the most of the idea? Very often the first good idea an entrepreneur has is not necessarily the best one they will have. Before committing yourself to one viable idea, it is a good practice to take some time and see if you can take that viable idea and innovate on it to create an even better—more profitable, more distinctive, harder to copy—idea.

Why worry about being innovative in your approach? Consider the ease with which you can get data over the Internet on industries and markets, such as your competition, and how small business research and how-to articles are at your fingertips with many journals and magazines available over the Web. Of course, everybody else who is thinking about starting a business similar to yours has this same information at his or her fingertips also. There are, however, some very creative methods you can use to help you generate ideas and opportunities that take you beyond what everybody else already knows. This is what can give you the innovative edge in business ownership, whether you are looking for ideas that are just a little bit different from the competition, or a world apart from what everybody else is doing or not even doing yet. These strategies are discussed later in the chapter.

Figure 4.2 provides one tool you can use to help you identify new opportunities. It is based on the work of Alex Osborne, a pioneer in the field of **creativity**, who first coined the word, *brainstorming*. The tool is known as SCAMPER, and it is an acronym for a set of cues that trigger new ideas for your business.

creativity
A process producing an idea or opportunity that is novel and useful, frequently derived from making connections among distinct ideas or opportunities.

S – Substitute
C – Combine
A – Adapt
M – Magnify or modify
P – Put to other uses
E – Eliminate
R – Rearrange

FIGURE 4.2
Using SCAMPER to Recognize Business Opportunities[14]

Substitute: Think of what you might substitute for something else to form a new idea. A feature that allows your customers to order directly from a Web site rather than visiting your store or ordering by mail is an example of substitution. Sometimes solutions derived through SCAMPER cues are very "way out" and lead people to some creative ideas for solving annoying problems. One city in the Netherlands, for example, was experiencing a growing litter problem (not unlike your own town or city, no doubt), and the civic leaders tried all the usual ways of fixing the problem: They increased the number of trash bins around the city, they posted signs reminding people not to litter, and they fined people for littering. Nothing seemed to help. Then they got a breakthrough idea: a tiny recording device was installed inside trash bins, and every time someone pushed the lid to deposit litter, a joke would play from the recorder! Not surprisingly, it was not too long before the litter problem declined.

Idea Trigger: What opportunities can you think of that come as a result of substituting or replacing something that already exists?

Combine: Think of possible combinations you can make that result in something entirely different. Not long ago, if you wanted to buy a book, you went to a store that typically carried only books, and if you wanted to buy a cup of coffee you went to a coffee shop, and if you wanted to hear music you went to a club or theater. Today, you can have all three under one roof at many establishments, including big ones such as Barnes & Noble, but also some smaller businesses such as Tattered Cover Book Stores in Denver, Colorado. Also, when you buy gasoline at the service station, you most likely can pick up some groceries along with basic auto supplies, and maybe even CDs or videotapes.

Idea Trigger: What separate products, services, or whole businesses can you put together to create another distinct business?

radical innovation strategy
Rejecting existing ideas, and presenting a way to do things differently.

Adapt: Think about what could be adapted from products or services that already exist. Many successful businesses are founded on the concept of adaptation. It's a popular innovation strategy that can be just as effective, and much more likely in the real world, than business opportunities that are the result of **radical innovations** such as inventions. You may remember the original Book-of-the-Month Club that sent members a different book every month. What adaptations can you find? How about beer-of-the-month, pasta-of-the-month, and many other variations? Did you know that one day a manufacturer of toilet tissue received a shipment of paper that was too thick to use? The manufacturer could have thrown it out, but instead the manufacturer improvised, and paper towels were introduced! Sometimes adaptations occur when entrepreneurs try their best to work with scarce resources.

Idea Trigger: What could you adapt from other industries or fields to your business?

Magnify or modify: Taking an existing product and changing its appearance or adding more features or increasing the hours your store is open or making its advertising more dramatic are some ways you could magnify or modify your idea. Ally Bank is a relatively small, new, online financial services company that is currently expanding nationally using ads proclaiming this in some very dramatic and humorous ways, poking fun at the traditional fees that banks and other financial service companies charge for checking accounts, for example. The goal is for such messages to be remembered by potential customers, and the effect is to make the business stick out among its competitors. There is much a small business can do to create memorable images and advertising for itself, and it does not need expensive television ads to do it. The letter M also can cue you to "minimize" something. The microchip industry was born, for example, when someone asked the question, "What if we shrunk them?"

Idea Trigger: What could I make more noticeable or dramatic, or different in some way from my competitors? It need not be in the product itself, but it could be the way you advertise or treat the customer during the transaction that becomes memorable.

Put to other uses: Think of ways you could generate a high number of opportunities for your product or service beyond what it is traditionally used for. A few years ago, Arm & Hammer Baking Soda was known as a product customers used by the teaspoonful every few weeks when they baked a batch of cookies or a cake. The problem for Arm & Hammer was that it wasn't selling a lot of boxes of the stuff since it tended to sit in people's kitchen cupboards for years. At 59 cents a box, that doesn't bring tremendous sales revenues. One day, the company brought together a group of employees and gave them the challenge to think of all the uses for baking soda (besides baking) that they could. Ideas took off, and today the company produces an entire line of baking soda–related products that bring a handsome return in profits. Can you think of some? (Hint: washing clothes, refrigerators that smell, a product cats use, etc.)

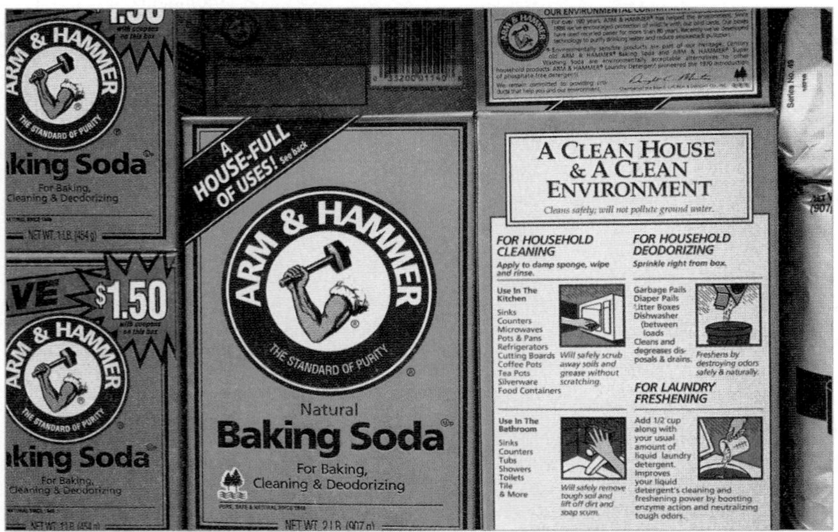

Arm & Hammer Baking Soda was put to another use when employees came up with absorbing refrigerator odors. What other uses can you imagine?

Antoine Fuerchtwanger sold frankfurters at the Chicago Exposition over 100 years ago, and his customers complained that they burnt their fingers when holding them. Fuerchtwanger tried gloves, but customers kept walking off with them. Finally, he took some rolls that a baker had made, cut them in half down the middle, and placed the frankfurters inside them. Hotdogs met buns, and today it's hard to imagine one without the other.

Idea Trigger: Suppose you learned that all the traditional uses for your product had disappeared and that you have trailer truckloads out back with tons of product. What other uses might there be? Aim for quantity, and allow outrageous ideas to flow along with more mundane ones. Who knows what new applications you may find.

Eliminate: Search for opportunities that arise when you get rid of something or stop doing something. What products or services emerged when these questions were asked: What if people didn't have to leave their houses to go grocery shopping? What if you could buy something (or do bank transactions) without leaving your car?

Idea Trigger: What could I get rid of or reduce that would eliminate something my customer has to do, and as a result give the customer more than he or she expected?

Rearrange or reverse: One of the best examples of this technique is shown in the opening vignette to this chapter. Magnetic Poetry is a product that by definition is about rearranging things to inspire ideas. Other examples include using reverse psychology or paradox to challenge old ways of thinking, for example, using stimulants to calm hyperactive children.

Idea Trigger: What can you rearrange or reorder in the way your product or service appears, or the way businesses in your industry usually look or are decorated or located?

SCAMPER is a very effective method for helping business owners and their employees come up with alternative solutions and opportunities. The method works because it helps you to step outside the usual way you look at opportunities or try to solve problems. It offers cues that push you outside your traditional areas of expertise, to consider what interesting new forms might be out there that you could try. We know that highly creative individuals are people who usually ask lots of questions. Creative business owners similarly question and challenge the way things appear, to see if they can find a new way of doing things. When you see a highly innovative business, don't think that there is something especially magical or lucky about the entrepreneur or the situation. It's more likely that the person or team behind the business is simply persistent about asking questions. Following are several recommendations to help you put yourself and your business in an innovative frame of mind.

THE THOUGHTFUL ENTREPRENEUR

The Creative Process

The creative process in individuals, teams, and organizations has been studied intensively for over 75 years. It is concerned with the way in which creativity actually happens. Much of what we know about creativity comes from understanding the process that highly creative people go through when they get their ideas. Artists, scientists, composers, poets, and inventors have attempted to describe their creative moments. Graham Wallas[15] developed one of the early descriptions of the creative process, and it is still widely used today to guide the creative process in business. This research suggests that creative thought includes four stages:

1. Preparation—exploring the problem or opportunity in all directions.
2. Incubation—thinking about the problem or opportunity in a "not-conscious" way, putting it on the back burner, so to speak.
3. Illumination—the lightbulb comes on, and ideas begin to flow.
4. Verification—testing of the idea and reducing it to its most exact form.[16]

This process is very useful when you want to explore a business problem, such as why you lost a customer, or when you want to identify further opportunities for your business, such as new markets or features for your product line. If you can pinpoint what stage of the creative process you are in, you can guide yourself through to an innovative solution by looking at things from different perspectives and allowing the issue to simmer in the background for a bit. This technique has worked for many famous creative people—from Leonardo da Vinci to Albert Einstein.

Get into an Innovative Frame of Mind

Regardless of whether you feel your business needs a subtle change or a drastic one, building "changeability" into a core business is possible if you actually practice change.[17] Here are some techniques you can try as you practice the business of innovation:

- Read magazines or trade journals outside your area.
- Invite someone you never included before to a meeting at which you are solving a problem or searching for a new opportunity. Try a supplier or a friend who works in a different field.
- Have a "scan the environment" day in which you discuss trends and happenings that could impact your business.
- Try a mini-internship. Ask a colleague or friend if you can spend a week at his or her business to see what you can learn that may be applicable to yours.
- Instead of trying to simply sell your product or service to customers, put yourself in their shoes and ask them what frustrates them most or what problems they cannot seem to solve that relate to your business.
- Redesign your work environment. Get a room with a view.[18] This doesn't have to cost a bundle in remodeling or even redecorating costs. Try to bring in some items from nature and add color and inspirational objects or quotations.

Avoid Pitfalls

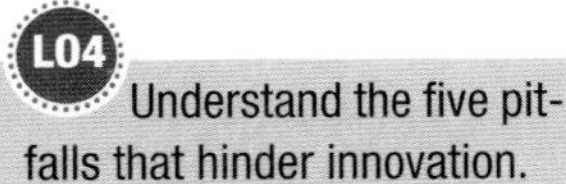

Understand the five pitfalls that hinder innovation.

In your quest for new business ideas, from time to time you may catch yourself rejecting ideas or jumping on the first good idea you get because you are excited and there is no time to lose.

There are five major pitfalls[19] that business owners can become victim to when trying to become more innovative. See if you recognize the ones that apply to you and your business, so that you can sidestep them at every opportunity:

1. **Identifying the wrong problem:** When a problem doesn't stay solved or an opportunity doesn't pan out as expected, it could be that the wrong problem was defined. For example, a synthetic-fiber producer brought a group of employees together to help find ways to reduce the manufacturing costs of a particular product. After spending a few days brainstorming and finding that the problem was not leading them to any interesting or useful solutions, the employees turned the problem around and began developing ways to increase the sales of a highly profitable part of the product line. How were they able to change their focus in this way? They simply examined the problem within the broader context of profitability (instead of costs) and discovered that the real problem was low profits.
2. **Judging ideas too quickly:** At many business meetings when someone suggests a new idea or approach, often the first reaction you hear is, "We've tried that before and it didn't work," "The boss will never go for it," "It's not in the budget," or the frequently heard, "Yes, but . . ." People tend to judge ideas prematurely, before they take the time to ask, "What's right about this idea?" or "How could this idea be made better?"
3. **Stopping with the first good idea:** The first good idea you come up with is rarely the best. That's because it was the easiest to think of, and so there is little doubt that your competitors have already thought of it, too. The very best ideas come a little later, after the ideas that are on the top of your mind come out. Using a tool such as SCAMPER, for example, encourages you to explore things more deeply than just rattling off the first thing you can think of and then doing that.
4. **Failing to get the "bandits on the train" and ask for support:** Imagine you are on a train in the American West in the late 1800s. At the time, bandits often placed dynamite on the tracks to hold up the train. How can you keep that from happening? One way is to get the bandits on your train. In modern business terms, this means figuring out whose support you must have or who could derail your project and then involving them early in the project. If you need an employee's involvement or a supplier's agreement, get them on board early to avoid failure later.

5. **Obeying rules that don't exist:** We sometimes put obstacles in front of ourselves because we think we can't do something, when in fact there is no reason we can't. Are you assuming that as the business owner you need to do all the work, or make all the sales calls, or solve everybody's problems (including your employees' or partners' problems)? Before you assume that you do, challenge the assumption.

Types of Innovations Small Businesses Develop

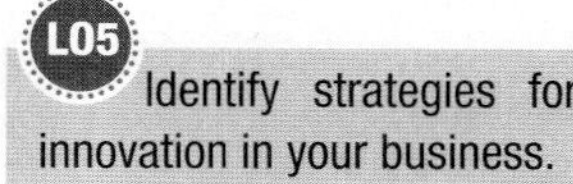

LO5
Identify strategies for innovation in your business.

Companies may find it easier to mimic the strategies of other firms because of the expense and intense effort required to make decisions based on a radical innovation strategy. In addition customers may view a new company as more legitimate if it imitates established practices in the industry.[20] This is the idea behind several of the methods for product-based legitimacy described in Chapter 3. It is also central to the idea of pursuing an **imitative strategy**, which is covered in detail in Chapter 7.

imitative strategy
An overall strategic approach in which the entrepreneur does more or less what others are already doing.

incremental strategy
Taking an idea and offering a way to do something slightly better than it is done presently.

But mimicking others is not the only strategy that an entrepreneur can pursue. Gaglio and Katz[21] offer a model for thinking about the business implications of opportunities. Called the *opportunity identification process* (see Figure 4.3), it has the entrepreneur assess whether the situation faced is one that is the same as it has been traditionally or if it is changing. Strategies that involve doing the same thing, or mimicking others, or pursuing an **incremental strategy** make a lot of sense when the business is continuing on a fairly steady course. Sometimes during these periods of stability, trying innovative ideas might help win more business from rivals, and "shake up" the industry, perhaps giving the innovator an advantage. During times of great change—whether from technological, political, economic, or cultural change—the potential for steady business declines, and the attractiveness of innovations increases. At times of great change, people become more willing to try extreme new ideas, so it becomes a great time to introduce extremely innovative ideas.

One unusual ability found in the entrepreneurs studied by Gaglio and Katz was that many of them can come up with new ideas given nearly any combination of resources. Sitting at an airport, entrepreneurs begin to look where lines are forming and wonder how to make money off that. Others can be given some everyday items and in a few minutes they are thinking up ways to combine them to make a profit. Their use of the opportunity identification process tells us that being creative can become a way of life.

FIGURE 4.3

Opportunity Identification Process

Source: Adapted from C. M. Gaglio and J. A. Katz, "The Psychological Basis of Opportunity Identification: Entrepreneurial Alertness," *Small Business Economics*, 16, no. 2, (March 2001), p. 99.

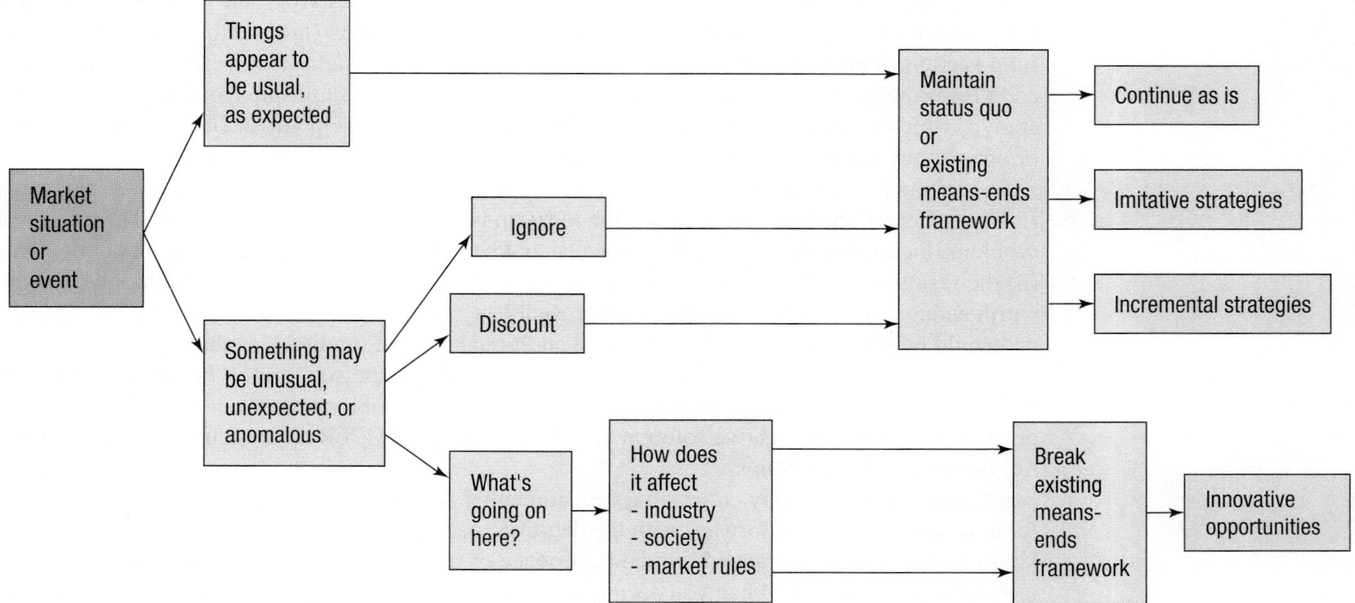

LO6 Describe how to conduct a comprehensive feasibility study for your business ideas.

Make Sure an Idea Is Feasible

Before you implement a business idea, you should test the idea for its **feasibility**, which means the extent to which the idea is viable and realistic and the extent to which you are aware of internal (to your business) and external (industry, market, and regulatory environment) forces that could affect your business. In this section, we examine the major criteria that will help you determine the feasibility of your business opportunity. Before we examine an outline for conducting a feasibility study, let's take a look in Table 4.2 at the results of a study in which entrepreneurs revealed what matters most to their business, with respect to the economic and community context in which their businesses are located.[22] The entrepreneurs were asked, on a scale of 1 (very confident) to 5 (very unconfident) how certain they were that the new business would be able to accomplish the following:

feasibility
The extent to which an idea is viable and realistic and the extent to which you are aware of internal (to your business) and external (industry, market, and regulatory environment) forces that could affect your business.

TABLE 4.2 What Start-Up Entrepreneurs Feel Confident About

Comply with local/state federal regulations	1.64
Keep up with technological advances	1.84
Attract customers	1.85
Obtain raw materials	1.95
Deal with distributors	1.95
Compete with other firms	2.10
Attract employees	2.29
Obtain working capital	2.70
Obtain start-up capital	2.84
Obtain a bank's help	3.15
Obtain venture capitalists' help	3.41

Source: Adapted from C. H. Matthews and S. E. Human, "The economic and community context for entrepreneurship." In *Handbook of Entrepreneurial Dynamics: the process of business creation*, ed. W. B. Gartner, K. G. Shaver, N. M. Carter, and P. D. Reynolds. Thousand Oaks, CA: Sage, 2004. Table 36.1, page 424.

Feasibility studies consist of careful investigation of five primary areas: the overall business idea, the product/service, the industry and market, financial projections (profitability), and the plan for future action. Within each of these areas you will examine the strengths and weaknesses (advantages and disadvantages) of your business opportunity. Exhibit 4.2 is a descriptive outline of a feasibility study,[23] which includes a brief explanation of the areas that will help you decide whether your idea or opportunity can be a feasible business or not.

In crafting a feasibility study, such as Pet Élan at the end of this chapter or the plans at the Online Learning Center, the goal is to assess if the idea can be profitably brought to market. The traditional problems facing new ideas are: (1) the idea cannot be economically made into a product or service, (2) the resulting product or service works, but does not appeal to a large enough market (or is not worth enough to them) to make the effort profitable, (3) the product or service works, has a market, and could be profitable, but you need to get additional people, funding, or other resources to make the idea into a business. Notice that each problem builds on the solution of the prior problem. As with idea screenings, having no solution for one of these problems may not spell the end of the process *if* you can use creative solution approaches like SCAMPER to come up with a new way to resolve or sidestep problems.

Often a feasibility study comes to a decision either to keep pursuing the opportunity, or to wait for a better time to move forward with the decision (perhaps in a better economy, or when the market matures, or after you get additional experience or training), or to stop working on the idea and look for something else. When you decide in a feasibility analysis to go with the idea, very often the

EXHIBIT 4.2

The Feasibility Study Outline

Guidelines for Completing Your Study

I. **The Business Idea**

- **Description of Your Business**

What business are you *really* in? Describe your product or service in the most concise way you can, and think beyond the characteristics of the product or service to the *experience* that you hope the customer receives from buying the product or service.

- **You, Your Firm, and Your Fit**

What do you bring to this idea or business? How well does this product or service fit with your knowledge, skills, abilities, networks and experience? How determined are you to bring this product or service to market? If you are already in business, how does this idea fit with the other products or services you sell?

II. **The Product/Service**

- **Unique Features: Benefits**

What are the unique features of the product or service? How do these features meet your customers' needs or preferences? What are the benefits of this product or service compared to the competition? Describe your product or service very simply, and use photos or drawings to illustrate how it works.

- **Unique Features: Limitations**

What are the specific shortcomings of the product or service? Can it become obsolete soon? Is it perishable, difficult to use or install, or are there legal restrictions? An honest assessment of your product or service is extremely important during this analysis. You do yourself no favor by being in denial, or failing to see the disadvantages *before* you go into business. Noting them now will help you prepare solutions or ways to minimize these issues.

- **Stage of Development**

Is the product still in the idea stage, or is there a model or working prototype available? Have any samples been manufactured? If it is still in the idea or prototype stage, what is the time frame for getting it ready for production?

- **Legal Restrictions and Rights**

List any patents, copyrights, trademarks, or licenses that apply to your product or service. If you are entering into a franchise agreement, partnerships, distributorships, etc., these should be discussed in this section. Seek the assistance of patent attorneys or intellectual copyright specialists for assistance. Also list the government regulations you must adhere to, such as FDA, EOA, OSHA, IRS, Secretary of State, etc., and research zoning restrictions carefully. If you will be home-based and your clients will be coming to your house, will this be impacted by your neighborhood's zoning restrictions?

- **Insurance Requirements**

Research the liability of your product or service and consult an insurance specialist to be sure you are protected adequately. This will depend on the nature of your business. A flower shop that sells floral arrangements is in a different liability situation than a pet grooming business, for example. If you have employees, you will need insurance to protect them from harm also, along with any insurance benefits you want to provide your staff.

- **Trends Related to the Product or Service**

How will you keep your finger on the pulse of change in your product or service area? What trends are likely to occur in the way the product is used, or what features it offers, for example?

- **Production or Service Delivery Costs**

Will you be producing or subcontracting out the manufacturing or delivery of your product or service? List all the costs, including labor, supplies, shipping, repairs, etc.

III. The Industry and Market

- **Current Industry**

Describe the industry as specifically as you can. There are some excellent sources in your college or public library that can help you determine the size of the industry, location of the industry (local, regional, national or global), and average sales and profitability for the industry. For example, the Risk Management Association provides industry-specific data based on the SIC (Standard Industry Classification Code) that can tell you what the average revenues are for a particular industry, and what profits you might expect to earn.

- **Market Potential for this Industry**

Is the industry in a period of decline, stability, or growth? What is the market demand likely to be for the next 1 to 3 years? Talk to people in the industry as well as potential customers for their ideas about where the industry might be headed. Consider how technology or the global economy might affect the market potential for the business. Research trends in the industry.

- **The Competition**

Who are your primary competitors, and what are their distinct advantages and disadvantages? Consider not only your direct competitors, but also your indirect ones who might be selling a substitute for your product or service or bundling your product with something else they provide. Check the Online Learning Center for help finding competitors.

- **Your Customers**

Who are your customers? Demographic information tells you all about your customers' personal characteristics, such as where they live, how much household income they have, and how many children they have. You can find very specific information in your library or on-line using zip codes for communities. What are your customers' preferences, values, attitudes that relate to your business? How will you find out what your customers think or intend to buy? How can you find out what problems they have, what they need, or what they want that they don't know yet! Use your creativity to learn as much as you can about your potential customers. If you have more than one target market, do this for each market segment. It's important to note the different benefits and limitations for each customer group.

- Market Penetration

How will you reach your target customers? What forms of distribution or selling will you use? How will your potential customers become aware of your business? How will you advertise?

IV. Financial Projections

- Pricing

How much will you charge for your product or service? Do a break-even analysis, and list all the assumptions behind your pricing.

- Sales Revenue Forecast

How much of your product or service will you expect to sell? What will your gross revenues be? What percentage of market share do you think you will reach in one year? Three years? Check the Online Learning Center for help making forecasts.

- **Cost Forecast**

What does it cost to produce, distribute, deliver, etc., your product or service? If you plan to manufacture goods, consider the cost of raw materials, labor, and delivery of goods. If you plan to retail or wholesale goods and services, consider mark-up, inventory costs, and freight. Refer to the RMA (Risk Management Association) studies for more information to help you compute these costs. See **www.rmahq.org**.

- **Gross Profit**

What are your sales minus cost of goods sold? Do this for each product or service and compare to industry averages.

- **Operating Expenses**

What marketing expenses (advertising, etc.), administrative (clerical and management), and general expenses do you expect to incur? Be sure to state your assumptions about these figures.

- **Profitability**

What is your expected net profit? After you have derived your gross profit above, subtract other expenses you expect to incur, such as rent, insurance, and salaries. This will help you determine your net profit.

V. Future Action Plan

- **Start-Up Capital**

How much money do you need to start the business? In addition to the cost of goods sold that you calculated and your marketing and administrative expenses, what additional costs do you have, such as renting space, utility expenses, and salaries?

- **Sources of Start-Up Capital**

Where can you obtain the money you need to start the business? Consider all the sources available to you, such as personal savings, family and friends, bank loans, investors, etc.

- **Further Information Needed**

What are you uncertain about? Whom could you ask? Where can you find this information? Your analysis is incomplete if you haven't considered what it is you don't yet know.

- **Writing a Business Plan**
  The feasibility analysis will help you get started writing your business plan. You will have the information you need to address the competitive advantages and disadvantages of your business and the strategies you will use to meet your goals.
- **Support Needed**
  List the individuals or groups you could consult for advice. Consider developing an advisory board consisting of people with experience in your industry and professionals from other industries who might be expert marketers, for example. Do you have an attorney, accountant, Web site designer, etc., who could help you when needed? Make a list of all the supporting actors your business may need in the future.

next step is to begin working on a full business plan, which capitalizes on many of the things you have written about in the feasibility study. Business plans are more involved than feasibility analyses, and in Chapter 8 you will not only see how to do a business plan, but also how business plans and feasibility studies relate to one another. On the Online Learning Center, we have a feasibility study for Serenity Spa. There is also a business plan for Serenity on the OLC, so you can begin to see how feasibility studies and business plans fit together.

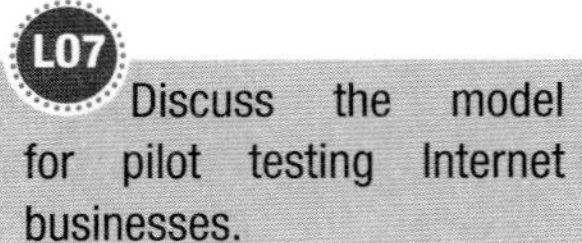

LO7
Discuss the model for pilot testing Internet businesses.

Assessing Feasibility by Pilot Testing

With so many sales and service businesses built using the Internet, a low-cost, low-risk approach for testing feasibility exists using the concept of a **pilot test**. Creating a basic e-commerce Web site can be done for $10 to $20 a month using e-commerce Web site software provided by major Internet Service Providers like 1&1.com or godaddy.com, with even lower costs for information-only Web sites (most often used for service providers). Check the Online Learning Center for help finding low-cost Web providers. Creating a sales operation on eBay (for products) or eLance (for services) are also low-cost ways to go operational (see Chapter 5 for details).

pilot test
A preliminary run of a business, sales effort, program, or Web site with the goal of assessing how well the overall approach works and what problems it might have.

conversion rate
The measure of how many visitors to your Web site (or people who click on your online advertisement) actually make a purchase from you.

Web companies like Google, Napster, Facebook, and others started with an approach built on four stages,[24] as seen in Figure 4.4.

In this approach, an entrepreneur like you or like Scott Wilson (see his Small Business Insight) create and bring online (deploy) a Web or crowdfunding site with the products or services you want to offer, and start advertising it. You then listen to customer feedback through tracking who comes to the site, from where, using what search terms and what referring sites, and most of all whether they buy or not (this is called the **conversion rate**). You can ask purchasers and nonpurchasers alike whether they liked the site or not via e-mail or quick Web surveys as they complete their purchase or leave the site, as well as giving visitors a discussion board or e-mail form to get feedback to you. This gives you active and passive ways to listen to your market.

FIGURE 4.4

Rapid Web site Prototyping Process

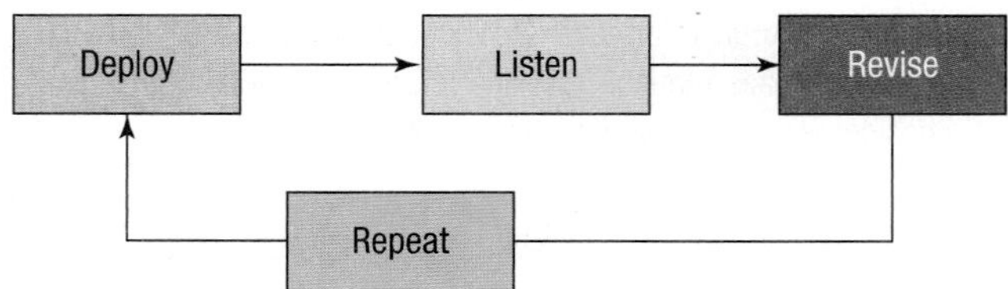

SMALL BUSINESS INSIGHT

TIKTOK+LUNATIK WATCHBANDS[25]

Scott Wilson was inspired when he saw the sixth-generation iPod Nano. When he saw it, he imagined it as a wristwatch. All it needed was a band—and maybe a market. While he was the head of a Chicago design firm called Minimal, he felt the idea needed some space of its own—and a pilot test. To pilot test his idea, he made a video pitch and posted it on crowdfunding Web site Kickstarter.com, hoping to raise $15,000 in a month to fund the development of the product. However, he hit the jackpot. At the end of the month he had raised $942,578 from 13,512 backers who contributed from $1 (for the good feeling that came from helping out) to 100 backers who gave $500 each (for a unique signed backers' LunaTik with five LunaTiks and five more TikToks to give friends). The customer reaction was so strong that the $500 backer level was sold out—Apple cofounder Steve Wozniak was $500 backer number 98—and the Apple Store approached Scott to get the product on store shelves. Even Kickstarter points up that results like Scott's are absolutely not typical, but Scott's story shows the power of design, crowdfunding, and pilot testing your ideas.

Based on the feedback from customers and visitors, you quickly fix (revise) what does not work and reinforce and promote those things which seem to work best. These changes are done quickly, usually over a few days, although if response is strong enough, over a few hours. And this process gets repeated continuously until it becomes clear that the idea is feasible or it becomes evident that the idea does not make a viable business regardless of the revisions tried. Generally you want the feedback on the Web site visitors and customers to move toward complaints or requests about minor issues to be able to be sure the Web approach is close to final form. The strategy for using the pilot test approach is to show potential partners, investors, or bankers that the idea can generate sales. In the spirit of "the proof is in the pudding" showing actual sales for a product or service, and being able to say how many visitors became customers—the conversion rate—is a powerful way to prove your idea is potentially feasible. For small-scale ideas or those which lend themselves to a Web-based approach, the Web pilot test model can give powerful results quickly and painlessly.

Ways to Keep On Being Creative

LO8 Recognize the value of building a creative culture in your business.

Once you have generated your business idea and evaluated it and determined whether or not it is feasible, you have completed the opportunity identification and evaluation process. But this process never really ends. Even after you are well on your way into business and even after your business is successful and you have met your initial goals, the nature of entrepreneurs and small business is that you will always be on the lookout for new opportunities. Successful business owners never rest on their laurels and assume that, since they have achieved success, it will always be there. One of the pitfalls small business owners can fall into is to fail to build a company culture—a way of thinking and behaving—that encourages new ideas and embraces change. This is especially important if you employ or plan to employ other people. There is nothing as discouraging as working for someone who feels there is nothing new you can possibly contribute to the business. And you would be surprised to learn how many business owners have this mentality. Here are some ways you can avoid this and build a company that is "idea prone." You will find that you can attract more creative employees and get more useful ideas out of them that affect your business's bottom line by following the recommendations given in Skill Module 4.2.

SKILL MODULE 4.2

Great Ideas for Making Idea-Prone Companies

1. Give yourself and your employees time to think of ideas. While it can seem that there is never enough time to get everything done and deadlines are always looming, you can't afford not to take the time to come up with new ideas. Allow even just a few minutes every day to discover what your customers or employees are thinking and what problems or frustrations they may be experiencing. Ask your employees what they are working on, where there may be problems, and what ideas they have for solving them.
2. Positively reinforce ideas[26]—avoid the automatic no. As discussed earlier, don't rush to judge ideas. It's the process of coming up with ideas that needs to be reinforced, not whether the idea is good or not. Evaluation can come later.
3. Look to unlikely sources of opportunities. You never know where creativity and innovation will emerge. Think beyond your age group, socioeconomic status, and education.
4. Get a room with a view. Give your employees—and yourself—varied experiences. Get away from the office, go visit customers, allow employees to learn one another's jobs, and so on. It enables people to get a different perspective, and it is when we can change our routine that breakthrough ideas often can be discovered.

An innovative company does not automatically develop out of an innovative business idea. You have to deliberately set your expectations and communicate them to your employees. Remember that recognition is fuel—it fans the fires of creativity and helps your business reach potentials that you may never have anticipated. Einstein said, "Creativity is contagious . . . pass it on." As the business owner, you are in a unique position to make sure that people's brains don't stop at your company's door.

Innovation is at the heart of entrepreneurship, because every time people start a business or become the owner of one, it is a new start and often a new experience for them. Some businesses are themselves built on new ideas or new twists on existing ideas. For these kinds of situations, taking some time before committing your money to think about which ideas make the most sense as a profit-maker can save a lot of grief later on. That is where the opportunity identification process, the idea screening process, and feasibility analysis come in to play. It is also true that one of the greatest challenges facing a business is getting control over the process of change—knowing when and how to change and try something new. Sometimes even thinking in new ways can be difficult, and that is when techniques like SCAMPER can make all the difference. The point is that while many people think innovation is a bolt from the blue, unpredictable and uncontrollable, in reality it is anything but that. That is good news, because it means that one of the most powerful techniques for building your business is under your control.

CHAPTER SUMMARY

LO1 Recognize the sources of opportunity entrepreneurs draw on to get business ideas.

- Opportunity recognition is one of the most basic entrepreneurial behaviors.
- Entrepreneurial alertness means that entrepreneurs have a special set of observational and thinking skills that help them identify good opportunities.
- A plurality of entrepreneurs studied knew they wanted to start a business and were very motivated to find business ideas.
- Ideas for new businesses come from a great variety of sources. These include work experience, seeing a similar business, hobbies or personal interests, a chance happening, discussions with family and friends, education and experience, and technology transfer and licensing.

LO2 Identify the ways ideas are screened for business potential.

- In assessing the potential value of your business idea, there are six major areas to consider:

- The product or service: Its description, underlying technology innovativeness, and uniqueness.
- The market: Target groups, their needs, and market size.
- The protection of intellectual property.
- The people behind the idea.
- The other resources needed.
- The profits likely to be generated.

LO3 Understand how creativity methods can help business owners recognize new opportunities.

- Creative methods help you identify opportunities beyond what everybody else already knows.
- SCAMPER is a tool you can use to trigger new opportunities for your business.
- Use techniques to help you get into an innovative frame of mind. Read outside your area, invite a "wild card" to a business meeting, have a "scan the environment" day, arrange a mini-internship, solve your customer's problem rather than selling a product, redesign your work environment to stimulate your innovative skills.
- The creative process has four stages: preparation, incubation, illumination, and verification.

LO4 Understand the five pitfalls that hinder innovation.

- Identifying the wrong problem.
- Judging ideas and opportunities too quickly.
- Stopping with the first good idea.
- Failing to get support.
- Obeying rules that don't exist.

LO5 Identify strategies for innovation in your business.

- There are three innovative strategies small business owners can select:
  - Imitative strategies take an idea that somebody else has already discovered and build a business around that idea.
  - Incremental strategies take an idea and offer a way to do something better than it is done now.
  - Radical innovation strategies reject existing ideas and present a way to do things differently.

LO6 Describe how to conduct a comprehensive feasibility study for your business ideas.

- Conduct an analysis to determine whether or not your business idea is feasible.
- Describe your business idea concisely, including the experience you wish to sell to potential customers, as well as details about your product or service.
- List the unique benefits and limitations of your product or service, at what stage of development it is now (idea or prototype), any proprietary restrictions and obligations, insurance needs, product or service trends, and any production costs.
- Describe your industry, including its size and trends. Provide the market potential for your product or service, the strengths and weaknesses of your competition, who your customers are, what their needs and preferences are, and how they will find you.
- Compute financial projections. Provide sales revenues, cost forecasts, gross profits, operating expenses, and net profit.
- Write a future action plan. Determine the start-up capital you need and where you can raise it. Consider any further information you need, and begin writing a business plan. Decide where you can find additional support, such as from attorneys, accountants, and other business advisers.

LO7 Discuss the model for pilot testing Internet businesses.

- For Internet-based sales and service businesses, it is possible to pilot test the idea online.
- In setting up a pilot test, use free open-source software or low-cost Web hosting services.
- Use a rapid revision process consisting of:
  - Deploy the Web site.
  - Listen to feedback from sales, customers, visitors, and the Web site's statistics.
  - Revise the Web site based on the feedback.
  - Keep repeating this process.
  - Evaluate the business after getting the Web site closer to its final form.

LO8 Recognize the value of building a creative culture in your business.

- Build a company culture that values new ideas and embraces change.

- Create slack time to enable employees to think of new ideas.
- Positively reinforce ideas others bring to you.
- Look to unlikely sources of opportunities.
- Get a room with a view and establish an environment that stimulates innovation.

KEY TERMS

opportunity recognition, 82
entrepreneurial alertness, 82
license, 85
licensee, 85
licensor, 85
royalty, 85
creativity, 89
radical innovation strategy, 90
imitative strategy, 93
incremental strategy, 93
feasibility, 94
pilot test, 98
conversion rate, 98

DISCUSSION QUESTIONS

1. How do entrepreneurs recognize new ideas for their business?
2. What are some common ways you can search for new business opportunities?
3. How can entrepreneurs evaluate the merit of a new idea?
4. How are creative methods for opportunity recognition different from traditional ways of searching for ideas?
5. What should you watch out for as you are searching for new opportunities?
6. What are the differences between imitation, incremental, and radical innovation strategies? How can you assess which one is right for your business?
7. What should a good feasibility study contain? What questions can it help you answer to determine if your business idea is a sound one?
8. How can entrepreneurs ensure that their business stays innovative and fresh? Why do you think some small businesses lose their creative edge as the business grows?

EXPERIENTIAL EXERCISES

1. As you go on errands or walk around your campus, notice all the things that you could improve. Make a list of things that frustrate you or things that could be made even better. Does your list surprise you in terms of how much you noticed?
2. List 15 new uses for a popular product or service. Try paper clips, or coffee mugs, or home delivery. Use SCAMPER to generate new uses and make connections to other uses.
3. Interview a local business owner and ask how he or she thought of the idea behind the business. How does the business develop new ideas now?
4. Do some research on innovative companies in your area. What sets them apart? How are they designed to take advantage of the innovativeness of their staffs?
5. Next time you are working on a problem or looking for new ideas (your major in college? Where to move on campus? What do to this weekend?), go to a museum, a park, or anywhere outside the ordinary places you frequent. Were any new ideas suggested to you?

6. Keep a journal in which you can record your ideas as they come. Sometimes we get breakthrough ideas while our brain is incubating as we sleep. By the time we wake up in the morning we have lost them, so keep your journal near your bed.
7. Pick a business idea and research its industry and market. What did you learn? What are some creative questions you might ask about contemporary trends in this business? How could you find out the answers?

MINI-CASE

AltiTUNES: FROM IMITATION TO CONTINUOUS INNOVATION[27]

Amy Nye Wolf had completed a backpacking tour across Europe in the mid-1980s when she saw a store selling music at London's Heathrow Airport. Wolf recalled that she was tired of the music she had and was very happy to see it. She purchased some music, and returned to the States excited to have found the store. At that time retail outlets in American airports consisted of food service restaurants and newsstands.

It wasn't until 1994, after Wolf had completed college and worked as an investment banker for Merrill Lynch, that she decided to go into business for herself. She never forgot the music store at Heathrow, and Wolf founded AltiTunes Partners LP, a chain of music stores that eventually grew to over 20 locations, mostly in airports. AltiTUNES' five year mission was to become the leading brand for small format, extraordinary location, music and electronics retailing with an expanding network of domestic and international locations.

Innovative plans included expansions to locations such as hospitals, hotels, and travel plazas and the EARport™ that features a series of interactive listening stations programmed to preview music and help customers decide on their music selections without disturbing other customers. With innovations like these coming and the number of sites growing, AltiTUNES grabbed the interest of one of their bigger competitors, Inmotion Entertainment, who bought the firm and the innovations it developed from Amy. Today Amy is on the lookout for other innovative firms in which she can invest and mentor.

CASE DISCUSSION QUESTIONS

1. How did Amy Nye Wolf discover her business opportunity?
2. How did she evaluate whether it was a good opportunity or not?
3. What did she copy from the store in Heathrow?
4. What innovations did Wolf add to AltiTUNES to make her idea unique?
5. How would you continue to identify new opportunities for AltiTUNES successor, Inmotion Entertainment?

SUGGESTED CASES AND ARTICLES

- Big Business in a Small Rural City, C-4

Available on McGraw-Hill Create™:

- *The Franchising Entrepreneur*
- *Creative Care*

SUGGESTED VIDEOS

www.mhhe.com/katz4e

Video Case:

- For a written video case and corresponding clip, visit the OLC at www.mhhe.com/katz4e and select "Chapter 4".
- From Granny's Kitchen to Tesco

SBTV.com Video:

- Fostering Innovation—John Winsor

STVP Videos:

- When Do You Know If You Have a Good Idea?
- When Not to Listen to Your Customer
- Using Your Whole Brain

APPENDIX

A Sample Feasibility Study[1]

Pet Élan

I. THE BUSINESS IDEA

Description of Your Business

In recent years, there has been an increase in the number of households that have pets, especially dogs and cats. Further, there is emerging a steadily growing group of pet owners that is willing to purchase upscale, unique products for these important members of their family. Pet Élan is an upscale boutique for these discriminating pet owners. Pet Élan will offer high-quality pet products to discerning individuals who wish their pets to enjoy a healthy, fun, and elegant lifestyle while being pampered. By carefully selecting luxurious accessories made with superior materials, Pet Élan will provide an elite product line that celebrates the uniqueness of each animal's personality.

Description of the Entrepreneur (or Team)

Randy Miller will be the owner of Pet Élan. Randy has been interested in pets since childhood, and has worked for vet clinics, the Humane Society, and a local zoo in pet care. Randy is currently employed full time at a local discount retailer. Randy's other retail experience includes work in local pet stores in animal care and sales, as well as retail experience at PetSmart. Randy's self-employment experience started as a teen, with child care and yard care businesses. Randy's education includes a BA in Entrepreneurship from DePaul University. Although employed full time, Randy will leave to give 100 percent effort to the start-up of Pet Élan.

II. THE PRODUCT/SERVICE

Unique Features: Benefits

Pet Élan will offer products that promote a healthy, fun, and elegant lifestyle for dogs and cats. Our products are grouped into three primary categories: dietary products, playtime products, and accessories.

Dietary Products

Pet Élan will offer all-natural pet food and treats, full of essential vitamins and nutrients to promote a healthy diet. We will carry two to three top-selling brands of organic pet food from the industry leaders such as Newman's Own Organics,[2] Natura Pet Products,[3] and Organix.[4] We will also feature snacks and treats from Old Mother Hubbard,[5] Three Dog Bakery,[6] Flint River Ranch,[7] and Howling Hound Bakery.[8]

Playtime Products

Playing with one's pet is also a key ingredient for a pet's healthy lifestyle. Pet Élan will offer products that enable owners and their pets to play in style. For dogs, we will offer toys for chewing, retrieving, tugging, and chasing. For cats, we will offer toys stuffed with premium grade catnip and other toys to chase and fetch. We will offer exclusive toy brands such as Happy Dog Toys,[9] KONG Toys,[10] and Fat Cat, Inc.[11]

Accessories

Pet Élan will make walking or traveling with a dog or cat an extension of the owner's unique style with leashes, collars, and travel bags that make a statement. We will also offer pet home accessories including food and water bowls, pet furniture and pillows, and pet clothing made from fine fabrics such as silk, suede, and faux fur.

Unlike other pet stores, Pet Élan will target clientele who demand top quality in pet couture. To fulfill this demand, Pet Élan will order pet clothing and accessories from the trendiest brands such as Woof: The Small Dog Company,[12] Dogz Togz,[13] and Ruff Ruff and Meow.[14]

Unique Features: Limitations

One of the largest threats to the luxury pet accessory industry is the presence of online stores. Pet Élan will compete with these online retailers, as well as other local pet stores. Consumers have the opportunity to comparison shop on the Internet, so Pet Élan will need to carefully determine the pricing strategy for each line of accessories to remain competitive. However, it is likely that pet owners will want to sample and view unique products we carry and will be willing to come to our store for its one-of-a-kind shopping experience—and bring their pets with them.

The rise of larger chain pet stores, like PETCO and PETsMart, has made it much easier for pet owners to satisfy all their pet needs in one place. These stores are now offering pet apparel, pet furniture, and natural pet food. Pet Élan will offer a higher quality, but more expensive, product mix that may overlap with these stores in some areas. To counter this, Pet Élan will showcase the products we carry that cannot be obtained at the larger retailers.

Competitive Advantage

Pet Élan's competitive advantage is quality and the ability to provide customers with the feeling that pampering their pets is an integral part of a healthy, fun, and contemporary lifestyle. Pet Élan must establish this reputation through *high quality products* and *selective advertising* and through *exceptional customer service*.

Stage of Development

Pet Élan is currently in the idea stage. This feasibility study is the first step in exploring the market potential for a luxury pet store. The current time frame for introducing Pet Élan is one year. Pet Élan has set the following milestones to accomplish prior to launch:

- Complete feasibility study: month 1.
- Begin and complete business plan and identify location: months 2–4.
- Pursue start-up capital: months 5–6.
- Receive start-up capital: month 7.
- Secure store location and secure appropriate permits: months 7–8.
- Plan and order inventory: month 9.
- Receive inventory and set up store: months 10–11.
- Store launch: month 12.

Legal Restrictions and Rights

Pet Élan will operate as a Sub-Chapter S Corporation to ensure limited personal liability and for tax advantages. Pet Élan will have one owner, who will have day-to-day responsibility for running the business. The corporation will receive all income generated by the business and pay the owner a salary and/or reinvest in the store. A board of directors will be appointed by the owner.

Insurance Requirements

Although business insurance may not be *required,* Pet Élan will purchase insurance to protect the corporation's assets and to benefit employees:

- Property insurance will cover the business in the event of damage or loss to the business property. The insurance will need to cover the store location's fixtures, cash registers/computers and any other equipment, any store furniture such as display tables and shelving, as well as inventory and supplies.
- Liability insurance will protect the business against the unfortunate situation of a customer or employee being injured on the property and suing.[15]

As an employer, Pet Élan will also need to secure additional insurance for:

- **Workers' compensation insurance:** The Workers' Compensation and Workers' Occupational Diseases Acts require employers to provide insurance for accidental deaths, injuries, and occupational diseases of employees arising in the course of employment. Temporary workers who normally do not receive company benefits are still provided workers' compensation. The Illinois Workers' Compensation Act requires all employers to post a notice in the workplace that explains workers' rights and lists the name and address of the workers' compensation carrier.
- **Unemployment insurance:** Since Pet Élan will most likely employ one or more workers in each of 20 or more calendar weeks, the business will be required to make unemployment insurance contributions to the Illinois Department of Employment Security.[16]

Trends Related to the Product or Service

Several studies show that pet ownership is at an all-time high and that people are taking better care of their pets and spending more money on them than previously. Surveys conducted every two years by the American Pet Products Manufacturers Association, Inc. (APPMA) show that 63.4 million households have a pet, compared to 52.6 million households a decade ago.[17] Pet Élan will cater to the increasing number of customers that consider their pets a full-fledged member of the family.

Trends in Customer Demographics

The demographics of the typical customers of the pet industry have been shifting over recent years from married with children, to younger, cohabitating couples who are waiting longer for marriage, as well as married baby boomers looking to fill their empty nests, and single households composed of divorcees and seniors looking for companionship. In fact, only one-third of all pet owners today are married with children.[18]

Trends in Pet Products

The pet products industry is booming. The upscale pet services industry was named as a hot market by *Entrepreneur* magazine in its annual prediction of the hottest business ideas for both 2004 and 2005.[19] The APPMA also cites luxury, natural, and hygiene products as the top three among its top ten trends in pet gifts.[20] In fact, the APPMA further notes that high-tech and high-end products such as luxury doghouses are showing the most growth.[21]

Similar to the human food industry, pet food trends are moving toward more organic and natural products. The Organic Trade Association reported that organic pet food sales are up by 63 percent from last year and are growing at almost three times the rate of human organic food sales.[22]

III. THE INDUSTRY AND MARKET

Current Industry

Americans spent a total of $34.4 billion on pet food, care, and supplies in 2004, and the industry is estimated to increase to $35.9 billion in 2005. Sixty-five percent of this estimated total was spent on food and supplies alone (*supplies also included medicine*).[23]

This growing industry is made up of a diverse customer base. Although families have been the traditional focal point of pet-related businesses, only one-third of all pet owners today are married with children.[24] Pet Élan plans to not only target this traditional market, but also to reach out to newer niche markets such as seniors, young unmarried, and middle-aged couples who are married but have no children.

Thirty-nine percent of Americans between the ages of 55 and 64 own a pet.[25] One of the largest percentages of pet owners is 18- to 34-year-old married Americans without children (52 percent). Of this group, 36 percent own a dog and 26 percent own a cat. In addition, this group is 33 percent more likely than the average American to own more than one pet.[26] Finally, 52 percent of married 35- to 54-year-olds without children have a pet and 31 percent have two or more.

Market Potential for This Industry

One out of three U.S. households owns a dog or cat,[27] and over 80 percent of pet owners purchased at least one accessory for their pet during the past year.[28] In 2003, MarketResearch.com predicted that the pet supplies industry would be an $8 billion market by 2007.[29] Business Communications Co. projects that the pet services industry as a whole (including pet food, pet services, and pet supplies) will grow to $36.3 billion by 2008.[30]

Despite this promising growth and if the economy continues to contract, customers may have less disposable income. The percentage they intended to spend on their cat or dog may be diverted for necessity purchases. However, according to pet industry analyst Julia Dvorko, "Owners tend to pamper their pets even when they have to cut back on [household] spending. After all, even during economic downturns, people give gifts to family members and buy special treats for their children."[31]

The Competition

Pet Élan plans to open in the 60657 zip code area of Chicago, Illinois, locally known as Lakeview. There are 23 pet-related businesses in this zip code: nine are veterinarians, three are pet sitting/walking services, three are pet grooming services, three large chain pet stores (one PetSmart, two PETCO), two combination pet grooming/accessories stores, a combination boarding/training store, a pet adoption/accessories store, and one boutique called "Sam & Willy's: A Bow Meow Boutique."

While not competing directly in the 60657 area code market, national companies including Paul Mitchell, Omaha Steaks, Origins, Harley Davidson, and Old Navy are now offering lines of pet products ranging from dog shampoo, pet attire, and name-brand toys to gourmet treats and food.[32] Although these companies have recognizable brand identities, they do not specialize in the pet retail market. They do not carry a full line of pet products as Pet Élan will, and they cater more to impulse buyers rather than discerning pet owners.

The table on page 108 compares the strengths and weaknesses of a subset of the competitor pet stores in the 60657 area code, as well as online retailers, and highlights the differentiating features of Pet Élan.

Customers

According to the APPMA, 62 percent of households in the United States own a pet, and 46 percent of households own more than one pet. Also, as mentioned earlier, dogs or cats are found in at least one out of three households (in the United States).[33] Data collected on dog owners show that they are likely to be married high school graduates who own their homes. As income increases, the percentage of households with a dog increases as well.[34] In fact, 75 percent of the households with dogs have a combined income of greater than $35,000. This is consistent with the specific market profile of the clientele Pet Élan plans to target in the 60657 zip code. Seventy-six percent of Lakeview households have a combined income of $35,000 or more (see chart on page 109).[35]

Additionally, 30 percent of Lakeview residents own their homes, and 94 percent of residents over age 25 are high school graduates. The average family size is 2.56 with 7,523 residents below the age of 16 and 7,706 senior residents (65+). The median household

Competitive Analysis of Pet Stores

Competitor Pet Stores in Zip Code	Strengths	Weaknesses	Differentiating Features of Pet Élan
Area pet grooming/ accessories stores	• Customers whose pets are being groomed can browse while they wait for their pets	• Limited selection • Pet grooming is core competency, not selling accessories	• Core competency and primary focus of store are on selecting and selling luxury pet products and accessories
PETCO[36]	• Well-established brand identity • All-in-one brick-and-mortar stores • Wide selection of basic pet necessities • Online shopping	• Does not sell pet food because of high shipping costs • Limited number of brands in pet clothing and accessories • Inexperienced sales associates	• Caters to discerning pet and owner tastes by providing high-end pet products and accessories • Store owner builds personal relationships with customers based on knowledgeable service that focuses on their individual preferences and pet's personality
PetSmart[37]	• Well-established brand identity • All-in-one brick-and-mortar stores • Wide selection of basic pet necessities • Online shopping	• Sells pet food online, but consumer faces high shipping costs • More pet clothing and accessories brands than PETCO, but not high-end brands • Inexperienced sales associates	• Caters to discerning pet and owner tastes by providing high-end pet products and accessories • Store owner builds personal relationships with customers based on knowledgeable service that focuses on their individual preferences and pet's personality
Omaha Steaks[38]	• Customers may add on pet treats as an impulse when shopping for themselves or for gifts	• Limited selection—only offers one variety of pet treats	• Pet Élan will offer a wider variety of pet treats (all organic)
Old Navy/Harley Davidson[39]	• Recognizable brand • Can target impulse buyers who are making other purchases	• Products are not currently available on Web site • Very specific target audiences	• Pet Élan will target customers that look for the latest pet couture by focusing on brands made exclusively for pets
Sam & Willy's: A Bow Meow Boutique[40]	• Provides accessories and gifts to pets and their owners in a boutique setting • Provides variety of organic pet food brands	• Static Web site • Sponsor local animal shelters but doesn't have social entrepreneurial mission	• Web site will provide tips and trends for hip pet owners • Five percent of pretax profits will go to a local no-kill animal shelter

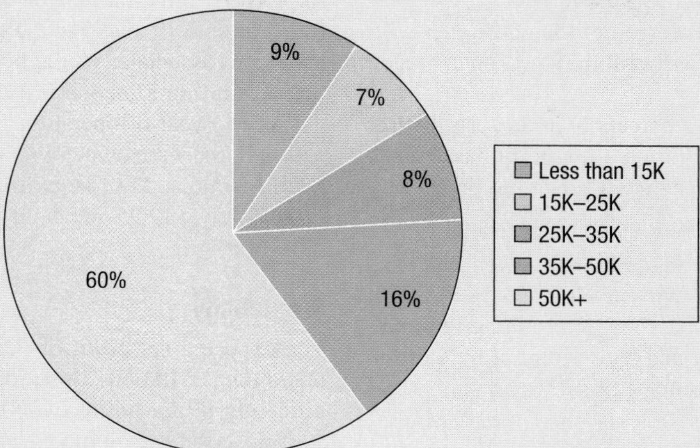

income is $63,695.[41] Of the approximately 49,534 employed residents 16 years and older in the 60657 zip code area (as of the 2000 census), 64 percent are in "management, professional, and related occupations."[42]

Market Penetration

Pet Élan will serve customers in a boutique setting where pets are welcome to browse along with their owners. The store will operate with a social entrepreneurial mission and will donate 5 percent of pretax profits to a local no-kill animal shelter. Consistent with this socially responsible mission, Pet Élan will work with other area pet-related businesses to form a network of highly qualified veterinarians, as well as well-established boarding, grooming, in-home sitting, and training service providers. By connecting Pet Élan customers with reliable service providers, Pet Élan will also benefit from the reciprocal referrals from these service providers.

Pet Élan will also maintain a Web site, but initially only to provide the location and hours of operation. As the business grows, the Web site could include tips and trends information for current and future consumers to keep up with the latest in pet fashion accessories. Pet Élan will seek assistance from a local college or Small Business Development Center for the Web site and market research assistance.

When the Pet Élan storefront opens, we plan to advertise by hosting a series of pet fashion shows, combined with an adoption event with local pet shelters. The events will raise awareness among clientele and would help a good cause. Until Pet Élan breaks even, the store will rely on the advertising and public relations from partnering with other service providers to draw customers into the store.

IV. FINANCIAL PROJECTIONS

Pricing

Pet Élan will price the merchandise it intends to sell using cost-plus pricing. The base cost will be the wholesale cost of the pet product, and the markup component will be the profit Pet Élan will make on each product. For purposes of this feasibility study, Pet Élan will assume a 54 percent margin on goods sold. Because Pet Élan will be selling luxury products and because the target clientele is customers with a large percentage of disposable income, we will work to maximize the profit from each item sold.

The store will also follow a price skimming strategy, meaning it will set relatively high prices on the newest luxury products when they are first released, and then lower the price over time. By maintaining a wide selection of the newest fashions and accessories for cats and dogs, Pet Élan will be able to charge a higher price for newly released items, reducing prices as the trend becomes more mainstream.

The social entrepreneurial mission is to donate 5 percent of pretax profits to a local no-kill animal shelter, and this amount will be donated quarterly based on pretax profits from that quarter. Pet Élan made the following assumptions in putting together the sales revenue forecast for the first three years of operations:

- Pet Élan will sign a three-year rental agreement for a 2,000 square-foot storefront location. The rental property will be priced at $35 per square foot, with an additional real estate tax of $9.50 per square foot per annum.
- Pet Élan will be open for business six days a week (Monday through Saturday) from ten o'clock in the

morning until seven o'clock in the evening. The store will be closed on Sunday.

- It is estimated that the average Pet Élan customer will spend $18 per visit and will visit the store, on average, two times per month.
- Pet Élan will contribute 5 percent of pretax profits to a local no-kill animal shelter on a quarterly basis. This contribution has been accounted for in the pretax net profit (loss) forecast.

Based on these assumptions and a break-even analysis, Pet Élan's break-even sales will be $263,699, or $21,975 per month. This was calculated by determining the total fixed costs in the first year and by dividing it by a gross margin expressed as a percentage of sales.

Sales Revenue Forecast

Pet Élan forecasts gross revenues during year one of operations to be $296,740. The gross revenues for year two and year three are predicted to increase to $404,448 and $458,304, respectively.

Cost Forecast

Pet Élan will maintain an inventory of products in each of the three primary areas of focus mentioned earlier: dietary products, playtime products, and accessories. As products are purchased, Pet Élan will reorder monthly to maintain a sufficient inventory to serve its customers' needs. Pet Élan has estimated that initial inventory will cost $20,000. The wholesale cost of inventory for the first year is estimated to be $147,000. As the customer base grows, Pet Élan will need to have a significantly higher amount of inventory on hand to support increased demand. The future cost of inventory is forecast to be $186,880 for year two and $211,730 for year three.

Gross Margin

The gross margin (sales minus cost of goods sold) for Pet Élan during the first three years of operation is estimated to be $159,620, $217,568, and $246,574 respectively.

Operating Expenses

There are several operational costs associated with running a pet store like Pet Élan, and these are also accounted for in the budget forecast for the first three years of operation. These operational expenses include items such as rent, utilities, advertising costs, and professional services assistance. These operational costs are summarized in total operating expenses and are forecast to be $147,907 for year one, $190,881 for year two, and $201,744 for year three.

The owner will be the primary employee of Pet Élan for the first three months of operation. Beginning in the fourth month of operation, Pet Élan will hire one full-time sales associate. As the business grows, Pet Élan anticipates hiring a second full-time sales associate during the second year of operation. The full-time sales associates will assist the owner with customer service and other retail functions. Pet Élan will pay the sales associate approximately $12.25 per hour (or $25,500 per year) for the work.[43]

Profitability

The expected net profit of Pet Élan for the first year of operation is $10,660. This profit is expected to grow significantly in the future two years as some of the initial start-up costs are defrayed and the customer base becomes larger. In year two the net profit is forecast to be $25,345, and in year three it is estimated to be $42,589.

V. FUTURE ACTION PLAN

Start-Up Capital

To start the business, Pet Élan will need to have enough start-up capital to cover leasing costs to secure the storefront location. The start-up capital will also need to cover insurance and operating expenses including appropriate licensing, store utilities, and professional services such as legal and accounting assistance. Initial inventory, as well as retail equipment needs (such as a cash register) will require a large initial investment. These needs will be funded through the start-up capital that Pet Élan secures prior to opening. The amount needed is estimated to be $70,000.

Sources of Start-Up Capital

The start-up capital of $70,000 is composed of 45 percent (or $31,500) of the owner's personal savings, 25 percent (or $17,500) of a bank loan, in addition to two equity investors (one family member of the owner and one local veterinarian), each with a 15 percent stake (or $10,500) in the company.

Further Information Needed

To ensure the successful opening of Pet Élan, we must have a deeper understanding of the customer needs in the area. Conducting market research in the 60657 zip code area, using techniques such as surveys and/or focus groups of customers in Pet Élan's target market, could assess these needs. Pet Élan should also begin to approach other pet service providers in the area to explore potential partnership opportunities that could help raise awareness about both Pet Élan and the partnering business. This would also allow the owner of Pet Élan to form a network within the local pet products and services industry.

Writing a Business Plan

Pet Élan's next step is to create a business plan to further explore the business model of Pet Élan from an objective point of view. By identifying strengths and weaknesses, opportunities and threats for Pet Élan as compared to other market competitors, the company will have a much better chance of reaching the business and financial objectives outlined in this feasibility study. The business plan will also provide vital information about the business to potential investors and allow them to evaluate the viability of Pet Élan's business model.

Support Needed

Pet Élan will seek guidance from a local Small Business Development Center. Pet Élan will review the initial draft of the business plan with a volunteer from the Service Corps of Retired Executives (SCORE), which is associated with the Small Business Association, to learn from his or her experience. Pet Élan will also form an advisory board made up of small business owners and members of the pet retail industry.

Financials-Summary

	Year 1	Year 2	Year 3
Revenue	$296,740	$404,448	$458,304
Cost of Goods Sold	137,120	186,880	211,730
Gross margin	159,620	217,568	246,574
Operating expenses	$147,907	$190,881	$201,744
Net profit (loss) pretax	$ 11,713	$ 26,687	$ 44,830
Net profit (loss) pretax and post contribution (5%)	$ 10,660	$ 25,345	$ 42,589

Financials—Year 1

	Month 1 September	Month 2 October	Month 3 November	Month 4 December	Month 5 January	Month 6 February
Sales	**$11,620**	**$16,900**	**$20,060**	**$27,460**	**$20,060**	**$21,120**
Less Cost of Goods Sold	$ 5,370	$ 7,810	$ 9,270	$12,690	$ 9,270	$ 9,760
Gross Margin	**$ 6,250**	**$ 9,090**	**$10,790**	**$14,770**	**$10,790**	**$11,360**
Operating Expenses						
Utilities	185	160	165	180	200	200
Salaries	2,500	2,500	2,500	2,500	2,500	2,500
Labor	—	—	—	2,125	2,125	2,125
Payroll Taxes and Benefits	313	313	313	578	578	578
Advertising	300	300	300	300	300	300
Web site	20	20	20	20	20	20
Office Supplies	150	75	50	50	50	50
Insurance	250	250	250	400	400	400
Maintenance and Cleaning	50	50	50	50	50	50
Legal and Accounting	350	350	350	350	350	350
Licenses	300	—	—	—	—	—
Bags, Paper, etc.	150	150	200	250	250	250
Telephone	85	85	85	85	85	85
Miscellaneous	200	200	200	200	200	200
Rent	5,833	5,833	5,833	5,833	5,833	5,833
Total Operating Expenses (Fixed Costs):	**10,686**	**10,286**	**10,316**	**12,921**	**12,941**	**12,941**
Gross Profit (Loss)	**(4,436)**	**(1,196)**	**475**	**1,849**	**(2,151)**	**(1,581)**
Contribution to Charity (5% of net):	—	—	***24***	***92***	—	—
Net Profit (Loss) Pre-Tax:	***(4,436)***	***(1,196)***	***451***	***1,756***	***(2,151)***	***(1,581)***

First year fixed costs (FC)	**$ 147,910**
Contribution Margin Ratio (CMR) ((sales – cogs)/sales)	**53.8%**
Annual breakeven sales (FC / CMR)	**$ 274,970**
Average monthly breakeven sales	**$ 22,910**

Month 7 March	Month 8 April	Month 9 May	Month 10 June	Month 11 July	Month 12 August	Total
$24,290	**$26,400**	**$28,510**	**$31,680**	**$35,900**	**$32,740**	**$296,740**
$11,220	$12,200	$13,170	$14,640	$16,590	$15,130	$137,120
$13,070	**$14,200**	**$15,340**	**$17,040**	**$19,310**	**$17,610**	**$159,620**
180	170	165	185	185	185	2,160
2,500	2,500	2,500	2,500	2,500	2,500	30,000
2,125	2,125	2,125	2,125	2,125	2,125	19,125
578	578	578	578	578	578	6,141
300	300	300	300	300	300	3,600
20	20	20	20	20	20	240
50	50	50	50	50	50	725
400	400	400	400	400	400	4,350
50	50	50	50	50	50	600
350	350	350	350	350	350	4,200
—	—	—	—	—	—	300
300	300	300	300	300	300	3,050
85	85	85	85	85	85	1,020
200	200	200	200	200	200	2,400
5,833	5,833	5,833	5,833	5,833	5,833	69,996
12,971	**12,961**	**12,956**	**12,976**	**12,976**	**12,976**	**147,907**
99	**1,239**	**2,384**	**4,064**	**6,334**	**4,634**	**11,713**
5	***62***	***119***	***203***	***317***	***232***	***1,054***
94	***1,177***	***2,265***	***3,861***	***6,017***	***4,402***	***$ 10,660***

Financials—Year 2

	September	October	November	December	January	February
Sales:	**$31,680**	**$33,790**	**$35,900**	**$35,900**	**$29,570**	**$32,740**
Less Cost of Goods Sold	$14,640	$15,610	$16,590	$16,590	$13,660	$15,130
Gross Margin	**$17,040**	**$18,180**	**$19,310**	**$19,310**	**$15,910**	**$17,610**
Operating Expenses						
Utilities	195	170	175	190	210	210
Salaries	2,500	2,500	2,500	2,500	2,500	2,500
Labor	4,250	4,250	4,250	4,250	4,250	4,250
Payroll Taxes and Benefits	844	844	844	844	844	844
Advertising	400	400	400	400	400	400
Web site	30	30	30	30	30	30
Office Supplies	100	100	100	100	100	100
Insurance	550	550	550	550	550	550
Maintenance and Cleaning	60	60	60	60	60	60
Legal and Accounting	400	400	400	400	400	400
Licenses	300	—	—	—	—	—
Bags, Paper, etc.	400	400	400	400	400	400
Telephone	100	100	100	100	100	100
Miscellaneous	225	225	225	225	225	225
Rent	5,833	5,833	5,833	5,833	5,833	5,833
Total Operating Expenses:	**16,187**	**15,862**	**15,867**	**15,882**	**15,902**	**15,902**
Gross Profit (Loss)	**853**	**2,318**	**3,443**	**3,428**	**8**	**1,708**
Contribution to Charity (5% of net):	**43**	**116**	**172**	**171**	**0**	**85**
Net Profit (Loss) Pre-Tax:	**811**	**2,202**	**3,271**	**3,257**	**8**	**1,623**

March	April	May	June	July	August	Total
$31,680	**$32,740**	**$34,850**	**$35,900**	**$33,790**	**$35,900**	**$404,448**
$14,640	$15,130	$16,100	$16,590	$15,610	$16,590	$186,880
$17,040	**$17,610**	**$18,750**	**$19,310**	**$18,180**	**$19,310**	**$217,568**
190	180	175	195	195	195	2,280
2,500	2,500	2,500	2,500	2,500	2,500	30,000
4,250	4,250	4,250	4,250	4,250	4,250	51,000
844	844	844	844	844	844	10,125
400	400	400	400	400	400	4,800
30	30	30	30	30	30	360
100	100	100	100	100	100	1,200
550	550	550	550	550	550	6,600
60	60	60	60	60	60	720
400	400	400	400	400	400	4,800
—	—	—	—	—	—	300
400	400	400	400	400	400	4,800
100	100	100	100	100	100	1,200
225	225	225	225	225	225	2,700
5,833	5,833	5,833	5,833	5,833	5,833	69,996
15,882	**15,872**	**15,867**	**15,887**	**15,887**	**15,887**	**190,881**
1,158	**1,738**	**2,883**	**3,423**	**2,293**	**3,423**	**26,687**
58	**87**	**144**	**171**	**115**	**171**	**1,334**
1,100	**1,651**	**2,739**	**3,252**	**2,179**	**3,252**	**$ 25,345**

Financials—Year 3

	September	October	November	December	January	February
Total Sales:	**$35,904**	**$33,792**	**$38,016**	**$42,240**	**$33,792**	**$35,904**
Cost of Goods Sold:	$16,590	$15,610	$17,560	$19,510	$15,610	$16,590
Gross Margin	**$19,314**	**$18,182**	**$20,456**	**$22,730**	**$18,182**	**$19,314**
Operating Expenses						
Utilities	205	180	185	200	220	220
Salaries	2,750	2,750	2,750	2,750	2,750	2,750
Variable Labor	4,674	4,674	4,674	4,674	4,674	4,674
Payroll Taxes and Benefits	928	928	928	928	928	928
Advertising	400	400	400	400	400	400
Web site	32	32	32	32	32	32
Office Supplies	120	120	120	120	120	120
Insurance	570	570	570	570	570	570
Maintenance and Cleaning	70	70	70	70	70	70
Legal and Accounting	440	440	440	440	440	440
Licenses	300	—	—	—	—	—
Bags, Paper, etc.	420	420	420	420	420	420
Telephone	125	125	125	125	125	125
Miscellaneous	225	225	225	225	225	225
Rent	5,833	5,833	5,833	5,833	5,833	5,833
Total Operating Expenses:	**17,092**	**16,767**	**16,772**	**16,787**	**16,807**	**16,807**
Net Profit (Loss) Pre-Tax:	**2,222**	**1,415**	**3,684**	**5,943**	**1,375**	**2,507**
Contribution (5%)	**111**	**71**	**184**	**297**	**69**	**125**
Final Net Profit (Loss) Pre-Tax:	**2,111**	**1,344**	**3,500**	**5,646**	**1,306**	**2,382**

March	April	May	June	July	August	Total
$38,016	**$40,128**	**$40,128**	**$40,128**	**$40,128**	**$40,128**	**$458,304**
$17,560	$18,540	$18,540	$18,540	$18,540	$18,540	$211,730
$20,456	**$21,588**	**$21,588**	**$21,588**	**$21,588**	**$21,588**	**$246,574**
200	190	185	205	205	205	2,400
2,750	2,750	2,750	2,750	2,750	2,750	33,000
4,674	4,674	4,674	4,674	4,674	4,674	56,088
928	928	928	928	928	928	11,136
400	400	400	400	400	400	4,800
32	32	32	32	32	32	384
120	120	120	120	120	120	1,440
570	570	570	570	570	570	6,840
70	70	70	70	70	70	840
440	440	440	440	440	440	5,280
—	—	—	—	—	—	300
420	420	420	420	420	420	5,040
125	125	125	125	125	125	1,500
225	225	225	225	225	225	2,700
5,833	5,833	5,833	5,833	5,833	5,833	69,996
16,787	**16,777**	**16,772**	**16,792**	**16,792**	**16,792**	**201,744**
3,669	**4,811**	**4,816**	**4,796**	**4,796**	**4,796**	**44,830**
183	**241**	**241**	**240**	**240**	**240**	**2,242**
3,486	**4,570**	**4,575**	**4,556**	**4,556**	**4,556**	**$ 42,589**

Initial Calculations

Cost Assumptions First Year of Operations

Fixed Costs (FC)		Monthly	Annually
Lease Payment ($35/sq. foot)		$ 5,833	$ 70,000
Utilities		200	2,400
Insurance		833	10,000
Salary of Owner		2,500	30,000
Salary of Sales Assistant		2,125	25,500
Advertising		200	2,400
General Supplies		300	3,600
Professional Services		667	8,000
Miscellaneous Expenses		417	5,000
Web site		20	240
Total		**13,095**	**157,140**
Variable Costs (VC)		**Monthly**	**Annually**
Cost of Goods Sold		11,427	137,120
Total		**28,250**	**339,000**
Break-Even Amount		**Monthly**	**Annually**
Contribution Margin Ratio (CMR)		53.8%	53.8%
Breakeven (FC \ CMR)		$ 24,340	$ 292,082
	Daily	**Monthly**	**Annually**
Breakeven Number of Customers	45	1,352	486,803

Assumptions:

Rental location will be 2,000 square feet.

Average customer spends $18 per visit and comes to the store on average twice per month.

One Time Start-up Costs	
Licensing & Permits	$ 300
Decorating	$ 800
Signage	$ 5,000
Beginning Inventory	$ 40,000
Fixtures and Equipment	$ 6,000
Professional Fees (accountant, attorney)	$ 5,000
Total	**$ 57,100**

PART TWO

2

Small Business Paths & Plans

CHAPTER 5

Small Business Entry: Paths to Part-Time Entrepreneurship

● Kathryn Otoshi works part time doing corporate graphic design and part time on her passion, children's books. What kind of business would you start if you went part time?

LEARNING OBJECTIVES

When you complete this chapter, you will be able to:

LO1 Describe when and why part-time entrepreneurship makes sense.

LO2 Assess the feasibility of opportunities to enter into a part-time business.

LO3 Describe the major paths to part-time entrepreneurship.

LO4 Use the BRIE model to describe what it takes to be successful in part-time entrepreneurship.

LO5 Describe the advantages and pitfalls of delegating and outsourcing.

LO6 Explain the benefits of bootstrapping methods for entrepreneurship.

LO7 Describe the ethical challenges of part-time entrepreneurship.

LO8 Describe the challenges of moving from part-time to full-time entrepreneurship.

Focus on Small Business: Kathryn Otoshi[1]

With the exception of a seven-year-stint at one exceptional full-time job (as Art Director at George Lucas' Industrial Light and Magic), Kathryn Otoshi has always been a part-timer. Trained as a graphic designer (BA in graphic design from Cal Poly San Luis Obispo, MFA from California College of Arts), she created her own design firm KO Design (for Knock Out Design) and alternated that with freelancing for companies like Seattle's Hornall-Anderson Design, working for them on projects like Boeing, Lexus, Starbucks, and Intel. Still, even when she was working full time at ILM, she continued to do occasional part-time design projects on the side. But all along she wanted to publish beautifully illustrated children's books. Eventually she decided to give this a try, leaving ILM in 2002 and starting KO Kids Books in 2003. Kathryn's work won rave reviews. Her first book, *What Emily Saw,* was a Borders' Original New Voice nominee. The next year her book, *Simon and the Sock Monster,* was also a best children's book finalist for the IPPY Award (Independent Publishers Award) in 2004. Despite critical acclaim and good sales for premium children's books, to keep cash flowing, Kathryn alternates between the book business and working part time through KO Design, continuing to work as a graphic designer on large scale corporate identity projects. Part-time author and illustrator, part-time industrial designer, Kathryn Otoshi remains the perennial part-timer, 20 years after graduating from college.

DISCUSSION QUESTIONS

1. What difference do you think it makes when you freelance for another firm vs. working entirely on your own?
2. What are the ethical concerns when you are working full time for one company and part time for yourself? How would you recommend managing these issues?
3. Producing one premium children's book a year, how long do you think it would take Kathryn to be able to do children's books as her only full-time work? Why?

LO1 Describe when and why part-time entrepreneurship makes sense.

Why Part-Time Businesses Are Important

Kathryn Otoshi's story is repeated millions of times a year. After graduation she took a full-time job with an existing firm, but also created a part-time business of her own. That first business became the template and learning ground for her later part-time businesses.

Today, Kathryn is self-employed full-time, but does so through two part-time businesses—KO Design and KO Kids Books. Because she works less than 35 hours a week at each business, she is practicing what is called **part-time self-employment**. Working part time means that the entrepreneur can do other work, such as have a job in another company, go to school, or take care of family. For people working more than 35 hours a week, the term is **full-time self-employment**. Working full time means that the majority of one's time is spent on the business.

part-time self-employment
Working for yourself for 35 or fewer hours a week.

full-time self-employment
Working for yourself for more than 35 hours a week.

When you enter business, you make a choice about pursuing a full-time or part-time approach. Full-time approaches include buying or inheriting existing businesses, franchising, or opening a new full-time business. Those approaches are discussed in Chapter 6.

This chapter focuses on part-time approaches to business. Why does it deserve a whole chapter? There are two reasons. First, most entrepreneurs start out working part time on their new business. According to the Panel Study of Entrepreneurial Dynamics (PSED), three-quarters of new businesses start on a part-time basis.[2] This includes the businesses shown in Table 5.1. The ease and low cost of entry and exit make part-time entrepreneurship a great way to try a variety of different businesses without "betting the farm" each time they start a business.

Second, the sheer number of part-time self-employeds makes them a major force in our economy, even if it is one we do not always recognize. Officially, of the 27.2 million small businesses in the United States in 2007, around half were part-time businesses.[3] However, that understates the situation. Remember Chapter 1 mentioned there were about 1 million new firms a year? Many people jump into and out of self-employment (a change called **volatility** by economists) for a few weeks at a time, perhaps because they do project-based work like taking on a single consulting project in their spare time, or doing someone's taxes, or selling an item or two on eBay or at a garage sale. These very short-term projects get missed in the "1 million starts a year" survey. The Kauffman Index of Entrepreneurial Activity reported that during 2011 approximately 543,000 new businesses were created each month. This is more than 6.5 million businesses per year–way more than the 1 million new starts counted by the SBA. The Kauffman Index may itself underestimate the true number of annual business starts by not including many of the more than 6 million people who are actively selling products and services through online sites.[4]

volatility
The frequency of business starts and stops.

When to Consider Part-Time Entrepreneurship

These days, the conventional wisdom is that if you are serious about starting a business, you ought to start a business full time and prepare for it by doing a business plan. That makes a lot of sense, since a business plan enables you to look at every aspect of your business. Business plans are also

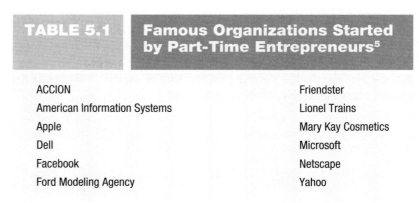

TABLE 5.1 Famous Organizations Started by Part-Time Entrepreneurs[5]

ACCION	Friendster
American Information Systems	Lionel Trains
Apple	Mary Kay Cosmetics
Dell	Microsoft
Facebook	Netscape
Ford Modeling Agency	Yahoo

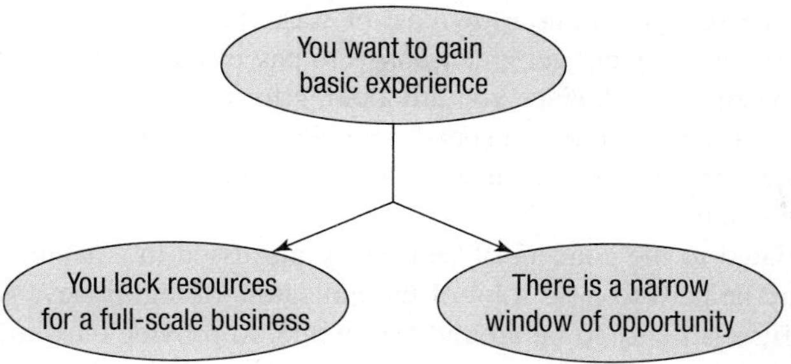

FIGURE 5.1

When to Consider a Part-Time Business

important if you intend to ask others for expertise or financial investments. However, running a business full time can be a major commitment and is not always the best way to go about becoming an entrepreneur.

There are three situations in which it might make better sense to first undertake a part-time business. One of these is when you are new to business and need to *gain basic experience*. If you have not been involved in pricing, buying, and selling, learning how to do such things makes a lot of sense before launching the business of your dreams. You might want to obtain other types of experience before starting a full-scale business or writing a business plan. These can include experience in the industry, in the line of business, in the locality of the specific market you plan to serve, in managing cash, or in managing yourself in self-employment.

A second type of situation is one in which you *lack resources* to pursue a full-scale business or create a business plan. Time is probably the ultimate resource, and starting a business can tax it heavily. Estimates suggest that a business plan may take anywhere from 50 to 200 hours or more if you are new to business and working on your own.[6] Starting a full-time business can absorb 70 hours a week or more in its early stages. You might not be able to commit the time to work that way, and pursuing a precursor makes a lot of sense. It also makes sense if you are missing other resources. Kathryn Otoshi originally lacked the funds and contacts to sustain a full-time design business of her own. By pursuing her own business part time, she gained experience, contacts, and savings while freelancing for Hornall-Anderson Design and working full time at ILM. Armed with experience, she was able to succeed in her own businesses.

The third type of situation is *a narrow window of opportunity*. For example, when teams are announced for tournaments like the NCAA Men's Basketball Tournament, there is suddenly a veritable flood on eBay of logo clothing and memorabilia from the selected teams. These eBay entrepreneurs are capitalizing on the increased interest in the newly announced teams. Within a few weeks, most of the selected teams will have lost and left the tournament, but in the meantime, they (and anything with their logo on it) are hot properties. Part-time businesses can generally be created quickly, and they offer a concrete example of a business to customers, suppliers, and others. When there is not enough time to do a business plan or get the entire business going, pursuing a part-time business to capture the attention of others makes a lot of sense. (See Figure 5.1.)

LO2 Assess the feasibility of opportunities to enter into a part-time business.

Key Considerations for Success in Part-Time Entrepreneurship

When you decide to pursue part-time entrepreneurship, there are usually two major questions: What kind of product or service do you want to offer and how do you want to organize your part-time business? Chapter 4 discussed the process for coming up with a good (and maybe even a creative) idea for your business. In this chapter we will focus more on how you would get that business started part time.

For the second question, about how to organize your business, there are usually three key considerations for part-time small business start-ups:

- The **cost to start-up** your new part-time business.
- The **time to start-up** your business.
- The **permanence** of the business you are creating.

cost to start-up
The amount of money it takes to start a new business.

time to start-up
How long it takes to start a new business.

permanence
The impression of long-term continuity a business gives others.

For part-time businesses, you want a low cost of start-up, since you probably will not have a lot of money to invest, and may not get great returns to pay off expensive start-up efforts. Time to start-up is also best when shortest, since you are looking for a basic idea of what might and might not work. The more time and energy you spend preparing for a small-scale part-time business, the longer it takes to make a profit. The good news is that in most cases, the cost to start-up and the time to market are closely related.

Permanence is related to the concept of legitimacy discussed in Chapter 2. For a small-scale, part-time firm, it may be hard to have a lot of the indicators of legitimacy. What customers want to know is that the firm is likely to be around for awhile, to provide customer service and future sales. That is the fundamental idea of permanence. The three considerations are at the heart of most peoples' decisions about their mode of entry to part-time entrepreneurship.

What Kinds of Part-Time Entrepreneurship Exist?

LO3 Describe the major paths to part-time entrepreneurship.

In this section we will look at the ways to start a part-time small business in most industries—retailing, wholesaling, most services, and even manufacturing (because most part-time manufacturing is based on either an artisan's small-scale production of products or on subcontracted manufacturing). How do we know what are the most popular industries? Knowing that small businesses range from 97 to 99 percent of nearly every industry, a quick look at the number of firms in each can give us an idea. We can see a listing by industry in Table 5.2.

Most part-time business starts with where you live—your home or dorm room, so home-based business is where we will start. A relatively new wisdom about part-time start-ups has emerged in the past few years. It is based on everyone's increasing use of the Internet as a source of information and as a replacement for traditional phone books. Today if you are trying to market beyond your immediate family, neighborhood, or circle of friends, you need to start your business with a web presence. Some businesses can in fact be done entirely on the web, and informational and e-commerce websites are the second and third techniques we will consider. The fourth start-up approach will be a

TABLE 5.2 Size of U.S. Industries by Major Sector, 2007[7]

NAICS	Industry	No. of Establishments	Percentage
54	Professional services	1,233,625	17%
44–45	Retail	1,122,703	16%
51–53	Business services	1,026,915	14%
61–62	Health & education, extraction, utilities	839,763	12%
21–23	Construction	784,318	11%
72	Accommodations	626,558	9%
81	Other services	537,819	7%
42	Wholesale	432,094	6%
31–33	Manufacturing	293,919	4%
48–49	Transportation	217,926	3%
71	Arts	123,965	2%
	Total	7,239,606	≈100%

Source: Special tabulation of the March 2007 Current Population Survey (2009) by Jerome Katz.

collection of other fast, low-cost approaches which can be helpful in a variety of situations. If you are looking for more ideas about the ways you can get started, consider jumping ahead to Chapter 11, Small Business Distribution and Location, which discusses some of the more involved techniques like direct mail, telemarketing, and direct-response advertising, which can be used in particular situations for a part-time business.

This is close to an ideal setup for a home office. There is space for files and equipment. The owner has the equipment needed to do her work, and there is a door to provide some quiet and privacy, but the glass lets her see what is going on at home, and lets her family know she is around.

Home-Based Business

Home might be where the heart is, but it is also where the part-time business starts. If yours is a retailing or wholesaling business, home is where you store your goods. If you are making furniture, toys, clothing, or food, it is probably where your work area is. And if you are in a service, it is where you retire to in order to get your work done. For nearly everyone, home is where you keep your office records, do your bookkeeping and taxes, and where you probably first receive your firm's mail. You may work away from home—in Chapter 11's section on location we consider service firms where you do part of your work at the client's location or at remote locations, but unless you get an office or other location from which you will base your business, you will probably start from home.

There were about 14.4 million home-based businesses in the United States in 2007,[8] and they represented 52 percent of all firms. The reason for these large numbers is because the home-based business meets at least two of the three criteria for start-up. It is inexpensive, since you are already living somewhere and you can quickly get your business going where you live. Although home-based businesses do not always give customers the strongest sense of legitimacy, the idea that a customer knows where the entrepreneur lives can be a point in favor of trusting in the potential permanence of the firm.

That said, with so great a number of firms, there are not many hard-and-fast rules that apply to everyone, but there are a few key ideas to keep in mind.[9] First and foremost is the location of your home-based business. Although the dining room table may be infrequently used, is it the best place for your work? Even though anything *can* work, the following suggestions come from home-based entrepreneurs and are likely to make your life a lot easier.

According to home-based entrepreneurs, the greatest problems they face come when there are zoning challenges or family challenges to the business. Cities, counties, neighborhoods, apartment complexes, and dorms pass regulations which limit the ways residents can use or modify their space. The government restrictions are called **zoning laws**, while the ones set up by other organizations are called **covenants**. Unfortunately there is no comprehensive free online national listing of zoning regulations,[10] but there are public records, and these can often be found online on your city's or county's government website. Otherwise, the local Chamber of Commerce or the local library may have the basic information.

zoning laws
Government specifications for acceptable use of land and buildings in particular areas.

covenants
The limitations imposed on your property by your neighborhood group.

It is best to carefully check out the zoning and covenant situation before fully committing yourself to a home-based business. Most of us live in areas zoned as residential areas. Typically, it is not legal to have a home-based business in a residential area—even an online business.[11] It may be tempting to simply ignore such restrictions. Doing so, however, raises ethical issues and may cause the imposition of fines and penalties on your new business.

Usually people get into trouble only if a neighbor, landlord, or dorm staffer complains or it becomes apparent to police or other public service employees that "something" is going on at your home. In either situation, what causes the problem, and makes it stick, are aspects of your business that "change the residential character of the neighborhood" through increased traffic, noise, parked cars, or smells.

To minimize problems, there are several alternatives.[12] If you are not concerned about the ethical implications, you can generally keep the web- and phone-based aspects of your business at home without neighbors becoming aware of (or disturbed by) your business—but be sure not to tell them you work from home! The way to handle large amounts of mail and packages is through the use of private mailboxes (from a company like PakMail, Mailboxes Etc., or PostalAnnex) and self-storage facilities (like Public Storage U-Haul, Storage USA, or similar local companies), rather than having them delivered to your home. Use the private mailbox address for your business on the web and on your stationery.

variance
Permission from a government organization to act differently that the laws state.

Another approach is to seek to get permission—called a **variance**—to have your business operating from out of your home. Often there are local lawyers who specialize in real estate and zoning law, and they can often advise you if a variance is a workable solution. While you can request a variance on your own, having a lawyer advocate for you can cost from hundreds to thousands of dollars, so this approach is only for those with determination and money.[13] The best way to find such a lawyer is through referrals from friends or businesspeople whose judgment you trust, but if that does not work, or you want to check into the lawyers suggested to you, you can use an online directory such as Martindale.com (www.Martindale.com) or FindLaw.com (www.FindLaw.com) to find and learn more about local lawyers. There is a video showing how to do this on the Online Learning Center.

Once zoning is handled, think about issues inside your home. The list below touches on many of the issues home-based entrepreneurs find most important to running their business:

- Choose a work location inside your home that is away from noise, distractions, and family traffic. It helps you concentrate and sound businesslike when on the phone.
- Be realistic about the amount of space you'll need for your equipment.
- An office door can keep business separate from family and the rest of life.
- Try your location out for a day or two to check out noise, traffic patterns, lighting needs, and distractions.
- Don't overload on hours of work, or on snacks from the refrigerator down the hall.
- Set up your work day to minimize distractions from household or family chores and, as much as possible, stick to the plan.
- Consider hiring help to handle household or family chores to free up your time.
- Set the ground rules early and stick with them. Watch out for family, friends, and visitors who don't understand home-based businesses. Both of the Peters were running home-based businesses. Their working-outside-the-home siblings didn't understand why they couldn't drop off their ill or vacationing children so that they "wouldn't miss work."[14] You'll be asked to do extra school or sports carpools, wait for service people, or other such things because of your at-home status.

One of the greatest challenges to making a home office work is getting family and friends to give you the privacy and time alone to do the work you need to do. How could this father have avoided this situation?

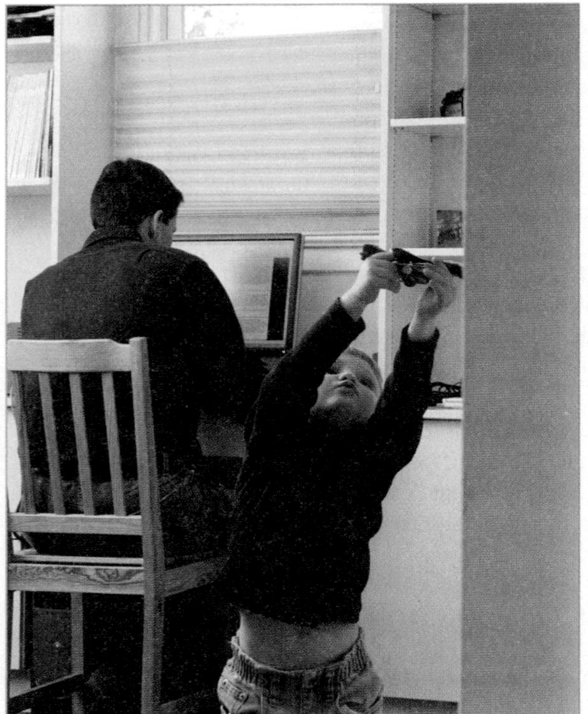

Exhibit 5.1 summarizes the most important 20 questions to ask yourself as you think about setting up a home-based business.

Once you've chosen your location, you'll need equipment. You'll need a comfortable, usable desk and chair and adequate lighting. Consider the tasks you'll perform most frequently and check out the ergonomic options that will serve you the best. Although you can store files in cardboard boxes, an inexpensive filing cabinet would be so much simpler. Think about the layout of the furniture for access to proper lighting, phone jacks, and electrical outlets. You may need to supplement some or all of these.

Tools typically include a telephone (these days most often a cell phone), high-capacity Internet service (like cable or DSL or 3G Wi-Fi service for your laptop), a business e-mail account, a high-speed desktop computer, a fax machine, a copier and appropriate software (look at Table 5.4, Essential Free Software and Web Services for Small Businesses, on page 147 for high-quality free programs and services). These days many multipurpose devices combine a printer, copier, fax machine, and scanner into one piece of equipment. These items reduce the amount of space you'll need. Consider the layout of the equipment and how you'll use each piece. You don't want to reach around your computer monitor to pick up the telephone or race across the room to catch printer pages.

You'll want to have a separate business telephone line with an answering machine, voice mail, or virtual PBX service so that you can get those

EXHIBIT 5.1

Twenty Questions to Ask Before Planning Your Home Office[15]

1. Do you want clients or visitors traipsing through your home to get to your office?
2. Do you want your family trooping through—or even past—your office?
3. Are you doing mostly desk work?
4. Do you need space to sort, store, and ship materials?
5. Are you producing and assembling a product?
6. Do you want or need to keep your work in progress on hand and available for tweaking at a moment's notice?
7. Does noise or activity easily distract you?
8. How much and what kind of sound can you tolerate while working?
9. Do you work more efficiently when you can see and touch reference materials?
10. Do you wilt in the absence of natural light?
11. Do you need a desktop computer, or would a notebook do as well?
12. Are you left- or right-handed?
13. Do you need a separate entrance to maintain clients' privacy or your own sanity?
14. Is your work life completely separate from or fairly integrated with the rest of your life?
15. Do you need help maintaining healthy boundaries around your work?
16. Is your work something in which your family can participate?
17. Will you be adding more equipment in the near future?
18. Does listening to music boost your creativity?
19. Do you need space to hold meetings?
20. Does your town or city have special zoning requirements for home-based businesses?

important calls after hours. Make sure your voice-mail message sounds businesslike and not like the message on your home answering machine. Consider a second phone line if you are limited to a modem-based Internet connection. Ideally, this space and its tools will be used only for your home-based office. In addition, totally separate space and equipment make tax deduction preparation much simpler.

When does a home-based business outgrow the home? For some companies, the answer is never. Some entrepreneurs opt for charging higher prices for their goods or services or limiting their sales so as not to outgrow the space available; being a home-based business is just too important to them to change. Others reinvest their profits into additions to their homes to accommodate their business growth or to upgrade to a roomier house with the extra space they need. Some die-hard home-based entrepreneurs faced with this decision have found creative ways of housing their staff and other operations in an outside office while continuing to telecommute as much as possible.[16]

More typically, a business will find the need for meeting rooms and employee accommodations or zoning restrictions will force the change. In other cases, family situations just aren't favorable to a home-based business. Some entrepreneurs find they aren't cut out for the solitude of working by themselves or find household chores, family, or other distractions disturb them too easily.

Home-based business is the easiest and fastest way to start a business, and the easiest and fasted type of business to move or close down. This ease of

Sometimes the success of a home-based business is what makes it necessary to move. This part-time entrepreneur's business completely overwhelmed the downstairs den. What started as a home office in the corner grew until it became an office warehouse and shipping center. How do you think his family is responding?

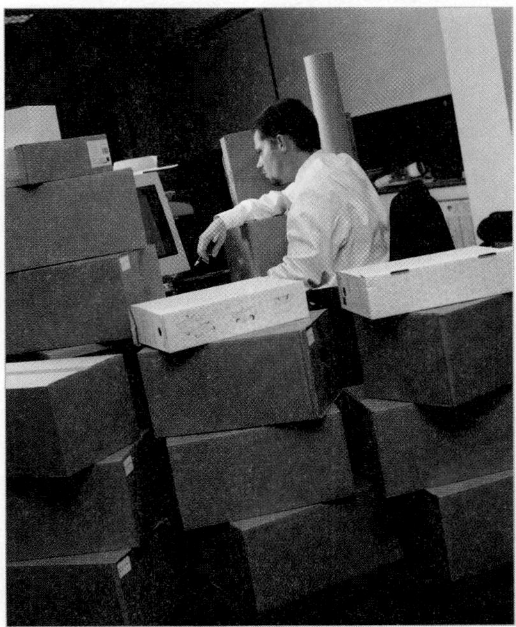

deployment, moving, and closing make the home-based business one of the volatile forms of part-time business. Even so, it is the core and greatest common factor in business start-ups.

Internet Informational Websites[17]

e-commerce
The use of the Internet to conduct business transactions.

informational websites
An Internet site designed to introduce and explain a business to others.

Perhaps the biggest change in part-time self-employment in the past five years has been the growth of the Internet as a major method for conducting business. Most of us have bought something online, which is what is called **e-commerce**. But another type of website, the **informational website**, is an even more important type of website which informs possible customers about your firm. For a part-time entrepreneur, a website can become a 24-hour-a-day, 7-day-a-week source of information and prospects, if not sales.

To get some idea about the power of the Internet for information and for e-commerce, consider this. The Pew Internet Project studied people who bought music or cell phones in 2006. Over half the music buyers (56 percent) used the Internet to check out the music, while 39 percent of buyers of cell phones got information online. Roughly one-third of those getting information online bought online (music 22 percent, cell phones 12 percent).[18] So these days having an Internet presence is key to letting customers know what you are selling, but those sales are still more likely to come from traditional means like face-to-face selling, telephone sales, mail order, or coming to where you are displaying your wares.

business-to-consumer (B2C)
Business-to-consumer transactions using e-commerce.

business-to-business (B2B)
Business-to-business transactions using e-commerce.

Products like music and cell phones are examples of the kind of goods we buy as individuals. That type of e-commerce is called **business-to-consumer (B2C)**. There is another type called **business-to-business (B2B)** sales where one firm sells to another firm. While our personal experience is in the B2C marketplace, all of those sales on iTunes, eBay, and Amazon account for only about 3 percent of all retail sales in the United States. For most of us, the B2B market is invisible, but when businesses buy, they buy big. In 2010, over 46 percent of all manufacturing sales were handled online as well as almost 25 percent of all wholesale trade between businesses.[19] You can see the difference, and the growth of these forms of e-commerce in Figure 5.2. The moral of this story? B2C e-commerce is large, B2B e-commerce is larger, but using an informational website to inform customers—whether they are individuals or businesses—is huge.

The Internet's power comes from its being a very cost-effective and efficient way to contact your customers. With the Internet, a small, part-time, one-person operation can compete with a

FIGURE 5.2

E-Commerce as Percent of Total Value: 2002–2010

Source: U.S. Census Bureau. "U.S. Census Bureau E-Stats: Historical Data."

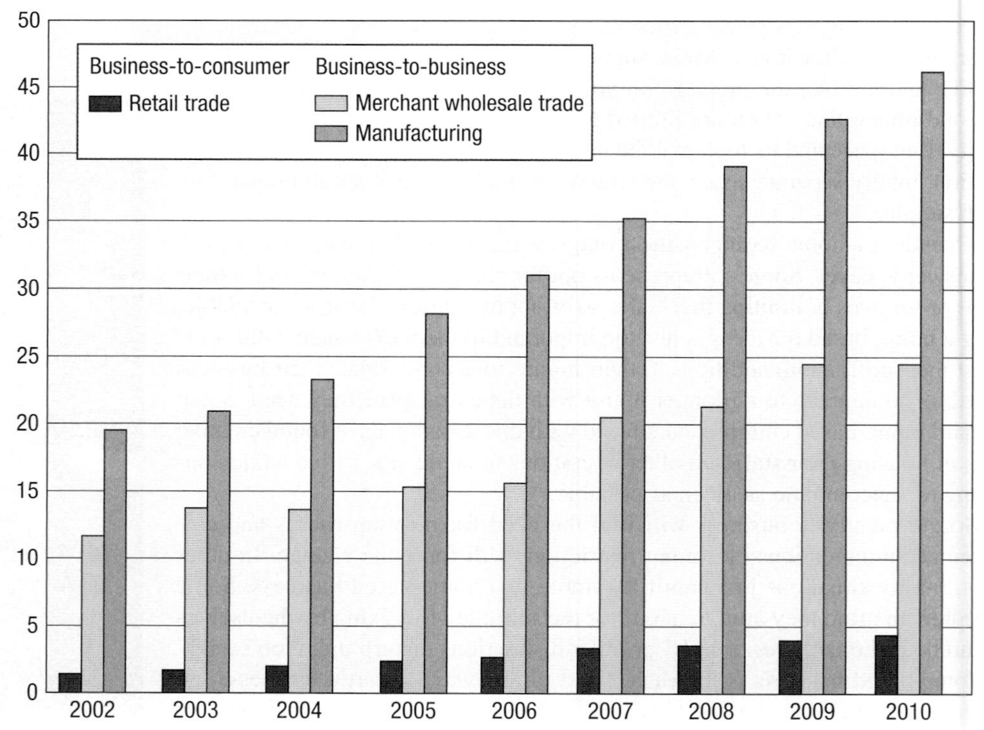

billion-dollar-a-year multinational. Whether your customers are other businesses or other **consumers**, getting a website together is essential.

consumer
A private individual or household that is the end-user of (the entity that "consumes") a product or service.

Most small businesses—even part-time ones—need to have a website regardless of whether or not they use it for actual sales. First of all, potential customers will use it to find you. Second, if they've heard about you from something other than the Internet, they will use your site to find out more information about you and to decide if they want to actually contact you. Letrah International, a firm specializing in international consulting for design and engineering projects, knew it should have a website, but it was a low priority and was worked on only when something else did not come up. Dave Peters, the firm's vice president at that time, asked a firm in the United Arab Emirates if there was anything he could do to help convince the firm to accept Letrah's bid. The firm expressed concern that Letrah was not a real company, because it didn't have a website, and "everybody knew real U.S. firms had websites." The website was running the following day.[20]

Letrah was able to develop and deploy an informational website in a matter of hours. That is not uncommon. The basics of an informational website can be set up within an hour. There are a number of very low-cost vendors, such as 1and1.com, iBuilder.com, and Godaddy.com, as well as the major web presence providers like Yahoo! and Google sites (just search Google for "cheap websites").

What you are looking for in a basic informational website package is a domain name of your own. Ideally you want your business's name in the domain name of your site. If you want to call your company Beachcomber Shoes, you would ideally look for the domain name beachcombershoes.com. If the dot-com version was not available, using .net or .biz or .us might work for you. Otherwise you can tweak the domain name, for example beachcombershoecompany.com or beachshoes.com. You want a name that reinforces your firm's name or your product's name, or something highly memorable, like ouch.com. Note that the price of domain names varies. An unregistered name is about $35 a year retail, but most of the discount website providers will charge only $7 or $8 a year, and some will include it for free when you buy a website (what they usually call a "hosting") package.

A hosting package for an informational site should include at least 1 gigabyte of traffic a month (this refers to people downloading your pages into their browser). It should give you at least 10 web pages of space to tell your story. It should also include templates to help you develop a website which has a professional look and an online website editor so you can make changes to your site without buying web-authoring software. The hosting package should also include at least five e-mail accounts using your domain name (e.g., info@beachcombershoes.com, support@beachcombershoes.com, jane@beachcombershoes.com, etc.). While using Beachcombershoes@gmail.com (which is a free e-mail service from Google) is good, having info@beachcombershoes.com is even better.

The material for your website can come from promotional material you have written. Every page should have the company name, your contact information (or a link to it), a site map link (which shows a directory of all your pages—don't worry, the template should generate this automatically), and a link back to the home page. Typically your home page (the first page people see when they type in your domain name), gives a quick (one or two paragraphs) introduction of the company and should prominently display your product or service. Other typical pages include:

- "About Us" which gives a brief background on the company and yourself.
- Product or Service pages which give a more detailed description of what you sell or what you do.
- Support page which gives customers or potential customers information on how, and reassurance that, their problems with your product or service will get solved.
- Resources page, which typically gives general information (e.g., "Five things you should know about buying ________").
- Press or Media page if you have received notice in the media.

Today many informational websites include the capability to add a **blog**, which is a web page in which entries are posted in reverse chronological order (i.e., the most recent at the top of the page). Many blogs let readers respond online, so the entrepreneur and the potential customers can interact directly. Today website packages include the ability to push content, like your blog, out to customers who register at your site. Some sites do this by using an **RSS feed**. RSS stands for "really simple syndication" and an RSS feed pushes or sends whatever web material you specify to subscribers to that feed. RSS feeds can be read in many browsers or with special readers.

blog
A web page in which entries are posted in reverse chronological order (i.e., the most recent at the top of the page).

RSS feed
An Internet messaging service that pushes (sends) whatever web material you specify to subscribers to that feed.

A similar approach uses an e-mail mailing list to send e-mails or online newsletters (sometimes called eNewsletters) to people on your subscriber list. To read these, subscribers have to use an e-mail program or a browser. Many web hosting packages offer a mailing list program as part of the package, but there are also for-fee specialized mailing list programs with more features, such as ConstantContact.com. The latest variation on push technology is Twitter.com. Twitter is a free service which lets a person send a 140-character or less message or **tweet** to people who subscribe to the person's Twitter account. You can see what Oprah is up to, or check out StockTwits.com, which uses tweets to inform members about up-to-the-second trends in the stock market. StockTwits started part time, and by May 2009 had four employees.[21]

tweet
A 140-character or less message sent using the Twitter web service.

Realize that while you can design your own site, there are also a lot of people who can do it for you as well, from your "techno-geek" teenage nephew who will do it for the cost of the latest computer game to firms that will not only design but also maintain your website for you—at a cost, of course. You can also hire professionals to set up and manage a site for you. The Google search would look for "managed e-commerce solutions."

There are volumes and volumes written about what things to consider when building your website. You probably have your own list of pet peeves about things some websites do that drive you crazy. That list is what you need to make sure your website does not have those properties, which probably include:

- Slow-loading graphics or pages.
- Too many layers of screens to get to what you want.
- Dead links within the website (when you see a "404 error").
- Hard to fill in online forms.
- Pop-up ads.
- Pages that only look or work "right" in one type of browser.

But you are likely to have many other complaints. The trick is to think of them before you deploy your website, and you'll make your customers and prospective customers happier.

Once you've got your website up and running and it is a masterpiece in design, how do you get your customers to find it? The first way is **multichannel marketing**. Have your website listed on your business cards and every piece of paper, advertising, and the like. The second and equally important way is to get linked to other web pages. If you were in the target market for your product, what web pages would you visit? Figure out what these are and establish **reciprocal links**. In a reciprocal link, you display a link to another website and that website displays a similar link to yours. Scan chat rooms and other electronic message boards to see if people are looking for your type of product or service and post your website. Discover what sorts of electronic newsletters they might read and get a mention in them.[22]

multichannel marketing
The use of several different channels to reach your customers, for example, a website, direct mail, and traditional retailing.

reciprocal links
A listed, live connection to a different website, which in turn displays a similar link to the first website.

The third way is online searching. Searching online is how about 85 percent of Internet users find websites, but users will seldom go beyond the first couple of pages of a search.[23] There are several ways to get your site positioned so that a person searching is likely to see it. The technique, which is free, is called **search engine optimization** (SEO) and refers to designing a website so that search engines like Google and Yahoo are likely to rank your site high (closer to the first listing). Many web hosting packages include programs to help you edit your website to improve your ranking. There are also books on SEO and websites like SearchEngineGuide.com, SearchEngineWatch.com, and SubmitCorner.com that are devoted to telling you the hundreds of secrets to mastering SEO.

search engine optimization
A general approach to website design intended to result in the site being displayed toward the beginning of a search engine's (e.g., Google, Yahoo!, etc.) listing for that term.

If you are willing to put up some money, you can pay for **sponsored links** (guaranteeing you a particular placement on the first page of a search) from the search engines at a manageable cost. Google and Yahoo! ask you what word you want to use and how much you are willing to pay (our suggestion is start with a low number). You then find out how often the word is used, and how often a searcher clicks on any sponsored link. Paying more will get your sponsored link closer to the top of the page. You can make multiple offers until you find one you can live with.[24] The problem you might face comes from what you sell. If you are a bookstore, the word "books" might come to mind, but that's true for lots and lots of other bookstores, publishers, and others. Maybe "first editions" is more appropriate, if that is indeed what you sell.

sponsored link
A form of paid advertising that gets your company's website at the top of a search list.

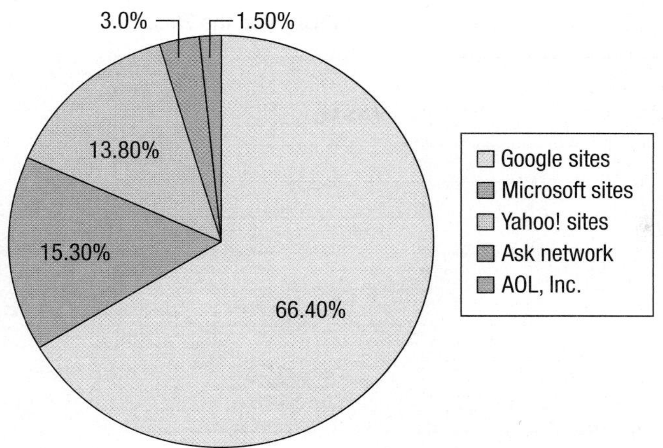

FIGURE 5.3

Search Engine Rankings—February 2012

Source: Adapted from comScore.com, "February 2012 Search Engine Rankings."[25]

On the other hand, if you have something somewhat more unusual like yo-yos, buying "yo-yo" is likely to get you on a page with limited competition.[26] Watch for jargon; think of what the average searcher might enter. A video showing how to find the terms on competitors' websites is available at the Online Learning Center. Your hosting service's SEO program or your own web page designer will understand where to place the keywords you select and can help you get listed on the major search engines. There are literally hundreds of search engines, but there are four very major ones—Google, Yahoo! Microsoft, and AOL. The next six largest search engines share 6 percent of the searches. You can see their relative shares of the search business in Figure 5.3.

With all of these details revolving around making a truly effective informational website, you may wonder if it makes sense to do it yourself. As we have discussed, many $10-a-month web hosting packages will give you access to the tools to create a basic template-driven website and do the basic work necessary to perform SEO and will push your information to others via e-mails, RSS feeds, or Twitter tweets. The advantage is that you can deploy the site within hours and the cost is very low. The downside of template-based sites is that they can look similar to one another. On the other hand, having an e-commerce website created for you can be a $5,000 to $10,000 effort, and is likely to take a couple of weeks as you and your designer talk through draft versions of the site. One way to strike a balance between these two extremes is to commission custom graphics to use at the top of your online store's pages, and as a background. Another approach is to seek bids for your e-commerce store design on sites like eLance.com or from local web designers.

For many part-time firms, an informational website is the essential starting point to get word out to the public, and to make your firm visible to those Internet search engines so many people use to find companies, goods, and services these days. Often, as the firm and its offerings mature, there is a benefit to moving beyond providing information via the web, and making it possible for customers to actually place their orders online. That takes you to the next step, e-commerce.

E-Commerce and eBay Websites

How big is e-commerce and how fast is it growing? As noted above, there is a growing use of the Internet for e-commerce. The number of e-commerce sites, shown in Figure 5.4, passed 1,000,000 in January 2009, doubling since the summer of 2006.[27] Meanwhile, Figure 5.2, on page 128, showed how e-commerce sales were growing at a steady pace for B2C retail and wholesale sales, and growing at a much faster rate for B2B wholesale and manufacturing sales. E-commerce in 2007 was more than $2.25 trillion sector of U.S. business.[28] So the answer is that e-commerce is big and getting bigger.

For part-time entrepreneurs, the lure of an e-commerce site is undeniable. Consider listing your products on the top two sites. eBay reports over 4 million sellers in the United States alone, and seven out of every eight sellers work on eBay only part time.[29] The cost of listing a $25 item on eBay is $1, plus an additional 8.75 percent of $25 if the item sells. The cost to open an eBay account?

FIGURE 5.4

Growth of E-Commerce Sites

Source: From Netcraft, "One Million SSL Sites on the Web," www.netcraft.com. Used by permission.

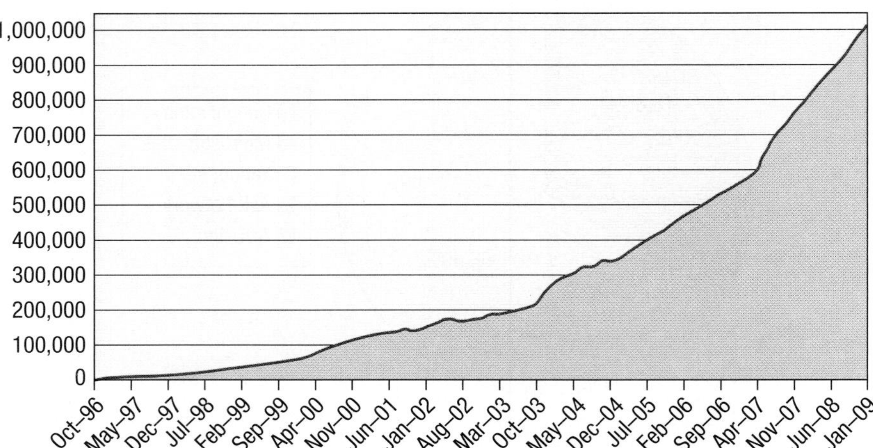

Nothing. eBay's biggest competitor, Amazon, offers a similar deal with slightly different terms. Between the two sites, nearly a half-billion computer users visit one site or another during the year.

With numbers like those it is no wonder that e-commerce on the Internet is an attractive approach for entrepreneurs looking to create a business. This is especially true for part-time entrepreneurs. For part-time entrepreneurs the online approach makes a highly attractive opportunity because it offers the advantages of a large market, 24/7 availability of your products, and a start-up which is quickly done and potentially inexpensive. For many part-timers, the online approach provides a great way to learn the business and the market, establish your reputation and business track record, and lay a foundation for a full-time business. For entrepreneurs looking to prospect for the right type of business, the online sales approach makes it possible to try out a range of industries quickly and with minimal risk. For entrepreneurs with highly specialized products, like a banana-shaped cell phone cover (**http://cellfoam.com/**), the idea that low-cost listings on two sites could reach half of 1.1 *billion* Internet users worldwide[30] opens up sales possibilities like never before.

There are two major approaches to online selling. One is using eBay or another online site to showcase your goods and handle the selling and payment process. The other is to do this through a website of your own. The two approaches can be complementary. As we saw with Paul Scheiter of Hedgehog Leatherworks in Chapter 4, eBay can be used to introduce your product to a large audience, to find an initial selling price, and to learn more about customers and competitors. Paul later set up his own website as his primary point of sale, and uses eBay to market to new customers.

Everything we have said so far about informational websites applies to a website enabled for e-commerce. Most of the hosting companies mentioned in this chapter can also provide you with an e-commerce site. In fact if you already have an informational site, they can set it up so everything you have posted to the web moves directly into the new, more capable site. What e-commerce sites add is the ability create and maintain an online catalog of products, create new database entries for orders, and handle the payment for products or services. The more tools and services you need and the larger the catalogs you post, the more you will end up paying. It is worth doing some serious comparison shopping for hosting services. Conduct a Google search for "cheap e-commerce" and "free shopping cart" (a *shopping cart* is the electronic version of a catalog with an ordering system) to find a large number of possibilities. Many offer do-it-yourself software to make the design of websites and shopping carts easy.

In addition to the keys to designing an effective informational website covered above, there are also two important financial issues for entrepreneurs who create their own e-commerce websites. These issues are payment and chargebacks.

- **Payment:** Most online transactions use a credit card or an online payment system like PayPal (which is a division of eBay). There are fees for the transaction itself, and there are often fees for currency conversions, or guaranteed payments. Unless you as the seller buys a payment guarantee at the time of the transaction, services will also make a chargeback (see below). Many online e-commerce packages come with a service that handles these transactions for a fee. Where you can specify another vendor, you may be able to get one who charges less. But as important as the fees charged is the service's handling of customer service. When problems crop up in payments, both buyers and sellers want to talk to a person immediately. Services with fast response rates and helpful people on the phone are valuable.

- **Chargebacks:** This is a fee the service levels on you for any of a variety of problems related to the sale, for example, a lost, stolen, or fraudulent card was used, the customer reports nothing was received, the product was not the one promised, or there were problems with the product. While chargebacks in stores is around 0.1 percent of sales, online chargeback rates can be as much as five times higher.[31] Techniques to control this include using the Address Verification Service or verifying their phone numbers or address yourself, getting proof of delivery from the carrier, and making sure your return policy is known by the customer before the sale is finalized.

eBay is a site offering a variety of ways to sell goods and services. To give you an idea of how varied are eBay's offerings, consider these ways eBay supports entrepreneurial efforts:

- For many just interested in selling a few items and moving to something else, eBay is like the largest consignment store or garage sale in the world. You can list a single item for sale, without creating a website or a company to support your effort.
- You can create an online store within eBay complete with your own online catalog and ordering systems.
- eBay has 34 major categories of goods ranging from "collectibles," which includes the Pez containers many erroneously believe was eBay's first item, to "Business & Industrial," where you can buy 75-ton construction cranes.
- You can sell services through Elance.com ranging from web design to business plans, accounting to translation, training to CAD projects, in a reverse auction format. In a **reverse auction**[32] the low bid gets the business.

reverse auction
An auction in which the low bid gets the business or wins.

Elance.com adapts the eBay model to services. Businesses post projects, review bids, use the message boards to keep up-to-date, and can even pay online, all for a small fee Elance collects once the provider is paid. Service providers are able to post information about their expertise

This entrepreneur is taking no risks with her product sales on eBay. Not only is she checking her product's listing for prospective buyers, she is also checking how her eBay online store is showing up in social media like Yahoo!'s groups and a set of photos of products she has uploaded to Flickr.

and experience as well. Cheri Rychlee Tracy was looking for a web designer. Local companies wanted between $1,500 and $7,500. She was able to find a freelance designer on Elance from the Ukraine for $750.[33]

While this section concentrates on eBay, it is important to know that there are competitors for every type of service eBay offers. While their traffic numbers may not match eBay's, they may have a better audience for your purposes. For example, freelanceseek.com has a strong programming and online art focus, and is a site often used by people in the e-commerce industry. Competing sites include:

- For Elance: ContractedWork.com, ScriptLance.com, GetAFreelancer.com, and Freelance Seek.com.
- For eBay's B2C auction services: Auction.com, Bidz.com, Ioffer.com, Ubid.com.
- For eBay's B2B auction services: Business.com, B2BToday.com.
- For eBay's online store services: Amazon.com, Godaddy.com, 1and1.com

Using e-commerce services like eBay or Elance can provide access to a wider range of vendors or service providers than most people would normally have. And many of the online services like eBay, Elance, and Amazon provide detailed feedback and ratings from prior customers, so as a buyer you can have a higher level of assurance that the online company you are dealing with is on the up and up, but problems can crop up. Two of the greatest ones for vendors—chargebacks and payment problems—were mentioned above. A customer can also face trouble, as seen in the Small Business Insight box: "My People Might Destroy Your Website."

SMALL BUSINESS INSIGHT

My People Might Destroy Your Website

Henry Richardson was a professor at a small college and had an active consulting business. A lot of the materials he created for individual clients he rewrote in a more general form and sold as pamphlets, short reports, and self-published trade books. He had an informational website, but as the technology advanced he realized he could cut his production costs dramatically by selling his pamphlets, reports, and books as downloadable PDF files. To control this process, he needed a different type of online store—one specialized for the electronic publishing industry. Such programs not only handle the order, but also control the downloading of files so that only bona fide customers can obtain the download. Not finding any electronic publishing sales packages he liked, he decided to have one custom designed.

Henry went onto Elance.com and put up a request for bids for his project. From the 23 responses (ranging from $11,800 to $450), Henry narrowed the field by looking at the customer ratings, track records, and portfolios of the companies. His chosen company had an American sales office and a team of programmers in India. Henry thought this would help provide better coordination for the project. The final negotiated price was $1,800.

Although the project was supposed to be completed in three weeks, Henry never heard from the U.S. or Indian offices, a definite bad sign. Henry got a call from the U.S. sales office in week 4 stating that the project was behind schedule but would be finished "soon." Excuses piled on for two more months. At the end of month 3, Henry sent an ultimatum to the vendor—finish the project or return the money.

This brought forth a call from the Indian office. The company's manager said because they had done "work" on the project, they would refund $1,200, but only if Henry would give a positive review for the firm on Elance! When Henry asked what would happen if he gave an honest rating, the manager said he did not know how his programmers would take such an insult. They *might* just destroy Henry's existing informational website out of anger. Not wanting to spend his days protecting his website, Henry agreed. He later had a local programmer do the site for $4,000.

People who sell on eBay or competing auction sites stores strongly suggest using the auction feature; after all that is what most people think of when they go to the site. Sherry Chase of Fancy That! started an eBay store as a means of getting rid of excess merchandise from her store. She had tried her own website with virtually no luck at first. She found that eBay sales exceeded her expectations. She also found that by auctioning items and including her link in the auction description she got people to her eBay store.[34]

eBay auctions themselves are legendary. On any day 12 million items are available with nearly 2 million new postings a day.[35] There are 150 new items for sale listed every minute, and 500 bids placed during that same minute. There are 69 million eBay users who spend $59 million a day.[36] The eBay method means you pay a fee for posting your product and a sales fee based on the final bid price when the item sells. You have the option of setting a bottom offer you will accept, a **reserve price** (if the bidding does not exceed the price, the sale will not go through), and the number of days the auction will run (out of several choices). Your posting can include pictures of the product and links to more data (like your website).

reserve price
A minimum acceptable selling price in an auction. If the bidding does not exceed the price, the sale will not go through.

eBay allows you a bit of anonymity—all buyers and sellers have screen names. E-mail addresses and limited personal information are only given out in certain circumstances. (Obviously, if you are a successful bidder, the seller needs to know to whom and where to send the merchandise.) eBay sellers may take checks, money orders, or credit cards, or accept payments through PayPal, eBay's own electronic payment system, reducing sellers' risk. eBay also allows buyers and sellers to post feedback about their transactions which produces a score that's displayed by the buyers' and sellers' screen names and allows others to get a feel for how reputable a certain buyer or seller is. This feedback is also available for the public to read. (See Skill Module 5.1 for more tips.)

Checklist for Maximizing Success on eBay[37]

SKILL MODULE 5.1

There are whole books written on how to do well on eBay, but what are the basics that can make the biggest difference? As you prepare for selling via eBay, test your ad and your approach to eBay selling against the checklist below.

DESCRIPTION

1. **Detailed Description?** Use detailed descriptions so that the buyer isn't expecting something different from what you are selling.
2. **Typpppos?** Watch out for misspellings and typos. Experienced eBay buyers use the search engine to find specific things and it won't find your misspelling. Besides, it doesn't look very professional.
3. **Factual Bad News Upfront?** Be honest and factual. Don't say, "slight damage." Instead state that there is an 8-inch chip on the upper right-hand corner and a faint scratch along one side. The buyer can make an informed decision, and there are no surprises.
4. **Got a Positive Feedback Rating?** Since most buyers are somewhat reluctant about buying from a seller with no feedback, try buying for awhile; your feedback rating will grow, and since there is no differentiation between buyer and seller feedback, this puts you in a better position as a seller.

PHOTOS

5. **Photo Present?** A picture is worth a thousand words.
6. **Photo Pretty?** Make sure the photo is not too dark or too light. Does it adequately display your product? Check out backgrounds, too. They can detract from the subject and might even show things you'd rather not display on the Internet.
7. **Photo Fast?** Don't use huge slow-to-download files.
8. **Photo Real?** Showing a photo of a box of commercial software is fine if that is what you are selling. If it is only the CD, without the box and the items included in it (like manuals, jewel cases, registration cards, etc.), it is better to take a photo of what exactly you are selling and include it on the eBay page.

(Continued)

COMPETITIVE ISSUES

9. **Price-Matched the Competition?** See what the competition is doing to see if you even want to try eBay auctions. If your product (or something fairly similar) is selling on eBay for less than you need to meet your profit goals, find another way to get to your customers.
10. **Shipping Not a Rip-Off?** Be honest and up-front about shipping. It is acceptable to charge for postage and a reasonable amount for shipping materials. If you are using recycled boxes, don't charge for them. Some sellers like to use a flat fee for all shipping charges (e.g., $5.00 per paperback book). Experienced eBay buyers will know that for regular U.S. media mail, that price is way out of line. If you're the only one selling that item, they may pay; but if there are a dozen others, they'll shop around or reflect their concerns in the top bid they place.
11. **Terms Match the Competition?** When you find similar products being offered by competitors, make sure you have the same terms on your product page, so people searching on those terms find your page when they find your competitors'.
12. **Time Matches the Competition?** If you are using auctions, try to time your auctions to end after your competitors'. Remember that most people will lose in an auction. If you are offering a similar product, which comes up on the same search with similar costs, and closing right after an auction from a popular seller, many buyers will come in to bid on your offering.

SALES-RELATED SERVICES

13. **E-Mail Ready?** If buyers have a question, they'll e-mail you. Respond as soon as possible, at least within 24 hours. Don't post auction items just prior to going on vacation.
14. **Shipping Promptly?** Package well. Notify your buyers when things have been shipped. If you need to wait for a check to clear and you'll be gone a few days during that time, let them know. Most buyers are prepared to be reasonable if they know what's going on.
15. **Quick Customer Response?** Customer service is very important. You want positive feedback. Dissatisfied buyers may either leave negative feedback or leave no feedback at all on your transaction.
16. **Gave Feedback Promptly?** Give feedback to your buyers, too. First of all, it helps them when making further purchases. Second, if you expect feedback yourself, do it for them. If they see you've posted positive feedback, they are more likely to do so themselves.

SCORING

Score 1 for each Yes answer and 0 for each No answer, then add up each category. 4 in a category is "Excellent"; 3 is "Adequate", and 2 means "Needs Improvement." A score of 1 or zero in *any* category is "Not Ready for eBay," and you should hold off selling on eBay until you have raised your score in this category.

There are restrictions on the types of products that may be sold—for example, anything that is considered fraudulent, illegal, or harmful, as well as anything that infringes on patent or trademark rules. eBay does enforce this policy. For more detailed information about doing business on eBay, check the website www.ebay.com or look at one of the numerous books about eBay, like *eBay for Dummies.*

Although the web traffic counts for eBay and Amazon are extremely high, a wise entrepreneur (even a part-time one) does not rely on customer searches on these sites alone to bring in business. The most successful web entrepreneurs keep using the multichannel marketing approach introduced earlier. Getting the name of your online store into newsletters (electronic or printed), newspapers, trade journals, blogs, or on mass media (local can be just as powerful as national) can help you promote your site to potential customers. Increasingly, entrepreneurs are using the social networking sites mentioned in Chapter 2, like Facebook, MySpace and LinkedIn, to get the word out to friends of your firm as well as potential customers interested in what you or your firm has to say. A quick listing of the other places to promote your site is given in Figure 5.5, The Multiple Channels of Business Promotion.

Figure 5.5 mentions a few other types of sites we have not discussed so far. These include free sites like the video site YouTube.com where you can post a video for free, bookmarking sites like Digg or Del.icio.us where you can identify websites and get these voted on or adopted by readers, and opinion sites like ePinions.com, where customers can post opinions about firms, products, and

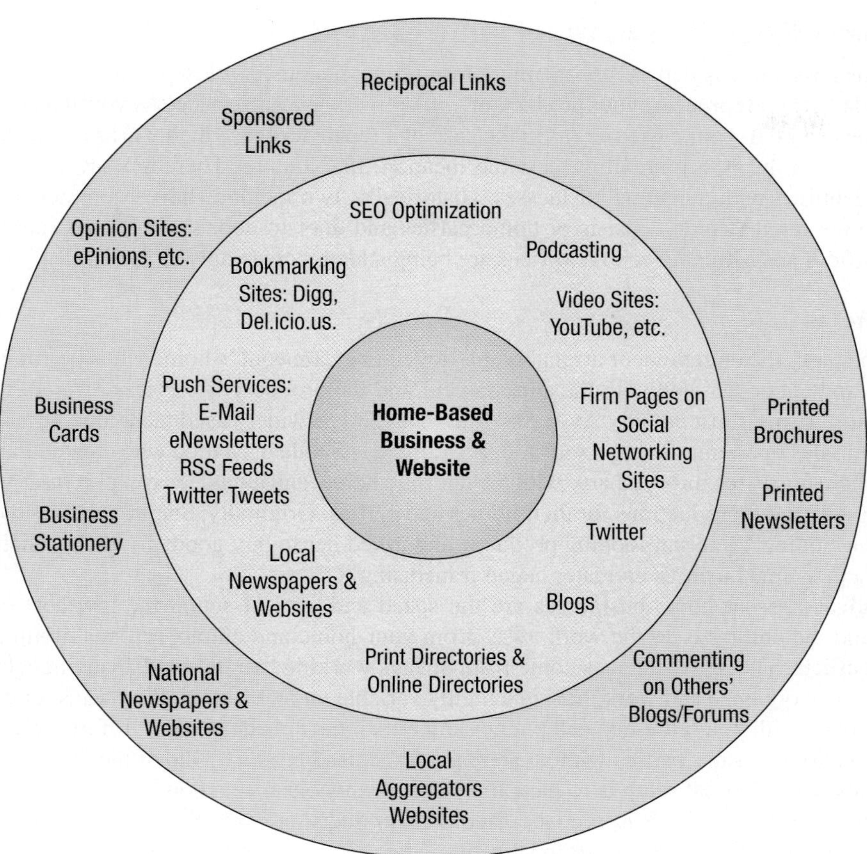

FIGURE 5.5

The Multiple Channels of Business Promotion

services. There is also a free way to get your name (and your business) known, and that is by making informed comments on blogs and discussion forums related to your business. For example, if you are selling laptops, key blogs to show your comments might include LaptopBlog.org or Laptop Advisor.com.

There are also several advertising channels that come with costs. Obviously, the traditional approaches to advertising, like business cards, stationery, printed newsletters, and brochures, cost money (although these days you can print just the quantity you need on a good color printer). There are also old media approaches which are still important. Local and national newspapers (like *The Wall Street Journal*) also have online versions (and online ads). The phone company's local directories also often come with an online version, and there is a new group of local aggregator websites like NewYork.com, which create local directories of members' sites, most often online, but sometimes in print form.

Given the cost of getting into e-commerce, especially with sites like eBay, you can't argue with the resulting success stories. Mark and Robin LeVine sell more than $1 million per year of bubble wrap and other packing materials. Sarah Davis sells over $4 million annually of designer handbags. Although "eBay millionaires" are a minority of eBay sellers, these two examples are by no means unusual.[38] eBay is also successful for business-to-business selling. Farmer Joel Holstad purchased a tractor, a combine, and a cherry picker for about half of what he expected to pay, although eBay no longer has a page "eBaybusiness.com."[39]

Home-based business and Internet business are the two core methods of getting started for part-time entrepreneurs. They can cover a wide variety of retail, wholesale, service, and even simple manufacturing situations (like artisans' work or custom electronics), but there are other approaches that offer quickly deployed, low-cost ways to start part-time businesses. Sometimes these approaches are next steps for home-based or Internet businesses, but in other cases, these approaches can be the first step for a part-time firm.

The Next Best Things to a Home-Based Business

Often, business success depends on getting close to the customer—close enough so the customer can see you, the entrepreneur, your product, or you delivering your service. As you'll learn in Chapter 11, you can go to your customer (as in the case of a repair service which works at the customer's site) or you can go to a mutually accessible location, like a store. There are several approaches closely identified with part-time businesses. Historically, two methods have been mentioned most often—home retail (which consists of home parties and door-to-door selling), and stands. Today mobile offices and virtual/executive offices are being added increasingly to the mix.

Home Retail

At a home party the entrepreneur arranges a get-together at someone's home where participants can socialize and get acquainted with the entrepreneur and the products or services offered. Pioneered by cosmetics firms, most notably Avon and Mary Kay, it is a widely used technique with dozens of franchised sales operations using it today. One example is Sheila di Matteo who created Parties Victorian, where hostesses throw a party with a Victorian theme, and attendees can purchase Victorian-themed goods and reproductions for their homes and parties. Originally, Sheila's friends recognized her skill at finding Victorian-looking products, and asked her to buy goods for them. Sheila turned this into a part-time business and later began franchising it.[40]

The advantages of home businesses are the speed and ease of setup, the low cost of getting started, and the ability to do the work away from your home and employer, thus minimizing potential conflicts. The disadvantages come from always working "on the road," lacking a base from which you can organize and work, having a highly variable income, and finding ways for customers to get in touch with you (although cell phones and e-mail have made a major difference).

You can arrange sales parties without selling a franchised product. One of the ways to make arrangements with minimal setup is to have the party at someone else's home. This person in return gets a portion of the proceeds in product discounts, products, or cash. You and the host work up a guest list, and the arrangements for refreshments and participation presents are agreed to in the early stages of the negotiation. Picking hosts with good contacts and a pleasant home is the key factor in party success. Often the opportunity for repeat customers and customers hosting later parties presents itself, and it's a great way to keep sales growing.

In door-to-door selling, the retailer goes to the home to demonstrate and sell the product. Matching the product to the community is a key factor. For example, it is hard to find good prospects for buyers of seeds if you are working an apartment community. Think about the income and lifestyle of the community with respect to your product.

The fundamental success factor in door-to-door selling is closing the sale. *Closing* means getting the customer to agree to buy. Amazingly, asking the customer to buy is often all that is needed. If the answer is no, the natural comeback is to ask customers what they need to know or have in order to buy. If they tell you something they need, your job becomes trying to meet that need. Meanwhile you continue to ask if they are ready to buy. Only if you cannot meet a need do you give up and go to the next customer.[41]

network marketing
An approach to selling in which the salesperson recruits customers to become distributors of the product or service to others.

Another variation on the home model is **network marketing** efforts, also called multilevel marketing or MLM. These are organized through a parent organization; agents sell in part using in-home parties and person-to-person sales. The added twist is that current salespeople are invited to recruit additional new salespeople. The recruiter gets a commission from the sales made by his or her recruits. Everything mentioned above also applies in network marketing, with the added need to carefully check into the parent organization and the terms of the recruiting. The extra caution is necessary because illegal pyramid schemes are often made to look like legal MLMs. For example, where the fees paid by newly recruited network members are paid directly to more senior network members, there is a good chance you are seeing an illegal pyramid scheme. You can check with the Federal Trade Commission (www.ftc.gov) and the Better Business Bureau (www.bbb.org).[42]

Stand Retail

Stand retailing—the roadside, flea market, farmers' market, or craft fair business—is one of the most ancient forms of small business. It is mentioned in the Bible, and marketplaces full of stands have been found in virtually all archeological digs. Today, stands tend to be either semipermanent ones that remain in one place and are built to be sturdy, like a farmer's roadside stand, or movable ones that can be quickly assembled and disassembled for use in farmers' markets, flea markets, and craft fairs. To get started inexpensively, people often start selling from the back of their cars or using a folding table or blanket laid out with wares.

The advantage of stand businesses is that you can start with little investment. Stands can be a box or ground cloth. They also do not require a lot of investment in inventory. There are a variety of locations where a stand can be set up, such as flea markets. Stands can also be quickly established and easily ended as a business. Stands vary widely in the products they sell. The disadvantages of stands are the variable income they provide; the difficulty of making sure your stand and business meet legal requirements such as compliance with registering, licensing, and zoning (for help with this look at the section "Exchange: Dealing with Others" later in the chapter); the problem of knowing how to price goods; and building up a customer base for your stand.

While stands can be among the least expensive ways to set up a shop, a high-end version exists too. It is the mall cart, if it is on wheels, or kiosk, when it is in a fixed location. Carts and kiosks cost between $2,000 and $10,000,[43] although carts can be rented from many malls. Carts and kiosks are often among the most expensive locations in the mall in terms of rent per square foot. A cart in a high-end mall like the Mall of America in Bloomington, Minnesota, can go for $2,300 or 15 percent of sales a month in rent.[44] Costs include rent (usually a percentage of sales with a base monthly rental), mall member fees, and cart design costs. On the other hand, carts can be rented for specific periods (holiday seasons, weekends). The advantage of carts and kiosks is that your products can be seen by more than 100,000 people a week as they walk through the mall. One idea to minimize rents is to consider placing your cart or kiosk away from the high-traffic locations, but near specific stores where your most likely customers would come from, for example, putting a trading card kiosk near a mall arcade or sporting goods store.[45]

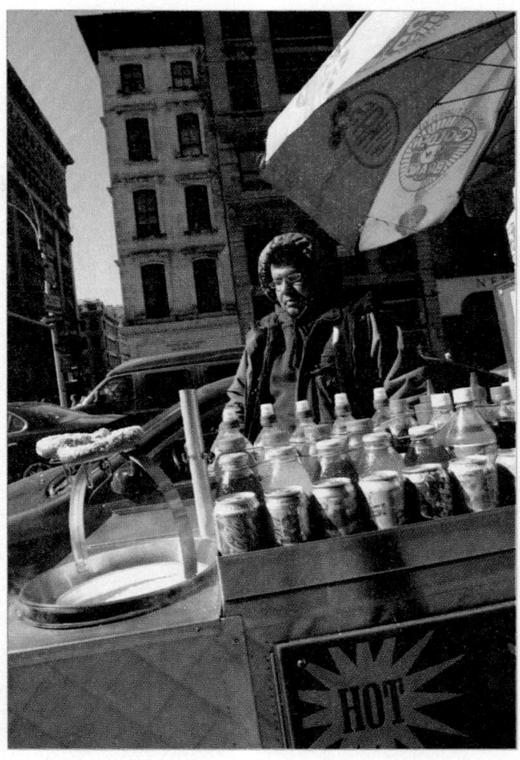

This part-time business worker has his finger on the pulse of a niche market, capitalizing on the limitations experienced by people on the streets of New York who are hungry for a snack. His signs and position on a street corner create visibility and boost market desire for his products. His stand allows him to easily move elsewhere as he perceives needs. If you were positioning in a downtown for lunch and dinner traffic, how would you decide where to move your cart?

The key success factor for a stand is having a location where there is enough foot or vehicle traffic to sustain the business. High traffic concentrations are why flea markets, farmers' markets, and craft fairs are popular locales for stands. However, even in these, locations will have traffic levels that vary. Try to locate on or near a major walkway, or near the food, entertainment, or major vendor areas to get the most traffic. Always make sure to keep your documentation (e.g., vendor's permits, licenses, tax numbers, etc.) handy for checks by police and venue officials.

The other success factor is inventory. You might be selling products you make yourself. The next best thing is to start with what you know. If you have seen someone's work and think it would sell, ask if you can be an agent or reseller. If you are looking for others' products to sell, there are a host of sources (like wholesalers shopster.com and Doba.com) or you can go online to search for products or services to resell at the Industrial Resource Network, or at Thomas Register's online site, which has a print version available in many libraries. You can also do a search online for the manufacturers of particular products.[46]

Mobile Offices

One recent survey suggested that one in six working Americans worked from their cars or trucks. The kinds of jobs that involve face-to-face selling and client services are the ones most likely to be done from a car or truck. There are advantages to this approach. There is no rent, and car expenses can be deducted from tax returns. It places the entrepreneur close to the customer, and typically close to the entrepreneur's printed materials or tools.

The key to a mobile office is a cell phone and a laptop with Internet access and a printer (especially one that can be run from a USB port on the laptop). To keep everything powered, getting a power converter with a lighter plug will usually do the trick. What many mobile teleworkers initially forget is how important it is to have a comfortable place to write and mark up written reports—working behind the wheel gets old fast. Berny Coffee was an early entrepreneurial leader

Today cell phones and laptops with wireless modems make it possible to run your business from your car. For a one-person, part-time business that wants to get close to customers, there is no better arrangement. What kind of features would you want in a car if you were going to use it as your primary office?

in teleworking. A yacht broker in Alexandria Bay, New York, Berny manages a network of 35 brokers from his car. The key for getting his work done is his cell phone, and a WavBoard wireless router, which connects him to Verizon's EV-DO wireless network from wherever he is located. He runs it through a power converter plugged into his cigarette lighter. With the router working, he can even ditch his cell phone and call around the world for free using Skype. With this approach, Berny was even able to stay in business from Florida during a hurricane when people had no electricity and few cell phones worked.[47] These days, if you have a 3G or 4G cell phone or one of the 3G/4G wireless modems for your laptop, you should be able to mimic Berny's feat.

In terms of the car or truck, make sure it can accommodate you, all your equipment and, files, and your telework equipment (and can handle the drain on the car's battery over the long term). It is also important that it provide adequate and comfortable accommodations for passengers. You may not drive them often, but you are likely to have them in the car for business discussions.

Virtual Offices, Executive Offices, and Incubators

When stresses in the home are making the home office problematic, but your business is not ready for a full-time rental, one approach is to look at outsourcing your office. A virtual office is actually the next step to most business web hosting packages. In addition to handling your e-mails and newsletters, a virtual office typically gives you access to your files, as well as web-based fax services and, most typically, full business telephone services including phone trees, voice mail services and often additional phone-based services such as reminders, and call forwarding based on the time of day. Major players include Regus.com, Onebox.com, and Hq.com.[48]

Executive offices provide small amounts of short-term space for an office or work area. They can be furnished or unfurnished, and provide basic utilities. They often have preferred vendor arrangements for phone services (which may not always be the best deal—keep using your cell phone) and low-cost shared services such as copying and telephone answering by a live receptionist. Regus and HQ also offer such services, as do InstantOffices.com and IntelligentOffice.com.

Another solution you might find interesting is to see if you can rent space in an incubator, which was introduced in Chapter 1. Incubators are community-based organizations designed to help small businesses. For-profit incubators are very similar to executive office operations, although usually with somewhat lower prices. Not-for-profit incubators are often sponsored by universities, economic development agencies, or localities themselves. They tend to offer heavily subsidized space, shared services like executive offices, and almost always offer on-site expert advice about running small businesses. The key online directory for incubators is run by the National Business Incubator Association at nbia.org.

Doing Business without a Business Organization

Artists, artisans, authors, inventors, small-scale manufacturers, collectors of antiques or other collectibles all have one thing in common. They possess something they would benefit from selling. Often, these people start small, often part-time, businesses to do that. However, many others prefer to stick to their creating or discovering and let someone else handle the selling process. The kind of businesses that do this are called a variety of names such as consignment shops, auctioneers, or sales agents.

Regardless of the name, the basic business model remains the same. The agent (we will use this term for the person running the consignment businesses) will take on the product of the creating or discovering or manufacturing part-time entrepreneur. Some agents charge a basic fee up front to cover initial expenses. Some do not. All agents make an effort to sell the product they were given. When sold, the agent gets a portion of the sale price, with the remainder going to the part-time entrepreneur who employed the agent.

Let's look at two different types of consignment situations—eBay consignment shops and intellectual property agents. An eBay consignment shop starts with you dropping off your item. The consignment shop photographs the item, prepares a description, and posts it on eBay. When the item is sold, they ship it to the buyer and send you your share of the sale price. There are several national franchise chains offering drop-off consignment services like 877isoldit.com, AuctionItToday.com, and SnappyAuctions.com. There are also hundreds of small, independent local consignment stores. An excellent listing of eBay drop-off stores can be found at consignmentpal.com. Although there is wide variation in pricing, the eBay consignment stores generally charge a percentage (around 40 percent for the smallest items, with less for larger sales) for their work.

Intellectual property (often abbreviated *IP*) refers to original works like inventions, visual and performing art works, books, and computer programs. We will learn about the many ways to legally protect IP in Chapter 18, but for now just think about how you might get money for some IP you have created. There are a variety of agents who specialize in different types of IP. Experts (often lawyers by training) called IP agents usually focus on placing inventions, computer programs, and manufactured products with companies willing to pay to add to their complement of new products. Sometimes companies will buy competing IP to prevent their competitors from getting it.

intellectual property (IP)
Property coming from some sort of original thought, for example, patents, trade secrets, trademarks, and copyrights.

For works of art, there are a variety of specialized art agents. You have probably heard of book agents (also called literary or publishing agents), and there are similar types of agents for designs and paintings. Recall the story of Aaron McGruder which started this book? Once he learned how hard it was to place a cartoon strip with newspapers and get a good deal doing so, he found the best artist agent he could to find the most motivated seller possible to help him structure a deal that got him the money, ownership, and editorial control he wanted.

Regardless of the type, you can find listings of agents through a Google search using the terms given above. Finding the right agent for you requires some additional research. While an agent close to where you live means you would be able to meet face-to-face, local agents may lack the contacts in the major corporate, manufacturing, media, or artistic centers where your work could get its best offer. Some suggestions for how to find a good agent include:

- Checking out the agent's biography and track record, as well as searching for articles confirming their accomplishments.
- Often there are a couple of local lawyers in the nearest big city who have experience dealing with agents from the major cities. It may be possible to get referrals from them.
- Don't be afraid to write someone in your field whom you respect and ask for their recommendation. They know a bit about their business, and may be able to give you some direction.
- Often faculty in your college or university may have experience with, or connections to, agents. Look for faculty who have done any mass media work (best-selling books, national TV, movies or radio, nationally sold designs or works of art, and faculty with patents, etc.).

In all forms of consignment relationships there are a few things you should always consider. For any consignment, make sure there is a written contract outlining what the consignment agent will do to sell your product, what the costs and fees are, and how they get paid (some will come out of the selling price, others may be paid up front). It is also crucial to have a clear description of the product and any variations, parts, pieces, and manuals included. For physical products and works of art, the description should mention the condition of the items and any blemishes—photos help.[49]

The advantage of consignment approaches is that they permit full-time sales with only a part-time involvement from you, low setup cost, a low risk level, and the flexibility that comes from the variety of consignment agents and agencies available to you. The disadvantages can include little effort being put forth to sell your product, high potential for competing offerings, long amount of time before payouts, and lower profitability because of agent's fees.

Success Factors for Part-Time Businesses

LO4 Use the BRIE model to describe what it takes to be successful in part-time entrepreneurship.

Research indicates that most service and retail firms typically start out as a hobby.[50] There are many different ways to start a part-time business. Consider for example the way Courtney Hennessey got CodiJewelry going. The BRIE model introduced in Chapter 1 can point out many of the key factors

SMALL BUSINESS INSIGHT

COURTNEY HENNESSEY AND CODIJEWELRY

Courtney Hennessey of CodiJewelry.com did not intend to go into the jewelry business. It just grew. During Christmas break of her junior year at Saint Louis University, Courtney decided to make stretchy crystal bracelets for her friends as holiday presents. When she left the bead store, she had another problem—she had spent $400 on beads and string, and she needed to make the money back before her father found out. Courtney became a walking ad for her bracelets and sold them throughout the holiday, including at a family wake. Eventually the business grew to have in-person and online retail sales as well as wholesaling to stores, including Neiman-Marcus. Eventually Courtney won a Global Student Entrepreneur Award for innovative thinking.

Courtney Hennessey, the founder of CodiJewelry.com, began her small business part time out of the necessity to recover her Christmas giftmaking costs. Like many others highlighted in this chapter, her part-time business afforded her the chance to earn a reasonable profit while carrying on with her other life priorities.

you need to think about. Intention is usually where part-time businesses start in the BRIE process, and we talked about key resources—such as inventory or competencies—earlier. Let's go further to address the other two other aspects of the model for part-time businesses: boundary and exchange.

Boundary: Separating and Balancing Business and Home

Time is central to balancing home and business. It is important to organize a business around a schedule that makes sense for you. Internet-based businesses let you work any time that is convenient for you. For Courtney, having time during Christmas break was critical. Operating on weekends at roadside stands or at flea markets or farmers' markets is the best way to structure time that is convenient for you and your customers.

Either way, time management, as discussed in Chapter 3, is the crucial skill for juggling your part-time business and the rest of your life. The key device for managing time is the to-do list. To be effective, the list needs to be with you at all times. You can get by with a small notepad, or can go for preprinted organizers, such as those from Day-Timer or Franklin Covey. You can even go electronic, using a personal digital assistant like a Palm PDA or cell phone with calendar and to-do list capabilities built in.

When using a to-do list, be sure to list the key information such as due dates and contact information if it applies. Most entrepreneurs find that it also helps to prioritize the list. One of the simplest ways to do this is 1-2-3 ordering. Those activities that are absolutely essential to your business or life are coded 1. Those that are current but of lesser importance or that can be rescheduled if necessary are assigned a 2. Activities that you want to do when you have some extra time or that have due dates far in the future get coded as 3. Typically, owners keep a to-do list of 6 to 20 items per week, and they reprioritize on a daily basis.[51]

For people with a part-time business, the to-do list includes items from business and personal life. For students, tests are probably a 1 priority. For parents, children's extracurricular activities are also 1s. Often family and personal lives make demands that put business and the rest of life in conflict.

Having some general rules to help sort out these conflicting demands helps. Fred Kiesner, an entrepreneurship professor at Loyola Marymount College suggests six key ideas:[52]

1. Do not waste time complaining; do something about a problem.
2. Do not aim for perfection; "good enough" really is good enough.
3. Do not dwell on the past; just plan to do better next time.
4. Minimize your time spent in meetings, or schedule meetings to be short.
5. Schedule and protect quality time with your family.
6. Schedule and protect some time for yourself to have fun.

The majority of part-time businesses are based in the home. The business takes space, uses resources the family also uses, and generally places stress on the household. Keeping a clean boundary, like an area known as the "business corner," helps make sure that family and business are protected from each other.

Exchange: Dealing with Others

There are two key groups outside your business with whom you must deal—government and customers. Even part-time businesses have to deal with government, and three issues pop up repeatedly: registration or licensing, taxes, and zoning which was discussed earlier in this chapter. For businesses run from a home or commercial venue like a fair or consignment shop, most states and localities require some form of **registration**, but the requirements vary so it is important to check. The U.S. government has a web page with links to state registration information at http://sba.gov. On the site, click on the menu item, "Register Your Business." Read through the article, "5 Steps to Registering Your Business." Links to state requirements are included within the article.[53] It is also important to check whether your business needs special **licensing**. For example, home-based beauticians need state licensing, and in many states home-based day-care providers need to get special registration and, in some cases, licensing.

registration
Information provided to the government concerning the existence of, name of, nature of, and contact information for your business.

licensing
Documented permission from the government to run your business.

Even when you do not have to register a business, you need to keep track of your sales in order to pay your income taxes later. Although taxes are discussed in Chapter 13, it is useful to mention here that you want to keep track of your costs, too, because if you itemize your deductions on Schedule C, you can deduct your costs from your income (and a lower income means lower taxes). In many states and localities, you must also pay sales taxes, and these often need to be kept in a separate bank account and tracked as well. Often, flea markets and craft fairs include temporary local tax numbers in the booth rentals, but it is important to check.

Pricing and Costing

Because exchange is the way businesses make profits, it is important to price your goods or services to make profits likely. Folks working part time can be prone to underestimate their costs. Using things found around the house or neighborhood or not adequately considering the cost of the time you contribute are typically what lead to underestimating the cost of a product or service. Taking some time to think through the real cost of your product or service is critical to your success. Central to figuring the real cost is recognizing that your own time has value. When you price your product or service to pay yourself what you could get working part time for someone else, then you have achieved a real milestone on the road to growing your business.

Pricing is also often seen as a challenge by part-time businesses. Even if the business is part time, that does not mean the prices have to be cut-rate. One good way to get an idea of realistic pricing is to price competitors' offerings. Doing some window-shopping in person, via catalog, or on the Internet is the classic way. Once you know the kind of price your product or service can get and once you know your costs, then you are in a great position to know the kind of profit it's possible to make in your business.

What Are the Challenges of Being an Entrepreneur Part Time?

LO5 Describe the advantages and pitfalls of delegating and outsourcing.

Four aspects of part-time entrepreneurship are very different from full-time business. Gaining legitimacy and trust among customers is discussed in Chapter 2. Three other key aspects remain: determining what you are able to delegate, the special ethical challenge that comes from juggling part-time entrepreneurship and other work, and the challenge you face when you try to move from part-time to full-time entrepreneurship.

Delegation and Outsourcing

delegation
The assignment of work to others over whom you have power.

outsourcing
Contracting with people or companies outside your business to do work for your business.

For part-time entrepreneurs, time is the ultimate resource. While the most successful entrepreneurs in high-growth ventures are those who learn to get and leverage other people's money (OPM), for entrepreneurs in part-time businesses the key is leveraging other people's time (OPT). There are two major ways to do this—delegation and outsourcing. **Delegation** happens when you assign work to those over whom you have power, usually people you employ, those volunteering to help you out, or family members. When you employ outsiders who are not your employees to handle all or part of a functional area of your business, it is known as **outsourcing**.

Delegation makes sense in two situations. The first is when others can do things better than you. For example, an entrepreneur who is a wizard at sales may be totally lost doing the books. The second is when you want your business to operate when you are not present, or operate in two places at once. If you have two people working in a store, you could be selling to two customers at once. Done well, delegation frees the owner to pursue those things that make the biggest difference in the business—key sales, strategic thinking, negotiating, or inventing. It is a powerful concept, and there are several tips that can help make any delegation effort more successful.[54]

- Start delegation with simple tasks to get you and your employee used to the process.
- Match the task to the person with the best skills and attitude for it.
- Be specific about what outcomes you want from their work.
- Solicit questions from your employees about the delegated work.
- Attach a motivating outcome to the delegated work—a chance to learn new skills or demonstrate leadership, increased visibility, or an opportunity to see more of the business or its customers.
- Allow time for the employees to learn the task and correct the inevitable early mistakes.
- Give employees feedback about their performance soon after they start.
- Hope for perfection in performance, but be satisfied with good enough.
- Once delegated, do not take responsibilities back. When problems arise, remedy them, rethink your approach, and retrain the employee.

Delegation is not for everyone and every situation. It makes the most sense when you have people who are good at their jobs and trustworthy, but with some additional steps, delegation can work in less than optimal situations. Even with these tips, being able to delegate depends on the owner's ability to trust others and on the quality of the people to whom the owner can delegate. When delegation is essential but it is hard to trust employees, checking up on an unpredictable schedule helps keep the employees on their toes and provides maximum assurance to the owner. When trust is high but employees lack skills, the owner should allow time to train them and monitor their work—frequently at first, but less often as they prove they know their jobs.

As noted earlier, when you employ outsiders who are not your employees to handle all or part of a functional area of your business, it is known as outsourcing. The most popular types of outsourcing among small businesses are shown in Table 5.3.

In the nineteenth and twentieth centuries, the idea behind automation was to save time. If you can get a computer program or another company to do work instead of you, you save time, and that is good. Table 5.3 shows that the most technical aspects of a business—issues such as law, computers, or financial records—are the areas in which outsourcing is most likely to occur. This provides some insight into how to think about outsourcing. In areas in which expertise is hard to come by, changes frequently, or is an important support to the functioning of the firm, it makes sense to outsource. The

TABLE 5.3 What Do Small Businesses Outsource?[55]

Legal issues, 78%	**Sales**
MIS	Advertising and marketing, 37%
Website hosting, 70%	Finding new customers, 29%
Computer technical support, 57%	Public relations, 21%
Website design, 55%	Customer service, 6%
Database management, 18%	**HRM**
Accounting and Financial	Payroll, 26%
Accounts receivables, 50%	Recruiting and hiring, 20%
Financial advice and management, 48%	Training, 16%
Bookkeeping and accounting, 30%	
Collections, 27%	

Source: Dun & Bradstreet (2002).

other key idea for outsourcing is to never outsource what *defines your distinctive competence*, what you think makes your business unique. Consider the example of Gourmet Gatherings.

Gourmet Gatherings' "symphony" suggests the kind of careful involvement and oversight needed to make outsourcing work. Activities that are central to the strategy of the business, like cooking and running the cooking groups for Gourmet Gatherings, stay inside the firm. Activities that are not strategically critical are outsourced, especially when they can be done better or more cheaply by outside firms.

Making Do When You Are Starting Out

LO6 Explain the benefits of Bootstrapping methods for entrepreneurship.

Bootstrapping—finding a low-cost or no-cost way to do something—is a popular approach for all businesses and essential for part-time firms. It is especially important for firms early in their lives because one of the major threats to the survival of firms is **undercapitalization**.[56] Running out of money before the business is self-supporting is a major threat. This can come from a shortage of

bootstrapping
Using low-cost or free techniques to minimize your cost of doing business.

undercapitalization
Not having enough money available to the business to cover shortfalls in sales or profits.

SMALL BUSINESS INSIGHT

GOURMET GATHERINGS[57]

Bibby Gignilliat has bounced from job to job. She was a programmer, bookseller, travel agent, bike tour guide leader, public relations representative, and marketing manager before she started as a cook teaching for HomeChef and later on San Francisco television. Her prior skills equipped her for a special project, using cooking as part of a team building exercise for a group of lawyers, and later for a group of 40 businesspeople. This led to the idea for Gourmet Gatherings, which provides culinary entertainment "designed to inspire conviviality, camaraderie and confidence in people who appreciate good food."

Armed with a strong network of contacts, Bibby partnered with longtime friend Shannan Bishop (their fathers were partners in a brokerage business). Bibby's varied experience had an interesting side effect—she knew all the kinds of work she did not want to do. So she and Shannan outsourced every function of the business except the recipes, menus, and leading the gatherings. Their financial, marketing, legal, and web work were all outsourced. They describe their role as "conducting a symphony of specialists" and argue that they could never have grown if they had to do everything themselves. Besides, it was the cooking that was fun, not the bookkeeping.

cash in the business or even from a shortage of cash in the owner's personal life, since for small businesses starting out the two are often drawing from the same resources.[58] The key ideas of bootstrapping are simple:[59]

- Do without as long as you can.
- Cut your personal and business expenses to the bone (e.g., no salary, work from home).
- If you need something, see if you can get it for free (like help from SCORE or former professors), borrow it, barter your time for it, or rent it before you buy it.
- If you need to buy outside services, consider offering **equity** instead, but be stingy with this.
- Before you buy, see if you can substitute a lower-cost alternative (e.g., a printing calculator and lock box instead of a cash register).
- If you buy, buy used or at a deep discount, and always ask if you can stretch out your payments to minimize cash flow.
- If you need money, borrow it from yourself first, then from family, then friends, and after that banks, credit card advances, and finally, credit companies, in that order.
- If mortgage rates are low, consider first or second mortgages to put money into the business, if you are comfortable risking your house.
- To minimize debt, use a cash card like American Express, which requires repayment in 30 days, instead of a credit card.
- When you use a credit card, limit purchases and keep your credit balance as clear as possible.
- And always, always keep track of your cash!

equity
Ownership of a portion of a business.

One key to making bootstrapping work is leveraging low costs with free expertise. One way to do this is to set up an advisory board. Andy and Chad Baker, founders of the CashCard Coupon Company, recognized the value of seeking advisers and were surprised at how easy it could be to find experts interested in helping a fledgling business.

The Baker brothers were able to obtain lots of help from advisers while keeping their business small. There are many people from whom you can get free expertise for your part-time business, such as: bankers, insurance agents, trade and professional association officers, former or retired entrepreneurs, and public business development organizations such as your local SCORE or Small Business Development Center. In Chapter 2, Skill Module 2.3 gives you the specifics for successfully getting others to help you.

One area of bootstrapping which is growing quickly is the availability of high-quality free software useful for small businesses. For example, 37signals.com got started using free open source programs to build applications such as a project management program, which they offered for free over the Internet. Today, a small start-up can get even more of the tools it needs for free. Look at Table 5.4 and the Online Learning Center for examples. Note that in many cases you can use web-based programs (using an Internet connection) or have the free programs reside on your personal computer.[60]

For more free software explore the Free Software Directory project (http://directory.fsf.org/) and sourceforge.net. Note that free programs and websites often have limited support. However, many offer help files and discussion groups, and some offer e-mail support if you can wait a day or more. If you choose a free program, consider picking one which offers pay-as-you-go support as an option, or better yet, bootstrap help by picking software or websites already used by friends.

Ethics and Part-Time Small Business

LO7 Describe the ethical challenges of part-time entrepreneurship.

It is impossible to gain legitimacy for your small business if your ethics are in question. There are two situations in which part-time entrepreneurs are particularly at risk: moonlighting and aggrandizing.

Moonlighting

Often, the most successful small businesses build from the business expertise and personal contacts of the entrepreneur. However, managing this without offending your current employer, or getting into legal or contractual trouble, is not easy. Working on your own part time after your regular job is called **moonlighting**, and it poses particular risks.

moonlighting
Working on your own part time after your regular job.

TABLE 5.4 Essential Free Software and Web Services for Small Businesses

	Open Source*	Web Based
Basic Business Suite (like Microsoft Office)	Openoffice.org	ThinkFree.com drive.google.com
Project Management (like Microsoft Project)	OpenWorkbench.org	Basecamphq.com
E-mail (like Outlook)	Mozilla Thunderbird	Zimbra.com
Knowledge Management (like PeopleSoft)	www.bitfarm-archiv.com/	Mediawiki.com
CRM—Customer Relationship Management	SugarCRM.com	Freecrm.com
Social Networking	Elgg.com	LinkedIn.com
Financial Projection Creation	Exl-Plan Free (www.planware.org/exlfree.htm)	Vpspro.com
Accounting Program (like Quickbooks)	Grisbi.org, Turbocashuk.org, freeaccountingsoftware.net	Waveaccounting.com Numia.biz
PDF File Creation (like Adobe Acrobat)	Openoffice or Pdfcreator (sourceforge.net/projects/pdfcreator/)	Pdfonline.com
Desktop Publishing (like Adobe Pagemaker)	Scribus.net	www.fatpaint.com
Paint Program (like Adobe Photoshop)	paint.net (get it at getpaint.net) Gimp.org	Sume.fm

*All open source software offer versions which will run under Microsoft Windows.

SMALL BUSINESS INSIGHT

CashCard Coupon Company[61]

Andy and Chad Baker operate a business called the CashCard Coupon Company. Initially selling advertising to businesses in Bloomington, Indiana, the company manufactures distinctive signs predominantly for restaurants and bars. Just after starting their business, they sold some products to Rodney Wasserstrom, a Columbus, Ohio, businessman, but their delivery times were very slow. Because they were feeling bad about their service to him, Andy and Chad sent him an explanatory letter along with free coupons to a trade show—not realizing that Mr. Wasserstrom was owner of a nearly $250 million business in Ohio. Getting a huge kick out of the letter, Wasserstrom became both a great customer and a mentor with unparalleled marketing experience. Since that time the Bakers have received mentoring help from others—in one case two brothers that they read about in an article in *Inc.* magazine. Having gone to the same college as these brothers, the Bakers had an immediate connection. The Bakers note that they "always seek out the best people in a given field when [they] get involved in that field." They note that if "you are not aware of anyone to advise you, just contact your local Chamber of Commerce or pick up a newspaper. We have found that simply sending a letter explaining that you are interested in some advice normally elicits an 'I would be happy to meet with you' response."

conflict of interest
A situation in which a person faces two or more competing standards or goals.

cannibalizing
Taking business away from your employer.

poisoning the well
Creating a negative impression among your employers' customers.

aggrandizing
Attempting to make your business or yourself seem more accomplished or grander than reality.

The major concerns are conflict of interest, cannibalizing sales, and poisoning the well. Conflict of interest crops up when people do work for their part-time business while they are at their full-time job, blurring the boundary between them. **Conflicts of interest** happen when what is best for your part-time business is different from what is best for your full-time employer or when people cannot be sure which of the two firms you represent. The key is to keep your full-time and part-time jobs clearly separate. For example, do not contact customers of your part-time business when you are at your full-time job.

Cannibalizing means taking business away from your employer. This can come from your taking sales away from your employer or taking working hours away to do your own business. This is a real problem if your part-time business is similar to your full-time occupation, for example, if you are a painter for a building contractor in your day job and do similar sorts of painting as your part-time moonlighting enterprise. In such cases, the usual course is to get your employer's approval at the start. This, however, may be easiest to get when the kinds of work you are doing, or the kind of clients you have, are *not* like those at your day job. In fact, it is often possible to get your boss to refer customers to you when they fit your type of schedule, pricing, or type of work a little better than that of the bigger enterprise.

Poisoning the well refers to creating a negative impression among your employers' customers. If you use your business contacts through your day job as the basis for your part-time self-employment, you will inevitably find some customers who do not want to hear your sales pitch. If, because of this, they tell your employer they are less likely to buy from him or her, your part-time business has hurt the full-time one. The traditional work-around for this is to develop a separate customer list without names from your full-time job and then wait for your employers' customers to ask you about this other business they hear you've started.

Aggrandizing

For a part-time small business, achieving legitimacy and business respect can become a driving force. Occasionally, the entrepreneur sees an opportunity that is possible, but a stretch. If it looks like a stretch to the customers, the entrepreneur may start thinking about making the firm seem bigger, more substantial, or more capable than it really is. This misleading impression, called **aggrandizing**, can spell the death of a firm if discovered at an inconvenient time. As discussed below, this was the lesson Jeremy Barbera encountered in the early days of his business.

Jeremy Barbera "got away with it." He lied quickly and easily, no one checked up on his firm, and he was able to meet his obligations. However, if his aggrandizing had been exposed before he could prove himself, he would have lost all credibility. Jeremy says that an entrepreneur has to take risks to get ahead. When Jeremy started his firm, checking up on a firm required time-consuming investigations or credit reports, so Jeremy's risk was perhaps not so great. Today, with credit reports and business directories available online in seconds, the potential for being found out is much higher, and the risk is greater.

The most typical form of aggrandizement is implying that a firm is a full-time one when it is only part time. Recall from Chapter 2 that it is hard for a part-time firm to achieve the legitimacy of a full-time firm, and there can be a strong temptation to make the firm sound like it is a regular nine-to-five business. Remember that in the end, however, the biggest risk is that of losing the trust of your current and potential customers. In a small business, especially a part-time one, the owner *is* the business. If you cannot trust the owner, you cannot trust the firm.

Moving from Part-Time to Full-Time Entrepreneurship

LO8 Describe the challenges of moving from part-time to full-time entrepreneurship.

Some people start their businesses part time with hopes of moving to full-time operations when the time is right. For them, landing a major contract or sale may be the financial and marketing indicator of the right time. Others start part time and want to stay that way, and they can face challenges when they achieve success. The strains of producing goods or services for a voracious market can make staying part time difficult.

In deciding whether to make the move to full time, the key question is usually financial. If you are already employed full time somewhere else, the move to full-time entrepreneurship means taking a close look at your financial situation. Can you afford to go on your own? This means having enough

SMALL BUSINESS INSIGHT

METRO SERVICES GROUP INC.[62]

Trained as a physicist and employed by NASA, Jeremy Barbera started Metro Services Group as a part-time business on his kitchen table with his "partner," his mutt Luka. Of the $900 he invested in the business, $200 went to rent a Madison Avenue mailing address at a local incubator to help his business look more professional. Selling direct-marketing services to financial and entertainment firms, Barbera was a one-person operation, but he consistently stretched the truth. For example, he used "we" and "us" when talking about the firm. He would promise a prospective client to have his secretary type up the proposal and courier it over before 5 P.M., but it was Jeremy who did both.

This once came close to backfiring. Jeremy had delivered the proposal in the afternoon, dressed as a delivery person, and reappeared the next morning for the follow-up meeting with the CEO, this time attired in suit and tie. An alert security guard informed the CEO's office that the delivery man claims to have a meeting with the CEO. Jeremy told the guard and CEO that the delivery man was his brother, down on his luck. Jeremy's favorite line was, "It all depends on the light you portray yourselves in." Jeremy made MSGI look bigger than it was until it landed its first contract—with American Express.

to cover personal and family expenses (typically for six months), as well as business expenses. There may also be new costs, as you scramble to replace employer-provided health insurance.

The way to determine the financial situation of a business is through crafting a business plan such as the one you will learn about in Chapter 8. Having a business plan helps you work out all the major details of the business and how you plan to organize it as you are growing it. For example, Nancy Bombace of Mill Valley, California, took the time to do a business plan before taking her part-time honeymoon registry service, HoneyLuna, full time. By doing the plan, she learned she needed to keep her full-time job and run HoneyLuna on the side to make ends meet.[63] In addition, bankers, lawyers, big corporate customers, consultants, and potential investors will ask you for your business plan, so it makes sense to do one to show you have done your homework in starting a full-time business.

There are several ideas to keep in mind to help in this transition. First, it often makes sense to wait until there is a solid income likely for the business before moving over to full time. Second, make use of any transition services your former employer offers, such as COBRA health coverage (look at www.dol.gov/dol/topic/health-plans/cobra.htm to get information on this from the U.S. government). Third, recognize that initially at least you will spend nearly all your time running and marketing the business, so it makes sense to change over when your family and personal obligations are at their lowest and support from family and friends is at its highest.

Often people move into full-time entrepreneurship by building their part-time work to longer hours, until they have, in effect, two full-time jobs. Done this way, sleep, family, and personal time take a hit, but as a financially secure way to operate, the two jobs approach is great when done for short periods.[64]

Like the work of Nancy Bombace, Jeremy Barbera, Pamela Williams, Sheila di Matteo, Courtney Hennessey, or Kathryn Otoshi, part-time entrepreneurship is around you all the time. Millions of people are working at part-time businesses of their own. Whether in retail or wholesale, selling service or products, they or their wares are in our stores and our markets, on our streets, and in our homes. Part-time entrepreneurship is important because it gives people a chance to learn the ropes in business and to test out their ideas. It also is often the only way people can engage in entrepreneurship amid their other responsibilities. Part-time entrepreneurship is important as a test bed for starting full-time, larger firms and as a means of self-reliance and self-expression. However, as long as a few minutes online or simply saying, "I can do that for you" to a neighbor is all it takes to start a part-time business, it will remain an option that lots of potential entrepreneurs are certain not to overlook.

CHAPTER SUMMARY

LO1 Describe when and why part-time entrepreneurship makes sense.

- It makes sense when you need to gain basic experience.
- It makes sense when you lack the resources for a full-time business.
- It makes sense when you face a narrow window of opportunity.

LO2 Assess the feasibility of opportunities to enter into a part-time business.

- Part-time entrepreneurs typically want a low cost to start the firm.
- Part-time entrepreneurs typically want a short time to start the firm.
- Part-time entrepreneurs typically want a firm to appear permanent.

LO3 Describe the major paths to part-time entrepreneurship.

- Home is where most part-time businesses start.
- Care for preparation of your home office and family are essential to home-based business success.
- For almost all part-time businesses, having an effective website is key.
- Websites can be informational and/or e-commerce in purpose.
- E-commerce can also be done through eBay or similar sites.
- Key issues are optimizing visibility and managing the payment process.
- Home retailing includes shopping parties, door-to-door selling, and network marketing.
- Key issues for home businesses include having a good hostess for shopping parties, or a solid technique for closing sales in door-to-door selling.
- Stand-based businesses include roadside stands, flea markets, farmers' markets, and fairs.
- Key issues for stands are location, where traffic is high, and having adequate inventory.
- It is possible to make money without opening a business by using the consignment process through shops or specialized sales agents.
- The key for success in using the consignment process is having your product presented to the right market.

LO4 Use the BRIE model to describe what it takes to be successful in part-time entrepreneurship.

- Use the BRIE model to help identify key boundary and exchange issues.
- *Boundary*—you need to manage your time carefully and keep business and home separate.
- *Exchange*—you will need to register with the government, pay your taxes, and comply with zoning regulations. You will also need to keep careful track of your costs including the cost of your own time.

LO5 Describe the advantages and pitfalls of delegating and outsourcing.

- Delegation is getting others to do your work. It can help an entrepreneur to get more done.
- Managing the delegated work and the people performing it is a key challenge for the entrepreneur.
- Outsourcing is paying experts to take on the functional tasks of your business.
- You may outsource to experts anything but the tasks that make your firm unique.

LO6 Explain the benefits of bootstrapping methods for entrepreneurship.

- Bootstrapping means making do with little or no money.
- Keep your costs down, do without, borrow instead of buy, buy used or at a discount, and check out the other bootstrapping techniques listed.
- Bootstrap expertise by creating an advisory board.

LO7 Describe the ethical challanges of part-time entrepreneurship.

- The two ethical challenges of part-time businesses are moonlighting and aggrandizing.
- Moonlighting can result in cannibalizing sales from your employer or poisoning the well by making your employer's customers angry.

- Aggrandizing can happen when a part-time firm tries to present itself as a full-time one or a bigger one than it really is.

LO8 Describe the challenges of moving from part-time to full-time entrepreneurship.

- The key challenges of moving to full-time self-employment are mainly financial.
- Do a business plan to assess your financial situation in the new business.
- When you make the move, do it when support from your family and previous employer are at their strongest.
- Consider increasing part-time work hours until you are working at two full-time jobs, and then quit to devote your full time to your firm.

KEY TERMS

part-time self-employment, 122
full-time self-employment, 122
volatility, 122
cost to start-up, 123
time to start-up, 123
permanence, 123
zoning laws, 125
covenants, 125
variance, 126
e-commerce, 128
informational website, 128
business-to-consumer (B2C), 128
business-to-business (B2B), 128
consumer, 129
blog, 129
RSS feed, 129
tweet, 130
multichannel marketing, 130
reciprocal links, 130
search engine optimization, 130
sponsored link, 130
reverse auction, 133
reserve price, 135
network marketing, 138
intellectual property (IP), 141
registration, 143
licensing, 143
delegation, 144
outsourcing, 144
bootstrapping, 145
undercapitalization, 145
equity, 146
moonlighting, 146
conflict of interest, 148
cannibalizing, 148
poisoning the well, 148
aggrandizing, 148

DISCUSSION QUESTIONS

1. What are the three situations in which it might make more sense to go into business part time rather than full time?
2. If you were going to start a home-based consulting business in a dorm room, what do you think would be the greatest challenge to face? What about if you were starting the same business from home?
3. The two major types of business websites are informational and e-commerce. What are the differences between them?
4. Is it possible to sell products on eBay without having an online store? What would be the advantages and disadvantages of doing so?
5. How would you use multichannel marketing to promote your part-time businesses? If you had to use one of the nonfree approaches, which would you choose and why?
6. What are the differences between party and door-to-door retailing?
7. When managing your time using a to-do list, how do you go about prioritizing the list? Why?
8. What kinds of tasks do small businesses most often outsource? Why do you think they are popular tasks to give to others?
9. Of the two ethical problems prevalent to part-time small businesses (moonlighting and aggrandizing), which do you think is the biggest problem for entrepreneurs? Why?

EXPERIENTIAL EXERCISES

1. Search for art fairs in your area using Google maps. In the search box type "art fair" (leave off the quotes when you type) and the city and state you are checking on. When you look at the results, try the links for category searches to see if you get a narrower set.
2. Check the kind of licensing you need for a part-time business in your state. Go to **www.business.gov** and click on "Register, Licenses & Permits." Type in your business's zip code or city and state and use the drop-down box to get the type of business. Note that there are several different types of permits, licenses, and certifications needed from nearly every level of government.
3. Research pricing your product or service electronically. Go to eBay.com (if you are selling a product) or eLance.com (if you are selling a service), and enter the term for your product or service. From the resulting list, note the offerings that most closely match yours and check the prices posted. If possible, look for recent sales or contracts for your offering to see what people paid for the goods or services.
4. Create your own first-pass customer base. List family members; friends; people you know from religious, fraternal, civic, and school organizations; and people who provide you goods and services. Look at the list again and select five people who you think are most likely to know the kind of person you would imagine would make your best customer.
5. Create a to-do list for the upcoming week using the technique described in the chapter. Prioritize your tasks using the 1-2-3 method, and use the list for a week. Ask yourself if you felt having the list helped you remember better what you had to do and if it helped you better decide what to do and when to do it.

MINI-CASE

TIM HAYDEN'S LAST VACATION

In the four years since missing St. Louis Cardinal Mark McGwire's 70th home run in St. Louis' Busch Stadium in 1998, Tim Hayden had been toying with the idea of creating some sort of electronic device to let people attending a sports event enjoy the same sort of video and informational graphics that people who watch the game at home enjoyed. He even figured out the technology needed. He would use a PDA with Wi-Fi capabilities, "hardened" through its construction and tough case to be able to withstand liquids and the kind of rough handling you would expect among spectators at a sporting event. He would call it SkyBOX. In his spare time, he pursued the SkyBOX idea with sports managers, advertisers, computer people, and with everyone he met.

A tech-savvy marketing manager by trade, Tim knew what the user interface would look like. Having no budget for his part-time business, he had to talk friends into putting together a flash graphic of what his service would look like. (You can see the graphic on the Online Learning Center.) He had also thought about how he could make money with SkyBOX, and how he could get the major sports leagues to support SkyBOX.

Meanwhile, he continued his day job as the director of marketing and sales for a local advertising firm. He knew to make SkyBOX work he would need to leave his employer, but he wasn't sure how to decide. He was making good money and liked his work, but he was also likely to get moved from straight salary to more of a commission basis to help grow the business. He had a girlfriend. A lifelong St. Louisan, he had an active social life with his friends. He was close to his family, and they lived nearby.

The moment of truth came during a vacation Tim and his parents took in the summer of 2002 to visit family in Florida. Trading introductions around a pool, the man to Tim's right turned out to be the entrepreneur who founded the multimillion-dollar Val-Pak mailer business, Terry Loebel. Hearing about SkyBOX from Tim, Terry was relentless: "What's your business model?" "What's in it for the league and teams?" "Are you the right person to carry this off?" Under the hot sun, beers in hand, Tim and Terry went back and forth. In the end, Terry gave Tim a look that said, "You done good kid." A little while later, Terry left.

For the rest of the afternoon, Tim kept thinking, "I did it. I really did it!" He held his own and showed his business off well enough to impress a very successful entrepreneur. He knew his business, and he knew his stuff. Maybe he was ready to go for it full time.

Over dinner, he mentioned his experience to his parents—a corporate entrepreneur and a self-employed HR consultant. Suddenly a raft of questions hit him he wasn't prepared for, questions like "What will you live on?" and "What about your girlfriend?" With a lot more difficulty than that afternoon, Tim started answering questions. As he got more into it, he felt maybe he was on top of the personal dimension of the prospect of going full time.

CASE DISCUSSION QUESTIONS

1. People talk about entrepreneurs depending on luck. Tim saw Terry Loebel only that one time. Their conversation was one of the factors leading Tim to decide to go full time with Vivid Sky and the SkyBOX. Was it luck on Tim's part? Was there anything Tim was doing to improve his luck?
2. Tim had concentrated on mastering the business and technology angles of the SkyBOX, but was slightly taken aback when asked about how his personal life would change if he went into entrepreneurship full time. If you were contemplating a full-time entrepreneurial career, what are some of the personal considerations you think might be important?
3. Why would Tim's employers' plan to change business directions make becoming a full-time entrepreneur more attractive?
4. Tim felt he needed to go full time to take the SkyBOX "to the next level." Can you think of ways he could have continued building up the SkyBOX while sticking with a part-time approach? What would have been the downfalls?

SUGGESTED CASES AND ARTICLES

- The Ambitious College Kid Who Just Can't Wait, C-5

Available on Create

- Virginia's Yarn Shop

SUGGESTED VIDEOS

www.mhhe.com/katz4e

Video Case:

- For a written video case and corresponding clip, visit the OLC at www.mhhe.com/katz4e and select "Chapter 5".
- Magno-Grip

SBTV.com Videos:

- Legal Issues for Home-based Business—They're All Illegal
- Selling Internationally on eBay
- Creating a Successful E-Commerce Website
- Small Biz: Breaking the Home Office Barrier
- Home Offices—Is It Time to Move to Office Space?
- 5 Ways to Get Your Home Office Organized

CHAPTER

6

Small Business Entry: Paths to Full-Time Entrepreneurship

● Thomas Caldbeck created a successful construction business in San Antonio, Texas. What problems and challenges would you expect to encounter in starting and growing a construction business in southern Texas?

LEARNING OBJECTIVES

After you complete this chapter, you will be able to:

LO1 Describe five ways that people get into small business management.

LO2 Compare the rewards with the pitfalls of starting a new business.

LO3 Compare the opportunities with the pitfalls of purchasing an existing business.

LO4 Explain four methods for purchasing an existing business.

LO5 Compare the advantages with the disadvantages of buying a franchise.

LO6 Explain the issues of inheriting a family-owned business.

LO7 Describe how hired managers become owners of small businesses.

Focus on Small Business: TLC Remodeling LLC[1]

Thomas Caldbeck was in an uncomfortable position for an owner of a small business. He had put in many years and untold hours in starting and growing a successful contracting business in San Antonio, Texas. Now, however, he was facing a shrinking real estate market and increasing competition from huge national builders such as Pulte Homes and KB Home. His business had been reduced to the point that he was seriously considering just walking away.

"I'm a third-generation builder," Tom said. "My grandfather was in the Army Corps of Engineers during World War II on Guam where he worked laying concrete for runways."

After the war, Tom's grandfather returned to Des Moines where he started a pre-cast concrete company. Soon the business branched out to on-site concrete finishing, which led to setting up a rough-in carpentry business.

Tom said, "I started working for Grandpa before I was 12 years old. As I grew, I did more and more different jobs. By the time I graduated from high school I was a skilled rough-in carpenter. I did pretty well at concrete finishing, too."

After high school, Tom moved to the Los Angeles area where he quickly found full-time employment with a rough-in crew. By his 21st birthday he was foreman of five rough-in carpentry crews. For a single man, the pay was generous, and Tom was living large.

Of course, romance got in the way.

"Once I started thinking about marriage and a family, I realized that I couldn't make it in LA. The cheapest house I could find that I would even consider buying was still over $220,000. This was 15 years ago, and even though I was making about thirty bucks an hour, I couldn't begin to afford a quarter-of-a-million for a house." Tom said. "I decided to move to San Antonio where one of my uncles lived. The cost of living was much lower, but the wages for carpenters was about the same."

In San Antonio, Tom went to work as a supervisor for Continental Homes. When new home sales sagged in 2001, Tom was laid-off, and then immediately hired back as an independent contractor. Tom was now a self-employed entrepreneur.

He found that he was making more money as a contractor than he had ever done as an employee. Even better, he was his own boss—able to turn down jobs that he did not want; and able to set his own hours and work schedule. Once again, things were looking up.

In 2002, with $7,000 of savings and a bank loan, Tom purchased power tools and a van body truck. He built racks in the truck to hold his tools and supplies. An unused bedroom was turned into an office and his two-car garage was converted into a workroom and storage area.

Things began to change in 2010. Although San Antonio escaped the worst of the 2008–2009 recession due to a backlog of long-term projects, by the middle of 2010 Tom was running out of work. He was forced to lay off employees, and he found himself accepting smaller contracts than he would even have considered just a year earlier.

Then in 2011 Tom encountered a set of serious setbacks that nearly broke his company. He took a contract to rebuild a historic house in the King William area of San Antonio.

"This job nearly killed me," he said. "I absolutely could not please the owner. It got to where I was doing every part of the job twice and still she would rant and rave and declare that the work was not acceptable. Of course, then she started holding back my progress payments. It was a nightmare!"

Finally, Tom and the owner agreed to disagree. Tom was paid wages for the work completed and he left the job. His next two jobs were also disasters. On the first, a plumber who contracted to lay new sewer and water supply disappeared for over a week, leaving open a 5-foot deep ditch and preventing any progress to be made on the job.

The next job required pouring and finishing a concrete slab for a local artist's studio.

"I really should have done the concrete work myself," Tom said. "But I just didn't want to mess with it. So I hired a contractor who had worked for me several times. Everything seemed ok."

But when Tom's framing crew began to rough-in the building, everything was off-square.

Tom said, "The slab was poured on a slant. The far back corner of the slab was more than 1 1/2 inches lower than the diagonal corner. Sure, it was my responsibility to check everything, but how does anyone make such a mess of a 24 by 48 foot slab? I had to break it out, reform, and repour the whole slab. I'm still trying to get something back from the sub."

Since then, Tom has been doing remodeling work. To his surprise, he has discovered that he likes the work, and he is able to make a profit doing it. In fact, he recently filed a Texas LLC under the name, "TLC Remodeling." He has had business cards printed, a web site published (www.tlc-remodeling.org), and new signs made for his truck.

Tom said, "Always in the past I refused to do remodeling. I often said that remodeling was just one terrible surprise after another. But I have found that I can show the problems to the owners and by working with them, arrange a fix even if it means billing them more."

"You know," he said, "I really like working alone. If I need muscle, I can always get it for a few hours or a day. I'm really considering just quitting the general contracting and specializing in remodeling. The jobs are smaller. I can finish each in much less time. It just doesn't have the headaches of running a contracting business."

DISCUSSION QUESTIONS

1. In what ways is Tom's story like that of a "typical" entrepreneur?
2. What experiences that Tom had in creating and growing his business would be considered bootstrapping?
3. If remodeling is such a pleasant and profitable business, why would Tom (or anyone else) be conflicted about "walking away" from a failing construction business?
4. Suppose you are a consultant to small business. What advice would you give Tom Caldbeck?

LO1 Describe five ways that people get into small business management.

The Five Paths to Business Ownership

There may be "50 ways to leave your lover,"[2] as the song states, but there are only five ways to get into small business management:

- You may start a new business.
- You may buy an existing business.
- You may **franchise** a business.
- You may inherit a business.
- You may be hired to be the professional manager of a small business.

franchise
A legal agreement that allows a business to be operated using the name and business procedures of another firm.

Although everyone gets into business by one of these five paths, the specific details of going into business are unique to each person.[3] **Start-ups** may be deliberate, well planned, and financed. On the other hand, many start-up businesses "just happen." Often a compelling hobby slowly morphs into a profitable business, or a chance occurrence leads to a new business venture. Purchases of existing businesses may occur in any number of ways, from cash purchases to "earn-outs" in which the business is bought over a period of time with money earned from the business. Franchises may range from "turnkey," in which every part of setting up the business is handled by professionals, to those in which the only thing that is franchised is the right to use the business name. Some business managers work their way to the top from a beginning part-time employee position. Other professional managers are recruited to become the chief executive. It is common for hired management to use leveraged **buyouts** or employee stock option plans to purchase the firms for which they work. This chapter examines the details of these paths of entry into small business: start-ups, purchasing, franchising, inheritance, and professional management.

start-up
A new business that is started from scratch.

buyout
The purchase of substantially all of an existing business.

Starting a New Business

LO2 Compare the rewards with the pitfalls of starting a new business.

Starting a new business is at once the most risky path into business and the path that promises the greatest rewards for success. The success rate of start-up businesses is a matter of some controversy. As we note in Chapter 1, while the Small Business Administration (SBA) reports that 66% of new employers survive two years or more, 50% survive at least four years, and 40% survive more than six years,[4] those businesses that get help last much longer. Eighty-seven percent of start-ups that begin in business incubators are still in operation five years later,[5] and the survival rates for students from entrepreneurship programs and entrepreneurs seeking help from Small Business Development Centers are about twice that of businesses in general.[6] Even for those who get help in starting their business, one must admire the courage and optimism of a person who chooses to start a new business (see Figure 6.1). Despite the rather high failure rate, creating a start-up is not, as some maintain, a triumph of hope over reality. Many businesses that end do so not because they failed, but because the owner took advantage of a better opportunity.[7] The rewards, both financial and personal, of starting a successful new business can be most impressive.

Advantages of Start-Ups

There are many reasons that people choose to start a new business rather than purchasing an existing business, franchising, or being an employee:

- A start-up begins with a "clean slate." There are no existing employee problems, debts, lawsuits, contracts, or other legal commitments that must be satisfied.

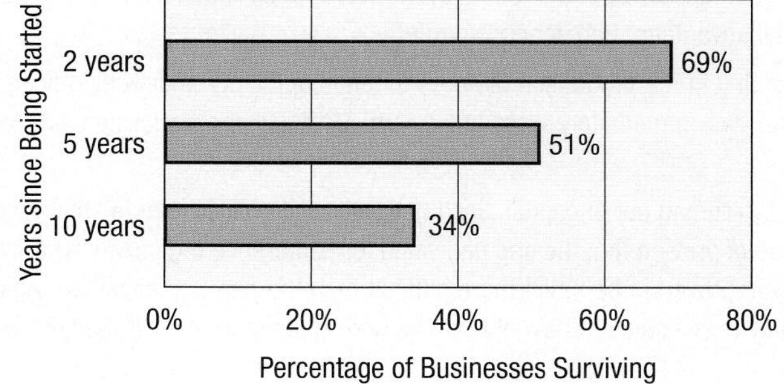

FIGURE 6.1
Survival Rate of Start-Up Businesses

- A start-up provides the owner with the opportunity to use the most up-to-date technologies. There are no "legacy" locations, buildings, equipment, or software that can hamper productivity.
- A start-up can provide new, unique products or services that are not available from existing businesses or franchises. Existing businesses and franchises exist because of their success in providing proven products and services.
- A start-up can be kept small deliberately to limit the magnitude of possible losses. A purchased business or franchise requires immediate and constant **cash flows** to meet ongoing obligations.

cash flows
The actual receipt and spending of cash by a business.

Disadvantages of Start-Ups

Offsetting the advantages of starting a new business are several disadvantages:

- A start-up business has no initial name recognition. An existing business or franchise has invested in developing its market. The brand rights can guarantee immediate acceptance of the business.
- A start-up will require significant time to become established and provide positive cash flows. An established business or franchise has built-in customers to provide immediate cash inflows.
- A start-up can be very difficult to finance. Established businesses and franchises provide immediate **assets**, sales, and cash inflows that can be used to obtain financing for the business.
- A start-up usually cannot easily gain **revolving credit** from suppliers and financial institutions. An existing business or franchise often has lines of credit that transfer with the business.
- A start-up may not have experienced managers and workers. Established businesses and franchises provide experienced workforces, training, and management support.

asset
Something the business owns that is expected to have economic value in the future.

revolving credit
A credit agreement that allows the borrower to pay all or part of the balance at any time; as the loan balance is paid off, it becomes available to be borrowed again.

SMALL BUSINESS INSIGHT

Surviving a Startup

While still in college, Josh Fraser and his roommate, Rob Johnson, were contracted to develop a social networking app for a single business conference. The resulting product used information from the attendees' registration, thus achieving 100% inclusion for the conference.[8] Information included profile pictures, biographical information, and tags to allow users to sort on common interests, sessions to attend, etc.

The partners put together a presentation of proposed features and were accepted by TechStars which provided mentoring and seed capital in the amount of $10,000. One of the mentors, Noah Kagen, agreed to use the product in an upcoming conference that he was producing. This led to a successful angel funding round in which approximately $500 thousand was raised.[9]

EventVue was on its way.

But sales did not materialize. The product, as designed, worked only among registered attendees of any specific conference. Although the app was popular with conference attendees, it did not provide conference organizers any financial advantage. Rob Johnson wrote:

> . . . instead of investing in the production features to [enable] EventVue directly driving people to events (hindsight: mistake), we immediately went out and tried to sell the social network tool to conference organizers.[10]

The firm was rapidly running out of capital. Josh and Rob made a last-minute "hail-mary pass" by attempting to address the issue of proving that the app had value for conference organizers who were the actual paying customers. Development proved to be much more difficult than the partners expected. Again they attempted to sell the app "as is," only to see sales remain elusive. As Rob Johnson wrote, " It really is too little, too late."[11]

Creating a New Business

The vast majority of start-up businesses are "me-too" enterprises. The business idea is simply to create another occurrence of a common business: a beauty shop, a restaurant, a bar or lounge, a rock band, a sign company, plumbing service, yard care, and so on. Starting a copycat business provides some protection from business failure. It is not necessary to define the business to the market because everyone knows what a beauty shop, restaurant, or lounge provides.

On the other hand, this type of start-up can be very difficult to differentiate from other similar businesses. Often, the only competitive advantage may be the location of the start-up. This is why owners of common businesses go to so much effort to try to make a difference between their business and other, essentially identical, firms. An example is how Morton's of Chicago and the Ruth's Chris steak houses operate. Careful sampling of each firm's steaks reveals no significant difference in price, quality, tenderness, size, or taste. The restaurants have similar menus and wine lists. Each, however, has distinctive interior decorating and presentation of their meals. Morton's brings a selection of huge uncooked steaks to each table for patrons to make their choices. The cooked steaks are served on oversized china plates. Ruth's Chris provides equally large steaks, selected from a printed menu, served on plates that are heated to a high temperature to create the trademark "sizzle."

Amy Conti, of San Antonio, provides an example of an accidental business start-up. She initially did babysitting for a few friends. When demand for her services exceeded her available time, she began having some of her friends, whom she knew to be competent, sub contract for her. She required her "subs" to have advanced Red Cross first-aid certification and she closely supervised their sitting engagements. Her strict standards and ability to pay for standby sitters has made her service unique. The high reliability of her service and the confidence that parents have in the abilities of her sitters have made a business that is usually considered to be a part-time thing for the girl next door into a professional and profitable business for its founder.

The specific concept that leads to a start-up business usually comes from the experience of the person starting the business. Two-thirds of all start-ups are based on ideas from prior work experience, hobbies, and family businesses.[12] These businesses are generally more likely to succeed than are businesses based on ideas from other sources. Research into the indicators of successful start-ups shows that one of the best predictors of success is the level of experience of the **founders**. Random events, suggestions from friends and associates, and specific education courses are the sources of only a relatively few start-up ideas.

founder
People who create or start a new business.

Increasing the Odds of Start-Up Success

The probability of creating a successful start-up is increased greatly when the founder has certain attributes and when the founder takes certain actions. Doing the following things has been shown to be the most effective route to success (see Exhibit 6.1).

EXHIBIT 6.1

Top 12 Indicators of Start-Up Success

1. Start the business in a business incubator.
2. Take part in a mentoring program.
3. Have a detailed start-up budget.
4. Produce a product or service for which there is a proven demand.
5. Secure outside investment.
6. Start with more than one founder.
7. Have experience managing small firms.
8. Have industry experience.
9. Have previous experience in creating a start-up business.
10. Choose a business that produces high margins.
11. Start the business with established customers.
12. Build trust in your "story."

- **Start the business in a business incubator:** A business incubator is an organization that provides financial, technical, and managerial help to start-up businesses. Most incubators are associated with economic development agencies and are integrated into the community. Incubators provide access to angel investors, public grants for seed money, and technology support.

  Business incubators are created to strengthen the local economy by helping create jobs through the establishment of successful small businesses. But incubators do much more than just create new jobs. They aid in the commercialization of new technologies, the revitalization of distressed neighborhoods, and the creation of wealth. The best incubators provide inexpensive office space with full-time on-site managers who can assist the entrepreneur in many ways. Incubator participants share common office services, such as telephone answering, and production and copying of documents. Perhaps most important, incubators provide legitimacy by furnishing the business with a location and with established business processes.

- **Take part in a mentoring program:** Successful business owners and corporate executives do well by doing good. They can, by helping others, in a way repay the many people who helped them achieve success. Executive volunteers contribute their time and energy to assisting start-up and struggling small businesses as a public service. Because of their experience, mentors can help you avoid mistakes and make good business decisions.
- **Have a detailed start-up budget:** The start-up phase is usually the most difficult time you will have in business. You are required to make myriad decisions concerning location, product, target market, promotion, sales, and all the facets of starting and operating a business. And you must juggle all these demands while simultaneously seeing that you have enough cash. A detailed start-up budget provides a road map for necessary spending during the start-up phase, when cash inflows are likely to be small or nonexistent. Companies that carefully plan their start-up activities and avoid any unnecessary spending are much more likely to succeed.
- **Produce a product or service for which there is a proven demand:** It is an unfortunate fact that most new products and services fail to gain acceptance. NewProductWorks of Ann Arbor, Michigan, maintains a "failed product museum" that contains samples of over 73,000 items, all of which were commercial failures. During the dot-com bubble of 1998–2001, many businesses started with novel and completely untested products and services. Examples are Beenz .com, which was started to facilitate Internet transactions; webvan.com and yourgrocer.com, both of which sold groceries online for home delivery; and estamp.com, which offered online purchasing of U.S. postage, to be printed on the user's printer. All four of these businesses failed to gain success with their products. None of these businesses survived the "dot-com" bust of 2001, although the domain and patents of e-stamp.com were purchased by the currently operating company, stamps.com.

  Large corporations, such as Procter & Gamble or Sony, spend millions of dollars annually testing the market acceptance of new products. Despite their huge resources and years

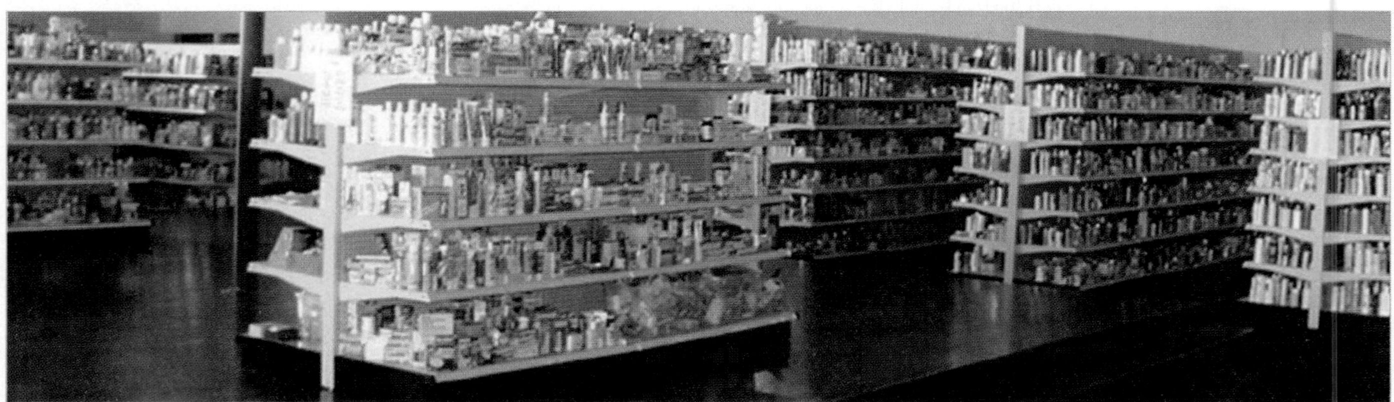

Keep your business's products and services out of NewProductWorks' failed product museum by testing the demand for your ideas before attempting to implement them. What are some ways and means available to small business owners that can help determine market needs for new products? [NewProductWorks Failed Products Museum Ann Arbor, Michigan.]

of experience, they regularly introduce products that fail. (Are you old enough to remember "New Coke"?) Your start-up business will not have either the experience or the resources to absorb the loss from product failure. By producing a product or service for which there is a proven demand, the risk of product failure can be reduced or eliminated.

- **Secure outside investment:** Securing outside investment accomplishes two things: First, the process of obtaining investment funds means that your business will be critically examined by outsiders who have no vested interest in your idea, product, or service. Second, the fact that you were able to convince outsiders to invest in your business indicates a level of belief in the business and you that provides legitimacy.
- **Start with more than one founder:** Starting with more than one founder provides the business with more experience, skills, and resources than can be furnished by a single individual. Having more founders in the business also provides an opportunity for **synergy**, in which the business results are greater than the sum of the input. Multiple founders can also provide a forum for examining ideas, evaluating information, and making good business decisions.

synergy
A combination in which the whole is greater than the sum of its component parts.

- **Have experience managing small firms:** Managing a small business requires attention very much like that displayed by a person spinning plates on sticks. As a performer must move quickly from plate to plate, many demands of small business management require that you have the ability to quickly move from task to task, without allowing any task to ultimately go uncompleted.

  The process can be overwhelming for inexperienced managers. Those entrepreneurs who have experience in small business management are more likely to be able to meet the many simultaneous demands of guiding a successful start-up than would a person new to small business.
- **Have industry experience:** Each industry has its own peculiarities. Only through experience can you learn the methods, sources, and markets for any specific one. Even simple tasks, such as buying necessary material, can be nearly impossible without industry knowledge.

  For example, suppose that you plan to start a quality steak house, similar to Ruth's Chris or Morton's of Chicago. Where do you buy prime beef of the required cut and quality? How do you cook the meat? Or, consider making high-tech, lightweight bicycles. Where can you buy titanium tubing? What does it cost? What do you need to cut, shape, and weld it? How will you sell the bikes? Are bicycles sold through wholesalers? Are they sold directly to bicycle shops? Or maybe you want to start a sign company to make sand-blasted signs. Where will you buy the resist material to protect the wood you don't want blasted away?

  The less you know about something, the easier it appears to be. A true expert makes a task seem effortless. Watching Tiger Woods play golf might lead you to believe that it is an incredibly easy game. Just stand up, hit the ball, and watch it fly to the green. Sure it's easy: So why do fewer than 2 percent of golfers ever make a course par? The same is true of business. Businesspeople, such as Michael Dell, Scott McNealy, and Warren Buffet, make the process of succeeding in business seem effortless. But if you have been in the business, you know better. Being experienced won't make your start-up easy, but at least you have firsthand knowledge of how your industry works that will make your task easier.
- **Have previous experience in creating a start-up business:** "Nothing succeeds like success." In the 150 years since Dumas made this famous statement, it has come to be an unquestioned part of our language. It is just succinct enough, just truthful enough, to seem like a universal truth. For entrepreneurs, it is fortunate that the statement is also not completely true. Although one may learn from successes, most learners acquire expertise through a process of repetition, which only occasionally results in successes. One study of entrepreneurs who had successfully created a start-up business found that on average an entrepreneur suffered three start-up failures before achieving success. Thus it is more nearly correct to state that no entrepreneur succeeds without having prior experience in failing.
- **Choose a business that produces high margins:** High margins, the amount by which sales prices exceed product costs, provide a buffer for lots of mistakes. The single greatest hurdle to a successful start-up is obtaining and maintaining sufficient cash to support both operations and growth. When margins are low, loss of any one sale or customer has an

immediate effect. However, the problem of replacing the lost margin is much easier if you have to make only one or two sales or get one or two new customers to make up for the lost business.

spin-off
A business that is created by separating part of an operating business into a separate entity.

- **Start the business with established customers:** When you start with established customers, you know that you will immediately have cash inflows. There are basically three ways that you can go about obtaining committed customers prior to start-up: (1) You can start your new business as a **spin-off** from your current employer's business. (2) You can start a business to specifically go into competition with your employer. (3) Or, you can start a business to subcontract services to your employer or to other established businesses.

  (1) Creating a spin-off is a regular business practice that is done by businesses of all sizes and at all stages of development. Some spin-offs are created to get rid of "noncore" activities. By disposing of the noncore activity, the parent firm reduces capital requirements and provides a tighter focus for management on the remaining businesses. Other spin-offs are created when the parent lacks either the interest or the resources to pursue the opportunity. By being spun off, the start-up can gain access to resources other than those of the parent.

  (2) Going into competition with your current employer is also a common practice. Of course, this almost always results in resentments and often ends in lawsuits over issues of trade secrets, rights to intellectual property, and abridgment of contractual provisions. You will have to make difficult ethical decisions. From a legal point of view, the contract between employer and employee is satisfied when all wages and other benefits have been paid in return for you accomplishing the tasks for which you were hired. Absent a specific contract providing otherwise, neither party, employer nor employee, is obligated beyond this exchange. However, not so easily answered are the questions: (1) Is it ethical to use your employment to build relationships with customers that subsequently can be used to start a new business? and (2) Is it ethical for you to use knowledge and skill received through training and education furnished by your employer to go into business competing with your employer?

  (3) Subcontracting services to an existing business is somewhere between doing a spin-off and starting a competing business. Services that are often contracted include sales, janitorial services, accounting, research, and product development. It is a common, accepted practice for the contractual relationship to be created prior to starting a business.
- **Build trust in your "story":** Building trust is essential to the success of all start-ups. You must be able to convince suppliers, employees, and, most importantly, customers that the business is now successful and will be in the future. Not only is there an understandable reluctance for people to be associated with a potential "loser," but customers, vendors, and employees all take risks by doing business with an unknown and unproven start-up.

  Suppliers are often reluctant to deal with start-ups, even if you make your purchases in cash. Most new businesses are small compared to established businesses in the same industry. There is a good reason why you, as the owner of a new business, would prefer to make numerous orders of small quantities of the goods and services you need. Doing so reduces cash flow requirements and reduces the risk of your being stuck with old or obsolete inventory. For the vendor, however, accepting your frequent small orders greatly increases the cost of providing goods and services to you. Most vendors, especially wholesalers, work on very small margins. The cost of accepting and filling numerous orders for a new customer may well make such business unprofitable. It is, therefore, essential that the vendor believes in your eventual success and that you will become a valuable customer in the future.

  Employees take on significant risks when they go to work for a start-up business. Not only may the start-up fail, but frequently the cash flow problems of start-ups cause payments for wages to be late or missed entirely. This is one reason why so many start-ups offer stock options and stock bonuses to employees. The start-up doesn't have enough cash to pay high wages right now, but if it's successful, employees will share the rewards in the future.

  Customers can similarly be at risk when purchasing from a start-up business. In the event that the start-up fails, there is no recourse for warranty problems, for maintenance, or for upgrades to the product. This risk is especially acute when the product or service of the start-up affects the core business of its customers. For example, the San Antonio Bed & Breakfast

Association contracted with a start-up business to develop and maintain a web-based availability and reservation service for the association's members. The start-up failed during the dot-com bust of 2001. When problems with the system subsequently developed, there was no one to fix them. The system was complex and the source code incomprehensible. As a result, the association lost a core service that provided value to its members.

The issue of building trust in your story is a catch-22. If customers, vendors, and employees do not have trust in the entrepreneur and in the business, quite simply, there is no business. However, there must be a business, or you don't need customers, vendors, and employees. There are several ways for a start-up business to build trust and legitimacy, and these are detailed in Chapter 2. Specific examples for the kinds of businesses discussed in this chapter include obtaining a performance bond that will pay vendors and customers if your business fails. Restaurants, lodging establishments, barbers, beauty shops, and other businesses that deal with issues of cleanliness as a business requirement can obtain licenses and join industry groups that perform inspections. Displaying licenses and certificates of inspection provides assurance that you are at least meeting minimum standards. Manufacturing businesses and construction businesses may hire engineers to certify design and construction details. Warranty service can be contracted to an independent company that specializes in providing such services. Rigorously maintaining business procedures that ensure on-time delivery of products and services and on-time payment of bills, wages, and loan payments will, in time, result in the start-up being trusted.

Many businesses have been successfully created which lacked one or more of these indicators. It is also true that many start-up businesses have failed, despite having all these characteristics. No one knows what makes the difference between such successes and failures. Some have speculated that the one indispensable trait of people who create successful businesses is determination to make the business work.

"LEAN" Entrepreneurial Methods

You may have read or heard about the currently popular idea of the "lean start-up." "Lean" is the latest name for a set of tried-and-true methods that can lessen the capital requirements and, as a result, reduce the financial risk of a start-up. We discussed the similar concept of bootstrapping in Chapter 5. You remember that bootstrapping includes methods for "finding ways to achieve desired business goals and objectives when start-up capital is limited." Both lean operations and bootstrapping are based on and share three underlying ideas:

1. **Waste not, want not.** That this thought appears in a 1576 book when Shakespeare was a mere 12-years-old tells you how old this latest fashion is. Avoiding waste is one obvious way to achieve this, but so is borrowing something rather than renting it, and renting rather than buying. Making do with an older but free laptop would be another example, as would saving every penny you can.
2. **Create, standardize, repeat.** About the same time as Shakespeare, shipbuilders in Venice created a ship made of standard parts. It made creating subsequent ships much faster and easier. You do this when you make a form letter to solicit customers, when you create a cell phone app that thousands of people can download, or when you buy in bulk to save money. Some firms standardize their most important characteristics so customers get the same result wherever they buy, for example, in franchise restaurants. If your most important characteristics are built uniquely, you can still benefit from standardizing by applying it to the supporting, repetitive aspects of your business.
3. **Keep in touch.** Central to the lean start-up is being close to your customer. It helps you know if your product or service is doing its job. It alerts you to problems earlier so you can correct them, and it is just a good business practice in general. Customers and their needs change, and to keep up, you need to keep in touch. As you learn what is needed, adjust your product or service to optimally fit needs. Most cell phone apps get updated every few weeks. This is because as the app makers find out about bugs or glitches, they can fix them and get the fixed version out to users.[13]

Today's lean start-up and bootstrapping stress the need for creativity and innovation in all aspects of business start-ups and operations. Eric Reis, the modern father of the lean start-up writes that

SMALL BUSINESS INSIGHT

JULIA DALTON AND ULTIMATEKEYCHAINS.COM

While Julia Dalton was a business student at Saint Louis University, she did an internship at a local Internet e-commerce provider, MonsterCommerce. One of the subsidiaries of MonsterCommerce was a website that sold keychains, UltimateKeychains.com. MonsterCommerce received the firm when business got bad and UltimateKeychain's founder defaulted on his bills to MonsterCommerce. Julia was assigned the business as one of her projects. The owners of MonsterCommerce, and now UltimateKeychains, had bigger fish to fry.

Julia realized that the business could be turned around. She asked what it would take to buy UltimateKeychains, and her bosses actually gave her the business for free. Julia restocked the inventory, updated the website, and began to make money almost immediately. She still kept working at MonsterCommerce and continued to bounce ideas off of her bosses to keep UltimateKeychains on top of its game. For her work, Julia won Saint Louis University's campuswide 2005 Global Student Entrepreneur Award.

start-ups should attempt to produce the "minimum viable product," ship it to paying customers, measure its success, apply what is learned to improving the product. There is an older quality control model that checks for problems before the product leaves the firm, and where safety is an issue, that is the best way to go. But for many other types of products or services, the minimum viable product approach is a better one.

Thomas Caldbeck, whose story introduces this chapter, exemplifies many aspects of the lean approach. He did not start into business until after he had mastered the basic management skills needed for success. His garage, van truck, and a spare bedroom in his home became his business location. He expanded into additional areas of business only after a customer had been obtained for that service. This way Tom relied on revenues to provide funds for growth. He maintained close contact with customers to ensure that they were satisfied with the work he was doing. He used his own funds for the start-up and leveraged their value by using bank financing for his truck and equipment. Part-timers and subcontractors who are paid only for work actually completed, met the need for employees.

Your current employer may provide assistance if your new venture is not going to be a direct competitor. Often, a new product or service idea arises from the work being done in the current employment of the start-up founder, as in the case of UltimateKeychains.com. The employer may, however, have no interest in pursuing the opportunity. In such cases, the start-up may well proceed with the employer's active support.

If at First You Fail . . .

What do you think of when you hear "KFC"?

Of course, you recognize the name of one of the world's largest restaurant chains. But do you know that the firm's grandfatherly logo, Colonel Sanders, is a real person? If you didn't know, you are among the majority of young Americans.[14]

In fact, the Colonel, Harlan Sanders, was an entrepreneur who overcame failure and went on to become a millionaire—and he did it at an age when most folk retire.

Sanders was thrust into financial ruin when his Kentucky restaurant failed. Rather than just giving up, however, Sanders, then 65 years old, took his first Social Security retirement check,[15] loaded his old Cadillac with pressure cookers and supplies of his "original recipe" coating, and began traveling the country, setting up franchises in existing restaurants.[16]

His persistence paid off. In less than 10 years his franchise operations became so successful that he was able to sell his company for $2 million.[17] Sanders, then 74 years old, did not quit. In fact, he remained involved in the business as its spokesperson until his death at the age of 91.

Buying an Existing Business

The second most common way to enter small business management is to purchase an existing business. Buying an existing business has important advantages over creating a start-up. However, purchasing a business has its own, unique set of risks.

LO3 Compare the opportunities with the pitfalls of purchasing an existing business.

Advantages of Purchasing an Existing Business

There are some advantages to buying an existing business:

- Established customers provide immediate sales and cash inflows. Because the business is already successful, it has proven that there is sufficient demand for its products and services to operate profitably.
- Business processes are already in place in an existing, operating business. This eliminates the need to hire employees, find vendors, set up accounting systems, and establish production processes.
- Purchasing a business often requires less cash outlay than does creating a start-up. The seller will often provide financing that makes it possible for you to buy the business.

Disadvantages of Purchasing an Existing Business

Disadvantages to buying an existing business include:

- Finding a successful business for sale that is appropriate for your experience, skills, and education is difficult and time-consuming.
- It is very difficult to determine what a small business is worth. The value of a small business can never be known with certainty. You must rely on analyses, comparisons, and estimates.
- Existing managers and employees may resist change. It can be very difficult to convince employees to adapt to new business methods, procedures, and processes that can provide increased profits.
- The reputation of the business may be a hindrance to future success. Sellers are usually reluctant to tell you about problems that the business has. Business owners are especially sensitive about discussing past disputes and lawsuits with vendors and customers.
- The business may be declining because of changes in technology.
- The facilities and equipment may be obsolete or in need of major repair.

Finding a Business to Buy

The first problem you must solve is finding a business for sale. Of course, you aren't looking for just any business. You are looking for one that is right for your own experience, education, and skills. The things that make a business appropriate for you are like those things that help create a successful start-up. The business should be in an industry in which you have experience. It should be producing a product or providing service that is in demand and that has high margins. Perhaps, most importantly, it should have adequate financing available so you can continue operations and make the business grow.

Finding a Business for Sale

SKILL MODULE 6.1

Although all businesses are for sale, *if the price is right*, finding that one perfect business is a difficult and time-consuming task. As you will find out by completing this skill task, businesses for sale that are easy to find usually are unsuitable. Businesses that are right for you are downright elusive:

1. Decide what type of business you would be interested in buying. Write a profile of your ideal business to buy, specifying its industry, product or service, size, location, price, and financing.
2. Search the Yellow Pages and the Internet to find business brokers active in your area.
   a. Contact each broker and inquire about businesses that meet your criteria. Be honest in your approach. Do not represent yourself as a serious buyer, unless you are one.
   b. Obtain copies of the information that the broker has concerning the businesses.

(continued)

3. Search your local newspaper, *The Wall Street Journal*, and *Barrons* classified advertisements for the headings "business for sale" and "business opportunities."
4. Make a list of businesses that seem to meet the requirements that you wrote down in step 1.
5. Contact the businesses that you have identified. Be honest in your approach. If you are doing this solely as a classroom exercise, explicitly say so. Remember that while the owner of the business may want to sell it, he or she is undoubtedly very busy and may not want to discuss the business with a student when there is no chance of your actually buying it.
6. Visit a business that is engaged in the industry you have identified as being right for you. Find out the following things:
   a. The title and publisher of the journals dedicated to the industry.
   b. The primary businesses of this type operating in your geographical area.
   c. Conventional business practices:
      i. Is business done on credit?
      ii. Who are the primary suppliers to the business?
      iii. What are the sales channels of the business (direct sales, catalog, etc.)?
      iv. How is technology changing in the business?
      v. Are there any industry rules of thumb for valuing businesses?
      vi. Does the owner know of any businesses that are for sale?
7. Obtain sample copies of the industry journals. Examine them for advertisements of businesses for sale.
8. Make an appointment with a loan officer in the commercial loan department of a bank in your area. Describe what you are looking for in a business to buy.
   a. Ask if the loan officer knows of any businesses for sale in your area.
   b. Ask if the loan officer can introduce you to anyone who might be able to help you find a business for sale.

Finally, write and present a report to your class that details the efforts and results of your research.

You will greatly increase your chances of finding the right business by using multiple sources. Make some calls: Contact business brokers and ply your own network. You should be actively reading advertising of businesses for sale in newspapers and magazines and on the Internet. You might consider asking your employer if his or her business is for sale. Keep in mind that *every* business is for sale at a high enough price. If you hear of a business that is interesting, contact the owners and ask what it would take to buy it.

Brokers advertise and facilitate the sale of businesses for a fee, most usually a percentage of the ultimate selling price. Most states have laws that require brokers to work solely for the interest of the seller and to obtain the highest selling price possible. This creates a conflict of interest between the broker and you. The broker is trying to get the highest price. You're trying to get the lowest.

The quality of broker services ranges from excellent to outright rip-offs. Only a few states have any education or licensing requirements, although some, such as Illinois, do require business brokers to register by filing a simple form. Accusations of misrepresentation and fraud by brokers are common in the business press.

Networking is an excellent way to find businesses for sale. While most businesses are for sale at any time, for competitive reasons most owners do not want to say so explicitly. Because customers, vendors, and employees are likely to feel threatened, openly advertising a business for sale can lead to the loss of revenue, credit from vendors, and key employees. For these reasons, it is common for business owners to make their intention to sell known only to trusted confidants in the industry and in the community. Attorneys, bankers, accountants, and insurance agents all will provide you with information only if they know that they can trust your discretion. You can usually get solid leads just by telling other businesspeople that you're interested in buying a business.

There is a trade journal for every industry that exists. People in the mortuary business bone up with *Embalmer* and *American Funeral Director*. The replacement window industry looks through *Fenestration*. The electric sign industry is energized by *Signs of the Times*. The folks who process dead and decomposing animals into useable products digest *Render* magazine. The construction industry digs *Rock and Dirt*. No matter what type of business you might be considering, there is a magazine for it. They all have advertisements of businesses for sale.

The Internet also has numerous sites that advertise businesses for sale. A search using Google with the keyword "business" and the phrase "for sale" resulted in over *38 million* pages listed. None of the advertisements that were inspected during the research for this book provided the name or the exact location of the advertised business. Rather, the sites have various ways you can obtain additional information. Some provide a link by which you can request more information. A very few listed phone numbers you can call. Others require becoming a member and paying a fee for access.

Your current employer is probably a ready source of information about businesses for sale in your industry. Most managers of small businesses are members of formal and informal groups of businesspeople, for example, the Chamber of Commerce, Rotary, Kiwanis, and other groups that have meetings and provide resources. Also, your employer probably has information about competitors and vendors in the area. Don't forget the example of UltimateKeychains.com—your employer just might be interested in selling his or her business, as well.

Investigating Entrepreneurial Opportunities: Performing Due Diligence

Suppose you've actually found a business you'd like to buy. Your job has just begun. Finding an appropriate business is merely the first, and easiest, step in the process. Buying a business is a lot like getting married—it is easy to get into, but if it turns out bad, it's very hard to get out. Now that you've found that "perfect" business, you must make an exhaustive investigation to tell if it is really suitable. Unlike residential real estate, which is highly regulated in the United States, sellers of businesses are not legally required to make disclosures of impairments or deficiencies. If you are outside the United States, your laws may be different. For example, in Canada, sales of businesses for a price less than $200,000 are tightly regulated. Sales for amounts greater than $200,000 are not regulated at all. As in the United States, it is *your* responsibility to fully investigate the business and to come to your own independent evaluation of its value.

Due diligence is the process of investigating to determine the full and complete implications of buying a business. During the process of due diligence every aspect of the business is examined in exacting detail. Nothing is taken for granted. No statement is accepted without evidence. Evidence is, itself, substantiated with sources external to the company. Properly performing due diligence minimizes the risk of failure and maximizes the probability of success by identifying the strengths and weaknesses of the business.

due diligence
The process of investigating a business to determine its value.

When a business is acquired, there is a clear order of steps that should be followed:

1. Conduct extensive interviews with the sellers of the business.
2. Study the financial reports and other records of the business.
3. Make a personal examination of the site (or sites) of the business.
4. Interview customers and suppliers of the business.
5. Develop a detailed business plan for the acquisition.
6. Negotiate an appropriate price for the business, based on the business plan projections.
7. Obtain sufficient capital to purchase and operate the business.

The first five steps together make up the process of due diligence.[18]

A basic tenet of business law is **caveat emptor**, or "let the buyer beware." This does not mean that a seller can freely lie to you about the business. Deliberate misrepresentations can lead to lawsuits and may be prosecuted as fraud. However, except for specific representations by the seller, you are responsible for understanding the condition and the facts of the business. It's kind of a "don't ask—don't tell." If you don't ask the right questions, the seller has no obligation to tell you the right answers. Thus, as the buyer, you must determine how the business is currently being operated, and you must substantiate (or disprove) representations made by the seller regarding the existence and value of assets, liabilities, financial performance, and the condition of the business.

caveat emptor
Latin: let the buyer beware.

Due diligence has two primary goals. *First,* you are attempting to find any wrongdoing: (1) fraud committed by the owners or managers; (2) misrepresentations of the sellers, such as improperly recognized revenues or expenses; and (3) missing information, including pending or threatened litigation, technological obsolescence of equipment, processes, product, or service, and unpaid taxes. *Second,* you are trying to find any inefficiencies, unnoticed opportunities, waste, and mismanagement. The first goal is information that greatly affects the value of the business and the advisability of purchasing it. The second goal is how you, as a new owner, can make changes to increase its value. Both goals can give you a negotiating advantage.

The first information that you get is usually a set of financial statements. There are four reasons why this is so: (1) the seller usually has financial statements available and incurs little added cost in providing them, (2) you, as a business person, are most likely familiar with financial statements and can extract useful information from them, (3) financial statements are accepted as representative of the business by bankers and investors, and (4) financial statements are considered to be indicators of future business results.

Financial statements should include (1) a balance sheet, (2) an income statement, and (3) a statement of cash flows. You should also examine the federal and state tax returns for at least the last five years. Information forms for partnerships, corporations, or limited liability companies should be examined also. Any financial statement prepared by or for the seller must be treated with skepticism. Some financial statements that you see will have been subjected to rigorous examination by professionals outside the business; some will have been dashed off by the owner at midnight on April 15. To be believable, the statements must be substantiated by external sources.

When you examine the income statement, you should focus on corroborating the amount and timing of revenues and expenses. Be aware that the income statements of small businesses are commonly misstated. To avoid taxes, owners often charge personal expenses to the business, such as cars, country club memberships, travel, and even home office expenses. On the other hand, when preparing to sell the business, owners are motivated to overstate revenues and understate expenses to show the highest profit.

intangibles
Assets, such as patents or trademarks, and liabilities, such as accounts payable, that have no physical existence.

Balance sheet items that are likely to be misstated are intangibles, that is, things that have no physical existence, but rather are legal rights and obligations. **Intangibles** include accounts receivable, patents, licenses, and liabilities. Assets claimed on the balance sheet must be examined to ensure that they exist and that the stated value is reasonable. Because liabilities are legal requirements to give up economic value in the future, such as debts for borrowed money or merchandise purchased on account, your risk is that there will be liabilities that are not disclosed. Your problem is that you are attempting to prove the absence of something. Once the examination is complete, you should adjust the amounts, contents, and format of the statements to reflect what you have discovered through due diligence.

During due diligence you should also try to answer many nonfinancial questions. Why is the business for sale? Who are key employees? What is the extent of obsolescence of equipment and key technologies? What are the prospects for the firm's products and services? What opportunities can the firm reasonably expect to have in the near future?

Determining the Value of the Business

After you have completed a thorough and exacting investigation, you need to analyze all the information you have gathered. This is the time to consult with your business, financial, and legal advisers to arrive at an estimate of the value of the business. Outside advisers are impartial and are more likely to see the bad things about the business than are you. You should make a decision to actually attempt to buy the business only after the evaluation process is complete.

discounted cash flows
Cash flows that have been reduced in value because they are to be received in the future.

It is very difficult to place a value on a small business. The most theoretically rigorous method of valuing an ongoing business, using **discounted cash flows**, is based upon estimates of future cash outflows and inflows, given the change in ownership. Making such estimates is highly problematic. Because of these difficulties, it is common to use other, less rigorous methods to place a value on a business, such as asset valuation, comparable sales, financial ratios, or industry heuristics.

Discounted Cash Flow Methodology

Discounted cash flow analysis is based on the concept that the longer you have to wait to receive money, the less valuable it is right now. The application of discounted cash flows to business valuation is similar to having an annuity. An annuity consists of some amount of money which is invested to earn interest. The interest that is earned and a portion of the capital invested is then paid back to the holder of the annuity in a series of equal cash payments. In a similar way, when one buys a business, an investment is made. The business then should provide a return sufficient to repay the investment and also provide a return on that investment.

A detailed explanation of the use and calculation of discounted cash flows is presented in the appendix to Chapter 14, beginning on page 450.

Asset Valuation Methodology

Asset valuation methods are based on the assumption that a business is worth the value of its assets minus the value of any liabilities. There are two major problems with using asset valuation methodologies. First, such estimates do not consider the value of an ongoing firm over the value of its identifiable assets; for example, the value of an established restaurant over the value of the building, signage, equipment, and fixtures. Second, it is very difficult and time consuming to separately identify and estimate the values of all the assets of a business—imagine a hardware store with tens of thousands of items.

There are three methods commonly used to estimate the value of a firm's assets, book value, net realizable value, and replacement value.

Book value is the the original acquisition cost of the asset, minus all depreciation expense recognized to date. There are three major problems with using book value

book value
The difference between the original acquisition cost and the amount of accumulated depreciation.

1. The original cost of an asset might bear no relation to its current value—for example, a computer bought five years ago may be worth next to nothing today.
2. Depreciation is an arbitrary, although systematic, method of transferring asset value to expense. Depreciation makes no attempt to measure actual loss of value of an asset. For example, for income tax purposes, a new car is depreciated over a five-year period of time, where in fact it loses 40 percent of its value when you drive it off the lot, but may well have significant cash value at the end of the depreciation period.
3. Internally developed assets, such as patents, trademarks, and trade secrets do not have book value. For an example, consider The Coca-Cola Company. Its single greatest asset is its rights to the names "Coca-Cola" and "Coke." However, if you examine the annual statement of the company, you will discover that no value for this right is shown in the balance sheet. To address such problems, you must make adjustments to the value of assets that are obviously worth more or less than their book values.

Net realizable value is an estimate of the amount for which an asset would sell, less the costs of selling it. If you were selling a building, the cost of selling would be the money spent on the real estate agent, advertising, and preparing the building for display.

net realizable value
The amount for which an asset will sell, less the costs of selling.

Replacement value is an estimate of what an identical asset would cost to be acquired and readied for service. Net realizable value is usually significantly less than the replacement value of any specific asset.

replacement value
The cost to acquire an essentially identical asset.

Comparable Sales

Comparable sales of other firms in the same industry are commonly used to estimate the value of a business. This method has two major problems. First, no two firms are exactly alike. Second, there are often no recent sales to use for comparison.

Financial Ratios

Financial ratios are often used to place a value on businesses, because industry ratios are independent of the size of the business. For example, the percentage food cost for the entire Pizza Hut chain is essentially the same as that of an independent pizza restaurant. Using financial ratios requires that you have an estimate of future income and tax flows. Businesses are never identical. At the minimum they occupy different locations. At the other extreme, they may be different in all measurable aspects: location, size, gross sales, profitability, condition of markets, and physical assets. The best source of industry financial ratios is from data collected by industry associations or industry statistic providers, such as BizMiner.

Some of the commonly used ratios are:

earnings multiple
The ratio of the value of a firm to its annual earnings.

The **earnings multiple** ratio is simply firm value divided by actual or expected annual earnings. Multiplying forecast earnings by the earnings multiple provides a quick estimate of firm value.

Pre-tax return on assets (ROA) is calculated by dividing earnings before income tax by asset value. Multiplying forecast earnings by the pretax ROA gives an estimate of net asset value, or total asset value minus liabilities.

Net income to equity is determined by dividing income by the equity owners have in the business. To estimate firm value, you must multiply your estimate of future earnings by the ratio. This ratio, however, can seriously understate firm value because it does not include the value of borrowed capital.

Net income to (equity + debt) is an extension of net income to equity that explicitly includes the value of borrowed capital as a component of firm value.

Income capitalization is calculated by dividing projected net income excluding depreciation, interest, and owner draws, by the best return that you could expect to obtain in other investments. For example, if you are forecasting that you will have a net income of $66,000 and your cost of capital is 11 percent then the estimated value of the business would be $600,000 ($66,000/0.11).

Industry Heuristics

heuristic
A common-sense rule, a rule-of-thumb.

Industry **heuristics** are simply rules of thumb that are commonly used to estimate firm value in relation to some easily observable characteristic of the business. Industry heuristics are similar to comparable sales in that they represent the combined experience of people active in the industry. For example, in the bed and breakfast and small inn industry, two heuristics are often used to estimate the value of an operating inn. The first is that an inn should sell for approximately $100,000 per rental room. The second is that an inn should sell for approximately four times its annual gross revenue.

Industry heuristics can be amazingly accurate. In a recent survey of 300 inns, the Professional Association of Innkeepers International found that the average selling prices of inns between 2000 and 2002 was $99,300 per guest room. The average gross revenue multiplier was 4.3.[19] Similar heuristics exist for nearly all industries and are usually available from the group's trade association. You'll learn how to find associations in the next chapter.

Structuring the Deal

LO4 Explain four methods for purchasing an existing business.

A buyer and seller get together to negotiate the final price for a business. The buyer should have performed the due diligence procedure and be confident about the assessment of the condition and value of the business. Along the way you, as the buyer, should have decided on the absolute highest price that you would be willing to pay. That highest price is called your **point of indifference**[20] in the negotiation process. The term comes from the idea that once that price is reached, you should be indifferent as to whether or not a deal is made.

point of indifference
The price at which a buyer is indifferent about buying or not buying the business.

Of course, you'll open negotiations with a price substantially lower than your point of indifference. The purpose of opening low is twofold: (1) you want to make the purchase at the lowest price possible, and (2) you recognize that the seller assumes that any opening offer is less than what you are actually willing to pay. A low opening bid allows both parties room to reach a compromise satisfactory to both.

In addition to negotiating for price, you also negotiate about the terms of the sale. When you are buying a business, everything is negotiable, not just the price. In fact, the terms of the acquisition, such as seller financing, payment periods, noncompete agreements, and the exact details of what is being acquired, all interact to affect the price that you are willing to pay and that the seller will accept. There are four basic ways that a business may be bought: (1) you may buy out the seller's interest in the business, (2) you may **buy in**, by acquiring some, but not all of the ownership, (3) you may *buy only the key assets* of the business such as the inventory or equipment of the business, and

buy-in
The purchase of substantially less than 100 percent of a business.

not the business itself, and (4) you may **take over** a public business by buying a controlling interest of its stock.

takeover
Seizing of control of a business by purchasing its stock to be able to select the board of directors.

Buyouts

Buyouts are restricted to businesses that have a formal legal form of organization, including corporations, limited liability companies, and some partnerships. Legal business organizations are artificial entities that exist separately from the owners. Buyouts are accomplished through purchasing the ownership interest in the entity. Technically, partnerships and sole proprietorships do not exist separately from the owners and thus cannot be purchased. Rather, the assets of the business must be purchased and the liabilities assumed in a process called *key resource acquisition* or *bulk asset sale*. The subsequent business is considered to be a new entity different from the selling entity. In practice, partnerships can continue in existence despite a change in ownership. Sole proprietorships cannot.

The primary advantage to a buyout is simplicity. The seller must only transfer his or her stock to the purchaser to complete the transaction. The business continues as an entity, owning its assets and maintaining responsibility for its liabilities. The primary disadvantage to a buyout is that all liabilities are transferred, including potential lawsuits that arise from actions and transactions that took place prior to the change in ownership. This has, as in the case of the widespread class-action suits concerning asbestos, led to bankruptcy for the purchaser.

A buyout may take place all at once, with all stock being transferred at a single point in time. Sometimes buyouts are made with ownership being transferred over some agreed upon time range. Buyouts made by employees are examples of changes of ownership over time. Employee buyouts were made legal in 1974 when employee stock ownership plan regulations were codified into law. An employee buyout occurs when the owners of a company sell a majority of stock to the employees through an employee stock option plan (**ESOP**) as was provided in the 1974 legislation. ESOPs are complicated transactions that require highly skilled professionals to implement them.

ESOP
Employee stock option plan: a method for employees to purchase the business for which they work.

Buy-ins

A buy-in results when someone acquires only a part of the ownership of an existing business. Any amount of ownership may be considered a buy-in, as long as less than 100 percent of the ownership is transferred. Buy-ins can be made in any form of business. Technically, if one buys into a sole proprietorship, it becomes a partnership. Corporations and limited liability companies may continue without a change of the form of entity.

There are two advantages to making a buy-in: (1) a buy-in allows the purchaser to leverage inside knowledge, and (2) it aids in keeping key employees. The seller and the managers of a successful business, by definition, have experience in operating that business profitably. The buyer, no matter how expert, does not have the same depth of knowledge of the business being purchased. One great threat to the buyer of a business is that employees who are key to its operations will leave the business. Keeping the current owner as an active participant of the business reassures employees that large changes are not likely to occur.

The disadvantages of a buy-in are the same as the advantages: the prior owner and management remain with the business. This often causes friction when the new owner wishes to make changes, and the old owner and managers do not.

Key Resource Acquisitions

Key resource acquisitions, also called *bulk asset purchases,* are the only way a sole proprietorship may be purchased. This technique may also be used with any other form of business. As the name implies, key resource acquisitions comprise purchasing only the assets of the business. Most usually, the seller will keep any cash and receivables and will retain responsibility for some short-term liabilities such as notes payable.

As we saw earlier, the most difficult issue in purchasing a business using this method is assigning a value to the intangible assets, such as the value of the business name, the value of having an ongoing business, the value of established relationships, and so forth. The value of the business in excess of the value of the identifiable assets is called *goodwill*. You should attempt to recognize a minimum amount of goodwill. One advantage of business ownership is the ability to shelter income by using noncash deductions to reduce income taxes. Prior to 2002, a business could reduce income taxes by deducting goodwill over a period of years. However, businesses purchased after December 15, 2002, are now prohibited from deducting for goodwill.[21] Thus the more of the business's value that is recognized as goodwill, the less income can be sheltered from income tax.

Key resource allocation provides one important advantage. Because only the assets are acquired, the subsequent business, regardless of its legal form, is not responsible for any of the acts or transactions made prior to purchasing the business. Although this does not completely relieve the successor business from all prior liabilities, it does protect it from action concerning any noncollateralized liabilities, such as a line of credit or a personal loan of the seller.

Takeovers

Takeovers are possible only of businesses that have stock which is freely transferable without the permission of management or other owners. In other words, only corporations and certain partnerships can, under any circumstance, be acquired in a takeover process. A takeover comprises purchasing enough of the target business's stock to gain control of the board of directors of the business. In a takeover, the buyer (often called a *raider*) seizes control of the business without the permission of all owners. Sometimes, only a few owners are involved, as takeovers can often be accomplished by purchasing or even borrowing a relatively small percentage of outstanding stock.

Takeovers are hostile events. There is the threat that current management will be replaced. Occasionally, the raider will explicitly state that the intention of the takeover is to sell off portions of the business, or even to liquidate it completely. In these circumstances, current management is likely to make strenuous efforts to prevent the takeover from occurring.

Because of the requirement that stock be freely transferable, only a few small businesses are vulnerable to hostile takeovers. Accomplishing a takeover of a small business is likely to result in the loss of key employees and the resentment and resistance of those employees who remain. As a result of these limitations and problems, takeovers are usually done on medium to large businesses. Only very rarely does anyone acquire a small business through a hostile takeover.

Franchising a Business

What Is Franchising?

LO5 Compare the advantages with the disadvantages of buying a franchise.

Franchising is a legal agreement that allows one business to be operated using the name and business procedures of another. The most ubiquitous franchise, worldwide, is McDonald's, which has over 30,000 restaurants in more than 100 countries. Approximately 85 percent of McDonald's restaurants are owned by independent businesspeople who operate them in a franchise relationship. The remainder are *company stores*, that is, stores that are owned and operated by the McDonald's Corporation.[22] Most franchisors are large businesses, most franchisees small: McDonald's Corporation is a large business; McDonald's franchisees are small businesses.

Franchises are agreements between two entities, (1) the franchisor who sets conditions and standards and who grants operating permissions, and (2) the franchisee, who pays a fee for the rights, and who agrees to abide by the conditions and standards.

Four elements are essential for an agreement to constitute a franchise:

1. The agreement provides the franchisee with a legal right to engage in the business of offering, selling, or distributing goods or services.
2. The agreement provides that the franchisee may engage in business using a marketing plan or system provided by the franchisor.
3. The agreement grants the franchisee use of a brand name, trademark, service mark, logo, or other commercial symbol which designates the franchisee as an affiliate of the franchisor.
4. The agreement requires the franchisee to pay a fee for the right to enter into the business.

Franchising a business, such as Auntie Anne's or McDonald's, may be the right avenue for starting your own business if you want to lower some of the risks involved in small business. Franchising gives owners the opportunity to cash in on an already developed, market-tested product. However, drawbacks include less creative control and greater reliance upon your parent company's financial status. Does franchising appeal to you? Why or why not?

The value of a franchise is determined by (1) the rights granted and (2) the cash flow potential to the franchisee. Each of these factors can be highly variable from one franchise to another. There are four basic forms of franchising:

1. **Trade name franchising** is an agreement that provides only the rights to use the franchisor's trade name and/or trademarks. Two examples of this are True Value Hardware and Associated Grocers, Inc.
2. **Product distribution franchising** provides the franchisee with specific brand named products, which are resold by the franchisee in a specified territory. Two examples of this type of franchising are Snap-On Tools and auto dealerships.
3. **Conversion franchising** provides an organization through which independent businesses may combine resources. An example is Century 21 Real Estate. Individual real estate businesses combine to create a nationwide brand name and enhanced advertising effectiveness.
4. **Business format franchising** is exemplified by the McDonald's Corporation. A McDonald's franchise includes the right to use McDonald's many trade names, specifications of the product to be sold, operating methods, marketing plan, and national advertising. Franchisees pay to the franchisor both an up-front fee to obtain the franchise rights and a percentage of gross sales.

trade name franchising
An agreement that provides to the franchisee only the rights to use the franchisor's trade name and/or trademarks.

product distribution franchising
An agreement that provides specific brand name products which are resold by the franchisee in a specified territory.

conversion franchising
An agreement that provides an organization through which independent businesses may combine resources.

business format franchising
An agreement that provides a complete business format, including trade name, operational procedures, marketing, and products or services to sell.

In addition to the above, some franchisors, such as Subway (sandwich shops), sell *master franchises* that require opening multiple stores within a specified area. Subway describes these franchisees as being "development agents." Master franchisees are required to open a minimum number of stores within a specified time period, which they may do by selling *subfranchises* within the development area.

Franchising has become the predominant method by which entrepreneurs open new businesses. Depending upon who is doing the counting, somewhere between 1 in 10 and 1 in 8 businesses currently operating in the United States are franchised operations. Today, in addition to fast food, nearly every product or service from accounting to zoology is available from franchised businesses.

The most important reason that franchising has become such a successful way of doing business is that a well-run franchise offers a "win–win" situation for both the franchiser and the franchisee. Franchisers have the opportunity to experience high growth and rapid market penetration without having the requirement to raise capital in huge amounts and to obtain skilled, experienced managers in large numbers. Franchisees are able to partner with an established business that has proven success.

Franchising provides an entrepreneur with the opportunity to own a small business quickly while avoiding the high risks of a start-up. As we have discussed, starting a new business from zero is very expensive in terms of demands on the entrepreneur. Most start-ups have limited capital resources, and very little room to make business mistakes while learning what is needed to make the business succeed. Franchisers have survived their own start-up phase of business, and have determined the "recipe" for success. For this reason, franchises (on average) have lower failure rates and shorter times to achieve positive cash flows and business profits.

Advantages of Franchising

Let's take a look at the specific characteristics of franchises that offer such advantages to would-be entrepreneurs.

Having a Fully Developed System of Doing Business

Perhaps the single greatest advantage of a franchise is that it comes with a complete business system. Many franchises are actually "turnkey." That is, the franchiser oversees (or even manages) the selection of location, the construction of facilities, the acquisition and installation of necessary equipment, and the initial inventory with which to open business. Many franchises come complete with computer software for budgeting inventory control, ordering, point-of-sale computerized cash register, and complete accounting application. So, what does the franchisee do? First, the franchisee must, in one manner or another, pay for all these services. Second, the franchisee will be required to complete training to become intimate with the details of the franchise business system. Third, the franchisee will be required to take an active part in opening and operating the franchise business.

Franchise Opportunities

There are more franchises available than you can count. Unlike finding a small business to buy, finding a franchise is easy. Every issue of *Entrepreneur* magazine contains the advertisements of dozens of franchisors eager to sell their franchises to you. *Entrepreneur.com,* the magazine's website, lists 500 franchises. The franchises are listed in rank by the number of new locations opened in the last year. The list of franchises is also broken down into more categories, including:

- Fastest-Growing Franchises
- Top New Franchises
- Best of the Best
- Top 10 Lists
- Top Home-Based Franchises
- Top Low-Cost Franchises
- Top Global Franchises

It is interesting that 8 of the top 10 franchises overall are in the service industry. The other two, which happen to be numbers one and two on the Entrepreneur Franchise 500 list, are the fast-food restaurants Subway and Dunkin' Donuts.

If you don't find one you like in *Entrepreneur,* the Internet contains thousands of resources for identifying franchise opportunities. A Google search of the web using the terms "franchise opportunity" returned 788,000 pages. Several of the highest listed pages were the sites of services that offer information concerning franchises of all types. Some offer free services. Some charge a fee for information.

Among the 788,000 sites listed by Google are two U.S. government agencies, the Federal Trade Commission (FTC) and the Small Business Administration (SBA), a British government site, Business Link (**www.businesslink.gov.uk**), and an Australian site, Smallbusiness.gov.au, (**www.smallbusiness.gov.au**). Similar government sources are available around the world.

Franchising's industry association, the International Franchise Association (IFA) (**www.franchise.org**) maintains a website that contains a database of over 800 franchises. The companies listed range from old familiars such as 7–11 stores to the really obscure such as Jet-black and Pop-A-Lock.

Once you've identified a potential franchise, you should perform due diligence, just as if you were buying an operating business. What you are most interested in with franchises is the stability, integrity, and financial performance of the franchisor. You really should interview current franchisees, and you should talk to competing franchisors and their franchisees. If you buy a franchise, you will invest thousands of hours and thousands of dollars. Be sure that it is really an opportunity for you and not just for the franchisor.

Legal Considerations

Before you sign on the dotted line, you should personally study two key documents you always receive from a franchisor—the uniform franchise offering circular (UFOC) and the franchise agreement. The UFOC is a standard document franchises use to explain their operations, requirements, and costs to potential franchisees. You can get a guide to help interpret the UFOC at the Federal Trade Commission site. The franchise agreement is the specific contract signed, often incorporating the information included in the UFOC. Both documents are complex. To make sure you have all your bases covered, it is important to get the opinion of an experienced franchise lawyer. You want to know several things, including (1) if and how you can transfer the franchise license to someone else, (2) how you may terminate the contract, (3) how the franchisor may terminate the contract, and (4) what disclosures you are required to make.

SMALL BUSINESS INSIGHT

When Your Franchisor Goes Broke[23]

Burt Benepal had just received a most unwelcome call. A business colleague reported that American Hospitality Concepts, Inc., had just declared bankruptcy. This news was delivered Friday the thirteenth, 2004, just before Benepal was to have opened his first-ever Ground Round Grill and Bar restaurant.

Because of the filing, American Hospitality had ordered all company-owned stores closed immediately. Timing could not have been worse for a restaurant. The announcement was delivered just as the Friday evening rush began. Diners were sent home with half-eaten meals in doggie bags. Over 3,000 employees were dismissed without any notice or severance pay. Their final paychecks bounced when they attempted to cash them.

Because he was a franchisee, Benepal did not necessarily have to stop work on his restaurant. However, he was under no illusion about the magnitude of the task facing him if he were to stay in business. He already had committed to a capital investment of $1 million. Would customers come to a restaurant that was involved in a bankruptcy?

"What should I do," he wondered.

In the subsequent weeks, struggling to stay in business, the franchisees organized. They formed a co-op, renegotiated contracts with suppliers, and even introduced a new lo-carb menu to capitalize on the Atkins Diet fad. Soon they realized that they were not so bad off. They no longer had to pay royalties or toe the line to meet franchisor requirements. Soon they developed a plan to buy Ground Round out of bankruptcy. On July 7, 2004, their offer to the bankruptcy court was accepted. The franchisees were now the proud owners of Ground Round Grill and Bar, Inc.

What about Burt Benepal?

He finally opened his restaurant in Richmond, California. He opened five months later than he had planned, but at least it was open and successful. Benepal stated that he expected his first full year of sales to be almost $2 million. He was actively searching for a location for his next Ground Round to be opened in 2005. He had plans to open five more before the end of 2006.

In many ways, Benepal was incredibly fortunate. Often when franchisors go bankrupt, franchisees soon follow. Even in the Ground Round case, not all franchisees fared so well. Mike Metz, owner of three Ground Round restaurants in Pennsylvania, had a sales decrease of 20 percent. According to attorney Craig Tractenberg, several franchisees were forced into involuntary bankruptcy. Similar stories of failed franchisors abound. Have you ever heard of Arthur Treacher's Fish and Chips, Griffs Hamburgers, 50 Flavors in a Tub, Spud Nuts, or Minnie Pearl's Fried Chicken? Probably not, but they represent just a tiny fraction of the scores of failed franchisors who not only went out of business but who took hundreds of franchisees along, as well.

If the contract restricts or prohibits you from transferring the franchise to another or if it requires that you achieve unrealistic results to be able to renew, an unscrupulous franchisor has an opportunity to take over your successful business at a bargain price. Your blood, sweat, tears, and life savings will have gone for naught.

The contract must specify the conditions under which it may be terminated. There have been lawsuits and allegations of fraud against some franchisors because of contract provisions that prohibit the franchisee from terminating the contract, but give the franchisor permission to cancel with specifying cause or giving advance notice. If you can't terminate the contract in the case that the franchisor goes bankrupt, most likely you will also be forced out of business.

Franchising has a long history of unscrupulous and fraudulent operations. Because of the many abuses, the U.S. government and the governments of all 50 states have passed regulatory legislation for franchisors. The minimum disclosure standards that a franchisor must meet are specified by Rule 436 of the Federal Trade Commission. Despite this law, however, abuses and frauds are still being perpetrated. In fact, the third item listed on the SBA's Hot List site is a document that details how to avoid being victimized by scam artists. In college terms, do your homework—know what the opportunity is and who the franchisors are. As is true of purchasing an operating business, caveat emptor.

Inheriting a Business

LO6 Explain the issues of inheriting a family-owned business.

Unless your parents or grandparents are small business owners, you might think that this section does not apply to you. However, the fact that you are taking this course indicates that you have at some interest in becoming a business owner yourself. Thus, someday you may well find yourself on the other end of the inheritance process: You may be the founder who wishes to pass your business to your heirs. Whether you are inheriting a business or bequeathing a business, you face the same problems of passing ownership. Only your point of view changes.

In Chapter 2, we introduced the topic of family businesses. As we point out there, family-owned businesses make up a huge percentage of all businesses in the United States. In fact, this pattern holds throughout the world. Ownership of all of these millions of businesses can potentially be passed through family succession, for example, by being inherited in one form or another.

Family Businesses Succession

Inheritance is not restricted to parent-child or grandparent-grandchild. Family businesses can be, and often are, passed from the current owner-manager to nieces, nephews, cousins, or in-laws.

One of the most difficult things that you will ever have to do is make a successful ownership transition. Turning over management authority is not easy for most founders, nor is it easy for the heir of the founder to assume the authority. However, if the firm is to prosper, you've got to find a way to do it. Research shows that family-owned businesses usually fail after the death or retirement of the founder. Fewer than 30 percent are successfully transferred to a second generation. Fewer than 13 percent succeed long enough to be inherited by the third.[24] Family businesses that successfully make the transition do so by taking specific actions to organize the business and ensure that it can run profitably when the founder is gone.

Developing a Formal Management Structure

To make the transition, you will have to establish a formal management structure. You will have to develop a comprehensive business plan that states clear goals and objectives. Most difficult, you must be able to clearly see the strengths and weaknesses of family members who will remain in the business.[25] You must then hire professional managers to run those functions that family members cannot. Once successors have been selected, they must be educated in all parts of the family business to develop experience and skills.

Whether you are the founder or the successor, you face an overwhelming task. The founder must impart his or her unique knowledge, skill, and experience that has made the business successful. The successor must learn all these things. While this is happening the founder and successor will have to work closely together.[26] Always there will be issues of who is in charge. No matter the skills and experience of the successor, as long as the founder is active in the business, many people will automatically turn to him or her for decisions.

Succession Issues for the Founder

To ensure that your business survives after you're gone, you must be proactive in bringing selected family members into the business as soon as you can.[27] The issue that must be faced in this process is selecting the appropriate family members. All members of the family business, whether being active in management roles or simply being silent owners, should have an open and ongoing dialog about the strategy, goals, and operations of the business. If you, as the founder-manager, take part in family dialogs about the business, you will gain insight into their values, ideas, and goals. Although family members usually share a set of basic values, there is inevitably some diversity in motivations and personal goals. This diversity can be a positive advantage when it brings new thinking to the management of your business. On the other hand, it can be a source of divisiveness which can lead to a failure to cooperate or even to angry confrontations to the point of mutual lawsuits among family members.

To avoid having the diversity of values, goals, and motivators from becoming the source of such intrafamily strife, you and the other family business members should respect one another's differences by:

- Being certain that all family members know and accept that they are not forced to enter the management of the business if they don't want to.
- Providing each member of the family business with the opportunity to obtain education and experience outside the business. Working in other businesses will provide knowledge and skills that cannot be provided solely from within the family business.
- Allowing each family member who does wish to enter the business to find out and do those functions and activities that he or she does best.
- Not assuming that the leadership of the business must come from within the family. Being part of the family does not guarantee business leadership skills. After all, almost all of us have at least one "black sheep" in our family.

Once you have brought a family member into the firm, you must provide opportunities for learning and growth. This is achieved by deliberately and methodically sharing both responsibility and authority. Often, the founder of a small business finds it very difficult to give up decision-making authority to family members, especially to children and grandchildren. Regardless, you have to "let go" and allow family members that you bring into the business to use their knowledge, skills, and experience to make decisions in the areas where they have special competence. It is only by doing that you and your heirs can develop stronger management skills necessary to ensure the future success of the business.

Successfully bringing family members into the firm, allowing them to find their areas of special abilities, and sharing both responsibility and authority for management decision making is an essential first step. Next, you need to set up specific avenues of access among family members to be able to share their ideas and challenges. One way to achieve this goal is to set up regular "family board" meetings—meetings where each family member listens carefully to the others, and each has a chance to express specific concerns. Openness and regularity in intrafamily communications ensure that you will develop your family managers into a learning community that will benefit from each other's mistakes and successes.

You should write out your specific decisions and desires concerning who inherits what. You should then personally inform everyone who is affected by your decisions. You must also explicitly state the reasons for selecting any one family member over another when there is competition for a specific job in the business. All too commonly the heir not selected challenges the succession after the founder dies. When this happens, the business often fails, and only the lawyers win.[28]

Succession Issues for the Successor

To ensure that the business thrives after you've taken over, you must be able to gain the loyalty of other family members, professional managers, and employees. You will be treading a fine line between acceding to the wishes of the founder, and making changes as all dynamic businesses require. When changes are necessary, you should take the time to involve as many of those affected as possible in the decision process. It is important that you neither allow the business to become fossilized—a monument to the founder—nor present yourself in such way that you are perceived as an "upstart"—determined to erase all signs of the founder.

In the best of all possible worlds, you will have started working in the family business while you were quite young. As you aged and matured, you would have been given increasingly more difficult and important tasks to complete. You would have worked in all parts of the company, from the most menial to the most demanding. As you learned these tasks, you would have been provided the same performance evaluations, training, and mentoring as would be provided to any employee being groomed for greater responsibilities.

Such a gradual and growing role in the business goes a long way toward reducing suspicion and resentment of workers that the "boss's kid" is being given the position despite any lack of competency. (Assuming, of course, that you are actually competent.) As you, the successor-to-be, gain greater responsibility and authority you will also gain experience and skills in the multiple activities and functions of the firm. Although the responsibility for teaching and grooming the successor lies with the founder, you, the successor, have a responsibility to know and to master the areas that are essential to the success of the business.

These essential skills include (but are not limited to):

- *Technical knowledge*—You must understand the science, technology, and methodology of the industry of which the business is part.
- *Financial knowledge*—You must understand the financial needs and resources of the business and industry, and be competent to negotiate with lenders, investors, vendors, and customers.
- *People skills*—You must be able to effectively deal with people, with other family members in the business, with employees, suppliers, regulators, and, most importantly, with customers.
- *Leadership skills*—You must be able to communicate your vision for the company to family members and to employees, getting them to "buy in" and make the business goals their goals.
- *Knowledge of your own limitations*—Nobody can know and be expert at everything. You must know your weaknesses, and be quick to obtain assistance in those areas.

Finally, you must determine just how final authority will be passed to you. Business succession is not always the result of the death of the founder. Often the founder simply realizes that it is time to "pass the torch" to the next generation. Your problem, as the successor, is to understand and to be comfortable with the role, if any, that the founder is to play in the business once you take over. Often, the founder takes an executive position, such as chairman of the board, while the successor becomes chief executive officer. Sometimes, however, strong-willed founders just can't keep from meddling. When this is the situation it is probably best that the founder leave the business altogether and allow the successor space to create his or her own management style in the business.

Ownership Transfer

Whether you are the founder or the successor, you certainly do not want to wait until the founder dies to transfer ownership. If you are the founder, once you're dead, your desires become irrelevant. If you are the successor, once the founder is dead, there is no authority figure who can help with issues of control and strategy. Rather than waiting for the founder to die, you should assist in completing a comprehensive estate-planning process while the founder is still healthy and in charge.[29] In most cases, a gradual transfer of ownership is preferable to a single inheritance.[30] This strategy may not be appropriate, however, if there are multiple heirs. Of greatest importance is determining who gets voting stock. If the heirs who are not involved in management receive voting stock, issues of who is in control can arise because of jealousy and intrafamily rivalries.

There is no easy answer to these issues. In fact, the transfer of ownership is highly complex and is unique to each family business. The larger and more successful your business is, the more complex and difficult the problem becomes. Using experts in law, accounting, and business can help identify the potential problems and help organize solutions. For family business succession plans, using specialists is essential. For family business experts, the major professional association is the Family Firm Institute. There are several organizations for business brokers; you can find them in the Google directory by entering "business broker association." In any case, it always pays to ask other entrepreneurs and advisers such as lawyers and accountants if they have recommendations and personal experience with these experts. Involving specialists also sends a clear message to creditors and suppliers that both old and new owners are determined to make a success of the transition.

Professional Management of Small Business

LO7 Describe how hired managers become owners of small businesses.

As small businesses grow, the requirements of managing them increase proportionately. If a business grows large enough, no matter how experienced or talented a business owner is, eventually the demands of managing will become too great to be handled alone. At this point, one of two things happens: (1) the business starts to decline, or (2) professional managers are hired to share the management load.

In the terms of small business, professional management is not an issue of education, titles, or credentials. A professional manager of a small business is one who has the experience and skills to use a systematic approach to analyzing and solving business problems.

These kinds of people are not easy to find. You may have to look to other businesses in your industry for experienced managers who are seeking new challenges and opportunities. You may find such people working for your vendors or your customers. In an ideal world these people would already be working among your employees, people who, because of their individual drive, personality, and skills, have learned your business quickly, and have taken on responsibility and authority.

An opportunity for you to get into small business while avoiding the many risks of start-ups or franchises, and at the same time avoid the difficulties of raising capital to buy an existing business, is to go to work for the business as a hired manager. If you have the skills and experience of a professional manager that will allow you to be hired, taking the position will provide a unique perspective of the business from the inside. Should the business prove to be one that you want to own, you are in a position to understand the business's worth and to negotiate terms that make it possible for you to acquire it.

Employee managers of small firms are often would-be entrepreneurs. The set of management skills needed to be an effective manager of small business is very similar, if not identical, to the set needed to be an effective business founder or owner. Because of this, it is common for a manager to become an owner—either of your business or of a competing business. Entry into ownership is accomplished through all the ways discussed in this chapter, including leaving employment to start up a new business, buying out or buying into an existing business, or contracting a franchise relationship.

There are only five paths of entry into small business management, although the details of how any one person gets started are unique. You may start a business, buy a business, franchise a business, inherit a business, or be employed as a manager in a business. Getting into business, for all its difficulties and problems, however, is the easiest part of small business management. Making the business successful and finding a graceful and appropriate way to get out is the true challenge, and that is what we look at in later chapters.

SMALL BUSINESS INSIGHT

ARE YOU ESPECIALLY INTERESTED IN FAMILY BUSINESS?

Here is a guide to the discussion of family business in *Entrepreneurial Small Business*:

1. What constitutes a family business, role conflict in family businesses, and an introduction to succession is presented in Chapter 2, pages 37–40.
2. Intergenerational succession in a family business, from the viewpoint of each—that of the founder who is giving up control and of the successor who is assuming control of the family business is discussed in this chapter, Chapter 6, pages 176–178.
3. The issue of managing the potential conflict between family issues and business issues is discussed in Chapter 19, pages 644–648.
4. Specific techniques of making intergenerational transfers of small businesses is discussed in Chapter 20, pages 662–666.

CHAPTER SUMMARY

LO1 Describe five ways that people get into small business management.

- You may start a new business.
- You may buy an existing business.
- You may franchise a business.
- You may inherit a business.
- You may be hired to be the professional manager of a small business.

LO2 Compare the rewards with the pitfalls of starting a new business.

- **Advantages:** A start-up begins with a clean slate and provides the owner with the opportunity to use the most up-to-date technologies and new unique products or services. It can be deliberately kept small to limit possible losses.
- **Disadvantages:** A start-up business has no initial name recognition, will require significant time to become established, can be very difficult to finance, cannot easily gain credit, and may not have experienced managers and workers.
- There are 12 methods for increasing start-up success.
- Starting a new business from scratch can be made easier by using methods to reduce initial capital requirements and to gain access to business and industry experience, such as starting a business in your home to reduce start-up costs, having a partner to share capital, and making an alliance with your current employer to gain access to industry sources.

LO3 Compare the opportunities with the pitfalls of purchasing an existing business.

- **Advantages:** Established customers provide immediate sales and cash inflows, business processes are already in place in an existing business, and purchasing a business often requires less cash outlay than does creating a start-up.
- **Disadvantages:** It is very difficult to determine the value of a small business, existing managers and employees may resist change, the reputation of the business may be a hindrance to future success, the business may be declining because of changes in technology, or the facilities of the business may be obsolete or in need of major repair.
- There are multiple sources to help find businesses for sale, such as business brokers, networking in the industry of interest, advertising of businesses for sale, and your current employer's business.
- You must do an exhaustive investigation to determine a business's suitability and value.

LO4 Explain four methods for purchasing an existing business.

- Buyouts are restricted to businesses that have a formal legal form of organization, including corporations, limited liability companies, and partnerships.
- A buy-in involves acquiring only a part of the ownership of an existing business.
- Key resource acquisitions, also called bulk asset purchases, are the only manner in which a sole proprietorship may be purchased.
- A takeover involves purchasing enough of the target business's stock to gain control of the board of directors of the business.

LO5 Compare the advantages with the disadvantages of buying a franchise.

- Franchising is a legal agreement that allows a business to be operated using the name and business procedures of another firm.
- There are four basic forms of franchising: trade name, product distribution, conversion, and business format.
- Master franchises require opening multiple stores within a specified area.
- **Advantages:** the benefit of a proven successful business model, training and management support, and less risk than in starting a new business or acquiring an operating business.
- **Disadvantages:** little control of business marketing and operations, and success determined to a large extent by the success of the franchisor.

LO6 Explain the issues of inheriting a family-owned business.

- Family-owned businesses tend to fail after the death or retirement of the founder.
- Those family businesses that make the transition from the founder to the next generation take specific actions to organize the business.

LO7 Describe how hired managers become owners of small businesses.

- Entry into ownership by employee managers may be accomplished in three ways: leaving present employment to start up a new business, buying out or buying into a business, or contracting a franchise relationship.

KEY TERMS

franchise, 156
start-up, 157
buyout, 157
cash flows, 158
asset, 158
revolving credit, 158
founder, 159
synergy, 161
spin-off, 162
due diligence, 167
caveat emptor, 167
intangibles, 168
discounted cash flows, 168
book value, 169
net realizable value, 169
replacement value, 169
earnings multiple, 170
heuristic, 170
point of indifference, 170
buy-in, 170
takeover, 171
ESOP, 171
trade name franchising, 173
product distribution franchising, 173
conversion franchising, 173
business format franchising, 173

DISCUSSION QUESTIONS

1. What is the best way to get into business? Why do you think so?
2. If you were able to enter into any small business that you desired, what things would you look for in the business?
3. Suppose you had arranged enough capital so that you could either buy into an existing Outback Steak House or could start your own independent steak house restaurant. What are the advantages and disadvantages of each alternative? Which would you prefer and why?
4. Suppose that you have developed an idea for a new business service. You have limited capital and you do not want to drop out of college. How might you successfully start up a new business using your idea?
5. One evening when you went to pick up your child at the KinderKare, the owner mentioned to you that she would like to sell the business. You have always wanted to run a day care facility and would like to try to buy her business. What facts should you consider in making this decision?
6. After discussing the KinderKare purchase with your banker, you decide to make a determined effort to purchase the business. To make a good decision, what information must you have, and how will you get it?
7. Based on the information you developed, you have decided that the maximum value of the KinderKare including the building and lot is $350,000. You have $35,000 that you inherited from your favorite great aunt. Your parents have promised to invest $25,000. Based on the $70,000 that you have available, the bank has promised to make you an SBA guaranteed loan of $70,000. What are your options if you wish to pursue this opportunity?
8. You took a job bagging coffee for a business that purchases directly from Guatemalan farmers, thereby getting the coffee at a bargain price, while still paying the farmers above market for the coffee. Working with all that caffeine has you charged up about going into business for yourself. The owner is only 60 years old, but he has told you that he'd like to slow down. He has offered to sell you all or part of the business. What things should you consider in making a decision about what to do?

EXPERIENTIAL EXERCISES

1. Using the resources of your library, find the name and address of an active business broker in your area. Arrange an interview with the broker. Write a report detailing what methods the broker uses to place a value on a business for sale.
2. Find out how the owner of the business where you are employed got into business.
3. Visit the Small Business Administration website franchising page at **www.sba.gov/starting_business/startup/franchise.html**. Using the links on that site, find a franchise business that you believe might be successful, were you to buy it. Contact the franchisor, explain your interest, and find out the specifics of the franchise opportunity. Report your findings to your class.

MINI-CASE

TOO HOT TO HOLD

Gwendolyn Bonnefille, a single mother, is barely scraping by. Although she earns a fair salary working in the accounts receivable department of a local business, she has to pay for child care for her two children, Samantha who is 5 and Merlin who is 3. While surfing the web, under a listing titled "businesses that can be moved," she found for sale a business that makes a great hot sauce called Caterwauling Coyote, with the slogan, "You'll howl at the moon!" The sauce is made in the kitchen of the owner, bottled, labeled, and then delivered to gift and specialty shops in south Texas. The equipment to make the sauce is commercial quality and appears to be in good condition.

The business financial statements and the owner's 1040 C business tax returns do not agree. The financial statements show that in the most recent year the business earned $60,000 on sales of $200,000. The 1040 C shows a profit of only $10,000, and a zero tax liability because of deducting losses suffered in prior years. The sellers are asking $240,000 for the business. They are willing to finance $190,000 at 10 percent for 15 years.

When Gwendolyn sat down with the owner, Sylvester Gatos, he attempted to explain the discrepancy between the accounting and the tax returns.

"You see," Sly said, "there are two things. First, some of the expenses on the schedule C aren't really business expenses, if you know what I mean. Second, when we did the income statement, we took out depreciation, interest, property tax, and the money that we used from the business because a buyer will not have those expenses."

CASE DISCUSSION QUESTIONS

1. What do you think about Sly's explanation of the differences between his income statement and his 1040 Schedule C?
2. Suppose that the income statement is reasonably accurate. What do you think about the purchase price?
3. What information should Gwendolyn obtain before making a decision to purchase the business?

SUGGESTED CASES AND ARTICLES

- The Grande General Store, Est. 1948—It's Time To Sell, C-6

Available on Create:

- A&W Brands, Inc.
- Badger Plastics: The Acquisition Process (A)
- Das Wiener Works (B)

SUGGESTED VIDEOS

www.mhhe.com/katz4e

Video Case:

- For a written video case and corresponding clip, visit the OLC at www.mhhe.com/katz4e and select "Chapter 6".
- Blue MauMau

SBTV.com Videos:

- Ontic Engineering
- Franchising: Do's and Don'ts

STVP Videos:

- How Do You Find Soul Mates?
- Do Whatever It Takes To Stay In Business

CHAPTER 7

Small Business Strategies: Imitation with a Twist

● Nick Tostenrude and Dennis Moulton took time to understand their idea's strengths, weaknesses, and their market. How did this thorough analysis lead to their success rather than an unfulfilled dream?

LEARNING OBJECTIVES

After you complete this chapter, you will be able to:

LO1 Describe the decisions needed to establish a foundation for strategic planning.

LO2 Identify the forms of imitative and innovative businesses.

LO3 Articulate the benefits that win over customers.

LO4 Assess how industry changes affect strategy.

LO5 Explain the major strategies of business—differentiation, cost, and focus.

LO6 Determine how to sustain competitive advantage through attracting customers and discouraging competition.

Focus on Small Business: Mindnautilus.com[1]

Nick Tostenrude was attending the University of Portland when he met Dennis Moulton in 1999. The two got to talking, and it turned out both wanted to get into business for themselves. Dennis offered an idea from his father—PC- and Internet-based programs to help the cognitive functioning of people recovering from traumatic brain injury. While Dennis' father had developed the software on the Apple II years before, its functionality was limited by the less capable hardware and software of that early computer. Dennis and Nick thought they would try again, with state-of-the-art technology. They incorporated in March 2000.

The fundamental idea made sense. Doing an industry analysis, they discovered some interesting opportunities. Most of the substitutes for their proposed product involved the person going to a hospital, rehabilitation center, or health professional's office for therapy. The alternative was working at home, but books were hard to use, and videotapes offered limited interaction. Research also showed a market of 54 million people with disabilities in the United States.

There were also some threats in the market. Numerous small mom-and-pop companies offered one or two products, but none had taken the market by storm, due largely to poor marketing, mostly confined to one locality. Another major market hurdle was that many people with traumatic brain injury did not have personal computers equipped with special features, like keypads, pointing devices, and screen enlargers. Without this equipment, even the best cognition software would be unusable. By far the biggest threat was technological. While Dennis' father had developed the software years earlier, creating software that met the demands of a market increasingly sophisticated about therapies and personal computer software was turning out to be a real challenge.

Mindnautilus looked like a promising idea, but one that would require three or four years of expensive research, development, programming, and debugging before any sales could be made. Neither Nick nor Dennis had the deep pockets it would take to fund the research and development effort. The problem was to find a strategy that would leverage what they could do now and use it to build toward their dream.

They knew there was a large market of potential consumers. They also knew there was a pool of firms making assistive devices and software for the market, but for the most part these firms had weak marketing and hence weak sales. Nick and Dennis realized that the Internet was the perfect way to sell these products to a market of families with one or more members with disabilities. Fortunately, the software for creating online stores was easy to master and inexpensive. So they started Enablemart.com, an online store specializing in selling assistive devices and software for people with disabilities. Sales of the Enablemart store would provide cashflow to support development of the program, Mindnautilus.

The business grew to customers in all 50 states and in over 20 foreign countries. The firm's expertise was great enough that it did contract work for Microsoft and Goodwill Industries. The firm gave 10 percent of its pretax profits to charitable causes nominated by its customers. All these together led the firm to its receipt of a 2002 Global Collegiate Entrepreneur Award for the Pacific Northwest region. It also happened that Nick graduated from the University of Portland in 2002 with his bachelor's degree in electrical engineering. How did Nick describe the secret to his success? A superior strategist to the end, he said, "Find a niche." With this track record of success, Nick and Dennis sold EnableMart in 2012 to School Health Corporation.

DISCUSSION QUESTIONS

1. What were the strengths Mindnautilus possessed? What were the weaknesses it faced?
2. What could Mindnautilus do better than its competition?
3. What kind of strategy did Nick and Dennis plan for Mindnautilus?
4. Do you think Dennis and Nick could have predicted they would start EnableMart when they started Mindnautilus? Why or why not?

Strategy in the Small Business

LO1 Describe the decisions needed to establish a foundation for strategic planning.

Strategy is the idea and actions that explain how a firm will make its profit. Whether you know it or not, all small businesses have a strategy. The strategy may be a blueprint for planning or a standard to compare actions against. Either way, strategy defines for you, your customers, and your competition how your business operates.

Good strategy leads to greater chances for survival and higher profits for a small business. What makes a strategy good is its fit to the particulars of your business and the resources you can bring to it. In this chapter, we consider how strategy can be created and applied to help your business be its best.

Strategy in small business is special because most small businesses are more imitative than innovative. If you are opening a home day care center, a machine shop, an Italian restaurant, or an online collectible figurine store, these types of businesses already exist. You can find examples, books, and often even magazines to study, as well as trade and professional associations to join. There are special strategies that aim to help imitative businesses be successful.

Getting to the useful strategies for a small business is a four-step process. Figure 7.1 shows the strategic planning process for small businesses. The first step involves reviewing and confirming the goals that define your firm and knowing your *magic number*. The second step is where you consider your customers and the benefits you want to offer them and plot these out in a procedure called *perceptual mapping*. The third step is to study the dynamics and trends of your industry using a technique called *industry analysis* in order to identify the best way and time to enter business. The fourth step involves building on the prior three steps to determine the best strategic direction and strategy for the firm. After this four-step process, there is a continuing effort called *post start-up* which aims to refine your firm's strategies and tactics in order to maintain a competitive advantage.

As you can see in Figure 7.1, strategy builds on four key types of decisions you make about your firm. These may be made formally or informally in your opportunity analysis or feasibility analysis. These decisions are:

1. The major goals you set for your firm.
2. The types of customers you seek and what benefits you plan to offer them.

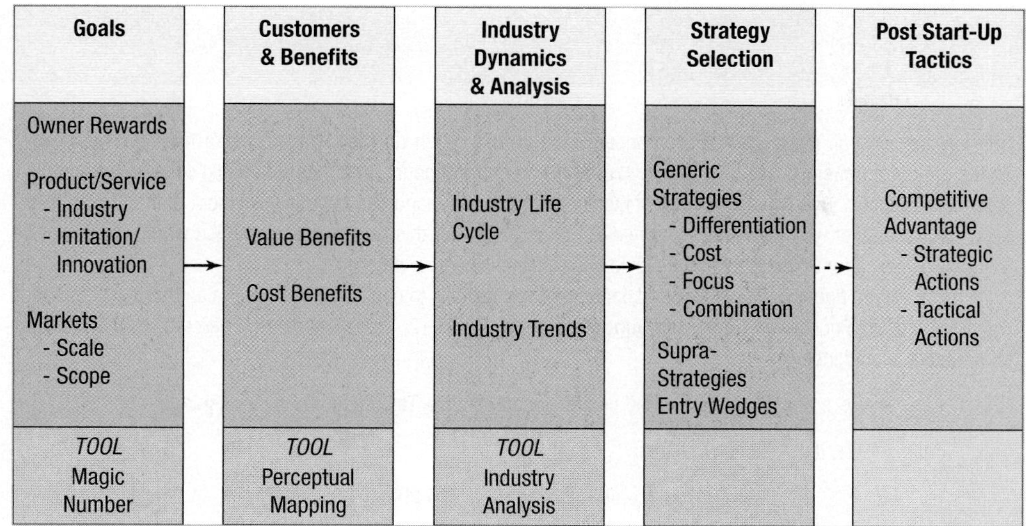

FIGURE 7.1

The Small Business Strategy Process

3. The stage and trend of your chosen industry.
4. The specific generic and supra strategies you choose to pursue.

Goals: The First Step of Strategic Planning

Before getting into industry analysis, you as the entrepreneur need to make some very basic decisions about your goals for your prospective business—you, your idea, and your firm. These **goal** decisions will set the stage for the kind of business you will have and are the foundation for further analyses. There are five initial key goal decisions:

goal
An intended outcome for your business.

1. As owner, what do you expect out of the business?
2. What is your *product or service* idea (and its industry)?
3. For your product or service, how innovative or imitative will you be?
4. Who do you plan to sell to—everyone or targeted markets?
5. Where do you plan to sell—locally, regionally, nationally, globally?

Owner Rewards

For a small business that is starting out, all strategy starts with the owner. As owner, what do *you* want out of your business? In Chapter 1 we introduced the rewards sought by entrepreneurs from their businesses. Some, like flexibility, personal growth, and a solid personal income, were pretty universal. Skill Module 7.1 looks at how you can determine your **magic number**, which is the income you personally seek from the business. Knowing that number from the start, you are better able to evaluate if your proposed business can deliver on that very basic need that everyone reports needing. Other rewards like great wealth and developing a new product or service was mentioned occasionally, while recognition, admiration, power, and family tradition get mentioned least often of all rewards. For EnableMart, the original reward was to generate the wealth necessary to bring Mindnautilus to market, and also provide a service that made it easier for America's 54 million disabled to get the products they need to make their lives better.

magic number
The post-tax income the entrepreneur personally seeks from the business.

Whatever the reward or rewards you seek—it is fine to want more than one—it should be central to your creating the business. In a very real sense, what you want from the business *is* the core of your and your firm's strategy. It is the "why" which drives the process of entrepreneurship.

SKILL MODULE 7.1 Finding Your Magic Number

One key decision all prospective entrepreneurs face is how much do they want to make from the business. That's the entrepreneur's "magic number." For full-time entrepreneurs, that number should cover your monthly personal expenses, give you some leftover money to invest, save, and add to your enjoyment of life. If you have ever made a budget, you know how to arrive at that number. For this example, assume you would like to have $24,000 a year, after taxes. How much would your business need to pay you?

A quick way to figure combined federal, state, and city taxes is to check the numbers related to Tax Freedom Day from the Tax Foundation (**www.taxfoundation.com**). For 2012, the rate was 29.2 percent, so the pre-tax computation would look like:

Pretax income = (Your desired posttax income) / (1 – Tax Freedom Day percentage rate)

For our example, it would look like this:

Pretax income = $24,000 / (1 – 0.292) = $33,898

That is what you would receive after the business taxes are paid. In your feasibility analysis you probably got an idea of what the costs are for your particular type of business. Let's say they are around 75 percent, not including any salary for you. At that level, for you to be able to take home $33,898, your firm would need to sell the amount in the equation (which is the same type of computation as we did on pretax income) below:

Company sales = $33,898 / (1 – 0.75) = $135,592

Now you have a starting goal. Here are some basic ideas what it would take to achieve those sales:

Business	Unit Sale	Number of Units	Number Per Day
Web Design	$50/hour	2,712 hours	13 hours/day
Hedgehog Knife Sheath	$200/sheath	678 sheaths	1.9 sheaths/day
EnableMart	$20/product	6,780 products	19 books/day

The "Number Per Day" gives you an idea of what you need to accomplish each day. For the web designer, we are looking at 250 days a year (5 days a week for 50 weeks). For the Hedgehog Leatherworks (see Chapter 1) and EnableMart, we are figuring an online store open year-round. As you can see from this analysis, the web designer is clearly facing a challenge. She will need to scale back her financial goals, or increase her prices, or rethink her approach in other ways, since few people want to work 13 hours every day. But that is fine, if a few minutes with a pencil and paper can help you get a sense of the task in front of you, it is time well spent.

What is your magic number?

Product/Service Idea and Industry

Along with this pursuit of rewards, there is often an idea for the business. Recall in Chapter 4 we saw that 37 percent of businesses start with an idea which energizes the entrepreneur to start a firm. For 42 percent the idea of starting their own business comes first, while for 21 percent the idea and the desire to start a business are simultaneous.[2] EnableMart was one of those cases where the idea (Mindnautilus) came first. This is an example of a pivot, described in Chapter 1. The feasibility study Nick and Dennis did showed that it would take time to bring this product to market (and for customers to be able to use it easily). Then came the idea for a business to support Mindnautilus, which became EnableMart. Whichever applies in your case, the fact is that the idea for a product or service and the idea to start a business to earn rewards make up the core of strategy—what you plan to do and why you are doing that. The process for evaluating ideas, called the feasibility study, was detailed in Chapter 4. For the purposes of this chapter, we will assume you know your idea is feasible.

Some entrepreneurs may start a firm to get the product or service out, while others may create the product or service and have agents find firms to use it, which is the consignment process described in Chapter 5. Either way, the idea gets made real as a *product* (something physical a customer buys) or a *service* (activities undertaken on a customer's behalf). It is possible to combine products and services, like a GM auto that comes with the OnStar cell phone service. You can learn more about that in Chapter 9.

If you have in mind a product or service, you also have an industry. **Industry** is the general name for the line of product or service being sold. Examples include the restaurant industry, the computer consulting industry, and the collectible doll industry. In addition to a name, industries have numeric codes, called SIC or NAICS codes,[3] which are discussed below. Industry is vitally important to your core strategy decisions because simply put, there are industries that are more profitable than others.

industry
The general name for the line of product or service being sold, or the firms in that line of business.

In fact, picking the right industry is key to the success of your small business. Stanley and Danko,[4] in *The Millionaire Next Door,* point out that two-thirds of all millionaires are self-employed. They say that the key to being successful is selecting an industry that offers good potential for making a profit and attractive opportunities to work with a minimum of risk and competition. These industries are described as having high *industry attractiveness.* Stanley and Danko were surprised to discover that most millionaires who owned businesses are in industries like scrap metal, coal mining, and dry cleaning. It turns out that industries that are attractive from a profit-making sense may not be the industries thought of as attractive places to work. But choosing one of these attractive industries can do a lot to help your firm survive and you to be successful.

Industries which do well in good times and poor historically include financial firms tied to banking, health-related firms, insurance firms (especially related to health), and business consulting.[5] When talking about the small business myths in Chapter 1, other occupations that came up included bookkeeping, credit counseling, and tax preparers.[6] Figure 7.2 gives information about a number of industry sectors and some popular individual businesses to help you get an idea of the relative attractiveness of industries (based on their profitability), and the expected level of sales.

If you know the industry's code number (see Skill Module 7.2 to find out how to do this), you can find out a tremendous amount of information about the industry. This is because most information is coded using the industry number. From the work done by marketing researchers Stanley and Danko[7] as well as BizMiner.com and others, we know there are between 15,000 to 30,000 different industries in the United States.

There are two major classification systems that code industries: the new NAICS (North American industry classification system) and the better-known standard industrial classification system, or SIC. SIC codes have four digits; NAICS have six. NAICS covers more industries and more of the newer types of industries. Skill Module 7.2 gives you help in finding the NAICS and SIC codes for the industry for your business. The Skill Module is also on the Online Learning Center.

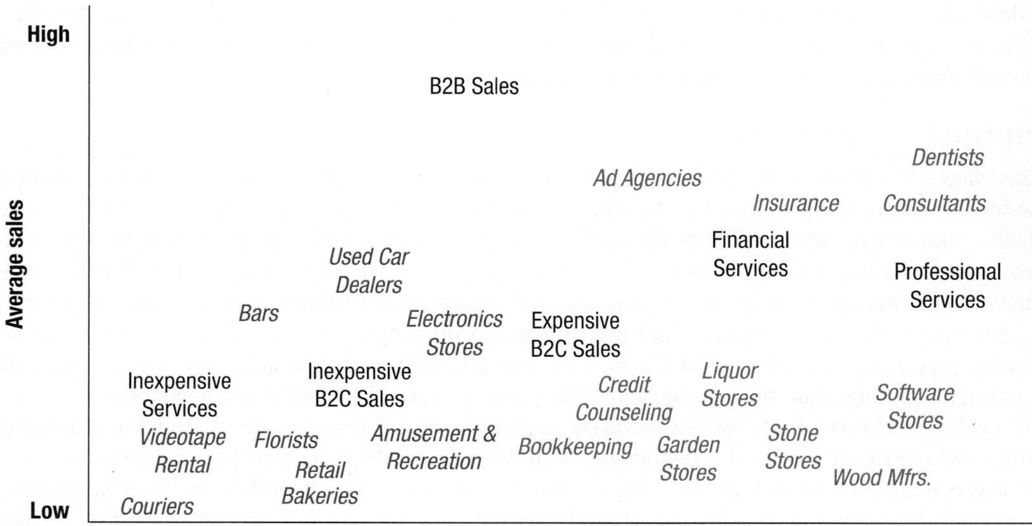

FIGURE 7.2

Attractiveness of Selected Industries and Lines of Business

Industries shown in blue are the most profitable, while industries shown in red are the least profitable. Averages for major industrial sectors are shown in black.

SKILL MODULE 7.2

Finding Your Firm's Industry

Finding the NAICS and SIC codes for your industry is essential to tracking down information about the line of business you want to pursue. Most libraries have reference works that you can read to find your industry such as the *Standard Industrial Classification Manual, 1987* (NTIS, 1987) and the *North American Industry Classification System: United States, 2012* (NTIS, 2012).

It's easier to search online. Go to **www.census.gov/eos/www/naics/** and find the text box that says "enter keyword." Enter the name of your industry. If you are not sure of the exact name, you can try using a part of the name. For example, you could enter comp in the box and get computers and compact disks. For today's example, think about opening a hamburger and fries sort of restaurant to compete with McDonald's. Enter *restaurant* and click on the *2012 NAICS search* button. The results give almost a dozen possibilities including "Fast food restaurant," "Restaurants, full service," and even related industries like "Restaurant Associations."

"Fast food restaurants" is the key. Its NAICS code is 722513. If you had tried the 2007 or 2002 NAICS buttons, the NAICS code would have been 722211.

To see what you can do with it, go to **www.census.gov** and click on "Economic Census," which is in the business section. In it there is another text box where you can enter an NAICS code or keyword. Enter 722211 (the 2007 code) or fast food restaurant or 722513 (the 2012 code) and click on the *NAICS search* button. The result on screen will give you a link to the statistics. Click on the hot link, and you'll find yourself looking at the results from the economic census. You can find out how many fast food restaurants there are nationally or in your state. You can find out how much revenue they had and how many people were employed by them. You can figure averages for per-store sales and employment to get an idea of how well these restaurants do.

For example let's use the 2007 data, specifically the 2007 Census Geographic Distribution, which is a tab on the "Industry Sampler" page. Texas had 16,501 fast-food restaurants (establishments), employing 321,735 people. So the average restaurant employed 9.5 people. Those 16,501 restaurants spent $3,491,573,000 in payroll in 2007, or $211,597 per fast-food place. That works out to around $10,851 in wages or salaries for each employee on average. Now you know a bit about the going rates for workers and the kind of money you'll need to budget.

Armed with the NAICS or SIC codes, you can go to library and online sources listed in Table 7.1 on page 200 to find more detailed information about the industry you're thinking of entering.

LO2 Identify the forms of imitative and innovative businesses.

The key to finding information about industries is knowing how to check the information, and NAICS and SIC codes are essential to that. It is also important to know that there are no "safe" industries. In much the same way that families and societies are living things—things that are born, mature, and can die—industries can be considered living too. Ten years ago, coffee shops were a dead industry in most of the country. However, today, with Starbucks, Panera Bread, Seattle's Best, and a host of independent coffee shops blanketing the country, the industry has been revived through franchises, company-owned stores, and innovative independents.

competitor
Any other business in the same industry as yours.

imitative strategy
An overall strategic approach in which the entrepreneur does more or less what others are already doing.

innovative strategy
An overall strategic approach in which a firm seeks to do something that is very different from what others in the industry are doing.

Imitation and Innovation

This chapter's subtitle is "Imitation with a Twist." The idea reflects the fact that for most small businesses, the owner wants to be a lot like others in the industry, but not exactly like them. Owners who elect to imitate their **competitors** still want to have *something* that distinguishes them from the others—something that makes the owner's firm special and better. That special and better element—that innovation amid a lot of imitation—gives us the kind of entrepreneurial thinking behind the chapter title.

The choice between imitation and innovation is truly important and often overlooked. Businesses, especially new firms, can do more or less what others are already doing—an **imitative strategy**—or they can start doing something that is very different from what others do—an **innovative strategy**. Imitation is the classic small business strategy. We know from the PSED that almost two-thirds of people starting businesses today plan to use imitation as their approach.[8]

There are several advantages to using an imitative strategy.[9] You benefit from being able to buy existing technologies, such as industrial grade washing machines for a laundromat, web servers for a hosting service, or calligraphy pens for greeting card publishing. Architects, builders, real estate agents, zoning boards, equipment manufacturers, equipment servicing companies, and banks are more likely to understand the industry and what is expected. Because of this, they can give you firm estimates of costs and schedules. With imitative approaches, there is also the possibility to buy existing businesses.

Perhaps the key benefit of an imitative strategy comes from your customers. Chances are they already know about the kind of product or service you are offering. This means your marketing efforts can focus on the benefits you offer instead of explaining the product itself.

When you elect an innovative strategy, you have the benefit of making your business precisely fit your own ideas and preferences. Take the example of snowboards. When Dimitrije Milovich built the first modern snowboard in 1969, he not only had to have the product available for purchase, but he also had to inform the customers that such a product existed and how it could be used. With highly innovative businesses, there is often not much opportunity to sell the business, and the owner spends a lot of energy in creating the processes and markets as well as informing suppliers, resellers, and investors about the new product or service.

In practice, most firms use imitation plus or minus one **degree of similarity**. Imitation minus one degree of similarity would be the business equivalent of cloning. It is franchising, first discussed in Chapter 6, in which you purchase a precise and complete copy of an existing business from the franchisor. Imitation itself involves patterning a business on existing firms and processes. Your imitation is not likely to match the precision or completeness of copying seen in franchising, since you are unlikely to have all the information about the model businesses or processes. You may also adapt your business to fit local situations or your current situation. You might pattern your new Italian restaurant after the Olive Garden, but you end up buying your equipment and food from different sources and add local favorites, such as toasted ravioli in St. Louis, barbeque pizza in Memphis, or deep-dish pizza in Chicago. This approach is called **parallel competition**.

degree of similarity
The extent to which a product or service is like another.

parallel competition
An imitative business that competes locally with others in the same industry.

Imitation plus one degree of similarity is where you look at existing businesses and pattern yourself after them, with the exception of one or two key areas in which you seek to do things in a

Chef Joseph Poon, of Philadelphia Chinatown, showcases Asian Fusion cooking, an innovation he helped to spearhead. What kinds of ethical challenges might a pure innovation product or service pose to a small business owner?

new, and hopefully better, way. This is called **incremental innovation** and is second only to parallel competition in frequency. You have seen it in the fast-food business where Burger King told customers "have it your way." This approach was bettered by Wendy's, which offered custom-built hamburgers that were, in addition, "hot and juicy." Hardees moved into the fray with supersized custom burgers. Each company makes custom-built hamburgers, but each added a small innovation to differentiate it from its competition. Small businesses do the same thing, whether they are offering haircuts or golf clubs.

incremental innovation
An overall strategic approach in which a firm patterns itself on other firms, with the exception of one or two key areas.

The last type is **pure innovation**, also called a **blue ocean strategy**, which results in a new product or service. These situations are rare. Typically with a new product or service, you also have a unique setting. For example, Philadelphia chef Joseph Poon was one of the early developers of a food style called *Asian Fusion,* which combined Asian food with contemporary American and nouvelle cuisine elements. His restaurant reflected the Asian Fusion theme with light woods, simple lines, and oriental details. Other Asian Fusion restaurants, such as Roy's of Seattle or the E&O Trading Company in San Jose, California,[10] added different wines, beers, and liquors, and even new types of mixed drinks developed to complement the food. After all this, the Asian Fusion chefs had to convince diners to try these new combinations of flavors.

pure innovation
The process of creating new products or services, which results in a previously unseen product or service.

blue ocean strategy
A strategy based on creating a new product or service which has no competitors.

These ideas lead to a simple set of strategic moves that can help you think about how to compete better as an imitator. Think of the case of the upstart Netflix, which became a major player in the video rental business, but was a relative latecomer.[11]

- Parallel Innovation
  - Use the standard-setter's approach for lower start-up costs: Blockbuster set the standard, so the software and basic inventory for video rental existed.
  - Don't make the mistakes the leader is making: Blockbuster customers complained about lack of selection, and out-of-stock movies, so Netflix had a larger selection and arranged to avoid stock-outs.
- Incremental Innovation
  - Take it to the next level: Pick one area important to customers to do much better than the pioneer. You can be easier, cheaper, or offer higher quality. Netflix offered avid movie renters a better financial deal and better selection.
  - Borrow from Outside: If another industry has a solution that works (and people know about and like), imitate that idea in your home industry. Netflix married the book clubs' use of mail and the video rental model of Blockbuster.

LO3 Articulate the benefits that win over customers.

Remember that a lot of research shows that imitators do better than pioneers in the long run.[12] For example, we know Boeing, Microsoft, and Google, but these are all imitative companies. The pioneers in their industries were companies like Wright or Curtis (airplanes), Digital Research (PC operating systems), Wandex (web searching), and Overture (keyword ad sales). When you do imitation well, it can do well by you.

Markets

A **market** is the business term for the population of customers for your product or service. If you know your market inside and out, you are likely to know much of the key information for how to be successful in your line of business. There are two market decisions you need to make early in the process of going into business. One of these is the **scale** of the market, which is the size of the market—whether you plan to aim for a mass market or a niche market. The other is the **scope** of the market, which defines the geographic range covered by the market—from local to global.

market
The business term for the population of customers for your product or service.

scale
A characteristic of a market that describes the size of the market—a mass market or a niche market.

scope
A characteristic of a market that defines the geographic range covered by the market—from local to global.

Scale: Mass or Niche

When you think about the market for your product or service, you typically have two choices. A **mass market** is a market that involves large portions of the population—all men, all women, all teens, all elderly, all families, all manufacturers, all restaurants. Mass markets are broad, and a mass-market approach targets the entire market.

A **niche market** is a narrowly defined segment of the population that is likely to share interests or concerns—25–34-year-old women, families with twins, Boy Scouts, Italian restaurants,

mass market
A customer group that involves large portions of the population.

niche market
A narrowly defined segment of the population that is likely to share interests or concerns.

manufacturers in your city. Niche markets are specific and narrow, and in a niche market approach, you try to target only customers in the niche.

Most industries have both mass and niche markets. For example, the greeting card industry has mass-market giants like Hallmark and American Greetings, which advertise nationally on TV (a sure sign of a mass marketer). However, the industry is also full of niche markets. For example, Maria Peevey and Lisa Bicker started SimplyShe with greeting cards targeting women going through trying life experiences such as breaking up, motherhood, or weddings. Having identified their niche and its needs, they market their cards through specialty fashion boutiques such as Henri Bendel, as well as online.[13]

Scope: Local to Global

Market scope is related to market scale. Market scope refers to the geography of your target market. It can be local (like a neighborhood or a city), regional (e.g., a metropolitan area or a state), national, international (usually meaning two to a few countries), or global (meaning everywhere). Owners of the businesses studied in the PSED[14] were asked how much of their business they thought would come from each of the geographic categories. Overall, they estimated that 58 percent of sales would be local (within 20 miles), 30 percent would be regional (from 21–100 miles), 22 percent would be national (from 100 miles out to the rest of the United States), and only 4 percent would be international (outside the United States).

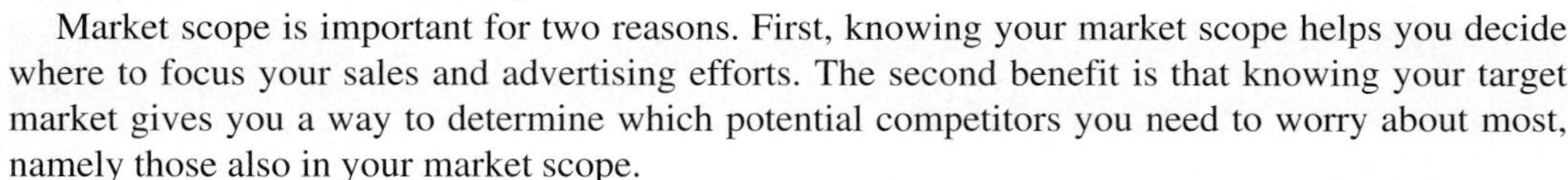

Market scope is important for two reasons. First, knowing your market scope helps you decide where to focus your sales and advertising efforts. The second benefit is that knowing your target market gives you a way to determine which potential competitors you need to worry about most, namely those also in your market scope.

In the Goal step, the key is to bring together the decisions that underlie the business you hope to own. This starts with you and the rewards you seek; the product or service you plan to offer for sale to achieve those rewards; and the industry and markets with which you and your firm will plan to deal. Armed with this basic understanding of your firm, you are ready to begin developing a strategy to achieve your goals. Very often, it starts with a closer consideration of your potential customers and what you can do with your product or service to best catch their attention.

Customers and Benefits: The Second Step of Strategic Planning

In this second step of the strategic planning process, the focus is on the kind of customer to whom you want to sell, and the benefits that will attract them. Just as there are industries that offer better and worse opportunities, there are customers that entrepreneurs prefer. Customers who offer the kinds of rewards you are seeking are generally those you are most likely to view positively. If you are interested in great wealth, having customers who are themselves wealthy and not very sensitive to price issues would be seen as rewarding. If growth is your goal, having customers from whom you can learn and who expect things to be constantly new and improved will help you meet your goal.

There are also some types of customers often seen as particularly attractive. These include:

- *Corporate customers:* Look at Figure 7.2 and compare the B2B (wholesale) to B2C (retail) sales. Selling to other businesses may produce greater profits.
- *Loyal customers:* Loyal customers return and are already presold, making your life easier. They also refer friends, another source of revenue.
- *Local customers:* This was originally true because as the owner you could keep tabs on the satisfaction of local customers more easily than distant ones; but in the digital age, it is less about geographic proximity than about you taking the time to stay in touch with your customers.
- *Passionate customers:* People who are not just loyal but are likely to rave about your business are likely to generate more potential customers than any other type.

There are literally dozens of beliefs about the best customers. Most of them have at least a germ of truth about them. You can learn about the types of customers in your intended line of business by talking to other entrepreneurs already in the business, and by researching the business in the trade press (to find these, refer back to Skill Module 3.1). Look for terms like "customer profile" and "preferred customers" as well as articles about "loyalty programs" and "repeat customers." These articles are most likely to have information about the most prized customers in your proposed line of business.

The point is that thinking ahead about the kind of customer with whom you want to deal is the best way to orient your strategic planning process toward finding those customers when you get to picking a strategy. As you decide on the type of customer you want to encounter, your next step is thinking about the kind of benefits you can offer them to help meet their needs with your product or service.

Value and Cost Benefits

Benefits are characteristics of a product or service that the target customer would consider worthwhile, such as low cost or high quality. The best way to identify desirable benefits is through potential customers. You can do this directly through interviews, focus groups, or questionnaires (see Chapter 12 for more details on how to do this), or indirectly through reviewing websites using the techniques given in Skill Module 7.3. Ratings and complaints for products

SKILL MODULE 7.3 Checking Customer Opinions Online

Today there are many ways to quickly assemble information about products or services from customers from online sources. For this exercise, imagine you would like to produce and market a new iPhone case. The list below will point you to online sources you can use to build a profile of customers and their opinions. The list starts with the most direct ways to find opinions, and shows more complex ways to find opinions as you work your way down the list.

1. When you have a particular product or service in mind, try to start with a website that specializes in it (or type the product name into Google). For example, there really is a site called iphone-cases.com. They sell iPhone cases, but do not have reviews posted. If you try Googling "iPhone case review" you will quickly find sites that include customer ratings and comments for many of the cases.
2. Along the same lines, Amazon.com does a better than average job of soliciting and displaying customer ratings on products.
3. You can go to the major customer opinion sites (epinions.com, yelp.com, and complaints.com) to see if they have anything on iPhone cases. For other sites of this type you can check Yahoo!'s directory (dir.yahoo.com) for "Consumer Opinion."
4. You can try a shopping site like eBay.com, Amazon.com, or shopping.google.com for iPhone cases and look for possible customer ratings of these.
5. Finally, you can look for blogs on the subject. Putting "iPhone case blogs" into Google or Yahoo will point to blogs with individuals passionate about a variety of topics and who along the way mention iPhone cases.
6. Increasingly, manufacturers provide a customer opinion web page and from that you can learn a wealth of information about your competitors' products.

With these reviews, you look for themes about what satisfies and dissatisfies customers. What these reviews miss are potential customers—people who did not buy. On the other hand, those who provide reviews tend to be the more passionate customers—pro or con. You can get a wealth of information from dozens of people for free in a matter of minutes.

Beware that one problem is the "fake review," often gushingly positive reviews which turn out to have been written by the manufacturer or reseller. That is why it is important to get reviews and comments from different sites and keep an eye out for similar-sounding reviews. When presenting your results, list the sites you visited and the number of customer reviews you analyzed. You can use the value benefits list to categorize your findings, or make a set of categories that fit the special features of your product or service.

These two burgers have very similar costs for raw materials and preparation, but one costs $2 more than the other because of the value benefits it offers.

and companies can give you valuable information on what benefits people want, and might want more of. Usually the benefits focus on value added to the product or service or on the cost of the product or service.

Benefits are usually characterized as value benefits or cost benefits. A *value benefit* displays characteristics related to the nature of the product or service itself. Things like quality, fashion, and reputation are elements that give a product or service value in the eyes of the customer. A complete list is given in The Thoughtful Entrepreneur box on value and cost benefits.[15] Value benefits are important because they are almost always what lead to higher prices and higher profits. For example, McDonald's Big Mac often costs $2 more than their double cheeseburger. The difference between them are some sesame seeds, a third piece of bun between the top and bottom patty, the "special" Big Mac sauce, and some lettuce. Both have two all-beef patties, two buns, and cheese, which you would figure (correctly) are the major costs of the sandwiches. But people pay far more for the Big Mac and pay it far more often. Next time, ask your friends why they do that. The answers you will get will tell you a lot about value benefits, and how much people will pay for them.

While value benefits refer to what the customer senses in the product or service, *cost benefits* refer to the ways by which a firm can keep costs low for the customer. These include scale and scope savings, and a full list is given in the same Thoughtful Entrepreneur box. It is often important for customers to know one of these cost benefit reasons why a product or service has a low price so that they do not erroneously conclude that your firm has cut price by cutting quality.

Benefits are central to how you appeal to your target customer base. Picking benefits customers find attractive makes your firm attractive to them. Picking customer-desired benefits that your competitors do not offer is a powerful way to make your firm stand out from the competition. Benefits drive your firm's offering to its customers and influence every part of the strategy process. As we will see later, benefits can be combined to offer themed strategic packages.

Offering the benefits your customers want opens up the possibility of your being able to charge a premium price and make higher profits, since people are willing to pay for value-based benefits they desire. Having cost-based benefits can also increase profits by lowering your cost of doing business, and thereby increasing your margin relative to your competition's. Therefore, it is easy to see how benefits help you select a strategy that improves your firm's profitability.

As you decide what benefits to offer, you open up the possibility of using a powerful strategic analysis tool called a **perceptual map**. Perceptual maps are a graphic display of products, services, brands, or companies evaluated in two or more ways at once. Very often one of these ways is cost or price or one of the cost-related ideas from the Cost Benefits list in the Thoughtful Entrepreneur box, since most consumers have ideas about what they are willing to pay. So price becomes one of the dimensions of your perceptual map.

perceptual map
A graphic display which positions products, services, brands, or companies according to their scores on important strategic dimensions.

The other dimension can be what you think you or your customer will think is most important. It could be the stylishness of an item of clothing, the speed of a cell phone app or car, any of the Value Benefit ideas mentioned in the Thoughtful Entrepreneur box. You are not limited to one idea. Entrepreneurs often make different perceptual maps to find a benefit that the competition is

THE THOUGHTFUL ENTREPRENEUR

Value and Cost Benefits

VALUE BENEFITS

Quality: Offering a quality level others do not. It can be the highest quality, just enough quality to meet the basic need, or a bit more quality than is typical for the price. Offering guarantees and warranties also reflects quality benefits.

Style: Items that are beautiful, fashionable, popular, or otherwise aesthetically pleasing.

Delivery: Sometimes simply offering delivery is enough, but other times you may need to deliver quickly, on schedule, or where others do not.

Service: Examples include the go-the-extra-mile sort, the personalized know-your-customer's-name sort, the we-serve-you-in-one-minute sort, or even the service-after-the-sale sort.

Technology: You can offer state-of-the-art or leading-edge technology, technology that others do not have, or technology that automates or simplifies tasks or that meets industry standards. Offering complementary technology such as voice mail or answering machines to people with telephones also fits in here.

Shopping ease: Providing one-stop shopping; having all of a product line; making ordering, returning, or upgrading easy for the customer are all benefits.

Personalization: This can come in building custom products or services, or personalizing the customer experience.

Assurance: Offering guarantees, warranties, or service that takes the risk out of buying your product or service.

Place: Being conveniently local is one example. Being willing to sell and deliver where others do not is another.

Credit: One key benefit small businesses offer customers can be extending credit where larger firms and chain stores will not.

Brand/reputation: This can come from the products or services that you offer, or from your own firm's reputation.

Belonging: Some products confer value because they make the customer part of a larger group, such as a member of a club or an online gaming community.

Altruism: If your product helps the community, a group, the environment, or the world, it is a benefit.

COST BENEFITS

Lower costs: Operating from your home, getting family members to contribute their time for free, or selling something you've already gotten your value out of are all examples of ways small businesses keep their costs low.

Scale savings: Buying in volume usually produces savings, so some firms buy in bulk and sell or repackage in smaller amounts, passing along some of the cost savings.

Scope savings: A multifunction printer has a broad scope—it combines a printer, a scanner, and a fax machine into one box. This is because they can share parts, and this sharing results in lower costs.

Learning: As a firm gets more experience, it can often work with fewer mistakes and greater efficiencies, thereby lowering costs.

Organizational practices: Possibly a small business has automated or professionalized or mastered a product or service to the extent it can do it more cheaply than others.

not delivering on, but their own company could. That kind of opportunity is the goal of perceptual mapping—a combination of Value and Cost benefits your firm provides and makes your firm stand out from others in your industry or market. Skill Module 7.4 takes you through developing a perceptual map.

Building Perceptual Maps

SKILL MODULE 7.4

Let's build a hypothetical perceptual map for EnableMart, the firm in the opening vignette for this chapter. As noted in the vignette, one of the key value benefits would be offering a broader selection of products than most local stores usually carried, so one dimension would be the number of products offered. And we will use price for the other dimension since people were concerned about how hard a hit their pocketbooks would take. This produces a two-dimensional grid like the following:

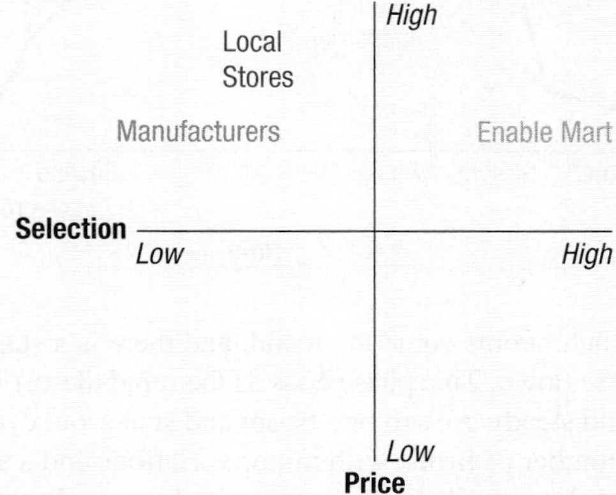

The local stores had high prices and limited selection, and manufacturers were not much better on either dimension. So with a broader catalog of products available for sale from one online site, EnableMart could occupy a unique competitive position. Note in this analysis they would set their prices only a little lower than local stores and manufacturers. Why? In this analysis the benefit EnableMart would be offering offers its customers is one-stop shopping. With that breadth of products and convenience of one-stop shopping, EnableMart would not need to compete entirely on price. This also meant that if this was the way they promote their business to customers, their profit margins could be larger.

Notice how there were no other firms in the high-high quadrant with them? To many strategists, that is the ideal outcome—offering high value with few or no competitors in the space, which justifies a higher price. That is the idea behind blue ocean strategies. In many industries, there are competitors in your space, so you need to focus on some combination of benefits on which your firm excels and less little competition, and that becomes your competitive advantage.

LO4 Assess how industry changes affect strategy.

Industry Dynamics and Analysis: The Third Step of Strategic Planning

Industry refers not only to your product or service, but also to all the firms also selling that product or service, in other words, your competitors. In setting strategy you need to look at your competitors in order to best position your firm, but you also want to look at the changes in competitors, sales, and profits in your industry—what are called the **industry dynamics**—to make sure it is a good time to enter it.

It turns out the fortunes of industries move in a predictable way. Figure 7.3 shows the two ways the number of firms in an industry change.[16] Most industries' **introduction stage** starts with only a few firms. These firms elected to be innovative in their approach, making a new product or offering a new service. The number of firms typically grows slowly at first. Sales are probably small, and most customers are largely unaware of the offering. When enough customers have bought the product so that it begins to draw the attention of the general public, there are two possibilities for the **growth stage**. Most products and services tend to grow at a regular rate, one at which the growth in the number of firms more or less meets customer demand. However, some products or services turn out to be extremely popular or "hot" and grow very rapidly. In these cases, the original firms are unable to keep up with consumer demand. Other firms jump in to take advantage of the growth; this stage is often called the **boom**. Firms begin to compete on features and price, and there may seem to be an explosion

industry dynamics
Changes in competitors, sales and profits in an industry over time.

introduction stage
The life cycle stage in which the product or service is being invented and initially developed.

growth stage
An industry life cycle stage in which customer purchases increase at a dramatic rate.

boom
A type of life cycle growth stage marked by a very rapid increase in sales in a relatively short time.

FIGURE 7.3

The Industry Life Cycle

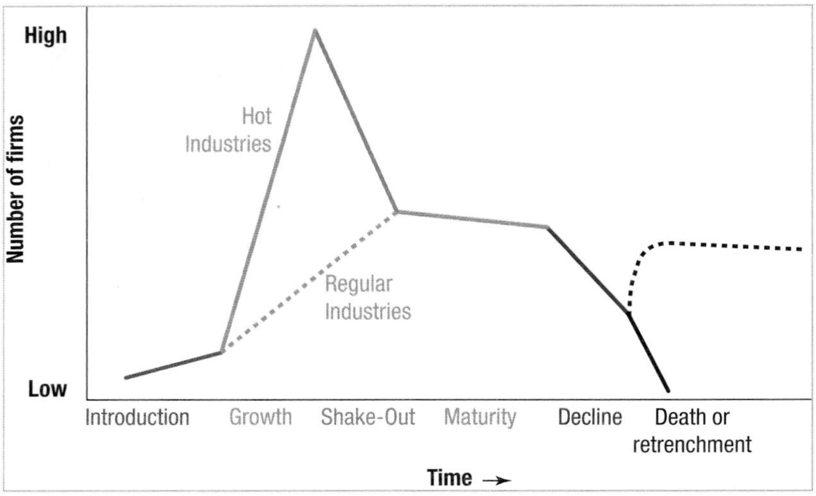

shake-out
A type of life cycle stage following a boom in which there is a rapid decrease in the number of firms in an industry.

maturity stage
The third life cycle stage, marked by a stabilization of demand, with firms in the industry moving to stabilize or improve profits through cost strategies.

decline stage
A life cycle stage in which sales and profits of the firms in the industry begin a falling trend.

retrenchment
An organizational life cycle stage in which established firms must find new approaches to improve the business and its chances for survival.

industry analysis (IA)
A research process that provides the entrepreneur with key information about the industry, such as its current situation and trends.

of choices. Eventually, all such booms come to an end, and there is a stage called the **shake-out** in which many of the firms close down. This phase ends as the rapid die-off of firms stops.

Whether through slow and steady growth or a boom and shake-out cycle, the industry eventually reaches a relatively stable number of firms, with minor variations and a slow drop in numbers. This is called the **maturity stage**. Eventually mature industries begin a **decline stage**. Some industries face death, while others find new life in a process called **retrenchment**. We will look at those later stages later in this chapter.

Starting early is not always a guarantee of eventual success. Consider cars—the original car companies were small businesses. Charles and Frank Duryea, brothers who created a family business, made the first production car in the United States in 1893. Firms from the start-up stage included Duryea, Winton, and Studebaker as well as Olds, Cadillac, and Ford. The boom started in 1905 and went to 1915 with over 75 auto manufacturers, many of them still small businesses. In the shake-out during World War I, the number dropped into the teens, settling into the maturity phase of the Big 3 (GM, Ford, and Chrysler) who survived into the 21st century.

Industry dynamics are important in telling you and potential partners or investors about the prospects for the industry as a whole. Obviously it is easier to sell people on your business when the whole industry is growing. But if the industry is not growing there are still ways to be successful, but as a start-up you need to have worked these through ahead of time. As mentioned before, the market relinquishment in the declining airline industry after 9/11 opened up opportunities for new small airlines in the cities abandoned by the major airlines. Remember, there are small businesses started in every industry at every stage of the industry life cycle. Knowing where your industry is in the life cycle helps you to craft the best strategy for success.

Tool: Industry Analysis

Armed with the concepts and preliminary information about the product/service and the market, you are ready to do a preliminary industry analysis. **Industry analysis (IA)** is a research process

SKILL MODULE 7.5

Short and Sweet Industry Analysis

The basics of industry analysis (IA) consist of knowing seven pieces of information.

1. **SIC/NAICS number and description (online):** Getting this information is detailed in Skill Module 7.2. It is important to know in order to search for other information about the firm.
2. **Industry size over time (online):** Getting this information is detailed in Skill Module 7.2 for 2007 data, but you can also get earlier years. These numbers tell you the overall trend (growing, stable, declining) and the degree of fragmentation of the industry (how many firms are in the industry, and how much of the market

the largest firms have). Fragmented industries—in which the largest four firms control 40 percent or less of the sales—are more likely to have active small business populations.

3. **Profitability:** This is key data. You can get the basic information for a wide variety of industries from the Bizstats website (**www.bizstats.com**). For this site you need to know the description of your business (you will find restaurant under "Retailing—Restaurant and Drinking Places") and an estimated total sales per year (put in what you would hope your sales would be if you do not have better information). You can pay for online reports at the Risk Management Association (RMA) or BizMiner websites, or you can check if your school or local library has a copy of the RMA's *Annual Statement Studies: Financial Ratio Benchmarks*. The key numbers are in the "Income Data" section in percentage form. Find the size of your firm above the "Number of Statements" number (for start-up businesses, the smallest size is often the best place to start). Then look down the column for the "Gross Profit," "Net Profit," and "Profit Before Taxes" numbers. **Gross profit** is what is left after deducting the cost of goods sold. **Net profit** is what is left after deducting the operating expenses of the business. **Profit before taxes** represents the amount of money the owner or owners take out of the firm annually and on which they pay taxes. When the business can sustain it, owners tend to put their salaries in the operating expense category. However, if the firm cannot afford the owner's salary, the only income is the profit before taxes.
4. **How profits are made (interview or articles):** Armed with the information from above, you can look for the last piece of the puzzle—how profits are made. There are usually four activities to evaluate. One is what can be done to generate more sales. Second is a judgment of whether it is possible to charge a premium for a product or service. Third is how to keep the cost of goods or services below the industry's average. Fourth is looking at ways to keep operating expenses below industry averages. Small businesses may use one or more of these approaches. Finding out which get used and the specifics of how they are used generally requires either talking to people in the industry or checking out the industry press. Skill Module 3.1 talks about where to find the trade and professional press for particular industries. If you go the interview route, you can talk to people at companies in the industry. Among the owners most willing to talk are those who have been officers in trade and professional associations or owners of businesses who would not see you as competition, such as owners in other cities. Many people have also found chat rooms, like those at **http://groups.google.com**, or discussion boards (via **www.boardreader.com**) to be useful in finding people and comments. Whenever possible, try to get at least five different sources to make sure you know what is really going on.
5. **Target market competitor concentration (directory checking):** By looking at the listings for local and commercial directories (and companies' websites), you can get an idea of the market scope and scale of the businesses with whom you'll be competing. By getting the number that matches your firm in scale and scope, you can get a clear idea of the concentration of competitors in your segment of the industry—and whom you will need to keep an eye on.
6. **Analysis:** In general, the data you have gathered is put into a report, which helps readers understand what the numbers mean for the industry under consideration. When analyzing the industry, give an overview of the industry (e.g., growing, stable, declining, does it have any major segments like fine-dining vs. quick service restaurants) in words and numbers, its size and profitability (as well as the trends for each over the past 3 to 5 years), and the major strategies by which businesses in the industry make money (e.g., cost or differentiation strategies, see "Strategy Selection" later in this chapter).
7. **Sources:** Let readers know where you obtained your information (e.g., books, websites, or personal interviews). It is important to assure them of the quality of your work. Without sources, you could be accused of plagiarism.

gross profit
Funds left over after deducting the cost of goods sold.

net profit
The amount of money left after operating expenses are deducted from the business.

profit before taxes
The amount of profit earned by a business before calculating the amount of income tax owed.

that provides the entrepreneur with key information about the industry, such as its current situation and trends. Most entrepreneurs initially do an IA to find out what the profits are in an industry in order to better estimate possible financial returns. Taking this one step further, finding out how those profits are generated often makes the difference between success and failure. Armed with this information, the entrepreneur can tell if the industry is growing, stable, or in decline and what the degree of competition is. Skill Module 7.5 provides a how-to description for gathering the key types of information needed to perform an industry analysis. It also explains how the information is useful. For a complete example of an industry analysis, see this chapter's appendix.

What are you looking for in your industry analysis? You want a business that can help you meet the magic number you determined earlier in the chapter. In looking at the other numbers in the industry analysis, you may see ways to cut costs, or leverage friends or expertise or other resources available to you to make your business more profitable than the average one. That can be a tremendously useful finding.

Knowing the stage and trend in the industry is important to thinking about how you will enter the industry. Going into an established industry means it is easy to find locations, equipment, and experienced people (think pizza parlors). Going into an industry early may mean you have to spend more time and money doing things for yourself. It is better to know these things early. If the analysis tells you that you are facing a lot of competition, you want to pay particular attention in building or rebuilding your perceptual map to find a set of benefits that will help your firm stand out. All in all, an industry analysis is central to your plotting of your firm's strategy.

Table 7.1 provides a listing of many of the key databases used in assembling industry analyses. Some are online, while others are in book form and available in local libraries. Armed with

TABLE 7.1 Sources of Data for Industry Analysis

Free Online Sources

BizStats.com—Offers profit and cost information for about 100 industries dominated by small businesses. Also has balance sheets and income statements as well as a calculator to project financials from the firm's sales and legal form of organization. BizStats has a for-fee companion called BizMiner (see below).

Bureau of Labor Statistics Consumer Expenditure Survey—One of the few databases that tracks buying habits (expenditures) of American consumers (families and individuals). Useful for determining market size. Also includes income and demographic information on consumers, **www.bls.gov/cex/**.

Census.gov's Industry Samplers—There are web pages, gathering together sales, employment, and establishment counts for 7,500 separate industries. The data are based on the 2007 Economic Census. Samplers based on the 2012 census will come out starting in early 2013. Type "Industry Statistics Sampler" (with the quotation marks) into Google or Yahoo! to find them. The best start page is the "All sector" one. When you find the page for your industry, remember to scroll down to the bottom. There you will find gems like "Business Expenses," which can tell you what firms actually spent their money on at the time of the survey.

Sources Likely to Be Found in a Library

Standard and Poor's Industry Surveys—This gives you the overall trend in narrative and statistical terms for 52 major industries.

Encyclopedia of American Industries—Provides detailed rundowns on major industries. Names leaders, gives upcoming trends as well as historic ones. Has two volumes, one for manufacturing and one for all other industries. (Also available online as the Business and Company Resource Center database.)

Industry Norms and Key Business Ratios, and RMA Annual Statement Studies—Each of these two competing products offers a rundown of the financials for hundreds of industries, along with the key ratios (see Chapter 15 for more detail on this).

Market Share Reporter—Compiles market share data on products and service market shares for public and private (i.e., small business) companies.

For-Fee (Not Free) Online Sources—Many school and local libraries already have access to these databases, so check with yours.

BizMiner.com—BizMiner covers over 15,000 industries including those most dominated by small business. For example, BizMiner has reports on more than a dozen types of restaurants and has similar coverage in other industries. In addition to financials, BizMiner offers market reports for thousands of industries in hundreds of U.S. communities.

Business and Company Resource Center—Database with an extensive listing of industries (along with industry reports), companies, and news articles linked to specific firms. Listings of small businesses give names, location, and in some cases sales. Competing databases with similar types of data (but in less organized form) include Lexis and ABI/Inform. Your library may have the hard copy version of this, the *Encyclopedia of American Industries.*

IBISWorld—Covers 700 industries in the United States along with economic and demographic (market) profiles.

Mintel Reports—Covers United States and Europe with an emphasis on market research (vs. industry analysis). Gives consumer segments and explains the competitive positions of companies in covered industries.

the information from your industry analysis, you are in a better position to decide if the industry meets your needs for income (which comes from profits and operating revenues), financial growth (depending on the trend of the industry as a whole), and competitive challenge (depending on the number and concentration of competitors). It can also help you determine if you have or can get the expertise needed to run a profitable business (comparing how profits are made to how you would run your business if you started now). If the IA outcomes do not look promising, there are thousands of other industries to try, and it is time to think about what you can offer to attract customers to your business.

Strategy Selection: The Fourth Step in Strategic Planning

LO5 Explain the major strategies of business—differentiation, cost, and focus.

There are three classic strategies for businesses of all types—differentiation, cost, and focus.[17] Because they are so widely applicable, they are called **generic strategies**. **Differentiation strategies** are aimed at mass markets—situations in which nearly everyone might buy your product or service. With this strategy, you try to show how your firm offers some combination of value benefits that is different from and better for the customer than those offered by competitors.

Relatively few small businesses use differentiation strategies, because it is hard for small businesses to have the resources to pursue mass markets. It happens most often when a small business offers a mass-market product or service locally. For example, a gas station offers a mass-market service, but its sales are naturally limited to a particular location. This business reality sets boundaries for where the firm competes, which help target advertising and pricing.

Cost strategies are also aimed at mass markets. In a cost strategy, you try to show how your firm offers a combination of cost benefits that appeal to the customer. Small businesses in a variety of industries make use of mass-market cost strategies. Typically, this comes when the small business can pursue a very low cost operation. For example, one gravel supplier in Memphis, Tennessee, was the undisputed low-cost provider. His secret? A farmer by trade, he discovered gravel under one of his farm fields. He sold directly to the users, cutting out intermediaries and their costs.

Focus strategies target a portion of the market, called a *segment* or *niche*. Instead of selling mass-market gravel for everyone, a focus strategy might target people seeking decorative gravel. For example, Scott Stone Company in Mebane, North Carolina, offers eleven different types of gravel that differ in color, stone size, and durability. By ensuring the quality and consistency of the gravel and knowing which types work best in specialized settings, such as oriental gardens or waterscapes, Scott Stone offers customers products and expertise not readily available elsewhere.

Small businesses often use a combination strategy that can use aspects of differentiation or cost approaches that are reformulated for the niche market. You identify a focus or combination strategy by figuring out what benefits your market most wants. This can be done by asking customers outright, through surveys, or by looking at what is working among your competitors locally or in more advanced markets. Often you will find that your market seems to want several benefits at once.

Building from this, strategy researchers such as Dean Shepherd and Mark Shanley as well as Michael Porter have identified classic benefit combinations which they call *supra-strategies* [18] which are given in Exhibit 7.1. All are designed to work where there are many small businesses in an industry, along with a few larger firms.

Tightly managed decentralization can also work in more conventional firms too. The Menlove family mastered the auto business in southern Utah with a Dodge dealership that started in 1962. Family members opened a Toyota dealership in 1986, and a Mitsubishi-Subaru dealership in 2002. Each one is highly rated in customer satisfaction and sales volume.[19] Part of the underlying reason for their success is their ability to transplant the skills they mastered in the first dealership.

generic strategies
Three widely applicable classic strategies for businesses of all types—differentiation, cost, and focus.

differentiation strategy
A type of generic strategy aimed at clarifying how one product is unlike another in a mass market.

cost strategy
A generic strategy aimed at mass markets in which a firm offers a combination of cost benefits that appeals to the customer.

focus strategy
A generic strategy that targets a portion of the market, called a *segment* or *niche*.

EXHIBIT 7.1

Eleven Small Business Supra-Strategies

Craftsmanship: Specialized product, localized business operations, high levels of craftsmanship (vs. competitors with scale economies).

Customization: Short delivery times, custom features, short production runs, high quality (vs. products that are mass produced).

Supersupport: Extensive, intensive, and personalized after-sales service.

Serving the underserved/interstices: Targeting markets forgotten by larger competitors.

Elite: High-quality products with high prices, backed up by high expenditures for advertising and R&D (vs. mass-market products).

Single-mindedness: Developing and demonstrating exceptional expertise in one product or service (vs. competitors with broad approaches or product lines).

Comprehensiveness: Offering one-stop shopping with complete inventory, immediate delivery, knowledgeable staff, and the major supporting services in one location.

Formula facilities: Use a prepackaged business (like a McDonald's franchise or a preconfigured restaurant package from Sysco) to offer a better or more consistent product or service.

Bare bones or no-frills: Keep prices super low by cutting back on décor (think warehouse stores), hours (think weekends only or flea markets), or employees.

Cutting out the intermediary: Today farmers at their roadside stands and bands selling their own tracks online are able to sell at lower prices and still make more money by eliminating wholesalers' and retailers' mark-ups.[20]

Tightly manage decentralization: Once you know how to efficiently run one type of business, it often becomes easier to open related firms. This is especially common for Internet businesses.

Armed with these strategic choices, it is possible to profile the most typical strategies for new businesses. Table 7.2 shows four types of start-ups and outlines how they align with the scope, generic strategies, imitation/innovation choice, and supra-strategies discussed above.

It might help to think about how Table 7.2 applies in a particular industry. Let's look at Italian restaurants (part of NAICS 72211). There are probably several Italian restaurants where you live or go to school. If you think about it, the vast majority offer the same sorts of dishes. They are fundamentally imitators of one another. Most of them differentiate themselves based on one or two menu items (one has cannoli, another has Italian wedding cake, etc.). That is their craftsmanship. Another may differentiate on the basis of atmosphere (i.e., best place to take a date) or location (close enough to walk to from class). They probably have nearly identical kitchens and bought most of their furniture and serving ware from the same restaurant supply store. That is their formula facility. Together, these restaurants are classic imitators.

There is also probably another Italian restaurant known as the place to go toward the end of the month, when money is tight. The menu has the same sort of items, but the quality of the ingredients may be less (e.g., more like institutional food) or the décor may be nothing to look at, but the prices are always low. That restaurant is your classic cost leader.

Last, think about the Italian restaurant that has the most different menu. It may be hard to find a marinara sauce on the menu. The décor may look more at home in a Scandinavian restaurant, and the menu may change with the season and what looks good locally. Here you have a firm pursuing

TABLE 7.2 Typical Strategies for Small Business Start-Ups

	Classic Imitator	Internet Imitator	Classic Cost Leader	Classic Innovator
Market Scope	Niche	Niche or mass	Niche	Niche
Optimal Strategy	Focus (differentiation)	Focus (differentiation or cost)	Focus (cost)	Focus (differentiation)
Imitation/Innovation	Imitation	Imitation	Imitation	Innovation
Organizational Goal	Match competition with one element different	Match competition but be online	Lowest price	Master technology
Supra-Strategy	Craftsmanship; formula facilities	Comprehensiveness (inventory); cutting out the intermediary; serving the underserved	Bare-bones; cutting out the intermediary; single-mindedness (cost)	Elite; single-mindedness; supersupport
Attractiveness	Moderate to low	Moderate to low	Low	Moderate to high
Life Cycle Stage	All	All	All except introduction	Introduction, growth, or retrenchment

an innovator strategy. It may appeal only to a few individuals. Because the food varies so much, they are more willing to tweak recipes to fit the customer's wishes. Some of the equipment in the kitchen or the seating area will probably be different from what the other local Italian restaurants have. That too is part of the innovator strategy. Innovators either grow enough to become mainstream, or they die out fairly quickly.

Innovators may also come along as drivers of the retrenchment of an industry. The growth of northern Italian cuisine (Italian without red sauce) revitalized the Italian restaurant industry by expanding the menu and reenergizing bored customers to come back and learn about new dishes. The growth of the wine industry in the United States also led to a revitalization of Italian eating. The Internet version of the Italian restaurant is the online ordering system pioneered by big chains like Pizza Hut, but is now available for small restaurants everywhere. The food is the same. The prices are the same, but the difference is the ability to order online. For some other businesses, the online inventory may be larger than the one at the store, because the entrepreneur can fill an online order through their supplier, without adding to their own inventory. So it is possible to be more comprehensive online than in the store.

Most of the time your preferences for a particular type of business or industry and the industry analysis you perform are closely tied together. But there are times when opportunities pop up unexpectedly, and suddenly you can find yourself trying to decide if the opportunity is the right business and industry for you. This ability to quickly pivot is one of the classic strengths of the entrepreneur. Retired entrepreneurship professor Karl Vesper[21] named these opportunities **entry wedges,** and he identified seven that come-up again and again:

entry wedge
An opportunity that makes it possible for a new business to gain a foothold in a market.

- **Supply shortages:** Supply shortages occur when a new product is in demand. The target audience is leading-edge buyers who are willing to pay a premium to be the first to have the product. This is a short-term market and one that changes rapidly. The key benefits are delivery, shopping ease, and style.
- **Unutilized resources:** Unutilized resources can be a physical resource like gravel in a farm field or even entire inner cities (see Small Business Insight: Initiative for a Competitive Inner City). It can also be a human resource. Tax Resources, Inc. was started in 1988 by people experienced in dealing with the IRS in order to advise taxpayers on legal strategies to minimize their taxes or handle audits.[22] The key benefits are lower costs, scale savings, or organizational practices.

- **Customer contracting:** Customer contracting occurs when a customer, most often a business, is willing to sign a contract with a small business to ensure a product or service. Because big businesses frequently downsize, they have ongoing needs to outsource work. Former employees are often the preferred source for independent subcontractors. The key benefits are quality, delivery, technology, shopping ease, brand/reputation, and assurance. Style and personalization are often factors too.
- **Second sourcing:** Second sourcing seeks out customers who are already being serviced by another firm. The strategy is to offer customers a second place to obtain goods or services. Often the advantage the small business offers is being locally based. Second sourcing provides the customer with greater certainty of supplies or services, and at its best provides a competitive pressure to keep both suppliers providing the best service and prices. Like customer contracting, the key benefits are quality, delivery, technology, shopping ease, brand/reputation, and assurance.
- **Market relinquishment:** Market relinquishment occurs when business firms leave a market. Since the 9/11 terrorist attacks, the major American airlines have dramatically scaled back their service. For small commuter airlines, these market relinquishments have been opportunities to expand and provide ongoing service to smaller airports. Key benefits are place, shopping ease, quality, delivery, and service.
- **Favored purchasing:** Favored purchasing occurs because government agencies, government-sponsored commercial contracts, and many big businesses have policies that provide for set-asides or quotas for purchases from small businesses. You can find out more at the SBA's online government contracting site. Key benefits are quality, delivery, service, assurance, place, and belonging.
- **Government rules:** Rule changes by the government can help small firms compete. For example, when the Environmental Protection Agency let small construction firms out of some of the water pollution treatment requirements that large firms must face, it gave the small businesses a savings of $1.5 billion, which made them more competitive. The Regulatory Flexibility Act of 1980 drives many of these rule changes in government.[23] Key benefits here are technology, service, personalization, lower costs, and organizational practices.

The industry analysis helps confirm that you have chosen the right industry, and also where your competitors are and the current industry stage. That and your own decisions earlier about the scope of your business and whether you plan to pursue an imitative or innovative strategy give you the fundamentals for deciding the type of small business strategy that makes the most sense for your start-up. With that information in mind, it is time to think about how you will set up your firm to implement the strategy.

SMALL BUSINESS INSIGHT

INITIATIVE FOR A COMPETITIVE INNER CITY

The inner city of Buffalo, New York, is an unlikely place to find a growing construction company. It is an economically depressed, gritty, urban center still on the long road to revitalization. Some folks, however, see a lot of potential in it. Sundra Ryce graduated from Buffalo State in 1996, and started SLR Construction Services Company. She knew the industry from working in her father's construction firm. She chose the inner city because it put her close to her clients in government and helped keep costs low. One of the few woman and minority certified construction firms in the United States, SLR was able to land major contracts with the Veterans Administration. Her drive led SLR to become number four on a national list of most accomplished inner city businesses[24] in 2003 when she was 28 years old.

Post Start-Up Tactics

LO6 Determine how to sustain competitive advantage through attracting customers and discouraging competition.

The goal of strategy after the start-up stage is to maximize profits (or any other reward you specify as meeting your criteria for success) and protect your business from the competition. To secure success, there is a step you need to take past picking and implementing the right strategy. It is the step of securing competitive advantage. **Competitive advantage** is the particular way you implement your customer benefits that keeps your firm ahead of other firms in your industry or market. Competitive advantage is your firm's edge in meeting and beating the competition.

competitive advantage
The particular way a firm implements customer benefits that keeps the firm ahead of other firms in the industry.

It can be harder than it looks. Why? In part because most small businesses face a lot more forms of competition than they initially realize. Strategy guru Porter[25] identifies five different threats of competition for any business, see Figure 7.4. Imagine you plan to start a web development firm in Pocatello, Idaho.

The first place to look at for competitive threats are *existing firms* in your industry. Pretty much all the other web developers in the Pocatello vicinity pose the threat of *rivalry*. Since web development is even being taught in high schools, another potential competitive threat will be *potential entrants,* other web development firms that open after yours. If you think about why people come to a web developer, you realize that there is a very broad threat of *substitutes* with which you compete. Prepackaged website templates are offered by many hosting services, companies like monstercommerce.com and Amazon.com sell whole e-commerce sites already laid out using templates, and people can buy their own templates from companies on the Internet like websitetemplates.com or even freewebsitetemplates.com. But *customers* can substitute whole other approaches, so you compete with free blogs from Blogger.com and Wordpress.com, and the growing possibility of running a company site from MySpace.com and other social networking sites.

Part of what will make your web development firm special might be the advanced services you offer. Perhaps you licensed one of the large archives of photos to include in your customers' Websites. If your *supplier* of photos raises prices, your profits could take a hit. Similarly, if your customers have done their homework and checked out what other local developers offer and are charging,

These five—rivals, entrants, substitutes, suppliers, and customers—are aspects of your industry which can change your profitability and give an edge to any of the many types of competitors you face. The major ways you cope with these competitive pressures is by undertaking some combination of **strategic actions** and **tactical actions**. Exhibit 7.2 shows some of the best-known

strategic actions
Competitive responses requiring a major commitment of resources.

tactical actions
Competitive responses with low resource requirements.

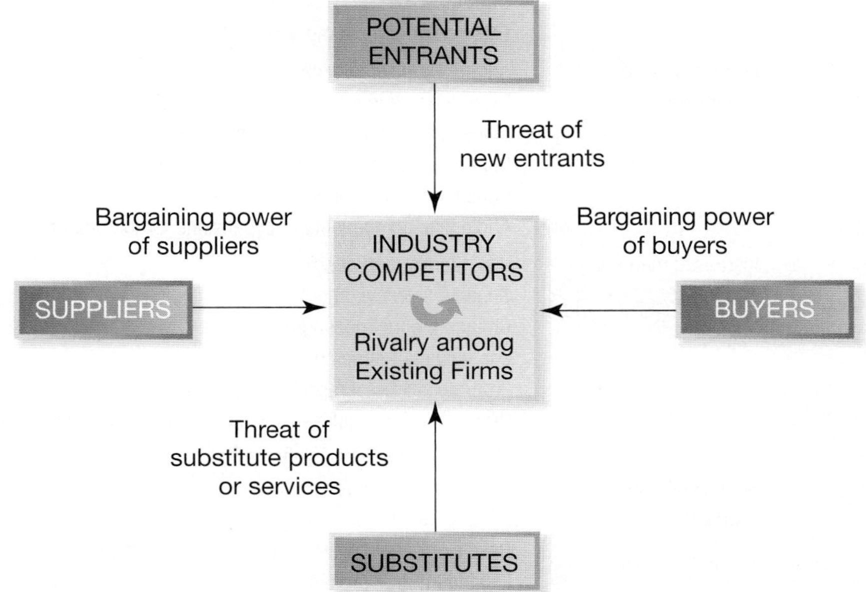

FIGURE 7.4

Porter's Five-Forces Model of Industry Competition

Source: Reprinted with permission of The Free Press, a division of Simon & Schuster Adult Publishing Group, from *Competitive Strategy: Techniques for Analyzing Indusries and Competitors* by Michael E. Porter. Copyright © 1980, 1998 by The Free Press, All rights reserved.

EXHIBIT 7.2

Strategic and Tactical Competitive Actions

Sources: Adapted from G. Dess, A. Eisner, and G. T. (Tom) Lumpkin, *Strategic Management: Text and Cases*, 5th ed. (McGraw-Hill/Irwin, 2009), Exhibit 8.2, page 300. M.J. Chen and D. C. Hambrick, "Speed, Stealth, and Selective Attack: How Small Firms Differ from Large Firms in Competitive Behavior," *The Academy of Management Journal* 38, no. 2 (April 1, 1995), pp. 453–482. M. Davies, "Sales Promotions as a Competitive Strategy," *Management Decision* 30, no. 7 (December 31, 1992), www.emeraldinsight.com/journals.htm?articleid=864603&show=abstract, accessed June 20, 2012. W. J. Ferrier, K. G. Smith, and C. M. Grimm, "The Role of Competitive Action in Market Share Erosion and Industry Dethronement: A Study of Industry Leaders and Challengers," *The Academy of Management Journal* 42, no. 4 (1999), pp. 372–388. R. A. Garda, "Use Tactical Pricing to Uncover Hidden Profits," *Journal of Business Strategy* 12, no. 5 (December 31, 1991), pp. 17–23.

	Specific Actions	Examples
Strategic actions		
	Entering new markets	Make geographical expansions
		Go global directly, by agents or by joint ventures
		Expand into neglected markets
		Target rivals' markets
		Target new demographics
		Expand Internet markets
	New product introductions	Imitate rivals' products
		Address gaps in quality
		Leverage new technologies
		Leverage brand name with related products
		Protect innovation with patents or trademarks
		Offer stripped-down versions as loss leaders
		Introduce older products in less sophisticated markets
	Changing production capacity	Create overcapacity
		Option others' capacity to keep it out of competitors' hands
		Tie up raw materials sources
		Tie up preferred suppliers and distributors
		Stimulate demand by limiting capacity
		Seek production certifications (e.g., ISO 9000)
	Mergers/alliances	Acquire/partner with competitors to reduce competition
		Flank your primary competitor by connecting with their competitors in other industries
		Tie up key supplies through alliances
		Obtain new technology/intellectual property
		Facilitate new market entry
		Seek protective legislation
		Seek favorable standards
Tactical actions		
	Price cutting (or increases)	Maintain low price dominance
		Offer discounts and rebates
		Offer incentives (e.g., frequent flyer miles)
		Enhance offering to move upscale
	Product/service enhancements	Address gaps in service
		Expand warranties
		Make incremental product improvements
		Copackage your product with related ones
		Bundle multiple products together
		Add online components or expansions for the product
	Increased marketing efforts	Use guerilla marketing
		Conduct selective attacks
		Change product packaging
		Use new marketing channels
		Promote stories of customer and employees
		Offer altruistic benefits—going greener, charity contributions, etc.
		Tie customers in via social media
	New distribution channels	Access suppliers directly
		Access customers directly
		Develop multiple points of contact with customers
		Expand Internet presence

examples of each type. Generally strategic actions require more time, money, and specialized expertise (which collectively are known as your firm's resources) than most tactical actions. That means a tactical response is most often your first response, with strategic actions building behind the scenes.

From all this, you can see that strategy represents the way by which an entrepreneur plots a path to success. For strategy to work, it needs to draw on most of the elements discussed in the chapter. When Nick and Dennis were putting together the idea for Mindnautilus.com, they were trying to strategize the right way. You know by now that they did an industry analysis that led them to see that Mindnautilus faced significant threats, and at that time, the partners lacked the strengths, especially financial strength, to overcome the threats. They kept thinking through what they could offer and eventually found an innovative option, creating EnableMart, which was ultimately a very successful firm.

Long term or short, every small business has a strategy, and successful small businesses have strategies that fit their industry, market, and resources. Strategy is one of those areas in which you can take charge and think through the options available to you and your firm. For all the ideas on which strategy touches, in the end there are some straightforward ways to help you decide on strategies, such as industry analyses and perceptual maps. These analysis techniques can help you narrow down your choices to a model of strategy that can help you succeed. For the vast majority of small businesses, the most powerful technique is to pursue an imitative strategy. By following the industry standard practices, with only one or two innovations to differentiate your firm from others, you can gain many of the benefits of established businesses and industries and still benefit from the power of innovation along smaller lines, which can make a real difference for your customers. For many owners, strategy *is* the grand game of business, but it is a game in which winning can make a major difference in the success of your firm and your life.

CHAPTER SUMMARY

LO1 Describe the decisions needed to establish a foundation for strategic planning.

- Strategy is the idea and actions that explain how the firm will make its profit.
- Strategic planning for small business is a four-step process.
- Consider the rewards you seek from your business when crafting and evaluating strategies.
- Choose whether your firm will focus on a mass or niche scale and a scope ranging from local to global.

LO2 Identify the forms of imitative and innovative businesses.

- Imitation is the classic strategy of small businesses.
- An imitative approach lets you build on existing products, services, and markets.
- An innovative approach lets you build a business in your own unique way.

LO3 Articulate the benefits that win over customers.

- Benefits are desirable characteristics of a product or service.
- Benefits can target value, such as quality or style, as well as cost.
- Situations and benefits can help clarify entry wedges that can offer exceptional profits.

LO4 Assess how industry changes can affect strategy.

- A successful start-up depends on knowing the industry's stage.
- Access to support depends on the industry's performance trend.
- An industry analysis combines trend, stage, and profit data to assess the firm's chances in a particular industry at a particular time.

LO5 Explain the major strategies of business—differentiation, cost, and focus.

- There are three generic business strategies—differentiation, cost, and focus.
- Most small businesses use a focus strategy, targeting a niche by combining cost or differentiation approaches.
- Particular combinations of benefits are called supra-strategies.

LO6 Determine how to sustain competitive advantage through attracting customers and discouraging competition.

- Competitive advantage is your firm's edge in meeting and beating the competition.
- Operating businesses deal with competition through a combination of strategic actions and tactical actions.

KEY TERMS

goal, 187
magic number, 187
industry, 189
competitor, 190
imitative strategy, 190
innovative strategy, 190
degree of similarity, 191
parallel competition, 191
incremental innovation, 192
pure innovation, 192
blue ocean strategy, 192
market, 192
scale, 192
scope, 192
mass market, 192
niche market, 192
perceptual map, 195
industry dynamics, 197
introduction stage, 197
growth stage, 197
boom, 197
shake-out, 198
maturity stage, 198
decline stage, 198
retrenchment, 198
industry analysis (IA), 198
gross profit, 199
net profit, 199
profit before taxes, 199
generic strategies, 201
differentiation strategy, 201
cost strategy, 201
focus strategy, 201
entry wedge, 203
competitive advantage, 205
strategic actions, 205
tactical actions, 205

DISCUSSION QUESTIONS

1. The book asserts "All strategy starts with the owner." Many of the gurus of strategy say strategy starts with the environment outside the firm. Which do you think is true? Be ready to back it up.
2. A lot of famous entrepreneurs brag how innovative their product is, when it is fundamentally like the competition, although better in one way or another. How do you classify such entrepreneurs in terms of the innovation/imitation balance?
3. Imagine you have developed a new two-way GPS system for trucks and their dispatchers. Trucking companies are all over the country. So are you looking at a mass market? Why or why not?
4. What are the differences between innovative and imitative strategies? Which is more likely to be something a small business can pursue?
5. Pick a small business with which all of the class is familiar. Discuss what are the customer benefits that business is trying to offer. Could they do a better job if they chose some other benefit?

6. Small businesses that pursue a cost (or cost focus) strategy often do so by using a location in a very low-rent district, with the store itself made up of used furniture, no decorations, and a very no-frills atmosphere. What is the problem with such an approach? Can you think of other ways to achieve low-cost without encountering similar problems?
7. What is the competitive advantage of a business, and how does it lead to success?
8. In the life cycle of an industry, how can you tell when it has left the introductory stage and entered the growth stage?

EXPERIENTIAL EXERCISES

1. Go to the Online Learning Center and look for the Skill Module, "How to Generate Local Statistics from National Ones." Develop a set of statistical estimates for an industry in your area. If the census reports numbers for your area already, try the exercise using the same industry, but do it for "Lawn and garden equipment and supplies stores" (NAICS 4442) for Brattleboro, VT. Be sure to remember to include nonemployer businesses (alias the solo entrepreneur).
2. Look at local hamburger restaurants. How do they pursue imitative strategies, and where do they offer their innovations?
3. Pick five online businesses in the same industry. From their websites, see if you can identify what *they* think is their competitive advantage. Do you agree with their assessment? Why or why not?
4. Think of the life cycle of an industry. Give examples of industries that are at the different stages, and be ready to defend your classification.

MINI-CASE

Ronnie Scales had his heart set on an Internet consulting business specializing in SEO (search engine optimization), which involves getting websites the characteristics that help them appear high up in search result displays. Being on the first screen that people see can be worth a lot to a company selling on the web.

Ronnie had a strong background, with a bachelor's degree in MIS with a marketing minor from a university in his hometown of Dallas. He had worked in the university's lab, and had done web design and SEO for campus organizations, local nonprofits, and a few students with online businesses. When he tried a perceptual map with cost and value benefits like expertise, his firm did not do well. After all, he was new to the industry so his experience was not as great as a lot of his competitors. Also, since SEO can be done remotely, he was competing with firms in India and Eastern Europe who charged less than he did. He felt there had to be some advantages of being physically near to the customer, but he was not sure how to leverage it.

What sort of tactics could he use to better position his SEO business for success in such a crowded industry?

CASE DISCUSSION QUESTIONS

1. Considering the Porter model, from what sectors would Ronnie's competitors be coming? What kinds of threats do they pose to his business?
2. Pick two tactics from the list in Exhibit 7.2 and explain how they could be applied to Ronnie's business. Explain why you think those tactics would work.
3. Industry experts say that SEO is an industry on the rise. What are the implications for Ronnie as he plans to run his business?

SUGGESTED CASES AND ARTICLES

- Scented Candles for Men, C-8

Available on McGraw-Hill Create™:

- Amy's Bread
- Sparta Glass Products

SUGGESTED VIDEOS

www.mhhe.com/katz4e

SBTV.com Videos:

- Innovative Small Business Strategy Tips
- Duct Tape Marketing—Creating Your Core Message: Differentiation

STVP Videos:

- Think Big and Act Small
- Emerging Long Waves of Research and Industry

APPENDIX

Five Steps to an Industry Analysis

Retail Shoe Store

HOW-TO'S

Finding the SIC and NAICS Codes

The first order of business is to find the NAICS and SIC codes for the industry of interest. This is done by going to the website www.census.gov/epcd/naics02/. Plug in your keyword, click the 2002 NAICS search tab, and a listing is displayed that will tell you the NAICS code. Find the code that you are looking for and click the link. This will lead you to the SIC code for the same industry. For example, for the retail shoe industry, the codes are SIC 5661 and NAICS 448210.

Industry Size

Step 2 is to find the size of the industry. First go to the site www.census.gov. Second click on "Economic Census" in the business section and enter the NAICS code to find this information. Click on the hotlinked 448210 on the resulting Industry Statistics Sampler page.

On the next page, labelled "NAICS 448210 Shoe Stores" click on the "2007 Census: Geographic Distribution" tab. From the resulting page, pull the number of "establishments" in the USA and their sales. Then click on the "Historical Data" tab and grab the numbers from 2002.

2002—there were 28,499 businesses in this industry with sales of $22,955,111,000 or $805,470 per store.

2007—there were 28,076 businesses in this industry with sales of $26,509,421,000 or $944,202 per store.

Profitability

Step 3 starts with going to the BizStats.com website and look under "Industry Financial Reports: Profit & Loss, Balance Sheet and Financial Ratios." Let's look at sole proprietorships, since those are where most small businesses fall. On the list of industries, select "Retail." In this case, a retail shoe store would fall under the category "Clothing and Accessories Stores." Click on the link and you will be taken to the report.

The BizStat report gives you the profitability (Gross Profit 43.55 percent, Total Expenses 32.31 percent, leaving a Net Operating Income—profit of 11.24 percent). It then breaks them down by sales. The report also gives a detailed breakdown of operating expenses, a balance sheet (using percentages), and a set of financial ratios (which are explained in Chapter 15).

Remember that these BizStat numbers give you an average based on a variety of different types of clothing stores. So it still makes sense to get specific numbers for shoe stores (including corporations, partnerships, and sole proprietorships), and so you should still get the BizMiner or Risk Management Association data.

Go to the library to find information about the profitability of the retail shoe industry next. Using the RMA's *Annual Statement Studies: Financial Ratio Benchmarks,* the following information was gathered for the smalles stores, with zero to $500,000 in sales.

Gross profit 38.6%

Operating expenses 35.0%

Operating profit –3.6%

All other expenses 0.9%

Profit before taxes –2.8%

Note that the RMA numbers are more specific to the shoe store segment than the BizStats.com numbers; also the numbers are more pessimistic. The rule of thumb in business is to use the most conservative or most pessimistic figures. In this case, the most conservative figures come from RMA, and are specific to your industry. From this you would conclude that the profit picture for the shoe store industry is potentially problematic. Note that the BizStats numbers suggest there might be some *other* type of clothing store which is posting superior profits, and looking for that type of business might make sense.

Ways to Make Profits

Information about making profits can be found by looking at trade articles and information or doing actual interviews. The following information came from two sources: One source is a trade site, National Shoe Retail Association (www.nsra.org/), and the other is from the home business site www.PowerHomeBiz.com. The answers to four key questions on profitability are given below:

- First is the question, What can be done to generate more sales?
  - Excellent service
  - Courteous and well-trained staff
  - Diversity in product selection

    - Competitive pricing
    - Functional store design
    - Location, location, location (more heavily populated cities have greater demands for shoes)

- Second is a judgment of whether it is possible to charge a premium for a product or service.
    - Depends on the market that you are catering to. If it is high end, then your target customer has the means to spend more money on more expensive (name brand) shoes. Also, if the store is located where families have higher discretionary income, the demand for brand name shoes will be higher.

- Third is how to keep the cost of goods or services below the industry's average.
    - Put adequate stock control in place to reduce inventory costs and increase stock turns. Loss prevention is critical in any retail establishment, as theft and shrinkage represent lost dollars for the retailer. Have systematized procedures for doing physical counts of your inventory as well as clear policies on employee theft. It is also important to choose styles that are hot to the consumer to avoid inventory costs.
    - Another cost saving tactic is to use "start ship" and "in store" completion dates on all orders. Start negotiating on everything received past completion date.

- Fourth is looking at ways to keep operating expenses below industry averages.
    - Always check your freight expenses against the freight charge on the packing slip. It is usually different. Charge the difference back to the vendor.
    - Join forces with other same brand concept stores for savings on your direct mail advertising. In direct mail, the higher the quantity printed, the lower the cost per unit. There are additional savings to be realized in the cost of mailing if all pieces are sent from the same location. Savings can be substantial.
    - Use co-op dollars to reduce costs. Use some of your co-op dollars to co-brand with suppliers on things like business cards, shopping bags, and so on.
    - If you're doing a profit and loss statement monthly, consider doing it quarterly. Chances are you are simply putting it in a file anyway and are not adjusting the operating budget that often. This can trim the accounting bill considerably.
    - Negotiating better terms and rates with your bankers and other service providers can really save on fees. For example, go to other banks to get competitive rates and then renegotiate with your bank or change banks. For a bank, this applies to bank transaction fees as well as interest and credit terms.
    - Bid or get multiple estimates for things like construction/repair projects, insurance, contract services (i.e., refuse removal), and so forth.

Competitor Concentration

The last step is using a directory provider to find out how many competitors there are in an area. Using YP.com's online yellow pages directory, there are 263 retail shoe establishments in the St. Louis metropolitan area.

ANALYSIS

Overview

It seems as though the retail shoe industry is shrinking. From 2002 to 2007 the number of stores in the industry decreased by 10 percent. Using the information from the Industry Size section, we can determine that although the number of stores has declined, the sales have increased and gone from an average of $805,470 per store to $944,202. The retail shoe industry is very competitive, and it is important for hopefuls to be able to distinguish themselves in a mature market.

Profitability

While the gross profit for this industry looks very good compared to other similar businesses (at 38.6 percent), operating profit and profit before taxes are low. Therefore, to be successful in this industry, it is important to differentiate and focus on customer service and other approaches which add value. Also, an owner should do everything possible to cut the cost of goods sold and expenses. Taken together, these strategies might result in a profitable firm, but it will be a highly risky venture.

Differentiation and Cost

There are several ways to differentiate in the retail shoe business. There are many different categories for retail shoes. An owner could choose to focus on men's or women's shoes, kid's shoes, or athletic shoes or include all these categories in one store. Then within these categories, there is low end, one price and discount, mass designer, and high end. Again, the shoe business is very competitive, so it is important to choose an image and stick to this image to establish and build a reputation with customers.

Once the image is established, there are six areas that must be covered to be successful and maintain a foothold in the industry. They are as follows:

- Excellent service—many a customer is won over by receiving great service.
- Courteous, honest, and well-trained staff.
- Diversity in product selection—offer a wide range of shoes appropriate for the surrounding environment. For example, if the location is near a beach, be sure to include plenty of sandals, thongs, and flip-flops in the inventory.
- Competitive pricing—be competitive with other stores in the area to maintain a loyal customer base.
- Functional store design so that customers may move around with ease.
- Location, location, location—locations in or near heavily populated cities tend to have higher sales.

Incorporating these elements well, along with a differentiating image, will help an owner to have strong placement and be most able to compete effectively in the industry. It would seem that with a solid business plan, a marketing edge, and great location, while a retail shoe business could be risky, it could also be viable and rewarding.

SOURCES

"Bright Ideas" From National Shoe Retailers Association's February 2005 Conference, www.nsra.org/brightideas.pdf.

Jenny Fulbright, *Starting a Shoe Retail Store,* n.d. www.PowerHomeBiz.com/vol136/Shoe.htm, July, 2005.

Risk Management Association, "eStatement Studies 448210—Shoe Stores", June 19, 2012, www.statementstudies.org.ezp.slu.edu/Help.aspx?id=8158&menuid=584 (accessed June 19, 2012).

U.S. Census, NAICS page, www.census.gov/epcd/naics02/.

Note: This industry analysis was written by Beatrice Emmanuel of Saint Louis University under the direction of Professor Jerome Katz.

CHAPTER

8

Business Plans: Seeing Audiences and Your Business Clearly

● Though small businesses thrive on creativity and less structure, sometimes these elements can be more of a liability than an asset. Hiring outside experts to analyze details can help produce more clarity and better results, as Global Fromage owners Gail Berman and Sara Lamont found when their financial dilemma was solved with the help of a CPA.

LEARNING OBJECTIVES

After you complete this chapter, you will be able to:

LO1 Understand why and when to develop a business plan.

LO2 Know how to tell the business plan story.

LO3 Learn the major sections of the classic business plan.

LO4 Focus business plan sections to meet specific needs.

LO5 Identify the major risks to business plan success.

LO6 Master presenting your business plan to others.

Focus on Small Business: Global Fromage

Gail Berman and Sara Lamont started Global Fromage, a specialty cheese shop in Kansas City's Westport, a revitalized entertainment and shopping district. Through discussion, they settled on a general plan for the company:

- Their products would be gourmet and specialty cheeses to be sold at a premium price.
- Their target market was to be people like themselves in the 20–50-year-old age range with middle to upper incomes.
- The Berman and Lamont families put up the nearly $100,000 it would take to secure a lease and pay for improvements and the initial inventory.

The shop had a steady flow of sales, but when it came time to pay bills at the end of the month, Global Fromage always seemed to come up short. Gail and Sara didn't know what the problem was. A certified public accountant (CPA) friend they hired quickly found the problem. Gail and Sara's "premium" pricing technique was simple. For any cheese they bought, they sold it for twice the price they paid for it. This seemed as if it should be enough, but in fact it was not. Because they never worked out the costs of running their business, they didn't know that the markup should have been closer to 200 than 100 percent. Armed with financials developed by the CPA, Gail and Sara repriced their cheeses and began to show a profit.

DISCUSSION QUESTIONS

1. What are the reasons you think Gail and Sara would have given for *not* doing a business plan?
2. What are the kinds of business costs that Gail and Sara are likely to have missed?
3. Since they got the money to start up from their families, who would have been the audience for the business plan?
4. Do you think it makes sense to create a business plan for a business *after* it starts? Why or why not?
5. Gail and Sara used a CPA to find the problem. Where else could they have turned for help?

Business Plan Background

LO1 Understand why and when to develop a business plan.

business plan
A document designed to detail the *major* characteristics of a firm—its product or service, its industry, its market, its manner of operating (production, marketing, management), and its financial outcomes with an emphasis on the firm's *present* and *future.*

external legitimacy
The extent to which a small business is taken for granted, accepted, or treated as viable by organizations or people outside the small business or the owner's family.

internal understanding
The extent to which employees, investors, and family members involved in the business know the business's purposes and operations.

Gail and Sara had a good idea, a good sense of their market, and a good location. They were great salespeople, and yet they were not making a profit. The reason was that they did not plan their business all the way through. When you are serious about your business or when a lot of money of your own or someone else's is at stake, creating a business plan is perhaps the most critical activity you can undertake. The plan is important, but what is even more important is the understanding you get from the planning process. This chapter will help you understand the thinking behind business plans and how to make and present your own.

A **business plan** is a document designed to detail the *major* characteristics of a firm—its product or service, its industry, its market, its manner of operating (production, marketing, management), and its financial outcomes with an emphasis on the firm's *present* and *future*.

There are two circumstances under which creating a business plan is absolutely necessary. One is when outsiders expect it. This is called **external legitimacy**. Creating a business plan is the acknowledged best way to build external legitimacy for your firm. When you are seeking outside support—whether financial or expert—you do a business plan to signal your professionalism and how serious you are about the business. Investors, whether they are venture capitalists, informal investors (called *angels*), government bureaucrats, bankers, or your two great aunts, are going to expect to see a business plan before considering investing in your business.[1] If you are pursuing a partnership or joint venture with a larger firm, a plan is the only way you are going to get the attention of outsiders. The kinds of benefits these different groups look for in a plan are given in Table 8.1.

Keep in mind how business plans get used. The most common use of business plans is when you are raising money for your business. In that case, the plan becomes a way to introduce your idea, your business, yourself, and your deal to the reader. The plan is a sales document, but also the first installment in the relationship you are hoping to build with an investor. You want your plan to be easy to read, to make clear who you are and what you are offering, both as your goods or service, and as a potential investment. Remember that many potential investors, especially family and friends, may not have an extensive background in your proposed business, so the plan needs to explain how your industry (i.e., you versus your competitors) works and how your business fits into and builds its opportunities in its market (i.e., with your customers).

The items for each type of audience in Table 8.1 can help remind you what parts of your plan are crucial for the intended audience. It is not uncommon to have different types of plans for different audiences. Your Aunt Mary may not be into the social media industry, but she wants to know how long you'll need her money and what she will get in return. And if she refers the plan to her accountant or attorney for an opinion, they will want to know these things for sure.

On the other hand, if you are presenting to accomplished angel investors individually or in groups, they will want to know a great deal about your business market potential. They want it to be big to assure the high returns they demand for their investment. They will want to know the projected growth rate, and since they probably don't know you as well as your Aunt Mary does, they will want a lot of information about you and your team, since most angel investment can be based as much on the investor's assessment of a venture team as on the product itself. Most angels believe a winning team can make the most of nearly any situation.

Remember that while Aunt Mary and the angels will require a full business plan (as we call it in Table 8.3) others in Table 8.1 would not expect to see everything about your business. For example, you might develop a version of the plan for potential key employees or key suppliers. Neither would expect to see your financials, but both would want to know what the business is about, who is in your market, and who is on the firm's team already. So when putting your plan together, flip between Tables 8.1 and 8.3 to make sure you get the right sections (from Table 8.3) and emphasize the right issues (from Table 8.1) to get the most from your business planning effort.

The other circumstance under which a business plan is needed is for **internal understanding**. This is when you want to get all the aspects of the business clear in your mind and the minds of others in the business, such as your partners or your key employees. For example, the La Terrasse Restaurant in Philadelphia has long had an extensive business plan. It talks about the history and vision of the restaurant and includes a detailed operational plan covering everything from table layouts to techniques for minimizing waste. For new hires, the plan offers insight and specific information on the La Terrasse way of doing things.

TABLE 8.1 Concerns of Different Business Plan Audiences[2]

Audience	Concerns
Family and friend investors	Amounts and Schedules for returns Stability of firm Funds use Your investment
Silent Partners/Angel Investors	Growth rate Market Business team Amounts and schedules for returns
Joint venture partners	Fit between the firms Competitive advantage Benefits Intellectual property protection R&D
Bankers	Cash flow and cash cycle Asset/collateral base Long-term prospects
Government agencies and institutions	Compliance with regulations and laws Monitoring compliance
Potential customers	Service/product quality Benefits Competitive advantage Responsiveness to customers
Key employees	Stability of firm Growth (as applies to increased opportunities within the firm) Long-term prospects

Is a business plan absolutely essential? If you are seeking a banker, investor, or partner, yes. Generally if you need outside support to get a business going, those you are seeking support from will want to see a business plan—and you will want to make sure the plan addresses their concerns.

Also, if you are trying to start or run your business in a professional or ambitious way, a business plan is vitally important. It is true that some of the most famous entrepreneurial firms—Apple, Microsoft, Dell, Holiday Inns—started without business plans. On the other hand, there are a lot more famous firms that started from the business plan—Amazon, eBay, Mrs. Fields, Red Hat, Xerox, and Federal Express to name a few.[3] When *Inc.* magazine polled 500 owners of high-performing small businesses, 54 percent had a plan and 41 percent did not.[4] Typically, the higher-performing firms in any industry (measured in profits) tend to be those who engage in planning.[5]

It is important to know that research suggests that firms without a business plan are more likely to close down than firms with plans.[6] While having a business plan does not guarantee higher profits,[7] it is essential to qualify to be considered by business professionals for investments, loans, or credit lines. For example, Apple and Microsoft drafted business plans when they wanted to go for venture capital funds.[8]

These days, more start-up businesses are doing business plans than in the past, which increases the importance of your doing one to stay competitive and look as legitimate as the other competing start-ups.[9] In your head or on paper, sooner or later most businesses need to do a plan.

The Business Plan Story: Starting Small and Building Up[10]

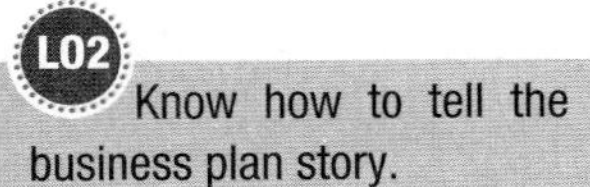

Know how to tell the business plan story.

Business plans are a type of story. In a business plan, you tell the reader about a future place—your business. Every business plan is a bit like fiction. The best fictional stories are based on what exists now, as a good business plan should be. The business plan tells a story that starts in the here and now and builds believably toward a better future.

Good storytellers know that you make the story fit the audience's time. Sometimes you have only a moment to get the story of your business across; sometimes you have hours. Entrepreneurs need to have a variety of versions of their business's story available.

Figure 8.1 shows the path or sequence of presentations entrepreneurs may create when planning to go into business. When you have only a moment to talk, your vision statement or a tagline you've developed is the way to go.[11] When you have more time to talk about your business, longer and longer presentations are possible. These range from the 2-sentence concept all the way to the 40-page business plan. The five types of business planning presentations are (1) vision statements, (2) mission statements, (3) elevator pitches, (4) executive summaries, and (5) business plans. We tell you how to do each below.

The Vision Statement

A firm's vision statement is perhaps its most important single idea held by the owner and employees.[12] The **vision statement** is a very simple 5–10 word sentence or better yet a **tagline** that expresses the fundamental idea or goal of the firm. As strategy professors Greg Dess and Tom Lumpkin suggest, a vision statement is supposed to be inspiring, overarching, and long term.[13] When Bill Gates and Paul Allen started Microsoft as teenagers, their vision was "a computer on every desk—running Microsoft software."[14] At the time, personal computers were being constructed by hobbyists and even lacked keyboards! So you can easily see how visionary their vision statement was.

vision statement
A very simple 5–10 word sentence or tagline that expresses the fundamental idea or goal of the firm.

tagline
(also known as a slogan) Memorable catchphrase that captures the key idea of a business, its service, product, or customer.

Taglines or slogans or what Guy Kawasaki calls a mantra, are a good way to present vision statements, because a good tagline or mantra is brief and memorable. The tagline can also serve as

FIGURE 8.1

The Path to the Business Plan

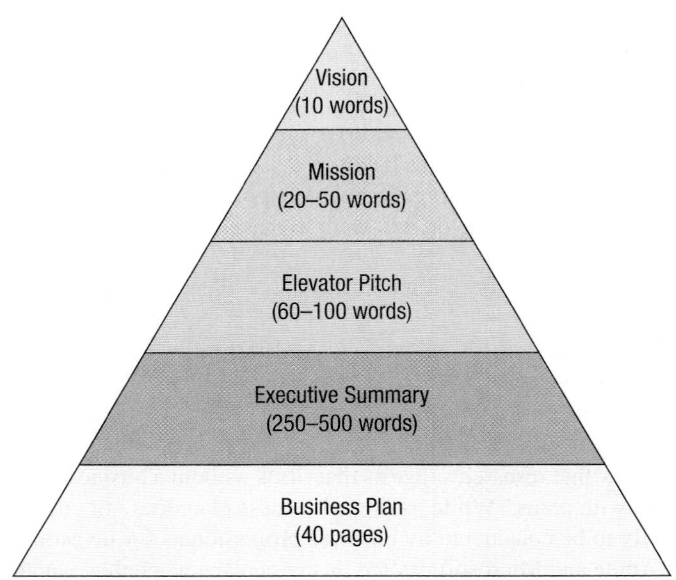

the company's vision statement.[15] Some examples of good taglines encompassing the firm's vision statement are:

- Book Passage (Corte Madera, California): The Bay Area's Liveliest Bookstore.
- Crum Electric Supply (Casper, Wyoming): Plug into Quality—People, Products, Service.
- Progressive Insulation & Windows (Chatsworth, California): Total Living Comfort.

The Mission Statement

The mission statement is closely related to the firm's vision statement. The **mission statement** takes the vision statement's description of the firm's goal and adds the competitive advantage information developed as part of the firm's strategy. For example, the Excalibur Seasoning Company says its mission is "to provide you, as a customer, with the highest quality products and service available in the seasoning industry."[16] Typically a mission statement talks in terms of what will make a difference for the customer or the industry. It rarely discusses profits, but it often mentions the entry wedge that follows from the firm's strategy[17] discussed in Chapter 7. A few more examples of mission statements from small firms are:

mission statement
A paragraph that describes the firm's goals and competitive advantages.

- BabyGenie.com (Fort Lauderdale, Florida): The mission of BabyGenie.com is to become one of the best online resources for young mothers and repeat parents.
- Bob Victor's (Topeka, Kansas): Our GOAL is to manufacture the finest solid American hardwood mouldings from hand-selected American hardwood with real wood finishes.
- Fantastic Gift Baskets (Raleigh, North Carolina): The family at Fantastic Gift Baskets puts the same care and love into designing our gourmet gift baskets as you would . . . if you had the time![18]

Mission statements can get long. Since they are usually oriented toward those inside the firm or to formal investors, mission statements tend to cover everything that is truly important. This might include the major competitive advantages of the firm, its position in the industry, and its attitudes toward customers, competitors, and the environment. Remember, however, that the best mission statements are simple, short, and direct.

The Elevator Pitch

An **elevator pitch** is an action-oriented description of your business that is somewhat longer than a vision statement or tagline. It is designed to open the door to a more in-depth dialogue. Even when it doesn't lead to any specific business, this information about your business should be memorable enough so that the listener can tell others about your business. The idea of the elevator pitch is that you are alone with a prospective customer or investor for the length of an elevator ride, say, around 30 seconds.[19] That comes out to 100 words or less. This description is used in one-on-one business settings and when someone asks for more detail after hearing your concept. In a time when politicians develop sound bites and a good phrase can make a product (Altoids, for example, are "curiously strong"), having a high-quality concept or elevator pitch for your business is more important than ever.[20]

elevator pitch
A 30-second (100 words or less) action-oriented description of a business designed to sell the idea of the business to another.

> In life there are "needs" and there are "wants." We think we can cover both in a single bite . . . At Red Jett Sweets we are intent on baking a cupcake that sends mind, body and soul to a whole new place. Whether you are a traditionalist or an adventurer, you will find a cupcake for every craving. We offer a number of crowd-pleasing flavors on a regular basis as well as a rotating menu of featured cupcakes that simply sparkle with innovation and wit. All that and we'll deliver our sweet sensations right to your door. So next time you encounter that "can't-live-without-it" impulse, give us a call! Red Jett Sweets. Have Sugar. Will Travel.

The above elevator pitch leads with the hook—luring us to think about needs and wants and food all at once. It follows up with the purpose of the service—providing outstanding cupcakes. For a familiar type of business like this one, you talk about what makes your firm unique or superior to the competition. If your pitch were for a new type of service, you would want to give the listener more details about how it works than may otherwise appear in an elevator pitch. The pitch ends with where the business is now—seeking sales from customers, although this could also be where you

Going up? Each year, Wake Forest University's Babcock Graduate School of Management holds its annual elevator pitch contest. Teams must progress through a rigorous weeding-out process to advance to the semi-finalist stage, where they get the chance to present their pitch to real venture capitalists and experts on a two-minute elevator ride. To read more about this year's contest, visit http://business.wfu.edu/elevator/.

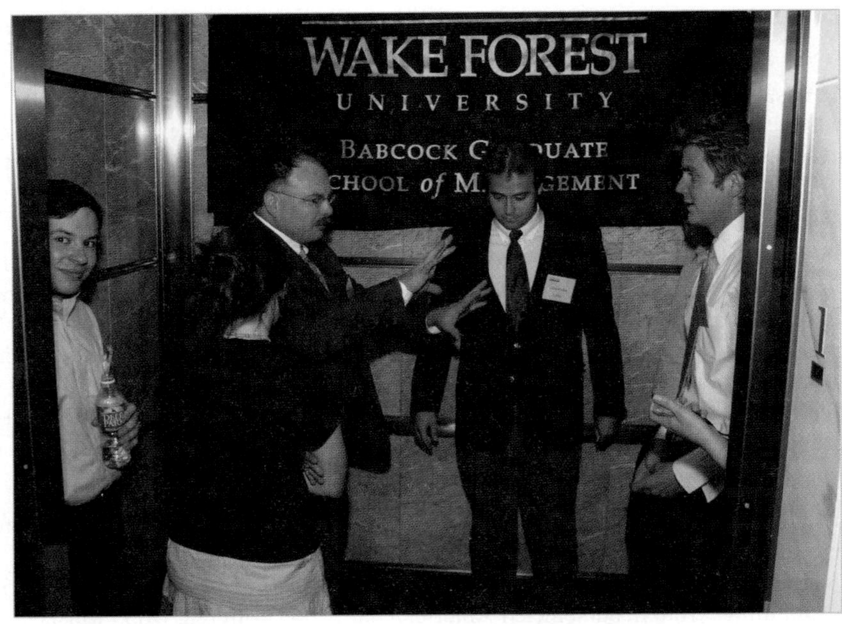

close asking for money from seed investors. This is about 115 words and would take about half a minute to say. Note that a lot of it sounds like a sales pitch, and that is intentional. Listeners might be customers or investors, but either way, the goal is to sell them on the idea and their need for it. With this background, Skill Module 8.1 explains how to craft an elevator pitch.

SKILL MODULE 8.1

How to Write Your Elevator Pitch

Elevator pitches have four success factors: the hook, the purpose, the what and where, and the delivery.

First, find a hook—something about your product or service that people would remember and take to heart. "We tutor kids others call too difficult." "When government or industry wants to find the newest businesses, they come to us." "We are one of the nation's biggest suppliers of parts for old Corvettes."

Stan Mandel supervises Wake Forest University's Elevator Pitch Competition, so he knows pitches. He suggests using analogies. If you're planning a large, discount pen store, you might say "We will be a Walmart for pens." For CellTunes, it might be "We'll be the Home Shopping Network for music." It helps people quickly understand your firm. Great pitches or concepts aim to get the listener to ask questions or take some other form of "next step." Stan suggests different pitches for different sorts of audiences—investors, customers, suppliers, and so forth.

Second, focus on the purpose your product or service serves for the customer. Do not talk skills ("I am a graphic designer."); talk about how you make customers happy ("I produce designs that sell books!").

Third, tell the listener the business's situation: where the business "is at"—if it's a start-up, state what the business is seeking (funding, partners, distributors, etc.). If it is operating, tell the listener where he or she can buy the product or service.

Once your elevator pitch is written, you need to become conversationally perfect in your delivery. You want to be able to give the pitch or concept dozens, even hundreds, of times. Yet it is important that the pitch does not sound memorized. It needs to sound like regular conversation, preferably a conversation whose topic excites you. To achieve this, you must master the material, and then keep working on it so that it becomes a natural part of what you say to others. Have family and friends listen to it. Consider using a video camera to see how natural you seem when making the pitch. Remember, the elevator pitch is often the first real insight people have about your business, so it is essential to have a pitch that flows and sells for you.

The Executive Summary

An **executive summary** is the key component of the written business plan because it is the one element that nearly everyone will read first when they receive a plan. An executive summary gives a one- to five-page (250–1,250 words) overview of the business, its business model, market, expectations, and immediate goals. (See Exhibit 8.1.) Typically, executive summaries start out written, and they remain the most popular item to send people who ask about your business. They comprise the core of a business plan presentation and form the basis for additional discussion when someone asks for more detail. Executive summaries are written in a formal style, suitable for investors, lawyers, and bankers to read. They give much more detail about the business than the vision or mission statements or elevator pitch. Executive summaries are usually organized in a series of short paragraphs (three or four sentences), each with a particular topic. These topics are:

executive summary
A one- to two-page (250–500 words) overview of the business, its business model, market, expectations, and immediate goals. It is typically put at the start of a business plan and is the most popular summary form for a business plan.

- **Product:** Describes the product or service and how it is used.
- **Market:** Describes the size and characteristics of the customer group and how it will buy the product or service (e.g., in person, online, catalog).
- **Competitive advantages:** Explains what makes the product or service unique, often in terms of an entry wedge.

EXHIBIT 8.1

Executive Summary for Red Jett Sweets

Red Jett Sweets, Inc., is a subchapter S corporation opening a mobile cupcakery in August 2011. Red Jett Sweets will build a reputation in Fort Worth as one of the best cupcakeries in the area. Red Jett Sweets will provide its clients with innovative flavors, high-quality ingredients, and the highest level of customer service and satisfaction found anywhere.

The mobile cupcakery will feature cupcakes that are freshly baked, have original and innovative flavors, use high-quality ingredients, and are fun, eclectic, seasonal, and traditional. Although Red Jett Sweets is targeting individuals with the disposable income to buy cupcakes, the mobile cupcakery will be welcoming a wide variety of income levels by competitively pricing cupcakes at $2.75. Other cupcakeries in the Fort Worth area sell their cupcakes for $2.50 and $2.95. Cupcakes will be the main focus of Red Jett Sweets, but a limited line of beverages will be sold to complement Red Jett Sweet's cupcakes.

Red Jett Sweet's management and staff will provide customer service that is friendly and helpful, but not pressured, with an emphasis on building ongoing relationships. The mobile cupcakery will provide extensive client service offerings such as home delivery, special orders, gift wrapping, private parties, and customization. The mobile cupcakery design will create an inviting atmosphere that customers will enjoy visiting.

Management

At the heart of Red Jett Sweets are the owners, Christina Meyer and Natalie Gamez. They will be responsible for all aspects of product selection, client relations, and day-to-day operations. Ms. Meyer has previous experience starting and running a small business, where she has demonstrated talent in most of the activities required to manage a small business. She has a strong passion for the business and swiftly builds personal connections and maintains strong relationships with people. Ms. Gamez has worked at many businesses in the restaurant industry and still maintains many connections in the industry. She is very detail oriented and well organized, and has a passion for baking.

Red Jett Sweets will be staffed with a baking assistant and eventually one or two sales associates. Ms. Meyer and Ms. Gamez have established relationships with several additional outside consultants, including an insurance agent, attorney, and graphic designer. Their accountant, Diane Hanley, will play an active role in financial management and reporting in the first year.

Target Market

Red Jett Sweet's primary target market includes people, ages 25 to 44, with household incomes of $75,000 or higher. Secondary target markets include people in younger (18–24) and older (45–54) age groups with household incomes between $40,000 and $75,000.

Red Jett Sweet's primary trading area will be west Fort Worth. The secondary trading area includes people living in the rest of Tarrant County. Red Jett Sweets may also be able to draw some clients from neighboring Parker and Johnson counties. In the 2001 census, the total number of households in our primary target market was approximately 29,000. The total number of households in both the primary and secondary target markets was 60,000.

Over 2,000 mobile and cart food vendors covered U.S. street corners and parking lots in 2010. Also, in 2010, mobile food operations were estimated to have earned $163 million in sales revenue nationwide.

Competitive Positioning

Similar businesses exist in other cities, but when Red Jett Sweets opens it will be the first and only mobile cupcakery in Fort Worth. Its customers will enjoy the best variety of products, best customer service, and best mobile food truck environment and experience, all available in accessible locations without paying more than at other storefronts in the area.

Some existing local cupcakeries, such as Cupcake Cottage and J' Raes, offer cupcakes similar to Red Jett Sweet's, but do not sell their products via a mobile cupcakery.

Red Jett Sweet's will focus on promotional strategies based on personal relationships, word of mouth, and social media marketing. Red Jett Sweets will use a client database to notify clients when new flavors become available. The mobile cupcakery will host events such as a large opening party with local newspapers and magazines invited to cover it, and special events with 10 to 15 percent of profits donated to local charities and organizations. Ms. Meyer and Ms. Gamez will leverage their diverse personal networks to build awareness and interest in Red Jett Sweets before and after the mobile cupcakery opens.

Projected Sales and Income

Red Jett Sweets expects to achieve sales revenues of $44,477 in the first year and up to $152,842 by the third year. It may be possible to achieve higher sales than this conservative estimate, which is equivalent to 160 cupcakes a day from August to December. This is lower than reported sales at similar cupcakeries in other cities. The local market is large enough to support a higher level of growth.

Break-even sales for the first year are $80,358 or 29,221 cupcakes. Net income after taxes is projected to be ($16,995) in the first year and over $10,000 by the third year. Note that during these first three years of business, the break-even sales is raised and net income is significantly lowered due to purchases of equipment and amortization of intangible assets related to Red Jett Sweet's start-up.

Financing

Ms. Meyer's initial equity investment of $50,000 will fund the start-up of Red Jett Sweets. This includes $29,000 for the mobile cupcakery and small renovations; $3,000 for marketing and advertising materials; $2,500 for equipment; $2,500 for research, development of recipes, and direct labor hours associated with the two; $13,000 in working capital. Please refer to the Start-up Costs table in the Key Assumptions section.

- **Management:** Describes the entrepreneur and start-up team in terms of expertise and track record.
- **Business:** Describes the current stage of the business and when major milestones of starting, sales, or profitability will be met.
- **Finances:** Describes the deal being offered investors and the schedule for payouts.

The order for the topics in an executive summary is not fixed, although most experienced readers will be looking for the same items—markets, advantages, and management. The summary is probably the single most important written part of the business plan for two reasons. First, it is the single most widely distributed written description of the business. Second, all readers of a business plan typically start with the executive summary of the plan, and then go on to the section of the plan where they can best apply their expertise. For example, accountants typically go to the financial projections after they've read the executive summary.

It also is typical to include the key numbers for the business, such as industry size, customer base, number of employees, or projected sales. However it is important to make sure that the numbers can be supported by a trustworthy source. Examples of such sources include the government, industry associations, and major commercial sources such as Dun & Bradstreet, the Risk Management Association, BizStats, or Bizminer. The sources may be included in the executive summary or made available to readers in footnotes.

Strategizing for the Business Plan

The business plan brings together every aspect of your business including your product and service, your market and your strategy. Before launching on the business plan, it makes sense to think through the approach you want to take in the plan—in particular how the plan ties together key elements like the vision/mantra or mission covered in this chapter, or the strategic objectives discussed in Chapter 7. It also helps to be clear in your mind about the plans you want the business to pursue *before* you start writing the plan. A great way to help organize your thinking and work so far is The One Page Business Plan® developed by consultant and entrepreneur Jim Horan.[21] This approach provides a great way to translate your ideas and strategies into components of a business plan and organize your thinking about the overall message of your business plan. With Jim's permission, we have adapted The One Page Business Plan® to fit with the approach you have read about so far. Our 5-M Model uses one-line bullet points in five areas to structure your thinking and your full business plan:

Mantra: This follows the Vision/Tagline/Mantra model discussed earlier in this chapter. Aim for 3–4 words, or 6 at most.

Mission: This also follows the approach described earlier focusing on competitive advantage and goals, with a definite time period in mind. Mission statements typically give the company name, product or service, and its customer or market. Mission statements also give the firm's major business goal, which can be stated quantitatively or qualitatively, but always with a time period or end date.

Measures: These are business goals given as measurable results, in terms of sales, market share, employment, locations, profits, growth, etc. It is typical to have multiple measures, and they are typically given in quantitative form. This section should reflect the Mission.

Method: These are the activities which would make your business successful over the time period given in the Mission section. It should tie in with the Measures and Mission. As with Measures, it is typical to have multiple methods. Methods in this exercise typically involve identifying qualitatively stated strategic achievements (vs. numerical outcomes in Measures) which would prove you have done what you set out to do as a business.

Mechanics: This last section ties into everything above, and gives several specific tasks the business needs to do to accomplish what is mentioned in the Method and Measures. These are often given as one-line project descriptions (e.g., "Open two locations by June 1," or "Hire an advertising firm by November 15.").

FIGURE 8.2

Janexia Waterproofing: A 5-M Model Example

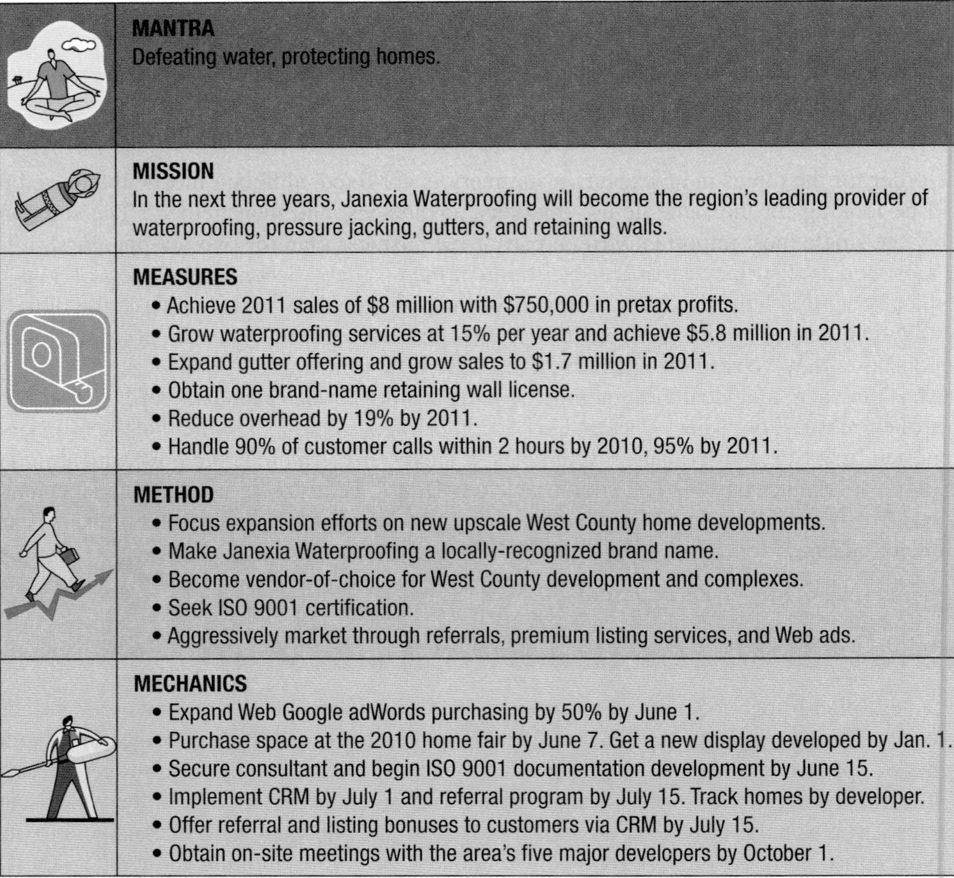

MANTRA
Defeating water, protecting homes.
MISSION
In the next three years, Janexia Waterproofing will become the region's leading provider of waterproofing, pressure jacking, gutters, and retaining walls.
MEASURES
• Achieve 2011 sales of $8 million with $750,000 in pretax profits.
• Grow waterproofing services at 15% per year and achieve $5.8 million in 2011.
• Expand gutter offering and grow sales to $1.7 million in 2011.
• Obtain one brand-name retaining wall license.
• Reduce overhead by 19% by 2011.
• Handle 90% of customer calls within 2 hours by 2010, 95% by 2011.
METHOD
• Focus expansion efforts on new upscale West County home developments.
• Make Janexia Waterproofing a locally-recognized brand name.
• Become vendor-of-choice for West County development and complexes.
• Seek ISO 9001 certification.
• Aggressively market through referrals, premium listing services, and Web ads.
MECHANICS
• Expand Web Google adWords purchasing by 50% by June 1.
• Purchase space at the 2010 home fair by June 7. Get a new display developed by Jan. 1.
• Secure consultant and begin ISO 9001 documentation development by June 15.
• Implement CRM by July 1 and referral program by July 15. Track homes by developer.
• Offer referral and listing bonuses to customers via CRM by July 15.
• Obtain on-site meetings with the area's five major developers by October 1.

An example of a completed 5-M Model is given in Figure 8.2. A downloadable blank form for doing your own 5-M Model is available from the *Entrepreneurial Small Business* Online Learning Center or your instructor.

With your 5-M Model completed, you have a roadmap for designing your business plan. With the results of this business plan strategizing process in hand, you are better positioned to develop a plan which not only meets the goals of important outsiders like investors or partners, but also your own goals for the business.

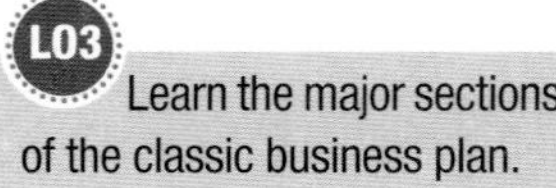

LO3
Learn the major sections of the classic business plan.

The Classic Business Plan

The business plan remains the standard for describing the business in detail. The business plan takes all the elements introduced so far and includes them in a complete description of the major elements of the business. The nine parts of the full business plan are detailed below and outlined in Table 8.2. The full (or classic) business plan contains a maximum of 25 single-spaced pages of text and 15 pages of financials and appendixes.[22] Plans for any business whose product or service is new, even revolutionary, or in which the entrepreneur is new to the industry, are the ones that really need these 25 pages. However, recall from our discussion of strategy that most small businesses are more imitative than innovative. When you are going into an imitative business, your business plan can be shortened considerably. Where the type of business is well established, such as a dry cleaner or word processing service, the market is well defined and well known, and the entrepreneur comes to the business with experience in the industry, the amount of necessary description drops dramatically. In such cases, these simple business plans may require only 10 pages of text.[23] Even so, the financial section remains its usual length, although the appendixes may be sparse.

TABLE 8.2 Business Plans Outline[24]

1. Cover letter (1 p., but is separate from plan)
2. Title page (1 p.)
3. Table of contents (1 p.)
4. Executive summary (1–2 pp.)
5. The company
    - 5a. Company description (1–2 pp.)
        - 5a1. Vision statement
        - 5a2. Mission statement
        - 5a3. Objectives (optional)
        - 5a4. Company background
    - 5b. Product/service and industry (1–8 pp.)
        - 5b1. Product/service description
        - 5b2. Industry description
6. The market
    - 6a. Market and target customer (1–3 pp.)
    - 6b. Competition and competitive advantage (1–2 pp.)
    - 6c. Marketing strategy (1–3 pp.)
        - 6c1. Overall strategy
        - 6c2. Sales plan
        - 6c3. Competitive plan
        - 6c4. Research and development or growth plan
7. The organization
    - 7a. Legal and organizational structures (1/2–1 p.)
    - 7b. Key personnel (1/2–3 pp.)
    - 7c. Related service providers (1/2–1 p.)
    - 7d. Location (1/2 p.)
8. The financials
    - 8a. Critical risks (1 p.)
    - 8b. The deal (1 p., if needed)
    - 8c. Income statement (2 pp.)
    - 8d. Cash flow projection (2 pp.)
    - 8e. Balance sheet (1 p.)
    - 8f. Start-up costs (1 p., if needed)
    - 8g. Assumptions (1 p.)
    - 8h. Schedule (1 p.)
9. The appendixes (optional)
    - 9a. Owner's résumé
    - 9b. Examples of other popular appendixes: Product or service pictures or specifications; customer/investor contracts; marketing studies or pilot sales efforts; industry reports; price lists; floor plans; advertising copy; customer or spokesperson testimonials; letters of opinion.

Table 8.2 summarizes the classic business plan in outline form, and page budgets are given for each content section. The shorter lengths are the typical page budgets for simple business plans, while the longer lengths are typical for full business plans.

Cover Letter

cover letter
A one-page document on business stationery (also called *letterhead*) that introduces the business plan and the business owner to the recipient and indicates why the recipient is being asked to read the plan.

When you send a business plan to someone, it is a good business practice to include a cover letter. A **cover letter** is a one-page document on business stationery (also called *letterhead*) that introduces the business plan and owner and indicates why the recipient is being asked to read the plan. It is typically the first written material someone sees about your business, so it needs to look and sound just right. The specifics of writing a cover letter are provided in Skill Module 8.2, and an example of a cover letter is given in the appendix to the chapter.

SKILL MODULE 8.2 How to Write a Cover Letter

We all know that first impressions are important. For business plans, the first impression is made by the cover letter, so having a good one-page letter is vital. Fortunately, writing a good cover letter is easy.

Step 1: Get the stationery. Since the cover letter shows off your firm, the paper it appears on is important. These days, you can print high-quality stationery from a color printer, using templates that come in word processing programs. For a more distinctive template, you can buy ready-made ones from companies like TemplateZone.com or from your local office supplies or computer store. You can also make a template on your own. Stationery should be heavier (at least 20-pound weight) paper. Printed on this should be your firm's name, address, phone and fax numbers, e-mail and Web addresses, and the firm's logo if it has one. Great stationery should be simple and eye-catching and leave a lot of space for your letters.

Step 2: Get all the recipient's address information. Find out the proper name, title, and address of the person to whom you are sending the plan. Call or e-mail this person's office to get the right information if you are not sure.

Step 3: Draft your letter. There is a classic format for cover letters.

a. **Salutation:** "Dear Mr. Monroe," "Dear Ms. Craft," or "Dear Dr. Jones" is how cover letters typically start. If you have a long-standing personal relationship with the reader, you can start informally, like "Dear Chris."
b. **First paragraph:** Here you introduce yourself and your business ("I am Edward Blankenship, owner of PROmote Advertising"). You explain how you got the recipient's name ("Brigit Hawkins at Security Bank suggested I contact you." Or "I am contacting you in your role as president of the Northside Investment Group.").
c. **Second paragraph:** Here you explain your company in a little greater detail. Typically this will be a variation of your vision statement in the first sentence ("PROmote specializes in increasing sales of small-lot professional and technical books through market expansion."). The next sentence describes the product or service in a sales-oriented manner ("PROmote's expertise gets books into specialty bookstores, online bookstores, and professional and trade association booklists for new sales."). The third sentence points up your competitive advantage, or what makes your product, service, or firm special ("PROmote is the only company in the industry that targets small-lot professional books on behalf of the authors, helping them increase sales.").
d. **Third paragraph:** Here you describe the current situation of the company and explain what you are seeking from the recipient ("PROmote is in start-up phase, having completed its pilot tests and secured its first customers. PROmote is currently seeking a $20,000 line of credit. I would appreciate your consideration of the attached business plan."). The typical requests are for investment, lines of credit, partnering or joint ventures, sales, or feedback on those areas of the plan in which the recipient is expert.
e. **Fourth paragraph:** In closing, you thank the recipient for his or her consideration, let the reader know you are available to answer any questions, and close with a mention of your future action, such as a promise to contact the recipient within a week.

f. **Signature block:** Typically you sign off with "Sincerely," and your name the way it appears in the business plan.

Step 4: Proofread. A cover letter with misspellings or grammatical errors sends the worst possible first impression. If the cover letter has problems, imagine what the plan must look like!

Step 5: Package and send. Print or type mailing labels for the recipients' addresses and your return address. Send the plan, with the cover letter clipped to the cover, in a 9- by 11-inch envelope. Make sure you put enough postage on it.

Title Page

The title page typically contains the following information:

- Company name (usually in large type, with a logo if you have one).
- Contact information (owner names, company address, telephone and fax numbers, e-mail and website addresses).
- Date this version of the plan was completed.
- Proprietary statement to protect your ideas: For example, "*This document contains confidential and proprietary information belonging exclusively to [your company's name goes here]. Do not copy, fax, reproduce, or distribute without permission.*" Often on the line following this statement is a copy number unique to each copy of the plan. This helps you keep tabs on individual copies.

There are three other possible items to include on the title page. One might be a securities disclaimer. If you are using a business plan to seek individual investors, it is important to state the following on the title page: "*This is a business plan. It does not imply an offering of securities.*" Typically this comes after or as part of the proprietary statement. The disclaimer is needed to comply with Securities and Exchange Commission (SEC) rulings. Another item to include is the name of the person who prepared the business plan, if it is someone other than the owner. The third possible item for inclusion is a notice of copyright for the plan or trademark for your brand name or logo, if you choose to pursue those forms of intellectual property protection. You can learn more about those in Chapter 18.

Table of Contents

The table of contents typically puts the major section headings (e.g., executive summary, company, market, etc.) in boldface type and the sections underneath each in regular type. Page numbers are given for every component, including financial statements and appendixes. Remember to put page numbers on every page of the business plan, even the financials.

Executive Summary

Many entrepreneurs write the one- to two-page executive summary first, using it as a guide, and then write the rest of the plan. (We discussed the executive summary earlier in this chapter.)

The Company

The first section of a business plan tells the story of your company. Ideally it should sell the reader on the company and the ideas and people behind it. It usually consists of two subsections—one that provides an overall description of the business and another focusing on its product or service.

Company Description (1–2 pp.)

Typically the first two subsections are the vision statement and mission statement of the business, which were discussed earlier. If you have specific goals or objectives for your business (e.g., "Third year sales of $50,000," "Picked-up by a major national chain by year 2"), they go in a subsection after the mission statement.

The next subsection is typically labeled "Company Background," or you can use the name of the business (PROmote Advertising, for example). This section gives a brief description of the business—its age and location, as well as the markets it serves or plans to serve. The firm's current status (start-up, seed stage, ongoing, expansion, and so on) is covered, and the most recent milestone achieved is often mentioned (received initial investments, finalized product design, tested a prototype, completed market testing, made first sales, and so on). For an existing business, the history of the business is briefly covered here.

The last part of the company background describes the business's competitive advantage and the way that it goes about making its profits and achieving its mission—its business model. These are the ideas covered in Chapter 7 on strategy. This is where the plan gets a chance to sell the key ideas about the firm's approach to business. The language should be upbeat and positive, and where there are numbers that support the operation of the business model, such as a 25 percent profit margin, 98 percent customer satisfaction, or double-digit growth, those should be included.

Product/Service (1–4 pp.)

The goal of this section is to describe your firm's product or service in order to help the reader understand what you are selling and how it could help your target customers. The best descriptions entice the reader to want to buy the product or service or get involved in the company that sells it. These descriptions often include pictures or graphics that help readers visualize the product or service. It is also common to explain how the customer uses the product or service or how it fulfills some need or desire or solves a problem for the customer. Often the descriptions explain how the firm is able to deliver value benefits to the customer (quality, style, delivery, service, technology, ease, personalization, assurance, place, credit, brand/reputation, belonging, and altruism), as discussed in Chapter 7.[25] If the product or service has protection through a **proprietary technology** or from patent, trademark, or copyright, you mention it here.

proprietary technology
A product or service or an aspect of one that is kept as a trade secret or is protected legally using patent, copyright, trademark, or service mark.

Industry (1–4 pp.)

The industry section tells the reader about the other firms producing this product or service—the competition. The goal is to position your firm so that it looks like a potentially solid competitor in an industry with potential. This section describes the industry in overall terms. Two sections later you will have a chance to compare your firm to the competitors' firms in detail. This is the overview.

Every product or service is part of an industry, and here is where you talk about it. Industry descriptions typically include the key information identified in the industry analysis, also discussed in Chapter 7. This includes the industry's SIC and NAICS codes, the size of the industry (in number of firms and sales), and some indication of the historical trend of growth, stability, or decline (how much it is growing, how long it has remained stable, or by how much sales overall is it declining over time). Industry profit margins are an important part of this section, as is how profits are typically made. Then you point up what your firm's projected or achieved profit margins are, and how your business model helps make this possible.

The Market

The market section talks about your customers—who they are and what they are like, who else is pursuing them, and how you plan to get or keep your customers. The market section builds on material you may have developed in the feasibility analysis (see Chapter 4), the industry analysis (see Chapter 7), and the marketing plan (see Chapter 12).

Market and Target Customer (1–3 pp.)

The market refers to the total population of people or firms to whom you plan to sell. Markets are usually described in terms of their size (both in numbers of customers and size of sales) and scope (local, regional, national, international, global). The major ways the market is organized are also covered. Professional, trade, or industry associations, special-interest clubs, major national gatherings, and media dedicated to the market (e.g., *Restaurant Business* magazine for restaurant owners, or *Simple Scrapbooks* magazine for people who are into scrapbooks) are all relevant.

The target customer section focuses attention on the individual who would buy your product or service. Target customers are described in terms of demographics (such as age, gender, education, income, experience), their relation to the product or service (will they use it themselves, gift it, re-sell it, etc.), how often they buy (once a day, once a week, twice a month, every three years, once in a lifetime, etc.), their past experience with your kind of product or service (new user, prior user of competitor's product, prior user of your product), and what they are looking for when buying your product or service. What they are looking for should be based on discussions with potential customers, and it hopefully matches closely with the value benefits your product offers. Providing a comparison of the two is often a good idea.

It is very common to have multiple target audiences. When this is the case, you should provide a separate description of each one. It often helps to give each target group a specific name when you refer to them in the rest of the business plan. For scrapbookers, the target audiences have names like "kiddies," "moms," "grandmoms," "hobbyists," and "historians." Since your marketing plan can differ dramatically among the different groups—imagine how to sell to "kiddies" and "historians"—you want to have an easy way to differentiate them.

Competition and Competitive Advantage (1–2 pp.)

Consider doing this section with one page of text and a one-page table. The table identifies the major competitors for your market by name and location. Remember from Chapter 7, the vast majority of businesses are imitative in nature, not new, and rarely disruptively new. If you think you don't have competition, think again! What do your customers use to achieve your goal now? Find those firms or products and list them here. Other columns mention the competing product or service, its market share, price, competitive strength, and competitive weakness. The accompanying page of text talks about your firm's competitive advantage—what makes your product or service or firm unique—and how your competitive advantage gives you an opportunity to win sales from these firms. Often this information is based on material gathered from the industry analysis (see Chapter 7). Some people prefer having this section included in the Industry section above. That works, too. The advantage of having it here is that it connects your market description to what you will do to sell your product or service against the competition.

Marketing Strategy (1–3 pp.)

A good marketing strategy section focuses on three ideas: (1) The overall strategy your firm pursues in the market, (2) the sales plan that shows the specific ways you apply strategy to secure sales from your customers, and (3) the longer-term competitive plan that shows how you protect your firm from efforts of the competition to unseat you. Much of the specifics are built from the ideas you develop in the marketing chapters of the book, Chapters 9 through 12.

The overall strategy subsection discusses your generic strategy (differentiation, cost, focus) as well as any supra-strategies (craftsmanship, customization, etc.) or fragmented industry strategies (no-frills, formula facilities, etc.) you pursue. Explain here how each is used in your firm and in your sales efforts.

The sales plan addresses the day-to-day specifics of how sales are achieved. It builds on the value benefits being sought by your customers and shows how these are turned into promotional efforts, pricing and incentive programs, distribution techniques, and location. Most of all, it emphasizes the way you or your employees go about selling. Examples of advertising materials, displays, coupons, or the like are useful and typically mentioned here, but details are put in an appendix. The proof that your approach is working comes from sales made using these approaches, so the strongest sales plans talk positively about the results of pilot tests, **preselling** efforts, or conventional sales already made. Being able to name customers (especially repeat customers) really builds up this section.

preselling
Involves introducing your product to potential customers and taking orders for later delivery.

Over the longer term, even with a clear competitive advantage, a sound strategy, and a good sales plan, your competitors are not likely to give up the market. They will fight back. When they do that, trying to match your sales plan features or competitive advantage, what are you keeping in reserve to help you fight back? Here is where you want to have several additional strategies that play against weaknesses in the competition, or further improve your product or service. These can include protections through patents and intellectual property protection or relationships with powerful partners. You may have contracts that tie customers to you long term, but most often advantages come from bringing out improved versions of your product or service before the competition introduces its own improved product or service.

Having these improvements ready requires some preparation on your part. In a business, this is often called **research and development** (alias R&D) or the *growth plan*. Most business plans add a section on R&D or growth here to explain how they are working to maintain an in-depth competitive advantage, with one or more additional generations of products or services ready to be used, or quickly brought to market, in order to keep the competition one generation behind your firm in meeting customer needs. Growth plans often talk about longer-term partnerships to be sought, new markets to be pursued, or ways to leverage the firm's assets, for example through licensing or franchising.

research and development
(often abbreviated R&D)—The part of a business (and a business plan) that is focused on creating new products or services and preparing new technologies, ideas, products, or services for the firm's market.

The Organization

In this section you lay out the components and supports for the firm itself. So far you have covered the product and the customer. The goal for this section is to convince the reader that the business will be successful because it has access to high-quality people both within the firm and within the larger business community, and the organization itself is structured to make the best use of those people.

Legal and Organization Structures (1/2–1 p.)

This subsection describes the legal form of the business (LLC, LP, sole proprietorship, etc.) and where it is formally registered (topics discussed in Chapter 18). It also describes the organizational structure of the firm. Often for big businesses these are drawn using organizational charts. For small businesses with an owner-manager and an employee or two, it is easier to just give the description in words. The typical format for this is to start from the top, with the highest-level manager, giving his or her title and major duties, as described in the human resource management chapter (Chapter 19). Successive sentences describe the positions and duties of workers at each level below. This section should make clear how many employees there are and whether they are full time or part time, permanent or seasonal, family or nonfamily. If you have schedules for seasonal hiring and if you have standards for hiring, they get mentioned in this section.

Key Personnel (1/2–3 pp.)

By now you have sold people on your vision, mission, product, service, competitive advantage, and even your sales approach. It is now time to sell the most important single element in the business plan—you! In any business and any business plan, everything hinges on the quality of the entrepreneur behind it. If we do not have confidence in the entrepreneur, there is no way to have confidence in the other parts of the plan. The goal for the key personnel subsection is to inspire that confidence in your reader.

Who are your key personnel? Any owners or senior managers count, as do people who will be handling key aspects of the business. For example, a salesperson with an extensive customer base would be a key employee, as would an employee who is locally famous for a skill the business will use. Often businesses have a circle of outsiders involved. This might include a local media personality who will be promoting your business, or the inventor or holder of a patent or trademark you are using, or the owner of a key outside venture partner.

While you might put in the résumés of one or two key people if you have the space, typically the key personnel are described in a half- to one-page description. Simply put, the goal is to impress the reader. What is impressive? Accomplishments, and the closer these are to the business, the better. Having been successful in the business in this industry in another firm or in your own firm (if this plan is for an existing business rather than a start-up) is the best proof. Having been successful in another line of business is a good second choice. Having experience in sales is always useful, as is experience managing projects or people.

Whenever possible talk about accomplishments rather than just experience. Achieving some mark of distinction, such as being a store's top salesperson, is best, followed by years of experience in some aspect of business, followed by education. Sometimes giving the specifics of the accomplishment does the job, even if no award was given. For example, being able to say, "In my five years at Hobbyco, my sales increased an average of 50 percent a year" shows your sales abilities are improving, which is good.

When looking for accomplishments, do not limit yourself to business. Particularly for students and stay-at-home spouses, there are often organizational accomplishments that are relevant. Activities undertaken or managed for schools, churches, social organizations, civic organizations, or community groups are often important indicators of expertise. For example, managing a team during a fund-raising event may help prove your skills in people management and making quick decisions.

Related Service Providers (1/2–1 p.)

These days, small businesses are rarely alone, and the quality of the professionals surrounding you tells people a lot about how good you might be. Taking a paragraph or two to identify your bank and banker, your attorney and legal firm, accountant or bookkeeper, and other consultants can help show that you have high-quality supports. If you have major relationships established with well-known suppliers or customers, list these here also. If you have a board of directors, members can be mentioned here or under key personnel. If you have a board of advisers made up of people who are not owners, they would be listed here.

Location (1/2 p.)

The other major organizational asset of a business is its location. This is given here, along with a description of the facility that focuses on how it meets the strategic and sales goals of the business. Also mention whether you own, lease, or rent the property. If you have investments in the property, either in terms of ownership or improvements made to it, mention those too. If there are plans to expand the facilities, mention them.

The Financials

When you are using a plan to find investors, the financials section starts with a page on critical risks and one on the deal being offered investors. For all types of business plans, a set of financial reports or projections then follows. For either approach, it is always important to develop the financials in the most conservative way possible—never overstate your sales or profits, always explain the assumptions you are making, and provide (or be ready to give) the source for every number you include. It is usually better to include fewer numbers, but ones you understand inside-out, rather than having lots of numbers, but knowing only in a general way how you arrived at them.

Critical risks are discussed in more detail below. The deal subsection typically talks about how much money is needed and how the funds will be used. This subsection goes on to address any prior or existing investments and the current ownership situation. Then it explains the equity being offered to investors, giving the price and the kinds of assurances offered (e.g., seats on the board of directors, buy/sell agreements, etc.). Here the plan details how investors will be able to sell or redeem their equity in order to harvest their investment and exit the business. The best plans explain how investors will be assured that management will be responsive to investor concerns. Typically the critical risks and the deal will each take about one page each.

The financial statements expected include: (1) income statements (also called a P&L for profit and loss) and its assumptions, (2) cash flow and its assumptions, and (3) balance sheet and its assumptions. For start-up businesses, it is also common to include a listing of the expenses incurred in the start-up process.

For an existing business, the financials report the last two years of actual data, and then offer three-year projections for the income, cash flow, and balance sheet. For a start-up business, the tradition is to offer three years of data projections. If you will take three or more years to show a profit, it makes sense to give projections for five years. In either case, income and cash flow are given monthly for the first year, quarterly for the second year, and annually for the third and any later years. Think in terms of a layout described in Exhibit 8.2.

EXHIBIT 8.2

Financials Layout for a Typical Business Plan

Page 1:	Critical assumptions.
Page 2:	The deal (if the plan is going to investors).
Page 3:	Income statement for year 1, by month. Assumptions marked as endnotes.
Page 4:	Income statement for year 2 by quarter and year 3 (and later if needed) by year. Assumptions marked as endnotes.
Page 5:	Cash flow statement for year 1, by month. Assumptions marked as endnotes.
Page 6:	Cash flow statement for year 2 by quarter and year 3 (and later if needed) by year. Assumptions marked as endnotes.
Page 7:	Balance sheet for years 1–3 (or 1–5) by year. Assumptions marked as endnotes.
Page 8:	Start-up cost budget. Assumptions marked as endnotes.
Page 9:	Assumptions (endnote) page for financial statements.
Page 10:	Timeline or Milestone List.

Note that each of the financial statements also includes its assumptions. Included as endnotes, the assumptions are often considered to be the most important part of the financials. Assumptions explain how the computations are made, which items are included or excluded, and whether there are any special considerations underlying the particular numbers. For example, key assumptions include how sales are computed, which items are expensed versus depreciated, and how inventory and business valuations are made.

A schedule of the major milestones or benchmarks the company plans to achieve is often included in the financials section, typically after the assumptions page. If significant milestones or benchmarks have already been achieved, these can top off the schedule, so readers can see how the firm has progressed.

The Appendixes

With approximately 10 pages used for financials, you have up to 5 pages left for appendixes. The most popular appendix is a one-page version of the owner's résumé (see Skill Module 8.3 and also see an example of a résumé for a student starting a business in the appendix at the end of this chapter). There are several other useful appendixes, listed below. The ones you select depend on what you are trying to highlight in your business plan. They can include:

- Product or service pictures or specifications (important when you stress features or style, or when your product or service is not familiar to readers).
- Copies of signed contracts, letters of intent or commitment, or contingency contracts from customers or investors (useful to show acceptance).
- Results of marketing studies or pilot sales efforts (useful for showing market acceptance).
- Industry reports (if there is significant information not included in the plan).
- Price lists for products or services.
- Floor plans of the location, if it is central to the business (e.g., a manufacturing facility or restaurant).
- Advertising copy, such ads, logos, catalog pages, brochures, sales letters, or press releases.
- Customer or spokesperson testimonials.
- Letters of opinion from intellectual property attorneys on prospects for patent or trademark protection or from manufacturers or consulting engineers about the viability of production processes for the product.

If readers want to know more about something that is not in the plan, they can ask you for the additional information. So do not worry too much about the many possible appendixes you cannot include. The goal of appendixes is to provide supporting information that helps detail or support the key selling points of your plan.

How to Write a Résumé

SKILL MODULE 8.3

Résumés are among the most popular and most frequently changed documents a student or businessperson ever writes. There are many forms of résumé, and many ways to prepare one. Every college's career center has booklets and workshops on résumé-building, and most will be glad to review any résumé you put together. The *Entrepreneurial Small Business* website has links and examples. Microsoft Word includes résumé templates (click File > New > On my computer > Other Documents or File > New > Templates on Office Online).

Simply put, résumés are summaries of you and your accomplishments. There is a strong business norm that résumés should be limited to one page. Résumés typically start with a block at the top identifying you: name, address, phone, e-mail. By the way, make sure your phone's voicemail message and your e-mail address sound "businesslike." An e-mail like **xtremedrift@hotties.com** is better replaced by "jsmith1811" at one of the free e-mail sites like Google's gmail, Yahoo!, or Hotmail.

After the identification block, it is good for students and those changing jobs to include a "Skills" section. Go beyond school-based skills. The ability to sell, to work in a team, to lead others, to communicate, to organize, to work exceptionally hard, or to solve problems for yourself or others count as much as knowing financial modeling or Web design. For any skill you list here, be ready to back it up with specific examples of when you demonstrated this skill.

For students (or newly graduated students) usually the next section is "Education" because it is the most important section. For people in the workplace already, "Work Experience" is usually here. Both sections are presented in reverse chronological order (i.e., most recent first). Entries give the college, its city, and your graduation month and year (even if it is in the future). On the next line, give your degree and major. If you have a good GPA (grade point average), put it in too. Generally, you do not list high schools, only colleges and up.

The "Work Experience" section is similar. For each company you worked for—in reverse chronological order—put your position, the company, city, state, and starting and ending dates. On the next line put two to four bullet points explaining what you achieved at work. We understand most jobs; what helps is for you to tell us how you helped the company and did superior work.

The last section covers any honors or awards you've received or earned (like Dean's List, scholarships, honorary society memberships, elected or appointed positions, etc.). Like in "Work Experience," give the organization on the first line, then bullets with the honor or award on the subsequent line.

Keep in mind the following. Résumés change often, so keep it handy. Make sure the résumé is easy to read (use 11 or 12 point type) and scan (keep colors and fancy formatting to a minimum). And remember, the purpose of a résumé is to sell you!

At this point, the writing of the classic business plan is done, but there is still work to be done assembling it. Plans are typically delivered as an 8 1/2- by 11-inch document or electronically as an Adobe Acrobat PDF file, which has been carefully and repeatedly checked to eliminate spelling and grammar mistakes. It has been checked to make sure all pages are included and cleanly printed. While your own copy of the plan might be kept in a loose-leaf binder to make insertions and deletions easy, the copies you give out should be spiral bound (so they lay flat when opened). Covers should be sturdy to protect the plan from the inevitable coffee stains of business. Cover letters are typically clipped to the cover, rather than included in the plan itself, so the reader opens the plan to see the title page.

Focusing Your Business Plan

LO4 Focus business plan sections to meet specific needs.

To be successful in telling the firm's story, a business plan needs to match the needs of the reader. Businesses face four situations in which reader needs are specific enough and distinct enough that it makes sense to write the plan with particular emphases in mind.

- **Plans for a pioneering business:** When your product or service is truly new to everyone, it is considered a **pioneering business**. With a pioneering business, your greatest problems are: (1) helping people understand how it works, (2) showing them how they would use it, (3) estimating how many people would want it, and (4) estimating how much they would be willing to pay for it. Anything you can do to help readers experience and understand the product or service helps demystify it. Plan on a detailed explanation of the product or service and

pioneering business
A firm whose product or service is new to the industry or is itself creating a new industry.

how it works. Make sure you explain the benefits customers would receive, and talk about the customer's personal experience in trying out, buying, and using the product. The value of preselling, pilot tests, or **test marketing** cannot be stressed enough. If 100 people tried the product and 10 bought it, you have a powerful proof of concept. Pioneering products also face a hurdle around manufacturing—can they be manufactured at a cost that leaves a chance for profit? Letters from manufacturers or consulting engineers confirming the viability and production costs of your product go a long way to alleviating fears in this area. Also, if your product is a minor variation on a product already made (for example, a consumer version of an existing industrial product), play this point up, since it means fewer problems are likely for your specific product.

test marketing
Selling your product or service in a limited area, for a limited time.

- **Plans for a new entrant business:** When your product or service already exists but your *firm* is the first of its kind in your market, it is considered a **new entrant business**. As such it is always harder to prove that your product or service will work. Just imagine trying to explain the idea of a $5 cup of coffee to people who had never heard of Starbucks! In response, help make the product or service seem more familiar by detailing how it is used by customers, and give more background on how the product or service has done in other markets, especially markets similar to yours. Also emphasize existing operations in your industry analysis. Seeing that it has worked elsewhere takes much of the mystery out of the question of whether it would work where you plan to market it.

new entrant business
A firm whose product or service is established elsewhere, but is new to this market.

- **Plans for an existing business:** Occasionally, entrepreneurs start a business before they write a plan for it. When writing a plan for an existing business, you have the benefit of knowing the history, the existing market, and the financial track record of the firm. These form a foundation for the plan, so the projections about future markets, sales, and profits should clearly build on these historical facts. It can make sense to gather information on existing customers to help clearly define the market, and often suppliers and trade associations can provide more in-depth information on market shares and competitors. Existing firms have assets to protect, such as the customer list, the firm's name, and any intellectual properties it has developed (e.g., a patented way of performing work, a trademark, a copyrighted report, a recipe protected as a trade secret). Showing how you plan to protect and perhaps even make additional profits from your intellectual property (e.g., through licensing patents or trademarks) strengthens the plan, as does talking about new ideas for increasing sales, which typically appears in the research and development section.
- **Plans for a business with significant government involvement:** Some businesses depend on government approvals to go forward. Examples include salvage yards, garbage dumps, companies using toxic chemicals, nursing homes, service stations, and even in many places, day care centers. When government gets involved in a major way, for example, having to approve the business license, zoning, or environmental impact, delays are inevitable. You need to build a plan that anticipates delays and either works around the parts of the business requiring approvals or is able to go into a type of sleep mode, using as few resources as possible until approval arrives. Working around approvals usually hinges on selling services or products that are part of the business but do not require specific approval. For someone starting a service station, it may be possible to do minor car repairs such as oil changes, detailing, or tune-ups at the customer's home or workplace. This helps spread word, build a customer base, improve skills, and keep cash flowing until approval for the service station comes.

Once you have written the complete business plan, you are positioned to create special-purpose versions of the plan to meet the needs of a wide variety of people important to your business. Usually these special-purpose plans use a subset of the total plan. In addition to the full business plan described above, there are seven other special-purpose types of plan:[26]

- If you intend to send your plan to professional funding sources such as private banks, investment clubs, or venture capital firms, it is common to send what is called a *mini-plan* or a **screening plan**. The idea is to give the basic overview of the firm and a detailed look at the financials. This is because funding sources typically start their decision process with clear ideas about the industry and the profit levels they want to pursue. Screening plans usually consist of the cover letter, title page, executive summary, and financials sections of the business plan. The only time any appendixes would be included is when it is important to prove the viability of contracts, intellectual property protection, or the product's ability to be manufactured. A screening plan can also be a useful way to get into the planning process.

screening plan
Also called a *mini-plan*; gives the basic overview of the firm and a detailed look at the financials.

Michael McMyne won one of the Global Student Entrepreneur Awards for his consulting business. When he started, all he used was his executive summary and the financials.[27]

- You may find that the business plan has a lot of information you would like to share with potential customers or suppliers, but you do not want them to see your financials. One variant of the traditional business plan is called the informational plan. **Informational plans** typically consist of company and organization sections. The cover letter, title page, executive summary, and table of contents are typically revised to reflect the differences. Relevant appendixes might also be included, such as detailed product descriptions or price lists.
- A special form of informational plan posted on the Internet is the **proof-of-concept website**. This kind of site is designed to solicit information on customer interest. They are particularly useful for demonstrating a technology or service that is new or novel (see VividSky's site on the Online Learning Center), or to reach a market that is very widely spread out, making conventional promotional techniques too expensive. The goal is to inform customers and partners about the firm and the product, so proof-of-concept websites consist of the vision and mission statements, the product/service description, and often an animated or interactive demonstration of the product or service. Short biographies of the key personnel replace résumés, and the site may also have price or product lists or testimonials. The site itself tracks information about the viewers. Visitors are asked for feedback on the concept and are offered the chance to be kept up to date as the product nears the market.
- In seeking a marketing or joint venture partner or a key employee, you need to provide more of an idea about your market and approach to it. In the early stages of finding a partner, however, it is usually too soon to share your detailed financial information. As a result, a **key employee/partner plan** (also called a *summary plan, concept plan,* or *idea plan*) can be drawn up to include all the materials of an informational plan, plus the market section and critical risks subsection of the regular business plan.
- An **invention plan** focuses on the market and operationalization of a new invention. Inventions are typically licensed to others, so the organization section simply describes the inventor and any business the inventor runs, to provide background. The product or service being invented is given a very detailed description, with diagrams or pictures to help the licensee understand it. While the plan helps to explain the market and competition to the prospective licensee, the marketing strategy is not typically included. Legal issues tend to focus on intellectual property protection (e.g., patents, trademarks, etc.) instead of on the legal form of organization, and the financials are limited to the prospective deal and risks, since the invention does not come with a firm that creates sales.
- There are only two types of plans that actually add material to a full business plan. **Operational plans** are designed to be used as working documents within a business. So in addition to all the material typically included in a full business plan, an operational plan includes detailed specifications of the major techniques, methods, recipes, formula, and sources used by the firm to do its work.
- The other type of plan which adds to a business plan is a **private placement memo** or PPM. PPMs are the official version of a business plan offered to potential investors. As such, it is a legal document, and should be drafted by a lawyer. PPMs build on a business plan, using information about the company, products and services, strategy and operations, and competition. There are also sections on the risks facing the business, the people and partnerships, the deal being offered, the financial statements, and the planned use of the investment money, although these are often longer (for the risks section, much longer) than in a business plan. There are also sections unique to a PPM such as a plan for the description and distribution of shares, compensation of managers and officials, and even the articles and bylaws of the corporation. In short, PPMs are complex and exacting, and should be left to lawyers. However, the basis for a PPM is the business plan that you create.

Table 8.3 provides an easy way to compare the different types of special-purpose plans and the components they take from the full business plan. Even though the table shows the business plan sections and subsections usually included, it is important to keep the specifics of your business and your readers in mind. If sections of the business plan seem inappropriate for your type of business or for the specific readers who will see the plan, it makes sense to leave them out. The business plan is first and foremost a sales document, and tailoring the plan's "pitch" to the specifics of your business and the readership is always a smart move.

informational plans
Give potential customers or suppliers information about the company and its product or service.

proof-of-concept website
An Internet-based type of business plan providing information or demonstration of a product or service designed to solicit information on customer interest.

key employee/partner plan
Provides information on the company, product/service, market, and critical risks to prospective business or marketing partners or to prospective key employees.

invention plan
A business plan that provides information to potential licensees. Invention plans focus on the details of an invention, including intellectual property rights.

operational plan
Business plans designed to be used internally for management purposes.

private placement memorandum
A specialized legal form of business plan crafted by lawyers for the purpose of soliciting formal investments.

TABLE 8.3 Types of Business Plans

Business Plan Sections	Full Business Plan	Operational Plan	Invention Plan	Key Employee/ Partner Plan	Informational Plan	Proof-of-Concept Website	Screening Plan
1. Cover letter	X	X	X	M	M		M
2. Title page	X	X	X	M	M		M
3. Table of contents	X	X	X	M	M		
4. Executive summary	X	X	X	X	M		X
5. The company	X	X	M	X	X		
5a. Company description	X	X	M	X	X	X	
5a1. Vision statement	X	X		X	X	X	
5a2. Mission statement	X	X		X	X	X	
5a3. Objectives (optional)	X	X		X	X		
5a4. Company background	X	X	M	X	X	X	
5b. Product/service and industry	X	X	X	X	X	X	
5b1. Product/service description	X	X	X	X	X	X	
5b2. Industry description	X	X	X	X	X		
6. The Market	X	X	X	X			
6a. Market and target customer	X	X	X	X			
6b. Competition and competitive advantage	X	X	X	X			
6c. Marketing strategy	X	X		X			
6c1. Overall strategy	X	X		X			
6c2. Sales plan	X	X		X			
6c3. Competitive plan	X	X		X			
6c4. R&D/growth plan	X	X	X	X			

7. The organization	X	X		X	X		
7a. Legal and organizational structures	X	X	M	X	X		
7b. Key personnel	X	X	X	X	X		
7c. Related service providers	X	X	X	X	X		
7d. Location	X	X		X	X		
8. The financials	X	X					X
8a. Critical risks	X	X	X	X			X
8b. The deal	X	X	X				
8c. Income statement	X	X					X
8d. Cash flow projection	X	X					X
8e. Balance sheet	X	X					X
8f. Start-up budget	0	0					
8g. Assumptions	X	X	M				X
8h. Schedule	X	X	X				X
9. The appendixes	X	X					
9a. Owner's résumé	X	X		0	0	M	0
9b. Other popular appendixes	X	X		0	0	0	0
10. Detailed specifications of work	0	X					

X = Included; M = Included in modified form; 0 = Optionally included. (Private Placement Memoranda are not included since they are done only by lawyers.)

The Most Common Critical Risks in a Plan

LO5 Identify the major risks to business plan success.

risks
The parts of a business or business plan that expose the firm to any kind of loss—profits, sales, reputation, assets, customers, and so on.

Every business faces **risks** in the real world, so every business plan needs to spend some time addressing them.[28] The exact issues raised by business experts, bankers, lawyers, and investors are often specific to your plan, but the themes they consider in assessing risks are actually quite common. Knowing these risk themes, you can go through your business plan, identify the risks, and determine how you want to handle them, the way Dan Watkins of DigitalFirst Productions did (see Small Business Insight box on page 239). Each of the risks can be handled, but the best test is to have people in your target audiences give you feedback on your plan.

1. **Overstated numbers:** Examples include sales or profits that are too optimistic, owner salaries above the minimum needed to live.
2. **Numbers that are wrong:** Examples include balance sheets that do not balance, numbers in the financials that do not flow from one section to the next (look at Figure 13.1 to see which numbers "flow" from one of the financial reports to another), no assumptions given for the financials, and ratios that do not match RMA or other standards (Standard & Poors, BizMiner), with no explanation given for the differences.
3. **Inadequate cushion:** The number one killer of young firms? Not enough money. Having enough cash to survive three months goes a long way to avoiding this risk.
4. **Inadequate payback:** There are always opportunities out there; is yours worth someone's time, energy, and (maybe) money? Any plan that does not clearly specify the key paybacks to readers will fail to sell them on the idea. Don't offer an investor a 10 percent return when corporate bonds offer nearly that with little risk of default.
5. **Narrative and financials do not fit:** If you have a plan that calls for a large marketing campaign, but financials do not show costs for one, there is a problem.
6. **No direct customer connection:** If it sounds like you have not actually talked to potential customers about your product/service, readers will consider that a major problem.
7. **Uncertain sales (especially conversion rates):** You need to prove your sales estimate. The best way is to know your *conversion rate* (alias *hit rate*), which is the percentage of people who buy out of the total population of people you approach. You get this from test marketing or preselling (introducing your product to potential customers and taking orders for later delivery).
8. **Overlooked competition:** You do not want to overlook a major player in your industry. If a search on the Web or in a phonebook can turn one up you could be in trouble. Also be broad in your search for competitors. For example, a student claimed there was no competition for his wireless cell phone headset because he didn't use Bluetooth, but the Bluetooth headset makers could quickly change radio types if it made business sense. Recall Porter's five forces (rivals, substitutes, etc.) to find competitors.
9. **Experience deficits:** Do you (or someone else in your firm) have experience in (a) the line of business, (b) the industry, (c) the locality, (d) managing?[29] Have it, find it, or say how you'll learn it.
10. **"What" problems:** For the product or service, make sure it is explained clearly enough so anyone could understand it. Also make sure the plan (or cover letter) is clear about what is being asked of the reader (e.g., invest, make a loan, give feedback, partner, etc.).
11. **Deadly aggravations:** Looking and sounding professional is key. A plan with misspellings looks amateurish. Lacking a table of contents or page numbers in the plan makes life harder for people you want to impress. Selling instead of summarizing in the Executive Summary comes across as hucksterism.

Ideally, you should have a circle of advisers who can review the plan and help identify the critical risks and your coverage of them. This circle might include successful entrepreneurs you know, lawyers, or accountants. Other good resources include the free consultants from the Service Corps of Retired Executives (SCORE), available via www.score.org, or your local Small Business Development Center (www.sba.gov/sbdc). There are even websites that make it possible for you to get a preliminary analysis of your plan. One of the most complete is Ibis Associates checklist at www.ibisassoc.co.uk/quiz/start-up-business-questionnaire.htm. The SBA also has an online self-assessment (http://web.sba.gov/sbtn/sbat/index.cfm?Tool=4) that is keyed to their resources

SMALL BUSINESS INSIGHT

ANALYZING RISKS AT DANIEL J. WATKINS PHOTOGRAPHY

Award winning photographer Dan Watkins of DigitalFirst Productions (www.digitalfirstproductions.com) started two businesses in the last decade—one succeeded, and one failed. In that first business, sales never seemed to take off, and the financial health of the business was not as clearly known as it should have been. Dan feels the major difference between the two was the presence of what he called "a good solid business plan" for the second business. Dan argues that a thorough business plan can turn great ideas into reality because it forces you, the prospective entrepreneur, to take a close 360-degree look at your business ideas. For Dan the plan became a basis for evaluation as his business grew, with detailed sections on the market, how to sell to them, and the financial projections those sales should generate. He knew he was getting the hang of business when the second business venture became profitable in the exact year, quarter, and month that his original business plan had forecast it would. The one element of the plan Dan credits with the most importance was the critical risks section. Dan claims, "If I hadn't considered some of the potential pitfalls associated with my original business ideas, my business venture probably wouldn't have been successful or profitable at all." For Dan, the plan made all the difference, and the critical risks section made the plan.

and is suitable for a wide range of businesses. A very popular self-assessment for Internet-based businesses is the Startup Genome Project (www.startupcompass.co). To get a quick check of your major financial measures, you can use the BizStats website (www.bizstats.com), and the Small Business Threat Index (www.entrepreneur.com/i/images/misc/threatquiz/threatquiz.swf). The key is to get as much feedback as possible before sending it out in hopes of money, sales, or people.

Presenting Your Plan

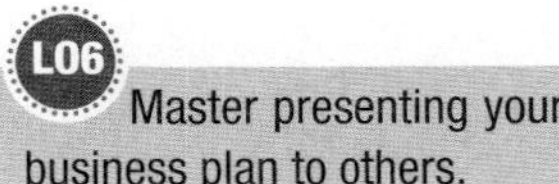

LO6 Master presenting your business plan to others.

When it works, a written business plan is the way to get on the schedule of someone who can provide the money, the expertise, or the markets you seek. In such cases, the written plan is followed by a chance for you to make a formal presentation of your plan and answer questions about it. The

Presenting your business plan as often as possible, to fellow students like you see here or to businesspeople, can help you become a more polished and professional presenter. What is the biggest challenge you feel you face in pitching your plan to others?

business plan presentation, like the plan itself, has a very clear tradition about how it is supposed to be done. Knowing this tradition can help you quickly learn what is expected when presenting a plan to others.

A business plan presentation usually lasts 10–15 minutes, followed by 15 or more minutes for questions. Usually the presentation provides an overview of key points of the business plan—a chance to sell your ideas and, most of all, a chance to sell yourself.

A major part of any business plan presentation is a chance for the listener to form an opinion about you as an entrepreneur. The key things an influential person looks for in you are: (1) your passion for the business, (2) your expertise about the business and the plan, (3) how professional you are in your work, and (4) how easy it would be to work with you. How do you show these?

- **Passion for the business:** When presenting, do not read. Think of yourself as telling a story—a fascinating story—about your business. Help listeners understand why you are excited about the business, proud of it, and ready to stake your reputation and assets on it. Learn your presentation so well that it comes out as an often-repeated, beloved story, not as a prepared statement.
- **Expertise about the business and the plan:** Practice answering questions about the plan. Expect really tough questions. Assume people do not trust your assumptions when they first read them. Be ready to explain where you get your assumptions, your numbers, and your ideas. Be ready to mention sources. Be ready with comparisons to competitors and their offerings. Know how every number in the plan came about and what it means. For example, it is not uncommon for a banker to ask, "In your cash flow statement for April in the first year, you say you will be spending $1,140 on sales promotion expenses. How did you get that number—and isn't it a bit high?" It is better to have less material and know it backwards and forwards than to have material in the plan you do not totally understand.
- **How professional you are in your work:** Your plan should look professionally done. It should be neat and orderly, with perfect spelling and grammar. When you present it, you should be in a business suit or dress, clean and pressed. Carry copies of your presentation slides to give the listeners. And have copies of your slides on acetates and on disk so that you can present no matter what technology is available. Have business cards ready, and bring a couple extra copies of the plan in case someone unexpected comes to the presentation. Meet all those attending the presentation with a smile and a firm handshake. Give them your card and take theirs if they offer one in return. Make sure you know the names of all the people in the room, and their position, so if there is a part of the plan you think might be of interest to them, you can mention it.
- **How easy it would be to work with you:** Typically when you are presenting a business plan, you are doing it with the goal of establishing an ongoing relationship with the listener. All relationships carry an element of liking. It is easier to see yourself establishing a relationship with someone you like than with someone you do not like. Part of the goal in the presentation is to get the listeners to like you. How? The techniques are simple—use eye contact, use peoples' names, remember what they might be interested in or in what they have shown an interest before, smile, and above all, be honest. When they ask tough questions, try not to get nervous, upset, angry, or defensive. If you do not have the answer, tell them so honestly, make a note about their question and name, and tell the person you will get back to him or her with the answer. Recognize that tough questions are the listeners' way of making sure they—and you—are protected from risks.

It may be hard to accept it when you are presenting, but no matter what the outcome, there are two points in the presentation where your listeners will be giving you value: in the questions they ask you and in the feedback they give you at the end of the session. Make sure you have someone taking notes for you (you will be busy answering questions) or ask if you can record the Q&A session. Knowing what kinds of questions are being asked can help you prepare for the next time, and can also inform you on how best to revise the plan. Recalling what the feedback was regarding you and your plan also gives you a powerful leg up for your next presentation.

Typically the presentation follows the content of the business plan. For different audiences, for example, potential partners or customers, you delete slides—just as you delete sections in the business plans for partnering or customer information plans.

Business, and the understanding of business you get from business plan writing, changes. Sometimes it changes quickly as you achieve new things or learn new things (including errors that crept into the plan you just finished). This means that parts of your plan may change from week to week. You handle this by creating handouts with the new information. These can be mailed to people reading your plan, or handed to them at the presentation. If there are detailed parts of your plan that you have left out, such as a market survey or a detailed cost breakdown, it makes a lot of sense to make copies to use as handouts during a presentation or question-and-answer period.

Dwight Eisenhower was not only the 34th U.S. President, but he was the general who planned the most daring effort in all of World War II, the D-Day landing. A master planner, Eisenhower said, "I have always found that plans are useless, but planning is indispensable." The best way to think about the business plan is as a way to get yourself to think through your entire business. Some parts will be so easy that you can instantly know how everything works. Things in the business you imitate from others are classic examples. For other aspects of the business, planning may become the way you get a handle on the complexities and risks you face.[30] Some results of the planning process you will write

THE THOUGHTFUL ENTREPRENEUR

Wisdom from the Front Lines

Those of us teaching at Saint Louis University have asked for short takes from students after the smoke clears from their business plan presentations. Here are some of the most memorable observations and thoughts:

I nailed my numbers, but this entrepreneur failed my plan because I misspelled his name in the cover letter!

It is a lot like playing poker for the first time, but you're playing against pros (for this student, bankers and angels) that have been doing this for years. You've got to bring your "A" game or it's all over!

Before you start pitching, walk over, look them in the eye, smile, and introduce yourself. It makes them more like regular people.

You don't have to have everything in the plan, just as long as you have it with you when you present. (This student's partner added—"And have it where you can find it. Tell your students, USE TABS!")

When they challenged me and I knew I was right, I stood my ground, but I was polite about it. I think that got me their respect.

After awhile, the judges could figure out which member of our team wasn't "into" the plan and they just kept hounding that person.

Passion pays! If you don't come across as totally believing in your plan, nobody will. Pitch it like your life depends upon it. My grade did!

How can an inexperienced kid stand up to those old guys? I figured I've got energy. I've got fresh knowledge. I've got a world of supporters I can get to on the Web, and nobody knows my business or cares about my business more than me. If they don't like it, I've got years to go find someone who does.

The best plan is one where you've already got sales. If you've got sales, you've proven everything. If you've got sales, you've got cash and you've got real financials, not financial projections. I got sales, so I had it made. Like my mom always says, where there is a will, there is a way.

down. Other parts will be kept in your head, ready to be used or amended as circumstances require. Many of the parts of the plan will quickly become outdated or need to be changed or adapted as the business is in operation.[31] In fact, the Eisenhower quote makes sense in another way too—business planning is a process you continue throughout your firm's life. Plans, once done, get revisited. Sometimes this is done formally, but more often you informally compare reality with the plan.

However you approach it, the idea of business planning is a powerful one, helping you imagine and then realize the business the way you want it to be. The techniques that contribute to creating a business plan—forming vision and mission statements, elevator pitches, financials, and marketing plans—can be used as stand-alone activities that help you meet the many demands you face as an aspiring entrepreneur. Whether you become an avid business planner or not, the process of business planning goes a long way to helping firms survive and prosper.

THE THOUGHTFUL ENTREPRENEUR

THE SEVEN SLIDES OF CLASSIC PITCH DECK

While 15 minutes sounds like a lot of time to talk, when summarizing a 40-page business plan, the time can go very quickly. From watching winning presentations in business plan competitions and in the real world, it is clear that a superior business plan presentation is usually built around seven slides.

1. **Introductory slide:** Has your firm's name and the names of the owners and presenters. While showing this slide, you thank your listeners for the opportunity to present and explain the purpose of the business plan (e.g., financial, partnering). Introduce your firm by name, as well as yourself and any other people from your firm that you have brought with you. (1 minute)
2. **Product/service slide:** This slide demonstrates the product or service in terms of the benefit it provides customers or the problem it solves. Often a picture is included. Your talk describes the product or service in detail. The slide also gives the size of the target or overall market. Although you mention this, spend more time showing how the market has already accepted your product/service or ones like it. (3–4 minutes)
3. **People slide:** Investors invest in people as much as in ideas. This slide presents the key people with the one or two skills they have that are most persuasive in proving their expertise or their contributions to the business. If you have partnerships or alliances with names the listeners would know and respect, these can be included (often as corporate logos) and briefly mentioned. (1 minute)
4. **Strategy slide:** This focuses on a one or two line explanation of your strategy as it relates to your making profits (your overall strategy). The slide also has one or two lines explaining how you plan to make the majority of your sales (your sales strategy). For both, think about specifics rather than general jargon. Saying, "We will get business because we offer faster service than anyone else," for your strategy sounds more persuasive than, "We leverage time-sensitivity in a manner superior to our competitors." (2–3 minutes)
5. **Risk slide:** Admit to the two or three greatest risks or challenges facing your firm, and for each, explain how you are preventing, insuring, repairing, or monitoring the situations. Your goal here is to head off the most threatening questions by showing you are working on the problems. (1–2 minutes)
6. **Financial slide:** Here you give the sales, breakeven, and profit projections for the firm for the period covered in the plan. Mention the worst-case scenario projections, but explain why you think the numbers on the screen are the most likely ones. (1–2 minutes)
7. **Summary slide:** This gives a one-to-two line summary of the firm in a positive, upbeat manner ("PROmote Advertising's quality service and large potential market will lead to excellent sales and profits"). Give this line in your most confident and sales-oriented manner and mention that you believe you have shown this in today's presentation. Include a line on the slide with the request from the listener ("Loan of $25,000," "Line of Credit of $100,000," "Investment of $50,000"). In covering this, explain briefly what the money's use will be. There is also a line on the slide for what is offered in return (savings moved to a bank, pledged securities, stock in the firm for investors). You conclude with a repeat of thanks, and then ask for questions. (2 minutes)

CHAPTER SUMMARY

LO1 Understand why and when to develop a business plan.

- Plans are done for external legitimacy and/or internal understanding.
- Plans are sometimes essential, and are often linked to improved firm survival.
- Different audiences seek different goals when reading business plans.

LO2 Know how to tell the business plan story.

- The business plan is a story you write about your firm.
- The story gets told in different ways and lengths, from vision statements, to mission statements, to elevator pitches, to executive summaries, to full business plans.
- The one-page business plan can be used to help organize the classic business plan.

LO3 Learn the major sections of the classic business plan.

- The full business plan gives the complete story of the firm and its major elements: the company's product/service, market, competition, marketing strategy, organization, key personnel, service providers, location, and financials.
- It is a maximum of 25 pages long, with up to 15 pages of supporting material.
- Plans for simple businesses can be shorter than those for innovative types of firms.

LO4 Focus business plan sections to meet specific needs.

- A full business plan is often modified for special circumstances the firm faces, such as pioneering technology, new markets, established operations, or significant government involvement.
- Parts of a full business plan are often combined to create shorter plans for particular audiences such as investors, partners, or others.

LO5 Identify the major risks to business plan success.

- All business plans face risks; part of the role of the business plan is to explain how the firm will handle these risks.
- The risks come from numbers or assertions that are not adequately explained or supported.

LO6 Master presenting your business plan to others.

- Most business plans are presented to others using a seven-slide show.
- Listeners check presentations for the presenter's passion, expertise, professionalism, and potential as a colleague.

KEY TERMS

business plan, 216
external legitimacy, 216
internal understanding, 216
vision statement, 218
tagline, 218
mission statement, 219
elevator pitch, 219
executive summary, 221
cover letter, 226
proprietary technology, 228
preselling, 229
research and development, 230
pioneering business, 233
test marketing, 234
new entrant business, 234
screening plan, 234
informational plans, 235
proof-of-concept website, 235
key employee/partner plan, 235
invention plan, 235
operational plan, 235
private placement memorandum, 235
risks, 238

DISCUSSION QUESTIONS

1. What are the reasons to write a business plan?
2. Imagine you were presenting your plan to a consultant who specializes in your industry. Your goal is to get her help. Using the ideas in Table 8.1, what kinds of issues do you think would be of interest to her as she reads your plan?
3. You are going to attend an after-work gathering sponsored by your local chamber of commerce. Which of the types of short business plan presentations (vision statement, mission statement, elevator pitch, executive summary) will you prepare for use, and when will you use them?
4. What is the most important part of a business plan in general? Considering the way you plan to use your business plan, what will be the most important part of it?
5. What are the differences in a business plan for a start-up pizza business and for an existing pizza business?
6. Students know people, including some who might invest in your business. What kind of business plan (e.g., informational, screening, key employee, full) would you give to other students?
7. For a business plan being put together by a student in his late teens or early 20s, what are the most likely risks?
8. Passion is clearly important in the business plan presentation. How can you display your passion for the business during the presentation?
9. What can you do to make the business plan easy to read and understand?

EXPERIENTIAL EXERCISES

1. **Evaluating a Business Plan** The goal of this exercise is to help you get used to scoring business plans the way bankers and investors do in the real world. Most financial professionals have checklists and scoring sheets that convert their accumulated wisdom into the factors that make a difference. Knowing how this scoring works can help entrepreneurs to bulletproof their plan, identifying problems before outsiders see them.

   One of the best business plan scoring systems is available to everyone for free on the Web. It comes from France's Ibis Associates. Originally built from a test of 57 firms, today it has been refined and is used on thousands of businesses, mostly from the United States and Western Europe.

   a. Go to Ibis Associates New Business Plan analysis page at **www.ibisassoc.co.uk/business-startup-analysis.htm**.
   b. Print out the checklist and familiarize yourself with it.
   c. Now read through the MyLibros.com business plan included in Appendix B of this chapter. When you see something that relates to the scoring checklist, mark it.
   d. After reading the plan, fill in 'no' for those items missing.
   e. Go to the website and fill in the questionnaire for the MyLibros.com, and check the score received.
   f. Be ready to discuss your findings (and defend your scoring) in class. Give some thought to what could be done better in the plan to achieve a higher score.

   Your score will vary from those of others in the class. You will find that some of the difference comes from how closely people read the plan and the checklist. But there will be times when everyone will agree on what was read, but disagree on the meaning or score. That happens in business too. That is why it is important to try your plan out repeatedly. Just because one person or firm or bank said no does not mean that every one will see it or score it the same way. (Scoring site used with permission of **alan.west@ntlworld.com** for Ibis Associates, January 25, 2004.)

2. **Business Plan Archives** See if you can find a plan for your business at one of the business plan archive sites, because there is no shortage of business plans available for review on the Internet. For example, **www.businessplanarchive.org** provides plans from the dot-com boom and bust, including some plans of businesses still operating today. The commercial site behind Business Plan Pro offers a number of example business plans on its site, **www.bplans.com/sample_business_plans.cfm**. This is the site the SBA refers people to when they seek example plans. The key academic archive comes from the Moot Corp competition, which pits MBA students against one another in an international competition. Their archive is at **www.businessplans.org/businessplans.html**, although the site is sponsored by another commercial company, Business Resource Software.

MINI-CASE

LOFT IN SPACE[32]

A student at the University of Nebraska—Lincoln (UNL), Michael Cain, built a loft for his dorm room bed. Others asked him to build one for them, and he started to think about making a business out of it. He had put together his marketing plan in his head and had even begun to think about operational details that would help make his business more efficient. He knew he needed to get some sort of official approval, since his business would be on campus. So he started checking with university officials about setting his business up, but it was here that he started hitting problems, such as:

- He could not run the business out of his dorm room.
- He couldn't use his UNL telephone or e-mail account for the business.
- His firm needed a $1 million liability policy to work on campus.

He needed to be able to address these problems and make sure the solutions would leave him with a profitable business.

CASE DISCUSSION QUESTIONS

1. If he was going to build a business plan to present to the university administrators, what type of plan should he develop (following the types mentioned in Table 8.3)?
2. What parts of the plan should he make sure are included?
3. What solutions would you suggest for his three problems?

SUGGESTED CASES AND ARTICLES

- The Early Stages of Paint Check Services, C-9

Available on McGraw-Hill Create™:

- Electrical Distributors, Inc.

SUGGESTED VIDEOS

www.mhhe.com/katz4e

Video Case:

- For a written video case and corresponding clip, visit the OLC at www.mhhe.com/katz4e and select "Chapter 8".
- Financing for Entrepreneurs

SBTV.com Videos:

- Business Plan Roadmap
- What to Worry About When Investors Come Calling

STVP Videos:

- Change the Business Plan in Response to a Changing Environment
- Tips for a Good Pitch
- Don't Write a Mission Statement, Write a Mantra

Your Business Videos:

- Elevator Pitch: Calendar Girl
- Elevator Pitch: Blow Dry Bar

APPENDIX A

Example Cover Letter and Résumé

Example Cover Letter

Mr. Michael Hansen
Vice President for New Accounts
Bank New Narwhal
1234 Main Street
Anchorage, AK 99501

Dear Mr. Hansen,

I am Abe Zabrowski, the founder of a new painting inspection company, Surety Inspections, LLC. I have been doing my personal banking at BNN for several years, and so you were the first people I thought about when considering establishing a business line of credit.

Surety Inspections evaluates the completeness and quality of commercial painting projects for the clients of painting companies. Because commercial painting is difficult to evaluate, we offer an objective evaluation to painting customers to make sure everything was done according to specifications, or industry standards. Our clients are industrial plants, commercial firms, and government organizations that buy major painting projects. We are the only full-time professional painting inspection business in Alaska, with most of our competition consisting of painting firms that work between jobs. As such, we offer a more consistent and higher-quality evaluation, and we are always available for inspections.

While we have funded our initial equipment and operations, it is possible that we will need a line of credit to draw against when we must rent or buy equipment specific to particular contracts, or to pay for travel and lodging for contract work away from Anchorage. Since work in our industry is paid for after the report is delivered, we could incur costs early in a project and need credit. We are looking to secure a $10,000 line of credit. We can offer the firm's equipment as collateral, and we would be willing to discuss other forms of collateral or conditions that would make this workable. You will see that my credit rating and bank history are very solid.

Thank you for your consideration. I am available to answer any questions you have. Please call me at 907-555-1213. I will call you later this week to schedule an appointment to discuss my business and what BNN can do to help me grow it.

Sincerely,

Abe Zabrowski, CEO
Surety Inspections, LLC

Example Résumé[33]

DANIELLE SHERWOOD
123 University Drive
St. Louis, Missouri 63101
(314) 555-XXXX
dsherwood@ggg.com

SKILLS

- Able to plan and organize self, others, and operations.
- Exceptional sales ability.
- Capable leader and team member.
- Excellent presentation and communications skills.

EDUCATION

Saint Louis University, St. Louis, MO, May 2012
Bachelor of Science in Entrepreneurship, Minor in Marketing, GPA: 3.6/4.0

WORK EXPERIENCE

Owner, CardinalAngelSales, St. Louis, MO, 2010–Present

- eBay Gold level reseller specializing in St. Louis Cardinals memorabilia and logo wear.
- Grew sales to over $15,000 in year one, with a 99.8 percent customer approval rating.

Student Intern, Saint Louis University, St. Louis, MO, 2009–Present

- Partner with program director in writing and editing brochures and advertisements on leadership.
- Trained 10 new student employees and facilitated orientation on job duties.
- Generated new ideas to update department's website.

Sales Associate, May Company, St. Louis, MO, 2007–2009

- Sold merchandise to clients, increasing monthly sales by 25 percent.
- Resolved customer complaints and problems in a positive manner.
- Implemented customer service questionnaire which helped improve buyer satisfaction.

Sales Consultant, J. C. Penney Co. Inc., St. Louis, MO, 2005–2007

- Made suggestions and sold clothing items to customers.
- Developed customer service procedures and training program for staff.
- Assisted in training new employees on store procedures.

HONORS/ACTIVITIES

Collegiate Entrepreneurs Organization

- Vice President, Membership (2010–present)
- Textfile Shift Manager (2009–2010)

Alpha Delta Pi

- President (2009–Present)
- Philanthropic Chairperson (2008–2009)

APPENDIX B

Red Jett Sweets Business Plan

May 2011

This document contains confidential information belonging exclusively to **Red Jett Sweets** and its owners. Do not quote, copy, or distribute without permission.

Table of Contents

[Note to students: You will notice not every heading given in the chapter is used here. If a section does not fit with your plan, it can be acceptable to leave it out. You should check with an expert though, to make sure you don't leave out a section important in your industry or to your readers.]

EXECUTIVE SUMMARY

Red Jett Sweets

Red Jett Sweets, Inc., is a subchapter S corporation opening a mobile cupcakery in August 2011. Red Jett Sweets will build a reputation in Fort Worth as one of the best cupcakeries in the area. Red Jett Sweets will provide its clients with innovative flavors, high-quality ingredients, and the highest level of customer service and satisfaction found anywhere.

The mobile cupcakery will feature cupcakes that are freshly baked, have original and innovative flavors, use high-quality ingredients, and are fun, eclectic, seasonal, and traditional. Although Red Jett Sweets is targeting individuals with the disposable income to buy cupcakes, the mobile cupcakery will be welcoming a wide variety of income levels by competitively pricing cupcakes at $2.75. Other cupcakeries in the Fort Worth area sell their cupcakes for $2.50 and $2.95. Cupcakes will be the main focus of Red Jett Sweets, but a limited line of beverages will be sold to complement Red Jett Sweets' cupcakes.

Red Jett Sweets' management and staff will provide customer service that is friendly and helpful, but not pressured, with an emphasis on building ongoing relationships. The mobile cupcakery will provide extensive client service offerings such as home delivery, special orders, gift wrapping, private parties, and customization. The mobile cupcakery design will create an inviting atmosphere that customers will enjoy visiting.

Management

At the heart of Red Jett Sweets are the owners, Christina Meyer and Natalie Gamez. They will be responsible for all aspects of product selection, client relations, and day-to-day operations. Ms. Meyer has previous experience starting and running a small business, where she has demonstrated talent in most of the activities required to manage a small business. She has a strong passion for the business and swiftly builds personal connections and maintains strong relationships with people. Ms. Gamez has worked at many businesses in the restaurant industry and still maintains many connections in the industry. She is very detail oriented and well organized, and has a passion for baking.

Red Jett Sweets will be staffed with a baking assistant and eventually one or two sales associates. Ms. Meyer and Ms. Gamez have established relationships with several additional outside consultants, including an insurance agent, attorney, and graphic designer. Their accountant, Diane Hanley, will play an active role in financial management and reporting in the first year.

Target Market

Red Jett Sweets' primary target market includes people, ages 25 to 44, with household incomes of $75,000 or higher. Secondary target markets include people in younger (18–24) and older (45–54) age groups with household incomes between $40,000 and $75,000.

Red Jett Sweets' primary trading area will be west Fort Worth. The secondary trading area includes people living in the rest of Tarrant County. Red Jett Sweets may also be able to draw some clients from neighboring Parker and Johnson counties. In the 2001 census, the total number of households in our primary target market was approximately 29,000. The total number of households in both the primary and secondary target markets was 60,000.

Over 2,000 mobile and cart food vendors covered U.S. street corners and parking lots in 2010. Also, in 2010, mobile food operations were estimated to have earned $163 million in sales revenue nationwide.

Competitive Positioning

Similar businesses exist in other cities, but when Red Jett Sweets opens it will be the first and only mobile cupcakery in Fort Worth. Its customers will enjoy the best variety of products, best customer service, and best mobile food truck environment and experience, all available in accessible locations without paying more than at other storefronts in the area.

Some existing local cupcakeries, such as Cupcake Cottage and J' Raes, offer cupcakes similar to Red Jett Sweets', but do not sell their products via a mobile cupcakery.

Red Jett Sweets will focus on promotional strategies based on personal relationships, word of mouth, and social media marketing. Red Jett Sweets will use a client database to notify clients when new flavors become available. The mobile cupcakery will host events such as a large opening party with local newspapers and magazines invited to cover it, and special events with 10 to 15 percent of profits donated to local charities and organizations. Ms. Meyer and Ms. Gamez will leverage their diverse personal networks to build awareness and interest in Red Jett Sweets before and after the mobile cupcakery opens.

Projected Sales and Income

Red Jett Sweets expects to achieve sales revenues of $44,477 in the first year and up to $152,842 by the third year. It may be possible to achieve higher sales than this conservative estimate, which is equivalent to 160 cupcakes a day from August to December. This is lower than reported sales at similar cupcakeries in other cities. The local market is large enough to support a higher level of growth.

Break-even sales for the first year are $80,358 or 29,221 cupcakes. Net income after taxes is projected to be ($16,995) in the first year and over $10,000 by the third year. Note that during these first three years of business, the break-even sales is raised and net income is significantly lowered due to purchases of equipment and amortization of intangible assets related to Red Jett Sweets' start-up.

Financing

Ms. Meyer's initial equity investment of $50,000 will fund the start-up of Red Jett Sweets. This includes $29,000 for the mobile cupcakery and small renovations; $3,000 for marketing and advertising materials; $2,500 for equipment; $2,500 for research, development of recipes, and direct labor hours associated with the two; $13,000 in working capital. Please refer to the Start-up Costs table in the Key Assumptions section.

PART I: THE COMPANY

Company Description

Red Jett Sweets, Inc., is a start-up company in Fort Worth, Texas, opening a mobile cupcakery in August 2011. The company, which is a subchapter S corporation, and the mobile cupcakery are both referred to as Red Jett Sweets throughout the business plan.

Mission Statement

Red Jett Sweets shares moments of joy with its customers by providing mouth-watering, quality cupcakes that delight the senses of young and old alike. Red Jett Sweets will be the premier mobile cupcake business in the area, widely known for its unique vehicle that offers convenient street sales and that delivers creative custom designs for special events.

Ingredients for Success

The following key elements of the Red Jett Sweets business will help it achieve its mission.

- **Mobile Cupcakery.** As Fort Worth's first mobile cupcake business, Red Jett Sweets will use the mobile cupcakery to make home deliveries and to sell directly to customers at scheduled stops in prime locations. A small box truck will be transformed into a unique cupcake sales vehicle, making a memorable impression on everyone who sees it.
- **Just Cupcakes.** Selling only cupcakes, and no other dessert items, creates a clear brand identity and a focus for operational excellence. More than a fad, cupcakes have timeless appeal as a uniquely portable, nostalgic, attractive, and affordable dessert served as a personal single serving in a range of flavors.
- **Top Quality.** Red Jett Sweets cupcakes are made from scratch daily with high-quality ingredients. They are sold fresh; any leftovers will be donated to shelters. Shipping, small sizes, or other new flavors will not be offered if they compromise Red Jett Sweets' high standard of quality.
- **Innovative Flavors.** The menu of flavors features a rotating selection of creative seasonal recipes, special flavors of the week, and year-round essentials such as vanilla, chocolate, and red velvet.
- **Special Events.** Red Jett Sweets caters parties and events with custom-themed recipes and decorations. Whether provided as a service to customers or as a donation to community organizations, these special events also generate word of mouth and future sales with attendees.
- **Visual Branding.** Red Jett Sweets is building strong brand recognition and appeal by using playful, memorable, and modern visual designs for its logo, cupcake decorations, packaging materials, sales vehicles, website, and printed sales materials.

PRODUCTS

Cupcakes

At Red Jett Sweets we are intent on baking a cupcake that sends mind, body, and soul to a whole new place. Whether you are a traditionalist or an adventurer, you will find a cupcake for every craving. We offer a number of crowd-pleasing flavors on a regular basis as well as a rotating menu of featured cupcakes that simply sparkle with innovation and wit.

Our customers will be able to call ahead if they wish to have more than two cupcakes packaged together and want to ensure their specific flavor choices are available to them.

- **Crowd-Pleasing Daily Flavors**
  - **Red Jett Velvet**—red velvet cupcake topped with cream cheese icing
  - **Chocolate Echo**—dark chocolate espresso cupcake topped with chocolate buttercream icing
  - **ChocoVan**—milk chocolate cupcake topped with vanilla buttercream icing
  - **VanChoco**—vanilla bean cupcake topped with chocolate buttercream icing

- **Featured Rotating Flavors**
  - **Beloved Banana Foster**—banana foster cupcake topped with vanilla buttercream icing and caramel drizzle

- **Dulce de Leche**—3-milk cupcake with a caramel center and topped with cream cheese icing
- **Peanut Better Cupcake**—milk chocolate cupcake topped with a peanut butter cream cheese icing

- **Featured Seasonal Flavors**
  - **January–February**
    - **Strawberry Champagne (cheers!)**—strawberry champagne cupcake topped with strawberry cream cheese icing and dark chocolate drizzle
  - **March**
    - **Irish Chocolate**—Guinness chocolate cupcake topped with Bailey's Irish buttercream icing
    - **Emerald Velvet**—our signature Red Jett Velvet cupcake tinted green for St. Patrick's Day
    - **Snickerdoodle O'Shea**—vanilla cinnamon cupcake topped with vanilla cinnamon buttercream icing
  - **March–May**
    - **24-Karrot Cake**—spiced carrot cupcake topped with cream cheese icing
    - **Hummingbird**—banana-pineapple cupcake topped with cream cheese icing
  - **October–December**
    - **Peter Pumpkin**—pumpkin spice cupcake topped with cream cheese icing
    - **24-Karrot Cake**—spiced carrot cupcake topped with cream cheese icing
  - **November–December:**
    - **Gingerbread Hug**—gingerbread cupcake topped with cinnamon cream cheese icing
    - **Cocoa Peppermint Cloud**—chocolate cupcake topped with peppermint buttercream icing
    - **24-Karrot Cake**—spiced carrot cupcake topped with cream cheese icing

Food Allergy Disclaimer: Red Jett Sweets is not a "nut-free" establishment and as such does not guarantee our products to be nut free. All products are made on equipment shared with milk, wheat, nuts, and eggs. Red Jett Sweets will take extra precautions when preparing products for customers with certain allergies.

Beverages

Red Jett Sweets will offer a variety of beverages that complement the taste of our signature cupcakes. We will have our everyday beverages, as well as seasonal beverages, including:

- **Water**
- **Milk**
- **Lemonade**

CUSTOMER SERVICES

- **Private Parties.** Customers will be given the opportunity to rent Red Jett Sweets' catering services for their private parties. This could mean a young child's birthday party, a baking class, or partnering with an additional catering company to provide for our customers' special event.
- **Special Orders.** Red Jett Sweets will offer our customers the opportunity to place special orders to ensure they can purchase their desired flavors. They will also be able to work with us to design the cupcake colors or flavors to fit their needs. Red Jett Sweets will also provide our customers with the opportunity to choose one of our standard toppers to tie our cupcakes to the theme of their event. Additional decorations are available for special occasions including holidays, weddings, birthdays, baby showers, and bridal showers. Extensive custom decorations will be offered at an additional charge of $5–$10 per dozen based on the amount of detail associated with their toppers. Search Engine Optimization will benefit this part of Red Jett Sweets' business. We will also rely on word of mouth and local party planners' referrals for large orders.
- **Delivery.** Red Jett Sweets will offer discounted delivery around certain holidays and for special promotions. At all times, we will offer delivery within our primary trading areas in Fort Worth for a small fee. If our customer is outside this area we will charge an additional fee to deliver his or her order if the customer does not wish to pick them up at our mobile cupcakery. For large orders over $150, Red Jett Sweets will provide free delivery.
- **Gift Packaging.** Gift packaging will be provided for all products upon request for a small fee to cover packing materials. Wrapping materials will be based on our Red Jett Sweets signature colors and will include a sticker with the Red Jett Sweets logo and a ribbon.

PART II: THE MARKETING PLAN

Industry Analysis

Nationally, the market for pastry and/or baking shops has expanded and contracted over the past 10 years. This growth was in part due to an increase in public awareness because of media coverage, such as The Food Network and TLC food shows. Consequently, this has led to an increase in demand for premium bakery products such as what Red Jett Sweets offers its customers. The reductions in growth can be attributed mostly to the drop in the economy, which caused consumers to restrict their level of discretionary spending. According to IBISWorld industry research, "The industry is sensitive to movements in real household disposable income, which is influenced by changes in employment growth (particularly adversely by the rapid spike in unemployment as has occurred since late-2007) and to increasing competition from other food service operators, including limited service restaurants, cafés, and other caterers."

Red Jett Sweets functions predominately as part of the bakery (pastry) industry, based on its products and clientele, but it is not precluded from also being a part of the newly arising food truck industry. The marketing strategy, selling prepackaged cupcakes, legally allows Red Jett Sweets the luxury of licensing itself as a "cupcakery" that utilizes a specialized vehicle as a means of distribution; in other words, selling prepackaged cupcakes offers Red Jett Sweets the opportunity of a loophole in a number of legal requirements required of food trucks. This distinction, while excluding Red Jett Sweets from the licensing requirements mandated to all-inclusive food trucks, does not prevent Red Jett Sweets from associating itself with the food truck market and industry. Currently, there is a steady, yet small, local industry for food trucks in the Dallas/Fort Worth area including, but not limited, to **Salsa Limón, Yum-Yum,** and **Taco Heads**, all of which are gourmet taco trucks in Fort Worth with prominent reputations among Fort Worth residents for their superior taste and quality. **Chef Point on Wheels** is famous for its fried chicken and bread pudding. **The Wiener Man,** which will serve as a partner to Red Jett Sweets serving gourmet hot dogs, but no desserts. **The Messy Cheesy Gourmet Food Truck:** As of March 15 2011, this is Fort Worth's newest food truck. They serve a variety of food, all with one ingredient in common, cheese.

IBISWorld market research indicates that the prospects for the mobile food industry appear brighter than recent years, with more solid growth in economic activity and general employment as predicted for 2015. The mobile food industry is estimated by IBISWorld to be in a mature phase of its life cycle based on sluggish industry revenue growth, as well as in employment and operators over the past decade. Over 2,000 mobile and cart food vendors covered U.S. street corners and parking lots in 2010, and mobile food trucks serving bakery-type products were estimated to have generated $163 million in sales. The food truck industry, however, is still expected to evolve, fueled mostly by competition and the ingenuity of the idea, both of which have given mobile food trucks a way to offer highly varied menus and food items. It is expected that in the next five years, rising retail sales and nonresidential construction activity will provide many new opportunities to developing food trucks, increasing their number of customers and thus their revenues and profits. According to IBISWorld, the greatest threat to the industry is local regulations on food trucks and high levels of competition from long-established brick-and-mortar restaurants.

Source: IBISWorld Industry Report 72233
Street Vendors in the United States
July 2010 Roman Zwolak

TARGET MARKETS

Primary Trading Area

The Red Jett Sweets mobile cupcakery will be located in Fort Worth, Texas. Red Jett Sweets' primary trading area will be west Fort Worth.

The primary trading area includes neighborhoods containing people who are close enough to come to our mobile cupcakery on a somewhat regular basis (rather than as a "special trip"). Our trading area is a bit larger than it might be for other cupcakeries, due to the fact that we are mobile and will be able to serve many locations around Fort Worth.

The primary trading area is shown on the maps on the next few pages. It is roughly based on a circle with a radius of 5 miles, that includes the zip codes found in the table on the next page. The table makes up the primary trading area and shows the number of households in each area in the primary and secondary target markets in terms of age and income.

Red Jett Sweets' primary target market includes people, ages 25 to 44, with household incomes of $75,000 or higher. Secondary target markets include people in younger (16–24) and older (45–54) age groups and with household incomes between $40,000 and $75,000. We have chosen these groups as our primary target market because of the disposable income the age group on 25–44 has and also because they are still young enough to be following current trends. The secondary market is important because the age group of 16–24 follows trends more than any other age group and the 45–54 age group has the desirable disposable income.

In the 2001 census, the total number of households in our primary target market was approximately 29,000. The total number of households in both the primary and secondary target markets was 60,000.

- **16–24, Secondary Target Market**. These young women and men will be attracted to Red Jett Sweets' cupcakes, but most of them do not have the disposable income to become consistent clients. However, Red Jett Sweets' products are priced competitively with other stores in the Fort Worth area. This will allow these women and men to purchase from Red Jett Sweets and help the mobile cupcakery to build relationships with these future clients. Note that there is a segment of teenagers in high school and college from very wealthy families who spend considerable amounts of money on food and entertainment and could be considered part of the primary target market for Red Jett Sweets. We will target this market segment using social media marketing.

- **25–44, Primary Target Market.** Red Jett Sweets will focus its attention on selling cupcakes to this age range of women and men, which includes generation X and the youngest baby boomers. They have growing spending power, strong interest in trends, and are knowledgeable about current trends found in local and national magazines, among celebrities, on television and social media outlets, and among their own peers. Part of this market segment is still young enough to be actively using social media websites, but our greatest source of marketing will be word of mouth and personal networking. When we park downtown we intend to attract this segment of potential customers.
- **45–54, Secondary Target Market.** The baby boomer generation is an attractive market due to its large size and large expenditures. These women and men definitely will be welcomed to the mobile cupcakery and the special orders side of the business as potential clients. However, many of them may be less interested in Red Jett Sweets. This group may be more likely to shop at businesses that have been in the community for many years. This age group is one that we don't expect to jump on the trend of food trucks; however, by donating to charities and organizations around Fort Worth, we hope to gain business from this group through special orders. We will also attract this group through local magazine and newspaper advertisements.
- **55 and older, Secondary Target Market.** This group will receive the least amount of our marketing attention. Red Jett Sweets hopes that they will purchase from us for special events and for the occasional treat or surprise for their grandchildren. This age range may also be more likely to shop at businesses that have been in the community for many years. Like the previous segment, we do not expect these people to make the trip to our mobile cupcakery; however, we hope to draw customers who attend charity events to the special-order side of the business.

	Number of Households in 2000		
Zip Code	**Primary Target Market (Greater than $75,000)**	**Secondary Target Market ($75,000–$40,000)**	**Comments**
76109	4,152	2,599	This area around TCU has the largest number of primary target market households and is therefore an important trading area for Red Jett Sweets. The owner, Ms. Meyer, lived in this area for nearly 20 years.
76116	5,763	6,160	The owner, Ms. Meyer, lived in this area for the past two years (2009–2011). Ms. Gamez has lived in this zip code for 22 years.
76132	3,759	3,500	This area contains several high schools that have students from wealthy families and high-traffic volume on several streets. Cousin's BBQ, a potential partner, is located in this zip code.
76107	3,232	3,429	Although many residents in this area are not wealthy, this zip code also includes Westover Hills, which is an exclusive enclave of "old money" residences. This area contains The Cupcake Cottage and J Rae's, our top two competitors. This zip code also contains Shampoo, a second potential partner.

76133	6,582	6,002	This area is important owing to the large number of households in the secondary target market. The commercial kitchen we rent to bake our cupcakes is located in this area. This is also where Ms. Meyer currently lives.
76110	2,136	2,832	This area is located right next to 76104 and 76109. The Fort Worth Zoo is located in this zip code.
76114	1,560	2,838	This is where we will have our mobile cupcakery logo wrap installed. This area does not have the large number of people in our target market like the ones listed above, but it is still important for us to target them because most of these people have jobs in other parts of town where we will be parked and selling on a daily basis.
76102	523	528	This area includes downtown Fort Worth. Although this area does not have a large number of households, there will be many more people downtown during the daytime while at work. This will be a great area for us to park our mobile cupcakery during their lunch hours.
76115	695	1,689	This will not be an area of our main focus, but it is important to consider this area due to the number of people in the secondary trading area.
76104	539	1,072	This area includes the hospital district and a developing area centered around Magnolia Ave. The coffee shop that will be selling Le Chat Noir–Cupcake Bordello cupcakes is located in the new developing area. Although this zip code has the least number of households, this area attracts a lot of people for work and personal reasons during the day. With its close proximity to downtown, this is a desirable location to attract downtown customers to the hospital district and vice versa.
Total	**28,941**	**30,649**	

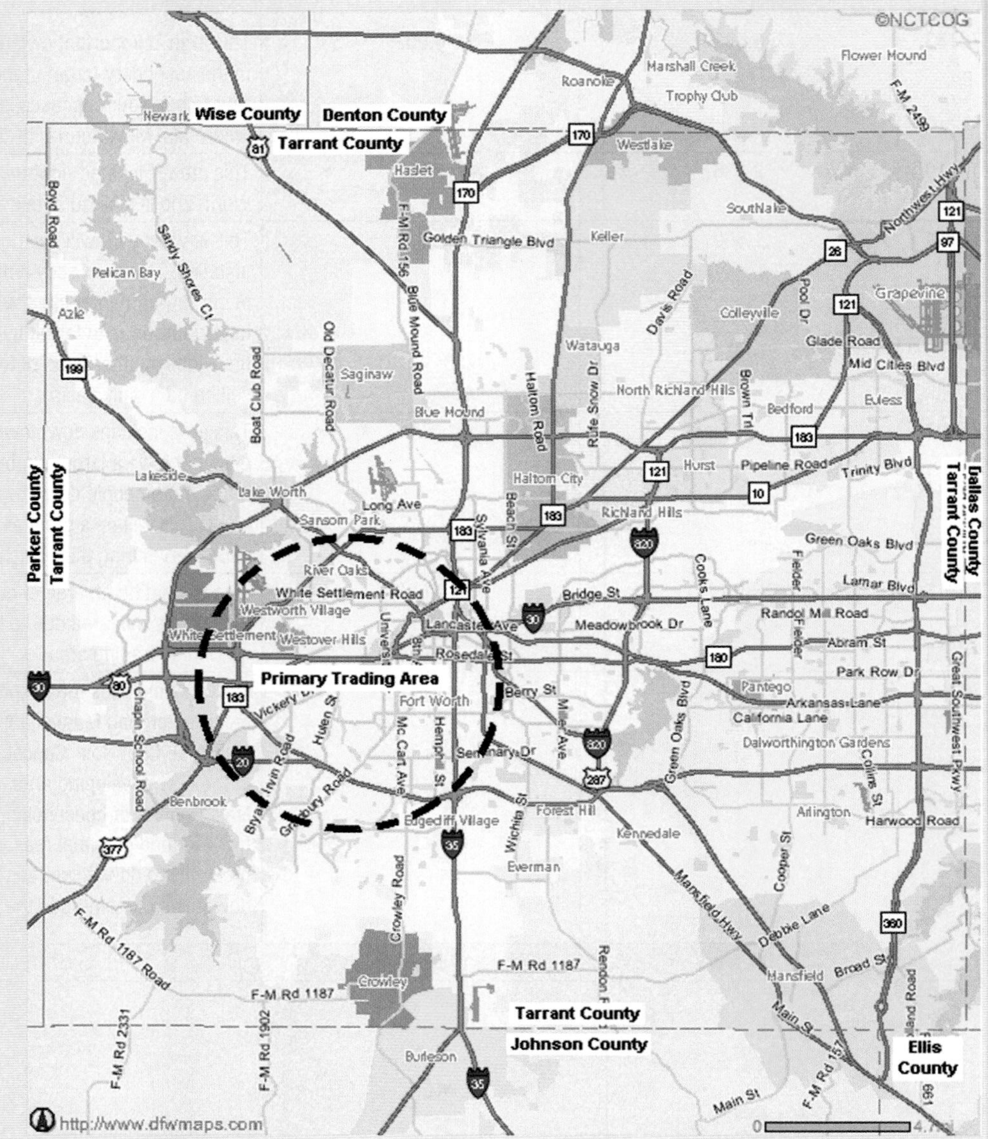

● Tarrant County and the neighboring Counties. (Johnson, Dallas, Parker, Wise, and Denton)

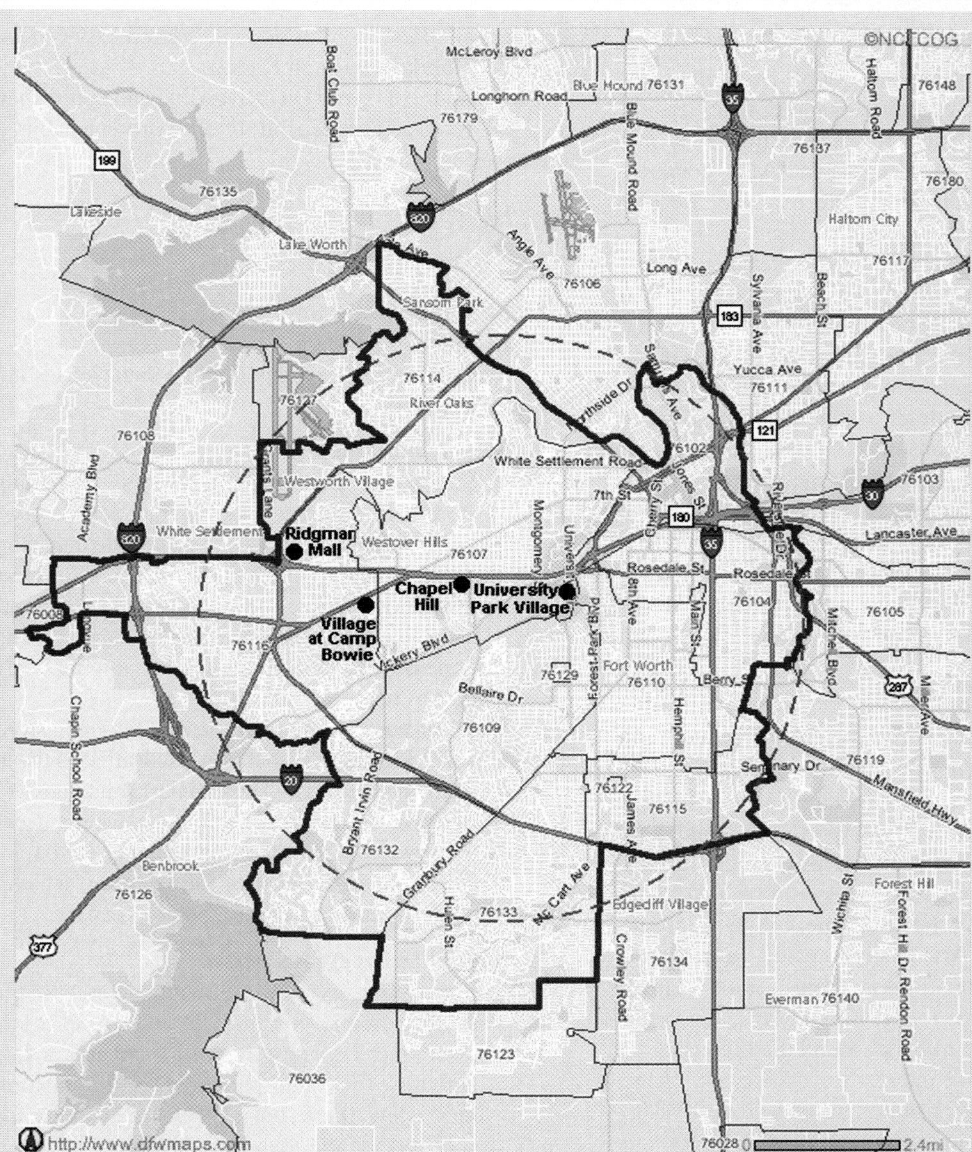

Primary Trading Area

Secondary Trading Area

The secondary trading area includes people living in the remainder of Tarrant County outside of the primary trading area. Red Jett Sweets may also be able to attract some clients from neighboring Parker, Johnson, and Dallas counties.

Several areas of Tarrant County are relatively wealthy and are more likely to contain potential clients for Red Jett Sweets. One of the largest concentrations of wealth in Tarrant County is in the northeast corner in cities such as Southlake and Colleyville. While Red Jett Sweets hopes to draw some clients from this area, it is not an ideal market because of the distance to the surrounding area and Dallas County.

Red Jett Sweets will attract a small number of customers from Parker and Johnson counties to the west and south of Tarrant County, as people from these areas make occasional trips to Fort Worth for various reasons. These two counties are not considered part of the secondary trading area, but they are still considered as feasible markets in this report. People in Denton and Dallas counties typically travel to Dallas more often than Fort Worth.

MOBILE CUPCAKERY PLACEMENT STRATEGIES

Red Jett Sweets will choose locations based on the type of people in the area and the amount of traffic in that area. We will focus mainly on areas around Texas Christian University (TCU), downtown Fort Worth, and southwest Fort Worth. We will also be researching special events in the Fort Worth area in which we would be able to attend and park our truck at. For example, Mayfest and the Fort Worth Main Street Arts Festival would be two good events for us to attend. In addition, there is a local brewery in town that hosts free tours on Saturdays. We could possibly find somewhere to park around the brewery.

TCU will be a point of interest for us because of the large number of 18–22 year olds. This age group likes to keep up on the latest trends, for example, cupcakes and food trucks. This will be a good place for us to park on Saturdays, particularly if there is a football game, because of the large number of people who attend the game in such a short amount of time.

Downtown Fort Worth will also be a focus point of ours because of the large number of people in a small area who typically take their lunch breaks from around 11:00 a.m. to 2:00 p.m. We would park down there on Mondays through Fridays during this time.

Southwest Fort Worth, specifically Hulen St. and Bryant Irvin Blvd. have high levels of street traffic. This is where Cousins BBQ is located. Bryant Irvin Blvd. is also home to two private schools in the area. These streets specifically have high traffic levels from 2:30 p.m. to 4:30 p.m. The types of families who attend these schools are mostly in our primary targeted income levels. This will be a good location for us to be parked between those times on Mondays through Fridays.

These hours of operation are flexible and could change on a day-to-day basis depending on customer habits and events around town.

COMPETITORS

Types of Competitors

Direct Competitors

- **Mobile Cupcakery**
  - Currently there are no mobile cupcakeries in the Fort Worth area.
- **Storefront Shops**
  - **Strengths:** One major advantage to having a storefront cupcake shop is that people always know where your building is. People may stop in on their way to another destination. Storefronts also allow people a place to sit down immediately to enjoy their purchase. Because baking is done on-site, customers might view their products as being fresher.
  - **Weaknesses:** One weakness of having a store in a fixed location is that you are limited to the area of town you serve. These types of businesses do not have the ability to easily go to where an event or crowd is. The major disadvantage to having a storefront is the cost of the location, which includes rent, utilities, and other expenses.
- **Special Delivery Businesses**
  - **Strengths:** By only allowing people to place special orders, you may be able to do a larger event more frequently, which creates a larger amount of revenue per order. Some customers may view these business's products as more specialized, and therefore these businesses may be able to charge more for a dozen cupcakes.
  - **Weaknesses:** These types of businesses cannot receive walk-up customers like storefront shops do. Although exclusivity is a strength, it can also be a weakness. These types of cupcakeries have a limited customer base, and orders are typically placed for special occasions or events.

Secondary Competitors

- **Other Desserts/Bakeries**
  - **Strengths:** Bakeries usually offer more than one type of dessert, giving customers many options to choose from and allowing every customer to find the product that is best for them. They also have a broader customer base and have the luxury of a readily changeable menu.

- **Weaknesses:** Having a broad selection of products forces the company to split their resources among all the different products. This can cause one product to be better or to have an unclear brand image to customers. Similar to storefront cupcakeries, bakeries incur the high costs of kitchen equipment, rent, utilities, and other expenses.

- **Cake Shops**
  - **Strengths:** Cake shops usually produce highly customized items. These tailored cakes usually provide large revenues per order.
  - **Weaknesses:** One weakness of cake shops is that cakes are usually purchased for large events, not just for one or two slices of cake. These cakes are typically large cakes.

Key Competitors

Primary Competitors		
Mobile Cupcakery		
Currently there is no other mobile cupcakery in the Fort Worth area.		
"Brick and Mortar" Cupcakeries		
Cupcake Cottage	• Opened first cupcakery in Fort Worth in 2007. • Set central location; people will know where they are. • Usually sells out around 1:00 p.m. • In-house kitchen. • Uses Facebook daily to inform customers of flavor options and when the last cupcake is sold.	• $2.95 per cupcake. • Unprofessional marketing material. • Only bakes a limited amount per day. • Stops selling cupcakes once they are sold out. • No intentions to expand beyond necessary capacity. • Location is surrounded by five other competitors.
J Rae's	• $2.50 per cupcake. • Set location in popular developing area of Fort Worth (7th Street). • In-house kitchen.	• Uninformative staff. • Location is surrounded by five other competitors.
Ultimate Cupcake	• Offers delivery for special orders. • Environmentally friendly.	• $3.00 per cupcake. • Located outside our target area. • Limited flavor options. • No customization.
Leah's Sweet Treats	• Many options for customization. • Minimum order of 1 dozen.	• Does not focus solely on cupcakes. • Unprofessional website. • Sole proprietorship. • $35.00 per dozen. • Location is surrounded by five other competitors.
Special-Order Cupcake Businesses		
Sugar Lush Cupcakes	• Wide variety of flavors. • Options for customization.	• Oriented more toward catering events. • $150.00 order minimum. • Bakes at a commercial kitchen with many other business.
Le Chat Noir—Cupcake Bordello and Bakery	• Upon completion of a new coffee shop on Magnolia Avenue, they will be selling their cupcakes at that location. • Minimum order of 1 dozen. • Offers gluten-free cupcakes.	• No content on website. • Can be adult oriented. • $32.00 per dozen.

(*Continued*)

Secondary		
Blue Bonnet Bakery	• Established in 1934. • Strong customer loyalty. • Wide ranging hours of operation. • Also sells cupcakes.	• Broad menu. • No innovation. • Location is surrounded by five other competitors.
Nothing Bunt Cakes	• Nationally recognized brand. • Does not sell cupcakes, but the bundtlets are a similar size to cupcakes. • Trendy.	• $3.99 per bundtlet. • Limited flavor variety. • Location is surrounded by five other competitors.
McKinley's Fine Bakery and Café	• Informative website. • $2.00 per cupcake. • Large variety of cupcake flavors. • Also sells cupcakes.	• Broad menu. • No options for customers to customize cupcakes.
Cake Shops		
Sublime Bakery	• People might order cakes from them instead of cupcakes from Red Jett Sweets for special events. • Offer vegan and gluten-free options • Also offers cupcakes.	• $36.00 per dozen cupcakes.
Crème de la Crème	• People might order cakes from them instead of cupcakes from Red Jett Sweets for special events.	• Custom cakes are expensive, usually purchased for large events.
Couture Bake Shop	• People might order cakes from them instead of cupcakes from Red Jett Sweets for special events.	• Custom cakes are expensive, usually purchased for large events.

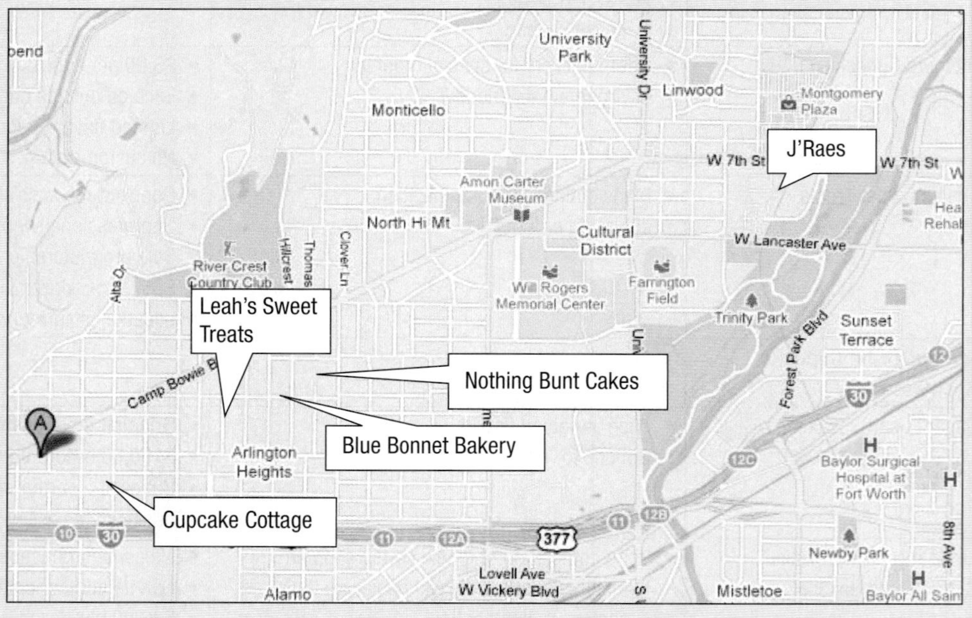

Leah's Sweet Treats has recently announced that they have leased a space for a storefront. This space is also on Camp Bowie Blvd., the same street as Cupcake Cottage, Blue Bonnet Bakery, and Nothing Bunt Cakes. It is less than .25 miles from Cupcake Cottage. Leah's Sweet Treats is scheduled to open in May or June. All three storefront cupcakeries in Fort Worth will now be within 3 miles of each other.

As the map shows, Camp Bowie Blvd. has a significant number of our direct and indirect competitors. Therefore, we will be focusing on other areas of the city more than on this area (76107). The areas we will focus more of our attention on now will be downtown, the hospital district, the TCU area, Hulen St., and Bryant Irvin Blvd.

COMPETITIVE ADVANTAGES AND VALUE PROPOSITIONS

Partnerships

- **The Wiener Man.** Red Jett Sweets has partnered with The Weiner Man, Fort Worth's newest food truck. The Weiner Man will serve only gourmet hot dogs, no desserts. We will be coordinating with them to park in the same areas a few times a week to help bring the food truck phenomenon to the DFW area. The Wiener Man's main strategy for locations is to get approval from certain businesses to park on their premises.
- **The Messy Cheesy Gourmet Food Truck.** This is Fort Worth's second newest food truck. They serve a variety of food, all with one ingredient in common, cheese. The Messy Cheesy Truck has an agreement to park in a businesses lot next to a hospital. They have been having problems because of their location due to the fact that they do not move around to different locations in Fort Worth.
- **Cousin's BBQ.** Through Ms. Meyer's networking throughout the Fort Worth community, Red Jett Sweets has been able to talk with the owners of Cousin's BBQ. Cousin's BBQ is a local family-owned barbeque restaurant that has expanded to many locations over the last 28 years. We are currently discussing the possibility of selling Red Jett Sweet's cupcakes in their primary location inside our primary target area (Bryant Irvin Blvd.) until we have our mobile cupcakery up and running. We are also in negotiations with them to be able to park in their parking lot to sell our products once we have our mobile cupcakery up and running.
- **Local Party Planners.** Red Jett Sweets will network and build relationships with several party planners in the Dallas-Fort Worth area to be known as the preferred cupcake provider for party planners. Cupcakes have become extremely popular for weddings, wedding showers, baby showers, and other special events arranged by party planners. It will be very beneficial to build and maintain strong relationships with party planners.

Red Jett Sweets is continuing to use personal networking opportunities to develop these and other partnerships throughout the Fort Worth community.

SWOT ANALYSIS

- **Strengths**
  - Cupcakes are made from scratch daily with high-quality ingredients.
  - Red Jett Sweets donates any cupcakes remaining at the end of the day.
  - Red Jett Sweets will pursue customer service excellence to ensure that each customer leaves fully satisfied.
  - Red Jett Sweets will be Fort Worth's first mobile cupcake business.
  - Being a mobile cupcakery will allow Red Jett Sweets to be able to serve many different areas around Fort Worth.
  - Selling only cupcakes creates a clear brand identity.
  - Red Jett Sweets caters parties and events with custom-themed recipes and decorations.
  - Red Jett Sweets will continue to develop new and innovative flavors.
  - Red Jett Sweets' cupcakes are competitively priced with primary competitors of "brick-and-mortar" storefronts in Fort Worth.
- **Weaknesses**
  - Since Red Jett Sweets is a new start-up company, we do not have an established reputation comparable to our competitors.
  - The trend of food trucks has not fully caught on in the Dallas-Fort Worth area.
  - We do not have our own baking facilities.
  - We sell only one product.
- **Opportunities**
  - Creating strategic relationships with other businesses and party planners will lead to repeat business and sustained long-term growth.
  - Since there are no mobile cupcakeries and few "brick-and-mortar" cupcake storefront shops in Fort Worth, Red Jett Sweets will have the opportunity to take a portion of their market share.
  - Producing products using high-quality ingredients, providing exceptional customer service, and differentiating our products will generate positive word-of-mouth marketing opportunities.
  - Cupcakes continue to be increasingly popular for weddings and large events.
  - Red Jett Sweets will start with a "blank slate" in our customers' minds; therefore, they will have a chance to create customer loyalty from

day one. Customer loyalty separates successful companies from unsuccessful ones.
- Cupcakes, food trucks, and mobile cupcakeries are current popular trends around the United States.
- After proving to be successful in the mobile cupcakery business, Red Jett Sweets will have the opportunity to expand to a storefront location with a private kitchen.
- Although the current economic situation has consumers looking for ways to cut spending and save money, hopefully even if consumers may resist large purchases, they may instead treat themselves to a small and relatively inexpensive indulgence.

- **Threats**
  - The cupcake industry has relatively low barriers to entry due to low start-up capital requirements and the possibility of new competitors selling to their existing networks.
  - Growth may be more rapid than expected. This would mean Red Jett Sweets would need to hire more employees, but only if they are marginally beneficial.
  - In the case that Red Jett Sweets is busier than expected, we will not purchase additional baking supplies such as mixers, cupcake tins, etc. until sufficient cash flow is generated to pay for such expenses.
  - New competitors may try to compete with Red Jett Sweets on the basis of price.
  - Consumers around Fort Worth might decide that cupcakes are a fad.
  - Since food trucks are not the norm in Fort Worth, there are many requirements and regulations we must follow and abide by.
  - Since Red Jett Sweets uses the finest ingredients, over time the cost of these ingredients may fluctuate, causing Red Jett Sweets to eventually raise the price of the cupcakes.
  - The current economic situation has consumers looking for places to cut spending; the food, dining, and restaurant industries have been greatly impacted by this.

MARKETING STRATEGY

Marketing Objectives

- **Build Awareness.** Various communication tools will be used to create awareness of Red Jett Sweets in the target markets and trading areas and to attract the attention and interest of potential clients.
- **Convert Sales.** When potential customers visit the mobile cupcakery, Red Jett Sweets' personal selling techniques, delicious cupcakes, and inviting environment will encourage customers to revisit to make purchases. The events that Red Jett Sweets will host will also create a setting in which clients are more likely to buy.
- **Exceed Expectations.** Red Jett Sweets will pursue customer service excellence to ensure that each customer leaves fully satisfied. Such customers are more likely to become loyal, repeat customers and to encourage others to visit our mobile cupcakery.
- **Build Loyalty.** Red Jett Sweets will maintain its relationships with customers after they leave the mobile cupcakery, encouraging them to not only become repeat customers, but also to build an emotional investment in the mobile cupcakery and their relationship with the owner. Such loyalty will help Red Jett Sweets maintain its customer base in the face of increasing future competition. Red Jett Sweets will do this by keeping a client database and interacting with customers on various social media channels.

Marketing Channels

- **Word of Mouth.** Interest in Red Jett Sweets has already been spreading by word of mouth a year before the store will open. In the long term, word of mouth will be the single most important means of building awareness and attracting new customers. A personal reference or recommendation speaks much louder than a newspaper or magazine article. Red Jett Sweets will further encourage word of mouth once the mobile cupcakery opens by exceeding customers' expectations, building loyalty, hosting events, and providing customers with delicious cupcakes that invite the question, "Where did you get that?"
- **Networking.** In addition to passive word of mouth, the owners will engage in active networking to build awareness of Red Jett Sweets during the start-up phase and after the mobile cupcakery opens. Ms. Meyer has developed an extensive personal network through her social, professional, and volunteer activities. She will ask friends and associates to help spread the word about Red Jett Sweets around Fort Worth and Tarrant County, including specifically targeted social groups such as local country clubs, parents at Fort Worth Academy, and Junior League. Ms. Gamez will help target the target age group of 16–24 through her connections at Trinity Valley School, All Saints

Episcopal School, and Fort Worth Country Day School. She will also help target parents at these schools. During May 2011 Ms. Meyer will order a set of stylish T-shirts with Red Jett Sweets' logo and sell them to friends to wear around town.

- **Search Engine Optimization (SEO).** By utilizing search engine optimization services of certain companies, Red Jett Sweets will be paying for our website to be featured when consumers type in certain keywords, such as "cupcakes," "Fort Worth cupcakes," "mobile cupcakeries," "Fort Worth food trucks," etc. These services ensure that www.redjettsweets.com will be more visible to consumers and that the website will generate more hits. We are currently working on maximizing this form of marketing. In the next few weeks we will be updating our website to include key words that will make it easier for consumers to find us online.
- **Guerilla Marketing.** Guerilla marketing is a type of marketing especially beneficial to small businesses with a small marketing budget. It is usually unconventional, interactive, and catches consumers at unexpected places. This type of marketing creates a unique image that usually is thought-provoking in order to create a buzz to pass along via word of mouth. Instead of spending large amounts of money on marketing materials, companies that use this type of marketing should invest time, energy, and imagination. Red Jett Sweets is currently brainstorming ways to promote ourselves using guerilla marketing.
- **Digital Marketing Materials**
  - ***Social Media.*** Red Jett Sweets will use all forms of social media marketing to keep our customers up to date on our location and daily flavor options. These outlets will also help Red Jett Sweets build a customer base and brand recognition.
  - ***Facebook.*** Facebook permits users to "like" certain business pages. By "liking" these pages, customers can view pictures posted by Red Jett Sweets or photos users "tag" Red Jett Sweets in. Users of Facebook can then invite or suggest other users to "like" our page. Users can also view other users' comments on the Red Jett Sweets page and any updates or posts Red Jett Sweets makes.
  - ***Twitter.*** Twitter is a great way to inform customers that "follow" us about where our mobile cupcakery will be parked daily and even hourly. This is a fast and effective way to notify customers what flavors we will be selling on a certain day, updates on the quantities of flavors for the day, if we run out of a flavor, or advertise upcoming promotions and special events. In the next week or so we will be changing the name on Twitter to @FortWorthCupcakeTruck. This will hopefully allow people to find us online more easily. Because there are no other mobile cupcakeries in the area, this will not post any problems.
- ***Four Square.*** Four Square enables users to "check in" at various locations and business to earn badges based on the locations and frequency of their "check-ins." Similar to Facebook and Twitter, users can find friends on Four Square and share and view other information.
- ***Yelp.*** Yelp allows customers to post pictures and write reviews on www.yelp.com. This website is also a great way to find new or nearby restaurants in nearly any city based on distance, type of food, or highest reviews.
- ***Social Coupon Websites.*** These websites have become a very popular trend over the past year or so. If given the chance to work with the right company, Red Jett Sweets will consider the opportunity. These websites reach a significant number of people; more than Red Jett Sweets could contact through our networks and mailing lists. When people purchase the coupon this will give them the opportunity to try our products at a discount price. Red Jett Sweets believes there is no better advertisement than the taste of our cupcakes. As a new addition to the Fort Worth community, this will help spread word of mouth and hopefully develop additional loyal customers.
- ***Website.*** The website will be very basic during start-up and phase I, including only static information such as contact information and directions. The website address will be included in most promotional materials during this time. The website will be expanded for phase II into a more interactive and dynamic site with additional information and pictures of the mobile cupcakery and regular updates with pictures of selected new flavors, event announcements, and the latest email newsletter. The current web address is www.redjettsweets.com; we have also secured www.redjetsweets.com that will redirect potential clients to our website.
- ***Emails.*** Once per month, Ms. Meyer and Ms. Gamez will send out a newsletter email to all customers in the customer database. The

newsletter will include a personal note from the owner describing new flavors for the season and upcoming events at the mobile cupcakery. During the start-up phase, Ms. Meyer and Ms. Gamez will send out email newsletters to an initial mailing list to provide updates and an announcement of the opening of the mobile cupcakery and to encourage advance word of mouth.

- **Personal Use/Charity.** By donating cupcakes to local charities and nonprofit organizations, people in the community will hopefully view Red Jett Sweets as a socially responsible and community-oriented company. In some cases we might be given media coverage opportunities at no cost. Another way to gain recognition while donating to various organizations would be to partner with a local business, organization, or school to allow Red Jett Sweets to park on its premises and donate a portion of sales from that day to the organization. By donating only some of our cupcakes, instead of money, we will be exposing ourselves to a new customer base while making a good impression on the community.
- **Events.** Opening day: Ms. Meyer and Ms. Gamez will invite a small, select group of close friends to a private event, which will give them and the staff an opportunity to gather feedback and test the point-of-sale systems before opening. Red Jett Sweets will then host a kickoff party, with mailed invitations sent to a larger group of selected people. This will be a lavish event with a budget of up to $2,000 and a great opportunity for publicity to build awareness of the mobile cupcakery.
- **Signage.** Our mobile cupcakery will have a full wrap with our logo and contact info. Please refer to Appendix D for an illustration of our mobile cupcakery.
- **Print Marketing Materials**
  - ***Magazine Advertisement.*** This will be the least used form of print marketing. As trends show, people are reading fewer magazines and newspapers, and relying more on the Internet and social media marketing outlets. Magazine ads can be costly and do not always reach the desired target. Ideally, Red Jett Sweets hopes to land interviews with small local magazines (for example: *Fort Worth, Texas*) and have the interview act as free advertising.
  - ***Newspaper Articles.*** Similar to magazine ads, newspaper ads don't always reach the desired market, especially with the declining number of readers. Again, Red Jett Sweets would like to earn an interview or a write-up in one of the Fort Worth newspapers, *The Fort Worth Star Telegram* or *FW Weekly*.
  - ***Business Cards.*** Business cards are relatively inexpensive and are very effective in leaving contact info and networking with business professionals. Refer to Appendix F for a picture of the front and back of Red Jett Sweets' business cards.
  - ***Stickers for Boxes and Containers.*** The smaller sticker will be placed on our individual containers and the larger sticker will be placed on our boxes that hold 4, 6, 12, or more cupcakes. Refer to Appendix F for a picture of the stickers.
  - ***Rack Cards.*** Rack cards will also be placed on tables at events in which we have donated our products and services or events which we are hosting. Rack cards are similar in length as the bookmark but are about twice as wide. If we were to set up a booth or table at any type of trade show, these would be placed on the table. Refer to Appendix F for a picture of a Red Jett Sweets' rack card.
  - ***Postcards.*** Direct mailings will only be used to send invitations for specific events (such as a private event or new flavors) to a targeted subset of the client database. Refer to Appendix F for a picture of a Red Jett Sweets' seasonal postcard.
  - ***Table Toppers.*** Table toppers will be placed at events to which we donate our cupcakes. This will increase our visibility and word-of-mouth marketing. Refer to Appendix F for a picture of the Red Jett Sweets' table toppers.
  - ***Car Magnets.*** Red Jett Sweets has purchased car magnets to place on personal vehicles to create word-of-mouth marketing until the mobile cupcakery is ready for use. We will be using these when we make deliveries around town and when running personal errands to create brand recognition in the Fort Worth area.

RESEARCH AND DEVELOPMENT

Market Research

Red Jett Sweets will continue to conduct industry research as well as research for new and innovative flavors or products as well as research on established competitors and any new entrants. Red Jett Sweets will conduct research through several channels.

- **Internet.** The Internet will be a vital channel to collecting new data on the industry and information about our competitors. This will allow us to identify how our competitors are selling, advertising, and how much they charge for a cupcake. In addition, this will allow us to learn how we are different and similar to our competitors.

- **Friends and Family**. Red Jett Sweets will also rely on experiences, recommendations, and knowledge from friends and family. Friends and family are a great way to find out what potential customers are looking for in a cupcake company.

Development

- **Start-up Phase.** Red Jett Sweets is currently in this stage. Red Jett Sweets has also completed work with consultants to develop the logo and visual identity, and has created the financial plan. Other key activities during the start-up phase will include minimal renovating of the mobile cupcakery, purchasing initial inventory, hiring a baking assistant, launching promotions, and establishing business systems.
- **Phase I.** Red Jett Sweets' goals for the first two years of operations (ending August 2013) will be to improve the effectiveness of operational and managerial systems and to achieve profitability and growing sales. The owners will be involved hands-on in building the mobile cupcakery's clientele and in operating and refining all aspects of the business.
- **Phase II.** In the next three years of operations, Red Jett Sweets plans to hire additional staff. Ms. Meyer will be able to focus on expanding the range of product lines and client services. Red Jett Sweets also plans to purchase its own building with a baking facility, which will also be home to a storefront location.
- **Expansion Phase.** Although not detailed in this business plan, Red Jett Sweets will explore the potential for additional expansion after five years of operations. One expansion strategy would be to open one or more additional Red Jett Sweets stores or mobile cupcakeries in the Dallas–Fort Worth area.

PART III: THE ORGANIZATION

Organizational and Legal Structure

Red Jett Sweets, Inc., is a subchapter S corporation (S-Corp) registered in the state of Texas. The owner, Ms. Meyer, will report profits and losses on her personal tax returns. The company will distribute money to the owner two to four times per year to pay this additional tax burden. Ms. Meyer's tax bracket in 2010 was 35%. One of several benefits of incorporating as an S corporation is that the owner has limited personal liability for business debts. Although the incorporation of an S corporation is more expensive to create and has similar advantages to a Limited Liability Company (LLC), Ms. Meyer will be able to use any corporate loss to offset income from other sources. Another major advantage of an S-Corp is that profits and losses are taxed only once.

INSURANCE REQUIREMENTS

- **Product Liability Insurance**. Product liability insurance protects the business from claims related to the manufacture or sale of products, food, medicines, or other goods to the public. It covers the manufacturer's or seller's liability for the losses or injuries to a buyer, user, or bystander caused by a defect or malfunction of the product, defective design, or a failure to warn.
- **Commercial General Liability.** Commercial general liability protects the business against liability claims for bodily injury and property damage arising out of premises, operations, products and completed operations; and advertising and personal injury liability.
- **Business Interruption**. Business interruption insurance provides loss of income coverage for the business by replacing the operating income during the period when damage to the premises or other property prevents income from being earned. This type of insurance will be a necessity for Red Jett Sweets. Inevitably in the future the mobile cupcakery will undoubtedly need maintenance repairs or upgrades. Hopefully, Red Jett Sweets will be able to find a local business to perform these services on the mobile cupcakery. In the case that we have to use a business outside of Fort Worth or outside of Texas, the mobile cupcakery will be out of commission for at least one day, or in the worst case scenario, weeks. This type of insurance will provide income for the loss in revenue while the truck is in the shop. Red Jett Sweets will need to conduct further research to decide if this cost of insurance will be worth the protection.
- **Automobile Insurance**
  - **Comprehensive.** Comprehensive auto insurance covers losses caused by injuries to persons and legal liability imposed on the insured for such injury or for damage to property of others.
  - **Collision.** Collision auto insurance covers losses caused by damage to or loss of the insured automobile.
- **Excess Liability**. Excess liability insurance provides an extra layer of coverage above the primary layer. The excess insurance does not respond until the limits of liability in the primary layer have been exhausted.

- **Property Insurance**. Property insurance covers the property of every description against loss caused by any covered peril such as fire, windstorm, or lightning.

PERMIT REQUIREMENTS

- **Business License.** Red Jett Sweets, Inc., is a subchapter S corporation (S-Corp) registered in the state of Texas. Red Jett Sweets also has a business license with the city of Fort Worth for special orders and will be obtaining a license for the mobile cupcakery.
- **Register for Tax ID number.** Red Jett Sweets has registered for a Tax ID number. The Tax ID number is 752891984.
- **Food Handler's Permit.** All employees of Red Jett Sweets will be required to obtain this permit. In addition, Ms. Meyer and Ms. Gamez will have a food manager's permit. Once this course is completed, managers and staff members will be aware of HACCP, Hazard, Analysis and Critical Control Points, Food Safety Management.
- **Mobile Unit Permit.** Red Jett Sweets is still researching the permit rules and regulations in Fort Worth. The type of mobile vehicle purchased by Red Jett Sweets will affect the type of permits necessary.
- **Texas Manufacturing Permit (TDSHS).** In order to serve prepackaged cupcakes and beverages on the mobile cupcakery, Red Jett Sweets will need to apply for a manufacturing permit in the state of Texas. This allows Red Jett Sweets to bypass some equipment needed in the mobile cupcakery in comparison to applying for a standard mobile food truck or street vending permit.
- **Fort Worth Health Permit.** Red Jett Sweets will need to apply and be approved for a health permit. This permit can be obtained at the Code Compliance—Consumer Health Division office in Fort Worth.

FORT WORTH MOBILE VENDING REQUIREMENTS

Application Process and Requirements

The following items are required at the time of application or renewal. All names must match on all documents. There are no exceptions for any of these documents. Items are in order to minimize processing time.

- **Assumed Business Name Certificate**. This can be obtained at the Tarrant County Court House.
- **Current State Sales Tax & Use Tax Permit.** This can be obtained at the State Comptroller of Public Accounts Office.
- **Current and Valid State Vehicle Registration** on the mobile vending unit we are using for the sale of our goods, if applicable. It must match the vehicle information located on the health certificate issued to us by the health department.
- **Current and Valid Vehicle Insurance on the Mobile Vending Unit** or vehicle pulling the unit that will be used for the sale of our goods, if applicable.
- **Current and Valid State Motor Vehicle Operators License** (state drivers license) for the owner of the mobile vending unit.
- **Property Owner Authorization Letter** authorizing applicant the use of the property the vending unit will be on from the property owner. These letters MUST be original and correctly notarized before we can accept them.
- **Copy of Health Department Letter** authorizing applicant the use of the property the vending unit will be on and specifically authorizing the use of the property's restroom access by the applicant. (This is verified by the Health Department. A copy will be needed by Development to put into the file.)
- **For Food Vendors, Original Current and Valid Health Certificate.** This can be obtained from the City of Fort Worth Health Department.
- **Basic Site Plan Sketch.** This must show the entire property and the location of the vending unit relative to the property boundaries, accesses, parking, fire lane(s), and any structures. This sketch should be drawn to scale, have labeled the "north arrow," and contain the property address and legal description, i.e., Lot, Bock, Legal Name/Subdivision.

Basic Restrictions

- No mobile vending unit shall operate at any time between the hours of 2:00 a.m. and 7:00 a.m.
- Transient food vendors may not stop for more than 60 consecutive minutes at any one location to sell or serve food.
- No more than one mobile vending unit per individual tract, parcel, or platted lot shall be allowed. A maximum of three mobile vending units shall be allowed on an individual tract, parcel, or platted lot in which a grocery store with a footprint exceeding 50,000 square feet may be located with a special exception by the board of adjustment, provided, however, that in granting any such special exception, the board shall consider the following:
  - The reason for the request;
  - The number of available parking spaces on the lot;
  - Whether an increase number of mobile vending units would be compatible with the existing use

and permitted development of adjacent properties; and
  - Any other issue the Board of Adjustment considers to be relevant.
- All food vendors must be inspected and approved by the City of Fort Worth Health Department prior to processing an application for a Vendor Certificate of Occupancy.
- Vending units must park on improved surfaces and may not occupy required parking spaces, obstruct traffic movement, or impair visibility or safety to the site. Units must also observe standard setback restrictions.
- All food-vending units permitted after September 24, 2002, must be certified by the Health Department as Commercial Vending Units. Units permitted prior to September 24, 2002, are waived for 5 years if an annual renewal is secured.
- With the exception of Sno-Cone Stands, Merchandise and Food Vendors shall remove the mobile vending unit daily from the property.
- No mobile vending unit may operate within 50 feet from a single-family or multi-family residential use. Single-family or multi-family residential use shall not include a residence that is part of a business or a mixed-use structure.
- All mobile vending units between 50 and 100 feet from a single-family or multi-family residential use must obtain the unanimous consent of all the owners of the of the single-family or multi-family residential property within 100 foot radius around the mobile vending unit.
  - Consent from the property owners must be original, signed, notarized, and dated within 30 days from the date the vendor submits an application for a vendor certificate of occupancy.

Merchant Fees

At this time, Red Jett Sweets is only accepting payments by cash and check. Allowing customers to pay with credit and debit cards will increase sales and/or average ticket price. Recent studies have shown that nearly 1 in every 3 consumer purchases in the United States is made with a payment card; of every \$100 spent by consumers, nearly \$40 is in a form other than cash or check; and the average ticket for card purchases is consistently more than cash. Red Jett Sweets has chosen to use Square as our method of accepting credit cards.

- **Benefits.** Square uses a card reader that is approximately the size of your thumb by plugging it into the headphone jack of an iPhone or iPad. You can use any iPhone or iPad by downloading the application for free and setting up an account with them. There is also no limit to the number of free card readers you can have. This way, we can help two customers at once and will not incur the additional costs of purchasing additional POS systems.
- **Disadvantages.** Requires cell phone reception in order to process the transaction.
- **Fees.** By swiping a credit or debit card through the card reader Red Jett Sweets will pay a 2.75% fee. If Red Jett Sweets were to manually enter the card number, there is a 3.5% + \$0.15 fee.

Management and Personnel

Staff

Red Jett Sweets will have one or two staff employees in the kitchen and mobile cupcakery to assist the owners. Hiring the best possible staff and maintaining a high level of employee satisfaction are essential for providing the highest quality customer service and for reducing, ideally avoiding, the costs associated with employee turnover.

Red Jett Sweets will attract and retain quality staff by providing them with the following:

- **Compensation.** Whether salaried or hourly, staff will be paid above-market wages (higher wages than they would typically be paid for similar jobs in Fort Worth). They will also receive discounts on our products. They will be rewarded for continued strong performance through raises. Staff will not receive health insurance through Red Jett Sweets for the foreseeable future.
- **Work environment.** Ms. Meyer and Ms. Gamez will create a positive, dynamic, and fun work environment for the staff of Red Jett Sweets (which will also help set a similar tone for the mobile cupcakery customers). They will strive to build personal, interactive, and supportive mentoring relationships with each individual.
- **Association with store.** Ms. Meyer and Ms. Gamez will look for employees with genuine enthusiasm for the mobile cupcakery and its products. For the right candidates, their involvement with Red Jett Sweets will be seen as its own reward. These individuals will take pride in their work, share their enthusiasm with clients, and help spread positive word-of-mouth advertising through their social networks.

Management

- **Ms. Christina Jett Meyer**
  Ms. Meyer's resume can be found in Appendix A. As a sales associate at Lord & Taylor in Houston from 1985 to 1987, she learned retail operations and achieved success in sales in multiple departments.

In 2004, Ms. Meyer opened She Boutique. She personally launched the store for women's clothing and accessories with annual sales of $1,200 per sq ft. Ms. Meyer was successful in building a large customer base through effective branding and marketing. She also organized innovative series of themed special events that generated high sales and positive word of mouth.

In addition to her experience, Ms. Meyer brings important personal strengths that will contribute to the success of Red Jett Sweets. She has the high energy level, strong organizational skills, and attention to detail necessary to succeed as an entrepreneur.

Ms. Meyer swiftly builds personal rapport and maintains strong relationships with a wide variety of people, which will help her to build the client base for the store and to attract, motivate, and retain high-performing employees. Ms. Meyer has developed diverse personal networks in the Fort Worth community through activities such as her extensive volunteer work with Fort Worth Academy and her acting roles with the Fort Worth Theater and Circle Theater. She will leverage these networks to help implement relationship-based marketing strategies for Red Jett Sweets.

Ms. Meyer's active involvement will be vital to establishing the mobile cupcakery, and she is fully committed to dedicating the time and effort necessary to make Red Jett Sweets succeed. She will be present in the store during most of its operating hours, especially during Phase I. She will continue some of her volunteer and community activities, but will greatly reduce her time commitments.

- **Ms. Natalie Gamez**
  Ms. Gamez's résumé can be found in Appendix A. Ms. Gamez has several years of experience in the restaurant industry. She has worked in many different areas in the industry. She has perfected her customer service, time management, and organizational skills that will be critical to the success of Red Jett Sweets. Ms. Gamez will be graduating from Saint Louis University in May 2011 and will use the accounting, marketing, and financial skill she learned to help Red Jett Sweets thrive.

  Ms. Gamez also has many ties to the community and will also utilize these relationships to Red Jett Sweets' advantage. Ms. Gamez will be actively involved in the day-to-day operations of Red Jett Sweets and is fully committed to dedicating time and effort to make Red Jett Sweets a successful business.

Related Service Providers

- **Accountant.** Diane L. Hanley CPA and firm is a tax and business consultant whose areas of expertise include small business financial management and business tax planning. Ms. Hanley will set up the QuickBooks accounting software package, and in the first year of operation will handle bookkeeping and the creation of financial, inventory, and sales tax reports. They will teach Ms. Meyer and Ms. Gamez how to perform these functions in the first year so they can then assume ongoing responsibility with only occasional assistance. Ms. Meyer and Ms. Gamez will meet with the accountants on a monthly basis in the first year, and quarterly after that, to analyze financial statements and discuss implications for the management of Red Jett Sweets. Payroll and tax accounting will be outsourced to the accountants on an ongoing basis. Diane Hanley CPA is located at 1320 S. University Dr. #808 Fort Worth, TX 76107
- **Attorney.** As the lead attorney for Red Jett Sweets, Aaron Moses, will be assisting with legal aspects of the property lease as well as with any other future legal issues that may arise. The unique legal issues expected for Red Jett Sweets concerns the aspect of the mobile "cupcakery."
- **Insurance Agent.** Eric Jones is a local insurance agent who has developed a quote for a business insurance policy for Red Jett Sweets through the Hulett Agency, Inc. Red Jett Sweets does have unique insurance needs associated with the mobile "cupcakery" aspect. Red Jett Sweets' insurance policy will be similar to those of a standard storefront "cupcakery" as well as a mobile food truck. The deductible for the basic policy is $2,500.
- **Graphic Designer.** Amy Devine is a graphic designer based out of Brookfield, Wisconsin. Ms. Meyer and Ms. Devine worked together in the initial idea stages of Red Jett Sweets to create a playful, memorable, and modern logo. Ms. Devine has also developed a wide variety of marketing materials. These materials can be found in the Advertising Copies section of the Appendix F.
- **Website Designer.** Amy Devine is also the website designer for Red Jett Sweets during the start-up and initial phases of business. The expenses for the website include $2,500 for the initial development and $25 per month for updating and maintenance. Ms. Devine created all the written copies on the website, as well as the format and interactions with GoDaddy. Once we have reached a specific level of sales and business we will need to hire a new website designer to develop a more interactive website, for example, www.georgetowncupcake.com.
- **Mobile Cupcakery.** Amy Devine will also be doing the graphic design work for the logo wrap on the mobile cupcakery. To bring the truck up

to Fort Worth health code we will need to install a generator, small drink refrigerator, and an air-conditioning unit. We have not yet found a company or person to install these items, but we will within the next few weeks. Lastly we will need to have a full logo wrap done on the mobile cupcakery. We have found a company out of River Oaks, Texas, (PS Dink) to do the logo wrap.

Advisory Board

Red Jett Sweets is currently looking for members to be on an advisory board. We are in contact with several professionals in the Fort Worth area, and will hopefully have an advisory board assembled by June 2011 with 4–7 members. In return for these professionals agreeing to sit on Red Jett Sweets Advisory Board, they will receive credit in the start up process of Red Jett Sweets, credit in bringing the mobile food truck phenomena to Fort Worth, Texas, and have access to new business professional and networking opportunities in the Dallas–Fort Worth area.

LOCATION AND FACILITIES

- **Kitchen**
  Red Jett Sweets will be renting an offsite kitchen in Fort Worth to bake the cupcakes. The kitchen is located at 7455 South Hulen Street #120 Fort Worth, TX 76133. This kitchen is owned by All In Good Taste, a Fort Worth catering company. This zip code is shown on the Primary Trading Area figure.
  We will be paying a monthly all-inclusive rent of $1,000 for full use of the kitchen, most equipment, utility payments, cleaning supplies, etc. In Appendix C is a layout of the kitchen. Red Jett Sweets will have designated areas in cool and dry storage to store equipment and ingredients. The only piece of equipment that Red Jett Sweets is not permitted to use is their mixers. Red Jett Sweets also has full use of the kitchen from 12:00 a.m. to 11:00 a.m. All In Good Taste will have the remaining time for use of the kitchen. In special circumstances in which we need to use the kitchen during times that All In Good Taste has rights to the kitchen, Red Jett Sweets will inform All In Good Taste and work with them to accommodate this need.
- **Mobile Cupcakery**
  Red Jett Sweets recently purchased a mobile cupcakery from Rosie's Cakes in Denver, Colorado. It is a 1997 Chevy 3500 Box Truck with 48,000 miles. The truck has had two previous owners. Rosie's Cakes, the most recent previous owner, owned the truck for less than a year and put fewer than 1,000 miles on the truck. Rosie's Cakes sold their truck because they could not handle the level of business generated by the mobile truck and the additional special orders. The owner of Rosie's Cakes felt it was more beneficial to sell the truck and to focus on special order business.
  Refer to Appendix D for photos of the mobile and also for a layout of what Red Jett Sweets mobile cupcakery will look like.

PART IV: THE FINANCIAL PLAN

General Risks

As with any start-up company, Red Jett Sweets must consider both internal and external risks that could contribute to the failure of the business.

- **Cancellation of Rental Agreement**
  Despite the many benefits of renting a commercial kitchen, there is one major disadvantage. In the case our lessor were to discontinue operations and terminate our contract, we would no longer have a baking facility and would need time to relocate. In the time it would take us to relocate, we would not be able to bake, which means we would be incurring other fixed costs and not earning any revenue. Red Jett Sweets does have a local restaurant, Terra Mediterranean Grill, which would allow us to bake in their kitchen in the morning from 4:00 a.m.–9:00 a.m. if this were to occur.

- **Inadequate Sales**
  There is the possibility that we can bake too many cupcakes for the day and not be able to sell them or that cupcakes don't "take off" in the Dallas–Fort Worth area. In this case we would not only lose revenue, but we would have lost direct costs of approximately $0.51 per cupcake. This includes ingredients, paper, and packaging costs. Choosing good locations can also play a critical role by making the mobile "cupcakery" visible and accessible in a high-traffic area to ensure that we sell as many cupcakes a day as possible.

- **Insufficient Inventory (cupcakes)**
  On the other hand, projected sales are based on a conservative estimate, and if actual sales are much higher than expected at start-up, then Red Jett Sweets may be left with an insufficient number of cupcakes baked per day. While a sign of early success, this would still cause problems because some potential customers may come to our mobile cupcakery, see a lack of cupcakes, and decide not to return.

- **Inadequate Working Capital**
  Even if Red Jett Sweets has the potential to become a profitable company in the long term, it may run out of cash and be unable to meet its short-term

financial obligations. The financing for Red Jett Sweets includes working capital to cover the first nine months of expenses, and access to a line of credit will help ensure liquidity until profitability can be achieved in the worst-case scenario.

- **Competition**
Red Jett Sweets could face additional competition if another similar store opened in Fort Worth. There is no strong barrier to new entrants, but Red Jett Sweets can create a competitive advantage in advance by building strong relationships and brand identity with its clientele. There is also a risk of existing cupcake stores expanding to a mobile cupcakery. Continually featuring new flavors will help Red Jett Sweets continue to stand out from other stores.

- **Dependence of Owners**
Ms. Meyer's and Ms. Gamez's active involvement will be essential to establishing the mobile cupcakery, especially in the first few years of operation. Both are fully committed to dedicating the time and effort necessary to make Red Jett Sweets a successful company.

- **Name Confusion**
Customers could become confused about the Red Jett Sweets' brand name and identity if another store named "Red Jett Sweets" were to open in Texas or were to build a national reputation. Red Jett Sweets will register its name as an exclusive trademark within the state of Texas. At least four other stores named "Red Jett," "Jett Sweets," or "Red Sweets" have been identified in other states, but not in Texas. None of these stores are recognized nationally or are part of a chain, but this situation could change in the future. In addition, since *Jett* is not the typical way to spell *Jet*, potential customers may be easily confused and not be able to locate us online or on any of our social networking web pages. We have secured the URL www.redjetsweets.com in the case that this happens. It will redirect the user to our proper website, www.redjettsweets.com. Below is a list of other businesses with similar names that are in the same industry.
    - Jett Cakes—San Carlos, CA
    - Jett's Sweets n' Eats Bakery—Englewood, CO
    - Red Jet Café—Grand Rapids, MI
    - Jet City Cakes—Kirkland, WA

- **Supply Cost Inflation**
At Red Jett Sweet we use high-quality ingredients; therefore, we cannot readily substitute more cost-effective ingredients and simultaneously be in accordance with our standards. For this reason we may at times be forced to absorb costs related to these increases or eventually raise the price of our cupcakes.

- **Truck is Out of Commission**
As already addressed, the mobile cupcakery will undoubtedly need maintenance repairs, or upgrades, on occasion. Hopefully Red Jett Sweets will be able to find a local business to perform these services on the mobile cupcakery. In the case that we have to use a business outside of Fort Worth or outside of Texas, the mobile cupcakery will be out of commission for at least one day, or in the worst-case scenario, weeks. We could prevent this by purchasing business interruption insurance. Red Jett Sweets will need to weigh the costs of this type of insurance against the potential profit losses.

- **Inclement Weather**
Due to the nature of our industry, food trucks are usually parked outside on busy streets. This means when there is bad weather (rain, snow, wind, hail, tornadoes, or excessive heat) our customer might weigh the pros and cons of venturing outside in order to purchase our products. The Fort Worth area will not need to worry as much about snow, but will need to worry about excessive heat in the months of June, July, and August. Tornadoes and hail could potentially be a problem around April and May, but this type of weather typically does not last for more than half-a-day increments.

- **Quality Control**
Red Jett Sweets prides itself on its high-quality cupcakes. If our customers do not get the same product every time they visit our mobile cupcakery, they might stop coming back. To prevent this we will regularly test our cupcakes at various stages in the baking process to ensure they consistently taste the same. In addition, we will continuously use the same brands of various ingredients in every batch and also make sure our ingredients are as fresh as possible.

- **City Laws and Regulations**
Fort Worth is still adjusting to the idea of food trucks. Fortunately, Red Jett Sweets is not the first food truck in Fort Worth, and will be able to watch as the two newest food trucks go through the process of obtaining and keeping city permits. In order to battle the possibility of city orders to immediately terminate street-vending sales, Red Jett Sweets will allow customers to preorder cupcakes days in advance, and will continue to strive to land large catering type and event orders.

3

PART THREE

Marketing in the Small Business

CHAPTER

9

Small Business Marketing: Product and Pricing Strategies

● How has the pricing strategy most likely changed for Beyond Fleece as the company has expanded? What might be the future challenges in terms of pricing and continuing to deliver customized products to its customers?

LEARNING OBJECTIVES

After you complete this chapter, you will be able to:

LO1 Recognize the characteristics of goods and services.

LO2 Define the total product.

LO3 Differentiate the stages of new product development.

LO4 Understand why pricing is an important but difficult task for small business.

LO5 Understand how elasticity, margin, and value impact pricing setting.

LO6 Apply different pricing strategies.

Focus on Small Business: Scott the Seamstress[1]

Scott Jones was a junior at the University of Oregon when he discovered that he had a problem. Eugene, Oregon, is cold and wet much of the year and Jones wanted a fleece jacket like those he saw popping up all over campus, but he couldn't afford one. So Jones went to the campus Craft Center, bought a pattern and two yards of fleece, and sewed his own. At that time, Jones said, "I didn't know the seams had to line up.... The whole thing was pretty mismatched, but everybody seemed to like it. All my friends were saying, 'Hey, I want one, too.' So I kept making them."

With that, Beyond Fleece was born. Beyond Fleece began in 1996 in Jones's room where he would sew every morning from 5:00 A.M. until 8:00 A.M. before his morning classes. Jones experimented with various patterns from the Craft Center, and each jacket was custom-made for his individual customer. At first, pricing was pretty easy. Scott needed to cover the costs of his materials plus a little extra for mistakes and enough profit to be worth the time he put in.

After graduation in 1998, Beyond Fleece's first website **www.beyondfleece.com** went live, and Jones began to sew full time while he coached in the University of Oregon's rowing program. The website began generating hundreds of orders, each one still individually customized, and Jones became a busy man. After he finished 20–40 jackets, Jones would load them into a large backpack and set off on his bike to ride the five miles to the embroidery shop.

Now Beyond Fleece offers dozens of basic pants, jackets, vests, and pullovers in fleece for both male and female weekend warriors. Jones allows customers to customize the product by offering several options. For example, the Classic Women's Jacket offers 5 colors and 16 feature options including armpit zippers, internal and external pockets, a hood, reinforced elbows, and thumb loops. Jones puts his target market between the ages of 25 and 45, estimates that about 70 percent are male, and says that they have to be comfortable buying online. Most orders come from the colder climates of the East Coast, although, ironically, he has noticed many from Texas and Georgia.

An effort with Navy SEALs in 2001 to design a new cold weather coat morphed into another line of custom cold weather gear for military and emergency service workers, called Beyond Tactical.

The company began to regularly do over $1,000,000 in sales, and pricing the product now meant covering overhead, including equipment such as laser cutting tables and computerized sewing machines. Also, as the popularity of his product has grown and customer loyalty has increased, Scott found that he did not have to be the cheapest product around. In fact, from March to June 2007 Scott was able to cease sales while the company retooled into a full-line cold weather clothing company, adding items like custom designed long underwear. In order to accommodate these expanded lines, he renamed the company Beyond Clothing, or simply, Beyond, at their new website, www.beyondclothing.com. Almost immediately, they received a contract to be the sole supplier of cold weather layer system garments to the U.S. Special Operations Command. Building off of this contract and referrals within the military, today Beyond Clothing provides tactical gear to the FBI, Secret Service, and Air Force Para-Rescue groups as well.

DISCUSSION QUESTIONS

1. How would you describe the pricing approaches used by Beyond Fleece when it started and as it grew?
2. As Beyond continues to grow, Jones will face several challenges. First and foremost, how can he continue to offer a unique, customizable product while he produces dozens of types of garments?
3. As more companies offer custom sizing, will consumers continue to pay higher prices for Beyond's clothing?
4. What directions do you see Beyond moving as a provider of custom clothing and how will the business's prices be affected?

The story of Scott and Beyond Fleece's clothing shows the power of marketing in the entrepreneurial small business. While Scott's first sales were inadvertent, just friends asking for a coat like his, Scott made a business out of his personal passion by some very shrewd marketing decisions and efforts. What exactly is marketing? Marketing is the process of planning and executing the factors of product, price, promotion, and placement to satisfy the goals of the entrepreneur and the organization. It is often confused with selling. Selling is the actual effort to pitch a product to a customer. Sales are essential to the business, because sales are the major way any business makes money. But marketing's goal is to lay out the best way to get sales, and set up the conditions so selling will be as successful as possible. The selling act and the marketing process need each other for the small business to be successful. Product, price, promotion, and placement mentioned above are called the **4 Ps of Marketing** or the marketing mix. The next section of the book covers these 4 Ps as well as marketing plans, starting with product.

4 Ps of Marketing
The four major components of a marketing effort—product, price, promotion, and placement. Sometimes called the marketing mix.

Product

Goods versus Services

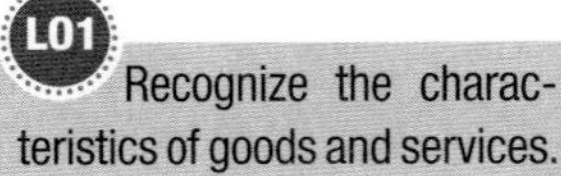

Recognize the characteristics of goods and services.

A *product,* in general terms, is anything that is offered to the market to satisfy consumer wants, needs, and demands. This can include **goods** (like Beyond Fleece's clothing, a car, a can of green beans, a CD), **services** (haircut, divorce), people (political candidates, celebrities), and ideas (a political platform, an environmental message). Most people's first thoughts are to think in terms of goods or services, but these days, most of the things sold are combinations of the two (see Figure 9.1) along what is called the *goods/services continuum.*

Let's talk autos for example. If you need transportation customized to your needs, you could start with buying a car. That seems at first to be a pure good, but it is not likely to be. The car has **tangibility**; it is something you can touch, but your check also covered the cost of a warranty on the car, which is a service, and something intangible. If you included a satellite radio, or a cell service like OnStar, or an extended warranty, you have bought more services. Still the vast majority of what you are paying will go for the car itself, so most car purchases would be an example of a *good-dominated product.*

goods
A physical product.

services
A nonphysical product.

tangibility
An item's capability of being touched, seen, tasted, or felt.

FIGURE 9.1

Goods-Services Continuum

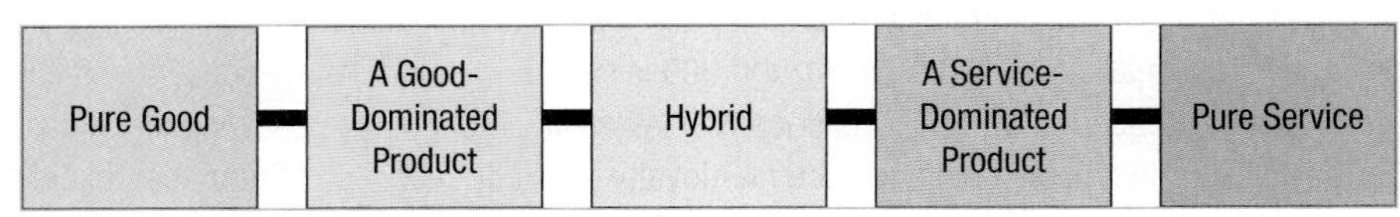

ZipCar autos for rent include all related services, like insurance, making these cars a service-dominated product.

perishability
A service exhibits perishability in that if it is not used when offered, it cannot be saved for later use.

inseparability
A quality of a service in which the service being done cannot be disconnected from the provider of the service.

heterogeneity
A quality of a service in which each time it is provided it will be slightly different from the previous time.

But what if, instead of buying the car, you lease it. Then the leasing company owns the car and you are getting the use of it (a service). While you have the car you are responsible for gas and maintenance, so you are taking care of the tangible product, but it is in the context of the lease. Leasing a car is an example of a *hybrid* good and service combination.

Taking this a step further, think about renting a car. The rental company takes care of maintenance and may even take care of the gas. You just pay and drive. New hourly rental car businesses like ZipCar.com and WeCar.com rent you a car for 1 to 24 hours at a time, and include all services, including insurance. With this model, the car becomes something more along the lines of a mobility service you control, or what marketers would call a *service-dominated product*.

At the other extreme, there is the pure service of a cab. You get it and get transported to the destination of your choice. A car is involved, but it is in no way your car. You pay for the service only. The cab driver is responsible for everything else. This is something close to a *pure service* and since when you have paid for the service you have nothing physical, that service you bought was an intangible product, where buying the car gave you a tangible product. Looking at these different types of personal transportation, you can probably see differences in how you would market these to customers. You may recall how these different products have been marketed to you (leasing versus buying, renting versus taking cabs, etc.).

There are also other differences among the five types of product. Car rentals show the problem of the **perishability** of services. If a cab goes without a fare for an hour, that is one hour of revenue that is lost forever—it literally perished. For the car sitting on the dealer's lot, whether it sells today or tomorrow, the dealer will recoup pretty much the full value of the car. These cars are nonperishable goods. That cab ride is also an example of the **inseparability** of services. The service you bought, the cab ride, can only get delivered when you get in the cab. The service, and your consumption of the service, happen at the same time so they cannot be separated. On the other hand, goods have separability of production and consumption. The car you bought could be a week old or six months old. For goods, production and consumption can be separated in time.

The fourth characteristic differentiating goods and services is **heterogeneity**. Products are generally thought of

This restaurant is making money from the two businesspeople eating, but the other two empty tables are not earning any money for the restaurant. Those empty tables reflect the perishability of service businesses. Those lost meals can never be made up. What other services do you see as highly perishable?

as homogenous or consistent. They should have the same quality every time you buy one. Services, however, can be more heterogeneous. The quality of your haircut depends on which shop you visit and which stylist you use, and may even vary day to day depending on the mood of the stylist, how busy the day has been, whether you are the first or last client, and a hundred other factors. To solve this challenge, service firms use employee training, identical—or nearly identical—store layouts, employee uniforms, services offered, prices, automation, and the like to reduce heterogeneity.

Those combinations fall between pure goods and pure services and have names, shown in Figure 9.1. The combinations also differ in how much they have of each of four characteristics. For most businesses, like Beyond Fleece, there are elements of both goods and services in nearly every offering. You can test out your ability to handle these issues by trying Skill Module 9.1. For almost every industry, there are ways to offer your customer a good, a service, or a mixture of the two. In reality most of what we buy, and what small businesses make, are combinations of goods and services. Knowing, understanding, and playing around with the particular blend of goods and services in your particular offering helps you find your product's differential advantage and communicate it better to customers.

SKILL MODULE 9.1

Facing Intangibility and Perishability

Because service industry businesses are so diverse, there can be no hard-and-fast list of characteristics to use in facing intangibility and perishability. For example, we want a quick service restaurant (like McDonald's or your local small business equivalent) to provide a meal in a couple of minutes, but at a premium restaurant (like Ruth's Chris Steakhouse or your local small business equivalent), we expect more leisurely service. Similarly, most of us want that meal at pretty much the same time, so restaurants often are their busiest around noon or 6:00 p.m. That time sensitivity means that restaurant sittings are perishable. If you had an empty table at lunch, you'll never make that money up again.

So put on your thinking cap and work in a team to come up with some ways to handle the problems of intangibility and perishability in one of the following service industries:

A restaurant specializing in soup
A website specializing in self-recorded music
A bookkeeping firm
A housekeeping service
A rooftop cell-phone tower rental service
An online sporting goods retailer
An 800-number health advice service
A home-based child care service
A house-sitting service
A business consultancy specializing in tax advice

For intangibility, what kinds of symbols would help make your service seem more tangible to potential customers, and what kinds of qualities would help strengthen the customer benefit or value of the service? Test these out with other groups in class.

For perishability, identify if there are times of peak demand for the service, and if there are limits to how many customers you can serve at once. If there are peak times or customer service limits, explain how you would organize your business to get the largest sales possible. Test these out with other groups in class.

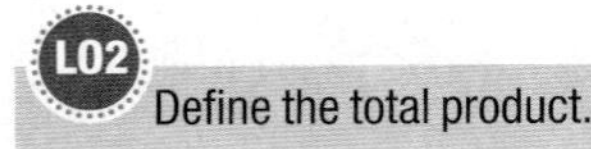
L02 Define the total product.

The Total Product Approach

total product
The entire bundle of products, services, and meanings of your offering; includes extras like service, warranty, or delivery, as well as what the product means to the customer.

Most products are combinations of goods and services. They have differing degrees of perishability, tangibility, heterogeneity, and inseparability. Understanding these characteristics of your good or service will help you better match it to your customers' needs and differentiate your product from those of competitors. But there can be aspects of your product that even you as its creator or distributor do not know about.

In marketing, this is the difference between the total product and the augmented or core products. The **total product** includes the entire bundle of product and services that you offer, but is based not only on what you as the small business owner thinks about the product, but also about how customers think about it. An Alabama bottle-making company discovered that one of the top 10 reasons customers liked their 16- and 20-ounce screw-top plastic bottles was because, when filled with water and a enough rocks to sink the bottle, it makes a safer toilet tank space filler than bricks, which can break down when left in water for years. People learned about this on several green living blogs.

We often know less than we think we do about customers, co-workers, or even those close to us. Try Skill Module 9.2 to test this out.

SKILL MODULE 9.2

Learning about the Total Product of You

Marketing is all about getting people to like your product enough to buy it. In a way, we market ourselves to others, doing a little bit of selling of ourselves in the hopes of getting another person to like us. When they do end up liking us, is it for the reason we pitched to them?

This one is simple. Pick your spouse, boyfriend, or girlfriend and make a note to yourself why they like you or love you. You can put down as many reasons as you want. This by the way is your augmented product. Put the note away, and when you have a chance, ask them why they like you. If they give you more than one reason, there is a very good chance it will be one not on your list. Those unlisted items are what distinguish the total product of "you" from the augmented product you described in your note to yourself. When you have a product for your business, repeat the procedure, this time asking customers why they like it. You will likely see the same thing happen.

The total product is how your customers describe your good or service, but there are two other ways to describe your product. What you describe as your product or service is your **augmented product** and has features that differentiate it from the competition. These features can include brand names, quality levels, packaging, and specific features of your product. In practice, it might sound like this when you are asked "What do you do?" "I run the Happy Housekeeper, a housekeeping business in the greater Chicago area."

augmented product
Core product plus features that tend to differentiate it from the competition.

Underneath the total product and the augmented product lies the **core product**, which is the basic description of what your company does. It is a variation of the NAICS code or industry description we discussed in Chapter 7. Beyond Fleece's core product is clothing, the bottle maker makes bottles, and the Happy Housekeeper is in the house cleaning industry. It is the most general description of your business, and the one which captures the smallest amount of what is special about your business.

core product
The very basic description of what a product is—a bar of soap, a house-cleaning service.

Why is the total product in particular important for you as a small business owner? First of all, your product means more to a consumer than just the core component. Sure, a housekeeper will clean your house, but this will give the consumer additional leisure time, might be a status symbol, and probably has other meanings for your customers. Merry Maids sends its personnel to your house in a distinctive van with the company's name plastered all over it; when your neighbors see the van in your driveway, they know that you are important/rich/busy enough to be able to afford this service.

Second, as a small business owner, using the total product approach can help you get inside your customers' heads and figure out the most cost-effective "bundle" of value and cost benefits (see Chapter 7) to give your **target market**. Last, when you're designing the rest of your marketing plan, knowing what your product really "means" to consumers will help you set an appropriate price (Would driving a BMW mean as much if it cost only $10,000?), design effective advertising ("We give you valuable free time" versus "We clean your house"), and select the distribution chain that will successfully carry out some of your service components (such as delivery, installation, repairs, etc.).

target market
The group of people on which a marketer focuses promotion and sales efforts.

Branding

Your brand sets the product personality and helps separate it from competitors.[2] For some small firms the brand name and the company name may be the same—especially if you are a service (Speedy Dry Cleaning) or have a limited product line (e.g., Beyond Fleece). There are certain guidelines for coming up with a company or brand name, but there are many exceptions. Here are some things to keep in mind:

- The first thought for many entrepreneurs is to name the firm after themselves. While that is not necessarily a problem, it is also not very clear to potential customers what it is that you do. What is the Smith Company? What products can I find at Brown's Emporium? Consider adding another descriptive word to your name—Smith Machining Company will attract a whole different clientele from Smith Beauty Supply. This isn't usually a problem with a product because we usually add the product category: Smith Dishwashing Detergent.
- Another issue with using your name concerns how to handle the name if you decide to sell the company. The new buyer of Smith Machining Company will become tired of explaining that there is no longer any Mr. or Ms. Smith with the business. If you decide later to reenter the business (or any business), your name is now on someone else's business; while "Smith" is common enough, customers may wonder why Mr. John Cuttlebrink doesn't work at John Cuttlebrink Machining Company. In addition, should the new owners have a bad reputation, it's your name that will be smeared.
- Is your name appropriate? If your name is Payne, you might not want to use it for a dental clinic. How many other firms are using the same name (with or without additional descriptors), and will that cause confusion? (City or place names can get overused as well.) Maybe you are the only Srivhantinivasthian in the phone book, but will your customers remember your name or be able to spell or pronounce it? Maybe you should consider a nickname or a first name, or forget vanity for now and go with something else.
- Be careful about infringing on trademarks. Even names relatively close can cause you trouble. Dr. Peter wouldn't work for a soft drink, but it could be used for other products.
- Something that describes your firm or product and is easy to remember is ideal. While plain old "Discount Furniture" certainly fills that bill, "Cheap Seats" is a little more catchy and memorable. Be careful, though: This technique isn't appropriate for every type of business. "Divorce Depot" or "Bankruptcy Barn" probably won't convince potential clients that you're a serious, competent attorney.
- Creative spellings are eye-catching, but don't go overboard; "Myk's Otto Groj" is certainly different, but Mike's customers won't have an easy time finding him in the phone book or on the Internet when they need their cars repaired. Product brand names, too, are often evocative of the benefits they offer—Vaseline Intensive Care—but they may also be simple names—Dove, Zest, and so on. The same guidelines about being relatively easy to spell (not too creative) and to pronounce apply here as well.
- Beware of selecting a name that's too narrow to allow your firm to grow. "Just Jams and Jelly" might work right now, but what happens when you expand into candy, juices, pies, and the like?
- Check that the name can be used as your firm's name on the Internet. If you decide on Rachel's Dog Care Products as your name you will want to be able to buy the domain name **www.rachelsdogcareproducts.com** or **www.rachelsdogcare.com** for your website and e-mail address. You can check what names are available at **www.whois.net** or at most web hosting companies' website (search for *cheap web hosting* to find one).

Of course, many firms use one name for their company and a separate brand name for their products. Procter & Gamble doesn't use its company name on a single item. Kraft uses its name on some products (cheese, for example) and not others (Jell-O). The nice thing about separating your company name from your brand name is that if you have a product that doesn't take off—or fails catastrophically—you can drop that product line with minimal impact to the company image. Dropping New Coke was a bigger problem for Coca-Cola than dropping the Edsel was for Ford Motor Company. The same basic rules apply here as well: catchy, easy to spell and pronounce, and descriptive are usually the best options.[3]

James Dyson's face, voice, and identity as the founder of Dyson, Inc. are as much a part of his firm's brand as Dyson, Inc.'s innovative products.

Remember that as the entrepreneur, owner, and founder, to many people you are the brand. What would Dyson vacuum cleaners be without the on-screen presence of inventor James Dyson? If chef Emeril left his restaurant, wouldn't you feel something important was missing? For small businesses, the entrepreneur and the business often start out as one and the same. As the business adds employees, the importance of the owner declines, but realize

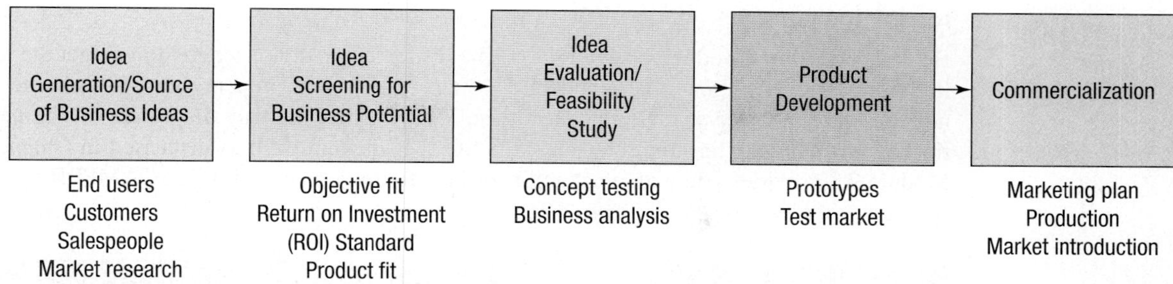

FIGURE 9.2

Stages of New Product Development

that the brand you have created will always be dependent on you. When Vince Shlomi, the pitchman for the ShamWow towels, was arrested for a hotel room brawl in Miami, his mug shots made the celebrity TV shows and magazines. Can you imagine how the ShamWow's target market reacted? Remember, for your small business, you are part of the brand, even when you have been careful not to put your name on the business.

New Product Development Process

LO3 Differentiate the stages of new product development.

An old *Far Side* cartoon describes an early (as in the cave dweller era) business failure. The product? Porcupine on a stick. Although meant as a joke, it should remind any entrepreneur that every product idea needs to go through the development process (illustrated in Figure 9.2) before it gets introduced. This process may take a few hours for simple products that are similar to existing products (commonly referred to as **me-too products**) or may take years and years of preparation and testing, such as introducing a new pharmaceutical product. For me-too products, steps may even be skipped.

me-too products Products essentially similar to something already on the market.

Regardless of the pace you are able to move at, this is a necessary process; the U.S. Patent Office issues about 100,000 patents a year, but only about 0.1 percent of those are profitable.[4] In a typical year, over 50,000 new products will be introduced in the U.S. market. Of those introduced by big businesses, the survival rate is between 20 and 55 percent after two years, while for small businesses the survival rate is estimated at closer to 5 percent. Marketing and new product experts believe that most of the small business failures could have been avoided by following the new product development (NPD) process.[5]

As discussed in Chapters 4 and 7, most businesses are imitative in nature, so the vast majority of new ideas for such businesses will be me-too products. If people are already using white ear buds for their music players, might they buy other colors? Probably, and the most likely colors are ones that match their clothes or their already-purchased music player cases. Does this require a lot of testing? Probably not.[6] Most of the testing has already been done and public acceptance is pretty much assured. Your me-too product needs to have a differential advantage over your competition—otherwise, why would you introduce it?—and this advantage may be the only thing you need to test. Customers are familiar with the product category, and some of them may already have been thinking about what they'd like to see different about the product or service. Much of the up-front testing can simply be polling existing users of the product and suggesting to them what you might see as an improvement. "I see you are using XYZ; what if I was able to sell you the same thing, but deliver and install it (or add or change features, etc.)?" Open-ended questions (If you could change one thing about XYZ, what would it be?) might confirm your potential improvement, might point out other new ideas, and won't necessarily tip off the competition as to what you are planning to do.

For goods, there is a cost for design and manufacturing as well as a delay, so trying out new products is more of a gamble. For service firms, it can be easier. Should a restaurant offer low-carb pasta? The cost is probably a case of pasta, or an even smaller amount of soy flour (used instead of the regular seminola flour) to make your own fresh. If no one likes it, it vanishes from the menu and blackboard. Cost? Twenty dollars for the case of pasta and reprinting the menus to drop low-carb pasta.

For small businesses planning to pursue an NPD effort for a highly innovative product, the steps start with the process described in Chapter 4; let's review them briefly.

Idea Generation[7]

Behind every great product is a great idea. The difficult question is where do you get the ideas? The traditional first idea generator—and often what gets an entrepreneur started—is something they need or want themselves and either can't find or can't find the way they want it. The new way to find opportunities is through the use of the SCAMPER approach as discussed in Chapter 4. Skill Module 9.3 provides you with an example of how to implement a simple SCAMPER application.

SKILL MODULE 9.3

Creating Your Idea Notebook

There are many products and services out there that we use regularly and often think that there's got to be a better way. Even with products and services we like, we can often think of improvements that we'd like to see:

1. Make a list of about 10 products or services you believe could be improved.
2. Specify exactly what it is about each one of them that you do not like.
3. Select three or four of them and think of ways that would "fix" the "defect." (Assume you have relatively unlimited money and technology.) Use the SCAMPER approach.
4. Talk to several friends and brainstorm to see if they have similar opinions about the product or service. Ask their opinion of your solutions and if they have any other ideas.
5. Add all these to your "idea" notebook—and who knows?

Many new products or services are "invented" because someone was unhappy with the available alternatives. Sometimes the technology isn't there yet; sometimes the solutions are too expensive to implement or make the product too expensive. Others are just waiting for someone to do something.

Idea Screening

Idea screening is the process of selecting the most promising ideas to be further evaluated for feasibility. Chapter 4 introduced the six areas which are important to consider when screening ideas to find the most promising ones. From the Idea To Product (I2P) model the initial three areas are (1) product—innovativeness and uniqueness, (2) market—customer need and market size, and (3) intellectual property. Even with promising results in all three areas, in order for your firm to be able to take the idea all the way, you need to assess three additional areas: (4) the people behind the idea, (5) the additional resources needed to bring the idea to market, and (6) the profitability of the idea.

Typically, the smartest idea is to generate multiple ideas and compare them head-to-head to help clarify what characteristics are important and which idea has the greatest potential. This comparison approach is shown in Exhibit 9.1 and is very simple. The ideas are listed across the top of the grid, and the important factors are listed vertically. Each idea is given a numerical score for each of the factors, and the scores are totaled. While you are likely to be one of the screeners, it is fine to let others in on this. One model that the World Innovation Network (**www.wini2.com**) uses has been to have purchasing managers look at a product. You can have friends with business expertise, or people in the target market look and offer their opinions. Done this way, it is possible to screen out the less promising ideas and identify the ideas you want to take to the next stage, idea evaluation.

Idea Evaluation

Idea evaluation is an exhaustive process of specifying the details of each idea's technological feasibility, its cost, how it can be marketed, and its market potential. Additionally, you should consider how the idea fits with the mission and goals of your business. A basic tool for idea evaluation is the feasibility analysis introduced in Chapter 4. Recall the components of a feasibility analysis: (I) Business Description, (II) Product/Service Description, (III) Industry and Market, (IV) Basic Financial Projections, (V) Future Action Plan. These topics follow on those you considered in the Idea Screening, but cover them in greater depth, based on library and Internet research, as well as discussions with experts and potential customers. As we saw in Chapter 4, while the hoped-for result is that the

EXHIBIT 9.1

Idea Screening Comparison

Factor	Scale	Idea 1	Idea 2	Idea 3	Idea 4
Product—Innovative	1(Low)–5(High)	2	3	4	5
Product—Uniqueness	1(Low)–5(High)	4	2	1	4
Market—Customer Need	1(Low)–5(High)	5	2	5	5
Market Size	1(Small)–5(Large)	3	2	1	3
Protectable Intellectual Property	1(No) & 5(Yes)	1	2	5	2
Product Team Quality	1(Low)–5(High)	1	2	2	5
Other Resources Needed?	Count of Res. Types Needed	2 (financial, materials)	2	1	2
Profitability	1(Low)–5(High)	5	2	2	5
Total		**23**	**17**	**21**	**31**

idea can be profitably produced and sold to a large and eager market, the more typical outcome of a feasibility analysis is one of these three:

1. The idea cannot be economically made into a product or service.
2. The resulting product or service works, but does not appeal to a large enough market (or is not worth enough to them) to make the effort profitable.
3. The product or service works, has a market, and could be profitable, but you need to get additional people, funding, or other resources to make the idea into a successful business.

Feasibility analysis is an essential step in the new product development process because it precedes a potentially large investment of your time and money into the creation of the key product or service of your business. Making sure the underlying concept is financially and competitively feasible is an important safeguard of your precious resources, and an important double-check of your own initial positive impression of an idea.

Product Development

Concepts that survive to this stage are ready for formal development. The first versions are called *prototypes* and are used in further consumer testing.

If you are just starting out (rather than adding a product to your product line), you may need to get a prototype made. Prototypes can be expensive, but there are a few shortcuts you can try. Study the manufacturing process necessary to make your product and see if you can't come up with a simplified "desktop" version. This is especially useful if you need to go through several iterations to debug your process. Jorge Lahens did just this to prototype a fragrance tab that hooks onto dog collars. He used Thomas Register (www.thomasnet.com/) to find companies dealing with scented plastics and learned all he could from them. He perused *Inventor's Digest* (www.inventorsdigest.com) and found information about how to set up a small-scale manufacturing model for just a few hundred dollars. Other sources of information include local inventor's clubs which are listed at the United Inventor's Association's[8] website (www.uiausa.org) and *The Inventor's Handbook* which is available online for free from the Lemelson-MIT Program (http://web.mit.edu/invent/).

Rapid phototyping machines, like the one pictured, can create a wide variety of products to help potential customers and investors get a clear sense of what the entrepreneur is marketing.

For many, getting a prototype or sample built is the toughest hurdle. One suggestion is to rough something out using products from home, or a craft or art store. Seen at a distance, it will help customers visualize, without having full details. Also, more and more universities have rapid prototyping equipment on campus. These machines can turn out a 3-D model of your intended product from a set of drawings. Today there are free programs for 3-D drawing such as Art of Illusion, Blender, FreeCAD, PythonCAD, and Wings3D that can produce the drawings necessary for a rapid prototype to be built. Often universities offer the services at low cost, especially for students.

If a university approach is not workable, take a look at the April 2011 issue of *Wired* magazine, whose section "How To Make Stuff" offers a quick primer of ways to build prototypes in plastic, wood, metal, and even silicon. Some manufacturers may be interested in developing your prototypes in exchange for a portion of your business.[9] Try the Job Shop Technology buyers guide (**www.d2pbuyersguide.com/**, type in *prototype* to find prototyping firms) to find local services. The Internet also makes it easier to find companies willing to bid on and build prototypes, for example, by searching for *prototype manufacturers*. Examples include *emachineshop.com* and *protonow.com*, or sites that represent multiple prototyping and manufacturing firms like *mfg.com*, *alibaba.com*, and *xpress3d .com*. When searching using Google, the terms to use are "rapid prototyping" or the more general "contract manufacturing."

For services, the same ideas apply. You develop your service, often first with example projects you think of yourself, or creating a mock-up as in the case of a website. Make sure you set the website up so that it is not indexed by search engines until you are ready to start selling.

Once the prototype is developed and tested, the product is ready for test marketing. Test marketing involves selling the prototype in either a real or simulated market environment. Standard test marketing introduces the product and the marketing strategy in the actual environment. Small businesses, for financial reasons, primarily choose smaller local markets and conduct fewer tests than their larger counterparts. While test marketing can reduce the potential for failure and can identify weaknesses in the product, advertising, price, or distribution method, there are also opportunities for astute competitors to "steal" your ideas and launch before you do. More recently, simulated test markets have also been computer-generated. While this is relatively safe from competitive interference, the biggest problem with simulations is that they are artificial and do not always reflect actual buying behavior. Also, for small businesses, simulations may be expensive—especially the traditional method.

Depending on your product, offering to deliver a service or giving samples to friends and family may be a convenient option for getting a test market type of feedback. They are less likely to tell your competitor, but they may try to spare your feelings if they don't like your product. If appropriate for your product and if you are patient, you could pass out samples or provide the services to friends and family and then wait to see if they come back asking for more or refer friends to you; that's a sure sign they liked it. Then see if they'll pay you the next time they want a replacement.

You may also be able to find (or belong to) a group that is willing to try your product and report back to you about how it works.[10] Sometimes nonprofit groups (a church's Ladies Aid, Friends of the Library, or something similar) might be willing to be a test market in order to gain a small donation toward one of their causes. If you are offering a service, they may be willing to let you test it out for them for free. Maybe the product would be appropriate for use at one of their activities, such as trying out your environmentally friendly detergent at a series of church suppers. Be sure to select a nonprofit that represents your target market as much as possible.

One of the ways to leverage social media is to invite participants in the test-marketing effort to share their opinions on a private group on Facebook[11] or LinkedIn. As they post their observations and see what others think, they are more likely to mention their experiences, and the exclusivity of their involvement as a tester becomes an additional benefit.

If you're not in business—or if you are in a very different business—prototyping and test marketing services are very difficult. Simulations work in some cases. Focus groups and concept testing, as discussed in Chapter 12, work in others.

Commercialization

Commercialization is the process of making the new product available to consumers. In reality, most businesses creating a new product will not face problems with this step. If a rapid prototyping model can be developed, the molds for manufacturing can be made inexpensively by most modern manufacturers. However, if your product requires a truly innovative manufacturing process, you are looking at what is likely to be a multimillion dollar undertaking. This is relatively rare.

When the technology underlying the product comes from a university or government funded research effort, the small business may be able to get government financial assistance for commercialization through the Small Business Innovation Research (SBIR) and the Small Business Technology Transfer (STTR) programs. Even adding qualifying intellectual property from a government-backed project to an existing technology you are developing might qualify your business for SBIR/STTR funding. Find out more at www.sbir.gov.

Even with support commercialization is a risky process. Many weaker ideas have dropped out of consideration by the point of commercialization, but still only about 60 percent of all new product launches are successful.[12] To play in this league, a small business may need to rent or purchase manufacturing space and equipment. Large companies may spend between $10 million and $200 million for advertising, promotion, and other marketing efforts during the first year of a product's introduction.[13] A small business, especially a young one, cannot afford to spend that much money. That does not mean, however, that a small business cannot compete. (See the Small the Business Insight box, "The Story of Kryptonite"). By using contract manufacturers (see www.mfg.com for an extensive listing) or sales agents like Inventor's Universe (www.inventorsuniverse.com) you are utilizing the consignment approach discussed in Chapter 5, so look at the advice on making the most of these sorts of arrangements.[14]

If you are doing it all yourself, know that smaller firms generally introduce their products city by city or region by region in a gradual fashion until their potential market is covered—a limited rollout. Mistakes made in earlier markets can be addressed before rolling out to additional markets. However, limited rollouts also have the problem of allowing competitors to anticipate your movement into their markets and to counterattack.

Before leaving commercialization, think about the augmented product idea introduced earlier in the chapter. Whatever your new product is, me-too or radically innovative, the key is going to be having something unique about it that separates it from everything out there. The Innovation Index[15] shows that since 1990, innovative products ran well under 10 percent of all new products introduced—and the index includes as innovative things such as reaching an unmet market, repositioning of a product, or even creative new uses. The point is that you can do—and probably will do—a me-too product, but it better have something unique about it that separates it from everything out there or you won't even get it on the store shelves.[16]

Pricing

> **LO4** Understand why pricing is an important but difficult task for small business.

The act of writing down a price on a tag and putting it on your product is one of the easiest and most quickly done actions an entrepreneur can take. But for most entrepreneurs, setting a price for your goods or service is one of the toughest decisions you will face. This is because price is central to how much you can make on each sale and that relates to your personal income. It can also determine how many sales you are likely to make. In addition, price can convey a sense about the quality of your firm and your product. So setting a price can be emotionally difficult.

It is also subject to various complexities and a lot of second-guessing. Since most goods and services are imitative, there are competing alternatives in the marketplace, so many potential customers

SMALL BUSINESS INSIGHT

THE STORY OF KRYPTONITE[17]

How do you build a strong brand on a small budget? The Kryptonite Lock Company (**www.kryptonitelock.com/**) has found the answer and now owns more than 60 percent of the North American bike lock market.

Back in 1972, Michael Zane founded Kryptonite and created a unique "U-shaped" lock which changed the face of bicycle locks forever. By mid-1972, Kryptonite was so convinced of its product's superiority that it began offering the first antitheft guarantee to protect against bike theft caused by lock failure.

In the early 1980s, the U-shaped locks were gaining acceptance as a strong security measure. Additionally, with its commitment to creating high-quality products, Kryptonite rose to become the leader of bike security technology. Competitors then began to aggressively target the company and captured the low-end market. Kryptonite's response was to introduce the lower-cost KryptoLok in 1988, again increasing market share. The KryptoLok helped offer a wider range of products at different price points.

In 1989, with the increased popularity of mountain bikes, Kryptonite introduced the ATB (all-terrain bike) model, further diversifying its product offerings. In 1992, the Evolution 2000 was introduced with a stronger Kryptonite steel.

In 1994, in response to a new method New York City thieves were using to break locks, the New York Lock was introduced with a flurry of hype. Zane locked up his own bike on the streets of New York and sat in a surveillance van for 48 hours with a *New York Post* reporter. Together they watched as several would-be thieves tried unsuccessfully to steal his bike.

Now known for product innovation and attention to customer needs, Kryptonite continues to add new products. In addition to bike locks, Kryptonite offers a complete line of security devices for motorcycles, sporting goods, skis, and snowboards as well as travelers' security locks, and it sells these products in over 50 countries. Attention to detail and to changing customer needs has earned Kryptonite the reputation as the number one bike lock brand in the world. Not bad for a bearded kid who started with only a VW van and a big idea.

Kryptonite's rise from idea stage to its current status of multimillion dollar market leader is a story of consistently innovative product development, competitive pricing, and creative marketing. How does Kryptonite's story reflect product development and pricing?

have an idea of what something should cost. There are computations you can do to help inform your decisions, but they take a bit of time and thought. However, computations cannot provide hard and fast answers because they are subject to the quality of the data put in, the assumptions you make and their fit to the reality of your firm, and the interpretation of the resulting answers. Price also depends on your magic number and strategy (see Chapter 7), your target audience and value proposition (see Chapter 10), and the costs of your business (see Chapter 13).

optimum price
The highest price that will produce your desired level of sales in your intended market.

Simply put, your fundamental goal should be setting the **optimum price**, the price that would generate the most income possible for the product or service you are selling over the course of a year. If your sales are less than you expect, you will end up asking yourself, "Are my prices too high?" On the other hand, if sales are exceeding expectations, you will end up asking, "Are my prices too low? Am I leaving money on the table?" There are four key factors for determining an optimum price:

1. **Demand for the product or service:** Where demand is high, you can charge a premium. Where it is low, you need to consider lowering prices to keep cash flowing into the business.
2. **Value delivered to the customer:** You can buy hair-coloring kits at the supermarket for $8.00, and a single use of professional products would not cost more, but having a professional do

the job with professional products and expertise can easily cost 10 times as much—and many people gladly pay it.

3. **Prices set by competing firms:** If a liter of Coke costs a dollar, few are likely to pay $2 for a liter of Pepsi.
4. **Your business strategy and product placement:** A company that prides itself on an environmentally conscious approach to manufacturing probably would not choose to use cheaper, unrecycled components, even if it helped profits.

Failing to set the right price is one of the greatest problems facing small businesses. Why does this happen? Often entrepreneurs set prices using some more or less arbitrary heuristic, or rule of thumb. In other words, they guess at what the best price should be using some formula such as "add 40 percent to what I pay for the product," or "set prices so that the cost of the food on the plate is no more than 35 percent of the menu price." But is that rule of thumb any good? Does it apply to the specifics of your business? Are you willing to risk your income and survival on that rule of thumb? Look back at the case of Global Fromage at the start of Chapter 8, where a bad heuristic led to business failure. A much better approach for you is to take the time to understand pricing, develop that optimum price, and then monitor and adjust it to work for you and your business.

In the following sections we will talk about the key ideas behind setting a price that is advantageous for you. We will start by talking about the fundamentals of setting a price—margin pricing and elasticity, value and contextual factors—and follow it up with a rundown of the amazing number of different tactics for adjusting price to fit the many situations your firm may face once it is in operation.

The Fundamentals of Pricing: Margin Pricing and Elasticity

LO5 Understand how elasticity, margin, and value impact pricing setting.

Recall in Chapter 7 we showed you how to find your magic number: the posttax income you wanted from your business. In that example, a person who wanted $24,000 a year after taxes, would need annual sales of $135,592. If you imagine yourself in a five-day-a-week business (i.e., 250 working days), that would work out to $542 of sales per day. Here is where you start making decisions.

Imagine you were selling custom-designed T-shirts and your first thought was to price them at $20 each, based on what you've paid for similar T-shirts in the past. Exhibit 9.2 shows you the costs. To get to your $542 in sales you would need to be able to sell 28 T-shirts a day—more than three T-shirts every hour! This assumes you are selling online or in-person wherever you are so you don't have to add costs for rent, displays, and the other things that go with a storefront.

The method shown in Exhibit 9.2 is an example of what is called **markup pricing** and is probably the most widely used of the many pricing methods out there. Knowing your costs and the

markup pricing
A price-setting method where an amount is added to the cost of a product to set the retail price and provide a profit.

EXHIBIT 9.2
Computing Margin and Markup

You can easily purchase all-cotton T-shirts for a unit price of	$ 3.00
Equipment, ink, and your time to screen them will add perhaps another	$ 2.50
Marketing costs (mostly flyers and a couple of shirts given away)	$ .50
If you then sell the shirts for	$20.00
You have a markup of $20.00 – 6.00 =	$14.00
Your markup as a percentage is the markup divided by the cost:	$14.00/6.00 or 233 percent
You have a **margin** on sales of the markup divided by the sales price:	$14.00/20.00 or 70 percent

margin
The amount of profit, usually stated as a percentage of the total price.

markup
The amount an entrepreneur adds to costs to provide a profit.

markup—what you would like (or need) to make from each sale—gets to the fundamentals of pricing and relating prices to your business. The computations also tell you what your margin of profit is, and that number is one asked by bankers and is one of the numbers you can often find in industry statistics, so it is a good number to know.

But when you apply the markup model and then figure out what your daily sales would need to be, you may need to refigure. If selling three $20 T-shirts an hour sounds like a difficult-to-achieve goal, one possible way to increase sales is to drop the price, figuring the less expensive the T-shirt, the more people will be willing to buy them. If you drop the price to $10, you might think that more people will be willing to buy them. But at $10 each, you will need to sell 55 T-shirts a day or nearly seven per hour.

elasticity
From economics, the idea that the market's demand for a product or service is sensitive to changes in its price.

inelastic product
Product for which there are few substitutes and for which a change in price makes very little difference in quantity purchased.

elastic product
Product for which there are any number of substitutes and for which a change in price makes a difference in quantity purchased.

If the idea of dropping the price to increase sales makes sense to you, congratulations! You understand what the economists call price **elasticity.** Something that is essential to how you live and does not have many substitutes or alternatives is called an **inelastic product.** Housing, basic food, basic clothing, basic transportation, and utilities are examples. The T-shirts you are planning to sell go beyond basic clothing and fall into the category of an **elastic product,** which has a lot of substitutes—cheaper T-shirts, used T-shirts, other types of shirts, digging deeper in your closet, and so on.

Economists have figured out that when you increase the price for an inelastic product, people might cut back, but only a little. Think about what happens to your driving when gas prices go up sharply—you cut back on your driving as much as you can, but you are stuck buying that high-priced gas. When you cut back on an elastic product, like your T-shirt, people buy a lot less. You might buy one T-shirt a month at $10 each, but at $20 you might not be willing to buy it at all, or if you are willing you will probably want to save up to buy it. The difference in elasticity is why in bad times you see clothing stores close down more often than you see gas stations close.

Figure 9.3 shows the difference in elasticity for your elastic product of T-shirts and for the inelastic product of gasoline. The difference in the slopes of the lines can help you think about the impact of dropping or raising the price. Remember to keep in mind how the general economy is doing for your customers. If money is tight, they will respond to price increases for elastic products much more negatively, because that is where their needs are more flexible, or elastic.

law of supply and demand
The economic theory that describes how the demand for products (or services) and the supply of them affect each other.

price gouging
Charging an outrageously high price for something.

You've heard about the **law of supply and demand** and this is where it applies in business. When the supply of a product or service is generally enough to meet the customer demand for it, the price is stable, and, over the long term, pretty average. If the supply suddenly shrinks (e.g., imports of basic T-shirts you sell in your business dries up because of a trade embargo, a typhoon, or any other reason), the prices go up. If demand suddenly grows (everyone wants to wear a red T-shirt on Monday to show support for the hometown team), the prices are likely to go up. While there is an ethical (and sometimes a legal) issue in charging too much in such situations—what is called **price gouging**—having a reasonable increase is expected. Figuring out what is "reasonable" is a case of looking at what your competitors are doing, considering what you feel is ethically right, and being ready to adjust your prices as you gain insight into the situation.

FIGURE 9.3
Pricing Elasticity

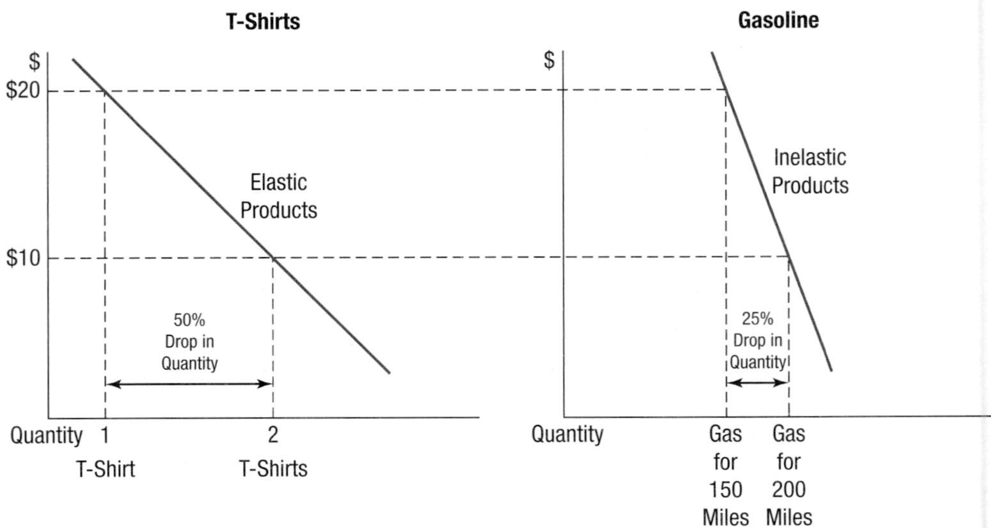

So as an entrepreneur, you can adjust your prices based on supply and demand, but you also need to keep an eye on the competition. As we noted earlier, if a liter of Coke costs a dollar in the store, few are likely to pay $2 for a liter of Pepsi in the store. But as an entrepreneur you have the potential to make choices that may justify a $2 price, for example, selling ice-cold liters of Pepsi on the street corner across from the baseball stadium on the afternoon of a game. Demand will be up because of the heat, and your $2 price might still look like a good deal compared to soda prices inside the stadium.

Gasoline is a product with almost no substitutes. If you need to drive, you need gas, no matter how high the price. That makes gasoline an inelastic product. Even when expensive, you will buy it.

As you can see, being an economic theory and not a law of nature, the predictive power of elasticity and the law of supply and demand can get watered down by a host of possible factors. Coke and Pepsi are brands people know about so they know what they are buying when they get a liter. T-shirts, however, are another matter. If you begin selling T-shirts for $20 and you don't get enough sales, you might want to see what happens when you drop the price of the T-shirts from $20 to $10. Sales may go up because of the lower price, but it is also possible that some customers will assume that you have started compromising on quality (maybe getting cheaper T-shirts on which to put your designs). Taking the price of the shirt as an indicator of quality, they may decide to buy fewer shirts at $10 than at $20. That means to make elasticity work, you need to also keep in mind the value people see in your product. Let's look at how that gets figured into pricing.

The Fundamentals of Pricing: Value

Elasticity is an important indicator, but it is not the only one you ought to consider. T-shirts and gasoline are products that almost everyone buys, and that results in a lot of competition and price pressure. However, there are other markets and products for which people will pay extra. Remember in Chapter 7 we talked about value and cost benefits. Those value benefits now come back into play as you think about price. We know that people will pay more for a product of high quality or high stylishness or leading-edge technology. That is why we all know that an iPhone typically costs more than the competing Android phone. But small businesses can offer products with the same sort of appeal.

Let's consider the example of Screaming Eagle wines from Napa Valley, California. This small business follows a strategy of deliberately remaining a limited producer of fine wines. The demand for high-end wines is so high that the winery sells solely by subscription. Even at $750 per bottle for newly released vintages, there is a waiting list of people wanting to be placed on the customer subscription list. There certainly is no pressure for the winery to reduce prices, as it currently sells its entire output before it is even bottled. In fact, there is pretty good evidence that Screaming Eagle could increase the winery price substantially and still sell its entire 600 to 750-case output before it is released. You only need do a Google search on the term "Screaming Eagle wine" to see that there is a very vigorous secondary resale demand. You will find individual bottles of older vintages of the wine priced over $5,000.

The value delivered to the customer is second in order of importance to the pricing decision. How can a boutique winery like Screaming Eagle charge $750 for a bottle of wine?[18] The answer is that the price customers are willing to pay is determined by their perception of value received. From the consumer's point of view, top-flight vintners are selling much more than a mere bottle of fine wine. They are also selling exclusivity. Only a few, very rich, people can buy Screaming Eagle directly from the winery, and they can only buy it if, and only if, they have been accepted to the subscription list. Also consider: "Would the wine have the very high demand that it currently enjoys if it were priced at a more 'reasonable' rate, say $50 per bottle?" Certainly it would not. The extravagant price is actually part of what creates and maintains the high demand.

In addition to demand and value provided, you must consider the prices set by your competition.[19] It is often tempting to set your price lower than that of your competitor in the hope that you can pull away some of her customers. This is often self-defeating for two reasons. First, if you lower your price, your revenue will decline as a percentage of your total sales. Often, the increase in sales is insufficient to make up for the lost revenue. Second, if your strategy works, it will not be long before your competitor realizes the drop in sales and lowers prices to meet yours. You both end up with lower prices, and no more volume than before the price cut. The issues of deliberately lowering prices for strategic reasons are discussed in detail later in this chapter.

The opposing temptation is to set your prices higher than that of your competition. For wines, the First Growth (Grand Cru) wines of Bordeaux actually sell for even more than $500, so why not raise the price of Screaming Eagle? For that matter, bottles for Screaming Eagle wine sell for more than $800 on wine-searcher.com all the time. The problem with this reasoning is that it is backward: it is considering the firm's competitive position from only the owner's point of view. A much better approach would be to determine what features your customers are actually willing to pay for. Setting prices higher than the competition without providing customers with the perception of receiving greater value can only lead to lower overall volume. For Screaming Eagle's connoisseur customers, a Grand Cru is an even better wine, so it should cost more. Some day, Screaming Eagle may have the vintage that makes the breakthrough in the world of wines, matching Bordeaux's best, and it is then they could safely raise their prices and keep their customers happy.

● Screaming Eagle sells their wines for $500 a bottle and sells all their wine before it is even bottled. How do you think they can do such a great job of convincing customers to pay a superpremium price?

With the lesson of Screaming Eagle wines in mind, go back to the list of value benefits in Chapter 7 and ask yourself if there is a way to tap into them to make a case for higher price. For the T-shirts, having designs by a known local artist or band, or offbeat designs featuring local schools could make it work. If you work it right, value benefits can turn into higher prices for your products.

The Fundamentals of Pricing—Contextual Factors[20]

The discussion up to here has covered why pricing is so important and the major factors that determine prices. Issues of the effects of demand and value upon pricing were analyzed. All this is necessary information for you to be able to set prices. However, it does not explain the "nuts and bolts" of how to use the information to actually set a price. Of course, one reason that this discussion is necessarily general and not specific is that the details of determining the "right" price differs among industries and businesses. Still, some practices are valid across industries.

As we've said, your first task must be to decide what is the optimum price. This can be a very different number among similar businesses, depending upon specific business goals. If you are operating profitably near your business's maximum capacity, the right price is most likely the one that maximizes the probability of a sale without leaving money on the table. For example, if your restaurant and lounge is the "in" place to be, and you cannot even begin to handle those Friday and Saturday night crowds, you just might want to impose a cover charge. Or if your business is the patent holder of a biopharmaceutical that will grow hair on bald men's pates, you will initially set the price so high that only a few can afford it. Then, as the patent approaches its termination, you will lower the price to capture the maximum market, and to establish a barrier to the entry of generic manufacturers.[21]

If you are operating below capacity, the right price might be one that is low enough to fill your production capacity and keep your key employees working. If you could throw a bowling ball through your restaurant without hitting anyone on a Friday night, you will want to consider $10 pitchers of margaritas, or perhaps (if local regulation allows) a "ladies drink free."

If you are trying to make your business grow, or if you are at the point that you are preparing to exit your business, the right price is the one necessary to capture a desired market share or to meet a specific profit target, given an anticipated level of sales volume.

Once you have decided what your pricing goals are, the next logical step is to examine the existing market prices for similar products and services. You should also make a comparison list of the similarities and differences among your competitors' offerings. If at all possible, you should attempt to determine which features of your competitors' products and services are actually desired by customers. This process will provide you with a range of prices and features to which you can compare your own product.

Now is the time to consider your business costs. The question that you must answer is, "Can I make a profit at the price that will meet sales volume goals?" If the answer is yes, you have established an acceptable base price. From this price, you can then experiment a bit. You probably should start by deliberately setting your price above the acceptable base. If your initial price needs to be adjusted, you will face much less customer dissatisfaction if your response is to lower your price rather than to raise it. If the answer is no, however, you are going to have to consider how you can lower your costs to the point that you can make a profit at the price that you have determined to be the "right" one.

SMALL BUSINESS INSIGHT

BLUE WATER BOATWORKS

Blue Water Boatworks is one of the business plans available on the Online Learning Center. The company, started by Saint Louis University student J. P. Keating, provided boat cleaning and detailing services to individuals, marinas, and boat dealers. One story which did not make the business plan arose when one of the biggest boat dealers negotiated a price for detailing dozens of boats in preparation for a boat show. With Bluewater in its start-up phase, J. P. was overjoyed to get the contract, and set a price based on his costs of materials and time. Being a student, he didn't think his time was worth that much. He set the cost at $100 for a 15-foot boat, and adjusted it as boat length became longer.

The boat dealer figured that it cost him almost $300 to detail the 15-footer in his organization. A part of him wanted to lock J. P. in for a long-term contract to get a great deal. But the dealer also realized he would be taking advantage of J. P., and once J. P. realized he had massively underpriced his service, he would not be a willing contractor.

The dealer called J. P. over to the office and actually showed J. P. what it really cost to detail a boat. He worked with J. P. to come up with a more realistic price, one that would help J. P. stay motivated and grow his business. In the business plan, J. P. set the price at $350. He felt he could charge more than the in-house cost because as a specialist, he could do a better job. In addition, he offered boat owners convenience, doing the detailing on the owner's schedule. For the boat dealer, this meant being able to do two things at once—a real help as the big boat show approached. He was glad to pay the $350, but J. P. gave him a discount price of $300 out of respect for the dealer's honesty and help.

J. P. was lucky to find such an ethical first customer. But from then on, he always worked through the mechanics of setting his prices before talking to customers. You can see his latest venture—a blanket for use in offices—at deskblanket.com.

Your Company Objectives[22]

For most small businesses, the early years are survival years, and the tendency is to sell your product for whatever you can get for it. Sure, you'd like $5,000 per desk, but if someone offers you $3,000, well, at least it'll help you to meet this week's payroll. While it may be a fact of life at certain times, it shouldn't be your firm's pricing objective.

More commonly, firms set prices to maximize profits or to increase market share. Increasing market share usually means pricing toward the low end of the competition in order to take market share from the competition. This strategy becomes more popular as a product reaches the maturity phase of the product life cycle. However, this shouldn't be an objective for a small business for several reasons.[23] Bigger, better-established companies have deep pockets, and often more geographic diversity, and larger product lines than you do. They can match or undercut your price in a heartbeat—even sell below cost because they're supported by sales of other products or in other regions.[24] Another reason why a small firm shouldn't try to compete on price is that it probably won't be working at full capacity for some time. Your building rent is the same whether you are producing at top speed or working only a few hours a week. If you cut your prices too low, you won't be able to cover costs during your nonproductive times. When you are up to full speed, you could drop your prices, or you might find other ways to please your customers, such as including free delivery or other services, and leave your price alone.[25]

Maximizing profits is a much better option for the small firm. This doesn't mean that you have to have the most expensive product out there unless you're worth it, but it does mean that your price should be above the average price.[26] First, this simply adds to your profit. If your business is profitable, a one dollar increase in price will add one dollar to profit. Second, as a small business, you do not have the volume of sales that would allow profitable operation with low margins.

Studies have also shown that companies that compete on product innovation and high quality achieve higher growth than those that try to compete on price. Firms that compete on price even tend to experience negative growth.[27] Another study of 1,000 firms shows that a 1 percent price increase converted to a 12 percent increase in profitability, all else being the same.[28] There are times and places to compete on price, but exhaust all other strategies first.

One more example: J. David Allen, now the director of a large entrepreneurship center, once owned a company that sold dominoes. He barely sold any at $3 per box. Then, he added a design for the Texas Sesquicentennial and couldn't keep them on the shelf at $19.95.[29] The product cost roughly the same—adding the design had minimal impact—but look at the difference in the profit. Be different, be better, but don't be too cheap. And remember: it's always easier to lower prices than it is to raise them.[30]

Marketing Strategy

Your price must be consistent with the rest of your marketing strategy. If you are advertising high quality or prestige but price your product lower than the competition, your customers will be confused at best, or at worst simply not believe your ads. If you're trying to get into Walmart, you don't want to have Rodeo Drive prices. If you package in a plain cardboard box, you're hinting at a different price point from a silk-lined, leather case. If you are making custom desks, they had better be higher priced than the pressed board, assemble-it-yourself ones you find at the discount stores. Consistency is key.

Channels of Distribution

Everyone who handles your product will be expecting to make something from it. If you are using a traditional retailer, your product may go through several middlemen (see Chapter 11 for more information) before getting on the shelf. The end price to your customer might be four times from what *you* got. This is called *price escalation.* You need to make sure that once all those involved get their cut, your product is still priced correctly to reach your target market. If the distribution costs price you out of the market, you may want to sell direct. (More information is available in Chapter 11 on this subject.)

Competition

We've talked a bit about pricing in relation to your competition, but you can't just look at the competition's price ranges and pick something at, oh, about 75 percent of maximum. Just as yours is, your competitor's products are a "bundle of satisfactions." How does their product bundle match up to yours? You may make athletic shoes just as good as Nike's, but you don't provide the prestige of the Nike logo (at least not to start). What other "extras" do customers get from your competition—additional service, brand recognition, prestige, bragging rights, comfort of knowing a big company will back up their product, and others? These intangible things are hard to price, but you need to really think about how your product or service matches up to theirs.[31]

Ultra Pearls, sold by Dan and Russell Schlueter, offer the ultimate in cat litter control. How does the Schlueter pricing strategy reinforce their product's known benefits?

Dan and Russell Schlueter sell pet products, including Ultra Pearls and Crystal Clear Litter Pearls. This cat litter offers a significant benefit over ordinary litters. About 4 pounds of the Schlueters' product lasts as long as 28 pounds of other litters. Competing brands sold 14-pound bags for $6 to $7, but the Schlueters priced their 4-pound bag at $14 to $16. Their 4-pound bag lasts a month—the same as two bags of the other litter. Still, they're at a premium to the competition. Which would you rather carry from the store—28 pounds of the old stuff or 4 pounds of Ultra Pearls? Add some awards from *Cat Fancy* magazine and PetSmart Outstanding Technology Achievement Award and in less than five years, they have a $10 million plus business.[32]

Legal and Regulatory Issues

There's a plethora of items that can fall under legal and regulatory issues. There are laws, for example, against price fixing and other collusion among competitors. The government sometimes establishes "acceptable" prices or price minimums or maximums—especially if you are selling to the government. Some forms of price discrimination are illegal.[33] It's okay to lower your prices during happy hour (effectively discriminating against those who work during that time period), but you can't charge different prices to customers of different races. You can offer a senior citizen's discount, but you can't charge a "skinny person" premium. In most states, you must collect sales tax for retail purchases. Usually, however, you are not required to do so for mail order and Internet sales. Sometimes there are special taxes or fees that must be collected, such as deposits or hazardous waste handling fees. Talk to your accountant and your attorney about specific rules pertaining to your product or service.[34]

The Pricing Toolbox

From the material above, you should now know what influences the setting of prices based on your magic number, your costs, the value you can offer, the elasticities of the market, and the contextual factors from your business environment. You should have a basic idea of *your* costs and needs, but there is still one key group that needs to be considered—your customers. For most people, their reaction to the prices they see is as much about their own perceptions and psychology as about the major market forces. In this section we provide you with the tools to make that final pricing decision, adding to the mix the customer's psychology, and the myriad of techniques that can help you couch a price in *just* the right way to appeal to your intended customer. Then we will give you practical examples of how pricing works when selling a product and a service.

Pricing Psychology: How Customers Perceive Prices

When you shop for products, you look at a price and make a judgment as to whether this is a fair price or too low or too high. Where you shop and under what circumstances you shop can also influence this judgment. We expect different prices at different places. We expect to pay more for emergency plumbing repairs or for certain conveniences. If your needs change, your willingness to pay changes. A submarine sandwich has little value to you if you have just completed a five-course meal, but if you haven't eaten in two days, you might pay almost anything for it. (Even though it is exactly the same sandwich.)

Consumers have what are known as internal and external reference prices. Basically these are expectations about what a price should be, based on their own knowledge (**internal reference pricing**) or from gathering information from outside sources (**external reference pricing**). External reference prices may come from looking at competitive ads, researching on the Internet, visiting several stores, or asking friends. Consumers will also pick up on external clues. If the product is sold at Walmart, they will expect to pay less than if it's sold at an upscale department store (expectations based on where it is bought). A Rolex watch sold by a street vendor in Beijing should cost less than a Rolex at Tiffany's in New York City (expectations based on perception of the likely quality and authenticity). You'd expect lower prices at a "going out of business" sale than at a "back to school sale" (perception of motivation of the seller—how eager he or she is to sell).

internal reference price
A consumer's mental image of what a product's price should be.

external reference price
An estimation of what a price should be based on information external to a consumer, such as advice, advertisements, or comparison shopping.

Consumers' internal reference price may be based on the last time they purchased something, recollections of what they might have read or heard in the past, their understanding of how much it would cost to make it (it's made in China, so it should be inexpensive; it's gold-plated, so it'll cost more), or their perception of the value the product has. If the last time you went to the movies you paid \$4 for a ticket and today you find out it costs \$10, you might just wait for the video to come out. (You're forgetting that the last time you went to the movies was 10 years ago.)

Perception of value varies from person to person. For example, if you can clean your apartment in two hours and figure your time is worth \$10 an hour, you won't want to pay someone else \$30 to do it for you. On the other hand, if it takes you four hours or if you figure your time is worth \$20 per hour, then \$30 sounds like a good deal. It doesn't need to be purely financially motivated either. If you find cleaning relaxing and a break from your regular job while other people rank it as their absolute least favorite thing to do, they are willing to pay something, while you may be willing to pay nothing at all. Skills may be involved: some people might be able to figure their taxes themselves; others may find any math involving more than three digits beyond their capabilities.

Expectations of future prices may be internal or external. The newspaper says interest rates are going up; consumers may decide to pay a bit more to get their new house now while rates are low.

You're going to the Bahamas next November; you'll wait for the end of the season sales to buy your vacation clothes because you remember end of the season sales from past experience.

Consumers also have a price range of acceptability. Any price within this range is really okay with them. How wide the range is varies by product, by consumer, and by situation. This price range of acceptability tends to be the inelastic parts—the "sticky" parts—of the elasticity curves, like the $30–$35 range in the jeans example above.

Setting a price somewhat above the competitive midpoint has a psychological impact on buyers.[35] If three sweaters appear to be identical but are priced at $30, $40, and $50 dollars, you are likely to feel that the more expensive one is of higher quality.[36] You can explore this in Skill Module 9.4.

SKILL MODULE 9.4 Pricing Psychology

Customers often view pricing as a proxy for quality, especially when it is difficult for them to truly evaluate the products:

1. Tell your friends that you are conducting a taste test and provide three samples of the same product in containers marked A, B, and C. (Choose products for which brands are not easily visually detected, such as pasta, soft drinks, etc.)
2. Predetermine three price points: one that is about average for the product, one that is relatively high compared to the competition, and one that would reflect the "discount" brand price.
3. As your friends sample each of the three, give them some data about the product. Include exactly the same data about each—in a different order—except for the suggested retail price. (For example, soft drink A might be sugar-free, vitamin-fortified, cola-based, only one calorie, manufactured in the United States, and available locally for 50 cents. Sample B sells for 75 cents and is cola-based, and is manufactured in the United States as well. It has only one calorie and is sugar-free and vitamin-fortified. Sample C is an American, cola-based, vitamin-fortified, soft drink with no calories. It retails for $1.00 and is sugar-free as well.)
4. Allow your friends to taste each product once, and do not permit them to go back and resample. Between samples, provide a sip of water or a cracker to remove any lingering taste—anything to separate the three samples slightly.
5. After tasting all three, ask them to discuss each one of them, stating what they did or did not like about the product.
6. If done in a classroom setting, provide a score sheet for each student to rate the product.
7. Often you will find that the more expensive product's characteristics are rated higher.

Note: This test often works with similar results on other "quality indicators" such as the store where something is purchased—the item bought at Walmart versus an upscale department store—or country of origin—products from a country with a good reputation versus a less-developed country (e.g., wine from France or Bulgaria).

How you define your product really determines your competitive advantage and affects your price. When you get right down to it, there are really only two competitive advantages: your product or service must be better (quality, features, distribution, etc.) or cheaper. Being better is sustainable, but someone else can always match or beat your price.[37]

Customers who are attracted to low prices will not be loyal and will switch as soon as something cheaper comes along.[38] Customers will always pay more for a product or service that stands out from the crowd. Treehouse Cuts Salons is a children's hair salon that has chairs designed as Barbie jeeps and other kid-friendly items such as televisions or Sony PlayStations at each chair. The salon charges about 30 percent more than the competition, but parents are willing to spend the money to make their child's haircutting experience more pleasant.[39] Consumers perceive Treehouse Cuts as a better value—regardless of the actual price.

Pricing Strategies[40]

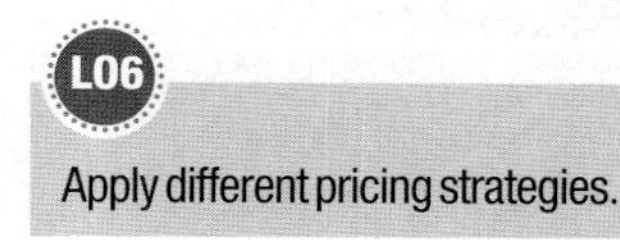

We have discussed all the "externalities" that can affect your price. These set the limits for what you are able to do with your pricing strategies. For example, if the government has set a price maximum, you may not be able to use a skimming or premium price strategy—strategies that mean setting prices relatively high compared to the competition. If you have determined that the price range of acceptability for a large pizza is between $8 and $15 and your costs determine that you need to charge $20, then the premium pricing route—with creating the correct mind-set through other parts of the marketing mix—is almost imperative.

To reiterate, it's almost always a bad idea for a small firm to try to compete on price. Competing on price may lead to a price war in which you just don't have the staying power of a big firm. Lower prices are "throwing away" profit you really need. They can signal your customers that your product isn't as high quality as your competitors'. There are, however, plenty of strategies available to small businesses that you can use as successfully as the larger firms.[41]

Skimming[42]

Skimming is charging the highest price the market will bear. This technique is usually only possible if you are absolutely the first product or service of your type in the market, and only if it's something people really want. Companies sometimes use this strategy in order to recoup research and development costs or heavy marketing expenses. If your product or service is truly innovative and at the beginning of the product life cycle (little or no competition)—for instance, plasma television—and if you can convince customers to try it through effective advertising, then skimming may be an option. This method will attract competition, so it's not a long-term strategy.

skimming
Setting a price at the highest level the market will bear, usually because there is no competition at the time.

Prestige or Premium Pricing[43]

Just as setting your prices low signals low quality, having a high price can signal great quality and an item that is prestigious to own.[44] When a consumer has difficulty assessing the quality of the item—for example, the first time he or she purchases a product in that category—price is used as a proxy for quality. Similarly with prestige. Consider average computer buyers: Do they really understand RAM and ROM and gigabytes and all those other terms or do they have the vague impression that "bigger is better"? The same goes for the price; that more expensive computer just *has* to be better than the less expensive, no-name brand. (If you needed a root canal, would you rather go to a dentist who says it'll cost several hundreds of dollars or one who states he or she can do it for $49?) Certainly most everyone would agree that a Toyota Corolla is a good-quality automobile, but if you ask people to what kind of car they aspire to own, you'll hear Jaguar, BMW, Mercedes. It's a prestige thing determined partly by a higher price tag.

Generally **prestige pricing** is for an item considered a status symbol, such as a Rolex watch or a Mercedes automobile. **Premium pricing** is used for nonstatus symbol types of products, such as toothpaste, shampoo, or laundry detergent. The idea behind both is the same.

prestige or premium pricing
Setting a price above that of the competition so as to indicate a higher quality or that a product is a status symbol.

A few warnings. If you are going to go for the high-end market, remember what we say about marketing mix consistency: Make sure your product, packaging, advertising, distribution—in short, everything—matches your price. If your product or service quality isn't appropriate, you'll not only not get a second chance, but you'll generate a lot of bad word of mouth as well. Also you may not want to be the very highest out there; a Lamborghini and a Jaguar are both prestigious cars, but the Jaguar market is much larger. Figure 9.4 shows a couple of ads that demonstrate a good use of prestige and premium pricing.

Odd-Even Pricing[45]

Odd-even pricing simply means setting a price that ends with a 9, 7, or 5. For example, don't charge $100; charge $99.99 (or $99.97 or $99.95). Numbers that are multiples of 10 are a psychological hurdle for consumers. Therefore, $9.99 seems much cheaper than $10, and the difference between $9.99 and $10 feels greater than the difference between $9.99 and $9.98. Consumers will set price limits in their minds; they'll want to spend under a thousand for a new computer. They may spend $999, before taxes and other extras are added on, and they'll feel that they've succeeded in

odd-even pricing
Setting a price that ends in the number 5, 7, or 9.

FIGURE 9.4

Prestige/Premium Pricing Ads[46]

meeting their budget—and will brag to their friends that they were able to buy "all this for under a grand."[47] Does odd-even pricing work? A recent study showed that when an identical dress was priced at $34, $39, and $44, a third more dresses were sold at $39 than at either of the other two prices.[48]

Partitioned Pricing

partitioned pricing
Setting the price for a base item and then charging extra for each additional component.

Partitioned pricing is alluded to in the computer example above—setting a base price and charging extra for all other components. You set the price for the main component—a computer for $999—but just about everything else you need is extra. You need a printer? That's another $100. How about cables to connect the printer to the computer? That's $29.95. Did you realize you could increase your computer's memory, add a read/write CD burner, or a DVD player? They cost more, of course. Extended warranty? $79.95. Don't you want to scan photos, add a digital camera, and upgrade to a flat screen monitor? What about some ink cartridges for that new printer? And several different kinds of paper? Don't forget to check out our excellent selection of software on your way up to the checkout. That $999 computer may end up costing twice that much (or more) before the consumer gets out the door.

Partitioned pricing works because once consumers make a decision that a certain product is the one they want, they are very reluctant to change their mind. It's sort of like saying that they made a bad decision or decided too quickly. They don't want to look stupid or cheap or settle for something less than they really "deserve." A number of products are sold that way: shipping, extended warranties, installation, training, additional services, and the like are not often included in the final price.

Captive Pricing

captive pricing
Setting the price for an item relatively low and then charging much higher prices for the expendables it uses.

For certain products and services, **captive pricing** works well. In captive pricing, you sell something, usually a base system, at a relatively low price, but the expendables it uses are relatively expensive. Computer printers are usually priced low for the technology—sometimes even thrown in for free when you buy a computer—but the cost of the replacement ink cartridges is high. By the time you purchase three or four, you've spent more money for them than the price of the printer. For services, something you can offer a low price for, such as first time membership to a health club, can be a candidate for captive pricing. Any extra classes, sauna, massage, and the like can be higher priced and more profitable. Although it's true that customers could get a massage elsewhere, they have already purchased this membership and it's convenient.

Price Lining

Price lining is an attempt to appeal to several different markets. In this situation, you might have three models of your product or service price to appeal to the high-, mid-, and low-end market. You might have a computer with all the bells and whistles priced at or near the top of the competitive price range, a bare-bones, stripped down version priced at or near the bottom, and a third model at a midrange price with midrange features. This way you appeal to customers with different budgets and different needs. Even if it's a product without a lot of features to add or remove, price lining can work. Next time you are at the store, find all the Procter & Gamble or Unilever products in the shampoo or laundry detergent aisle; they'll have products at every price point with different brand names. For example, Unilever manufactures both Suave hair care products at the low price end and Helene Curtis products at the high price end. Procter & Gamble has Gain (low price) and Cheer (high price) laundry detergents.

price lining
The practice of setting (usually) three price points: good quality, better quality, best quality.

Price-Lowering Techniques[49]

Even though all-out price competition is not usually the best strategy for smaller businesses, there are times when a company needs to reduce its prices in order to attract more business, smooth service cycles, build loyalty, move excess inventories, alleviate temporary cash flow problems, and the like. "Sale" is a powerful term. A recent study shows that even just the word "sale" can drive up demand by 50 percent without any actual price change.[50] The following techniques can generally be used without starting price wars, or reducing the quality perception of your product or service. The complete list is given in Table 9.1. Some of the less obvious techniques get a bit more coverage below.

TABLE 9.1 Pricing Strategies

Pricing Technique	Description	Example
Secondary market pricing	One price for the primary market and a different one for secondary markets	Computer priced at $2,000 for U.S. business markets and at $1,500 in Mexico
Periodic discounting	Patterned or systematic price reduction	Holiday sale, back-to-school sale
Random discounting	Nonsystematic price reduction	Sales without a discernable pattern
Price skimming	Charging the absolute highest possible price due to inelastic demand	Prices of plasma televisions
Off-peak pricing	Lower prices during off-peak periods in order to even out purchases	Happy hours or late night specials at restaurants
Loss leaders	Selling a name brand at or near cost in order to attract traffic to a retailer	Toys R Us selling Pampers at cost and locating them at the back of the store, hoping a customer might pick up other items while in the store
Price discrimination	Charging different prices to different groups, usually to attract a different demographic	Senior citizens' discounts
Penetration pricing	Setting a low price in order to get market share	A later entrant into the market may set prices below all competition in order to steal market share
Limit pricing	Extremely low penetration price to discourage competitors from entering a market	Instead of skimming, the first on the market may price just above cost until it feels the competition has given up on the market
Price signaling	Setting a high price on a product in order to imply high quality or similar quality to a competitor	If I set my price the same as Levi's jeans, people will assume they are the same quality
Going rate	At or near industry average	Competitors price from $5–$10 and your price is $7.50
Captive pricing	Selling one item at a very low price (even below cost) when there are necessary supplies that you can sell for a high price	Low-price ink-jet printers, but high-priced replacement ink cartridges

Pricing Technique	Description	Example
Bait pricing	Advertising an inexpensive product and placing it near better, more expensive models. The idea is to get the consumer to buy up. Sometimes the product will be intentionally ugly—unpopular color, etc.	The ad shows a $300 computer, but to see it you have to walk by all the other computers that have many more features, better quality, etc.
Reference pricing	Two similar products displayed side-by-side in ad or at the store but at different prices. Implies the same product but at a better price	Walmart brand aspirin next to Bayer, but at half the price
Everyday low price	Implying that the price stated is always low and it's always a good deal	The Walmart strategy; even when its prices are higher than the competition's, the consumers feel that they are not
Odd-even pricing	Ending a price with a 9, 7, or 5	This book is $69.99
Customary pricing	Prices based on tradition; it's very difficult to raise above this limit	Penny gumball machines, 50-cent candy bars
Prestige/premium pricing	Setting a high price to imply that this product is a status symbol and/or of much better quality than others	Pricing of luxury cars, the best perfumes
Professional pricing	Fees set by doctors, lawyers, and other similar professionals that tend to be uniform in a geographic region	Lasik eye surgery runs about $499 at all eye doctors
Product line pricing	Selling products at different price points to attract the low-, mid-, and high-end customers	Marriott hotels are high priced, but the Marriott Courtyards are moderate priced
Bundling/bonus pack/Multipack	Putting two or more of the same or different products or services together and selling for a price somewhat under the products' individual prices	An oil change is $49 and tire rotation is $69, but if you do them both, it will only cost $99
Partitioned pricing	Pricing each piece separately; the consumer gets "hooked" on the core component and then pays extra for everything else needed	The computer is only $699, but the printer is another $100 and cables are $30 and the modem is ...
Coupons/rebates	Temporary price-reduction strategies	This coupon is worth $1 off the next visit
Loyalty programs	A reward given to repeat customers	Buy nine sandwiches and the tenth one is free
Referral discounts	A reward to customers who encourage others to buy from you	If one of your friends signs up at our health club, you'll get one month free

Periodic and Random Discounting

periodic or random discounting
Sales conducted at either predictable or nonpredictable intervals.

Periodic discounting refers to sales that happen regularly, such as the January White Sale or the special on Christmas cards on December 26. You may need to do one of these to keep up with your competition, since savvy customers often expect these sales. An alternative is **random discounting** where you run a sale unexpectedly. Random discounts shouldn't be too frequent because consumers begin to realize if they stock up in this sales period, they can probably wait until the next sales period.

Off-Peak Pricing

off-peak pricing
Charging lower prices at certain times to encourage customers to come during slack periods.

What do happy hours and using your cell phone late at night have in common? Both can be examples of **off-peak pricing**. Services have busy periods and slow periods. Restaurants give wait staff split shifts with time off between lunch and dinner, but not every service can do this. By putting on a sale during slack periods, you may cover part of the cost of staying open. Happy hours are designed to attract business in the late afternoon slump just before the dinner crowd arrives. The reverse of this is *peak pricing*. Hotels charge more during their busy tourist season for example. Movie tickets also cost more on weekends. When demand is higher, people are less concerned about paying a premium to get the service when they want it.

Bundling or Multiple-Packs or Bonus-Packs Pricing

This works equally well for services or products. Let's say a haircut is $25 and coloring is $50. For this week, if you do both, you'll pay only $60. The beauty salon has " **bundled** " haircuts and coloring for a price lower than the two would cost separately.[51] This technique is particularly effective for promoting the sales of a second product or service that might not be doing as well or is newly introduced.

A variation of this is selling **multiple or bonus packs**, such as buying five bottles of hand lotion for the price of three—the kind of packaging that has made Sam's Club so famous. People are creatures of habit, and the more you can get them to use your product, the more likely they are to internalize it—it becomes their brand.

bundling
Combining two or more products in one unit and pricing it less than if the units were sold separately.

multiple or bonus pack
Combining more than one unit of the same product and pricing it lower than if each unit were sold separately.

Coupons, Rebates, Loyalty and Referral Programs

These three related methods are used to reduce prices and promote sales. Most coupons are delivered in newspapers (80 percent),[52] but magazines, mail, on packages, handbills, door hangers, Internet, and in person are all other ways of delivery. The higher the value of the coupon, the more likely it is to be redeemed. But even so, coupon redemption runs only 2 percent in the United States. About 64 percent of all Americans are willing to switch brands if they have a coupon.[53] Coupons are a great way to get people to try new products as well (reduces the risk). Even if coupons aren't redeemed, they serve an advertising purpose. Consumers see them and their brain registers a lower price. Even if they forget to clip the coupon or use it, their subconscious remembers the product favorably. In the same way, a rebate—even one that is not redeemed—leaves people with the impression they saved (or could save) money. Rebates are so powerful that many people, seeing there is a rebate on a product, might buy it even though it was not something they were in the market for at the time.[54] Loyalty programs are intended to tie customers to your business. Most often, these take the form of a card (see Figure 9.5) on which each purchase is stamped, and when a certain number of purchases or visits have occurred, the customer gets a free service, a discount, or a gift. Again, people may lose or not use the card in their purse, or wallet, but in their minds, though, they hold the perception that they are getting a good deal. If that's not a good enough incentive for you, how about the fact that 45 percent of all consumers spend more money in stores with loyalty programs?[55]

FIGURE 9.5
Typical Loyalty Program

referral discount
A discount given to a customer who refers a friend to the business.

A variation on the loyalty discount is the **referral discount**, in which a current customer refers a new customer to use the service or buy the product. The older customer then gets a discount for referring the new business. Since, for services, the recommendation of a friend or relative is often a deciding factor in a purchase or in trying a new service, referral bonuses can be a powerful technique.

Pricing in Practice

Price setting is one of the more complex decisions an entrepreneur faces. It certainly is one of the most studied, and it is one of the most crucial. So let's look at how entrepreneurs use these materials and their own judgment in setting prices. We saw one example previously in the chapter with our T-shirt entrepreneur. We will return to that example of selling something tangible and also include an example for a service.

Pricing T-Shirts

In Exhibit 9.2 we saw our T-shirt entrepreneur—Janeen—pick a price of $20 a shirt for online and in-person sales. Janeen's quick check of the Internet showed her that a lot of designed T-shirts are in the $15 to $20 range, and a check of local stores showed a range from $15 to about $25. Taken together, this gave her some confidence in her $20 price. To finalize her price and make it more attractive, she applied the technique of odd-even pricing to price her T-shirts at $19.99, and then, exercising her entrepreneurial judgment, dropped the price further to $19.89. This had the benefit of odd-even pricing, seemed just a little less expensive than the competition, and would fit with some of her plans for future shirts and branding efforts. Janeen thought 1989 was a good year for what she felt was important: world changes that promoted freedom, like the Solidarity movement getting elected in Poland, apartheid starting to be dismantled in South Africa, Israel and the PLO starting their talks, and the first Chinese youth promoting freedom taking to the streets. She is toying with the name "1989 Tees" or "89 Tees" since the domain names are available, and it would reflect some of what makes her T-shirts special.

She is also looking for opportunities to build her brand using price. She hopes to connect with a local band and sell T-shirts with their logo. She realizes that means the band will get a cut, and some online research and discussion with friends in the local music scene tell her their share would be about $2 to $3 per shirt, with part paid up front, which she can't afford right now. On the other hand, if she gets the deal and can sell at the band's local shows, she can sell the $20 tees for $24.89 or even $29.89, with $1 a shirt going to the owner of the local venue and another dollar going to the band itself. She is also thinking about when to offer a sale, like when she opens up, or for a week early in the Christmas season to grab shoppers early. For those sales, she will be aiming for $17.89 (the year George Washington takes office, first Congress convenes, France gets rid of feudalism) and if she is closing out a shirt, $9.89, even though she cannot think of anything freedom-related in that year.

Pricing Web Design Services

Antonio has designed websites for friends and students starting businesses from their dorm rooms, but now that he's graduating, Antonio wants to make web design his business. He found a calculator for helping him set rates at freelanceswitch.com/rates/ and went through the computations. You can see the full workup of his numbers on the Online Learning Center. Central to this was the belief that starting out, he would only be able to sell half of his available hours, with the rest taken up with business upkeep, and for a start-up marketing the business to drum up sales. After figuring out his own needs (rent, food, insurance, etc.) and his business expenses, he came up with a break-even rate of $45.21 an hour, but if he wanted to make a target $20,000 profit for the year, he would need to charge $66.49 an hour. The summary of his computations are included in Exhibit 9.3. His first thought was to drop his hoped-for profit down to $10,000 for the year, which brought his target rate to $55.85 an hour, which Antonio rounded up to $60 an hour.

What does this exercise do for him? Antonio now knows the lowest price he can take and cover his costs is $45.21 an hour. He knows that his target hourly rate should be $60 an hour. This

EXHIBIT 9.3

Computing Hourly Rates

Business Costs	$11,500
Personal Costs	$31,000
Desired Profit/Tear	$20,000
Target Income	$62,500
Billable Hours/Year	940 (235 days × 8 hours/day × 50% unbillable hours)
Break-Even Hourly Rate	$45.21 (Business Costs + Personal Costs/940)
Target Hourly Rate	$66.49 ($62,500 / 940)

computation was the equivalent of what Janeen did in Exhibit 9.2. How do these numbers work when we factor in the real-world issues? Antonio found results online from a 2007 survey of web design prices that ranged from $25 an hour to $350 an hour with an average of $68 an hour.[56] In addition, when Antonio looked online for local competitors, those who gave rates generally had rates of $70 to $90 an hour, so he thought his numbers were good for now but that he would keep evaluating them.

But web design is sold two ways. One is based on an hourly rate, while the other is based on selling a package of services at a fixed price. Antonio checked online (a Google search of *web design pricing*) and found companies who posted their prices as well as an online design quote wizard (www.designquote.net/html/dq_estimate_wizard.cfm). Antonio built a model package consisting of the items in Exhibit 9.4, which is what he thought a business might want in their first professionally designed website.

For the kind of package he thought he could sell locally, the cost range the wizard produced was between $3,740 and $5,060 for small firms like his. No local companies posted package rates, so while Antonio did not have a solid basis for estimating how his prices stacked up locally, he also thought he might be able to aggressively market a package price to fill the opening left by his competition. He decided on a package price of $4,500, which put him in the mid-range for this type of service. Notice that this works out to $56.25 an hour, which is very close to the hourly rate he computed separately, and which he knows fits with what local competitors are charging.

With Antonio's $4,500 package, he has some other options open. He obviously could apply odd-even pricing to make the price $4,499. Another method that fits well is partitioned pricing, adding additional desirable services to the basic package at different price points, like a basic blog for $150, or $750 to add an iPhone or Android App, or a complete e-commerce shopping cart for an additional $2,000. He will also offer different types of post-installation supports, as well as web server packages so he can be their one-stop for all web needs.

Antonio was lucky to find a website that goes through the types of work possible and provides estimates of how long each takes, but you need to take those estimates with some skepticism. For example, DesignQuote estimates the time to make a Flash banner is 4 hours, but Antonio has never used Flash very much so he could easily spend 12 hours making his first banner. The best basis is to use your own experience, but when you have to use estimates from others, always treat them as tentative and be quick to adjust your estimates and rates based on your own experience. Some other ways to find out what competitors are charging is to ask their customers. Telling someone you liked their website and asking who did it and for how much can help you get a feel for local costs. But in the end, there is no substitute for building estimated costs from your real-life experience. Taking on jobs for free to build your reputation, to create a portfolio of projects, and to give you a more solid basis for estimating your costs is a good idea to build many service-oriented businesses.

EXHIBIT 9.4

Antonio's Basic Professional Website Package

Completely custom site	15 hours
Template-based, needing minor customization	6 hours
A few stock photographs integrated	4 hours
Flash banner	4 hours
Integrate 7 pages of typed content (3 hrs/page)	21 hours
Contact form	3 hours
Site search	4 hours
E-mail auto-responders	2 hours
Google Adsense integration	2 hours
Off-the-shelf content manager	2 hours
Traffic statistic reports	1 hour
MetaTag keyword optimization	5 hours
Search engine submission	3 hours
Twitter integration	3 hours
Facebook page	5 hours
Total number of hours	80 hours
Estimated budget:	\$2,300–\$7,480
Comparison price ranges: Professional firm	\$7,480–\$10,120
Small Firm / freelancer	\$3,740–\$5,060
Student or offshore	\$1,700–\$2,300

Source: Computed using the DesignQuote.com Web Design Wizard at www.designquote.net/html/dq_estimate_wizard.cfm.

Pricing Strategy Wrap-Up

Entrepreneurs agonize about price, but perhaps for the wrong reason. Too often owners figure since they run a small business, their prices should be smaller too. But that is highly dangerous. Ellen Rohr, the financial management expert at *Entrepreneur* magazine, estimates that 99 out of 100 small businesses in financial difficulties have set their prices too low.[57] As this chapter has tried to show, it makes more sense to find ways to charge more than to charge less. And when it's all said and done, only 15 to 35 percent of consumers decide on a product using price as the number one factor, depending on the product. In fact, nearly 80 percent cannot accurately recall the price on something they purchased a week ago.[58]

So, goal number one in pricing is to set the price as high as you think you can, using your competition and customers' responses as a check. If the higher price was working, but has tapered off, consider pursuing goal number two—use the pricing strategies given in Table 9.1 to drive more sales. Customers recognize sales for what they are, a temporary reduction in price, and these won't tarnish your product image. Even if the competition matches a sale or offers some other promotion to match your offering, it's not as aggressive an action as a price war. Your customers will feel smart about buying something at a better price, and even if your prices are higher than the competition's and you offer a sale that brings you in line with its pricing, customers are still likely to buy from you—all else being equal—and feel they got a great deal.[59]

Believe it or not, Table 9.1 only scratches the surface of pricing strategies. If you are fascinated by these, grab a marketing textbook and learn about even more methods for saying "sale!" New pricing strategy ideas crop up all the time. For example, Amazon, Priceline, and eBay let the customer set the price,[60] so there are always new methods to learn about.

To wrap up this chapter, remember that the marketing effort in small businesses starts with the idea for the product or service and builds from there to include the key benefits that customers will want, the price they are willing to pay, and also some larger issues such as innovativeness and where the product or service is in terms of its life cycle. Together, these issues can help you craft a pricing strategy that can lead you to success. Even if your product or service is imitative, your profits do not need to be. The secret is in understanding the market, the cost of doing business, and the prices your customers are willing to pay.

CHAPTER SUMMARY

LO1 Recognize the characteristics of goods and services.

- Goods differ from services in tangibility, inseparability, perishability, and heterogeneity.
- Very few true goods or service exist; most products fall somewhere along a goods/service continuum and have components of each.

LO2 Define the total product.

- A product is a bundle of services and goods and has three basic levels: core, augmented, and total product.
- Understanding the total product allows you to concentrate on the features and aspects important to the customer and to coordinate your other marketing activities.

LO3 Differentiate the stages of new product development.

- The stages include idea generation, idea screening, idea evaluation, product development, and commercialization.
- During the product development phase, prototypes can be developed in order to do additional screening, and test markets or test market simulations can be run.
- The last stage, commercialization, involves developing the final marketing plan, getting the product into production, and the start of sales.
- "Me-toos" are products similar to competitive products that need a much-abbreviated new product development cycle. In this case, only the aspects that are different from competition need to be tested.

LO4 Understand why pricing is an important but difficult task for small business.

- Owners of small businesses give a great deal of attention to issues of pricing.
- The price of a product is a function of the value placed on the product by the customer.
- Price is directly related to revenue, and is indirectly related to volume.
- Price is the easiest marketing variable to change.
- Price is an essential part of competitive strategy.

LO5 Understand how elasticity, margin, and value impact pricing setting.

- Products tend to be price elastic or inelastic, that is, the quantity sold may vary considerably due to changes in price (elastic) or not (inelastic).
- Prices are also influenced by the effects of the law of supply and demand, the margins you set, and the value you can show to your customers.
- In addition to costs and consumers, price setting is influenced by five other factors: Company objectives, marketing strategy, channels of distribution, competition, and legal and regulatory restrictions.

LO6 Apply different pricing strategies.

- Consumer psychology has an impact on pricing as well. Through a number of ways, consumers get ideas about what is an acceptable price and what is not.

- Firms may use a variety of different pricing strategies. Some of the more common ones include: skimming, prestige or premium pricing, odd-even pricing, partitioned pricing, captive pricing, and price lining.
- Dropped prices are hard to raise. Rather than dropping prices, firms should consider using periodic or random discounting, off-peak pricing, bundling, coupons, rebates, and referral discounts.
- There are different methods for setting product prices, hourly rates, and service package prices.

KEY TERMS

4 Ps of Marketing, 274
goods, 274
services, 274
tangibility, 274
perishability, 275
inseparability, 275
heterogeneity, 275
total product, 276
augmented product, 277
core product, 277
target market, 277
me-too products, 279
optimum price, 284
markup pricing, 285
margin, 285
markup, 286
elasticity, 286
inelastic product, 286
elastic product, 286
law of supply and demand, 286
price gouging, 286
internal reference price, 291
external reference price, 291
skimming, 293
prestige or premium pricing, 293
odd-even pricing, 293
partitioned pricing, 294
captive pricing, 294
price lining, 295
periodic or random discounting, 295
off-peak pricing, 296
bundling, 297
multiple or bonus pack, 297
referral discount, 298

DISCUSSION QUESTIONS

1. A college education comes pretty close to being a true service. Discuss the four main characteristics of service—intangibility, inseparability, perishability, and heterogeneity—as they pertain to a college education.
2. What is the core component, the augmented product, and the total product sold at your college or university? How does it differ from your institution to others in the area?
3. List all the products/services you have seen lately that are promoted as new, different, improved, or otherwise changed from what has been available before. What percentage of these are actually me-too products? Identify the differential advantages these companies believe they have over the competition.
4. Why do owners and managers of small businesses spend so much time on issues of pricing?
5. Suppose you are operating a copy service. You learn that FedEx Kinkos is going to open an outlet just a few blocks away. You are concerned that you cannot compete with the marketing power of FedEx. What is likely to happen to your business if you lower your prices and place colorful advertising banners in the windows announcing the lowered prices?
6. How do the four primary factors of optimum price work together to determine what price should be? Draw a diagram of the relationships.

7. Imagine you can make a $75 retail Christmas wreath in two hours at a variable cost of $25 per wreath and a fixed cost of $800. Marketing consists of a booth at the local craft fair (rent: $100 for the month before Christmas), where five other competitors already sell wreaths nearly identical to yours in cost and quality. Annually they sell 300 wreaths, so if you join in, your target share would be about 50 wreaths. Should you sell your product? If one competitor lands the coveted spot by the door, capturing half the market, what is your decision?

8. While displaying at the craft fair, a representative of a mail order catalog company wants to put your product in the catalog. It will pay you $40 and mark the product up to $55 for the catalog. It estimates that your market share could be substantial and should be dependent only on your production output. You decide to quit your real job and devote all your time to making wreaths, but you want to match your current $50,000 salary. You really don't want to work more than 40 hours per week in actual wreath manufacturing (assume all paperwork, material purchasing, and such takes place beyond those 40 hours). You want four weeks a year for vacation, holidays, and sick days or personal days. Taking into consideration time constraints, the price you will get from the catalog company, and your revised costs, does this make sense?

9. Describe a situation in which you have been influenced by consumer buying psychology toward considering a price too high or a real bargain.

10. Think of two products in the same product category—one high priced and one low priced. How do the other parts of the marketing mix—the product itself, the advertising message, and the distribution—support or detract from the message the price tag gives?

EXPERIENTIAL EXERCISES

1. At this time, you are fairly experienced with college education. What could you suggest could be done in order to reduce intangibility, inseparability, perishability, and heterogeneity of this service?

2. BMW automobiles call themselves "the ultimate driving machine." The advertising tagline attempts to capture the total product package—what driving a BMW means to its owners. Review other advertising and come up with a list of five other products that do the same thing. What do their products mean to their consumers?

3. With a group of friends, brainstorm a list of ideas for a service you could provide for your college professors. Design an idea checklist to evaluate this list.

4. Select a service you know. Brainstorm a list of potential incremental changes—whether technologically feasible or not—that might extend the product life cycle for it over the next several years.

5. Set up several selling scenarios for the same product displaying different cues about the value of a product (e.g., where it's sold, whether it's on sale), the motivation of the seller, prices of competitive products (external reference price), and other possibilities appropriate for your product. Ask several people what they would pay under the circumstance you've set up.

6. For one week collect all the coupons you find in newspapers, magazines, mail, and so on. What percentage are for products or services or brands that you would really buy? Typically, how many coupons do you actually use in a week? Pull all the coupons for one product category and visit a store. Are there other brands of that same product that do not have coupons? Is the store engaging in any other methods to attract customers—rebates, sales, contests, multipacks, and so on?

7. You've heard about Paul Scheiter and his firm, HedgehogLeatherworks.com. One of his customers, Ian Atkinson, is a big fan and also a leatherworker, and provided his analysis of the pricing behind one the Hedgehog's most popular sheaths. See the video at www.youtube.com/watch?v=NYqmSzx_LRs. Based on this example, explain in your own words how elements like design and quality of construction make a product worth more than just the cost of raw materials and an hourly wage for leatherworking. The first 14 minutes give you the pricing discussion. The last 7 minutes show you what you would have to do to make a similar sheath of your own.

MINI-CASE

YAK MILK[61]

Dongzhou Gongbu saw a golden opportunity, only he wasn't quite sure what to do with it at first. A native Tibetan, he had worked in the Chinese government for a number of years and had witnessed the difficulties the Chinese government was facing feeding its people. While China is quite a large country, over 60 percent of its landmass is unsuitable for agriculture. Those areas that are suitable are also where China's huge population lives, further reducing available land. Dongzhou remembered the vast Tibetan plateau dotted with yak, the only animal suited to the severe climate found there and knew there had to be a solution.

Yak are "low maintenance" animals needing no feed that they can't gather themselves and living on the open range herded by nomadic Tibetans. While yak are milk producers, the quantities produced are much less than that produced by dairy cattle. In addition, because of its remoteness, bringing milk from the plateau to the population centers is an expensive proposition. A quick look at the prices on existing milk products and yak milk cost structure showed that yak milk just couldn't compete, because it would need to be about 50 percent more expensive than cow's milk.

Dongzhou didn't let this stop him, though. He consulted a specialist and found that yak milk was higher in certain nutrients than cow's milk. In addition, the Tibetan plateau is well respected in China for being pollution-free. Dongzhou capitalized on these features plus the fact that the yak was truly organically raised and revered in Chinese mythology. He positioned his product not as just another milk but as an extremely healthy alternative to other products—almost a nutritional drink—and priced it at a premium level.

CASE DISCUSSION QUESTIONS

1. How did Dongzhou Gongbu "discover" his new product?
2. What was his "total product"?
3. How did this help him with his pricing strategy?
4. How might he use this in advertising?
5. Can you think of another product that is basically the same as the competition and has been positioned much differently in order to command a higher price?

SUGGESTED CASES AND ARTICLES

- The House of Wine—Grand Opening, C-9

Available on McGraw-Hill Create™:

- Alma Products, Inc.
- Whale Printing Company
- Giberson's Glass Studio

SUGGESTED VIDEOS

www.mhhe.com/katz4e

Video Case:

- For a written video case and corresponding clip, visit the OLC at www.mhhe.com/katz4e and select "Chapter 9".
- Craft Beer Boom

SBTV.com Videos:

- Howard Wright, Inventor of the Storm Safety Whistle
- Market Research

STVP Videos:

- The Product Vision
- Role of Market Research

CHAPTER

10

Small Business Promotion: Capturing the Eyes of Your Market

● Addie Swartz's lifestyle brand, Beacon Street Girls, is aimed at two market audiences. What challenges are posed to this small business by its double-pronged approach? How might this approach work to Swartz's advantage?

LEARNING OBJECTIVES

After you complete this chapter, you will be able to:

LO1 Describe the marketing funnel and why promotion is so important.

LO2 Develop your value proposition.

LO3 Segment and further define your target audience.

LO4 Recognize the different approaches and methods you can use to craft and convey your promotional message.

LO5 Describe how to develop a press relations program.

LO6 Explain how to develop a public relations program.

LO7 Apply the key skills involved in personal selling, especially closing the sale.

LO8 Recognize the major approaches to customer relationship management.

Focus on Small Business: Addie Swartz and Accessories for Girls Who Are "Between Toys and Boys"[1]

As Addie Swartz's two daughters approached the pivotal "tween" years, she—like many mothers—struggled to find something to help her girls bridge the gap between Barbie and Britney. Frustration stoked her entrepreneurial spirit, and the Beacon Street Girls, a new lifestyle brand for girls ages 9 to 13, was born.

NO DOLLS OR ICONS

The Beacon Street Girls invites tweens into a rich and exciting contemporary world in which values matter, friendships are everything, and community service is important.

In promoting the brand, Swartz comments that all of Beacon Street Girls marketing initiatives need to understand and speak to two audiences: tween girls and their parents/older gift-buying relatives. Their goals are to:

- Build awareness among stakeholders.
- Create interest and desire in tweens to engage with the brand and share with their peers.
- Drive customers into the stores to seek and purchase Beacon Street Girls products.
- Encourage tweens and their parents to come to the website.

Marketing programs are aimed to promote retailer presence, push to the web, and leverage the tween consumer to promote the brand via web-based viral marketing programs. In describing her market further, Swartz divides the market into two segments, the primary and secondary. The primary market consists of girls ages 9–13 years, with the "sweet spot" being the older, 11–12-year-old tween. These girls are entering middle school, a time of new friendships, body changes, and growing-up experiences. They are media-savvy, looking for fun and possibilities, admiring of teenagers, but still want to be kids. They are in the early stages of navigating the often rocky waters of adolescence and desperately want to fit in. The secondary market consists of their mothers, fathers, aunts, uncles, and grandmothers who seek positive role models and messages for their daughters/relatives.

DISCUSSION QUESTIONS

1. What are some ways that Beacon Street Girls can promote its brand in order to meet the company's goals?
2. What ways can Beacon Street Girls market to the tween girls?

3. How can it also reach the parents of the tweens? In what ways is the marketing message different or the same?
4. How can Addie Swartz continually develop and promote the brand that has meaningful, value-driven tween girl properties that are also relevant, cool, and realistic?

LO1 Describe the marketing funnel and why promotion is so important.

impression
What it is called when someone notices a promotional effort.

sales leads
People who receive a promotional impression and who give some thought to buying the product.

prospects
Sales leads who actually make some sort of effort to learn more about the product, service, or business in anticipation of a possible purchase.

marketing funnel
The rule of thumb in marketing is that it takes a large number of people to be made aware of your product in order to find a purchaser.

The Need for Promotion

You've experienced your business "light bulb" idea for a terrific new product or service. You've organized an office complete with desk, phone, and computer, and you may possibly even have a small storefront or service vehicle. By all accounts, you are in business. Now ask yourself this: Does your target market know you exist?

In order for customers to purchase your goods and services, you must first go to them. You need to advertise and actively promote your business before you can expect inquiries into what you have to offer. While there are a handful of promotional means that are standard for all business ventures, entrepreneurs' limit to promotions is their own creativity.

Unless you know enough customers to keep you in business from the day you open up, you need to gain customers. To some extent, that is a game of numbers. To get people to buy what you are offering, you first need to make an **impression** on them, letting them know who you are and what you are offering. Those who have some interest become your **sales leads** and the most interested ones become your **prospects** for a sale. So at a fundamental level, promotion drives sales. How many prospects? Marketers talk about the **marketing funnel**, a rule of thumb about how many prospective customers it takes to find one who will actually make a purchase. For mass market and Internet advertising, the typical ratio is 1000 to 1. Figure 10.1 graphically shows you the promotion process and how the marketing funnel fits into it.

FIGURE 10.1

The Promotion Process and the Marketing Funnel

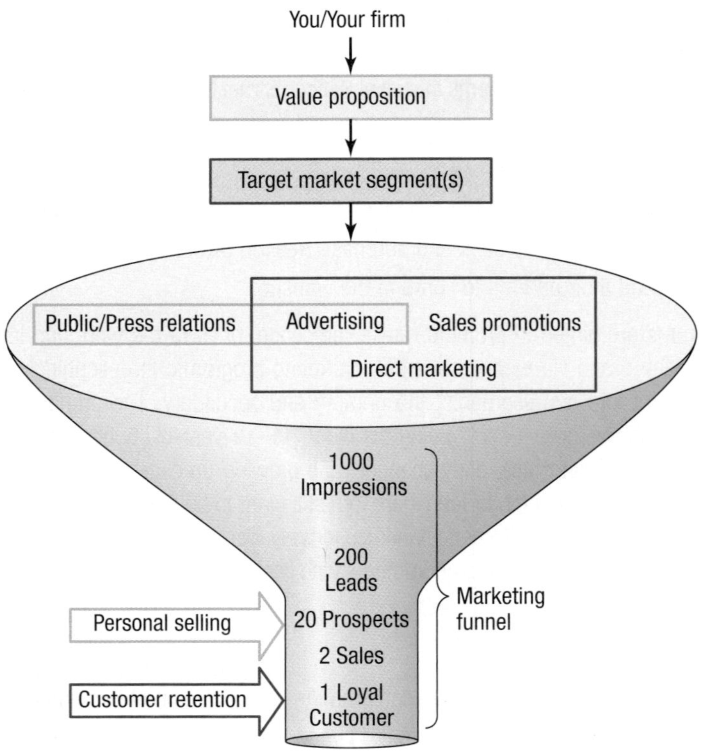

Promotion is essential to gaining the attention of people in the general audience, and anything you can do to improve your marketing will improve your chances of making a sale. The funnel provides some insights into recognizing what is truly important in the marketing process. For this funnel, every customer you keep saves you from having to contact 1,000 new people in the general audience to find a replacement customer—so improving customer loyalty is tremendously important. We will talk about loyalty and other postsale issues later in this chapter.

The funnel illustrates selling to the general public, but what if you could target people you already know have a reason to be interested in your goods or services? Maybe one or two people in a thousand would buy a baseball glove, but what if you could target people playing baseball? Instead of two sales per thousand, with *qualified leads* like people already playing baseball, you might be able to sell 10 times as many gloves, or more.

Following Figure 10.1, in this chapter we will talk about defining your target market and determining how to identify segments like those already playing baseball. We then discuss the methods of promotion including social media, public relations, and press relations. We conclude the chapter with a discussion of personal selling, and managing postsale relations in order to retain as many customers as you can. But first, as is true in so much of entrepreneurship, it all starts with you, your ideas for your business, and its goods or services. Because all promotion is about the value you can provide your customer.

The Basics: Crafting Your Value Proposition

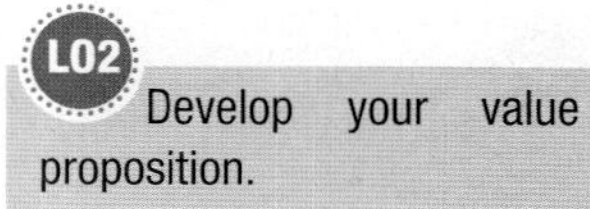
LO2 Develop your value proposition.

Chapter 7 introduced the idea of value and cost benefit. This was further developed by talking about your total product in Chapter 9. As you recall, your total product is not just the bare bones object or service you provide, but what it means to your customers. You don't just do a great job cleaning houses; you provide free time to your customers. You don't just sell desks; you handcraft beautiful and functional desks in exotic woods. You can talk about your competitive edge—what you do better than your competition—or your distinctive competency—what you do that no one else does, but what it all boils down to is your **value proposition.**[2]

value proposition
Small business owners' unique selling points that will be used to differentiate their products and/or services from those of the competition.

You can think of defining your value proposition along the same categories of value and cost benefits of quality, style, delivery, service, technology, shopping ease, place, and scale and scope. For each of the categories mentioned in Chapter 7, think about how your company, product, or service is different from anyone else's. Under each category, answer a few questions as objectively as you can:

- Why would someone want your product or service? What need does it fill? List the benefits and the problems it solves. In what way does it improve the life of the user?
- Would you personally buy this product? Why or why not? The "why nots" may give you an insight into potential weaknesses or categories of differentiation that you need to work on.

From there, you can then start to determine who will most benefit from your product or service. Begin with these questions:

- Who, in your opinion, is most likely to buy it? Be as specific as you can. How old are they? Male or female? Where do they live? Where do they work? These people are your primary target market. It doesn't mean that you don't have second-or third-tier markets.
- How does your primary target market currently go about buying existing products or services of this type? What are its sources of information? **Word-of-mouth?** Trade publications? Yellow Pages? The Internet?[3]

Word-of-mouth?
A means of spreading information about your business through the comments friends and customers make to other potential customers.

By answering these questions, you can start to further develop the value of your product and ways you can find and communicate with your customers. Once you know who needs your product or service, you can begin to craft your value and message directly to where your market would look to find information related to your small business. Skill Module 10.1 will help you develop a value proposition.

SKILL MODULE 10.1

Developing a Value Proposition

Choose one small retail business (e.g., children's clothing store, pet store, independently owned beauty salon, restaurant, etc.). Using promotional and advertising material, level of service, in-store displays, location, and any other information available (website), create a value proposition for that business. The goal of this value proposition is to create and occupy a space inside the target customer's head. Create a value proposition for your chosen small retail business by replacing the text in parentheses below as it reflects the product, market, and strategy.

- **For** (target customer)
- **Who** (statement of the need or opportunity)
- **The** (retail business name) **is a** (product or service category)
- **That** (statement of key benefit–that is, compelling reason to buy/purchase)
- **Unlike** (primary competitive alternative)
- **Our business** (statement of primary differentiation)
- **Is available** (where)

Now place the answers in paragraph format to arrive at the overall value proposition. Feel free to share your perception of the proposition with the actual small business owner.

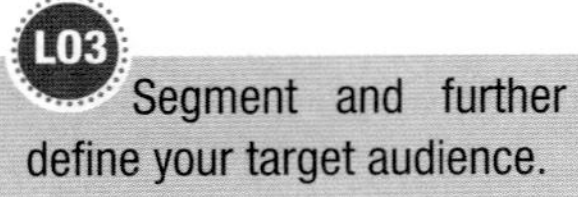

LO3 Segment and further define your target audience.

Segmenting Your Market

Many entrepreneurs have trouble answering the question, "Who is your target market?" Most entrepreneurs assume that everyone is their target market. Why should an entrepreneur care who buys their product, as long as it's sold? If pressed, the entrepreneurs can usually tell you who is most likely to buy their product or service and why. When they can tell you this, they have targeted their market. Although targeting and market segmentation are more fully discussed in Chapter 12, there are some concepts that are important to know in order to understand promotion.

segmentation
The process of dividing the market into smaller portions of people who have common characteristics.

target market
The segment or segments selected for concentrated marketing efforts.

Segmentation is the process of dividing the market into smaller portions of people who have certain common characteristics. Your **target market** is the segment or segments you select on which to concentrate your marketing efforts. A marketer can chose more than one target market, but it is customary for a smaller business to concentrate its efforts on one target market at the beginning and consider secondary ones later. Marketers use information on the target market's wants and needs in order to tailor the product or service, as well as its price, distribution, and promotion.[4]

Dividing the market into different segments can be done in a number of ways. Some of the more typical ways include geographically (in a certain city or neighborhood), demographically (income, age, religion, ethnicity, and many others), or by the benefits sought (clothing that is practical, stylish, for a particular sport, etc.). Most companies will use several ways of segmenting to come up with their final target market. For example, the Beacon Street Girls products were segmented by gender (girls) and age (9–13). In addition, the fact that they were into values and community service would be a form of benefit segmentation. Beacon Street Girls also had primary and secondary target markets—the girls and their parents and other gift givers.

Let's start with an example: you run a day care center. Who is your market? For starters, it is small children, or at least, the parents of small children. You have segmented by life cycle position; that is, you have eliminated children, teenagers, senior citizens, and parents of older children. But this really does not eliminate very many potential customers. How else could you limit your potential customers? Driving distance, say 15 miles, is a popular limit since parents are unlikely to want to drive too far. Income, or disposable income, is also a key segmentation device. Families need to be rich enough to afford your service but not so rich as to hire nannies. Other segmentation ideas include schedule (parents who work evenings and nights) or children's hobbies (e.g., offering soccer or music lessons). The more accurately you define your segment, the closer you come to defining your target market.

What are the benefits to both your primary and secondary market customers if you open a bilingual day care center in the middle of a largely Hispanic neighborhood? How would you promote to both of these markets?

Using our example from above, let's say that you are located in a town with a large Hispanic population (Phoenix) and all of your day care workers are fluent in Spanish. Your day care center is located in a middle-class, Hispanic area where most households are dual income parents with several children. Your research has shown only a couple of nearby competitors and none of them have the bilingual staff that you have. This opens up the opportunity for the business approach you have in mind, targeting a bilingual day care center for the Hispanic parents needing day care. A potential secondary market might be non-Hispanic families who desire their children to be fluent in Spanish—a market that could be considered at another time.

With the target market defined, it becomes easier to determine what information customers need in order to make a decision to buy your service. The Juarez family (as we imagine our typical customer) needs to find a day care center for little Tomas, who speaks a mix of English and Spanish. Good news! At your center he is not likely to be misunderstood. Other benefits include being able to leave instructions in English or Spanish or having children get a mix of both cultures, such as holiday and birthday celebrations, stories that are read, decorating colors, the day care center's name, and such. These are things that an entrepreneur could use to make this day care center "perfect" for a bilingual clientele.

Promotion includes getting the message out to the target market so that they can make decisions about your product or service. When advertising, your day care center will want to mention the language abilities and other benefits likely to be important to the target market. In order to catch the eye of the audience, the advertising might make use of Hispanic music, a Hispanic model/spokesperson, or symbols that will resonate with the Hispanic culture. (In the Phoenix area, perhaps a Mexican flag would work well.) It is likely to run ads in Spanish or at least partially in Spanish. It is also likely useful to use local Spanish television, radio, or newspapers depending on its budget and the ability of these media to reach the target market. Your day care center may send out mailers in the local area and other predominately Hispanic neighborhoods.[5] Parents who visit the day care center would likely hear a sales pitch that was directed to cares and concerns of this target market.

Consider, for a moment, promotion for the secondary market mentioned earlier: the non-Hispanic parents that wanted their children to be fluent in Spanish. Now the ads are likely to be in English. They are likely to run in different media. Mailings would go out to other areas. The sales pitch that the prospective parents would hear would likely be much different.

An advantage of segmenting a market is that is means you can target your message better. Also, with a targeted audience, your advertising dollars stretch farther. This is the home page of the website for KLNZ-FM in metropolitan Phoenix, which is a Spanish-language station, potentially focusing on a portion of your target market.

So how do you do this for your particular product or service? First of all, consider where your target market gets the information they need to make purchasing decisions. Is it the Internet? From their friends? From magazines such as *Consumer Reports*? From television or radio ads? From talking to the clerks at the stores? Or is your product something they will buy without much prior thought processes—an impulse purchase. These all have implications on where you will put your message in order to make sure they see it.[6]

Secondly, what features about your product or service are important to your target market? That is, what is it they are looking for when considering buying this product or service? Is it cost? Reliability? Technology? Appearance? Fitting in with their peer group? Convenient location? How do what the customers deem important fit in with your product or service? (If your customers are motivated by price and your product's distinction is style, technology, or other factors that increase price, maybe you have the wrong target market—or the wrong product for that market.) Knowing what the customer wants will help you determine what to say about your product or service. If you really aren't sure about where they get their information or what they want, try checking out your competitors' ads—your successful competitors, that is. While you'll want to be different in your message content, you can get a lot of hints from what is already working.[7]

Next, what will get your target market to pay attention to your message? Are you going to use rap music or classical music? Will the people in your message be wearing grunge or high fashion, business professional or jeans and a T-shirt? Will you use bold colors and exotic fonts, or will you use understated elegance? One of the major mistakes an entrepreneur can make is to choose an appealing (to them) message or media, instead of picking one which matches the demographics—and tastes—of the target market.[8]

The answers to these questions are determined by a person's age, gender, ethnicity, education, income level, profession, geographic region, personality, and a myriad of other factors. This is what makes defining your target market accurately so important. While many entrepreneurs have difficulty selecting only one target market, it is nearly impossible to design a message that will appeal universally or to find media that will reach all consumers. These rather generic messages often end up appealing to nearly no one and can be a considerable waste of marketing dollars.

A word of caution: unless you are particularly artistic, do not create your own promotional pieces. It is quite acceptable to sketch out concepts, suggest colors, symbols, and other features and to retain final approval, but expect to spend a little money getting professional artistic help. A graphic artist is well worth the investment. If you have an exceptionally tight budget, consider asking a graphic design department at a local university to use you as a class project or for a student who is willing to do the work for minimal cost and a chance to include the results in his or her portfolio.[9]

Once you have a clear idea of who your target customer is, a world of data is available to help you think about their habits. Many of the large marketing firms offer information on **predetermined market segments** based on their own unique approaches. Nielsen, a company you probably recall is famous for television ratings, has several types of segmentation analyses. The one that fits for most consumer-oriented firms is called Prizm (www.MyBestSegments.com). For nearly any zip code in the United States, Prizm can tell you the predominant groups in it.

predetermined market segments
Professionally compiled target audiences based on shared demographic, financial, shopping, and psychographic characteristics.

For the day care center, our entrepreneur defined the target market based on personal contacts, discussions, and first-hand research. With the target market defined and the likely areas (specifically zip codes) identified, it is possible to supplement the personal work with information on predetermined market segments. Prizm, for example, will identify the five largest market segments within a specific zip code for free. For each segment, Prizm provides a free, detailed, rundown about the buying habits and demographics of this group. For the day care center, one of the likely zip codes is 85008. In that zip code the Prizm segment "New Beginnings" is one of the top five. The information on the segment is shown on this page.

The information in these predetermined market segments can help you identify the financial and shopping characteristics of the group, which can be difficult questions to ask people face to face. These segments can also be a useful check on your own analyses of your target market.

Competitors to Prizm include Esri's Tapestry model (www.esri.com/data/esri_data/tapestry.html) and Strategic Business Insights' VALS survey (www.strategicbusinessinsights.com/vals/). Each provides descriptions of their segments, as well as the opportunity to see some data for free by

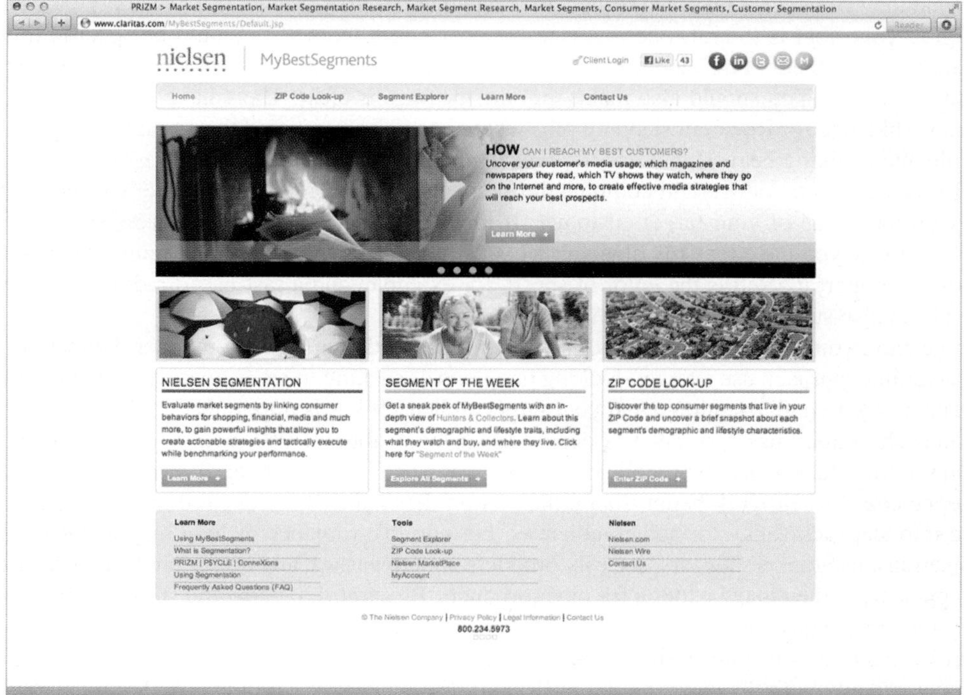

Nielsen's segmentation model, PRIZM®, found at MyBestSegments.com provides profiles like this for 66 different consumer segments based on extensive research. Why should predetermined market segments like the one shown here be used only after you've identified and learned first-hand about your target market?

Source: Nielsen PRIZM (as seen on www.MyBestSegments.com).

zip code. Additional data requires a fee. If you want to know the general characteristics of particular zip codes without the addition segmentation analysis, you can use any of the new crop of free zip code data sites, like www.zipwho.com, www.censusscope.org, www.zipskinny.com, or www.city-data.com, the use of which are shown in Skill Module 11.2. There is also a mountain of free data available at www.census.gov for areas, businesses, and households.

Why don't we recommend using these carefully crafted segments first? Because the essential strength of small business owners is that they are close to their customers. Good entrepreneurs understand their customers and their needs at a personal level. It actually hurts your ability to define your own target market if you first rely on some other group's or firm's idea of who the target audiences are. The only certain way for you to know your customers is to start looking for them personally, finding out what they are like personally, and hearing what they have to say personally. Then you have a basis for deciding if and how these predetermined market segments fit any of your real customers. If they do, then these commercial products can help you know more about your customers, but they can never really replace the knowledge you first build about your customers on your own.

LO4 Recognize the different approaches and methods you can use to craft and convey your promotional message.

Crafting Your Message

American consumers are bombarded by messages all day, for example, a Yankelovich Advertising Agency study reported the average person was exposed to 5,000 ad messages a day.[10] However, many of us screen out most of the commercials we see or hear. Even when an advertisement catches our eye, we are likely to spend only a few seconds at most considering it unless it is of special importance to us. For example, if you are in the new car market, the car advertisements suddenly become more visible to you, but even when you are interested and move down the marketing funnel from having an impression to becoming a sales lead, you may have a poor recall of any ads you've seen. Was it the funny ad or the one with the special effects? Ad recall is a major problem for all advertisers.

The bottom line consists of two questions: How can you get the attention of your potential customer? If a potential customer sees or hears your message and walks away with only one thought about your firm, your product, or your service, what do you want that to be?

The how has been addressed somewhat by thoroughly investigating your target market and finding out what they like. This will give us a good idea of where they are likely to be exposed to our messages. This will also give us a good idea of how our messages should be designed.[11] So if you did a good job on the target market analysis introduced earlier, you should know where they look and what they want. That leaves crafting a message that fits their needs.

Figure your goal is to craft one message for your target market. It should be specific to them and appealing to them. You should plan to repeat it, because a message repeated is more often the message recalled. You should also make sure the message is clear. There have been famous commercials (like one for Rozerem sleeping pill) where people remembered the commercial (with Abe Lincoln and a talking beaver), but had little recall about the product.

The message you craft should combine the elements of your product or service's value proposition with the needs of your target customer. If they want speed, you should stress speed in your message. Once you have that key element, what can you do in the message to reinforce, repeat, or otherwise support it? Red is the color of speed, for example, and a fast-paced radio, television, or web ad can also support the impression of speed.

In general, you can structure messages to be similar to the target customers or distinctive. Ads with a similar approach use average-looking people. Ads seeking to be distinctive may opt for models. This is where understanding what your target audience likes is important.

Along the same lines, you need to decide the voice or tone of your message. Tones or voices include humor, fear, patriotism, collegiality, sex, romance, love, and nearly every other emotion. Some, of course, will work better than others, often depending on your product. Humor may degrade into slapstick (okay for some audiences, but not all); romance or love may become sappy. Medications, insurance, safe cars, security products, mouthwashes, and breath mints may be fine for fear appeals, but they may be tough for other products. Be careful of being too strong. A fear appeal that is too strong may cause the audience to react negatively.

Will your ad show a real-life situation (think ads for paper towels) or will you exaggerate (the less-than-average guy with the super-model girlfriend), use fantasy or cartoons? Will you demonstrate

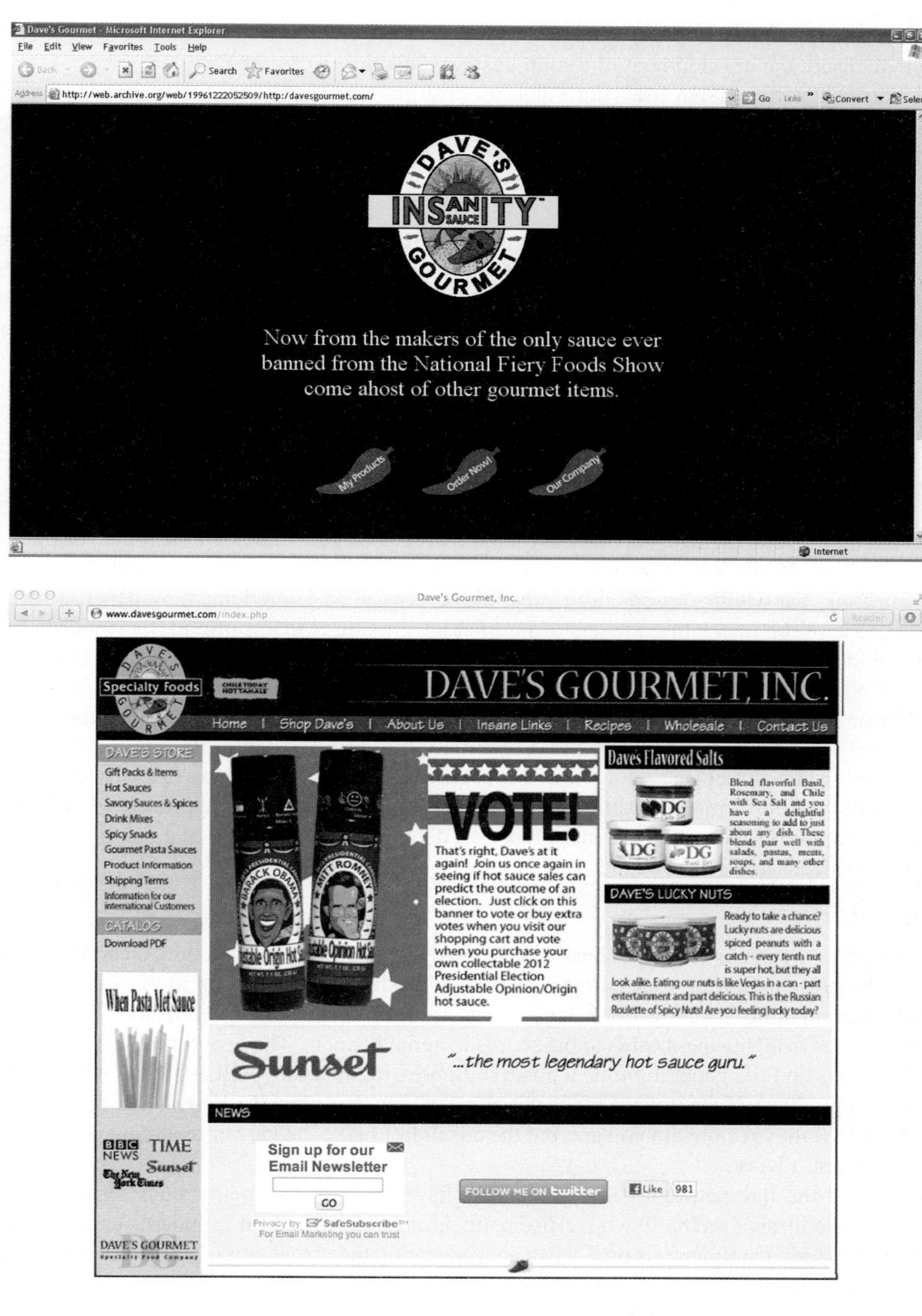

In crafting your message, the owner's job is making sure the important aspects are present. The smart owner then goes for expert help in graphic design and presentation. These two web pages are from the maker of Dave's Insanity Sauces. In the original 1996 site (top), the logo was visible and the website was very simple. By 2012, the website (bottom), had gone through three rounds of makeover and, as the company and its offerings grew, the need to share more about the brand and make customers aware of the broader range of products grew too. The message had to be recrafted to match the company's needs.

your product or compare it to competition? If you compare, will it be overt (We are better than Company A) or not (We are the best)? Will you use rational arguments about the size and speed?

The answers to these questions vary based on product/service and target market; there are not always hard and fast rules. Car commercials, for example, range from the excitement of the speeding car on the curving road to rational appeals about miles per gallon and other features of the automobile. They use comparisons to others, humor, sex, fear (safety), and feel-good family themes.

Effective messages are **succinct messages** that will make your business clear to potential clients and customers. You will use more general messages to convey your firm's overall image.

succinct message
Your key point in as few and as memorable words as possible.

A great example is Mary Kay's slogan "Enriching women's lives." If used consistently, these messages will ensure the development of a solid business identity.

To start initially, you can use your value propositions for each identified market to help you develop your overall message or slogan. Try to think of three to five key words that would describe your business to anyone. What words capture the essence of what you do and why you exist?

Specific marketing messages use the same principle: What is the key idea I want the potential consumer to leave with? Sometimes these messages are pretty straightforward like "We are having a sale on May 24 through May 26." Others may take more time to craft your value proposition or other distinct features of your product in a form that will resonate with your target audience. Start out with a strong first mental image—the first thing your client will see in his or her mind when exposed to your message. Avoid overworked verbs; use action wherever you can but pick unexpected words. Saying "We beat the competition" is fine, but how much more interesting is "We wallop the competition"—and even adds a bit of alliteration as well.[12]

Conveying Your Message

The challenge of conveying your message is knowing that your intended customer has actually heard or seen it. If you are selling face to face, you can be more sure that you and your message are connecting, but when you send out a press kit or have an ad printed in a newspaper, it is harder to know. One of the interesting aspects of Internet advertising is that it provides a somewhat more detailed understanding of who looked at a page, and if a viewer clicks on an ad, you can learn a lot about the potential customer. However, away from the Internet, it is hard to be as sure.

Traditionally marketers think in terms of five types of avenues for getting your message out: advertising, sales promotions, public/press relations, and personal selling that will be covered in this chapter, while direct marketing, will be covered in Chapter 11 as part of distribution. The **promotional mix** essentially describes how much of each of these five approaches you will use. The key to promotion for you as the entrepreneur is deciding on the promotional mix that works best to meet your needs and your budget.

promotional mix
How much of each message conveyance you will use to sell your product as well as your objective in using each one.

Advertising

Advertising is the major way most businesses convey their message to potential customers. Advertising is the presentation of your company's image, products, and services to potential customers and the general public. It can be done in print outlets, or electronically via mass media or the Internet, or via signs from business cards to billboards to aerial banners. The goal for any advertising is to give customers and the general public a positive impression that they will associate with you, your firm, and its products. If the impression is positive but they don't recall who you are, the advertising did not work. If they recall who you are, but the ads didn't make the viewer feel more positive about you, the ad didn't work.

advertising
Advertising is often used to support the corporate identity and value propositions that are established through public relations efforts. Part of conveying your message to your customers, advertising outlets include newspapers, magazines, billboards, television, and Internet banner ads, to name a few.

Because of the Internet, today's entrepreneurs have never had so many ways to promote their businesses. Traditional media like advertisements in magazines and on billboards can now appear all over web pages. Commercials on TV can also appear on the web. Door hangers with your coupon can be supplemented with local campaigns on Groupon or with Google Local to focus on particular cities or even neighborhoods. There are more places to put the name of your firm or product than ever before—from every square inch of a NASCAR racer's uniform, to the poles of turnstiles at the amusement park, to pop-ups inside of your YouTube video. Table 10.1 gives you an overview of the many forms of promotion available to you.

As you can imagine, given the enormous number of ways to advertise, it is impossible to give you detailed information on the ins and outs of each type of advertising technique. In fact there are semester-long courses in advertising in most business programs, with whole textbooks going through the many forms. You can get a lot of information online from reputable sources such as www.entrepreneur.com, www.inc.com, www.itsyourbiz.com, www.mashable.com, and www.ducttapemarketing.com. What we can do here is help get you started in advertising your business. So we will talk about the first steps you take—those you need to pay for and those you can do for free.

TABLE 10.1 Traditional and Online Promotional Techniques

Promotional Effort	Traditional Media	Online Equivalent (and Companies)
Video (Good for Building Awareness)		
Commercials	15/30/60-second spots	Online/YouTube video
On-screen logo overlays	Overlayed on-screen ads	Overlay ads in videos, hotlinked logos in videos and photos
Dedicated programming	Infomercials	Online infomercials, podcasts
Product placements	In movies, TV	In online games, videos
Audio		
Radio	Commercials, infomercials	Audio commercials, Infomercials, podcasts
Print (Best for Complex Information)		
Forms with company identity	(See Exhibit 10.1)	Company website, Facebook page, LinkedIn page, Twitter page, Custom URLs for these, custom e-mails with firm's name
Ads	1/8–full page ads	Online ads
Paid specially placed ads	Newspaper or magazine ads placed By section and day/edition, code for ad-responses, phonebook ads	Placed By search results or matched to content (e.g., Google Adwords, Facebook Likes), track click-through-rates, cookies, or code for ad responses, targeted e-mail, opt-in options on websites
Search results	Phonebooks	Websites appearing as a result of a search
Included ads	Blown-in/copackaged ads	Pop-up ads
Classified ads	Classified ads	Craigslist (and competitors) ads
Customer newsletters	Mailed newsletters	Emailed/online newsletters, Rss feeds, blogs, Facebook postings, Twitter tweets
Sponsorships	Sponsorship in ads and commercials	Sponsorship on websites, e-mails, videos, links, online games
Sales promotions	Coupons (in newspaper, Valpak, etc.), customer sales mailings, contests, sweepstakes, etc.	Online coupons (Retailmenot, U-pons or Groupon), e-mailed sale announcements, online contests sweepstakes
Locational Promotion		
Basic location design	Store, storefront	Website
In-store promotions	Sales displays, in-store coupons, in-store scannable QR codes	Pop-up displays and coupons, store-specific mobile apps with coupons and sale info
Ad placements	Shelter ads, wall posters, transit placements, billboards	Search engine and portal ads
Network Advertising		
Referral promotions	Coupons for friends, shopping together specials	Invite/refer a friend, share links, Facebook "Likes", Twitter hashtags, social bookmarking (e.g. digg, reddit)
Mass exposure	Billboards	Banner ads on major websites
Reciprocal advertising	Reciprocal ads	Reciprocal links
Affiliate marketing	Franchise and buying groups' ads	Affiliate marketing programs, e.g. CommissionJunction.com
Customer opinions		Yelp, ePinions, Google places, Amazon, eBay

EXHIBIT 10.1

Basic Elements of Business Identity

domain name
The specific name of a Internet site, consisting of a name followed by .com, .net , or a similar code.

- **Domain name and website.** Today the selection of a company name that can become your **domain name** (what is typed after "www" in a web address) is essential to building your corporate identity. Most website packages will also let you use the domain name for your emails so Jerome@Telesell.com becomes your e-mail instead of Jerome6073@gmail.com. Using your domain name in your e-mail address makes it look more professional, and helps reinforce your company's identity. Once you have this nailed down, open up a Facebook page for your business, which you can do for free at **www.facebook.com/business/**.
- **Business cards and stationery.** These should have your firm's name, slogan, website, e-mail, and Facebook company page on them. Your business card may very well be your first advertisement. Use every opportunity to pass it out, not only to potential customers but to friends and family who may also pass your card along (word-of-mouth advertising). Many places offer bulletin boards where you can put your card. Place several if permitted, in case a potential customer takes one along. Your stationery puts your name and message in front of potential clients, existing clients, suppliers, and others. You need stationery and business cards anyway; you might as well make them work for you.
- **Brochures and flyers** can be produced on your computer and printed with good results on a high quality desktop printer. Or they can be run off rather inexpensively at many copy centers. They both will give more information about your firm and products than your business card. The brochures and flyers can be as simple as a photocopied take-out menu or as complex as glossy four color printed mini-catalogs. They can be passed out, posted on bulletin boards, enclosed in other mailings, or mass-mailed by themselves.
- **Sales packets or marketing kits** provide potential customers an education in your product or service, including stories of customers whose problems were solved, an FAQ (Frequently Asked Questions) list, as well as a page on your products or services, and a page on you and your firm. These sheets can be printed on nice paper and put into a pocket folder with a sticker with your firm's name and address on it.
- **Signs** are also a form of advertising. They need to be large enough to read by passing traffic and should reflect your firm. Homemade signs do not indicate high quality and professionalism. Consider lighting it at night—a must if you do business in evening hours. Changing messages keeps your customers' interest.[13]
- **Promotional novelties** range from key chains, pens, and coffee mugs to more expensive embossed briefcases and the like. Something like a pen or small calendar can be produced with your company's name and slogan for pennies in quantity. Fancier items may be given to key customers or potential key customers or as gifts to your employees. T-shirts, golf shirts, or other clothing can be given as gifts or worn by employees and your message goes wherever the clothes are worn. Staples developed a whole marketing plan around the succinct message "Staples: That was easy" and created the Easy Button. This promotional novelty was so successful that they now sell them in their stores.[14]

Paid Advertising

The first thing you need to do when starting your business is to establish your company identity. While some elements are free, others will take some money up front. Exhibit 10.1 gives you a listing of the key elements of creating your corporate identity. Central to the identity is picking your company name, which we discussed in Chapter 9.

You will want a name for which you can get a matching domain name. That domain name is necessary to get your own website, and most websites with domain names also give you the ability to get an e-mail address with your company's domain name. You can check if prospective names are available at any online firm selling hosting packages or domain names, but if you find that a name you like is available, plan to buy it that day. There are firms paying each day to see what names were looked for, and they buy the names up for the purpose of reselling them. Search for *cheap domains* to find low-cost vendors. Many web-hosting companies will give you the domain name free with a web-hosting package. Unless you're planning to do e-commerce from day one, you can open up a "starter" type website (usually around five pages) for a low fee and upgrade as you get an idea of what your business really needs.

Armed with these you can start making business cards, and then websites and brochures (the print equivalent of your website). If you think a professional-looking logo would help, there are free do-it-yourself sites like www.logomaker.com or www.logosnap.com, or you can post for proposed logos on a site like www.elance.com and offer a price ($25 is typical) for the logo you select. Most marketing and web design firms can help you in this area as well.

Although regular phone service is not free, you need it, and you need the number to include on your business card and website. Think about getting a number that reflects your business—one tile company snagged a phone number they could display as 555-868-TILE (8453). One free service to consider is Google Voice, which will let you program one number to ring in multiple places or across multiple phones. With these basics in place, you can get down to the serious business of advertising your product and service offerings.

From your prior workups of value proposition, target market, and market segmentation, you should have a clear idea of your intended audience. You should have some idea of where they get their information—from TV, radio, newspapers, magazines, direct advertising like mail, or the Internet—and how much they use and trust each of these vehicles. From this, you can begin to think about how to structure your mix as soon as you add one more item—price!

Advertising costs are usually based on cost per thousand (CPM—the M is the Latin *mille* or thousand). Figure 10.2 shows you CPMs for a number of different forms of paid advertising. What the chart doesn't show, but you need to keep in mind, is that one ad impression is unlikely to do the job. Marketers talk about needing 15 to 20 impressions for people in the general audience to notice and remember who you are. This is why you will notice that commercials are repeated so often on TV and radio. The companies are trying to get enough impressions to you so that you recall their product.

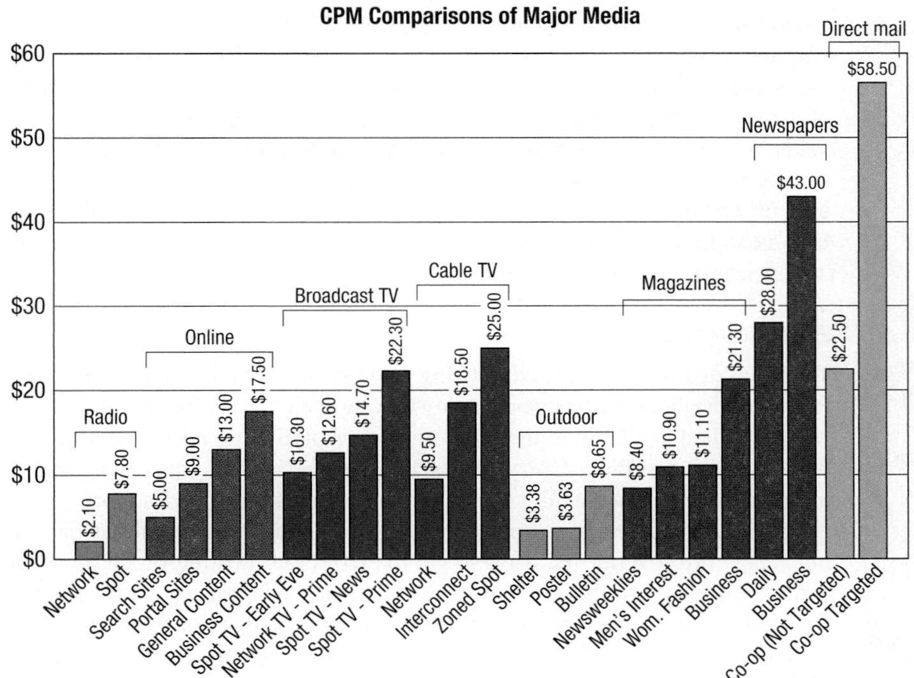

Source: Wells Fargo Securities, 2007–2008, Nielsen Out of Home Figures, 2011

FIGURE 10.2

Cost Per 1000 Impressions For a Variety of Paid Media Used in Promotional Campaigns

Taking a look at the graphic; knowing the underlying need for ad repetitions, you can quickly see that major advertising campaigns using traditional media are problematic for small businesses—they are just too costly for most start-ups. How can you build an advertising campaign on a limited budget?

For companies whose products have a regional, national, or global audience, there is no real competition to the Internet. Ads bought on the major services like Google, Bing, and Yahoo can be seen by millions around the world every hour. But because Internet ads depend on how often they get shown, you will want to limit who sees the ad to people in particular localities, or people who have searched for a term linked to your product, or people online on certain days or times of day. You will be able to check how many people react to the ad by their click-through rate, the frequency with which they click your ad for more information or to buy the product. You can also test multiple forms of the ad in a day, and adjust the ad as you learn what works best with your target audience.

search engine optimization
Techniques applied to web pages in order to obtain favorable placement on Internet search page results.

keyword and description tags
Terms included in the hidden portion of a web page (called the *document head*) which are used by search engines such as Yahoo! and Google to describe your website and evaluate its focus and category placement.

But as great as web-based advertising is, it is only worthwhile if your intended target audience is on the Internet on sites where you can advertise to them. The story of AO Rafting in the Small Business Insight box shows a powerful way to leverage the web. For our day care center in Phoenix, we could limit online ads to people in Phoenix who search for terms like *day care*. Services like Google Adwords Express let you focus your paid ads in a relatively small geographic area. Services like Valpak and competing local coupon mailing or door-hanging services offer a similar service using traditional print media. For our day care center, we could use Google Adwords for people searching for "day care" or "child care" in the local area and supplement that with mailed coupons in areas of town we know have families with children. We could then supplement these with the free techniques discussed below. We also could check locally for neighborhood newspapers where we might place ads, as well as church and school newsletters, which tend to be very low cost.

When you think about spending money to buy advertising space, especially when we are talking about traditional media like TV, radio, and print, it can make a lot of sense to also allocate some money to have advertising professionals prepare your ads. There are small advertising and marketing agencies virtually everywhere (and if you are comfortable working with an online ad agency, they literally could be virtually everywhere). Most good ones will show you a portfolio of their work, and hopefully you can check them out with their other clients. Most will also give you a cost estimate to help you determine quickly if you can afford them.

Entrepreneurs have promoted their businesses for ages. This baker's sign dates from medieval days, before reading was common, but it still wroks today. What kind of eye-catching sign could you create for your business?

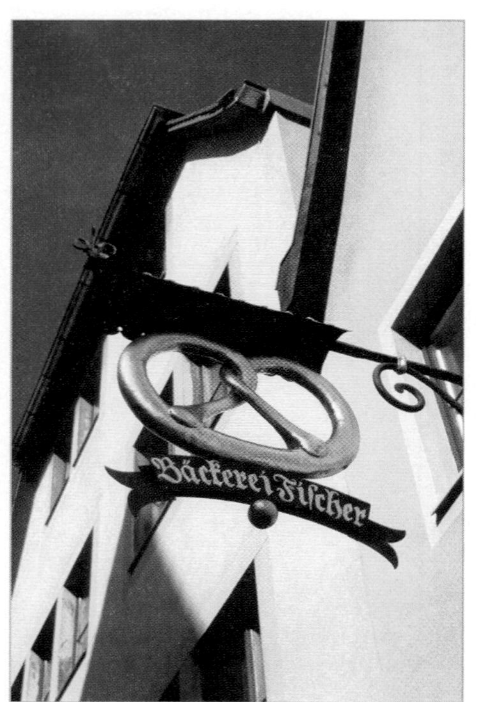

This can also apply to your Internet ads, especially if you are planning to develop videos or want interactive websites with state-of-the art graphics, or if having a stylish site is central to the image you want your firm to project. Otherwise, many people using the Internet seem to prefer the less professional ads that give you the sense of a personal connection to the entrepreneur at some other computer on the World Wide Web. On the other hand, you may want to hire some professional help in order to make your website appear high up on search results, through the techniques of **search engine optimization** (SEO). Identifying the best **keywords and description tags** to your web pages can be extremely useful, especially if you are new to the intricacies of the World Wide Web.

Free Advertising

There has always been free advertising. It probably started with entrepreneurs telling their friends about the business while working their "day jobs," or people calling out what they had available in the marketplace, or putting up a self-made sign showing what they were selling. Every one of those forms of free advertising remains very much in force and they still work! But today there is more—a lot more.

For our Phoenix day care center, we already have talked about paid advertising. There are several free ways to get the word out. Posting brochures or business cards on the bulletin boards of supermarkets and pharmacies or other stores in the targeted neighborhoods is one way. Passing out brochures or flyers in local areas or at meetings (e.g., PTO) is very inexpensive, but make sure you get permission first! Think about places families might go and pass out cards and brochures there—think of parks and playgrounds on weekends, for example. The idea is to think, "Where does my target market go?" and be there to advertise your business. We could look for local bloggers on family topics and send materials about our new day care center to them in hope of getting a mention on the blog. In other words, wherever we can get the word out, we do it. This kind of thinking will be used when building press and public relations programs later in the chapter.

We can make free websites for our business on Facebook (useful if you sell to consumers), LinkedIn.com (useful if you sell primarily to businesses), and Twitter (popular with both groups). These sites give you ways to get involved with customers and with groups as part of an online social exchange, making them feel more connected to your firm. On all three websites, there are groups of people with shared interests, and there is also sharing with the members' network connections. So if a customer of yours "Likes" your Facebook page, all of their Facebook connections will see that, which can explosively add to your growth. Typically these social networking websites are linked back to our main website, so that customers can easily use all your web resources.

While these sites are free and interactive, giving you a way to exchange ideas and opinions with one another, if you are going to be serious about using these free networks, you need to be consistent about living up to your social obligations. Checking Facebook, LinkedIn, or Twitter every 24 to 48 hours is necessary, and you need to not only check what is happening, but to keep the site's content fresh, with new postings at least a couple of times a week. A dormant Facebook or Twitter account actually hurts your business reputation because it seems like you don't care.

The other opportunity that opens up with these social network driven sites is the possibility of buzz or **viral marketing**. You or one of your customers on your Facebook or Twitter account may post a message, upload a picture or a video that people start sharing, and the sharing becomes explosive, with thousands or even millions of people seeing and sharing the material. Having something "go viral" is not easily done. Some say that it can only occur naturally. But you could get a small-scale virus going. For example, imagine our day care center owner posts on her Facebook page a short video on "How to get your child ready for his or her first day at day care." The customers on the Facebook page like it enough to pass it on to their friends, who pass it on, and suddenly a reporter at the local TV station sees it and asks the owner for an interview. In the interview, the reporter mentions the video and links to it from the TV station's website. Suddenly the owner is the top day care expert in Phoenix. Think about that when you see the local news. There are stories like this happening every few days. The two major sources for these are viral marketing and press relation efforts.

viral marketing
Any electronic equivalent of word-of-month advertising, in which the advertiser's message spreads quickly and widely via e-mail, website, blogs, and other online tools.

Getting other people to talk about you and your business is one of the best ways to get potential customers' attention. Since the days of newspapers, this has been called **free ink** because getting the local gossip columnist to mention your restaurant got your name in ink but didn't cost you hard dollars (although it might have meant the gossip columnist got a free meal from you). Today there are more ways than ever to get free ink, and it goes far beyond newspapers.

free ink
Mentions of your company or products in the media for which your firm did not pay.

Again the Internet is a major player. For example, NM Incite reported the existence more than 186 million blogs worldwide at the end of 2011.[15] There are even blogs like Squidoo (www.squidoo.com/sumbit-startup) or KillerStartups.com that are focused on spotlighting new start-ups.[16] With that many blogs, there are bloggers focused on every topic, locality, and industry. There are even directories of blogs, search for *blog directory* on Google or Bing to help narrow your search.

Whether you are seeking free ink from traditional media or the Internet, you have to do your part, mainly providing them with information ready to be used. For example, Internet marketer Kipp Bodnar[17] suggests blog-ready materials might include answering customers questions, aggregating an interpreting industry statistics, or making lists or charts the blogger can quickly incorporate in their next posting. We'll get more into the details of press releases in the section on press relations later in the chapter.

If you can get the bloggers to like your product or service, they are more likely to mention it. Sending them your press release might work if it is relevant, but a sample of your product might be better. Do some research on the sites to decide which to target. For example, there is Coolhunting for urban living products, Kevin Kelly's CoolTools for tools and gizmos of all sorts, DailyCandy for fashionable clothing, Gizmodo for electronics, Luxist for luxury items, MoCoLoco for modern furniture, and Treehugger for environmentally friendly products.[18]

The whole idea of connecting businesses to blogs has itself spawned entrepreneurship opportunities. PayPerPost—which is blog focused but not free—is a firm that connects firms hoping to be featured on blogs with bloggers who don't mind some extra cash for mentioning their products. The company's founder counters implications that this is unethical by stating that the firm doesn't specify whether the content needs to be positive or not; in other words, you can even get paid for complaining about a product or service.[19]

Another of the original forms of free advertising is word-of-mouth (WOM) advertising because it is passed when one person speaks to another about a product or service they like, or when the entrepreneur makes a personal pitch about their business to someone they just met.

SMALL BUSINESS INSIGHT

White-Water Marketing[20]

A business website doesn't win awards because it has cool features and bells and whistles that are part of many websites. It has to work for both the customers and the company. Rated as one of the top sites according to *Inc.* magazine, that's what really distinguishes the website of AO Rafting (**www.aorafting.com**). Established by a schoolteacher over 40 years ago, the company All-Outdoors Whitewater Rafting or AO Rafting is a multigenerational family business. It's a regional company in a seasonal business, with about $2 million in annual revenues and fewer than 20 permanent employees year-round. However, during its eight-month annual season, AO Rafting employs more than 100 people including some 75 part-time guides. Based in Walnut Creek and Lotus, California, right by the mother lode that drew the forty-niners out west for the Gold Rush, this business seems isolated, deep in canyon country. Yet, it has built a web presence that puts to shame a lot of other small businesses that may be more tech-savvy and have greater resources. Prospective customers can tour the Klamath and Tuolumne rivers through the site's virtual tours. They can also plan trips right on the site, check the availability of tours, make reservations, access real-time information on water conditions, refer the company to friends, and find discounts on trips. The site has virtually replaced almost all the traditional marketing and promotion that All-Outdoors Whitewater Rafting used to do.

When it comes to promoting a small business that is just starting out, spreading the news by word-of-mouth remains one of the surest ways to build a client base. Whether a potential customer meets the owner directly or hears of the business secondhand, a connectedness is established that cannot be matched by advertising or other marketing methods. Entrepreneurs should make use of every opportunity to meet potential clients and expose them to their products or services.

Network advertising includes referrals as discussed in Chapter 9, but also the information you spread through your own network of family, friends, and business associates, who are described in the social networking discussion of Chapter 3. Ask those clients you've satisfied to pass your name along. If possible, give them an incentive—a discount on their next purchase, for example—to do so. Another example is by passing out your business card at every opportunity. (You may even want to print special ones offering the carrier to some token gift—an advertising novelty, perhaps—a free estimate, sample, or discount when they visit your business.)

While a business card goes a long way, prepare yourself to sell your business at every opportunity. Join local groups such as Rotary or Toastmasters. Get involved with trade associations, chambers of commerce, or even local government. If you are able, offer to speak at organizations; perhaps you can share some of your funniest start-up stories and the lessons you learned.[21]

If you ask most service providers how they get business, the answer is usually referrals or word-of-mouth.[22] Carter Prescott, head of New York-based Carter Communications, which provides high-level writing and speaking services for Fortune 500 clients, doesn't even have a listed phone number. "I've never needed one," she says. "It's better to have people call you on their own, rather than soliciting calls anyway. You get a better client that way." She only gets calls when a current client gives her number to a potential client.

One cold call to a dealer can start *word-of-mouth advertising*[23] and get your product into stores. Lynn Gordon, proprietor of French Meadow Bakery in Minneapolis, Minnesota, started her bread-making business in her kitchen, producing 40 loaves a week for local co-ops. One day she made a cold call to a local gourmet shop, which started a word-of-mouth snowball. As luck would have it, the buyer was on a special diet, and Gordon's bread was just what she was looking for. Soon other grocery stores signed up. Meanwhile, customers sent loaves to friends around the country, who called to order more.

Under pressure from stores, distributors started asking for French Meadow bread. Next, Diane Sawyer and the *60 Minutes* crew showed up to do a story about the Women's Economic Development Corp., a program for women entrepreneurs in which Gordon was involved. Sawyer highlighted Gordon and her gourmet bread on the show. Then the state helped subsidize a trip to the International Fancy Food & Confection Show in Chicago, where 300 stores placed orders. Will Steger, the tundra explorer, ordered Gordon's bread for the international trip he was leading across the Antarctic. Even Neiman Marcus bought French Meadow bread to include in a $5,000 Ultimate Cocktail Buffet. As a result of that first cold call, Gordon moved her operation into a 13,500-square-foot storefront bakery in Minneapolis, where she eventually employed 15 people.

Another effective way to create word-of-mouth marketing is to give your product away. Yes, you read that sentence correctly: give your product away. You start by making a list of the top people you would like to have as your customers. Who is your target market? Who do these people listen to when trying to make product decisions? What if these influential people had your product—and didn't have to pay for it? If your product is as great as you think, won't these influencers be excited about it and tell everyone else they know?[24]

Sales Promotions

Sales promotion is a form of communication that encourages the customer to take immediate action. Good examples of sales promotions include coupons, sales, contests, sweepstakes, giveaways, samples, "buy one get one free," and other gimmicks. They range from inexpensive—sales flyers photocopied—to expensive—all-expenses-paid vacation. They are relatively easy to manage—sales and coupons—to much more complex—contests and sweepstakes. Frequent buyer programs (as described in Chapter 9) are also examples of sales promotion. When using contests and coupons, it is a good idea to check into local and state laws, since there are some places that prohibit or limit

sales promotion
A form of commvunication that encourages the customer to act immediately, such as coupons, sales, or contests.

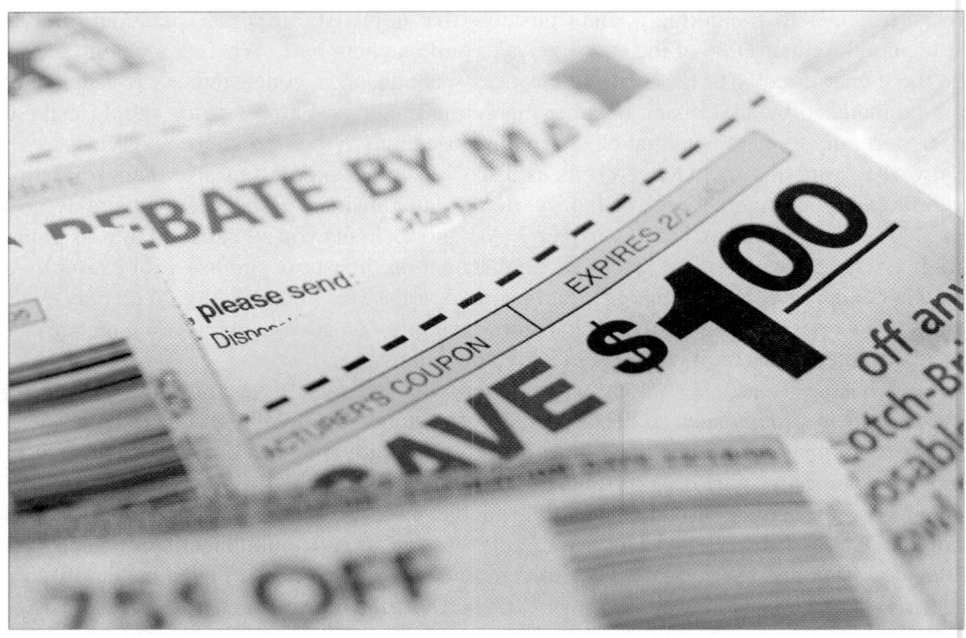

Coupons are one of several sales promotion techniques small businesses can use. These coupons were sent by mail, but you can also provide coupons online through your firm's website or coupon aggregator sites like CouponMountain, DealCatcher, and FatWallet.

how these are used. For example, if you use a sweepstakes in Florida or New York, you need to post a bond equal to the amount of the prizes.

Building a Press Relations Program

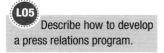

LO5 Describe how to develop a press relations program.

Press relations are those activities you do to influence or increase media coverage of your business. Media include newspapers, magazines, websites, blogs, radio, and television. These can be targeted to the general public or for specific groups like industry or trade associations, professions, neighborhoods, or lines of business (e.g., gas stations, restaurants, etc.). In this section we talk about how to target media outlets that can do your firm the most good, how to develop the keys to any media strategy—your press release and press kit—and even how to determine what a media outlet might find newsworthy.

press relations
Activities used to establish and promote a favorable opinion by the media.

Targeting Media Outlets

Building a press relations program is a lot like planning any other aspect of marketing. It starts with your target. In public relations, determining your target is determining which media are likely to reach your customer. This may include radio, newspapers, magazine, television, and newsletters. Since you are a small firm and perhaps local in scope, national media are probably not for you (unless you have invented the next Google, YouTube, or other breakthrough technology). Most communities have local publications promoting local businesses. Local television stations won't offer you *60 Minutes* slots, but like to feature stories as fillers in their newscasts—especially if the story is newsworthy, of human interest, humorous, or generally "feel-good."

As with personal selling, make a list of these media and then determine which ones are most likely to carry the sorts of news you offer. Treat them as if they are your customers. Find out the main contact people, their phone numbers, and do a Google search to see what stories they cover and find out more about them. Ask if they have any preferences as to how they like the information delivered. Send them your press kit and ask for theirs.[25] Some will prefer that you write the story and let them edit. Others will prefer to send out their own reporters.

Additionally, the press release can be used on your website, as handouts to clients, or included in direct mail. If you are a presenter at a meeting or conference, pass it out as background information. Frame it and hang it in your place of business. (Many restaurants hang favorable reviews where

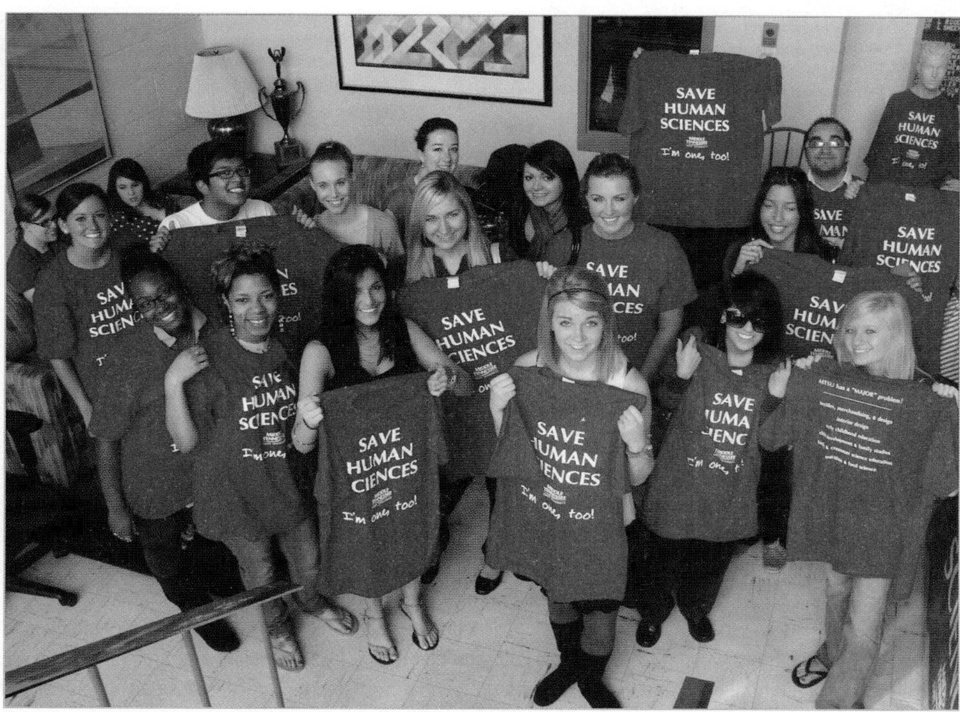

One of the techniques of buzz marketing, which started with student entrepreneurs and has grown, is the campus T-shirt campaign. Pick a product, service, or cause, print up T-shirts (the more striking the better), and get friends or groups on campus to wear them around to drum up awareness.

clients can see them as they wait for their table.) And, as with personal selling, continue to build your relationship with the media. Include a link to the article as part of your signature.[26] Now, you need to determine which story you will send out and write the press release.

The Basics of a Press Release[27]

The **press release** (see Skill Module 10.2), like the one seen in Exhibit 10.2, is the key method for telling your business story. Entrepreneurs can use the AIDA (attention, interest, desire, and action) formula to write press releases well.

press release
A written announcement intended to draw news media attention to a specific event.

- Attention: Get their attention with a catchy headline. Something clever or a play on words may do the trick. It needs to be short—no longer than ten words and preferably less. Sometimes a subtitle may be used, especially if the attention-getting title may not give enough information. For example, "Udderly Delicious: Dairy Marketing in Venezuela"[28] is the example of a clever title—a pun—and a subtitle to explain what the article is really about. Try to strike an emotional chord with your readers. Empathize or address a problem they have and you may draw their attention further.[29]
- Interest: While the title should start to pique their interest, the opening paragraph should really capture them. This first paragraph should include the *who, what, when, where, why,* and *how* of the story. If you are really good, you can get all that in the opening sentence. The idea is to "hook" them and get them to read further.
- Desire: Now provide the meat of the press release—details that tell us more about the opening information and increase our interest. Depending on what your press release is about, this could include features of your new products, or some biographical information on the new person you hired. Start with the most important information in the story because editors frequently delete ending materials to fit space. Quotes from key people from outside the company can imply third-party endorsements.
- Action: At the end you put contact information. Where can they find out more about your wonderful new product, your exciting new vice president, or this fantastic company that just won an award? The goal is to get them to be potential clients; kind of hard if they don't know where to find you!

SKILL MODULE 10.2

Writing a Press Release

One of the best-known sources for press releases is called PR Newswire. They offer what is seen as the gold standard in press release layout, consisting of seven items:[30]

- A top heading which says: **FOR IMMEDIATE RELEASE**
- Then your **Headline** below that
- Below that is your **Dateline (your city and the date you sent the release)**
- Now you start your **Lead Paragraph (giving the *who, what, when, where, why, how*)**
- Next comes the **Body (most important information and quotes first)**
- Below that is the **Company Boilerplate (generic information about the company and its history, your products, and the like)**
- Last is the **Contact Information (name, phone, e-mail)**

Now that you know what the media expects in a press release (and you can see an example of an excellent one in Exhibit 10.2), you have the opportunity to actually write one. Start by going to **www.pressbox.co.uk/Sports/index.html**. This website has thousands of press releases that are submitted to the pressbox newswire and directory every day. It also has several categories of press releases ranging from arts, business, sports, and technology.

Pick one of your favorite categories and start reviewing several of the newly posted press releases, some good and some needing improvement. Your task is to find one that is less appealing and probably would have a difficult time catching the editor's eye. Given the information provided in the press release along with any additional information (website address, additional contacts), rewrite the press release so that it would capture the attention of the media. Again, consider how the information provided in the press release benefits the individual reader. Using all the recommendations mentioned, make sure you get the five Ws and one H of the story—*the who, what, when, where, why,* and *how*. When you're finished, take the original press release and your revised one to one of your classmates. Have him or her critique both and ask which of the two he or she believes would grab the attention of the press and other readers.

EXHIBIT 10.2

Sample Press Release

8minuteDating.com, the pioneer in offering speed dating services, started small and now reaches over 60,000 customers in 55 major cities. What elements of their Cupid Party press release illustrate how 8minute successfully attracts and relates to its market audience?

Source: Reprinted with permission of 8minuteDating.com.

Draft release: Jan. 23

Contact:	Chris Perkett	Tom Jaffee
	PerkettPR, Inc.	8minuteDating.com
	781-555-5852	617-555-7764, x201
	chris@perkettpr.com	tom@8minutedating.com

8minuteDating.com Hosts "Biggest Dating Event in History" on February 11

8minuteDating.com Cupid Parties provide singles in 47 cities across the U.S. and Canada with a unique alternative for Valentine's Day

Boston, Mass. — Jan. 27, 2013 — 8minuteDating.com, the world leader in round robin dating, today announced it will be holding the largest recorded dating event in history on Tuesday, February 11. The "8minuteDating.com Cupid Party" will be held in 47 cities at 59 venues across the U.S. and Canada, providing singles with a fun new way to enjoy the Valentine holiday, as well as the opportunity to meet someone. The marquee event will be held at the Hard Rock Café on 57th Street in New York City.

Single people often dread Valentine's Day because they want something fun to do that offers the possibility of making a romantic connection. The 8minuteDating.com Cupid Parties are not only a great party, but using the automated 8minuteDating.com matching system, participants are likely to get a date in time for Valentine's Day.

"Today's singles are busier than ever and they need help meeting people to date," said Tom Jaffee, CEO and founder, 8minuteDating.com. "8minuteDating is the 'bar scene made better' because participants get to meet like-minded people every eight minutes, rather than staying clustered with their friends in a smoky bar. It's a fun party, and we expect about 60 percent of the participants to find a date in time for Valentine's Day."

Appealing to America's 82 million singles of diverse ages, ethnicities and sexual orientations, 8minuteDating.com provides a fast, fun, safe and comfortable way to meet people for dating, friendship or business. 8minuteDating.com is the first and the largest company to bring together the best of today's most popular dating services, combining the ease of the Internet with the opportunity to meet a room full of like-minded people, face-to-face, before committing to a lengthy one-on-one date.

How does it work?

— An equal number of single men and women gather at a restaurant or other venue.
— Each person has eight one-on-one dates that last eight minutes each.
— To keep the conversations comfortable for everyone, participants do not ask anyone for their last name, for their phone number or for a date.
— An intermission enables participants to meet everyone at the event, in addition to their pre-determined eight dates.
— After the event, participants log on to www.8minuteDating.com and enter the names of the people they want to meet again, whether it's for dating, friendship or business.
— Whenever two people enter each other's names in the same category, 8minuteDating.com automatically sends the contact information to both people so they can set up another date.

Guaranteed Success

More than 99 percent of 8minuteDating.com attendees report that they enjoyed their evening of 8minuteDating. Of that number, 81 percent had a "very good" or "excellent" time. An overwhelming 96 percent of attendees say they would attend another 8minuteDating.com event, and 95 percent recommend 8minuteDating.com to others. Most importantly, more than 90 percent of participants meet someone who they want to see again. In fact, the company guarantees that if a participant does not meet someone who they want to see again, their next event is free.

Cupid Party Information

For information regarding the nearest 8minuteDating.com Cupid Party, please visit www.8minutedating.com.

About 8minuteDating.com

8minuteDating.com, part of Match Events Inc., is the world leader in round robin dating. 8minuteDating.com's mission is to create a fast, fun, safe and comfortable way for singles of all ages, religions, ethnicities, sexual orientations and other special interests to meet for dating, friendship or business. Match Events, Inc. was founded in 2001 by Tom Jaffee, a successful high tech entrepreneur. The company is headquartered in Boston, Mass., and can be reached online at www.8minutedating.com.

Resources for E-Mailing Press Releases[31]

Once you have developed your press release, there are a plethora of websites that can assist you in sending or e-mailing your press release to the appropriate media. These include:

- ABYZ News Links—contains links to more than 17,200 newspapers and other news sources from around the world: www.abyznewslinks.com
- Gebbie Press—where you will find a wealth of media information: www.gebbieinc.com
- American Journalism Review—a great link to media sources that are on the Internet: www.ajr.org

This basketball tournament will raise money for and awareness of the needs of amputees, and was put on by an entrepreneur whose friend is an amputee. What other ways can small businesses generate positive publicity?

press kit
A type of sales kit sent to media outlets which is focused around a press release.

newsworthy events
To garner serious attention from the media and the public, a news story needs to deliver certain essentials that will hold their attention and keep your news in their thoughts. It should have public recognition, importance, and interest.

public recognition
Being recognized or acknowledged by large numbers of people, similar to "fame."

issue recognition
A concept in public recognition which alludes to the extent to which the public is familiar with the issue or problem at hand.

trendiness
A concept in public recognition which alludes to the fit of the topic to current fashion or public interest.

proximity
A concept in public recognition which alludes to the impact level of the issue being discussed.

public importance
(1) Things that are considered important to large numbers of otherwise unrelated people, (2) things that are of civic importance, as opposed to private or corporate entities.

The press release is often included as part of a **press kit**. Press kits are a variation of the sales kit mentioned earlier. Press kits include brochures, business cards, product information, and other materials that can provide background material for a reporter. They should include a letter of introduction and may include a brief history of the firm and information about the owner and other key managers. Include other press releases, articles, and other newspaper clippings about the firm and other such material. Consider including a "frequently asked questions" page, information about awards, audio and videos of television, or radio interviews. Financial statements, if you are publicly traded, are a must. If appropriate, include samples of your products, camera-ready logo art, statistics specific to your industry or target market, photos, and even an order form—they could be your next customer![32] Whenever you run across a new media outlet appropriate to your clientele, add it to your media list.

What Is Newsworthy?[33]

Press releases are meant to draw the attention of the public to something that's new and **newsworthy** which could be a range of things, from products and people to services and solutions. To further garner serious attention from the media and the public, a news story needs to deliver certain essentials that will hold readers' attention, and keep your news in their thoughts. It should have public recognition, public importance, or public interest.

Public recognition includes **issue recognition** (Have you solved a problem that is an at-large issue? If your problem is not familiar to the public, people need to be familiarized with it before they understand your news), **trendiness** (Is your news a low-carb diet or a Cabbage Patch Kid? That is, will you be able to ride the wave of fashion or will you be just another in a long and dated line of related stories?), famous faces (If the news is connected to one or more recognizable people or organizations, the public will already feel a connection to the story.), and **proximity** (News is sure to attract attention if it can potentially affect a number of people. The more people it will affect, the further your story will spread.). **Public importance** includes **power** (Does your news represent a power struggle or shift? Power affects the community, and the farther its potential reaches, the more newsworthy the event.) and **currency** (Your event will have its greatest importance while the issues are current. Will your news be connected to other recent events?). Finally, **public interest** includes a **good story** (Does your news present a good conflict and resolution? Nothing grabs attention and memory better than a good story.), **human interest** (A character with whom the public can relate helps generate interest and attention. Can you pull human interest into your news? The human interest story line helps connect the news to the audience with emotion.), **visuals** (graphics—action, photography, and so on—draw attention to the piece, making another connection between viewer and the news. Are there interesting visuals in the piece?), and **cultural resonance** (Broad cultural themes expose the event or news to a wider audience. Does the event or campaign speak to a wide demographic range? Is it meant to?).

Even though something is "new," it might not have enough of the three "essentials" above to grab the attention you had hoped. For example, hiring nonexecutives doesn't hold importance for the media. Even new products aren't newsworthy unless they are something new and innovative on the market.

Leveraging the Press and Generating Publicity

How do you further leverage the press to grow your business? The press can be extremely valuable in helping businesses of all sizes succeed and gain market share by generating a high level of exposure to a wide audience. As discussed above, the first challenge is to develop that unique story or angle, but once that is done the next task is to find the appropriate person at specific press outlets that would be interested in this news. All reporters or editors have their own beat, so it's imperative that you do your research before approaching them to find out what kinds of stories they typically write, what trends might be interesting to the audiences they write for, and whether or not they just did a similar story last week.

For a small business, mentions in the "corporate notes" sections of the daily and local business papers are a good way to start. These are great places to list new client acquisitions, project completions with substantial results, and new hires—all reflective of a solid, growing company. Consumers and companies want to buy goods and services from a company that has demonstrated it's going to be around in a few years, not one that has an interesting idea but can't properly articulate why the idea is good.

power
A concept in public importance which alludes to potential shifts in control or influence.

currency
A concept in public importance which alludes to the degree to which the issue is immediate in its impact.

public interest
(1)Things that are generally considered to be beneficial to large numbers of people, (2) civic causes and benefits, as opposed to private and corporate benefits

good story
A concept in public interest which alludes to an incident with good triumphing.

human interest
A concept in public interest which alludes to a character to whom the public can relate.

Building a Public Relations Program[34]

Public relations include **publicity** and other forms of communication to the public in general in order to promote a favorable opinion by the public about your firm. For example, corporations send out shareholders' reports in order to provide information and create a favorable impression about the firm with the shareholders who may never be one of their customers. Other publics that are routinely the target of these messages include government, education systems, special interest groups, neighbors to the firm, competition, other business in general, employees and potential employees, investors, and, of course, potential clients.

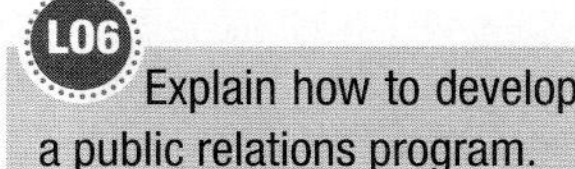
LO6 Explain how to develop a public relations program.

Public relations have some weaknesses as a tool. Many people regard public relations stories skeptically: "Of course they will tell us only the good things and not the bad." Some feel that these stories are a thinly veiled advertisement. Also, these are very difficult to control. A firm may spend many hours and resources developing and submitting press releases or other publicity and the news media may never use them. Or, often worse yet, the news media will edit the press release to the point that the original intent is totally distorted.

Public relations are those things you do to help create a favorable opinion of your firm in the mind of people in general. For most businesses, the more people who know about your business the better, but this only works if people have a positive opinion about your firm. Often it is easy to do things which help get you a favorable opinion from others. Activities you undertake which show your willingness to help others, through pitching in or sharing time or expertise, can do a lot to build favorable public opinion.

To show your expertise, consider writing articles for magazines[35]—not press releases, but an article addressing a problem you can solve, a human interest story, or something about which you are an expert. If it relates to your business, this will help establish you as an expert in your field.[36] (College professors do this all the time.) This gets your name out among potential clients, generates referrals and strengthens your competitive advantage. You can also offer different media to consider you as an expert opinion on related news articles. Include the articles in your press kit or use them as you would other public relations materials.[37]

To show your good will, consider sponsorships or donations. For example **sponsorships** can be a good way to get the word out about your firm. Your budget will not cover renaming a local major league baseball stadium, but it might put your name on the back of a T-ball team's uniforms

visuals
A concept in public interest which alludes to the graphic interest held by an event.

cultural resonance
A concept in public interest which alludes to events with a broad appeal within the market or population.

public relations
Activities used to establish and promote a favorable opinion by the public.

publicity
Information about your company and its activities that is disseminated to the public in order to going their good opinion.

sponsorships
Paying for a local organization's needs in exchange for recognization.

THE THOUGHTFUL ENTREPRENEUR

Tips for Generating Publicity[38]

Okay, you are convinced that publicity is great for your firm; what can you do that's newsworthy and likely to be picked up by the news media? The following are based on suggestions by Margie Fisher, the president of Zable Fisher Public Relations:

- Create a holiday: Why shouldn't February be National Roofing Month—even if it's only on your signs, banners, and advertising?
- Write a book: So what if it is self-published and you give it away rather than sell it? It still establishes you as an expert.
- Win a business award.
- Get on a reality show or game show: Even a three-sentence introduction can mention that you are the owner of XZY Plumbing in Sarasota, Florida.
- Put on an educational workshop: Ginger's Quilt Shop of Upland, California, offers all sorts of free or reduced price classes in quilting or related activities and if you happen to want to buy your supplies at her shop, that's fine.
- Produce an electronic newsletter: Realtors are great at sending out newsletters all about buying, maintaining, and selling houses and just mentioning that if your plans include buying or selling, to let them know.
- Create a contest with a twist: A camera shop could run a contest for the worst picture ever taken. A veterinarian could offer a free checkup for the homeliest pet.
- Do pro bono work: Clients who get your service for free also practice word-of-mouth advertising.

in a neighborhood where your target market lives and plays. This spreads good will among the local community and might even be picked up in the press. If a community group has a program which would attract your target market, approach the group about sponsorship. Unexpected money is often the most persuasive to sponsored organizations.

donations
Monetary or other gifts to organizations or people who are in need.

Donations are the other paying forward approach, and do not need to be millions of dollars. Products that are nearing expiration, returns, or slightly out of specification may be donated to shelters or other nonprofits. Time maybe donated to read books for the blind; small cash or product donations to local theaters will get your name in the program. Some of these will not result in instant publicity, but can be worked into company history or biographical information.[39] In addition, donations can have tax benefits for your business.

There is another approach for building positive public awareness of your business—creating a publicity event. This works best if it is tied into what you sell. Additionally, it is likely to get more press if the idea is not seen as self-promotion. For example, Immaculate Baking Company baked the world's largest cookie—100 feet in diameter and 40,000 pounds. This put it in the *Guinness Book of World Records* but also generated publicity. What made it even better was that Immaculate Baking tied this into a fundraiser for the construction of a local folk art museum. Sales went from about $500,000 to over 7 million and the museum gained $20,000 in donations.[40] Even simple approaches can pay handsome dividends. Hold an open house or a tour. Have a booth at a local street fair. Celebrate Grover Cleveland's birthday with special activities throughout the day. You can even hold seminars or programs on issues of immediate interest when your firm has topical expertise, or you can give your site to the media as a place to film outside of the studio, but if you do, make sure your signs are visible. These approaches are not the only ones possible. Others can be found in The Thoughtful Entrepreneur: Tips for Generating Publicity.

Two Ways to Generate Publicity[41]

Even though it may be the latest innovation on the market, a newsworthy product, event, or service always benefits from well-planned publicity. Aside from advertising, there are several tools that can help your news gather a piece of the limelight.

1. Write or provide materials:

- Offer exclusive articles, photos, or columns to publications that are read by your target audience.
- Offer (through a national service) ready-to-reproduce, typeset feature stories to smaller newspapers (**mat releases**, color pages).
- Not-for-profit organizations can produce public service announcements for broadcast, print, and other media.
- Produce and distribute video or audio news releases for the broadcast media.
- Produce your own program or short feature for the broadcast media. Depending on distribution rights, this might also be used as a video brochure or for other groups.
- Include your products as props for films and TV shows (consider whether the show's message would help or hinder your product's image).

mat release
A news release that is typeset and thus may be photographically reproduced for inclusion in a newspaper.

2. Conduct interviews:

- Appear on local TV talk shows or radio call-in shows.
- Hire a professional spokesperson to make appearances and talk about your product or service.
- Take your message to the media on a multicity media tour.

Having a great product or service does not do you or your business any good if potential customers do not know about it. Getting the word out about your business and its offerings is the purpose of promotion in small business. The avenues for getting the word out are fairly well known—current or potential customers, the press, and these days the Internet—but because everyone knows those avenues, crafting and distributing a message that people will notice and respond to amid all the ads they face is an ever-increasing challenge. This chapter focuses on preparing you with the basic skills of press and public relations, as well as advice on what makes promotion efforts pay off. Armed with these ideas, you *can* make your business stand out and be noticed. The other key role of this chapter is to discuss the specifics of selling—how to get started and how to close sales. In the end, sales are everything, because everything in business depends on sales. If you can master promotion and selling, your business will have gone much of the way toward eventual success.

Vermont Teddy Bear Company, whose products are pictured, promotes their merchandise primarily through radio spots. What marketing and promotion research factors do you think have motivated their choice to focus on radio advertising as their main avenue of generating publicity?

LO7 Apply the key skills involved in personal selling, especially closing the sale.

The Process of Personal Selling[42]

One of the most important jobs an entrepreneur can do is being a good salesperson for his or her product or service. Who knows more about your firm than you do? Who believes in it so much to put all the time and effort into getting it launched?

Personal selling has the advantage that you can be flexible in your presentation. If the current customer is a technophobe, emphasize ease of use. If he loves technology, let him know that he'll be on the cutting edge. Personal selling allows you to find out the buyers' main concerns and address them; in advertising you can only guess. Personal selling allows you to find out from clients what future features they may want to see.

personal selling
The process of selling your products and service; includes prospect and evaluate, prepare, present, close, and follow-up.

While selling may be thought of as an art, there is a general formula for generating interest in your product or service:

1. **Prospect and evaluate:** A good salesperson will collect background information and prepare to present. This could start months ahead of a sales call by making sure that you are thoroughly informed about your product and what it can or cannot do. Of course, the entrepreneur knows all that, but may need to study up on some of the technical terms used in the field. In hiring a new salesperson, this step may be lengthier. In addition, putting together a list of potential clients (called "prospecting") takes place. Here is another case when thoroughly knowing your target market is key and critical. In some firms, this may be as simple as who walks in the door. How do you find these prospects? Here's where using a referral form can be a good idea. Ask all satisfied customers of the names of people they know who may potentially need or want your product. Customers may prospect themselves by asking for more information after finding your website

Entrepreneurs are, in a sense, always selling their company/product/service. Being skilled in personal selling is important for many reasons. What elements of the process of personal selling are you confident in? Are there elements you think you need to practice?

or responding to a direct mail advertisement. You may buy mailing lists of prospective clients as well. (See Chapter 11 for more information about direct mail and mailing lists.)

2. **Prepare:** Preparation means finding out what you can about the clients before approaching them. In business-to-business selling, you may be able to check out their website and find out more about what sorts of products the potential client makes. This will help you decide how you may want to pitch your product. What seems to be critical to them? Is it state-of-the-art technology or quality or cost? Prequalifying means cleaning up your list to remove potential clients that are unable or unlikely to buy your product. The reasons for excluding will vary from firm to firm but might include financial status, having just purchased a competitive product, legal issues (e.g., to whom you can or cannot sell), and the like. At the end of this phase, the initial contact is made or the appointment is set up. Once again, check your intended sales pitch for jargon or terms and phrases the customer is unlikely to understand. You want your argument to be compelling and logical for the customer and the sooner the customer can see the potential advantages, the more likely you are to successfully close the sale. What do you offer that is better than the competition? Go back to your value proposition and make sure you are correctly communicating it.[43] This stage is certainly a bit harder than consumer selling where the potential customers may often just walk into your place of doing business. Some of the best salespeople in handling these sorts of clients are found in the computer and electronics industry. They usually start off with a few questions to hone in on information to help them make their pitch. ("Will you use your new computer for gaming, Internet searching, or word processing?" "Do you have a budget in mind?" "Who will be using this computer: you or your child?")
3. **Present:** During the presentation phase, the salesperson presents a logical and compelling argument for purchasing their product. The more information he or she is able to obtain in the preparation phase, the better she or he is able to address potential concerns and point out specific features. Most salespeople emphasize the needs or wants their product can satisfy. You don't sell features; you sell benefits. Presentations should be rehearsed and facts memorized, but the presentation should never appear canned. A good salesperson can and will adapt his presentation to his audience. Note that this is similar to suggestions in Chapter 8 on how to prepare and present an elevator pitch. It is much the same type of selling. Establishing a personal relationship helps. Take an interest in what the client likes. Be prepared to spend a few minutes in idle chitchat (but don't waste their time; if they want to chat, fine, but when they want to get to business, switch gears immediately). For walk-in clients, introduce yourself and if they give you their name, use it. Find out a little bit about them in the approach. (Remember the computer salesperson mentioned above.) Try to establish rapport—an emotional connection between you and the other person. Even simple statements like "I know what you mean; I hate that, too" make the client feel that you understand. Use technological language appropriate for your audience.
4. **Close:** As you begin to wrap-up your presentation, you will likely encounter objections as customers also anticipate the close of the sales pitch and the coming request for purchase. Customers nearly always have objections and the good salesperson is prepared to answer these objections. "Certainly the price is higher than our competitor's, but we have 20 percent less downtime, making our product much more cost effective." Once the material has been presented and the objections answered, the salesperson needs to close the sale. The close is the commitment from the customer. There are a number of techniques including:

   - **Trial close** ("Which credit card would you like to use to pay for that?")
   - **Assumptive close** ("I'll just need your credit card for payment.")
   - **Urgency close** ("This rate will end at the end of the day.")
   - **Alternate choice close** ("Would you prefer the standard or deluxe model?")
   - **Chances-are close** (Customer asks to think about it and you say "What are the chances you will buy later?")
   - **Make-a-suggestion close** (Offer a waffling customer suggestions on why it is a good idea to buy.)
   - **Try-before-you-buy close** (Offer a trial period, if your business can handle that.)
   - **What-will-it-take close** ("What will it take to close this deal?")

   Additional closing techniques are discussed in the Skill Module 10.3.

SKILL MODULE 10.3

The Art of Closing[44]

Columnist Cord Cooper of *Investor's Business Daily* has made a career of gathering tips on closing sales. His suggestions include:

- **"Restate the need."** As Barbara Corcoran, chairman of The Corcoran Group, a $2.5 billion New York City real estate firm, and author of the book *Use What You've Got* suggests, get the customer's requirements and restate them. If you can do a better job of explaining the customer's needs, so much the better. Other examples of Cooper's widely respected advice include:
- **Listen.** It seems obvious, but it is the key to everything. Don't interrupt and listen for what seems important to the customer. Note needs your product can meet (and those it can't) and include the former in your response.
- **"When would you want it?"** This question is a great way to determine the degree of urgency the customer faces. Something needed "tomorrow" means making the sale now and could help the customer feel better.
- **Get feedback.** The more a customer will tell you about what they like and dislike, the better you can tailor your sales effort.
- **Handle buyer's remorse.** If someone is buying a big-ticket item, they might get nervous about the money they're spending. While you're there, reinforce their desire for the product by going over the benefits. Consider telling them of others' positive experiences, and think about calling them the next day to reinforce the benefits and value.
- **Sell the result.** Show customers specific beneficial outcomes from their use of your product.
- **Use more than one outcome.** High quality items last longer and are more prestigious—use both benefits if they fit your customer's needs. Consider outcomes like service, delivery, financing terms, warranties, and extras in addition to cost.
- **Take strategic advantage.** This is done in several ways. Bring your assistant along to show you're important and to have another pair of eyes. Ask to be last so you don't have to compete with anyone else. And above all, practice. "Role-playing puts your inhibitions to rest and results in a well-prepared, confident delivery," says Corcoran, who started her firm with just $1,000.
- **Be patient.** Often if you ask for a decision before they are ready, the answer is "No."
- **Accumulate "yeses."** The more items you and the customer agree on, the more likely they are to agree to the sale. Arrange the discussion of needs and benefits to generate a lot of information, and a lot of yeses.
- **Counter positively.** When you hear something that makes you want to say "No," or "Yes, but," try instead to phrase your response as "Yes, and ... " to show agreement.

5. **Follow-up:** Finally, the close is not the end of the sale. The important objective of follow-up is to make your customer feel at ease. Do this by staying with the clients for a few minutes postsale and get to know them. Have you ever bought something only to start second-guessing yourself in a couple days? Maybe you should have at least checked out the competition? Maybe you should have waited until it was on sale? This is known as **cognitive dissonance** and happens frequently especially with more expensive items or purchases that are considered risky. A good salesperson will often contact you during this time to reiterate all the good qualities of your purchase and to reassure you that you did indeed make a good decision. This is also a good time to ask for referrals. Follow-up may also include activities from others in your firm such as installation, warranty work, financing, and the like. Building long-term relationships is the key to successful business and taking care of a customer postpurchase goes a long way to building them.[45]

cognitive dissonance
Doubt that occurs after a purchase has been made. An inconsistency between experience and belief.

LO8 Recognize the major approaches to customer relationship management.

Customer Retention: Succeeding after the Sale

Every sale gives you the most valuable resource any business can get—a customer. It sounds obvious, but once you have been in business awhile you will learn that it is easier and more profitable to sell to existing customers than to prospect and attempt to sell to people who are not your customers. How much easier? Literally five times easier, according to the research. Research shows it costs five times as much to get a purchase from a new customer compared to an existing one.[46] Or try it this way—what is the easiest way to increase your profits 100 percent? Again, according to the research, just keep one more customer out of every 20, i.e., increase your retained customers by 5 percent.[47]

The name for the general approach to keeping customers is called **customer retention** (CM) for short. CM focuses on satisfying your customers after the sale, and managing your marketing efforts with customers to maximize their loyalty to and purchases from your business. There are two major elements to CM. One is handling problems that crop up after a sale, and the other called **customer relationship management** (CRM), which focuses on the longer-term monitoring and promotion of customer interest and loyalty.

customer retention
Techniques that focus on efforts to promote satisfaction with and interest in the firm.

customer relationship management (CRM)
The process of tracking the customer's different contacts with the firm, and using this data to help improve sales as well as the customer's experience.

Handling Postsale Problems

While "customer service" is one of the truisms of why small businesses are better than large ones, this is hardest to sustain when dealing with postsale complaints. Small business is usually a personal business, so it is hard not to take complaints personally. But in the end, the ultimate test of any business is how it handles adversity, and complaints are probably the most frequent example of that ultimate test.

In reality, some complaints are justified[48]—a product or service arrived late, did not live up to (or worse yet match) the description, did not reflect the quoted price or discounts, was lower quality than the customer was led to expect, or was delivered by an impolite, uncaring, or unprofessional worker. When this happens, your job is to make things right. Find out the details of what went wrong. Here your job is to sit and take it (and ideally ask for more) as your customer vents their frustration at you—it helps them to get it all out. Once they are done, talk to them about what you are prepared to do to make things right. Your goal is to come to an arrangement that the customer thinks is fair. Keep in mind the value of a lifetime of this customer's purchases to help you realize how far you should go to keep them happy. A few days later, follow up with a call to make sure the customer is satisfied—in fact, see if you can leverage it into another sale.

But it is also true that you will face customers with unjustified complaints. There is no magic phrase which disarms these explosive situations.[49] Your job is to remain calm and stay focused on what you are willing to do. Some ways to handle this sort of problem include:

- Appeal to the customer's sense of fair play, saying you want to do what is right.
- Consider offering a compromise, giving them some (but not all) of what they seek.
- Suggest involving a third party like the Better Business Bureau to arbitrate.
- Consider politely standing firm only when the facts unquestionably back you up.
- Also consider politely standing firm when the demand is clearly unreasonable.

Upset customers, like this woman, can get overwrought. How can you handle postsale problems when they arise?

When handling these complaints as a small business owner, it does not work to talk about "company policy" as a reason for inaction—as owner, you make the policies. It also never works to lose your cool and yell. It backs the customer into a corner (where you are likely to lose business if nothing else), and makes you look less professional. Finally, it does not work to argue with a customer. Winning these sorts of arguments may mean a rockier road with the customer in the future.

In the end, marketing is about sales, and in most businesses, the goal is to sell to the same customers again and again, as well as get those customers to recommend your business to their network. Doing this well over the long run requires mastering the 4 Ps (price, product, promotion, and place) as well as the postsale behaviors of CRM and handling complaints, but the goal is more and more satisfied customers, and in the end that is what business is all about. As Babson's Jeff Timmons says, "Happiness is a positive cash flow." And nothing generates cash like sales.

Strategies of CRM

What are the strategies behind CRM? These depend on what kind of customer you are seeking—new or existing—and what you are trying to sell them—a new product or one you already have. These variables lead to four approaches, seen in Figure 10.3. Selling the same products to the same customers is called a **market penetration** approach (this is what customer loyalty programs focus on developing), while selling the same customers a new product is called **product expansion** (this is central to the process called "upselling"). When selling to your existing customers, you have the benefit of being able to use data you have gathered in your prior customer contacts.

market penetration
A strategy whose goal is growth, based on selling more of the firm's product or service to the existing customer base.

product expansion
A strategy whose goal is growth, based on selling existing customers a product or service they have never bought before.

market expansion
A strategy whose goal is growth, based on selling in areas or to groups previously not served by the business.

diversification
A strategy whose goal is growth, based on adding new products or services to the firm's existing collection of offerings.

If you are looking at people who have not been customers, you might seek a **market expansion** strategy to sell your existing products to them (this is where prospecting comes in), or a **diversification** strategy if you are trying to sell them newly developed products (e.g., your new lines). In such cases, you might get prospects' contact information from referrals by existing customers (the approach likely to give you the best results), purchases of mailing or customer lists from marketing list big businesses like Dun & Bradstreet or Donnelly or from smaller specialized list firms like Direct Media or USADATA, or from organizations whose members might be particularly interested in your product or service (e.g., a local kennel club's member list if you had a pet grooming business).

Steps in CRM

Entrepreneurs have always tracked their customers. It could be as simple as a 3 × 5 index card with the customer's name and contact information on it, their family members' names, perhaps their sizes, and what major items they've bought and when. Today, of course, we use computers or web-based services to handle these kinds of chores, but the basic ideas remain the same, and the analysis of customer data is easier and more powerful than the previous generation of entrepreneurs could ever have imagined. This modern computerized approach is called customer relationship management (CRM). As in the old days, the necessities are pretty much the same: (1) Gathering the data, (2) Analyzing the data, and (3) Delivering CRM-driven marketing efforts to increase sales.

FIGURE 10.3

The Strategies of Market Growth

Source: William O. Bearden, Thomas N. Ingram, and Raymond W. Laforge, *Marketing: Principles and Perspectives* (4th ed.), (Burr Ridge: McGraw-Hill/Irwin, 2004), p. 57.

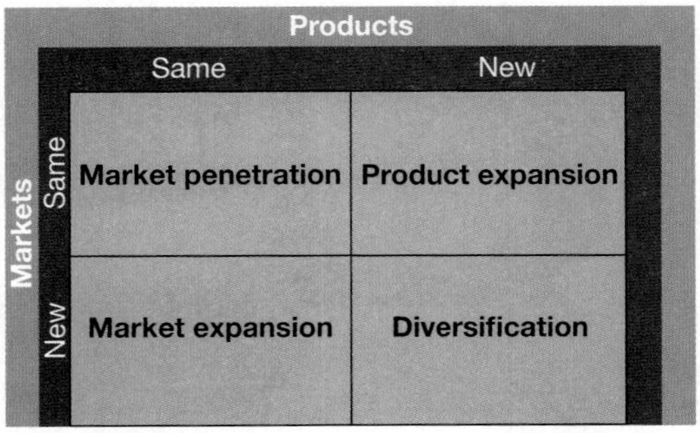

Markets \ Products	Same	New
Same	Market penetration	Product expansion
New	Market expansion	Diversification

Step 1: Gathering the Data

The key to CRM is the data on current or prospective customers. Given the power of repeat selling, the most valuable data comes from your existing customers. For all existing customers you want two kinds of data—contact data and performance data. Contact data gives you the particulars on your customers while performance data gives you information on the date and type of contact, since in many sales situations, it can take repeated contacts before a sale is made.

Some of this information might be entered by the customer, for example, when they are buying online or filling out a delivery form in your store, or it could be done by you or an employee. As noted above, when you are building a prospect database for your CRM efforts, the names and contact data usually come from a variety of sources outside of your firm.

If you look at the contact data in Table 10.2, you will see that many of the contact fields are the ones you find in an Outlook contact record. For contact data, Outlook or related software can provide a ready-made starting point; also note that Microsoft offers an Outlook add-on called Business Contact Manager and a stand-alone program called Dynamics CRM which add more functionality. However, today there is a tremendous range of software available for CRM.[50] For example, people use specialized software such as Sage's ACT! Software for managing contact data, often connecting it with accounting software like Peachtree or Quickbooks to tie contact and performance data together. You can also build your own database in Microsoft Access or Excel (or in the free open source alternatives found in OpenOffice).

If you prefer a polished solution, you can use the sophisticated CRM offerings from companies like Salesforce.com or Siebel, which typically offer a web-based approach for a monthly fee. There are also open source solutions for CRM such as Sugar (www.sugarcrm.com) or OpenCRX (www.opencrx.org). There are also free versions of commercial packages like the personal version of Etelos CRM for Google Apps. A Google search for "open source" CRM will get you a quick listing of free open-source, as well as for-fee, commercial CRM applications.

In designing your database, separate the items which only need to be entered once (like most of the Contact Data) from items which need to be added each time, like the purchases and especially promises made to a customer (such as additional materials or information, or some action like help). This reduces the time burden on you and your employees when recording the sale, and increases the likelihood that the data essential to your CRM effort actually makes it into the database. Often, you can tie in your inventory (which has the product or service information) and point-of-sale system (which records the sale, method of payment, etc.) to the CRM system so the number of fields you need to enter for each sale is dramatically reduced.

Step 2: Analyzing the Data

In the end, the kind of analyses you want to be able to perform are ones which give you a **customer vector** which is a type of data report from your CRM database which lets you summarize information by date, by product or service being sold, by groups of customers (e.g., all firms in NAICS 453310—antique dealers, all customers from California), or by the purchases of an individual person or firm. An example of a customer vector for individuals is given in Figure 10.4.

customer vector
A type of CRM report which segments by customer (or customer group) on purchases or dates of purchase.

Reports such as this can help you decide how to operate several key aspects of your marketing effort. If you track sales by purchase basis, you can tell which of your advertising efforts resulted in the most sales, so it makes it easier to decide which marketing efforts to continue or expand. If you link sales and purchase basis to the type of customer (by industry, location, education, or age) you might figure how to better target ads or promotions to particular types of customers. If you look at customer source basis and purchase, you might be able to tell which mailing lists produce the best returns. You could also find a product which has low quality by tracking sales organized by product and customer satisfaction. As these varied examples show, the possibilities are nearly endless, even with the basic data outlined here.

But perhaps the simplest and most important analysis is sales by customer. In marketing, there is a strong belief that 20 percent of your customers give you 80 percent of your sales. The key is identifying which customers are in that 20 percent and once you have, doing everything you can to keep them, and keep them happy. In the hustle and bustle of the day, you might come to believe that

TABLE 10.2 The Key Data of a CRM Database

Contact data

- **Person**
  - Unique customer ID number
  - Customer Name
  - Honorific (Mr., Ms., Dr., etc.)
  - Title (e.g., Purchasing Manager)
  - Firm Name (if it is a business customer)
  - NAICS or SIC code (if it is a firm)
  - Unique firm ID number (if it is a firm)
  - Basic Demographics (age, gender, and other data specific to your business, such as sizes for clothing firms, education for professional training firms, etc.)
- **Location**
  - Mailing address (business and personal if possible)
  - Preferred mailing address
  - Phone numbers (work, cell, and home if possible)
  - E-mail
- **Source**
  - Sales
  - Referral from Customer (give customer ID)
  - Mailing List (specify which one)

Performance Data

- Purchases
  - Date
  - Product or Service
    - Product/Service Name
    - Product/Service ID Number (e.g., Model N475, Service 16—this helps if you plan to do quantitative analyses)
    - Quantity Purchased
    - Price
    - Any Discounts/Coupons/etc. applied
    - Sales setting (online, in-store, at a show or fair, etc.)
  - Related Purchases (e.g., delivery, set-up, refills, warranty)
  - Purchase basis (walk-in, saw paper ad 1, paper ad 2, online ad 1, online ad 2, handbill 1, handbill 2, referral from customer—and give the customer's ID number)
- **Relations**
  - Other visits without purchases
  - Website visits without purchases
  - Telephone contacts
  - Other personal contacts
- **Follow-Through**
  - Follow-up
    - What was done, when
    - Was customer satisfied? If not, why and how was it handled?
  - Materials or actions promised to a customer
  - Reasons (new product arrival) or times (e.g., start of school year) to contact this customer

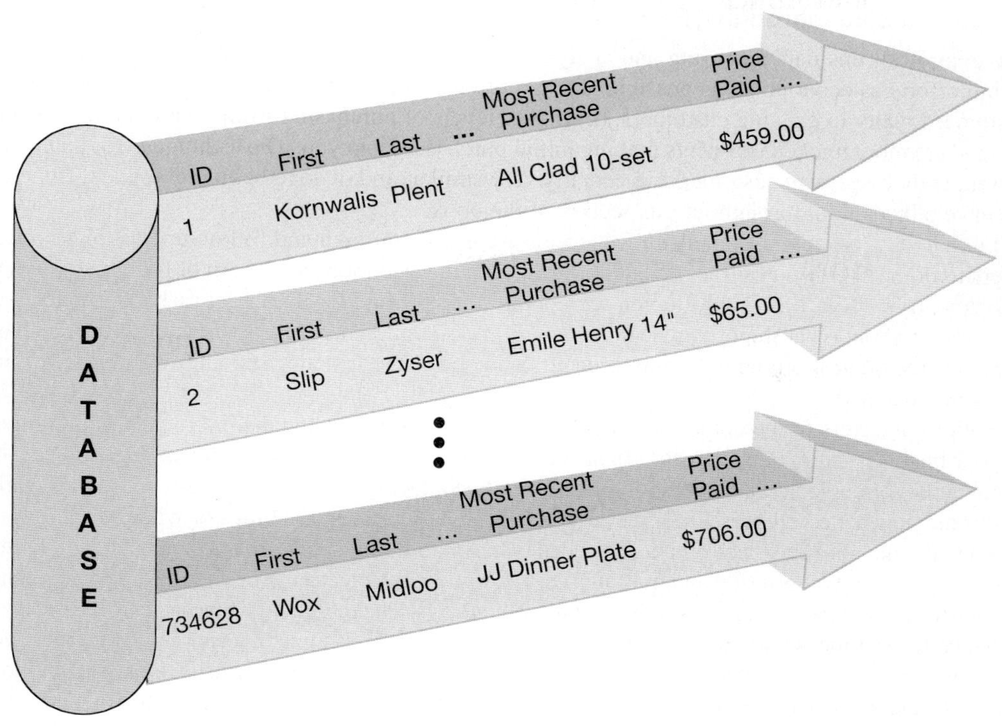

FIGURE 10.4

Example of a Customer Vector Report from a CRM Database

Source: Rafi A. Mohammed, Robert J. Fisher, Bernard J. Jaworski, and Gordon J. Paddison, *Internet Marketing* (2nd ed.), (Burr Ridge: McGraw-Hill/Irwin, 2004), p. 658.

the loudest or most demanding people are your biggest customers, but often a sales-by-customer analysis lets you identify quiet, easygoing customers who are nonetheless major purchasers, and who are the ones you would otherwise be most likely to overlook.

Customer analysis can get significantly more complex, and there are whole courses and segments of the marketing profession focused on performing and interpreting those complex analyses. However, you can get your own 80 percent of benefit from performing the simple basic 20 percent of analysis outlined here.

SMALL BUSINESS INSIGHT

UNION NATIONAL COMMUNITY BANK[51]

Union National Community Bank (UNCB) in tiny Mount Joy, Pennsylvania, was founded in 1853, and pretty much had the local market to itself until the big national banks moved in during the 1990s. Facing competitors offering more and better services and lower rates, UNCB lost customers. Although they lowered their loan rates and offered higher returns for deposits, they could not make up the lost business. Then the bank installed a CRM system and had a revelation when they saw a report of customers segmented by how profitable they were. With this information in hand, the bank identified the customers most important to the bottom line, and offered those people more of the services they had shown they liked. Less profitable customers were directed to services like electronic banking, which in turn helped make even this segment profitable. The CRM approach helped turn the bank's fortunes around, with more than $1 million in increased revenue, and a profit increase of 35 percent. For UNCB, CRM made a big difference.

Increasing Sales through CRM

The goal of all this data gathering and analysis is to increase your sales and help make your marketing efforts as economical as possible. The proof of a CRM effort is seen in (1) higher levels of customer loyalty in existing customers, (2) higher levels of purchasing from your existing customers, and (3) more tracked prospects making initial purchases from you. The techniques for managing current and prospective customers are actually very similar, and tie together many of the techniques we have talked about throughout this section of the book.

Fundamentally, the keys to customer service are follow-through and follow-up. Follow-through refers to doing what you said you would do. If a customer mentions a concern or problem, you will of course try to fix it. But too often entrepreneurs or their employees can get rushed, and delay or even forget about what they promised customers. If you remember to keep up your CRM database (which is the biggest problem for entrepreneurs), a good CRM system will remind you of the promises you have made.

Follow-up refers to the contacts you periodically make with customers in order to remind them of your business, and your interest in their business. This can be done through personal contacts by phone, mail, or personal visits, although increasingly contact is done electronically through e-mails, electronic newsletters, discussion lists, or interactive web services like blogs or wikis.

The advantage of the electronic approaches is they can dramatically lower the cost of marketing efforts, by saving you printing and mailing costs. Additionally, electronic marketing aids can get into your customers' hands in minutes or hours rather than days. The interactive approaches also give you a chance to hear ideas and concerns from customers directly and immediately, giving you a chance to resolve problems quickly and even get new prospects for products and services to offer from those who have the need. The essential aspect of follow-up is to take the initiative to stay in contact.

If you can get a customer's e-mail address, there are a wide variety of low-cost or free services you can use. For electronic newsletters, there are services such as Benchmark, StreamSend, or Constant Contact, which run from $5 to $30 a month for a mailing list of 1,000, and offer free trials. These services can also be used for e-mail campaigns, along with free services like Google Apps (www.google.com/a/) or BlueTie Free (www.bluetie.com).

Note that there are ethical and legal concerns in doing mass e-mailings to current or prospective customers. While the CAN-SPAM act lets you contact people with whom you have done business, sending unwanted e-mail is not something which will endear you to your customers. It works best if you ask customers' permission to e-mail them. It also means they are more likely to treat your e-mails as real and not spam to be blocked by their e-mail service. There are other aspects of e-mailing you should check on, and you can get the latest details at the Federal Trade Commission website (http://business.ftc.gov/advertising-and-marketing/online-advertising-and-marketing).

Follow-up can be periodic, based on the time elapsed since a customer's last purchase, or based on a fixed schedule, such as Spring/Summer/Fall/Winter or a holiday schedule. It can also be based on aspects of your firm, for example, when your new shipments arrive, or when you are the first in town to have a particular product. It can even be based on targets of opportunity. For example, if a big movie event occurs like the opening of one of the *Pirates of the Caribbean* movies, you might do a follow-up promotion based on pirate-themed products or a pirate-themed gathering.

By linking follow-up efforts to customer sales, you can identify which follow-ups work best—and even how long they take to work. When you convert a prospect into a customer through your follow-ups, the CRM data can tell you how you found them, and from there you can even figure out which approaches give you the most value (in terms of sales made) for the money spent on the promotional effort.

Remember that the goal of CRM is to increase sales. One way is to remind customers about your business. Anything which reminds existing customers of prior positive purchasing experiences helps bring them back to you. Anything which helps you open, maintain, or expand your relationship with the customer eventually helps bring them back for additional purchases. And anything that helps you identify your most profitable customers helps you concentrate your most valuable resource, your time, on those people and firms whose business can make the biggest difference in your business's bottom line.

CHAPTER SUMMARY

LO1 Describe the marketing funnel and why promotion is so important.

- The marketing funnel relates promotional impressions to firm sales.
- The value of promotion is directly tied to the sales it produces.

LO2 Develop your value proposition.

- Craft your value proposition to present your firm's unique selling points.
- Tailor your value proposition to the needs of your intended customers.

LO3 Segment and further define your target audience.

- Aim for a narrow segment (or portion) of the market.
- Develop a profile of the needs of your target market.
- Match your product or service and promotion to your target market's needs.

LO4 Recognize the different approaches and methods you can use to craft and convey your promotional message.

- Follow the basic methods for conveying your message.
- The Internet provides a variety of free ways to advertise your business, such as blogs, and free business pages on Facebook, LinkedIn, and Twitter.
- Other free approaches include word of mouth, referrals, using local bulletin boards, and going where your customers are to pitch your business.
- The basic paid methods include:
    - Business cards, brochures, flyers, and signage.
    - Advertising in the media outlets.
    - Publicity and press kits.
    - Website.
    - Network advertising.

LO5 Describe how to develop a press relations program.

- Small businesses want to positively influence or increase media coverage.
- It helps to focus on media seen by your target market.
- A press release is the critical way to inform the media about your business.
- Press kits add material to the press release that reporters or editors would find useful.
- The structure of a press release includes:
    - Headline.
    - Opening paragraph.
    - Body.
    - Closing paragraph.
- Make your press release draw attention and catch the eye of the average reader.
- Make use of the resources for e-mailing press releases.
- The essentials of determining what news is newsworthy include:
    - Public recognition.
    - Importance.
    - Interest.

LO6 Explain how to develop a public relations program.

- Contribute stories, sponsorships or donations to help build public relations.
- Create a publicity event to focus attention on your business.
- There are two ways to generate publicity coverage:
    - Write or provide materials.
    - Conduct interviews.

LO7 Apply the key skills involved in personal selling, especially closing the sale.

- Recognize the importance of personal selling.
- Key processes of personal selling include prospect and evaluate, prepare, present, and close.
- The art of closing the sale includes:
    - Restate the need. "When would you want it?"
    - Get feedback. Forewarn customers about buyer's remorse.
    - Practice.
    - If your buyer gets cold feet, unfurl more benefits.

- Weigh the angles before you start. Don't outbid yourself when bidding on a project—counter with care.
- Accumulate "Yeses."
- Follow up the sale (in order to stimulate referrals, encourage repurchasing, and prevent cognitive dissonance).

LO8 Recognize the major approaches to customer relationship management.

- Handling complaints impersonally is a particular challenge in small businesses.
- Complaints can be justified or unjustified.
- The goal in resolving all complaints is to keep good customers satisfied with your firm.
- Post-sale success depends on customer relationship management (CRM) and handling complaints.
- CRM today is driven by keeping and analyzing data on existing and prospective customers.
- CRM analyses can identify the most profitable customers and products.

KEY TERMS

impression, 308
sales leads, 308
prospects, 308
marketing funnel, 308
value proposition, 309
word-of-mouth, 309
segmentation, 310
target market, 310
predetermined market segments, 313
succinct message, 315
promotional mix, 316
advertising, 316
domain name, 318
search engine optimization, 320
keyword and description tags, 320
viral marketing, 321
free ink, 321
sales promotion, 323
press relations, 324
press release, 325
press kit, 328
newsworthy events, 328
public recognition, 328
issue recognition, 328
trendiness, 328
proximity, 328
public importance, 328
power, 329
currency, 329
public interest, 329
good story, 329
human interest, 329
visuals, 329
cultural resonance, 329
public relations, 329
publicity, 329
sponsorships, 329
donations, 330
mat release, 331
personal selling, 332
cognitive dissonance, 334
customer retention, 335
customer relationship management (CRM), 335
market penetration, 336
product expansion, 336
market expansion, 336
diversification, 336
customer vector, 337

DISCUSSION QUESTIONS

1. What are some ways that you see small business owners promote their products or services? Provide examples of your perception of their value proposition to each of the markets they are currently targeting. In your opinion, how effective do you think some of their messages are?
2. In your opinion, what do you think is the most effective and efficient way for small business owners to promote and market their products or services? Why?
3. How have you seen the use of referrals and word-of-mouth advertising work to the benefit of a small business owner? Provide examples. How have these methods worked in reverse

(to the disadvantage of the owner, but possibly to the benefit of the competition)?

4. Recall the last time you purchased a product or service from a small firm. Did it use any of the techniques or skills involved in personal selling? How did the salesperson close the sale with you?

5. If you were consulting for a small firm, what advice would you give to the owner on how to write a press release? What specific tips would you give him or her on ways that they could generate publicity for the business?

6. Imagine you sold someone a new movie DVD in a factory-sealed package, and a day later they bring it in for a refund, saying the movie does not play, and they no longer want to see it. It works fine on the DVD players in your store. You suspect they just pirated the DVD and want their money back. How would you resolve their complaint? If the DVD had an obvious scratch on its playing surface, would it make any difference in how you would resolve the complaint?

EXPERIENTIAL EXERCISES

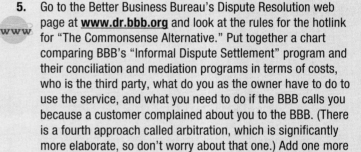

1. Collect promotional materials from a small business in your area. These can include coupons, loyalty programs, special tie-ins, special events, advertisements, or any other promotional materials. Using these materials, answer the following questions:
   - What is the owner trying to achieve with these promotions? What are the goals and objectives of each? If you take the various promotions as a portfolio, what overall goal do they have?
   - What incentives (for the customer) are embedded in the promotion materials?
   - What business image or business characteristics do these promotions convey or imply?
   - Assuming limited funds, how would you improve the promotions for this business? Be sure to tie your ideas to specific goals.
2. Compare the promotional materials from two competitive (small) businesses. What are the goals and objectives of the promotions? How well do you think they fulfill these objectives?
3. Visit three independently owned small retail establishments in the same industry or business. Ask the manager of each business the following questions. What target market(s) does your store appeal to? How are the target markets different? If I were a member of your target market, why would I shop at your store? What new information from your research about the industry can the owners use to improve and enhance what they are currently offering? Or how are they promoting their business based on the latest trends within the industry?
4. Read your local newspaper for information about a small business that you think stems from a publicity effort (e.g., new location or management, product line shift or expansion, special events, or promotions). Compare the information in the article to website information and to business advertisements for the same business. What are the differences and similarities? Advantages and disadvantages (for the business and for the customer)?
5. Go to the Better Business Bureau's Dispute Resolution web page at **www.dr.bbb.org** and look at the rules for the hotlink for "The Commonsense Alternative." Put together a chart comparing BBB's "Informal Dispute Settlement" program and their conciliation and mediation programs in terms of costs, who is the third party, what do you as the owner have to do to use the service, and what you need to do if the BBB calls you because a customer complained about you to the BBB. (There is a fourth approach called arbitration, which is significantly more elaborate, so don't worry about that one.) Add one more row comparing what steps you would take from the start to be ready to use each of these BBB services if you needed them.

6. Imagine that you own a small independent bookstore. You are holding a special reading and book signing by a well-known author:
   a. Describe what your goal(s) might be in arranging this event.
   b. Write a press release for the event.
   c. What other events might support the same goal(s)?
   d. Describe how you might use this information in crafting a newspaper advertisement for the store.
   e. Compare the press release, the ad, and any other events arranged in terms of overall promotional strategy for the store.

MINI-CASE

GOING VIRAL MAKES FOR A HEALTHIER FIRM[52]

Dr. Bob Wagstaff (a biochemist and nutritionist) developed the Orabrush to scrape bad breath–causing particles off of our tongue. He got the Orabrush patented and approved by the FDA. He got it manufactured and worked hard to get it onto the shelves of drugstores and supermarkets. He had some success with smaller chains, but sales were below his expectations. He tried making an infomercial, which cost him around $40,000, but it produced only a few hundred more Orabrush sales. Thinking bigger marketing clout would make the product into a success, he tried marketing the patent to oral hygiene companies, but no one took him up on his offer.

He went to a marketing class at Brigham Young University and received advice from students in the class. He hoped that the young people could tell him how to sell more Orabrushes over the Internet. A survey a class team conducted showed 92 percent of the respondents wouldn't buy an Orabrush online, and the students on the team concluded that the Internet approach was not workable. However, another student in the class, Jeffrey Harmon, had a different interpretation. Jeffrey suggested that with millions of people watching videos on the Internet every day, getting 8 percent of that group to buy an Orabrush would still be an enormous market. After class "Dr. Bob" asked Jeffrey to help him market Orabrush on the web, giving Jeffrey his old motorcycle as payment. Jeffrey recruited a coworker named Austin Craig to be the video's pitchman for $100. He got scriptwriter friend Joel Ackerman to write the script and film major Devin Graham to film the video. Total cost? About $500. It was actually recorded in the back room of a pool hall—so that really is a clinking sound in the background of the video. The video went viral on YouTube, racking up millions of views and igniting sales of the Orabrush, with close to 1 million brushes sold over the next 2 years.

Note: Videos related to the case:

Story of Orabrush: **www.youtube.com/watch?v=p4tuTi8_z6Q&feature=relmfu**

Original YouTube Video:

www.youtube.com/watch?v=nFeb6YBftHE&feature=list_related&playnext=1&list=SPB73276F91DD26C78

CASE DISCUSSION QUESTIONS

1. Why do you think a YouTube video worked better than a professionally done infomercial?
2. How were Dr. Bob and Jeffrey able to get so much done for so little money? How could you apply this in starting your own business?
3. Dr. Bob had tried traditional media and pursuing traditional outlets for the Orabrush. Why do you think his sales were not up to his expectations?
4. Explain how having 8 percent of the potential market to draw from could still be a worthwhile strategy for a small business.

SUGGESTED CASES AND ARTICLES

- Business Demise, C-11

Available on McGraw-Hill Create™

- Colonial Traditions, Inc.
- Pamela Spencer: Is the Customer Always Right?
- Benjamin's Bagels

SUGGESTED VIDEOS

www.mhhe.com/katz4e

Video Case:

- For a written video case and corresponding clip, visit the OLC at www.mhhe.com/katz4e and select "Chapter 10".
- Antipreneurs

SBTV.com Videos:

- Duct Tape Marketing—Marketing Materials That Educate
- Duct Tape Marketing—Lead Conversion
- Trade Shows—SEMA 2006 Miller Robbie Knievel Segment

STVP Videos:

- Understanding Your Customer
- How Do You Compete Against More Established Competitors?

CHAPTER

11 Small Business Distribution and Location

● Steve Niewulis's original marketing efforts focused on major sports stores. When that wasn't successful, he altered the way he marketed his product. Can you think of other methods which he might have employed to create interest in his product?

LEARNING OBJECTIVES

After you complete this chapter, you will be able to:

LO1 Recognize the different types of direct marketing and their pros and cons.

LO2 Learn how to do nondirect distribution.

LO3 Differentiate the types of international strategies.

LO4 Identify the factors to consider in selecting your business location.

LO5 Recognize the key issues in leasing.

LO6 Know what to look for in evaluating a potential site layout.

LO7 Understand the pros and cons of buying, building, or leasing.

Focus on Small Business: Steve Niewulis and Tap It!

Steve Niewulis, a minor league baseball player, came up with a solution to a problem all baseball players have—keeping the baseball bat handle dry between pitches. He invented Just Tap It!, a rosin bag attached to a wristband so a player could dry the bat handle between pitches. While it seemed like the perfect product for all the major sports stores, the stores were not interested because they prefer to buy from companies with several products in their product lines. Undeterred, he began attending trade shows and association meetings for high school coaches, tennis association meetings, and other similar venues. He was able to set up a booth displaying his product for just a few hundred dollars, and he created interest, recognition, and sales. At one show, he met up with Baseball Express, a catalog that targets high school, college, and minor league teams. Since he already had orders and customers using the product, he was able to show Baseball Express that this was a product it should carry. Niewulis's company, Tap It! now sells thousands of units to not only baseball players, but also to other sports, such as basketball, tennis, golf, and rock climbing.[1]

DISCUSSION QUESTIONS

1. Niewulis's original intent was to market to major sports stores. How would you describe the market he finally targeted? Is there a commonality?
2. What other methods could Niewulis use to get this product to his customers?
3. Would this method have worked as well had the product been something like baked goods? Or mural painting? What methods would work better for these sorts of products?

LO1 Recognize the different types of direct marketing and their pros and cons.

Distribution[2]

Other chapters have answered a lot of the "who," "what," "how," and "why" questions about small business; this chapter deals primarily with the "where." There are two basic "where" questions to be considered. The first one is, "Where are my customers?" In answering this question, you are primarily interested in figuring out how to get your product or service to them so that they have the opportunity to buy it. *Distribution* is the process of getting your product to the customer. The second question is, "Where should I be?" This question can be closely tied to the first—if your business is a restaurant, you need to be exactly where the customers are. Other businesses can be located at a distance from their customers—and often find advantages in doing so.

To help explain why **channels** are important to your marketing strategy and profits, think about the implications of the different channels shown in Figure 11.1. They differ in terms of the number of intermediaries between you and the eventual customer. Keep in mind that every one of the intermediaries will want to make a profit for selling your product or service, so they will each add their share to the price you sold to them. So you created a product that cost you $5 to make and sold it to an agent or to a retailer for $10 to resell. They want their profits, so they mark the price up to $20.

Realize that the more intermediaries you add, the higher the eventual price of your product. Also keep in mind that all of your profits are based on your first sale of the product. Hold that thought a second.

As the **manufacturer** of the good or service, you have the ability to set the **manufacturers' suggested retail price** of your product. To do this, you need to think of how many intermediaries are likely to be in the channels for your product. In the example above, with a single intermediary, your $5 product costs end consumers $20. That approach is called **direct sales,** and is a part of **direct marketing.** But what if there is a second intermediary, for example, from you to a wholesaler or distributor, who in turns sells to retailers? Not everyone doubles the price they paid for a product, but for this exercise, if they do double the price, then your $5 product costs consumers $40. If your product is popular, then everyone is happy—the consumers certainly are and because of their happiness, the retailers, wholesalers, and you are probably happy, too.

Because of the math of intermediaries in channels, the possibilities for direct marketing becomes more and more attractive. Why? Well, it would not be fair to all those intermediaries if you sold your product to the public for $10. In fact, doing so would pretty well assure that few intermediaries could compete with you and make a profit. But because you have set the retail price at $40 to keep your intermediaries happy, you too would sell to the public for $40, in which case instead of your usual $5 profit per product sold to other resellers, you are suddenly making $35 profit per sale! Done this way, your resellers are happy and not overly worried about you as a competitor, and you are happy because direct sales can be some of the most profitable ways for you to make sales. We go into direct marketing and direct sales in this chapter.

channels
People and firms who connect producers of goods and services with customers.

manufacturer
The entity which produces a product or service to be sold.

manufacturers' suggested retail price
A target price set by a manufacturer for a product or service intended to provide profit for each intermediary in the distribution channel.

direct sales
Methods of going directly to your customer in order to sell your product. Vending machines, door-to-door salespeople, leasing space at a craft fair, farmers' markets, party sales, and most industrial sales are methods of direct selling.

direct marketing
Selling your goods or services to consumers without intermediaries, typically to select customer groups and typically with tracking of the results.

FIGURE 11.1

Typical Distribution Channels

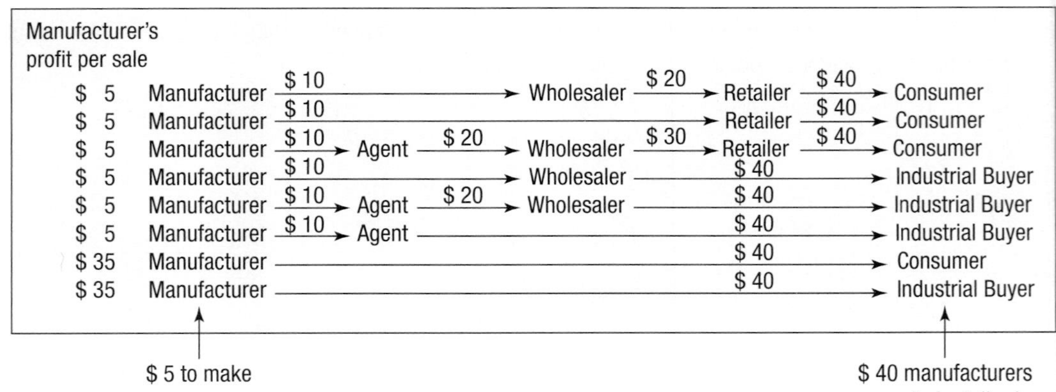

1154 Lill Studio began as a direct sale-based business, offering their custom-made handbags at parties, open houses, and direct appointments before branching out into stores and an online center. Building a strong customer base with the agility of direct selling helped owner Jen Velarde grow 1154 Lill into a successful business that truly taps into its market.

Direct Marketing

For many entrepreneurs—and larger firms as well—direct marketing is the way to go. It can be as simple as the child who sets up a lemonade stand in front of her or his home, or as complex as a four-color printed catalog with a mass mailing. Direct marketing can be relatively inexpensive. It also provides more control over where your product or service goes, the information that gets passed along to the consumer, how the product is used, and final pricing. You have already been introduced in Chapter 5 to several forms of direct marketing through the Internet, including eBay. Even having learned these, there remain about as many forms of direct marketing as there are entrepreneurial ideas, and some of the other more common ones are discussed below.

Word-of-Mouth[3]

This is a great way to get customers and is usually the first technique an entrepreneur uses. Word-of-mouth[4] is discussed in detail in Chapter 10.

Direct Sales

Direct sales (industrial, door-to-door, party sales, vending) can take several forms. This is the primary way of selling to businesses. A salesperson (often you) contacts industries, churches, schools—whatever type of business is likely to use your product or service—directly. The salesperson meets with the decision maker, presents the product, and hopefully makes a sale.

The lemonade stand mentioned above is also a form of direct sales, albeit a little less professional than you may want to be. A more polished approach is a booth at a local fair, cultural event, flea market, craft fair (all of which are discussed in Chapter 5), trade show, or association event. The cost of leasing space can be less than $100 for a local flea market to quite expensive for national trade shows. For a flea market, a simple card table may be appropriate, while the cost of a professional booth at a major trade show could easily be $100,000. The key here is to pick the event most likely to attract your target market and least likely to make a serious dent in your pocketbook. Start small and move up as you get more sales revenues.

Some of the other techniques discussed in Chapter 5 that are also direct sales methods include door-to-door sales (remember the Avon lady?), party sales (think Tupperware or Mary Kay), and vending machines. For products that need demonstrations or detailed explanations, door-to-door selling allows you to show consumers how your product works in their home. Part of the success of home sales is that it is hard for consumers to say no after the salesperson has spent some time in their home—it's just not hospitable. This method is made more difficult these days with dual-income families, because evenings are usually the only time to catch people. Consumers are often reluctant to invite strangers into their home, but you might be able to at least introduce yourself and leave behind information about your product or service. Avon used to sell predominately through door-to-door sales but has branched out into Internet, mail order, and mall kiosks sales in order to combat declining door-to-door sales for the reasons just mentioned.

Vending machines aren't appropriate for every product, but they do offer the flexibility of having your product available around the clock and at convenient locations for your customers. Vending machines are typical for less expensive, convenience products. The key to success is volume achieved with machines located everywhere. People are willing to pay extra in order to have the product readily available. Compare the price of a can of your favorite beverage from a vending machine to what you would pay in the grocery store. The disadvantages of vending machines are their high maintenance and vulnerability to vandalism.

Party sales usually require a range of similar items to be sold, and this kind of selling is not appropriate for every product. Typically, a host or hostess invites a number of friends and family members to his or her house, while a company representative (you, at first) demonstrates the product. Samples of the products as well as catalogs are available for all the guests to browse through, and orders are taken at the party for later delivery. Typical party sales products include everything from laundry aids to makeup to lingerie to cookware to housewares. Two of the disadvantages are the sanctity of the home and the reluctance of people to open up their homes to strangers (salespeople). As these parties take several hours of a salesperson's time and can usually be held only in the evening, one person is limited to how many parties (sales) a week he or she can handle. Generally, the successful companies using this method have hundreds of salespeople who earn a percentage of each sale they make. Many entrepreneurial firms have grown tremendously from a party sales approach—Mary Kay, Amway, Pampered Chef, and others.

Direct Mail and Its Variants[5]

direct mail
A method of selling in which catalogs, brochures, letters, videos, and other pieces of marketing materials are mailed directly to customers from which they can mail, call, or e-mail an order. Direct faxing and direct e-mailing are more modern forms of direct mail.

mail order
Sales made from ads in newspapers or magazines, with purchases made online or by phone as well as by mail.

Direct mail can take many forms—postcards, catalogs, videos, **mail orders**, sales letters, brochures, leaflets, CD-ROMs, faxes, e-mails, and many others. A variant of this, Internet-based direct mailing, is introduced in Chapter 5.

There are several advantages to the direct mail approaches: the ability to sell on your schedule, low costs for getting started (especially if you place your goods in others' catalogs or online), the ability to get by without major inventory investments, and the potential for selling to large markets. It plays well with customers too because they tend not to see direct mail as a form of home invasion (as they often do with door-to-door sales or telemarketing); they can read it at their leisure, and they have something they can set aside until they need it.

Of course, there are challenges to this approach including adequate preparation before selling, the need for writing and photography skills, and a way to get customers' attention. Perhaps the greatest challenge is the need to find the right market for your offering. In direct mail, market translates into getting the right mailing list or sales vehicle.

There are many companies that will sell you a list of addresses (even a list already typed on labels), and these are often available for virtually any target market you may choose. The cost of these lists can vary, but current rates are about $60 to $75 per thousand names. Try Focus USA (www.focus-usa-1.com), or Practical Marketing (www.practicalmarketing.net) or do an Internet search for direct mail lists. Also, professional organizations and clubs sometimes will sell their mailing lists for a relatively modest fee.

There are also low-budget ways of getting a mailing list. Often membership rosters are distributed to members of certain organizations. If such an organization meets your target market, you can have the list for the price of membership. One caution, though: Sometimes members are expressly forbidden to use these lists in any commercial way. However, if it truly is a product or service that a number of these members are likely to want and if it is a one-time "soft sell" mailing, you're probably okay.

Those sales vehicles mentioned above refer to the magazines, newspapers, or websites you select to display your mail order ads. If you are targeting doctors, advertising in the local newspaper would get you most of them, but you would also be paying for the ad to be seen by 98 percent of the readers who are not doctors. There are magazines and websites that focus on particular groups. These include the trade magazines you learned to find in Skill Module 3.1. For websites, a quick Google search of "doctor's websites" will get you quickly started. You can use a service like Alexa.com to check on the overall traffic to sites, although the magazines and sites themselves should give prospective advertisers like you more detailed information on their visitors.

The other challenges mentioned above relate to preparing an ad that does a good job of answering the customers' questions and entices them to buy. There are best practices for writing copy for ads and they are discussed in Skill Module 11.1.

Making Mail Order Ads Work[6]

SKILL MODULE 11.1

WRITING AD COPY

1. **Headlines are key:** Focus on the customer's needs, benefits, problems, or goals. Keep the headline short—five words or less. Scan the mail order ads of your newspaper or magazines to see what attracts your attention, and check the headlines of your competitors. Unless your company name is famous, its name should not go in the headline.
2. **Put the payoff up front:** If the customer doesn't see the payoff to them for using your product in the first sentence or two, they will give up and look elsewhere.
3. **Offer incentives:** In the body of your ad, consider putting in a discount ("Save 20 percent if you mention this ad!") or coupon to spur customers to action. Put an end date on the offer to move them along. A variation of this is to register customers in a drawing for a prize. This helps keep promotion costs down.
4. **Visuals:** While adding pictures can be prohibitively expensive, check out lower-cost options such as different font styles or sizes to make your ad distinctive. Sometimes line drawings are possible, and they are usually less expensive than photos.

PLACING ADS

1. **Newspaper ads:** You can always place classified ads, but for ongoing sales, you will want to use column ads in the regular sections of the paper. Think about what section of the paper is the one most likely to be read by your customers. Also, think in terms of what days of the week make sense. If the big automotive ads are in the Wednesday paper, that may be when you want to advertise your car repair service.
2. **Finding magazines:** In order to find the appropriate magazines in which to place your ads, consider the following: Oxbridge Communications offers an online database of 75,000 magazines and newspapers you can search by keyword or title. At your library, you can find hard copy magazine directories from Burelle and Bacon.
3. **Get the media kit:** Contact the magazine or newspaper of interest and ask for its media kit. These kits tell you about the types of ads, placement options, and costs. They're a great way to get an understanding of the basics of the ad business.
4. **Monitor:** Put a code in every ad, and ask customers for the code in their orders. That way you can track which ads work best for you.

Everyone is familiar with catalogs. They offer customers a description and often a picture of the product and tell the customer how to order it by mail, phone, or online. Catalogs are usually targeted at particular types of consumers and focus on particular types of products.

You can start a catalog of your own. Depending on the size and quality of the catalog, costs for print versions start at around 50 cents each and can rapidly go up to $2, $5, or more. Typically, the number of catalogs you will have to order is 5,000 at a minimum. Online catalogs are a less-expensive approach. Creating and disseminating a catalog online saves you the cost of printing and mailing. Generally, web-hosting services offer shopping baskets that are in fact online catalog-making programs.

However, most part-time entrepreneurs typically try to get their products into existing catalogs. Here the catalog firms function as your first customer; you want to convince them to carry your product. You can find catalogs through the www.catalogs.com site, from the Online Learning Center, or from print directories in the reference section of your local library.

When you have found the catalogs, try to obtain copies and check to see how your product would fit. Once you've identified your target catalogs, the key person you will be trying to find (by phone, mail, or online at the websites) is called a *buyer*. For the bigger catalogs, there will be several buyers, each specializing in a few product areas. Buyers usually require pictures of the product, and some will want to see the actual product. Buyers are used to buying based on preproduction models and prototypes. This works well with part-time entrepreneurs trying to maintain a microinventory. A **microinventory** is a set of goods or services that consists of only one or a few items. Microinventories are the small business's answer to **just-in-time inventory** methods in big business. In micro-inventories, you try to buy your product or prepare your service only after you get an order. For this to work, you need a stable, consistent, and secure source of inventory supply.

microinventory
A set of goods or service that consists of only one or a few items.

just-in-time inventory
Having just enough product on your shelves to meet the immediate purchases. This usually requires frequent shipment from your supplier.

When possible, try to talk to the buyers by phone first to make sure your product would fit their needs. Also make sure you check out each catalog's requirements for companies listing with them. There are many factors to consider such as whether the catalog charges for a listing; whether they hold the inventory (and if so have they bought it), or do they expect you to drop ship it; and whether the catalog gets an exclusive on your product and the right of first refusal for future versions or even your entire line. While these are policies, with thousands of catalogs, there are always other catalogs, probably with different policies, so negotiation may be possible. Also, check the catalog out with the Better Business Bureau (www.bbbonline.org) to make sure they have a solid track record among entrepreneurs like you. Entrepreneurs typically send buyers a packet with ad copy and pictures of the product. It often helps to provide different versions of the ad copy and different pictures to maximize the chance buyers see something they like. If possible (or if asked), send a sample product.

Catalog sales, like most business-to-business sales, are rarely immediately successful. Be prepared to come back repeatedly to catalogs that best fit your product or market. Persistence shows you are serious about the business.

Also, think about local wholesalers. The phone book or business directory at the library can point you to wholesalers who supply local businesses with products. If you know a business your product would fit, you can ask the owner who the wholesaler is and build on that. The materials developed for the catalogs work in terms of introducing your product to wholesalers too. The product description and photo for a catalog can quickly be made into an offering circular that you send to wholesalers to test their interest.

Three other direct mail sorts of activities are worth mentioning: direct faxing, e-mail, and daily coupon sites like Groupon. Particularly for business sales, direct faxing can be a way of reaching potential clients. Fax numbers can be obtained in the same way as mailing lists. Unfortunately, frequently faxes are of relatively poor quality, and often the person receiving the fax is not a decision maker.

Anyone who has an e-mail account is subject to this form of direct mail, commonly known as *spam*. E-mail addresses can be purchased just as can regular addresses from the same companies. There is also inexpensive software (see www.emailsmartz.com, for example, or do a search for "e-mail marketing software") that can easily generate millions of possible addresses. E-mail is one of the least expensive forms of direct mail, and the cost per recipient is, by far, the lowest. There is now a nationwide "can spam" law that overrides the 35 different state rules direct marketers had to consider previously.

However, in some cases state laws are more stringent and must be followed as well. For example, in California, the e-mail must state "ADV" in the subject line. Most of the requirements of the national law are fairly straightforward:

- Don't in any way falsely misrepresent who you are, where the e-mail is from, or that the e-mail is anything other than a sales pitch.
- Randomly generated e-mail addresses or harvested e-mail addresses are not to be used.
- All e-mails should allow recipients the opportunity to "opt out" of receiving further e-mail correspondence from you—and you must obey their wishes on this.[7]

Spam is a hot topic, and legislation changes are likely, so be sure to check on current rules. "Opt-in" e-mail, where recipients allow you to e-mail them, is legal and much more acceptable to the potential client.

One of the areas of explosive growth on the Internet has been around daily deal sites. Groupon.com was the first to strike it big, but today there are literally thousands of sites. There are two major types. One is coupon sites, where you can buy a coupon that entitles customers to a discount on a product or (more often) a service, for example, getting a $50 massage for $10. These are intended largely as a way to build awareness of and traffic to your business. But be ready to manage a major spike in customer demand immediately after a coupon comes out. Many businesses find that they have trouble meeting demand if there are too many coupons in customers' hands.

The other type of daily deal site is called a group buying site, like 1saleaday.com, which usually offers viewers a chance to buy a product at a discount. This is a way to get rid of excess inventory, but keep in mind that the discount levels for such sites can be very high, squeezing the profit margin severely. For either type of daily deal site, make sure that you can limit the numbers of coupons or products that you offer. Also look for sites that have success with your type of offering and your target market. Today there are thousands of local sites, and they, as well as most of the major national daily deal sites, will let you focus your listing in particular geographic areas.

Telemarketing

We have all received telephone calls from salespeople (or worse yet, recorded messages) wanting to sell us everything from aluminum siding to vacations. While most consumers find this method particularly annoying, **telemarketing** still remains a viable form of direct marketing because it works. It is, however, the most expensive form of direct marketing. Currently, many states have adopted "do-not-call" lists, and there is a national do-not-call list as well. The Direct Marketing Association maintains a comprehensive listing of national and state do-not-call lists (see www.the-dma.org/government/donotcalllists.shtml). These are currently facing some legal challenges, and the present situation should be checked out before you consider a telemarketing campaign. Target market telephone lists may be purchased from the same companies as mail or e-mail addresses—theoretically cleansed of all do-not-call registrants—or random dialers (computers that use random number tables to generate possible phone numbers) may be used.

telemarketing
Contact via telephone for the express purpose of selling a product or service. Telemarketing can either be inbound (customer calls company) or outbound (company calls customer).

Inbound telemarketing is a different story. Here, the customer calls the manufacturer or service provider. This may be in response to a direct mail piece, direct response advertising, or other methods. A major consideration for the entrepreneur is handling the phone lines. Your California customer calling at 8 P.M. reaches your home in Connecticut at midnight. This is where an answering machine with a message stating working hours (located far from your bedroom or with the sound turned off) is a necessity.

If inbound telemarketing is your primary way of doing business and if there are enough calls (and profit) to warrant it, there are firms that will answer these calls for you. You can find them by searching for "call center services" on Google. Generally these firms can take orders or send on additional information; more technical problems or special situations will require your personal attention. The cost varies, again, based on the amount of service and volume of calls. These centers can also provide services in several languages if this is critical for your firm.

Direct Response Advertising

direct response advertising
Placing an advertisement in a magazine or newspaper, on television or radio, or in any other media. The ad contains an order blank with a phone number and e-mail or regular mail address with the intent of having the customer place an immediate order.

In **direct response advertising**, you place an ad somewhere—magazine, newspaper, radio, billboard, or television, for example—that includes a phone number, e-mail address, or snail-mail address and wait for the orders to come in. (Placing a website in the ad is technically part of Internet marketing, which we get to in a moment.) This can be as simple as a classified ad in the newspaper or as elaborate as a half-hour infomercial—and the costs associated vary as much as the type of ads. A chart showing the cost per thousand (CPM) for a variety of media is given in Figure 10.2.

The pros and cons of your media choice are just about what you'd expect. Television can be expensive, but it attracts a large audience and is a good way to demonstrate what your product is capable of doing. Try cable channels for the cheapest rates. Many stations offer discounted advertising for small businesses. This might not amount to much more than an announcer reading your ad over the credits of the local news, but it's a starting point.

Some of the home shopping networks may be appropriate if your product meets their criteria. These networks publish their standards on their websites and may offer days for inventors to demonstrate their products to studio personnel—a chance to sell your concept. Products that work well are those that have a wide appeal and have advantages that are easy to demonstrate.

A magazine allows for very specific targeting—a hobby, sporting interest, a certain age, or other demographic group—and often offers classified type ads (less expensive) or multipage, full color ads (much more expensive). Newspapers allow geographic segmentation; that is, they are a great source if you want to attract people in a specific geographic region (think restaurant, day care center, and the like).

Magazines are also very appropriate places for direct response advertising for business-to-business selling. Virtually every industry, trade, and profession has a magazine dedicated to it. Finding the correct one and placing your direct response ads will give you high contact with your target market. Try *Gale's Directory of Publications and Broadcast Media* or the *Encyclopedia of Associations,* probably at your library, for lists of industry trade magazines and trade associations. You can also refer back to Chapter 3 or the Online Learning Center for Skill Module 3.1, "Finding Your Trade or Professional Association and Their Magazines," for some help along these lines.

Radio ads provide both geographic and demographic segmentation; if you do custom designed cowboy boots or train horses, a radio ad on the local country western station might be just the right place. On the other hand, radio audiences are generally highly distracted; people listen to the radio while driving, or doing housework or other tasks and might not be able to drop everything to write down your phone number. Billboards reach local people but do not permit a lot of details. Other possibilities include signs in buses and cabs or at bus stops.

SMALL BUSINESS INSIGHT

Floppy Sprinkler USA[9]

Jeff Pettit, the founder of Floppy Sprinkler USA, LLC (**www.floppysprinkler.com**) used television to get the word out about his unique water sprinkler called Rain on Demand. The idea was so different from traditional water sprinklers that a demonstration seemed the logical way to convince customers of the product's worth. Pettit found information for submitting ideas on the QVC website (**www.qvc.com**) and got his opportunity. His company started in 2000. With the QVC push, sales reached $250,000 by 2002. Today, his product is patented in 34 countries and is being marketed worldwide by a South African firm who has licensed the rights to the product. Today they sell it not only as an improved lawn sprinkler, but a water-saving, yield-increasing irrigation system for farms—a highly lucrative additional market.

For a start in direct response advertising, consider a classified type ad—no pictures, limited graphics (if any), and relatively low cost. If your target market is a specific geographic region, newspapers might work best. If it is specific to a hobby, job, sport, or other interest, try a magazine catering to that interest. If the budget allows, try a quarter- or half-page ad with some color or modest graphics. Magazines will sell you an eighth or sixteenth of a page ad.

Remember that there are also the relatively low-cost methods of Internet advertising, such as videos, blogsites, postings on Facebook or Twitter, and a host of other techniques (described in Chapter 10) that can be as effective or even more so than the traditional marketing vehicles.[8]

Guerilla Marketing[10]

guerilla marketing
The use of creative and relatively inexpensive ways to reach your customer. Examples include door-knob hangers, flyers under windshield wipers, T-shirts, balloons, and messages written on sidewalks.

Guerilla marketing is a relatively new concept in marketing, but the start-up company's best friend. Guerilla marketing is a term for unusual and nearly free advertising. While it can be simply advertising—stating why your product or service is great—it's extremely effective as direct response advertising when you add your phone number, address, website, or other contact information. Guerilla marketing includes everything from placing flyers under windshield wipers of cars to waving signs at passing cars to hanging information on doorknobs to placing business cards on bulletin boards at the grocery store. For the cost of copying and a bit of shoe leather, you can get your message out to a lot of potential customers. Then again, if you aren't interested in delivering the message yourself (How valuable is your time?), there are many companies that will do this for you. CIPS Marketing Group (www.cipsmarketing.com), owned by the *Los Angeles Times,* will distribute a newspaper "ride-along" advertisement, doorknob hangers, flyers, or product samples to selected target neighborhoods for as little as $35 to $130 per thousand. It will even design and print your advertisements for you for an extra fee.

The key here is to catch the customer's attention. We talked a little earlier about daily deal coupon sites, but when it comes to couponing, there are a myriad of ways to get the word out to your consumers. Susan P., moving into a new house in a new subdivision, became part of the target market for landscapers, house cleaners, blinds and drapery manufacturers, pool installers, satellite television installers, painters, decorators, local restaurants and merchants, and a plethora of other such small businesses. Daily there are several pieces of advertising trying to get her attention. A few—very few—are slick four-color brochures or in-mail catalogs and coupons. The majority are low budget or homemade. What attracts her attention? "Coupons are a good bet; I'll try out a restaurant or neighborhood merchant if I get a discount or free dessert or some other gift. Others that catch my eye are those that are different. For example, a landscaper left his business card—just like several dozen before and after him—but his was in a small plastic sandwich bag with a few samples of decorative gravel and bark. It cost him only the time to make these, but this was much more appealing than

Guerilla marketing, as in the photo, attracts potential customer attention while helping small businesses keep marketing costs down. Which guerilla options seem most effective to you and why? Do you see any ethical concerns with guerilla marketing techniques?

SMALL BUSINESS INSIGHT

Courtney Hennessey Revisited—Guerilla Guru[11]

We met Courtney Hennessey of Codi Jewelry (**www.codijewelry.com**) the first time in the chapter on part-time self-employment. While Courtney might not have realized that she was a guerilla marketing expert, her experience speaks for itself. Her first products were stretchy bead bracelets, and she generated interest by wearing them around town. People would ask about them, and she'd take orders. If they didn't place an immediate order, she had business cards to pass out "for future reference." She gave out business cards with all her sales, too, so her customers could pass them along to people who commented on their new jewelry. One of these cards ended up with a Neiman Marcus associate, which resulted in several trunk shows at the store, where she was allowed to present her merchandise directly to the jewelry buyers. One of her more unusual marketplaces—and possibly a marketing first—was her great aunt's wake where she brought samples of her jewelry and walked away with $800 in orders. During a vacation in the Bahamas, she happened to be eating at the same restaurant as Regis Philbin of *Live with Regis and Kelly,* and worked up the courage to approach him with her story and samples of her jewelry for his wife, daughters, and co-host Kelly. Regis presented the necklace to Kelly during the show, telling the story about Codi Jewelry, resulting in well over 100,000 hits on her Web site the next week. None of these "marketing ploys" cost her very much, but all were incredibly successful at generating publicity for her firm and getting resulting orders.

just sticking a business card in my door." In another case, a decorator printed her ad on a wallpaper sample—colorful and different![12]

Find unusual and unique places to display your products. Can you wear your own creations? Can you pass out samples of your homemade fudge to your bridge club? Could you display your product alongside complementary products or services, such as a custom jewelry maker who arranges to display her product at the checkout counter of a local hairdresser, with both of them splitting the profits. Give your product as gifts, along with your business card or other contact information, and encourage the recipients to pass along that information to anyone who asks. A variant of this is to try a barter arrangement with local TV and radio stations. You give them your product or service for free or at a significant discount in return for their mentioning it, or preferably endorsing it, on the air. All of these approaches share the common quality of guerilla marketing—they are low-cost ways to gain a potentially high impact on your market. One popular recent idea is paying college students to wear T-shirts with a message on them, such as Shirtsinschool.com.

Multichannel Marketing

multichannel marketing
The use of several different channels to reach your customers, for example, a website, direct mail, and traditional retailing.

The term **multichannel marketing** refers to using several outlets for contacting your customers. If you include in your classified ad your phone number, your website, and your e-mail address, then you are a multichannel marketer. One customer may pick up the phone. Others will e-mail or browse your website. This simply allows your customers to contact you in the way they feel most comfortable. Having your phone number, website address, and e-mail address on your packaging ensure that your customer can find you again should a retail outlet decide not to carry your product any longer.[13]

Distribution Issues for Direct Marketing

Even when your shippers pay postage, you'll need to know where to go to find the information you need to add that to the amount the seller pays. You'll need a decent postage scale and rate tables. These tables can be downloaded from UPS (www.ups.com), Federal Express (www.fedex.com), or the U.S. Postal Service (www.usps.com). *Tip:* Charge a shipping and handling fee that includes postage as well as packaging materials. Most catalogs have a shipping and handling fee based on the dollar amount of the order. These companies also offer tracking software that can be downloaded and installed on your computer to track your shipments.

Another option to consider, especially if you are doing quantity shipping, is to use a **fulfillment center**. These centers will warehouse your products, pack and ship them, and send an automated e-mail to your customers to let them know your product is on its way. Other services include credit card processing, supplying inventory levels to your website, reordering products, offering call center services, and handling returns.[14] Fees vary, but they should be less than 10 percent of sales plus freight costs. Distributors are a good idea if you want to offer a whole line of products that you don't have to buy or warehouse. In this case, the distributor services several **retailers** or e-tailers.[15]

How do you find these fulfillment centers or distributors? A good starting place includes www.fisglobal.com/products-retailpayments-ecommerce. There are also several companies that exist specifically for Internet sales businesses, such as Shipper.com for larger businesses and ifulfill.com for those companies with fewer than 50 products.[16]

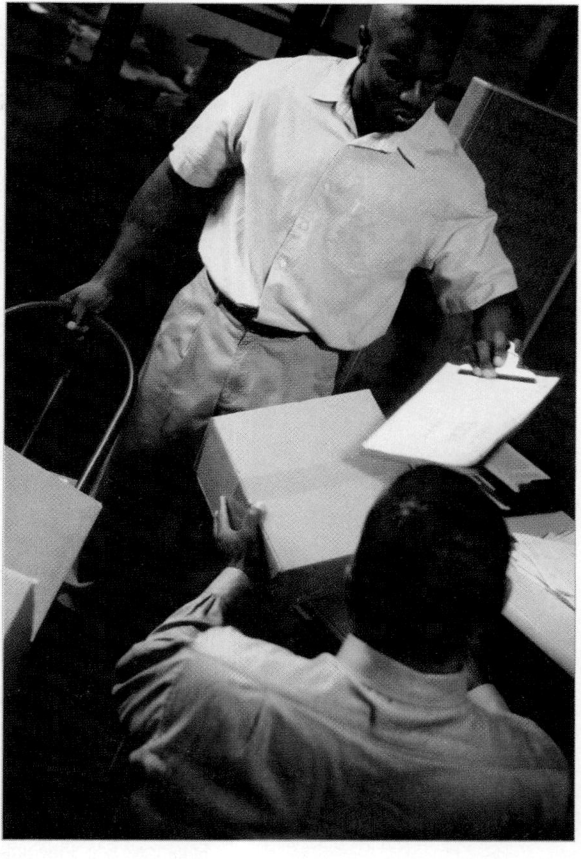

Arranging for fast and low-cost delivery is essential to successful distribution. Where would you go to compare shipping costs?

Nondirect Distribution

LO2 Learn how to do nondirect distribution.

In Figure 11.1 at the beginning of this chapter you saw **wholesaler**, retailer, and **agent**. These, along with distributors and a dozen or so others not mentioned above, are commonly referred to as intermediaries. Intermediaries—frequently small businesses themselves—provide the service of getting the product to the end consumer, including such functions as inventory control, advertising and promotion, delivery and warranty services, to name a few. For these services, they take a percentage of the profit. As a result, the final price the end user must pay is often four (or more) times the manufacturing cost.

How do you find out which distribution channel is correct for your product? One suggestion is to start at the end and work your way up by asking each link from whom they buy.[17] At that point, you can determine other wholesalers or distributors that carry similar products and begin interviewing them to find the best fit for your product and target market. Another way to locate possible distributors is to attend trade shows. The Manufacturers' Agents National Association publishes a *Directory of Manufacturers' Sales Agencies,* available in many libraries.

Unfortunately for the entrepreneur, many distributors and wholesalers are not interested in taking on a start-up product. They are concerned about an unproven source and market, setup charges, and a multitude of other possible problems. On the other hand, talking to distributors—especially in product development stages—may often give you ideas on what to do and what not to do.

One way to get a distributor interested in trying your product is to be able to prove that it does sell. In this case, you may have to convince a single retailer to give the product a try. Dr. Bob Wagstaff, the inventor of the Orabrush, had gotten it into stores by literally walking in and talking to managers. As noted in the Small Business Insight, he faced a rocky road, but he persevered, working his way through the system.

Getting your product into a catalog may also convince a distributor that it's a product worth taking, but how do you get into that catalog? One way is by showing your product at trade shows and gaining sales and recognition. This is the route that Steve Niewulis from the chapter's opening vignette used. Sources for finding trade shows include the quarterly magazine, *Job Shop Technology,* or the website www.tscentral.com. You can also search using Google and the terms "trade show directory."

Another way to get into a catalog is to find one that carries the type of product you have and for about the price you'll want to charge. Call for their guidelines for submitting new products and follow the information you get carefully. If you aren't already receiving such a catalog, you can check out resources such as the *National Directory of Catalogs* or *The Catalog of Catalogs V: The*

fulfillment center
A company that will warehouse your products and fill your customers' orders for you.

retailer
A middleman business which sells to consumers or end-users of a product (typically in single or small quantities).

wholesaler
A middleman business which buys (typically in large quantities) and sells (typically in smaller quantities) to businesses rather than consumers.

agent
A middleman business which represents a manufacturer's product or service to other business-to-business middleman firms.

SMALL BUSINESS INSIGHT

How Orabrush Pitched Itself Into Walmart[18]

You recall how Orabrush went from an also-ran on the toothbrush aisle to the darling of the Internet when its YouTube went viral. Online sales skyrocketed, but the firm still had trouble getting the Orabrush into major chain stores. Their target was Walmart, the nation's largest retailer. It turns out the Walmarts around Provo, Utah, where Dr. Bob Wagstaff lived and worked had Orabrush on sale in their stores. A Walmart manager took the plunge, and other local Walmart managers liked the point-of-sale display and the product enough that they brought them into their stores, too. Those managers recommended Orabrush to Walmart's headquarters. Orabrush sent the buyer at Walmart a customized video on DVD, with statistics, media coverage, and customer comments, but no decision was coming. In the end, they decided to build some support around Walmart headquarters. They created an ad (tied to a video, of course) saying Walmart employees had bad breath and need the Orabrush, which ought to be sold at Walmart. They targeted Walmart employees around Bentonville, Arkansas, where the headquarters is. After spending $28 on Facebook ads, they got the e-mail they were hoping for, asking if Orabrush could deliver 735,000 Orabrushes in a couple of months.

Complete Mail-Order Directory in your local library. Some will charge you a fee for warehousing your product, while others will simply pass the orders along to you.[19]

Virtually every industry, sport, hobby, or interest has its own trade shows and events. Regional events are usually a better place for the entrepreneur because you have lower expenses and less competition. Hit the library or Internet to find them, and be sure to have all the answers about cost, delivery, product advantages, and the like.

e-tailer
An electronic retailer; a store that exists only on the Internet.

If catalog sales do not feel right and retailers do not seem interested in your product, an **e-tailer**[20] might be willing to take a chance. Because of e-tailers' low overhead and unlimited shelf space, they can afford to take a chance on an unknown firm or product. Sometimes, they will carry inventory, but often they just pass the orders on to you for fulfillment. You can find potential sites by doing an Internet search for "e-tailer." Sometimes they will post information on how to submit product ideas, while other times be prepared to dig for phone numbers and names. Craig Winchell, the inventor of Conscience, an interactive board game for teaching children right and wrong, tried the American International Toy Fair, a trade show, with disappointing results. He found that EToys was willing to take a chance. EToys' (www.etoys.com) initial order was six games in 1998; in 1999, Winchell shipped close to 10,000 units.[21] With the kickstart from the EToys sales, by 2007 Conscience was sold at ten online catalog sites and more than ten retailers in the United States and Bermuda. In the end, though, Craig felt the board game would not give him the financial independence he needed. Today you can find Conscience on sale in several Internet sites, but Craig remains an entrepreneur making his money as a management consultant in Dallas.

International Strategies

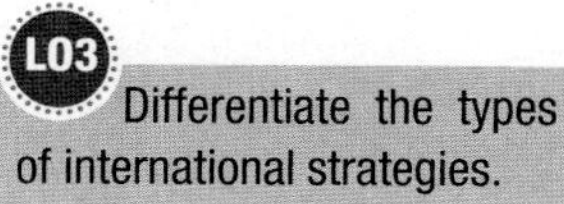
LO3
Differentiate the types of international strategies.

When you are struggling to get through that first year of business, international sales are about the last thing on your mind. The U.S. Department of Commerce, however, indicates that large companies account for only about 4 percent of all exporters, meaning the other 98 percent of the exporters in 2010 were small businesses.[22]

Entrepreneurs typically fall into three categories. There are those who realistically will never go international (for example, a restaurant owner or dry cleaner working from a single site). There are those who intentionally start international businesses[23] (for example, import-export businesses), such as Peter P., the director of procurement for a Russian trading company, who saw a trading opportunity with the opening up of Eastern Europe and the former Soviet Union. Educated in the United States, he is of Ukrainian descent and speaks both Russian and Ukrainian.[24] Last, there are those who think international business might be something they'll do someday way off in the future. This section is primarily for the last two categories.

Thanks to the Internet, once a company has a website, it is essentially an international business, a whole new breed of firms known as **born internationals.**[25] Potential foreign customers see the website and before you know it—or before you are prepared—the first international order rolls in. Even "website–free" companies aren't exempt. A foreign visitor comes across your products and sees a need for it in his or her country, and here comes that order.

born international
A new firm that opens a website immediately, thus being exposed to customers from around the world.

Some international orders aren't all that difficult to handle. If the order is small enough, if the product or service is not highly regulated domestically, and if the country is one with which the United States has rather liberal trade such as Canada, the order processing may offer few or no headaches. The customer may use a credit card or international money order, and the product ships in the mail without much more effort than figuring the extra postage. That's okay for the occasional order, but more complex situations will require more time and effort on the part of the entrepreneur. The ideal situation is to consider and prepare an international strategy before it becomes a hit-and-miss method that is too cumbersome or before serious and costly mistakes are made.

Entrepreneurs have available to them the same options as large companies including wholly owned subsidiaries, joint ventures, licensing, franchising, and exporting. For most, though, an export strategy is sufficient and is all that is covered in this section. It's usually inexpensive, quick to start, easy to change, and less risky than other ventures. It has the additional advantage of allowing the entrepreneur the opportunity to learn about doing business abroad in case the company reaches the point of moving further. For U.S. entrepreneurs, the U.S. government offers detailed and useful help for exporters, including seminars and other training, export assistance, websites and reports, financing, insurance, and legal and collection assistance.

Exporting[26]

Putting together an export strategy involves answering three questions:

1. Are we ready?
2. Where should we go?
3. Whom do we contact over there?

There are many sources for assistance in answering these questions, and many good ones are free or almost free. One excellent resource is the U.S. Commerce Department's report entitled, "A Basic Guide to Exporting" that can be found at www.unzco.com/basicguide.

Question 1: Are you ready to export? Exporting requires a different kind of thinking and preparation from selling locally or even nationally. Are you going to target one country, a region, or the whole world? Do you know what customers want? Do you know what the import requirements are? What aspects will you handle, and which ones will you contract out? Are you ready for the costs and headaches of exporting? To see how you are coming along, you can check your readiness online at the U.S. government's exporting site www.export.gov/, which provides extensive exporting basics, including a "readiness test" at www.fas.usda.gov/agexport/exporttest.asp.

Consider your product as well. Will your U.S. designed product fit an international lifestyle or needs? Clothing sizes are different—both in how they are numbered and what the sizes mean. A woman's medium in the United States is an XXL in mainland China. Electrical currents are different, as are various other safety and product standards, and the United States is one of only two countries that's not on the metric system.[27]

There are several ways you can export. One is to use online services such as eBay. Approximately one-fifth of eBay's sales are out of country.[28] If you're handling your international business this way, a lot of the rest of this section isn't really for you until you want or need to change methods. Another is to work from personal contacts gained through school, travel, or family. Most exporting small businesses start with countries where they have had personal experience or support.[29] These two methods are called **direct exporting**, since you are selling *directly* to foreign buyers or distributors.

direct exporting
Exporting using no intermediaries.

indirect exporting
Exporting using intermediaries such as agents, export management companies, or export trading companies.

freight forwarders
Firms specializing in arranging international shipments—packaging, transportation, and paperwork.

If you want to use outside experts, there are three intermediaries who can help. With **indirect exporting**, you use agents, export management companies, or export trading companies as intermediaries to handle most of the exporting process. Direct exporters can also get help from freight forwarders. **Freight forwarders** are specialists in export-related activities including tariff schedules, shipping, insurance, packing, transportation arrangements, customs clearing, and other export details. (By the way, many agents, export management companies, export trading companies, and freight forwarders are themselves small businesses. They know exactly what problems you've faced and are much easier to approach than some megacompany.) The Small Business Administration's Export Assistance Center can help you find one.

Question 2: Where should we go? The United Nations has 193 member countries in the world; chances are not all of them are right for your product. Even if your product should have wide appeal, it makes good sense to pick one or two as first markets. One of the safest bets is to consider countries that are similar to the United States—Canada, United Kingdom, Australia, for example. In those countries, you have few language issues, the culture is pretty close, the governments and economies are stable, and the people there are likely to want or need about the same kinds of products as people in the United States do. Should you decide to go further afield, those are the same sorts of things you want to look for—language and culture issues, government and legal situations, economic situations, and peoples' wants and needs. Here's a good time to use those personal contacts mentioned earlier; if they live there, they are likely to be able to tell you if the product makes sense or not.

International marketing research isn't cheap and can be difficult to do. Contacts are a valuable resource. Additionally, the U.S. government and world trade centers can give a lot of free or low-cost assistance. See Table 11.1 for a list of some of the major ones.

TABLE 11.1 Sources of Export Assistance

Agency	Website	Assistance Offered
Small Business Association	www.sba.gov	U.S. Export Assistance Centers offer help in virtually all areas of exporting, much for free or at very low costs.
U.S. Department of Commerce	www.export.gov	U.S. government's main exporting site with extensive exporting basics.
	www.unzco.com/basicguide/	This extensive guide is available for downloading and contains virtually everything a beginning exporter needs to know. Includes copies of most paperwork and how to fill it out.
Regional U.S. Department of Commerce offices		Offer export seminars on various topics; many are free or under $50.
Ex-Im Bank	www.exim.gov	Offers seminars on export financing.
Bureau of Industry and Security	www.bis.doc.gov	Offers seminars on export licensing and compliance issues.
International Trade Administration	www.ita.doc.gov	Has detailed information about U.S. trading partners.
World Trade Centers Association	www.wtcaonline.com	Networks hundreds of local world trade centers, which provide export/import assistance.
State and local governments		Often offer convenient seminars and other export assistance programs.

Question 3: Whom do we contact over there? You may already have international contacts through school, friends, travel, or other methods. If so, you're ahead of the game. Even if they cannot help you with specific questions, they probably know someone who can. On the other hand, if you do not have any contacts, a lot of the government services you have already used can provide lists of potential intermediaries or end users. In addition to the free services available, U.S. Commercial Services (www.export.gov) provides a number of levels of fee-based customized services. For $500, they offer their International Partner Search service, which will identify up to five potential businesses to work with you as licensees, agents, distributors, or strategic partners, and prequalify them based on your criteria. The government's www.export.gov site offers a database of sales leads that can be searched for free by industry, region, or country. They also are the point of contact for catalog exhibitions which can get your product or service catalogs into the hands of potential buyers in specific markets (or at specific trade shows) overseas.

Other good ways to make international contacts are to participate in trade shows and trade missions. In a trade mission, a U.S. government official takes a small group of business owners to different foreign countries in order to help establish relationships and promote exporting. There are not a lot of these missions, and they are usually specific to a particular type of business and region of the world, so they are not always appropriate. At an international trade fair, similar to domestic trade fairs, you have a booth displaying your products or services and the opportunity for exposure to thousands of potential clients. Again, some fairs are industry-specific, while others are more general. The U.S. government often has a U.S. pavilion featuring export-oriented companies. These companies often have the opportunity to tie into other U.S. government services such as meeting with local U.S. embassy officials, prearranged meetings with qualified customers, market research information, trade barrier information, transportation and customs information, and assistance and access to U.S. trade show experts. Even if you can't exhibit in the fair, attending the fair may give you a chance to meet the sort of people you need to know.

The U.S. government through www.export.gov also provides such services as printed and video catalogs, online databases, and personalized (fee-based) contact services. The U.S. Commercial Service will also assist a company in arranging private promotional activities, including exhibitions, press releases, and receptions when appropriate.

Still another way is to look for foreign companies with a resident representative in the United States, a type of private importing agent. Often these representatives are interested in bringing U.S. products back to their home countries and will already have a good idea if your product is right, and how to promote and distribute it.[30] To find these resident representatives, try a Google search with the terms "resident representative" US, importing-site:.gov.

The next step is to export your products. But there are a few other things to consider first. Pricing becomes complicated as you need to cover transportation, the additional documents you may need,

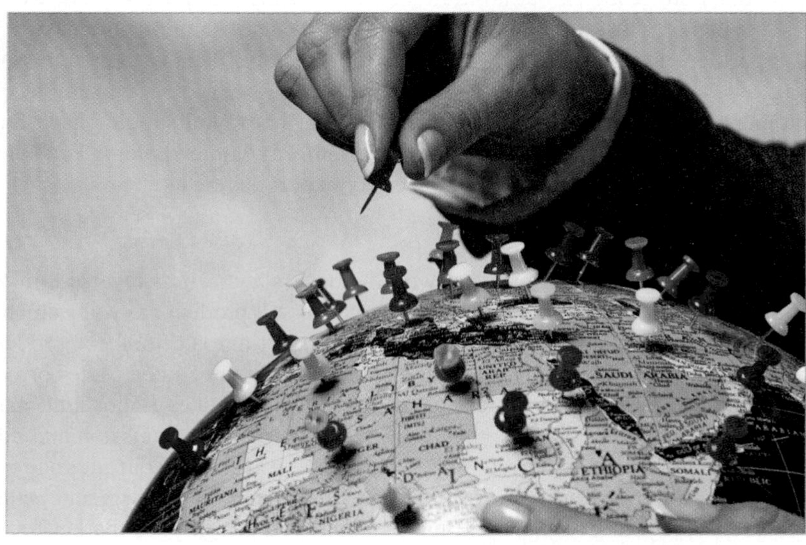

Exporting is a major way for small businesses to grow, and today there are more resources than ever before to help you find markets overseas. What would be some of the first websites you would check to find help?

possible tariffs (taxes on incoming goods), potential currency valuation changes, the cost of converting currencies, and the additional packaging necessary to ship abroad. The importer usually covers foreign taxes, tariffs, additional shipping charges, port handling fees, and the like, but this must be carefully spelled out in your contracts in order to avoid potential differences of opinion.

Shipping documentation and other paperwork are very specific to the product and the country to which it is going. The International Trade Administration (www.ita.doc.gov) provides extensive information about tariffs, taxes, specific country information, and other general exporting information. The U.S. Country Commercial guides also provide some assistance in this area, as do some country government websites. The Bureau of Export Administration (www.bxa.doc.gov) provides information about when export licensing is necessary and also information on exporting of politically sensitive products. In addition, companies such as NetShip (www.netship.net) have arisen specifically to handle shipping and documentation issues for e-commerce.[31]

There are a variety of payment procedures available. The easiest for you is to require up-front cash payment prior to shipment (or credit card if appropriate). This eliminates your risk, but puts the customer at risk. Providing credit to your customers reverses the risk, and puts it all on you. Both of these are possible methods of receiving payments, but less often used. More typical methods include **letters of credit** or **documentary drafts**. In both cases, the payment procedure now includes four parties—you, your customer, and both of your banks—and payments are made upon proper presentation of certain documents, including the letter of credit or draft, bills of lading, and other paperwork. Although the system is somewhat complex, it provides a lower level of risk for all parties than cash in advance or an open account. You can find assistance about these methods at your current bank.

letter of credit
A document issued by a bank that guarantees a buyer's payment for a specified period of time upon compliance with specified terms.

documentary draft
A draft which can be exercised only when presented with specified shipping documents.

Financing and insurance become important because of the length of time it may take for international payments to be processed and the risk of default, as well as the difficulty of recovery in case of default in international transactions. The Small Business Administration (www.sba.gov), the Ex-Im Bank (www.exim.gov), and the Overseas Private Investment Corporation (www.opic.gov) provide loans and insurance to cover exporting. In some cases, these loans may also be used to finance trade show participation, to translate brochures and catalogs for international distribution, to renovate or expand existing facilities necessary to produce products for export, to set up lines of credit for potential customers, to provide export working capital, and to provide funding for developing an export program.

Last is the consideration of conflict resolution. Although the possibility exists for pirating, product misuse, and other unfortunate occurrences, the primary areas for conflict resolution include nonpayment and contract default issues. There is no universal court of law that can handle these situations. The U.S. Department of Commerce can provide advice and offer reputable local counsel, but only for sizable losses, typically several thousand dollars or more. The U.S. Council of the International Chamber of Commerce (www.iccwbo.org) provides international arbitration services and offers some other suggestions, but arbitration, too, is costly and probably not worthwhile unless the loss is significant. This difficulty in international dispute resolution underscores the need to carefully select partners and to do a thorough job of prescreening. This is an area in which various government agencies can help you. The U.S. Commerce Department, for example, prequalifies potential customers in many cases prior to recommending them; you should check the particular program specifics to verify. Ex-Im Bank provides credit information on potential customers and, as mentioned earlier, many agencies provide insurance for export payments.

Importing

Importing strategy is similar to exporting, but with the buyers and sellers reversed. Instead of customers to buy your products, you are looking for sources to sell products to you (which, of course, you'll eventually resell). If you have the opportunity to travel abroad, look for products that are selling well in the country you're visiting and aren't available in the United States or products that are considerably cheaper than similar ones found in the United States (labor and manufacturing costs are often cheaper in other countries than the United States). Trade mission and domestic and international trade shows are also good sources. If you can't travel, ask your international contacts for this information. Next, find out who manufactures them and write the manufacturer a letter, introducing yourself and your company and the potential you see in your market for its product.

You're selling yourself, so be sure to tell the producer why you are the best person or company to be representing the product (i.e., experience in that product or in importing, contacts and distribution systems already in place, familiarity with the market, etc.). International mail can be painfully slow, so a fax or e-mail letter is probably best. Also, avoid slang terms (e.g. "your product is da bomb!") and idiomatic expressions (like "break the ice") that are likely to be misunderstood. Since English is rapidly becoming the language of business, a translation is usually not necessary. Follow up with a phone call or visit in which you can pitch the specifics of your marketing plan for the product.[32] One way to conduct international calls for free is to register for Skype, an Internet service which lets you use a broadband connected computer to call other Skype users for free (www.skype.com). If you and the overseas company both use Skype, having long conversations to get an understanding of each other will not pose a financial problem. Along the same lines, it is worthwhile these days to check to find out whether an overseas company has video capabilities. Video cameras for PCs are inexpensive, and videoconferencing services are often available on campuses or at commercial locations such as FedEx Kinko's for low costs.

With importing, many of the paperwork and insurance details will be your source's responsibility. Import buying works the same way as export selling, that is, the same sorts of paperwork and procedures are followed only in reverse.

Concluding Thoughts on International Business

One of the major mistakes commonly made by U.S. businesspeople (entrepreneurs or major companies) is being insensitive to cultural differences. You're likely to make some mistakes, but take time to learn at least the basics about the culture you're dealing with to avoid the biggest errors. Travel guides and U.S. government country reports often offer brief cultural assistance as do books such as *Kiss, Bow or Shake Hands* and a plethora of "doing business in ———" guides.[33]

Although international business might seem a little daunting with all the paperwork and regulations, small businesses just like yours do it every day. There's a lot of free or very inexpensive help out there; make use of it.

Location

LO4 Identify the factors to consider in selecting your business location.

When you ask real estate agents the best three things to look for in a house, they will tell you, "Location, location, location." The same holds true in your business. What location—in particular, *good* location—means for your business is highly dependent on what your business is, the amount of money you can afford to budget for it, your particular business philosophy, and the marketing niche you are seeking. Let's start with some general information about location, then move onto specific issues for services (including retailing) and manufacturing businesses. We then discuss some specific choices such as site selection and layout and the buy, build, or lease option.

The first choice, and often only choice, for many entrepreneurs is their hometown because it offers convenience and a familiar setting, and it eliminates a lot of possible family issues. There may also be valid business reasons for this choice: The local banker knows you and is more likely to loan you money; you know your market—the potential customers in the area—and understand their wants and needs; you have seen an unmet need that you can fill; and, for many entrepreneurs, friends and family (usually local) are often the first customers and are great at spreading the word about your business. (Remember that word-of-mouth is often the first method of getting to your customers.)

There may also be some compelling reasons to consider a different location. What are the business laws like in your area? Local zoning ordinances specify what sorts of businesses are allowed and not allowed in specific locations.[34] Certain types of businesses—usually those deemed hazardous or that produce foul odors—may be banned or severely restricted. State and local pollution standards, worker's compensation, wage rates, and other such legislation might increase the cost of doing business to the point that other locations become much more favorable. State and local taxes in particular vary considerably from state to state. For example, Wyoming has no personal or corporate income tax, while California has relatively high rates. On the other hand, certain locations often offer attractive incentives for new businesses ranging from tax credits to low-interest loans, from favorable business laws to business incubators (discussed later).

Most of this information can be found on the Internet. Try the state or city business development office (a good place to start is the Federation of Tax Administrators' state list at www.taxadmin.org/fta/rate/tax_stru.html) or the local chambers of commerce (look in the phone book or at www.uschamber.com/chambers/directory/default to find your local Chamber affiliate). There is also information by state available for your state at business.USA.gov, and the Small Business Administration offers links to state-based resources at www.sba.gov/category/navigation-structure/counseling-training. *Site Selection Magazine*'s website (www.siteselection.com) has a number of tools that can help you find the right location. Many of these require being a registered user, but registration is free.

Other reasons to consider other locations are tied to your customer. Your hometown may not be the best place for you to find your target market customers. Are you close to the people who will use your product or service? Other considerations include population growth or decline (especially in your target sector), income levels, and predicted increases or decreases in income. Is the location expanding economically or slowly dying? Perhaps the best source for this information is the US Census Bureau. State and local municipality business development offices may also carry such information, but they are likely to be slanted toward attracting new businesses. Being positioned to benefit your customer can also be key. Zappos's primary distribution hub was placed in Louisville, Kentucky, to be close to a major UPS air cargo hub in order to speed delivery.

Also consider the type of business you are planning. Do you need skilled labor? If so, what areas will provide you with the necessary employees? Do you need to be near raw materials or particular methods of transportation? These issues will help determine your choices. Where are your competitors? Certain industries tend to be clustered in certain regions where they can make efficient use of services and employees. Think of California's Silicon Valley or the financial district of New York City.

Doing business in your hometown may be perfectly appropriate; however, the cost of moving a company—whether across town or across the country—can be very expensive. It pays to plan ahead.

Service Firms

There are three typical locations for services: at the client's location, at a mutually accessible location, and at your firm's location. Traditionally, services may have been tied to one or another of these, but marketing niches have been carved out by people daring to be different. Typically, dry cleaning and restaurant dining are services provided at a place accessible to both parties, but some dry cleaners now offer pick up and delivery from the client's home, and not only pizza restaurants offer delivery these days. Thanks to the Internet, video rental like Netflix.com and other services are handled electronically, and the customer and service provider may never meet face to face. Whatever innovative niche you select, there are a few things to keep in mind.

At the Client's Location

Typically, these services include things such as house or office cleaning, pest control, remodeling, lawn and gardening services, carpet cleaning, and similar services which must be performed at the client's location. Business headquarters can be a home office with enough room to store and maintain any necessary equipment used in the service. Reliable transportation, preferably modified to organize and store tools efficiently, is imperative. More importantly, the range of your client's locations must be planned to prevent transportation times from being unmanageable. For example, facing a one-hour drive to a client's location might mean you have tied up two hours in commuting. If you cannot charge for travel and do not have other clients nearby, it means you have two hours in which you cannot make any money that day.

If you've done your homework carefully, you already know the geographic area(s) most likely to use your service. Certain services may be organized into a rotating schedule. For example, a house cleaning service may clean a certain set of neighborhoods on Monday, different set on Tuesday, and so on. In other cases, more remote clients may be charged a transportation fee. In some cases, a mileage fee may be appropriate for your business (delivery services, for example).

SMALL BUSINESS INSIGHT

LINDZEY PATTERSON AND HOME COOKING

Lindzey Patterson had a real passion for cooking. Even as she was finishing her degree at Saint Louis University, she was planning her next classes at a local cooking school. Her idea was to offer cooking classes in the client's own kitchen. Her business could operate from a van equipped with her cooking equipment and refrigerators for storing food. Reservations could be handled by cell phone. This way, Lindzey had taken a business usually based in a mutually accessible location and made it into a business conducted at the customer's location. In doing so she was able to minimize her costs and personalize her service, called Home Cooking. This, in turn, served as the launch pad for her next business, Coffee Girls Cafe in Kansas City, **www.kccoffeeegirls.com**.

As the firm grows, it may outgrow its home-based headquarters. As your clients seldom, if ever, visit you, you have more latitude in where you can be located and the ability to seek out low-cost space (see site selection section below). Reasonable distance to the clients and adequate storage room for your expanded fleet and equipment are key to choosing a site.

Mutually Accessible Location

Services using this approach often have too much specialized equipment to be readily transported and a need for at least some client involvement. Barbershops, dentist offices, video rental stores, and restaurants are services typically located at a site that is extremely convenient for the client and reasonably so for the owner and employees.

Even though your service may be traditionally located in a mutually accessible area, consider what you might do to make it home-based (see Chapter 5). Your watch repair shop might generate clientele by being located in a shopping center, but will the added sales be offset by the high cost of rent, utilities, insurance, and other payments? Can you offer pickup and delivery and do the work at

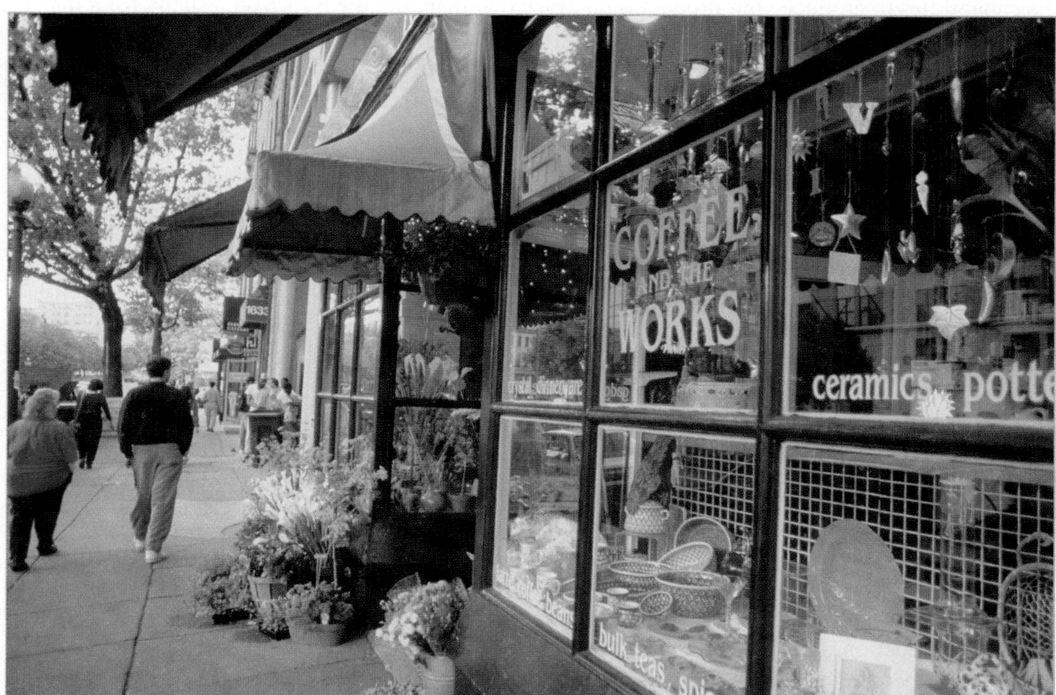

Finding a truly convenient space is one of the challenges to placing one's business in a mutually accessible location. In the example pictured, the owners offer an expanded product line in order to attract passers-by on a busy downtown street. Locating several different kinds of related items in one street front store gives customers the ability to shop for several needs at one time and place.

home? Your restaurant idea might work as a catering service. Instead of a specialized clothing shop, why not try mail order or Internet-based sales?

Remote Location

In this type of service, face-to-face meetings with the client are infrequent. Typical services that meet this criterion include medical transcription, data processing, fulfillment centers, and some consulting work. These services generally are ideal for home-based businesses. Certain services, for example, fulfillment centers, generally take more space—at the minimum, an attic, garage, or basement. The biggest advantage of these sorts of businesses is that they can be located anywhere in the world. U.S. hospitals, for example, use medical transcription services located in India. One such company, Infoflow/TSVI, operates from a U.S. sales base (which makes handling calls from U.S. hospitals easier) with transcription being done in India, managed there by a co-owner, who is a cousin and long-time friend of one of the two American owners (www.tsviinc.com).[35] Other than perhaps some initial sales meetings, all business is transacted via phone, fax, electronic exchanges, or mail.

Manufacturers

What if you are selling a product and not a service? What are your considerations about location now? Where you make the product is really dependent on the product. Some products that do not require a lot of specialized or bulky equipment can be produced at home unless zoning ordinances forbid it. In addition to whatever office space is needed, adequate work space is also required. The basement, a garage, or a home workshop may be adequate for some time. As business expands and as you add employees, it will become awkward if not illegal to continue production at home (see Chapter 5).

Some products require bulky and specialized equipment, utility demands atypical of homes, or sizable warehousing requirements and are never suitable for home businesses. Certain production characteristics—for example, use of hazardous materials and materials with strong odors or noisy operations—may make a home-based business undesirable. Many cities have zoning ordinances prohibiting manufacturing in residential areas. When you start to hire employees, providing the amenities they will expect or that are required by law will usually require moving the business from your home.

contract manufacturing
An existing firm with the correct manufacturing capabilities makes your product for you.

sheltered workshop
A nonprofit organization or institution that provides business services by using handicapped or rehabilitated workers.

Contract manufacturing might be a better option, at least for awhile. In this case, a firm with the capabilities to produce your product is contracted to manufacture it for you, usually for a flat per unit fee and a possible setup charge. Some firms will also assist in marketing and sales as well. Trade magazines in your field often list ads for contract manufacturers. An interesting possibility here is to use **sheltered workshops** to perform light manufacturing or assembly sorts of businesses. These workshops exist in nearly every state and offer very competitive pricing, often including tax benefits for the business.

Site Selection

Once you have determined the general location of your business, you need to determine the exact location for your operation. What you should look for falls into three main categories: home-based businesses (covered in Chapter 5), high customer contact (e.g., retail), and low customer contact (e.g., manufacturing). Each has certain criteria to be considered.

High Customer Contact Businesses

Businesses with high customer contact include such diverse operations as medical or legal offices, restaurants, retail establishments, dry cleaners, and other businesses that are highly dependent on being convenient to the customer. For these operations, there are three critical site selection considerations: traffic, customer ease, and competition.[36]

First of all, you want a site that is convenient to your target market and to enough of the customers to make you profitable. If you are considering a franchise, many will offer site criteria to help you make your selection. If you are going it alone, consider the population density of the area and how many of the people in the area meet your target market criteria. The U.S. Census Bureau website and a number of free nongovernment sites like www.zipwho.com and www.city-data.com can be a good starting place for free information. See Skill Module 11.2 and the Online Learning Center. If plowing through the Census Bureau website doesn't get you what you want, several commercial services mentioned in Chapter 10 including Prizm and ESRI will sell you data about the population in a particular zip code for several hundred dollars. More detailed and specific commercial information is also available and can range in price from several thousand dollars to over $100,000 and is probably not an option for most entrepreneurs.[37] Again, the website of *Site Selection Magazine* (www.siteselection.com) mentioned above has tools and additional articles that can help.

Finding Demographic Information By Zip Code

SKILL MODULE 11.2

In Chapter 10 we mentioned **www.zipwho.com**, **www.censusscope.org**, **www.zipskinny.com**, and **www.city-data.com** as websites that offer a variety of demographic information organized by zip codes. When looking for basic information on potential customers, this kind of information can be extremely valuable.

In Chapter 10 we talked about a bilingual children's day care center in Phoenix. The primary target market is Hispanic families with children and working parents. One way to advertise to these parents would be to do a traditional flyer, like those mailed out by Valpak and similar companies. For such coupon-sized flyers, you can select the zip codes in which your target audience would receive them. So in Phoenix, which zip codes would it be?

For this search we will use **www.zipwho.com** because it provides the most ability to specify demographics and localities in searching. Selecting Arizona and typing in "Phoenix" gets us precisely where we want to be. Because we are looking for Hispanic families we selected "Hispanic Ethnicity (%)." While there isn't a demographic category on zipwho.com for families with children, we used instead "Average Household Size Rank," figuring families with children will be larger, and should rank higher.

The result is a list of 38 Phoenix zip codes ranked by Hispanic ethnicity. For each zip code, there is a hotlink that takes us to a demographic breakdown of the area. Let's look at the first zip code, 85034.

The population in this area is poor, with $21,168 in the second percentile (meaning 98 percent of Americans are making more than the median income in this zip code). Household size is at the opposite end of the spectrum, at the 97th percentile. So it is likely the people in this community have children but would probably be able to afford only the least expensive child care. Note also that this zip code has a small population, 8.539 (80.3 percent Hispanic), so there would be fewer people responding than in more heavily populated zip codes. For example, zip code 85008 has 56,368 people, 58.5 percent who are Hispanic, so a target market of 32,975, or almost five times the size of the Hispanic market in zip code 85034. This number is important because direct mail firms usually have minimums, for example, 10,000 households, and at, say, 4 cents per home, making sure you can make back your $400 initial outlay is a key consideration.

Advanced Demographics Search

State: Arizona

Advanced Search

City: phoenix (optional)

Hispanic Ethnicity (%)

between 0.0 and 100.0

Average Household Size Rank (0–99)

between 0 and 99

(continued)

This is where the marketing funnel described in Chapter 10 comes into play. So you send out to 10,000 households. If the funnel's return rate holds, you could get 20 customers, 10 of whom would be loyal. To make this advertising program work, you would need to make a $20 profit from each family.

Repeat this with the other zip codes in the listing and identify at least two zip codes that you think look promising, with a large enough number of Hispanic families in the area and an area with a high enough family income to give the mail-out the possibility of being financially worthwhile.

85034: Phoenix, AZ

		National Percentile Rank (0-99)	
Median Income ($)	21,168	2	BOTTOM 10%
Cost Of Living Index	58.9	11	
Median Mortgage To Income Ratio (%)	22.7	72	
Owner Occupied Homes (%)	37.3	4	BOTTOM 10%
Median Rooms In Home	3.7	2	BOTTOM 10%
College Degree (%)	4.9	2	BOTTOM 10%
Professional (%)	10.8	0	BOTTOM 10%
Population	8,589	52	
Average Household Size	3.5	97	TOP 10%
Median Age	26.1	2	BOTTOM 10%

traffic generators
Other businesses that bring customers (generate traffic) to the area.

Another consideration is the presence of **traffic generators** in the area. These are other businesses that draw customers to the area and may include supermarkets, office complexes, schools, and malls. If the customers are drawn there, for example, to grocery shop, might they not stop at your video store next door? Reflect on the type of customer you are seeking and the likelihood of these businesses in attracting them. If you want a teen customer, a location near a high school works well. If you are looking for evening clientele, offices that close at five aren't the right traffic generators for you. Drive around likely areas and locate possible sites. Visit during the hours you anticipate to be peak times for your business and evaluate foot and car traffic.[38] Look at the crowds or lines in similar businesses and decide whether there is room for you. If most businesses seem empty, you probably will be too.

Intersections of major streets offer high automobile traffic, but because of divided roads and other barriers, they may not make it easy for your customers to get to you. Businesses along interstates have high visibility, but the frontage roads can be so convoluted that the clients seek easier-to-get-to competitors. Even some malls and shopping centers have such tortuous access problems that customers avoid them when possible. Sometimes entry is easy, but getting out is difficult. For example, no signals for left turns when most of the traffic needs to head in that direction can turn off customers.

Parking is also an issue. Is it conveniently located to your place of business? Do customers need to cross busy streets to get to you? Is parking free or paid? Are parking areas well lit and safe? Are there wheelchair ramps or other accommodations for disabled customers?

Customers have strong ideas about how far they should have to drive for things. These vary somewhat from major metropolitan areas to more rural towns and from one region of the United States to another. Generally convenience stores, fast-food restaurants, and gas stations need to be close to consumers. Grocery stores and banks can be somewhat farther away, but not much. Discount stores and midscale restaurants can be even farther away, while specialty stores, upscale restaurants, and malls can be relatively remote. Where does your business fit? How far are customers willing to drive to get to you?

Malls are great traffic generators, but space at malls is costly. If it is appropriate for your product, you might consider a kiosk or cart in the mall as a way of testing the market and location without making a large investment.[39] Neighborhood shopping centers (those anchored by a supermarket, drugstore, or major retailer) or strip centers (shopping centers without major anchors) are more modestly priced, but lack the drawing power of malls.[40]

SMALL BUSINESS INSIGHT

STEAK-OUT RESTAURANT[41]

Mark Dukes thought he'd found the perfect location for a restaurant that specialized in the delivery of burgers, chicken, and steaks when he found a location in the middle of the University of Tennessee in Knoxville. Students are always hungry and love delivery. However, during school breaks there are no orders—and also no employees. In addition, there was no parking at his location on campus. After seven years of struggling, Mr. Dukes moved his failing franchise off-campus to a free-standing building with a parking lot. His sales went up 100 percent. He still delivered to students, but he got a lot of community business, and a family order would average $30 compared to the student order of $7 or $8. Today he also owns several Steak-Out franchise outlets and Fork River Foods, Inc.

Generally, competition in the area can draw away valuable clients, but this is not true in every case. Many cities have a restaurant row, an antique district, or an automobile mile (as well as other business types) where many competitors cluster. Clients wish to comparison shop or have choices and are drawn to areas where they can see several similar businesses at one time. Locating far from these will mean that you are free from competition, but this benefit may easily be offset by the cost of attracting customers to a different place. Additionally, you can capitalize on competitive advertisements that bring potential customers to the area. Your competitor's high-budget TV ad might get customers to the neighborhood, but the "sale" sign in your window may get them to stop at your place instead.

Another instance when you want to be near competitors is when your business provides a strong contrast to the competition in the area. Do you offer better assistance, additional services, unique advantages, or other benefits that can easily be seen by customers? They may be drawn to the area by a well-known competitor's name, but they may select your establishment instead because of what you offer that differentiates you.

Low Customer Contact Businesses

Generally low customer contact businesses are manufacturing businesses, the headquarters of client location-based services, or remote location services. Customer access is relatively unimportant. More critical are access for your employees, reasonable cost, and the space necessary to do your business. Certain manufacturing operations will need adequate utilities and specialized transportation too.

Chicago's jewelry row is an example of clustered competitors whose proximity to each other gives customers added convenience and more options. What are some reasons you can think of that illustrate how clustering helps bring more interest and business to an entire area?

Unless you plan to use some of this space as a high-traffic showroom, commercial space in a business park or light industrial park might be appropriate. These parks are located near major transportation routes, often have rail spurs, and are designed for industrial utilities; that is, they have adequate electricity, gas, water, waste water treatment, and the like. Frequently, support businesses will be located in or near the park such as warehousing, shipping firms, copy centers, and office supply stores. Industrial or business park space tends to be cheaper in smaller cities and rural towns than in major metropolitan areas. If distribution to customers can be arranged, these locations are certainly cost-effective.

Some major metropolitan areas offer *empowerment zones.* These zones, often in economically depressed areas, offer businesses low-cost space and tax advantages for locating there. For more information, see www.rurdev.usda.gov/BCP-EZEC-Home.html or www.siteselection.com.

A third possibility is a business incubator. The National Business Incubator Association (www.nbia.org) shows over 1,400 business incubators in North America sponsored by government, universities, or private investment groups. These business incubators are specifically designed for the entrepreneur, and, in addition to relatively low cost space, they offer a multitude of small business support services. These services range from copy machines, faxes, and conference rooms to accounting, finance, and consulting services. Since the building is populated by other entrepreneurs, it's a great place to talk to others who might have had some of the same problems or to brainstorm new ideas. Most incubators require a stake in your company in exchange for their assistance—maybe as much as 50 percent—and often have quite a bit to say about how you run your business. Opinion is mixed on how much real help a company can get; just like all businesses, there are better and worse incubators, so do your homework.[42]

General Comments on Site Selection

How do you go about finding potential sites? Looking for "for sale" and "for rent" signs is a start, but not all space will be advertised that way. Just as a good real estate agent can warn you about the proposed freeway project going through the backyard of the house you are considering or let you know about houses not yet listed but likely to be, an experienced real estate broker will also be able to assist you in your search for your business location. Many have relationships with landlords that can work to your benefit. They are also likely to have at least some of the market statistics you may need to help you decide if the location is right for your business.[43] Level with them about what you can spend. You have your business plan and know the cost per square foot you can afford and be profitable. If you are looking at property more expensive than that, you'll need to cut corners elsewhere.[44]

Leasing

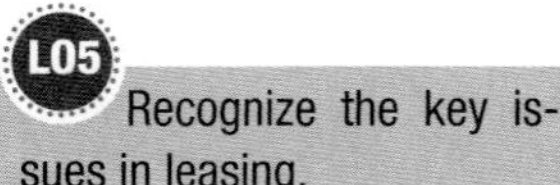
LO5 Recognize the key issues in leasing.

It is rare that a small business start-up buys its first location. The reason is financial. It takes a lot of money to buy a place, and beyond that a long-term commitment to pay for it. For most small businesses, it is not a worthwhile risk. It makes more sense to rent or lease your facility to leave more money for other aspects of the business. But leasing is one of the most complex of the issues an entrepreneur faces when starting a business.

In reality, most landlords (especially those from big national commercial real estate and mall companies) have fairly standard contracts which they don't like to change. These typically start out as very pro-landlord. That said, in many cases they are also likely to accept certain standard clauses that are more tenant-friendly. However, it is unlikely they will offer those. You will need to ask for them. In this section you will learn about the major types of tenant-friendly clauses you might want to seek. However, it makes tremendous sense to get a real estate lawyer involved to help you. They should be able to tell you what kinds of clauses are typical, and who else offers them in your area, and if there are any other likely traps in the lease. You can learn how to choose a lawyer in Chapter 18.

You should start the leasing process by looking for locations. You can start using the local newspaper's or business journal's classified ads for commercial real estate. If you know of a great location, but there is no "for rent" or "for lease" on it, consider asking the owner or current renter about subleasing a portion of the location. If your product or service complements the current tenant, you could find a home. Local real estate websites may also have listings, and there are national websites like LoopNet.com which compile listings from a variety of sources. There is a how-to video for using LoopNet on the Online Learning Center. You may contact a real estate agent with commercial experience to help you, but make sure you know how the agent is making his or her money. You want the agent to work in your best interests.

It helps to have two or three possibilities identified before you begin negotiating leases. This is a use of the idea of the power of rivalry from Chapter 7. This gives you a basis for comparison, and an alternative for leasing when negotiating. But note that the more alike the properties, the greater your power at the negotiating table. Also, if you are opening a franchised operation, you will want to contact your franchisor before you start looking for locations. Most franchisors have specifications for locations, and advice on costs and other features. They often have a lease review department to help you with this process.[45]

The best way to start thinking about the clauses is to separate them into those clauses related to choosing a property, day-to-day operations, and endings. In reality, though, all of these clauses will get negotiated when you and the landlord discuss the lease agreement.

There are several issues that could pop up as you are narrowing your choices and trying to decide which location and deal is the best for you. These are:[46]

- **"As is" versus compliant property:** If the location has problems, who should fix them? The landlord would like to have you do it, and will try to push you to accept the property "as is." You, of course, want the landlord to fix it before you move in, so you would ask the property to be "in compliance with all applicable laws, rules, and regulations." Realize that the landlord will get back the money paid for repairs eventually, through fees or higher rents, but it can save you money on the front end.
- **HVAC:** This is the commercial jargon for "heating, ventilation, and air conditioning." It can be the most expensive type of repair, and since it is mechanical, one of the types most likely to go wrong. The landlord wants it to be your responsibility. You want it to be the landlord's. This is particularly important if the location has a central air system so everyone shares the same air conditioner and heating equipment. This type of equipment needs to be the landlord's responsibility. For any type of equipment, you want the landlord to at least guarantee the first year of operation.
- **Signs:** Called "signage" in the business, it can be on the street, on the building, or around the door. You probably have ideas for your signs. If you are a franchise, you face signage requirements from the franchisor. You want a landlord who will work with you on the size, placement, and visibility of signs. Make sure you have written agreement on the signs and, if possible, a clause that says approval cannot be unreasonably denied for future changes.

This is what no one wants to see—repairs needed for an air conditioner. But who is going to pay for it? What kind of air conditioners are likely to be your responsibility?

There are other benefits possible if you know to ask for them. Often these are called concessions. Examples include "leasehold improvements," which are permanent changes made to the location to fit your business's needs. You cover these by seeking a "tenant improvement allowance" or "construction allowance" which are rent dollars (typically $5 to $25 a square foot) they agree to let you put into improving your location.[47] This amount should be based on a firm estimate from a construction professional. Another concession is a "rent-free use period" which covers the time while you prepare your location prior to opening.

As you start thinking about how you would operate day-to-day, there will be several different issues you will face. These include:

- **Hidden charges:** Many leases include charges that do not have to be listed in the term sheet given you for the property. An example is a monthly operating expense. This may be justified. You may be leasing a thousand feet of space, but there are also common areas, restrooms, parking and the like that the landlord keeps up for everyone. Ask specifically for a list of all expenses or charges for which you will be liable, and compare to other locations. Also make sure to learn the conditions under which you can lose all or part of your security deposit.

- **Use of premises:** You specify in the lease what you will sell or do at the leased location, but too exact a description could prevent you from expanding the products or services you offer. Try to add the clause "and related goods and services" to any description you give to provide reasonable flexibility.
- **Noncompete:** If you have a pet store in a strip mall, you'd like to be the only one there. For many types of businesses, you negotiate a clause limiting the landlord's ability to lease to a competing business. This can be just for your facility or for a radius. You should expect to pay for the exclusivity and the farther you want it, the more it will cost. Note that competition in terms of different types of restaurants, or another store selling some of your products, is still likely.
- **Hours of operation:** Mall landlords want stores open the same hours and days, and landlords of other types of properties may have some of the same desires. You need to negotiate times that fit your business model. Look for stores in the landlord's properties that match your hours. Precedence helps here.
- **Rent default:** When you are late paying rent, all sorts of penalties and problems emerge. It also hurts your credit rating. Some leases require the renter to keep track. Ask to change the lease to specify the landlord needs to alert you immediately on the rent due date in written or telephonic (usually fax) form, and get the 5–10 day default period for paying rent before default starts from that notice.
- **Moves and remodels:** There may be a clause that gives the landlord the right to move your business elsewhere, at their discretion. If this is to update or repair an area, fine, but what if it is to get a higher-paying tenant in your space? Set time limits and return rights on any forced move. Similarly, if the landlord decides to remodel, you should not have to pay for it.

As an entrepreneur negotiating a lease, you need to prepare for the good and the bad as time moves along. The good is the prospect your business grows and you need more space. The bad is that your business doesn't do well, and you need to get out of your lease before the end of the term. Dealing with these issues is like worrying about a prenuptial agreement while you are taken with the romance of getting married. It might be painful to imagine, but it is important to keeping what is yours.

If your business falters, you are obligated to continue paying your monthly rent and fees for the duration of the lease. A landlord has the power to let you out of a lease, but he or she is only likely to do this if a better tenant is lined up. Once you tell your landlord you may need to vacate the premises, she or he is supposed to look for a replacement tenant, but not all do, or do a good job of it. If you can find a replacement tenant, it can help this process along, but you need to make sure there is a clause that lets you sublease the property, and further, that the landlord can't unreasonably deny the sublease. If your pet store is closing, finding a dress shop is probably reasonable (as long as it doesn't violate some other tenant's noncompete clause), but finding an adult book store is probably not a reasonable replacement.

Three other ways to handle an early termination are to set up a short-term (e.g., 6 months) lease initially, ask for a bailout clause, or for a "cap" or limit on how long you need to continue paying rent. The bailout clause lets you out of the lease if sales do not meet an agreed-to level. You negotiate this with the landlord up front. To understand a cap, think about a three-year lease. If you close down after only six months, you are still obligated to pay 30 more months' rent. With a one-year cap you are only obligated to pay 6 months' more rent. This is like a type of insurance, and like insurance policies, you will probably have to pay a slightly higher rent from the start to cover this possibility.

Realize there can be problems you face caused by the property itself. What if you move into a mall with a major chain like Sears, Penny's or Macy's, or a strip mall with a major supermarket or discount store. Part of what you are paying a premium for is the traffic and reputation these anchor stores bring. What if they leave? Your location's quality could dramatically drop. To get out of your lease under these unfortunate circumstances, you want to ask for a cotenancy clause.

Although we've segmented a renter's concerns by stage of the leasing process, all of these issues need to be negotiated at the start when crafting a lease. Although landlords often start with a lease they call "standard," nearly everything about it can be negotiated. But be fair; the space may mean a lot to you, but it is a drop in the bucket to large commercial realtors. You can learn more about negotiating in general in Chapter 18, but there are some special considerations for lease negotiations. Because so many aspects are potentially negotiable and areas have different norms for what are typical tenant-friendly clauses, work with a real estate lawyer of your own to help you in the negotiation and phrasing of the lease terms.

Layout

LO6 Know what to look for in evaluating a potential site layout.

Since so much of this is particular to the type of business you are in, what you'll read below is a general guide. Check out competitors or similar types of businesses to see what you like and don't like, what seems to work well, and what seems to cause a lot of problems. In addition, certain categories—restaurants and retailing, for example—have numerous books from college textbooks to do-it-yourself books, like the "For Dummies" series. Try your local library or bookstore.

The layout of a potential site must be considered carefully. Is the building setup appropriate for your use? A restaurant will have different needs than a retail area or a manufacturing plant. The amount of area allocated to the "front room" (e.g., eating or retail areas) versus "back room" (storage, kitchen, warehouse, and office areas) needs to be adequate for the purpose of your business. If you are operating a restaurant or retail operation, how important is space in the front room? A coffee shop or fast-food restaurant squeezes in more customers per square foot than a gourmet restaurant. Do you need specialized areas, such as a kitchen or laboratory that are expensive to retrofit into existing buildings? Is there adequate storage area? How much dock space is appropriate for your business? A manufacturing firm usually needs more dock space and storage than a retailer or a restaurant, while a service company may need very little of either. Retail operations need display windows, while manufacturers do not. For restaurants or other services, this need varies. Is there room for expansion should the business grow? Remember: Moving can be expensive. A good strategy is to rough out the desired layout of your operation on graph paper to get a basic idea of the square footage needed and how it should look. What exactly you want may not be out there, but you'll be able to see what's close and what's impossible to live with.

Consider the amenities that are already there. Carpeting may be appropriate for a retail area and perhaps the office or dining area of a restaurant, but not appropriate for manufacturing or cooking areas. What about the walls? What sort of ceilings and lighting is appropriate? Again, a visit to the competition will help you decide what works and what doesn't, as well as where you want to be different.

Check the exterior, too. Is the building attractive and inviting? Are the sidewalks and landscaped areas in decent shape? Is parking adequate, well lit, and safe? Is employee parking separate from customer parking? What about handicap accessibility? The 1990 Americans with Disabilities Act (ADA) specifies that businesses (with few exceptions) must accommodate persons with disabilities. Many buildings have been brought up to code, and all new construction should meet the requirements of this act, but keep your eyes open.

Once the building has been selected, how you lay out the interior also needs to be considered. While retailers, restaurants, offices, and manufacturers all have different layout needs and considerations, two facts hold true: (1) layouts need to be designed so as to eliminate unnecessary and excessive employee movement, and (2) the layout says something about who you are to your customers, employees, and visitors. In retailing, this last factor is called *atmospherics*. While the opportunities for variation are limitless, let's consider the major types of retail and manufacturing layouts as well as what atmospherics might mean to a business.

Traditionally, manufacturing processes are laid out in one of two formats: production line layout and process layout displayed in Figure 11.2. In the production line layout, material flows in on one side of the operation and continues to the other end of the operation. Most assembly manufacturing is done this way, often with conveyors moving subassemblies from one station to another. Although a rather rigid flow, it works well for mass production and high-volume manufacturing. The second method, process layout, groups similar machines/or functions together, not unlike a typical machine shop. This format is much more appropriate for lower-volume, flexible manufacturing.

FIGURE 11.2

Typical Manufacturing Layouts

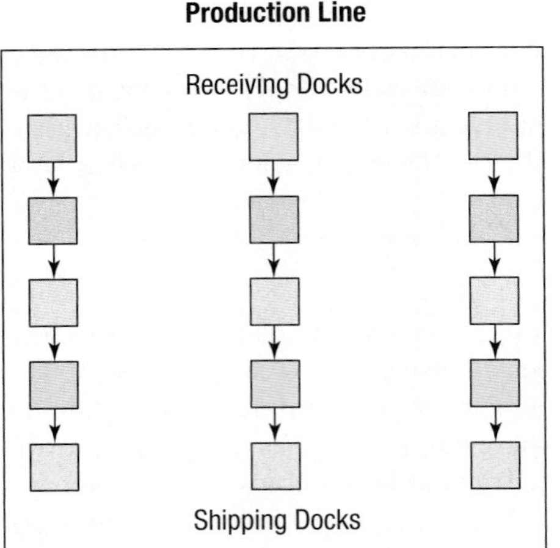

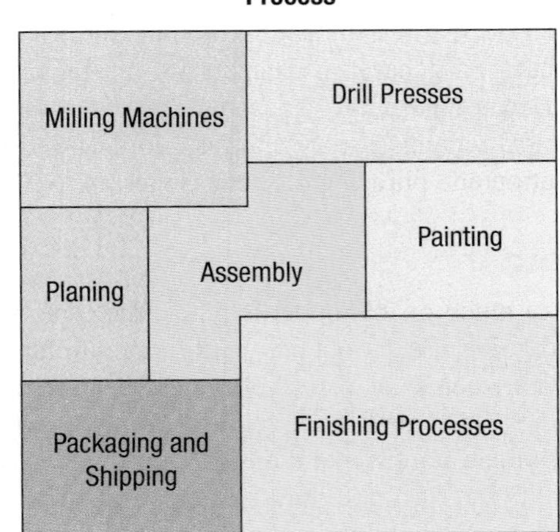

There are also two traditional layouts for retail operations, which are shown in Figure 11.3. The first one, the grid layout, has aisles running from the front of the store to the back like the typical grocery, discount, or convenience store. It's a very efficient and organized layout although it lacks some visual impact. The second layout, the free-form layout, alleviates this problem. In this layout, the store is laid out in sections with aisles that angle or meander through the store. This is the layout more typically found in upscale department stores, clothing stores, and the like.

Atmospherics include all the ambiance items that might be considered in your business. An upscale women's clothing store is likely to have wider aisles, deep carpeting, soft "elevator music," indirect lighting, and, perhaps, a lightly perfumed aroma. These are appropriate atmospherics for the target market. A shop catering to edgy teen fashions may be done in black and chrome with loud rock or alternative music and strobe or black lights. Both of these send a message about whom the store is likely to appeal to. Restaurants use atmospherics, too. Compare a family restaurant to a gourmet restaurant to an ethnic restaurant. Services and the office and public areas of manufacturing firms do this as well in their choice of colors, furniture styles, and background music.[48]

Build, Buy, or Lease[49]

LO7 Understand the pros and cons of buying, building, or leasing.

Ultimately, there are three choices available to the business: build, buy, or lease. Building has the advantage of having the perfect layout in the perfect location and the street appeal of a new building, but it is costly and slow. Buying something already in existence shortens the time and may be

FIGURE 11.3

Typical Retail Layouts

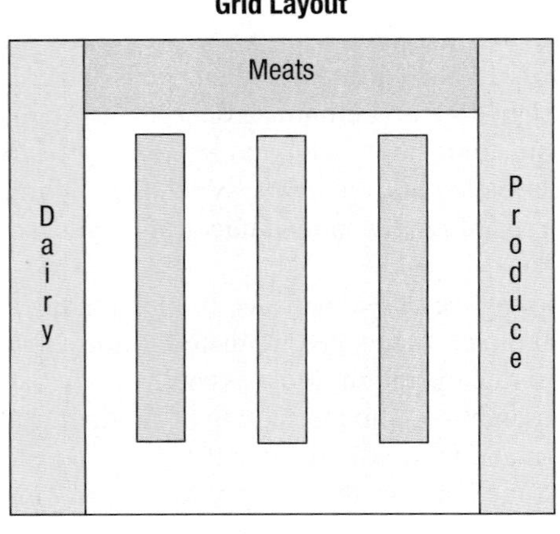

somewhat cheaper, but any remodeling or retrofitting that needs to be done may overshadow any time or money savings. In both cases, though, business owners have an asset that they can leverage, as well as the depreciation tax advantage. They have the flexibility to make the changes they need and know what the long-term costs will be.

Leasing, which we detailed earlier in the chapter, is an option with a considerably lower initial cash outlay, and it is often the only feasible choice for new businesses. Lease expenses are deductible business expenses. One of the main downsides of leasing is that you are usually limited in the renovations you can do. Another one is that leases tend to get higher with each renewal contract, and your landlord may choose not to extend a lease, forcing you to move before you are ready to do so.

The issues of location and distribution are decisions that business owners make only occasionally. Many businesses operate from the same location for their entire existence. Distribution decisions may come up more often. For example, a business started on eBay develops its own website, and then grows into a store in the city's commercial center. Regardless of how often these decisions are made, they are central to the success of the small business, because placing a business in the right location and equipping it with the right channels of distribution are essential to finding and connecting with customers. Done right, managing the issues of location and distribution can turn an average firm into a major success.

CHAPTER SUMMARY

LO1 Recognize the different types of direct marketing and their pros and cons.

- Word-of-mouth is a good starting point and is low cost, but is not controllable and is limited in reach.
- Direct sales fall into a variety of categories:
  - Most business-to-business sales are conducted by the personal contact of a salesperson calling on the potential customer.
  - Door-to-door sales are becoming less popular with the small amount of time to find people at home and privacy issues. On the other hand, they are particularly effective for product demonstration.
  - Party sales also face some time limitations, but are popular ways of selling products from detergents to personal care products and from housewares to lingerie.
  - Vending machines provide 24-hour-a-day convenience for certain types of products.
- Direct mail encompasses catalogs, flyers, letters, videos, mail order, and anything else that can be mailed.
  - Address lists—even lists on labels—can be purchased to match particular demographic or geographic targets.
  - Direct faxing and direct e-mailing are variations on this. Unsolicited e-mail, known as spam, is subject to restrictions from the national CAN-SPAM law and local and state legislation.
- Telemarketing has two forms:
  - Outbound telemarketing is when the company calls the customer. It is severely restricted by "do not call" lists and other legislation.
  - Inbound telemarketing is when the customer calls the company; this is often in response to a piece of direct response advertising.
- Direct response advertising is any ad that prompts the consumer to make contact with the company by phone, mail, or e-mail.
  - In addition to straight-out direct advertising spots, television offers opportunities to reach customers through home shopping networks.
  - Magazines offer targeted audiences and four-color printing opportunities as well as less expensive classified types of ads.
  - Radio direct response advertising is possible, but audiences are highly distracted and frequently unable to immediately respond or write down telephone numbers or addresses.
- Guerilla marketing is a term used to describe extremely low-cost or free alternative marketing. It covers things such as doorknob hangers or flyers stuck under windshield wipers.
- Multichannel marketing refers to giving your customers multiple ways of contacting you—phone, website, or mail-in order forms, for example.

- Direct selling distribution issues include:
  - Federal Express, UPS, and the U.S. Postal Service offer shipping software and services for small businesses.
  - For larger shippers, fulfillment centers or distribution center partners may provide better services.

LO2 Learn how to do nondirect distribution.

- Nondirect distribution requires using wholesalers, distributors, or retailers as well as other intermediaries.
- The appropriate channel may be discovered by tracing similar products back to their sources.
- Getting distributors interested may mean starting with direct sales through catalogs or trade shows to establish your product, demand, and reputation.
- E-tailers—Internet stores—may be willing to take on unknown suppliers and products because they have low overhead.

LO3 Differentiate the types of international strategies.

- Entrepreneurs generally fall into three categories in using international strategies: some will always remain local; some are founded specifically to be international; and most believe that international business might be right for them some day, but do not worry about it until that day comes.
- Small businesses have the same options as large businesses in the international area (licensing, joint ventures, etc.) but most will start with—and may always stay with—an exporting strategy.
- Exporting has four main steps:
  - Determining whether you're ready to export. This includes knowing if your product is appropriate, understanding whether you have the expertise or need outside help, and deciding exactly how you prefer to export.
  - Determining where to export. This step helps select the market or markets best suited for your product.
  - Determining whom to contact. This step explores ways to find appropriate contact people internationally.
  - Determining how to begin. Considerations at this stage include:
    - Shipping documents and paperwork.
    - Payment procedures.
    - Financing and insurance.
    - Conflict resolution.
- Importing: While many of the steps are similar to those for exporting, it is important to know how to find potential products to import and how to make the initial contacts.

LO4 Identify the factors to consider in selecting your business location.

- While most entrepreneurs assume they'll operate in their hometown, this isn't always the best location for their businesses.
  - Key consideration 1: What's the best business climate for your operation?
  - Key consideration 2: Where's the best location for getting to your customer?
  - Key consideration 3: Where's the best location for access to the raw materials, labor, and other factors necessary to conduct your business?
- Service firms may perform work at the client's location, at a mutually accessible location, or be remotely located and have limited customer interface.
- Manufacturers may be home-based, but most will be located away from the home. Contract manufacturing is a low-cost way to get started.
- Site selection choices include home-based businesses, high customer contact locations, and low customer contact locations.
- High customer contact considerations include:
  - Traffic:
    - Where is your best-sized target market?
    - What are traffic generators, and which ones are appropriate for you to use?
  - Customer ease: Consider traffic barriers, parking, and distance from the customer.
  - Competition:
    - Competition clusters are typical in some locations and for some types of business.
    - Having a noticeable differential advantage may make you look good compared to the competition.
- Low customer contact considerations include:
  - Business or light industrial parks provide lower-cost space and nearby amenities.
  - Empowerment zones, available in some areas, may also provide tax breaks.
  - Business incubators are an option that is good for networking with other entrepreneurs, generally at the cost of a portion of your equity.

LO5 Recognize the key issues in leasing.

- Standard leases are designed to be landlord-friendly.
- Entrepreneurs seek changes, added clauses, or concessions to make the lease fit their needs and circumstances.
- There are issues around choosing a property, operating the firm, and terminating the business which need to be negotiated up front.
- The changes, clauses, and concessions typical in one situation or locality will differ for another.
- Because leases are so complex, the help of a real estate attorney is essential.

LO6 Know what to look for in evaluating a potential site layout.

- The first consideration is the physical layout of the building. Is it large enough and laid out appropriately for your business?
- Second, consider the amenities. Remodeling is possible, but expensive.
- Last, take into account the exterior of the building. Does it have street appeal?
- Manufacturing typically is laid out in one of two ways: production line or process layout.
- Retailing also has two primary layouts: grid or free form.
- Atmospherics tell customers a lot about your business and the type of customers you are likely to service.

LO7 Understand the pros and cons of buying, building, or leasing.

- Buying offers you complete control of your facility and tax advantages, but it comes at a high cost with limited flexibility should you need to move. Remodeling costs, should the building not be exactly right for your business, may add considerably to your overall costs.
- Building offers some of the same advantages and disadvantages of buying; however, you are able to design the building perfectly to your specifications. Customers are likely to be attracted to new buildings and tend to feel that a company in a new building must be successful.
- Leasing is the low-cost option and still has some tax advantages, albeit different ones. Leasing allows you the flexibility of moving at any time, but subjects you to increasing rents and landlords who don't renew leases.

KEY TERMS

channels, 348
manufacturer, 348
manufactures' suggested retail price, 348
direct sales, 348
direct marketing, 348
direct mail, 350
mail order, 350
microinventory, 352
just-in-time inventory, 352
telemarketing, 353
direct response advertising, 354
guerilla marketing, 355
multichannel marketing, 356
fulfillment center, 357
retailer, 357
wholesaler, 357
agent, 357
e-tailer, 358
born international, 359
direct exporting, 360
indirect exporting, 360
freight forwarders, 360
letter of credit, 362
documentary draft, 362
contract manufacturing, 366
sheltered workshop, 366
traffic generators, 368

DISCUSSION QUESTIONS

1. Some of the most innovative start-ups have been firms that have dared to buck tradition in their distribution choices, like Netflix.com which distributes rental videos through the mail from its website. Select four small businesses and come up with unique distribution systems for them. Beyond the differential advantage, what other advantages might this give a firm?
2. What would be good traffic generators for a fast food restaurant? For an office supply shop? For a tattoo parlor?
3. What competitive clusters can you identify in your hometown or school location?

4. What products could be sold in vending machines that currently are not? What about party sales?
5. The chapter mentioned several unique guerilla marketing pieces that stood out from the rest—the landscaper who used a plastic sandwich bag of decorative stones with his business card and the decorator whose ad was on a wallpaper scrap. Come up with two or three innovative ways of presenting your message.
6. What direct response ads can you recall seeing or hearing lately? Which ones were more effective? Why?
7. Pick a hobby or sport you enjoy. If you had developed a product related to that hobby or sport, what are likely groups, associations, or other organizations that have meetings which might be a good place to set up a sales booth?
8. Assume you have developed innovative new business software and want to sell it internationally. Without doing any research, come up with a list of likely countries. Why did you choose the ones you did? If the product had been a nutrition bar or soft drink, would the list be different? Why?

EXPERIENTIAL EXERCISES

1. Select a product or service and pretend you are able to start that business anywhere in the United States. Using Skill Module 11.2 in the chapter, find a location different from your hometown or school location that would be appropriate to situate your business. What criteria did you use to make your selection?
2. Choose a business that you might someday like to start. Try one of the direct marketing address providers' websites listed in the chapter and locate a list that you feel would be appropriate to reach your market. Which list did you select and why? What would it cost?
3. Select a major high customer contact business category (restaurant, retail, dry cleaning, beauty salon, etc.)—and visit two or more different providers. What do you see in their store layout that seems to work well and what suggestions do you have for things that might work better?
4. Visit two stores, one where you belong to the target market and one where you do not. Make a list of all the atmospherics you detect and explain how they appeal to the target market.
5. Keep a list of direct marketing you experience for a week. Which messages did you find particularly appealing? Why? Which ones were you more likely to ignore?

MINI-CASE

THE RISE AND FALL OF AUCTIONDROP[50]

Randy Adams had a garage full of stuff too good to throw away. It was so bad that his car would no longer fit. His wife suggested selling some of the things on eBay, but Adams wasn't sure it was worth the effort. He'd have to take digital photos of everything, post auctions, wait for bids, arrange shipments, hope payments came in, and hopefully eventually get rid of everything. Also, as a new "eBayer," he had no feedback from previous sales, something that can make or break a seller as buyers are sometimes reluctant to use untested sellers. Of course, if he had these problems, so would a lot of other people. This sounded like an entrepreneurial opportunity to Adams, and so he started AuctionDrop in San Carlos, California, in March 2003. For a percentage of the selling fee, AuctionDrop will do all the work for you—photos, posting, monitoring, packaging and shipping, and payment collection. When the firm started, it amazed customers by selling 92 percent of everything it had listed compared to the typical eBay average of 50 percent. If the item isn't sold, AuctionDrop would ship it back to you or donate it to charity and provide a tax receipt for you.

AuctionDrop wasn't the only company doing this. Isoldit (**www.i-soldit.com**), Quik-Drop (**www.quickdrop.com**), Auction Wagon (**www.auctionwagon.com**), Door to Door Auctions (**www.doortodoor.com**), and PictureitSold (**www.pictureitsold.net**) jumped into the market, creating a nationwide industry of drop-off centers offering similar services.

At first the future seemed rosy. In less than a year, AuctionDrop had five stores with plans for 15 to 20 more. They slowed this expansion schedule down when Randy realized that the stores weren't bringing in a lot of profit. A city needed only one location to get the work done efficiently. Having multiple locations just meant more fixed costs and less profit. His thought was that arranging for places where customers could drop off their goods would be a better way to go long term. So he negotiated an agreement with The UPS Stores that provides more than 3,800 sites, worldwide.

But to fund his original plans for growth involved taking outside money, and those investors wanted to see returns. Randy estimated 10 items a day per UPS store, but while UPS was willing to receive, pack, and ship the goods, it was only one of a myriad of services they provided. AuctionDrop did not get anywhere near the volume they expected from these stores, and Randy couldn't afford to advertise nationally. Meanwhile the clock was ticking and the investors getting impatient.

CASE DISCUSSION QUESTIONS

1. If you were starting a similar service, where would you locate? What sort of building would you want?
2. Compare the costs and benefits of AuctionDrop's original store-based model with the model using UPS for drop-offs. What was needed to make each work? What would you imagine to be the impact on AuctionDrop's profit margins of each approach?
3. How could AuctionDrop let eBay and UPS users know they are available?

SUGGESTED CASES AND ARTICLES

- The Story of Signs & Signifiers, C-12

Available on McGraw-Hill Create™:

- Sidethrusters, Inc.
- Delavoie International

SUGGESTED VIDEOS

www.mhhe.com/katz4e

Video Case:

- For a written video case and corresponding clip, visit the OLC at www.mhhe.com/katz4e and select "Chapter 11".
- Fresh-Baked Entrepreneurs

SBTV.com Videos:

- Build a website to Go Global
- Shopping Center Leases (Part 1 of 2)

CHAPTER 12

Marketing Plans: Saying How You'll Get Sales

● Kwok-Foon Lai knew the food in his restaurant would be liked. What other market considerations did he take into account when opening his restaurant?

LEARNING OBJECTIVES

After you complete this chapter, you will be able to:

LO1 Understand the importance of a marketing plan.

LO2 Recognize the major methods for conducting market research.

LO3 Use sales forecasting methods.

LO4 Find or create a product's differential advantage.

LO5 Identify the critical components of a marketing plan.

Focus on Small Business: Kwok-Foon Lai and the Kwok Kee Restaurant

The problems of small business marketing are universal. For example, whenever the Lais would serve their family's porridge recipe, their Hong Kong friends raved about it. If all their friends liked it, it seemed reasonable that others would too, and the idea for Kwok Kee, a porridge restaurant founded in 1968, was born. Porridge is an everyday food—almost the Chinese version of fast food—and Kwok-Foon Lai needed a way to be different from the restaurants already out there. He knew that good-tasting food alone would not be the key to success, so he systematically considered his options. Lai decided to stay in the local area—Yuen Long, a small city now one of the "satellite cities" of Hong Kong. There were several good reasons for this. First, it was convenient for him. Second, although the nearby Mongkok district of Hong Kong was a popular location for restaurants, Lai knew that the rent expense would drive up his prices. He selected a location on a major street near a large complex of apartments and across from a park. This way, he was in a place where his competition was not, but yet a place with a lot of foot traffic. Also, because his costs were much lower than the competition's, he was able to keep his prices very low. Extensive advertising was beyond his budget, so he used word-of-mouth and backed this up with exceptional customer service. If customers thought the serving size was a bit small, Mrs. Lai would give them more. If a loyal customer was short on cash, she would say with a smile, "Pay when you come to eat next time."[1]

DISCUSSION QUESTIONS

1. A success is more than having the right product or service. What other things did Kwok-Foon Lai consider?
2. What kind of generic strategy did he use, and how did he implement it in his planning for the restaurant?
3. How did choices in one area of the marketing plan impact other areas of the plan?

The Importance of Having a Marketing Plan

LO1 Understand the importance of a marketing plan.

marketing plan
A systematic written plan of all phases of marketing for a business, including information on the product, price, distribution, and promotion strategy, as well as a clear identification of the target market and competition.

You've got your idea for a new business, whether product or service, and you know it's a great idea and you'll be successful beyond your wildest dreams, but to convince a bank or private investor to loan you money or a store or distributor to carry your product, you'll need more than just "gut instinct."[2] Even if you plan to use only your own personal savings and direct marketing, you're going to need some way to determine whether you are accomplishing your goals, something to make sure you're on the right path. At the absolute minimum, a **marketing plan** will help you articulate what it is that you are going to do.[3]

Every year, somewhere between 30 and 50,000 new products are introduced.[4] If history holds, about 75 percent of these will fail.[5] A few were simply bad products, but the majority were good. Why did they fail? They were at the wrong place at the wrong time and were sold at the wrong price or to the wrong people. Sometimes failure is the result of external factors beyond a company's control—economic recessions, bad weather, or unexpected legal changes—but many are the result of the entrepreneurs not giving enough thought to how they'll sell their product. You wouldn't take a trip without a map or directions, so why would you start your business without the same consideration?[6]

The marketing plan is the basic tool for this. This plan examines your current situation, including what your existing competition is doing, and states how you define your product or service, to whom you will sell it, at what price, with what advertising, and how you will get it to your customers. By systematically considering these issues, you can plan for most contingencies and greatly reduce your risk of failure. Creating the marketing plan is the first step in putting together your business plan.

Market Research

LO2 Recognize the major methods for conducting market research.

marketing research
Systematic collection and interpretation of data to support future marketing decisions.

While gut instinct, mentioned above, has its place, there is nothing like specific numbers and hard facts to give entrepreneurs confidence that a plan will actually work. Getting these facts is market research.[7] **Marketing research** can verify the size of the potential market. It can show what the competitors are doing correctly or what their weaknesses are. It can also reveal where potential customers are likely to shop, likely to see advertisements (as well as how they feel about different sources and types of advertisements), and what they consider a reasonable price. You may believe that your product or service has some tremendous advantages over the competition, but marketing research might show you that the customers really aren't willing to switch providers, do not think your features are worth the extra cost, or do not even like these features at all. Without this sort of information, you cannot put together a coherent business plan.[8] Marketing research is where and how you get the facts to support your plan and the proof that what you are planning to do has a reasonably good chance of succeeding.

primary research
New information collected to solve a problem at hand or answer current questions.

secondary research
Information already collected for some other purpose than the current problem or questions.

Research falls into two major categories. **Primary research** is research gathered to answer a specific marketing question. **Secondary research** is research already gathered for some other reason than your specific question, but can be just as useful. The Skill Module in Chapter 11 on using U.S. census data is a good example of using secondary data.

Secondary Research

Secondary research is often free and quick; there is no need to design questions and gather information yourself. Problems with secondary data include that the data may not be timely and you don't always know why the data were gathered and whether they were gathered correctly (biases). Sometimes it is hard to find the exact details you need. Secondary data are always a good starting point and will at least tell you if you are in the ballpark.

The challenge in secondary analysis is finding data. The most useful websites for finding fast and reliable secondary data for marketing research include:

- *BizStats.com:* Benchmarks, statistics, and financials for industries and the economy.
- Economic Census (*census.gov*): Sales, payrolls, employees for all industries. Also contains considerable detail on costs and characteristics (e.g., type of cuisine for restaurants) for individual industries.

- Business Expenses Survey (www.census.gov/econ/bes/): Covers wholesale, retail, and some service industries.
- Capital Expenditures Survey (www.census.gov/econ/aces/): Covers major expenditures for most industries. A companion survey is on Information and Communications Technology Expenditures (www.census.gov/econ/ict/).
- E-commerce Industry Reports (www.census.gov/econ/estats/): Overviews of performance and prospects of the Internet industry.
- Population and Household Statistics: Following the technique used in Skill Module 11.2, you can look at a wide variety of household statistics obtained by the government (e.g., income, education, computer ownership, health insurance, housing costs, number and age of family members, etc.) and made available to us on the Census website as well as on many commercial websites, including some free ones like www.zipwho.com and www.city-data.com.

There are also compendia which list secondary data sources with focused interests like the WWW Virtual Library in Economics' listing of worldwide economic statistics (www.helsinki.fi/WebEc/EconVLib.html), Intute's catalog of data sources (www.intute.ac.uk), and KnowThis' (www.knowthis.com) comprehensive website of databases and articles, the Canadian Government's Strategis website (www.canadabusiness.ca/eng/ for marketing information), and compendia sites linking to commercial resources like *Valuationresources.com.*

There are also commercial services which offer information (and in some cases may be the only source for the data you need). Examples include *Mintel.com* (focused largely on consumer data), *Freedonia.com* (B2B focus) as well as general purpose business data sources like Gale's Business & Company Resource Center, Lexis/Nexis, or ProQuest's ABI/Inform. Check with your school's library to see which databases they subscribe to and obtain a quick introduction to using them from your library's reference librarian.

Let us take a moment and see how you can use these resources to determine the three most important numbers for a marketing plan—the total size of the market (in terms of sales, or failing that, customers) for the geographic area of your focus, the typical price of a product or service like yours, and the typical profitability of that product or service.

Size of Market: When you are looking at a store level (for example, a women's shoe store), the Census can often give you what you want. Look at Figure 12.1 (copies of these Census and BizStats reports are available on the text's Online Learning Center). For a women's shoe store (NAICS code 4882102—look at the Chapter 7 Skill Module "Finding Your Firm's Industry" if you need to recall how to find this), the total market across the United States in 2007 was $2,561,825,000. There were 3,445 women's shoe stores, so they averaged sales of $743,636 each. These stores employed 22,276 people (6.5 employees per store on average), and paid these folks $386,916,000 in payroll or $17,369 each, which suggests these were mostly part-time positions.

If you are thinking of a shoe store employing only you, you can look at the nonemployer numbers lower on the same page, which apply to all types of shoe stores (they are not broken down by type of store like the employer numbers). Figure 12.2 shows that sales for these solo entrepreneurs' stores were $60,002 ($319,393,000/5323 firms; for shoe stores with employees the equivalent figure is $944,202). So a one-person women's shoe store is going to have a relatively low level of sales. For nonemployers and employing firms, we could get numbers specific to your state, and in some cases even your region, by clicking on the Census "More" down arrows. The one you would use for shoe stores is circled in Figure 12.1.

It has gotten easier to get numbers for a product or service line (for example, a women's cross-country athletic shoe). Sticking with the Census, we can look at the "Census: Product Lines" link circled in Figure 12.1 and from that discover that women's athletic shoes overall were a $2,949,233,000 market segment. Women's athletic shoes represented about 11 percent of all sales. (Note that results from the 2012 Economic Census will become available in 2013.)

Notice that we did not find any measures of the number of customers. For those, we would need to look at the commercial databases like Mintel or contact one of the trade associations (e.g., National Shoe Retailers Organization, found using a Google search for two words—association and shoe). You could also look for a trade magazine on the shoe or fashion or athletic wear industry and find a report on the industry (these often occur yearly in a particular issue).

FIGURE 12.1

2007 Economic Census Report on Shoe Stores with Employees

Source: *U.S. Census Bureau, "Industry Statistics Sampler: NAICS 448210—Shoe Stores," n.d., www.census.gov/econ/industry/hierarchy/i448210.htm (accessed June 30, 2012).*

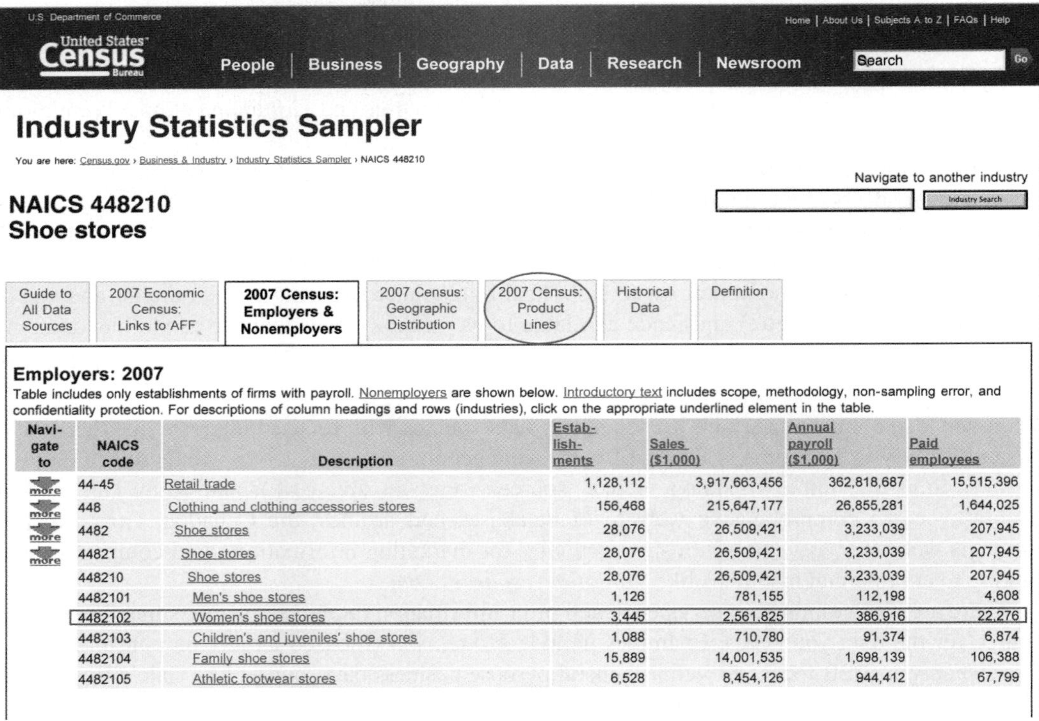

Industry Statistics Sampler

You are here: Census.gov › Business & Industry › Industry Statistics Sampler › NAICS 448210

Navigate to another industry

Industry Search

NAICS 448210
Shoe stores

Guide to All Data Sources | 2007 Economic Census: Links to AFF | **2007 Census: Employers & Nonemployers** | 2007 Census: Geographic Distribution | 2007 Census: Product Lines | Historical Data | Definition

Employers: 2007

Table includes only establishments of firms with payroll. Nonemployers are shown below. Introductory text includes scope, methodology, non-sampling error, and confidentiality protection. For descriptions of column headings and rows (industries), click on the appropriate underlined element in the table.

Navigate to	NAICS code	Description	Establishments	Sales ($1,000)	Annual payroll ($1,000)	Paid employees
more	44-45	Retail trade	1,128,112	3,917,663,456	362,818,687	15,515,396
more	448	Clothing and clothing accessories stores	156,468	215,647,177	26,855,281	1,644,025
more	4482	Shoe stores	28,076	26,509,421	3,233,039	207,945
more	44821	Shoe stores	28,076	26,509,421	3,233,039	207,945
	448210	Shoe stores	28,076	26,509,421	3,233,039	207,945
	4482101	Men's shoe stores	1,126	781,155	112,198	4,608
	4482102	Women's shoe stores	3,445	2,561,825	386,916	22,276
	4482103	Children's and juveniles' shoe stores	1,088	710,780	91,374	6,874
	4482104	Family shoe stores	15,889	14,001,535	1,698,139	106,388
	4482105	Athletic footwear stores	6,528	8,454,126	944,412	67,799

Prices: The easiest way to find selling prices for products these days is on the Internet, using the Google product search service (www.google.com/shopping), *Pricescan.com*, or *MySimon.com*. Today even industrial products can be found using these comparison shopping engines, especially Google. For services, there are sites like *eLance.com* or *SmarterWork.com* which sell services online, and let you get some idea about prices, although these will be far more variable. Typically you can see what contracts have been posted, and get an idea of the basic charges for services. A better approach is to ask potential customers what they are currently paying (and what do they get for their money).

Profitability: While the profitability of any particular store is nearly impossible to find, industry standards for profitability are easier than most people realize. For example, we have talked repeatedly about *Bizstats.com*. Go there and look at the benchmark box at the lower half of the page, scroll down to the closest category. In the "Annual Sales" box enter the average sales for stores obtained from the Census for "All Firms" in Figure 12.2 below, $803,282. Select "Corporations" as the form of business and click "Submit." The major industry is "Retail Trade" and the specific industry is "Clothing-Clothing accessories stores." The resulting table tells us the net profit is 7.45 percent.

This number is a ballpark estimate, since it is not specific to shoe stores, much less women's shoe stores, and does not even consider location. The numbers it gives are averages. More important to your plans, the profits reflect an average of stores where the vast majority of them are older and more experienced than you are at this point. As a result, the 13.7 percent tells us what you *could* make once you learned the business and solved the problems that others have mastered. Still, as a starting point, the BizStats numbers can give you an idea. *BizStats.com* also provides a breakdown of financial information for major categories and includes a report for "Clothing & Accessory Stores." In that report, they give overall profits of 12 percent for profitable stores.

It is wise not to depend entirely on one source when performing secondary analysis. In fact, there are other, more detailed sources available in your college or public library. These include the Risk Management Association's (formerly Robert Morris Associates) *Annual Statement Studies,* Dun &

Nonemployers: 2007

Data based on 2007 Nonemployer Statistics. Table includes only firms subject to federal income tax. Nonemployers are businesses with no paid employees. Introductory text includes scope and methodology. For descriptions of column headings and rows (industries), click on the appropriate underlined element in the table.

		All firms		Nonemployers				Employers	
				Establishments		Receipts			
NAICS code	NAICS Title	Establish-ments	Receipts ($1,000)	Number	% of all	$1,000	% of all	Establish-ments	Sales ($1,000)
44-45	Retail trade	3,107,688	4,005,806,374	1,979,576	63.7	88,142,918	2.2	1,128,112	3,917,663,456
448	Clothing and clothing accessories stores	297,990	221,591,815	141,522	47.5	5,944,638	2.7	156,468	215,647,177
4482	Shoe stores	33,399	26,828,814	5,323	15.9	319,393	1.2	28,076	26,509,421
44821	Shoe stores	33,399	26,828,814	5,323	15.9	319,393	1.2	28,076	26,509,421
448210	Shoe stores	33,399	26,828,814	5,323	15.9	319,393	1.2	28,076	26,509,421

N = Not available

Nonemployer Impact for NAICS 448210
Shoe stores

Establishments

Sales

Nonemployers
Employers

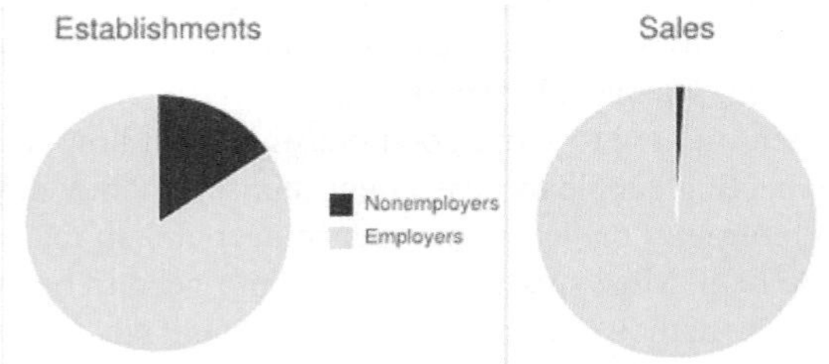

Note: Nearly all other statistics shown or linked on these pages are limited to employers, leaving out the nonemployer firms shown above. The only other statistics that include nonemployers are from the Survey of Business Owners. See the "2007 Economic Census: Links to AFF" tab.

Measuring America—People, Places, and Our Economy

FIGURE 12.2

2007 Economic Census for Shoe Stores without Employees

Source: *US Census Bureau, "Industry Statistics Sampler: NAICS 448210-Shoe Stores," n.d., www.census.gov/econ/industry/hierarchy/i448210.htm (accessed June 30, 2012).*

Bradstreet's *Industry Norms and Key Business Ratios,* or Leo Troy's annual *Almanac of Business and Industrial Financial Ratios.* All of these sources offer breakdowns of financial information based on the sales of firms, which can help you get a better idea of costs for the newest and smallest businesses. Also, they are widely recognized and respected by bankers, and are probably the sources for the financial ratios and sales numbers they will look up when they benchmark your business, so it makes sense to check those sources too.

Primary Research

Primary data are specific to the problem you are solving. You decide what you need to know and how to get that information. This information is extremely current, but it will take somewhat more time and money to gather it. There are marketing research firms that could do this for you, but the cost—usually several tens of thousands of dollars—tends to put it out of reach for small businesses. A much more reasonable option is an online survey. (See Table 12.1 for some cost comparisons.) Of course, an online survey works only if your target audience is likely to be online and if the questions you want answered are suitable. (Try doing an online taste test, for instance.) Companies such as Zoomerang (www.zoomerang.com) and Survey Monkey (www.surveymonkey.com) will help you do professional work. Both offer free surveying for small samples and short questionnaires. For serious surveying (with unlimited respondents), both offer packages around $200 per year. Also check out your local Small Business Administration office or the local SCORE (www.score.org); they can suggest local research companies that might be more reasonable and that are used to working with small businesses.

There are also new online services offering low-cost research opportunities with samples selected according to your criteria. SurveyMonkey, Zoomerang, and sites such as Ask Your Target Market (www.aytm.com) let you select groups from their survey panels and then pay them to take

In a focus group, the goal is to get participants to talk about their impressions of a product, service, company, or concept. How would you select focus group participants to give you the best feedback for your business idea?

TABLE 12.1 Cost Comparisons for Various Survey Methods[9]

	Mail	Phone	Online
Setup	$40,000	$6,000	$1,500
Invitations	34,800	66,667	500
Processing	38,560	72,000	0
Total	$113,360.00	$144,667	$2,000
Cost/response	$4.72	$6.03	$0.08

(Based on 12 surveys with 2,000 responses each.)

your survey. GutCheckIt.com offers a similar service when you want online interviews. These services can generate results in one to two days based on your criteria, often for $500 or less. If you are flexible as to who is answering, you can also try online.

There are volumes written on how to write good questions and how to gather and analyze data scientifically. If you are expecting people to invest huge sums of money in your business, your data had better be accurate and correctly gathered. In order to accomplish this, study a good marketing research text or hire outside help. Most small businesses don't need to be quite so formal; potential investors will let you know where they need more information and what they want to see. For help in designing your questionnaire and collecting and analyzing data, the Small Business Administration office, SCORE, or a marketing professor will often be good sources for free or relatively inexpensive help. Many community colleges, technical colleges, and university marketing classes are often looking for projects for their students to do as part of the course. They may not only write the questions, but also gather the data and help analyze them for you. Of course, this is somewhat dependent on your time frame fitting the quarter or semester. In other words, classes may not be a good source if you need the information this week. Many of these schools will also have marketing clubs whose members would love to do a project for a modest donation—well supervised by their adviser.

ethnographic research
Data gathered by simple observation—seeing what consumers do, rather than asking them.

focus group
A form of data gathering using a small group led by a moderator.

There are a number of methods for gathering data. One category consists of observation methods. For example, I could go to the local grocery store and watch people shop. I could make lists of the products they choose and the time they spend making decisions.[10] This is called **ethnographic research** and has its place. For example, if I was considering opening a restaurant in a particular location, I could stand in front of the location and count foot and automobile traffic. I could visit a competitive restaurant and observe what people ordered, how long they stayed, and the time of day they visited. I could listen to the customers' comments about what they like or don't like.[11]

Another method is the **focus group**, which is a small group (8 to 20 people) that is asked to meet to discuss a series of questions about a particular product or service. A skilled researcher, who can make sure the questions are asked the right way and the data are systematically collected, conducts these meetings. Because participants are paid for their time, this can be an expensive prospect for many small businesses.[12] On the other hand, gathering a few friends and neighbors over for dinner and quizzing them on their ideas about your product may be just as productive, if not quite so formal. (See Skill Module 12.1 for a brief explanation of how to conduct a focus group.) This more informal approach is also a good way to test your questions to make sure your audience understands exactly what you are

SKILL MODULE 12.1 How to Conduct a Focus Group

Focus groups are one of the most widely used techniques for getting information, especially at early stages, when you may not know everything you need to know about your product, service, or market. While it is probably best to have professionals run your focus group, you can do a passable job on your own if you follow these steps:

1. **Background:** Take a look at a book on how to conduct a focus group to familiarize yourself with the technique. Some examples are books like *Focus Groups: A Practical Guide for Applied Research* by Richard A.

Krueger and Mary Anne Casey (Thousand Oaks, CA: Sage Publications, Inc., 2000), or guides put out by Omni (www.omni.org/docs/focusgrouptoolkit.pdf) or Duke University (**http://assessment.aas.duke.edu/documents/How to Conduct a Focus Group.pdf**) or the brief guide from the Australian Museum Audience Research Center (**http://australianmuseum.net.au/How-do-I-conduct-a-focus-group/**).

2. **Questions:** Determine the three things you'd like to know about how potential customers think about their purchases of your product or service. Aim for open-ended questions.
3. **Moderator:** To help people feel at ease, it is better to get someone other than you to moderate the focus group. If you have a friend with experience, that's great. If not, a friend who works as a salesperson, especially the sort who travels, has many of the needed skills, such as getting people to explain their reservations, dealing with a variety of customer reactions, and thinking on his or her feet. You can also check with the local university to see if there are students or professors with experience whom you can hire.
4. **Location:** Get a location that is comfortable and offers few distractions. In order to hear what is going on, buy or borrow a child's in-room monitor, so you can listen from a distance to the focus group as it happens. Get a tape recorder to keep all the comments.
5. **Participants:** Think in terms of friends and friends of friends. Look for people who like to talk and are likely buyers of your product or service or who are already using a competitor's product or service. Offering dinner and perhaps a small gift or a drawing for a larger gift is suitable for this kind of setting.
6. **Scheduling:** Aim for a two-hour block of time. Take a break after around 60–75 minutes so you can talk to the moderator if you need to adjust the questions or probe for answers. Greet the participants as they arrive and leave, and be ready to answer their questions. It is a nice touch to come in and answer participant questions at the end of the session, if you can do it graciously and without sounding defensive.
7. **Analysis:** Have an adviser or mentor listen to the tape separately from you, and discuss what he or she noticed and what you did. Where possible, build a poll of responses to see how many people felt one way or another. Be on the lookout for concerns or problems people raised.

asking. This is especially important with close-ended questions, because there may be alternatives you hadn't considered or ambiguities you hadn't noticed. (This is sort of like the yes/no question, "Have you stopped spanking your children?" How do you answer that if you *never* spanked them?)

A more typical data-gathering tool is the **survey**—some form of questionnaire. The questions may be written, asked in person or asked on the telephone. In person tends to be the most expensive method, with telephone coming in second, and mail the least expensive. On the other hand, mail has the lowest return rate and does not allow for much flexibility. In person, you can ask for clarification, have people expand on their answer, or even change the next question based on the response. Internet surveys, mentioned earlier, are gaining in popularity and have the advantage of being able to collect data from a large geographic area inexpensively. By using multiple screens of questions, respondents can select the screen they will see based on their responses to an earlier question (known in Internet survey terms as *branching*). For example, if a respondent is currently not using a particular product, the next questions he or she sees may go after the reasons for not using it. If respondents do currently use the product, the next questions may ask about their current provider.[13]

survey
A data-collection method using a questionnaire—in person, on phone, on paper, or on the Internet.

Having a set of predetermined written questions has certain advantages whether responses are oral or in writing. If you ask the same questions to each respondent, you can accurately compare answers and even statistically analyze these answers. You can come up with an average answer or compare answers between two (or more) specific groups (and conduct more complex statistical analysis, if the situation warrants it).

Surveys can be done online, by mail, or in person like the entrepreneur and prospective customer here. What kinds of questions would work well in face-to-face interviews?

For example, suppose you ask people to rate your product on a scale of 1 to 10. The average rating might be 6.5 with 10 being high. This is nice information to know, but what could you find out by reexamining the data? What is the range of answers? If it is 5 to 8, you know that most people have similar feelings about your product—better than average but not perfect, with those at the 8 level being relatively pleased. It might take just a few tweaks of your product to move that average up to 7.5 or higher.

What if the range was from 1 to 10? Now you have people who love your product and others who hate it. It would likely take tremendous changes to convert those 1s to higher scores, and those changes might end up alienating the 10s. You now have a whole different scenario from when the range was small. What if you subdivided the answers based on some demographic value? For

scalar questions
Questions that are answered by some sort of scale; for example, "On a scale of 1 to 5, how do you like this book?"

dichotomous questions
Questions that have only two possible choices; for example, "Have you shopped here before?"

categorical questions
Questions that are answered by selecting the proper category; for example, "What is your ethnicity? White, African American, Hispanic, Asian, American Indian, Other."

open-ended questions
Questions that allow respondents to express themselves as they choose; for example, "What do you like about this book?"

example, maybe you could sort by sex, age, wealth, or race. If we subdivide our answers into male and female, for example, we might find out that the average male response was 3.4, while the average female response was 7.8. If our product were a new skin lotion with a floral fragrance, we would expect women to like it better than men. If we thought the fragrance was neutral (and we should have asked this in our questionnaire), maybe we want to revise the scent or simply focus on the target market that likes it, the women.

There are two major types of questions used in surveys: open- and close-ended questions. One frequent type of close-ended question—the **scalar question**—is illustrated above: "On a scale of 1 to 5, how would you rate XYZ?" **Dichotomous questions** are those with two choices—sex, employed or not, and so on. **Categorical questions** give you several predetermined groups from which to choose—for example, age levels (under 20, 20 to 29, 30 to 39, etc.). **Open-ended questions** allow the interviewees to answer any way they wish. Instead of asking, "Do you like XYZ?" (a question that can be answered, "yes," or "no,"), you could ask, "What are the advantages of XYZ?"

With close-ended questions, which can be answered only in certain ways, it is much easier to compare groups and to statistically analyze. However, they can limit the information you get. Let's say that your research shows that many people are concerned with the quality of their lawn service. What does this mean? One woman may believe that the trimming isn't as accurate as she would like, while a man is upset because the service ruined his in-ground sprinkler system. A simple 1–5 scalar, close-ended question wouldn't capture this information. Open-ended questions—"What do you dislike about your current lawn service?"—would.[14]

Open-ended questions, which can be answered in many ways, can help you find new niches and perfect your product or service before you introduce it. Stephanie Kellar (www.lashoutpro.com) had an idea for a new eyelash curler. She posted open-ended questions on a Usenet newsgroup called alt.fashion. In just a few months, she had collected information from over 100 people with minimal effort. She also used this venue to find people willing to test her new product in the development phase.[15]

As Stephanie Kellar found out, polling a group of consumers with common interests on the Internet is an inexpensive way to do marketing research and to find potential new customers for both test markets and the real thing. To find Usenet groups appropriate for your product or service, try Google, or more specifically, Google's group search at http://groups.google.com.

Open-ended questions provide data that are more difficult to tabulate; they take considerably more time to ask and evaluate, and answers can be difficult to compare. For example, if you asked, "How often would you use this product?" you might get answers such as "some of the time," "two or three times a month," or "whenever I have guests." Are those answers the same? If not, which one reflects a heavier user? In this case, a categorical question (once a month, 2–3 times a month, 4–5 times a month, etc.) would be easier to interpret. Open-ended questions are best for gathering preliminary information, when samples are small and when there are data that are difficult to get any other way. You can get a feel for the strengths and weaknesses of each type of question from Skill Module 12.2

SKILL MODULE 12.2 Open- and Close-Ended Questions

With a partner, design two questionnaires about a service business you are considering—dry cleaning, restaurant, and so on.

1. One questionnaire should have only open-ended questions, while the other one should ask similar things using closed-ended questions.
2. Each of you should submit your questions (orally or in writing) to 10 people (different sets of people).
3. Compare your results. What are the pros and cons of each set of data?

Lastly, you need to recognize that there is no such thing as perfect information. People say one thing and do another. They may like your product but consider it a luxury item that they may or may not purchase. Things are constantly changing, and no one can understand all the interrelationships and how they might affect a business. There are always more questions that could be asked, and more data that could be collected. Look for support for your ideas, but understand that the best you will have is a good, educated guess.

SMALL BUSINESS INSIGHT

GrandKids[16]

Irene Viento thought she had done things right. She decided to start a retail outlet, GrandKids, to target grandparents—especially those who had money to buy extra special things for their grandchildren. Viento had experience with this target group, being a grandmother herself. She studied the demographics of Pelham, New York, her hometown, and relying on school data and information from an advertising circular company, she estimated that there were about 10,000 families in the area. Although there were 10 direct competitors within eight miles, there were none in Pelham, an upscale New York City suburb. She found a location just outside of town and started her business in 1994, but she had to close her doors by 1997. Basically, her research was flawed: Pelham had only slightly more than 3,200 families and the largest age group was in the 22–49 range—not the grandparents Viento needed. She also didn't know whether her potential customers were willing to drive to her out-of-town location, and if they were, wouldn't they be just as apt to visit her competitors?

Sales Forecasting[17]

One of the most important pieces of the marketing plan—and of the business plan—is knowing what your sales will be. This determines your profitability and, ultimately, whether you will stay in business or not. Often companies base sales forecasts on historical sales, but since you're new, you can't do that. Just as with marketing research, there are costly mathematical or computer-generated models that can be used. There are also much simpler ways of coming up with a reasonably good estimate, such as the one shown in Skill Module 12.3 and the techniques described below it and on the Online Learning Center.

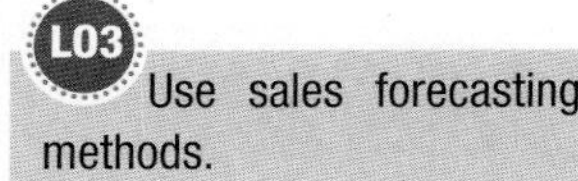

LO3 Use sales forecasting methods.

SKILL MODULE 12.3

Sales Forecasting from a Fixed Inventory

Let's start with a simple reselling example. You will buy St. Louis Cardinals' Adjustable Baseball Caps (with the MLB logo sticker showing it is official) from a St. Louis area Walmart. The caps retail for $5.00, but you talked the store manager into giving you a deal on 100 of them for $4.25 each.

Go to shopping.google.com and type in "St. Louis Cardinals' Cap." In summer 2012, around 905 possibilities came up, with prices ranging from $3.76 to $203 including shipping. Limiting prices to adjustable caps cut the range only slightly, from $3.76 to $35.00.

Now look at the types of caps being offered. The red cap you got from Walmart is the most distinctive of the types, and only two vendors sell a similar cap. One is on eBay and the other has an online store. Both sell it at $9.98, shipping included. This is your baseline price, unless you think you can sell at a premium. Since you have 100 caps, your forecast is how long it will take to sell them. You can track the cap seller on eBay to see how long it takes for the "in stock" number to drop, and then multiply that number of days by 100 to get how long you can expect your stock to last. (If you track sales of the other types of caps, you can learn which are the most in demand and perhaps buy a different type of cap next time.)

You could speed up your sales by going to stores around Cardinals' Stadium on game day and selling the store owner some additional caps, or (if your peddler's license is valid) even sell caps outside the stadium itself. At $10 a cap, you will be undercutting the competition, and should be able to sell all 100 in one afternoon or evening game. A quick Google check shows the stadium seats 43,975, and most games are at 70 percent capacity, so you're looking at 32,981 people. If one person in 300 bought your hats, you'll sell out in one game. By the way, if you're selling out too fast, raise the prices until your hats keep moving, but at a 100-hats-a-game rate.

Some products or services are tied to others. For example, if your company lays sod for new lawns, you can estimate the total market by looking at projected new homes being built in your geographic area. From there, you'll need to calculate what percentage of that market you can get. In other words, what's the competition like, and how do you measure up? If the market is underserved and all the competition is relatively equal in terms of size, product, price, service, and such, you might be able to divide the total market by the number of competitors, and maybe deduct a percentage "just to be safe" since you are relatively new. For example, perhaps the three existing firms will cover 85 percent of the business, and you'll only get 15 percent the first year. On the other hand, if you, or your competitor, offer unique products or services or have other advantages (or disadvantages), these can factor in. Using the same example, if you are the only firm offering in-ground sprinkler installation as well, you may be able to capture a larger portion of the market, or maybe most of a subsection of the market, in this case perhaps the more expensive homes.

Other products are not tied as neatly to others. If you are opening a restaurant, looking at the number of people who eat out in your particular geographic area just won't cut it. Some folks eat only fast food. Others don't like Chinese cuisine. Some go out only for breakfast. As a result, there are many different types of restaurant customers.

This is a good situation for some marketing research. You could conduct traffic counts during the hours you'll be open. You could stop a number of people to ask them how often they eat out and what type of restaurant they are likely to choose (and whether they think they'd like to try yours—a little word-of-mouth advertising). You could stop by your competition and see how long the waiting lists are or pick up a menu and see what prices they are charging. From these items you can get an idea of how many customers you might get.[18] This is certainly "softer" than the first method of estimating and is slightly more subject to error (both overestimation and underestimation). However, for most products this is the best information you can get.

This is also the time to verify that the potential market you've identified meets your capacity. If your restaurant will serve only 120 people over the hours you are open and the potential market is 300, you need to use your capacity figure, *not* your potential market figure. (You may also want to consider a larger space, more tables, more hours, more staff, or other ways of handling this unexpected extra market, if not immediately, at least for the future.) On the other hand, if your potential market is only 50, is that enough to be profitable? (Or can you lease a smaller, less expensive place or cut costs elsewhere to make your business profitable?)

Once you have figured out the number of customers, the next step is to estimate the average amount of sales per customer. This is usually a little easier; if your lunch prices range from $10 to $15, you could select the average price, or, more conservatively, assume everyone will eat the least expensive meal.

If you are selling a product, see what competitive products are going for in the market. Using traditional retailers and distributors nearly always quadruples the price you set "at the factory." You know what your costs will be and you know what profit you need; does this price the product beyond the competition? If so, can you find a way to convince your customers of your extra value, to cut your costs in production, or to use a different distribution channel? (More about that is covered in the other marketing chapters.) Are your prices below that of the competition? While this doesn't sound like it could be a problem, it might be a signal for you to double-check all your assumptions to make sure you didn't miss an important step. (Also, lower prices sometimes cause customers to doubt the quality; you expect more from a $10 T-shirt than from a $2 one.)

bot
A Web-based program that uses artificial intelligence techniques to automate tasks such as searches.

If you are selling online, a search will bring up competitive products. Or use some of the pricing **bots** such as Google product (google.com/shopping) and MySimon (www.mysimon.com) for products, or Elance (www.elance.com) and Smarterwork (www.smarterwork.com) for services to come up with the best prices. For other products, try an Internet search of "your product price bot." eBay is also a good place to check out what the competition is charging. If your prices seem too high or too low, rethink how you calculated your costs, your product, and your method of distribution, or determine how you can create enough value for your customer to choose you over the competitive products out there.

In many cases, the best sales forecast you can come up with is another educated guess. Consider the assumptions you made and try to justify why you made them. Try to anticipate questions that you will be asked and consider your answers beforehand. In some cases you may want to look at several levels of sales forecast—an optimistic, average, and pessimistic view.[19]

Differential Advantage

LO4 Find or create a product's differential advantage.

What makes your product or service different from the competition? In marketing terms, this is called a **differential advantage**, or what strategists call a *competitive advantage*, as discussed in Chapter 7[20] and demonstrated in Skill Module 12.4. When you first envisioned your product or service, chances are that you had a reason for thinking it would succeed in the marketplace. It could be that you found a target market that wasn't being served or was underserved. More commonly, though, this differential advantage is the result of something we do differently in one area of the four Ps—product, price, place, and promotion. Perhaps there is something different about your product or service, maybe something you identified when you analyzed your competition.[21]

differential advantage The characteristic that separates one company from another in product, price, promotion, and/or distribution.

Determining Differential Advantage

SKILL MODULE 12.4

This module works best when using a product or service with which everyone is familiar. Hamburgers or pizzas work very well. We will describe the process with pizza.

1. **Select a product category and target market:** For this demonstration, we will pick pizza delivered to your door. Our target market are students at Saint Louis University.
2. **List four or five competitors in this category:** Obviously you can include the big chains like Domino's and Pizza Hut. But also include some local firms. We will pick two more pizza restaurants from the area around Saint Louis University—Vito's and Imo's.
3. **Use the 4 Ps** (product, price, place, and promotion) to carefully consider how the competitors differ. Since we are talking about delivered pizzas, place is going to be excluded, but look at the other 3 Ps.

	Domino's	Pizza Hut	Vito's	Imo's
Product				
Free delivery	Y	Y	N	Varies
Sicilian style	N	N	Y	N
Superlarge	Y	Y	N	N
Sweet sauce	N	N	N	Y
Price				
1-Topping 14-inch	$14.38	$13.46	$16.44	$16.68
Promotion				
Online coupons	Y	Y	N	N
On-campus coupons	Y	N	Y	Y

The selection of specifics for the 3 Ps used here is one version; you would pick the kinds of issues you think would be important to your target market, such as other food items, trust in the brand, or how "in" the brand is.

4. **Analyze your results:** Obviously, Pizza Hut leads on price. Vito's offers a Sicilian-style pizza and Imo's offers a sweet pizza sauce. Highest-priced Domino's offers little differential advantage compared to the competition. In your comparison, you want to see where competitors are alike, and especially, where they are different. Are those differential advantages likely to make a big difference in sales or profits? A "yes" is great news for that competitor. Are they tough for competitors to copy? A "yes" here can make the originator happy.
5. Repeat this process with a product/service and target market of your choosing.

Let's say your Census Bureau research identified a large Chinese population in the area, most who still speak Cantonese at home (true for areas in or near Los Angeles and some other parts of the country). It could be that few of these people use housecleaning services because of real or perceived language problems. Maybe you have Cantonese language skills and can use this to your advantage. Or maybe as

SMALL BUSINESS INSIGHT

RUTH FERTEL AND RUTH'S CHRIS STEAK HOUSE[22]

Steak houses have been around forever, and steak house franchises come and go. So one can forgive the "experts" who didn't back Ruth's Chris Steak House when it started franchising in 1977. Of course, Ruth Fertel, founder and owner until her death in 2002, had been going against "good" advice since she mortgaged her house and purchased her first restaurant against the advice of her lawyer and banker. Ruth's Chris Steak House differentiated itself by using only the finest ingredients, serving gourmet steaks in an upscale setting, with a good bottle of wine available. Currently, the restaurant has over 115 locations and is patronized by those appreciating the ambience and great food.

a result of rapid new home construction in the area, there are not enough housecleaning services to take care of all the new potential clients. Possibly your research will show people who work evenings and would rather have their houses cleaned then, while they are at work, while most services clean during the days. These would be examples of an underserved or unserved market.

Alternatively, you could create a differential advantage with one of the parts of the marketing mix. (These are the entry wedges discussed in Chapter 7.) Here are some ideas for differentiating based on your product:

- Instead of simply cleaning the house, your service will do grocery shopping, drop off dry cleaning, and run other errands for customers.
- You will provide a homemade meal that can be popped in the microwave once the client returns from their busy day.
- You will offer specialized cleaning services—window cleaning or carpet shampooing.

The possibilities are limited only by your imagination and the customer's perception that you can fill a need.

Your differential advantage could be in pricing. While the lowest prices may attract customers, they are also subject to retaliation by bigger, better-established companies and are usually not a good idea for start-up companies.[23] However, if your cost structure is lower, you may succeed this way. But if your cost structure is not lower, you will not be able to compete in pricing. The key is not necessarily to be cheaper than your competition, but to be different from your competition. For example if the housecleaning services in your area price by the size of house (typical in the industry), you might price by the jobs to be done. Dusting will cost so much, and vacuuming another price; washing dishes is a certain price, while changing bed linens is another. A customer may choose to have your service only vacuum and do laundry.

Why do people pay more to shop at some stores, drive certain cars, or purchase certain brands? While there are differences in products and services, often the differences cannot be justified by the costs. What we have in this case is *prestige pricing*. With prestige pricing, people will pay more for a particular name brand because of the perceived benefits of driving a Jaguar car or wearing a

Rolex watch. If you are able to create a prestige image in your customer's mind, you can charge much higher prices than the going rate. As a matter of fact, unlike other firms, prestige firms often lose customers by lowering prices because the product is perceived to be not quite so good. If you offer a custom product or extra service, you may be able to claim this pricing strategy and use it as a differential advantage.

Place is another area in which your firm may have a differential advantage. While a housecleaning service is somewhat limited as to "place" decisions, other product and service firms have carved market niches for themselves by their place decisions. In the computer industry, Dell—by direct marketing—and Gateway—by its stores carrying only Gateway products—bucked tradition by doing something different. (This attempt at differentiation had mixed results as the Gateway stores proved to be too expensive and needed to be closed.) Smaller operations have done the same—dry cleaners with pick up and delivery services, mobile dental offices, renting videos via the Internet (www.Netflix.com) and mail, and many others.

Promotion, too, can create a differential advantage, although more likely it will be the means by which you convey this advantage to your customers. Creative advertising can woo clients from existing competition or encourage clients not currently buying a product or service to try it. By careful targeting, your promotions will appeal to the wants and needs of your potential customers. A money-back guarantee or free first time consultation encourages customers to try new companies. Discounts for client referrals can grow your business through word-of-mouth. Your housecleaning service could offer free carpet cleaning for a one-year commitment. You could offer a "friends and family" discount of 10 percent off the regular cleaning price for up to five new friends or family members who sign up for your services, plus a discounted cleaning to the original client for each successful referral.

In the vignette at the beginning of the chapter, Kwok-Foon Lai used differential advantages in several areas. He started with a better-than-average porridge and combined it with outstanding customer service (product differential advantage). He was able to keep his costs low and pass these savings on to his customers (price advantage). He selected a location away from his competition, arguably an area that was underserved (place advantage). His word-of-mouth strategy may have been a slow way to get started, but it kept his costs down and helped his pricing strategy (promotion advantage). As time passed, however, his excellent reputation passed on by word-of-mouth kept his customers coming back years after they had moved away from the area.[24]

The Marketing Plan

LO5 Identify the critical components of a marketing plan.

The components of a marketing plan are fairly straightforward.[25] First, you discuss your target market—the people who will be buying your product. Second, you explain your current situation vis-à-vis your competition. In the third section, detail your marketing strategy and objectives. Finally, you explicitly address the 4 Ps: product, promotion, price, and place.[26] Let's discuss each of these components in detail.

Target Market

Target market has been mentioned several times, and defined and described in Chapter 9. It is an essential element of your entire approach to business. It is easy to say that your target market includes "everyone," but that is true for very few products or services. Think of your circle of friends. How many foods or drinks or movies do you all agree on? How would those choices play with your parents? In reality, most products and services work best with some markets. The successful entrepreneur uses this to identify the best market for a good or service.

In developing your product or service, what competitor did you have in mind? Who is the target market for that firm? Which of their customers might agree with your improved approach? That group would be a potential target market.

What if you have a new product or service? Why do you think it serves a purpose? What other people might share the same thought you have? Describe them and you have a possible target market. At other times your target market will get defined geographically, if you have a small neighborhood store or, demographically, if your product or service appeals to only one demographic

● If this photo were used in an advertisement, what markets might it be targeting? What types of products or companies might try to appeal to so many market segments?

segment. For many products and services, however, the appeal might be broader than to a single demographic group.

Marketing professionals like to talk about **market segmentation**, which is also shown in Skill Module 12.5. Segmenting is simply a way to divide the total market—everyone in the world, essentially—into manageable pieces that have some common characteristics. Although you could divide by virtually any method imaginable (by middle initial, month of birth, number of cavities, last book read, etc.), marketers look for segments that are likely to have similar needs and buying behavior. *Geographic segmentation* is one method frequently used. Many businesses, large or small, choose to operate in one country, while even the biggest multinationals choose a manageable number of countries.[27] People who live in cities often have different needs from those in rural areas. People who live in Minnesota have different needs from those in Arizona, particularly in the winter. New Yorkers have different preferences from Los Angelinos. Many service industries have no choice but to segment geographically; if your car wash is located in Phoenix, you aren't going to attract too many customers from outside the city.

market segmentation
The process of dividing the market into groups that have somewhat homogeneous needs for a product or service.

SKILL MODULE 12.5 Identifying Target Market Segments

Marketers select their target market (or markets) first and then design their advertisements to attract and appeal to these customers. While there are "universal" advertisements, more effective ones are those that tempt a specific audience. Here's how you can identify your target market:

1. Go to the library and browse through several magazines. Choose several that appeal to very different audiences, for example, different ethnic groups (*Latina, Ebony*), different age groups (*My Generation, Seventeen*), different hobbies or sports (*Skiing, American Philatelist, Opera Today*), different income levels (*Forbes, Rosie*), different sexes—or sexual orientations (*GQ, Ladies Home Journal, Out, Girlfriend*), different life stages (*Brides, Pregnancy, My Generation*), and the like.
2. Review the ads and look for clues that would cause you to believe that the ad is focused at a particular group.
3. Show several of these ads—without identifying the magazine—and see if your classmates can determine the possible target market. (Figure 12.3 shows a couple of examples.)

FIGURE 12.3

Target Market Ads

These Burger King ads are aimed at targeting two different markets. Can you identify which market(s) each ad is geared toward? Is each ad successful in meeting its market's needs? Why or why not?

Demographic segmentation is also a valuable way to divide the total market. Teenagers have different needs from toddlers, as do other age groups. Where and how people shop and what they buy varies because of income, ethnicity, sex, education level, marital status, and virtually any demographic variable you choose. Life cycle position—unmarried, married without children, married with small children, married with teenage children, empty nesters, retirees, and so on—also determines the types of products a person may be interested in buying.

Benefit segmentation divides customers into groups based on what benefits they seek when making product or service decisions. For example, one customer buys a certain brand of toothpaste because it is a cavity fighter. Another customer wants the toothpaste that gives him fresher breath. A third may be looking for whitening power, while a fourth may want something that fights plaque. Many cars are segmented this way—speed, safety, capacity, and the like. Frequently used categories include those shoppers interested in a good value versus those more interested in reputation and prestige—think of Walmart shoppers versus those frequenting designer dress shops.

Another category for segmenting has to do with an individual's personality. Adventure seekers buy different products (or for different reasons) than more timid people. Hobbies, sports interests, religion, cultural interests, and similar individual factors can determine the likelihood of people purchasing certain products. For example, you are unlikely to purchase Showgard mounts unless you are a philatelist or Salomon SNS Pilot Equipe Skate bindings unless you are a Nordic skier.

A target market is the population segment or segments that are likely to buy your product or service. If you design dresses, you'll want to focus your efforts on women; if they are expensive, custom-designed, evening gowns, you'll want to narrow that focus to wealthier women (demographics, benefits) and those who engage in activities requiring the wearing of evening gowns (hobby, cultural interest).

Generally, marketers choose one of three targeting strategies: undifferentiated, differentiated, and concentrated. An **undifferentiated strategy** is useful when there is really no difference in the reasons why customers buy your products, that is, when it makes no sense to try to segment or target a particular market. Imagine selling bottled water at an outdoor fair on a hot summer day. Folks don't care what brand of water it is, and they are unlikely to go someplace specific for the water. Being at the right place with any reasonable product will get the job done. A lot of entrepreneurs are prone to fall into this trap ("My market is everybody!"), but as you can tell from the example, it is a rare situation in which an undifferentiated strategy works. While it may be true that you have a product that everyone wants, we can find different ways of promoting, distributing, or pricing the product that often attracts different segments. Even for bottled water, someone could say their water is purer, their bottles are bigger, their price lower, and so forth.

undifferentiated strategy
A marketing strategy that uses no segmentation; assumes that all consumers have virtually identical needs and can be reached by the same marketing mix.

A **differentiated strategy** is used when there is more than one market segment likely to need a product or service. By slight differences in how we make the product, promote it, distribute it, or price it, we can appeal to different markets. For example, both women and men use razors, but the color of the razor, the brand name, and product shape and how it is advertised (who uses it and how) are different.

differentiated strategy
A marketing strategy in which a marketer selects two or more distinct groups of consumers and designs specific marketing mixes to meet their needs.

A **concentrated strategy** is used when a firm chooses one particular segment on which to focus all its efforts. Entrepreneurs often are able to locate a particular niche that the larger companies ignore, and by focusing their efforts on them, are able to do extremely well. For example, Dale Bathum was tired of playing golf in shoes that just didn't fit, so in 1996 he formed Bite Footwear to make fashionable yet comfortable golf shoes (concentrated strategy). In later years, he expanded his product line into other shoes—hiking, fishing, running—and added a women's line as well (differentiated strategy).[28]

concentrated strategy
A marketing strategy in which a marketer selects one specific group of consumers and designs a marketing mix specifically for that group.

Why bother with targeting? The main reason is so that you don't waste a lot of effort and money. Once you know who your target market is, you can determine their purchasing behavior. You can find out where people in that group shop, where they are likely to see your advertisements (e.g., what television shows they watch, what magazines they read, what websites they visit, etc.), what prices they expect, what messages are likely to appeal to them—in short, everything you need to know to successfully market to them. If you are trying to sell handmade baby clothes, you could buy a banner ad on the CNN website, but one on the Mommy Mall website is less likely to be wasted on nonpurchasers. It's just logical to be where your potential customers are.[29]

In Chapter 11, you had the opportunity to do a skills module using U.S. census data to locate potential areas for a child day care service. Continuing with this scenario, we decided that certain areas in Phoenix had a concentrated population of Hispanic households with children and enough income to afford child care. People living in these areas would be a likely target market. Using the census data, we could find out more demographic information about them that might be helpful in putting together our marketing plan. For example, looking at their languages spoken at home might give us some clues for how we will want to do our advertising. The key is to be as specific as we can be about who these people are.

We can also start identifying the best ways of reaching these potential clients. Are there supermarkets, car washes, dry cleaners, or other businesses in the area where it might be appropriate to post notices? Is there a local magazine or newspaper that reaches a majority of those people? For example, in this area, there is a monthly magazine called *Presna Hispana* that contains local news and business ads. The *Arizona Republic* newspaper provides a Spanish language version name *LaVoz*. We may be able to find local community events where we can distribute information (guerilla marketing) or we may be able to capitalize on local issues or news for our advertising.

While defining your target market is important, it also pays to think about secondary target markets.[30] These are customers who might be interested in using your product or service, but are not whom you probably start out targeting. You need to at least consider who they are and how you might respond to them, and certainly keep them in mind for future expansion. For example, what will you do if a Chinese parents call your child care center and ask if they can enroll their child so that she might learn more Spanish along with her English? Roy "Bud" Davis, one of the co-founders of Bert and Bud's Vintage Coffins (www.vintagecoffins.com), builds custom coffins designed to be works of art that make a statement about the person who will be buried in them. His target market is wealthier people over age 55 who have "an independent streak, a sense of humor about their mortality, and the practicality to plan ahead." He found secondary target markets in Civil War reenactors who want authentic looking recreations of historical caskets, heavy metal music fans who use them as beds, and pet owners looking for a way to remember a special pet.[31]

Current Situation

The second step in creating your marketing plan is to examine your current situation. If you are an ongoing business, this means examining what you have done over the past year and how effective these actions were. Ongoing and new businesses also need to reflect on the political, economic, cultural, and other external environments and consider how they may affect the business. For example, are you located in a high-population growth area? Then it may be reasonable to expect your business to grow (if the growth is in your target market). Is the unemployment rate growing? Good news if you are an employment service, but bad news for many other services. Ask yourself, "What's going on and how might that affect my business?" What are the challenges you'll face this next year? What unique attributes does your business have to combat these challenges?

Often a SWOT analysis is a good tool for organizing this material. What things do you do very well and what things do you do less well (strengths and weaknesses)? What "gaps" are there in market coverage—specific markets not covered, new technologies not exploited, features competitors ignore, and so on—that you can fill (opportunities)? How could your competition, new laws, the economic environment, or other outside forces negatively affect your business (threats)?

direct competition
Other companies that make a similar product or provide a similar service; for example, direct competition for Coca-Cola includes all other soft drink providers.

indirect competition
Companies that provide alternatives that are dissimilar to your product/service that consumers might choose to meet a similar need; for example, indirect competition for Coca-Cola includes any other company providing items to quench thirst.

Probably the key component in your situational analysis will be to consider your competition. Certainly, you will need to consider **Direct competition**, those providing the same product or service. But **indirect competition**, what people use if they do not purchase the product or service category, is also important. In other words, if you are going to clean houses, what other housecleaning services (direct competitors) are doing business in the area? Also, if potential clients do not purchase housecleaning services, what is their alternative? In this case, the indirect competition would be cleaning themselves, having their children or other family members do it, or simply ignoring the dust and cobwebs—an extreme alternative, to be sure. Watching for ads, checking the Yellow Pages, and asking people in the area are all good ways to gather this information for your housecleaning business. Exhibit 12.1 shows a questionnaire that could be used to do this. Some of the items will be more or less important depending on your particular business, and there will probably be additional questions you will need to add.

EXHIBIT 12.1

Competitive Analysis[32]

	Competitor A	Competitor B	Competitor C
Where is your competitor located?			
What are your competitor's annual sales?			
Is the company owned or in partnership with any other corporations?			
What are the competitor's strengths?			
What are the competitor's weaknesses?			
What is the company's product line?			
How do the products compare to yours, in terms of functionality, appearance, and any other criteria?			
What is the price structure?			
What are the company's marketing activities?			
What are the company's supply sources for products?			
What are the strengths and weaknesses of its sales literature?			
Is the company expanding or cutting back?			

Identifying competition does two things for us. First, we can get an idea of how crowded the market is. The Census Bureau tells us how many potential households are out there. An informal poll of residents in the area can give us an idea of what percentage might use a housecleaning service. For a rough estimate, we could simply divide the households who use cleaning services by the number of competitors we've identified and come up with an idea of the number of clients per service. If we add our company to the mix, will the resulting number of clients per service be enough to be profitable? (This is exactly some of the same information needed for your sales forecast discussed earlier.)

The second piece of information identifying competition gives us is a chance to find out what its strengths and weaknesses are. Weaknesses in particular can identify opportunities for our company to excel. Are competitors ignoring certain sectors of the market? Are their clients 100 percent happy with them? If not, what aren't they doing that you could? Are they late to their appointments? Do they cancel too frequently because they are understaffed and an employee illness means that something doesn't get done? What prices do they charge, and do the clients feel they are getting their money's worth?

The 4 Ps

Your written marketing plan will contain detailed information about the 4 P's-your product or service, how you will promote and price it, as well as how you will get it to the customer (the "place" part of the 4 Ps). In defining your target market, you have already determined likely courses of action in these areas. For your marketing plan, though, you will be more specific.

In defining your product, you need to describe all the details. What features does it have? Are any of these options? Does it come in different sizes, flavors, or colors? What service elements do you include with the product (for example, delivery, setup, training, warranty, etc.)? If you are providing a service, again, what specific tasks will you do? Will you sell this as a bundled service (e.g., complete housecleaning), or will you sell it in units (e.g., vacuuming separate from windows, cleaning bathrooms, washing windows, etc.)? What short-term (next few years) improvements or changes do you foresee?

An example or photo of your product or service is a great visual aid in helping you sell your plan. If you are a restaurant, have a sample menu, photos of some prepared food, and a photo of the building you'd like to lease. If you write business plans for other companies, a sample table of contents of a business plan might be adequate. Blueprints, color chips, sketches, and fabric samples are other things that could be included for other types of businesses. In addition, the cost structure (e.g., materials, labor, overhead) needs to be included. If the marketing plan is part of an entire business plan, cost details can be left for the financial section, but the total should be identified here.

Price will be determined by your cost structure. In addition to identifying the actual price you will be asking, include information about additional expenses the customer may incur (for example, shipping or installation). Why do you consider this amount of profit to be appropriate? How does your price compare to that of the competition? If it is higher or lower, how do you explain or justify this?

In advertising, for example, you may have determined that a print ad is a good method for reaching your target market; now you will want to consider in which magazines to place the ads (e.g., a hobby magazine, a local magazine, etc.), and what their cost will be. What tools will you use (flyers, Internet, print ads in magazine or newspapers, television or radio, banners and posters, etc.)? How will you schedule your advertising efforts (weekly radio spot, daily newspaper ad, twice a year distribution of flyers, etc.)? What are the various costs of these and how successful are they at reaching your target audience? (In other words, consider costs versus benefits.) What is your advertising budget?

Identify what your message should contain—slogans, promises, photos, and so on. A rough mock-up of a print piece or a script of a radio or television ad should be included, explaining how you feel these will resonate with your target market.

Are you using any promotional tools (e.g., coupons, referral discounts, sales, giveaways, etc.)? If so, what are they? How much will they cost? How often will you do this?

The distribution system of your product or service can vary considerably depending on what you are doing. For example, if you are doing some sort of mail order sales, will you be taking the boxes to the local post office or to UPS or some other shipper? Will you go daily or weekly or on some other schedule? Will you be using a fulfillment center? What will your costs be for shipping boxes, packaging materials, and the like?

If your product or service will be in a store or other building or space you lease, what will this cost you? Why did you choose this place (e.g., traffic counts and other indicators that it is a good spot for your particular business)? If it's the Internet, are you going with eBay, other e-malls, or on your own? Why? What sort of hit rates do you expect?

This is a partial list of the questions that should be answered in writing this part of the marketing plan. What you include will be specific to the type of business you are planning. How do you figure all this out? A very useful tool to consider is called the *filtering process.*[33] Put yourself in the shoes of your prospective customer and consider that you are searching for something to solve the problem your particular product or service will solve. What are the steps you would take to find a solution? Would you first look in the phone book? Then you'll want to make sure you have a Yellow Pages listing. Would you ask friends? Now you may wish to consider some sort of referral bonus to customers who recommend you. What sorts of information would you want to know about the company, product, or service before you made your decision? These may be things to put in your ad (e.g., address and hours of operation) or, for more complicated items, things that should be addressed in your sales pitch (like more detailed information on technical aspects of your product, why you are better than the competition, or specifics about your guarantee). What are the features customers are likely to want (and how will they know you have them)? Where would they likely shop? How far would they drive to get your product or service? Since you are now the expert on your product or service, you might be a little too close to the process and this, too, might be a good place to do a little marketing research by identifying a few potential customers and asking them these questions.

The Written Plan

Your written marketing plan will include the specific details about your target market you consider useful as well as information about your present and near future situation including competitors. The plan will also identify your differential advantage and how this will be conveyed through your product or service, your pricing, your place (your way of getting your product/service to your customers), and your promotion. For a new company, this provides your justification for going into the market. If there aren't enough customers out there to make a reasonable profit or if you have no clearly defined method of finding them, you'll have trouble convincing anyone to loan you money. For an ongoing establishment this is your action plan for the near future, usually the next year.

In addition to the sections mentioned above, the written plan may include financial projections (if not part of an entire business plan). The plan will also include your budget for doing the things you plan to do, the schedule of when you'll do them, and how you will evaluate your progress. This last item will include measurements against your objectives and will include things like matching monthly sales projections and goals against actual sales and similar evaluations. Indicate what you'll measure and when you'll measure it.

Since your marketing plan is essentially your action plan, write it as such. List the major overall goals you have for your company and then the specific tactics you need to achieve them. Make your goals simple, concrete, and measurable. For example, if you plan to open a child care service in Phoenix, Arizona, your goal or objective could be to have 20 children within six months (determined from the sales forecasting you did earlier). How are you going to achieve that? What specific tactics will you use? Perhaps, you'll advertise in XYZ local magazine and in ABC newspaper. You'll distribute 1,000 flyers door-to-door or place them under the windshield wipers of cars in grocery store parking lots (where legal and permitted). A cooperative mail program (those envelopes containing ads or coupons from a number of sources, such as Valpak's blue envelopes) can print and deliver coupons to 10,000 houses for under $500. Break down and outline the costs for doing each of these activities. Set a time schedule.[34]

What should the written plan look like? There are nearly as many formats as there are companies writing marketing plans. There are software packages that help you work through the plan step by step and will create a high-quality, professional-looking plan, such as Marketing Plan Pro (www.marketingplanpro.com) by Palo Alto software. Even the basic version comes with about 70 sample marketing plans, the idea being that they can serve as templates for whatever business you may be planning.

Another consideration is whether the marketing plan is to be part of a business plan or whether it is to stand alone. In the first case, there are a number of items that will be covered in the other parts of the business plan and do not need to be duplicated. For example, the financial section of the business plan will include balance sheets, income statements, and such and do not need to be duplicated, but only referred to in the marketing plan section. For a stand-alone marketing plan, at least a summary version of these would need to be included.

Table 12.2 is a suggested layout of things to be included.[35] Two types of marketing plans are considered—a full stand-alone marketing plan and the marketing section of the business plan, like those described in Chapter 8. You'll notice that the categories for the marketing analysis follow the same elements outlined in Table 8.3 in Chapter 8, which gives the different types of plans and the sections of each. Here we add the details of how the 4 Ps fit into the sections of the marketing analysis and plan.

What's Next?

The marketing plan has been discussed almost as though it's a one-time process, and it's not. It's the basic building block for your business plan and your road map to what you want to do, but it shouldn't be set in concrete.[36] Successful businesses are constantly tweaking their marketing plan to

TABLE 12.2 Marketing Plan Outline

	Stand-alone Marketing Plan	Marketing Section of a Business Plan
1. Table of contents	X	
2. Executive summary	X	
3. Company description, mission, focus, structure	X	
4. Situation analysis	X	
a. Company SWOT analysis	X	
b. Product/service SWOT analysis	X	(in Competition section)
c. Competitive analysis	X	(in Competition section)
d. Customer analysis	X	(in Competition section)
5. Marketing analysis	X	X
a. Market and target customer	X	X
b. Differential/competitive advantage	X	X
c. Marketing objectives	X	X
d. Overall marketing strategy (the sales plan)	X	X
i. Product strategy and Description	X	X
ii. Pricing strategy	X	X
iii. Promotion strategy	X	X
iv. Place/distribution strategy	X	X
v. Contingency plans	X	X
(1) Reaction to competitors	X	X
(2) R&D/growth plans	X	X
6. Financial data and projections	X	
7. Implementation plan or schedule	X	X
8. Evaluation and control	X	
9. Appendixes	X	

accommodate necessary adjustments found during evaluation and control reviews, or to reflect new research, changes in the environment, changes in competition, new target markets, new opportunities in promotion, new anything.[37] In addition, on a regular basis (at least once a year),[38] you should take the time to decide what you want to accomplish next—increase sales, introduce a new product, move into a new market, and the like—and revise your marketing plan to reflect this next step. Caryl Felicetta started her business, The Argyle Studio, an advertising and graphic design firm, without a marketing plan. After a year of haphazard growth, she and her partner did their first systematic review and marketing plan. With this plan, their business grew by 100 percent the next year and has averaged about 50 percent growth each year after that.[39]

If you are uncomfortable with the prospect of doing a marketing plan yourself, there's low-cost help for you available in a number of ways. First, try the Small Business Administration (**www.sba.gov**) or the Service Corps of Retired Executives (SCORE) (**www.score.org**) for advice. *Entrepreneur* magazine (**www.entrepreneur.com**) has examples and a number of worksheets you can use to help you gather and organize your information. Last, contact a local community, technical, or four-year college (small business or entrepreneurship department if they have one, otherwise, the marketing department) or campus club in those areas and offer your company as a class project.[40] (A small donation to the class or club should be considered.)

CHAPTER SUMMARY

LO1 Understand the importance of a marketing plan.

- The marketing plan helps you articulate how you are going to sell your product or service.
- The marketing plan is a necessary piece of the business plan.
- The plan examines your current situation and competition and specifically identifies what you will do with your product, pricing, promotion, and distribution.

LO2 Recognize the major methods for conducting market research.

- Secondary research is data already gathered for some other purpose than the question you are trying to answer.
  - Internet, libraries, newspapers, and magazines offer free data; data are also for sale and can range from relatively inexpensive to very expensive.
  - While using secondary data is quick and often free, it may not give you exactly what you need.
- Primary data is that which you gather to answer your current questions.
  - Primary data can be gathered through observation, focus groups, or questionnaires.
  - Questionnaires can be administered via mail, phone, Internet, or in person and can consist of close-ended or open-ended questions.

LO3 Use sales forecasting methods.

- If your product or service is a component of another product or tied directly to another product or service, your estimated sales can be calculated as a portion of this known number.
- Most products and services, however, will require "softer" estimates such as traffic counts or questionnaire results.
- This sales forecast is critical to and must be checked against your capacity.

LO4 Find or create a product's differential advantage.

- A differential advantage is that which sets you apart from the competition.
- The differential advantage can be in your product, promotion, distribution, or pricing.

LO5 Identity the critical components of a marketing plan.

- Who is your target market?
  - Typically, markets are divided by demographic, life style, or personality traits.
  - The target market is the group that is likely to buy your product or service and that has distinct purchasing behaviors.
  - Secondary target markets should also be considered.
- What is your current situation?
  - Ongoing businesses must reflect over the recent year and how effective their actions were.
  - All businesses must consider likely changes in political, economic, cultural, and other external environments and how these may affect the business.
  - Direct and indirect competition must be identified and its actions and likely actions analyzed.
- What are your specific plans for your product, promotion, pricing, and distribution?
- The marketing plan needs to be written, but the format can vary depending on who is going to use it.
- The plan should be revised regularly—whenever something significant occurs to change a piece of it or at least once a year.

KEY TERMS

marketing plan, 382
marketing research, 382
primary research, 382
secondary research, 382
ethnographic research, 386
focus group, 386
survey, 387
scalar questions, 388
dichotomous questions, 388

categorical questions, 388
open-ended questions, 388
bot, 390
differential advantage, 391
market segmentation, 394
undifferentiated strategy, 395
differentiated strategy, 395
concentrated strategy, 395
direct competition, 396
indirect competition, 396

DISCUSSION QUESTIONS

1. Consider that you are planning to open a self-service car wash in town. What sorts of secondary data might be helpful in creating your marketing plan?
2. What are some of the ways that you could use secondary research to better understand the various segments of your market and to develop promotional materials?
3. What sorts of primary data could you collect using observation for your car wash?
4. Create a questionnaire that could be used to gather data for your car wash. Use both closed- and open-ended questions.
5. With your classmates, make a list of products or services that are or could be tied to other products or services. To which products or services are they tied? How could this be used to predict sales?
6. With your classmates, make a list of several products or services unlikely to be tied to other products or services. How might you estimate sales with these?
7. Is it ethical to pose as a customer in order to gather data from a competitor? What sort of behaviors do you believe to be ethical and justifiable, and which ones cross the line?
8. Going back to our car wash example, list all the ways you could differentiate your product, price, promotion, and distribution from the competition.
9. How could you segment your car wash market? Brainstorm as many different ways as possible. (Remember that some of the most successful businesses are those that have found unique ways to segment and reach a particular market.)
10. Use the filtering process and consider the steps you would take in trying to resolve the dirty car problem. What does this tell you about the product, price, promotion, and location of your potential new business?

EXPERIENTIAL EXERCISES

1. Visit your school's library or your local public library and investigate the reference section. Make a list of resources that might be useful if you were opening a new dry cleaning business.
2. Revisit the U.S. Census Bureau website (**www.census.gov**) and list secondary data that might be useful in opening your dry cleaning business.
3. Select a local shopping mall to do some observation and primary data collecting. (Try a food court or bench in a waiting area where you can be comfortable and unobtrusive.) Make a list of the sorts of observational data you could collect.
4. Select an item from your list in question 3 and collect data for 15 minutes. What does your information tell you, and how could you use it?
5. Assume your dry cleaning business is a service that you've found the average person will use once a month in your area. You also discovered that customers want to drive less than three miles for dry cleaning. Get a map of your city and select a street corner at random. (We'll assume that you will be able to build your dry cleaners there.) Use the Census website to estimate the population in your three-mile radius. Consult the phone book to find other dry cleaners within that radius. Assuming you will evenly split the customers, what would be your market share?
6. Make a list of the competitors of the company for which you work. What are their strengths and weaknesses? Are you aiming at the same target market(s)?
7. Using the competitors identified in question 6 (or choosing a different product or service), attempt to identify the target marketing they have selected. (Good ways of doing this is by identifying advertising or distribution aimed at particular groups.) Do any of them have secondary markets?
8. Interview someone at the company where you work. What kind of marketing plan does the company have (formal, informal, detailed, etc.)? How often is it reviewed?

MINI-CASE

INFOGLIDE[41]

David Wheeler got into business in order to ease his anger about his father's murder and in an attempt to see justice done. A computer database expert, he designed a program that would sift through crime reports in an effort to link and pinpoint criminals. The first trial of the product connected several seemingly unrelated crimes and located a suspect.

In 1991, Wheeler formed InfoGlide, Inc., to sell this software program to law enforcement agencies throughout the country. While the agencies found it a valuable tool and indeed used it to investigate successfully a number of crimes, as government agencies, few could afford it. Wheeler had a product that just didn't have a market.

In 1996, after struggling for several years to attract venture capitalists, InfoGlide reexamined all possible and potential markets. It discovered that hundreds of millions of dollars a year were lost because of insurance frauds—frauds that could be linked with Wheeler's software just as police cases were. InfoGlide immediately retargeted its product and revamped its marketing plan, and by 1998 had raised $5 million in venture capital. Today, the company has 38 employees and is worth $100 million.

CASE DISCUSSION QUESTIONS

1. In selecting a new target market, InfoGlide would have had to adjust all parts of the marketing plan as well. What changes could you envision in the product, the price, the promotion strategy, and the distribution?
2. Can you identify other markets that could benefit from the basic concept of Wheeler's software? What changes might need to be made for these markets?
3. Researchers call this process *transmigration,* changing a company so it can enter a peripheral or related industry. Select a firm you know and brainstorm several transmigrations it could make.

SUGGESTED CASES AND ARTICLES

- The Wallingford Bowling Center, C-13

Available on McGraw-Hill Create™:

- Creemore Springs Brewery: Branding without Advertising
- Optical Distortion, Inc. (A)
- Sealed Air Corp.

SUGGESTED VIDEOS

www.mhhe.com/katz4e

STVP Videos:

- You Must Have Real Sales and Customers to Be in Business
- Customers Will Say What They Need

APPENDIX

A Marketing Plan: PizzMo[42]

A marketing plan intended for inclusion in a business plan. Section numbers correspond to Table 12.2 on page 400.

3. STORE'S MISSION

Here at *PizzMo*, our mission is to deliver an entire evening's worth of enjoyment directly to your home. *PizzMo* will deliver the freshest, most appetizing pizza right along with the most entertaining movie or video game, straight from RedBox. By bringing dinner and a movie or video game right to your doorstep, we want to take the hassle out of your evening and give you a worry-free night.

Customers can first order their RedBox selection online, or start with the call to *PizzMO*. If they are on the RedBox site, customers in our delivery zip codes who rent are asked if they need a *PizzMO* code, and if they say yes, they are given a code number to give *PizzMO* when ordering the food, as well as a hotlink to the *PizzMO* online ordering site.

When a customer connects with *PizzMO* online or by phone, we input the code number to identify the kiosk, and the video game or movie is picked up by a *PizzMO* driver, either coming back from a delivery or by the driver with the food on the way to the house. All *PizzMO* drivers have a special *PizzMO*-RedBox card to use in place of a credit card on the RedBox machine. Using the card and inputting the customer's code number, the driver receives the movie or video game and makes the delivery. It is the customer's responsibility to return the movie or video game to any RedBox, or incur additional expenses.

4c. COMPETITIVE ANALYSIS

While there are pizza delivery services in every community, none can offer the combination of pizza and RedBox delivery that *PizzMO* can. Through our exclusive arrangement with RedBox, we will be able to pick up movies or video games at nearby RedBox locations and deliver these to homes with items from an outstanding menu of pizza, sandwiches, salads, sides, and beverages. For families interested in an evening at home with the food and entertainment taken care of for them, there is no competitor to *PizzMO*.

While there have been pizza and movie delivery services in the past, these have depended on having an inventory of videos or an arrangement with an independent video store in place. However, these were hampered by problems in knowing which videos were available at the time of the pizza ordering. Neither arrangement has worked out, as the lack of such surviving firms testifies. Through our partnership with RedBox and the use of their online systems to identify what movies are available, *PizzMO* does not need to carry the inventory cost, and will always know what movies or video games are available.

5a. TARGET MARKET

Our target market is between the ages of 18 and 35, both college students and young, middle-income families. College students will be prime candidates because of the easy and quick indoor date night that *PizzMo* provides. Our delivery service will be the best way for these scholars to get a break from their studies without diverting from them for too long. An average college student in our target market would earn at least $15,000 per year. Families with young children will be another main targeted group. These prospects will find *PizzMo* irresistible because of the immense benefits. A common family in our target would make a combined income of no less than $40,000 a year. The tremendous assistance that we will provide them with a worry-free night will be irreplaceable, because these people would prefer not to leave the comfort of their own home. Taking children out to eat can be a very daunting task; with *PizzMo,* worries are over because we bring dinner and entertainment to your door. *PizzMo's* typical customer will order from us at least once a month, but up to six times a month, spending an average of thirty dollars each time.

5b. DIFFERENTIAL ADVANTAGE

As mentioned before, we will be the first company in the area to offer delivered pizza plus a RedBox movie or video game of the customer's choice—fast, easy and convenient.

5c. MARKETING OBJECTIVES

As we are a new company, *PizzMo's* first marketing objective is to get information about our product/service out to our customers—name/brand recognition. Second, we want to develop brand loyalty among these customers.

5d(i). PRODUCT STRATEGY

PizzMo will offer a full menu—salads, sandwiches, pizzas, sides, and beverages. A customer can choose from an individual or a family-size salad with a choice of Italian, ranch, or honey-mustard dressings. Sandwich choices include: roast beef and cheddar, meatball, ham and Swiss, Italian sub, or a turkey melt. We'll make seven specialty pizzas: bacon cheeseburger, meat cravers, veggie, meatball, parmesan chicken, tostada, and the ultimate. Or you can create your own pizza with these toppings: pepperoni, sausage, pork sausage, beef, Canadian bacon, bacon, diced ham, black olives, onions, mushrooms, bell peppers, tomatoes, jalapenos, fire-roasted vegetables, and pickles. On the side, customers can order bread sticks, cheese bread sticks, little smokies, and toasted ravioli. To drink, we'll offer Coke and Pepsi products, in addition to bottled water.

5d(ii). PRICING STRATEGY

At ***PizzMo*** our pricing strategy will be to establish a family restaurant feel and an honest appeal to our customers. However, ***PizzMo*** wants to lead the market with a low-price strategy in an attempt to secure loyal customers with our wholesome values, and we also want to appeal to cost-efficient buyers. We will set up a pricing orientation with roughly 65 percent of our products in the inexpensive range, which consists of items under $9, and 35 percent in the medium-priced range of $10 to $15. There will be no items priced over $15; however, buying any combination of products will lead to a higher overall price. In addition, customers will be able to build their own pizzas, which could easily go over $15 if many toppings were added. In these instances, the price will be less of a factor and will be second to the amazing quality of the pizza. We will also carry the usual breadsticks, chicken wings/fingers, salads, sandwiches, and other Italian foods and will price these comparable to our competition.

5d(iii). PROMOTION STRATEGY

In our advertising and promotional scheme, our goal is to get the word out about our delicious pizza, fast and friendly service, and reliability. We will attempt to do this using minimal, but effective advertising that really reaches our target market and transforms them into loyal customers.

We will not neglect traditional media either. One of our big campaigns will be to use mailers with coupons attached as well as an offer for a free small pizza with no strings attached. Customers using the coupon can also arrange for a RedBox delivery with their first order. We hope that by offering a sample of our delicious pizza in combination with a coupon, we will create a repeat purchase that will turn into a lasting relationship. Since 85 percent of all pizza consumers use some form of coupons, ***PizzMo*** hopes to acquire many of its original customers through the use of this technique. We will also use electronic coupons on our website that customers can print directly and redeem with their purchase. Since these types of coupons typically have a higher redemption rate, ***PizzMo*** hopes to reach people who will adopt us as their pizza and entertainment company of choice.

Our major vehicle for promoting ***PizzMO*** will come through our partnership with RedBox. Every RedBox customer who is ordering a movie or video game online, on their PC, pad, or smartphone, will be asked if they want to order from ***PizzMO***. ***PizzMO*** will also be spotlighted in local RedBox advertising. At this point, RedBox is not charging ***PizzMO*** for mentions, providing the equivalent of free advertising and recommendations by a company our prospective customers already trust.

Supporting this is an aggressive social media campaign. ***PizzMO*** will have its own informational website, which will include an online ordering function, with an always live connection to the RedBox site, which can be accessed within the ***PizzMO*** site—with the RedBox redemption code automatically being forwarded to ***PizzMO***. In addition, we will have a Facebook business page, with a discount for customers who Friend or Like us. We will also have a Twitter business page. We have established a schedule for promotional specials to help increase business and will actively use our social media connections to promote ***PizzMO*** and keep it fresh in the minds of our customers.

We plan to use state-of-the-art web supports. Our website and Facebook page will be search-engine optimized so that we appear as high as possible in regular search results. In addition, we plan to have an active adword campaign on Google, Bing, and Facebook, with all three localized to our key zip and trade areas, focused on people who search for pizza, pizza delivery, or RedBox. We will work on variations of our online ads to make sure the ones we are using are the best possible, and we will monitor these carefully to make sure our online ad spending is working optimally.

Catchy bus and bus shelter ads and local signage will also be used by ***PizzMo*** to reach motorists who are trying to plan their evening. One of our innovations will be to work deals with local stores to post a ***PizzMO*** sign in their store for customers to see. In return, ***PizzMO*** will provide a free pizza delivered at least once a month. As more ***PizzMO*** customers mention seeing the sign at a particular store, we will increase their free pizzas, up to one a week. The advertisements will not be overly distracting, but will aim customers in the direction of our website by either suggesting free pizza, as in the mailers mentioned above, or promoting the unique and hassle-free service, without saying too much. Ideally, we would like to keep the people guessing, so that they are forced to look at the website and would be more likely to buy as a result.

Our costs associated with promotions and advertising for the first year are represented in the following table.

Advertising Costs

Promotion Type	Total Expense
Mailers w/coupons	$5,000
Online (website, SEO, adwords)	$10,000
Signage	$5,000
TOTAL	**$20,000**

5d(iv). LOCATION STRATEGY

Our main focus as a start-up organization will be to direct our business to our immediate service area, until success allows us to expand in partnership with RedBox. Given RedBox's geographic presence, we expect to expand initially into adjoining trade areas or zip codes, with additional stores added as needed. If RedBox seeks a more aggressive schedule of expansion, we hope to parlay our collaboration with them into third-party funding for expansion.

PizzMo will most likely be located in a strip mall, since with the current economic downturn there are a variety of sites available at low rents, including many with the necessary hook-ups for a pizza operation, and will need relatively small square footage to perform daily operations. One of the prime locations found for the first of our stores is a 1,500 square foot location at 1704 E. Washington Boulevard and is located in a strip center along with a salon and a liquor store. The prior tenant was a fried chicken take-out, so there will be no additional funds required to transform the location into a kitchen-friendly retail outlet. The location is one of the most optimum found because of its proximity to a large residential area, and the presence of seven RedBox kiosks within 1 mile of the location and another 11 within 2 miles, virtually guaranteeing adequate access to videos and video games our customers are ordering. The neighborhood has many young families, as well as college students, who are our precise target market. The median household income of the area is $72,889, and the average household size is 2.99 people. The area is 69.4 percent families and has an average of $28,140 in retail expenses and another $2,577 in entertainment expenses. This is an affluent area, whose residents fit ***PizzMo's*** target market to a T with 57 percent working in a white-collar job and 38.9 percent with a college education or better.

The retail configuration of the area around the storefront includes a beauty salon, jewelry store, insurance and auto leasing establishment, a nail salon, laundry, delicatessen, wholesale tobacco store, and a preschool. There are a few small restaurants several blocks away, but since ***PizzMo*** is a delivery business, these are not direct competitors. We understand that sometimes people want to go out to eat, but ***PizzMo*** caters to those evenings when the same people want to stay in and have a pleasant experience in their own home. Most of the other stores in this area are family-owned, which may help ***PizzMo*** since we too will be this type of retail outlet. We are hoping that the community welcomes us into the neighborhood with open arms and that the surrounding homeowners enjoy our honest offerings.

5d(v). CONTINGENCY PLANS

There are a lot of pizza places out there, and certainly if RedBox made similar offers to other pizza stores, anyone could add the ability to offer RedBox deliveries along with their pizza. This is perhaps our biggest threat. We hope to do everything we can to keep RedBox happy in the hopes they would prefer to grow with a company that shares their outlook. Coinstar, the parent of RedBox, bought out co-owner McDonald's, and our hope is that this bodes well for partnering to grow small businesses into bigger ones, and develop customer loyalty so that our customers will not switch when someone else offers a better deal. In addition, as we are delivery only, we can locate in low-rent areas and should always be able to compete on price.

While we will offer many pizzas similar to our competition, ***PizzMo*** also intends to experiment with local flavors and preferences. We will accumulate information about the "make your own" pizzas to see if there are some local favorites we can add to the menu, things that the large chains usually do not do.

7. IMPLEMENTATION SCHEDULE

Securing the lease, forming the company, and all the related paperwork can be done in the first month. Equipment will be ordered and remodeling started immediately afterwards, along with designing the website, packaging materials, and promotional materials. About 1 month before the store opens, advertising and promotion will begin and the website will be activated. We expect to be in business within 5 months.

PART FOUR

4

Cash, Accounting, and Finance in the Small Business

CHAPTER 13

Small Business Accounting: Projecting and Evaluating Performance

● Debbie Dusenberry seemed to have all the qualities that make a successful entrepreneur. She was passionate about her business, which, through hard work and an artistic sensibility, she had made into an internationally recognized source for unique decorating items. So, how did she find herself with a business that after years of growth was suddenly experiencing a huge sales decline and was racking up unsustainable losses?

LEARNING OBJECTIVES

After you complete this chapter, you will be able to:

LO1 Describe the basic concepts of accounting.

LO2 Specify the requirements for a small business accounting system.

LO3 Explain the content and format of common financial statements.

LO4 Use accounting information as a tool for managing your business effectively.

LO5 Develop a complete set of budgets for your business.

LO6 Use accounting information to make better business decisions.

Focus on Small Business: Debbie Dusenberry and the Curious Sofa

The Curious Sofa[1] was an off-beat but beautiful store, filled with one-of-a-kind items. The store was designed to look old with a black-and-white color scheme, columns made of used brick and distressed plaster, and a ceiling of antique tin tiles. All in all it was a for-real incarnation of Edwardian design. But then what would you expect of a store named after a novel by Edward Gorey, whose works (like the animation at the start of PBS's *Mystery!*) exemplify the Edwardian period?[2]

Debbie Dusenberry created the Curious Sofa just as we have encouraged our students *not* to do. She had no business plan, no specific measurable business goals, no regular reports of how the business was doing. In other words, she largely ignored the business aspects of her business.

That said, Debbie did do many other things right. She worked hard, spent long hours, and built on skills she had gained through years of designing sets for television commercials and working as an art director for movies. Her talent for choosing just the right antique (and sometimes just the right old thing) soon made Curious Sofa the go-to place for top designers. Debbie and the Curious Sofa were the topics of articles published in the *New York Times* newspaper, *Forbes Small Business, Romantic Homes, Better Homes and Gardens,* and incredibly, in *The National-Dubai,* a newspaper for expats in the Mideast.

So, it came as a shock when Debbie realized that her business was failing. Her first surprise came after she had moved into a location twice the size of the original shop. She wrote in her by-invitation-only blog, "If my sales were up 15 percent, why did I take a 20 percent salary cut three months ago when the rest of my staff got their raises?"[4] The next shock came with the recession.

> This year sales are down 28 percent, and it is killing me. I have laid off much-needed help, cut salaries, cut expenses, juggled the numbers so much I am OVER IT. I have laid my business out there naked to the landlord, my bank and advisers.[5]

● The Curious Sofa in Prairie Village, Kansas 2010[3]

Debbie was at that cross roads where many entrepreneurs meet failure. She had run her business for 8 years without ever having created a business plan, without ever having analyzed the economics of her business. She succeeded to this point by having phenomenal growth. But now the growth had stopped, even reversed. The only way to succeed from this point was to operate at a profit. Debbie not only had inadequate knowledge of accounting, no understanding of profit versus cash flow, inaccurate calculations of costs, nonexistent internal controls, she truly believed that she did not need it.

"I'm an artist. I want somebody else to do that stuff," she said.[6]

DISCUSSION QUESTIONS

1. What is the difference between profit and cash flow?
2. Where might Debbie Dusenberry find help to save her business?
3. Does a good accounting system guarantee entrepreneurial success?
4. In what ways does an inadequate accounting system impede entrepreneurial success?

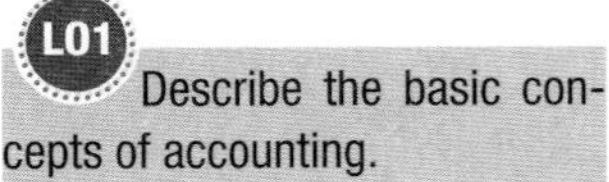
LO1
Describe the basic concepts of accounting.

Why Accounting Matters to Small Business

The way many people think of it, what makes a business businesslike is its focus on making money, and in the end, the only way an owner knows or can prove to others that money is being made is through keeping careful accounting records. Accountants themselves think of five reasons why accounting is important to a small business:

- It proves what your business did financially.
- It shows how much your business is worth.
- Banks, creditors, development agencies, and investors require it.
- It provides easy-to-understand plans for business operations.
- You can't know how your business is doing without it.

managerial accounting
Accounting methods that are specifically intended to be used by managers for planning, directing, and controlling a business.

tax accounting
An accounting approach based on specific accounting requirements set by governmental taxing agencies.

financial accounting
A formal, rule-based set of accounting principles and procedures intended for use by outside owners, investors, banks, and regulators.

There are three types of accounting, **managerial accounting**, which is used by managers for planning and control, **tax accounting**, which is used for calculating and reporting taxes, and **financial accounting**, which is used by banks and outside investors.

Managerial accounting is forward-looking and attempts to predict the results of management decisions.

Tax accounting is used to produce tax returns and schedules. Tax accounting is important for avoiding penalties for noncompliance and for minimizing how much money you have to pay in taxes.

Financial accounting is a formal, rule-based system intended primarily for absentee owners, bankers, investors, and regulators.

Basic Accounting Concepts

If you, as do many folk, have an aversion to even thinking about accounting, let alone trying to *do* accounting, then you are about to gain a new perspective on the topic. As you read the next couple of pages you'll come to realize that accounting is actually a very simple process that is based on common sense.

The most basic concepts of accounting are:

1. The idea that a business has an existence that is separate from its owner, called "business entity concept."
2. The expectation that a successful business will stay in business, or the "going concern concept."

3. An extremely simple equation called the "accounting equation."
4. The premise of revenue and expense.
5. The principle that accounting information must be useful to the owners and managers of businesses.[7]

Business Entity Concept

Because of the **business entity concept**, it is possible to separate business transactions from your own personal transactions. Thus we can distinguish between money that your business borrows, and money that you borrow for personal needs. It is the business entity concept that underlies the legal forms of establishing businesses, such as corporations, limited partnerships, and limited liability companies. (These are explained in detail in Chapter 18.)

business entity concept The concept that a business has an existence separate from that of its owners.

Does It Belong to the Business, or Is It Mine?

Mauro Padilla III, a San Antonio, Texas, builder, ran afoul of the law because of bad accounting said his lawyer, Adam Cortez.[8] U.S. Attorney James Blankinship agreed, writing in a presentencing court filing that more than $18 million of down payments and loan proceeds from different projects had been commingled with Padilla's own funds to the point that it was impossible to determine from the bank records what belonged to Padilla and what belonged to the various projects.

Cortez conceded that there should have been better segregation of the funds. But he also maintained that the failure was, in his words, "not a federal crime, ... just bad accounting."[9]

In this case, bad accounting, specifically not keeping a "bright line" between business funds and personal funds (a violation of the business entity concept) led to very serious results. Padilla received a 12-year prison sentence, 5 years of supervised release, and was ordered to pay more than $6 million in restitution to banks and investors.[10]

Going Concern Concept

The assumption that a successful business will stay in business enables long-range planning and strategy. Accounting assumes that this year's business results will affect next year's, and that the intent of business is to make money over a period of many years. The **going concern concept** also implies that, as a separate entity, the business may continue in business even if it is sold to other owners.

going concern concept The accounting concept that a business is expected to continue in existence for the foreseeable future.

Mario Padilla III leaving the Federal Courthouse in San Antonio, Texas.

The Accounting Equation

accounting equation
The statement that assets equal liabilities plus owners' equity (assets = liabilities + owners' equity).

Of all the concepts and ideas of accounting, the **accounting equation** is the simplest, but least understood. The entire system of accounting entries, reports, and financial statements is developed from this simple equation. The primary value that accounting produces for owners and managers is that of keeping records. The accounting equation is the method that is used to place these records into understandable categories that are useful for managing your business.

This equation has its basis in keeping track of everything that the business owns, while at the same time keeping track of what the business owes to others and what it is worth to its owners. This is done as a simple two-part equivalence, which is best understood by presenting an example.

Suppose you decide to start a business making executive desks of fine hardwoods. You already have a hobby of woodworking, and have collected tools during the pursuit of your hobby. These tools, especially the power tools, are very valuable, and you want to transfer their ownership to your new business. You will also need some cash for working capital, and your local banker (who already has one of your desks) has agreed to loan money to your business. Let's take a look at how these transactions are recorded, using the accounting equation.

First, you give up ownership of your tools, transferring them to your new corporation:

What the Business Owns		=	Claims on the Business	
Woodworking tools	$50,000		Capital donated by owner	$50,000

Notice that the business now owns the tools worth $50,000, but you as the owner have a "claim" on the business equal to the value you gave up. Should you change your mind right now, and dissolve the business, you could take back the tools. Or, were you to sell the business to someone else, you would expect to receive no less than the value of the tools.

Next, the bank makes a $50,000 loan to the business:

What the Business Owns		=	Claims on the Business	
Cash	$ 50,000		Loan payable to bank	$ 50,000
Woodworking tools	50,000		Capital donated by owner	50,000
Total value	$ 100,000		Total claims	$ 100,000

Now the business owns money and equipment. The total value of what it owns is $100,000. At the same time, the business owes $50,000 to the bank, and once the bank debt is paid, there will still be $50,000 value left for the owner. It may be hard to believe, but this is the entire accounting equation. The value of everything that the business owns is exactly equal to the sum of what the business owes to others plus any claims the owner has. Of course, the accounting equation is stated a bit differently. Its formal expression is:

$$\text{Assets} = \text{Liabilities} + \text{Owners' Equity}$$

So, let's take a look at the equation in the example, rewritten to use accounting terms:

Assets		=	Liabilities = Owners' Equity	
Current Assets			***Current Liabilities***	
Cash	$ 50,000		Loan payable to bank	$ 50,000
Long-Term Assets			***Owners' Equity***	
Woodworking tools	50,000		Capital donated by owner	50,000
Total assets	$ 100,000		Total liabilities & equity	$ 100,000

liabilities
Legal obligations to give up things of value in the future.

owners' equity
The difference between assets and liabilities of a business.

Notice that, except for using different terms, this is exactly the same as the earlier example. The only part that might be confusing is understanding what the terms "assets," "liabilities," "equity," "current," and "long-term" mean. An *asset* is simply something the business owns that will have value in the future. A **liability** is a legal obligation to pay some amount (or to give up product or services) at a time in the future. **Owners' equity** is simply whatever value is left after all liabilities have been paid. "Current" means that the value of the item can be realized, or must be paid as cash within one year. "Long-term" simply means that the asset will still be valuable more than one year in the future, or that the business may take longer than one year to pay the amount owed. The format used here is called a *balance sheet* because assets *must* equal the sum of liabilities and owners' equity. Simple, huh?

Costs, Revenues, and Expenses

Now suppose you purchase $10,000 of hardwood and $5,000 of supplies. What does this do to the accounting equation?

As you can see, making these purchases of inventory and supplies does not change the value of the business. All that you did was trade an asset called "cash" for assets called "inventory" and "supplies." However, the inventory has a cost of $10,000 and the supplies have a cost of $5,000. You gave up $15,000 in cash to obtain them. So, a **cost** is the value of what you *give up* to gain something you need or want.

cost
The value given up to obtain something that you want.

Assets		=	Liabilities + Owners' Equity	
Current Assets			***Current Liabilities***	
Cash	$ 35,000		Loan payable to bank	$ 50,000
Inventory	10,000			
Supplies	5,000			
Long-Term Assets			***Owners' Equity***	
Woodworking tools	50,000		Capital donated by owner	50,000
Total assets	$100,000		Total liabilities & equity	$100,000

To explain revenues and expenses it is best to continue our example. Suppose that, having started the business and purchased inventory and supplies, you produce and sell one desk to a local attorney. In making the desk, you use $1,000 of your inventory. You pay your employee $400 in wages. You present the attorney with an invoice for $2,500, and he promises to pay you in 10 days. How do these transactions affect the accounting equation?

First, recognize that only $400 has changed hands. You used inventory that you'd already paid for, and you accepted the attorney's promise to pay in lieu of cash. It should be obvious to you that the value of inventory has gone down by $1,000. But what do we do with the $2,500 sales price? We recognize $2,500 of revenue, and we deduct $1,400 of expenses in this manner:

Assets		=	Liabilities + Owners' Equity	
Current Assets			***Current Liabilities***	
Cash	$ 34,600		Loan payable to bank	$ 50,000
Accounts receivable	2,500			
Inventory	9,000			
Supplies	5,000			
Long-Term Assets			***Owners' Equity***	
Woodworking tools	50,000		Capital donated by owner	50,000
			Revenues earned	2,500
			Expenses for inventory used	(1,000)
			Expense for wages paid	(400)
Total assets	$101,100		Total liabilities & equity	$ 101,100

Now we can see the differences among costs, revenues, and expenses. Costs are the value of whatever you give up to get what you need or want. **Revenue** is an increase in owners' equity that is the result of selling your product or service. **Expenses** are reductions in owners' equity that recognize the value of goods (inventory) and services (labor) used to produce your product or service. When you sold the desk, the business received the attorney's promise to pay, which is called "accounts receivable." The business gave up the value of the inventory used and the value of labor expended.

revenue
An increase in owners' equity caused by selling your product or service.

expense
A decrease in owners' equity caused by consuming your product or service.

Of course, if we continued to record transactions in this way, pretty soon the owners' equity part of the balance sheet would become unreadable. Just imagine a year's worth of sales and expenses being recorded as in the example, above. So, as a matter of practicality transactions are not actually entered directly into the balance sheet. Rather, we create an *account*. An account is simply a record of transactions that are similar in nature. Thus we have an account for sales revenue where we record each sale as it is made. Similarly, we have an account for wage expense in which we record wages as they are incurred. At the end of the accounting period, whether it is a day, a month, a quarter, or a year, we simply add up all revenues and all expenses. We then subtract expenses from revenues and the remainder is our profit (or our loss if it is a negative number).

A complete discussion of basic accounting is available as a set of interactive slides in the online learning website for this text: www.mhhe.com/katz4e.

Information Usefulness

There are only two reasons to do accounting: first, to produce information that is useful to you for managing your business, second, to meet legal or contractual requirements. To be useful, information must be accurate and relevant.[11] You can ensure that your accounting information is accurate by using a computerized accounting program, as discussed in the following section. Relevance of information must be evaluated for each decision as it is made. If having the information helps you make a smarter decision, a faster decision, or a decision you feel more comfortable about, then the information was relevant.

The skill module shown below illustrates the issues discussed in this section.

LO2 Specify the requirements for a small business accounting system.

Accounting Systems for Small Business

The primary reason to acquire and use a computerized accounting system is to ensure the accuracy of your accounting information. Computerized systems also simplify the accounting process by providing automatic error checking, entry screens that look like the common business forms, and automatic production of financial statements and management reports.

The most commonly used small business systems are QuickBooks, Sage 50 Accounting, Simply Accounting, One-write, and Microsoft Dynamics ERP. All these systems automatically produce financial reports that meet legal requirements for content and format. Although, as with any computer program, you will have to invest some time in learning to use it effectively, each of these accounting programs is very user-friendly. Its use can be mastered in a very short time, a matter of a few hours. Most community colleges offer night and weekend classes in QuickBooks and Sage 50 Accounting, and you may have (or have even taken) similar courses at your school. There are also numerous online sites that offer tutorials. Each program itself includes a tutorial, help files, and a printed manual to help you master its use.

SKILL MODULE 13.1 Why Does Accounting Matter?

Suppose you are operating a buffalo wings restaurant, and you purchase a high capacity fryer as discussed in the text above. Suppose you have estimated the following costs of operating your restaurant for one month:

Variable costs:	
food (chicken, potatoes, etc.)	$ 15,000
beverage (soda, tea, beer)	4,500
supplies (napkins, cleaning materials, etc.)	2,000
labor	21,600
Total monthly variable costs	$ 43,100
Fixed costs (rent, insurance, depreciation, etc.)	$ 21,900

Now suppose that you are currently using a battery of three fryers that you originally bought used for $4,000. Because the purchase price was small, you recognized the entire $4,000 cost of the fryer as an expense in the year it was purchased.

The Vulcan representative is trying to sell you a new four-basket computer-controlled battery fryer. The purchase price is $25,000 and the costs of shipping, installation, and testing will be $5,500. The representative has shown you how the new fryer, because of its improved insulation, safety features, and cooking capacity will save you $1,000 per month in reduced electricity use and lowered insurance premiums. The fryer also has much greater capacity than the one you are currently using, so you will be able to cook more wings and serve more people.

You have spoken with your accountant, and she told you that for tax purposes the fryer will have to be depreciated in six years, using the "5-year **MACRS rate**" set by the IRS. The amount of **depreciation** expense you will recognize will be the following:

Year	Depreciation
1	$6,100
2	9,760
3	5,856
4	3,513
5	3,513
6	1,758

1. What is the cost of buying the new fryer?
2. How will your expenses change if you buy the fryer?
3. How will your fixed costs per year change if you buy the fryer?
4. If you predict that sales will increase by 10 percent per year, should you buy the fryer?
5. Suppose that your accountant called you and said that the fryer could be depreciated for seven years, using straight line depreciation of $4,357 per year for the first six years and $4,358 in the last year. Would this change your decision of whether to buy the fryer?
6. Under what conditions is the amount of depreciation expense relevant to deciding whether to buy the fryer?

MACRS rate
An Internal Revenue Service acronym for the Modified Accelerated Cost Recovery System. The MACRS approach lets taxpayers depreciate more of the cost earlier in the life of a capital expense.

depreciation
Regular and systematic reduction in income that transfers asset value to expense over time.

To ensure that your accounting information is accurate, reliable, and useful, the accounting system that you choose should easily and efficiently accomplish the following tasks:

- Provide a simple, easy-to-understand user interface.
- Have an exhaustive context-sensitive help function.
- Produce an income statement that clearly lists revenues and expenses by appropriate categories for your industry and type of business.
- Produce a classified balance sheet that clearly shows the financial position of your business.
- Facilitate the development of a cash budget.
- Facilitate the task of developing operating and investment budgets.
- Produce financial statements in approved formats to be furnished to outside investors, bankers, and regulators.
- Produce multiple-year comparison financial statements for management use.
- Provide a method for you to define and produce custom reports to meet your management needs.
- Be able to export financial data in a form that can be used by your accountant and can be imported into tax preparation and spreadsheet programs.
- Maintain an internal "audit trail" that records all entries and changes to the accounting system in order to facilitate the identification and correction of errors.
- Enforce security measures to reduce the opportunity for employee misuse or fraud.
- Have provisions that will either allow the program to grow with your business or to easily export its data into programs that can handle larger businesses.

Key Software for Small Business Accounting Systems

1. Quickbooks www.quickbooks.com/
2. Sage 50 Accounting (formerly Peachtree) http://na.sage.com/
3. One-write www.one-write.com/
4. Microsoft Dynamics www.microsoft.com/en-us/dynamics

Setting Up an Accounting System

Your specific accounting needs are largely determined by the industry you're in and by the size of your business. The smallest businesses often need little in the way of accounting records beyond an accurate check register. As businesses become larger, the difficulty of any one person being able to remember all its details increases exponentially. When a business is large enough to have one or more employees, formal record keeping is a must.

Regardless of your business's size, the one essential element of an accounting system is *cash accounting* that is accurate, easy to use, and tracks all checks written and all deposits made.

As your business grows the following accounting functions will become important to your success:

- *Accounts payable* records to track what you owe and to make timely payments in order to capture prompt pay discounts and to maintain a good credit rating for your business.
- *Payroll* records to ensure that payroll and employment taxes are kept current.
- *Fixed asset* accounting that automatically calculates and accumulates depreciation.
- *Inventory* accounting that facilitates maintaining the appropriate levels of inventory and aids in calculation of appropriate stocking and reorder levels.
- *Credit card sales* function to enable reconciling your sales records with the amount of discount and charge backs taken by your credit card provider.
- *Accounts receivable* records if you provide credit to your customers. Accurate and timely accounts receivable records are essential for making decisions concerning the extension of credit. Accurate records also help produce accurate billing of customers, and thus help to maintain good customer relations.
- *Insurance register* to ease the problems of keeping necessary insurance coverage current and in force.
- *Investments* records if your business keeps surplus cash invested in securities.
- *Leasehold* records if your business has made improvements to leased property or equipment.

The actual task of setting up a computerized accounting system for your business is quite easy. All the small business accounting systems listed above include all the functions that you are likely to need. Additionally, each program has a method to establish a set of records that is appropriate for your specific business. Should you have a business that is unique, setting up a set of records from scratch takes less than an hour. Quickbooks and Sage 50 Accounting include an "interview" function that will guide you through the setup process by furnishing a series of questions and prompts.

Often in such situations, you can get help for free from your local Small Business Development Center (**www.sba.gov/content/small-business-development-centers-sbdcs**) or SCORE (the Service Corps of Retired Executives; **www.score.org**). Alternatively, for a small fee (generally $200 to $1,000) many CPAs (certified public accountants) will set up any of these accounting programs for your specific needs. You can find CPAs in your phone book (hard copy or online) or even through Google searches for an accounting consultant. As when you choose any other professional (like doctors or lawyers), it makes sense to check with others about a professional before making a major commitment.

Financial Reports

LO3 Explain the content and format of common financial statements.

financial statements
Formal summaries of the content of an accounting system's records of transactions.

The final output of a computer system is a set of **financial statements** and reports. Although there is certainly room for you to customize financial reports in many ways, the overall content and form of financial statements have been made standard by long usage. Bankers and investors are familiar and comfortable with standard financial statements. When you apply for a loan or seek equity investment, you will be expected to present financial information in the format and containing the information that is standard for your industry.

Figure 13.1 shows examples of the most common formats. When you are familiar with them, you will find that you can easily understand and adapt them to the differences unique to your industry.

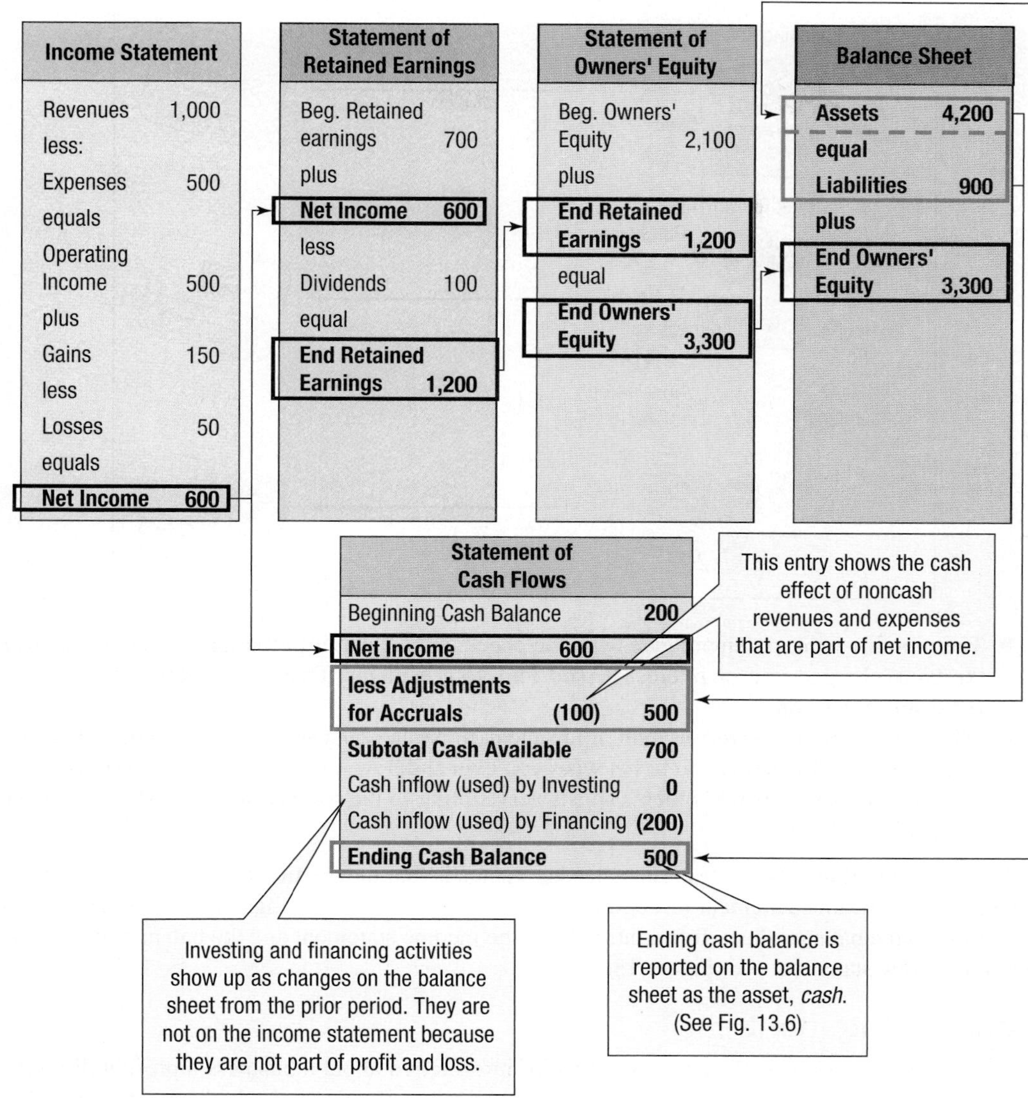

FIGURE 13.1

Flow of Information in Financial Statements

There are five common financial statements:

- Income statement
- Statement of retained earnings
- Statement of owners' equity
- Balance sheet
- Cash flow statement[12]

To the uninitiated these financial statements can seem almost alien, but in reality each type is similar in concept and operation to financial records we use in everyday life (see Figure 13.2):

- Think of your checking account or the account tied to your debit card. You put money in and write checks or use your debit card to take money out. That is similar to the use of the income statement.
- The exact amount you have in the account at any moment depends on the deposits credited to your account (which can take anything from minutes to days, depending on how you made the deposit and the speed of your bank) and which checks have been handled by the bank. Figuring that exact amount (which some people do with their check registers or by keeping a running tally in their heads) is the idea behind the statement of cash flow.

FIGURE 13.2

Everyday Financial Documents and Similar Financial Reports

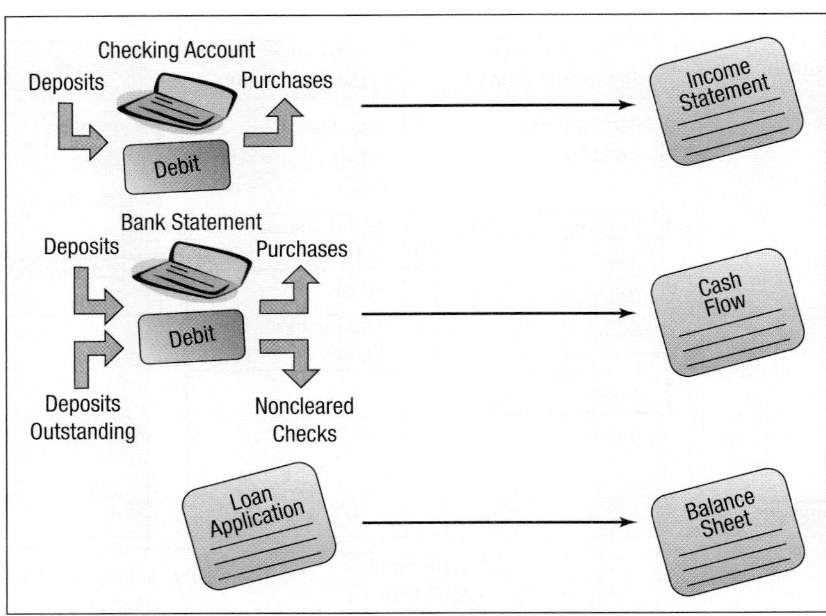

- The monthly bank statement gives you the check and deposit information as well as any fees the bank charged you or interest it paid into your account. That parallels the statement of **retained earnings**.
- When you apply for a student loan or for a loan to purchase a car, you must fill out a loan application. This form asks you to list what you own and how much it is worth. It also asks you to list all debts you owe to others. This is very similar to the balance sheet on which financial accounting is based.

retained earnings
The sum of all profits and losses, less all dividends paid since the beginning of the business.

The important thing about these financial statements is that they **articulate**, that is, information flows from the income statement through the statement of retained earnings, the statement of owners' equity to the balance sheet. Information from the income statement and the balance sheet flows to the cash flow statement (see Figure 13.1).

articulate
The concept that information flows from the income statement through the statements of retained earnings and owners' equity to the balance sheet.

Income Statement

The **income statement** is the primary source of information about a business's profitability. The income statement shows the amount of revenues earned minus its expenses which equals net income:

income statement
A statement that lists revenues and expenses and shows the amount of profit a business makes for a specified period of time.

$$\text{Revenues} - \text{Expenses} = \text{Net Income}$$

All income statements follow the same simple general format. Reading from the top down, the income statement presents answers to the questions shown in Figure 13.3.

The usefulness of the income statement for managing a small business is related to the amount of detail available in the statement. There are two formats for income statements: (1) a *single-step* format, illustrated in Figure 13.4A, which provides little detail—it simply lists all revenues and gains together, then lists all expenses and losses together, and (2) a *multiple-step* format, illustrated in Figure 13.4B, which lists revenues from operations separately from other income and gains.

Most owners and managers of small businesses prefer the multiple-step format because of its greater detail. Notice that in Figure 13.4B operating income of $105,800 is reported separately from the nonoperating gains and income from leasing. The two most commonly used computerized accounting systems for small businesses, QuickBooks and Sage 50 Accounting, by default produce income statements in the multiple-step format.

Difficulties in Understanding the Income Statement

There are two typical difficulties that arise in understanding and interpreting the income statements. First, there are disagreements about *what* exactly should be reported as revenue. The second problem arises from disputes over *when* to recognize revenues.[13]

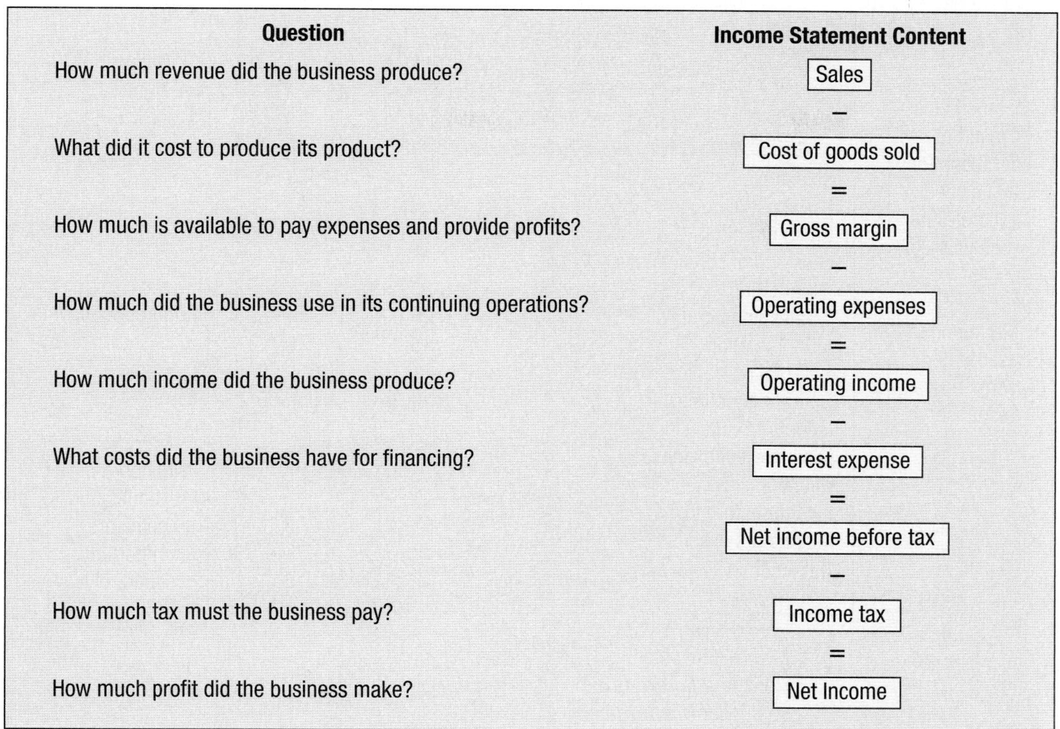

FIGURE 13.3
Organization of the Income Statement

Suppose your business is a water park that is open for only 120 days between June and September. In the late fall you run a promotion to sell season tickets as holiday gifts. Through this promotion, you sell for cash $200,000 worth of season tickets. Have you realized a revenue? No, to be recognized as revenue, you must have earned the money. This means that even though you have $200,000 in your bank account, it really isn't yours until the holders of season passes use them to visit the park. In fact, the amount of the season passes would be shown on your balance sheet as a liability—you owe the pass holders either access to the park or their money back.

Similar problems arise in determining the amounts and timing of gains, losses, and expenses. Suppose your business sells motor scooters. Customers who buy one will expect to receive a warranty.

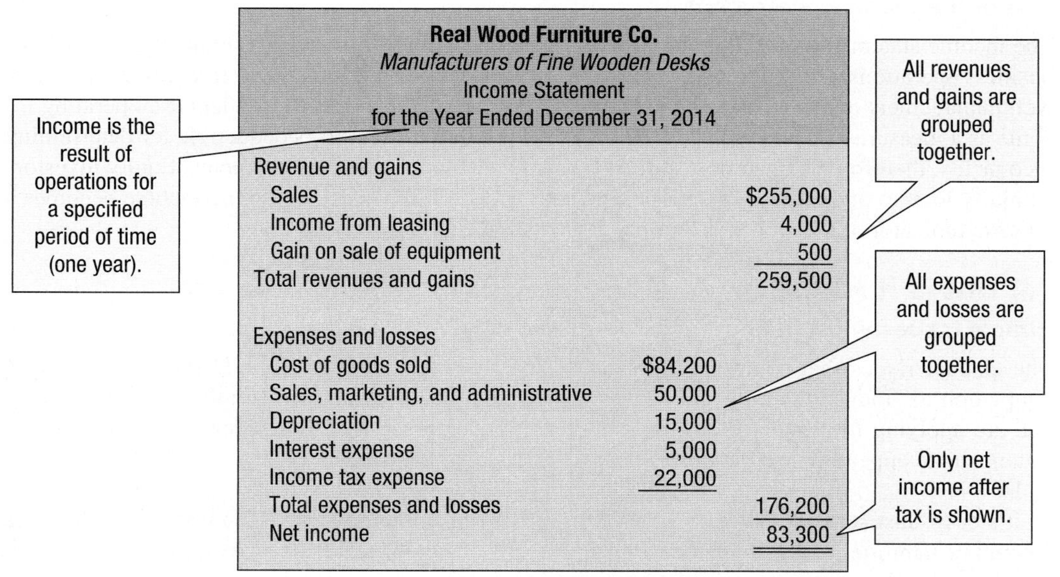

Real Wood Furniture Co.
Manufacturers of Fine Wooden Desks
Income Statement
for the Year Ended December 31, 2014

Revenue and gains		
Sales		$255,000
Income from leasing		4,000
Gain on sale of equipment		500
Total revenues and gains		259,500
Expenses and losses		
Cost of goods sold	$84,200	
Sales, marketing, and administrative	50,000	
Depreciation	15,000	
Interest expense	5,000	
Income tax expense	22,000	
Total expenses and losses		176,200
Net income		83,300

FIGURE 13.4A
Typical Single-Step Format Income Statement

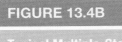

FIGURE 13.4B

Typical Multiple-Step Income Statement

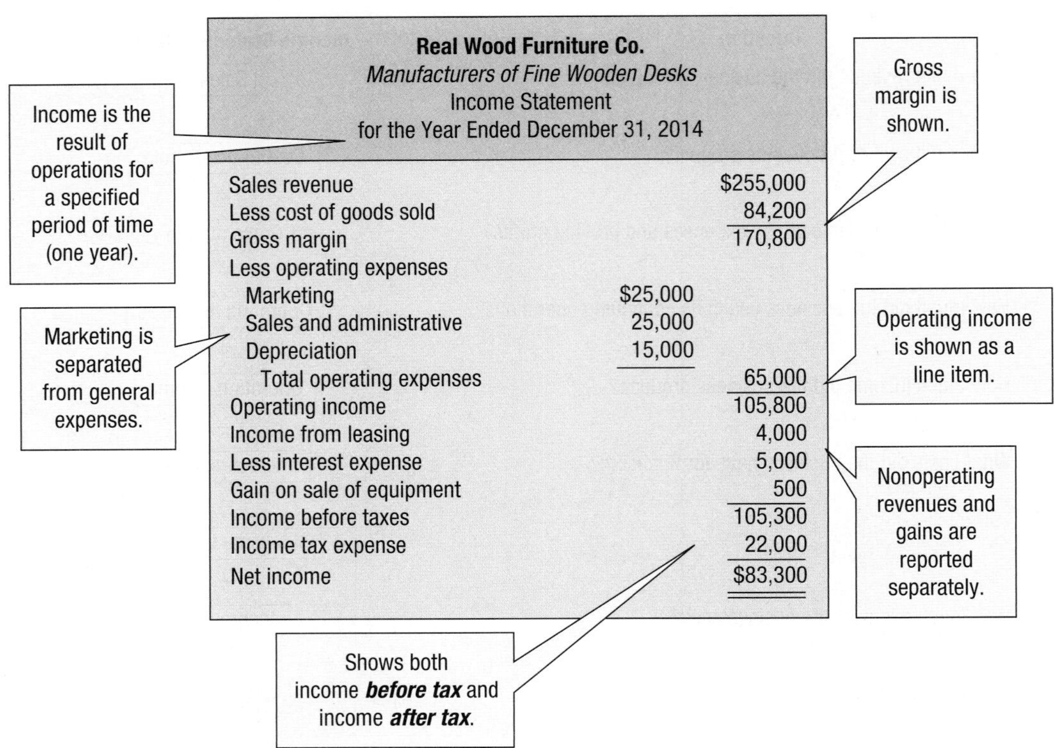

Real Wood Furniture Co.
Manufacturers of Fine Wooden Desks
Income Statement
for the Year Ended December 31, 2014

Sales revenue		$255,000
Less cost of goods sold		84,200
Gross margin		170,800
Less operating expenses		
Marketing	$25,000	
Sales and administrative	25,000	
Depreciation	15,000	
Total operating expenses		65,000
Operating income		105,800
Income from leasing		4,000
Less interest expense		5,000
Gain on sale of equipment		500
Income before taxes		105,300
Income tax expense		22,000
Net income		$83,300

Income is the result of operations for a specified period of time (one year).
Marketing is separated from general expenses.
Gross margin is shown.
Operating income is shown as a line item.
Nonoperating revenues and gains are reported separately.
Shows both income **before tax** and income **after tax**.

If they have a problem within the warranty period, they will expect that the scooter will be promptly repaired or replaced. So how much expense should you recognize for warranty? And when should you recognize it? When you sell the scooter, or when it comes back for repair? The amount of warranty cost and the timing of returns are not known at the time of sale.

Despite the difficulties and limitations of the income statement, it provides valuable information. Most small businesses do not have any difficulty deciding how much and when revenues and expenses occur. In many small businesses, all sales to customers are made either for cash or as credit card transactions that are essentially the same as cash. Subscriptions and warranties are not an issue. So in many cases, the income statement of a small business is a reliable report of just how well the business is doing in producing profits.

Use of the Income Statement

The income statement is used by you, by lenders, and by investors to analyze the effectiveness of business operations. *Operating income* is the most used item on the statement. It represents just how well management achieved sales and controlled costs to produce profits. Lenders use operating income as a measure of how much debt a business can support. Interest is deductible for determining income tax, therefore net income before tax is available to make interest payments. Equity investors similarly look to operating income as an indication of future sales, so operating income becomes a favorite indicator of the value of their investment.

. . . but is it *Right*?

Ethical Issues with the Income Statement

The characteristics that sometimes make the income statement hard to understand also provide temptation to "fudge" the numbers. Consider the example of a water park in the section above. If you are applying for a loan to install a new water slide, you can easily "clean up" your financial statements to appear to be a better credit risk.

How?

It's easy. Just state the $200,000 of advance sales as being a revenue. You instantly reduce the amount of liabilities and simultaneously increase owners' equity. Here is an example:

Honest Financials

Income Statement for November 2013	
Sales	-- 0 --
Expenses	10,000
Net income	(10,000)

Balance Sheet as of November 30, 2013	
Current assets	
Cash	$ 200,000
Current liabilities	
Accounts payable	10,000
Unearned income	200,000
Owners' equity	(10,000)
Total liabilities & equity	200,000

Misstated Financials

Income Statement for November 2013	
Sales	200,000
Expenses	10,000
Net income	190,000

Balance Sheet as of November 30, 2013	
Current assets	
Cash	$ 200,000
Current liabilities	
Accounts payable	10,000
Owners' Equity	190,000
Total liabilities & equity	200,000

Of course, any change in your financial statements has many implications; consider what effect changing your income statement from a loss of $10,000 to a profit of $190,000 would have on income taxes. In this case you would end up paying taxes on $190,000 in the current year. This would be a very expensive way to get a loan.

It could work the other way, though. You could immediately recognize warranty expense, for example, and reduce stated income and thus the amount of tax due. But then, the IRS takes a dim view of manipulating your financial statements to reduce your income tax.

So, the question remains, "Just because you can make your business results look better, should you?"

Balance Sheet

The **balance sheet**, also called the *Statement of Financial Position,* presents a "snapshot" of the financial holdings and liabilities at the close of business on a specified date. The balance sheet explicitly details the accounting equation for your business. The balance sheet provides answers to the questions shown in Figure 13.5.

balance sheet
A statement of what a business owns (assets), what it owes to others (liabilities), and how much value the owners have invested in it (equity).

The usefulness of the balance sheet is determined by the detail it includes. As shown in Figure 13.5, the minimum level of detail is to report both assets and liabilities in two categories: current, which will either produce or use cash within a year, and long term, which will convert to cash over a period of time greater than one year. However, your balance sheet may be made in greater detail if there is a need to do so. A common practice is to present multiyear balance sheets to facilitate analysis, as is shown in Figure 13.6.

Use of the Balance Sheet

The information in the balance sheet is used to determine the liquidity, financial flexibility, and financial strength of the business, which are detailed below. These measures of a business's financial position are used by owners, lenders, and equity investors in making financial and investment decisions.

liquidity
A measure of how quickly a company can raise money through internal sources by converting assets to cash.

Liquidity is a measure of the expected time before an asset can be converted into cash, and of the expected time before a liability must be paid. A completely liquid asset is one that can be converted instantly to cash, at its full value.[14] Cash is the most liquid of assets, as it does not have to

FIGURE 13.5

Organization of the Balance Sheet

Question	Balance Sheet Content
What does the business own that can be turned into cash within one year?	Current assets
	+
What does the business own that will produce revenues for more than one year?	Fixed assets
	+
What other things does the business own, such as investments, patents, and copyrights?	Other assets
	=
What is the value of everything that the business owns?	Total assets
What debts does the business have that must be paid within one year?	Current liabilities
	+
What debts does the business have that will take longer than a year to pay?	Long-term liabilities
	+
How much is the business worth to its owners?	Owners' equity
	=
	Total liabilities and equity

FIGURE 13.6

Typical Balance Sheet

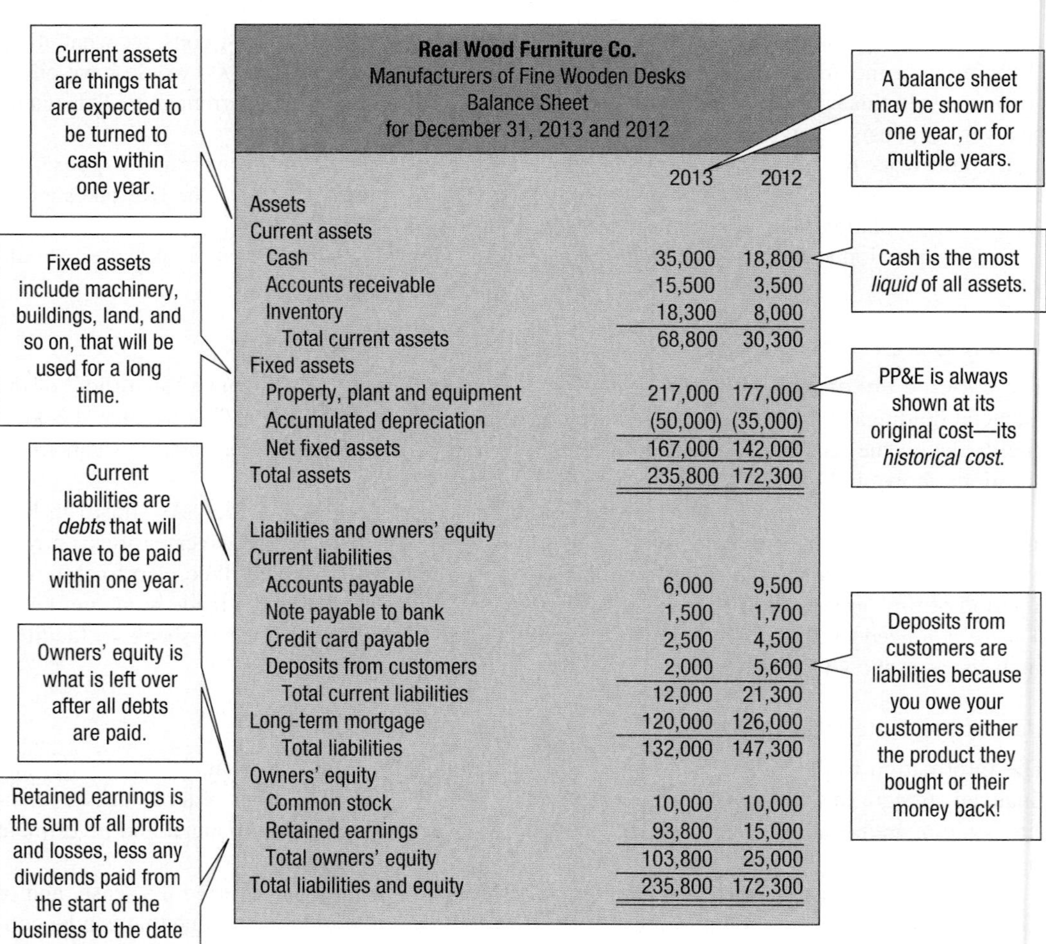

Real Wood Furniture Co.
Manufacturers of Fine Wooden Desks
Balance Sheet
for December 31, 2013 and 2012

	2013	2012
Assets		
Current assets		
Cash	35,000	18,800
Accounts receivable	15,500	3,500
Inventory	18,300	8,000
Total current assets	68,800	30,300
Fixed assets		
Property, plant and equipment	217,000	177,000
Accumulated depreciation	(50,000)	(35,000)
Net fixed assets	167,000	142,000
Total assets	235,800	172,300
Liabilities and owners' equity		
Current liabilities		
Accounts payable	6,000	9,500
Note payable to bank	1,500	1,700
Credit card payable	2,500	4,500
Deposits from customers	2,000	5,600
Total current liabilities	12,000	21,300
Long-term mortgage	120,000	126,000
Total liabilities	132,000	147,300
Owners' equity		
Common stock	10,000	10,000
Retained earnings	93,800	15,000
Total owners' equity	103,800	25,000
Total liabilities and equity	235,800	172,300

Current assets are things that are expected to be turned to cash within one year.
Fixed assets include machinery, buildings, land, and so on, that will be used for a long time.
Current liabilities are *debts* that will have to be paid within one year.
Owners' equity is what is left over after all debts are paid.
Retained earnings is the sum of all profits and losses, less any dividends paid from the start of the business to the date of the balance sheet.
A balance sheet may be shown for one year, or for multiple years.
Cash is the most *liquid* of all assets.
PP&E is always shown at its original cost—its *historical cost*.
Deposits from customers are liabilities because you owe your customers either the product they bought or their money back!

be converted. An illiquid asset *cannot* be sold quickly without suffering a significant discount from its true value. Specialized machinery is not a liquid asset. Certainly, given enough time, specialized machinery that is not technologically obsolete can be sold. However, it is not likely to be sold quickly, and is quite likely that when sold, it will sell for only a portion of its true value as a productive asset. Think of a hot rod automobile. You might spend $20,000 or more building it. But if you must sell it, you are unlikely to get more than a tiny fraction of your cost. The same is true for any custom asset, and the more illiquid it is, the greater the discount.

Liquidity is a measure of the ability of a business to meet both short-term and long-term obligations. Lenders are concerned with liquidity because it indicates the level of risk that a loan will not be repaid as contracted. Equity investors are concerned with liquidity because it affects a business's ability to pay dividends.

The most common ratio used to estimate liquidity is the **current ratio**. The current ratio is calculated by dividing the value of current assets (those assets expected to be converted to cash within one year) by the value of current liabilities (those liabilities that must be paid within one year). The rule of thumb for evaluating current ratio is that the minimum acceptable ratio is 2.0, and higher is better. The calculation and use of financial ratios are discussed in detail in Chapter 15.

current ratio
The value of current assets divided by current liabilities.

Financial flexibility is an indicator of the business's ability to manage cash flows so that the company has the financial ability to respond appropriately if an unexpected opportunity or problem arises. There are no accepted financial ratios that are indicators of financial flexibility. Financial flexibility is a matter of judgment, usually based on experience. What owners, managers, bankers, and investors look for to help indicate levels of financial flexibility include (1) the ability to sell nonoperating assets, (2) the ability to obtain loans or to sell additional stock, and (3) the ability to increase efficiency and to lower costs of operation.[15] You can see that what is similar across the three indicators is the business's ability to rapidly and efficiently raise additional capital.

financial flexibility
A business's ability to manage cash flows in such a manner that the company can respond appropriately to unexpected opportunities and needs.

The **financial strength** of the business is also a matter of informed judgment. The balance sheet provides information about the nature of the assets and liabilities of the business. In evaluating financial strength, more cash and cash equivalents indicate higher strength. Current assets that comprise cash, short-term investments, and accounts receivable are more indicative of strength than are inventories and prepaid expenses. In fact, excessive amounts of inventory in the current assets are indicative of management problems and financial weakness. For example, a large inventory may indicate lagging sales or products that have become obsolete or fallen out of favor with customers—all indicators of out-of-touch management. Long-term assets that are relatively new, low current liabilities, low long-term debt, and fully funded retirement plans for employees are all indicative of financial strength.

financial strength
The ability of a business to survive adverse financial events.

Problems in Interpreting Balance Sheet Information

For all its usefulness to the owners and managers of businesses, the balance sheet has several limitations. First, all values listed in a balance sheet are *historical* values—the cost of the asset when it was acquired. In the case of long-lived assets, such as land, buildings, and equipment, the value recorded in the accounting records can be widely different from the asset's current value. Given even a small level of inflation, the original cost of such assets is likely to be a much smaller number of dollars than its current value. On the other hand, cash is always current. This means that ratios such as return on assets (current income/net average asset value) have a current value as numerator and a denominator that, at best, is measured in older dollars of greater purchasing power. At the extreme, the true value of the asset may have changed because of changes in population density, demographics, highway access, and economic development.

Additionally, every balance sheet typically contains estimated amounts, such as estimated loss from uncollectible accounts receivable, estimated warranty cost, accumulated depreciation, depletion, amortization, and income taxes. Sometimes these estimates can be significantly wrong, such as when an unexpected product defect appears.

Finally, certain assets and liabilities are omitted from the balance sheet. Assets that are not listed include the value of licenses, established business with vendors, established customers, organizational knowledge and expertise, employee loyalty and morale, and research and development. When such assets represent a major strength of your company, the balance sheet will underreport your firm's financial strength.

SKILL MODULE 13.2 Applying for a Loan

You are going to apply for a loan for your business. Your banker told you that you will need to bring him a set of financial statements that show your business income, your business's financial position (balance sheet), and your cash flows for the year to date. To complete this task, you have collected the following information from your accounting records, which you keep manually in a three-ring binder.

Use the information to make a balance sheet in the format shown in Figure 13.6. (You can complete only the current year balance sheet.)

Account	Balance
Accounts payable	2,500
Accounts receivable	5,000
Building and equipment	112,000
Note to bank	27,500
Customer deposits	3,000
Cash	15,000
Accumulated depreciation	35,000
Capital portion of owners' equity	50,000
Retained earnings	14,000

1. What is the amount of current and long-term assets that you have?
2. Can you pledge the retained earnings of $14,000 as collateral for the new loan? Why or why not?
3. Calculate the current ratio. Using the rule of thumb given in the text, is this a good or bad ratio?
4. Why would the current ratio matter to your banker?

Cash Flow Statement

cash flow statement
A statement of the sources and uses of cash in a business for a specific period of time.

GAAP
Generally Accepted Accounting Principles are the standardized rules for accounting procedures set out by the Financial Account Standards Board and used in all audits and submissions of accounting reports to the government.

You compute the **cash flow statement** in order to see the sources and uses of cash by the business. Cash flow statements can be either direct statements or indirect statements. The direct statement is developed solely from the cash records of the business (only those things bought and sold) and does not make any reconciliation to the income statement. **GAAP** (Generally Accepted Accounting Principles) now specifies that the direct method should be used. The indirect statement of cash flows starts with net income and adjusts the accruals and deferrals to provide cash flow information that can be easily reconciled to the other financial statements. Most owners, lenders, and investors prefer the indirect method because it explicitly links net income and the balance sheet to cash flows.

There are six items that must be reported in the statement of cash flows (see Figure 13.7A):

1. Cash flows from operating activities.
2. Cash flows from investing activities.
3. Cash flows from financing activities.
4. Net effect of foreign exchange rates.
5. Net change in cash balance during the period.
6. Noncash investing and financing activities.

Common *cash inflows* (receipts) and *outflows* (payments) are shown in Figure 13.7B.

operating activities
Activities involved in producing and selling goods and services.

investing activities
The purchase and sale of land, buildings, equipment, and securities.

Operating activities include all the functions that are performed to create your product or service. Thus the receipt of cash from customers is an operating activity. Funds received from obtaining a loan at a bank is not an operating activity; rather, it is a financing activity.

Investing activities include the acquisition and disposal of property, plant, equipment, and investment securities of other firms. The outflows are the cash investments made by the business to acquire noncash assets. Investing outflows arise from the sale or disposal of noncash assets acquired from prior investments.

FIGURE 13.7A

Organization of the Cash Flow Statement

Question	Cash Flow Content
Cash flows from operating activities	
1. How much money did I receive from my customers?	Cash collected from customers
2. How much did I pay for merchandise?	(Cash paid for merchandise)
3. How much did I pay for leased equipment?	(Cash paid for equipment leases)
4. How much did I pay my employees?	(Cash paid for wages and salaries)
5. How much did I pay for other expenses?	(Cash paid for miscellaneous expenses)
6. How much cash did I receive from interest earned?	Interest received
7. How much did I pay in interest on borrowed funds?	(Interest paid)
8. How much cash was provided (used) by operations?	Net cash provided (used) by operating activities
Cash flows from investing activities	
9. How much cash did I receive (use) from disposing of obsolete or surplus equipment?	Cash proceeds (use) from disposal of equipment
10. How much did I use in paying credit deposits?	(Cash paid in security deposits)
11. How much cash did I receive from selling stock in another company?	Cash proceeds from security sales
12. How much cash did I pay to acquire equipment?	(Acquisition of equipment)
Cash flows from financing activities	
13. How much money did I invest in my own business?	Owner's contributions
14. How much did I borrow from banks?	Proceeds from bank loans
15. How much did I pay back to banks on loans?	(Principal payments on bank loans)
16. How much money did I take out of the business for personal use?	(Owner's draws)
Net effect of foreign exchange rates	
17. How much money did I gain (lose) through foreign currency conversions?	Gain (loss) due to foreign currency exchanges
Net increase (decrease) in cash	
18. Do I have more or (less) cash now than at the beginning of the year?	Net increase (decrease) in cash
Noncash investing and financing activities	
19. What was the value of barter transactions that I made?	Schedule of noncash investing and financing activities

Financing activities are those actions taken by management to finance the operations of the business. Thus cash inflows come only from investments by owners and from money borrowed through notes, mortgages, and bonds. Cash outflows from financing activities comprise capital repaid to owners and repayment of the principal amount of borrowings.

financing activities
Activities through which cash is obtained from and paid to lenders, owners, and investors.

Net effect of foreign exchange rates is becoming ever more important to small businesses. The Internet has opened foreign trade to businesses of all sizes. Exchange rates often vary rapidly, affecting the value of contracts and sales made in currencies other than the currency of the home nation of the business.

Net change in cash balance simply reconciles the net increase or decrease with the beginning cash balance and the ending cash balance.

Noncash investing and financing comprise transactions in which an exchange of value other than cash takes place. An example of a noncash transaction is when a debt is settled by issuing stock to the creditor. These types of transactions are rarely made by small businesses. A more common transaction for small businesses is a barter transaction, which is discussed in detail in Chapter 14.

FIGURE 13.7B

Typical Cash Inflows and Outflows on the Cash Flow Statement

Inflows	Outflows
Cash Flows from Operating Activities	
1. Cash received from customers	1. Cash paid to purchase inventory
2. Interest received on accounts receivable	2. Salaries and wages
3. Dividends received on investments in other firms	3. Cash paid for rent, utilities, royalties, and license fees
4. Cash refunds from vendors	4. Income taxes, duties, and fines
5. All interest received from loans to other entities	5. All interest paid on liabilities
Cash Flows from Investing Activities	
1. Disposal of property, plant, and equipment	1. Acquisition of property, plant and equipment
2. Disposal of investment securities	2. Acquisition of investment securities
3. Receipt of the capital amount of loans made to customers and vendors	3. Loans made to other entities
	4. Acquisition of assets other than inventories
Cash Flows from Financing Activities	
1. Cash received from owners of the business	1. Cash paid to owners as dividends and draws
2. Cash received from borrowing	2. Cash paid to acquire the firm's own stock
	3. Repayment of the principal of borrowed funds

LO4 Use accounting information as a tool for managing your business effectively.

Uses of Financial Accounting

Although financial accounting is not specifically designed for management purposes, it can be a highly valuable aid in decision making. Financial and business managers are familiar with the format, content, and interpretation of financial statements. Obtaining loans, answering Internal Revenue Service inquiries, and satisfying the reporting requirements of regulatory agencies are all made easier when an appropriate set of financial statements is provided.

As the accounting scandals of recent years have made evident, the existence of financial accounting statements, even when audited by major accounting firms, does not guarantee that the representations of management are complete, accurate, or even true. In this respect, financial accounting is much like a lock on the door. A lock will keep honest people honest. Crooks will pick the lock, jimmy a window, or find another entry to commit burglary. Similarly, a business manager who is determined to commit fraud might be inconvenienced by accounting standards, but will find some way to do the crime.

Thinking about the lock idea, if you have locked something, doesn't it just make sense to double-check that the lock is in fact locked? Doing that just shows a healthy skepticism. Similarly for owners and managers of small businesses, all representations by owners, managers, employees, and providers of business outsourcing should be examined with an attitude of informed professional skepticism. It is just a healthy attitude to have.

Reporting to Outsiders

The greatest value of financial accounting for small business owners and managers is reporting the results of operations and the financial condition of the business to entities outside the business. Outsiders can include absentee owners,[16] creditors and lenders, unions, and taxing and regulatory agencies. Each of these groups has some interest in the conduct of the business. Each has either or both legal rights and political power to enforce honest disclosure of your business's finances. You are less likely to be accused of misrepresentation if your disclosures comply with accepted accounting principles.

Record Keeping

The primary criteria for a small business's record keeping system are: (1) simplicity of use, (2) accuracy of detail, (3) timeliness of reports, (4) understandability to the manager of the business, and (5) security of data. An appropriate accounting system keeps records of the details of financial transactions that facilitate the task of corroborating the conduct of the business. The most convincing evidence that can be provided to outsiders is a set of complete and accurate records that can be substantiated by third-party sources.

Taxation

Current Internal Revenue Service (IRS) regulations require that employers withhold federal income, social security (FICA), and Medicare taxes from the wages of each employee. Employers must also pay the federal unemployment tax (FUTA). The amount withheld, and the employer's share of taxes, must be paid to the IRS regularly, on a schedule determined by the amount of withholding. At the year's end, each employer is required to submit summaries of each employee's total earnings and withholdings for the year and to report the information to the IRS and to each employee on a Form W-2. This process can be automated by using one of the small business computerized accounting systems mentioned earlier.

Similarly, businesses need to pay taxes each year, and having the financial records makes the task dramatically easier. In fact many of the computerized accounting packages have tax modules or are designed to feed information to tax programs such as Intuit's TurboTax or H&R Block's TaxCut.

Control of Receivables

Accounts receivable—money owed your business by customers—is often the key to survival. An appropriate record-keeping system provides detailed reports of amounts due from customers including purchases, payments, and current contact information. The key in controlling receivables is to have them *aged,* by sorting them into groups of those that are 30, 60, 90, and over 90 days past due. If you don't receive payment when due, you should take immediate and appropriate action to collect it. Often businesses step up collection efforts when the receivables are more than 30 days overdue, with many businesses treating receivables more than 90 days old as delinquent. In such cases the owners may refer the account to a collection agency or even factor the account, selling it (at a substantial discount) to a company that will take aggressive actions to collect the entire amount owed and keep all the money it obtains.

Analysis of Business Operations

Your accounting records contain information that can be easily used for analysis of the results and state of your business. Experience in your business provides a benchmark to which all items may be compared. Those items that appear unrealistic—either too high or too low—should be carefully examined. The examination should attempt to answer the following:

- What are the appropriate levels of sales and expenses?
- Why do certain expenses appear too high or too low?
- Can any expenses be reduced or eliminated?
- Are profits appropriate for your investment, risk, time, and effort?

Uses of Managerial Accounting

Managerial accounting—the forward looking form of accounting—is one of the three types of accounting, along with tax and financial. Mastering certain managerial accounting techniques will make you a better small business manager.[17] The techniques of managerial accounting will help you become more accurate at forecasting profits, planning operations, and conserving scarce resources. Managerial accounting information and reports are used in the conduct of all managerial functions: planning, organizing, staffing, directing, and controlling.

Managerial accounting is based on understanding how costs change as a result of business changes. Some costs, such as the cost of food for a restaurant, change because of increases or decreases in gross sales. If you sell more steaks to customers, you must buy more steaks from your meat supplier. Other costs, such as rent on your building, do not change when you sell more or when you sell less. Rent is usually determined by a contract called a lease. For most stores outside of malls, leases have a specified term (for example, one year) during which rent will not change.

Many things both external to the business and internal can cause costs to change. External forces that cause cost changes can be anything from inflation, to changes in supply and demand, to economic shocks such as war. Internal forces are functions of how your business works. Consider a commuter airline. The amount of fuel used changes as a result of how long, how high, and how fast the airplane is flown. Flying a long trip at a low altitude and a high speed will use much more fuel than flying a short trip at high altitude and low speed. The cost of fuel, therefore, changes with (1) **external factors**, the cost per gallon that you have to pay, and (2) **internal factors**, how you decide to operate your planes. Other costs of your airline will change according to the operating decision you make. For example, costs of landing the airplane are caused by the cost of a landing fee at the airport, wear on the tires and brakes, and fees for parking and using airport facilities. Costs for ticket agents, baggage handlers, and onground fleet service are largely driven by the number of airports which the airline serves.

external (cost) factors
Aspects of the world outside the business which could cause the business's costs to change.

internal (cost) factors
Aspects of or choices within the business which could cause the business's costs to change.

Notice that none of the costs for this commuter airline are related to the revenues paid by passengers. Fuel burn is very nearly the same whether the airplane is empty or full. Landing costs are based on landing, no matter how many passengers are aboard. Costs for ground crew are determined by how many people are working, and how many hours they work, not how many passengers they help.

Cost-Volume-Profit Analysis

The most common application of managerial accounting, called **cost-volume-profit analysis** (CVP) is based on sorting costs into only two categories: **variable costs** and **fixed costs**. The total cost is the sum of variable costs and fixed costs. To make this analysis, all costs that change with changes in output (which can be units made or sold, or sales revenue) are called variable costs. All costs that do not change because of changes in output are called fixed costs. In the example of the commuter airline, which uses a measure of the number of passengers for output,[18] every cost listed is considered to be fixed. None of them change as passenger loads change.

cost-volume-profit analysis
A managerial accounting technique which looks at the fixed and variable costs of a business to arrive at a number of unit sales (volume) to maximize profits.

variable costs
Those costs that change with each unit produced, for example, raw materials.

fixed costs
Those costs that remain constant regardless of quantity of output, for example, rent.

Fixed costs are those costs that cannot be (or are very difficult to be) assigned to a specific item sold or manufactured. Imagine that Red Jett Sweets, whose business plan you examined at the end of Chapter 8, rents an office. The firm pays for utilities to heat or cool the building, for lighting and operating their computers. Red Jett Sweets has all the paperwork expenses of running a virtual business that relies on other entities for supply and distribution. It has legal fees and accounting fees. Eventually, Red Jett Sweets will have to hire additional workers, secretaries, office managers, web programmers, purchase agents, and salespersons. Red Jett Sweets must pay for security, cleaning, or other services. None of these items is directly connected to the sale of any single cupcake, but Red Jett Sweets cannot do business without them. The effect of variable costs and fixed costs is shown graphically in Figure 13.8.

FIGURE 13.8
Total Costs

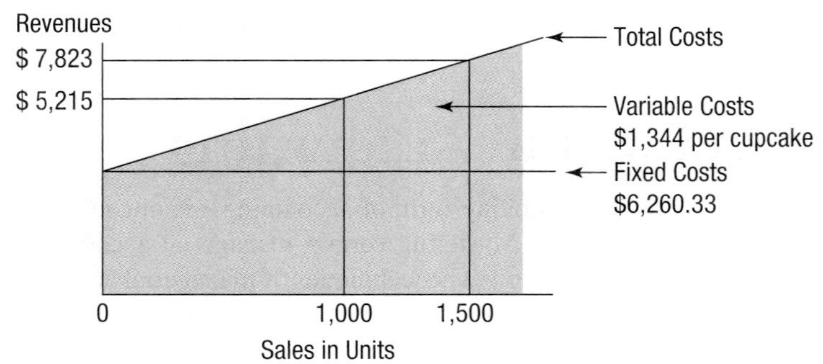

It is important to understand that fixed costs are paid whether you sell or make one product, one million products, or no products. If Red Jett Sweets hires an office manager, he or she will want to get paid whether anything is sold or not. The electric company expects to be paid regardless of what Red Jett Sweets' sales are.

Most variable costs are the costs directly related to the production or sale of one item. For example, Red Jett Sweets must purchase raw materials for each cupcake that they make and sell. The more cupcakes sold, the greater the cost of cupcakes sold will be. The same is true for beverages and any other products that the business sells. Red Jett Sweets is also paying Internet sites for "click through" advertising. Each time an Internet user clicks on the Red Jett Sweets link to go to Red Jett Sweets's website, the company is charged $0.15. As does Red Jett Sweets, most retail businesses usually have primarily variable costs for the goods they sell. In contrast, many businesses have very few variable costs. An airline, for example, has minimal variable costs, which include a small addition to fuel burn due to the added weight of carrying more passengers or cargo, the food and service item that a passenger consumes en route, and sometimes a per-person fee for using airport facilities.

Expendables are often variable costs. Expendables (also called indirect materials) are products used in the sales, manufacturing, or delivery that are not part of the finished product. Red Jett Sweets may need a $0.25 cardboard carton in which to pack the cupcakes, disposable cups for beverages, and other costs. These items are necessary, but Red Jett Sweets's product comprises the cupcake and beverages these items contain.

Other variable costs are not directly related to an individual product but still change in proportion to changes in output. For example, there is usually some amount of waste or scrap in a production process. Red Jett Sweets may have to discard shipping boxes that are dirty, torn, or have become wet. Cupcakes may be dropped, or may be under- or over-baked. Bonuses paid to salespersons as a percentage of sales, the cost of creating and fulfilling an order for product, and the costs of shipping product commonly vary with changes in output, and thus are variable costs. See Figure 13.8. Generally, both fixed and variable costs are averaged over a year. For example, Red Jett Sweets might have a clogged drain that causes several shipping boxes to have to be discarded in a single day. The business will not charge a greater scrap rate for that event but will expense the average scrap rate for the year over time. Legal fees might be paid only once a year, but part of this cost will be shown as a cost for each month of the year, not just for that particular month. There are some accounting exceptions to this, but using averages is both perfectly acceptable and about the only reasonable way to handle the situation.

To understand how this works, consider Red Jett Sweets's cost structure. (These numbers come from the **Master Budget Red Jett Sweets Example.xlsx** Excel workbook on the textbook Internet site, www.mhhe.com/katz4e.) In Figure 13.9, we reorganize the business costs as either variable or fixed. Variable costs are those costs that will increase as Red Jett Sweets makes and sells more cupcakes. Fixed costs are costs that will not change, no matter how many cupcakes are made and sold.

Suppose for a moment that Red Jett Sweets sold only a single cupcake in the month. How much revenue would be received, and what would the net income be? Red Jett Sweets would have $2.75 in revenue, less $1.34 in cost of goods sold, less $6,260.34 of fixed costs. Net income would be a **loss** of **$6,258.93.** If Red Jett were to sell 1,000 cupcakes in the month, net loss would decrease to $4,850.34 (1,000 × [2.75 − 1.34] − 6,260.34). If 2,000 cupcakes were sold, the loss would decrease even more to only $3,440.34. Indeed, as Red Jett Sweets sells more cupcakes each month, the loss will decline, and eventually a profit will be made.

So, it is obvious that at some level of sales, revenues will exactly equal costs. Red Jett will neither lose money nor make a profit. This level of sales is called the break-even point. To figure out what the break-even point is, you simply must answer the question, "How many cupcakes must Red Jett Sweets sell in one month so that gross revenues exactly equal total cost?" The easiest way to do this is by converting the question into an equation like that in Figure 13.10.

FIGURE 13.9

Example of Fixed and Variable Costs Based on Red Jett Sweets

		Cupcakes
Revenues		
Price		$ 2.75
Variable costs		
Cost of Goods Sold (COGS)	1.30	
Spoilage (3% of COGS)	0.04	1.34
Contribution margin of one cupcake		1.41
Monthly Fixed Costs		
Marketing		240.75
Rent		1,000.00
Salary		2,941.67
Wages		1,200.00
Insurance		250.00
Legal & accounting		35.00
R&D		208.33
Supplies & fixtures		163.75
Depreciation		
12 quart mixer	7.42	
6 quart mixer	2.50	
Other equipment	24.00	
Mobile cupcakery	186.92	220.84
		6,260.34

FIGURE 13.10

Breakeven Analysis

At Breakeven, Revenues Exactly Equal Total Costs, Thus

Revenues	=	Variable Costs	+	Fixed Cost
Quantity Sold × Price	=	Quantity Sold × Variable Unit Cost	+	Fixed Cost
Quantity × $2.75	–	Quantity × 1.34	=	6,260
		Quantity × (2.75 – 1.34)	=	6,260
		Quantity × 1.41	=	6,260
		Quantity	=	6,260 / 1.41
		Quantity at breakeven	=	4,440 cupcakes

Note that 6,260 / 1.41 actually equals 4,439.716. Because we cannot make and sell 71.6% of a cupcake, we round up to the next highest whole number of units. This makes little difference for Red Jett Sweets ((1 – 0.716) * 1.41 = 0.40). But suppose you are manufacturing carbon-fiber bicycle frames, each providing $1,000 of contribution margin. Rounding up from 71.6% of a unit would overstate breakeven by $284.

Breakeven with More Than One Product

SKILL MODULE 13.3

1. Suppose that Red Jett Sweets, on average, sells one beverage for each three cupcakes sold. In this situation, an average (typical) sale would be 3 cupcakes × $2.75 plus 1 beverage × $1.35, for a total sale of $9.60. If the variable cost of one cupcake is $1.34, and the variable cost of one beverage is $0.52, how many cupcakes and beverages must be sold to attain breakeven?
2. How would you calculate breakeven for a restaurant that sells 50 different items, each with a different price and different variable cost?

Key points

- Fixed costs plus variable costs equal your total cost.
- Fixed costs remain constant in total, but variable costs increase as output increases and decrease if output decreases.
- The more cupcakes that Red Jett Sweets sell, the less its fixed cost per item becomes. In our example, at one cupcake, the entire fixed cost of $6,260 is applied to that one item. At 1,000 cupcakes, the fixed cost per item is only $6.26. This truism is called **economy of scale**.

economy of scale The idea that it is cheaper (per item) to make many of an item than few.

break-even point The point at which total costs equal gross revenue.

You have certainly encountered these concepts before. The point at which gross revenue exactly equals total costs is called the **break-even point**. At breakeven you neither make any money nor lose any. In the example above, Red Jett Sweets must sell 4,440 cupcakes to break even. These relationships are shown graphically in Figure 13.11. Of course, no one goes into business to break even. For this reason, the concept has been expanded into cost-volume-profit analysis (CVP). Red Jett Sweets has determined that the best price for their cupcakes is $2.75. Suppose management would like to earn $100,000 per year. How many cupcakes must Red Jett Sweets sell to make a $100,000 profit? There must be enough sales to cover all Red Jett Sweets' costs, then to produce $100,000 in profit:

Total Revenue		Total Variable Cost		Total Annual Fixed Cost		Desired Profit
Quantity × $2.75	=	Quantity × $1.344	+	6,260 × 12	+	$100,000

If you solve this equation as in Figure 13.10, you will find that Red Jett Sweets must sell 75,362 cupcakes to earn an annual profit of $100,000. These relationships are shown graphically in Figure 13.11. This formula can easily be expanded to account for income taxes. If Red Jett Sweets's management wants to have $100,000 after tax, and the firm's tax rate is 25 percent, then the formula would become:

Calculate Sales to Make $100,000 *AFTER* Taxes

Total Revenue		Total Variable Cost		Total Annual Fixed Cost		Desired Profit
Quantity × $2.75	=	Quantity × $1.344	+	6,260 × 12	+	$100,000 / (1 − .25)

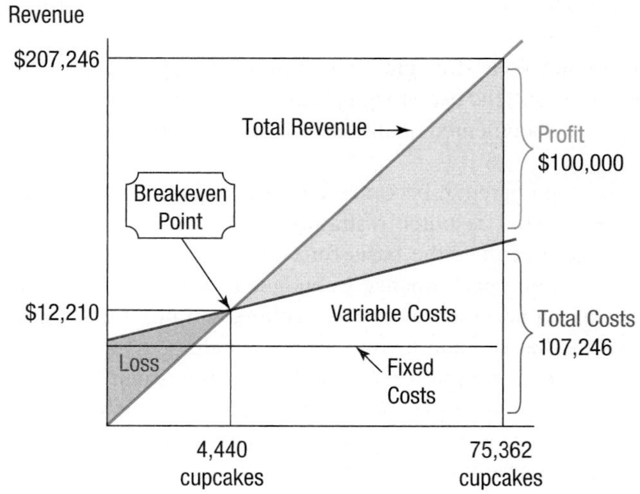

FIGURE 13.11

Red Jett Sweets's Break-Even Graph

This discussion has been simplified by assuming that Red Jett Sweets will sell only cupcakes. In fact, the firm is currently selling cupcakes and beverages. In practice, having more than one product greatly complicates the determination of breakeven. In a two-product situation like that of Red Jett, the business can break even with either product, alone. There is a near infinite number of combinations of the two products that will provide breakeven. To handle this problem, you must do one of two things: (1) assume fixed proportions of each product, as Red Jett Sweets does, or (2) use a percentage average of each, sales price and variable cost.

No one starts or buys a business for the purpose of losing money. Rather, you go into business for the express purpose of making profits and creating wealth. It is unfortunate that, as business failure statistics show, a significant number of small business owners do not achieve this basic goal. One of the underlying causes of financial failure of small businesses is the lack of a coherent plan to produce the profits necessary for continued existence and growth.[19]

Accounting data contain the information necessary to create detailed plans of how to make a desired level of profit. The problem is coaxing the information out of the data.

The process of profit planning comprises creating a *model* of the business which will allow you to test various situations, assumptions, and occurrences without risking financial loss. If the model "crashes," simply reset it and try again.[20] Models can be as simple as a schedule of expected profits at differing levels of sales, or as complex as a full, interactive computerized simulation of the business and the economy.

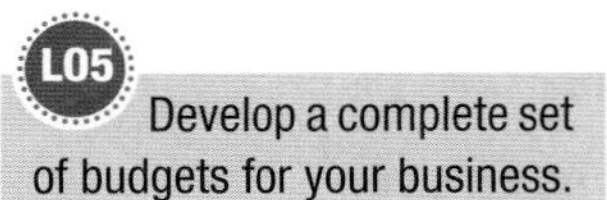

LO5
Develop a complete set of budgets for your business.

The Business Plan and the Budget Process

The most common model used for small businesses planning is the familiar business plan, like those described in Chapter 8. Looked at the managerial accounting way, a business plan specifies the amounts and types of inputs required to achieve a set of desired outcomes. It is based on assumptions concerning how costs will change in response to changes in the business operations, how risks can be controlled, and what opportunities can be taken. The financial projections in your business plan are a form of a budget which can easily be expanded to be useful for day-to-day management of your business. In fact, the budgeting techniques we show here use exactly the same estimates and calculations as you must make to create pro forma financial statements for a business plan. The budgets here, however, have the advantage of being comprised of a series of small, easy-to-understand schedules. When they are linked and printed as a single set of financial statements, they are identical to the familiar business plan **pro forma** statements.

pro forma
Latin for "in the form of" when used to describe financial statements, indicates estimated or hypothetical information.

Planning/Budgeting

Strategic planning, as discussed in Chapter 7, results in statements that are expressed in broad terms. For example, your strategic marketing position may be a price strategy, a luxury strategy, or a value strategy. However, if your broad strategic goals are to be achieved, you must take specific tactical steps. Budgeting is the process through which strategy is mapped into a series of tactical and operational actions.[21]

The process of achieving your strategic goals requires complex activities, cooperation among the people in your business, and the use of significant valuable resources. You will be better able to direct all this if you have a documented quantitative plan of action for your business. Such a plan is called a **budget**.

budget
A financial plan for the future, based on a single level of operations; a quantitative expression of the use of resources necessary to achieve a business's strategic goals.

Once a budget has been prepared, it becomes a standard against which performance can be measured.[22] Your budget establishes resource restraints within which your managers and employees must operate. Your budget becomes the basis for controlling activities and the use of resources. By constantly comparing actual performance to budgeted amounts, determining the causes of the inevitable differences, taking necessary corrective action, and providing feedback concerning performance, you may ensure that you attain your business goals.

Despite the many benefits to comprehensive budgeting, few small business owners consistently budget.[23] Those who do create budgets often set them aside in the rush of business activities.[24]

Let's face it, budgeting is seen by many entrepreneurs as a tedious and difficult job. We are going to try to convince you otherwise. In fact, business planning is a *simple* process of applying

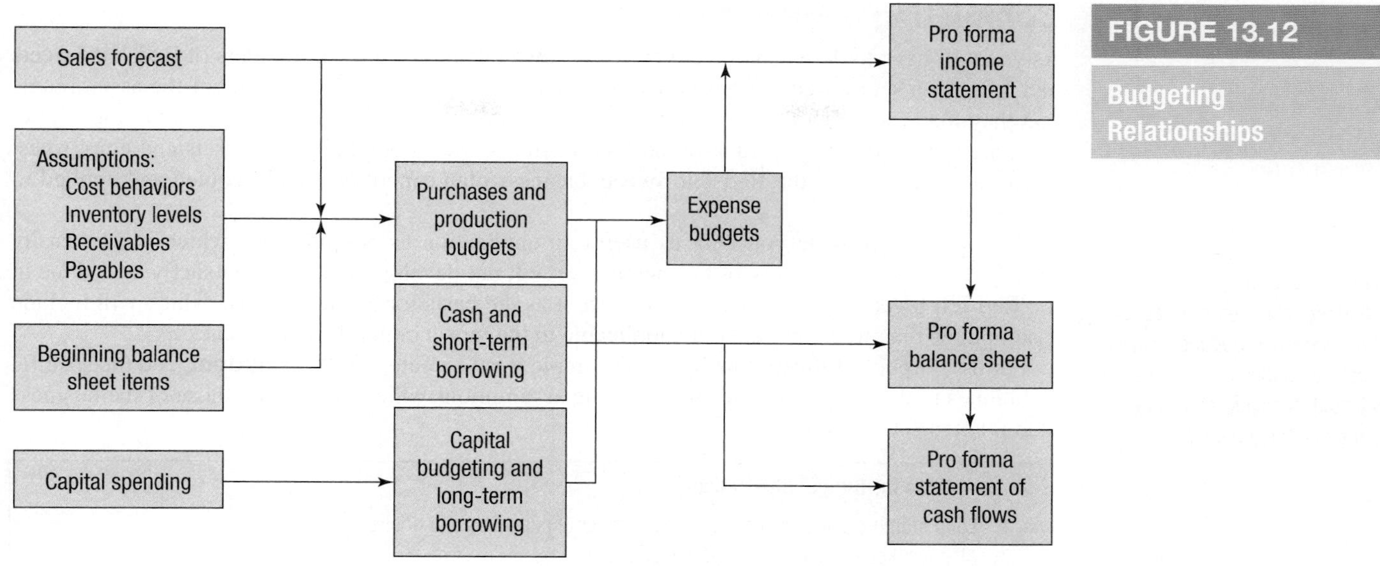

FIGURE 13.12 Budgeting Relationships

your knowledge of your business to make estimates of future operations and results. In many ways it is little more than an expanded application of the break-even analysis that was discussed earlier. However, business planning uses more detail than break-even analysis, and thus provides a basis for analyzing, directing, and controlling your day-to-day business operations at the level of detail that is most effective for you.

The first step in budgeting (as in any other method of business planning) is to make a forecast of your future sales. From the sales forecast, and from your knowledge of cost behaviors, collections, payments, and expenses, a complete business plan will be developed. Although this sounds daunting, in practice, you can adjust the level of detail you need to provide a comprehensive budget that is both compact and understandable (see Figure 13.12).

You may create as many or as few supplemental budgets and schedules as you need to model your business. The budgets and schedules that you will find most useful are listed in Table 13.1.

TABLE 13.1 Useful Budgets and Schedules

Budget for a Manufacturing Business	Budget for a Retail or Wholesale Business
1. Sales budget	1. Sales budget
2. Schedule of budgeted cash receipts	2. Schedule of budgeted cash receipts
3. Production budget	3. Purchases budget
4. Direct materials budget	4. Cost of goods sold budget
5. Direct labor budget	5. Labor budget
6. Manufacturing overhead budget	6. Overhead budget
7. Cost of goods manufactured and sold budget	7. Selling and administrative budget
8. Selling and administrative expense budget	8. Cash disbursements budget
9. Cash disbursements budget	9. Cash budget
10. Cash budget	10. Budgeted income statement
11. Budgeted income statement	11. Pro forma cash flow statement
12. Pro forma cash flow statement	12. Pro forma balance sheet
13. Pro forma balance sheet	

Completing a Master Budget

As you will have to do when you develop your own business plan, the founders of Red Jett Sweets had to make a set of assumptions about how their business would work. Some of the assumptions that they made were for the purpose of simplifying the task of planning. Other assumptions, however, are unique to doing a truck-based food business with limited physical assets and employees. Because of these facts, the Red Jett Sweets business plan cannot be simply copied and applied to most other businesses.

Therefore, to provide you with as useful an application as possible, one which can be easily modified to fit a wide variety of businesses, we will not develop budgets here exactly as is done in the Red Jett Sweets plan. Rather, we will use it as the basis for a teaching case which will include assumptions that are more generally applicable to the most common small businesses.

master budget
A budget, also referred to as a *comprehensive budget*, consists of sets of budgets that detail all projected receipts and spending for the budgeted period.

For the purpose of illustrating both how simple it is to create a **master budget**, and the specific techniques to do so, we will use the following assumptions which differ from those of the business plan for Red Jett Sweets.

Assumptions for Budget Illustration

1. Each month's sales will be a specific number of cupcakes and drinks.
2. All cupcakes have the same cost of goods sold.
3. All beverages have the same cost of goods sold.
4. All sales will be made by credit card.
5. Credit card processing fee will be 2 percent of sales.
6. Any ending inventory of cupcakes will be donated to a food bank. The cost will be absorbed in a 3 percent spoilage allowance.
7. Ending inventory of beverages will be 15 percent of the next month's budget sales of beverages.
8. Ending inventory of raw materials will be 20 percent of the next month's required material

The master budget that is developed from these assumptions contains the budgets and schedules for a retail business, as is shown in Table 13.2. The specifics of producing these budgets are detailed below. Because the way that the Red Jett Sweets business plan projections are developed, it is necessary to use different assumptions to show examples of more common budgeting techniques and

Note: April sales projection is used in inventory calculation.

TABLE 13.2 Sales Budget

Red Jett Sweets, Inc.
Sales Budget
1st Quarter, 2014

	Jan	Feb	Mar	Quarter 1	Apr
Projected sales					
Cupcakes in units	4,160	4,160	5,480	13,800	5,480
Unit sales price	2.75	2.75	2.75		
Revenue from cupcakes	11,440	11,440	15,070	37,950	
Beverages	416	416	548	1,380	
Unit sales price	1.35	1.35	1.35		
Revenue from beverages	562	562	740	1,864	
Gross sales revenue	12,002	12,002	15,810	39,814	
Less credit card processing	240	240	316	796	
Less spoilage allowance	360	360	474	1,194	
Net revenue	11,402	11,402	15,020	37,824	

formats. ***Thus, while these budgets are based on Red Jett Sweets, they are not actual projections made by Red Jett Sweets's founders.***

Copies of the entire Excel workbooks for each of the original Red Jett Sweets financial projections and this teaching case, can be downloaded from the website for this textbook. In each workbook you can see all the details of the assumptions and calculations used.

Sales Budget

The first step in preparing a master budget is to prepare a sales budget. The sales budget shows the projected future level of sales in units multiplied by the sales price per unit. Chapter 12 discusses the many methods you may use to project future sales. For teaching purposes, we assume that a specific number of cupcakes will be purchased in each month. This simplifies setting up the spreadsheet formulas.

Notice also that unit sales prices are stated in dollars and cents, while revenues are stated to the nearest whole dollar. This may seem inconsistent, but remember that all the numbers both in an initial business plan and in later budgets are based on lots of estimates. There simply is no way that you are ever going to estimate the exact "correct" amount. For the purposes of planning, controlling, and directing, it is sufficient for any small business to carry calculations only to whole dollar amounts, or even to round to the nearest one hundred dollars.

Purchases Budget

Once sales have been projected, the next step is to plan for inventory purchases.

The business plan for Red Jett Sweets was designed as if there were no inventory of raw materials. (Flour, sugar, butter, milk, eggs, etc. are expensed directly as cost of goods sold.) Nor does the business plan provide for an ending finished goods inventory. (All leftover cupcakes are donated to a food bank). These are reasonable simplifying assumptions because of the nature of the raw materials required and because of the marketing value of having absolutely fresh cupcakes each day.

However, there are almost as many patterns of buying and holding inventory as there are businesses that need inventory. Restaurants and bars usually purchase food and alcoholic beverages, especially meats, fish, and beer, two or three times per week. It is common for restaurant food suppliers to require payment in cash when the goods are delivered. The common practice for consumer electronics (stereos, DVD players, car radios, etc.) is for the retailer to place annual orders for products that will come in the form of only a few future deliveries. This annual ordering is usually done at the Winter Consumer Electronics Trade Show, held in Chicago every January.

Most often a retail business will start each month with some amount of inventory already in hand (often around 60 percent of projected sales) and the rest is ordered for delivery in that month.

If Red Jett Sweets operated this way, what would its purchases budget look like? Table 13.3 shows this more common approach, which can easily be modified to fit any pattern of ordering and holding inventory.

The purchases budget shows the number of units that are expected to be acquired during the budget period. The specific number of units that must be bought in each period is a function of how many units are on hand at the beginning of the period, how many are projected to be sold, and the desired number of units to be held in inventory at the end of the period.

To provide an illustration that applies to the widest range of businesses, we are going to show how a purchases budget is developed using four raw materials, flour, sugar, butter, and milk. We will use the quantities and prices from the Restaurant Depot sheet in the Red Jett Financial Planning Excel workbook. (This simplification results in the budget projecting the cost of one cupcake to be approximately $0.015 less than that in the Red Jett Sweets business plan.)

Examine the column for February. Sales are projected to be 4,160 cupcakes (346⅔ dozens). Each dozen cupcakes requires 4 cups of flour weighing 1.325 pounds. It takes 459.3 pounds of flour to make 346⅔ dozen donuts. Management has decided to keep 30% of the next month's requirement for flour on hand at the end of each month. Thirty percent of the March requirement is 3.63 bags. However, there are 2.8 bags of flour left from January. Red Jett Sweets must purchase 10.1 bags of flour to meet planned production. To get wholesale pricing, flour must be bought in 50-pound bags. You can't buy 1/10 of a bag of flour, so the amount to be purchased must be rounded up to 11 bags.

TABLE 13.3 Purchases Budget

Red Jett Sweets, Inc.
Purchases Budget
1st Quarter, 2014

	Jan	Feb	Mar	Quarter 1	Apr
Sales in units					
Cupcakes	4,160	4,160	5,480	13,800	5,480
Flour					
Bags needed to meet sales need	9.19	9.19	12.10	30.48	12.10
Plus ending inventory (30% of next month needs)	2.76	3.63	3.63		
Less beginning inventory	1.60*	2.76	3.63		
Flour to be purchased	11	11	13	35	
Cost per bag of flour (50 lbs)	16.67	16.67	16.67		
Total cost of flour purchased	183	183	217	583	
Refined sugar					
Bags needed to meet sales need	3.04	3.04	4.01	10.09	4.01
Plus ending inventory (30% of next month needs)	0.91	1.20	1.20		
Less beginning inventory	1.60*	0.91	1.20		
Refined sugar to be purchased	3	4	5	12	
Cost per bag of flour (50 lbs)	30.70	30.70	30.70		
Total cost of refined sugar purchased	92	123	154	369	
Butter					
Cartons needed to meet sales need	2.41	2.41	3.17	7.99	3.17
Plus ending inventory (30% of next month needs)	0.72	0.95	0.95		
Less beginning inventory	1.60*	0.72	0.95		
Butter to be purchased	2	3	4	9	
Cost per carton of butter (36 lbs)	83.38	83.38	83.38		
Total cost of butter purchased	167	250	334	751	
Milk					
Cartons needed to meet sales need	21.67	21.67	28.54	71.88	28.54
Plus ending inventory (30% of next month needs)	6.50	8.56	8.56		
Less beginning inventory	1.60*	6.50	8.56		
Milk to be purchased	27	24	29	80	
Cost per carton of butter (36 lbs)	2.71	2.71	2.71		
Total cost of milk purchased	73	65	79	217	
Total cost of raw materials inventory purchased	515	621	784	1,920	

*Note that beginning inventory for January, given as 1.6 units, is an arbitrary number used here for illustration only.

TABLE 13.4 Cost of Goods Sold Budget

Red Jett Sweets, Inc.
Cost of Goods Sold Budget
1st Quarter, 2014

	Jan	Feb	Mar	Quarter 1	Apr
Units sold					
Cupcakes	4,160	4,160	5,480	13,800	
Cost of goods sold per cupcake	0.688	0.688	0.688		
Cost of cupcakes sold	2,862	2,862	3,770	9,494	
Beverages	416	416	548	1,380	
Cost of goods sold per beverage	0.275	0.275	0.275		
Cost of beverages sold	114	114	151	379	
Total cost of goods sold	2,976	2,976	3,921	9,873	

This simple formula is used over and over to produce most of the schedules of a master budget:

The amount to be bought = The amount to be used + Desired ending amount − Beginning amount

Other inventory items to be purchased are estimated in exactly the same manner.

The **cost of goods sold budget** shows the predicted cost of product actually sold during the accounting period. The calculation is simply the quantity of goods sold times the price that you expect to pay for each product.

cost of goods sold budget
A schedule that shows the predicted cost of product actually sold during the accounting period.

Labor Budget

The labor budget shows both the amount and cost of labor needed to meet output goals. As is common for most small businesses, such as plumbing companies, electrical contractors, restaurants, and the like, Red Jett Sweets's single largest cost is labor. Notice that Red Jett Sweets chose to treat both wages and salaries as fixed costs. In other words, the cost of labor does not change as sales increase or decrease. This is a bit unusual—salaries are usually considered fixed and wages are usually variable. Regardless, it's a reasonable simplifying assumption for Red Jett Sweets both because the amount of wages is immaterial ($\approx$ 4% of sales) and because Red Jett Sweets is budgeting a fixed number of labor hours for each day.

There are small businesses, especially online businesses, that have very little cost of labor. Management often chooses not to show labor as a separate amount and includes it in administrative or overhead costs because the cost of separate budgeting and accounting is greater than the value of these processes for the management of the firm.

So, how would you predict labor costs if they do vary with the amount of output? First, you would have to estimate the amount of production labor required for each unit of production. Second, you would then multiply the unit labor cost times the number of units actually produced. A common way to make this estimate is to take total annual estimated production labor costs and divide it by total annual estimated units of output. This provides labor cost per unit. Using Red Jett Sweets's third-year projections provides \$17,800 / 55,600 = \$0.32 per cupcake.

The budget shown in Table 13.5 is an example of the most commonly used method to forecast labor cost.

TABLE 13.5 Labor Budget

Red Jett Sweets, Inc.
Labor Budget
1st Quarter, 2014

	Jan	Feb	Mar	Quarter 1	Apr
Number of cupcakes sold	4,160	4,160	5,480	13,800	
Production labor per cupcake	0.32	0.32	0.32		
Total production labor cost	1,331	1,331	1,754	4,416	

TABLE 13.6 SG&A Budget

Red Jett Sweets, Inc.
Sales, General, & Administration Costs Budget
1st Quarter, 2014

	Jan	Feb	Mar	Quarter 1	Apr
Selling expenses	610	649	610	1,869	
General	173	173	173	519	
Administrative					
Executive wages (including FICA)	2,941	2,941	2,941	8,823	
Legal & accounting	35	35	35	105	
Total Sales, General, & Administration costs	3,759	3,798	3,759	11,316	

Selling, General, and Administrative Expense Budget

The selling, general, and administrative (SG&A) budget illustrated here contains both costs that change with production and costs that do not. Selling costs, including freight, are a variable cost in respect to sales. General and administrative costs are fixed.

Overhead Budget

Traditionally, all overhead costs have been treated as fixed, not changing with changes in output as measured by either volume of production or gross sales. It is becoming more common for managers to use **activity-based cost estimates** for overhead. As previously discussed, many costs that do not vary in proportion to output levels do vary in response to changes in other business activities. If the cost behaviors are known, they can easily be included in the budget process. For simplicity, the example given here assumes that overhead costs are fixed with respect to sales.

activity-based cost estimates
An accounting method which assigns costs based on the different types of work a business does in order to sell a particular product or service.

Budgeted Income Statement

The budgets that have been completed to this point can now be combined into a "pro forma" budgeted income statement. It is common to create the budgeted income statement in only a fiscal period format (one quarter or one year) as is done here. While the income statement could be produced in months or even in days, that level of detail, while possibly helpful for management, is not helpful to bankers, investors, or others outside management for which the income statement is intended.

TABLE 13.7 Overhead Budget

Red Jett Sweets, Inc.
Overhead Budget
1st Quarter, 2014

	Jan	Feb	Mar	Quarter 1	Apr
Rent	691	691	691	2,073	
Depreciation					
Mobile cupcakery	358	358	358	1,074	
Baking equipment	100	100	100	300	
Repairs	83	83	83	249	
Permits	257	257	257	771	
Liability insurance	167	167	167	501	
Telephone	127	127	127	381	
Total overhead expenses	1,783	1,783	1,783	5,349	

TABLE 13.8 Budgeted Income Statement

Red Jett Sweets, Inc.
Budgeted Income Statement
For the Quarter Ending March 31, 2014

Sales revenue		39,814
Less credit charges & spoilage		1,990
Net revenue		37,824
Less cost of goods sold		9,873
Gross margin		27,951
Operating expenses:		
Labor	4,416	
Sales, general, administration	11,316	
Other expenses		
Rent	2,073	
Other overhead items	1,902	19,707
Income before depreciation, Interest & Income tax		8,244
Interest		--0--
Depreciation		1,374
Net income before provision for income tax		6,870

Thus the detailed planning that is included in the budget is condensed for the income statement. The entire budgeted income statement is based on the assumption that all budgeted items, sales, production, purchasing, labor, overhead, and SG&A will be incurred exactly as planned in the supporting budgets. During the year, comparisons of actual results are made to the budgeted items. If the budget is met, then the projected profit will be realized.

Completing a Comprehensive Budget

The final schedules to be completed to produce a master budget are (1) a cash receipts budget, (2) a cash disbursements budget, and (3) a cash budget. From these schedules, a pro forma cash flow statement and a pro forma projected balance sheet are prepared.

The management of cash is so important to small business that it deserves a chapter to itself. Therefore, the discussion of cash and cash budgeting is included in the next chapter.

Controlling

Managerial accounting, primarily through the budget process, provides information that allows managers to determine how well the business is doing in attaining its goals. This is done by comparing actual results to budgeted results. The difference between actual and budget is called a **variance**. Management can determine where the business is not meeting goals through examining a report of variances.

variance
The difference between an actual and budgeted revenue or cost.

Variances should be evaluated to determine the significance of a particular variance. Small variances from budget are expected to occur, as the budget is a collection of estimates. No business manager, in fact, no person, no computer, is capable of making estimates that are exactly what future results will be. For this reason, it is customary for management to determine a range of acceptable variances. Individual variances that fall within the predetermined acceptable range are ignored. Variances that exceed the acceptable range are examined in detail, with the manager tracing the activities that drive the cost to determine the cause of the variance and appropriate methods to deal with it.

variance analysis
The process of determining the effect of price and quantity changes on revenues and expenses.

Variance analysis is a topic that is simple in concept but complex in execution. At the variance analysis most basic level, variances occur because of one of two events: (1) Prices are different from what was estimated, or (2) Quantities are different from what was estimated.[25]

You can see from this that variances can measure two things: (1) the effect of changes in prices and (2) the effect of changes in the quantity used or produced. The specifics of variance analyses are detailed in the Thoughtful Entrepreneur box below.

SKILL MODULE 13.4

Preparing a Master Budget

Go to the McGraw-Hill website for this textbook (**www.mhhe.com/katz4e**) and download the Excel file, "Master Budget Red Jett Sweets Example.xlsx." Using the information in the downloaded spreadsheet, complete a monthly master budget for the remainder of 2014, following the examples shown in this chapter.

THE THOUGHTFUL ENTREPRENEUR

Performing Variance Analyses

Suppose that you operate a business that produces aluminum window frames for the replacement window industry. You have used all your expertise to budget the next year's operation of your business. Based on prior years' results, the current state of the economy, and projections for the replacement window industry, you developed the following budget items:

Materials to produce one window frame	Budget
Aluminum extrusions 16 ft @ 1.20 per ft	$19.20
Sheet aluminum 25 sq in @ $ 0.08	2.00
Screws 22 @ .06 each	1.32

For the past month, you estimated total production to be 6,000 window units. You actually produced 5,800 window frames. You used 93,960 feet of extrusion that cost $109,933 in total. As a manager, how would you answer the questions, "How did the price of aluminum affect us?" and "Did we use the extrusions efficiently?"

Logically, the answer to the first question can be found by answering the question, "What would I have paid for the aluminum I actually used if the price had been what I expected?" The difference between that and what you actually paid is the difference caused by price changes.

The second question, "Did we use the material efficiently?" can be answered by asking, "How much material should I have used to make the number of window units that were actually completed?" The difference between what you should have used and actually did use multiplied by the price you expected to pay for aluminum is the difference resulting from efficiency.

These questions are answered by variance analysis, which uses the information mentioned above to produce quantitative results. The equations that make up variance analysis are given in Figure 13.13. Figure 13.14 shows how the calculations are made.

Thus we can see that the actual cost of material was $2,819 less than the expected cost for the amount actually used. This is called a **favorable price variance**. On the other hand, the cost of the amount of materials actually used is greater than the budgeted cost of materials to make 5,800 window frames. This is called an **unfavorable quantity variance**. The terms *favorable* and *unfavorable* are determined by the variance's effect on profits, all other things being as budgeted. Paying 3 cents a foot less for extrusions than was budgeted would cause a greater profit than budgeted, if all other budget items were exactly correct. Conversely, using more extrusions to make 5,800 window frames than was budgeted for that level of output would cause a decrease from budgeted profit.

Note that although the variances are labeled as favorable or unfavorable depending on the direction of the variance from budget, no value judgment can be made from the label. A favorable price variance could be a bad event for the company; if, for example, the reason for the lower price was lower quality of materials that would prevent the business from attaining its strategic goals. Additionally, managers must use judgment to determine if the variance is worth the effort to investigate. For example, the price of aluminum extrusions is set by the world price for aluminum. It is not likely that any amount of investigating would result in determining a way to get a lower price. On the other hand, using 0.2 feet more of material than was budgeted might indicate that cutting tools are out of adjustment or that worker efficiency is not as great as expected. Management could reasonably expect to find the cause and to devise a way to improve the use of this resource.

favorable/unfavorable variance

A label applied to variances to indicate their effect upon the income statement; favorable variances would result in profits being greater than budgeted, all other things being equal; unfavorable variances would result in profits being less than budgeted, all other things being equal.

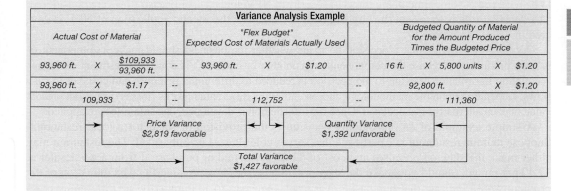

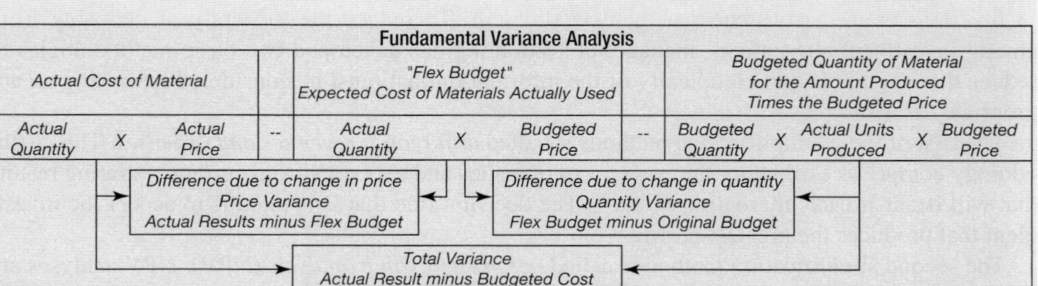

FIGURE 13.13
Fundamental Variance Analysis

Variance Analysis Example				
Actual Cost of Material		*"Flex Budget" Expected Cost of Materials Actually Used*		*Budgeted Quantity of Material for the Amount Produced Times the Budgeted Price*
93,960 ft. X $109,933 / 93,960 ft.	--	*93,960 ft. X $1.20*	--	*16 ft. X 5,800 units X $1.20*
93,960 ft. X $1.17	--		--	*92,800 ft. X $1.20*
109,933	--	*112,752*	--	*111,360*

Price Variance $2,819 favorable

Quantity Variance $1,392 unfavorable

Total Variance $1,427 favorable

FIGURE 13.14
Variance Analysis Example

Decision Making

LO6 Use accounting information to make better business decisions.

Managers have five primary functions in a business: planning, organizing, staffing, directing, and controlling the combined efforts of the firm. Each of these functions requires making decisions, both large and small. The primary purpose of managerial accounting is to support good decision making.

To use accounting information for decision making, you need to have some understanding of the processes by which people make decisions.

All current theories of decision making are based on the belief that people are rational, that is, people think, reason, and consider alternatives before they act. Although this assumption may be a bit optimistic, it applies (or *should* apply) to decision making in business situations. The assumption of rationality itself comes in several "flavors." At one extreme are theories that assume that the human mind has essentially unlimited reasoning powers. At the other extreme are theories that assume that people have limited abilities to obtain and process information.

The theories of unlimited reasoning powers have been largely discredited. Research shows that people use incomplete information and incomplete analyses of alternatives to make decisions. Today, it is generally assumed that people are inefficient processors of information. Theories based on the assumption of limited human abilities are called *bounded rationality models*.[26] One implication of the assumption that people are limited in their ability to use information is that the more information available to be included into the decision process, the less efficient that process will be.

Thus to make good decisions we need (1) good information, (2) efficient ways to condense information so it is understandable, and (3) methods to help compare alternatives.

Managerial accounting is both a source of information that is used in decision making and a methodology to reduce the complexity of the information used to make a decision. By definition, managerial accounting deals with only financial information. By limiting the information being considered to financial concerns, the complexity of the alternatives is reduced. Managerial accounting further reduces information complexity by evaluating information for relevance to the decision to be made. For financial purposes, any decision that was made in the past cannot be changed and is therefore irrelevant to any decision to be made today. Information that is the same for two or more alternatives cannot be used to choose between them. For these reasons, managerial accounting decision support is based solely upon the differences in expected financial outcomes among identified alternatives.

Examining some of the common management decisions that can be aided by the use of accounting information and procedures will illustrate these concepts.

Investments are a constant management problem. To reduce the difficulty of choosing from among investment alternatives, managerial accounting has developed two basic methodologies to reduce the magnitude and complexity of the information that must be considered in making an appropriate decision.

The first of these simplification methods is called *differential revenues and expenses*. This methodology comprises estimating the *changes* in revenues and expenses from current operating results that will occur if each alternative is taken. The decision rule that is applied is to accept the investment that produces the greatest profit.

The second simplification method is called *net present value analysis* (NPV). NPV analyses are based on the concept that a dollar to be received right now has more utility (value) than does a dollar to be received at some time in the future. To perform NPV analyses, only cash flows are considered. The decision rule is to accept the largest positive NPV. The theory and application of NPV is covered in detail in Chapter 17.

Outsourcing requires that a decision be made whether the business should make a component of its own product or purchase the component from another business. As is done in investment decisions, accounting information relevant to the decision is reduced to differential revenues and costs, or to cash flows. Depending upon the methodology chosen, either the differential profits (losses) or the net present value of each alternative is calculated. Once the information is developed, decision rules are applied.[27]

A simple example of an outsourcing decision is the provision of salad for a local restaurant. Suppose that the restaurant is a barbeque that serves cole slaw as its only salad. The restaurant may either make the slaw on premises at a cost of $2.87 per pound or purchase it from a wholesaler at $2.40 per pound. Should you make the slaw or purchase the slaw? A superficial examination of the problem would indicate that purchasing it is less expensive. Examining only the differential costs offers a very different conclusion (see Exhibit 13.1).

EXHIBIT 13.1

Using Differential Costs to Make an Outsourcing Decision: Make or Buy?

Current Costs to Make Slaw on Premises		
Pounds of slaw served per month		900
Materials per pound		$0.87
Direct labor per pound (2.4 hrs @ $10 per 30 lbs.)		0.80
Variable overhead per pound		0.20
Allocated fixed costs per pound		1.00
Total cost per pound		$2.87
Differential Costs between Alternatives		
	Alternatives	
	Make	Buy
Materials	$0.87	–0–
Direct labor	0.80	–0–
Variable overhead	0.20	–0–
Purchase price	–0–	2.40
Total	$ 1.87	$2.40

The difference arises from the fact that fixed costs will not change if the decision is made to purchase the slaw. By definition, fixed costs are costs that do not change with changes in output (here output is slaw). As a result, the amount of fixed cost allocated to making slaw is irrelevant to the decision. If you have trouble understanding this, simply put a line for fixed cost into the decision criteria above. Put the allocated amount of $1.00 in the columns for making and buying the slaw. Add the columns and see if your decision would change.

Accounting is useful for managers of small businesses, for record keeping, for reporting to absentee owners and other stakeholders, for substantiating assertions made to regulators and taxing agencies, for support of the five functions of management, and for decision making. Accounting information is a financial model of the operations of the business and provides a wealth of useful reports, analyses, and measures that are valuable to the management of small businesses. Accounting is a rich source of information. It is not, however, the only source of information needed by managers.

CHAPTER SUMMARY

LO1 Describe the basic concepts of accounting.

- Accounting matters to small businesses because:
  - Accounting proves what your business did financially.
  - Accounting shows how much your business is worth.
  - Banks, creditors, development agencies, and investors require accounting statements.
  - Accounting provides easy-to-understand plans for business operations.
  - Accounting provides information about how your business is doing.
- There are three types of accounting:
  - Managerial accounting attempts to predict the results of management decisions.
  - Tax accounting is used to produce tax returns and schedules.
  - Financial accounting is a formal, rule-based system intended primarily for absentee owners, bankers, investors, and regulators.
- Accounting is based on a few basic concepts:
  - A business is believed to have an existence that is separate and different from the owner's (business entity concept).

    - Because a business exists, it is expected to continue to exist (going concern).
    - The accounting equation is simply an expression of the common sense statement that your net worth is whatever is left over after all your debts are paid.
- To use accounting effectively for management purposes, you must understand the difference between costs and expenses:
    - Costs are real changes in the value of what you own.
    - Expenses are simply entries made in your accounting system to record your use of goods and services in the conduct of your business.
- There are only two reasons to do accounting:
    - To produce information that is useful to you for managing your business.
    - To meet legal or contractual requirements.

LO2 Specify the requirements for a small business accounting system.

- The primary reason to acquire and use a computerized accounting system in your business is to ensure the accuracy of your accounting information.
- Your accounting system should easily and efficiently accomplish the following tasks:
    - Provide a simple, easy-to-understand user interface.
    - Have an exhaustive context-sensitive help function.
    - Produce financial statements in the format used by your industry and type of business.
    - Facilitate the development of a cash budget.
    - Facilitate the task of developing operating and investment budgets.
    - Provide a method for you to define and produce custom reports to meet your management needs.
    - Be able to export financial data in a form that can be used by your accountant and can be imported into tax preparation and spreadsheet programs.
    - Maintain an internal "audit trail" that records all entries and changes to the accounting system in order to facilitate the identification and correction of errors.
    - Have provisions that will either allow the program to grow with your business or to easily export its data into programs that can handle larger businesses.
- Your specific accounting needs are determined by the industry you are in and by the size of your business.
- When a business is large enough to have one or more employees, formal record keeping is a must.
- Essential elements of an accounting system are:
    - *Cash accounting* that is accurate, easy to use, and tracks all checks written and all deposits made.
    - *Accounts payable* records to track what you owe and to make timely payments in order to capture prompt pay discounts and to maintain a good credit rating for your business.
    - *Payroll records* to ensure that payroll and employment taxes are kept current.
    - *Fixed asset* accounting that automatically calculates and accumulates depreciation.
    - *Inventory* accounting to facilitate managing inventory.
    - *Credit card sales* function to enable reconciling your sales records to those of your credit card provider.
    - *Accounts receivable* records if you provide credit to your customers.
    - *Insurance register* to ease the problems of keeping necessary insurance coverage current and in force.
    - *Investments records* if your business keeps surplus cash invested in securities.
    - *Leasehold records* if your business has made improvements to leased property or equipment.

LO3 Explain the content and format of common financial statements.

- The final output of an accounting computer system is a set of five financial statements and reports.
    - Income statement.
    - Statement of retained earnings.
    - Statement of owners' equity.
    - Balance sheet.
    - Cash flow statement.
- It is common for these statements to be presented as only three separate documents by combining the statements of retained earnings and owners' equity into the equity section of the balance sheet.
- The income statement is the primary source of information about a business's profitability.
- The primary difficulties in understanding and interpreting the income statement arise from two causes:
    - Disagreements about what should be reported as revenue.
    - Disputes over when to recognize revenues.

- The income statement is used in the following ways:
  - The income statement is used to analyze the effectiveness of business operations.
  - Lenders use operating income as a measure of how much debt a business can support.
  - Equity investors similarly look to operating income as an indication of future sales and thus the value of their investment.
- The balance sheet presents a snap-shot of the financial holdings and liabilities at the close of business on a specified date.
- The balance sheet is used in the following ways:
  - The balance sheet is used to determine the liquidity, financial flexibility, and financial strength of the business.
  - These measures are used by owners, lenders, and equity investors in making financial and investment decisions.
- The following are problems in interpreting balance sheet information:
  - All values listed in a balance sheet are *historical* values—the cost of the asset when it was acquired.
  - A balance sheet contains several estimated amounts.
  - Certain assets and liabilities are omitted from the balance sheet.
- The purpose of the cash flow statement is to disclose the sources and uses of cash by the business.
- There are two primary formats of cash flow statement:
  - The direct statement is developed solely from the cash records of the business and does not make any reconciliation to the income statement.
  - The indirect statement of cash flows starts with net income and adjusts the accruals and deferrals to provide cash flow information that can be easily reconciled to the other financial statements.

LO4 Use accounting information as a tool for managing your business effectively.

- Financial accounting is useful for decision making.
- Financial and business managers are familiar with the format, content, and interpretation of financial statements.
- Obtaining loans, answering Internal Revenue Service inquiries, and satisfying the reporting requirements of regulatory agencies are all made easier when an appropriate set of financial statements is provided.
- Financial accounting is used for reporting to outsiders.
- Managerial accounting is used internally for management purposes.
- By mastering managerial accounting techniques, you will become more accurate at forecasting profits, planning operations, and conserving scarce resources.
- Managerial accounting information and reports are used in the conduct of all the managerial functions of planning, organizing, staffing, directing, and controlling.
- The most used managerial accounting technique is cost-volume-profit analysis.
- Accounting data contain the information necessary to create detailed plans of how to achieve a desired level of profit.
- The process of profit planning comprises creating a model of the business which will allow you to test various situations, assumptions, and occurrences, without risking financial loss.
- The most common model used for small businesses planning is the familiar business plan.
- The financial projections in your business plan are a form of a budget which can easily be expanded to be useful for the day-to-day management of your business.

LO5 Develop a complete set of budgets for your business.

- Budgeting is the process through which strategy is mapped into a series of tactical and operational actions.
- Once a budget has been prepared, it becomes a standard against which performance can be measured.
- Business planning is a *simple* process of applying your knowledge of your business to make estimates of future operations and results.
- The most common budget schedules are:
  - The sales budget which shows the projected future level of sales in units multiplied by the sales price per unit.
  - The purchases budget shows the number of units expected to be acquired during the budget period.
  - The cost of goods sold budget shows the predicted cost of product actually sold.
  - The labor budget shows both the amount and cost of labor needed to meet required output.
  - The overhead budget details both fixed and variable overhead costs.
  - Selling, general, and administrative expense (SG&A) budget shows both costs that change with production and costs that don't.
- These budget schedules are combined into pro forma financial statements.
- The difference between actual results and budgeted amounts is called a variance.

- Variances occur because either actual prices or volume is different from what was budgeted.
- To understand the effect of price changes, you must answer the following questions:
  - What would I have paid for the amount I actually used, if the price had been what I expected?
  - How much material should I have used to make the number of units that were actually completed?

LO6 Use accounting information to make better business decisions.

- The five primary functions in a business—planning, organizing, staffing, directing, and controlling—are combined as input for decision making.
- To make good decisions we need:
  - Good information.
  - Efficient methods to condense information so it is understandable.
  - Methods to facilitate comparing alternatives.
- Managerial accounting is both a source of information that is used in decision making and a methodology to reduce the complexity of the information used to make a decision.
- Common management decisions that can be aided by the use of accounting information and procedures include investments and outsourcing.
- Managerial accounting uses two primary simplification methods to handle information: differential revenues and expenses and net present value analysis (NPV).

KEY TERMS

managerial accounting, 410
tax accounting, 410
financial accounting, 410
business entity concept, 411
going concern concept, 411
accounting equation, 412
liabilities, 412
owners' equity, 412
cost, 413
revenue, 413
expense, 413
MACRS rate, 415
depreciation, 415
financial statements, 416
retained earnings, 418
articulate, 418
income statement, 418
balance sheet, 421
liquidity, 421
current ratio, 423
financial flexibility, 423
financial strength, 423
cash flow statement, 424
GAAP, 424
operating activities, 424
investing activities, 424
financing activities, 425
external (cost) factors, 428
internal (cost) factors, 428
cost-volume-profit analysis, 428
variable costs, 428
fixed costs, 428
economy of scale, 431
break-even point, 431
pro forma, 432
budget, 432
master budget, 434
cost of goods sold budget, 437
activity-based cost estimates, 438
variance, 440
variance analysis, 440
favorable/unfavorable variance, 441

DISCUSSION QUESTIONS

1. Which of the three types of accounting is most important to small business? Which is the least? Why do you think so?
2. How does the accounting equation relate to the balance sheet?
3. How are costs and expenses different?
4. Why should you, as a business owner, care about the distinction between costs and expenses?
5. Defend the statement, "The function of accounting is to produce information that is useful for decision making."

6. What are the three most important characteristics of a small business computer accounting system? Why do you think these are the most important?
7. What are the three most important functions (think cash, accounts payable, owners' equity, etc.) that a computerized accounting system should have? Why are they the most important?
8. Which financial report is most important for managing a small business? Why?
9. You can sell your product (have revenues) without receiving any money. You can receive money (customer deposits) without having any revenue. Because revenue, expenses, and cash are so different, why should a small business owner care about the income statement?
10. Why would a small business ever need an accounting system more complicated than a simple checkbook register?
11. A budget is a collection of estimates—a big word that means the same thing as "guess." If you are guessing what future results will be, what value can a budget really have?
12. How are budgets related to business plans, as described in Chapter 8?
13. Is there any advantage to making a series of budget schedules, rather than just producing a pro forma income statement and balance sheet? What are the advantages, if any?

EXPERIENTIAL EXERCISES

1. www Assume that you have decided to purchase a computerized small business accounting system. Visit the website of each of the accounting systems named in this chapter. From the information there determine:
   a. The price of the accounting system.
   b. The minimum computer requirements for the program.
   c. The availability and cost of training to learn to use the program.
   d. The availability of trained accountants and consultants in your geographic area who can be retained to assist you in setting up and using the program.
2. www Choose an industry in which you would like to own a small business. Use the Internet, the university library, and the public library to find the names and addresses of industry trade associations. Examine the websites of the trade associations for availability of financial statistics of your industry. Examine governmental agency sites, such as those of the Department of Commerce, Department of the Treasury, Securities and Exchange Commission, and the Small Business Administration, for benchmark statistics.
3. www Choose a public business that is in the same industry as the business you would like to own. Go to the company's website and find "investor relations." Download a copy of the business's most recent annual report. Examine the financial statements in the annual report. Make a list of the ways in which their content and format differ from the examples in this text.
4. Either by yourself or in a group of other students, select a business that you could reasonably expect to be able to start and run right now. (This could be as simple as a T-shirt company.) Using the techniques learned in exercises 2 and 3, above, develop a set of estimates of (a) sales, (b) variable cost of product or service and (c) the amount of other costs (rent, electricity, transportation, etc.) that you would expect to incur. Using these estimates, create a set of budget schedules through the schedule of cost of goods manufactured and sold.
5. www Go to either the QuickBooks or the Sage 50 Accounting website. Download and install a demonstration copy of its accounting program. Using either the budget schedules you developed in exercise 4, or the Red Jett Sweets, Inc. example from the text, set up the program to do accounting as if this were a real business.
6. www Do a Google search on the terms "accounting system" and "small business." Follow the Google returns to the websites of the companies (other than the ones named in the text) that you can find that sell computerized accounting systems. Examine the site to determine if its program would be suitable under the criteria specified in the text.

MINI-CASE

PHIONIA'S FINICKY FELINE GOURMET CAT DINNERS

Phionia Phelps has developed a gourmet cat food. Not only is this food eagerly eaten by the most finicky felines, but it is specially formulated to prevent the many health problems of aging cats. Phionia has been making the food on her kitchen range and selling it at $250 per case only to close acquaintances who are also cat lovers. One of her wealthy acquaintances has now offered to invest in her business if Phionia will begin selling the product through her website. However, the investor wants Phionia to produce a budget for the first six months of operation.

Based on her experience to date, Phionia predicts the following sales in cases:

Nov	Dec	Jan	Feb	Mar	Apr	May	Jun	Jul	Aug
4,300	4,600	5,000	5,500	6,100	6,800	7,000	7,200	7,400	7,500

Each case of Finicky Feline Gourmet Cat Dinner requires 5 pounds of prime lamb meat, 10 pounds of short grain Chinese rice, 2 pounds of wild caught Alaskan salmon, and 1 pound of secret vitamins and supplements. Phionia plans to maintain end-of-month inventories equal to 10 percent of the next month's projected sales, to meet expected sales growth. All the ingredients inventories are to be maintained at 5 percent of the production needs for the next month, but not to exceed 1,000 pounds of any one ingredient. January will begin with all inventories at the projected levels.

Phionia has the following price quotes good for the following year:

Item	$ per pound
Lamb	$15.00
Rice	1.20
Salmon	24.00
Vitamins	45.00

The production process requires direct labor at two skill levels: (1) ingredient preparation, $18 per hour, and (2) cooking and canning, $24 per hour. Two workers are willing to work part days if there is not enough demand for them to work full time. It takes one hour to process one batch. Because of preparation and cleanup time, only six batches can be produced per day. Each batch produces enough food to fill 100 cases. Manufacturing overhead is $6,000 fixed per month plus $15 per case.

CASE DISCUSSION QUESTIONS

1. Prepare the following budgets for the period, January through June:
   a. Sales budget in dollars.
   b. Production budget in units.
   c. Direct materials purchases budget in pounds.
   d. Direct materials purchases budget in dollars.
   e. Direct manufacturing labor budget in dollars.
2. Comment on the viability of this business and the advisability of the investor making a $50,000 investment to get it started.

SUGGESTED CASES AND ARTICLES

- Parker Mountain Products, Inc., C-14

Available on Create:

- Lexington Valley Medical Associates
- Michaels Ballet Company
- Thermal Remediation, Inc.
- Majsperk
- Wilmont Chemical Corporation
- Ratios Tell a Story: 2003
- ENTERTAINMENTNOW.COM
- Belle Air Charter

SUGGESTED VIDEOS

www.mhhe.com/katz4e

SBTV.com Videos:

- Start-Up Costs
- Three Tips for Accounting

STVP Video:

- Keeping a Financial Focus

CHAPTER

14

Cash: Lifeblood of the Business

- Chuck Bidwell and Jennifer Guarino faced the failure of their business, J. W. Hulme, Inc. of Minneapolis, Minnesota. Faced with declining sales and inadequate cash flow, they borrowed heavily to modernize their factory to gain efficiency while maintaining the highest quality standards.

What would you do in their situation?

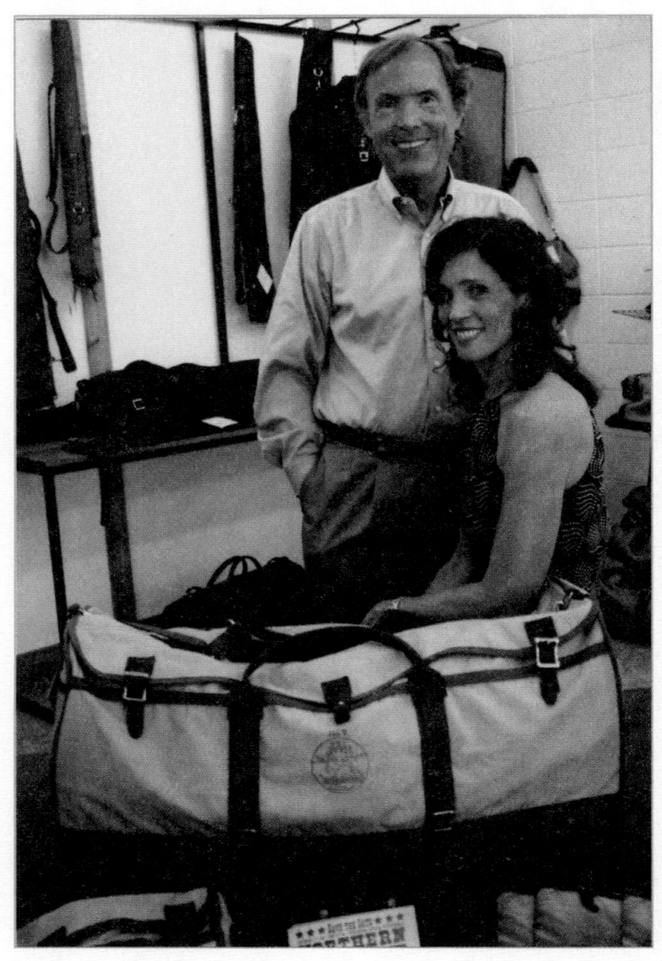

LEARNING OBJECTIVES

After you complete this chapter, you will be able to:

LO1 Explain the importance of managing your business's money.

LO2 Explain the concepts of money, cash, and cash equivalents.

LO3 Explain the basics of managing cash flow.

LO4 Reconcile bank and company book balances.

LO5 Develop a cash budget.

LO6 Develop strategies for preventing and coping with cash flow problems.

LO7 Implement strategies for coping with cash shortages.

Focus on Small Business: Chuck Bidwell and Jennifer Guarino of J. W. Hulme, Inc.

Chuck Bidwell and Jennifer Guarino were in the business equivalent of the pilot's dilemma: what to do when you're out of altitude, airspeed, and ideas all at the same time.

In 2003, the partners purchased J. W. Hulme, Co., a small (three-employee) manufacturer of duck-hunting gear and fishing-rod bags. At the time they bought it, the company was losing $150,000 per year on gross sales of less than $450,000. Confident of their ability to turn the company around, they agreed to pay $600,000 to the owners over 7 years.

They believed that the firm could be remade into a manufacturer of luxury leather products: women's handbags, briefcases, and luggage. To employ this strategy, however, required money, and lots of it. Within a short time of taking over the business, they had hired an additional six workers, purchased high-capacity industrial sewing machines, a leather splitting machine, and numerous mailing lists.

To raise the needed funds for this expansion, Chuck Bidwell took a $130,000 second mortgage on his house. The Maple Bank in nearby Champlin, Minnesota, loaned the company $70,000 and provided a line of credit for up to $200,000.

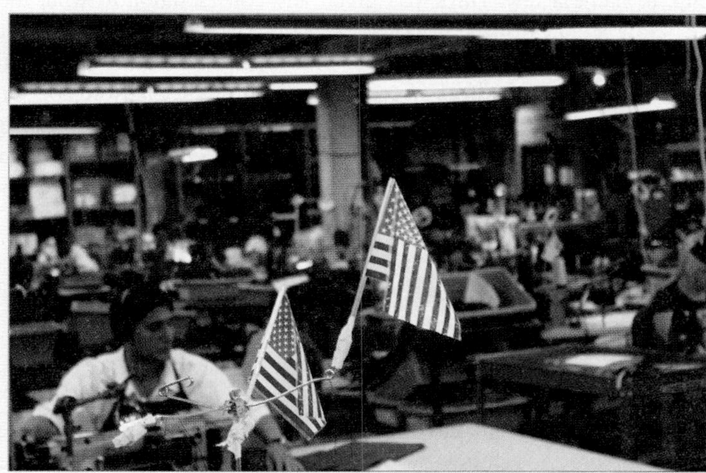

J. W. Hulme, Co production area

At first, the strategy worked. Within 3 years gross sales exceeded $1.4 million. The firm was profitable and had a positive cash flow. So, of course, the partners expanded. They applied for a $700,000 SBA insured loan. When the loan was delayed, they raised $500,000 from the famous "three-f's," (friends, family, and fools).

And then . . .

One of the really nasty realities about the mail-order business is that mailing dates for catalogs are critical. This is why you will be receiving dozens of catalogs starting in late September. J. W. Hulme was dependent on mail order. There simply was no retail organization from which merchandise could be quickly sold.

But Hulme missed critical mailing dates. Sales lost altitude at a sickening rate: actual sales were a half-million dollars short of projections.

It was obvious that the business was losing speed as well. Although profitable, the firm was not generating anywhere near enough cash to meet its needs. Total debt exceeded $2 million. The debt-to-equity ratio hovered just above 5.5. There was a $1 million inventory of finished products. Cash flow was headed toward the ground.

After ending their own salaries and laying off half the workforce, the partners were turned down for an additional loan. In desperation they sold personal property. Bidwell's wife put up $50,000 of her personal funds. Having tapped all sources, the pair were out of ideas, as well.

With no cash for operations, no cash for debt service, no cash for advertising, just no cash at all, it appeared that the firm was destined to fail.[1]

DISCUSSION QUESTIONS

1. What would you recommend to salvage this critical situation?
2. How can a business be profitable but still have insufficient cash flow to stay in business?
3. What do you believe is the rest of this story?

The Importance of Money Management

LO1 Explain the importance of managing your business's money.

Have you ever considered the question, "What is money?"

Certainly you have thought about money. It is a rare small business person who does not think about money—making money, investing money, spending money, having enough money. In fact, money can seem so important to business that sometimes people make the error of believing that money is all that business is about. Of course, as you have already learned in the earlier chapters, business is about many important things, of which money is only one.

But this still leaves the question, "What is this *'money,'* and why is it so important?"

Throughout this book, terms that refer to money are tossed about: money, cash, cash equivalents, profits, and banking, to name a few. Have you given any consideration to what these terms mean? How are they alike? How are they different? How are they related to each other? The differences are important because in the end money in its different forms represents the lifeblood of the business, and knowing which form to use, and when to use it, can make the difference between boom and bankruptcy.

In this chapter, the meaning of these terms and how they are important to managing small businesses is discussed. If you are like most people, this chapter will contain some surprises. Things that you think you know are going to turn out to be false. Things you might think are trivial will turn out to be of great importance. It is part of what makes cash and money fascinating.

Money In/Money Out—Just How Important Is It?

A recent poll conducted by the National Federation of Independent Business (NFIB Foundation) found that almost two-thirds of small businesses experience money problems (see Figure 14.1). Businesses either do not have enough money, or if they have money, they cannot get to it when it is

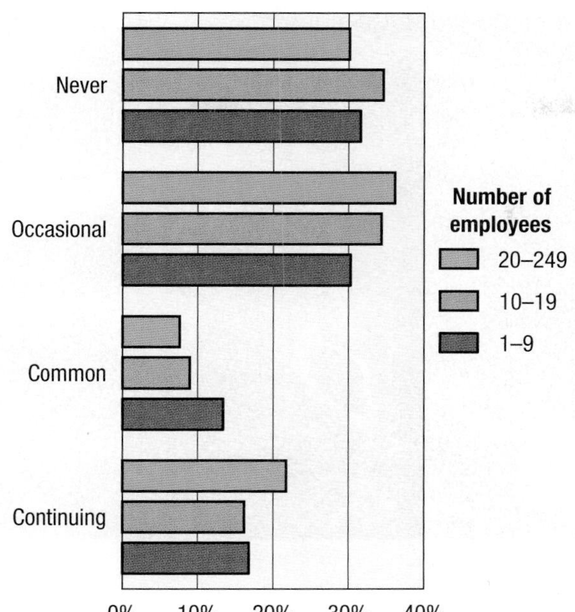

FIGURE 14.1

Percentage of Small Businesses that Experience Cash Shortages by Number of Employees

needed. Nearly one-fifth of small business managers reported that cash flow—*how much* and *when* money will come into and go out of the business—is a continuing problem, one they face daily. The owners reported that the three primary causes of cash flow problems were (1) difficulty collecting money due from customers, (2) seasonal variation in sales, and (3) unexpected decreases in sales.[2] Approximately 55 percent of small businesses that fail do so because of cash flow problems with an immediate impact, not because of lack of profitability.[3]

Cash flow management is a problem for small businesses because of the difficulty of matching the *timing* of the *receipt of cash* to the *timing* of the need to *expend cash.* Figure 14.2 illustrates the flow of money into and out of your business as you buy what you need and sell your product or your service. This repeating flow of money is called the **cash-to-cash cycle** or the **operating cycle** of your business.

cash-to-cash cycle
The time that is required for a business to acquire resources, convert them into product, sell the product, and receive cash from the sale.

operating cycle
See cash-to-cash cycle.

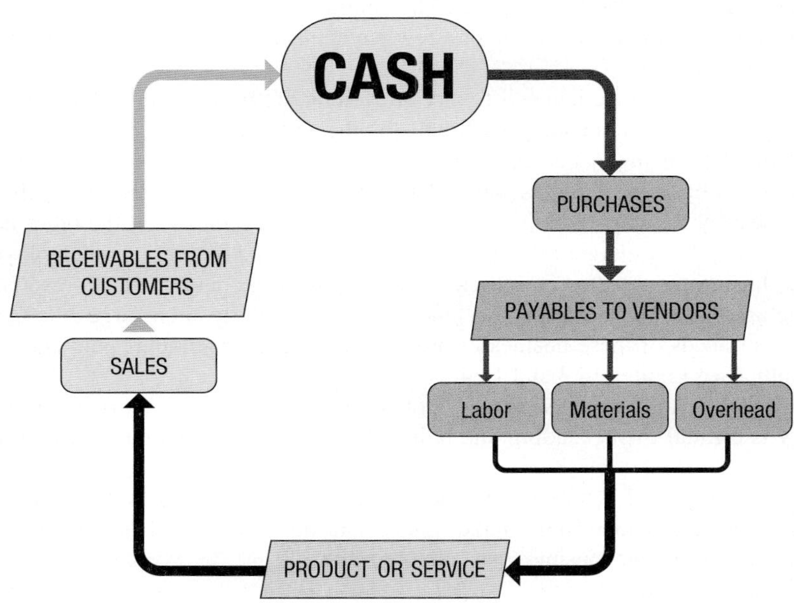

FIGURE 14.2

The Cash-to-Cash Cycle

Pushcart vendors, such as the ones pictured here, enjoy a very short cash-to-cash cycle, due to the nature of their business. Each day, their receipt of cash from sales enables them to then expend cash back to their suppliers for exactly what has been sold. Though small in scope, the simplicity of their business set-up allows for the immediate assessment of their profitability. Does this kind of a set-up appeal to you?

payables
Amounts owed to vendors for merchandise or services purchased on credit (see receivables).

receivables
Amounts that are owed to a business for merchandise that was sold on credit (see payables).

When you start a new business, you put in some money. You then buy all the things necessary to run the business, such as materials, supplies, rent, and labor. Some of these you purchase for cash. Other things you may buy on credit, creating **payables**, which you will have to pay next month. You then use labor to convert materials and supplies into your product or service, which you sell to your customers. Your customers then either pay you immediately, or agree to pay you soon. The promises of your customers to pay are **receivables**, which you will collect in the future. The money you collect will then be used to buy the things necessary to run your business, and thus the cycle repeats.

The time that it takes to complete this cycle can be as short as a few hours or as long as several years, dependent upon the type of business you are in. The ubiquitous pushcart vendors of hot dogs in New York City purchase inventory on credit every morning. They sell their product for cash during the day. Each evening they pay for the merchandise sold that day. The cash-to-cash cycle of a pushcart vendor is only a few hours. Construction projects, on the other hand, can easily take years to complete. A contractor will borrow money to begin construction. That money is paid out across the time that it takes to complete the project. The contractor, however, receives from his customer either a single payment upon completion or a few payments as prespecified completion targets are met.

Many small businesses experience difficulty or even failure because of (1) the mismatch in time between receiving cash and spending cash and (2) the mismatch between the size of payments received and the size of payments that must be made. In some businesses, such as restaurants, cash comes into the business in a reasonably dependable pattern that is affected by the state of the economy, the season, the day of the week, and the weather. Expenses, on the other hand, tend to occur less frequently but in larger amounts, as suppliers are paid monthly, and employees are paid weekly. Other businesses, such as construction firms, plumbing contractors, ski resorts, and equipment manufacturers, have cash receipts that tend to occur irregularly but in large amounts. However, the cash payment needs of these businesses are relatively smaller amounts paid consistently from month to month. (See Figures 14.3 and 14.4.)

Although maximizing your wealth may not be your highest priority, managing your business's money is critical to succeeding and being able to attain goals that are more important to you.

John Mackey, founder of Whole Foods, Inc., said, "Business is the most transformative agency in the world. [Business leaders] can make money and do good. . . . I always wanted to make money. . . . To be sustainable, business has to be profitable."[4]

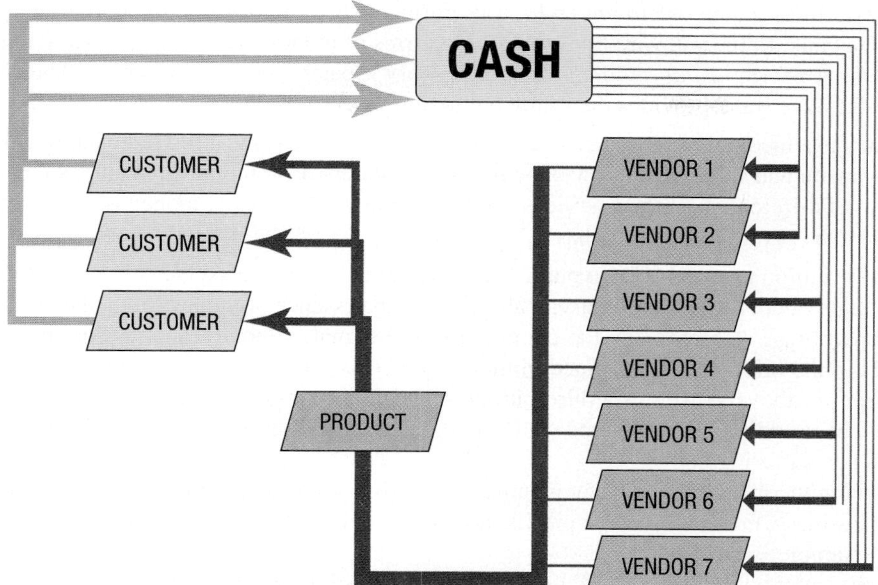

FIGURE 14.3

Cash-to-Cash Cycle

Many vendors, few customers.

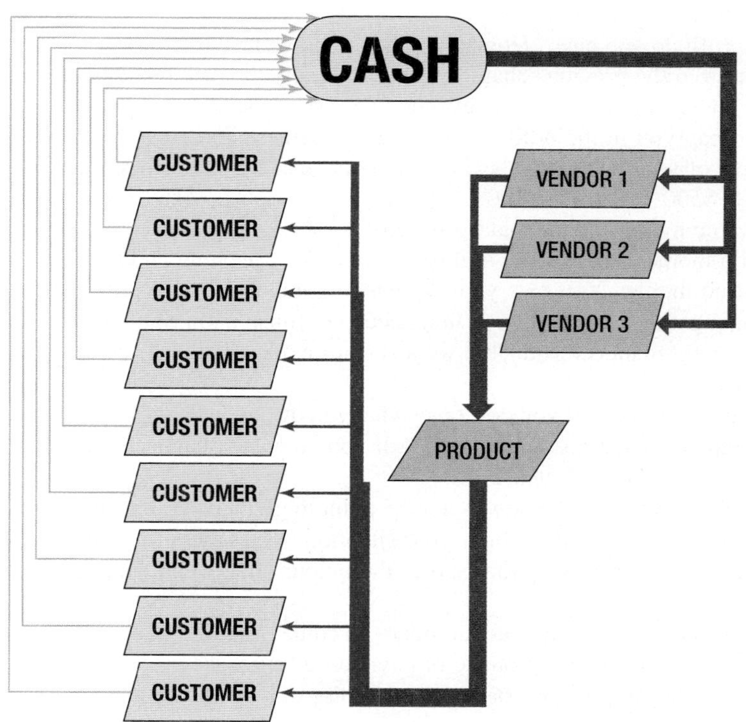

FIGURE 14.4

Cash-to-Cash Cycle

Few vendors, many customers.

Money as the Key Idea

LO2 Explain the concepts of money, cash, and cash equivalents.

Ask people, "What is money?" and most likely they talk about currency—the bills and coins that you use to make purchases. That answer is right, but it tells only part of the story, because while all currency is money, all money is not currency.

Today we use many electronic and plastic forms of money: debit cards, online bill payments, electronic bank drafts, and wire transfers. These forms of money make an important point—money in the end is a form of *information.* Money is a very special type of information. The U.S. Dallas Federal Reserve Bank provides the following definition:

> Money is a medium of exchange accepted by the community, meaning it's what people buy things with and sell things for. Money provides a standard for measuring value, so that the worth of different goods and services can be compared. And lastly, money is a store of value that can be saved for later purchases.[5]

money
An accepted medium of exchange.

This definition gives us the two purposes of **money**: (1) to make exchanges and (2) to keep track of wealth or value. More importantly, it also defines the essence of money. In the Federal Reserve's qualifying phrase, "accepted by the community," what makes money "*money,*" is the *belief* users have about the information contained in the money. This information (and belief in it) reflects the two purposes above as well as a third purpose—wealth accumulation as in saving money. Money can even be used for quantifying the value of nonmonetary assets, such as when juries make awards for pain and suffering.

Knowing the meaning of money is important so that you can recognize where you have money in your business. For example, are profits money? You might think so at first, but consider the following example.

Suppose you own a business that details used automobiles to prepare them for sale. You complete work on a car, removing dings, rubbing out scratches, shampooing the carpets and upholstery, and giving the car a hand-buffed wax job. You promised your brother-in-law that for his help you would pay him \$100 when you received payment for the work. When you delivered the car to the dealer, you presented an invoice for \$500.

How much profit do you have? How much money do you have?

As is discussed in the previous chapter, profit is simply the difference between two accounting items, revenue and expense. You have revenue of \$500, because the work is finished and you trust the customer to pay you in the ordinary practice of business. You also have an expense of \$100, which is the cost of your brother-in-law's help. Your **profit** is the difference between the revenue and the expense, \$500 − \$100 = \$400.

profit
The amount that revenues exceed expenses.

But you have no money, at all. Nada, zip, zero!

Suppose for a moment that you're in this situation. Your heating and air-conditioning company has profits, but no money. You owe your equipment wholesaler for last month's purchases. As a result, you cannot get the air conditioner unit needed to finish a job right now.

"Sorry," the credit manager said, "but we just can't extend any more credit until you bring your account up to date."

What are you going to do? If you don't pay what you owe, you cannot get equipment. If you cannot get equipment, you cannot stay in business. If you do not stay in business, you cannot pay what you owe. You are in a classic "catch-22!"[6]

You're in a bind, certainly, but now is not the point to give up. You have several options to help you deal with this problem. Think about your situation. You have profits that are not money, but they are information about money that shows the amount of revenue and expense your business generates.

Your problem is that information about money to come is not the same thing as the money itself. You cannot use your customer's promise of payment to purchase groceries at a supermarket, any more than your brother-in-law can spend your promise of payment to him at the local tavern. You will receive money if and when your customer pays you. You will give up money if and when you pay your brother-in-law.

The identical situation exists for your heating and air-conditioning company. You have promises to pay from customers, and you have made promises to pay your vendors. The promises of your customers, your receivables, can be quickly turned into money by using them as collateral to obtain a loan from your banker or a factor.

Remember: a profit on your accounting spreadsheet or in your account book is *not* money in your hand. Money is a medium of exchange, store of value, and measure of wealth. Until backed by the actual money, profits in your account books are none of these things.

Cash and Cash Equivalents

To this point we've been throwing around the terms *money* and *cash* as if everyone knows just what they are; just how they differ. Although we have carefully defined the meaning of money, we have not done so for cash.

Cash is money, but it's only one form of money, a subcategory of money that is immediately available to be spent. Not all money is "spendable." For example, think of certificates of deposit. Although you may well have a lot of money in CDs, you may have very little cash because your money is tied up in the CDs and would take time to convert into cash. Cash is composed of the three forms of money that can be immediately used to make payments: currency, demand deposits, and traveler's checks.

cash
Money that is immediately available to be spent.

Businesses, on the other hand, use a concept called **cash equivalents** to measure how much money is available to be spent. Cash equivalents are assets that may be turned into cash in a slightly longer time, from a few hours to a few days, such as marketable securities, commercial paper, and debt investments that mature in less than three months. Businesses use cash equivalents because they provide a better measure of the resources available to pay current bills than is provided by cash alone.

cash equivalents
Assets that may be quickly converted to cash.

Currency is the most familiar form of cash: bills and coins that represent money. In December 2003, the Federal Reserve Bank of St. Louis reported that the supply of currency in circulation was $663 billion, or approximately $2,300 of currency for each individual living in the United States.

currency
The bills and coins printed by governments to represent money.

Demand deposits make up most of the noncurrency cash. Demand deposits are accounts that let you withdraw (what bankers call demand) any amount of the balance immediately, without any advance notice to the institution: That is, owners may withdraw money on demand by using a check, draft, currency, or electronic transfer. Checking accounts and savings accounts are the two most common forms of demand deposit accounts.

demand deposits
Money held in checking and savings accounts.

Marketable securities are made up of stocks and bonds for which there is an active auction market, such as the NASDAQ or the New York Stock Exchange. Marketable securities represent either ownership or debt of publicly held firms and government issued debt, in the form of bonds, notes, and bills.

marketable securities
Stocks and bonds that are traded on an open market.

Commercial paper and **short-term debt** are two forms of short-term financing (30 days to 1 year) whereby a company with good credit can issue a note for cash to another company. Commercial paper is issued to be paid to the **bearer** of the note, and thus is fully transferable. Short-term debt is expected to be collected in less than a year, but it can be sold to other investors at any time.

commercial paper
Notes issued by credit-worthy corporations.

short-term debt
Any debt that must be paid in less than one year from the date of the financial statement on which it is reported.

bearer
Any person or business entity who possesses a security.

Managing Cash Flow

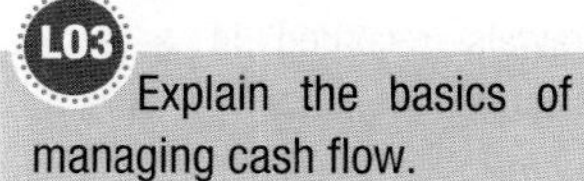

LO3
Explain the basics of managing cash flow.

Suppliers, vendors, employees, and lenders all demand payment in cash. Because of this, a small business must have access to cash to be able to remain viable. Cash can come from only three sources: (1) Cash can be obtained by selling the products and services of the business and collecting cash from customers. This is called *cash flow from operations.* (2) Cash can be obtained from investments the business has made, such as stocks, bonds, land, buildings, or equipment. This is *cash flow from investing.* (3) Finally, a business may obtain cash through financing. Financing may be in the form of cash donated to the business in return for ownership or in the form of money borrowed from other entities.

Just as many businesses have failed by failing to manage cash, many businesses have credited their success to good cash management. Baby Einstein is a case in point. Because of the careful cash management of the founders, Julie and Bill Clark, Baby Einstein was able to grow to a $25 million company without once using outside investment.

The starting point in understanding cash management is understanding how banks, and especially your own bank account, work. This is because the vast majority of small businesses depend on banks to store cash, handle checks and credit cards, and finance their debt through credit.[7] You can see how much debt the banks support in Figure 14.5.

FIGURE 14.5

Sources of Credit and Debt for Small Businesses

Share of outstanding debt for all small firms, by supplier of credit, 1998. (Total value = $700 billion)

Source: U.S. Small Business Administration, Office of Advocacy from data provided by the Federal Reserve Board's 1998 SSBF. Table 1.5a. www.sba.gov/advo/stats/ssbf_98.pdf, page 14.

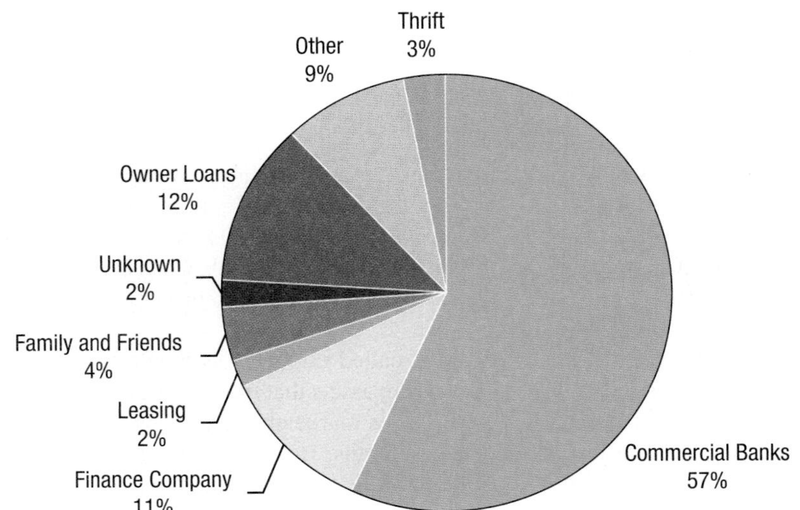

Company and Bank Cash Balances

Because most cash is held as bank deposits, understanding how banks actually work is essential. For example, money you have deposited today may not be immediately available to you. Money that you have spent by writing a check may well remain in your bank account for days after you have made payment. The first step in managing your cash flows is to understand how the bank's idea of your business's cash flow and your own view of the business's cash flow differ.

company book balance
The sum of cash inflows and cash outflows recorded in the firm's accounting records.

Let us start with the company. The **company book balance** is the name given to the sum of the company's internal accounting record of all transactions that affect cash. This account (usually called the *cash account*) includes records of all inflows of cash, such as cash from sales, receipts on receivables, checks received from customers, and deposits made directly to the bank through electronic transfers. The cash account also includes records of all outflows of cash, such as checks written to pay for wages, salaries, inventory, services, taxes, and so on. The difference between inflows of cash and outflows of cash is called either *company book balance*, or simply *book balance*. Book balance usually does not reflect the actual amount of cash that is available to the firm at any specific time, because the actual cash amount depends on which checks have cleared or been cashed.

bank ledger balance
The sum of deposits and withdrawals recorded in a bank's accounting records.

Now let us consider the bank's side. The **bank ledger balance** is the name given to the bank's accounting system for all recognized transactions that affect the account, including deposits, electronic transfers, service fees, and checks presented to the bank for payment. However, just as a company book balance may differ significantly from the actual value of cash of the firm, a bank ledger balance may vary significantly from the actual value of cash that the bank is holding for the depositor because of delays in collecting deposits and delays in making cash transfers.

bank available balance
The sum of money that has actually been received and paid out of a depositor's account.

The key measure is called the **bank available balance**, which is the actual cash value of the account and can vary significantly from the ledger balance. The bank available balance is the amount of money that has been received from or on behalf of the customer less all amounts of money that have actually been paid out of the depositor's account by the bank. Bank policies, such as how long checks are held, or when new deposits are added to your account, determine a great deal of the difference between the two balances.

clearinghouse
An entity that processes checks and electronic fund transfers for banks and other financial organizations.

Deposits of cash, electronic transfers, and cash withdrawals result in immediate changes in the available balance because money has been received or disbursed by the bank. Checks, drafts, and automated **clearinghouse** payments result in receipts or disbursements of money only after some

SMALL BUSINESS INSIGHT

THE BABY EINSTEIN COMPANY[8]

When Julie and Bill Clark started The Baby Einstein Company to produce videos for infants, they made a conscious decision to fund the business using only their own resources. They had been involved in an earlier business that produced educational software.

"I struggled through the experience of dealing with a venture capitalist. Julie lived through it with me and wanted to avoid a repeat experience at all costs," Bill said.

They started the business in their home with an initial capital of $10,000 from their savings. Their determination not to use bank debt, private placements, or venture capital meant that they had to have strict control of cash. They had to budget carefully and conduct constant oversight to prevent spending from exceeding cash receipts.

To conserve cash, marketing was initially conducted by word-of-mouth. As the company grew, the product line was gradually extended to include discovery cards and audio CDs.

How well did they succeed? By setting conservative revenue projections and carefully monitoring cash flows, Baby Einstein was able to grow rapidly, financed solely with internally generated cash. By the fourth year of the company's existence, annual sales were approximately $17 million.

In November 2001, the Clarks sold The Baby Einstein Company to Disney. Their one splurge has been to buy a share in a business jet. "We want the kids to see the world," Julie said.

Julie Clark of Baby Einstein knows what it means to strictly manage cash flow. By adhering to conservative revenue projections and rigorously monitoring their cash intake and outtake, she and husband Bill got to experience first-hand both the substantial growth of their company and the eventual personal payoff it granted them.

delay. The delay can range from as little as a single day up to several days in the event of a check paid across national boundaries. (See Figure 14.6.)

Banks differ in how the ledger balance and available balance are used. Some banks will allow established customers to **overdraft** their accounts by paying a check when the available balance is not sufficient to cover the check amount, but the ledger balance is.

overdraft
A negative balance in a depositor's bank account.

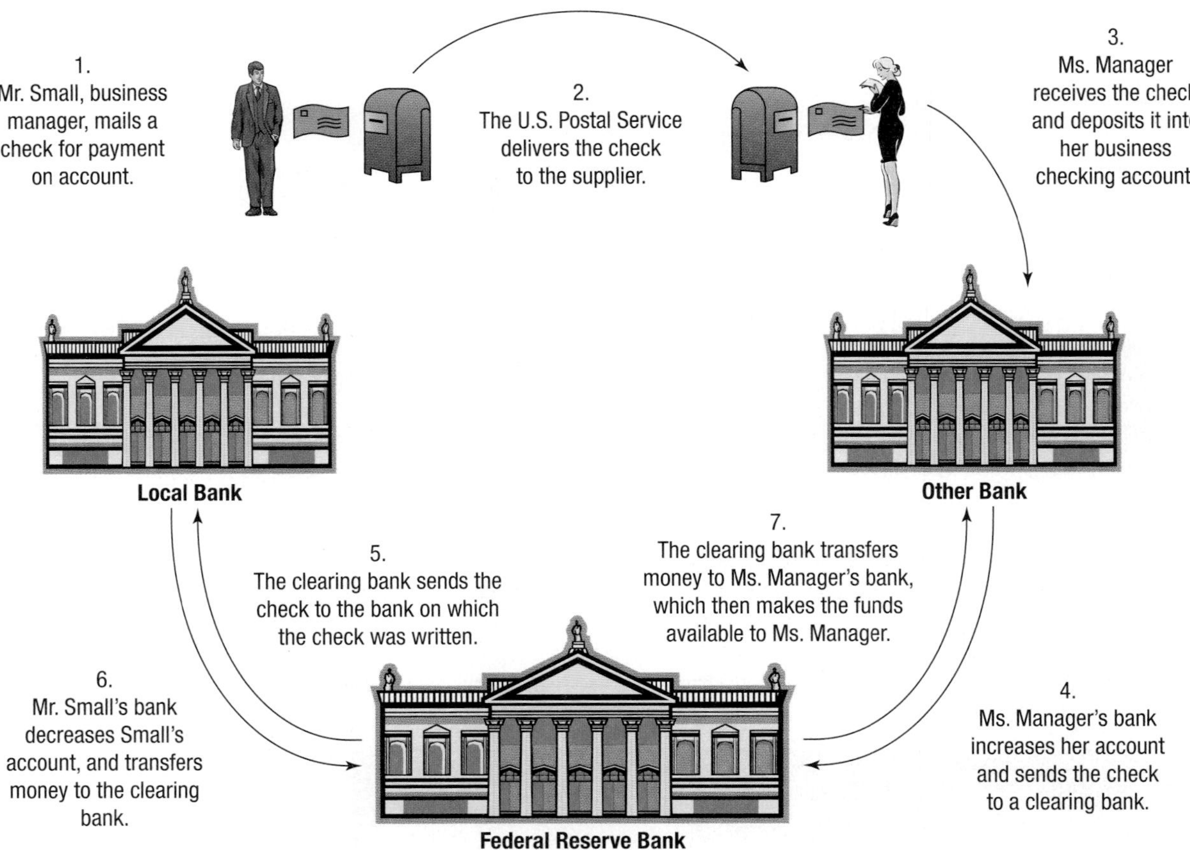
1.
Mr. Small, business manager, mails a check for payment on account.
2.
The U.S. Postal Service delivers the check to the supplier.
3.
Ms. Manager receives the check and deposits it into her business checking account.
Local Bank
Other Bank
4.
Ms. Manager's bank increases her account and sends the check to a clearing bank.
5.
The clearing bank sends the check to the bank on which the check was written.
6.
Mr. Small's bank decreases Small's account, and transfers money to the clearing bank.
7.
The clearing bank transfers money to Ms. Manager's bank, which then makes the funds available to Ms. Manager.
Federal Reserve Bank

FIGURE 14.6

How Checks Get Cleared

float
Delays in the movement of money among depositors and banks.

Float is the term used to describe the delay in movement of money among depositors and banks. There are two primary causes of float: (1) delays in transferring money among banks due to internal procedures, called *availability float,* and (2) delays in delivering checks from the writer of the check to the recipient's bank, called *processing float. Processing float* is the time required to move checks among payers, payees, and banks. Processing float is what individuals refer to when they say, "The check is in the mail."

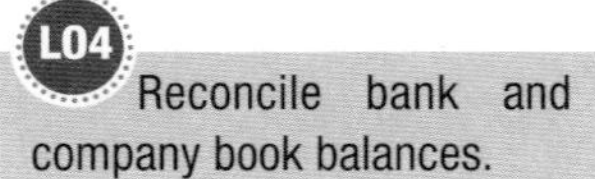

LO4 Reconcile bank and company book balances.

reconciling
An accounting process that identifies the causes of all differences between book and bank balances.

Reconciling Bank Balances with Company Book Balances

The key to managing your daily cash flow is knowing how much cash is available to you in your bank account at that moment. Some banks report available balances only once a day, so that amount can be misleading. To get a more realistic number, you need to **reconcile** the differences between bank and book balances caused by float to know how much cash is currently available and how much will soon be available for your business needs. Most small business managers concentrate their attention on maintaining a positive book balance and assume that this means there will be an adequate available balance. However, when this assumption is not correct, it often leads to cash flow crises.

If you want to be able to manage your cash flow in real time, it is important to choose a bank that gives you online access to account information that is continuously updated. Check to make sure how quickly transactions get posted and are reflected in your online account statement. If you feel you can afford a more leisurely approach to cash flow management, remember that day-old information is much more timely than the month-old information furnished by a traditional bank statement. A manager can, with a bit of effort, use yesterday's bank transactions and the current business book information to estimate cash availability and demands with reasonable accuracy.

The process of reconciling bank balance and book balances is quite simple. There are only two reasons why the balances differ:

1. The bank knows information about your account that you cannot know until the bank tells you.
2. You know information about your account that the bank cannot know, because relevant transactions have not yet reached the bank.

Information that the bank knows about your account that you do not know includes (1) the amount of service charges taken from your account, (2) the amount of any direct payments made to your account by your customers, (3) the amount of any interest received or charged, (4) and the amount of any checks that were returned because of **nonsufficient funds** (NSF).

Information that you know about your account that the bank does not know includes (1) the number and value of checks that you have written and mailed but that have not been received by the bank, and (2) deposits that you have mailed or made after bank closing.

nonsufficient funds
A situation that occurs when a check is returned to a depositor because the writer of the check did not have a bank available balance equal to or greater than the amount of the check.

The process of reconciling the bank and book balances is, therefore, a two-step process:

1. Add (subtract) to the bank balance those things that you know about your account that the bank does not know.
2. Add (subtract) to your book balance those things that the bank knows about your account that you do not know until you receive the bank statement.

When this is done the *corrected* bank balance and the *corrected* book balance will be identical. The appendix to this chapter presents a complete example of performing a bank reconciliation.

Accepting payments by credit card causes significant differences between the bank and book balances for three reasons:

- Your business will record the gross amount of each credit card sale, while the credit card service provider will deposit to your account the sale amount less the credit card service fee.
- Your business will show the amount of the sale deposited on the date of the sale, while the service provider will take up to three working days to actually make the deposit to your account.
- Credit card clearing services also will reduce the amount deposited, or will **charge back** the amount, removing it from the business's account in the event of fraud or customer challenge.

charge back
A reduction in the bank account of a merchant by a credit card company.

Similar patterns of the timing and the amounts of various deposits, fees, and transfers exist for other electronic transactions. A bank may accept payment, charge a handling fee, and deposit only the net amount, or it may deposit the gross amount and show a separate charge for handling fees. Regardless, the use of electronic payment systems, of all types, creates significant differences between bank and book balances.

Why go to all this trouble? Because reconciling differences in the bank and book balances serves four purposes:

- Reconciliation gives you a way to estimate the bank's available balance for the purpose of managing your cash flows.
- Regular reconciliation of bank and book balances identifies any mistakes that were made by either the bank or by your own bookkeeper—and those mistakes happen.
- Performing a reconciliation checks the accuracy of both the bank and business records, providing an accurate statement of the value of cash held by the business.
- A reconciliation lets you know about items on the bank statement that would not otherwise be included in the business's accounting records.

Planning Cash Needs

Develop a cash budget.

For small businesses, the key to cash planning is the **cash budget**. Simply put, the cash budget identifies when, how, and why cash is expected to come into the business, and when, how, and why it is expected to leave. The quality of those expectations is important. Making more realistic or accurate estimates about expected incomes and expenses means that the budget becomes a more useful tool for understanding and managing your cash flow and financial situation.

cash budget
A cash budget identifies when, how, and why cash is expected to come into the business, and when, how, and why it is expected to leave.

TABLE 14.1 Sales Budget

Red Jett Sweets, Inc.
Sales Budget
1st Quarter, 2014

	Jan	Feb	Mar	Quarter 1	Apr
Projected Sales					
Cupcakes in units	4,160	4,160	5,480	13,800	5,480
Unit sales price	2.75	2.75	2.75		
Revenue from cupcakes	11,440	11,440	15,070	37,950	
Beverages	416	416	548	1,380	
Unit sales price	1.35	1.35	1.35		
Revenue from beverages	562	562	740	1,864	
Gross sales revenue	12,002	12,002	15,810	39,814	
Less credit card processing	240	240	316	796	
Less spoilage allowance	360	360	474	1,194	
Net revenue	11,402	11,402	15,020	37,824	

All business budgeting begins with a forecast of sales. As is discussed in Chapters 12 and 13, there are several methods that are used to make sales forecasts. We will illustrate the process of creating a cash flow budget for the first quarter of the second year of business based on the predicted sales of Red Jett Sweets. However, as we did in Chapter 13, we are basing the cash budgets on selling a specific number of cupcakes and beverages. For this reason, the projections in this text do not exactly match the original Red Jett Sweets Inc. business plan. The sales forecast is shown in Table 14.1.

THE THOUGHTFUL ENTREPRENEUR

THE BUSINESS COSTS OF USING CREDIT CARDS

Credit card use fees quickly add up to material amounts. Consider a successful restaurant that grosses approximately $80,000 per month, with an average per-customer ticket of $20. If 90 percent of customers pay with a credit card, 3,600 credit card charges will be made in a month ($80,000/$20 × 0.9). Assume that the credit card company charges 20 cents per transaction plus 2 percent of the amount charged. The credit card fee for the month will equal $2,160 (3,600 transactions × 0.20) + (80,000 × .9 × .02). The restaurant will also pay the 2 percent fee on any tips that are added to the bill. If the average tip added is 15 percent, then the added fee on tips charged per month will be another $216. Thus the restaurant will average paying an amount greater than $28,000 in credit card fees per year.

So why, you may ask, do small businesses use credit cards? First, accepting credit cards creates increased sales. Second, the credit card issuer assumes the cost and risk of determining credit/worthiness.

Sales Budget: Forecasting Sales Receipts

For many small businesses, the sales forecast *is* the cash receipts forecast. Businesses such as barbershops, muffler repair shops, restaurants, and all kinds of retail merchandisers do not provide credit to customers. All sales are made either in cash or by credit card. Despite this, this type of business *can* have cash flow problems created when sales are insufficient to cover required payments. Each type of business has a different pattern of sales and cash receipts. Some businesses, whose customers make heavy use of credit cards, can face serious cash drains as a result (see The Thoughtful Entrepreneur: The Business Costs of Using Credit Cards).

Many businesses have either relatively few large sales events or highly seasonal sales that complicate forecasting cash inflows. Examples include:

- Retailing
- House builders
- Custom electric sign shops
- Machine shops
- Providers of custom software
- Real estate brokers
- Consultants
- Ski resorts
- Water parks
- All businesses that depend upon tourism

Cash Receipts Budget

As we discussed earlier in this chapter, how much and when money will come into your business is of critical importance. Later, we will discuss specific techniques that you can use to help control both how much and when you will receive money. However, the basis to being able to control your business's money is to understand and be able to predict the patterns of cash flows. Understanding and predicting begin when you prepare a **cash receipts budget**.

cash receipts budget
A schedule of the amounts and timings of the receipt of cash into a business.

Many small businesses operate on pretty much a cash basis, as does Red Jett Sweets customers who purchase and pay at the same time. If, on the other hand, you do provide credit to your customers, sales and cash receipts can be very different. If you provide credit, you will always wait some period of time for some of your money—that's what providing credit means, after all. You also, sooner or later, will have some customer who never pays. These two facts about selling on credit create significant differences between the amount of sales and the amount of cash received in any month.

The pattern of collections greatly affects the timing of cash flows. For example, assume that, on average, 10 percent of your sales are made for cash, collected immediately. The remaining 90 percent of sales are made on credit. You collect 60 percent in the month following the sale and the remaining 40 percent in the second month following the sale. To forecast cash receipts, simply combine the expected collections by months. To illustrate this, assume for a moment that Red Jett Sweets, instead of using credit cards, sells its product on credit as described above. The cash receipts budget for the last quarter of the second year and the first quarter of the third year would look like Table 14.2a, on the next page.

Of course, Red Jett Sweets is NOT making sales on credit. The Red Jett Sweets business plan explicitly states in the section titled "merchant Fees" that Red Jett Sweets will use "Square" as its credit card provider. Credit Card Sales are expected to be 40% of total sales at a fee of 2.75%. For this example, however, we will assume that 100% of sales are made by credit card with a 2% transaction fee.

The business plan also assumes that all revenue will be collected in the month of the sale. This assumption is reasonable, to simplify the business plan projections. However, it is not exactly correct. It takes approximately three to five working days for credit card charges to be transferred into the merchant's bank account. Thus, sales made in the last few days of the month will be collected in the following month. For this reason, the cash budget in Red Jett Sweet's business plan at the end of Chapter 8 is slightly inaccurate. The inaccuracy is *not* material to the business plan. But, for purposes of illustrating how this cost could be explicitly included in your planning, consider what the cash receipts budget for their actual operation would be if these two effects were included in the

TABLE 14.2a Cash Receipts Budget When Offering Credit

Red Jett Sweets, Inc.
Cash Receipts Budget
1st Quarter, 2014
Assuming that credit terms are provided to customers

		2013		2014				
		Nov	Dec	Jan	Feb	Mar	Quarter 1	Apr
Month of Sale	Amount of Sale	Cash collected in November from sales made in November	Cash collected in December from sales made in November and December	Cash collected in January from sales made in November, December, and January	Cash collected in February from sales made in December, January, and February	Cash collected in March from sales made in January, February, and March	Total cash collected in the first quarter	Cash to be collected in April from sales made in February and March
Nov	12,635	1,264	6,823	4,548			4,548	
Dec	11,733		1,173	6,336	4,224		10,560	
Jan	11,440			1,144	6,178	4,118	11,440	
Feb	11,440				1,144	6,178	7,322	4,118
Mar	15,070					1,507	1,507	8,138
Collections by Month				12,028	11,546	11,803	35,377	12,256

40% of 90% of November sales

60% of 90% of December sales

10% of January Sales

Account receivable

cash receipts budget. To make the changes explicit, we put the credit card fees on the cash receipts budget. We also assume that the credit card processor takes the full five days to transfer cash into Red Jett Sweets's account.

You can compare the numbers in Table 14.2a above and in Table 14.2b on the next page, with the numbers in the Red Jett Sweets business plan at the end of Chapter 8. You will see that the effect of not including the credit card charge results in Red Jett Sweets slightly overstating cash receipts. Because Red Jett Sweets is forecasting even daily sales, the delay in receiving payment for the last few days of the month has no material effect. Over time, Red Jett Sweets will collect for all sales.

Businesses for which the delay in receiving cash from credit card sales is important are those which make most of each week's sales on Friday and Saturday evenings, such as theaters, restaurants, bars, and lounges. Purchases made over the weekend usually will not be transferred to the business's bank account before the next Wednesday.

You can never know exactly when you will collect cash. However, your experience in business, the experience of other businesses in the industry, and careful monitoring of your credit process lets you make very good estimates. While resort owners may on occasion get advance bookings a year or more in advance, on average, deposits are received about one month in advance. Thus a reasonable estimate of their amount and timing can be made.

Forecasting Cash Disbursements

A similar approach is used for the forecasting of cash disbursements. The estimates of expenses that you develop in your budget, and your knowledge of your business's payment patterns are combined to predict how much and when cash must be paid out. (See Table 14.3.)

TABLE 14.2b Cash Receipts Budget All Credit Card Sales

Red Jett Sweets, Inc.
Cash Receipts Budget
1st Quarter, 2014
Assuming all credit card sales

				2014				
Month of Sale	Amount of Sale	Credit card fee (2%)	Net Sales	Cash collected from sales made during the last 5 days of December and the first 26 days of January	Cash collected from sales made during the last 5 days of January and the first 23 days of February	Cash collected from sales made during the last 5 days of February and the first 26 days of March	Quarter 1	Apr
Dec	11,733	235	11,498	1,855			1,855	
Jan	11,440	229	11,211	9,403	1,808		11,211	
Feb	11,440	229	11,211		9,209	2,002	11,211	
Mar	15,070	301	14,769			12,387	12,387	2,382
Apr								
Collections by Month				11,258	11,017	14,389	3,664	

$11,498 / 31 × 5

$11,211 / 31 × 26

$11,211 / 28 × 23

$11,211 / 31 × 5

TABLE 14.3 Cash Disbursements Budget

Red Jett Sweets, Inc.
Cash Disbursements Budget
1st Quarter, 2014

	First Quarter of 2014			
	Jan	Feb	Mar	Total cash disbursed
Purchases of inventory	515	621	784	1,920
Marketing	241	241	241	722
Rent	1,000	1,000	1,000	3,000
Salary	2,942	2,942	2,942	8,825
Wages	1,331	1,331	1,754	4,416
Insurance	250	250	250	750
Legal & accounting	35	35	35	105
R&D	208	208	208	625
Supplies & fixtures	164	164	164	491
Total Disbursed	6,686	6,792	7,377	20,855

From Labor Budget

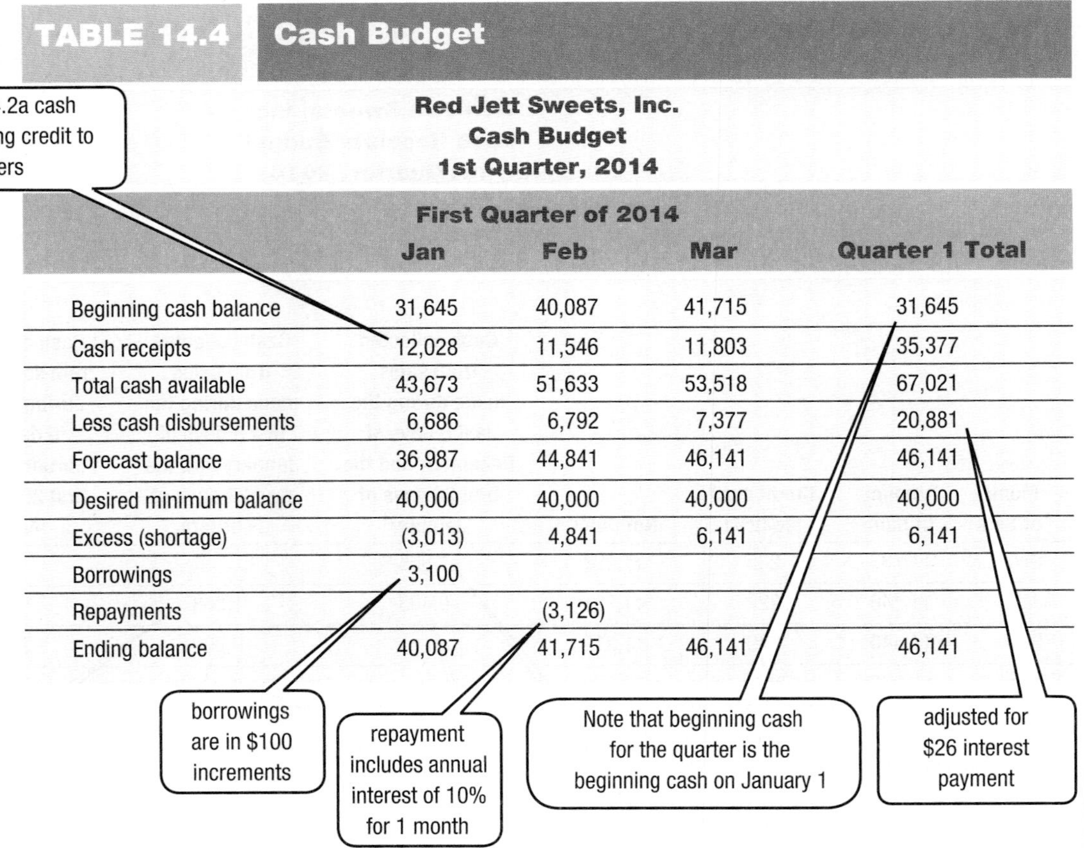

TABLE 14.4 Cash Budget

Red Jett Sweets, Inc.
Cash Budget
1st Quarter, 2014

	First Quarter of 2014			
	Jan	Feb	Mar	Quarter 1 Total
Beginning cash balance	31,645	40,087	41,715	31,645
Cash receipts	12,028	11,546	11,803	35,377
Total cash available	43,673	51,633	53,518	67,021
Less cash disbursements	6,686	6,792	7,377	20,881
Forecast balance	36,987	44,841	46,141	46,141
Desired minimum balance	40,000	40,000	40,000	40,000
Excess (shortage)	(3,013)	4,841	6,141	6,141
Borrowings	3,100			
Repayments		(3,126)		
Ending balance	40,087	41,715	46,141	46,141

Red Jett Sweets states in the business plan, "Inventory is paid for and delivered in the month prior to sale." In other words, the management of Red Jett Sweets intends to prepay for all inventory. This is a reasonable assumption for many small businesses including online retailers, restaurateurs, liquor stores, and bars. If we follow this assumption, but use the more common inventory purchases practice developed in Chapter 13 (Table13.2), then Red Jett Sweets's **cash disbursements budget** would be as shown in Table 14.3, on the previous page.

cash disbursements budget
A schedule of the amounts and timings of payments of cash out of a business.

With the cash receipts and cash disbursements budgets complete, we need to know only how much money we expect to have on the first day of the year to put together a cash budget for the first quarter, as shown in Table 14.4. The amount of cash we will have at the beginning of the year is simply the amount of cash we had at the end of the prior year. We can get this number from either of two sources: (1) the balance of our cash account after the year end reconciliation is complete, or (2) the amount of cash shown on our year-end balance sheet. You will find the beginning cash balance for December 31, 2013 in Red Jett Sweets business plan on the balance sheet for the end of year three: $31,645.

To illustrate how projected cash shortages may be handled, assume that Red Jett Sweets desires to have a minimum ending cash balance of $40,000 each month. If the projected cash balance is less than this, money will be borrowed from a line of credit. If the projected balance exceeds the desired minimum, then the surplus may be used to pay back some or all of the outstanding line of credit. Because most business lenders will not make loans for "odd" amounts, we assume here that any money borrowed will be the amount of the shortage, rounded up to the next higher $100.

The Comprehensive Budget—the Pro Forma Cash Flow Statement

It is a fact that no matter how daunting, you will budget, one way or another. The budgeting process presented here is specifically designed to feed directly into your business plan. The final step in this part of business planning is to put everything together to create a complete set of pro forma financial statements that you can use for raising money, for evaluating your operations, and for managing your business. All the budgets from Chapter 13 *and* the cash budget developed here are combined at this point to make the **comprehensive budget**. (Comprehensive budgets are also often referred to as "*master budgets.*")

comprehensive budget
Comprehensive budgets are often referred to as *master budgets*.

Planning Cash Needs

SKILL MODULE 14.1

1. How would sales for custom electric sign shops, machine shops, providers of custom software, real estate brokers, and consultants vary with (a) changes in the economy and (b) season of the year?
2. Use the spreadsheet, ComprehensiveBudget.xls, from the text website, **www.mhhe.com/katz4e**, to complete the following tasks:

   a. Complete the cash collection forecast for Red Jett Sweets for the current year.
   b. Complete the cash disbursement forecast for Red Jett Sweets for the current year.
   c. Complete the cash budget for Red Jett Sweets for the current year.
   d. Complete annual (i) income statement, (ii) statement of retained earnings, (iii) balance sheet, including statement of owners' equity.

(Note: All needed data and step-by-step instructions are included in the spreadsheet.)

The statement of cash flows, as shown in Table 14.5, is essentially a restatement of the cash budget, but with the cash coming into your business and the cash going out of your business placed into the categories of cash from operations, cash from investing, and cash from financing. The format illustrated here is the direct method, which is the format now required by GAAP. Many owners of small businesses prefer the indirect method, which explicitly links net income to cash flows. An example and explanation of the indirect method of cash flow statements is available on the website for this text: www.mhhe.com/katz4e. Notice also that although we did the budgeting process to the nearest dollar, when pro forma statements are prepared, they are usually stated with an accuracy no greater than whole dollar amounts. In fact, for businesses that gross in excess of $10 million per year, pro forma amounts are usually rounded to the nearest one thousand dollars.

The Comprehensive Budget—Pro Forma Balance Sheet

The final step in preparing a master budget, and also in preparing the pro forma financial statements for a business plan, is to prepare a balance sheet for each accounting period. As discussed in Chapter 13, the balance sheet provides a "snapshot" of the financial position of your business as of the date it is prepared. The sample balance sheet shown in Table 14.6 illustrates how the various schedules of the master budget are collected and reported.

The spreadsheets used to prepare the budget examples are available on the website for this textbook, www.mhhe.com/katz4e. They may be used as models to develop other planning spreadsheets appropriate for businesses other than retail.

A Comprehensive Budget

SKILL MODULE 14.2

Choose a business that you are interested in owning.

1. Prepare a complete list of the costs of operating this business. To determine the costs of your selected business, examine sources such as *Entrepreneur* magazine's start-up manuals (**www.smallbizbooks.com/cgi-bin/SmallBizBooks/index.html**) or perform a Google search on the term "business startup guide" for other books, manuals, and websites. You may also obtain cost information from the Internal Revenue Service, audit guides, franchisors, and industry organizations.
2. Place each cost that you identify into one of the following categories: fixed cost, variable cost, or mixed cost. (Remember: variable costs are costs that vary with changes in sales or production.)
3. From industry sources, determine what the customary payment terms are from vendors and what terms, if any, your business will be expected to provide to customers.
4. Use this cost information to produce a comprehensive budget, based on the ComprehensiveBudget.xls from the McGraw-Hill website, **www.mhhe.com/katz4e**.
5. From the cash budget that you have prepared, identify any cash flow shortages. Prepare a plan to deal with the expected shortages.

TABLE 14.5 Statement of Cash Flows

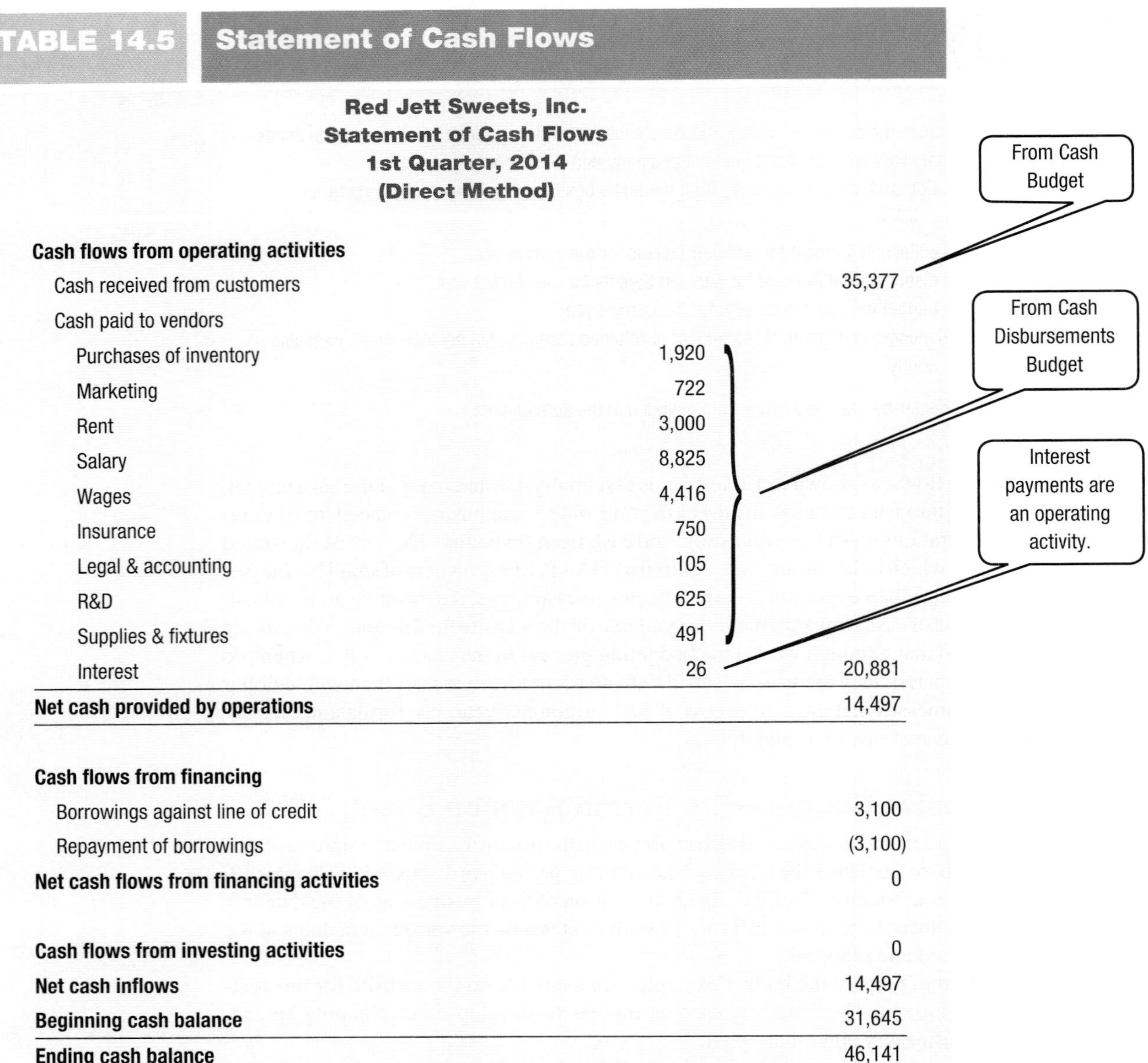

Red Jett Sweets, Inc.
Statement of Cash Flows
1st Quarter, 2014
(Direct Method)

Cash flows from operating activities		
Cash received from customers		35,377
Cash paid to vendors		
Purchases of inventory	1,920	
Marketing	722	
Rent	3,000	
Salary	8,825	
Wages	4,416	
Insurance	750	
Legal & accounting	105	
R&D	625	
Supplies & fixtures	491	
Interest	26	20,881
Net cash provided by operations		14,497
Cash flows from financing		
Borrowings against line of credit		3,100
Repayment of borrowings		(3,100)
Net cash flows from financing activities		0
Cash flows from investing activities		0
Net cash inflows		14,497
Beginning cash balance		31,645
Ending cash balance		46,141

Preventing Cash Flow Problems

LO6 Develop strategies for preventing and coping with cash flow problems.

Benjamin Franklin's adage, "An ounce of prevention is worth a pound of cure," truly describes the best way to manage cash flows in a business. It is much, much easier to prevent such problems than to solve them once they begin.

Several techniques can help prevent getting into a cash flow problem in the first place. The best prevention is attending to and understanding your business's operations—its patterns of generating cash inflows and outflows—which should help you maintain an accurate forecast of cash needs. However, planning alone usually is not sufficient to ensure that cash flow needs are met. The assumptions made may be incorrect. The economy may suffer an unforeseen shock, such as a natural disaster, war, or energy shortages. Fashions and preferences change, often in unexpected and unpredictable ways. As airline pilots often point out, "Careful planning is no substitute for full fuel tanks."

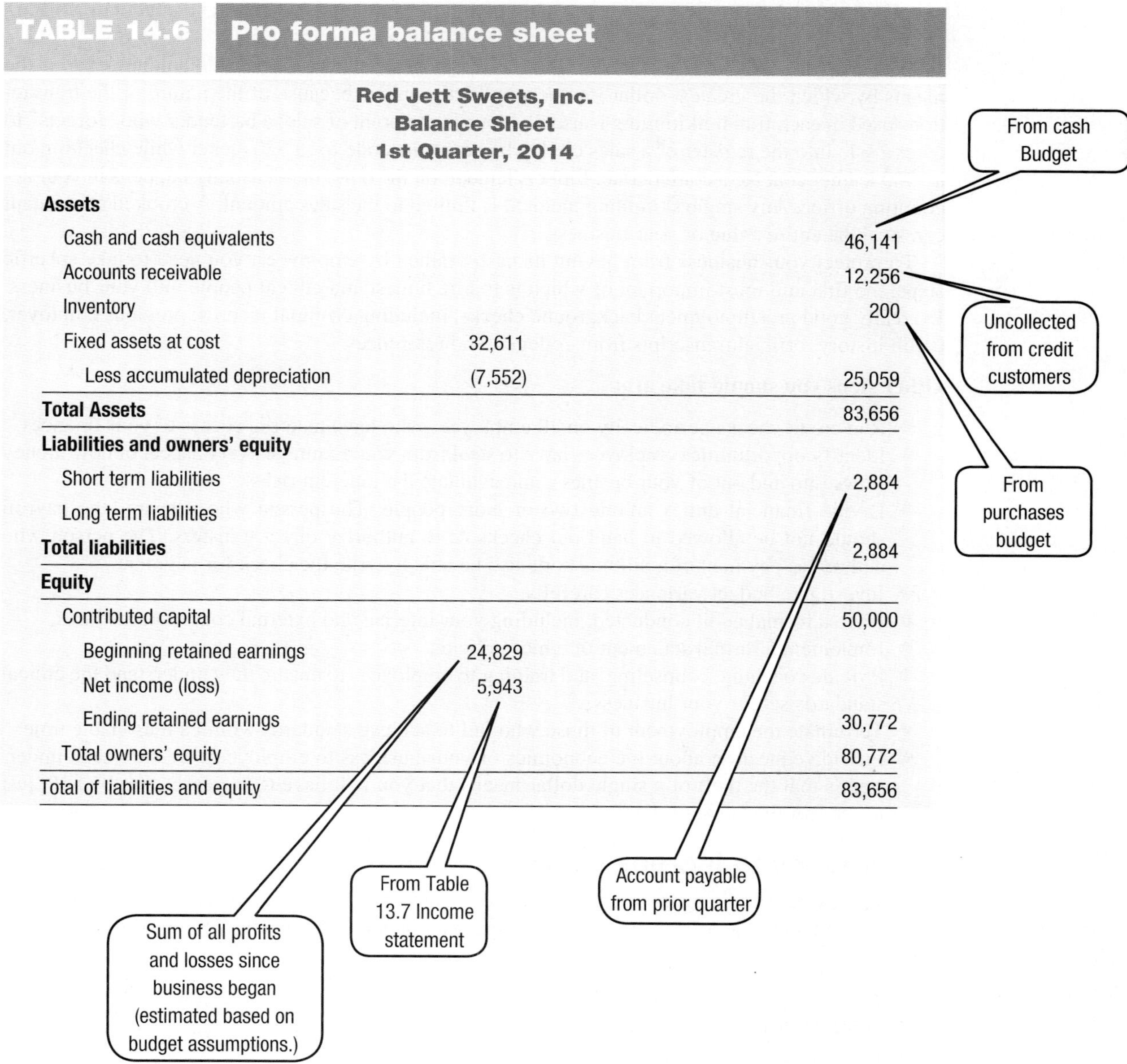

TABLE 14.6 Pro forma balance sheet

Red Jett Sweets, Inc.
Balance Sheet
1st Quarter, 2014

Assets		
Cash and cash equivalents		46,141
Accounts receivable		12,256
Inventory		200
Fixed assets at cost	32,611	
Less accumulated depreciation	(7,552)	25,059
Total Assets		83,656
Liabilities and owners' equity		
Short term liabilities		2,884
Long term liabilities		
Total liabilities		2,884
Equity		
Contributed capital		50,000
Beginning retained earnings	24,829	
Net income (loss)	5,943	
Ending retained earnings		30,772
Total owners' equity		80,772
Total of liabilities and equity		83,656

Protecting Cash from Being Stolen

Cash is the most desired asset and easiest asset to steal from your business. While there is some chance that theft will be committed by criminals coming into your business carrying a gun, the vast majority of business theft is committed by employees. This is so for two reasons. First, employees have access to cash in the course of doing their jobs. Second, employees are often in a position to be able to hide the theft.

According to the U.S. Chamber of Commerce,[9] the most common means by which employees steal cash from their employers are through misappropriations of cash accomplished using one of three categories of theft: (1) Larceny and embezzlement, which are methods employees use to steal cash after it has been received and recorded in your books. (2) Skimming, which is the practice of "pocketing" money from customers and hiding the theft by not recording the sale. (3) Phony disbursements, which are most commonly accomplished by making fake invoices that are subsequently paid by your ordinary cash disbursement procedure. There are many, many variations on these broad categories, including such practices as creating "phantom employees," whose paychecks go to the accounts of the thieves, tampering with legitimately processed checks, and conducting billing scams.

Of these three broad categories, skimming is the most prevalent. Embezzlement, however, is the means by which the greatest dollar loss occurs. Partly, this is because of the nature of the transactions used in each fraud. Skimming is usually done at the point of sale: a bartender who "forgets" to enter a sale into the register or a sales clerk who scans the code for a $20 jacket while checking out a $500 leather coat for a confederate. Embezzlement, on the other hand, usually happens in your accounting office. Any single skimming incident is limited to the sales amount. A crooked accountant can steal the entire value of your business.

To protect your business from having its cash drained by employees, you need to take specific steps, the first and most important of which is to hire honest and ethical people into your business. Do really good preemployment background checks, including criminal records, previous employer, credit history, official transcripts from colleges, and references.

Other steps you should take are:

- Run credit checks periodically on all employees who have material access to your finances.
- Identify opportunities employees have to steal from you. Examine every aspect of how money flows into and out of your business, and evaluate the inherent risks.
- Divide financial duties among two or more people. The person who prepares the payroll should not be allowed to hand out checks or to authorize direct transfers. The person who authorizes payment of a bill must not also be able to write the check for payment.
- Investigate budget variances carefully.
- Have a formal audit conducted, including your internal and external control procedures.
- Implement a formal statement of ethics policies.
- Provide coaching, counseling, and training to employees to ensure they understand the ethical standards set for your business.
- Terminate the employment of those who fail to achieve standards within a reasonable time.
- Provide education about the economics of your business to employees. Be sure each understands that the theft of a single dollar means that you will have to increase sales by $10, just to recover the value of the theft.

Techniques to Increase Cash Inflows

There are several simple methods that can be used to increase the amount of cash flows while simultaneously reducing the effects of irregular or seasonal patterns of receipts. Five proven techniques are:

- Taking deposits and progress payments.
- Offering discounts for prompt payment.
- Asking for your money.
- Taking on noncore paying projects.
- Factoring receivables.

deposits and progress payments
Cash payments received before product is completed or delivered.

Deposits and progress payments can greatly smooth the receipt of cash in businesses which otherwise have highly variable levels of cash flows. For example, many businesses that involve summer activities, such as water parks, are open as few as 100 days per year. However, many costs, such as rent, taxes, maintenance, security, and utilities, continue year-round. These types of businesses often choose to obtain cash flow during the closed season by selling season tickets or other forms of advance purchase.[10] Progress payments are payments that are received from your customer as you achieve predetermined goals in a lengthy project. Progress payments are very common in the construction industry where individual projects may take years to complete.

Requiring deposits is advisable in many kinds of businesses in which the process to fulfill a contract with a customer requires significant amounts of time or additional capital. Examples of this type of business are building contractors, consultants, and manufacturers of custom machinery.

discounts for prompt payment
A reduction in sales price provided to credit customers for paying outstanding amounts in a timely manner.

Discounts for prompt payment will often motivate your customers to make payments in a timely manner. It is common for wholesale suppliers to offer their customers terms of a 2 percent discount for payment within 5 to 10 working days. You must carefully balance the cost of providing

TABLE 14.7 Effect of Prompt Payment Discounts on Gross Margin

Gross sales amount	$100.00
Less cost of goods sold	78.00
Gross margin	22.00
Less prompt pay discount of 2 percent	2.00
Net margin	$20.00
Percentage reduction in margin ($2/$22)	9.1%

the discount with the cost of obtaining needed cash from other sources.[11] The cost of a discount for prompt payment is deceiving. Consider that you are operating a wholesale distributorship of plumbing supplies, with an average margin on sales of 22 percent, and you provide a 2 percent discount for prompt payment. A customer purchases $100 of supplies on account. What is the effect on your profitability? Your profit margin will decline from $22 to $20, a decline in gross margin of 9.1 percent. (See Table 14.7.)

Asking for your money is at once the most simple and the most effective way to obtain payment from customers.[12] Surprisingly, many owners and managers of small businesses are loath to call customers and request that they pay what they owe. However, you will find that few, if any, businesspeople will be offended by a polite phone call requesting payment. This is especially true of the owners and managers of small businesses who have encountered cash flow difficulties themselves. Very often, a request for prompt payment will be honored, if possible. Of course, there is an implied obligation that, if at some time in the future the customers encounter cash flow problems, you will also be understanding and cooperative, helping them through their own rough spot.

Taking on **noncore projects** can often provide desperately needed cash during slow business periods. Possibilities are limited only by your imagination. Many sign installers, during slow times in early spring, often will send a crane truck and operator to hoist air-conditioning and other equipment onto the roofs of buildings. Bill Millers' Barbecue of San Antonio, Texas, for a fee, deep-fries whole turkeys for customers during the slow restaurant periods immediately preceding Thanksgiving and Christmas. Rowan Oak House B&B in Salisbury, North Carolina, as do many bed and breakfasts, during its slow seasons, sells "murder mystery weekends" that include lodging, breakfast, dinner, and a role-playing mystery game, complete with costumes and props.

noncore projects
Revenue-producing tasks and activities related to, but not part of, the primary strategy of a business.

Factoring receivables should be considered only if other, less expensive methods to increase cash flows have not been sufficient.[13] Factoring is a method of borrowing against receivables. The factor will usually lend between 75 percent and 80 percent of the amount of uncollected receivables. As the receivables are collected, the factor deducts a proportional principal amount and remits the remainder, less its fee, typically 5 percent of the gross receivables, to the business.[14]

factoring receivables
Borrowing money secured by a firm's accounts receivable.

To factor your receivables, your customers must have good credit ratings. Your credit rating is irrelevant because it is the customers who pay the factor, not you. To provide for losses on uncollectible accounts, some factors either hold back some of the remittances or charge back any uncollected amounts at the end of a specified contract period.

Techniques to Decrease Cash Outflows

Decreasing cash outflows is as important as increasing cash inflows. Regardless of how much money you're making, conserving cash is essential. All companies have certain costs that cannot be avoided and cannot be financed. Examples of unavoidable cash payments include payroll, rent, utilities, and withholding taxes. If you do not have enough cash to pay your employees, keep the door open, the lights burning, and the tax collector at bay, the business will fail, no matter its potential or paper profits. As with cash inflows there are two factors of cash outflows that must be controlled: (1) the amount of cash being paid out and (2) the timing of cash being paid out.

THE THOUGHTFUL ENTREPRENEUR

DANGERS OF TAKING ON NONCORE BUSINESS PROJECTS

There are several caveats to be considered in taking on noncore projects:

- First, any noncore project should be such that it can be completed in a reasonable time.
- Second, the project should be clearly specified, with clearly defined outcomes or stopping points.
- Third, no noncore project should be taken solely for the purpose of "churning dollars."

Noncore projects can sometimes provide desperately needed cash. However, the time for such projects is taken from time that otherwise would be used for your core business. When the environment for the core business improves, noncore projects can become very costly distractions.

Specifying outcomes and stopping points prevents making noncore projects into permanent business, which then competes for limited resources with the core business.

It is always tempting, when faced with a need for cash, to offer deep discounts to gain cash inflows. This is counterproductive, however, for two reasons: (1) discounting in either your core or in an associated business devalues your product or service, which will limit the price that can be charged when conditions improve, and (2) accepting business that does not provide an adequate margin reduces profitability for the entire year, which can negatively affect your ability to arrange financing and investment when business conditions improve and additional funding is needed for growth.

THE THOUGHTFUL ENTREPRENEUR

EFFECT OF BORROWING AGAINST YOUR RECEIVABLES

Although it is tempting to use your receivables to obtain immediate cash, doing so is quite expensive. Suppose, for example, your business has $100,000 in accounts receivable. If you factor these receivables, you will obtain an immediate $75,000. Now suppose a customer who owes $10,000 pays the full amount. The factor will deduct 75 percent in repayment plus 5 percent of the gross payment amount. You will receive the remaining $2,000:

Customer payment	$10,000
Repayment to factor	(7,500)
5% factor fee	(500)
Balance received	2,000

If your factored receivables are all collected within 90 days, you will have paid $5,000 to receive $75,000 immediately plus $20,000 over three months, a total of $95,000. On an annual basis, this is essentially the same as paying 22 percent interest.

Controlling the amount of cash being paid out is primarily a function of making good purchasing decisions and avoiding waste. By purchasing in the appropriate quantities with the appropriate quality at the appropriate times, the need to make cash payments can be aligned with the receipt of cash, to the extent that the nature of the business allows.

Every business that maintains inventory has an optimal level that minimizes the total cost of (1) carrying inventory, (2) processing orders, and (3) losing sales due to being out of stock. The optimum level of many other business resources can similarly be determined. Setting reasonable standards and carefully monitoring usage and stocking levels reduce the amount of cash required for these essential business resources while maximizing revenues. The determination of optimum stocking levels is fully discussed in the appendix of Chapter 16.

Waste also affects cash outflow. Resources that are wasted represent cash that was paid out with no economic benefit. Almost any resource can be wasted. You can waste the time of your employees by requiring procedures such as record keeping and reporting that are not useful for management. You can waste primary materials by inefficient cutting and by allowing materials to spoil, break, or be stolen. You can waste rent by maintaining space that does not produce revenue. The list of potential waste is endless.

Most of us become so accustomed to our ways of doing business that we often do not recognize waste when we see it. For years, restaurants paid people to haul away old cooking oils and grease. If there was no one to haul the oil, it was often dumped onto gravel parking lots or poured into solid waste dumps. The oil was indeed *scrap*—it had no further economic use in the restaurant. The oil was not *waste,* however, until it was poured out. There was an economically valuable use for the oil in making cosmetics, animal feed, paint, and chemicals. Today, the waste oil from restaurants and commercial food manufacturers is so valuable that not only is there an active market for waste oil, but organized bandits often steal the oil at night. Oil that once was considered trash is today a significant source of revenue.

It takes insight into your particular business to determine what constitutes waste.[15] Suppose you have a sizable store of the leftovers from cutting plywood to make your product. It is certain that the plywood pieces are scrap. But are they waste? To determine if these odd pieces of wood are waste, you need to find out (1) if there is a cutting pattern that will reduce the amount of leftover wood; (2) if you cannot reduce the amount of scrap, is there an economically valuable use for it; and (3) what it is costing you to keep the scrap pieces on hand. You may find that the wood is scrap, but the waste is the space that it occupies—space that you could otherwise put to productive use.

In addition to making wise purchasing decisions and avoiding waste of resources, there are several strategies that will provide savings in cash outflows, including:[16]

- Trade discounts.
- Noncash employee incentives.
- Use of temporary agencies.
- Consignment.
- Barter.
- Control of the timing of paying out cash.
- Negotiation of terms with suppliers.
- Timing of purchases.
- Gaming of the payment process.

Some of these should be familiar, because they are mentioned in the discussion of bootstrapping in Chapter 5, where bootstrapping is introduced as a way to make possible a part-time business operating on a very limited budget; but the ideas of bootstrapping, as we can see below, also apply to more established kinds of small businesses.

Trade discounts are given by suppliers and vendors to encourage customers to make timely payments on account. In effect, you are borrowing from the vendor at the discount rate for the number of days that you may wait to pay after the cutoff date for receiving the discount. The rule of thumb for trade discounts is that you should always capture discounts of 1 percent or greater, if the billing period is less than 30 days.

trade discounts
Percentage discounts from gross invoice amounts provided to encourage prompt payment.

If the supplier provides payment terms exceeding 30 days, then you must perform a quick analysis to determine whether taking the discount or delaying payment provides the greater value. To decide whether to take the discount, compare the annual effective interest rate of the discount to your cost of borrowing from other sources. Then choose the one with the lower annual effective rate.

Noncash incentives for employees is the most widely used technique to reduce the amount of cash that must be paid out of the business. The most common such incentive is to grant stock options, which give the employee the right to purchase company stock at a fixed price in the future. The hope of the employee is that the stock will go up significantly in price and, that upon either selling or exercising the option, the employee will realize large gains. Other noncash incentives include autonomy, a chance to be creative, flexible hours, telecommuting, praise, training, career

noncash incentives
Rewards that do not require payment of cash, such as stock options, compensating time off, or added vacation days.

THE THOUGHTFUL ENTREPRENEUR

SHOULD I TAKE A SUPPLIER'S DISCOUNT FOR PAYMENT?

Assume that Red Jett Sweets can borrow from the bank at 11 percent. The supplier of baking ingredients provides credit terms at a 1 percent discount, if paid within 10 days of the receipt of the invoice, and the full amount must be paid in 30 days. To see if the heuristic ("take any discount of 1 percent or greater when the payment period is 30 or fewer days") holds in this case, calculate the annual effective interest rate:

Annual effective rate = discount/(100% − discount) × 365/(payment period − discount period)

$AER = .01/(1.00 - .01) \times 365/(30 - 10)$
$AER = .01/.99 \times 365/(20)$
$AER = 0.01010101 \times 18.25$
$AER = 18.43\%$

Yes, indeed, the heuristic holds. 18.43 percent is much greater than is 11 percent. Red Jett Sweets should pay within 10 days, taking the 1 percent discount on the goods.

Suppose, however, that the vendor's terms were 1 percent discount if paid in 10 days, due in full in 45 days after receipt. If you do the same arithmetic, the result is 10.53 percent. With the more generous terms, it is better for Red Jett Sweets to delay payment to the full 45 days.

opportunities, the chance to work with (or learn about) advanced technology, responsibility, benefits packages (health, vacation, retirement, etc.), a supportive or protective culture, and even small prizes and awards.[17]

Use of temporary agencies is another way to reduce the cost of employees. If you do not need a full-time, permanent employee, agencies can provide educated, trained, and skilled workers who will work only as much as you need. It is common today for small businesses to contract with agencies to provide all sorts of temporary employees, from unskilled labor to a chief executive officer.

consignment
The practice of accepting goods for resale, without taking ownership of them and without being responsible to pay prior to their being sold.

Consignment is the practice of accepting goods for resale without taking ownership of them and without being responsible to pay prior to their being sold. Consignment sales are the norm in the operation of art galleries. Living artists usually make an exclusive contract with a specific gallery to display their works. When a piece of art is sold, either by the gallery or by the artist, the gallery arranges for receipt of payment, delivery of the art, and guarantee of the provenance of the art, in return for a percentage of the sales price.

Other industries that use consignment sales include the distributors of salty snacks (potato chips, corn chips, peanuts, etc.), specialty food items, used furniture and antiques, sporting goods, and used automobiles. The advantage of receiving goods on consignment is that they remain the property of the consigner and do not have to be paid for until sold, thus matching cash receipts with cash disbursement.

barter
The practice of trading goods and services without the use of money.

Barter is the practice of trading goods and services without the use of money. For example, an accountant may trade accounting services to a sign company in return for the sign company manufacturing and installing a sign at the accountant's place of business. Barter alleviates the need for cash by trading good for good, service for service, or service for good. Barter is legal in the United States and is widely practiced among small businesses.[18] Although money is not used in the transaction, the legislature, the IRS, and the courts have consistently ruled that barter is a taxable transaction, except in case of trades of "like-kind" goods or services. In other words, you may trade real estate for real estate, or machinery for machinery without creating a taxable transaction. However, if you trade your airplane for real estate or if you use any amount of money in the trade, the transaction is subject to tax.

Because of the provision for tax-free treatment of like-kind trades, barter transactions are susceptible to misuse to avoid paying taxes. As a result, the rules for reporting barter transactions are restrictive and quite complex. Misuse of barter is usually considered fraud by the IRS and can lead to criminal penalties.

There are numerous services, organizations, and websites that facilitate barter transactions. For example, the Open Directory Project, www.dmoz.org/search?q=barter, lists over 60 online barter clubs, organizations, brokers, exchanges, and for-profit companies that support barter, using the Internet. There are even trade associations for the barter industry such as the International Reciprocal Trade Association (www.irta.com) or the National Association of Trade Exchanges (www.nate.org).

Controlling the timing of paying out cash can be accomplished through a number of methods. The strategy is not to unnecessarily delay paying, but to arrange payment schedules in such a way that due dates match the times when cash is available.

Negotiating terms with suppliers is a common, acceptable method for controlling when payment must be made for goods and services. For example, many building contractors who build single-family houses expect to complete and sell a house in a 90-day period. Most builders negotiate with primary suppliers such as lumberyards and plumbing wholesalers to finance the materials needed to build a house. The suppliers are protected by having a lien on the house that must be paid before title of the house can be passed to the buyer.

Similar arrangements are made to finance many types of long-term projects, as well. Often the winning bidder on a large project will make the major suppliers subcontractors who agree to accept payment when the general contractor is paid.

Timing purchases is a method of controlling the timing of cash outflows that is invisible to suppliers and vendors. Your specific reason for placing any certain order on any certain day is not apparent. However, knowledge of the payment policies of suppliers can provide considerable leeway in when bills must be paid following delivery of goods. For example, it is common for wholesale suppliers to have payment terms that define an on-time payment as being any payment made on or before the tenth day of the month following purchase. Knowing this term, you can gain additional time to pay by delaying purchase until the first day of the month. This provides up to 41 days before payment must be made without being classified as late. Were you to purchase on the last day of the month, you would have only 10 days to make a timely payment.

timing purchases
A method of controlling the timing of cash outflows that is invisible to suppliers and vendors.

Gaming the payment process is a common, if a bit underhanded, method of controlling cash outflows. Methods range from simply not paying a bill when it is due to sending checks that you've "forgotten" to sign, to sending checks in payment and then stopping payment after the payment has been recorded, but the check has not yet cleared. Very few business owners and managers are proud of taking such measures, but most will, if promised confidentiality, admit to having done one or another in times of cash crises.

gaming the payment process
Using methods to appear to be paying bills on time, when in fact payment is being delayed or avoided.

Gaming payments can be quite costly, however. You may well get away with any one of these strategies with any single vendor one time. The more often you game payment, the more certain it becomes that your business credit rating and reputation will suffer as a result. Being consistently late in payment, regardless of gaming strategies, will cause a decrease in your business's credit worthiness. It is not uncommon for suppliers and vendors to refuse to do business with customers who regularly attempt to game the process.

. . . and Then Came the Turnaround: The Rest of the J. W. Hulme Story

When you discussed the J. W. Hulme story, which opens this chapter, did you predict that the company would ultimately succeed?

Well, it did. Here's how.

You'll remember that when we left Hulme, the owners, Chuck Bidwell and Jennifer Guarino, had stopped their own salaries, laid off over half of their workers, missed a critical mailing date for their catalogs, tapped out their friends, family, business acquaintances, their own funds, and bank lending. Failure seemed inevitable.

But then, through an association with WomenVenture (a business incubator) Jen Guarino and J. W. Hulme Inc. became the topic of a *Wall Street Journal* article.[19] Dean Vanech, one of the principals of Olympus Capital Investments read the article.[20] Olympus subsequently purchased a 49 percent interest in the firm, providing a cash infusion of $550,000.[21]

By following Olympus's advice, J. W. Hulme's debt was reduced by nearly half. Private lenders were convinced to convert their debt into a 15 percent ownership stake. A deal was made with New York–based Steven Allen Showrooms to act as sales agent in North America, Europe, and Japan. Hulme bags are now available in Barneys, a retailer of high-end fashions and accessories.[22]

So, J. W. Hulme is soaring again. With the added boost from Olympus and Steve Allen the firm has regained its airspeed and altitude. Good ideas just keep rollin' in.

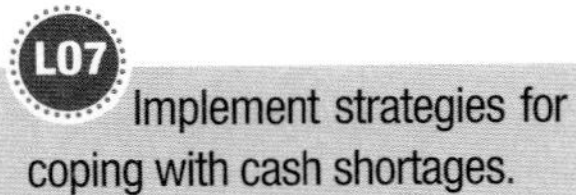

LO7
Implement strategies for coping with cash shortages.

Controlling Cash Shortages

No matter how well you plan or how well you manage your business, sooner or later you will experience a significant cash shortage. Causes of cash shortages range from the obvious, a customer fails to make an expected payment or goes out of business without paying at all, to the obscure—an economic shock, such as a plant closing, natural disaster, or political turmoil like an oil embargo or war. During a time of economic shock, you may not attain your sales goals, *and* you may not be able to collect from customers as they suffer from the same bad economy. However, many, if not all, your bills go on, demanding payments that you no longer have the money to make.

Another often overlooked cause of cash shortages is a surplus of good news: Your business has proven to be wildly successful, and sales are growing at an exponential rate. This situation is often referred to as the **growth trap**.[23] Because of increased sales, you need more labor, more materials for your product, more factory space, and more warehouse space to store completed products until they can be shipped to your customers. All this growth requires money, and lots of it. However, as discussed above, sales take time to convert into money. The product must be made and shipped before any customer will pay. If you are offering credit to customers, you will have to wait even longer to receive that payment. You are in a "trap" made by growth: Growing will produce more money, but right now you need money to grow.

growth trap
A financial crisis that is caused by a business growing faster than it can be financed.

There are numerous strategies to handle cash shortfalls, including laying off employees, slowing payments for purchases, stepping up collection efforts, selling investment securities, or using your own money. A survey of small business owners (see Figure 14.7) found that there are at least eight strategies employed by small businesses for handling money shortages. These are, in the order of their frequency of use:

1. Use personal money.
2. Borrow.
3. Adjust scheduled purchases.
4. Adjust scheduled payments.
5. Try to collect money due.
6. Sell investments.
7. Sell receivables.
8. Lay off employees.

Of the strategies employed, the three most common, in order of use, are (1) use personal money, (2) borrow, and (3) adjust scheduled purchases. Together, these three strategies were used by over 60 percent of the respondents to the survey.

FIGURE 14.7

Eight Top Strategies for Handling Cash Shortages

Strategies for Small Business Managers to Handle Cash Shortfalls

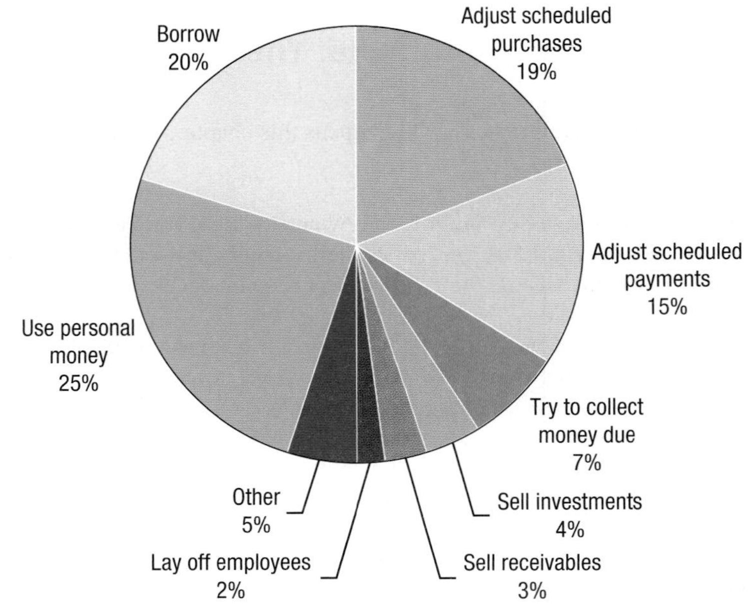

In Review

Managing cash flows is at the same time the most important and most difficult task faced by owners and managers of small businesses. What makes it so difficult is the constant juggling act between the timing of cash coming into the business and cash going out of the business.

You now have the basics of understanding what constitutes money, cash, revenue, and expense. You know that they are related, but very different concepts. Money and cash are economic realities that are essential for business operation. Revenues and expense are solely accounting concepts that are used primarily as tools to measure business activities.

Revenues and expenses are used to predict the amounts and timings of cash inflows and outflows primarily through the budgeting process, which starts with forecasting sales and ends in a cash budget.

Since most small businesses depend on their bank checking accounts as a money management tool, the most basic money management skill becomes a bank reconciliation. The best way to go about this is to reconcile the bank balance for items that you know about but are unknown to the bank, and adjust your book balance for those items that are reported by the bank, such as their fees. When done accurately, this type of reconciliation results in the bank and book balances reporting the identical "true" cash position of the firm as of the date of the bank statement.

There are numerous ways that both the amounts and timings of cash flows can be managed, to some extent, by the owner or manager of a small business. Some cash management techniques are very inexpensive and really a matter of common sense, such as not wasting resources and not buying anything that is not absolutely needed for the business. Other techniques incur costs in the form of interest expense and use of management time. All of the techniques discussed in this chapter are used daily by small business managers across the world.

CHAPTER SUMMARY

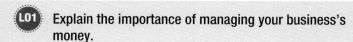

Explain the importance of managing your business's money.

- Almost two-thirds of small businesses experience money problems because of:
  - Difficulty collecting money due from customers.
  - Seasonal variation in sales.
  - Unexpected decreases in sales.
- The cash-to-cash or operating cycle is the time it takes for a business to obtain resources, produce and sell its product, and collect cash from sales:
  - The cycle can be as short as a few hours or as long as several years, depending upon the type of business.
- Many small businesses experience difficulty or failure, because of:
  - The mismatch in time between receiving cash and spending cash.
  - The mismatch between the size of payments received and the size of payments that must be made.

Explain the concepts of money, cash, and cash equivalents.

- Money is a special type of information with three primary purposes—making exchanges, keeping track of wealth or value, and storing wealth for future use.
  - What makes money "*money,*" is the *belief* users have about the information contained in the money.
  - Profit is not money. Rather profits are information about money derived from the difference between two accounting items, revenue and expense.
- Cash is composed of the three forms of money that can be immediately used to make payments: currency, demand deposits, and traveler's checks.
- Cash equivalents are assets that may be turned into cash in a few hours to a few days. Cash equivalents include marketable securities, commercial paper, and debt investments that mature in less than three months.
- Currency is the most common form of cash and is composed of bills and coins that represent money.

- Demand deposits, which include checking accounts, savings accounts, and traveler's checks, are the second most common form of cash.
- Marketable securities are made up of stocks and bonds for which there is an active auction market.

LO3 Explain the basics of managing cash flow.

- Cash can come from only three sources:
    - Operations which comprise selling the products and services and collecting cash from customers.
    - Investing, which comprises buying and selling stocks, bonds, land, buildings, or equipment.
    - Financing which is either cash donated to the business in return for ownership or money borrowed from other entities.
- The starting point in understanding cash management is understanding how banks work, because small businesses depend on banks to store cash, handle checks and credit cards, and obtain financing:
    - Money you have deposited today may not be immediately available to you because deposits, checks, and electronic transfers take time to complete.
    - Bank available balance is the amount of money that has been received into the account, less all amounts of money that have been paid out of account by the bank.
    - *Float* is the term used to describe the delay in movement of money among depositors and banks. Business managers often use float as a cash management tool.

LO4 Reconcile bank and company book balances.

- Reconciling the differences between bank and book balances caused by float lets you know how much cash is currently available and how much will soon be available.
- The process of reconciling bank balance and book balance is quite simple.
    - Add (subtract) to the bank balance those things that you know about your account that the bank does not know.
    - Add (subtract) to your book balance those things that the bank knows about your account that you do not know until reported by the bank.
- Accepting payments by credit card causes significant differences between the bank and book balances for three reasons:
    - Credit card service providers deposit the sale amount less the credit card service fee.
    - The service provider will take up to five working days to make a deposit to your account.
    - Credit card clearing services reduce the amount deposited in the event of fraud or customer challenge.

LO5 Develop a cash budget.

- A cash budget identifies when, how, and why cash is expected to come into the business, and when, how, and why it is expected to leave:
    - For businesses that make sales by cash or by credit card, the sales forecast *is* the cash receipts forecast.
    - If you provide credit to your customers, you will always wait some period of time for some of your money. You also, sooner or later, will have some customer who never pays.
- Cash receipts and cash disbursements budgets are used to put together a cash budget.
- All budgets are combined at this point to make the *comprehensive budget*.

LO6 Develop strategies for preventing and coping with cash flow problems.

- The best way to prevent cash flow problems is to pay attention to and understand your business's operations and patterns of cash flows.
- Five proven techniques to even out cash flows are:
    - Taking deposits and progress payments.
    - Offering discounts for prompt payment.
    - Asking for your money.
    - Taking on noncore paying projects.
    - Factoring receivables.
- Controlling the amount of cash being paid out is primarily a of making good purchasing decisions and avoiding waste.

LO7 Implement strategies for coping with cash shortages.

- No matter how well you plan or how well you manage your business, sooner or later you will experience a significant cash shortage.
- Causes of cash shortages include a customer failing to pay or going out of business, and economic shocks, such as a natural disaster or war.
- The growth trap causes cash flow problems when the rate of growth is faster than the operating cycle.
- The three most common ways to handle cash shortages are (1) using personal money, (2) borrowing, and (3) adjusting scheduled purchases.

KEY TERMS

cash-to-cash cycle, 453
operating cycle, 453
payables, 454
receivables, 454
money, 456
profit, 456
cash, 457
cash equivalents, 457
currency, 457
demand deposits, 457
marketable securities, 457
commercial paper, 457
short-term debt, 457
bearer, 457
company book balance, 458
bank ledger balance, 458
bank available balance, 458
clearinghouse, 458
overdraft, 459
float, 460
reconciling, 460
nonsufficient funds, 461
charge back, 461
cash budget, 461
cash receipts budget, 463
cash disbursements budget, 466
comprehensive budget, 468
deposits and progress payments, 470
discounts for prompt payment, 470
noncore projects, 471
factoring receivables, 471
trade discounts, 473
noncash incentives, 473
consignment, 474
barter, 474
timing purchases, 475
gaming the payment process, 475
growth trap, 476

DISCUSSION QUESTIONS

1. Why is it important to plan for the amounts and timing of cash inflows and outflows?
2. What is money, and how does it differ from profits?
3. What are the primary purposes of money?
4. How do the economic and accounting definitions of cash differ?
5. What are the relationships among planning, budgeting, and forecasting?
6. Discuss five methods commonly used to increase cash inflows.
7. Discuss four methods to decrease cash outflows.
8. The text calls the practice of gaming the payment process, "underhanded." What is your opinion of this common practice? Does it have any ethical implications?
9. How does using the float as a cash management method differ from deliberately writing NSF checks?

EXPERIENTIAL EXERCISES

1. Make an appointment with a loan officer at your bank who handles small businesses. Conduct an interview to find out the following:
   a. Will the bank lend to small businesses, using receivables for collateral?
   b. Does the bank ever factor receivables or act as a collection agent for receivables?
   c. Present the example of the air-conditioning company in the section Money as the Key Idea, of this chapter. Ask what help from the bank would be available in such a situation.

   Write a report of your findings.
2. Form a group from your classmates who completed Exercise 1 above. Collect your findings into a chart. Compare and contrast bank offerings. Present your findings to your class with a recommendation of which banks in your area offer the best small business support.

3. Do a Google search, using the name of your city and "online banking." Examine the sites returned to determine:
   a. How often is the account balance updated online?
   b. Are monthly account statements available online?

   c. How far back (one month, two months, one year) can you retrieve statements and transactions?
   d. Can you electronically transfer funds among your accounts?
   e. Can you electronically pay bills?
   f. Can you download bank account information into your small business computerized accounting system? If so, which systems are supported?
   g. What is the cost of online banking?

   Make a chart of your findings and report to your class.

4. Do a telephone survey of banks in your area. Ask:
   a. Do they use electronic check clearing?
   b. If they use a clearing bank to manually clear checks, ask what bank they use.
   c. Ask what the average period of float is for the bank.
   d. Ask what the bank's policy is for nonsufficient funds: Does it pay to the limit of ledger balance or to available balance?
   e. What other provisions does the bank make to help small businesses avoid having checks returned NSF?
   f. When does the bank make available funds from deposited checks?

   Write a report of your findings and present it to your class.

5. Form a group from your classmates who completed Exercise 4 above. Collect your findings into a chart. Compare and contrast bank offerings. Present your findings to your class with a recommendation of which banks in your area offer the best overdraft protection to small businesses.

6. Use the resources of your library and the Internet to identify five credit card processing providers. Contact each and determine the following:
   a. The cost of equipment to be able to accept credit card charges.
   b. The transaction cost, if any.
   c. The amount of discount charged for:
      i. Physically swiped card charges.
      ii. Charges accepted over the telephone.
      iii. Online charges taken on the Internet.
   d. How long does it take between accepting a credit card for payment and receiving the cash in your bank account?

   Report your finding to your class.

7. Assume that you are preparing to open a new business. You need both an on-location sign and professional accounting services. Do a web search and examine your local telephone book to find (a) a sign company and (b) an accountant who is willing to provide its product and services in a barter transaction for the product or service of your business.

MINI-CASE

BULLTUFF STOCK TRAILERS, INC.

Hal Carrier, of Bulltuff Stock Trailers, Inc., has asked you for help. In the last four months, he has had several checks written to suppliers that were refused by his bank because of nonsufficient funds. Now his main supplier, Alcoa Aluminum Supply Co., has cut off credit.

"We're sorry, Hal," Alcoa's credit officer said, "but we simply cannot keep accepting your checks. Every time one bounces, it costs us at least $100 combined in processing fees and our internal accounting. You simply will have to pay cash or bring a cashier's check for future purchases."

Hal simply cannot understand why his checks keep bouncing. "We've plenty of sales," he said, "and our customers pay pretty much as agreed. Right now, I have only one customer who is as much as 60 days past due. My accountant, Brill Yant, assures me that our cash balance never goes negative. So why are my checks bouncing?"

To try to understand Hal's problem and to advise him how to correct it, you have collected the following information about Hal's business:

1. Cash sales are 10 percent of total sales.
2. Credit card sales are 10 percent of total sales and are collected the week following the sale. The credit card provider deducts 2.5 percent of the gross amount of each credit card sale. (For example, on a $100 sale, $2.50 is deducted.)

3. Sales on account are 80 percent of all sales. All credit sales are to dealers. Terms for dealers are "30-30-30," that is, three equal payments made in each of the three months following the sale. Payments are considered late if they're not received by the tenth of the month in which they are due.
4. Direct materials, primarily aluminum, are 60 percent of the cost of building a trailer. Before credit was cut off, Bulltuff paid 30 percent on delivery and the remainder in 30 days. Now it must pay cash on delivery.
5. Total cost of direct labor is 15 percent of the cost of building a trailer. Workers are paid each Friday for work performed the previous week. Withholding and employment taxes are paid each Friday, also.
6. Variable costs combined (e.g., materials and labor) are 50 percent of gross sales. Fixed costs are *not* allocated to the cost of trailers but are expensed evenly across the year.
7. All other costs combined are treated as fixed costs, and total $1 million per year.
8. Bulltuff leases its building and equipment and has no depreciation.
9. Sales for the year were originally projected to be $2,450,000. However, given the current growth in sales, Hal now estimates that sales will be $5,000,000.
10. Sales for the first four months of the year have been:

January	$208,000
February	261,000
March	293,000
April	328,000

CASE DISCUSSION QUESTIONS

1. What is causing Hal's cash flow problems?
2. Develop a plan to address the problems.

SUGGESTED CASES AND ARTICLES

- Nate Mower & Son, Residential Plumber(s), C-15

Available on Create:

- Patriot Electrical Manufacturing Corporation
- Le Parisien

SUGGESTED VIDEOS

www.mhhe.com/katz4e

Video Case:

- For a written video case and corresponding clip, visit the OLC at www.mhhe.com/katz4e and select "Chapter 14".

- Credit Squeeze on Small Business

SBTV.com Videos:

- Credit Concerns
- eBay: Avoid Bad Payers

STVP Video:

- Importance of Cash Flow

APPENDIX

Completing a Bank Reconciliation

One very useful skill you can have for managing cash in your business is being able to quickly and accurately reconcile your own cash records with your bank's records.

To illustrate the process of reconciling a bank statement, we will use a fictitious company, Languid Lizard, Inc. Languid Lizard is a manufacturer of aluminum lawn furniture. Their primary material costs are for aluminum tubing and nylon webbing for the chairs and lounges.

Carefully examine the copy of Languid Lizard's December bank statement on the next page.

Of special interest are the amounts that are highlighted with the red labels. These are amounts added to and subtracted from the account directly by the bank. Languid Lizard's owner has no way of knowing these transactions have occurred, except to be informed of them by the bank. These amounts are one of the two reasons that the bank balance and book balance differ.

Now take a look at Languid Lizard's cash records: Notice five things: (1) According to Lizard's accounting records, there is a cash balance of $42,038.19. Compare this with the bank balance of only $34,220.22. This is an $8,000 difference. (2) Lizard made a deposit of $7,233.99 which the bank has not yet recorded. This may be because the deposit and the bank statement were both made on December 31. Normally, deposits made after 3:00 P.M. will not be recorded by the bank until the next work day. A deposit made at 3:01 P.M. on Friday will not show up as an addition to your bank account until the bank updates accounts *after 3:00* P.M. *on the following Monday.* (3) Lizard has received a check from a customer that has been recorded in the company's books, but has not yet been taken to the bank for deposit. (4) Lizard has written two checks to suppliers that have not yet cashed them. (5) None of the items flagged in red that were added and subtracted by the bank show up in Lizard's books in any way.

No wonder that the bank and Lizard have very different opinions of how much money Languid Lizard has.

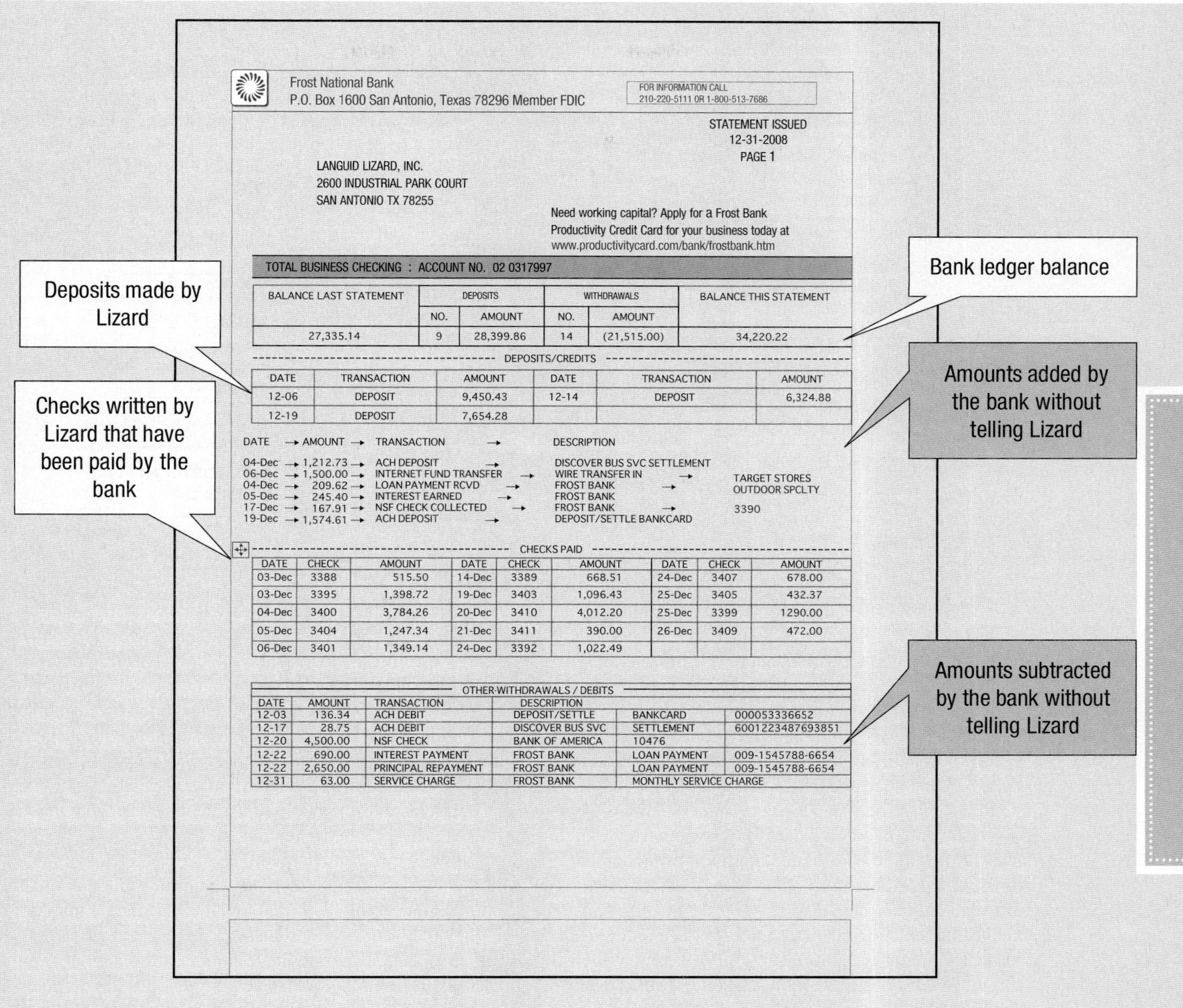

Frost National Bank
P.O. Box 1600 San Antonio, Texas 78296 Member FDIC

FOR INFORMATION CALL
210-220-5111 OR 1-800-513-7686

STATEMENT ISSUED
12-31-2008
PAGE 1

LANGUID LIZARD, INC.
2600 INDUSTRIAL PARK COURT
SAN ANTONIO TX 78255

Need working capital? Apply for a Frost Bank Productivity Credit Card for your business today at www.productivitycard.com/bank/frostbank.htm

TOTAL BUSINESS CHECKING : ACCOUNT NO. 02 0317997

BALANCE LAST STATEMENT	DEPOSITS		WITHDRAWALS		BALANCE THIS STATEMENT
	NO.	AMOUNT	NO.	AMOUNT	
27,335.14	9	28,399.86	14	(21,515.00)	34,220.22

DEPOSITS/CREDITS

DATE	TRANSACTION	AMOUNT	DATE	TRANSACTION	AMOUNT
12-06	DEPOSIT	9,450.43	12-14	DEPOSIT	6,324.88
12-19	DEPOSIT	7,654.28			

DATE →	AMOUNT →	TRANSACTION →	DESCRIPTION	
04-Dec →	1,212.73 →	ACH DEPOSIT →	DISCOVER BUS SVC SETTLEMENT	
06-Dec →	1,500.00 →	INTERNET FUND TRANSFER →	WIRE TRANSFER IN →	TARGET STORES
04-Dec →	209.62 →	LOAN PAYMENT RCVD →	FROST BANK →	OUTDOOR SPCLTY
05-Dec →	245.40 →	INTEREST EARNED →	FROST BANK	
17-Dec →	167.91 →	NSF CHECK COLLECTED →	FROST BANK →	3390
19-Dec →	1,574.61 →	ACH DEPOSIT →	DEPOSIT/SETTLE BANKCARD	

CHECKS PAID

DATE	CHECK	AMOUNT	DATE	CHECK	AMOUNT	DATE	CHECK	AMOUNT
03-Dec	3388	515.50	14-Dec	3389	668.51	24-Dec	3407	678.00
03-Dec	3395	1,398.72	19-Dec	3403	1,096.43	25-Dec	3405	432.37
04-Dec	3400	3,784.26	20-Dec	3410	4,012.20	25-Dec	3399	1290.00
05-Dec	3404	1,247.34	21-Dec	3411	390.00	26-Dec	3409	472.00
06-Dec	3401	1,349.14	24-Dec	3392	1,022.49			

OTHER-WITHDRAWALS / DEBITS

DATE	AMOUNT	TRANSACTION	DESCRIPTION		
12-03	136.34	ACH DEBIT	DEPOSIT/SETTLE	BANKCARD	000053336652
12-17	28.75	ACH DEBIT	DISCOVER BUS SVC	SETTLEMENT	6001223487693851
12-20	4,500.00	NSF CHECK	BANK OF AMERICA	10476	
12-22	690.00	INTEREST PAYMENT	FROST BANK	LOAN PAYMENT	009-1545788-6654
12-22	2,650.00	PRINCIPAL REPAYMENT	FROST BANK	LOAN PAYMENT	009-1545788-6654
12-31	63.00	SERVICE CHARGE	FROST BANK	MONTHLY SERVICE CHARGE	

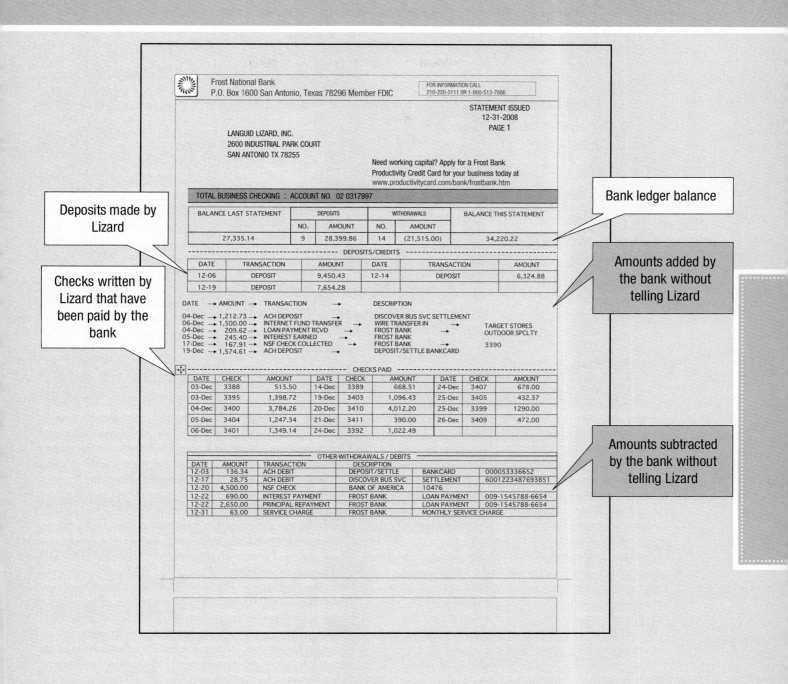

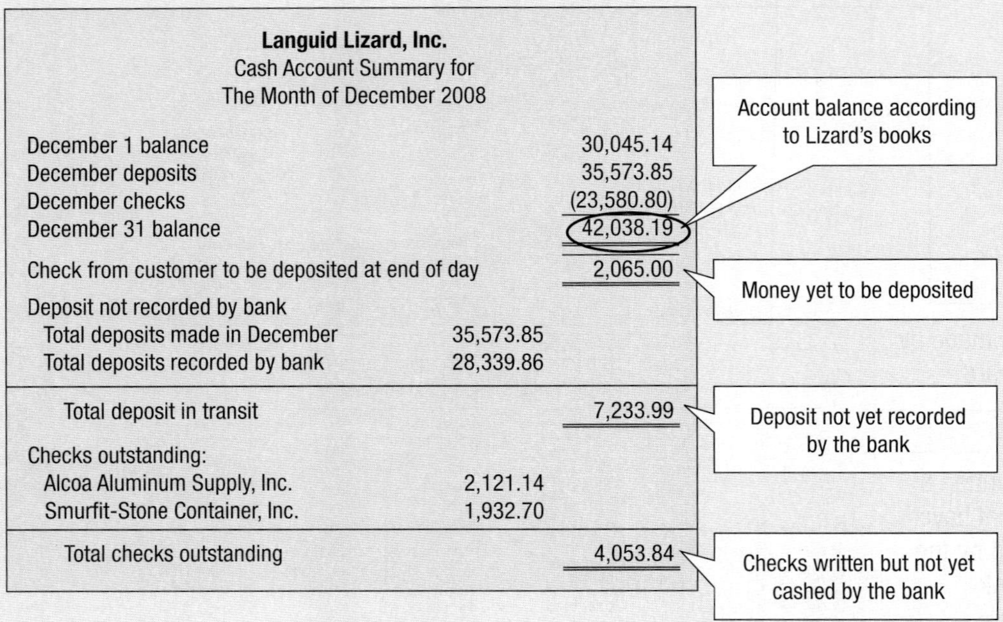

Languid Lizard, Inc.
Cash Account Summary for
The Month of December 2008

December 1 balance		30,045.14
December deposits		35,573.85
December checks		(23,580.80)
December 31 balance		42,038.19
Check from customer to be deposited at end of day		2,065.00
Deposit not recorded by bank		
Total deposits made in December	35,573.85	
Total deposits recorded by bank	28,339.86	
Total deposit in transit		7,233.99
Checks outstanding:		
Alcoa Aluminum Supply, Inc.	2,121.14	
Smurfit-Stone Container, Inc.	1,932.70	
Total checks outstanding		4,053.84

Fixing these differences is incredibly simple. We are going to do two little tasks. (1) We are going to add and subtract from the bank's balance those transactions Lizard has done that the bank currently knows nothing about. (2) We are going to add to and subtract from Lizard's balance those things the bank has done, that until now Lizard knew nothing about. When we are done, the *adjusted* bank balance and the *adjusted* book balance will be identical. This process is detailed on the next page.

We start on the bank balance by (A) entering the balance shown on the bank statement into our reconciliation worksheet. To the bank balance we add (B) the things Lizard added that the bank can't know—the undeposited check and the deposit which has not yet been recorded by the bank. Finally, we subtract (C) the checks written by Languid Lizard that have not yet gotten to the bank for payment.

We finish up on the book balance by (D) adding the items that the bank added, but Languid Lizard did not know until it received the monthly bank statement—deposits from the credit card provider, wire transfers in, collections on notes, interest earned, bad check collected, and a check that was incorrectly entered into Lizard's books. Then we subtract from Languid Lizard's balance (E) those things the bank subtracted that Lizard could not know—a bad check from a customer, charges made by the credit card provider, a payment on borrowed money taken directly from the account, and the bank service charge.

To complete the reconciliation, add each of the bank adjustments and the book adjustments, and as predicted, the resulting balances are identical.

Now Lizard's owner simply enters the adjustments into the accounting records. This brings the recorded book balance to $39,465.37, which is the amount of money the business really has.

This one business function, tracking and managing cash, is itself enough reason to buy and use a computerized accounting system. Although such systems cannot make reconciliations automatically, they have very powerful and very easy-to-use built-in functions to complete this important business task. With just a little bit of attention, you can always *know* just how much money your business has.

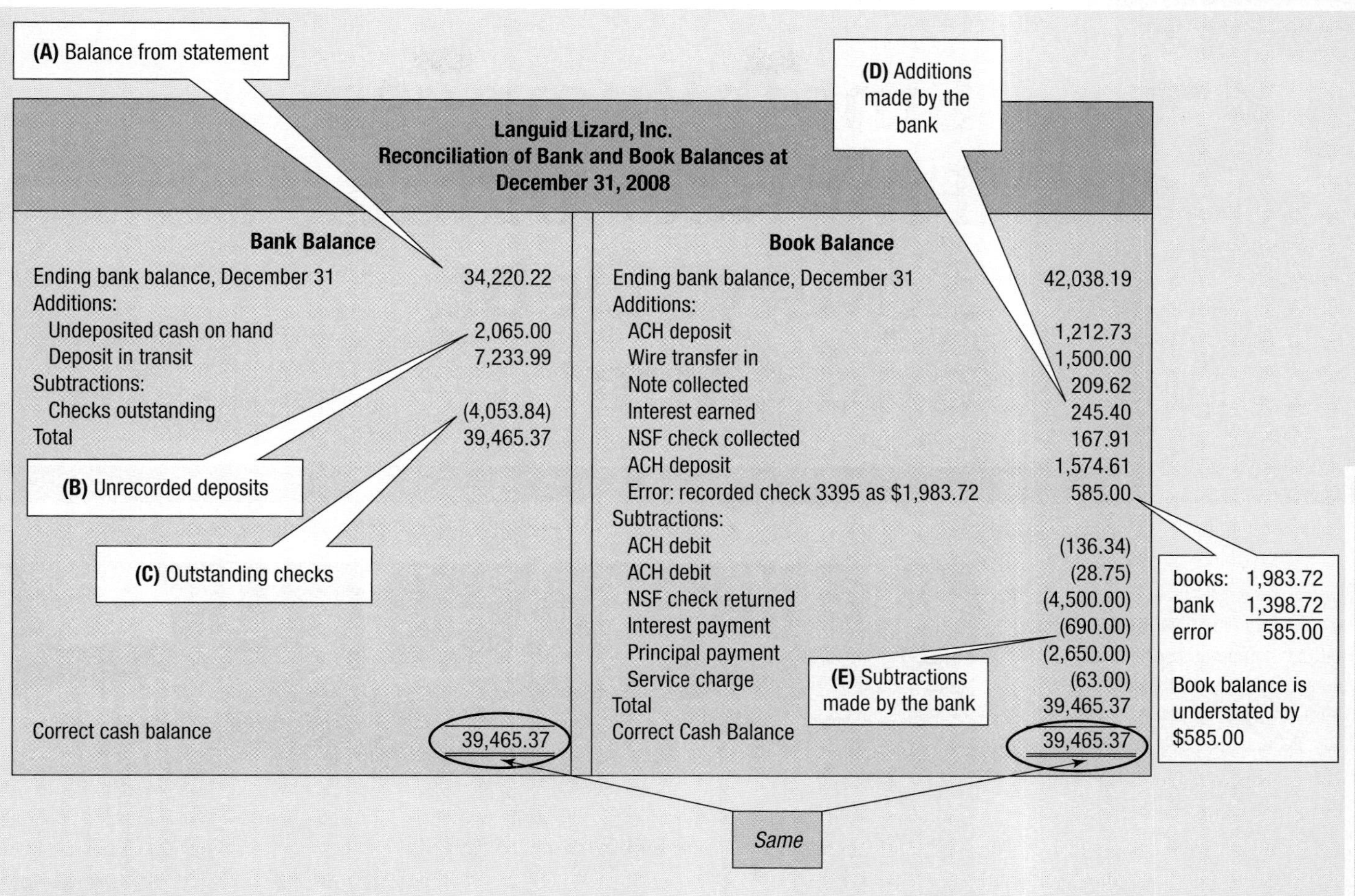

Languid Lizard, Inc.
Reconciliation of Bank and Book Balances at December 31, 2008

Bank Balance		**Book Balance**	
Ending bank balance, December 31	34,220.22	Ending bank balance, December 31	42,038.19
Additions:		Additions:	
Undeposited cash on hand	2,065.00	ACH deposit	1,212.73
Deposit in transit	7,233.99	Wire transfer in	1,500.00
Subtractions:		Note collected	209.62
Checks outstanding	(4,053.84)	Interest earned	245.40
Total	39,465.37	NSF check collected	167.91
		ACH deposit	1,574.61
		Error: recorded check 3395 as $1,983.72	585.00
		Subtractions:	
		ACH debit	(136.34)
		ACH debit	(28.75)
		NSF check returned	(4,500.00)
		Interest payment	(690.00)
		Principal payment	(2,650.00)
		Service charge	(63.00)
		Total	39,465.37
Correct cash balance	39,465.37	Correct Cash Balance	39,465.37

CHAPTER

15 Small Business Finance: Using Equity, Debt, and Gifts

● Dr. Mary Pat Moyer began INCELL Corporation solely with personal savings and cash flows from selling her products. To this day, INCELL has never received any outside equity funding. This has limited the growth of INCELL and increased Dr. Moyer's financial risk. Suppose you were building a biotech company. What would you do?

LEARNING OBJECTIVES

After you complete this chapter, you will be able to:

LO1 Describe the three types of capital financing and their costs and trade-offs.

LO2 Explain the characteristics of a business that determine its ability to raise capital.

LO3 Explain which type of financing is best for your business.

LO4 Describe the differing needs for financial management at each stage of business life.

Focus on Small Business: Dr. Mary Pat Moyer and INCELL Corporation

Dr. Moyer ("Call me Mary Pat," she says.) began the biotech firm INCELL solely with her own financial resources. The business has since grown without ever receiving equity investment from either angel or venture investors.

"I've used my own savings, borrowed from banks and credit card companies, and obtained grants from both the U.S. government and the state of Texas. If I had depended solely on the traditional sources of investment for small businesses—angel, seed, and venture capitalists—INCELL would not have survived its first year. In fact," Mary Pat continued, "INCELL may be the only biotech in the world to be bootstrapped."

"From day one we bootstrapped growth by carefully using personal credit cards, accounts payable, and revenues from sales. We 'played the game' by collecting as fast as we could and paying as slowly as our personal ethics would allow. Still, we barely scraped by."

About a year after INCELL was founded, it received the first of several grants through the Small Business Innovation in Research program of the U.S. government. These grants supported, among other efforts, the development of an oral smallpox vaccine. Later development has led to INCELL adapting the oral delivery method to a number of fragile molecules that otherwise could only be given by injection.

Mary Pat did seek venture capital to fund testing of the oral vaccine delivery medium. "I've been to Philadelphia, Orange County, San Francisco, even Ft. Atkinson, Wisconsin—pretty much everywhere in the U.S. where there are venture capitalists specializing in biotech and pharmaceuticals. And I've not raised a penny, at least not at a price we're willing to pay! We have given up on the venture capital route for now," she said. "While a venture capital investment seemed like an easy way to raise growth funds, the interest rates and amount of equity that were demanded were much, much too high."

Mary Pat's husband, Jim Janowiak, who is a CPA and the CFO of INCELL, said, "Financial management is a daily, constant, ongoing process for INCELL. We regularly remind ourselves that every dollar must be made to work. We do not tolerate any waste, because we quite simply cannot afford to do so."

DISCUSSION QUESTIONS

1. What did Dr. Moyer mean when she said, "INCELL may be the only biotech in the world to be bootstrapped"?

2. In what ways does financial management for small start-up businesses differ from that of academic organizations and businesses?
3. What did Dr. Moyer mean when she said, "We've not raised a penny, at least not at a price we're willing to pay!"?
4. How can raising money from venture capitalists be said to be expensive?
5. How would you categorize investment from government sources such as grants, that do not require repayment or giving up equity?

Sources of Financing for Small Businesses

LO1 Describe the three types of capital financing and their costs and trade-offs.

Getting the money to start or grow a business seems like one of the greatest challenges, but in reality most people who try find the means to get their business going. There are two reasons for this. First, financing is often easier than people think, because most of us have many assets and financial resources that we take for granted. Second, the range of financing resources available to us is so varied that few people just starting out in business know more than a fraction of the options available to them. The more you learn about your personal finances and the financing options, the greater your chances of finding the financing you need to start your business.

However, getting money to start is only the tip of the iceberg of finance for small businesses. Once you have started your business, you must continually work to keep up a constant flow of money and capital assets to meet the strategic and operating goals of your business. As Jim Janowiak of INCELL Corporation said, constant, careful management of money and other capital resources is essential for success throughout the existence of any business. A business's needs for financial management change as the business develops, as economic conditions vary, and as your needs and goals change. Although the details of financial management are unique to each business, there are patterns that can be seen as a business develops from start-up to exit. We examine these patterns, first getting money for start-up and growth and second using strategic financial management to reach your goals.

Where *does* financing come from for most small businesses? The number one source is from the owners (or potential owners) themselves. (See Figure 15.2.) The other major sources include family and friends, credit cards, trade credit, banks, and other commercial lenders. There are also a number of other sources that exist but are used very rarely. These include angel investors, government programs, community-based financiers, stock sales, and venture capital. As Figure 15.1 shows, startups are funded about half from equity and half from debt.

Table 15.1 lists sources of financing as debt, equity, and gifts. **Debt** can take many forms. A business may borrow money directly from banks, development agencies, governments, or individuals. When you sell part of your business, the money you receive is **equity capital**. Any valuable assets or services, including money, that are donated to your business without any obligation to repay or to give any ownership interest, is a **gift**. Each of these three types of financing requires a different approach, which we cover below.

debt
A legal obligation to pay money in the future.

equity capital
Money contributed to the businesses in return for part ownership of the business.

gift
Valuable assets or services donated to the business without any obligation to repay or give up any ownership interest.

FIGURE 15.1

Use of Debt and Equity in Start-Ups from the PSED

Source: Adapted from Michael Stouder and Bruce Kirchhoff, "Funding the First Year of Business," in William B. Gartner, Kelly G. Shaver, Nancy M. Carter, and Paul D. Reynolds, (eds.), *Handbook of Entrepreneurial Dynamics: The Process of Business Creation* (Thousand Oaks, CA: Sage, 2004), p. 368.

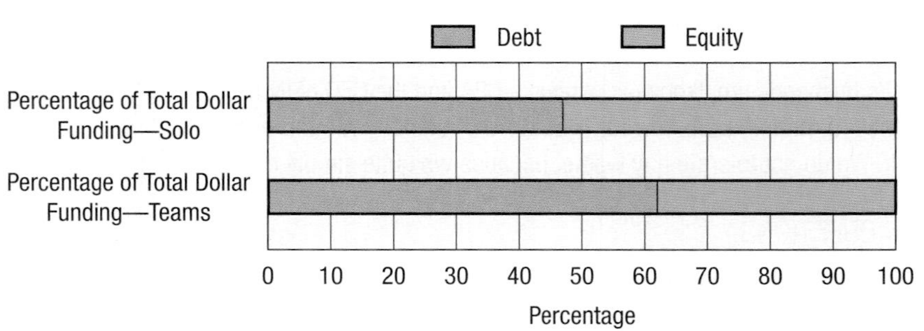

TABLE 15.1 Financing for Small Business by Phase, Type, and Source

Phase of Business/ Financial Management Need	Sources of Capital Financing: Debt Financing	Equity Financing	Gift Financing
Financing for start-ups Profits are secondary to cash flow Need cash to pay employees Need cash to pay suppliers Need cash to live on	Consumer banks Commercial banks SBA insured loans Economic development agencies Small business investment companies Incubators Accelerators Leasing companies Personal credit cards	Friends, family, and "fools" Angels Venture capital Public stock offerings Direct public offerings Crowdfunding (for equity)	Institutional: Grants don't exist for start-ups Personal: Cash, picking up the tab, accelerated cash-outs, free use, free work/unpaid labor, overpayment, favored status/sweetheart deals, forgiveness, deferral, piggybacking Crowdfunding (non-equity)
Financing for growth Profits consistent with risk levels Funds for investment in equipment Cash for marketing Cash for building inventory levels	Commercial banks Small Business Administration Private placement loans Economic development agencies Small business investment companies Suppliers Leasing companies Personal credit cards	Self-generated funds Venture capital Direct public offerings Mergers Acquisitions	Institutional: SBIR, STTR grants State grants Incubators, accelerators Donated capital Tax abatement Personal: Same as for start-ups
Financing for operations Profits consistent with risk Build owner wealth Cash flow "smoothing" Reinvestment for maintenance	Factor receivables Business credit cards Commercial banks Small Business Administration Private placement loans Suppliers Leasing companies	Self-generated funds Venture capital Direct public offerings	Institutional: Same as for growth Personal: Same as for start-ups
Financing for exit Investing to build equity and firm value Reinvestment to replace worn assets New technology Productivity Quality	Consumer banks Commercial banks Small Business Administration Private placement loans Economic development agencies Small Business investment companies Suppliers Leasing companies Lines of credit	Self-generated funds Venture capital Direct public offerings	Institutional: Same as for growth Personal: Same as for start-ups

Which of these financing sources is right for you? The answer depends largely on whether you are trying to start a new business or are trying to get financing for an existing business. Existing businesses have a track record of financial performance, which lets investors and lenders make better guesses about the firm's ability to pay back a loan or pay off an investment. This means that more forms of financing are available to existing firms than to start-ups. Even when the same form of financing is available to start-ups and existing firms, existing firms that are profitable or have made profits in the recent past are likely to get better terms for debt or equity. They may pay a lower interest rate on debt or give up a smaller part of ownership.

We start with equity capital because for most businesses the owner's own resources are the first source of funds. Then we consider **debt capital** and conclude with a look at gift capital. After that, we look at some of the decisions entrepreneurs make in the financing process.

debt capital
Money borrowed for the purpose of investment in a business.

Financing with Equity

Equity can come from the entrepreneur or from others. In general the entrepreneurs' own pockets are the first source of financing for most businesses. Because of this, understanding your own financial situation and the opportunities available to free up personal capital for use in your business become the foundation for any effort to finance using equity.

Personal Equity

How much are you worth? How is that value held? Often people underestimate their personal worth, because many parts of their wealth are seen or thought about only occasionally—such as retirement funds—or because they use it so much that they forget about it having value, like a car, home, or personal collection. But when starting a business, knowing your personal wealth is critical to your ability to fund yourself. Also, if you plan to get investments or loans from other people or banks, they may ask to see your personal financial statements to understand *your* commitment to the business. Skill Module 15.1 has you determine your personal financial situation.

SKILL MODULE 15.1

Determining Personal Net Worth

Use the worksheet below to determine your personal net worth. You may either copy the form or go to the website for this text, **www.mhhe.com/katz4e**, and download it in Excel format. Enter into the column labeled "Cash Value" the amount of money you could get if you were to sell what you own. Enter into the next column any amount that you owe to pay off your debt on the item. Then, in the third column, enter the difference between what you could sell it for and what you owe on it (the difference could be a negative number). After you have listed all that you own and all that you owe, the difference is what you are worth financially.

Lenders and investors usually require that you furnish a personal net worth statement. You can find two different common formats for the report on the text website.

	Cash Value (A)	Amount Owed (B)	Net Value (A – B)
Cash			
Your personal checking account		0	
Your spouse's checking account		0	
Other checking accounts you own		0	
Money in all savings accounts		0	
Cash value of money market account		0	
Total money in other accounts		0	
TOTAL CASH			

	Cash Value (A)	Amount Owed (B)	Net Value (A – B)
Cash Equivalents			
Cash value of stocks owned (net of selling commissions)			
Cash value of bonds owned			
Cash value of annuity			
Cash value of IRAs			
Cash value of other retirement funds			
Cash value of life insurance			
TOTAL CASH EQUIVALENTS			
Personal Property			
Automobile 1			
Automobile 2			
Motorcycle			
Bicycles			
Personal watercraft			
Boat and motor			
Airplane			
Guns and rifles			
Cameras			
Sports equipment (binoculars, skis, parachutes, etc.)			
Art and collectibles			
Antiques			
Jewelry			
Shop tools			
Furniture			
TOTAL PERSONAL PROPERTY			
Real Estate			
Primary dwelling			
Second or vacation home			
Lot at the lake			
Farms, ranches, development property			
Houses, duplexes, apartment buildings that you rent to others			
Business lots and commercial buildings			
TOTAL REAL ESTATE			
Intangible Assets			
Copyrights on books, songs, videos, movies, etc., that you own			
Patents you own			
Trademarks			
URLs			
TOTAL INTANGIBLE ASSETS			

(Continued)

	Cash Value (A)	Amount Owed (B)	Net Value (A – B)
Unsecured Debt			
American Express credit card			
Master Card 1			
Master Card 2			
Visa card 1			
Visa card 2			
Discover card			
Unsecured loan from credit union			
Unsecured loan from bank			
Loan from your brother-in-law			
TOTALS			

Outside Equity

outside equity
Money from selling part of your business to people who are not and will not be involved in the management of the business.

Outside equity is money from selling part of your business to people who are not and will not be involved in the management of the business. People who buy ownership rights in your business are considered *outside equity investors*

- *Outside* because they are not part of the management of your business.
- *Equity* because they have legal ownership rights to your business.
- *Investors* because they are letting you use their money now in order to get wealth in the future.

partnership
Two or more people cooperating to conduct a business enterprise.

corporation
A legal "artificial" entity that is formed by filing specific documents with a state government.

limited liability company (LLC)
A legal form of business organization that is created by filing required documentation with a state government. LLCs have a choice, under federal tax law, of being taxed as either corporations or partnerships.

limited partnership
A legal form of business organization that is created by filing required documentation with a state government; within a limited partnership, one or more partners may have no liability for the debts and actions of the partnership.

You can sell ownership in your business only if your business is organized as one of three broad types of legal forms of business: a **partnership**, a **corporation**, or a **limited liability company**. We start the discussion of legal forms of business here, because the choice of legal form does make a difference in taxation, a critical issue in your efforts to secure financing. The other legal factors driving the choice of a form of organization are discussed later in Chapter 18 on small business law.

The decision of which type of business organization is best for you depends on a lot of factors, including tax treatment, business conduct, and legal liabilities. There are seven forms of organization commonly used by small businesses: sole proprietorship, general partnership, **limited partnership**, C-corporation, limited liability company, professional corporation, and S-corporation. You may need a different form of business organization at different times as your business grows and develops. A detailed comparison of the seven forms is given in Table 18.5 in Chapter 18, but two of the factors are introduced here because they are relevant to financing a business. (See Table 15.2.)

Businesses are either taxed as entities or the revenues and expenses of the business are "passed-through" to the owners who report them on their individual income tax forms. Limited Liability Companies (LLCs) are a relatively new form of organization whose primary advantage is that owners may easily choose whether to be taxed as an entity or have tax items pass through. Corporations, S-corporations, and partnerships have no choice of tax treatment.

In general, all the forms of business organization can be categorized along two dimensions: (1) how much responsibility owners have for the organization's liabilities, and (2) how the business is taxed. In business and in law, responsibility is called *liability*. In terms of the form of the organization, the amount of responsibility (liability) the owners personally face for the debts of the business can be all or "none." If the owners have *all* of the responsibility for business debts, they are *fully liable,* and they face the potential of having to pay business debts from their own wealth. If the owners bear *none* of the responsibility for the business debts, they have *limited liability,* and may lose only what they have invested in the business, and not any other assets they own. Business organizations that provide limited liability are corporations, limited partnerships, and LLCs. However, in limited partnerships, at least one partner, the *general partner,* is fully liable. In general partnerships all partners are fully liable as is the owner of a sole proprietorship, who is completely responsible for all debts of the business.

TABLE 15.2 Legal Forms of Business Organization

	Taxed as an Entity	Tax Passed Through to Owners
Owners personally liable for debts and actions of the business		Sole proprietorship General partnership
Owners *not* personally liable for debts and actions of the business	C-corporation LLC	S-corporation Professional corporation Limited partnership LLC

Sole proprietorships are not separate from their owners, and thus there is no specific documentation that creates their existence. The business and the owner are inseparable. Similarly, partnerships do not *have* to have a written agreement. If they don't, then they are assumed to be equally owned by the partners. However, partnerships should have a written partnership agreement covering key issues such as ownership, profit splits, buyouts, and other matters important to the partners. Thus partnerships may or may not be separate from their owners, depending upon the provisions in the written partnership agreement and the laws of the state in which they are formed. Corporations, and limited liability companies, are required by law to file specific forms with the state in which they are organized. Ownership of corporations is established by stock certificates. Ownership of partnerships is determined by partnership share agreements. Ownership of limited liability companies is shown by member share certificates.

sole proprietorship
A business owned by a single individual who is responsible for all debts and claims against the business.

LO2 Explain the characteristics of a business that determine its ability to raise capital.

Getting Equity Investment for Your Business

Small businesses get started and stay in business because their owners want to make money. Investors want to make money, too. Lenders expect a return on this money from making loans, by getting back the amount they had plus more money in the form of **interest**. In the same way, people invest in a business to get back the money they invest plus extra money, a **gain on investment** or a **dividend**. Governments also expect their gifts of grants and tax abatements to make a return for the people they represent. The only difference is that governments expect to be repaid in the form of the owner creating more jobs and paying more taxes. When a business succeeds and grows, it contributes to the *economic development* of an area.

interest
A charge for the use of money, usually figured as a percentage of the principal.

gain on investment
The percentage amount that the payout of an investment differs from original cost: calculated as (payout − investment + dividends) / investment.

dividends
Payments of profits to the owners of corporations.

Equity Capital from the Investors' View

Look at it from the investors' point of view. They have money to invest. They may lend it or put it to work by buying a share in someone's business. They do this to make money, so they want to invest in a business that will succeed and thereby provide them with returns. But of course, all businesses are not equal. Every year thousands of people start new restaurants. Every year, thousands go out of business. Of all the businesses that they could invest in, how do they choose the right one?

One way to decide is by analyzing the business's prospects. Investors want to know just how likely the business is to succeed and produce a gain. In other words, they want to know the business's **risk**. Unfortunately, they can't see risk directly, so they have to look at other things that are associated with risk. Investors know that some of their investments will fail. They just don't know exactly which ones. To protect themselves from losing everything, they **diversify**—invest in several businesses so that the ones that do succeed provide gains that more than offset the losses from those that don't.

risk
The level of probability that an investment will not produce expected gains.

diversify
To invest in multiple investments of differing risk profiles for the purpose of reducing overall investment risk.

THE THOUGHTFUL ENTREPRENEUR

DIRECT PUBLIC OFFERINGS

While initial public offerings (IPOs) are limited to those few start-ups with billions of dollars in potential sales and a powerful start-up team, other types of public offerings are more accessible to more conventional types of small businesses. They are called direct public offerings (DPOs). These can be used for raising equity by selling stock (for C-corporations) or membership units (for LLCs), or for raising debt by selling a note (also known as a bond). There are four forms of DPO: Section 504 or SB-1 offerings (for under $1 million), a 505 offering (for up to $5 million), the more complex 506 or SB-2 offering (for more than $1 million), and the still more complex Small Corporate Offering Registration (SCOR) program for up to $1 million. These are designed for selling securities nationwide and over the Internet. There is also a DPO limited to sales within only one state (i.e., the entrepreneur offering the DPO and the investor both live in the same state), called an Intrastate, or Rule 147, Offering.

On April 5, 2012, the *Jumpstart Our Business Startups Act* was signed into law. This law specifically provides for raising equity funds by crowdfunding. The final rules for using this new equity market are not known as we write this, but will be implemented on or about January 1, 2013.

All offerings, with the exception of the still-unknown JOBS regulations, require the creation of a private placement memorandum (a specialized type of business plan discussed in Chapter 8), a subscription agreement, and for a debt offering a promissory note. They also require government filings, sometimes with the federal SEC, often with your own state's security regulations office (a good directory of state offices is given at the North American Securities Administrators Association website—**www.nasaa.org**—search the site for its "Directory of Securities Laws"). Not many small businesses use this approach because of the extensive regulatory requirements. There is no substitute for engaging a securities lawyer to make sure the filing is done correctly.

Thus to get money from other people, you've got to show them that your business probably can make gains for them. Of course, you're not the only one looking for those investment dollars. You have to convince them that your business is a better place for their dollars than some other business. You do this by promising high enough gains. The minimum potential gain necessary to get someone to invest in your business depends mostly on the amount of risk they are taking by purchasing part of your business. Your investors could put their money into a bank savings account earning 1 percent, a CD earning 1.5 percent, or a government bond earning 1 percent. For these there is no risk at all.[1] Corporate bonds might offer higher rates of return, but they also offer a higher risk of default—think of Borders, Washington Mutual, or other corporate failures. The riskier the business investment, the higher the return investors expect. Most investors, certainly those who aren't your parents, insist that they take no risk other than the potential loss of their investment. To ensure that nothing other than their investment is at risk, they will invest only if your business is organized to limit the liability of outside owners.

To estimate how much gain they might get from investing in your business, investors consider the growth potential of your business, how long it will take for them to see a return on their investment, and the options they have to receive back the original investment and their gains.

Growth potential is a primary concern for equity investors. Equity investors buy part of a "pie" of a known size. The more slices into which the pie is cut, the smaller each slice is, unless somehow the pie can be made larger. For this reason, it is much easier to get equity financing to develop a new factory to make flexible liquid crystal displays or to produce a treatment for obesity than it is to get someone to invest in a lawn care business in a city of 50,000 people. Lawn care in a small city has a limit to its growth, but there are millions and millions of computer users and of overweight people who want to be slim. Family and friends may be pleased to get back their investment and a 10 to 50 percent bonus, while business angels and angel groups are looking to receive 5 to 10 times their investment, and preferably even more.

The time required to receive gains can be a deal killer for potential investors. The longer they have to wait, the greater their risk that the business will fail. Also, all other things being equal, an investment that pays sooner is more profitable than one that pays later. Consider two simple situations.

You are going to sell 25 percent of your business for $100,000. Your deal with the investor is that you will buy his or her share back at the end of one year for $150,000. In the second situation, you agree to buy back the investor's share for $150,000 in two years. Investors in the first case realize a 50 percent gain on investment, but investors in the second realize only 22 percent.[2] Waiting an extra year reduces the rate of gain by more than half. This is why business angels want to know when you plan to pay the investors their profits (called the harvest or exit) before considering investment. Letting family and friends, who may be more financially strapped, know how long it will be until they see a profit is also a nice thing to do, and for everyone, the sooner the better when it comes to getting money back.

Arrangements for paying gains to owners is an essential, but often ignored, facet of small business finance. Once more than one person owns equity in a small business, it *cannot* be a sole proprietorship. By law, lacking any specific legal business filings, it instantly becomes a general partnership. By making a legal filing, the business entity may become a limited partnership, a corporation, or a limited liability company. Regardless of what business form you choose, the issue of how to pay the owners is suddenly much more complex. Issues arise because of tax considerations, fairness to investors, and compensation for manager-owners. There is certainly no one right way to provide for returning gains to owners. It can take the form of salaries, stipends for serving on the board of directors, dividends, or stock repurchases. In those few cases in which a small business becomes a large business, equity investors often realize their gains by selling stock. Having a plan in place greatly aids in the process of acquiring outside equity capital.

Methods to Obtain Equity Capital

Bootstrapping

The practice of using one's own capital and funds generated by operating the business to finance start-up and growth is generally called **bootstrapping.**[3]

bootstrapping
Using funds generated by business operations to capitalize growth.

Bootstrapping is how the great majority of small business start-ups are funded. Various studies completed over the last several years have reported that anywhere from 90 to 95 percent of all start-up businesses are initially funded by the entrepreneur's resources and cash flows from the business.[4]

There are good reasons that bootstrapping is so common among small business start-ups. Consider the following business "facts of life":

- External equity capital is not available for most small business start-ups.
- Banks do not loan to start-up businesses.
- Owners often do not want to share ownership.
- Owners usually want to be their own bosses. They do not want to have to answer to others concerning their businesses.
- Owners typically do not want to be responsible to others for losses of the business.

For these reasons, most start-up small businesses get going by some combination of bootstrapping methods. Also, there is a growing body of evidence that highly effective small businesses continue to use bootstrapping for growth throughout operations.[5] Table 15.3 lists the most commonly used bootstrapping techniques.

So, how do you use bootstrapping to get your businesses going and to keep it going?

First, realize that bootstrapping is not simply going without. Rather, as Jeffery Cornwall defines it, bootstrapping is "the process of finding creative ways to exploit opportunities to launch and grow businesses with the limited resources available to most startup ventures."[6] In other words, bootstrapping means getting necessary things done using what you have right now. Here are four areas in which you can profit from bootstrapping.

Minimize Overhead Costs

All the stories that you've heard about businesses being "started in the garage" are examples of entrepreneurs using the bootstrapping method of minimizing overhead. You are already paying for the garage. It costs very little or nothing more to use it for your business. But, there are many, many other ways you might not have thought about, such as the following:

- **Cloud computing** can save your business hundreds, even thousands, of dollars each year. A five-user copy of Microsoft's Office Professional costs at least $1,700. You can use Google

TABLE 15.3 Percent of Women Business Owners Who Used Specific Bootstrapping Strategy During 2011

Delayed purchases	71.3%
Delayed compensation of business owners	64.9
Used credit cards	64.9
Used personal savings	55.3
Delayed hiring employees	54.3
Asked for discounts from vendors	35.1
Used a line of credit	35.1
Used creative compensation (stock, merchandise, etc.)	27.7
Requested vendor or customer financing	22.3
Applied for bank loans	19.2
Received loans from family and friends	17.0
Sold receivables	6.4

Source: *Bootstrapping—Financial Strategies* (Center for Women's Business Research, February 2012).

Apps for Business for $5 per employee per month. Or you can use Open Office for free on as many computers and with as many users as you want.

- **Virtual storefronts** provide you with a business "location" at a very low cost. Examples for retail are eBay stores and Amazon webstore.
- **Business incubators** often offer office space and services at a very low cost, compared to renting space, obtaining equipment, and hiring workers.
- **Business office co-ops** extend the idea of incubators to established businesses. Businesses rent individual offices, but share common space, business equipment such as high-volume copiers, and sometime clerical help such as phone answering or office assistant services.

Maximize Returns from Employee Expense

Maximizing what you get from your employees does not mean that you have to be a Simon Legree, demanding excessive work. Rather, it means that you will match employee costs to getting the optimum levels of services or products.

FIGURE 15.2

The Pecking Order of Funding Sources for New Firms

Source: Adapted from Charles Ou and George W. Haynes, "Uses of Equity Capital by Small Firms—Findings from the Surveys of Small Business Finances (for 1993 & 1998)." Presented at the 14th Annual Conference on Entrepreneurial Finance and Business Ventures at the De Paul University, Chicago, Illinois, on April 30–May 2, 2003, **www.sba.gov/advo/stats/wkp03co.pdf**, and from correspondence with Dr. Ou.

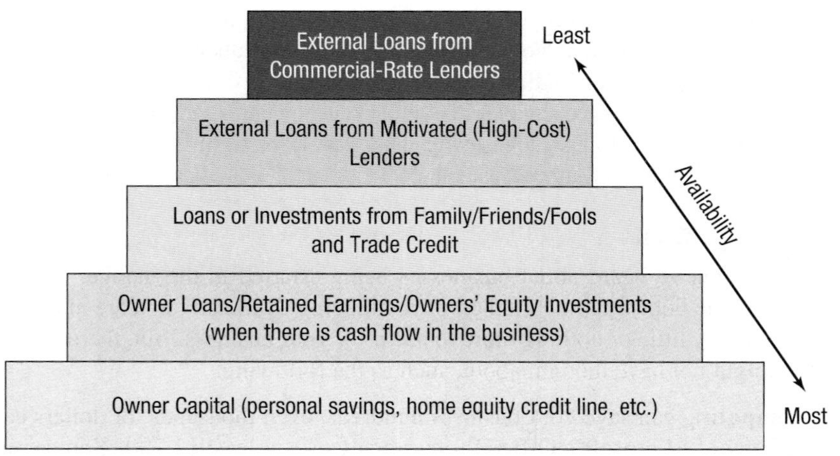

Here are some examples of maximizing the value of employees:

- **Student interns** often provide high talent and strong motivation at a low cost to you.
- **Overtime** is usually much less expensive than hiring more full-time workers during times of increased business.
- **Contractors** exist to complete tasks that have a clear beginning, middle, and end, such as developing a company website or producing sales reports, brochures, and other advertising materials. When the project is complete, the cost ends.

Minimize Operating Costs

Business space is expensive whether you are getting office, retail, or manufacturing space. Then there are the expenses of licensing, insuring, stocking, and all the other costs of keeping a traditional business operation going. It is easy to set up a business in such manner that it can never generate enough activity to provide you with a profit. You can get a lot of mileage from minimizing these costs, at any level of business. Here are a few "tried-and-true" ways to do this.

- **Outsource** the production of your service or product. If you outsource, you do not have to maintain inventories of raw materials. You do not have to pay for full-time employees, with all the attendant employee taxes and costs. You do not have to maintain expensive equipment and buildings.
- **Subcontract** parts of your business that are not your core competency. This is a common practice in construction. If you are a carpenter, you most likely will be more efficient if you stick to carpentry and subcontract painting and landscaping.
- **Rent space** that is unused or underutilized by other ongoing businesses. Suppose your business requires freeze-drying product. Rather than spending a half million dollars for your own equipment, you can rent time on the equipment of the biopharma down the street.
- **Rent equipment**. If you have a sign company that rarely makes an outdoor installation, when you do, rent a crane rather than buying one. If you have a catering business and you get a contract for a whole-hog barbeque party, rent a portable cooker/smoker for that one event.
- **Work from home**. This simple bootstrapping method has become widely accepted by Internet and software development businesses. When you allow work from home, you do not have to pay for office space for your employees. You may also be able to negotiate pay for specific output, rather than paying employees by the hour.

Maximize the Results of Marketing

Marketing is a prime area to use bootstrapping techniques. When you are starting and growing your business, it is essential that you make every dollar spent on marketing and advertising count in the form of increased revenue. This pretty much rules out the traditional advertising avenues of radio, television, and print advertising where the typical response rate is only 1 or 2 percent. To get the biggest bang for the buck, bootstrappers do marketing in tightly focused ways.

- **Word of mouth** is the bootstrapper's best marketing technique. How many times have you purchased something because a friend told you how good it was? When you made that purchase, you were responding to word-of-mouth marketing. The challenge for you is to get your customers to tell other potential customers just how great your service or product actually is. Some ways to encourage your customers to tell others about your business include:
  - **Discounts** for customers who recommend your business to other customers.
  - **Local signage** placed in customer's business locations, such as a web designer placing a notification on a customer's website or a remodeler putting a sign in a customer's yard.
  - **Facebook** "like" links can be done reciprocally—you tell your customer, "I'll 'like' your website, and you 'like' mine."
  - **Cooperative advertising** with your customers and vendors often allows you to reach people likely to become your customers, also.
- **Publicity** can provide a huge boost. "There's no such thing as bad publicity," P. T. Barnum once said. This may not be true in all circumstances, such as the local restaurant that makes the news because of health violations, but regardless, publicity is at the same time cheaper and more effective than advertising. The problem is how to get favorable publicity.

- **Press releases** often result in media attention. Reporters are always looking both for local news and for good news. A well-designed press kit about your business can provide the 10 o'clock news team with a needed filler item.
- **Public speaking** will give you an opportunity to stand before an audience and make a pitch for your business. You can present a 10- or 15-minute speech about your business's contribution to the local economy to meetings of the Rotary Club, Kiwanas, Chamber of Commerce, and the like.
- **Donate your service or product** to worthy groups and efforts. Is your new restaurant not doing as well as you'd like? Call the local business journal or newspaper and give them a heads up that you will be providing lunches to the Habitat for Humanity workers. Or, for certain exposure, contribute some of your product to your local public television station for inclusion in their annual fund-raising on-air auction.

Crowdfunding for Equity

A new way of getting people to invest in your business is to use the web for crowdfunding. Crowdfunding was created to provide a way for artists to obtain backing for their individual projects.[7] It has, however, emerged as a method for entrepreneurs to obtain public financing.

Using crowdfunding to raise equity capital is currently not well established. When you sell ownership in your business to people who are not going to help manage nor work in the business, you are selling a security. All developed countries have laws that require you to meet certain filing and disclosure requirements before you can legally sell a security.[8]

Most places, however, have some exceptions to this general rule. For example, in the United States you do not have to list your security with the Security and Exchange Commission (SEC) if you follow certain rules that limit how much money you may raise and that specify the nature of the investors to whom you may sell.

The U.S. Congress passed, and on April 5, 2012, President Obama signed a new law, ***Jumpstart Our Business Startups Act*** (JOBS Act).[9] This law specifically makes it legal for startup businesses to use crowdfunding to raise equity capital without having to meet the reporting requirements of the Sarbanes-Oxley Act (SarBox) or the registration and reporting requirements of the current SEC regulations. As we write this, the final regulations are not in place. The SEC has until January 1, 2013, to develop and implement regulations. Until the regulations are implemented, crowdfunding as an equity investment is illegal.

If you think that crowdfunding might work for you, there are some things that every business is going to have to do to succeed in this new market. These are the following:

- **Document your business**. Your business will have to be either a corporation or LLC to be able to use JOBS Act equity funding. You should have your articles of incorporation, minutes of the board of directors, and operating rules ready for potential investors to examine.
- **Make a business plan.** You are going to have to show investors how your business will work to make profits and create wealth.
- **Create a compelling story**. You are going to have to convince strangers of the value of your plan and of why they should trust you to implement it.
- **Create a professional-looking video.** Crowdfunding has a 15-year history in the arts. One thing that has been shown over and over is that projects that have snappy videos are much more successful raising money than those that don't.
- **Develop a list of potential investors**. Just having a plan, a sales pitch, and an Internet video is not enough to ensure success. You will be competing with thousands of other businesses for funding. You are going to have to work your contacts, and get your contacts to tell others if you are to meet your funding goal.

Angel Investors

angel investor
A wealthy individual who invests in companies in relatively early stages of development.

For a few very high-quality (or perhaps just very fortunate) business start-ups, there is a source of start-up capital beyond the entrepreneur's own resources. There are a number of high-wealth individuals who make a practice of investing in first- and second-stage funding of new businesses. These people are commonly called **angel investors**. Table 15.4 illustrates the characteristics of the three types of angel investors.

TABLE 15.4 Types of Angel Investment

	Individual Angel	Angel Network	Angel Fund
Ease of Finding Angels	Hard to find	Easy to find: formal networks Hard to find: small private networks	Publicly known, so easy to find
Legal Form	Private individual	Formal networks, corporation; informal networks vary	Corporation
Source of Funds	Invests own money	Each angel invests their own money	Fund invests on angels' behalf
Typical Size of Investment	$50–100K	$50–$250K	$50–$500K
Geographic Proximity Preferences	Very close proximity is preferred	Very close proximity is preferred. May invest remotely via syndicate	Very close proximity is preferred. May invest remotely via syndicate
Why Invest?	Equity growth and personal interest	Equity growth and personal interest	Equity growth, sometimes regional development
Reporting Requirements	Varies by individual	Varies, set by investing angels	Formal, set by the fund
Involvement Level and Method	Low to extremely high; informal	Low to extremely high; informal	Low to extremely high; more formal
Angels Exit Expectation	Often unplanned, Trade sale	Cash-out when firm bought or VCs invest	Cash-out when firm bought or VCs invest

Source: Parts of this table were adapted from Dirk De Clercq, Vance Fried, Oskari Lehtonen, and Harry J. Sapienza, "An Entrepreneur's guide to the venture capital galaxy," *The Academy of Management Perspectives, 20*, 2006, pp. 90–112.

It is impossible to get reliable statistics concerning the number of angel investors and the number of start-up businesses that obtain angel funding. Wealthy people generally do not want a lot of public exposure, thus they often require that their involvement in a new business be kept confidential. Entrepreneurs similarly are often reluctant to disclose information that might provide competitors an advantage. Compounding the resulting scarcity of information about angels and angel investing is a similar lack of reliable information about the number of start-up businesses. The Bureau of Labor Statistics reports that 698,000 businesses were founded in 2009, the last year for which the bureau has statistics.[10] On the other hand, the U.S. Census, in the 2012 Statistical Abstract,[11] reports that only 388,000 businesses were started in 2009.

And, as if these problems with getting reliable statistics were not bad enough, it is not only start-up businesses that seek angel funding. One of the characteristics of businesses that actually get funded by angels and angel groups is that the business actually exists: it has a legal form, a product or service, a large market potential, actual customers, a management team, and a plan for growth, success, and ultimate cash-out. Thus, a business that successfully gets angel funding may be a start-up or may have been in business for a year, 2 years, perhaps up to 4 years.[12]

Although we cannot provide specific numbers, we can confidently say that only a tiny percentage of businesses that seek angel funding actually get it. A typical angel group receives about 30 to 50 business plan submissions each month. Of these unsolicited plans, approximately 5 to 10 will be selected to be presented to the angel group in person. Of the plans that are presented, no more than one or two will be funded in any quarter. Putting this into percentage terms, we can state that of 600 business plans presented for angel funding, no more than 1.3 percentage will ever get the money.[13] However, this low percentage still amounts to nearly 60,000 angel investments made each year. From these numbers, we can infer that some 6 million submissions are made annually, and there must be somewhere around 10,000 individuals and groups making angel investments.

This might lead you to think that an awfully large number of great business ideas and great entrepreneurs are not being funded. This may be so. But, consider that of 100 businesses funded by angel groups, only about 60 percentage ever repay the original investment. The other 40 percentage provide net losses to the angel investor![14] So another way to understand the results of angel investing is to conclude that all worthy business ideas are being funded. In fact, it appears that more than half of the businesses that are funded actually are poor business ideas led by incompetent entrepreneurs.

The truth is most likely somewhere between these two extremes. It's probable that few really good business ideas go undeveloped, and that a large percentage of what seem to be good ideas prove not to be in the long run. It's also likely that some really great ideas fail because of less than stellar entrepreneurs, and that a very few really effective entrepreneurs make a success of a less than wonderful idea.

Equity Capital from the Owner's View

From the point of view of an existing owner, financing with equity is (1) expensive and (2) guaranteed to create problems of control and decision making.

Equity capital is not free, as many entrepreneurs think. Suppose you sell half your business to raise capital. You have just sold half of all your future profits, half of all your future growth, half of all your future wealth. If, on the other hand, you were to borrow the money, your cost will be only the cost of acquiring the loan and making interest payments. In addition, owners of your business (even those who own only a small part) have a legal right to know how you're managing *their* business. As a matter of fact, most equity investors in small businesses insist upon having the right to inspect the accounting records *at any time they choose.* Once you accept equity investors, you will find that you'll have to keep careful records of transactions, and you'll have to make regular reports to your investors. If those investors disagree with your running of the business, they can challenge your decisions, even to the point of suing you for supposed damages, or replacing you as manager. Many, many entrepreneurs have found themselves forced out of their own businesses by minority equity investors.

Why Use Equity Capital?

There are three primary reasons to use outside equity in your business: (1) you will reduce your own exposure to financial loss, (2) your business will not have increased costs in the form of interest, and (3) bringing outside investors into an existing business can often reenergize it by providing new ideas, procedures, and processes.

Financing with Debt: Getting a Loan for Your Business

The most common source of capital for established ongoing small businesses is borrowed funds. This is the case for several reasons, including all the reasons discussed above, and the simple fact that small businesses do not have easy access to equity financing. Additionally, national, state, and local governments all encourage small business borrowing. This is done in three ways: (1) direct loans of cash, (2) guaranteeing loans made by commercial banks, and (3) reducing taxes by allowing interest to be deducted. However, when it comes to borrowing significant amounts of money, all firms are not created equal. Established businesses that have valuable assets that are separable from the owners are able to borrow more easily than are start-up or knowledge businesses.

So, where can a small business actually get loans to start and grow? As you might expect, your best source is the bank where you are currently doing business. After all, it is in the business of making loans. You are a customer. As such, you are a known commodity—you pay your bills, you keep your account balance positive, you don't bounce checks. Start where you're known.

But if your bank turns you down, you are not out of luck. In fact, in the Small Business Administration guaranteed loan programs, you *must* be turned down by a bank before you qualify. So, maybe your bank did you a favor. Having been turned down, you can apply for an SBA guaranteed loan. Through this avenue, you will still borrow from your own bank, but the SBA will guarantee the bank that if your business fails, the SBA will pay off your loan. Other sources for SBA guaranteed loans include **community development organizations**, and for small loans, *microlenders.*

A third source of SBA guaranteed loans is the numerous **small business investment companies** (SBIC). A directory of SBICs is maintained on the SBA website: www.sba.gov/content/sbic-directory. All SBIC's are listed by state. Click on the "hot link" to open the appropriate list. The directory provides not only a list of active SBICs, but also an outline of the business requirements.

community development organization
An organization authorized by the SBA to make insured loans to small businesses that are expected to increase economic activity within a specific geographic area.

small business investment companies
Private businesses that are authorized to make SBA insured loans to start-ups and small businesses.

Character of the managers of the business.	**Capacity** of the business to repay both principal and interest on time.
Conditions of the industry and economy in which the business operates.	**Collateral** that can be used to secure the loan.

FIGURE 15.3

The Four Cs of Borrowing

You may also have access to *incubators* or **accelerators** in your area. These organizations exist solely for the purpose of facilitating the start-up and growth of new businesses. They provide advice for finding loans, and, in some cases, have the ability to make loans to member businesses.

accelerator
An organization that supports start-up technology businesses by providing inexpensive office space, a variety of support services, and resources; most accelerators are associated with universities.

The main things that lenders want to see before they give businesses their money are the Four Cs of Borrowing, listed here and shown in Figure 15.3:

1. Character of the managers of the business.
2. Capacity of the business to repay both principal and interest on time.
3. Conditions of the industry and economy in which the business operates.
4. Collateral that can be used to secure the loan.

No matter how you have organized your business, the bank is going to look at it as an extension of you. The simple fact is that you have the power to make decisions, good or bad, about all facets of operation regardless of its form, whether sole proprietorship, partnership, or corporation. Thus, although technically the loan may be made to the business entity, from the point of view of the lender, a loan is not made to a small business, a loan is made to the *owner* of a small business. The owner's character and business reputation are important considerations for lenders when they decide whether or not to let a business have money.

Owner character is judged largely by the owner's personal credit rating and by that of the business. All lenders want some assurance that a loan will be repaid as agreed. There are several private agencies called consumer **credit reporting agencies** (CRAs) which exist solely to collect, collate, and report the credit histories of individuals and businesses. Lenders pay a fee to join a credit agency, and then pay for each report received. Lenders also promise to provide information about you back to the agency.

credit reporting agency
A business that collects, collates, and reports information concerning an entity's use of debt.

There are four primary CRAs: Equifax, Experian, Innovis, and TransUnion. There are also many specialized agencies that provide special services for landlords, medical providers, and resellers of information who create customized reports from data acquired from the four primary CRAs.

The information collected and reported by the CRAs is limited to three areas:

- Identifying information.
- Credit information.
- Public record information.

Race, religious preference, medical history, personal lifestyle choices, political affiliation, criminal record, or anything not related to credit is prohibited from being reported. Of course, for a price, all this information can be obtained from sources other than credit reporting agencies.

The **Fair Credit Reporting Act** requires that all information reported by CRAs be accurate. However, the law does not require that CRAs independently confirm any information. It is incumbent upon you, the consumer, to obtain a copy of your credit report and to notify the CRA in writing of any inaccurate information. The CRA has 30 days in which to investigate. The CRA must also forward copies of all relevant information that you provide to the source of the inaccurate information. The source must then make its own investigation and report any inaccuracies to all nationwide CRAs.

Fair Credit Reporting Act
U.S. federal legislation specifying consumers' rights vis-à-vis credit reporting agencies.

Eventually you will get a report of the outcome of the investigation. If the information is still inaccurate, you have to send a notice of dispute to the provider. The provider does not have to change the information, but a copy of your dispute must then be included with any future credit reports.

SKILL MODULE 15.2

Obtaining Your Credit Report

Under the Fair and Accurate Credit Transactions Act consumers can request one free credit report in every 12-month period from each of the three national credit reporting agencies, Experian, Equifax, and TransUnion. You must use the toll-free telephone number, (877) 322-8228, the **www.annualcreditreport.com** website, or a special mailing address—Annual Credit Report Request Service, P.O. Box 105281, Atlanta, GA 30348-5281. You will have to supply a Social Security number and date of birth and answer a few personal questions to get instant access online. Credit agencies have up to 15 days to send out reports that are requested by phone or mail.

Use one of the methods listed here to obtain copies of your credit report. Carefully examine each report for accuracy. If you find any incorrect information, contact the CRA and have it corrected.

Commercial credit reporting agencies began in the 1830s when a silk merchant, Lewis Tappan, began to collect extensive records concerning customers of the business. Tappan eventually offered credit reports to other merchants. Through a series of mergers, Tappan's business today is known as Dun & Bradstreet (D&B).

Providers of commercial credit reports are much more entrepreneurial and less rule-bound than are CRAs. For example, Dun & Bradstreet allows businesses to self report gross sales, profits, numbers and types of customers, numbers of employees, and so on. D&B does, however, make extensive efforts to confirm the accuracy of information and also makes independent investigations of midsize to large businesses, including interviewing management.

You can create a credit file for your business with D&B by filling out an online application and paying an initial fee of $500. Once your file is established, D&B maintains it, using a sophisticated computer system to confirm accuracy. Visit https://mycredit.dnb.com/make-informed-business-decisions/

Although D&B is the best known provider of commercial credit reports, it is by no means the sole provider. Experian provides commercial reports as well as consumer reports. Additionally, there are numerous other commercial credit reporting agencies, including National Information Bureau, Ltd, Veritax Business Information, Inc., and Fair Isaac's Small Business Scoring, to name a few. Finally, there are industry-specific reporting agencies; for example, Seafax provides credit reports for the seafood, poultry, meat, and associated food industries.

The capacity of the business is the most important single factor for being able to borrow significant amounts of money. Your capacity to repay loans is measured primarily by two factors: profitability and cash flows from operations. **Profitability** that has been maintained over time indicates that you are an effective manager who will produce future profits to repay the borrowed money. *Cash flows from operations* that have been constant and reliable indicate that you can reliably convert profits to cash.

profit, profitability
The amount that revenues exceed expenses.

Condition of the industry and economy includes such factors as technology, competition, and economic growth. For example, right now the telecommunications industry is undergoing huge changes. Cable providers are offering telephone service, and telephone companies are offering movies. Satellite operators are adding broadband to their television and radio services. Copper wire connectors are being replaced with fiber optic cable directly into businesses and homes. Cell phones have rendered pay phones obsolete. Now is not a good time to try to raise money for a telecommunications business.

Collateral value is simply the estimated market value of the assets of your business. Tangible, long-lived assets are the best **collateral**. Auction markets for automobiles, trucks, and commercial machinery provide both a source for estimating value and an immediate market in which they can be sold.

collateral
Something of value given or pledged as security for payment of a loan; collateral may consist of financial instruments, such as stocks, bonds, and negotiable paper, or of physical goods, such as trucks, machinery, land, or buildings.

Intangible assets, other than patents, copyrights, and trademarks, are not good collateral. For example, *goodwill,* the value of a business that exceeds the sum of the value of all individual assets, cannot be sold separately from the business. The same is true of other intangibles, such as experience, education, institutional knowledge, and customer relations. These things can be very valuable, but none can be transferred to a lender to satisfy debt.

Other factors affecting debt worthiness include why you want to borrow the money and just how much money of your own is invested in the business. Lenders eagerly loan money to purchase capital equipment. After all, if you default, they will just repossess your truck and sell it to someone else. If you are willing to pay high enough interest rates, they will even lend you money to finance marketing efforts or business growth. They will not, however, lend you money to make up for financial failure. They will not loan money to finance consumption or extravagance. In fact, it is quite difficult to even borrow working capital to finance ongoing operations of all types. Also, most commercial lenders will not make a loan in an amount greater than that which, when added to existing debt, will bring the debt-to-equity ratio above 50 percent. (See discussion later in the chapter for an explanation of debt to equity.)

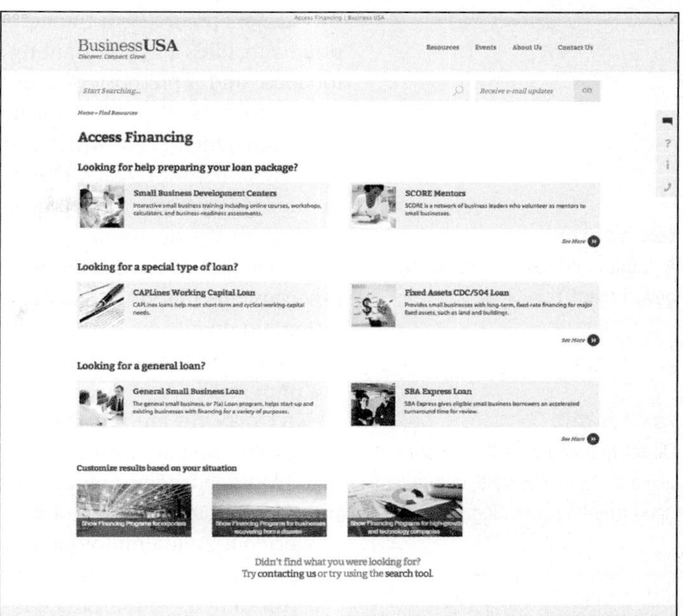

Government sites like business.usa.gov can help connect your to government grants and loans. What are the other major federal sites for finding grants?

Gift Financing

Gift financing has a special allure. It seems to many people as if they are getting something for nothing. The impression might be that a government or a foundation hands out money that never has to be repaid, or a family member magnanimously offers a present at just the right time. It is unfortunate that anything that seems too good to be true usually is. Gift capital is often anything but free. Often it costs time and money to obtain; and it often requires time and money for accounting and reporting to the granting agency, family members, and government. There are two general sources of gift financing: one is institutional, from government agencies and foundations, and the other is personal, from family or occasionally from friends.

Institutional Gifts

The most common form of institutional gift financing is in the form of reduced taxes, either through tax abatement or in the form of a credit against taxes payable. It does seem a misnomer to call reducing the amount taken from a business a gift, but as taxes are a cash cost to businesses, reducing tax burden has the same effect as receiving that same amount of cash would have.

THE THOUGHTFUL ENTREPRENEUR

When Uncle Sam Is a Soft Touch

It is hard to even begin to grasp how many government tax abatement programs exist. They are provided to businesses both large and small.

Many small businesses have taken advantage of the U.S. government's program that encourages building low-income housing and rebuilding historic structures through reduced income taxes.

The city of Kansas City, Missouri, once forgave all property tax on Trans World Airlines' aircraft overhaul facilities.

Right now, the city of San Antonio, Texas, and Bexar County agreed to forego property taxes on a new Toyota pickup truck factory. In addition, the state of Texas, Bexar County, and San Antonio together contributed over $23 million for the building of an 8-mile-long railroad spur from the main railroad line to the Toyota factory site.

The city of Flagler, Colorado, and the state of Maine are currently offering commercial land free to businesses that will agree to bring employment to specific areas.

Homestead, Florida, has established an enterprise zone in which there are property tax abatements, a direct refund of sales taxes, direct credits of property tax up to $50,000, as well as tax credits for job creation. Portland, Maine, offers tax increment and tax-exempt bond financing for firms that will relocate to the area.

Provo, Utah, is spending $7 million of tax money to build a new rendering[15] plant some distance from town. The city council explained this gift by pointing out that moving the plant would remove a source of unpleasant odors from the city, while keeping the taxes from the plant, which employs several hundred people.

Farmers receive gift financing from the U.S. government in the form of direct cash payments and price subsidies for not planting crops, for planting cereal grains, apples (but not peaches), cotton, tobacco, and a plethora of other crops, for raising mohair goats, and for producing lamb meat and dairy products. Payments for not growing crops are made through a program called "conservation reserve payments," in which farmers contract to not plant specified plots of erosion-prone land for a specific number of years. Direct subsidies and price supports are made through numerous programs, including payments for wetlands protection.

tax abatement
A legal reduction in taxes by a government.

Tax abatements are provided by state and local governments, primarily to encourage specific activities that are expected to improve blighted areas or to provide additional employment. Most governments that impose a tax on real estate have some form of tax reduction to encourage rehabilitating old dwellings, providing housing for low-income citizens, and maintaining buildings that are deemed to be historic. Tax abatements can take many forms, depending upon the type of taxes that are imposed.

tax credits
Direct reductions in the amount of taxes that must be paid, dependent upon meeting some legal criteria.

Tax credits are provided by the U.S. government and some state governments for the purpose of encouraging investment in specific types of assets, to increase economic activity in specified disadvantaged geographical areas, increase the welfare of specific groups of citizens, or support industries that are held to be of national strategic interest. Credits provided include those for empowerment zone employment, employing (American) Indians, purchasing electric automobiles, or using ethyl alcohol for fuel. The list of available tax credits and the details of how to claim them is too voluminous to reproduce in this text. Also, the credits change with each Congress, and thus any specific information would be sorely out of date by the time this text is published.

grants
Gifts of money made to a business for a specific purpose.

Grants of money are available from the U.S. government, most state governments, and semiprivate and private economic development agencies. The purpose of the grants varies with the entity that makes the grant. U.S. grant programs for small business are primarily a response to political pressure brought upon Congress. The stated purpose of the grant programs is to encourage development of small businesses, thereby increasing the economic activity of the country. Various states also have grant programs. As with the federal program, the rationale for providing grants to small business is to increase economic activity, provide job growth, and provide increases in the overall standard of living of the citizens of the state.

To find federal government grants, there are three good sources: (1) The Small Business Administration offers a loan and grant search tool (www.sba.gov/loans-and-grants) optimized for small businesses. (2) You can go to www.grants.gov and use the basic search. If you type in *small business* you will find hundreds of grants that mention small businesses as potential grantees. (3) Another great resource is http://business.usa.gov. Sections such as "Start a Business," "Grow a Business," and "Access Financing" can connect you to federal resources, grants, and support programs. This site also has a tab for "State and Local," which can connect you to resources and support organizations in your state.

While there is no single federal site that will direct you to the government resources for small business in your state, About.com (http://usgovinfo.about.com/od/smallbusiness/a/stategrants.htm) keeps up a page with the links you need.

Grants from governments are highly structured and require very accurate record keeping and reporting. Agencies that issue grants first publish a request for proposal (RFP) that specifies the conditions of the grant. Interested small businesses may then create a proposal, which must be submitted by the specified date and time, in the *exact* format specified. Grant proposals are then judged in a "blind" process. Winning proposals receive notification within about 30 days and funding within 6 months.

The two largest governmental grant programs that are specifically intended for small business are (1) the Small Business Innovation Research (SBIR) program and the Small Business Technology Transfer (STTR) program. These two programs require that every U.S. agency that makes research grants provide a minimum of 2 percent of its grant budget to small businesses, as defined by the SBA. Two percent may not sound like much, but in 2002, the SBIR program resulted in over $1.5 *billion* in grants made to participating small businesses. These programs are each three-phase programs. A winning proposal will initially receive about $100,000 to conduct a feasibility study, as detailed in the grant proposal. Depending upon successful completion, additional funds, which can range up into millions of dollars, are provided for stage II and stage III activities.

SKILL MODULE 15.3

Finding SBIR Grants

What kind of business are you interested in? Do you have any new ideas or procedures for this business that might lead to better ways of solving problems of health, national security, threats of terrorism, or any other area in which the U.S. government has an interest?

If you do, there is probably an SBIR grant for you.

Assume that you have come up with an idea that might result in stopping would-be terrorists at airports outside the United States. Your idea, if it works, will stop terrorists from getting to the United States in the first place. Do a Google search using the search terms: SBIR grants "national security."

Follow the leads returned by Google (more than 10,000) to identify agencies and programs that will provide funds through SBIR grants for ideas that might help national security.

1. Write a report of your findings to be presented to your class.
2. Use the skill you have now developed to find an SBIR grant that would apply to a business that you are actually interested in starting.

Grants from foundations are rarely made to for-profit businesses. **Foundations** exist for the purpose of addressing some identified social need that cannot be adequately met by market forces. The Ewing Marion Kauffman Foundation supports *education* and *research* concerning entrepreneurship and small business. The Ford Foundation supports the arts, including public television programs. The Rotary Foundation supports efforts to eradicate hunger and polio worldwide. All these foundations were founded by successful entrepreneurs and business managers, but they do not specifically support the start up, expansion, or operation of for-profit enterprises. Rather, their (and those of about 30,000 other private foundations) missions clearly state that grants are made to nonprofit organizations.

foundation
An institution to which private wealth is contributed and from which private wealth is distributed for public purposes.

However, occasionally private foundations will make grants to for-profit businesses, *if the purpose of the grant is to address some goal of the foundation.* If your business is such that it addresses a pernicious social problem, then you may be able to find private foundation grant funding for specific, limited projects.

Personal Gifts

While the type of gifts governments and foundations offer are relatively consistent, stable, and publicly known, the forms of personal gifts are as varied as human imagination and need can make them. Remember from Chapter 14 that not just money has value; goods and services can provide tremendous value to a start-up business. The most popular forms of gifts are shown in Exhibit 15.1.

Personal gift financing is tremendously popular. In the Panel Study of Income Dynamics,[16] fully one-third of the firms reported having unpaid labor contributed by family members. In business plan classes, the same one out of three ratio of personal gifts to start-ups in general is a fairly common occurrence. These gifts range dramatically in size, but the commonality of personal gifts as a major source of funding for start-ups is fairly well known.[17]

Gift giving seems so easy and straightforward that it is hard to imagine how complex it really is—for the giver and the recipient, as well as the business. Consider gifts from the standpoint of the recipient and then the giver.

You are trying to get your business off the ground, and your favorite uncle offers to provide you with start-up capital. Not just any start-up capital, not an investment, not a loan. He is going to *give* you that boost that you need to get into business. It is an entrepreneur's dream—capital without any strings.

Do you take the money? Not so fast. The simple fact is that although Freud may have believed that "sometimes a cigar is just a cigar"[18] you can bet that a gift is *always* much, much more than just a gift. Gifts are loaded with special meanings and hidden purposes. Robert Cialdini wrote that gifts "create and cement alliances, allegiances, and partnerships."[19] Are you ready to enter into an alliance or partnership with your beloved uncle?

Accepting money from family members and friends entails some real risks. That favorite uncle might really mean it when he says that he is *giving* you start-up capital. But gifts like this have a

EXHIBIT 15.1

Forms of Personal Gifts

Cash—always useful, but also the gift most likely to have tax implications.
Picking up the tab—when someone buys something on behalf of your business and lets you benefit from it.
Accelerated cash-outs—where you might be given the funds for your business from an account your family set up for your future education or first home. Some cash-outs come when family or friends cash out their retirements or home (often via taking out a mortgage).
Free use—your family has an empty storefront, apartment, van, car, or other useful product which they let you use for free, or at a severely reduced price, for your business.
Free work—you get family or friends to help you out in the business for free, or for pizzas and drinks, or for wages significantly below minimum wage. This is sometimes called **unpaid labor**.
Overpayment—where family or friends "hire" you at higher than market rates, to help you generate cash for your business. A variant of this is **favored status** or **sweetheart deals** where family or friends give you contracts to help you fund your business, instead of giving their work to the most qualified candidate.
Forgiveness—where family or friends give up on collecting debts you owe them, so you can use the money for the business. A variant of this is **deferral**, where the repayment of debts is delayed until the business is doing well.
Piggybacking—where family or friends let you add (i.e., piggyback) your purchases with theirs in order to get lower prices.

nasty way of morphing into very real expectations that you may quickly come to hate. Meanings, especially in spoken messages, are slippery little devils. Your uncle may well be saying "gift" but thinking "loan," or "investment." If you are successful, you may suddenly find that the "gift" has now transformed (at least in your uncle's mind) into something very different. So here you stand—you *accepted* a gift, but your uncle *gave* you a loan.

Lawsuits are made of just such differences of opinion.

Accepting gifts is difficult for many people. Especially when the gift is substantial. Before you accept your uncle's offer, you should examine your own feelings. Can you accept a gift? Or do you have some secret plan that you will repay the money when you become successful? If you do not like being beholden to anyone, you probably should think twice about accepting an outright gift. Taking one most likely will lead to guilty feelings and resentment.

No need to immediately refuse your uncle's offer, but you should be absolutely certain that both you and he understand just what is being given and just what is expected in return.

Now turn the example on its head. Assume now that you are the uncle who is going to give a gift of cash to your favorite niece to start her business.

Do you just write out a check and forget it? If you wish to keep your niece as a favorite, you probably shouldn't. Giving a gift is risky, just as is receiving one. Any gifts that you make had better be equitable among those who expect to receive from you. It is a simple fact that brothers, sisters, nieces, and nephews all expect to be treated fairly by their parents, grandparents, aunts, and uncles. Overtly favor one heir, and you will trigger resentment in all the others.

Giving a gift also has tax implications. Currently, any gift that exceeds $13,000 may be subject to U.S. Gift Taxes. Depending upon the size of the gift, and your own situation, current gift taxes can be as high as 47 percent of the amount given. So if you are planning to finance your niece's start-up with $500,000, you'll probably need some creative financial planning to avoid the tax implications.

You should carefully consider just why you want to make this gift. Perhaps you are one of those very rare people who are true Santa Clauses: You get real satisfaction from giving away your wealth. This is unlikely, however. Komter and Vollebergh showed that gifts given to extended kin are usually made because of feelings of obligation and rarely because of feelings of affection.[20] Probably, you are expecting to receive gratitude. If so, you'll more than likely be disappointed. Or do you think that your niece's business idea is the next Microsoft and that your support will result in untold wealth? In this case, you should not make your support a gift. Structure it as an investment in her business—make it a loan or a purchase of stock.

Given the many problems of gift giving, should you change your mind about supporting your niece's new business?

No, but you should understand exactly what you are giving, and what you expect in return. You should also be sure that your niece also understands.

For both of you to be certain that you agree, you should:

1. **Put your agreement into writing.** As is said in Mexico, "Words walk. Paper talks." This has the same message as the saying, "Oral agreements are just as valuable as the paper they're written on!" There simply is no better way to be certain that everyone understands a transaction than to write it out, then have each party read, sign, and date the document. When disagreements arise later, the written agreement provides a permanent, immutable record of your original intentions.
2. **If it is a gift, have the agreement specifically say so.** "This is a gift, freely given between uncle (grantor) and you (recipient). No repayment is expected, and none will be accepted."
3. **If it is a loan, have the agreement specify the exact interest and payment terms.** A good idea from the point of view of the recipient is to make repayment a percentage of positive cash flows. Ideally, payments will be made either (a) until the principal amount plus accrued interest has been paid or (b) until the giver has received a specified return on the original amount. In the real world, loans between family members often go unpaid. Be clear concerning the circumstances under which the loan will be forgiven.
4. **If it is an equity investment, consider nonvoting stock.** One common problem with family and friends as equity investors is that they want to have a say in the management of your business. This may be fine if they have appropriate talents and experience. It can be a kiss of death if they just want to meddle. Nonvoting stock provides the opportunity for capital gains, but pretty much precludes interference in business operations.

Even when gifts are given to help a family member or friend's business, common sense and clear communication are essential. Make sure both parties understand and assent to what exactly is being given, under which conditions, and with what kind, if any, of repayment plan.

Gifts Via Crowdfunding

Today you can fund your business online through gifts made to your business. The technique is called crowdfunding, and there are two types: a nonequity model and an equity model. Groups like KickStarter.com and IndieGogo.com pioneered the nonequity model. At such sites, you post your business idea, along with descriptions, photos, and if at all possible a video about your business. You set a gift target goal, say $10,000 and a deadline (like 30 days).

For example, the Ramos alarm clock (www.ramosclock.com) is a super-loud alarm clock that can be turned off only by getting out of bed. The inventors posted on KickStarter seeking $75,000 to develop the product. To get one of the clocks you would have to donate at least $160. Lesser donations received a T-shirt or a listing on the Ramos website. They went out on social media to drum up support and also began to receive some media attention—both of which are best practices you would want to follow. In the end, they had 525 backers from all over the world and had raised $153,585, or more than twice what they sought. This support also helped prove that there was a market for the clock, helping Ramos get the attention of stores and catalogs. Best of all, as gifts, the Ramos founders still owned all of their business, despite $153,585 of funding.

What Type of Financing Is Right for Your Business?

LO3 Explain which type of financing is best for your business.

Consider the simplest case in which a small business owner has the alternatives of using personal equity funding or borrowing funds. The business may be 100 percent capitalized by either equity or debt, or any mix of equity and debt. Equity capital costs are estimated to be 20 percent per year—the investors expect $200 in interest or dividends for every $1,000 invested in the business. Debt capital costs are estimated to be a net of 6 percent after tax, or for every $1,000 borrowed, the entrepreneur owes the bank $60 a year (plus the $1,000 will need to be paid back as agreed).

cost of capital
The percentage cost of obtaining future funds.

weighted average cost of capital (WAC)
The expected average future cost of funds.

If the owner chooses to use a capital mix of 70 percent equity and 30 percent debt, the weighted average **cost of capital** is approximately 16 percent. At a 50–50 mix of equity and capital, the **weighted average cost of capital** is 13 percent and at 30 to 70 percent equity, and debt is approximately 10 percent. The more debt that is included in the capital mix, the lower the weighted average cost will be. The lower your cost of capital, the more profits you can keep for yourself. The more money your business generates for its owners, the more the business is worth. Thus, firm value is inversely related to cost of capital at any level of operations.

In reality, you will never have such alternatives. Although you may choose to use 100 percent personal funds for equity capital, no lender will agree to loan 100 percent. In fact, most lenders, without having some sort of guarantee such as collateral or Small Business Administration insurance, will not lend an amount that exceeds the amount you have invested. Even with guarantees, as the amount of debt increases, so does the risk of default. Because of the added risk, lenders will demand higher rates of interest for those later loans. For these reasons, the cost of both equity and debt capital changes as their relative percentages of total capital change.

A more realistic case is a small business that is 100 percent funded from the owner's own personal wealth. In this case, the value of the firm can be described as the amount of profit divided by the owner's cost of capital. For now, assume that your business is producing $100,000 per year and that the cost of capital is 20 percent. The value of the business is $500,000 ($100,000 cash flow divided by 20 percent). Now suppose you have an opportunity to purchase a productive asset which will return 20 percent per year for its life, such as a computer-controlled 5-axis milling machine. The asset costs $50,000, which you decide to borrow at 8 percent interest. Firm value will increase. Profits will increase to $106,000 [$100,000 + ($50,000 × .20) − ($50,000 × .08)]. The weighted average cost of capital will be 19 percent ($500,000 at 20 percent plus the additional investment of $50,000 at 8 percent). The value of the business is now $560,600.

A few weeks later, you have an opportunity to purchase another asset which will cost $50,000 and will also produce 20 percent returns. Again, you can borrow the money, but because of the added debt and greater probability of default, the lender requires 10 percent interest. Making the same set of calculations shows that profits will now be $111,000. The weighted average cost of capital is 18 percent, and the value of the business is now $611,000.

financial leverage
A measure of the amount of debt relative to total investment.

Notice that the first investment increased the value of the firm by $60,600 (12 percent), while the second investment increased the value of the firm by only $50,400 (9 percent). As debt increases as a percentage of total investment (called **financial leverage**), *the value of the firm increases at a decreasing rate.* At some debt-to-equity ratio, the firm value peaks and then begins to decrease as added debt is incurred. You may make a series of such calculations, each time increasing the interest rate to convince yourself. You will initially see firm value increase. It will eventually reach a maximum value, and then start to decrease as debt and the cost of debt increases.

optimum capital structure
The ratio of debt to equity that provides the maximum level of profits.

Few, if any, small business owners, however, even attempt to estimate the **optimum capital structure** of their business. Making such calculations takes too much time for the value provided. If you understand the concept that having debt in your capital structure works to increase your profits and you know that interest rates do not increase smoothly as financial leverage increases, you can find that level of debt that works for you.

A similar argument holds for obtaining outside equity investors. The difficulties and costs of obtaining equity capital are so great that most owners of small businesses don't even try. A study reported in 2003[21] found that so few small businesses raised capital by selling equity to outsiders that no statistical analysis could be done. Given these facts, it is reasonable for you to approximate cost of capital by examining only a few specific debt-to-equity ratios which are reasonable for your business and which you expect to persist for significant periods of time.

The owners and managers of small businesses are quite diverse. Entrepreneurs come from all social classes. They have different levels of education ranging from no formal schooling to those with advanced degrees. People of all major religions, of every race, and from every part of the world are represented among small business owners. As you would expect, such a diverse group of people have very diverse attitudes toward work, toward investing, toward management.

Some people gleefully jump out of airplanes; others are determined to "keep one foot on the ground." Business owners similarly differ in their response to financial risk. A few seek risk, thriving on the pressure of attempting to make the big strike. Most prefer to avoid business risk to the extent possible. In academic terms, some business owners are *risk seeking,* although most small business owners are *risk averse.* The personal preferences of each owner of a small business affect choices concerning financial risk, debt, sharing of ownership, and interaction with private and governmental foundations and agencies. Because of this, the optimal capital structure for one entrepreneur may well be anathema to another. Each owner of a small business must find the levels of equity, debt, and financial risk with which he or she is comfortable.

Financial risk is the probability of financial loss. Business opportunities, projects, and assets that have a greater chance of producing a loss are considered more risky than those that have a smaller chance. In a very real sense, risk is synonymous with uncertainty. If you purchase a 30-day U.S. Treasury bond, the return is certain. On the thirtieth day the government will issue a check for the amount of the bond plus interest. Because the government has the power to create money, there is no uncertainty and thus no risk of financial loss. If, on the other hand, you use the same amount of money to invest in a business, the return is very uncertain. You might succeed greatly or the business might fail and you lose your entire investment.

financial risk
Uncertainty of returns; the probability of losing money.

Borrowing money increases financial risk. In effect, borrowing money for a business is very much like selling the business to an investor and simultaneously buying back an option to repurchase the business on specific terms of payment. If the terms of payment are not met, the lender has the right to keep the business. The lender may enforce this right through either repossession if business assets were pledged as collateral, or involuntary bankruptcy, mediated by the court system. Payments on debt must be made as agreed without regard to the cash position of the business.

Selling equity in the business provides neither the opportunity to repurchase nor the obligation to make payments to owners. If the business does not provide sufficient profits and cash flows, an equity investor must accept the situation and hope that future operations will be profitable.

So why should you borrow, if doing so increases the probability of financial loss? Borrowing money for capital investment provides two benefits: (1) Borrowing enhances the potential for higher rates of return for the owners. (2) Borrowing allows the owners to keep a greater level of control of the business. For these reasons, the majority of small business owners prefer to borrow over accepting outside equity investment.[22] The interaction of the effects of choosing between equity and debt capital results in a small business owner having to compromise among the levels of potential profits, financial risk, and control of the business. This is depicted graphically in Figure 15.4.

Borrowing increases potential profits by (1) lowering the weighted average cost of capital and (2) providing capital funds that allow the business to consider additional opportunities. To illustrate how this works, consider the following:

- Nucleodyne, LLC, is a biopharmaceutical start-up that owns intellectual property rights to a protein that will treat male pattern baldness. The science is sound, and the molecule grows hair on laboratory mice.
- The founders of the firm have already invested $1 million.
- To complete trials on human beings, the company must raise an additional $1 million. The owners have an agreement with a venture capital group to provide the money in return for 40 percent of the equity of the business.

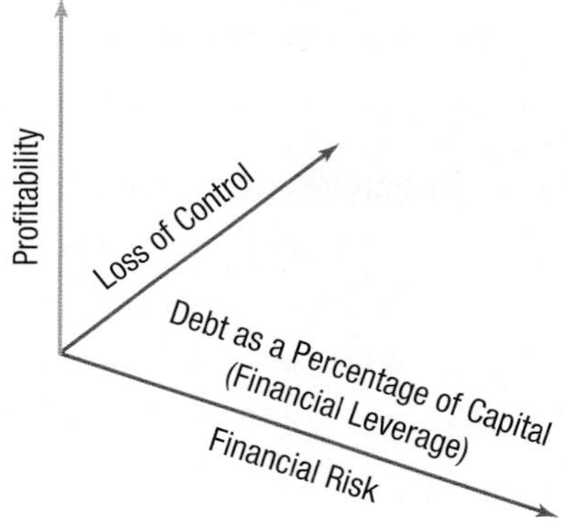

FIGURE 15.4

Interaction among Profitability, Control, and Risk

FIGURE 15.5

Effect of Financing Sources on Financial Results for Nucleodyne, LLC

EFFECT OF FINANCING SOURCES UPON FINANCIAL RESULTS

100% Equity Financing		50–50 Debt-to-Equity Financing	
Balance Sheet			
Total assets	$2,000,000	Total assets	$2,000,000
Debt	0	Debt	$1,000,000
Equity	$2,000,000	Equity	$1,000,000
Total of debt and equity	$2,000,000	Total of debt and equity	$2,000,000
Income Statement			
Operating income	$300,000	Operating income	$300,000
Interest expense	0	Interest expense	100,000
Net income	$300,000	Net income	$200,000

- Alternatively, the money may be borrowed from a local investment bank at 10 percent annual interest.
- Based on projections of sales and expenses, the company expects to realize a profit of $300,000. Using these facts, compare the balance sheet and income statements in Figure 15.5.

It is immediately apparent that the business makes a greater profit if all capital is equity capital. What is not so apparent is the effect on the owners of the business. When investments are made, they are not evaluated by the number of dollars that are returned. Rather, investments are evaluated on the *percentage of return* that is realized. In this case, compare the **return on equity** (that is, the percentage of return on the amount actually owned) for each of the original founders of the business and new equity investors as we can see in Table 15.5.

return on equity
The ratio of profits to owner investment in a business.

If the *original* owners solely use their own funds, then they will realize a return of only 15 cents on each dollar invested. If they sell 40 percent of the business to outside investors, the *original* owners will realize 18 cents on the dollar (60% of $300,000 divided by $ 1,000,000). If, however, they borrow the additional funds, then they realize a 20 percent return on their investment. The total original owners' return on each dollar invested in the business is one-third greater if the needed capital is borrowed than if the business is 100 percent financed by owners' personal funds.

This analysis, of course, does beg the question, "If the owners have the additional personal funds, why not invest them into the business because the total profit realized will be greater?" There are two reasons that making the additional investment might not be the best alternative. First, obtaining

TABLE 15.5 Owners' Return on Equity in Three Business Situations

$$\text{Owners' Return on Equity (ROE)} = \frac{\text{Net Income}}{\text{Owners' Equity Investment}}$$

Alternative 1 Use Personal Funds for Capital		Alternative 2 Issue Stock for 40% Equity		Alternative 3 Borrow Capital Funds	
Net income	$300,000	Net income	$300,000	Net income	$200,000
Original owners' equity	$2,000,000	Original owners' equity	$1,000,000	Original owners' equity	$1,000,000
New owners' equity	0	New owners' equity	$1,000,000	New owners' equity	N.A.
Original owners' ROE =	15%	Original owners' ROE =	18%	Original owners' ROE =	20%
New owners' ROE =	N.A.	New owners' ROE =	12%	New owners' ROE =	N.A.

equity investment from others reduces the potential loss for any single investor. Second, it is often possible to borrow at interest rates substantially lower than the opportunity cost of using the business owners' own resources. For example, you may have money invested in an IRA, 401(k), or other tax-sheltered retirement fund. Suppose your retirement is earning near the long-term market average of 10 percent. Interest rates for borrowing are currently about 8 percent. If you take money from your retirement funds, you are giving up a 10 percent tax-free gain. On the other hand, interest on money borrowed for your business is deductible for tax purposes. If you are in the 25 percent tax bracket, you will, in effect, pay interest of only 6 percent [(.08 × (1 − tax rate of .25)]. Thus, as a rule, even if you have enough money to finance your business solely with equity, you still should consider borrowing in order to get the greatest total profits.

Control issues arise under both alternatives of issuing equity to outsiders or borrowing funds. When outside investors acquire equity, they also acquire some level of influence over the operations and strategy of the firm. In the example above, Nucleodyne gave up ownership of 40 percent of the firm. The original owners retain 60 percent ownership. This provides majority voting control only so long as the original owners vote as a bloc. Should disputes arise, it is quite possible, depending upon the number of owners and their percentage of ownership, that disgruntled stockholders could form a coalition and take control of the firm from the original founders. Alternatively, disgruntled minority owners may sue majority owners. For these reasons, many owners of small businesses are loath to sell any ownership shares. They prefer to accept the added financial risk of borrowing rather than deal with stockholders.

Borrowing capital, however, is not without its own issues of control. Lenders have to trust your management to operate the business efficiently, generating sufficient cash flow to meet the repayment terms of the loan. It is common, therefore, for lenders to require borrowers to provide regular documentation of the financial condition of the business. Many banks require that a copy of each year's income tax return, income statement, and balance sheet be furnished during the term of the loan. Loan contracts may also impose restrictions on the operation of the business, such as requiring that a specific minimum net worth be maintained, a specific debt-to-equity ratio not be exceeded, no dividends be paid to stockholders, executive salaries not exceed a specified amount, no capital assets be acquired or disposed of without the concurrence of the lender, and so on. These types of restrictions, called *loan covenants,* can seriously limit management's freedom to operate the business and can make taking on shareowners seem like less of a burden. It could also make do-it-yourself funding more attractive.

Financial Management for the Life of Your Business

Tools for Financial Management

Financial management requires that you have some method to measure and compare your financial position and financial results. Your financial position is reflected on your balance sheet, your financial results on your income statement. The problem is how to interpret the information on these two reports.

As with any analysis, you must have something to compare with your position and results. The obvious comparisons are (1) with your planned position and results (your master budget), (2) with prior years' position and results, and (3) with the position and results of other firms. The difficulty is in how to understand the comparison. Suppose last year you had a net business profit of $50,000 and this year your profit was $55,000. Did you do well in the current year? You did make 10 percent more this year than last. But it is often misleading to compare dollars to dollars for a financial result. You did not do well for the year if you invested an additional $100,000 into your business: Your return on your added investment is only 5 percent: added income / added investment = 5,000 / 100,000 = .05.

For these reasons, most financial comparisons are made using ratios. You made $55,000 in profit. You have a competitor who also made a net profit of $55,000. So, were the two of you equally effective business managers? Perhaps so, perhaps not. You made the same profit, but what was your respective inputs to the business? Suppose you had $110,000 invested in your business. Your competitor has $550,000 invested. Your return on investment is $55,000 / 110,000, or 50 percent. Your competitor's return is $55,000 / 550,000, or 10 percent. It would certainly seem from this analysis that you are the better business manager.

There are four broad categories of financial ratios: (1) Activity ratios, (2) Profitability ratios, (3) Liquidity ratios, and (4) Leverage ratios. Activity ratios measure how productive a particular asset is in producing sales activity. Profitability ratios measure management effectiveness in creating wealth from sales and from invested funds. Liquidity ratios measure the business's ability to pay debts and expenses that are due in the current accounting period. Leverage ratios measure the relative risk that a business setback could cause bankruptcy. Commonly used ratios are explained in Table 15.6. The three most commonly used ratios are Return on Investment (ROI), Current Ratio, and Debt to Equity Ratio. The value of these ratios for management depends to a large extent on the type of business you are conducting and the stage of your business in the business life cycle.

The ratios are the key way businesses are evaluated. You have seen many of these key ratios in reports from BizStats.com, BizMiner.com, and the Risk Management Association *Annual Statement*

TABLE 15.6 Common Ratios for Financial Management Using Ratios to Analyze the Income Statement

Ratio Name	Interpretation	Decision Criterion	Formula
Activity ratios	Measures of how productive a particular asset was in producing sales activity		
Asset turnover ratio	Measures how efficiently a business uses all its assets to produce sales	A higher ratio is better than a lower ratio	$\frac{\text{Net Sales Revenue}}{\text{Average Total Assets (Beginning assets + ending assets) / 2}}$
Accounts receivable turnover ratio	Measures the frequency with which receivables are converted to cash	Higher turnover provides faster access to cash that can be used in the business	$\frac{\text{Net Credit Sales}}{\text{Average Net Accounts Receivable}}$
Inventory turnover ratio	Indicates how quickly inventory is sold and thus the relative efficiency of both the sales and purchasing functions	Higher turnover is preferred	$\frac{\text{Cost of Goods Sold}}{\text{Average Merchandise Inventory}}$
Average holding period	Indicates the same as inventory turnover, but is easier to understand	Shorter period is preferred	$\frac{\text{365 Days}}{\text{Inventory Turnover Ratio}}$
Profitability ratios	Measures management effectiveness in creating wealth from sales and from invested funds		
Gross margin ratio	Measures the percentage of sales revenue available to pay operating costs and to provide profits after paying for inventory	Higher is preferred	$\frac{\text{Gross Margin}}{\text{Sales Revenue}}$
Profit margin ratio, also called return on sales (ROS)	Measures management's effectiveness in managing all costs relative to sales	Higher is preferred	$\frac{\text{Net Income}}{\text{Sales Revenue}}$
Return on equity	Measures management's effectiveness in using investor funds to provide profits	Higher is preferred	$\frac{\text{Net Income—Preferred Stock Dividends Declared}}{\text{Average Common Stockholders' Equity}}$
Return on assets	Measures management's effectiveness in using the assets of the business to provide profits	Higher is preferred	$\frac{\text{Net Income}}{\text{Average Total Assets}}$

TABLE 15.6 (Continued)

Ratio Name	Interpretation	Decision Criterion	Formula
Return on investments (ROI) (Discussed on pp. 519–521)	Measures management's effectiveness in using the invested capital of the business to provide profits	Higher is preferred	$\frac{\text{Net Income}}{\text{Average Investment}}$
Earnings per share	Measures profitability per share investment	Examined over time, a trend of increasing per share earnings is preferred	$\frac{\text{Net Income—Preferred Stock Dividends Declared}}{\text{Weighted Average Common Stock Outstanding}}$
Liquidity ratios	Measures the business's ability to pay debts and expenses that are due in the current accounting period		
Current ratio (Discussed on p. 413)	Measures how much money can be made available to pay obligations within the fiscal year	Higher ratio is preferred	$\frac{\text{Current Assets}}{\text{Current Liabilities}}$
Acid test or Quick ratio	Measure of how much money can be made available very quickly to pay obligations within the fiscal year	Higher ratio is preferred	$\frac{\text{Current Assets} - (\text{Inventories} + \text{Prepaid Assets})}{\text{Current Liabilities}}$
Leverage ratios	Measures that indicate the relative risk that a business setback could cause bankruptcy		
Debt to assets ratio	Measures the extent to which the business can meet its obligations for the long haul	A lower ratio indicates greater solvency. A greater ratio indicates increased business risk	$\frac{\text{Total Liabilities}}{\text{Total Assets}}$
Debt to equity ratio	Measures the extent to which the business can meet its obligations for the long haul	A lower ratio indicates greater solvency. A greater ratio indicates increased business risk	$\frac{\text{Total Liabilities}}{\text{Total Owners' Equity}}$
Times interest earned	Measures the risk of being forced into bankruptcy for not meeting required interest payments	Higher is preferred	$\frac{\text{Operating Income before Interest and Income Tax}}{\text{Interest Expense}}$

Studies mentioned in Chapters 7 and 8. Sources like those can provide important comparisons to help you determine if your key ratios are better or worse than the norms for your industry. While you are in the start-up phase, there can be considerable volatility in your business, and looking over a month or two's results can lead to confusing results using ratios. That is why for start-ups ratios are usually based on annual figures, or at least a six-month period.

In addition, the kinds of ratios that add important information to your business decision making will change as the firm matures. As we have said, initially your concerns are less with profitability and more with having enough cash on hand to meet your immediate needs (what we call the "short term"). That is why initially Liquidity Ratios are the most important to you. As your firm gets past its initial trial-and-error period and develops its standard operating procedures, Activity Ratios help tell you if your use of the firm's assets in those standard operating procedures is giving your firm the kind of results it needs to be successful.

As the firm reaches its break-even point, profits become a reality, and Profitability Ratios become increasingly important to the firm. At this point, Leverage Ratios also become more important because they look at the longer-term success of the firm, as well as its ability to weather threats leading to bankruptcy. Table 15.6 provides the major financial ratios, and tells you how they are computed and interpreted.

LO4 Describe the differing needs for financial management at each stage of business life.

Financial Management for Start-Up

During the start-up phase of your business, you will use the **financial management** techniques described in the bootstrapping discussion. The emphasis is on conserving what little cash your new business has.

financial management
A set of theories and techniques used to optimize the receipt and use of capital assets.

Financial Management for Growth

Many small businesses successfully start up only to find that the need for financial management is greater than ever as the business enters a phase of rapid growth. This situation is like a lame "bad news-good news" joke. The bad news is that the business has greater capital needs than ever. The good news is that more sources of money are available to meet those needs. The emphasis of financial management during periods of growth is to obtain increasing amounts of cash inflows to pay for added inventory, productive assets, and employees needed to meet growing levels of business operations.

Financial Management for Operations

Most small businesses eventually reach a size that is relatively stable: not too small to generate sufficient profits, not too large for the preferences and abilities of the owners. At this stage of the business, the emphasis of financial management is to build owner wealth, to conserve assets, to match cash inflows to outflows, and to maximize the return on capital assets by making optimal investing decisions.

Financial Management for Business Exit

Eventually, you will face the necessity of leaving the active management of your business. This may be because you want to take advantage of a different opportunity, the business needs professional management, you want to pass ownership to family members, or you want to retire. You might become ill or disabled. Regardless why, successfully leaving your business requires maximizing the value of your business for your successors.

The goals of financial management in preparation for exiting the business depends, in part, on the nature of the exit that is planned. Business exit can entail a transfer to your heirs. Another common exit is to sell the business, either to outside investors or to the employees. Finally, business exit can come from terminating the business through bankruptcy, a "work-out," or simply closing the business and disposing of its assets.

If your plan is to transfer the business to family members, then you will want to ensure that the business is in sound financial condition. You should be working to minimize debt and to increase asset value. It is essential that you establish internal controls over assets by establishing policies and procedures that are clearly stated and understood by everyone involved in management.

If you plan to sell your business, your goals should be to optimize capital structure for profits. Investors usually will not pay to "buy" cash in your business. Therefore, you should be removing all surplus cash and tightening the cash-to-cash cycle to the shortest time possible. The condition and age of assets will greatly affect the final selling price, so now is the time to ensure that all equipment is in good working order, that the facilities are clean and organized, and that accounts receivable and accounts payable are up to date.

Termination of a business is also very common. Many small businesses are extensions of the owner. For example, CPA firms, beauty salons, real estate brokerages, indeed any business that provides personal services, often depend solely on the reputation and personality of the owner. In reality, there is no business to sell. In cases such as these, exit usually involves finishing all outstanding projects, collecting all money due, disposing of all business assets, and finally (if possible) paying off any outstanding debt. Thus, the goals of financial management are to recover all asset value possible, cover any indebtedness, and use the remainder for personal purposes.

Refer to Chapter 20, "Achieving Success in the Small Business," for a more comprehensive discussion of the many issues of business exit.

CHAPTER SUMMARY

LO1 Describe the three types of capital financing and their costs and trade-offs.

- Most people have many assets and financial resources that can be used to finance their business.
- Financing can be in the form of equity, debt, or gifts.
- An entrepreneur's own funds are the first source of financing for most small businesses.
- Forms of business organization can be categorized along two dimensions.
  - How the business is taxed.
  - How much responsibility owners have for the liabilities of the business.

LO2 Explain the characteristics of a business that determine its ability to raise capital.

- Investors put money into a business to make money for themselves.
- Lenders expect a return from making loans, by getting back the amount they loan plus more money in the form of interest.
- Equity investors expect to get back the money they invest plus extra money, a gain on investment.
- To get money from other people, owners must show them that their business probably can make gains for them.
- Financing with equity is expensive and creates problems of control and decision making.
- Other than the owner's own funds, the most common source of capital for established ongoing small businesses is borrowed funds.

LO3 Explain which type of financing is best for your business.

- As debt increases as a percentage of total capital, total cost of capital declines.
- Lower cost of capital results in higher firm value, all other things being held equal.
- Borrowing money increases financial risk because payments on debt must be made as agreed without regard to the cash position of the business.

LO4 Describe the differing needs for financial management at each stage of business life.

- You can use financial ratios to evaluate your business.
- There are four broad categories of financial ratios: activity ratios, profitability ratios, liquidity ratios, and leverage ratios.
- During the start-up phase of a small business the primary financial management need is to obtain sufficient funds to pay for equipment, buildings, inventory, and indeed, all the costs of starting and running a business.
- During the growth phase, the need for financial management increases to pay for added inventory, productive assets, and employees to meet growing levels of business operations.
- During the mature phase of the business, the emphasis of financial management is to build owner wealth, to conserve assets, to match cash inflows to outflows, and to maximize the return on capital assets by making optimal investing decisions.
- Successfully leaving your business requires maximizing its value for your successors by creating effective internal controls and developing business systems to replace your specific skills and knowledge.

KEY TERMS

DISCUSSION QUESTIONS

1. Why does a business require a constant flow of money and capital assets during its existence?
2. Explain how a sole proprietorship differs from a corporation.
3. What things do you need to do to convince an investor to make you a loan or purchase equity in your business?
4. In what ways does accepting outside investment change the ways you manage your business?
5. Why do you have to give up more ownership to get outside investment if your business is risky?
6. Explain why investors prefer investments that pay back sooner to those that pay back later.
7. Name four ways that an investor can receive payment from a business. Describe the advantages and disadvantages of each.
8. Many small business owners prefer to borrow money rather than sell equity. Why is this so?
9. In what ways do the Four Cs of Borrowing differ from the requirements for being able to obtain equity capital?
10. Explain why it is easier to borrow money to buy a semi truck than to purchase rights to a business process.
11. Explain how borrowing money (1) increases firm value and (2) makes more money for a business owner.
12. Explain the differing financial management needs of a small business during the start-up, growth, mature, and exit phases.

EXPERIENTIAL EXERCISES

1. Go to the SBA directory of SBICs **www.sba.gov/content/all-sbic-licensees-state**. Search through the directory, specifically looking for SBICs that will invest in businesses in the industry in which you are interested. Make a chart of the minimum and maximum investments that the SBICs will make, and their requirements to invest. Present your findings to your class.
2. Contact the owner of a business you would like to own. Arrange an interview. Ask how the owner arranged for start-up financing. What sources of financing does the owner use today? Report your findings to your class.
3. Find out if your city has an office of economic development. (Almost every city with a population greater than 100,000 does.) Contact the office and inquire about the programs that it supports. Ask specifically how the office would provide support to you for start-up and operations.
4. Find out if your city or county has any tax abatement economic development zones. What must you do to be able to take advantage of the tax abatement?
5. Make an appointment with a commercial bank loan officer who handles business loans. Ask about the bank's documentation requirements. Determine what commitment, if any, the bank has for making loans to local small businesses. Present your findings to your class.
6. Do a search of *Entrepreneur, Inc.*, and *BusinessWeek Small Business* websites looking for information about businesses that were successful in obtaining financing. Write a report detailing how the businesses arranged financing.

MINI-CASE

VIVID SKY IN 2008

Vivid Sky's sole product, SkyBOX, was designed to provide sports fans in a stadium with continual access to videos, sports statistics, info-graphics (e.g., pitch locations and hit/out locations), maps, chats and concession-ordering capabilities—giving the fan in the stadium "the best seat in the house."

To reach this point, Vivid Sky's founder, Tim Hayden, had achieved numerous developmental milestones since 2003 using nothing but bootstrapped help and his own cash (and very much his own credit cards). The software was ready for deployment on iPhones and other 3G cell phones and laptops/desktops. The back-end programs to run in stadiums to gather and tie together the many data streams and feed them to SkyBOX users were ready to go. What was needed now was $1 million to deploy the programs in the baseball, football, basketball, and hockey stadiums in North America starting with the 2009 baseball season.

Through an innovative product, a positive attitude, and tireless networking, Tim had convinced four Fortune 1000 companies to seriously consider investing $500,000 toward the million-dollar round. The companies were all in the entertainment business, and all saw the SkyBOX as a vehicle for selling content on a new platform, the cell phone. Tim still had to raise $500,000 before any of the big players would put their cash in.

Despite presentations from 2003 to 2007 to angels in St. Louis, Seattle, Chicago, Detroit, and Boston, and even a couple of presentations to Silicon Valley and Seattle venture capitalists, in the end his funding came from the people who knew him the longest and trusted him the most.

Tim's first investors were his parents, who invested $100,000 explaining to Tim that the money was his inheritance. That investment led to a friend of the family investing another $100,000, not based on the business plan, but on knowing Tim, the person. Once these two investors were aboard, a friend of the second investor wanted to get involved so an additional $130,000 was injected into Vivid Sky. When all was counted, Tim had raised $530,000 by the end of April 2008 from six partners who were all one degree separated from Tim.

Each $100,000 was set up as a convertible note (i.e., it starts as a loan, and when funding is complete, converts to stock) worth 2 percent of the stock, for 20 percent of the company total when all $1 million was raised. Twelve percent of the stock was held for the developers and executives, with Tim holding 68 percent. Those percentages put the valuation of the company at $5 million.

It was a great moment for Tim, with continuing successful deployments in baseball and hockey, international corporate sponsors signed up, iTunes Store sales exceeding projections, and four Fortune 1000 companies ready to do their due diligence now that they knew who their potential partners would be.

Sitting back, Tim started wondering, "What could go wrong now?"

CASE DISCUSSION QUESTIONS

1. Why might the investors want a convertible note instead of getting straight stock in a start-up?
2. From the standpoint of the smaller investors, what are the advantages or disadvantages of having a single large investor (like one of the entertainment companies) along with the smaller ones?
3. If the large firms decide not to invest, what are the options available to Tim and how likely will he be to raise the capital needed?
4. Finally, what do you think is the answer to Tim's question—What could go wrong now?

SUGGESTED CASES AND ARTICLES

- The Landlords: Investments in Commercial Real Estate, C-17

Available on Create:

- Fabricare, Inc.
- Circle Electronics Corporation

SUGGESTED VIDEOS

www.mhhe.com/katz4e

Video Case:

- For a written video case and corresponding clip, visit the OLC at www.mhhe.com/katz4e and select "Chapter 15".

- Women Entrepreneurs

eClips Videos:

- Mark Brandt Discusses Options for Funding When You Start as an Entrepreneur
- Mac Cummings Discusses Options for Funding a Start-up

SBTV.com:

- Distributors of Seafood P&G Trading—Credit Line
- Raising Capital: Fundraising for the Risk Averse

STVP Video:

- You Need Too Little Money

Your Business Videos:

- Elevator Pitch: Sunshade
- Elevator Pitch: Entertainment Humvee Pitch

CHAPTER

16

Assets: Inventory and Operations Management

● Curtis Graf's company lost a significant amount in assets when a thief disguised as a worker literally walked onto a construction site and drove off in a backhoe. Managing your business's property can be a challenge. What are some of the security measures Curtis could have put into place that would have deterred this theft? What measures do you think you would need to implement for your dream business?

LEARNING OBJECTIVES

After you complete this chapter, you will be able to:

LO1 Describe techniques to manage short-term assets.

LO2 Calculate the value of the assets in your business.

LO3 Describe techniques for managing fixed assets.

LO4 Calculate ratios used to analyze capital investment decisions.

LO5 Describe the advantages of renting or leasing capital equipment.

LO6 Describe techniques to manage and improve the operations of your business.

Focus on Small Business: Curtis Graf and the Nightmare on Construction Street

It's every contractor's nightmare. You arrive on a job site at six in the morning and find that hundreds of thousands of dollars of construction equipment was stolen overnight. Work comes to a halt. Expenses escalate as workers stand around while you make a frenzied effort to buy, borrow, or rent replacement equipment.

Curtis Graf in the Dallas suburb of Mesquite, Texas, encountered something even worse. A bold thief, in broad daylight, simply walked onto one of his construction sites, started up, and drove away in a $40,000 backhoe. A worker on the site saw the whole thing, but because the thief looked and acted as if he belonged, mistook him for another worker.

"I paid $3,000 to have it burglar-proofed," Curtis said, "but they stole it anyway!"[1]

Most unfortunately, equipment theft is a nightmare that all too often comes true. Despite all efforts—those of law enforcement, the owners, and industry groups—500 pieces of heavy construction equipment are stolen in the United States *each week*. Fewer than 15 percent of the machines stolen are ever recovered.[2]

Curtis did not get his machine back. He faxed a report to the local police and called numerous times to see if it had been found. Curtis said that the only reply from the police was, "We will call you when we find something." He added, "That's short for, 'We don't have time to talk to you anymore.'"[3]

His insurance company was little help, as well. It not only delayed payment as long as it could, but it also canceled his policy, which resulted in his changing insurance carriers for the third time in three years. He did finally receive a payment of $24,000 nearly a year after the machine was stolen, leaving him $16,000 shy of the cost of a replacement.

DISCUSSION QUESTIONS

1. Why do you think that thieves target heavy construction machinery?
2. To what extent do you think that Curtis Graf's negative experience with insurance coverage for theft is commonly encountered by small business owners?
3. Why do you suppose that fewer than 15 percent of stolen heavy machines are ever recovered when the FBI reports that 62 percent of stolen automobiles are recovered?
4. Think of the business that you own or would like to own. How and to what extent would the theft of machinery or equipment be a threat to your business?

Managing Short-Term Assets

LO1 Describe techniques to manage short-term assets.

In many ways, you can think of your business as a collection of assets: things you own that will provide value in the future. The things that you own include the obvious, such as cash, inventory, tools, machinery, buildings, and land. Less obvious things are also owned, such as legal claims to collect money from customers in the future, patents, copyrights, trademarks, expertise, and your reputation.

Because your business *is* its assets, if you allow them to be damaged, lost, stolen, or destroyed, your wealth diminishes. At some point, if your business loses enough value, it will cease to exist. It will be bankrupt, and you will have lost your investment.

Managing your business assets to obtain their maximum value is critical to ultimate business success. Chapter 14 is dedicated to the issues of managing cash, the most liquid of all business assets. This chapter discusses managing the critical short-term assets of accounts receivable and inventory, and managing the essential long-term assets of property, plant, and equipment.

Accounts Receivable

accounts receivable
Money owed to your business by customers who purchased your product on credit.

Accounts receivable are money that is owed to your business by your customers. As was discussed in Chapter 14, relatively few small businesses today provide credit to customers. Current practice is for small businesses to provide credit only by accepting bank-issued credit cards. However, there are still some small businesses, especially those involved in wholesale distribution, that provide direct credit to customers. For these firms, managing receivables is an essential activity.

The Pros and Cons of Offering Credit to Customers

Credit is provided to customers for marketing reasons. Providing credit usually results in higher sales revenue because of increased repeat business. Providing credit also reduces the cost of selling, because it is much less expensive to obtain repeat business than it is to get new customers.

On the downside, selling your product and then allowing customers a month or two to pay has three negative effects that are often overlooked when business owners make the decision to extend credit. First, providing credit delays the receipt of cash. If your small business is like most, you exist in a state of constant cash shortages. Anything that delays receiving cash makes the problems of meeting payrolls and paying suppliers and vendors even worse. This causes the second problem: You must somehow replace the "missing" cash. Most often this means borrowing. Borrowing, of course, is expensive. You spend time to arrange a loan, and then must make regular payments of interest. Third, if you give credit to your customers, sooner or later one of them will not pay. Although you provide credit only to those customers who you believe will pay, despite careful monitoring and despite strenuous collection efforts, eventually someone won't. The reasons why people don't pay can be almost anything, from inability to pay because they have no money to low ethics to outright fraud. Regardless of the cause, your business loses when customers don't pay.

Managing Accounts Receivable to Receive the Greatest Benefit for Your Business

As stated above, providing customer credit usually results in increased sales revenues and lowered transaction costs, which usually more than offsets the costs of interest and uncollectible accounts, resulting in greater profits. To realize this benefit, you must establish and enforce efficient and effective policies and procedures for extending credit. Your goals are to: (1) minimize the time that passes between when a credit sale is made and when the cash is received, and (2) keep the number of bad accounts as low as possible. Exhibit 16.1 provides a list of standards that should always be followed if you provide credit to customers.

Using Your Accounts Receivable as a Source of Financing

You can often get immediate cash from third-party finance companies if you have established and enforced policies to maintain a high quality of receivables. Having high-quality receivables lets you quickly get cash to meet unexpected needs.

You can use your receivables in two ways to quickly lay your hands on cash. First, you can pledge your receivables as collateral for a commercial loan. Depending on the finance company,

EXHIBIT 16.1

Policies for Managing Accounts Receivable

If you want to collect the money owed you from credit sales, you must be very careful to give credit only to those customers who are likely to pay. To make credit work for your business, you must work consistently to collect what you are owed. The following nine policies are minimum standards for managing customer credit:

1. Make an extensive credit check prior to authorizing credit sales to any individual customer.
2. Promptly bill each customer following each credit purchase.
3. Provide cash discounts for making timely payments.
4. Enforce significant late fees and interest on past due accounts.
5. Maintain constant "aging" of accounts to quickly identify customers who become delinquent.
6. Make consistent, vigorous efforts to collect from customers, including dunning letters and phone calls.
7. Discontinue credit sales to customers who become significantly late in paying.
8. File suits and liens against the assets of customers who default on payment.
9. Use your bank as a **lock box** for the receipt of payments.

lock box
A locked receptacle for money, the keys to which are not available to those who physically handle the receptacle; a common example of a lock box is the coin receptacle for parking meters which cannot be opened by the workers who are responsible for collecting the deposited coins.

SMALL BUSINESS INSIGHT

Put Your Bill on the Top of the Pile

Dwight Cooper, CEO of PPR Travel,[4] a nurse-staffing firm in Jacksonville, Florida, was in a quandary. Average time to collect payment on accounts was a crippling 60 days from the time the bill was sent. For two months, Cooper had to cover all the costs of his nurses—wages, benefits, and tax withholdings—as well as his own operating expenses. In effect, Cooper was financing the operations of his customers. On the other hand, if he pressed his clients for payment, he risked creating bad will and perhaps even losing business.

"What should I do?" he asked himself.

Owners of small businesses commonly face the same dilemma. A recent study by REL Consultancy Group of Purchase, New York, found that fully one-third of big businesses are habitually late paying vendors' bills.[5] Sooner or later, if you provide credit to customers, you too will have difficulties in collecting what is due. Customer accounts will slip ever farther into arrears. Past due accounts will accumulate: 90 days, 120 days, even 6 months in arrears. Cooper took a unique approach to his problem. He asked his customers why they paid late and what he could do to help them speed payment.

Dwight Cooper shaved 15 days off his company's average time for collection of bills receivable. Which of his steps could you see yourself imitating in your own business? What ideas might you add in improving your company's collection process?

Even more unusually, he *acted* to implement the things that his customers said would help them pay more quickly. First, he established procedures to ensure that every bill was accurate. Second, he issued a single invoice to each hospital for all nurses provided, rather than sending multiple invoices, one for each nurse provided. Third, he started printing his invoices on blue paper, making them immediately recognizable. Fourth, he began sending a reminder when a customer was only one day late. To take the sting from the reminders, each is addressed by hand.

The results of Cooper's efforts is that average collection time has been reduced from 60 days to 45.[6]

customer payments on pledged receivables may be collected either by you and forwarded to the lender, or may be directly collected by the lender. Second, you can *sell* your receivables to a finance company in a process called **factoring**. A factoring company will usually pay you about 75 to 80 percent of the total amount that can be collected. The factor then collects the receivables. The difference between the gross amount of the receivables and the amount that is ultimately collected is the factor's profit margin. Skill Module 16.1 gives you a chance to work through the ways a factor might structure a deal for you.

factoring
Selling the rights to collect accounts receivable to an entity outside your business.

pledging receivables
Giving a third party legal rights to debts owed your business in order to provide assurance that borrowed money will be repaid.

Pledging receivables to a commercial lender is usually less expensive than factoring. When you pledge receivables, your business is liable only for the borrowed amount and accrued interest on the loan, regardless of the amount that is subsequently collected from your customers. You have the opportunity to collect it all. On the other hand, a commercial lender will loan you only one-half of the amount that can be collected. When you factor receivables, you immediately get 75 to 80 percent of the amount due. But, you forever give up all rights to the factor's discount. Of course, for this amount, the finance company assumes your bad debt risk. If a factor does not collect enough to make a profit, it's the factor's problem, not yours.

SKILL MODULE 16.1

Using Receivables to Raise Immediate Cash

Suppose that you need $50,000 immediately in order to purchase welded steel roof trusses for a building that you have contracted to construct. Normally, you would simply purchase the materials on account from an established supplier, but two things prevent this. First, you have reached your credit limit with your supplier, and the supplier refuses to provide more. Second, your regular supplier is operating at maximum possible output and cannot deliver the trusses within the time required by your contract.

You have found a supplier who will manufacture and deliver the trusses when you need them. However, this supplier does not offer credit. Further, the supplier demands an immediate deposit of one-half of the cost of the trusses, $25,000, with the remaining $25,000 paid on delivery. You have approached your bank, but the bank has refused you a loan because (1) you are at your borrowing limit, and (2) the business with which you have contracted is embroiled in a lawsuit with the bank, and the bank therefore will not accept the contract as collateral.

You have current receivables of $67,000. You have contacted a factor in your area that has proposed two financing deals.

1. The factor will purchase your receivables for 75 percent of their collection value. You will receive 95 percent of the cash immediately, and the factor will retain the remaining 5 percent until all the receivables are collected. If the entire $67,000 is collected, then the remaining money will be paid to you. However, the money being held will be reduced by any amount uncollected at the end of 120 days from the date of the factoring contract.
2. The factor will lend you $54,000 discounted at 12 percent interest for 90 days. You must pledge 100 percent of your receivables as collateral for the loan. The factor will collect your receivables, applying 100 percent of the amount collected against the $54,000 until it is completely repaid, dollar for dollar.

What should you do? Show calculations to support your decision.

Managing Inventory

inventory
Products that are held for sale to customers.

Inventory is a constant, everyday problem for most small businesses. It is the largest current asset that most manufacturing, wholesale, and retail firms have. Manufacturing firms, wholesalers, and retailers simply cannot operate effectively without a minimum level of inventory on hand. Even service firms such as restaurants, beauty shops, automobile garages, plumbing businesses, electrical contractors, sign companies, and so on also have to have some inventory to function efficiently. It is a rare business, indeed, that has no inventory at all.

The amount and type of inventory held for resale is important for small businesses because (1) the supply of inventory and demand of customers cannot be precisely matched at all times, and (2) holding inventory requires a nonproductive cash investment. While inventory sits on your shelves, the money required to buy it is tied up and is not making a return for you.

Determining the Appropriate Level of Inventory

The *right* amount of inventory to keep on hand and the *right* amount of inventory to order at one time is determined by (1) the cost of processing an order, (2) the cost of keeping merchandise in inventory, (3) the cost of lost sales if you run out, and (4) the time it takes to receive inventory after it's ordered. These factors vary widely with the location and type of business. Small retailers and service firms that also sell products (such as a beauty shop) and are located in urban areas usually have easy access to wholesalers and can make frequent small purchases. If the business is in a small town or if it needs hard-to-get resources, then it may have to keep a lot of merchandise on hand. For example, our manufacturer of fine wooden desks, from Chapter 9, may well need hardwood, such as mahogany, teak, or burled maple, which is produced in only a few places and for which there are only a few wholesalers, worldwide. The distribution system for hardwoods is such that, except in very large cities, you have to buy a lot of it at one time and then keep it in stock until it is used.

There is a way to know how much you need to order so that you have an adequate supply of inventory on hand. It is called **economic order quantity (EOQ)**, and it helps you think in terms of ordering costs and carrying costs.

economic order quantity (EOQ)
A statistical technique that determines the quantity of inventory that a business must hold to minimize total inventory cost.

The total cost of keeping inventory is the sum of:

- The cost to buy the inventory.
- The cost to store, protect, and maintain inventory.
- The cost of making an order to purchase inventory.[7]

(See Exhibit 16.2.)

If the cost of carrying inventory were the only factor in making the decision of how much inventory to obtain, it would make the most sense to purchase the smallest number of units possible at any single time. On the other hand, if ordering costs were the only consideration, you would order the largest number that you expect to sell. But if you consider both these *and* purchase price, as we do in Figure 16.1, you get the economic order quantity (EOQ)—the quantity at which the total cost of inventory is minimized.

You do not have to derive the EOQ equation to use it. You can simply substitute your business's projected annual sales demand, cost of placing one order, and cost of holding one unit in inventory

EXHIBIT 16.2
Inventory Costs

Costs of Carrying Inventory	Costs of Ordering Inventory
1. The opportunity cost of the funds invested in inventory	1. The transaction costs of preparing and transmitting the order
2. The cost of keeping inventory secure and in sellable condition	2. Investigating and selecting an appropriate vendor
3. Cost of warehouse or other storage facilities	3. Receiving inventory
a. Utilities	
b. Physically moving inventory into, within, and out of the storage area	
c. Security guards, fencing, access control, etc.	
4. Insurance and taxes on inventory	4. Time required to travel to suppliers to pick up inventory
5. Inventory shrinkage, i.e., loss from waste, spoilage, and theft	5. Inspecting shipments
6. The transaction costs for counting and record keeping	6. Record keeping

FIGURE 16.1

Economic Order Quantity Graph

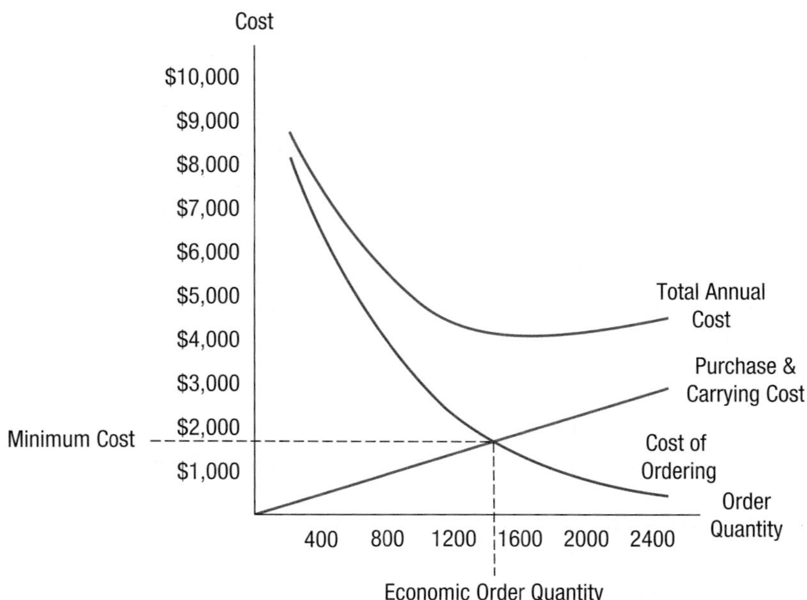

to calculate your unique optimum order quantity and the number of orders that you should place each year. If you are interested, Appendix A of this chapter, entitled "Economic Order Quantity," provides a detailed explanation of how the EOC equation can be used.

Scheduling Ordering and Receipt of Inventory

Determining the right quantity to order is only part of the problem of inventory management. You also need to know *when* to place each order. The EOQ tells us only how many units to order and how many orders to make. It does not tell us *when* to place each order. Deciding when to place an order is determined by (1) the rate of sales and (2) the time required to receive new stock.

optimum stocking level
(Also known as the *reorder point.*) The amount of inventory that results in the minimum cost, when considering the cost of lost sales resulting from running out of stock, the number of units sold per day, and the number of days required to receive inventory.

The **optimum stocking level** (also called *reorder point*) is the amount of inventory that results in the minimum cost, considering (1) the cost of lost sales resulting from running out of stock, (2) the number of units sold per day, and (3) the number of days required to receive inventory.

If everything worked perfectly, you would receive new inventory just as you sold the last unit from the prior order. But in business as in most things in life, things are never perfect. Delivery times vary. Sales volumes are not constant. Sometimes demand exceeds your estimate. Sometimes your estimate exceeds demand.

If you know how demand for a particular product or part changes, you can calculate the probability of being out of stock, given any initial level of inventory and time between receipts of inventory. Computing the reorder point tells you the minimum stock level at which you would place an order. Ordering at that time would ensure that you do not run out of inventory before you run out of customers, and at the same time would minimize your holding unnecessary amounts of stock.

In practice, managers of small businesses rarely attempt such statistical analyses. Rather, they use a heuristic (rule of thumb) developed from experience. Unless you are selling a product that has very high unit costs, such as automobiles, tractors, or airplanes, the effect of having too little inventory is worse than the effect of having too much. For this reason, most businesses deliberately time the placement of orders to keep some extra amount of inventory on hand as **safety stock** to provide for the possibility that sales might be greater than forecast, or that deliveries might be delayed.

safety stock
An amount of inventory carried to ensure that you will not run out of inventory because of fluctuating levels of sales.

One interesting use of optimum stocking levels comes when an entrepreneur starts to use it as a sales tool directed toward customers. If you compute customers' reorder point, you start to have an added reason to contact them and check to find out whether it is time for them to reorder your product.[8]

Just-in-Time Inventory Systems

The cost of owning and holding inventory is far greater than the cost of ordering inventory. As a result, most businesses try to acquire and keep on hand the minimum amount of inventory possible while still being able to meet customer needs. At the extreme, a few businesses hold no inventory at all. Rather, these businesses order and receive inventory only after a customer purchase has been made.

The practice of acquiring inventory only in response to a completed sale is called a **pull-through system**. Once a customer sale is made, an order is placed to either obtain or produce the product. Each stage of the production process operates in response to this order, ultimately reaching back to the acquisition of the raw materials from which the product is made.

pull-through system
A term for just-in-time inventory systems in which product is ordered and placed into production only after a sale has been completed.

The ultimate extension of pull-through processing is **just-in-time inventory** management. A just-in-time (JIT) inventory system attempts to reduce inventory levels to the absolute minimum by (1) accepting inventory only as it is sold, (2) assembling product in the absolute minimum time possible, and (3) shipping product to the customer immediately upon completion. In this way, the three primary inventories of manufacturing, (1) raw materials, (2) work in process, and (3) finished goods, are all kept at the minimum levels possible.

just-in-time inventory
The practice of purchasing and accepting delivery of inventory only after it has been sold to the final customer.

One of the best-known examples of just-in-time manufacturing is Dell Computers,[9] but small businesses use the approach too. Consider Alienware, a maker of high-end PCs for game enthusiasts started by two lifelong friends in Miami, Alex Aguila and Nelson Gonzalez. Their model is simple: "First you pay. Then we build." Having started with only $13,000, they could not afford to spend a lot on inventory. When Alienware receives a computer order from its website, a work order is generated that specifies each individual component to be assembled. Alienware maintains a just-in-time delivery system for needed parts, and leverages its relations with suppliers to ensure speedy delivery. With the parts together, the computer is assembled, tested, and then sent to the packing and shipping department. The use of the JIT approach originally meant that Alienware had no receivables to underwrite, no inventory to depreciate, and no bad debt.[10] Today Alienware still gets the same benefits, but it has grown to over $100 million in annual sales, and even has an arrangement with Best Buy.

Alienware, a subsidiary of Dell, Inc., uses just-in-time inventory management in order to keep costs of its high-end PCs at a reasonable level

Adoption of just-in-time inventory management requires an extreme degree of cooperation with your vendors. The location, scheduling, and transportation of inventory must be as carefully choreographed as is a Broadway dance routine. A single misstep in process can result in the shut down of production and in lost sales. To ensure against this, most businesses that adopt just-in-time inventory management compromise between the theoretical "best way" and the exigencies of real-world business management and maintain some level of safety stock.

The development and growth of the eBay online auction service has provided many small businesses with the ability to practice just-in-time inventory management. Buyers on eBay know that there will be a period of a few days between winning a bid and receiving the product. Numerous eBay sellers use this time to obtain the product. Often, it is shipped directly from the wholesaler to the buyer. This practice is the ultimate just-in-time process: The eBay seller never owns or handles the products being sold. It is called **microinventory** and is a very special form of JIT found in Internet-based businesses[11] such as Alienware.

microinventory
The purchase of inventory only after a sale is made; very typical with Internet firms.

Other Approaches to Inventory Control

There are three approaches to maintaining records of inventory which are very common in small businesses: (1) periodic inventory, (2) perpetual inventory, and (3) point-of-sale systems. Any one of these, applied conscientiously, can help control inventory and inventory costs.

Periodic inventory is the process of physically counting business assets on a set schedule. The time between counts is usually one business year, although periodic inventories may be conducted twice per year, quarterly, monthly, or as often as your business needs require. Most small businesses use the periodic inventory method because it is relatively inexpensive and meets the requirements of both local and federal taxing agencies.

periodic inventory
The process of physically counting business assets on a set schedule.

Perpetual inventory is a system of recording the receipt and sale of each item as it occurs. A perpetual inventory system maintains a constant record of the amounts and value of inventory that

perpetual inventory
A system of recording the receipt and sale of each item as it occurs.

FIGURE 16.2

The Stock Card

Stock Card					
Type of product:			Unit of measurement:		
Date	Reference	Designation	Receipts	Disbursements	Stock in hand
Total to be carried forward					

has been sold and the amounts and value of inventory on hand. Perpetual inventory systems provide you with instant access to accurate inventory records, thus greatly easing the problems of managing inventory levels. The main drawback to using perpetual inventory systems is the high cost in time needed for constant record keeping. (See Figure 16.2.)

bar coding
Obtaining a Universal Product Code number and scan-ready visual tag, and printing it on the product or its packaging. Bar codes can then be scanned and recognized by others.

Bar coding is one method used to reduce the cost of perpetual inventory systems. Bar codes are computer-readable tags that are unique to each item of inventory. The most common bar codes (those that are used every time your retail purchases are scanned at the register) are called universal product codes (UPCs) in the United States and EANs elsewhere. The system is administered by a not-for-profit standards organization, GS1, which has a presence in all large countries, for example, GS1 US (www.gs1us.org). Manufacturers pay an annual fee to participate. Each member of the system licenses a "company prefix," a variable-length code unique to that company. To that prefix, the member then adds on a unique code for each product, creating a number that includes all but one digit of the UPC or EAN. A GS1-provided tool creates a final "check digit," which ensures that the number scans correctly. Each UPC or EAN is therefore unique to the product for which it is issued. As a member of GS1, you have access to the database of all codes and the corresponding manufacturer information. The company maintains an extensive website that explains the system, the use of bar codes, and information necessary to join.

You may also create private bar codes of any number of digits for your internal use. Because the private codes are for your internal use, they do not have to be registered with GS1 US.

To use bar codes effectively in your business, you need (1) a method to create bar codes, (2) a means to print the codes on the items that you wish to track, (3) a scanner that can read the codes, and (4) a computer software program that can interpret the codes and update a database of information associated with each code. There are hundreds, if not thousands, of businesses that provide all the elements necessary for you to use bar codes internally in your business. A search of the Internet's open directory (DMOZ) on the term "bar codes" returned 229 individual listings for firms that provide bar code software and hardware.

point-of-sale (POS) system
Hardware and software combinations that integrate inventory management directly into accounting software.

Point-of-sale (POS) systems comprise both hardware and software to integrate inventory management directly into your accounting system. You are very familiar with POS, whether or not you are aware of being so. The familiar supermarket scanner and the multibutton registers at fast food restaurants are examples of point-of-sale systems. In these systems, every sale is immediately recorded in the accounting system. Revenue is increased and inventory is decreased simultaneously.

Point-of-sale systems have recently become inexpensive enough to be used by small businesses. Today, you may acquire complete systems, including a cash drawer, credit card scanner, bar code scanner, computer, monitor, and software for less than $2,000. There are numerous providers of POS systems, including such well-known companies as Intuit, Hewlett-Packard, Sony, and Panasonic.

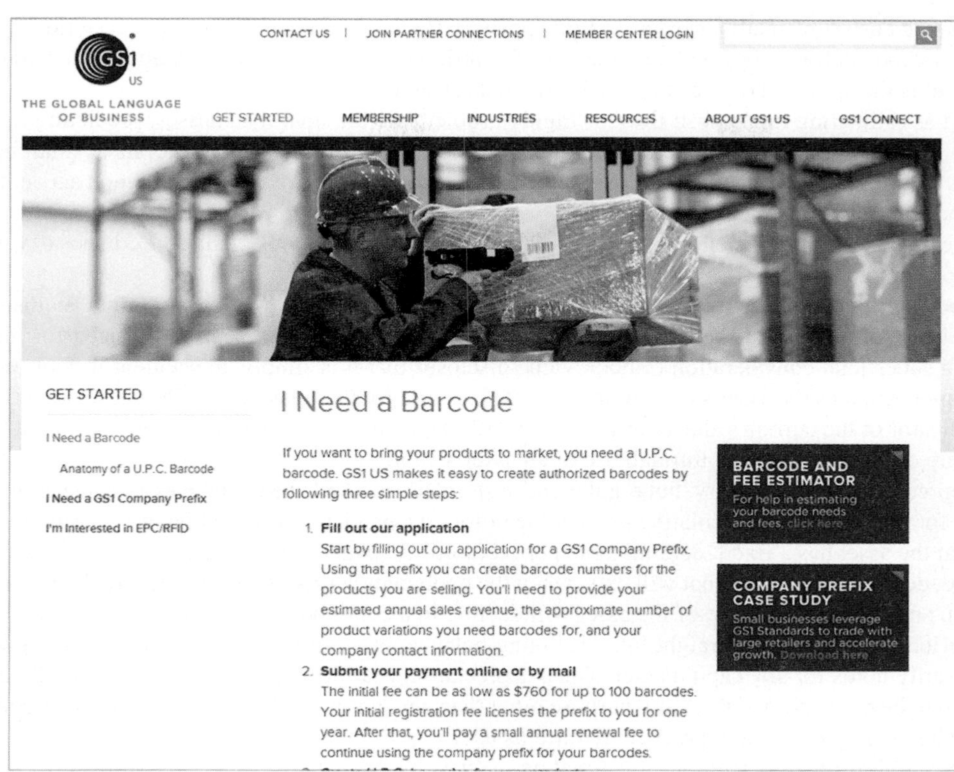

● If it is important to you that your product be recognized universally, be sure to apply with GS1 US in order to receive your product's UPC.

Value of Assets in Your Business

LO2 Calculate the value of the assets in your business.

There are two fundamental kinds of assets in a business—short-term, which includes inventory and accounts receivable, and operating or **capital assets**. The methods for determining the value of each are similar in many respects. Many small businesses need little in the way of capital assets. However, transportation, manufacturing, automobile repair, mining, ranching, and farming businesses all require the use of substantial capital assets in the form of land, buildings, and machinery. The value of such businesses is largely determined by the value of the physical capital assets that they own.

capital assets
Assets that are expected to provide economic benefits for periods of time greater than one year.

The value of assets for use in your business usually far exceeds the value that you might realize if you were to sell them. An example of such an asset is fencing for a ranch or farm. A four-strand barbed wire fence on steel posts can easily cost $4,000 per mile. However, no rancher can ever realize the value of the fence by selling it. At least half the cost of fencing is in the labor required to install it. Once installed, it would cost a similar amount to uninstall. Used barbed wire and posts will bring only a fraction of their cost new. In fact, farmers and ranchers often cannot even give away old fencing; rather, they incur significant costs to safely dispose of it.

Similar situations exist in other businesses such as manufacturing, in which equipment, especially custom-made machinery, is much more valuable as an operating asset than can ever be realized from disposal. Even restaurant equipment such as deep fryers, cooking grills, and ventilation hoods have a much greater value being used in a restaurant than they do sitting in a restaurant supply store.

Determining the Value of Your Operating Assets

The value of operating assets is a function of their utility. In other words, your assets are worth the sum of the future benefits that the assets will produce. It is this definition that is the source of the discounted cash flow methods discussed in Appendix B of this chapter. Discounted cash flow valuation methods define *utility* as being the net cash inflows that the asset will produce. The value of the asset is the sum of these cash flows discounted for time and cost of capital.

Just as estimating future cash flows is highly problematic for small businesses, predicting future utility of capital assets is so uncertain that it is largely a waste of time. Therefore, most small businesses determine the value of capital assets using some combination of the four common accounting methods of assigning asset value.

The four accounting methods to value capital assets are (1) book value, (2) disposal value, (3) replacement value, and (4) fair market value.

book value
The difference between the original cost of an asset and the total amount of depreciation expense that has been recognized to date.

Book value is an accounting term that describes the difference between the original acquisition cost of capital assets and the amount of depreciation expense that has been recognized for them. Even a superficial consideration of book value discloses that it is simply an accident if book value even approximates the asset's economic value. This is true for two reasons: (1) Purchase price is not an indicator of the current value of any asset, and (2) depreciation is not, nor is it intended to be, any measure of the consumption through use of an asset's value.

Depreciation is an arbitrary, but regular and systematic, method used to take asset value as an expense for the purpose of calculating net income or loss. Depreciation is based on three assumptions: (1) that the asset has a fixed, determinable period of utility (called useful life), (2) that the asset has a fixed, determinable value that will exist when the depreciation process is complete (called *salvage value*), and (3) that the value of the asset will decline in a continuous and predictable manner over the period of utility (e.g., straight line, declining balance, etc.). In fact, none of these assumptions necessarily holds for any capital asset. Thus, depreciation is arbitrary. Book value is generally considered to be not very useful for any purpose other than accounting and income taxes, each of which, through law, regulation, and practice, require its use.

disposal value
The net amount realized after subtracting the costs of getting rid of an asset from its selling price.

arm's length transaction
A business deal where the parties have a prior relation or affiliation, but where the business is conducted as if they were unrelated. This approach is done to help guard against potential conflicts of interest.

Disposal value is a method of estimating asset value by calculating the net amount that you would realize were you to sell the asset in an **"arm's length" transaction**. This is accomplished by subtracting from the estimated sale price the estimated costs of selling, disassembly, shipping, indeed, all costs necessary to dispose of the asset. Disposal value is the residual of many estimates. At best, you must consider the value to be a rough approximation. At worst, the value may hold no relationship to the asset's unknown, "true" economic value.

replacement value
The cost incurred to replace one asset with an identical asset.

Replacement value can be determined with much greater confidence than can be given to either book value or disposal value. In effect, you are estimating the value of a currently owned capital asset by determining the cost that would be incurred to replace it with an identical asset. Unlike disposal value, in which you must estimate an essentially unknowable selling price for a used asset, replacement value is based on determining the price of either a new asset or a used asset for which there is an organized market. For many assets, such as machine tools and vehicles, this is done quite easily by obtaining quotes from dealers. Custom-made assets require a bit more work, but still can be accurately priced through an engineering approach.

The primary advantage of replacement value is that you can be quite confident of its accuracy. The disadvantage is that the price of a new asset is often much greater than the price of an essentially identical asset already in your business.

fair market value
The price at which goods and services are bought and sold between willing sellers and buyers in an arm's-length transaction.

Fair market value lies somewhere between disposal value and replacement value. Fair market value is an attempt to determine the price that the asset would bring, in its current location and condition, in an arm's length transaction between a willing buyer and a willing seller. In contrast to disposal value, fair market value is assigned from the point of view of the buyer, and thus includes the selling price and all costs to install, test, and prepare the asset for productive use.

The appropriate valuation method is largely determined by the purpose for which the valuation is being made. As stated above, laws, regulations, and the requirements of GAAP require that book value be used for financial reporting and income tax purposes.

For any other purpose, you may use the valuation method that best meets your needs. If you are offering assets as collateral, lenders are most interested in disposal value, as that best approximates the amount that would be realized if the asset were repossessed. If you are considering an investment opportunity, disposal value provides an estimate of the timing and amounts of cash flows that can be used for net present value and internal rate of return calculations. If you are offering your business for sale, as the seller of a business you would view disposal value as a "lower limit" for the selling price because it approximates the amount that would be realized were the business to be liquidated. On the other hand, potential buyers and investors are most interested in replacement value. Replacement value sets an "upper level" for the value of your business assets as an approximation of the cost that would be incurred to equip a start-up business.

Determining the Value of Inventory

If your business holds inventory for sale, you are faced with the problem of determining its value. The value that you assign to inventory sold and on hand affects (1) the amount of profit that you recognize and (2) the value of your business.

Inventory valuation begins with knowing *how much* of *what* you are holding. All too often owners of small businesses purchase inventory items which are stored out of sight. These items somehow never get used or sold. Over time such "forgotten" items accumulate, tying up scarce funds. At the minimum, you should conduct a **physical inventory**—a type of periodic inventory—at least once each year, identifying and counting all items that your business owns. Items that have not been sold or used for significant periods of time should be disposed of to free their value for productive use. Slow-moving and dated inventory may be disposed of by discounting or "dumping" it to overstock resellers such as Big Lots, Dollar Stores, or junk dealers.

inventory valuation
Determination of the amount of assets held by the firm for sale or production.

physical inventory
A count of all the inventory being held for sale at a specific point in time.

SMALL BUSINESS INSIGHT

JAMES P. SMITH OF SIGNGRAPHICS, INC.

James P. Smith, owner of Signgraphics, Inc., of Blue Springs, Missouri, had just learned that a contract to produce signs for a chain of convenience stores had been lost to a competitor. As a result, Signgraphics was now stuck with twenty 8 ft × 12 ft polycarbonate plastic sign faces. The faces could not be used for any other purpose because they were vacuum molded and internally painted with the logo and name of the store chain. Each sign face, molded and painted, cost over $1,300. That meant Signgraphics had $26,000 of scrap.

Signgraphics, as would most small businesses, would be severely damaged by such a loss. Something had to be done, and done quickly.

Biting the bullet, James called the competitor who had just won the contract. The competitor quickly agreed to purchase the faces for $22,000. Although still a painful loss, $4,000 was not great enough to threaten the survival of the business. In fact, Signgraphics continued to be successful for an additional four years until the business was sold to yet another competitor in the area.

Sooner or later, you are likely to be stuck with surplus, slow-moving, or obsolete inventory. If you are like most entrepreneurs, you'll be tempted to keep the inventory, "just in case you find a use for it." Over time, such surplus inventory can build up to astonishing levels, tying up money that could and should be used in the business.

A better strategy is to constantly monitor the use of inventory and quickly dispose of any "dated" items before they become obsolete or otherwise unsellable. Such inventory items may, as in the case of Signgraphics, find a ready buyer in a competitor. If you are a wholesaler or retailer, you can offer steep discounts to existing customers. You may sell to a company that specializes in buying surplus and distressed items. Finally, you may, as a last resort, scrap such inventory, and take its acquisition cost as a business deduction against profits.

Signgraphics had to make a tough call on selling their extra sign faces inventory to a competitor. Having an inventory handling approach that allows for quick and easy adaptation is key to successfully managing your small business. What are some ways you think owners can build flexibility into their inventory management procedures?

Once you know what inventory you have, you can then assign it a value. One of the unpleasant surprises that many small business owners experience is the discovery that inventory is often worth far less than it cost to acquire. Inventory loses value in many ways. It can lose value because of changes in fashion or changes in technology. Some inventory items, especially food items, spoil with the passage of time. Some things get broken, dented, scratched, dirty, or otherwise shopworn. Determining the value of items being held for sale is essential to efficient inventory management.

The value of inventory items held in stock is highly problematic, especially when prices are rapidly changing. You must answer the questions, "Is inventory worth what I paid for it? Is it worth what I must pay to replace it? Or is it worth only the amount for which I can sell it?" Any of these methods, **acquisition cost, replacement cost**, or fair market value, respectively, can reasonably be used to determine the value of your inventory. However, your choice of valuation method affects the profit you recognize and thus the amount of taxes you must pay.

acquisition cost
The total cost of acquiring an asset, including such costs as purchase price, transportation, installation, testing, and calibrating in order to ready it for its first productive use.

replacement cost
The total cost of replacing an asset with an essentially identical asset.

If you assign a high value to inventory, you increase the amount that you deduct for cost of goods sold which results in decreased sales margin and reported profit. Less reported profit means less will be paid in income taxes. However, lowered reported profits makes your business worth less to investors, lenders, and potential buyers. On the other hand, if you assign the lowest acceptable value to inventory, you will make the results of operations of your business look better, but at the price of paying increased income taxes.

Property, Plant, and Equipment

LO3 Describe techniques for Managing fixed assets.

The importance of the issues of the acquisition and maintenance of real estate, buildings and machinery varies among businesses. If your business is wholesale or retail merchandising, the issues of **property**, **plant**, and **equipment** (PPE) are most likely of relatively minor importance to your success. If your business is manufacturing, mining, farming, ranching, or transportation, your greatest investments and your greatest costs are consumed by land, buildings, and machinery. Obtaining, maintaining, and efficiently using these expensive capital assets is critical to your success.

property
A general term for real estate, but it can also be applied as a legal term for anything owned or possessed.

plant
A general term for the facilities of a business.

equipment
Machinery, tools, or materials used in the performance of the work of the business.

All capital assets cause you to incur four costs over time: (1) the cost of acquiring the asset, (2) the cost of owning the asset, (3) the cost of operating the asset, and (4) the cost of disposing of the asset.

It is common for owners of small businesses to consider only the first of these costs in making an investment decision. This narrow focus on acquiring an asset is unfortunate because although you make such decisions infrequently, the ramifications of the decisions are critical to your success. Making a correct decision will increase the value of your business, and thus your wealth. Making an inappropriate decision will lead to suboptimal returns, even to your business going bankrupt. The probability of making a good capital investment decision is greatly increased when all the costs of the asset, called **whole of life costs**, are included in the decision process. In Skill Module 16.2 you will analyze the whole of life costs for one asset.

whole of life costs
The sum of all costs of capital assets, including acquisition, ownership, operation, and disposal.

Acquisition cost of a capital asset is the sum of *everything* that you spend to acquire and prepare the asset for its first productive use. Thus, the cost of engineering to specify the details of the asset, purchase price, shipping, insurance during shipping, setup, testing, and interest on any borrowed funds are all accumulated to determine the cost of the asset.

Costs of owning an asset include interest on funds borrowed and the opportunity costs of funds invested to acquire it. Costs of ownership also include insurance on the asset, property taxes, value of the space that the asset occupies, and the cost of record keeping and security for the asset.

cost of owning
Cost incurred in financing, insuring, taxing, or tracking an asset.

Costs of operating the asset include the energy the asset consumes, maintenance, loss of economic value resulting from wear and obsolescence, and any necessary training of operators.

cost of operating
The direct cost incurred in using an asset for the purpose for which it was intended.

Costs of disposition are composed of the value of the activities necessary to get rid of the asset. Such costs include meeting environmental regulations, disassembly, advertising, commissions, shipping, insurance, and fees. The cost of meeting environmental requirements can be huge for some assets. For example, it is nearly impossible to find affordable means to dispose of radioactive tools, anything that contains mercury or lead (e.g., computer monitors), electric motors and transformers that contain polychlorinated biphenyls (PCBs),[12] and personal computers which contain significant quantities of several poisonous heavy metals.[13]

cost of disposition
Cost incurred in the activities necessary to get rid of an asset.

Understanding Whole of Life Costs for Capital Budgeting

SKILL MODULE 16.2

You are the owner of the Real Wood Furniture Company. Business has grown to the point that a bottleneck has formed at the point where the 4-ft × 12-ft lumber-core plywood sheets are cut to finish size. You have identified two automated panel saws that have identical capacity sufficient not only to eliminate the bottleneck, but also to be able to keep up with projected growth for the next 10 years.

Each machine has a useful life of 10 years. However, each will have to be rebuilt at the end of the seventh year to be able to get the final three years of use. At the end of 10 years, either machine will be technologically obsolete, and thus you will have to dispose of it at that time. Estimated cost data for each saw are shown in the chart at the left.

Real Wood Furniture Co.
Manufacturers of Fine Wood Desks
Data Concerning Automatic Panel Saw

	Kyrobi	**Delta**
Purchase price	$110,000	$80,000
Shipping	3,500	1,000
Installation	6,500	4,000
Testing	3,500	4,500
Total acquisition cost	$123,500	$89,500
Maintenance cost per year	$12,000	$14,900
Energy costs per year	8,500	13,000
Rebuilding in seventh year	25,000	35,000
Disposal cost end of tenth year	4,850	6,000

1. Examine the data in the chart. Without doing any specific mathematical analysis, state which saw you would purchase, and why you made your choice.
2. Assume that every desk to be produced for the next 10 years will be made from wood that is cut by the saw that is purchased. Sales for the year the saw is purchased are projected at $260,000 and are expected to increase by 15 percent per year for the next 10 years. Use Real Wood Furniture Co.'s cost of capital to perform a discounted cash flow analysis of purchasing each saw. Now which saw would you choose, and why?
3. **Advanced topic:** Assume that Real Wood Furniture Co. is profitable and will pay 30 percent income taxes each year of the life of the saw purchased. Repeat the discounted cash flow analysis, only this time make adjustments for the effect of income taxes. Now which saw would you choose, and why?

The Capital Budgeting Decision

capital budgeting
The process of deciding among various investment opportunities to create a specific spending plan.

LO4 Calculate ratios used to analyze capital investment decisions.

Eventually small businesses get to the point where they can begin to make investment choices—do you open a new location or expand the one you have? Do you buy new machinery or invest in real estate? The process of deciding among various investment opportunities to create a specific spending plan is called **capital budgeting**. The goal of capital budgeting is to improve the quality of decisions about how to best use the scarce resources of the business. Capital budgeting works by determining the costs and benefits of each alternative investment, such as machinery or real estate. The question that must be answered to make a decision is, "Which of the available investment alternatives provides the greatest benefit relative to the cost of the investment?"

To do this, the alternatives are simultaneously compared by examining various financial ratios or by applying the concepts of the time value of money. The time value of money is the concept that a dollar received today is worth much more than is a dollar to be received at some time in the future.

The two most commonly used financial ratios for comparing investment alternatives are (1) **payback period** and (2) **return on investment (ROI)**. There are also two significantly more complex approaches called *net present value (NPV)* and *internal rate of return (IRR),* which are discussed in Appendix B of this chapter. Each of these measures has both advantages and disadvantages. Not one of them is appropriate in all circumstances, although each can be useful in the capital budgeting process.

payback period
The amount of time it takes a business to earn back the funds it paid out to obtain a capital asset.

return on investment (ROI)
A capital budgeting equation used to measure the relationship between initial investment and the profits that are expected to be received from making the investment.

To illustrate each of these investment analysis tools, consider the following: The owner of a sign shop has the opportunity to contract with a rapidly growing franchise operator to install signs at all new locations. To be able to complete this contract, she will need to invest in a heavy truck and a truck-mounted crane. She has reduced the decision alternatives to two different truck-crane combinations: a Skyhook 85-foot heavy-duty crane with a service ladder mounted on a Ford diesel truck and a Sponco 87-foot medium-duty crane with a service bucket and remote controls mounted on a GMC diesel truck. The cost of the Ford-Skyhook combination, ready for use, will be \$150,000. The cost of the GMC-Sponco combination will be \$185,000. Each truck and crane will have a useful life of 10 years.

Each crane has certain advantages and disadvantages. The Skyhook crane can lift 2,000 pounds to its full extension height. However, it does not have remote controls, and thus requires a crew of two people. The Sponco can lift only a 950-pound load, but its service bucket with remote controls allows it to be used by a single operator as a "cherry picker" to lift the operator into position, obviating the need (and dangers) of working from a ladder. Based on these facts, the owner has estimated future cash flows that will be provided by each alternative.

The owner has determined the following criteria to aid in making a decision:

1. The business's weighted average cost of capital is 20 percent.
2. The maximum acceptable payback period is four years.
3. Depreciation is recognized using a **straight line for a useful life of 10 years**.
4. Salvage value of each combination will be \$0 (zero).
5. Cash flows and profits will differ by the tax effect of depreciation recognized.[14] Depreciation for the Ford-Skyhook is \$15,000 a year, for the GMC-Sponco \$18,500 a year.

straight line for a useful life of 10 years
Depreciation is computed using a straight line method over 10 years, so an asset would lose 10% of its value each year.

Payback Period

The payback period measure is a statement of how much time must pass before your business receives back the same number of dollars in cash flow as you must pay out to obtain a capital asset. Only cash flows are considered.

Two decision rules are applied in choosing from among alternative investments:

1. Accept only those alternatives for which the time required to recoup the original investment is equal to or less than a maximum allowable time determined by management.
2. Accept the alternative with the shortest payback period among those that meet the first criterion.

Consider the following example: Using the data in Table 16.1, we can calculate that the Ford-Skyhook combination pays back in 2 years and 11 months. In the first year, \$35,000 is paid back. Another \$60,000 is received in year 2, leaving \$55,000 to be recovered. If we assume that the money is received evenly across the year, then it will take 55,000/60,000, or 0.917, of one year to recoup the final \$55,000.

Using the same method, we find that the GMC-Sponco combination will require 3 years and 2.7 months to pay back its initial investment.

Following the decision rules, we find that both alternatives meet the minimum hurdle of paying back in four or less years. However, the Ford-Skyhook alternative payback period is 3.7 months shorter, and thus we would choose this alternative.

The main advantage to using the payback period analysis is its simplicity. Also, it allows easy comparison of alternatives that are dissimilar in magnitude of cash flows and overall project life. The primary disadvantages of the payback method are that (1) it disregards the time value of money and (2) it disregards all cash flows that occur after the payback period. These disadvantages often result in managers making suboptimal investment decisions.

Rate of Return on Investment

Rate of return on investment (ROI) is a measure of the relationship between the initial investment and the profits that are expected to be received from making the investment. The calculation is straightforward:

$$\text{ROI} = (\text{average annual profits})/(\text{average investment})$$

TABLE 16.1 Data for Capital Budgeting Decisions

Estimated Cash Flows and Accounting Profits of Each Alternative

	Ford-Skyhook		GMC-Sponco	
Years	**Cash Flows**	**Accounting Profits**	**Cash Flows**	**Accounting Profits**
0	$ (150,000)		$ (185,000)	
1	35,000	20,000	45,000	26,500
2	60,000	45,000	62,500	44,000
3	60,000	45,000	62,500	44,000
4	65,000	50,000	67,500	49,000
5	70,000	55,000	77,500	59,000
6	75,000	60,000	87,500	69,000
7	75,000	60,000	92,500	74,000
8	80,000	65,000	95,000	76,500
9	80,000	65,000	95,000	76,500
10	80,000	65,000	100,000	81,500

As with the payback method, two decision rules are applied to choose from among alternative investments:

1. Accept only those alternatives for which the return on investment is equal to or greater than the business's weighted average cost of capital, which is the expected average future cost of funds and is discussed in Chapter 15.
2. Accept the alternative with higher ROI among those that meet the first criterion.

We can then calculate the ROI of each alternative:

	Ford-Skyhook	GMC-Sponco
$\dfrac{\text{(Sum of profits/length of project)}}{\text{(initial investment + salvage value)/2}}$	$\dfrac{(530{,}000/10)}{(150{,}000 + 0)/2}$	$\dfrac{(600{,}000/10)}{(185{,}000 + 0)/2}$
	$= 0.707$	$= 0.649$

Both alternatives meet the first decision rule as the ROI of each exceeds the business's weighted average cost of capital of 20 percent. We accept the Ford-Skyhook alternative because it has the greater ROI of the two.

Return on investment analysis has two advantages: (1) It is easy to calculate, and (2) it relies on accounting information with which business owners, lenders, and investors are comfortable. ROI's disadvantages are (1) profits are not the same as cash, and (2) the method ignores the time value of money.

Net Present Value

Calculation of net present value (NPV) and its application to this investment decision is explained in Appendix B, beginning on page 549.

Rent or Buy

LO5 Describe the advantages of renting or leasing capital equipment.

It is often not necessary, or even advisable, to purchase capital assets. Many capital assets for which there is an active market, such as real estate, trucks, tractors, and airplanes, can easily be obtained through rental agreements.

Renting such assets provides several important advantages. First, renting requires little or no cash investment on your part. Purchasing, however, often requires that your business be able to pay cash of 20 percent or more of the purchase price in order to be able to borrow funds to finance your purchase. Second, renting usually does not require an extensive (and expensive) application process as does borrowing money. Third, renting usually protects you from unexpected costs of repairs. If you are renting a truck for your business and it breaks down, you can quickly obtain a replacement vehicle. Fourth, renting capital equipment provides an easy method to avoid ongoing costs if business conditions change. If a sudden loss of business makes the asset uneconomical, you can return it to its owner, thereby avoiding the costs of ownership, operation, and disposal.

Making the decision to rent rather than to buy an asset provides a partial answer to the problem of projecting future cash flows. You may make the same analysis that you would in order to decide to buy. However, in making this analysis, renting provides two advantages over buying: (1) The exact amount and timing of cash **outflows** is specified in the rental contract, and (2) renting provides a fall-back position should your projections prove to be incorrect. If actual cash flows fall short of your projections, you may be able to return the rented property, avoiding future rent payments. If you still wish to pursue the opportunity despite lower cash flows than expected, you can make provisions for a less expensive alternative. Should actual cash flows exceed your projections, you have the options of either purchasing the rented asset or returning the asset and purchasing a higher-capacity replacement.

outflow
Funds being paid to others by the firm.

The disadvantages to rental are, first, you do not have an ownership position. The value of a rented asset does not ever show up on your business's balance sheet. Should you need capital, rented assets cannot be used as collateral to obtain borrowed funds. Second, rental requires that you make regular, timely payments. If you own an asset, you may be able to exercise some control over cash outflows for costs of ownership and operations, such as maintenance and upgrades. These options do not exist for rented assets. Third, the number of dollars paid in rent usually exceeds the number of dollars you would spend to own the asset. The owner of the asset you are renting bears the risk of breakdowns, obsolescence, and disposal costs. Because of these risks, the owner must receive a premium over the costs that you would incur if you were to buy the asset.

Financing with Leases

A lease is simply a rental agreement that specifies a minimum period of time for which you must make rental payments. Lease periods range from as short as a few days to 99 or more years, and leases can include other sorts of provisions or specifications for how the business deal or the leased property is to be handled. Thus, as lessee, you may agree to bear the costs of maintenance, insurance, and taxes on leased assets. Alternatively, any of these costs may be born by the lessor. Leases provide a middle ground between renting and owning assets.

There are two basic types of leases, operating leases and capital leases. The two types of leases differ primarily in how the property is disposed of at the end of the lease period.

operating lease
A long-term rental in which ownership of the asset never passes to the person paying for the lease.

Operating leases are leases that are similar to renting. In an operating lease, ownership of the asset never passes to you as the lessee. At the end of the lease period, you either return the asset to its owner, or you may purchase the asset at its then current fair market value.

All other aspects of maintaining and operating the asset can be negotiated between lessor and lessee. Either party may be contractually responsible for maintenance and operating costs.

capital lease
A lease in which at the end of the lease period the asset becomes the property of the lessee, possibly with an additional payment.

Capital leases are leases that are essentially the same as buying the asset. At the end of the lease period the asset becomes property of the lessee, either without any additional payment or by the lessee paying a nominal amount. The test to determine if a lease is a capital lease, rather than an operating lease, is the existence of provisions for title of the asset to pass to the lessee at a price less than the asset's fair market value.

The benefits of leasing are numerous. First, you can usually obtain a very low down payment. Second, the process of negotiating and closing a lease is usually less complicated and expensive than making a purchase and obtaining borrowed funds. A third benefit is that it is usually much easier for you to replace leased assets than it is to replace assets you own.

Because actual ownership of the asset remains with the lessor until the provisions of the lease contract are fulfilled, the owner is not faced with the expensive and time consuming process of repossession. As owner of the asset, the lessor may simply take it back, should you default on the contract. Because of this, a lessor is less concerned with your ability to pay than is a lender and is willing to accept a lower initial investment from you in return for higher periodic lease payments. Similarly, because the lessor is in the business of acquiring and disposing of assets, the lessor assumes the responsibility of disposing of obsolete assets and providing new ones.

The primary disadvantage of leasing is that it usually costs more than would purchasing. A secondary disadvantage is that leased assets are usually subject to numerous restrictions on how they may be used, maintained, and disposed of. Restrictive lease covenants are intended to provide protection to the owner by preventing the lessee from allowing the asset to lose value through misuse, neglect, or abuse. A typical lease restriction is a prohibition on driving or flying leased transportation equipment across an international border. Were you the lessee of a business airplane, such a provision could become a serious inconvenience should you develop business that requires you to regularly travel to Monterrey, Mexico, and no airline offers such service from your home city.

Fractional Ownership and Other Forms of Joint Ventures

A less used method of reducing the costs and risks of acquiring capital assets is the process of joint venturing. A joint venture is simply a formalized partnership between two or more businesses for some specific purpose. Joint ventures are quite common among medium to large businesses and are growing among small businesses.[15]

Joint venturing makes economic sense when each party to the venture has limited use of an expensive asset or faces major investments that could be sidestepped by partnering with another firm that already has made that investment. One area in which joint ventures are relatively common among small businesses is the ownership of airplanes. Airplanes are quite expensive. Even a 30-year-old Beech King Air turbo prop airplane can easily sell for $1 million. Although old, and by some standards obsolete, a King Air can still produce more than 6 million seat miles per year: the equivalent of 1,600 transcontinental trips. Very few small businesses need even a fraction of the transportation capacity produced by such an airplane. Because of these facts, it is common for airplanes to be owned by partnership arrangements among several businesses that share the costs proportionate to their use of the plane.

Recently, some leasing companies have created an ownership structure similar to joint ventures, called *fractional ownership*. These companies offer buses, airplanes, and yachts under arrangements in which a small business may buy only that share that it can reasonably use during the course of business. In this manner, many small businesses now have access to business jets by having purchased as little as one-sixteenth of the ownership rights.

"Once bought, forgotten" might be the sort of saying that reminds all entrepreneurs about why managing assets is critical to being successful in managing a small business and its finances. Whether inventory or operating assets, most firms have substantial value tied up in the assets of the business. It is possible to make sure that these assets are being managed to be financially useful, and this chapter outlines the techniques—ranging from simple to complex—to do that. The simple techniques of inventory tracking and management can be easily grasped and implemented in a wide variety of settings. The more statistically driven approaches are increasingly workable, because they use functions built into spreadsheets or accounting programs' inventory routines. Like so much in small business, asset management works if you take the time to do it or have it done for you.

Managing Operations

LO6 Describe techniques to manage and improve the operations of your business.

No matter what your business is, the functions of management are always the same: planning, organizing, staffing, directing, and controlling. You and your managers must establish the goals and objectives of your business. Once you have a set of coherent goals, you must make plans on how to attain them. You must organize and direct your business to attain the desired goals. You must also analyze the working of your business to be able to control it and to correct any variations from the planned procedures in order to reach the predetermined goals. These functions interact and it takes skill to coordinate them so you can accomplish your business goals, often through the efforts of others.

Although the preceding paragraph was easy to write, and is easy to read, putting it into practice is far from easy. You must be able to determine which management functions are most important and be able to organize them by priority. Although all five functions are important parts of a manager's job, just how imperative each is varies with changes in the business, such as during the stages of a product life cycle. One simplifying fact for operations management is the fact that operations management is concerned primarily with directing and controlling. Planning, organizing, and staffing are primarily the responsibility of executive management.

Operations management is focused on all of the activities of the business, such as producing product and moving it to customers. Throughout the book, you have seen examples of the operations management decisions small business owners must make. These include managing your time in Chapter 5, optimizing your business's value chain in Chapter 7, managing the product and service life cycles in Chapter 9, and optimizing the location and physical layout of your business

SMALL BUSINESS INSIGHT

Cabot Mills: A Turnaround Story

Ric Cabot was wrestling with a common business problem: competition from foreign suppliers who had much lower costs than Rick's business, Cabot Mills, could ever attain. Long-time customers were choosing other suppliers. Sales and profits were on an unsustainable downward trend.

Cabot had few choices. He could close the business. He could contract with sock knitters in China or Thailand. Or he could somehow come up with an idea that would allow him to continue making socks in Vermont.

Few hosiery firms remain in the United States, and even fewer of these are in New England. In fact, Cabot Mills is the only sock maker left in Vermont. Cabot was primarily a custom manufacturer, producing socks for several apparel firms including Bass Shoes, Eddie Bauer, L.L. Bean, and Orvis. But, by the early 2000s most of Cabot's former customers had outsourced their sock knitting to offshore firms, primarily in China and Thailand.[16]

in Chapter 11. Similarly, much of this chapter deals with optimizing the use of your assets, like inventory and property. Along the way we have mentioned the kinds of strategic operational choices owners have to make about product design, process choice, capacity, quality, productivity, technology, workforce, and job design. The overriding goal of operations management is to be constantly improving the organization, through a more efficient use of resources and through improved or expanded service to customers, where "customer" means the next process as well as the final, external user. Because there is an operations element in every function of your business, people in all jobs should work together to improve their own operation efficiency.

Market research conducted for Cabot disclosed that there was a sizeable percentage of people engaged in outdoor work and outdoor sports who were less than satisfied with the socks that were then available. To that end, Cabot developed an entire new line of premium socks made solely from marino wool, nylon, and Lycra.[17]

"Darn Tough has been a fantastic product for the company all over the United States and Canada. It's our brand and it will propel the company into the fourth generation. It's the most sustainable thing we do. We have wonderful private-brand customers, but the most important thing is to produce our own brand," Ric Cabot said.[18]

In fact, the Darn Tough Vermont sock has been way more successful than even the Cabots hoped. In the first quarter of 2012, Cabot Mills reported all-time record profits on gross sales that are fully 260 percent higher than in the same quarter of 2010.[19]

Inputs into Your Business

The **inputs** of a business are determined by its objectives. Your business objectives establish which raw materials are needed in what quantities. Your objectives will determine whom and how many people you must hire. For you to keep your business running smoothly, you must have information (feedback) concerning the essential processes that comprise your production system. This is as true for service industries, as it is for retail and manufacturing.

inputs
The materials, labor, and energy put into the production of a good or service.

Business Operations Comprise Converting Time and Materials into Service and Products

Business, to a great degree, comprises **operations,** or taking materials, the time of workers, and the investment of owners and changing these things into a desired product or service. This is illustrated in Figure 16.3. The specifics of your manufacturing, marketing, and distribution must be known in detail. You must also have some understanding of the ways your employees act and react. Some people will be interested in all the fine details. Others will be indifferent to the details as long as the

operations
The process of transforming materials, labor, and energy into goods or services.

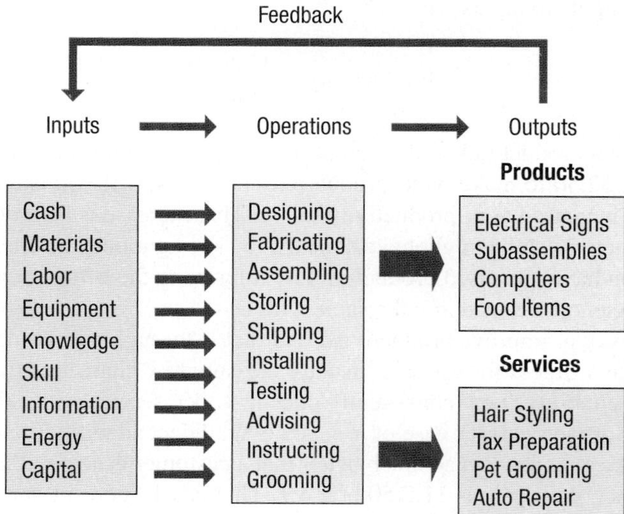

FIGURE 16.3
The Operations Process

desired result is obtained. For example, a manager may not know or care about the details of how a report is created and circulated. He or she is interested only in the information that the report contains. On the other hand, your accountant will be concerned with the details of each step: gathering data, preparing the report, and communicating it to those who need it.

Business Outputs

outputs
The service or product that is produced for sale.

What constitutes the **outputs** of your business depends upon what your business is. The output for a Liberty Tax franchise is completed income tax returns. The output for an automobile garage is properly repaired cars. Generally speaking, output is the quality and quantity of goods and services produced, those things that produce revenue for your business. The entire system of your business should be designed to produce something that is desired in a market. Business customers of all types want goods and services that will make them more efficient, more effective, or more profitable. Individuals as customers will buy those things that provide greater comfort, improved health, enhanced entertainment, etc.

Feedback

feedback
The process of communicating within or to the organization about how the outputs worked or were received.

Any control system must have **feedback**. All inputs, material and labor, must be compared with a predetermined standard. If there is variation between the output and the standard, management action can be undertaken to correct the situation.

A business that has multiple systems requires complicated feedback. Information must be communicated among all managers and employees who are part of the system. Operations control depends upon three types of feedback: (1) informational feedback, (2) corrective feedback, and (3) reinforcing feedback. Informational feedback is just that: information about the processes of your business. Corrective feedback is evaluative and judgmental. It comprises a value judgment about processes and behaviors. Inefficient work processes and undesirable employee behaviors are provided with various correctional actions. The manufacturing line may be redesigned. Misbehaving employees may be given training or punishment. Punishment ranges from a "dressing down" to termination of employment. On the other hand, reinforcing feedback rewards efficient processes and desired employee behaviors and can range from a simple statement, "Good job," to tangibles such as money or paid time off.

Measuring and Improving Productivity

productivity
The ratio measure of how well a firm does in using its inputs to create outputs, literally, productivity is outputs divided by inputs.

The essence of production management is to ensure that the factors of production, materials, labor, machinery, land, and capital, are used efficiently to produce your business's product or service. Simply put, the major outcome of operations and production management is improved **productivity**. Productivity applies what you have just learned about inputs and outputs, because productivity is simply the ratio of outputs to inputs, or:

$$\text{Productivity} = \frac{\text{Outputs}}{\text{Inputs}}$$

efficiency
The comparison of productivity ratios to see the extent that an organization has generated more outputs with fewer inputs.

quality
Quality is a product's or service's fitness for use, measured as durability, reliability, serviceability, style, ease of use, and dependability.

If you are creating a product (a.k.a. the output of your production process) that you can sell for \$10 and it costs you \$2.50 to make, your productivity ratio is 4:1. If you can cut your production cost to \$2, you have increased your productivity to 5:1. That increase is hard dollar proof you have improved your productivity. You might have done this by saving money on energy or raw materials or labor. In short, you have increased productivity by improving the **efficiency** of your production process—where efficiency means doing the same with less.

There is another way to improve productivity, and that is through improving **quality**. Quality is a product's or service's fitness for use. It is usually measured by characteristics such as durability (how long it lasts), reliability (how consistently does it work), serviceability (how easily can it be repaired), style (how attractive is it), ease of use, and overall dependability (how much you can rely on it). If you can make your product so much better that a customer is now willing to pay \$11 for the new improved product, your gain is 11:2.50 or 4.4:1. That is a 10 percent gain in productivity due to quality improvements.

Outsourcing to Improve Productivity

Entrepreneurs have long considered **outsourcing** to be a management method that could be used only by large firms. After all, entrepreneurs reason, where would I get the time, the contacts, the money to be able to oversee foreign contractors?

outsourcing
Outsourcing comprises obtaining a needed business process from a firm that is independent of the entrepreneur's business.

This reasoning no longer holds for two reasons: first, technology has made outsourcing available and second, outsourcing does not necessarily require dealing with foreign firms. In fact, your best choice for outsourcing to achieve better productivity for yourself and for your employees just might be in the office next to yours.

To get the greatest benefit from outsourcing, you need follow four simple rules:

1. **Know yourself.**
   Nobody is good at everything. This is a truism that is often lost on entrepreneurs who are notorious for believing "if anyone can do it, I can." Misplaced self-confidence has in the past, and will in the future, cause many otherwise excellent ventures to fail. Before you decide what business functions to outsource, you must carefully examine your own weaknesses and strengths.
2. **Keep strategy decisions in-house.**
   No one is likely to have the knowledge of your business and customers that you do. The success of your business is dependent on strategy. Outsource business functions and businesses activities, but keep strategy at home.
3. **Fully specify tasks that are to be outsourced.**
   The single greatest cause of failure of outsourcing is lack of clear communications between the entrepreneur and the contractor. You will get the best results when you provide your contractor with exact details of the specifications to be met, methods to be used, outcomes to be delivered.
4. **Know with whom you are contracting.**
   You will be satisfied with the results of outsourcing if, and only if, you choose competent contractors. Companies and individuals to whom you may outsource have specific competencies, just like you do. Not all CPAs are expert in small business issues. Not all biotech research labs can produce and purify proteins. You must perform careful investigation of the contractors available to choose the best one for your business.

The most commonly outsourced functions of small businesses are legal and accounting. Most entrepreneurs are neither lawyers nor accountants, and many quite frankly will tell you that they have no interest in attempting either area.

There are many functions other than legal and accounting where you could benefit from outsourcing. To identify these functions you need to identify things that you are currently doing in-house that could be done less expensively or more efficiently by expert contractors. In the final analysis all business functions and activities are potential areas for outsourcing.

Finding Outsourcing Contractors

As you would expect, the web provides a multitude of websites to help you find competent companies to which you can outsource services and manufacturing.

The oldest and best-known of these sites for manufacturing is alibaba.com. Alibaba was started in Hangzhou, China, by Jack Ma and a group of 17 other investor-founders. It initially was intended to be a trading platform something like eBay for small Chinese manufacturers to sell their products. Since its founding alibaba has grown to be the largest business-to-business trading site in the world. Skill Module 16.3 requires you to examine the Alibaba web site.

The best known website for contracting with individuals is Elance, based in the United States and in Norway. Elance claims to have over 1.4 million registered contractors and to have generated more than $500 million in contract fees.

Websites for Outsourcing Services and Manufacturing

www.alibaba.com
www.Elance.com
www.Freelancer.com
www.Getafreelancer.com
www.Greatlance.com
www.Guru.com
www.oDesk.com
www.paragonsourcing.com
www.VWorker.com

SMALL BUSINESS INSIGHT

OUTSOURCING BLUES: CELLDYNE LABORATORIES, LLC

The difficult task is not finding a business to which you can outsource. The difficult task is investigating the potential contractor to determine its reliability.

Scams do exist in the outsourcing industry. A San Antonio firm, Celldyne Laboratories, LLC, contracted with a Chinese pharmaceutical firm to provide a specific hormone precursor. When the product was delivered, tests found substantial levels of insulin, which rendered the product unusable.

Despite high ratings by the Federation of Chinese Trade Associations, Celldyne has not been able to get restitution for this very expensive quality failure.

Areas Where Outsourcing May Be Right for Your Business

- Support services
  - Legal
  - Accounting
  - Tax preparation and compliance
  - Website development and maintenance
  - Payroll services
  - Safety and OSHA compliance
  - Human resources / employee benefits
  - Food service
  - Janitorial
- Noncore business functions
  - Marketing and advertising
  - Customer fulfillment/shipping
  - Research and development
  - Customer service
  - Technical support
  - Warranty services
- Repetitive business activities
  - Data entry
  - Day-to-day bookkeeping
  - Accounts payable entry
  - Cold calling for new business leads
- Core business functions
  - Manufacturing
  - Packaging
  - Product design
  - Sales

Finding an Outsourcing Partner

SKILL MODULE 16.3

As an avid crossworder, I would like to have a lap desk that I could use to complete crosswords while in my easy chair. I've done market research that has convinced me that a market exists for such lap desks. A lap desk might look like this:

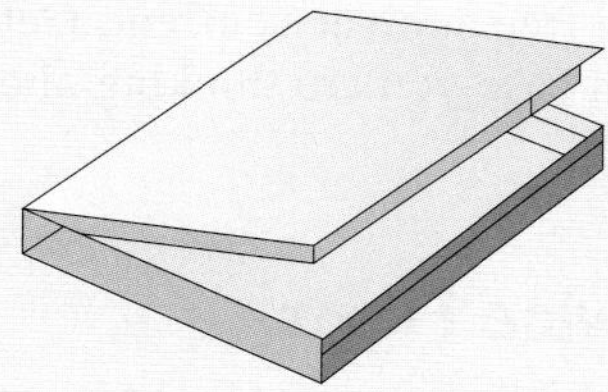

It is a simple plastic box 12 inches wide by 15 inches long by 1 ½ inches deep. It has a hinged lid that provides the writing surface. A magnet fastens the lid when it is closed. The inside of the box has molded dividers. The largest division is 8⅝ inches by 11⅛ inches to hold puzzles. Another section will hold a Webster's travel-size paperback crossword dictionary that measures 8¼" by 5¼". The remaining inside area will hold erasers, pencils, pens. For comfort in use, there is a foam pad attached to the bottom of the box.

I want to have this lap desk produced by an independent manufacturer. The lowest-cost manufacturers are located in Asia, so to find an outsourcing partner, I will use alibaba.com to obtain bids.

Go to **www.alibaba.com**. Examine the site to determine the requirements for posting to get bids for the production of 10,000 of these lap desks. Prepare a scale drawing and a list of specifications that conform to the requirements of the ailbaba site. Turn in to your instructor the completed documents for getting a bid on alibaba. Your instructor will grade your submission for accuracy, completeness, and clarity and will report back how your project compares to an actual ailbaba bid posting.

Do not post this project to the alibaba website for bids unless you actually expect to buy 10,000 lap desks.

Operations Management Challenges for Product-Based Firms

In talking about productivity above, the examples were primarily of product-based firms. Product-based firms take some sort of materials—groceries for a restaurant, crude oil for a refinery, or wood and pen parts for a high-end pen manufacturer like Michel Perchin ($1,000 and up) or David Oscarson ($4,000 and up) and add labor and technology to create a product. There are places for efficiencies all along the production process (or as we saw in Chapter 7, along the entire value chain, for that matter).

Consider high-end pens. One way to improve the efficiency of the production process is to use advanced technologies like lasers to help cut and drill quickly and precisely. Or using computerization with the laser to combine several steps into one, making it possible to produce more perfect pens faster. Another approach is to get the latest raw materials first when they are "hot" in the market. If moon rocks became commercially available, imagine what a pen made from moon rock would be worth. As more moon rocks would enter the market, the price would drop, so the best profits would come to the pen maker who gets the moon rock first into production and first into the hands of rich status-conscious buyers.

From this you can see the two major sources of efficiencies for product-based firms. One is to increase the amount, speed, or accuracy of work done for every day of operations. This can be done through scheduling improvements within the firm like those seen in the time management approach described in Chapter 5 or in this chapter's approach to inventory management. Another approach is to improve parts of the **supply chain** outside the firm so that raw materials get into production faster and that finished products get into customers' hands faster too.

How do you figure out ways to improve operations? There are several sources of expertise you can use. Our reliable friends at the SBA and SCORE can offer help, much of it low-cost or even free. Other major and relatively inexpensive sources are trade and professional associations. They often publicize "**best practices**" which represent the most productive ways found in your industry.

Often, top-performing firms will share their secrets of success with the rest of the industry to help improve the overall quality. It also does not hurt in advertising to say that "our procedures are now the industry standard, but we know more about them than anyone else!"

supply chain
Like the value chain, the line of distribution of a product from its start as materials outside the target firm to its handling in the target firm to its handling by sellers into the hands of customers.

best practices
Activities identified by authoritative bodies as examples of optimal ways to get things done in a particular industry, profession, or trade.

Another interesting source of free advice can be your vendors. For example, UPS, DHL, and FedEx will be glad to consult to you (for free) on ways to improve your supply chain. Although many of the answers will end with "we will be glad to do it for you" followed by a price quote, the analyses they can offer, as well as information about how other companies like yours have benefited from supply chain efficiencies, can help open new ideas to you. Similarly, raw material suppliers or equipment vendors will also be glad to consult with you on ways you could improve your productivity in areas where they have expertise—and possibly some equipment or supplies to sell you. The advice is often free and very current. Get it from competing firms to make sure you get the best ideas, and in case you are thinking about buying, also get the best price.

Operations Management Challenges for Service Firms

Service firms face several challenges in obtaining and maintaining efficient processes. Three characteristics of services—intangibility, inseparability, and perishability—impact operations choices and decision making, creating challenges for the managers of service operations. These characteristics confound and limit strategic choices and tactical decisions available to you.

The intangibility of services is a fundamental difference from goods. Services cannot be seen, felt, or tasted in the manner that goods can be. In contrast, tangible goods are produced, shipped, sold, and consumed in separate places. Another characteristic of a service is its inseparability: a service is produced and consumed at the same time. This exposes the entire production process to customer examination. In the manufacturing processes, the customer is rarely present. When producing services, however, the customer is usually present, preventing any clear distinction between the production stage and the consumption stage. Services are also perishable. In services, unused capacity is lost forever. Empty airline seats, vacant motel rooms, and unfilled theater seats not sold cannot be stored and sold later. Because of the characteristic of perishability, providers of services face great difficulty in managing capacity, and scheduling personnel.

However, despite intangibility, inseparability, and perishability, services can be improved. Part of the answer is deciding on a part of the service on which to focus. Services (let's use bowling as an example) tend to have differing degrees of four components. One component is called the explicit service. In bowling, rolling the ball and counting the pins dropped is the explicit service. The bowling takes place in a bowling alley, and that building with its balls and pins and equipment is what is called the supporting facility.

Part of the bowling experience depends on how you are treated—the friendliness of the staff, the process for which you are charged, and the cleanliness of the alley are examples. These aspects of what we usually think of as customer service are called implicit service. The fourth element, called a supporting good, refers to some tangible material outcome (remember that products were called "goods" in Chapter 9) you get from the service. In bowling, there are no tangible outcomes, unless you ask for a receipt. Because there is no real supporting goods in bowling, it is an example of a nearly pure service. Recall that in Chapter 9 we talked about pure services, pure goods, and the hybrids that include elements of both.

With these four elements in mind, it can become easier to target a way to improve the service. For a bowling alley, the owner could improve the supporting facility by getting faster pin-setting equipment, or adding more parking. The owner could add lights and sound equipment for "cosmic bowling" to improve (or at least expand) the explicit service. Improving cleanliness of the facility or getting the staff to be friendlier are ways to improve the implicit service, while a supporting good could be offered by giving bowling related tangibles, such as coupons for future games.

Also take a moment to consider innovative ways to improve service. For example, you could use the Internet to expand service delivery. Offering to post bowlers' pictures and high scores online, or sending them an e-mail with their scores, or letting customers network online for scheduling, or offering video analysis of a person's bowling stance are all implicit services which could add value to the customer and improve (as well as expand) the bowling experience.

The techniques for learning more about how to improve services are identical to those discussed for product-based firms. And if you have employees, there is one more great resource for improving productivity—asking them and putting their ideas into action. Employees of your business each have unique skills and knowledge. As your business grows, you most likely will find that certain employees have a greater understanding of certain functions of your business than do you. By including these people in the management process, you (1) ease your own work burden and (2) gain the advantage of expert input into the management process.

The point is that almost every service (and product) can be improved. In the long run, desirable operational improvements make your customers more loyal and your company more able to withstand competitive pressures. Operations management can add to the bottom line through efficiencies, through revenue growth, and when done right, to both at the same time.

CHAPTER SUMMARY

LO1 Describe techniques to manage short-term assets.

- Two short-term assets other than cash are critical to the success of most small businesses: accounts receivable and inventory.
- Offering credit can benefit a business in many ways, if the credit process is well thought out and carefully managed.
- High-quality receivables provide a means to quickly get cash to meet unexpected opportunities and problems.
- Inventory management is critical because for many small businesses inventory is the single greatest asset.
- Inventory requires significant cash investment that ties up capital that could be used for other business purposes.
- Careful management of inventory involves keeping the right amount of inventory available for sale and ordering the right amount of inventory at the right time to avoid both having too much on hand and running out of inventory, and thus losing sales.
- Techniques of inventory management include economic order quantity, just-in-time inventories, optimum stocking level, periodic inventory, perpetual inventory, bar coding, and point-of-sale systems.

LO2 Calculate the value of the assets in your business.

- Assets in use usually have a value greater than can be realized by selling them because of the value present in the assets' future use.
- Because the value of future use is very difficult to determine, accounting methods used to value capital assets are (1) book value, (2) disposal value, (3) replacement value, and (4) fair market value.
- Of these four methods, only book value and replacement value can be accurately determined.
- Each of the four accounting methods is useful in different situations:
  - Book value is used for financial reporting to outsiders.
  - Lenders prefer disposal value for the purpose of accepting collateral for a loan.
  - Disposal value is useful for estimating cash flows for discounted cash flow analysis.
  - Replacement value is useful for estimating sales prices for individual assets and for the business as a whole.

LO3 Describe techniques for managing fixed assets.

- Capital assets create four costs across their useful lives: (1) the cost of acquiring the asset, (2) the cost of owning the asset, (3) the cost of operating the asset, and (4) the cost of disposing of the asset.
- Better decisions result when all the costs above, called *whole of life* costs, are considered in the investing analysis.

LO4 Calculate ratios used to analyze capital investment decisions.

- The two most commonly used financial ratios for comparing investment alternatives are (1) payback period and (2) return on investment (ROI).
- There are also two significantly more complex approaches called net present value (NPV) and internal rate of return (IRR).
- Discounted cash flow methods (NPV and IRR) are the most complete, because they include the greatest amount of data in the analysis.

LO5 Describe the advantages of renting or leasing capital equipment.

- Renting requires little or no down payment. It therefore preserves cash.
- As a renter, you usually do not bear the costs of maintenance and repair.
- Leasing provides the same advantages as renting, but also provides assurance the asset will remain available for your exclusive use.
- Joint venturing for assets that have limited use allows you to obtain the benefits of the asset, but reduces the cost of ownership by sharing with other businesses.

LO6 Describe techniques to manage and improve the operations of your business.

- Operations management seeks ways to improve productivity.
- Increasing efficiency and increasing quality are the two ways to improve productivity.
- Product-based firms can improve the amount, speed, or accuracy of work, or improve the supply chain.
- Service-based firms can improve their explicit service, implicit service, supporting facility, and supporting good.
- You can get operations management advice from a variety of high-quality free and for-fee sources, as well as your own employees.

KEY TERMS

accounts receivable, 520
lock box, 521
factoring, 522
pledging receivables, 522
inventory, 522
economic order quantity (EOQ), 523
optimum stocking level, 524
safety stock, 524
pull-through system, 525
just-in-time inventory, 525
microinventory, 525
periodic inventory, 525
perpetual inventory, 525
bar coding, 526
point-of-sale (POS) system, 526
capital assets, 527
book value, 528
disposal value, 528
arm's length transaction, 528
replacement value, 528
fair market value, 528
inventory valuation, 529
physical inventory, 529
acquisition cost, 530
replacement cost, 530
property, 530
plant, 530
equipment, 530
whole of life costs, 530
cost of owning, 530
cost of operating, 530
cost of disposition, 530
capital budgeting, 531
payback period, 531
return on investment (ROI), 531
straight line for a useful life of 10 years, 532
outflow, 534
operating lease, 534
capital lease, 534
inputs, 537
operations, 537
outputs, 538
feedback, 538
productivity, 538
efficiency, 538
quality, 538
outsourcing, 539
supply chain, 541
best practices, 541

DISCUSSION QUESTIONS

1. Discuss the pros and cons of providing credit to customers. If you do decide to provide credit, what policies should you establish and enforce?
2. Discuss how the use of economic order quantity (EOQ) and reorder calculations can benefit a retail business. What are the drawbacks in using these calculations?
3. Which of the asset valuation methods (book value, disposal value, replacement value, and fair market value) is the best for determining the value of your business's assets? Explain your choice, detailing how your preferred method is better than the other three.
4. How would you estimate the whole of life costs of an expensive capital asset, such as an executive airplane?
5. Discuss the advantages and disadvantages to payback period and to return on investment (ROI) as analysis tools for making capital investment decisions. Which do you prefer and why?

EXPERIENTIAL EXERCISES

1. Choose a local business in the industry in which you would like to own a firm. Visit the business that you choose, and walk about to observe the amounts and types of inventory on display. Interview the owner or manager. Determine the approximate value of inventory kept on hand. Find out the average time that any single item stays in inventory before it is sold. Also find out the minimum order quantities and delivery times of inventory. Use this information to estimate the amount of working capital necessary to maintain inventory. Make a report to your class.

2. Make a search, using your library, the Internet, and your business contacts, to find factors in your area. Interview the factor and determine the terms offered. Ask what things about the receivables are considered in pricing the factor contract. Contact a commercial banker in your area and find out the bank's policy for lending against receivables. Report your findings to your class.

www

3. Contact a dealer who sells expensive capital assets, such as earth-moving or transportation equipment. Find out the costs of acquiring, owning, operating, and disposing of the asset. Use a spreadsheet program to estimate the amounts and timing of the whole of life costs of the asset. Estimate the cash inflows that the asset will produce. Use your estimates of costs and cash inflows to calculate the NPV, IRR, ROI, and payback of the asset. Make a presentation to your class, detailing the calculations you have made.

4. Assume that you have a plumbing business that requires the use of a backhoe. Contact equipment rental businesses in your area and find out the rental cost and terms for a suitable machine. Contact leasing companies to find out the cost of leasing a similar backhoe. Assume that, on average, you need the machine for 12 hours weekly. Which is more advantageous, renting or leasing? How would your answer change if you needed the machine an average of 20 hours per week? At what level of usage would renting and leasing not matter?

5. Assume that you own a 2005 Ford F750 Super Duty truck. The truck has been driven 32,000 miles. What is a reasonable disposal value for this truck? (Be sure to reduce your estimate of sales price by the costs of selling the asset.) What is the replacement value of this truck (in other words, how much would another F750 with 30,000 miles cost to find, buy, finance, deliver, and license?) Peruse newspaper ads, search the Internet, and talk with truck salespeople to estimate the truck's fair market value. Make a report to your class of your findings.

MINI-CASE

QUALITY SIGN COMPANY

The Quality Sign Co. of Visalia, California, provides credit to customers. The firm is currently averaging receivables of $34,500. The business needs an additional truck-mounted crane to keep up with its rapidly growing business. Quality's owner, George McElroy, has worked up an estimate of the cost of a suitable crane, which is presented in the chart below. Quality's bank is willing to loan 90 percent of the purchase price of the truck, crane, and equipment. All of Quality's currently available cash is needed as working capital and is not available to invest in this project. As a result, Quality must find a way to finance the 10 percent that the bank will not loan, plus the other costs of acquisition.

Quality has contacted a factor who has offered to pay 80 percent for all accounts that are less than 60 days past due. The factor is also willing to act as a collection agency for those accounts that are 60 or more days past due for a fee of 25 percent of the amount collected. Alternatively, Quality's bank has agreed to make a 90-day loan discounted at 12 percent interest in the amount of $32,100, secured by 100 percent of outstanding receivables. The sum of $32,100, which includes accrued interest, is due on the 90th day after the loan is made. During the 90 days, all new receivables will be pledged to the bank as they are incurred. Quality will continue to collect the receivables in the normal course of business. Examine the financial information provided below and prepare a recommendation to Mr. McElroy.

Cost of Acquiring Mobile Crane	
Ford F750 Tandem truck	$ 73,000
120-ft heavy-duty crane	67,000
Hydraulic outriggers	12,500
Hydraulic pump	8,000
30-ft truck bed	5,000
Installation of bed	1,500
Delivery	1,500
Sales tax	12,338
License	1,000
Total acquisition cost	$181,838

Accounts Receivable	
Current	$34,500
>30 days	6,000
>60 days	5,000
>90 days	4,000
Delinquent	4,000
Total receivables	$53,500

SUGGESTED CASES AND ARTICLES

- Richard Harris and Harris Homes LLC, C-18

Available on Create:

- Meyers & Morrison

SUGGESTED VIDEOS

www.mhhe.com/katz4e

Video Case:

- For a written video case and corresponding clip, visit the OLC at www.mhhe.com/katz4e and select "Chapter 16".

- Wine Entrepreneurs

eClips Videos:

- Cheryl Francis Discusses Aspects for Measuring the Value of the Company
- Malia Mills Discusses Importance of Creating a Budget, Monitoring Inventory and Cash Flow

SBTV.com Video:

- Owning Your Product Formula

APPENDIX A

Economic Order Quantity

To solve for the quantity at which total inventory costs is minimized, consider the following definitions:

EOQ = economic order quantity in units (quantity that minimizes total inventory cost)
Q = quantity in units to be ordered at one time
P = price of one unit of inventory
O = cost of placing one order
C = cost of carrying one unit in inventory for one year
D = number of units to be sold in one year (demand)
D/Q = number of order cycles per year
Q/D = length of one order cycle as a fraction of one year

The total cost of making a single order is calculated as:

$$\text{Total cost of one order} = O + P \times Q$$

The total cost of holding inventory is the cost of holding one unit in inventory times the average number of units held during one order cycle times the number of order cycles in one year. If the number of units at the beginning of an order cycle is Q, and the number at the end of the cycle is 0, and sales are made at a constant rate, then the average number of units held is $(Q + 0)/2$, or simply $Q/2$. The length of one order cycle, as a fraction of one year, lies between 1 and 1 divided by the number of units to be sold in one year.

$$\text{Holding cost per order cycle} = C(Q/2)(Q/D) \text{ which can be simplified to: Holding cost per cycle} = CQ^2/2D$$

The total cost of ordering and holding inventory for one order cycle is the sum of these two equations. The total cost of inventory for one year is the cost for one cycle times the number of order cycles per year:

$$\text{Total annual cost} = [(O + P \times Q) + (CQ^2/2D)] \times D/Q = (O\,(D/Q) + DP + C(Q/2)$$

The purchase price of inventory (DP) is independent of how many units are ordered at any one time and how many orders are made, and thus may be disregarded. This provides the total cost of ordering and holding inventory:

$$O\,(D/Q) + C\,(Q/2)$$

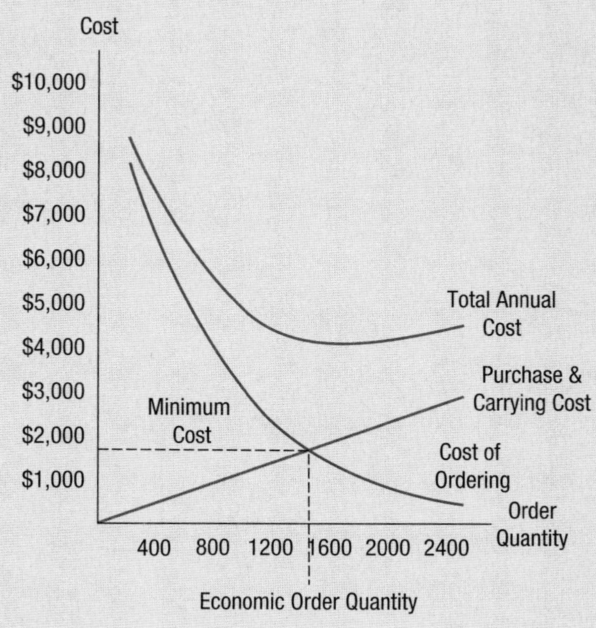

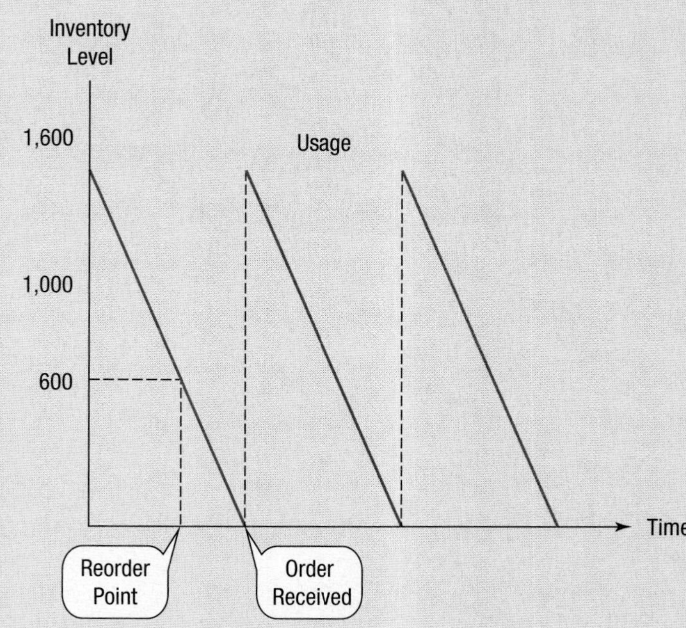

The minimum value of this equation is found by setting the first derivative equal to zero and solving for Q:

$$Q = (20D/C).5$$

The EOQ calculation indicates how much to order at one time. It does not tell you when to order, however. To make this decision, you have to know how much time will pass between when the order is placed and when the inventory will be received. Suppose that the lead time is one month and that your business uses 600 units of inventory each month. You, therefore, must reorder when inventory levels fall to 600 units, leaving you with one month's supply on hand.

But what if your usage fluctuates, say, between 400 and 700 units of product each month? If you wait to reorder until inventory drops to 600 units and you then have a high-sales month, you could run out of inventory long before you run out of month. To protect from this, you can set a policy of maintaining a safety stock of surplus inventory over the minimum. You will reorder when inventory drops to 700 units. This will increase the cost of carrying inventory, but for almost all businesses, the cost of carrying inventory is a fraction of the cost of lost sales. Thus, for you, the cost of holding safety stock is offset by the advantages of not having a stock-out situation.

As you can see from this explanation, deriving the economic order quantity equation requires the use of calculus. Additionally, there are two simplifying assumptions that are unrealistic:

1. Ending inventory quantity is zero for each order cycle.
2. The purchase price of inventory is not affected by the number ordered at one time or by the number of orders placed.

In reality, neither of these assumptions is likely to be true. However, providing for a positive ending inventory and for a price that varies with changes in order quantity and number of orders complicates the solution so much that nobody bothers to do so.

Thus, EOQ determination is another example of an accounting or finance calculation that is approximately true, but precisely wrong. This is why it is necessary to apply common sense to the mathematical solution.

APPENDIX B

Time Value of Money and Discounted Cash Flow Analysis

Which would you prefer? One dollar right now, or one dollar to be received one year from now?

Certainly, you'd prefer to have the dollar today. Anyone would. But consider this: Suppose you were offered the choice between one dollar now or a U.S. savings bond that will pay you $10 one year from now. Which of these would you prefer? Most people immediately see the savings bond as being more valuable.

Now ask yourself, "Why is a dollar right this minute preferable to receiving a dollar in the future, but an iron-clad guarantee of 10 dollars one year from now is preferable to one dollar now?"

Almost everyone, even young children, have an instinctual grasp of the concept that waiting for a benefit somehow lessens the immediate value of that benefit. Given the alternatives of a benefit to be received immediately and a benefit to be received later, the delayed benefit must be of significantly greater value if it is to be chosen. This simple concept is the basis of the concept of the time value of money.

Suppose you knew for a fact that to save your life, you would need to have exactly one dollar one year from today. You can make an arrangement with a bank to deposit any amount of money. The bank will pay 10 percent interest. How much must you deposit to have the one dollar when it is needed?

Let "x" represent the amount that you will deposit. Then $10\%x$ is the amount of interest that the deposit will earn in one year. The sum of the amount you deposit plus the interest earned must equal one dollar:

$$x + 10\%x = \$1$$
$$1.1x = \$1$$
$$x = \$1/1.1$$
$$x = \$.91$$

In finance terms, we would state that the *present value* of one dollar, *discounted at 10 percent for one year,* is $0.91. Alternatively, we could say that the *future value* of 91 cents, *compounded at 10 percent for one year,* is $1.00. The term *present value* simply refers to the amount of money that would have to be deposited now to grow into a specified amount, given an interest rate and period of time. *Future value* is the inverse: the amount that a specific amount of money would grow to be, given a specific interest rate and period of time.

With just a little bit of effort, this concept can easily be expanded to calculate the amount that you must deposit now, at any stated interest rate, to accumulate any amount desired to be received at any time in the future. For example, consider the problem of accumulating for four years:

Value at the End of Year 1	Value at the End of Year 2	Value at the End of Year 3	Value at the End of Year 4
$(1 + r)X$	$(1 + r)(1 + r)X$	$(1 + r)(1 + r)(1 + r)X$	$(1 + r)(1 + r)(1 + r)(1 + r)X$

Where X = amount to be deposited
r = interest rate to be earned

The property that in years 2, 3, and 4 interest is being earned on interest from the prior years is called *compounding.*

PRESENT VALUE AND FUTURE VALUE OF 1

Notice that the value at the end of each year is equal to the amount deposited multiplied by 1 plus the interest rate, raised to the power of the number of the period. This allows us to develop an equation that can be easily solved for any amount deposited, any interest rate, and any number of compounding periods:

$$FV_n = PV(1 + r)^n$$

Where:

FV_n = future value of the investment at the end of n years

PV = present value (the amount to be deposited)

r = annual interest rate (also called *compounding rate, or discount rate*)

n = number of periods that the deposit is compounded

By solving the equation for PV, we can develop a general equation that will answer the original question, "How much must you deposit now, at a stated interest rate, to accumulate a desired amount at a specified time in the future?"

$$PV = FV_n \times 1/(1 + r)^n$$

Thus, if you need one dollar four years from now, and you can earn 10 percent compounded annually, you must deposit $1/(1.1)^4$ dollars, or 1/1.4641, which equals 68.3 cents.

The calculated value of $(1 + r)^n$ is called the *future value of one,* and can be calculated for any discount rate, r, and any period of time, n. Similarly, the calculated value of $1/(1 + r)^n$ is the *present value of one.* You can easily calculate either the future value or present value of any amount by simply multiplying that amount by the appropriate future value or present value of 1. Thus, if you needed to have available $68,301.50 five years from now and you can earn an interest rate of 8 percent, you would multiply 68,301.50 times the present value of 1 for five years at 8 percent:

$$68{,}301.50 \times 1/(1.08)^5$$
$$68{,}301.50 \times 1/1.4693$$
$$68{,}301.50 \times 0.6806$$

The amount that you would have to deposit today is approximately $46,485.75.

PRESENT VALUE AND FUTURE VALUE OF AN ANNUITY

As the owner of a small business, you will often need to know information about the value of a series of equal payments over time. A series of equal payments made regularly over a set period of time is called an *annuity.*

For example, suppose you know that in three years you will have to replace an essential piece of equipment for your business. Your best estimate is that you can deposit $500 per month for three years at 8 percent interest in order to have sufficient money to make a down payment. How much would you have at the end of three years? The answer to this question can be easily, but tediously, solved by making a series of calculations. First, you must calculate the *monthly* compounding rate by dividing 8 percent by 12 months. Then, you use this monthly rate of .00666 to calculate the *future value of each payment,* then simply sum all 36 values:

$$FV = \$500 \times (1 + .00667)^{36} + \$500 \times (1 + .00667)^{35} + \$500 \times (1 + .00667)^{34} + \cdots + \$500 \times (1 + .00667)^{1}$$
$$635.119 \quad + \quad 630.912 \quad + \quad 626.734 \quad + \cdots + \quad 503.333$$

There is, however, a much less tedious, although slightly more difficult, means to calculate the future value of an annuity. The above summation equation can be solved algebraically, providing the following:

$$FV = C\left[\frac{(1 + r)^n - 1}{r}\right]$$

Where:

C = cash payment per period
r = number rate
n = number of payments

Substituting values into this equation provides:

$$FV = 500\left[\frac{(1 + .00667)^{36} - 1}{.00667}\right] = \$20{,}403$$

rounded to the nearest whole dollar.

The present value of a series of equal payments may be similarly solved by discounting each payment and summing all the payments. However, this summation equation has also been reduced to a formula:

$$PV = C\left[\frac{(1 - (1 + r)^{-n}}{r}\right]$$

Thus, by substituting in the appropriate values, you may easily calculate the present value of an installment contract, a lease, indeed, any series of equal payments.

DISCOUNTED CASH FLOW ANALYSIS

These simple concepts and calculations are the basis of all discounted cash flow analyses. Estimated current cash expenditures and net future cash inflows are discounted by some appropriate rate to derive *net present value* and *internal rate of return.*

NET PRESENT VALUE

To perform a net present value analysis, you must:

1. Estimate the *amount* and *timing* of all cash flows of the project.
2. Select an appropriate discount rate.
3. Discount to present value each cash flow using the selected discount rate and timing.
4. Sum the discounted cash flows.

As you can see from the steps above, net present value (NPV) is simply the sum of all cash flows, both negative and positive, discounted by an appropriate discount rate. The difficulty of NPV analysis lies first in accurately estimating future cash flows and second in selecting an appropriate discount rate. Performing the calculations is trivial.

Estimating future cash flows is basically a process of guessing the revenues and expenses that the project will create. Revenues and expenses are then netted for each time period, usually by month, quarter, or year. The estimating process can be as simple or as complex as you believe necessary to produce reliable numbers and dates.

Selecting an appropriate discount rate is absolutely essential to the utility of the analysis. If you select too high a discount rate, desirable projects will be rejected. Select too low a discount rate and money-losing projects will be accepted. Arguments can be made for using any of three very different discount rates: (1) cost of capital of your business, (2) the incremental cost of capital (or marginal cost of capital), and (3) a management-selected minimum acceptable rate of return.

The computation of NPV is accomplished by the following algorithm:.

$$NPV = -CF_0 + \frac{CF_1}{(1 + r)^1} + \frac{CF_2}{(1 + r)^2} + \frac{CF_3}{(1 + r)^3} + \cdots + \frac{CF_n}{(1 + r)^n}$$

Where:

NPV = net present value of the project
CF_0 = initial investment in the project
CF_n = cash flow at period n
r = discount rate

To illustrate the calculation of *NPV,* consider the following: You are thinking about purchasing for your restaurant a pressurized fryer that will allow you to rapidly prepare spicy deep-fried chicken wings. You believe that the demand for this product will peak within a year, then decrease to zero over three years. The total cost of the fryer, installed and ready for service, is $25,000. The cost of disposing of the fryer at the end of its useful life will be equal to its value at that time. In order to make an NPV analysis, you have determined that your weighted average cost of capital is 24 percent. You estimate that the fryer will provide the following cash flows to your business:

Cash flows	($25,000)	$20,000	$8,000	$4,000	$2,000
Time period	Right Now (t_0)	One Year from Now (t_1)	Two Years from Now (t_2)	Three Years from Now (t_3)	Four Years from Now (t_4)

Net present value of these cash flows is calculated thusly:

$$\frac{\text{Cash flows}}{\text{Discount factor}} \quad \frac{(\$25{,}000)}{(1 + .24)^0} + \frac{\$20{,}000}{(1 + .24)^1} + \frac{\$8{,}000}{(1 + .24)^2} + \frac{\$4{,}000}{(1 + .24)^3} + \frac{\$2{,}000}{(1 + .24)^4}$$

You may easily calculate the present value of the individual cash flows by using a financial calculator, any calculator that does powers, or a computer spreadsheet such as Lotus 123, Quattro Pro, or Excel.[20] The calculated NPV is ($724.16). Because the NPV is less than zero (a negative number), you should reject this project because it would not provide a return as great as your business's weighted average cost of capital.

Although the decision rule for NPV indicates that the project should be rejected, remember that all the numbers on which the analysis is made are estimates. No matter how carefully you attempt to estimate future results, you can never do so with certainty. In fact, were you to purchase the fryer, you might find that the product was either much more successful or much less successful than you would ever have expected.

There are several ways to deal with this inevitable uncertainty. You can change your estimates slightly up or down, a process called *sensitivity analysis,* to determine the effects of small changes in your estimates. For example, if you were to increase your estimate of the first year cash flows by just $898, the decision would change to "accept." If you enjoy doing math, you could adjust each of your estimates for the probability of their being correct, then use the *expected* values in the analysis. You might reconsider using weighted average cost of capital for the discount rate. Perhaps you should consider using the cost at which you can borrow funds. Or you might consider using a discount rate that is the sum of the cost of borrowing and some minimum return that you are willing to accept. In fact, in this example, reducing the discount rate by less than 3/10 of one percent reverses the decision.

INTERNAL RATE OF RETURN

Another way of dealing with the uncertainty of NPV analysis is to ask the question, "If this project does not provide a return equal to the discount rate, then what rate of return does it provide?" Internal rate of return (IRR) provides the answer to this question by disclosing the actual rate of return, based on the amount and timing of the cash flow.

The internal rate of return of a project is that rate at which NPV = zero. In other words, IRR is the discount rate at which the present value of the cash inflows of the project exactly equals the present value of the cash outflows. Thus, in this example, you must solve the following equation for the value of the discount rate (IRR):

$$\frac{(\$25{,}000)}{(1 + \text{IRR})^0} + \frac{(\$20{,}000)}{(1 + \text{IRR})^1} + \frac{\$8{,}000}{(1 + \text{IRR})^2} + \frac{\$4{,}000}{(1 + \text{IRR})^3} + \frac{\$2{,}000}{(1 + \text{IRR})^4} = \$0$$

It is unfortunate that there is no way to directly solve this equation for IRR. The only way to find the value of IRR is to try different numbers in a reiterative process until you find a number that provides a solution sufficiently close to zero. Financial calculators, such as those provided by Hewlett Packard and Texas Instruments, all provide an automated means to derive the answer. Computer spreadsheet programs also provide functions to find the IRR of any series of cash flows.

If you do solve the above equation, you will find that the IRR is approximately 21.59 percent. Compare this number with your estimate of your cost of capital, 24 percent. The question you must answer is, "How confident am I that my cost of capital actually exceeds 21.6 percent?" If you are confident, reject the project. If, on the other hand, you are not so sure, perhaps you should reconsider the assumptions and estimates that you have made.

APPLYING THESE APPROACHES TO THE TRUCK AND CRANE PROBLEM

Earlier in the chapter we discussed the problem of deciding whether to buy a Ford-Skyhook or GMC-Sponco truck and crane combination. We worked through two simple methods for making a capital budgeting decision—the payback period approach and the ROI or rate of return on investment approach. We noted then that NPV and IRR approaches could also be used.

Using either NPV or IRR will avoid the shortcomings of both the payback period and the return on investment methods. Discounted cash flow methods make specific numeric adjustments to approximate the lower value of money to be received as compared to the value of money received now.

Net present value (NPV), like the payback period method, is based upon estimates of the cash flows that an investment will cause and utilizes your business's weighted average cost of capital. It is like ROI in using the weighted cost of capital, but unlike ROI because NPV uses cash flows, not profits. When Warren Buffett is deciding if he will buy a company, he uses this technique. In his case he looks at the cash flow the business generates in a year and then figures how much it would be worth—after being discounted—at some point in the future. For buying businesses, he uses a U.S. Treasury long-term bond rate[21] for the period of time that he decides is appropriate. The final result of NPV calculation is a single dollar value, which can be of any magnitude, even a negative number, although the more positive the number, the better.

For our truck and crane example, the time period is the 10 years the truck and crane would be used. We know from the owner's earlier calculations that her weighted cost of capital is 20 percent, and we saw the cash flows in Table 16.1. The computations are complex, but spreadsheets like Excel can do them quickly and easily.

As with payback period and ROI, two decision rules are applied to decide among alternative investments:

- Accept only those alternatives for which the net present value is equal to or greater than zero.
- Accept the alternative with the greatest value among those that meet the first criterion.

Ford-Skyhook	GMC-Sponco
Net present value = \$108,112	Net present value = \$107,544

Both alternatives meet the first decision rule. Applying the second, you would accept the Ford-Skyhook alternative because it provides the greater positive net present value.

Internal rate of return (IRR) is a special case of net present value. IRR focuses on the return to the company, but also factors in the cost of the project. What is distinctive about the way IRR does this is that it statistically makes the net present value equal to zero, so the discount rate is thrown out as a consideration.

The decision rules for using IRR are:

1. Accept only those alternatives for which internal rate of return is equal to or greater than the business's weighted cost of capital.
2. Accept the alternative with the greatest IRR among those that meet the first criterion.

Ford-Skyhook	GMC-Sponco
Internal rate of return = 36.5197%	Internal rate of return = 33.37265%

As with net present value, both alternatives pass the first decision test. Of the two, you would choose the Ford-Skyhook alternative because it has the greater IRR.

It is important to note that NPV and IRR are considered some of the most complex of financial equations. The advantages of discounted cash flow analyses for evaluating investment alternatives are (1) all cash flows of each investment are explicitly included in the analysis, and (2) the time value of money is specifically calculated. Discounted cash flow methods do have serious drawbacks, however. First, a discounted cash flow analysis has the appearance of being extremely accurate. This appearance is highly deceiving, however. Every number in the calculation is, at best, an estimate. The weighted cost of capital, the amounts, and the timings of cash flows cannot ever be known with certainty. Second, the calculation uses a single estimate for each projected cash flow. Although cash flows that will occur soon may be reasonably accurately estimated, the longer the period of time over which projections are made, the greater the uncertainty of each estimate. Third, making good estimates of future cash flows requires considerable expertise and effort. Few owners of small businesses have either the time or the resources to do the necessary projections. All in all, discounted cash flow analyses are theoretically sound but are empirically highly problematic.

CHAPTER 17

Small Business Protection: Risk Management and Insurance

● Chimney sweeping is an example of an industry that is risky to insure. Read the chapter opening scenario to learn how two chimney sweeps catalyzed change by motivating a large group of fellow workers to get involved with the insurance company. Why do you think it is so important that small business owners and workers belong to a guild or similar industry group?

LEARNING OBJECTIVES

After you complete this chapter, you will be able to:

LO1 Explain the meaning and nature of business risk.

LO2 Describe the specific types of risks associated with different aspects of business operations.

LO3 Describe techniques to manage risks to stay within your level of risk tolerance.

LO4 Explain how insurance can be used to manage business risk.

LO5 Describe techniques for sharing risk with other businesses and organizations.

Focus on Small Business: The Massachusetts Chimney Sweep Guild[1]

Faced with paying twice as much for liability insurance as last year, Mike and Michelle Elliott decided to take action. Instead of simply paying the rates demanded and then griping about it, the couple prodded their industry group, the Massachusetts Chimney Sweep Guild, to use its bargaining power to get better rates for its members.

Chimney sweeps, like roofers, rough-in carpenters, and house movers, are difficult businesses to insure. Many large insurance companies do not want to deal with small businesses at all. Others will insure small businesses, but do not want to deal with businesses that involve heavy physical work, climbing ladders, and the presence of hazardous materials such as the soot and creosote that sweeps remove from flues. Such businesses have high risk of employee illnesses and injuries and high risk of damage to customers' properties—characteristics that are great disincentives for insurance companies.

The Elliotts sent a questionnaire to each of the 35 small business owners who comprised the Guild, asking for information concerning past claims, their volume of business, number of employees, and so on. Armed with the results of the survey, their own independent insurance broker, Tom Coonan, went to work to find appropriate insurance.

"Standard companies won't touch the Guild, because they have so few members. The total premium has to be over $1 million before the larger insurance companies will underwrite a group," Coonan says.

Coonan was able to find an insurance carrier that combined the desired coverages with affordable premiums. Overall, members of the Guild are highly satisfied with the insurance package. Plans are being made to obtain the group policy as an ongoing contract.

Operating a risky business such as chimney sweeping without the security of good insurance is a recipe for financial disaster. The cost of care for just one seriously injured worker or of repairing just one seriously damaged building can easily bankrupt a small business owner. On the other hand, if insurance coverage itself is excessively costly, the business cannot be profitable. By banding together, the members of the Guild were able to use their combined bargaining power to obtain appropriate coverage at affordable prices.

DISCUSSION QUESTIONS

1. The case mentions two kinds of risks faced by chimney sweeps. Name some others.
2. What is the risk to the small business owner of operating without insurance?
3. Why do you think the data on claim experience were useful for the insurance broker in negotiating the deal?

Risk in Small Business

LO1 Explain the meaning and nature of business risk.

We have discussed two kinds of risk in the previous chapters—financial risk that comes from your capital structure and investment risk caused by accepting or providing debt, and by holding debt or equity funds. Here we discuss other kinds of risk that small business owners face.

People define risk in many different ways, depending upon their unique situations and upon their own tolerance for uncertainty. You might define risk as the likelihood of getting an A in this course. A smoke jumper might consider risk the possibility of being trapped by a rapidly advancing forest fire. A surgeon who is to perform an operation might consider risk to be the level of probability that the patient will be no better after the surgery and will sue for malpractice. The person facing major surgery might think of risk as the chance that the operation will result in death.

For business owners, risk is the very real likelihood that the business may not succeed, that they may not only *not* become wealthy, but that they may well lose part or all of their investment in the firm.

We all know that people vary widely in their response to risk. Some people will run the bulls in Pamplona, others will not touch a calf in a petting zoo. As we pointed out in the previous chapter, business owners similarly differ in their response to business risk. Some seek risk. Most prefer to avoid risk to the extent possible. In academic terms, some business owners are *risk seeking*, although most small business owners are *risk-averse*.

To the extent that small business owners are risk-averse, as part of every business decision, they consider what they could lose. If they can't reduce the level of risk to where they're comfortable, then they make arrangements to either insure against future losses or to spread the risk among other people or businesses.

Thinking about Risk

Generally speaking, risk is the probability that future states of being will be worse than you expect. For example, folks who build houses on or near the San Andreas fault expect those houses to survive the inevitable earthquakes. However, there is a small, but measurable, probability that an earthquake will be violent enough to destroy any building that can be built. The risk of building in an earthquake area is the *level of likelihood*, or the *probability*, that a strong earthquake will damage or destroy the house, an outcome that is definitely a worse state of being than the homeowner expects.

business risk
The level of probability that the future economic state of the business will be worse than expected.

Business risk is the probability that the future state of the business will be less successful than planned, resulting in the loss of value of business assets. No person enters a business for the purpose of losing money, but it can and does happen. The next quarter's business does not meet expectations. Investments go bad. Sales projections are not met. Products do not meet specifications. All of a sudden, investors find themselves the owners of assets that are worth much less than expected. The likelihood of this bleak outcome is the essence of business risk.

Among the most commonly identified sources of risk are:

- Financial risk that is a result of choosing among sources and types of capital investment.[2]
- Nonpayment of debts owed to the business.
- Changes in technology that render the business's product or service obsolete.
- Injury and illnesses suffered by employees as a result of their employment.

- Injury from accidents incurred by customers, vendors, and others while on business property.
- Loss or harm incurred because of the use of the business's product or service.
- Natural events, such as storms, floods, fire, and earthquakes.
- Violation of any of the multitude of laws and regulations that apply to small business.
- Theft of business property.
- Misbehavior by employees.

Risks Associated with Specific Business Operations

There are three general types of events that cause business risk. These are (1) events related to the property of the business, (2) events related to personnel, and (3) events related to customers and others.

LO2 Describe the specific types of risks associated with different aspects of business operations.

Property of the Business

Every business owns things of value. A retail or wholesale business owns inventory. A manufacturing business owns production machinery. A consulting company owns reputation, skill, and experience. Many businesses own furniture, office equipment, vehicles, buildings, and land. Some businesses own valuable patents, copyrights, trademarks, or trade secrets.

Each and every one of these types of property involves specific forms of risk. Inventory can be stolen, spoiled, or become obsolete. Production machinery can break down. Institutional skill and experience can be diminished or lost as key employees die, retire, quit, go to work for competitors, or start their own competing businesses. Furniture, office equipment, vehicles, and buildings can be damaged or destroyed by vandalism, accidents, fire, flood, or wind. Land may become contaminated by spills of hazardous materials or rendered unsafe by cave-ins or landslides. Patents may be infringed upon. Trademarks and brand names that are not properly protected may pass into the public domain. A trade secret may be disclosed.

Events Related to Personnel

There are three main types of risk related to events involving personnel: (1) theft, (2) violation of governmental regulations, and (3) loss of key employees.

Employee Theft

Employee theft is a fact of life for almost all businesses. Theft by personnel may involve direct stealing of money or other assets of the business, or may be the conduct of an illegal act that is intended to provide personal benefit at a cost to the business. The most common form of employee theft is the pilfering of items of small value, such as office supplies and small hand tools, or actions such as making copies for their children to use at school or otherwise using company resources to make personal items. Thought of this way, some experts estimate that 95 percent of small businesses face at least some of this sort of loss annually.[3] Losses of these types are usually insignificant in their effect upon the financial results of your business. However, theft losses of cash and inventory can be of such magnitude that your business is significantly damaged or even fails. As we discussed in Chapter 14, large losses usually arise from embezzlement or fraud.[4]

employee theft Misappropriation of business property by employees of that business.

Violation of Governmental Regulations

Violation of government regulations has become a source of significant business risk over the last 30 years. **Regulation of the workplace** has increased, resulting in employer violations that range from having an employee one time "forget" to use required safety equipment to failing to provide required accommodations for handicapped employees and others to discrimination against a protected class (race, religion, color, national origin, age, disability, or gender). The cost of violating any of the many workplace regulations can range from as little as losing a few hours of your time completing paperwork, up to huge dollar fines and judicial awards.

regulation of the workplace Laws and governmental rules that limit the freedom of business owners to manage their businesses as they please.

Violation of some of the regulations is probably inevitable, given the complex, ambiguous, and sometimes contradictory nature of the regulations. The federal rule-making agencies of which employees may run afoul are countless, including the U.S. Food and Drug Administration, the Environmental Protection Agency, the Securities Exchange Commission, the National Transportation Safety Board, the Federal Aviation Agency, the U.S. Coast Guard, the Federal Drug Agency, and the Department of the Interior, to name only a very few. In addition, most states have similar business-regulating agencies that promulgate rules which often conflict with federal standards. The Small Business Administration estimated in 2001 that small businesses had to spend roughly $1,200 per employee per year to file and keep up with all the regulatory requirements. This rate was twice what large businesses had to spend.[5]

Although there are numerous government agencies that issue business regulations, those small businesses find most problematic are the rules from three agencies: the Internal Revenue Service, the **Equal Employment Opportunity Commission (EEOC)**, and the **Occupational Safety and Health Administration (OSHA)**. The problems arise because each agency has rules that are so complex that compliance problems are almost a certainty, if enough aspects of the business are reviewed. For example, the Americans with Disabilities Act has rules that govern the furnishings, size, placement, and clear space of public toilets and those run to over four pages and include more than 10 architectural drawings to specify exact maximums and minimums to the inch. Any violation of any of the specific accessibility measurements can result in civil fines or litigation awards. We discuss the IRS and the problems of tax code compliance later in this chapter.

Equal Employment Opportunity Commission (EEOC)
A commission established to enforce the provisions of the Equal Employment Opportunity Act.

Occupational Safety and Health Administration (OSHA)
A government agency created to enforce safety in the workplace.

The risk of noncompliance with OSHA and EEOC regulations is further increased by the continual growth in the scope of government regulations. For example, the Equal Employment Opportunity Commission's rule-making authority has grown from the agency's start in 1964. At that time, EEOC established five **protected classes**: "race, color, religion, sex or national origin."[6] Since then the authority of the EEOC has grown through the passage of (1) the **Age Discrimination in Employment Act** of 1967 (ADEA), (2) the **Rehabilitation Act of 1973**, (3) the **Americans with Disabilities Act of 1990** (ADA), and (4) the **Civil Rights Act of 1991**, all of which grant additional rule-making and enforcement powers. The commission has made thousands of rules that are ambiguous and, at times, contradictory.

protected classes
States of being that are expressly prohibited from suffering discrimination: race, color, religion, sex, national origin, gender, age, or disability.

Age Discrimination in Employment Act
An act of Congress that makes it illegal to discriminate against people who are older than 40 years of age.

Rehabilitation Act of 1973
An act of Congress that provides training for workers who are injured on the job.

Americans with Disabilities Act of 1990
An act of Congress that requires that businesses make provisions for access by disabled people.

Civil Rights Act of 1991
A series of acts by Congress that prohibit discrimination on the basis of race, color, religion, sex, or national origin.

Strategies for Dealing with Compliance

One strategy many small businesses use in coping with these rules is to stay small enough to remain below the thresholds for which these agencies' rules apply. For example, if there are no employees, there cannot be any discrimination in hiring. OSHA rules in most industries[7] do not apply to firms with fewer than 10 employees.

Some firms take the ultimate in risky strategies—indifference. Some owners figure it makes more sense not to spend time on compliance, and when they face government action, close the business. This sounds fine in theory, but government agencies can come after the owner of a business for damages and fines even after the business itself is bankrupt or closed. More often, the owner is fined and required to comply. The fines and time spent dealing with the agency are often said to cost more than complying ahead of time. You can see why indifference is the riskiest of strategies.

Another strategy is being proactive. Government agencies must post their rules and most make available summaries focused on the concerns of small business. For example:

EEOC's Small Business Page: www.eeoc.gov/employers/smallbusinesses.html.
EEOC's Americans with Disabilities Act Handbook: www.eeoc.gov/ada/adahandbook.html.
OSHA's Small Business Page: www.osha.gov/dcsp/smallbusiness/index.html.
OSHA's Small Business Handbook: www.osha.gov/Publications/smallbusiness/small-business.pdf.

A great listing of government small business resources can be found on the IRS's small business page, at www.irs.gov/businesses/small/content/0,,id598864,00.html. Perhaps the key resource for entrepreneurs trying to be proactive is www.reginfo.gov, the combined national website for federal, state and local regulation.

While many government agencies offer free reviews of a business for compliance, many small business owners are leery of such efforts, because they will be obligated to quickly fix any problems identified. A useful alternative is to have private contractors do assessments to check for compliance. Lawyers, especially labor lawyers, have experience in preventing EEOC compliance problems. Many consulting engineers can perform OSHA checks. In addition some of the major small business trade associations such as the NFIB and even local Chambers of Commerce offer classes on compliance for OSHA, EEOC, and other regulations.

One other strategy, which is not for the faint of heart or short of cash, is to fight for what you believe to be right. This usually entails first dealing directly with the agency's representative. Often this direct dealing is best done with an attorney present or only after being prepared by the attorney about how to handle your side of the meeting. If that meeting does not lead to a resolution, there are administrative reviews and even court actions at which the firm can stand up to the government. One famous example is that of Clint Eastwood (see Small Business Insight, below).

SMALL BUSINESS INSIGHT

ITS NOT JUST A "FIST FULL OF DOLLARS"!

Clint Eastwood may not quite match your idea of a small business owner, but, in fact, Mr. Eastwood owns several small businesses, among which is the 32-room Mission Ranch Hotel in Carmel, California.

In 1997, the Mission Ranch was sued for alleged violations of the Americans with Disabilities Act. The lawyer, Paul Rein, and his client, Diane Zum Brunnen, demanded that Mr. Eastwood widen some doors and make the bathrooms more accessible. They also asked for $577,000 in legal fees, and an unspecified amount of damages for the plaintiff.

Unlike many owners of small businesses, Mr. Eastwood is wealthy, politically savvy (he had been mayor of Carmel), and willing to bear the costs of litigation. The *Wall Street Journal* wrote:

> These "sleazebag lawyers," the veteran actor says, his voice constricting, messed with the wrong guy when they "frivolously" sued him and hundreds of other small-business owners for failing to comply quickly enough with the Americans with Disabilities Act. Mr. Eastwood states that he is not in any way against the ADA. Rather, he will not "roll over" for trial lawyers whom he believes are using the ADA to extort money from small businesses by filing unwarranted lawsuits.[8]

Mr. Eastwood also joined forces with U.S. Representative Mark Foley to pass a bill that would provide business owners with 90 days to comply with the bill's requirements before being sued. Mr. Eastwood actively lobbied members of Congress to pass this bill.

The provisions of Americans with Disabilities Act distinguish between those accommodations that must be made for employees, and those that must be made for nonemployees. If you violate any provision, you are liable for three costs: (1) all legal costs, both your own and those of the person suing you, (2) any damages awarded to the plaintiff, and (3) the cost of rectifying any noncompliance. By far the most expensive part of this is the legal fees. Without regard to what your own attorney may charge you, the plaintiff attorney is allowed to demand $275 per hour, based on that attorney's statement of how many hours we spent on the lawsuit.[9]

SO WHAT BECAME OF THE LAWSUIT AGAINST CLINT EASTWOOD?

The trial finally took place and was given to the jury on September 29, 2011, nearly 14 years after being filed in California. The jury, as is common in civil suits, "split the baby." It found Mr. Eastwood in noncompliance because of inadequate signage and no ramp access to the hotel office.[10] However, no damages were awarded to the plaintiff. Only Mr. Eastwood knows just how much this lawsuit cost him, but you can be certain that it far exceeds the original $577,000 demanded.

AND WHAT ABOUT THE PROVISIONS OF THE ADA?

Despite nearly 15 years of trying to get changes to the ADA that would provide business owners with a required notification period before being sued, no change has been made. As recently as March 2011, yet another bill to modify the act was introduced to Congress. It, as have all other similar attempts, died without ever being considered by the full Congress.[11]

The Eastwood situation hints at one other strategy, what the original lawyer suing the hotel hoped to achieve—capitulation. In capitulation, often unscrupulous people use the threat of bringing a charge of noncompliance against a firm as a means of getting a cash settlement not to file. This type of person actively looks for minor violations of OSHA, ADA, or other laws. They then write the owner of the "offending" business, demanding a cash settlement for the alleged damage. The business owner is placed into an untenable situation: Either pay the "complainant" as demanded, or be stuck with the costs of litigation, and the risk that a jury will award even more. Many small business owners choose to pay rather than face the risk of losing. Because these payments are never recorded in any central location, it is possible for the individuals to repeat the process.

Loss of Key Employees

key employees
Employees whose experience and skills are critical to the success of a business.

Loss of **key employees** is a particularly acute risk for small businesses. Because of the simple fact that there are only a few employees in a small business, invariably one person or a very few people are essential to the successful operation of the business. If such a key employee quits, retires, becomes disabled, or dies, the business faces a crisis. In many cases, the loss of a key employee has led to the bankruptcy and dissolution of the business.

Competition from former employees is also a constant risk. Good employees who understand the business, who successfully sell products and services, and who are skilled at the operations of the business are often tempted to become competitors. This can happen several different ways. A key employee may be "hired away" by an existing competitor who offers a higher salary and greater perks. A key employee may start her or his own business, using the knowledge and skills gained from working in your business. Customers may offer to back a key employee to establish a competing business in order to obtain lower prices and greater negotiating leverage. Vendors may offer a key employee dealerships or exclusive sales territories in a bid to increase sales of their specific products.

This risk is especially acute in knowledge and service businesses, such as accounting practices, medical practices, barber and beauty shops, and restaurants. All of these businesses have relatively low barriers to entry for qualified people. Each type of business depends upon personal relationships engendered with customers. When a key employee of a knowledge firm leaves, it is common for several customers to change to the new firm.

Events Related to Customers and Others

Although customers are, by definition, the "reason for being" of any business, they also are the source of considerable business risk. In addition to customers, you are also at risk from vendors and even trespassers on your property. This risk from customers and others primarily arises from (1) injuries suffered while upon business property and (2) injury or damage that is caused during the use of the business's products. These risks are, of course, in addition to the familiar risk of customers, who are sold products or services on credit, not paying as they have agreed.

Injuries suffered while on business property may or may not be your fault. People at times do stupid things, such as climb on shelves to get items that are "just out of reach." If the shelf collapses and dumps the customer onto the floor, you're going to pay twice: once for the broken shelf and spoiled merchandise, and once for the "pain and suffering" of the customer. A reasonable person might believe that the customer was responsible for his or her own acts and the business should not be liable. It is most unfortunate that juries are composed of "peers" and not of "reasonable persons."

Injuries on business premises may also arise from the actions of trespassers. In many cases, a business has been held responsible for harm experienced by a trespasser, as well as harm inflicted by the trespasser upon employees, customers, and vendors. An extreme example of this type of event is robbery and assault that occurs on business property. In many cases, injuries suffered by employees and customers at the hands of the criminals have been held to be the fault of the business. The rationale given has been that the business didn't provide good enough security. Again, the business pays twice: once when the robber steals money and other assets; again when the robber, employees, and customers are paid for pain and suffering caused by the robbery.

Payment for injury or damage that occurs during the use of the business's products is referred to as *product liability*. The magnitude of losses resulting from product liability claims has

Retailers can be held responsible for damages caused by goods that have been tampered with and placed on the store's shelves. Constant vigilance is required to assure that inventory is free of any impairment.

increased greatly in recent years with an increase in class action lawsuits. This is an issue that you must take very seriously if you are a manufacturer. Although individual customers usually get very little money from class action suits, the lawyers who pursue them often receive payments of millions of dollars, as occurred in the case of asbestos producers and tobacco companies. Certainly, the smaller your firm is, the less exposure you have to class action product liability suits. This is true for two reasons: A small business has fewer customers who can claim harm, and a small business does not have the "deep pockets" of cash and other assets that can be raided by rapacious law firms.

Individual lawsuits may also be filed when a single user claims to have been harmed by the product. Such lawsuits are actually more common than class action suits. Although the amount paid in settlement is usually a tiny fraction of that of a class action suit, a manufacturer must still take the issue very seriously. In the 1970s a rash of individual lawsuits against manufacturers of small (under 12,000 lb. gross weight) airplanes resulted in the demise of the industry. Many small businesses that either made small airplanes or made parts and subassemblies for airplanes were forced into bankruptcy. The production of small airplanes did not resume in the United States until Congress passed a law that limited the exposure of manufacturers to product liability suits.[12]

Risk of nonpayment by customers is experienced by all businesses that offer credit. This is true whether you directly provide credit or it is provided through a third party. You have to balance two conflicting things when you decide to offer credit: (1) giving credit to customers will increase your sales, and (2) offering credit guarantees sooner or later some customer will not pay as promised. How big this risk is depends on how many customers you give credit to and how much you let any single customer charge.

Restaurants, clothing retailers, barbers, and beauticians face relatively low risks of loss from nonpayment. First, most of these businesses provide credit only by accepting credit cards, which reduces the risk of nonpayment. Second, the amount that any one customer charges is unlikely to be big enough to threaten your business if it is not paid.

If you sell large-ticket items, such as signs, house remodeling, boats, and the like, you incur large risks by offering credit to customers. Few people have credit cards that have charge limits big enough to buy such things. Therefore, you have to give credit directly to your customer. When the inevitable default occurs, the amount of the unpaid debt can be large enough to threaten the survival of a business.

SMALL BUSINESS INSIGHT

BUT IS IT RIGHT? CELLDYNE BIOPHARMA

In late fall 2008, Celldyne Biopharma, LLC, after more than 4 years of research, had determined a way to concentrate a naturally occurring avian follistatin. Follistatin is part of the body's mechanism to regulate the growth of skeletal muscles. If you take active follistatin into your bloodstream, muscle cells quit dying and you will bulk up without exercise.

As exciting as this might be to body builders, it is even more important for people with wasting diseases. A regular supply of follistatin will reduce, and in some cases reverse, cachexia.

There was only one problem facing Celldyne Biopharma. The cost of raw materials and of the process to concentrate the amount of follistatin was so expensive that to make a profit, the food supplement would have to be priced like a cancer chemotherapy drug. As the product existed, it contained measurable amounts of follistatin. Tests on healthy male subjects found that ingesting the product resulted in elevated follistatin in the blood. It worked. But it could be made only in small quantities at great cost.

The chief medical officer of the LLC who was himself an M.D. sports physician, demanded that the product be packaged and put onto the market. He maintained, "It can be diluted to make the price acceptable." The chief science officer, a Ph.D. in cellular chemistry disagreed, as did the CEO and the CFO. They wanted to tweak the process to reduce costs and improve the concentration of follistatin available to be absorbed by those who took the product.

The managers came to an impasse. The chief medical officer and an outside marketing contractor (who had already started advertising the product) demanded that the product was good enough. "Forget further development and sell what is in hand," they urged. The other members of the executive committee balked at selling what they believed to be a less than optimum form of the product. "Beside which," they argued, "we can't make enough of it at this time, anyway."

The physician and marketer threatened to sue the other manager members if their demands were not immediately met. This put everyone into a quandary. What should they do?

1. Given that the product had been shown to be safe and at least slightly effective, should the managers agree to start selling it?
2. If they decide to sell a diluted version of the product, what obligation do the managers of the LLC have to the customers?
3. Was the CMO right to sue the other members of the LLC because they refused to begin immediate sales?
4. Whom do you suppose benefited most from Celldyne Biopharma, LLC?

If you want to know what the final outcome of this was, read the "Rest of the Story" box on page 581.[13]

Managing Risks

LO3 Describe techniques to manage risks to stay within your level of risk tolerance.

Although none of the risks discussed above can be completely avoided, there are strategies you can use to minimize the likelihood and magnitude of losses. The best strategy is to develop a business environment that minimizes (1) the probability of the event occurring and (2) the amount of loss that can be experienced if the event does occur. You do this by (1) making specific plans for and arrangements to deal with foreseeable events, (2) creating and enforcing an appropriate code of conduct for yourself and all employees, (3) ensuring that valuable assets are physically secure, and (4) actively working to get rid of any physical hazards in your workplace.

You should develop disaster plans for events which are unlikely, but that have a finite probability of happening. For example, those businesses that are located in the Missouri and Mississippi River flood plains near St. Louis have a very real probability of significant flooding in any year. Prudent business management for these firms includes creating a plan of action to remove valuable assets to high ground, making plans for temporary business locations, and creating provisions for subcontracting work in order to minimize the effect of business interruption from the inevitable flood. Disaster planning like this can also work to minimize the effects of fires, storms, and earthquakes upon business operations.

A written code of ethics and business conduct (like those discussed in Chapter 2) make explicit what you expect of your employees. By obtaining employee acceptance of the code, you can create an environment in which peer pressure works to discourage inappropriate behavior and works to encourage desired behavior. To be effective, it is essential that you abide by the code, leading your employees by your example of integrity and honesty.

Valuable assets of the business must be kept in secure areas. When valuable assets must be used, access to them should be carefully controlled and monitored by management. Only those employees who have a business need should be allowed access to valuable assets at any time.

Working proactively to ensure that your physical place of business is (1) free of potential hazards and (2) secure from intruders will prevent on-premises injuries and violations of EEOC or OSHA rules. It is easier and much less expensive to anticipate and prevent potential lawsuits than it is to defend yourself against them once they have been filed.

Managing Risk to Tangible Property

Managing risk to the tangible properties of your business depends upon the nature of the property. Land and buildings aren't subject to theft, but they can be damaged or destroyed by a variety of events. Equipment can be stolen, vandalized, or allowed to fall into disrepair. Small items of high value may be stolen by employees, customers, vendors, or others. The specific measures to control for each type of risk are particular to the specific asset at risk.

Managing Risk to Buildings and Land

Protection from fire for buildings may be obtained through such measures as installing smoke alarms and sprinkler systems and having a fire plug nearby. Other control measures include removing flammable ground cover such as brush, leaves, and fallen branches from proximity to all buildings.

Protection from flood can, first and foremost, be accomplished by not locating on a flood plain. Although this seems like a common sense directive, unimaginable numbers of businesses are built on flood plains, and new construction continues. In 1993, the entire flood plain of the Missouri and Mississippi Rivers in the St. Louis area, from Kansas City on the west, Hannibal, Missouri, on the north, to the confluence of the Mississippi and Ohio Rivers on the south, was inundated with water up to 50 feet deep. Hundreds of businesses in the areas around St. Louis and St. Charles, Missouri, were destroyed. Despite this experience and despite a second round of severe flooding in 1994, the flood plain of the Missouri River from St. Louis upstream for over 30 miles is the site of extensive building. It is only a matter of time until the river again rises, the levees fail, and hundreds of businesses are flooded with tens of feet of muddy water.

Flooding also occurs for reasons other than streams and rivers overflowing their banks. Floods often occur from breaks in water supply pipes, from accidental activation of fire suppression sprinklers, from blockages in storm and sanitary sewers, and from runoff of water that is sprayed upon burning buildings. You may protect yourself from these hazards through performing regular inspection and maintenance of the plumbing and fire suppression systems of your buildings.

Protection from storms can be accomplished by rigorously enforcing building standards concerning attachment of buildings to foundations, types and construction of roofs, and by choice of building materials and construction techniques. The specifics of storm proofing a building depends upon the geographical location of the building. Specific storm hazards, wild fire, wind, flood, or snow load are determined primarily by geography. Each geographic area has its own risk. California has frequent floods and mud slides. The mountains of the West are subject to winter snows, spring floods, and summer wild fires. The Gulf and Eastern shores south of New York are subject to frequent hurricanes. The Midwest, especially Oklahoma, Kansas, Nebraska, Iowa, Missouri, Illinois, Indiana, and Ohio, experiences thousands of tornados every year. On May 22, 2011, a category 5 tornado struck Joplin, Missouri. The storm destroyed homes and businesses in a path nearly a mile wide and fully 6 miles long. Total damage has been estimated to be $3 billion. The upper Midwest, including northern Ohio, western Pennsylvania, and western New York, is annually buried under tons of snow. Specific building techniques to withstand tornado winds are useless against five feet of snow on the roof, just as structure to withstand snow loading is useless when the entire building slides down the hillside.

Managing risks to tools, equipment, inventory, and other physical assets is largely a function of developing and enforcing appropriate business policies and procedures. Tools and equipment should be maintained on a schedule that prevents serious wear or damage. Frequent inspections should be made to ensure that any problem is detected as soon as possible, allowing repairs to be made in a systematic manner.

Physical assets that can be stolen must be kept in locked storage areas when not in use. Small items of high value should not only be kept locked away, but a procedure should be rigidly enforced that requires employees to sign for removing them from storage. A manager's signature should be required to confirm that the item has been returned to the proper storage when it's no longer needed.

Managing Risk to Computers and Data

One of the riskiest areas of business today involves computers, especially those connected to the Internet. Today hackers use programs which seek out unprotected computers connected to the Internet, and once identified, take them over through spyware programs. Some spyware may use your computer to send out advertising spam on behalf of the hacker's clients. Other spyware lets the hacker actually see and even steal data on your PC, including passwords and credit card information. If you

SMALL BUSINESS INSIGHT

The Medicine Shoppe Joplin, Missouri

On May 22, 2011, a massive multiple-vortex tornado tore through the Midwest town of Joplin, Missouri. Among the hundreds of business locations destroyed was the Medicine Shoppe, owned by David and Sherree Starrett. All that they could salvage from the wreckage was the safe that held controlled drugs, some computer equipment, and a few filing cabinets. All their pharmacy files were destroyed by being submerged in water.

The Starretts, however, did not give up. Only two days after the storm, they managed to lease an undamaged storefront. They moved in the few things salvaged from the storm. With fixtures donated by other Medicine Shoppe owners The Starretts set up for business. The DEA issued a new provider number and the state of Missouri provided a disaster waiver. They received an expedited shipment of drugs and medicines from their supplier. On May 28, 6 days after the storm, the Starretts reopened for business in their new location.

David and Sherree Starrett are recovering from a disaster of a magnititude that few will ever experience. Their resilience, determination, and hard work (along with business insurance and an effective business network) have enabled them to literally "rise from the ashes.[14]

have your business data on the computer, your customer lists (including *their* credit card numbers and identifying information) can get hacked.

The best way to think of protecting your PC is a lot like how you think about protecting your car. Locking the door and taking the keys with you prevents the vast majority of car thefts, those done by kids who find keys in the ignition or open an unlocked door and hot-wire a car. What is the equivalent for a PC?

1. A firewall: Firewalls are programs or pieces of equipment called routers which serve as a barrier between your PC and the Internet.
2. An antivirus program: Viruses are malicious programs designed to damage PCs.
3. Antispyware programs: Spyware are programs designed to report on your keystrokes or data, or give remote control of your PC to others.

The simplest answer is to buy an all-in-one collection of security programs like Norton Internet Security or ZoneAlarm Internet Security Suite. You can often find good deals on these packages (usually via rebates) at discounters like Office Depot or Office Max. The advantage of these programs is that all their installation and updating is done at the same time, so it is easier to maintain.

The least expensive alternative is to find a free stand-alone program. However, to be ethical in protecting your computer, you need to select programs that are free for use in business (profit-making) situations. Some great programs, like the free version of the ZoneAlarm firewall or AVG's free antivirus are not free for business use. One company which makes a complete set of programs (firewall, antispyware, and antivirus) available is Comodo (**www.comodo.com**). These can be used by businesses for free. The disadvantage of stand-alone programs is that each needs to be installed and updated individually (although many programs can be set to update themselves automatically).

Going back to our car thief analogy, if a professional car thief sets out to steal your car, the lock-and-take-keys approach will not deter them. Here you step up to a higher level of deterrence such as the use of an alarm system. The same is true for determined hackers. You may not be able to stop them from getting around a firewall or antispyware program, but you can protect your data by encrypting it. Encryption is the recoding of your data so that only people who know the unlocking code can see the data correctly. Windows comes with a way to encrypt data, but its approach does not let you move or share an encrypted file. A better approach is to use an encryption program like AxCrypt (**http://axcrypt.sourceforge.net/**) or Inferno (**http://inferno.sourceforge.net**), both of which are free. One caution though—if you encrypt a file, make sure you use a password for your encryption that you can easily recall. Once encrypted, if you lose the password, you lose the ability to decode the file!

That brings us to the final issue in Internet security—the human element. Many people reading about the problem of password loss probably think, "I'll write my password down." The problem is that most data theft comes from *inside* businesses. Writing your password down and leaving it where others can see it is the equivalent of leaving your keys in the car. Even with all the programs running, a computer can only be secure if the people using it practice safe surfing—using complex passwords, changing them frequently, and keeping passwords to themselves (or written down and hidden away from others), not opening downloads from unknown, unexpected, or untrustworthy sources, and having your PC set to lock itself up after a few minutes of inactivity (as when you leave your desk), so others cannot use your computer when you are not there.

Remember the car analogy? If your car is broken, it is of as little use as when it is stolen. That brings us to one other type of concern you should have about your data—preserving it. We have all heard the line, "my computer crashed and took my project." As your contact list in Outlook or your customer database or inventory and accounting records become more important to your business, the cost of a loss of data to *your* business increases. The cost is not just lost revenues—since you cannot charge people if you lost the information on what they owe—it is also lost time. Imagine how long it would take to recreate your complete list of contacts? Now repeat that for all the data files generated by your business. The result is frightening.

The solution is called backup. These days it is easier than you might expect. If you have Internet access, you can use Mozy (**www.mozy.com**), which gives you 2 gigabytes of backup space for free, and unlimited space for $50 a year. Their software can be set up for automated backup of key files when you are online. You can find other services by Googling "online backup." Many offer a mix of free and for-fee services like Mozy. Figure 17.1 graphically details this process. Another alternative

FIGURE 17.1

How Online Backup Systems Works

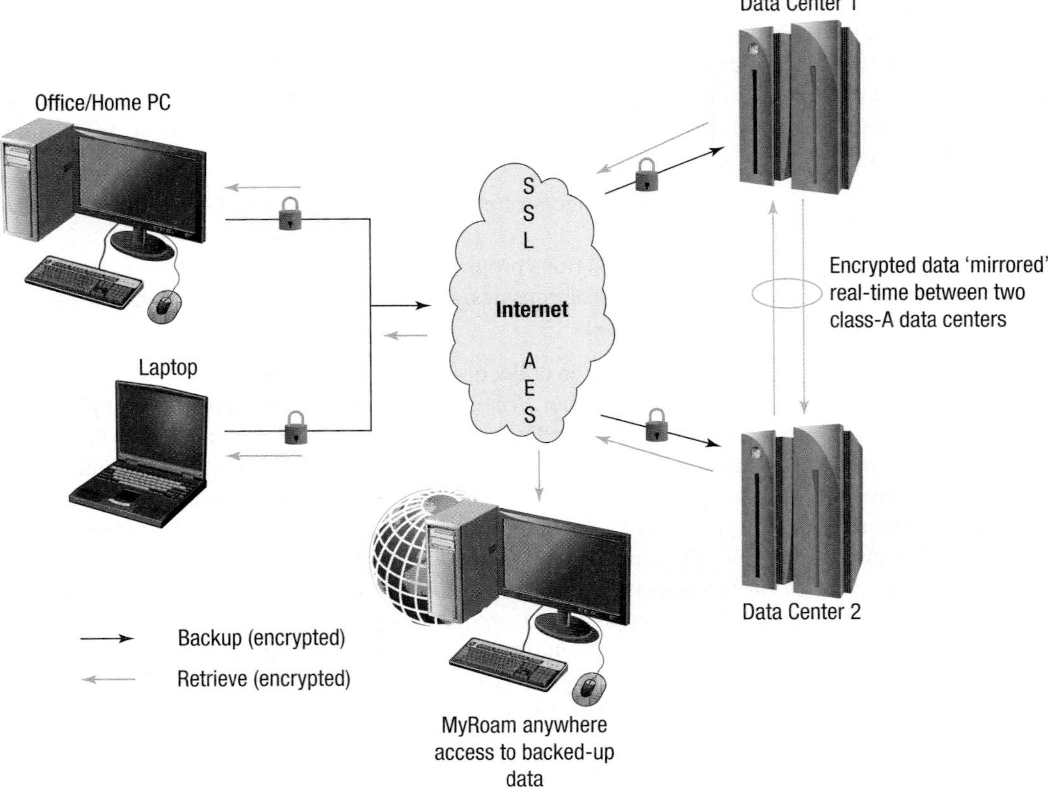

is to use an external hard drive that gets its connection and power through a USB cable. Get an external drive which comes with backup software. With these drives, you plug it in once a day to your PC and back up your files. Then disconnect the hard drive. This protects your data from electrical storms or other failures of your PC's power system or motherboard. If the PC does not work, you still have your current (or at worst, day-old) data to work with, and your business can operate almost normally from another computer with the right software.

Today the biggest risk to most businesses comes when using computers, and as more and more of your business's most valuable information are in the files on your computer, the importance of protecting it grows. The basics are relatively simple, but the quality of the protection depends on following through on the basics, and backing them up with behaviors that don't undermine your other efforts to secure your computer and data.

Managing Risk to Intangible Property

Intellectual property rights comprise the legal rights to use unique features of products or services that provide competitive advantage. The rights to use unique features may be legally protected in several ways, including establishing precedence, keeping the process secret, filing for a copyright or trademark, or obtaining a patent. However, if the feature is successful, competitors will eventually find a way to either lessen its competitive advantage or even to render it worthless.

The problem with legal protection methods for intellectual property is that there is no governmental agency that will assist you, as the owner of a small business, in maintaining your legal rights. Copyrights, trademarks, and patents do not automatically provide any protection. Anyone may copy any of these items at any time. If, and only if the holder of the intellectual property rights promptly reacts to infringement by making written objections to any and all infractions, can the legal rights be maintained. In other words, holding legal rights to intellectual property provides the owner solely with grounds to pursue lawsuits against infringement. Immediately upon learning of any infringement, a certified letter should be sent to the suspected violator, clearly specifying the nature of the intellectual property rights held and demanding an immediate cease and desist of the infringement.

If the infringement continues, a lawsuit is your only recourse. If you do nothing, you get nothing, as was the case for Harvey Ball, the inventor of the smiley face (see Small Business Insight, below).

Guarding against obsolescence is best accomplished by maintaining a diligent watch on business intelligence concerning developments within the industry. If you own a small business that depends upon valuable intellectual property, you should regularly read the journals and magazines that are unique to your industry. You also should subscribe to clipping services, such as those provided by WestLaw (www.westlaw.com) and Dow Jones (www.wsj.com).

Additionally, you should carefully listen to customers and vendors for information concerning developments in your industry. Although it sounds paranoid, the truth is that intellectual property is constantly under attack. Very smart people are diligently working to develop better products and processes from which they will gain wealth at your expense if you move too slowly reacting to threats to your business.

Protection from theft of business property also depends upon the type of property held. Although land is not subject to being physically stolen, you can lose your property rights through a process called *adverse possession.* Adverse possession occurs when the owner of real property does not enforce property rights and allows a nonowner to use the property as if it were his or her own. Just as land cannot be stolen, buildings and large equipment for which there is no ready market are similarly free from theft because of their physical nature. The property most at risk is cash and small items of high value that can be quickly and easily sold.

You need to do two things to protect yourself from theft: (1) physically protect your property, and (2) develop and enforce rules that prevent the employee responsible for the asset from being able to account for the asset. This is called **separation of duties**, and is a core management technique to safeguard money and other valuable assets of a business.[15]

separation of duties
A type of internal control that separates the physical control of an asset from the person accounting for that asset.

SMALL BUSINESS INSIGHT

Harvey Ball and the Smiley Face[16]

How could Harvey Ball have profited from his design? How can a citizen of France register a design created by an American artist?

You see them everywhere—yellow circles with a smiling caricature on them. The amazing thing is that as much of a cultural icon as the smiley face is, its inventor never got any money for it. Harvey Ball was a freelance designer working at state Farm Mutual Insurance in Worcester, Massachusetts, in 1963. He was asked if he could provide a design to boost morale after a merger had left some people upset. He designed the circle and smile, and he added the eyes so disgruntled employees couldn't easily turn the smile into a frown by wearing the button upside down. Ball was paid $45. He did not trademark it (which, as the designer, he could have done), nor did State Farm. State Farm gave them away—first to the employees, but then to customers who clamored for them. As the buttons spread, it got copied and copied. Franklin Loufrani of France registered the design in 1971 in over 80 countries and did receive royalties, and eventually Ball registered a version with his name on it. In the end, Loufrani made the money from the design, while Ball never got anything else for it, except a lot of satisfaction. As he said, "Never in the history of mankind or art has any single piece of art gotten such widespread favor, pleasure, enjoyment, and nothing has ever been so simply done and so easily understood in art."

FIGURE 17.2

Sources of Theft

Source: Richard C. Hollinger and Amanda Adams, 2008 National Retail Security Survey, University of Florida, 2008, p. 7.

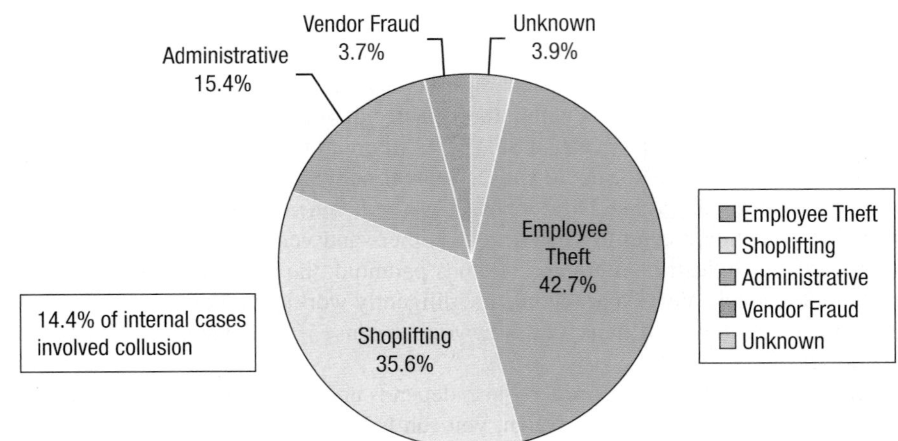

Although separation of duties will keep any single employee from stealing, nothing will keep two or more employees who decide to cooperate from stealing company property. Employee collusion is the source of the largest amount of employee theft.[17] When employees agree to defraud, "one lies, and the other swears to it!" This is the way that common frauds are perpetrated, such as sales of nonexistent advertising, payments to nonexistent vendors, and purchases of inventory and supplies from a vendor who will pay a kickback to the dishonest employees. As Figure 17.2 shows, employees account for the single largest source of business theft.

Managing Risk Resulting from Events Involving Personnel

Managing risks created by personnel starts with the hiring process, as is discussed in Chapter 19. Efforts must be made to identify people of high moral character and ethical standards. Owners of small businesses are well advised to use employment services to screen potential employees. Employment services can perform background checks, administer drug tests, and conduct psychological tests that are designed to measure an individual's level of integrity.

When potential applicants have been identified, they should be brought into the business to meet the people with whom they will be working. Current employees can participate in an informal interview with the job candidate. The purpose of these practices is to hire honest people who will become active and enthusiastic employees who consider themselves to be part of a team.

However, no hiring process is 100 percent foolproof. For that matter, no human being is 100 percent reliable. Ultimately, no one is able to withstand all temptation, regardless of ethical standards. Because all people are fallible, owners of small businesses have an obligation to employees to make theft difficult and honesty easy and rewarding. If you tempt employees with easy access to valuable property and with little likelihood of theft being detected, sooner or later most employees will succumb to temptation in ways great or small.

The Association of Certified Fraud Examiners found in a 2004 study (the Wells Report[18]) that the most costly employee frauds compared to total business assets occur in businesses with fewer than 100 employees. The median loss to these businesses was a staggering (for the owner of a small business) $98,000. This finding is interesting for two reasons: (1) The vast majority of small businesses have fewer than 100 employees, and (2) it contradicts the belief that people do not steal from people they know. The fact is that thieves come from all social classes, all levels of education, and all ethnic backgrounds. It is an unfortunate fact that the difference between many a thief and many an honest citizen is only that the citizen has not yet been caught. For these reasons, all owners and managers of small businesses must be aware of and guard against dishonesty in employees.

internal control
A set of rules and procedures that work to limit the opportunity for employee theft or malfeasance.

Internal control is the primary method of ensuring honesty in employees. Internal control is a matter of establishing policies and procedures that work to make dishonesty difficult and honesty easy. The most basic technique of internal control is to separate the duties of maintaining the security of assets from the duties of maintaining records of those assets.

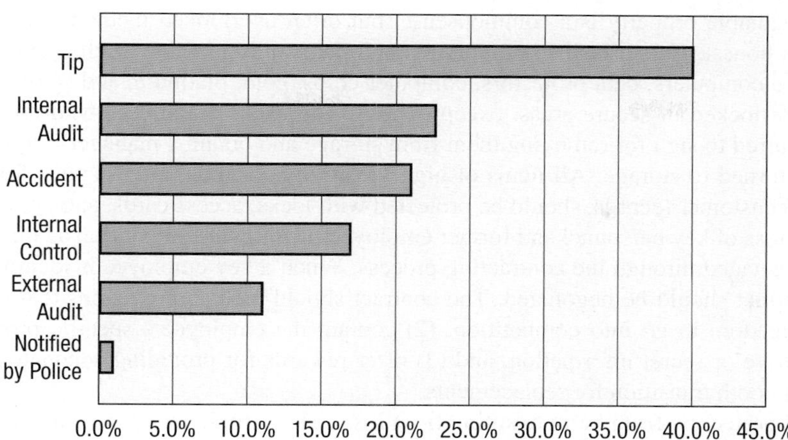

FIGURE 17.3

Percentage of Frauds by Method of Detection

Note: Total exceeds 100 percent because of multiple responses.

Source: Association of Certified Fraud Examiners, 2004 Report to the Nation on Occupational Fraud and Abuse, 2004.

While internal control will reduce the opportunity for employee fraud, it is not sufficient to disclose frauds that are currently taking place. The Wells Report found that internal controls were the fourth most likely method to discover fraud, following accidental discovery. As Figure 17.3 shows, nearly 40 percent of all frauds that were detected were found because of a tip. About one-fourth of frauds were detected by an internal audit, and one-fifth were found by accident. Internal controls were responsible for disclosing only 18 percent of the frauds that were detected during the study period.

Separation of duties is most important for intangible assets—those things of value that have no physical "reality," such as money, accounts receivable, patents, and licensing agreements. Consider the problems of keeping money secure. Money exists primarily as an entry in the accounting records of your bank. The employee who has authority to write checks and to make deposits has free access to the things related to embezzlement. All that person needs to do is write a check made payable to a fake entity, and then cash the check and pocket the money. If one employee both writes checks and keeps accounts receivable records, theft is even easier to commit and harder to detect. The employee merely mails an invoice from a fake entity. When the fake invoice is received, the employee creates a payable account for the fake vendor. Subsequently, during the ordinary course of business, the employee writes and mails a check which will be delivered to an address held by the employee. The accounting records of the business are in perfect order. The only problem is that you are out the money that was stolen.

Such simple frauds can amount to huge amounts of money over time. The 2004 Report to the Nation on Occupational Fraud and Abuse reports on 508 cases of fraud that combined resulted in over $761 million in losses to the defrauded companies. Nearly 93 percent of the frauds detected involved misappropriation of business assets, but fewer than one-fourth of those involved assets other than cash. Fraudulent disbursements of cash comprise 74 percent of all misappropriations with an average loss to a business of $125,000.

The greatest threat of loss from employee dishonesty occurs when two or more employees *collude:* agree together to defraud your business. Employee collusion is both very common and very difficult to detect. The most common form of employee collusion is the theft of cash and inventory. Cash is most usually stolen by making false disbursements. Inventory is stolen through false employee sales.

Many small businesses allow employees to purchase inventory at cost for personal use. When two employees agree to steal, one purchases merchandise from the other. The employee who is "selling" records the sale as being less expensive items. For example, Andrew wishes to buy a complete computer from his employer's business. Brenda makes the employee sale, but records the merchandise as a hard drive. Andrew pays only the $40 cost of a hard drive, not the $400 cost of a complete computer. The owner is out the $360 difference. Of course, at some point the computer will show up as an inventory shortage. But by the time inventory is taken, there is no way to determine if the missing computer was taken by an employee or stolen by a shoplifter.

Securing valuable property is a commonsense, but often overlooked method, of keeping honest employees honest. If your business involves small items of high value, such as precision tools, jewelry, laptop computers, data projectors, computer chips, gold, platinum, and so on, those items should be kept locked in secure areas, except when being used. Employees who use such items should be required to sign for removing them from storage and obtain a manager's signature when the item is returned to storage. All items of high sensitivity, such as trade secrets, formulas, and employee and customer records, should be protected with locks, access cards, and passwords.

Risk from loss of key personnel and former employees setting up competition against your business can be managed through the contracting process. When a key employee is identified, an employment contract should be negotiated. The contract should include provisions that (1) limit the employee's freedom to go into competition, (2) contain the employee's specific promise not to disclose sensitive or secret information, and (3) offer rewards for providing adequate termination notice and a smooth transition for replacements.

Additional protection from harm resulting from loss of key employees can be obtained by cross training among employees. Although any specific employee may not be able to be directly replaced, the needed skills and talents can certainly be found within a group of employees. If employees are cross trained, the loss of one individual can be alleviated by drawing upon the diverse abilities of other employees. Finally, any truly key employee, including yourself as the owner of a small business, should be actively grooming his or her own replacement to be able to step in on an instant's notice.

Managing Risk from Violations of Tax Regulations

tax codes
Laws and regulations that specify the requirements of taxation.

It is a rare business that has never run afoul of a taxing agency. Small businesses are subject to taxation from cities, counties, states, and the U.S. government. The **tax codes** of all levels of government have become ever more complex, placing more and more responsibility on businesses for calculating, collecting, and paying various taxes. Taxes imposed on small business include franchise or corporation taxes, income taxes, employee taxes, sales and use taxes, and property taxes. The regulations that relate to all these taxes are so voluminous that it is impossible for any individual to know them all. In fact, the regulations are so complex that even the enforcement personnel of various taxing agencies are often ignorant of the myriad details of the code and regulations. Perhaps then it is not surprising that the government estimates that 15 percent of taxpaying businesses are not complying with the rules.[19]

Although there is no magic formula that will prevent financial loss that arises from being the subject of a tax audit, there are some fairly simple techniques that will work together to limit your exposure. First, you must keep complete, *accurate* accounting records. If you use a computerized accounting system, be certain that the audit trail function is enabled. Control access to the functions of the accounting system by issuing and regularly changing passwords. File all source documents, such as purchase orders, bills of lading, requisitions, and invoices, in a systematic manner that will provide easy access if you are called upon to "prove" any transaction. Carefully document all cash transactions. Ensure that employees properly enter all cash sales into the cash register, and then reconcile the cash register tape to the cash register contents every day. Insist on receiving a *signed* receipt from vendors when you pay in cash.

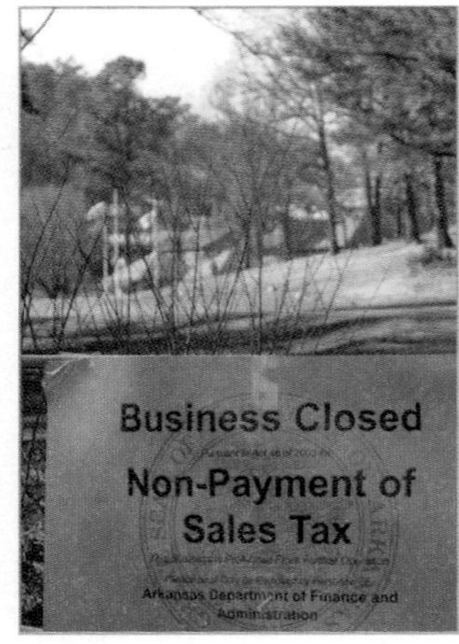

● You won't go to jail for failure to pay your creditors, but you will spend some time behind bars if you do not pay your taxes. Keep your business in financial shape by making timely payment of taxes your first top priority.

The simple fact is that many, if not most, owners of small businesses "skim" in ways small and large by taking cash from their businesses before it is recorded as a revenue. Many owners also inappropriately charge personal expenses to the business as a way of extracting money without paying income taxes. Tax agents know these facts very well. As a result, when your business is audited, the agent will assume that you have understated your revenues and overstated your deductible expenses. It is your responsibility to prove that you have not.

Second, you should establish a relationship with both an accountant and a lawyer who are expert in tax issues. Although attestation by an accountant or lawyer is not evidence of lack of criminal activity (think Enron), an accountant or lawyer whose practice comprises issues of small business taxation will most likely do a much better job of representing you than you can ever do for yourself.

Third, and most important, make paying your taxes your first financial priority. The temptation to "borrow" from tax money is at times overwhelming, especially when you are being hounded by creditors for payment. Do not give in to this temptation. You can go to prison for not paying

SMALL BUSINESS INSIGHT

WHEN CAREFUL PLANNING AND PREPARATION AREN'T ENOUGH

"Neither Rex nor I expected any problems when we found out that the Texas Sales Tax Commission was going to conduct an audit," said Jay Hall.

Rex said, "When the auditor came, we set up a desk for him. We kept him in coffee and gave him every record he requested. He worked for about three days checking through the last five years of our business."

"We were cool with it. After all, we have always kept our taxes squeaky clean. We knew that we had nothing to worry about."

"Little did we know," said Jay.

Rex Stone and Jay Hall are the owners and managers of Rex Stone Associates. Their business comprises planning, producing, and managing events, primarily in the San Antonio, Texas, area. They have a highly diverse client list, including businesses, unions, academic associations, and church groups. In the last few years, they have conducted training sessions, provided trail rides and chuck wagon dinners, conducted motor tours of the Hill Country, and put on numerous balls, dances, and hops for their clients.

"We were stunned when he told us that we owed the state over $125,000 in unpaid taxes, penalties, and accumulated interest. It just couldn't be so!" said Jay.

Rex continued, "When he left, we immediately called our lawyer. The issue boiled down to taxes on the services of bands and combos we had furnished for events. The auditor claimed that we had to collect sales tax on the amount that we charged our client for the music group."

"The problem was," Jay said, "we had already gotten an opinion from the Tax Commission that held that if we did not sell tickets to the event, no sales tax was due. In our business, we never sell tickets. We charge our client a fixed bid price, and only members and guests of the client group attend. Thus, no tax was due, and we had never collected for any music group."

"It took a year and cost us over $24,000 in legal fees, but finally we got a ruling that we had complied with Texas law. We did not owe the tax."

"Of course," Rex said, "we were out the twenty-four thousand. But you know, it could have been a lot worse."

employee withholdings, for not paying sales taxes when they are due, for not paying your income taxes. If you do not pay your creditors, your credit rating will suffer. Your business may fail. But you won't go to jail for not paying your bills.

Managing Risk from Employee Violation of Government Regulations

Reducing risk from events involving employees who violate business regulations is best accomplished through a proactive program of training and enforcing appropriate policies and procedures. The courts have consistently ruled that it is the responsibility of the employer to police employee compliance with regulations. Ignorance of either the regulations or of employee violation of regulations is not a defense against administrative action. You are financially responsible for employee violations, intentional or inadvertent. Those few cases where the employer has been held harmless all involve employers who (1) have a written policy provided to each employee, (2) have conducted training of managers and employees concerning those policies, and (3) have immediately and consistently acted upon receipt of any complaint.

Risks from violating the requirements of Equal Employment Opportunity Commission are best managed, as with risks from violations of any government regulation, by the owners being proactive:

- Know the EEOC rules that apply to your business.
- Obtain assistance from experts in EEOC regulations to assess the level of your compliance.

- Establish policies and procedures designed to prevent violations.
- Educate and train employees to know the policies and procedures and to understand the importance of following them explicitly.
- Enforce the policies and procedures by immediately dealing in a systematic manner with any employee complaint.

Knowing the EEOC rules is a daunting task for any business owner. As stated above, the rules are voluminous, ambiguous, and arcane. There are, however, many sources of information that are written to be easily understood. Most such third-party information is provided by industry associations, and thus is usually specifically written for the problems you are most likely to encounter.

Assistance can be obtained from experts in several different ways. One source that is often overlooked is the employment agency that you use to screen applicants. Employment agencies must be highly knowledgeable of the EEOC rules in order to remain in business. Often, such agencies can provide sample policy manuals and advice concerning compliance. Other sources of expert help include SCORE (www.score.org) and the EEOC, itself.

The EEOC maintains a website that contains myriad resources for small business owners. The commission also publishes numerous books and pamphlets that are available from www.EEOC.gov.

Alleged violations of the Americans with Disabilities Act are best handled through a proactive threefold approach: (1) Determine if you are subject to any of the provisions of the ADA. (2) Obtain the services of experts on the ADA to evaluate the level of your compliance. (3) Work diligently to meet the requirements to which you are subject. Although these actions will *not* prevent you from being the target of frivolous lawsuits, you may use records of your actions as evidence of your intent to comply. This is often sufficient to persuade a mediator to pressure the complainant to either reduce the amount demanded or to withdraw the complaint entirely.

The Department of Justice maintains an ADA Technical Assistance Program which provides help directly to interested parties. By using these services, a small business owner can be assured of having current information. The Technical Assistance Program provides specific advice for your business concerning how to comply with the pertinent requirements. This program is specifically aimed at the needs of hotels, motels, restaurants, and other affected small businesses. The program provides an information hot line, printed materials, and a speakers bureau. It does not provide any inspection or affirmation services. Visit www.usdoj.gov/crt/ada/adahom1.htm for more information.

Managing risk from violations of OSHA standards and regulations is also best accomplished through proactive efforts. As with risks from EEOC and ADA enforcement, you should first ascertain the standards to which your business is subject. The OSHA Act covers all employees except those in mining, transportation, state and local governments, and self-employment. If your business is in any other industry, you are subject to the standards of OSHA for employee health and safety. Also remember that while *you* are self-employed, anyone you hire is not. Thus, while OSHA standards and regulations do not apply to you, they do apply to your employees.

The best way to meet the basic laws of OSHA is to provide a place of employment that is free of recognized hazards and to:

1. Maintain tools and equipment in good condition.
2. Provide appropriate safety equipment and training in its proper use.
3. Provide medical examinations.

OSHA also offers free consultation services to employers who want help in identifying any deficiencies and in developing appropriate solutions. Consultations begin with a conference among the consultants and managers of the business where the scope of the consultation is set, and all parties agree on a set of working rules for the engagement. The conference is followed by an on-site inspection for hazards. The business's health program is also assessed. A final conference is held during which all findings are presented, along with suggested solutions to each identified problem. No report of any deficiency is made to OSHA for enforcement. However, if significant hazards are found, you can count on a follow-up inspection by OSHA after a reasonable time during which you must remedy the problems.

A directory of OSHA-funded consultants can be obtained by requesting OSHA Publication No. 3047, *Consultation Services for the Employer.*

You must also keep accurate records of all employee job-related illnesses and injuries. You must report within eight hours any accidents that result in a fatality or in the hospitalization of three or more employees. If your business has fewer than 10 employees or if your business is in one of the OSHA-defined "low- hazard" industries, you are exempt from the record keeping requirements of the regulations. Low-hazard industries include automobile dealers, apparel and furniture stores, eating and drinking establishments, finance, insurance, real estate, and legal, educational, personal, and business services, as well as cultural and membership organizations.

Using an Internal Audit as a Tool to Manage Risk

A valuable process that can greatly help you with the issues of keeping risks at acceptable levels is completing an internal audit. You probably are somewhat familiar with public business's external audits, which are conducted by CPA firms and which must comply with a set of standards called Generally Accepted Audit Standards (GAAS). An internal audit is similar in conduct; however, because it is strictly a management tool which is not provided to outsiders, it can be structured and conducted in any systematic manner you find acceptable.

It is unlikely that you (or any owner of a small business) have the time, experience, or inclination to attempt to conduct an internal audit on your own. Rather, you should consider outsourcing the conduct of an audit to an expert in the process. Your own accountant may be able to conduct such an audit. But if not, he or she will, in any case, be able to recommend a reputable and reliable firm that can do so at a reasonable cost.

A properly conducted, independent internal audit will give you:

- An evaluation of your overall level of business risk.
- An objective evaluation of your risk control structure.
- A systematic analysis of your business processes and controls.
- Information on irregularities detected during the audit process.
- Review of your firm's compliance with relevant regulations.
- A review of the existence and value of the assets of your business.
- Review of operational and financial performance.
- Recommendations for more effective and efficient use of resources.
- Assessments of how well your business is accomplishing your goals and objectives.
- Information about your employees' adherence to the organization's values and code of ethics.

As the owner of a small business, you must assume much of the task of conducting oversight of all aspects of your business. Activities that make up oversight include listening, asking questions, assessing and challenging answers. This is exactly what an effective internal audit will do for you.

To be sure that the audit effectively meets your goals in having it conducted, you should:

1. Meet (without the presence of other members of your management) with whomever is going to conduct the internal audit.
2. Establish with the auditor that you and your board of directors (if you have a board) have the final authority to review and approve the audit plan.
3. Write an engagement agreement with the auditor that clearly establishes the scope of work to be done.
4. Provide sufficient authority to the auditor to ensure that he or she can accomplish the goals of the audit.

Once the audit is completed, you must make positive steps to address any findings that indicate an unacceptable level of business risk.

Insuring against Risks

Although it is impossible for the owner of a small business to avoid all business risks, it is possible, through the use of insurance, to minimize the damage that such risks can cause. However, insurance can be expensive. Because of its expense, many small business owners choose too little insurance. When the inevitable occurs, an underinsured business may well face bankruptcy and liquidation.

LO4 Explain how insurance can be used to manage business risk.

The key to using insurance is to obtain the "right" amount of insurance at an affordable rate. Having too little insurance leaves the business open to unsupportable losses. Carrying too much insurance wastes money.

Using Insurance to Manage Risks

insurance
A contract between two or more parties in which one party agrees, for a fee, to assume the risk of another.

Insurance is a contract between two businesses in which one, the insurance company, for a fee, agrees to indemnify the other for specific losses that are likely to occur in the future. In other words, the insurance company contracts to pay money to your business if a specific "covered" event occurs that causes your business to suffer financial loss.

Not all risks are insurable. Insurance provides a benefit by requiring a relatively small fee compared to the amount of loss that is possible. The insurance company makes a profit by collecting premiums for coverage from many businesses for the same set of risks. In effect, you and the insurance company are taking opposite gambles. You are betting that your business will be damaged or destroyed. The insurance company is betting that it won't. The insurance company wins by collecting more from all the covered companies combined than it has to pay out to those few businesses that do, indeed, suffer damage. You win (if it can be considered a "win") by having the insurance company pay when your business suffers a covered loss. Thus, the more likely an event is to occur, and the greater the potential amount that the insurance company must pay, the higher the price that you must pay for coverage. For this reason, insurance coverage is either not available or is excessively expensive for common events.

Developing a Comprehensive Insurance Program

Developing an appropriate insurance program for your business requires that you understand the risks to which your business is vulnerable. You must then know the amount of loss that your business could suffer as a result of the adverse events. Finally, you must obtain appropriate rates from reliable insurers, rates that are not too high for your business to pay but that do provide sufficient payouts if the insured event occurs.

Identifying risks is the first task to be completed before a comprehensive insurance program can be developed for your business. Risks, as discussed above, vary with the nature of your business. Risks that are common to most small businesses include fire, flood, storm, theft, business interruption, and loss of key personnel. Business-specific risks include product liability claims for manufacturers, malpractice claims for dentists and physicians, and errors and omissions claims for lawyers and accountants.

Determining which risks are to be covered is the next step. Not all identifiable risks can be or should be covered by insurance. The risk of events that are certain to occur cannot be insured at any price. Risks of events that are highly likely to occur but that have indeterminable payouts can be insured, but only at a very high price. Extremely unlikely events (being struck by a meteorite, for example) can be insured, but why would anyone do so?

Events that should be insured are those that are likely, and the economic cost of which would create a severe burden upon the finances of the business. Such events include natural disasters, liability to others, and the death or disability of key employees.

coverages
Contractual provisions of insurance policies that specify what risks the insurance company is assuming.

Coverages required by law exist to provide social protection from harm caused to employees, customers, and uninvolved individuals. The most common mandatory insurance coverages are liability for damages caused by vehicle accidents and illness and injury caused by employment. Most businesses are also required to pay for unemployment insurance for employees to help defray the personal cost of having one's employment terminated.

Vehicle liability insurance is mandated by the legislatures of all the states and territories of the United States. Minimum amounts of coverage are specified for property damage caused by the vehicle and for injury suffered by anyone other than the driver of the vehicle.

Workers' compensation insurance is mandatory in some states. In others, it is discretionary. In all states, the workers' compensation laws provide fixed monetary awards to employees who are injured or disabled on the job. Workers' compensation is enforced through administrative procedures which preclude employees suing their employers. Federal statutes are limited to workers who are employed in some interstate commerce.

THE THOUGHTFUL ENTREPRENEUR

WHAT RISKS CAN BE INSURED?

Not all business risks can be covered by insurance at a reasonable cost. Insurance companies, just like you, are in business to make profits. An insurance company must charge competitive prices to be able to sell policies. At the same time, the insurance company must charge enough to be able to pay legitimate claims of its policyholders. To be able to balance these conflicting needs, an insurance company must be able to accurately predict the amount of payments that will be made to settle claims for insurable events.

The amount that an insurance company must pay out in claims is a function of (1) the frequency with which an event occurs, (2) the amount that must be paid according to the terms of the contract, and (3) the number of policies that have been issued.

- **The risk must be calculable:** An insurance company estimates the amount of potential claims payments by performing statistical analyses of the number and frequency of the occurrence of the event for which the insurance is being provided. For example, the probability of an individual business being flooded can be calculated from information concerning its location relative to sources and frequencies of floods. Although a specific flood may not be predictable, the number of businesses that will encounter floods in any one year can be predicted with reasonable statistical confidence, which allows an insurance company to determine the appropriate price for a flood policy.
- **The value of any loss must be measurable in dollars:** Insurance companies contract to pay only specific amounts of money for specific types and amounts of losses. In order to determine the amount that will be paid, it must be possible for the loss to be stated in a dollar amount. Thus, an insurance company will insure you for physical damage from fire. It will not insure you for the loss of your beautiful view, should the fire burn your neighbor's property across the road.
- **The policyholder must have an insurable financial interest:** Insurance companies will not insure losses for individuals who do not suffer a financial loss from what is being insured. This requirement acts to prevent fraud by persons deliberately "creating" the event in order to profit from it. In the same vein, an insurance company will not pay more than the actual amount of the loss, regardless of the amount of the policy terms.
- **The pool of potential policyholders must be of sufficient size:** Insurance works because the insurance company diversifies its risk by insuring numerous businesses in widely separated locations. This ensures that no single disaster will result in the insurance company having to pay an excessive number of claims at any one time. Of course, this strategy occasionally fails. In August 2005 Hurricane Katrina became the most costly catastrophe on record. The extensive damage to a relatively large area has seriously tested the ability of several insurance companies to pay required claims and to remain in business.

Unemployment insurance is collected by the IRS and state agencies as a percentage of tax upon payroll. The amount collected varies among industries and among businesses within an industry. Industries and businesses that have frequent seasonal layoffs pay higher amounts of unemployment premiums than do those that have stable employment.

Desired coverages beyond mandatory insurance include general liability, product liability, catastrophe, and various types of malpractice coverage. Liability insurance protects your business against claims from harm caused by inadvertent consequences of actions of the business or its employees. The list of potential causes of harm to customers, vendors, or others is nearly endless. Customers fall while on business premises. A careless worker can splatter paint on a stranger's automobile. Sparks from welding can start fires on others' property. A faulty valve can release noxious or even deadly fumes into the atmosphere. Your sewer can plug and cause flooding in your neighbor's place of business. Commercial liability insurance covers losses that are the result of such mishaps and accidents.

Product liability insurance covers losses resulting from claims made by persons who use the products of your business. The risk of customers and others being harmed by your product is largely a function of (1) the nature of your product and (2) the intended users. Those products that have historically given rise to the largest claims for injury and illness are (1) transportation equipment, such as automobiles, airplanes, and bicycles, (2) health products, such as pharmaceuticals and body implants, and (3) appliances, such as toasters, vacuum cleaners, and kitchen ranges. However, examples of huge cash settlements for product liability exist for a multitude of products that would seem to be harmless by nature. Examples of such cases include insulating foam that was discovered to emit formaldehyde, asbestos-containing products that are believed to be carcinogenic, and a multitude of toys that are alleged to cause choking and other hazards to children.

Errors and omissions insurance and malpractice insurance are examples of special types of liability insurance that cover losses from harm caused during the performance of your profession. Errors and omissions insurance covers claims made by clients of attorneys, accountants, and other consultants. Malpractice insurance covers claims made by patients of physicians, dentists, nurses, and other medical practitioners. The primary value of this type of insurance is the access to highly competent specialist lawyers that is provided by the insurance company. The insurance companies employ cadres of lawyers to represent professionals who are accused of incompetence or wrongdoing. These lawyers are usually successful in negotiating reasonable settlements with clients who have been harmed. Should a settlement be impossible, the same lawyers will vigorously defend the accused professional in the subsequent court action. Of course, in the event that the professional is held responsible for a client loss, the insurance company will pay the claim, up to the limit of the insurance contract.

You, as an individual owner or manager of a small business, can obtain a general liability insurance, which is often called an *umbrella policy,* or a *success protector policy.* General liability policies exist to pay losses that are not covered by other liability insurance. It is a sad fact of our current legal climate that actual culpability is irrelevant to many damage claims. If you are successful in your business, your success makes you a target for lawsuits because you are considered to be able to pay a judgment, either through your personal wealth or through seizure of your business property. Claims against general liability policies are usually a result of such litigation.

Insuring the Property of the Business

Commercial property insurance covers losses to the business property from causes such as fire, storm, vandalism, and theft. Other property insurance exists to pay losses resulting from floods or earthquakes. The cost of property insurance is determined largely by (1) the property's insurable value, (2) the amount of deductible loss, (3) the amount of co-insurance required, and (4) the loss limits of the policy.

insurable value
The amount of an asset for which a company will write an insurance policy.

All the value of a property does not have **insurable value**. For example, as a general rule, the value of land, excavation, and basement is not insurable. This is because even when a disaster occurs, the land remains. Only a very few types of disasters, such as earthquake or landslide, can change the nature and topography of land.

Additionally, some property has value that cannot be stated in dollar amounts. The value of the historical significance of a building often cannot be determined. For example, in Clarksville, Tennessee, the Hachland Hall Bed and Breakfast has a log cabin that was the home of President Andrew Jackson during the time that he was building the famous Hermitage. Were this cabin to burn to the ground, its replacement cost for logs, timber, and finish lumber could be no more than a few tens of thousands of dollars. However, no matter how carefully rebuilt, the replacement would be a replica, not the actual cabin. As such, it might be interesting, but it would not have the special character that now makes it unique. Placing a dollar amount on the historical value of this cabin is highly problematical.

deductible
An amount of loss that will not be paid by an insurance company

A **deductible** is an amount of loss that is specifically excluded by the insurance contract. It is common for vehicle policies to specify that in the event of loss, the insurance will pay the amount of the loss, less a deductible of $250 to $1,000. Policies on buildings and equipment usually have similar deductibles ranging from $1,000 to $10,000 or more. As a general rule, the higher the deductible, the lower the policy premium payments will be.

THE THOUGHTFUL ENTREPRENEUR

HEIDI KLUM'S UNIQUE INSURANCE POLICY[20]

In 2004, the model Heidi Klum had her legs insured for $2 million.[21] This may seem a little strange, but it is not unprecedented. During World War II, the then-famous actress and pinup girl, Betty Grable, received widespread publicity from insuring her legs for $1 million. More recently, the soccer player, David Beckham, had his legs insured for a cool $70 million.[22]

Given that the loss of a leg is not a common occurrence, why would a model, an actor, and a sports star seek such insurance?

Given that there is not a sufficient pool of models, actors, and athletes to allow an insurance company to diversify its risk, why would an insurance company write such a policy?

In actuality, such policies are not as unusual as you might think. Insurance companies routinely write policies that place a dollar value on the loss of a person's appendages. While the occurrence of the maiming of actors is low, nationwide a significant number of people lose arms, legs, hands, feet, and eyes in a variety of accidents and illnesses. Thus, the risk of such loss is well understood by insurance companies, and the cost of paying claims for such policies can be reliably predicted. Provisions for specific dollar payments for the loss of appendages is commonly included in insurance policies that cover disability.

Despite the ordinariness of disability insurance, it is clear that the purpose of these insurance policies for Ms. Klum and Ms. Grable was the publicity value to be gained. In both cases, they and the insurance companies all received lots of press coverage. It is interesting to note that while the amount of the insurance coverage is reported, no mention is ever made of the cost of the premium or of the term of the insurance contract.

There is a popular perception that any risk can be insured. This perception has arisen because of highly publicized events that were not actually insurance transactions but were publicity stunts. While it might be comforting to be able to insure against any loss, the fact is that businesses must constantly weigh the cost of insurance coverage. In many cases, the cost of insurance coverage greatly exceeds any benefit for small business.

Co-insurance is a contract requirement that works to prevent property owners from deliberately underinsuring. Co-insurance requires that the owner carry insurance in an amount equal to a stated minimum percentage of the market value of the property, most usually 80 percent. If the owner allows insurance coverage to fall below this amount, then the amount that the insurance company will pay in the event of loss is reduced by an amount proportional to the amount of underinsurance.

co-insurance
A contract stipulation that requires a policyholder to carry insurance in an amount equal to a stated minimum percentage of the market value of the property insured.

The reason for such arcane provisions is to increase the amount of premium that the insurance company collects relative to the risk that the insurance company is taking by insuring the property. The higher the value a property has, the greater the likely payout an insurance company will have to make in the event of loss.

Consider that property losses are highly correlated with the value of the property. At one extreme, the loss can never exceed the market value of the property. At the other extreme, loss cannot be less than zero. In between the two extremes, losses are often a function of the value of the property. For example, suppose two businesses each experienced a fire that destroyed the roof of a warehouse. A 43,000-square-foot warehouse worth $3.5 million has a much more expensive roof than does a 10,000-square-foot warehouse which is worth less than $750,000. Similarly, losing your 1,600-square-foot retail space will be a much greater dollar loss if the store is located on Rodeo Drive in Beverly Hills, California, than if it is located on Main Street in Beckwourth, California.

Business interruption insurance provides funds to pay the ordinary operating expenses of your business should it be forced to close temporarily because of an insured event. Although business interruption insurance can be purchased as a stand-alone policy, it is most usually acquired as a provision of commercial property insurance.

When disasters hit, like this fire, most small businesses depend on insurance to make up for the loss. What factors should you consider when seeking insurance?

fidelity bonds
Bonds, also called *dishonesty bonds*, that repay employers for losses caused by dishonest or negligent employees.

surety bonds
An agreement with an insurance or bonding company that will pay a specified amount in the event that the entity bonded fails to comply with specified contractual requirements.

Crime insurance offers protection against losses from crimes committed against your business. It is an unfortunate fact that the greatest number of crimes of which you are likely to be victim are committed by trusted employees.

Theft insurance is normally included in insurance on physical assets. However, the greatest threat of loss because of employee dishonesty is the misappropriation of cash, as was discussed earlier. Cash cannot be insured. An approach to obtaining insurance against employee theft of money is to require all employees with access to money or to accounting for money to be *bonded.*

Fidelity bonds, also called *dishonesty bonds,* repay employers for losses caused by dishonest or negligent employees. Fidelity bonds cover losses from employee fraud, theft, forgery, and embezzlement. Unlike **surety bonds**, fidelity bonds are purchased only for the employer's benefit.

If you have any employee who handles large amounts of cash or other valuable assets, you should consider bonding that person. Some businesses, including insurance companies, securities brokers, real estate brokers, and businesses that hold escrowed cash are required by law to carry fidelity bonds. All employees who have direct access to a company's cash, securities, and accounting records, or who handle investment or retirement funds, should be bonded. Bonds are available to cover individual specific key employees, or as blanket bonds that cover all employees.

When obtaining fidelity bonds, you should consider the following:

- The scope of coverage.
- All exclusions.
- Types of employee dishonesty not covered (e.g., salary, benefit, or computer fraud).
- Coverage for employee actions off-premises.

Credit insurance covers abnormal losses from credit customers not paying their bills. Abnormal losses are carefully defined within the insurance contract. Typical covered events include customers who cease business because of bankruptcy or business interruptions caused by fire, storm, wind, floods, and earthquakes. Less common and more expensive coverage exists that will pay for losses that arise from general economic conditions such as recession, war, or trade embargos.

Credit insurance can be obtained that covers all credit accounts or that covers only specific accounts. General credit insurance is expensive, and it is common to choose to cover only very large accounts, the loss of which would threaten survival of the business.

All credit insurance requires the merchant to provide co-insurance in the amount of 10 to 20 percent of the credit loss. The co-insurance provision works to prevent both frivolous claims and to provide a disincentive to companies to issue credit indiscriminately.

Credit insurance companies provide mandatory collection services. The insured business is required to promptly report all past due accounts. When an account is determined to be delinquent, usually after 90 days of no payment, then the account must be assigned to the insurance company which will make vigorous efforts to collect.

Credit insurance is available only for manufacturers and wholesalers. At this time no insurance company will write coverage for retailers who offer credit to customers.

Retailers who provide credit are protected in two ways. First, those few retailers who offer credit directly to customers usually have a large number of relatively small accounts receivable. This provides a greater diversification of the risk of loss than is available to wholesalers who usually have a relatively small number of large value receivables. Second, most retailers today provide credit only through credit cards, including Master Card, Visa, Discover, and American Express. Credit card companies perform credit checks before issuing cards, and thus limit the risk of nonpayment. Additionally, the credit card companies have developed rules which include checking cards for customer

THE THOUGHTFUL ENTREPRENEUR

BRING IN THE CLOWNS

Imagine a fair without a midway. Can a fair even be a fair without a carousel, a roller coaster, or a Ferris wheel? Carnivals are hugely popular entertainments. Over 500 million people attend amusement parks, fairs, and carnivals in the United States each year (which is quite impressive, given that the entire population of the nation is only 300 million).

As you might expect, carnivals experience numerous accidents each year, ranging in severity from bruises and abrasions to permanent maiming and death. According to the U.S. Consumer Product Safety Commission (CPSC),[23] approximately 11,000 people are injured on amusement rides each year. Of these, about five die.

There are approximately 500 carnivals that travel the United States each year, ranging in size from 1 to over 100 portable amusement rides. The vast majority of carnivals are small family-owned businesses with second and third generation members involved in management and operation.[24]

If your carnival is large enough and you expect to have about 1 million riders in a year, then you should expect to experience approximately 20 to 25 injuries, based on CPSC statistics. If the people injured are representative of the national experience, all of them will be younger than 16. Not one will have an injury severe enough to require more than outpatient treatment. However, there is a small, but measurable risk that you will be among the unfortunate carnival operators who have patrons seriously injured to the point of maiming or death.

As the owner of a carnival, what insurance should you carry to cover the injuries of customers on your rides? Insurance to cover the potential medical expenses for twenty-some minor injuries would be prohibitively expensive. It would, on the other hand, be quite risky for your business to carry no insurance at all. A reasonable strategy is to obtain insurance that will cover only serious injury and death. Your carnival will then absorb the cost of treating minor injuries, the number of which can be reduced by a safety program that prevents customer horseplay, requires operator training, and enforces regular rigid safety inspection of the rides. Taking such measures not only reduces the probability of serious injury, but also reduces the cost of accident insurance.

signatures, requiring a government-issued picture ID, and obtaining a transaction authorization prior to providing the credit sale. Retailers who follow the rules are not liable for any future nonpayment by the credit card holder.

Personnel insurance is available to protect both you and your employees from specific risks. Personnel coverages include key person insurance, life, disability, and medical coverage insurance.

Key person insurance protects you in the event that a key employee dies or is disabled and cannot work.

Life insurance is the most common kind of coverage on key persons. Usually key person insurance names you, as the owner, or your business as the beneficiary of the policy. Life insurance also is often provided to employees to provide security for their families. Life insurance provided by you, the employer, is usually term insurance. *Term insurance* is a form of insurance that does not accumulate any value over the contract term. Rather, only specific events, including disability, dismemberment, and death, are insured events. Term insurance is very inexpensive for healthy young people. The premiums increase with age, and with specified risk factors such as obesity, heart problems, and a history of driving while intoxicated.

Disability insurance is usually provided as part of life insurance, although it can be obtained as either a stand-alone policy or as part of medical coverage. You as the owner of a small business should carefully consider obtaining disability coverage not only for key persons but also for yourself. Statistics provided by the American Association of Retired Persons (AARP) show that between the ages of 22 and 65, there is a greater than 25 percent probability that you will be disabled for a period of 12 months or more.[25] Statistics provided by the Social Security Administration indicate that the greatest probability of becoming disabled for this period of time occurs between ages 50 and 65.[26] The probability of shorter periods of disability is, of course, much higher. Given the high probability of temporary disability and the devastating effects it can have upon a small business, it is becoming ever more common for disability coverage to be included in business insurance plans.

Disability insurance can take several forms. The most common disability coverage provides the insured person with funds to replace income lost because of the inability to work. While this coverage is important to the disabled person, it provides no direct benefit to your business.

Some insurance companies now offer disability coverage that provides direct benefits to small businesses and to owners of small businesses. The most common of such disability coverage is **buyout insurance** which provides funds to the business to purchase the ownership position of a disabled partner. Less common, but of similar value for small business owners, is disability coverage that will pay specific fixed costs of the business, such as rent, salaries, and utilities, in the event that the owner or other named key person becomes disabled. Even less common is disability coverage that will pay specific dollar amounts to the business to replace lost revenue caused by the disability of a key person.

buyout insurance
Insurance that provides money to owners of a business to buy the shares of any deceased owner from that owner's heirs.

Medical coverage is the most highly desired form of insurance for most employees. Medical coverage is quite expensive, and the cost has been increasing rapidly in recent years. There are many reasons, however, that you, as the owner of a small business, might wish to provide such coverage for your employees. First, receiving medical coverage is a strong retention incentive for employees. Second, if you provide medical insurance for all employees, you can obtain reduced rates and can include yourself and your family. Third, the least expensive way to obtain key person insurance is as a part of a comprehensive medical insurance plan that covers all employees.

Sharing Risk

LO5 Describe techniques for sharing risk with other businesses and organizations.

One very effective method to reduce and to control business risk is to share that risk with other entities. As discussed above, one way to share risk is through insurance programs which, in effect, diversify risk across industries, businesses, and geographical areas. Additionally, risk can be directly shared without the intermediary of an insurance company, by forming joint ventures, by joining industry groups, and by obtaining government grants and guarantees.

Joint Ventures

Joint ventures are partnerships through which two or more businesses combine to undertake a specific economic activity. Each business involved in a joint venture keeps its own identity and conducts its own business separately from that of the other partners. The businesses are partners only for the activities specified in the joint venture contract.

joint venture
An agreement between two or more entities to pool resources in order to complete a project.

Joint ventures are most usually formed and taxed as partnerships. This allows for disproportionate allocation of revenues and expenses among the partner businesses. The ability to assign tax items to the partner for which they are most advantageous eases the problems of dissimilar businesses forming a partnership. A relatively large, profitable partner can be assigned the deductible costs of the joint venture, while revenues are simultaneously assigned to the smaller, less profitable (or even unprofitable) partner who will pay taxes at a lower rate.

Another advantage of joint ventures is that each partner can lose no more than its investment in the venture. The joint venture is a separate entity from any of the partners that own it. Thus, if the joint venture fails, only the resources of the joint venture are lost. The partner companies can continue in their individual businesses.

Industry Groups for Insurance Coverage

One of the primary reasons that there is at least one organized group for every conceivable industry is that joining in groups provides benefits of scale to members. The most common benefit is low-cost group insurance. The cost of insurance, as discussed above, is partly a function of the risk that the insurance provider assumes. Insurance companies diversify risk by insuring large numbers of similar businesses. It is obvious that the National Electric Sign Association can provide a much larger pool of people to be insured than can any single sign shop member. Because of the larger pool of potential insured people and because of its greater bargaining power, the NESA can obtain much lower insurance rates for its members than the members can obtain individually.

SMALL BUSINESS INSIGHT

THE REST OF THE STORY: CELLDYNE BIOPHARMA, LLC

Ultimately, the chief medical officer and the owner of the marketing firm both sued the other member-managers, and the LLC itself. The sad facts for the other members were that the CMO was wealthy and was a long-time associate of the owner of the marketing group. They coordinated their suits, filing them in federal courts in Connecticut and New Jersey.

The other members had to retain attorneys in both states because litigants are not allowed to represent themselves in federal court. The initial retainer was in excess of $80,000. Before the case was ever considered by a federal judge, another $80,000 of legal bills, over and above the retainer, had accumulated. Ultimately, the fee for defending against the suit exceeded $250,000.

The LLC and the manager-members were rendered insolvent. Celldyne Biopharma, LLC surrendered its corporate rights and ceased business.

The CMO and the owner of the marketing firm attempted without success to produce a version of the product. Subsequently they had a falling out and sued each other, also in federal court.

The original follistatin product has never been completed nor brought to market. The patent for the production process was never completed, thus effectively remanding it to the public domain.

Only the lawyers profited.

Government Funding of Risky Ventures

The final source for sharing risk is governments. Townships up to the federal government have programs to encourage economic activity. Governments do not have the profit-making requirements of businesses, but they do have the power to extract money from citizens. As a result, risk for a government is very different from risk for private business. Governments often subsidize very risky ventures that private companies would otherwise never attempt.

One example of government subsidizing risky ventures can be seen in the building of sports arenas, convention centers, and convention hotels. Cities across the nation have imposed taxes upon citizens and tourists to subsidize the building of such facilities. St. Louis has three such publicly funded arenas: one for the Cardinals baseball team, one for the Rams football team, and a half-million-square-foot convention center. Houston recently demolished an old facility and built a new one for the Houston Oilers football team. The City of San Antonio, Texas, and Bexar County recently enacted one of the nation's highest taxes on hotel rooms and rental cars to finance a new arena for the Spurs basketball team, despite having the largely unused Alamo Dome.

It is important to realize that the cities do not directly profit from these facilities. Nationwide, arenas, convention centers, and convention hotels operate at losses, which are covered by taxes imposed on nonusers of the facilities. In those rare instances in which the facilities are profitable, the profits go to private businesses which lease or operate the facilities on contract. Absent government subsidies, few, if any, of these facilities would exist.

Small businesses can obtain their share of government subsidies through direct contracting and grants. Opportunities exist for small businesses to obtain government funding for recycling of waste materials, for research and development of products for health, security, and defense, and for providing services directly to government entities.

All businesses operate in varying states of risk. The most careful planning and the best management in the world cannot remove all uncertainty from business operations. Storms, earthquakes, tsunamis, famines, recessions, and wars are facts of life with which you must sooner or later cope.

Although business risk cannot be eliminated, it can be controlled. Management techniques including security devices and internal controls can reduce the risk of misappropriation of business assets. Those risks that cannot be controlled can be insured. Insurance works to reduce the amount of loss that any individual business experiences because of natural events, dishonesty, or negligence. Because the environment in which business operates is constantly changing, you, as the owner and manager of a small business, must constantly reassess your risk controls, your exposure to disaster, and your insurance coverage.

Ben Franklin said long ago "A penny saved is a penny earned," and that adage is truly important for small businesses. Money saved means more flexibility and more profit. The point of spending time on risk, insurance, and protecting yourself and your business is to help you identify the ways to minimize your losses. Often, thinking about the potential sources of risk and loss ahead of time makes it possible for you to take action to minimize the risk or handle the loss should it come. The whole concept of insuring against risk works best when you can think objectively about the potential risk, loss, and cost to your firm. Only then can you be sure that you are spending your insurance dollars wisely. Despite all the talk about financial loss, it is important to note the human and emotional cost of loss. Whether through injury or criminal action, loss focuses our attention and can make us sad, angry, guilty, or a combination of the three. When it causes harm to employees or customers, it can derail a business and its owner. For all these reasons, taking the time to protect your business, its assets, and people always makes sense.

CHAPTER SUMMARY

LO1 Explain the meaning and nature of business risk.

- Business risk comes from many sources, including financial risk from capital structure, economic risks from business decisions, and the environment.
- Business risk is the probability that the future economic state of the business will be worse than is projected.

LO2 Describe the specific types of risks associated with different aspects of business operations.

- Economic risks arise from events related to the property of the business, to the personnel of the business, and to the customers, vendors, and visitors to the business.
- Violation of government regulations has become a significant business risk due to the many laws, rules, and regulations of the ADA, OSHA, the EEOC, and various tax agencies.
- Businesses are usually held liable for injuries suffered on business property, regardless of the cause.

LO3 Describe techniques to manage risks to stay within your level of risk tolerance.

- The loss from various events can be reduced by making specific plans and arrangements to deal with them, should they occur.
- Disaster plans can reduce losses by reducing the time that business operations are interrupted when the event occurs.
- Following building codes, locating away from flood plains, and keeping property clear of flammables can reduce loss from natural events.
- Risk to computers and data can be controlled by protection software, backups, and password use.
- The best control for risks from personnel is to hire qualified people of high integrity.
- Conducting an internal audit can provide an independent analysis of the levels and types of business risk.

LO4 Explain how insurance can be used to manage business risk.

- Keeping the right types and levels of insurance can minimize a business's loss from adverse events.
- You should not try to insure against all risks, rather only those that have economic consequences great enough to threaten the survival of your business.
- Some insurance coverages are required by law.

Describe techniques for sharing risk with other businesses and organizations.

- Risk may be reduced and insurance made affordable by joining with other similar businesses.
- The risky activity can be separated from the main part of your business through joint ventures and placing the risky activity into a separate legal entity.
- Industry groups can obtain lower insurance rates than can a single business.
- Government agencies can provide protection from risk by limiting the potential loss and by subsidizing risky ventures.

KEY TERMS

business risk, 556
employee theft, 557
regulation of the workplace, 557
Equal Employment Opportunity Commission (EEOC), 558
Occupational Safety and Health Administration (OSHA), 558
protected classes, 558
Age Discrimination in Employment Act, 558
Rehabilitation Act of 1973, 558
Americans with Disabilities Act of 1990, 558
Civil Rights Act of 1991, 558
key employees, 560
separation of duties, 567
internal control, 568
tax codes, 570
insurance, 574
coverages, 574
insurable value, 576
deductible, 576
co-insurance, 577
fidelity bonds, 578
surety bonds, 578
buyout insurance, 580
joint venture, 580

DISCUSSION QUESTIONS

1. Discuss the types of risk encountered by small businesses. Are these risks different in any way from risks facing big business?
2. What are the risks to small businesses caused by personnel issues?
3. How are the risks from personnel affected by government business regulations?
4. How does disaster planning help a small business cope with risk?
5. The text discusses methods to protect against weather. What might a business do to protect itself against an earthquake?
6. Which is easier to steal, money from an employer's bank account or secret business processes? Why?
7. What types of insurance should a small business have? Give your reasons for maintaining each type of coverage.
8. Suppose you are in the business of making ladders. A customer places a board plank between two of your ladders as a scaffold. One of the ladders fails, causing your customer to fall and break a leg. Are you responsible for your customer's losses? How can you protect yourself from lawsuits in such cases?
9. You are considering offering credit to good customers to increase sales. What things should you consider to limit your risks if you do?
10. One of your partners has special skills that would be very difficult to replace. His great joy in life is single-track bicycle racing. How can you protect yourself from the probability that he will be injured and unable to work?

EXPERIENTIAL EXERCISES

1. Identify a business you would like to own. Make a list of the risks that are specific to that business. Contact an insurance broker to find out what coverages are available and what they would cost. Make a report to your class of your findings.
2. Identify a business you would like to own. Go to the OSHA website and find out what rules and regulations apply to this business. Create a chart of hazards of this business and the applicable OSHA rules. Make a report to your class of your findings.
3. Suppose you are going to open a consulting business. You are going to finish half of your garage to use as an office. Go to the ADA site and determine what accessibility requirements you must meet. Make a report to your class of your findings.
4. Identify a specific location (street address) where you would like to operate a business. Visit your city's planning and zoning office (or its website, if it has one) and determine if this site is in a flood plain. Make a copy of the city's map of flood plains. Make a report to your class of your findings.
5. Identify a business you want to own. Use the resources of your library and the Internet to identify what insurance you are legally required to carry. Contact an insurance broker to determine how and for how much you can obtain the required coverage. Make a report to your class of your findings.

MINI-CASE

RISKY BUSINESS

Vicky Volare fell in love with motor scooters on her vacation trip to Aruba. "They're a blast!" Vicky said, "They are convenient, safe, inexpensive, and fun to ride." Now she is planning to buy 30 Vespa Scooters to provide scooter rental in Vail, Colorado. Vicky will need four employees, in addition to her own services. She has completed a business plan, except for determining what types and amounts of insurance coverage she should have. As soon as she completes the insurance planning, she can complete the financial section of her business plan. Vicky will invest $50,000 of her own funds and is borrowing $230,000. $180,000 of the loan will be secured with the 30 scooters. The other $50,000 is a personal note to her from her bank. She hopes to start her business within 90 days, to catch the beginning of the summer.

CASE DISCUSSION QUESTIONS

1. What financial risks is Vicky assuming?
2. What are the risks that are specific to renting motor scooters?
3. What are the risks specific to motor scooters as physical assets?
4. What risks will Vicky face because she is hiring four people?
5. What regulatory risks will Vicky face in operating a vehicle rental service in the state of Colorado?
6. What insurance coverage will Colorado require Vicky to have?
7. What insurance must Vicky have for her employees?
8. How should Vicky structure her business to minimize the potential loss she can suffer if a customer or bystander is injured or killed by one of her scooters?

SUGGESTED CASES AND ARTICLES

- The House of Wine (Revisited), C-19

Available on Create:

- Daniel Dobbins Distillery, Inc.
- Play Time Toy Co.

SUGGESTED VIDEOS

www.mhhe.com/katz4e

Video Case:

- For a written video case and corresponding clip, visit the OLC at www.mhhe.com/katz4e and select "Chapter 17".
- New Orleans Biz

eClips Videos:

- Kathy Koultourides Discusses Importance of Taking Small Risks
- Alison Gerlach Discusses Different Risks That Face Companies

SBTV.com Videos:

- Stopping Employee Theft
- Legal Protection for Business Owners

STVP Video:

- Fail Fast Forward: Appreciating Risk

PART FIVE

Management and Organization in the Small Business

CHAPTER

18 Legal Issues: Recognizing Your Small Business Needs

● A top-notch turntable scratcher, like B-Money Hughes, could make a good royalty income from getting one of his tracks included on a commercial CD. But in order to get that royalty, you need a good lawyer negotiating on your behalf. How could you tell if a lawyer is right for the negotiation you face?

After you complete this chapter you will be able to:

LO1 Know when you need legal information and how to get it.

LO2 Understand legal structures in setting up a new business.

LO3 Learn how to master the process of negotiating.

LO4 Recognize potential legal liabilities for your business.

LO5 Know contract terms and when a contract is needed.

LO6 Understand the basics of intellectual property.

LEARNING OBJECTIVES

Focus on Small Business: Brian "B-Money" Hughes[1]

Brian "B-Money" Hughes has a tip for budding hip-hop producers: "The best advice I can give to anyone that's coming up: Make sure you get yourself a good lawyer." He knows of what he speaks.

B-Money was a turntable scratcher good enough to get credits on Jennifer Lopez and Murphy Lee CDs. He scored big in street cred when he produced 50 Cent's "Hustler's Ambition," the lead track to the soundtrack of *Get Rich or Die Trying*. This did not translate into much money, though. Two weeks before the film's release, 50 Cent's team offered a small flat fee rather than a larger royalty. B-Money was told to take it or leave it, but do it now. An experienced lawyer would have realized that the cost to 50 Cent to redo the film's soundtrack without B-Money's contribution would have been a lot more than what was offered. But as B-Money put it, "I had way more leverage, but my lawyer wasn't poised and let it slide."

B-Money took the flat fee offered, but he replaced that lawyer with an industry veteran. So later, when Jay-Z's producer asked for a B-Money-produced track called "The Prelude," this time the artist and lawyer were ready to negotiate. The track was the lead for Jay-Z's *Kingdom Come* CD. The new lawyer delivered, and B-Money finally came into some of the money he deserved for his work.

DISCUSSION QUESTIONS

1. Given B-Money's experience, if you were interviewing a potential lawyer, what sort of questions would you want to ask?
2. Can you think of anything you could have said to your lawyer to get a better outcome during the negotiation with 50 Cent?
3. Did B-Money have any recourse when it turned out his first lawyer was just not very good at the music business?

You and the Law

LO1 Know when you need legal information and how to get it.

Business and law are inseparable. For B-Money, the two predictably merged when he was negotiating a deal for his tracks. At other times, the merger is unpredictable, like when your business faces an unexpected auto accident, product recall, or government regulation change. In either type of situation, when business owners know the law, they can better protect themselves and sometimes even avoid the problems completely. This chapter will help you spot important legal issues for small businesses and provide guidance for dealing effectively with those issues.

The United States is one of the most *litigious* (from the word *litigate,* meaning to sue) societies in the world, along with countries such as Germany, Sweden, Israel, and Austria.[2] On the other hand, in a 2002 National Federation of Independent Business poll of small businesses, less than 1 business in 10 had been sued in the prior five years. No matter what the perception, the law affects everything about business. Despite all the negative comments about attorneys, attorney jokes, and general resentment of the legal profession, the fact remains that if you are going to start a small business, you are going to be stuck with the legal system—virtues and faults both.

Because of that, it is important for you as a prospective small business owner to understand our legal system. Understanding the legal system will help you be less intimidated by attorneys and the law. And that knowledge can help move you from being a passive victim of the legal system, merely reacting to legal threats, to an empowered owner able to use the law to your advantage in a proactive way. Starting a business is risky enough. With the right knowledge about the law and the use of legal counsel, many of those risks can be significantly reduced or eliminated altogether.

It is easy to underestimate the number of laws that apply to a new small business because it is hard to believe how many laws apply—federal laws, state laws, even county and city laws. Let us take a moment and get an overview of the laws most likely to apply.

Table 18.1 provides an overview of some major federal laws in the areas of taxation and environmental health and safety. Intellectual property laws are considered later in this chapter, and labor and employment laws will be considered in Chapter 19. Even so, what Table 18.1 does not consider are state laws. There are some areas which only states legislate, for example, workers' compensation and employment security, which we will cover in Chapter 19. There can also be areas where there are overlapping state and federal laws, most typically in civil rights, and in such cases, the more demanding law is the one you should obey.

While the scope can be overwhelming, the good news is that not all laws apply to your business on the day you open. Many laws only start to apply as you reach certain thresholds. For example, tax laws tend to focus on financial thresholds, while environmental laws look at how much waste you produce.

Meanwhile, the state laws applicable to a small business are extraordinarily varied. It is truly a case where one size does not fit all. In Chapter 19 you will see the additional state laws that apply to labor and employment. For any category of laws, it is important to check what is applicable in your state. The Online Learning Center shows how to begin your check on the Internet. State laws can vary dramatically, so one state's laws are unlikely to be of much use anywhere else.

There is no central online starting point for finding the relevant state laws. One of the best ways to get a complete rundown of the relevant laws is to contact your closest state Small Business Development Center (to find it, type your zip code into the "Get Local Assistance" search box at the SBA website, www.sba. gov). Also, your local SCORE chapter (www.score.org) should be able to help, or at least point you to the right resources. Obviously, you can also work with an attorney to get expert help personalized for your business.

In the next portion of this chapter we start with your key legal expert—your attorney. We talk about how to select and work with an attorney. We also cover how to make some key legal decisions, such as choosing a legal form for your business, how to negotiate, liability issues, and contracts (in person and online), that come up in business. We conclude the chapter with a discussion of the latest hot topic in law—intellectual property.

You Need a Good Attorney

Setting up a business requires some familiarity with several areas of law—forms of organization, contracts, and licensing, for example. Usually with legal issues, as with health issues, it is best to confront potential problems before they have a chance to get serious. Timely decisions and action

TABLE 18.1 Selected Laws Applicable to Growing Businesses

Benchmark	Law/Regulation	Ramification
Business and Taxation		
Employer's portion of federal employment taxes plus federal income and employment taxes withheld from employees' total wages: • Less than $2,500 during a quarter. • Under $50,000 during the four quarters in the "lookback period" applicable to the calendar year of withholding. • More than $50,000 during the "lookback period." • $100,000 or more during a monthly or semiweekly period.	Circular E-Employer's Tax Guide	Employer must deposit withheld taxes: • Quarterly (if paying with Form 941) • Monthly • Semiweekly • Next banking day after $100,000 threshold is reached
Gross receipts up to $5,000,000.	Section 448 of Internal Revenue Code	The business may qualify for an exception that allows it to compute taxable income using the cash method of accounting rather than the accrual method.
More than 100 shareholders of a corporation, more than one class of stock, certain prohibited shareholders.	Section 1361 of Internal Revenue Code	Corporation could lose or be ineligible to elect "Subchapter S" status.
Filing requirements for an employee benefit plan with: • One participant (with plan assets more than $100,000) • 2–99 participants • 100 or more participants • Reporting to participants: Summary Annual Report	Internal Revenue Service/ Department of Labor Reg. §2520.104(b)-10	• Generally must file form 5500EZ annually with IRS. • Form 5500 must be filed annually with IRS, with some exceptions if the plan is unfunded or insured. • Form 5500, with some exceptions, must be filed annually including a report by an independent qualified accountant. • Annually provide to participants no later than 8½ months after the end of plan year.
Qualifying depreciable tangible personal property (and certain computer software) purchased for use in the active conduct of a trade or business in excess of $500,000.	Section 179 of the Internal Revenue Code	Reduction of the $112,000 maximum amount of qualifying property that can be expensed in the current year instead of depreciated over several years.
Environmental/Health & Safety		
Conditionally Exempt Small Quantity Generators of Hazardous Waste: • Generators of less than 1 kilogram of acute hazardous waste in a month, or less than 100 kilograms/month of hazardous waste may accumulate up to 1 kilogram of acute hazardous waste or 1,000 kilograms of hazardous waste on-site. Small Quantity Generators: • Generates at least 100 kilograms but less than 1,000 kilograms of hazardous waste in a month, may accumulate 6,000 kilograms of hazardous waste before accumulation period begins.	Hazardous Waste Regulations under RCRA (Resource Conservation and Recovery Act) and Missouri Hazardous Waste Law	• Conditionally Exempt Small Quantity Generators do not require an EPA Hazardous Waste ID number. Manifests, reporting, personnel training, contingency planning, emergency procedures are not required. DOT transport labeling, however, is generally required. • Exceptions for the small quantity generator relax handling requirements. Allows the generator to accumulate hazardous waste on site until the amount of accumulated waste exceeds the small quantity exclusion limits. After this amount is exceeded, the time period allowed for accumulation of hazardous waste begins to run (180 or 270 days). ONLY if the generator exceeds this time period, are they required to obtain a RCRA Part B permit to store the waste.

TABLE 18.1 (Continued)

Benchmark	Law/Regulation	Ramification
Environmental/Health & Safety		
Facility has hazardous chemicals present at the facility at any one time in amounts equal to or greater than 10,000 pounds, or extremely hazardous substances present in an amount greater than or equal to 500 pounds, 55 gallons, or the threshold planning quantity (if lower).	Hazardous Chemical Inventory Reporting under §311 of the Emergency Planning and Community Right-to-Know Act	Requires owner or operator to submit reports on inventories of various chemicals based on certain threshold levels.
Process involves one of over 130 listed chemicals in an amount exceeding a listed threshold level or involves any flammable gas or liquid in a quantity of 10,000 pounds or more.	Process Safety Management Rule under the OSH Act 29 CFR 1910.119	Requires owners to perform a process hazard analysis and develop written operating procedures, employee training, emergency action plans, evaluation of mechanical integrity of critical equipment and written procedures for managing changes in process or procedures.
Employs 100 or fewer individuals on a companywide basis.	EPA's Interim Policy on Compliance Incentives for Small Businesses	EPA will eliminate or mitigate its settlement penalty demands against small businesses based on: (1) good faith effort to comply with applicable environmental requirements; (2) this is the business's first violation of this requirement (no previous enforcement of that requirement within last 3 years); (3) the violation has not caused or does not pose a serious harm or threat to health or the environment; (4) the violation does not involve criminal conduct; and (5) the violation is corrected within a specified period.
An employer with more than 10 employees on a company-wide basis (except those in Standard Industrial Classification codes 52-89).	OSHA's Recording and Reporting of Occupational Injuries and Illnesses	Employer is required to record occupational injuries and illness on a log with a separate supporting record for each injury or illness and post in the workplace the log for the previous calendar year during the following month of February.

The chart is not, nor is it intended to be, a comprehensive summary of the threshold levels at which the statutes and regulations cited therein take effect, and it is qualified in its entirety by reference to the appropriate statute and regulations.

Chart compiled in July 2012 by: Joseph D. Demko, Daniel K. O'Toole, Robert B. Reeser III and Roger A. Walker, all with the law firm of Armstrong Teasdale LLP.

may avoid a problem altogether or may make solving the problem much easier and cheaper. Think of legal knowledge as a form of insurance. The key is finding the right lawyer.

First, look for an attorney who is experienced in forming new business entities and handling the needs of small businesses.[3] Where can you find such a person? If you do not have someone in mind, get suggestions from small business owners you know and respect. Bankers involved in commercial financing on a regular basis often know which attorneys handle small businesses well. In addition, a trade association for your industry may have suggestions.

These days, it is typical to be involved with more than one attorney. As with doctors, where you might work with one generalist and several specialists, today most businesses need to depend on one general purpose lawyer and several specialists. The law is so complex that no one can be an expert in all areas. Beware of the attorney who tells you he or she can handle all your legal needs. However, if the attorney is in a group practice, there may well be others in the firm who specialize in the other areas where you need specialized help. Ask about the legal specialties covered within the firm when you call to make an appointment. You may make several calls and visits. If one attorney does not meet your needs in terms of qualifications, work ethic, or pricing, there are many others who would like to have your business.

Again, like with physicians, once you have chosen an attorney, having an ongoing relationship helps him or her to know you and your situation when something comes up and you need legal advice on short notice.

Clients and attorneys start with a natural conflict of interest. The attorney wants to make money for the services, and you would like the services for as little cost as possible. In reality, all entrepreneurs know they will have to pay, so the key issues are how and how much you will be charged for legal services.

Typically you and the attorney will discuss and decide on the type and rate of charges up-front, before you engage his or her professional services. The attorney-client agreement should definitely be in writing and signed by both parties.[4] Take the time to read the agreement before signing. Ask for it to be sent to you to review. If the agreement is hard to understand, think about what other work from the attorney will look like, and consider whether that attorney is right for you. There are four ways attorneys typically charge:

1. **Hourly fees:** **Hourly fees** can vary greatly from one part of the country to another, as well as from firm to firm and even within a firm. Attorneys with more experience often charge more than new law school graduates. Prestigious law firms often charge more than smaller, less recognized firms.
2. **Flat fees:** **Flat fees** are a fixed amount paid for a certain task. For example, an attorney may have a flat fee for handling all the paperwork to establish a corporation.
3. **Retainers:** When using a **retainer**, the attorney will be paid a specified amount every month regardless of the workload for that month. Usually there is a retainer agreement which specifies what types of work that monthly fee covers and when and how much additional fees are when circumstances change.
4. **Contingency fees:** You have seen the attorney ads on television announcing, "I don't get paid unless you get paid." That ad is describing a contingency fee. **Contingency fees** are typical in accident (especially personal injury) situations, but are not usually used in everyday contract and business-related matters. With a contingency fee, the attorney will take a percentage of your recovery (if your side wins) as his or her fee.

hourly fees
A basis for legal charges in which the rate is based on a price per hour. Often lawyers will charge for fractions of an hour.

flat fees
A method of billing for lawyers in which a fixed amount is paid for a certain task.

retainer
A fee paid by a client to an attorney to engage the attorney's ongoing services.

contingency fee
Fee paid by a client to an attorney for legal services that is dependent upon the outcome of a case.

Just like anything else, pricing of legal services is based on supply and demand, especially your negotiating demands. Do not be intimidated by having to negotiate price with an attorney. Regardless of what the attorney says, the attorney's fee schedule in all four types of pricing of services may be negotiable, particularly if the attorney is a more senior member of the firm with the authority to negotiate. Diplomacy is recommended in these negotiations because once the original issue of pricing is resolved, it is in your best interest for you and your attorney to have a positive working relationship.

Can I Do This for Free?

There are three elements to most aspects of business law—finding the right information, negotiating the specific outcome you want, and then taking care of the paperwork associated with it. The three elements are what you pay your lawyer to do, but when you look at paying lawyer's fees, you probably want to know if there are things you can do yourself. The good news is that you can.

These days there are many sources of reliable legal information on the Internet for small business owners who want to do the legal work themselves. Also be aware that your local library and bookstores are brimming with titles on business law and how to start your own business.

There are two basic categories of information available to small business owners: free and paid. If you are paying a nonattorney for legal services, such as using an Internet company to set up your business as a corporation, you may not be saving that much money over what an attorney would charge. Consider whether you would be better served in seeking out an attorney and getting individual, custom-tailored advice. Falling between free and paid are the do-it-yourself products. Nolo (www.nolo.com) is one well-known company that has been established for some time and offers do-it-yourself products.

Of the free information available, some are more reliable than others. Government websites, such as www.reginfo.gov (the regulatory information site), www.dol.gov (for labor laws), and www.sba.gov (the Small Business Administration site), provide information to business owners that is reliable, and the government does not have the conflict of interest of wishing to make money from the business owner. State government sources can be very valuable in helping you choose a business entity; check your state's secretary of state website. You can easily find the sites by searching Google with the term "secretary of state" followed by a comma and your state's name, or you can go to http://business.usa.gov/stateandlocal to find your state's resources, or the commercial site Coordinate Legal Technology's listing at www.coordinatedlegal.com/SecretaryOfState.html. Skill Module 18.1 and on the Online Learning Center offer help on finding legal information.

● Visit **www.nolo.com/legal-encyclopedia/small-business-resources** to take advantage of the government's free legal resources. Looking at this and related websites can help you determine which legal aspects you can manage on your own and which require a paid attorney's involvement.

SKILL MODULE 18.1 Getting Started on Legal Issues Online

The Internet can be a great source of information in helping you determine which various governmental requirements apply to a business. On the state level you can go to the website for the state and obtain all sorts of information on starting a business in that state, required licenses, and the like.

Pretend that you wish to start business as a debt collector in Spokane, Washington. You have questions on professional licenses required of debt collectors, and you are considering hiring a high school student to work parttime after school. In addition, you have concerns about safety and health rules that apply to businesses in Washington.

Start with Nolo's state information finder at **www.nolo.com/legal-encyclopedia/small-business-resources**. Select "Business Licenses and Permits" from the list of topics, and then "Washington" from the resulting list of states. For Washington State, the Nolo link takes you to the state of Washington's Business Licensing Service. To learn what is involved, select "Get a customized business license guide sheet" and then click "Get a Business Licensing Guide online." From the resulting search page type *debt* and hit "Search." You'll find *Debt Collector* as one of the results. Click on it.

The website asks where the business is located. For the exercise we'll pick Spokane. The next screen asks for the type of business (sole proprietorship) and type of employee (we'll pick minor for our high school student). The website provides you a customized list of agencies and forms.

While the Nolo site lists all states, each state's own website is different. So when you leave Nolo, what each state might offer or what information they will ask of you, will probably be different.

Trade associations are another source of information for business start-ups. Many trade associations compile legal information for their members, including laws particularly applicable to certain types of businesses in various jurisdictions and proposals for changing the laws that affect your industry. As you may be aware, these organizations also hire lobbyists to push the agenda of an industry or trade group within the various branches of government, both federal and state. Because of the limited resources of small businesses, membership in one of these organizations can be particularly valuable in informing the business owners and giving them more power as a group to influence legislation that affects them. In addition, through these trade associations it is possible to meet others in your industry and make noncompetitive connections that help you network and keep up with industry trends. Remember that you learned how to find your relevant trade, industry, or professional association in Skill Module 3.1 in Chapter 3.

Be wary of legal information on matters such as statutes or agency regulations offered by individuals who seek to profit from doing business with you. For instance, if you are looking for space to locate your business, be wary of what real estate agents tell you regarding the law. Never forget, these folks make their money when you buy something or if they arrange some lease agreement for you. It may not be in your best interest to buy property, but real estate agents are not likely to tell you that because they will make money by getting a percentage when you buy.

For example, in the issue of zoning, go to your local governmental unit and check on the zoning of the property before you seriously consider it.[5] Do not take the real estate agent's word on the zoning. Be sure that the business you plan may be legally operated in that location. If the building will need any remodeling to suit your purposes, be sure to contact the local government regarding safety standards, exits, entrances, and so on so that the property will pass inspection once the remodeling is done. In the contract with your remodeler, it is best to insert a provision that the remodeling has to be done according to applicable building codes before the contractor is fully paid.

In the contract to purchase or lease the property, insert a provision that the property has to be zoned such that your business can be legally operated in that location. By contacting the local government, you should be able to get guidelines on zoning, placement, and size of signage, parking, property tax, and other matters related to the location.[6] Also, be sure to inquire about future plans regarding street repairs, expansions, and closures in the area, which could affect your ability to do business. Do not rely on the real estate agent for any of this information.

As noted at the start of this section, there are three elements to the law—finding the right information, negotiating the specific outcome you want, and then taking care of the paperwork associated with it. Often as businesspeople become familiar with the legal specifics of their business, they take on more of the responsibilities. Most often they do the negotiating themselves (you will see how later in this chapter), and where the paperwork is standardized (as we see below with standard contracts) even handle aspects of the paperwork themselves. Even some legal research can be done, especially when the business owner is made aware of new legal concerns by the trade or professional association. But for all of these things you can eventually do for yourself, when learning the business or when facing a new or unusual situation, it makes sense to go with the pro. When in doubt, call your lawyer.

● One key legal issue for small business owners is the matter of real estate. Before you purchase a space for any of your business's activities, make sure the site is zoned appropriately and that you can legally undertake any planned remodeling, expansion, or re-zoning of the area.

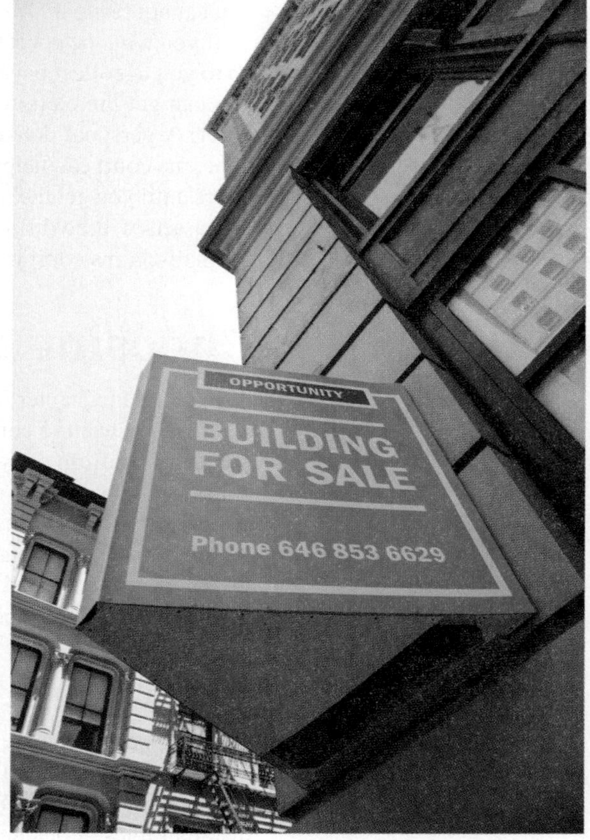

Small-Claims Court

There is also a legal option available to entrepreneurs that does not involve an attorney. It is typically called small-claims court. Despite the name, many of these courts will accept cases where the stakes are as large as $10,000. Most are designed so that ordinary citizens can bring their cases in. Yes, this is the sort of court you see on afternoon television—*Judge Judy, The People's Court, Judge Joe Brown,* and the like include a lot of small-claims court cases.

Believe it or not, you can learn something about preparing yourself for small-claims court by watching the television shows: (1) evidence helps, (2) have everything ready and with you when you go to court, (3) practice your explanation, (4) be on time, (5) stay calm, and (6) above all, stay respectful to the judge and court.

Small-claims courts work only when you are owed money, can prove it (proof you did the work, and that your customer did not pay—think of purchase orders, contracts, invoices, past-due letters, etc.), and have exhausted other procedures like calls and letters to the customer. If there is a reason the other party did not pay—for example, they said your work was late, shoddy, or not as promised—you need to prove you are in the right, otherwise you will have a tough day in court.

The typical next step starts with finding the right court—either where your business is located or where the person (or business) you want to sue lives or works. Realize this means small-claims court is not really useful for problems in other states, unless it is a short drive for you. To find the right court for your state, look at nolo.com lists of small-claims courts on their website. Go to nolo .com, select "Rights & Disputes," and then select "Go to court or mediate." Look for "Small Claims Court" to find the listing and help by state on the process. Most state bar associations also have pamphlets on small-claims courts. There is a video showing this on the Online Learning Center.

Contact the court to find out the specifics and costs of filing. These fees are typically less than $50, and are something you can charge the customer for if you win. You will probably have to fill out a form and give a written explanation of the problem. Make copies of your evidence to include in the packet. If you have potential witnesses, list them and get their testimony written down. Take the packet and the originals of your evidence to court to file the complaint with the clerk.

When you get to court, the TV lessons apply. Look the judge in the eye as you talk. Speak up and sound confident. Stick to what you wrote. Answer questions directly, briefly, and politely. Don't get angry at the other party, especially if they get angry or they insult you or the court. If you have a court date, be there no matter what. In case of emergency, it might be possible to get one postponement (called a continuance)—if the other party agrees. Otherwise, the case will be thrown out and you cannot refile it.

If you win, the court will give you official support to get your money; however, it remains mostly up to you to collect payment. The customer will have a fixed amount of time to pay up. If they don't, you can get the clerk to serve the losing party with a certified letter reminding them of the court order. A personal delivery can often be arranged for an additional fee. If that doesn't get the job done, the court can help garnish the loser's income or attach assets of the losing party, making them yours until you get the payment the court ordered. But realize that a defendant with little income and few assets will be difficult to collect from, regardless of the decision, so it only makes sense to go to small-claims court if you think you will be able to collect, should you win.

Choosing a Business Name

trade name or assumed name or doing business as (dba)
The name under which a business is operated.

assumed name filing or fictitious name filing
Filing made with a state(s) in which the business operates disclosing the trade name or assumed name of the business along with the owners of the business.

As we saw in Chapter 4, some entrepreneurs start out with the goal to start a business, others with an idea they want to commercialize. The legal issue for either approach is protecting the business's name or idea from copycats. Both of these are issues of intellectual property. At this point, we will consider the ways you can protect the identity of your business, while later in the chapter we will consider the other forms of intellectual property that can protect your idea.

The name of your business is called its **trade name**. It can also be called an **assumed name** or a **doing business as (dba) name**. If you use something other than your own name (e.g., The Jerome Katz Company), then the trade name must be registered in the states in which your firm does business. The filing is typically called an **assumed name filing** or a **fictitious name filing**. In most states, this filing is made with the Secretary of State's office. You can find these at the SBA website (www .sba.gov/content/register-your-fictitious-or-doing-business-dba-name). The same office usually offers a public database to see the names of the people behind other businesses using trade names.

There may be more than one business using the same name within a state. Most states allow several firms to use the same trade name, as long as the firms are in different parts of the state, or are in different lines of business (e.g., Courtesy Cleaners, Courtesy Pharmacy, etc.) in the same town, and

● St. Louis Bread Company® really did start out in St. Louis, but when they wanted to expand outside the region, they felt they needed a name that was place-neutral. They came up with Panera Bread, which is what the company is known as everywhere except St. Louis, Missouri, where the original name is still used.

as long as none of the firms have received a trademark or service mark in that name. You can check this using the Secretary of State database mentioned above, as well as the trademark search at the U.S. Patent Office (**www.uspto.gov**).

When selecting a trade name, you want to find one that is memorable and descriptive. "Social Networking Experts, LLC" tells customers who you are, better than "Darlene Jones, LLC" does. If you have plans to grow, factor that in too. Since St. Louis is known for baseball and beer, but not bread, the founders of the St. Louis Bread Company had to create a new name when they left their home market. Now the country knows them as Panera Bread. Given how Panera's menu has grown, it is possible that "Bread" may someday get dropped from the title, too.

In the end, the other key element in picking a trade name is your own goals. It can be very satisfying to have your name on a successful business—think of Donald Trump! But also realize that it can make it hard to sell the business. Imagine the Trump Companies without Trump. On the other hand, for a family-owned business, having the family name visible can be a benefit. Part of what makes Ford a bit more personal brand compared to General Motors is that there are members of the Ford family who own stock, sit on the board, and occasionally even run the place. The Ford family stands behind the Ford line, even today.

Choosing a Business Form

LO2 Understand legal structures in setting up a new business.

Most often choosing the *form* of your business is the next legal decision you need to make. Except for sole proprietorships, business forms are types of separate, legal entities. A **legal entity** is a unit recognized as having rights and duties apart from the owners of the company. Legal entities can own property, sue, and be sued.

legal entity
A being, human or nonhuman, such as a corporation, that is recognized as having rights and duties, such as the right to own property.

plaintiff
Person or other entity filing a lawsuit.

defendant
Person or other entity being sued.

The original type of legal entity recognized in England, the source of United States law, was the individual. An individual may hold property ownership and be a **plaintiff** (the party who files a lawsuit) or a **defendant** (the party who is sued) in a lawsuit. As time passed, the law recognized other legal entities that were not human beings. For example, about 1600 the corporation was recognized as a separate entity in England. In other words, a corporation itself, without its shareholders (or owners), could hold title to property and could sue or be sued in its own name, without its owners being sued.

Today there are seven general types of business form—sole proprietorships, general partnerships, limited partnerships, C corporations (commonly known as just "Corporations"), S corporations (also known as Subchapter S corporations), professional corporations, and limited liability companies (commonly known as LLCs). Each general form has advantages and disadvantages, which are outlined in Tables 18.2, 18.3 and 18.4. For start-ups, the most popular form is the sole proprietorship, although the approach is not always optimal for a small start-up, as we see below. General partnerships are the second most popular, and C corporations are third. These results are shown in Figure 18.1.

Unless you are going to see a lawyer for advice on what legal form of business makes sense in your situation, or you are using an interactive guide (like the "Formation Assistant" at **www.bizfilings.com/wizard.aspx**) to get a general idea about the best type of business form to use, the best choice for a new small business is a limited liability company (LLC). This is because LLCs are simple to set up and relatively easy to maintain once started. They can be used for an individual or a group of partners. If you have partners, it makes sense to create an agreement specifying ownership,

TABLE 18.2 Advantages and Disadvantages of Corporations

Advantages	Disadvantages
Can have representative management	Impersonal
Ease of raising large amounts of capital	Owners have limited interest in firm's activities—except profits
Legal entity separate and distinct from its owners as individuals	High incorporation fees and high taxes, especially double income taxation
Relatively permanent, since life of firm not affected by loss of any shareholder	Burdensome procedures, reports, and statements required by governments
Owners' liability for the firm's debt limited to their investment in it	Powers limited to those stated in charters—may be difficult to do business in another state

Source: Adapted from Megginson/Byrd/Megginson, *Small Business Management* 5th edition, 2006, p. 61. Copyright © 2006 by The McGraw-Hill Companies, Inc.

articles of organization Document setting forth information about a limited liability company that is filed with the state to establish an LLC.

profit splitting, buyouts, and the like, called **articles of organization**. When properly structured, an LLC offers legal protection to owners for assets they personally hold outside the LLC. It also gives the owners the benefits of single taxation, if they choose to go that route. (See Table 18.5.)

The major advantage of the sole proprietorship is that it is extremely easy to set up. There are no forms to file; you just start doing business. The problem is one mentioned in Chapter 17 when discussing risk. In a sole proprietorship, the owner and the firm are one and the same. If an employee has an accident while at work, the business is liable for the damages—*and the owner is personally responsible too.* This means the sole proprietor's home, stocks, savings, and even personal property could be taken to pay damages. (See Table 18.3.)[7]

articles of partnership Agreement between the partners of a firm on matters pertaining to the formation and operation of the partnership.

Partnerships can vary dramatically. They can be set up quickly with nothing more than with a handshake or with a formal legal agreement called **articles of partnership** (the latter is usually safer). They can be set up so all partners are equally and fully responsible for the business's obligations (called a *general partnership*) or where most partners are liable only for the amount they invested in the partnership (called a *limited partnership*—but every limited partnership has at least one general partner). The total liability issue in general partnerships is like that of sole proprietorships, so although easy to start, partnerships are something to avoid. (See Table 18.4.)

FIGURE 18.1

Legal Forms of Start-Ups from the PSED

Source: Paul D. Reynolds, "Nature of Business Start-ups," in William B. Gartner, Kelly G. Shaver, Nancy M. Carter, and Paul D. Reynolds (eds.), *Handbook of Entrepreneurial Dynamics: The Process of Business Creation,* p. 250. Copyright © 2004. Reprinted by permission of Sage Publications, Inc.

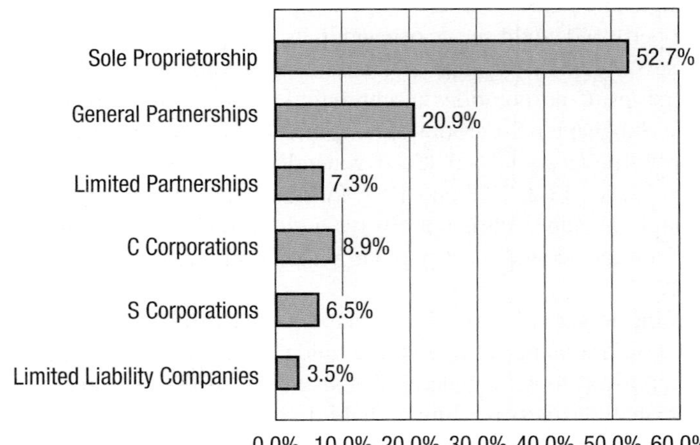

TABLE 18.3 Advantages and Disadvantages of Sole Proprietorships

Advantages	Disadvantages
Secrecy	Limited capital
Unique tax advantages	Difficulty in obtaining credit
Owner doesn't have to share profits	Inadequate management and employee skills
Relative freedom of action and control	Unlimited liability for the firm's debts
Easiest and simplest form to organize, operate, and dissolve	Limited life because business and owner are legally the same

Source: Adapted from Megginson/Byrd/Megginson, *Small Business Management* 5th edition, 2006, p. 58. Copyright © 2006 by The McGraw-Hill Companies, Inc.

Maybe you are not sure that an LLC is right for your situation, or your lawyer has suggested another form. How do you go about thinking through the issues? There are six major factors at play in the decision on the form of a business organization to set up:

1. Personal liability of the business owner—how much the owner can lose if there are problems arising from the business.
2. Taxation of both the entity and its owners—do owners get taxed as well as the business?
3. Complexity and organizational costs in setting up the business and maintaining that entity—how difficult and costly is it for the owner to maintain the legal form of the business?
4. Control of the business—who runs the business and how is decision making split among various people?
5. Continuity of the business—how long that particular form of business can continue and under what conditions the business could end.
6. Ability of the business to raise capital—can the business borrow money, issue stock, or issue bonds?

Table 18.5 provides a simple summary of how the forms of legal organization differ on the six issues. After going through the characteristics of these various entities, you can easily see how some

TABLE 18.4 Advantages and Disadvantages of Partnerships

Advantages	Disadvantages
Easy to form	Limited life
Division of labor and management responsibility	Unlimited liability for debts of the firm
Can use ideas and plans of more than one person	Each partner is responsible for the acts of every other partner
Specialized skills available from individual partners	An impasse may develop if the partners become incompatible
Can raise more capital since good credit may be available	Death of any one of the partners terminates the partnership
Obtains financial resources from more than one person	A partner cannot obtain bonding protection against the acts of the other partner(s)

Source: Adapted from Megginson/Byrd/Megginson, *Small Business Management* 5th edition, 2006, p. 59. Copyright © 2006 by The McGraw-Hill Companies, Inc.

single taxation
Earnings of the business are taxed once with the owners paying the taxes.

double taxation
Earnings of the business are taxed twice with the business as well as its owners being subject to tax.

pass through (taxation)
Earnings of the business are distributed to the business owners and those owners (rather than the business) pay individual tax on the earnings.

check the box taxation
A choice LLCs can make on their tax returns to be taxed as a corporation or a partnership.

operating agreement
A contract among LLC members outlining how the LLC will conduct itself.

TABLE 18.5 Forms of Legal Organization

Factors	Sole Proprietorship	General Partnership	Limited Partnership
Personal liability of owners	Unlimited personal liability.	Unlimited personal liability of partners if partnership has insufficient assets to cover partnership liabilities.	A limited partnership has to have at least one general partner and one limited partner. The general partner has unlimited personal liability. The limited partner can lose "only" his or her investment in the business.
Taxation	**Single taxation** of income to sole proprietor.	Single taxation of income to individual partners.	Single taxation of income to individual partners.
Control or management of business	Complete control by sole proprietor.	Authority shared equally between partners unless otherwise stated in articles of partnership.	Written articles of partnership generally are required for limited partnerships. Authority of various partners is set forth in the articles.
Continuity of business	Ends at death of sole proprietor.	Whenever mix of partners is changed, that partnership is dissolved.	Whenever mix of partners is changed, that partnership is dissolved.
Raising capital	Dependent upon assets and credit of sole proprietor.	Dependent upon capital contributions of the partners, credit of the partnership, and credit of the individual partners.	Dependent upon capital contributions of the partners, credit of the partnership, and credit of individual partners.
Complexity of setup and maintenance of business form	No government permission required, few (if any) legal costs.	May be formed by conduct of the parties, no government permission required, optional cost of articles of partnership.	Limited partnerships have to meet state statutory requirements which may vary from state to state. Filings with the state are generally required. In addition, states usually require that the business always identify itself to the public as a limited partnership.

Corporation	S Corporation	Professional Corporation	Limited Liability Company
Shareholders are not responsible for debts of the corporation. If the corporation fails, the shareholders can lose, at most, the value of their investment in the corporation.	Shareholders are not responsible for debts of the corporation. If the corporation fails, the shareholders can lose, at most, the value of their investment in the corporation.	Shareholders are not responsible for debts of the corporation. If the corporation fails, shareholders can lose, at most, the value of their investment in the corporation.	Members (owners) are not responsible for debts of the LLC. If the LLC fails, the members can lose, at most, the value of their investment in the LLC.
Double taxation of earnings generated by the corporation. Corporation is taxed on its income at the corporate rate, and shareholders are taxed on dividends at their individual rate.	There is no taxation of the S corporation, itself. The earnings are **passed through** to the shareholders who are taxed at their individual rate on their individual tax returns.	There is no taxation of the professional corporation (PC) itself. The earnings are passed through to the shareholders who are taxed at their individual rate on their individual tax returns.	**"Check the box taxation"** An LLC can choose whether to be taxed as a corporation or as a partnership (pass through taxation).
Shareholders elect directors who set broad corporate policy. Directors appoint officers to carry out that policy, aided by employees.	Shareholders elect directors who set broad corporate policy. Directors appoint officers to carry out that policy, aided by employees.	Shareholders elect directors who set broad corporate policy. Directors appoint officers to carry out that policy, aided by employees.	Members enter into an **operating agreement** under which the division of management rights, e.g., committees, voting, is established.
The corporate entity can continue indefinitely if the corporation is properly formed, regardless of changes in ownership of shares.	S corporations may continue as long as the business qualifies under the Federal Tax Code and the rules and regulations of the Internal Revenue Service.	PC can continue as long as the business qualifies under state law.	Depends upon state statute creating LLCs. Some states allow perpetual existence.
Corporations may issue securities such as stocks and bonds, and/or borrow money based upon the corporation's credit.	S corporations may issue securities such as stocks and bonds, and/or borrow money based upon the corporation's credit.	PC may issue stock although ownership may be limited by state law.	In addition to the capital contributions paid in by members, the LLC can borrow money as a separate entity.
Corporations are created by the state. Incorporators must submit articles of incorporation and pay appropriate fees to the state.	S corporations are created by the state. Incorporators must submit articles of incorporation and pay appropriate fees to the state. In addition, the S corporation must elect this tax status with the Internal Revenue Service.	Professional corporations are created by the state. The incorporators must qualify under state law. An application and fees are submitted to the state.	In some states a single individual may form an LLC. In other states two or more members are required. To form the LLC, articles of organization must be filed with the state. The members also need an operating agreement. There will be minimal state filing fees.

of the newer and nontraditional business forms, such as S corporations and LLCs, can offer the best of both worlds, that is, limited liability of owners as well as single taxation. Of these newer forms, the easiest to form and the most user-friendly is the LLC or limited liability company. As a result, LLCs should be viewed as a default of sorts, so select an LLC unless there is a compelling reason to choose another form.

If you choose any of the forms other than the sole proprietorship, please be careful to treat your legal form of business as if it were a being separate from the owner(s). When you keep the business separate from you personally, that business entity can have liability apart from its owners. If you fail to keep them separate, such as using personal funds for business purposes or using the business's car or equipment for personal purposes, there is a chance that a court may hold that there is no distinction between the entity and its owners in practice. If this happens, called **piercing the veil**, the court may hold that the owners have some personal liability for debts of that business entity. A good place to start in this area is to keep the finances of the business entity and those of its owners entirely separate. Company bills should never be paid from the owners' personal accounts using an owner's personal check. An asset of the business, such as a car, should not be used for personal use without accounting for that nonbusiness use.

piercing the veil
The dissolution of a corporate form, making it back into a sole proprietorship or general partnership, if the court finds that the owner carelessly mixed up personal and business assets or finances.

Another essential caution comes from recognizing that *no* form of LLC or corporation will make the owner(s) bulletproof. No matter what form of business a person owns, if he or she causes a traffic accident or accidentally hurts another person in some way (causes a tort), that person may be found "personally liable" in a lawsuit. That person may have to sell his or her car, home, or other assets (including the business) to pay the judgment. On the other hand, if the owner's employee causes the loss, as mentioned before, the business may be held liable. This is when it makes a huge difference what the structure of the business is in terms of what the owner can lose. If the business is a sole proprietorship or a partnership, the owner may lose personal assets as well as business interests. If the business is a corporation or an LLC, the owner can "only" lose what he or she has in that business.

Similarly, for a newly created LLC or C corporation going to the bank for a loan, it is unlikely that the new corporation will have the collateral base, asset base, or cash flow to convince a banker to issue a loan to the corporation. Regardless of your efforts to shield yourself from liability, the likelihood is that a bank giving a loan to your new corporation will require that you *personally* sign for the loan, in addition to the corporation's signing for it. From a banker's view, a corporation is only as strong as its balance sheet.

Taxation Issues

As you can see in Table 18.5 (and saw in Table 15.2 earlier), the legal form of organization you choose can have an impact on the taxes you pay. For every type of legal form except the C corporation and limited liability company, the taxes are paid by the owner on the basis of the income received from the business. This income can consist of a salary you pay yourself and any profits made by the firm. In these cases, you are being taxed at the applicable personal rate, shown in Table 18.6.

For C corporations, as a shareholder, you get taxed on the income you receive from the firm. This income can be in the form of dividends and profits. The good news is that tax rates for these are lower than for individuals. The bad news is that those profits face double taxation. The C corporation files taxes as an entity, and pays taxes on its profits and dividends. When the remaining posttax profits are paid to you as the owner or shareholder, you personally pay taxes again on the income, again at your individual rate. In 2011, dividends had have a rate fixed at 15 percent. But for dividends or profits you are looking at the double taxation mentioned in Table 18.5.

For the other forms of organization (except the LLC), the money you take out of the business is taxed at your individual rate. The firm itself does not pay taxes. This is the idea of single taxation. The good news here is when your business is unprofitable, these losses can also be applied to your personal taxes. So if you are employed somewhere else full time, and run your own business part time, the loss you have from your small business can be used to reduce your overall taxable income for the year.

One thing to watch for is the issue of paying yourself a salary. In a C corporation and S corporation, the IRS expects you to pay yourself a salary that is roughly at market rates. Why would you pay yourself less in salary? Because salary has the added costs of Social Security and Medicare taxes. But paying no salary is one of the red flags that draws IRS auditor attention.

TABLE 18.6 2011 Tax Rates

Sole Proprietors, General Partnerships, Limited Partnerships, S Corporations, Professional Corporations, and LLCs Not Filing Form 8832	C Corporations and LLCs Filing Form 8832
10% < $8,700 (single) < $17,400 (married)	15% up to $50,000 15% on all dividends
15% on $8,700–$35,350 (single) $17,400–$70,700 (married)	25% on $50,000–$75,000
25% on $35,350–$85,650 (single) $70,700–$142,700 (married)	34% on $75,000–$100,000
28% on $85,650–$178,650 (single) $142,700–$217,450 (married)	39% on $100,000–$335,000
33% on $178,650–$388,350 (single) $217,450–$388,350 (married)	34% on $335,000–$10,000,000
35% on $388,350 and up (single) $388,350 and up (married)	35% on $10,000,000–$15,000,000
	38% on $15,000,000–$18,333,333 35% on $18,333,333 and up

The LLC has been curiously absent in this discussion, but it can operate using either of the approaches described here. To use the C corporation taxation approach, you need to file a Form 8832 with the IRS. Otherwise, a one-person LLC is taxed as a sole proprietorship and a multiperson LLC like a general partnership. Once a Form 8832 is filed, you can't change it for 60 months, unless the business changes ownership and the IRS agrees.

Because the legal form of organization can make a difference in the taxes you (and the firm) pay, it makes sense to think about which legal form can make the most difference in your annual income. For many small businesses in their first years, losses are typical and profits are not, so it helps to have a form that provides for single taxation. As the firm becomes profitable, the advantages of the C corporation or LLC organized with Form 8832 as a check-the-box corporation can make a lot of sense.

Everything Is Negotiable, and Negotiation Is Everything

Some people argue that business is all about negotiation. While customers go into stores, find price tags, and pay the amount all the time, deals between businesses and even deals between businesses and consumers are often handled through a negotiation. Negotiations are discussions aimed at coming to an agreement about a particular outcome.

LO3 Learn how to master the process of negotiating.

The ideal goal in a business negotiation is for each side to feel it got what it wanted. Leaving one side feeling a loss, particularly if someone thinks he or she lost and the other side won, only paves the way for future bad feelings, bad reputations, and bad negotiations. Often small businesses entering into negotiations worry that their youth, lack of experience, lack of track record, or lack of resources mean that there is no way they can win. Experience has shown that small businesses, even *new* small businesses, can do well in negotiations.

Use these four steps to structure a negotiation to achieve a winning solution for you and the other party: prepare, position, propose, and pounce.[8]

- **Prepare** what you need to achieve, what you are ready to give up, and what it takes to close rapidly once agreement is reached. Learn as much as you can about the other side, its track record, current situation, and possible needs.
- **Position** by putting your best foot forward, show confidence in yourself, your firm, and your prospects. Don't lie or mislead, but do not apologize. All businesses started small. With the right deals some small businesses grow large and bring their trading partners along with them. Talk about where you see your business in a couple of months or years. Position your firm as a good partner with which the other firm can ally.
- **Propose** solutions that provide value and balance for both you and the other party. This is often the hardest part of the negotiating process, but it is also the aspect which has received the most attention. Consider using these techniques for finding mutually winning propositions:

  - **Seek to create value:** Listen to what *drives* the other side's needs and seek alternative ways to solve the problem. For example, it says it needs money, but it may be able to work with more time, more flexibility, or a preferred treatment later. Adding new acceptable factors enlarges the negotiated pie.
  - **Seek long-term solutions:** Today you are small, but tomorrow you may be bigger, so think longer term.
  - **Seek balance:** Ideally, each side's contributions should closely balance. Where close balance is not easily achieved initially, structure contingent contracts to ensure balance later. For example, pay a small amount now to get started, but agree to pay a larger amount (e.g., a balloon payment) or a percentage of sales when sales reach a higher level.
  - **Seek mutual safety:** Where risk is faced, consider sharing risks and rewards so each party is providing some of the safety net for the other, and each shows commitment to the deal working out.
  - **Seek outcomes commensurate with investment:** Scale returns or considerations according to the size of the contribution of the party to your success. Aim to satisfy people or organizations that are major factors in your business, and realize you cannot accommodate every small contributors' every need.

- **Pounce** when agreement on any part of the negotiation appears at hand; move to close the deal on that issue. When you have an agreement, even on small issues, pounce on it as a positive outcome, an indicator of future deals to be made. Then get the deal down in writing. When stalled, ask the other party how to move forward.

One fear some people have is being dealt a dirty trick by the other side. Preparation and a long-term view help here. A dirty trick only works when the other party can be confident you will not be able to retaliate or tell others about the dirty trick, since publicizing it will ruin negotiations with others. One-time deals are more prone to dirty tricks; long-term arrangements make them harder to sustain. Also, knowing if the other party has done dirty tricks in the past can help you prepare for them. Being well networked (and letting the other party know you are) can also help since if you are tricked, you can let others know, making the chance of the other party playing dirty tricks on others much less.

What makes all negotiations work is honesty. No one expects you to give up your secrets, but to build trust, you need to offer some information that helps the other side determine where to start negotiating. The optimal strategy is called *tit-tit-tat.*[9] Give up one piece of information on what you need or are willing to offer. Wait for an equal response. If you get one, your negotiation is off to a good start. If you do not get a response, offer one more piece of information. Wait for a response. If you do not get one, bring up the point that so far in the negotiation you have made all the overtures. If the other side is serious about coming to a fair deal, it needs to step up to the table and start talking seriously. If not, then it is clear it is not interested in striking a fair deal, and the negotiation must obviously be over.[10]

Along these lines, another negotiating tactic that lets you be open about your goals without giving away your secrets involves prioritizing your goals. Let us say you know three key goals you hope to achieve. Go into the negotiations asking for 5 or even 10 goals. In the bargaining process, you can "give up" some of your demands to show the other side you are willing to compromise.

As long as you gain some or all of the three key goals you wanted, you are ahead of the game by negotiating.[11]

Always keep issues of legality in the back of your mind when negotiating without a lawyer present. Let's say you negotiate a trade of services with another business—you print its ad brochure, it waterproofs your parking lot. Legal? Yes, *but* in barter arrangements, you are trading something of value. That means you need to count it when tax time rolls around. If you fail to account for it, you *have* done something illegal. Twists like that are a good reason to get lawyerly advice until you know enough to go solo.

Legal Liabilities

A huge concern for business owners is liability arising from the business. The simplest form of liability is direct liability. Simply put this means the business entity is responsible for something the entity has done. For example, when a customer goes into a fast-food restaurant and places an order, the restaurant employee is there representing the restaurant. The contract formed is between the customer and the restaurant, not between the customer and the employee. The employee is an agent of the entity, in this case the restaurant. The employee represents the entity. Through that employee's actions, the restaurant is now bound in contract to provide certain food at a certain price. Failure of the restaurant to honor its contractual obligations will bring direct liability upon the restaurant. The liability could apply through contract or tort law, each of which is described below.

LO4 Recognize potential legal liabilities for your business.

Torts: Responsibility for Your Actions and the Actions of Employees

Torts here are not fancy French desserts, but are civil, not criminal, wrongs. Torts can arise when a person's legal rights are violated in ways other than from a breach of contract. For example, where a person is hurt in a car accident caused by your driver, the tort issue is that the victim's right to travel down the road was impaired by the wrongful actions of your driver. Often when this happens, the driver faces direct liability for causing the accident, but the employer can also be sued by the injured party for what is called **vicarious (indirect) liability**. Vicarious liability against a business is possible if the employee involved was an agent of the business and at the time of the accident doing work for the employer.

vicarious (indirect) liability
Indirect liability or responsibility for the actions of another.

If your business is facing vicarious liability, there are two typical arguments you can try to deflect the liability: (1) the actor is not an employee, but an independent contractor, and (2) the actions were outside the scope of agency/employment. If you can prove that either one applies, your firm is not likely to be held for vicarious liability. The employee as an individual would face the liability alone.

The Independent Contractor Argument

Sidestepping the problem of agency is one of the reasons businesses often use **independent contractors**. If your firm publishes a cookbook series, and you sell it door-to-door through independent contractors, and one of those contractors accidentally damages a person's home while doing the sales pitch, your publishing company is not responsible for the damages—the independent contractor is.

independent contractors
Persons working to achieve a certain goal without being subjected to substantial controls by another.

That kind of distancing makes independent contracting attractive to small businesses. The fact that the entrepreneur doesn't pay benefits for an independent contractor makes it even more attractive still. It is so attractive that the IRS takes claims of independent contractor arrangements very seriously. According to the IRS, to be an independent contractor the person has to display three characteristics:[12]

1. **Behavioral:** The contractor solely decides how the work is to be done.
2. **Financial:** The contractor pays his or her own expenses (e.g., benefits, tools, purchases) directly rather than having the employer pay them.
3. **Relational:** The independent contractor is employed for a project or a distinct term and the service the contractor provides is not central to the operation of the business.

Protect yourself and your business from unnecessary lawsuits, which can quickly cripple your best-laid plans. The very first step in doing so is to develop clear guidelines for your employees to follow in regulating their conduct on the job and give them complete training programs on how to apply the guidelines.

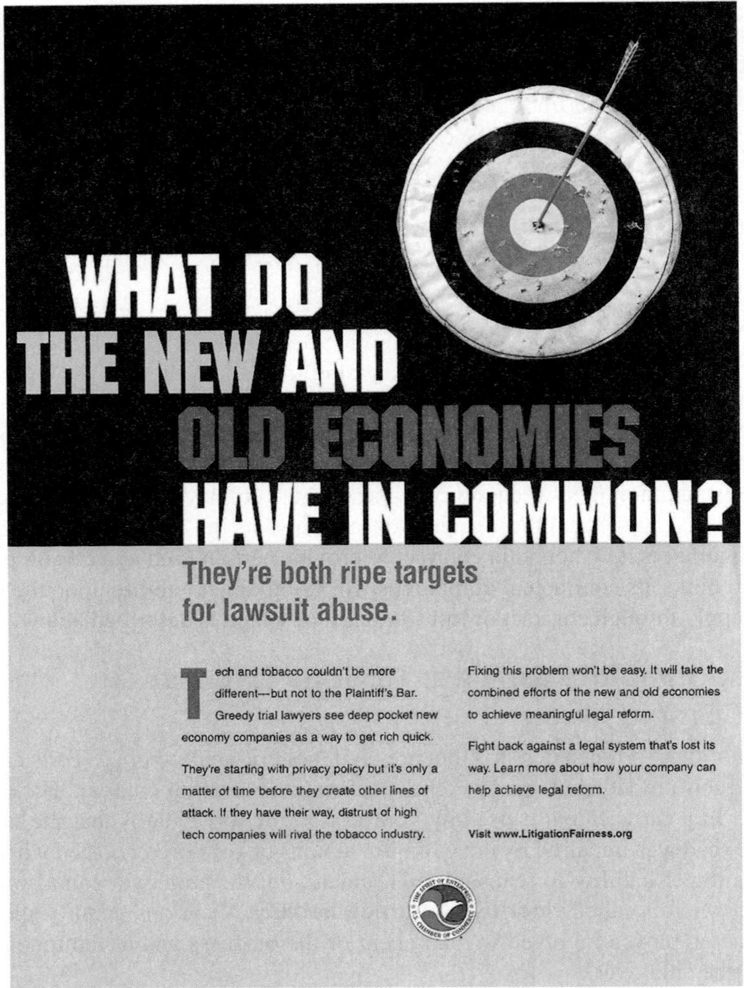

There are many ways to show these three characteristics, and the IRS can look beyond the three. For example, if the entrepreneur is not paying the contractor benefits, but also pays no or almost no benefits to employees, the contractor could look to the IRS like another employee. If the IRS classifies the independent contractor as an employee, the firm becomes responsible for damages, but also for benefits not paid, and for the taxes and workers' compensation sidestepped—the latter two with penalties possibly added. Checking with a lawyer ahead of time to make sure you are going to use independent contractors correctly is most often the right way to go to make sure you can benefit from using independent subcontractors.

Another approach to protection against liability is to train employees to avoid problems. Training employees on diverse issues such as safety measures, including spotting hazards at the business and how to treat customers, can drastically lower the exposure to liability for a business.

The Scope of Authority Argument

Another important part of agency law involves the amount of authority given to each agent. Employees differ in their job descriptions and responsibilities, so it is common for them to also differ in the amount of authority they have to handle their jobs. In practice this relates to the activities an employee can do and make decisions about without checking with their boss for approval. If employees make a decision requiring more authority than they really possess, the business can argue it was not liable for the problem.

For this argument to work, the firm needs to show that it fully trains or informs the employees of the exact authority they possess—when they can decide for themselves, and when they need approval from higher-ups. It also helps to include informing employees that they may face personal liability for problems which arise from their exceeding their authority. The business also ought to take steps to convey to its customers what the authority level of an employee is. For example, calling a sales clerk a "retail manager" would give the wrong impression of how much authority the clerk possesses.

Similarly it is important that management take appropriate steps to listen to employees. This is because one of the rules of agency law is that notice to an agent can serve as notice to the business itself. For example, if a customer comes into a retail store and announces to the employees that sleet has started falling on the steps outside, the business itself is now on notice that there is a hazard. If someone subsequently falls on that slick, frozen surface, the question may arise as to whether the business was negligent in clearing the icy area. The business will be unable to argue that it was unaware of the hazard. The court will be looking at what would be reasonable to expect of the business in terms of how quickly the area was cleaned up after any member of the business had notice of this problem. It is important to note that these issues work only where the concerns revolve around civil law. If it is a case of criminal law (see Thoughtful Entrepreneur: Dealing with Criminal Companies), another, tougher standard applies.

If you have involved business dealings with a publicly traded company, or are subcontracting with one, partnering with one, or being bought by one, or if you have plans to become a publicly traded company, or even if you have government contracts, you need to be aware of the **Sarbanes-Oxley Act** or SOX for short. SOX is legislation resulting from the Enron and other scandals, and its purpose is to make the financial activities of companies more visible to the shareholders, government, and public.

Sarbanes-Oxley Act
A federal law describing the steps publicly traded businesses must take to protect and provide their key financial information.

THE THOUGHTFUL ENTREPRENEUR

DEALING WITH CRIMINAL COMPANIES

Here's an example to think about. Suppose a business markets some sort of medical device used to close wounds. Assuming this device is widely sold and used, many thousands of patients may come in contact with the device. If the device is poorly designed or manufactured, one can imagine situations in which infections could result from the use of this product. Assume further that employees of the business know of the problem and do nothing to improve the product or to warn the users of this product. Perhaps the company has even been issued a warning of some sort from a governmental agency on this matter.

Even though the business entity itself cannot form criminal intent like a human being, if that entity produces or sells a product that is widely used, the potential to harm a great number of people is certainly present. The prevailing thought is that such businesses are subject to criminal prosecution in order to protect the public from harm and secondarily as a warning to others who might contemplate similar actions.

In other words, nowadays, there are cases in which the business itself (e.g., the corporation, partnership, or LLC) or management can be held *criminally* liable for damages caused by the actions of its employees. If management directs, encourages, knows of, or in some cases should have known of criminal behavior of others in the organization, the company and management may be held criminally liable. Of course, a nonhuman business form cannot be put in jail, but in such cases the business can be, and often is, fined a substantial amount of money as punishment.

There are also specific statutes which provide criminal penalties against businesses (as well as managers and under certain circumstances, owners) if those statutes are violated. Examples of these statutes are laws that protect the public health and environment, certain tax laws, and certain employment laws protecting employees from sexual discrimination and harassment.

SOX has requirements for preserving data and tracking its use, as well as extensive financial reporting requirements and external checks on all of these. Since its inception in 2002, the SEC (Securities and Exchange Commission) has focused its enforcement of SOX on large publicly traded businesses. While the SEC has considered giving exemptions for publicly traded small businesses, this is far from a done deal. Small businesses that are not publicly traded are not covered by SOX.

However, many large businesses are requiring their subcontractors to meet SOX standards, so all of the actions of the larger firm are seen as in compliance. Similarly, big businesses thinking about buying smaller firms look at the SOX liabilities they will be taking on when they buy the smaller firm, so compliance helps make a firm more saleable. Right now, at a practical level, SOX officially applies only to the small group of publicly traded small businesses, but if you find you are being asked by big corporate partners or investors to start operating under SOX rules, the only way to handle it is to get legal and accounting advice on how to do it correctly. It is not something that works as a do-it-yourself project.

Litigation vs. Arbitration vs. Mediation

litigation
A formal dispute resolution method that operates using the court system, typically with a lawyer representing each party.

Problems of contract or tort law can be handled either through litigation, through arbitration, or through mediation. **Litigation** uses the court system to settle differences. Whether you go to a small-claims court or go through a lawyer and the regular courts, the litigation approach is draining, both financially and emotionally, on both sides in a lawsuit, so before pursuing the litigation route, think through these issues to decide if litigation is right for you.

Either form of litigation means that prior efforts—letters, calls, or even visits—have failed. That will increase the emotional stakes for the entrepreneur and the defendant. While small-claims court is lawyer-free, it is not stress-free. It is a rare entrepreneur who really wants to play attorney when his or her own money and reputation is on the line. It is true that litigating going the lawyer route in the regular courts will cost money, time, and aggravation. It can cost to have the attorney handle correspondence and recovery efforts. If these don't solve the problem, you will pay additional fees for your attorney to take the case to court. And if you lose in regular court, you can be responsible for both sides' attorney's fees.

Our approach here is to recommend using an attorney from the start when creating contracts and setting up major deals or deals new to you and your firm. Why? There are four good reasons. First, in litigation, the only guaranteed winners are the attorneys. That is how they make their living, and particularly in business litigation, the case is not emotionally draining for them. Second, remember that good attorneys keep their clients *out* of court by writing better contracts and negotiating on behalf of their clients. If you are going to court, it means you have failed to win at the bargaining table. Third, remember that since litigation is so expensive, large, well-funded companies have a definite advantage over small businesses. And finally, beware of any attorney who guarantees a certain outcome in a case, particularly a jury trial. Human beings are not always predictable, and it is not all that unusual for a case to be decided in an unforeseen way. Of course, litigation can have wonderful outcomes for participants, but the point is that litigation can be risky, it often is expensive, and it always is emotionally demanding for the small business owner.

arbitration
A dispute resolution process held instead of court cases in which both sides present their case to a legal professional.

Given these cautions, if litigation does not make sense, a growing alternative is called *arbitration*. **Arbitration** is a way of settling disputes in place of going to court. Often it involves the two sides of a case presenting their perspective, facts, and materials to a private judge. If you agree to submit your dispute to arbitration, you are giving up a legal right to sue if you do not like the result. For that reason, an agreement to arbitrate should be in writing and should be given in exchange for something (a contract) if it is to be enforceable. Many of us unwittingly sign such agreements all the time. In a standard contract, such as an agreement with a brokerage firm to open an account, a contract for wireless service, and even in employment agreements, a closer look at the written contract terms may show that the parties have agreed, as part of the contract, to settle their disputes by the use of an arbitrator rather than by litigation.

A third choice is *mediation,* in which the dispute is put to a neutral third party who is not a judge. While arbitration and court cases have decisions that are binding, mediation works only if the two sides agree to the decision and settlement. If mediation fails, arbitration and litigation are still possible. Mediations are generally much faster to complete than either arbitration or litigation, and it is the least expensive of the three approaches. Mediation can even be used with the government, based on the

TABLE 18.7 Litigation versus Arbitration versus Mediation

Litigation		Arbitration	Mediation
Regular Courts	**Small-Claims Court**		
Uses court system	Uses court system	Works outside the court system	Works outside of the court system
Both parties represented by attorneys	Both sides represent themselves	Both sides represent themselves	Both sides represent themselves
Formal	Informal	Informal	Informal
Public judges	Public judges	Private judges	Attorneys or mediation specialists
Multiple levels of postdecision appeal	Appeal to regular court possible (varies by state)	Limited appeal possibilities	Full range of appeals
Can force the other party into court	Can force the other party into court	Occurs by agreement or accepting clause to arbitrate	Occurs only by mutual agreement
Binding decisions	Binding decision	Binding decision if agreed to beforehand	Nonbinding decision
Public	Public	Confidential	Confidential
Most costly	Least costly	Costly	Less costly
Slowest	Moderately fast	Moderately fast	Fastest
Favors those with more money for legal help	Friendly format for small businesses	More balanced than courts	Friendly format for small businesses

Adapted from John R. McGinley, Jr., "Arbitration or Litigation? Having Trouble Choosing between the Two? Here Are Some Factors to Consider when Making Your Decision," *entrepreneur,* April 01, 2002, www.entrepreneur.com/article/0,4621,298318,00.html. Steven C. Bahls and Jane Easter Bahls, "Stuck in the Middle: You're Jammed between a Court and a Hard Place. Get Free with Third-Party Mediation," *Entrepreneur,* November 2000, www.entrepreneur.com/article/0,4621,281851,00.html.

rules set out in the Administrative Dispute Resolution Act, which is handled by the Federal Mediation and Conciliation Service (www.fmcs.gov). Outside of government, mediators and arbitrators generally come from the same sources, such as the American Arbitration Association (www.adr.org).

A comparison of the three approaches is given in Table 18.7. Generally, the optimal situation is to include a clause in your contracts requiring binding arbitration. If an issue arises, you can see if you can handle it yourself. If you cannot get satisfaction, think about asking for mediation, since it is the fastest and cheapest of the procedures. If mediation does not work, exercise the binding arbitration clause. If there was no clause, the route is negotiate on your own, mediate if possible, and then go to litigation.

Commonsense Ways to Avoid Torts

In addition to the obvious ways of avoiding being sued, such as making sure there are no hazards on your property, not infringing upon another's trademark, and impressing upon your employees the importance of safe driving, there is another method to avoid a lawsuit that is rarely mentioned. When it comes right down to it, transactions between businesses and customers are an interchange of communications between people.

You know from personal experience that there are various ways of dealing with conflicts besides suing, the most obvious being communication and negotiation. You might think that lawsuits come as the result of a careful decision-making process, since they are so costly and time consuming, but in reality lawsuits are often filed out of frustration or anger. It sounds simplistic, but people are less likely to sue someone they like or someone they perceive to be willing to work the problem out with them.

Take a moment to think about the actor Tom Hanks and former *American Idol* judge Simon Cowell. Both are wealthy. Imagine each caused a car wreck. Which one do you think is more likely to be sued? If Hanks and Cowell are at all like their screen personalities, Hanks is much less likely to be sued. Being perceived as a likable and genuinely concerned person can sometimes save you from an angry reaction. How do you achieve this? Try to develop client loyalty and give personal service. Listen to your customers. Besides helping the bottom line of your business, developing such relationships can keep you out of court.

Contracting

LO5 Know contract terms and when a contract is needed.

The vast majority of business law in the everyday operations of a business is contract law. Contracts are essentially agreements in which the parties exchange promises. Not all contracts have to be in writing to be enforceable. For example, one neighbor wishes to buy a snowblower from the other neighbor who is relocating to Hawaii. The two discuss the purchase agreement and decide on a price of $800. Nothing is put in writing. It is a spoken promise to pay $800 in exchange for a spoken promise to give possession and title to the snowblower. If it works out as described, fine. But if there is a problem, how can it be resolved? There is likely to be a difference of opinion on what was intended. Without a written contract, there is no way to be sure what should have happened.

Oral agreements are as legally binding as written ones, but when the two sides disagree, how can a court decide which of the two versions to believe? In reality, it is very difficult to enforce oral agreements (also called handshake agreements). Sometimes oral agreements are unavoidable, but even in those cases, you can make the oral agreement written.

It works best if you specify you will write up the agreement and send it to the other person as you are shaking hands on the deal, but even if you did not mention it, write up what you thought the two of you agreed to and mail (use certified mail if possible), fax, or e-mail it to the other person. Mention in a note or letter accompanying the written form of the agreement that if the other person's recollection of the agreement is different, you would like to clarify what they thought was agreed to before either of you go further on the business deal—putting a deadline on the response can help move the work along. Follow up with the other person (preferably by certified mail or e-mail so there is a record of your sending it) if you don't hear back by the deadline. Should you continue the business if the other person does not respond? That is up to you, but at least you know that the situation is risky, and you have also taken the initiative to clarify what the responsibilities are for you and the other person.

In business, there are several kinds of situations in which you want a lawyer to take charge in making things work, for example:

- **Standard contracts:** If you are going to use one type of contract over and over, such as a purchase order, have your attorney draft that contract so that agents of the company can just fill in the blanks as needed.
- **Specialty contracts:** Unique contract terms and/or large dollar amounts at stake usually require careful drafting and legal counsel.
- **Interstate contracts:** When doing business outside your home state, it makes sense to have your lawyer draw up the contract because state laws vary. Charging 20 percent interest on financed purchases may be all right in your state, but this rate may be illegally high in another.
- **Noncompete clauses:** In a **noncompete clause** someone promises not to open a competing business or to go to work for a competitor.[13] Such clauses are tricky because they need to be part of another agreement and cannot stand alone. They also have to be reasonable. You cannot keep people out of their line of business forever, nor can you force them to leave town to practice their business. A lawyer can tell you what is reasonable for the kind of situation you face.
- **Exculpatory clauses:** **Exculpatory clauses** say that a party to the contract will not be responsible for certain things. An example of an exculpatory agreement is the statement on the claim check for dry cleaning that says that the dry cleaner will not be responsible for any damages to clothing. This may not be true, but such statements are "cheap" to make, just the cost of the ink and paper. The only chance for having one that works is to have a lawyer draft it.
- **Hold harmless agreements:** By agreeing to a **hold harmless** clause in a contract (also called a **waiver**), one party is agreeing not to hold the other responsible for his or her actions. In other words, one party is giving up legal rights to sue or otherwise enforce his or her rights. Courts tend not to like such agreements, so again the best chance to have an agreement that holds up in court is to have a lawyer draft it. If you see such a clause in a contract, let *your*

noncompete clause
Part of a contract in which a person agrees not to open a certain type of business or seek employment doing certain things in a particular area for a period of time.

exculpatory clause
Part of a contract in which a party to the contract states that he or she will not be responsible for certain actions.

hold harmless
A type of waiver in which a party agrees not to hold another party responsible for certain events.

waiver
Part of a contract in which a party intentionally gives up legal rights or claims.

SMALL BUSINESS INSIGHT

ANN WILLIAMS AND HEAD OVER HEELS[14]

Ann Williams and her husband Craig bought Head Over Heels, a children's gym in Birmingham, Alabama, in 2000. Ann had been a gymnast at Auburn University and had worked for another gym in town gaining experience. A key problem facing any gym—but especially one that focuses on children—is liability. Young bones and muscles are easily hurt, and while children are resilient, parents often are not.

The Williamses have liability insurance, but to keep it reasonably priced and to provide assurance to the parents (which is far more important in the long run), Ann makes sure parents know that every instructor is trained on safety issues and puts the safety of the children first. Additionally the gym has only the finest equipment. With all these in place, it is easier for Ann to get parents to sign a lawyer-drafted agreement, in which parents recognize the possibility of injury to their child and hold the business harmless for injuries.

lawyer advise you what to do. A workable clause makes it possible for Ann Williams to run a children's gym (see Small Business Insight: Ann Williams and Head Over Heels).

Contracting often seems intimidating, with all the small print and often official sounding language. But the point in contracting is to make sure *your* needs and goals are covered. Three ways to help take some of the fear out of contracting include:[15]

- Putting in a binding arbitration clause to minimize the possibility of court expenses (and because small businesses often do better before arbitrators than judges).
- When sued, call your insurance agent first. Your business liability insurance may not only cover the settlement costs, but often even your legal fees.
- Consider getting extra liability insurance if you fear you will be facing added business risks. For example, if you expand your business into a wealthy neighborhood, you might want to have an extra $1 million in insurance coverage.

Subcontracting

As the term indicates, a **subcontract** may be necessary to fulfill the promises of a "larger" contract. Particularly in small businesses, many support types of tasks such as human resources and marketing are often subcontracted, thereby allowing for fewer employees and thus lower salary and benefit costs to the business. Generally speaking, the same contract principles apply to both regular and subcontracts.

subcontract
A contract by which a new party agrees to perform a duty that one of the original parties to a contract was already legally obligated to perform.

Subcontracting has one unique aspect: Saying that the subcontractor did not perform does not get you off the hook. Imagine you get a contract from Ford to make rearview mirrors. You subcontract out making the glass, while you concentrate on the housing. Your subcontractor does not deliver. Who gets sued? It is you. Your firm signed the Ford contract, so you are responsible. You can sue the subcontractor, but you still have obligations to Ford, and can be sued by Ford.

Internet Issues in Contracting

Small businesses have blossomed through the Internet. They have taken their place in commerce alongside brick-and-mortar establishments. Contract law that has existed for hundreds of years is now being applied to Internet transactions. Courts are being asked to apply this old, standard, contract law to new situations arising in e-commerce as legislatures try to enact new statutes specifically addressing contract law as applied to e-commerce. In the meantime certain problems can be anticipated.

In business to business (**B2B**), contracts are often transactions involving electronic data interchange (EDI). These systems link suppliers of raw materials and components with wholesalers and retailers, often using dedicated lines or satellites. In this way, for example, an order for new inventory may be submitted electronically. B2B systems are generally used in situations in which repeat transactions are entered into and there is generally a master contract or umbrella contract that states

B2B
Business-to-business transactions.

EXHIBIT 18.1

Sources of High-Technology Alternatives to Signatures

Digital Certificates (also called SSL Certificates)	Encryption Programs
Entrust: www.entrust.com	OpenSSL (a free open source program): www.openssl.org
GeoTrust: www.geotrust.com/	PGP: www.pgp.com
Thawte: www.thawte.com	Comodo: www.comodo.com
Verisign: www.verisign.com	eOriginal: www.eoriginal.com
	And the digital certificate companies

the terms of the transactions covered, leaving for example, quantity and prices to be determined in each transaction. These master agreements between the parties are known as *trading partner agreements.* You need to have your lawyer review these before you enter into any major EDI effort.

B2C
Business-to-consumer transactions.

Another type of Internet contract is the business-to-consumer (**B2C**) contract. This is commonly used by small businesses to sell over the Internet. Here are a couple of pointers for setting up the websites. First, if you want to ensure control over the selling process, make it very clear on the website that the representations of merchandise or services are not actual offers to the buyer. Direct wording to that effect is common on many websites. The reason for this is so that the seller is not tied into a certain price and that the buyer cannot create the contract simply by accepting in the form of placing an order. In setting up a website, in addition to stating that information on the website is merely informational and not an offer, the website might also contain a statement to the effect that the seller reserves the right not to sell to everyone and that the website seller need not accept the buyer's offer. This gives the seller some control over pricing and also in this new world of terrorism allows the seller to not sell certain merchandise if he or she considers it a risk.

Another issue with online contracting is how to handle contracts that are required to be in writing to be enforceable. For a contract written on paper to be enforceable, it must contain the "wet signature" of the party to be held to his or her contract promises. An alternative is to use technology such as encryptions, third-party certificates, or passwords to guarantee that the parties to the contract are who they say they are. The law does not yet dictate what precise technology must be used, just that there be protection from imposters purporting to be someone else. See Exhibit 18.1.

Although not an issue in business contracting, there is one other Internet-related issue with legal overtones—how a business handles e-mail. As business e-mail becomes more important, more problems have arisen with employee misuse of these tools. For that reason, it is very important that businesses, big and small, establish policies for employees on usage of the Internet and e-mail.

LO6 Understand the basics of intellectual property.

If your employees have access to the Internet at work, make it very clear how that access can be used both in terms of amount of time spent and sites visited. Employees should be informed (ideally through a written communication such as an employee handbook or written notice) about the company's policy regarding usage of the Internet for personal business. For example, are employees allowed to access Internet sites for sports scores, sexually explicit materials, stock quotes, and online shopping while "on the clock"? If not, you need to specify this.

intellectual property
Property coming from some sort of original thought; for example, patents, trade secrets, trademarks, and copyrights.

intangible property
Property that has no value of its own but that represents value, such as a stock certificate.

For e-mail, the essential message that must be conveyed (again, ideally through a written communication such as an employee handbook or written notice) to employees is that the business owns the e-mail system and has full rights to monitor that system. This even includes e-mail in outside ISPs (like a personal e-mail account) that is accessed from work. In fact, over 50 percent of U.S. companies monitor employee e-mail, and 22 percent of companies have terminated an employee for misuse.[16]

Employees should be informed of policy regarding personal use of the e-mail system at work. For example, are employees allowed to send e-mails at work informing co-workers that their children are selling cookies for scouts or candy bars for the baseball team? In addition, employees should be told explicitly what is considered inappropriate content of e-mails. Clearly, unauthorized transfer of trade secrets is a huge concern of business owners and should be prohibited as well as e-mail that contains offensive sexual, ethnic, or racial messages. Besides monitoring e-mail for misuse by employees, it can be very beneficial for a company to monitor its system as a way to ensure proper customer service. A good rule of thumb is that nothing should be sent by e-mail that you wouldn't be embarrassed to read on the front page of the newspaper. Once that send button is clicked, it may be impossible to limit access to that message.

patent
A grant by the U.S. government to an inventor for an idea that is new, useful, and nonobvious, giving the inventor the exclusive right to make, use, or sell his or her idea.

trade secret
Confidential information within a company that gives that company a competitive advantage.

copyright
Exclusive right given to the creator of a literary or artistic work to make use of that work.

trademark
Distinctive word, slogan, or image that identifies a product and its origin.

Intellectual Property

When you worry about making copies of books or songs, you are dealing with issues of **intellectual property**. Intellectual property is a type of **intangible property** in which what is being protected is an idea or a form of expression. This includes the law of **patents**, **trade secrets**, **copyrights**, and **trademarks**. It also touches on the creation of a trade name for a business. In reality, a start-up will create a large number of properties that could be protected. Table 18.8 provides a checklist of many of the most common sorts of intellectual properties a start-up might create and offers some of the ways these typically get protected. Intellectual property laws are most active at the federal level, although trademarks and service marks can be registered with any state also. Remember, state level laws vary dramatically, so check what laws apply (and how) in your state.

TABLE 18.8 IP Checklist: Finding and Protecting IP in Your Business

Aspect of Your Business	Form of IP Protection
Business Identity	
Business name and logos	Trademark/service mark Fictitious name registration, incorporation (C-corp, LLC, etc. – consider in your home state versus an "away" state) URL in multiple domains (.com, .net, .org, .biz, .us, etc.) Digital watermarking for logos, TM/SM
Business Materials	
Brochures, sales materials, publicly visible pages on your website	Copyright (or Creative Commons) Digital watermarking for your photos, logos, audio, and video
Documents, forms and spreadsheets used internally by your firm to make decisions or perform evaluations	Trade secret
Your customer list or database	Trade secret
Your catalog	Copyright (or Creative Commons) [design may be covered by Trade dress], digital watermarking for the electronic copy
Your price list	Trade secret
Your investors or funding sources	Trade secret (except where disclosure is required by law)
Interactive web elements like Tweets, postings, blogs, videos, podcasts, etc.	Copyright (or Creative Commons) [design elements may be protected by trade dress or design patents or both], digital watermarking for your photos, logos, audio, and video
Uniforms or décor specialized for your business	Trade dress
Specialized designs used elsewhere in your business (e.g., magazine covers, custom packaging)	Trade dress

(Continued)

TABLE 18.8 (Continued)

Product/Service and Its Design	
Name of your product or service	Trademark/service mark, URL in multiple domains (e.g. ,dietcoke.com, .net, etc.)
Distinctive product design (e.g., a Coke bottle)	Design patent
Your product (if it does something new or in a new way)	Patent
Your type of business service if it new or different (e.g., Amazon's one-click ordering)	Business method patent
The process underlying your service (if it is new or does things in a new way)	Business method patent
Internal code of your website, esp. code that "does the work" of the website	Trade secret (also use techniques like server-side scripting so the user cannot see the code that contains your "secret sauce"). Patent (where possible)
Web mash-ups, widgets, gadgets (if does something new or different)	Business method patent, Permission from data sources
Your method for legally decreasing or deferring taxes	Tax patent
A new chemical process or product	Chemical patent
A new circuit or computer chip	Electrical patent
A biological organism or a new gene sequence	Biological/gene patent
Business Partnering	
Use of brand names (and/or logos) of components or services used by your firm	Permission of the vendor
Use of brand names (and/or logos) of customers of your firm	Permission of the customer

* *[Consider getting common misspellings of your business name to protect it, along with [businessname]online, my[busnessname], or [businessname]isgreat.]*

Patents and Trade Secrets

New ideas can be protected from being used by others by the owner obtaining a patent issued by the U.S. Patent Office (www.uspto.gov) or by keeping the information as a trade secret. A **design patent** (which lasts 14 years) covers the look of a product and those parts that are essential or a part of the design. **Utility patents** cover processes and functions and last 20 years. There are even **plant patents** for newly created strains of living matter, which last 20 years from when the patent application is filed. A great first stop at the Patent Office website, (www.uspto.gov) is the Inventor Resources page, at www.uspto.gov/web/offices/com/iip/index.htm. It can tell you most of what you will want to know.

design patent
A 14-year patent for a new, original, and ornamental design for an article of manufacture.

utility patent
A 20-year patent covering a process, machine, article of manufacture, composition of matter, or any new or useful improvement of an existing one.

plant patent
A 20-year patent that covers new strains of living plant organisms, algae, or macro fungi.

infringer
Someone who uses intellectual property without the permission of the owner.

Patents are essentially monopolies granted to inventors by the U.S. government giving patent owners the exclusive rights to make, use, or sell that invention for a certain period of time. Once the patent is issued, anyone can have access to the information covered by the patent, but people cannot make use of that information without the consent of the patent holder. Persons doing so are known as **infringers** and are subject to being sued by the patent holder. Because of the complexity in this area of the law (starting with the question of whether an idea *is* patentable), it is highly unlikely that an inventor could obtain a patent without the services of a patent attorney. See Figure 18.2.

Whether an idea is patentable and whether it should be patented or whether an idea can or should be protected as a trade secret are questions for a patent attorney. There are certain ideas that can be patented and also would be suitable for protection as a trade secret. Once again, a patent attorney is the appropriate source to help the business owner make that determination.

Here is an important word of warning: Be extremely wary of companies stating that they will assist you in finding financial backers to develop your new idea or that they will assist you in patenting your new idea. Do not deal with these companies. They are often out there to steal unprotected, new

FIGURE 18.2

Section of a Patent Application

Patents protect designs, processes, or plants but are complex documents which should be handled by a patent attorney. This patent was granted to Paul Scheiter, whose story started *Entrepreneurial Small Business*. It is for a strap on his knife sheaths that automatically retracts when opened. It is important to remember that patents don't require the item to be high tech, just a new way of doing something useful. What ideas do you hope to get patented?

Source: www.google.com/patents/US7587827?pg=PA1&dq=paul+alan+scheiter&hl=en&sa=X&ei=RoXjUJH50tSdqQHJIICQDg&ved=0CDgQ6AEwAA#v=onepage&q=paul%20alan%20scheiter&f=false.

US007587827B2

(12) **United States Patent**
Scheiter

(10) **Patent No.: US 7,587,827 B2**
(45) **Date of Patent: Sep. 15, 2009**

(54) **AUTOMATIC SWING-AWAY KNIFE SHEATH RETAINING STRAP**

(75) Inventor: **Paul Alan Scheiter**, St. Louis, MO (US)

(73) Assignee: **Hedgehog Leatherworks LLC**, St. Louis, MO (US)

(*) Notice: Subject to any disclaimer, the term of this patent is extended or adjusted under 35 U.S.C. 154(b) by 242 days.

(21) Appl. No.: **11/481,715**

(22) Filed: **Jul. 6, 2006**

(65) **Prior Publication Data**

US 2008/0006660 A1 Jan. 10, 2008

(51) **Int. Cl.**
B26B 29/02 (2006.01)
B65D 25/10 (2006.01)

(52) **U.S. Cl.** **30/151**; 224/232

(58) **Field of Classification Search** 30/156, 30/162, 298.4, 151; 224/192, 193, 198, 232, 224/238, 243, 911; D3/228; D22/118
See application file for complete search history.

(56) **References Cited**

U.S. PATENT DOCUMENTS

2,859,516 A *	11/1958	McQueary	....	30/151
2,870,947 A *	1/1959	Hendry	....	182/221
3,307,756 A *	3/1967	Brunosson et al.	....	224/232
3,533,540 A *	10/1970	Carinci	....	224/232
3,958,330 A *	5/1976	Hutchens	....	30/151
3,977,582 A *	8/1976	McMahon	....	224/246
4,414,744 A	11/1983	Collins		
4,886,197 A *	12/1989	Bowles et al.	....	224/243
5,002,213 A	3/1991	Newton et al.		
5,201,447 A	4/1993	Bumb et al.		
5,388,740 A *	2/1995	Garland	....	224/675
5,450,993 A	9/1995	Guerrero et al.		
5,779,114 A *	7/1998	Owens	....	224/193
5,794,347 A	8/1998	Serpa		
6,109,496 A	8/2000	Andrew et al.		
6,202,908 B1	3/2001	Groover		
6,364,187 B1	4/2002	Castellano et al.		
6,412,674 B1	7/2002	Lipke		
6,695,704 B2 *	2/2004	Parsons	....	463/47.2

* cited by examiner

Primary Examiner—Hwei-Siu C Payer
(74) *Attorney, Agent, or Firm*—Polster, Lieder, Woodruff & Lucchesi, L.C.

(57) **ABSTRACT**

A knife sheath is provided. In various embodiments, the knife sheath includes an automatic swing-away retention strap that includes at least one biasing device. The biasing device is adapted to automatically pivot a detachable distal end of the retention strap about a fixed proximal end of the retention strap to swing the retention strap from a fastened position to an open position.

3 Claims, 8 Drawing Sheets

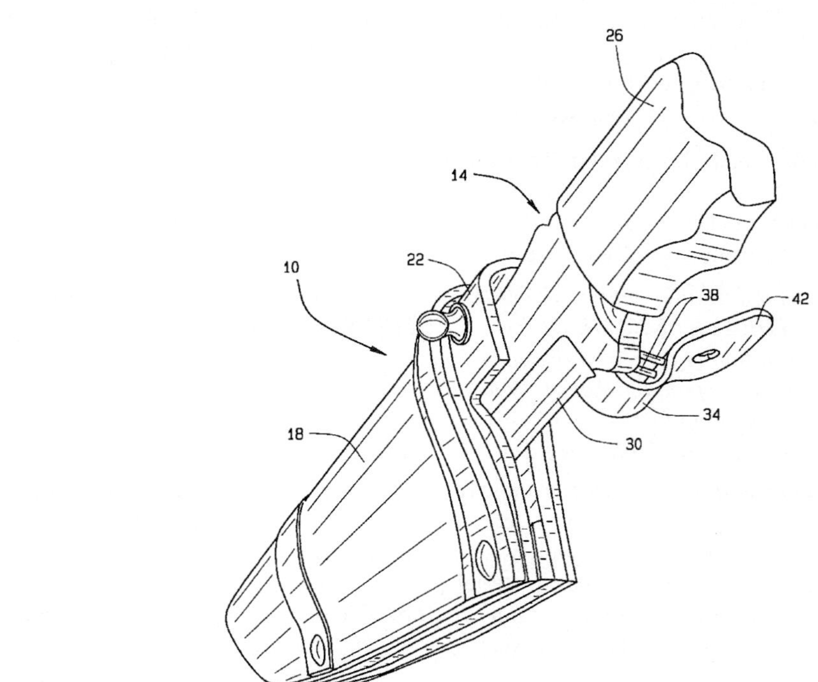

ideas from inventors. Before sharing information on a new idea to obtain financing or marketing assistance, that idea must first be protected as a trade secret or by a patent.

Also be aware that the United States and the rest of the world run with different laws regarding patents. One of the key differences between the two approaches is when you need to file your patent applications in order to qualify for patent protection if and when a patent is granted. In the U.S. you have one year from the first time you disclose your idea outside of your firm or to the public (via the web, printing, or a public presentation), while in the rest of the world, you need to file your patent application *before* you disclose it publicly. So if you plan to file patents in Europe, Asia, Africa, or South America, start your patent filings before you disclose to the public. Also check the World Intellectual Property Organization's database at www.wipo.int/wipogold/en/ to see if your idea has popped up elsewhere. Outside the United States, patent applications are publicly available, while in the U.S. only granted patents can be searched.

In general, it makes a lot of sense to file before you talk about your idea to anyone, other than a patent attorney. Anyone to whom you disclose an idea could beat you to a filing, and then you would find yourself trying to prove you had an idea first—not easy and unnecessary if you file before speaking. Filing a provisional patent application electronically with the U.S. Patent Office is a good way to start—*after* you talk to a patent attorney (the U.S. Patent Office lists them). Do not worry, talking to your attorney does not count as a public disclosure. While there are books showing patent filing as a do-it-yourself project, in reality the vast majority of patents granted to individuals are those filed by professional patent attorneys and patent agents. To give your patent the best chance of surviving, this is a case where you want to go with the pros.

A *trade secret* is not created by the government but is information known to certain people in the company that makes that company more competitive. Trade secrets include more than patents. A trade secret can be a formula (e.g., the formula for the KFC "13 herbs and spices" chicken coating), the name of the company's top salesperson, or details of (or even acknowledgment of) the upcoming ad campaign. One rule of thumb when considering whether certain information is a trade secret is to ask whether a competitor would be willing to pay for that information. If the answer is yes, then you may have an idea that is protectable as a trade secret.

To protect a trade secret, the secret must literally be kept a secret from all except those who need to know to operate the business. The most famous example of a trade secret is the formula for Coca-Cola Classic. Had that recipe been patented back in the late 1800s, the company would have had exclusive rights to it for 17 years under the patent laws in effect at that time (today it would have had the rights for 20 years). Then, after 17 years, anyone could follow the recipe and make the beverage known to us as Coca-Cola. However, by treating the formula as a trade secret and successfully keeping the formula a secret from outsiders for all these many years, Coca-Cola still has exclusive rights to its use. There is no expiration date for trade secrets. There are five steps to protecting trade secrets:[17]

1. **Trade secrets must really be secrets:** They cannot be shared with others or be likely to be known by others.
2. **Use warning labels:** Put "confidential" on *every* page that contains trade secrets. The full legal version can go on the front page of the document, and it looks like this:

   This item/document/material contains CONFIDENTIAL TRADE SECRET INFORMATION owned by [THE LEGAL NAME OF YOUR COMPANY] and/or its affiliated companies. This information is protected by applicable state law and may be protected by the federal Economic Espionage Act of 1996 (18 U.S.C. Sec. 1831), which provides for criminal penalties of up to 15 years in prison and/or a $5 million fine for stealing, receiving, possessing and/or duplicating any information contained herein.
3. **Restrict physical access:** Coca-Cola has a big vault. You can get by with a locked cabinet or a password protected file, but if you have a secret, it should be locked up when not in use.
4. **Confidentiality agreements:** Only people who sign one of these (have your lawyer draft it) get to handle, see, or hear the trade secret material.
5. **Keep doing Steps 1 through 4:** A trade secret is enforceable only as long as you take positive steps to protect it. If you get lazy, the secret may get out, and you have no protection.

Wrongful acquisition of a trade secret is a tort and if certain behavior, such as trespassing or bribery, is involved in getting the information, criminal violations may also have taken place. Concern over protection of trade secrets can justify use of a noncompete agreement to help protect against former employees taking that information to new employers.

Copyright

Copyright involves the expression of ideas, not (as with patents and trade secrets) the ideas themselves. For example, if a greeting card company creates a picture of a single sunflower for use on a greeting card, what can be copyrighted is that particular rendition of a single sunflower. Copyright does not mean that no one else can create a card with a single sunflower (which would use that idea). That *particular* image of a sunflower is protected, so another person or company cannot use that same image without permission. Copyrights for new works last for the creator's life plus 70 years. If it is a "work for hire" bought from the creator, the copyright lasts for 120 years after creation or 95 years after its first publication, whichever is less.

Writers, artists, and others who create unique expressions of ideas automatically copyright those expressions by creating their work. Even though it is not now required, it is a very good idea to place a notice upon your original creation such as a book, painting, sculpture, computer program, or musical score that the work is copyrighted. Placing a notice on the work is done by using the word "copyright," "copr.," or "©," the creator's name, and the year of creation. Because original works are automatically copyrighted, this notice does not create the copyright, but it puts others on notice that the materials cannot be copied without permission of the copyright holder and will prevent any infringer from successfully arguing that he or she didn't know the materials were copyrighted.

The government does not create copyrights. However, copyrights on works can be registered with the federal government (www.copyright.gov) for more complete protection of the work(s). Registration with the government of copyrighted materials will establish a presumption as to ownership of the work. However, registration is not generally done unless wide distribution of those materials is planned.

One of the recurring issues for self-employed professionals, Web designers, and artists is who owns the work they do for others. Unless there is a contract giving the hiring individual rights to the material (making the project into a "work for hire" in copyright law), the creator owns the material. Often freelancers have developed a set of materials, templates, or designs which they adapt for a variety of clients. If that is your plan, you need to make sure you retain the intellectual property rights to the materials you develop. You can grant the client rights to the specific products from your project, while retaining the rights to the underlying intellectual property for use in other projects. In these work-for-hire contracts, the typical approach is to license to the hiring party the particular creative materials produced. The license can be limited by duration (it is yours for a year), territory (you can use it in your city), media (you can use it only on the Web), or exclusivity (others may not have a logo similar to the one made for you). There are work-for-hire templates available, and it is a good idea to get with a lawyer early in your business to sort out how to create a standard contract to protect your ideas and your business.

Trademarks

One last area of intellectual property, *trademark,* can be of particular significance to small business owners. Trademarks identify certain goods. A trademark will indicate the source of particular goods, for example, a Mini Cooper automobile, and not just any automobile. A related concept using the same law is a service mark. Service marks identify services. Some words or groups of words such as Weight Watchers® can be both trademarks (applicable to foods sold under this name) and service marks (identifying services such as programs of instruction on dietary management).

Once a mark is established as identifying certain goods or services, the owner of the mark can keep others from using a similar or identical mark to identify similar or identical goods. As with other intellectual property, anyone using the mark without permission is an infringer and is subject to legal action such as Ty, Inc., learned in 2004 when it was sued by a small business (see Small Business Insight: Peaceable Planet and "Niles"). A trademark once granted lasts for 10 years and can continue to be renewed for another 10 years at a time.

Trademark issues can come up at the very beginning when a name is being chosen for a new business. It is very important to check to see what marks are already being used to identify goods and services similar or identical to yours, *before* a mark is selected. Skill Module 18.2, "Checking Out Trademarks Online," can help you get a start on this.

SMALL BUSINESS INSIGHT

Peaceable Planet and "Niles"[18]

Peaceable Planet is a very small toy maker from Savannah, Georgia, that makes a line of plush toy dolls. In 1999 it created a camel it called "Niles," named for the Egyptian river. Niles had a name card with information on it about Egypt. Peaceable Planet trademarked the name, and it sold a few thousand in the first year. The next year, Ty, Inc., the maker of Beanie Babies bean bag dolls, introduced its camel, who also happened to be named Niles, and sold more than one million of them in the first year.

Peaceable Planet sued for trademark infringement, and lost in the U.S. district court. Peaceable Planet appealed and won. In the complex world of intellectual property protection, what this meant was that Peaceable Planet got another chance to prove in district court that Ty took advantage of the Niles name. Peaceable Planet faced another round in court, with the attendant legal fees and time spent on depositions and briefings. However, in pursuing the case to the appeals court and getting a favorable ruling, the chance of getting an out-of-court settlement increases. In reality, sometimes that is what a "win" in intellectual property lawsuits looks like. In the case of Peaceable Planet, it did win on the rehearing of the case.

SKILL MODULE 18.2

Checking Out Trademarks Online

Before you settle on a name for your business or product, it is very important to determine how that word or group of words is already being used in the United States to avoid trademark infringement challenges. Assume you are starting a business doing detailing work on vehicles. You are considering the name "Clean as a Whistle." In checking the name, one source of information is the U.S. Patent and Trademark Office listing of federally registered trademarks. While that list shows only federally registered marks and there may be an identical or similar name used that is not registered, this listing is a start. Go to the U.S. Patent and Trademark website, **www.uspto.gov**, then to "trademarks," then to "search," then to "new user form" and search for "Clean as a Whistle." According to the information in this site, is this name currently being used for a car detailing business?

All too often with small businesses, a name is chosen and used, and the business incurs all sorts of expenses in terms of labels, signs, and even advertising without considering trademark issues. Before selecting a business name, an Internet address, or the mark for products or services, an attorney should be consulted. An attorney can do a trademark search to determine what use is being made of the words or groups of words a business may want to use. Researching the desired name(s) ahead of time can avoid liability for infringement in which someone already using or having rights to that name sues the business, as well as financial costs (including loss of goodwill) in changing names. Once an attorney has established that it is unlikely that your choice of name is infringing on another's, consideration can be given to obtaining state or federal trademark registration to get additional rights for your mark.

Any size business may own valuable intellectual property such as patents, trade secrets, copyrights, and trademarks. Understanding and protecting these assets by seeking qualified, professional counsel cannot be overemphasized.

Whether you think we have too many laws or not enough, the stability and success of the United States' business community is based, in large part, upon our legal system. Laws guarantee rights to individuals and companies. Those rights are upheld every day in courtrooms across America. Caveat emptor (let the buyer beware) is *not* the motto in twenty-first century America. Knowing the law or even knowing when to ask for advice concerning the law gives business owners more power in pursuing their dreams. Knowledge is power. After reading this chapter, you should have a greater understanding of our legal system and particular areas of interest for business owners. This should give you more confidence in pursuing those dreams.

CHAPTER SUMMARY

LO1 Know when you need legal information and how to get it.

- There are many federal, state, and local laws applicable to any small business.
- Get a good attorney with experience in your areas of concern. You may need more than one attorney for various issues that arise over time.
- You can use online sources from the government or trade associations for certain legal information.

LO2 Understand legal structures in setting up a new business.

- Trade names exist when a firm uses something other than the owner's name as the name of the business.
- The most common business forms are sole proprietorships, general partnerships, limited partnerships, C corporations, S corporations, professional corporations, and limited liability companies.
- Each of various types of business entities has pros and cons in terms of personal liability of the owners, creation and maintenance of the organization, management of the organization, continuity of the organization, the raising of capital, and taxation.
- Unless there is a compelling reason to do otherwise, an LLC is probably the best choice of business entity because of its ease of formation, limited liability of owners, and flexibility in taxation.

LO3 Learn how to master the process of negotiating.

- Nearly everything in business is negotiable.
- Negotiating successfully depends on mastering four steps: prepare, position, propose, and pounce.
- The goal is to create outcomes where you and the other party win.
- Be honest in your presentation and balanced in your approach.

LO4 Recognize potential legal liabilities for your business.

- You and your business may be held responsible for the actions of agents, including employees.
- Avoid lawsuits by properly training employees, using independent contractors, or submitting disputes to arbitration.

LO5 Know contract terms and when a contract is needed.

- You are free to contract for anything that is not illegal or unethical.
- Put agreements in writing and have them reviewed by legal counsel.
- Make use of special contract terms such as noncompete clauses, exculpatory clauses, and hold harmless agreements to avoid litigation.
- The primary contractor is responsible for a subcontractor's failure.
- On the Internet make sure to specify that your site is informational and arrange for secure alternatives to "wet signatures."
- Design and implement a company e-mail policy.

LO6 Understand the basics of intellectual property.

- Intellectual property is composed of patents, trade secrets, copyrights, trademarks, and trade names.
- Ideas can be protected as patents or trade secrets.
- Expression of ideas can be protected as copyrights.
- Trademarks uniquely identify products and their origin.
- Intellectual property is a business asset and can be extremely valuable. For that reason protection of intellectual property should be taken seriously.

KEY TERMS

hourly fees, 593
flat fees, 593
retainer, 593
contingency fee, 593
trade name or assumed name or a doing business as (dba), 596
assumed name filing or a fictitious name filing, 596
legal entity, 597
plaintiff, 597
defendant, 597
articles of organization, 598
articles of partnership, 598
single taxation, 600
double taxation, 601
pass through (taxation), 601
check the box taxation, 601
operating agreement, 601
piercing the veil, 602
vicarious (indirect) liability, 605
independent contractors, 605
Sarbanes-Oxley Act, 607
litigation, 608
arbitration, 608
noncompete clause, 610
exculpatory clause, 610
hold harmless, 610
waiver, 610
subcontract, 611
B2B, 611
B2C, 612
intellectual property, 612
intangible property, 612
patent, 613
trade secret, 613
copyright, 613
trademark, 613
design patent, 614
utility patent, 614
plant patent, 614
infringer, 614

DISCUSSION QUESTIONS

1. How would you go about finding a lawyer for your business?
2. Which form of business structure would be best for your new business and why?
3. In what ways could the owner of a parking lot limit his or her potential liability?
4. How could you keep your employees from going to your competitors after you have trained them?
5. How can you protect your company's trade secrets?
6. What issues should be addressed in a company policy on e-mail?

EXPERIENTIAL EXERCISES

1. Find your state's Secretary of State home page on the Internet. Find information on forming LLCs. Can the form(s) be submitted online? If not, can the form(s) be downloaded or filled in using the computer?

2. In most states you can contact the state bar, the state supreme court, or a state commission to check on whether a particular attorney has been disciplined for professional conduct violations. To find out whom to contact in your state, go to the American Bar Association listing at **www.americanbar.org/content/dam/aba/migrated/cpr/regulation/directory.authcheckdam.pdf** or on the **Americanbar.org** site search for *directory of state disciplinary agencies* and check it out.

3. You may be able to represent yourself on small matters by going to small claims court. These courts of limited jurisdiction have different names in different states. Go to **www.nolo.com/legal-encyclopedia/lawsuits-court**, click on "State-by-State Small Claims Court Laws," and select the state of Indiana as an example and there you will find information on small-claims courts in Indiana.

4. Would you like more information on LLCs? Go to **http://nolo.com**, click on "Get Informed" at the top of the home page and then on "Business Formation: LLCs and Corporations" to learn more.

MINI-CASE

VIVID SKY AND MAJOR LEAGUE TROUBLE

Entrepreneur Tim Hayden had created a service called SkyBOX which could stream videos and statistics to sports fans over their 3G cell phones (like the iPhone). It had taken four years to launch the service, which originally was going to require military-grade hardened wireless PDAs and wiring stadiums for Wi-Fi, but had been reconfigured to run on Internet-ready cell phones.

Professional teams in baseball, football, basketball, and hockey had seen SkyBOX and were enthusiastic about its deployment. However, there were competitors to the SkyBOX. One of the largest was Major League Baseball, who was developing their own iPhone application to tie fans into MLB video feeds and statistics.

Executives at Apple liked the SkyBOX so much they made it their Feature Product on the iTunes home page.

It wasn't clear if MLB's team saw this or not, but it was at that moment that they served Vivid Sky with a cease-and-desist claiming that the SkyBOX used content that was copyrighted. In addition, MLB contacted Apple and demanded that the SkyBOX application be pulled from the iTunes Store. Executives from Apple refused to pull the SkyBOX application. However, they wanted Vivid Sky to work out a solution with MLB.

While Tim knew that Vivid Sky conformed to all copyright issues and were legally within their rights, he suspected that MLB might be going this route to disrupt Vivid Sky and the sale of their applications in the iTunes Store. He could make a stand and hire lawyers, which would cost a small business like his lots of money. Or he could look for a mutually agreeable solution.

Tim thought, "What is an entrepreneurial way to handle this?"

CASE DISCUSSION QUESTIONS

1. What are Tim's choices at this point?
2. What do you think Tim means when he asks if there is an "entrepreneurial way to handle this"?
3. If there is no infringement, but the injunction was brought to slow down a fast-moving new competitor, would it make any difference in the strategy Tim should employ?

SUGGESTED CASES AND ARTICLES

- The Dreaded Letter, C-19

Available on McGraw-Hill Create™:

- Integral Vision Ltd. (A)
- Jack Schofield, Fast Food Franchisee (A)

SUGGESTED VIDEOS

www.mhhe.com/katz4e

SBTV.com Videos:

- How to Choose the Right Business Structure—LLC or C-Corp or LLP
- Protecting Your Company or Product Name
- Get It in Writing (Simple Letter of Agreement, 1 of 2)

STVP Video:

- When and How are Patents Important?

CHAPTER

19

Human Resource Management: Small Business Considerations

● Chris Perkett switched from part-time, virtual employees to full-time ones to staff her firm PerkettPR, Inc. What do you think she could do to ease that transition?

LEARNING OBJECTIVES

After studying this chapter, you will be able to:

LO1 Evaluate the decision to hire full-time or part-time help.

LO2 Understand how to recruit good employees on your budget.

LO3 Know how to match the right person to the job.

LO4 Describe employee training methods and resources.

LO5 Recognize how to meet employees' needs and expectations.

LO6 Develop a fair compensation and benefit plan.

LO7 Explain the complexities of managing family within your business.

Focus on Small Business: Chris Perkett and PerkettPR, Inc.[1]

As a former consultant herself, Chris Perkett had a fairly easy time deciding whether to hire independent contractors when she started her Marshfield, Massachusetts, virtual public relations agency in 1998. "I wasn't ready to hire employees because there's so much involved with doing that," says the CEO of PerkettPR, Inc. "I wanted to make sure I was [building the company] right and wasn't biting off more than I could chew."

Perkett admits she initially appreciated the temporal nature as well as the flexibility of having independent contractors, but as she began to increase her client base, those very aspects began to concern her. "I needed more of a commitment from my staff," she explains. "The knowledge that they could leave at any time was always looming over my head. I needed to show my client base that I had a staff that was as committed to serving them as I was."

So at the end of that year, Perkett decided to switch to an employee-based staff, hiring many of her former consultants as full-time employees. Since then, Perkett says there's been an increase in the level of excitement in the company's projects, and her clients now feel the company is growing and stabilizing, two things that weren't happening with the contractors.

Still, employees aren't necessarily the only way to achieve a common vision and commitment for a business, according to Jennifer Johnson, principal of Johnson & Co., The Virtual Agency. With 15 contractors and only 2 employees on board, Johnson encourages dedication to her Salt Lake City public relations firm by requiring all contractors to attend regular business meetings and retreats and to meet with a senior consultant mentor. "I think it's a myth to believe that because someone is an employee, it means they're more dependable," says Johnson. "In today's fast-moving, competitive market, the best talent needs to stay motivated and driven whether they're a consultant or an employee."

According to Johnson, the ever-changing nature of today's business world has left traditional job descriptions by the wayside and forced companies to have a more flexible structure. "Consultants are used to change; they thrive on [that]," she says. "They understand they're getting paid to deliver tangible results as opposed to just punching a clock."

As for Perkett, although she's had to adjust to the variety of personalities that now exist in the core of her company, she's confident that hiring employees was the right choice for her growing business. "If you're not sure where or how you want to grow, then it's a lot to take on," she says. "But I think it helps our clients feel like we're growing, we're adding clients, and we're committed to this business."

DISCUSSION QUESTIONS

1. What are some potential advantages as well as drawbacks of having contractors in Jennifer Johnson's firm attend meetings, retreats, and be mentored by senior consultants?
2. Do you agree with Johnson's assertion that "In today's fast-moving, competitive market, the best talent needs to stay motivated and driven whether they're a consultant or an employee"? Why or why not?
3. What do you think Chris Perkett means when she mentions that "I wasn't ready to hire employees because there's so much involved with doing that"? As a small business owner, what do you think is involved in hiring that first employee to your firm?
4. How does Chris Perkett's hiring and retaining employees perspective compare or differ from Jennifer Johnson's perspective?

The Bigger Small Business: Hiring Employees

L01 Evaluate the decision to hire full-time or part-time help.

Of all the decisions that differentiate the types of small businesses, no decision is as important or complex as the decision to hire an employee. Many small businesses never do. Of the more than 27.3 million businesses in the United States in 2010, over 21.7 million had no employees at all—only the owner. Another 5.6 million firms had one or more employees.[2] For the economy, those firms that hire employees are an important source of job generation.[3]

For the owner, adding employees is important for several reasons. Adding employees increases the amount of work that can be done—serving more customers, producing more, or staying open longer. It also increases the demands on the owner. Now sales need to be made to cover the employee's wages or salary, and, when adding employees, the owner and business become responsible for the safety and well being of the employee, as well as face legal requirements as an employer. Some owners look at the pluses and minuses and decide to stay a solo operation for as long as possible, like Chris Perkett in the early stages of her business. Others take on the opportunity and responsibility, as Chris did later. For those entrepreneurs, the next key decision is what work should be done, who the best person is to do that work, and how the firm should take care of them. Those areas are where the field of human resource management comes into small business. In this chapter we look at those three areas.

Let's start with the decision of what kind of work needs to be done. Generally we start by thinking about how much work we want to cover. As a small business owner, you can hire either part-time or full-time employees. Which one will be best for you? You need to consider the pros and cons and expand with care. Full-time employees make it possible for you to take significant time away from the business. They get to understand the business sooner, and often are willing to take on more responsibility. They provide the ability to dramatically increase your hours open, material produced, or sales. But there are many additional expenses to having a full-time employee on staff as opposed to a part-time employee. The cost of adding an employee includes compensation, training time, and employee tax and accounting costs. Presumably, such costs are outweighed by greater productivity, but you need to carefully balance the ledger. "Probably the biggest mistake I made in my early hires was hiring too early," says Louis Gudema, former president of Magic Hour Communications, a marketing agency in Watertown, Massachusetts (www.magic-hour.com). "As a result, we were not as profitable as we might have been if I had been slower to hire."[4]

"While every business has its own rhythm, it's usually wise to go through the first year without hiring. Get a feel for the sales cycle and the downturns. Measure the 'just right' temperature of income and outgo. Experts suggest squirreling away at least a year's worth of expenses and overhead before hiring in order to see you through any rough patches," says Joanna Krotz, co-author of the *Microsoft Small Business Kit*.[5]

employee fit
The match between the needs, expectations, and culture of the small business with the expectations and the skills of the individual employee.

Not only are there additional expenses to consider, but also **employee fit**.[6] You can ease into an eventual full-time employee by first hiring part-time help and if he or she works well and the demand for additional help is present, you can ease into a full-time position weighing the additional expense.

Before making a full-time offer, let the applicant work part time for awhile so you can see how she or he fits. Likely as not, this will be learning period for you, too. You can ease someone into the business as a part-time worker. Or, if you go ahead and hire a full-time applicant, set up a **probationary period** or set up the job as an internship or a temporary one.[7] Usually, state law dictates how long such trials may last, so check with your state employment office. Typically, a probationary period lasts 30–180 days. A trial period can be important, and if your first choice turns memorable in all the wrong ways, chalk it up to experience and keep recruiting.[8]

probationary period
Trial period in which an employee has temporary status before a formal offer to work full time is presented.

Whether you hire a part-time or full-time employee, it is important that each type of employee values your company's mission. Don Dymer, a former Scotland Yard police inspector, started his preemployment screening business in Jacksonville Beach, Florida, in 1995. He emphasizes the need for "employees to take on the mission and values that you want the business to take on." You do that by setting an example and making sure to define those values for every new hire.[9]

One of the challenges facing entrepreneurs who want to grow is understanding the many laws that apply to small businesses as their number of employees grows. Figure 19.1 provides a simple graphic to see which employment laws begin to apply at what size of firm, while Table 19.1 gives a quick rundown of the major Federal laws.

There is some help for determining if the federal employment laws will or do apply to your business. The U.S. Department of Labor has created a set of interactive online exercises to help you determine which laws apply in your situation, and they have gathered them all in one location—www.dol.gov/elaws. In particular, use the FirstStep Employment Law Advisor to get an overview

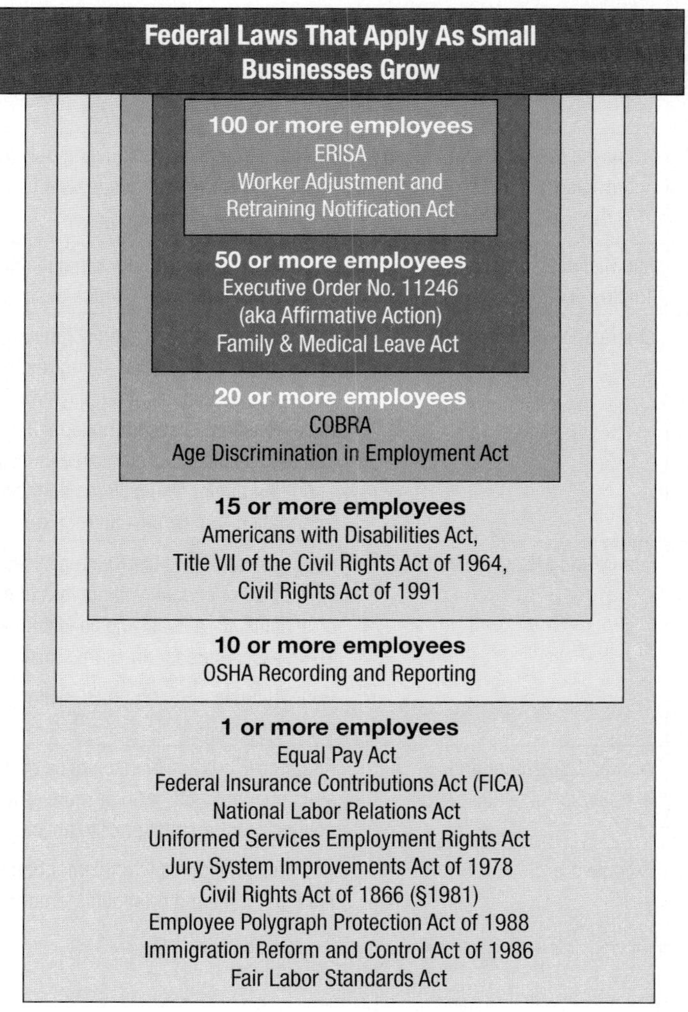

FIGURE 19.1
Federal Laws That Apply as Small Businesses Grow

TABLE 19.1 Federal Employment and Labor Laws Applicable to Growing Businesses

Labor and Employment		
Employers engaged in interstate commerce or engaged in the production of goods for interstate commerce (almost all employers).	Fair Labor Standards Act	Requires payment to most hourly employees of minimum wage and time and a half for overtime hours. Requires payment of same wage to males and females for work requiring equal skill, effort, and responsibility in similar working conditions. Notice posting requirements.
Employers who have 15 or more employees for each workday in each of at least 20 calendar weeks in the current or preceding calendar year (federal).	Title VII of the Civil Rights Act of 1964	Prohibits discrimination with respect to any condition of employment based on race, color, sex, religion, or national origin, except where religion, sex, or national origin is a bona fide occupational qualification which is reasonably necessary to the conduct of a particular business. Includes a prohibition on harassment, including sexual harassment. Notice posting requirements.
All employers.	Immigration Reform and Control Act of 1986	Prohibits hiring of unauthorized aliens. Prohibits employment discrimination based on national origin or citizenship status. Requires employers to complete I–9 forms for each employee. Notice posting requirements.
All employers.	Employee Polygraph Protection Act of 1988	Prohibits employers from using polygraph results as basis for employment action with limited exceptions. Notice posting requirements.
Employers with 20 or more employees for each working day in each of 20 or more calendar weeks.	Age Discrimination in Employment Act	Prohibits employment discrimination against individuals 40 years old and older. Notice posting requirements.
Employers with 15 or more employees.	Americans with Disabilities Act	Employers must have nondiscriminatory application procedures, qualification standards, selection criteria, terms and conditions of employment. Employers must make reasonable accommodation for limitations of qualified applicant or employee unless to do so creates undue hardship. Also governs confidentiality of medical information. Notice posting requirements.
Employers with 50 or more employees (within a 75-mile radius) each working day for 20 weeks in the current or preceding calendar year.	Family and Medical Leave Act	Requires employers to give employees up to 12 weeks leave, paid or unpaid, without loss of position, seniority, or benefits, for a qualifying condition or event, or up to 26 weeks to care for an injured military service member. General notice requirements, including posting requirements.
Employers with 100 or more employees.	Worker Adjustment and Retraining Notification Act	Requires 60 days advance notice prior to a plant shutdown or layoff of 50 or more employees. Notice posting requirements prior to action.
50 or more employees and contracts or subcontracts of $50,000 plus.	Executive Order No. 11246	Requires employers to implement an affirmative action plan for hiring and promoting females and minorities.

The chart is not, nor is it intended to be, a comprehensive summary of the threshold levels at which the statutes and regulations cited therein take effect, and it is qualified in its entirety by reference to the appropriate statute and regulations.

Chart compiled in July 2012 by: Joseph D. Demko, Daniel K. O'Toole, Robert B. Reeser III and Roger A. Walker, all with the law firm of Armstrong Teasdale LLP.

of which laws apply. eLaws also provides a host of other interactive advisors to help you determine eligibility for more than two dozen laws and programs.

To be fair, there are always more laws that apply. In addition to those detailed in Table 19.1, there are related laws that apply to small businesses. For example, the Civil Rights Act of 1991 kicks in at 15 employees. Some of the other laws applicable as soon as you hire one employee include at least two big issues—the Federal Insurance Contributions Act (FICA) which is the Social Security and Medicare withholding law, and the Uniformed Services Employment and Reemployment Rights Act of 1994 (USERRA) which gives veterans the right to the jobs they left behind when called up for service.

Meanwhile, the state laws applicable to a small business are extraordinarily varied. For example, in Missouri, there are laws such as the Missouri Genetic Testing Law, jury-release laws, a Voting Leave Act, the Political Activities of Employees Act, the Final Wage Payment Statute, Missouri's own Equal Pay Act, an Indoor Clean Air Act, and at the other extreme a Smokers and Alcohol Users Rights' Law. This is by no means a comprehensive list, but it gives you an idea of the range of laws that apply to businesses.

When it comes to state law, it is truly a case where one size does not fit all. Even when two states use similar names for laws, the specifics of the law in each state are likely to differ. Being in the same region doesn't mean two nearby states will be similar. To give you an idea of the laws you might have to deal with, take the example of two adjoining states, Missouri and Illinois. There are a lot of firms in either state that might consider expanding into the adjoining state, but the laws to run firms in the two states differ. Table 19.2 shows laws from the two states for three types of human resource practices a small business would typically need to consider.

Remember, most states have laws protecting citizens in the same general ways. But the names of these laws can differ—and more to the point—have slightly different starting sizes, requirements, processes, and penalties. You want to be sure to determine the laws that apply to you as you start hiring.

To find this out, as noted in Chapter 18, your can get help from your local Small Business Development Center (remember, to find it, type "SBDC Locator" into the search box at the SBA website, www.sba.gov or type in your zip code in the search box under "Get Local Assistance"), your local SCORE chapter (www.score.org), the local chamber of commerce, or the local branch of the trade or professional association for your line of business. Probably the best source for employment law questions is the state employment security office for your area. While the Federal government no longer provides a comprehensive national online listing of state sites, you can find a very well done list of state offices at the Job-Hunt.org website, (www.job-hunt.org/state_unemployment_offices.shtml).

The point is that hiring more employees makes your organization a more professional one, and with that professionalism comes a need to deal with more laws and regulations. While the best way is to work with a lawyer to make sure all issues are covered, these days you can get much of the work done at little or no cost by yourself, using the resources and free advice available to you. For example, RocketLawyer.com offers a free basic employee handbook you can develop online. While it is not a

TABLE 19.2 **Differences In State Laws: The Case of Two Adjoining States**

	Illinois	Missouri
Legal holidays	Traditional holidays	Traditional holidays plus Truman Day
Minimum wage	$8.25	$7.35
Wages must be paid	Monthly (for executive, administrative, and professional personnel) or bi-weekly (for everyone else)	Bi-weekly

Source: www.findlaw.com, www.google.com.

replacement for having a lawyer's advice specific to your company, the free handbook can be useful as a way to start thinking about the issues you will need to deal with when you start hiring. With the legal side under control, you are ready to go out and find those employees who will help you grow.

Attracting Employees

LO2 Understand how to recruit good employees on your budget.

A lot of the time a smaller firm can actually outperform large businesses in attracting high-quality employees.[10] To attract and hire new talent into a medium to large growing organization, help wanted ads in regional newspapers or the use of an employment service have been traditional methods. For small business owners, these methods tend to be expensive and have a long turnaround time. Today there are less expensive alternatives to consider.

Networking is a relatively low-cost, although time-intensive, method of recruiting. There are many benefits such as receiving a credible critique of a potential candidate's work experience and personal character. People to network with include colleagues, business professionals (your attorney or accountant), friends, vendors you have strong relationships with, alumni, and advisory board members. You can also use online social networking sites like LinkedIn (introduced in Chapter 2) to recruit, either by directly posting for a job or asking if people on LinkedIn know someone who might want the job you are offering.

Internet recruiting
Method of recruiting that allows you to search a résumé database or post a job description to the web; a small business owner who knows exactly what he or she wants can use filters to search vast numbers of résumés with pinpoint accuracy.

employee referral
An underused, low-cost method for finding workers that rewards your employees for recommending potential candidates that would be a great employee fit.

Internet recruiting allows you to search a résumé database or post a job description to the web. The main contribution of a recruiting website, such as Monster.com, has been to speed up hiring and vastly increase the accuracy of the job-search process. You can post a job at 2 P.M. and get your first response a minute later. An employer who knows exactly what he or she wants can use filters to search vast numbers of résumés with pinpoint accuracy.[11]

Employee referral is an underused, low-cost method which rewards your employees for recommending potential candidates that would be a great fit. Even for small businesses, to work successfully, referrals should be handled formally, with guidelines such as following up on all leads within 24 hours.[12]

Company websites can be used to post job openings. This method would be effective if your site receives a fair amount of traffic, and it would incur only a small incremental cost to your website budget.[13] If your business does not have a company website, the investment of website development and maintenance may be a limiting factor, but when a website can cost $50 a year, it is a worthwhile investment. Search Google for "cheap web hosting" and you will find plenty of services offering template-based design and hosting services. The Online Learning Center showed how to do this.

Many universities have *career service offices* that encourage companies to post openings to their job bank to recruit at both the undergraduate and the graduate levels. This service is commonly offered at no cost to companies and allows businesses to set up an account to manage résumé selection.

Attracting the best talent to your company can be encouraged by the strategic use of networking. Spend time in conversation with colleagues in the field, friends, vendors, and others to learn of possible employee leads.

Universities can often help you evaluate if it makes sense to offer an internship to their students. Internships are jobs in businesses like yours, arranged through the university. Some internships are done as a for-credit class, some are not. Some internships are paid by the employer, some are not. Interns usually work for only one semester, and the best internships involve a mix of simple and challenging work as well as time to talk with you, the entrepreneur, about what they are learning and what is the best way to do things. If you feel like teaching a little and working a little, an internship could work for you.

Professional groups can be a resource for recruiting new talent. Many associations publish newsletters or post openings online or at their meeting locations. Try sending a one-page job description to associations to which you belong.[14]

Outsourcing may be the answer if your small business is not ready to hire employees, but you have a growing need to meet workload demand. Consider, as an example, outsourcing to an assistant who is an independent entrepreneur and provides administration, creative, or technical support. The assistant works on a contractual basis online and handles such functions as keeping your schedule, customer intelligence, or database up to speed.[15] Assistants can be people from your neighborhood or city, or

SMALL BUSINESS INSIGHT

Go Virtual

Virtual employees or assistants can change the way many small businesses are operated and managed. This field is growing tremendously and is offering employers and small business owners alike an attractive new alternative to hiring and managing employees. Virtual employees are independent contractors who provide specialized business services or support from a distance, through the Internet, telephone, fax, or another method of communication. A virtual assistant can assist a small company that needs extra people to meet seasonal demands; step in to meet the demands of business growth, locally, domestically, or globally; or provide unique skills for a special project.

In the small business, virtual employees are not hired as full-time employees. They can be business owners themselves and are hired on a contract basis. Small business owners who work with a virtual employee have the distinct advantage of not having to deal with taxes, unemployment insurance, sick leave, vacation pay, or benefits. Rather than having to provide additional office space and be responsible for the development and supervision of an employee, they can enjoy the support and assistance of a professional without the headaches of hiring and managing employees.[16]

Here are some guidelines and methods for managing and fostering productivity among virtual employees:[17]

- Hire virtual employees who have experience with being self-motivated and disciplined, including former consultants, freelancers, and salespeople who are accustomed to dealing with deadlines and working independently. As a small business owner, this is critical, given that you already have multiple deadlines and responsibilities.
- As you manage your virtual employees, make sure to spend time developing a system of task lists, schedules, and goals with varying time frames and clear deadlines. Invest in spreadsheets and project scheduling software that will help your virtual employees organize tasks. Be sure to consistently review status reports with virtual employees to ensure that tasks are completed on time and on budget.
- Maintain communication with virtual workers via voice, fax, and other electronic methods. Don't become reliant on e-mail since it is too easy to misinterpret or misunderstand the written word. Speak on the phone and schedule face-to-face meetings occasionally.
- Micromanagement is nearly impossible with a remote staff, and it will unnerve anyone who attempts it. Trust that your employees are doing the right thing until evidence proves otherwise. If you are paranoid about slacking, hire salaried, rather than hourly, workers or pay per project.

THE THOUGHTFUL ENTREPRENEUR

Low-Cost and No-Cost Employees

If your budget does not allow for a paid employee, consider three alternative methods to hire an employee at no cost.[18]

1. **Barter:** Trade your products or services for those of another business, for example, a maid service trading its house-cleaning services to a designer in return for a new logo. For this method of recruiting, you must be flexible in services rendered and received. Bartered services may add great value to a particular function of your small business and can be particularly useful when money is in short supply.
2. **Internships:** Hiring students to work at no cost in exchange for work experience may be a great way to get the assistance you need. Generally, students who intern are looking to use specific skill sets or be exposed to a particular functional area of a business. If you can provide valuable work experience, offering internships may be an appealing way to attract temporary help.
3. **Volunteers:** Volunteers are a wonderful resource if your business is strapped for cash, although the search process may be time consuming. Who will work for free? Family members are always the first source, with friends a close second, although people who need relevant work experience might give a few hours to have an entry on their job applications, such as stay-at-home spouses who are looking for work experience while children are at school. Also, individuals committed to your company's mission are possible candidates. If your firm is doing a promotion for a charitable organization (like operating a stand at a fair), you may be able to get customers or members of the charity to contribute their help.

virtual employees
Independent contractors who provide specialized business services or support from a distance, through the Internet, telephone, fax, or another method of communication.

virtual assistants working over the Internet. The nonprofit Virtual Assistant Association can be found at www.ivaa.org, and the major websites for outsourcing are eLance Online (www.elance.com) and Smarterwork (www.smarterwork.com).[19] Advice for hiring and managing **virtual employees** can be found in the accompanying Small Business Insight: Go Virtual.

Employee leasing is a hybrid between outsourcing and having a paid staff. In employee leasing, your "employees" actually work for the leasing company, who handles recruiting, training, compensation, and government filings. You lease employees from the leasing company, paying a fixed amount for the employee as well as an annual fee, usually 2 percent to 7 percent of the dollar value of your annual payroll. Leases can be set for periods of a few weeks to a year or more. For employing the same people part time but repeatedly over a long period of time, or keeping the total number of full-time employees low, this can be a good way to handle the complexities of employment.

Other traditional and nontraditional hiring sources to consider include:

- Contact *local churches* and the pastors and see if they have parishioners who are looking for a new job.
- Visit local *high schools* for entry-level jobs, local *community colleges* for those interested in management or a technical career.
- Finally, *state unemployment offices* are a great resource, with no cost to the employer.

Matching the Worker to the Work

LO3 Know how to match the right person to the job.

Even before your first hire, you will need to know what your basic needs are and what roles this new employee will fit into. Ultimately, you would like to "match" the job with the ideal individual who can fulfill the responsibilities of the job and grow with the business. Your first step is to define and describe all the work that will be part of the new job. Then you'll need to know how to evaluate the potential employees to see how well they match your ideal set of requirements.

JOIN THE REVOLUTION:
BUSINESS/ENTREPRENEURSHIP/MANAGEMENT INTERNSHIP

Company or Recruiter	Make Me Heal	**Position Level**	Entry Level
Industry	Health Care	**Position Type**	School Year Internship
Function	Corporate Business Development	**Intern Paid**	Yes
Location	Los Angeles, CA	**Intern Type**	Undergraduate

BUSINESS/ENTREPRENEURSHIP/MANAGEMENT/FINANCE INTERNSHIP

Make Me Heal Internship Associate Program

Please e-mail your résumé and cover letter to: interns@makemeheal.com

We offer paid internships during the entire year (summer, fall, winter, spring) in all areas of the company, from business, marketing/press relations, to writing, journalism, and research. The nationally renowned The Princeton Review has honored our Internship Program by selecting it for inclusion in its prestigious Internship Bible, the book profiling the top U.S. internships.

Join The Revolution: The Internship Associate Program and the people who make part of this important team at Make Me Heal are an essential part of our "revolution." We are proud to have created internship positions that will not involve brainless tasks and will not only serve to try to impress or fill space on your résumé. Rather, our internships are designed to actually educate, empower, challenge, inspire, and accelerate your growth before you join the workplace.

Exposure and Growth in Several Disciplines: An important element of our Philosophy is to enable our team members to acquire expertise in a number of areas of our business. If we were to align together, you would be exposed to and learn about a number of disciplines. So during the scope of the Internship, team members can be expected to delve into various facets of our business as they grow with us.

Leap from an Internship to a Full-Time Career: Due to our philosophy of cultivating long-term connections with everyone in our team, it is entirely possible that an internship may evolve into a full-time career with us if the internship experience proves to be meaningful, productive, happy, and fun for you and all of us at Make Me Heal.

We're Family: Whether one is an Internship Associate or a full-time employee with us, we care about all of our MMPeople and are dedicated to offering everyone incredibly rewarding, meaningful, and fun career opportunities. Indeed, when you become an Internship Associate with us, you also become a part of our extended family.

Selected for Inclusion in the Internship Bible: It is worthwhile to note that the nationally renowned The Princeton Review (the U.S. leader in the educational/school services industry) has selected our Internship Associate Program to be included in its prestigious Internship Bible, which is indeed the "bible" profiling the top internship opportunities in the United States.

We're looking to connect with highly entrepreneurial, ambitious individuals who thrive in an ever-changing, multibillion dollar industry where rewriting the rules is the law.

Roles involve researching, analyzing, and formulating innovative business strategies and implementing them, conceiving strategies to build our brand name to a national/international scale, creating strong operational infrastructure, assessing financial issues, among other functions. Work directly with CEO (former investment banker and Wharton Business School alum) to formulate business strategies and plans, implement new product and service lines, initiate supplier relationships with multinational cosmetics companies and leading manufacturers, devise innovative marketing and publicity initiatives, devise financial forecasts, strengthen quality of consumer experience, develop financial statements and forecasts, participate in deal-making, make presentations to institutional/high-net worth individuals and strategic business partners, and create quality controls, accounting, and legal structures for transacting with consumers.

FIGURE 9.2

Sample Job Description

Source: Copyright © 2005 Vault.com: Item posted by an employer, job/internship listing on the Vault.com Job Board.

Writing a Job Description

job description
Defines and discusses all the essential knowledge, skills, and abilities that are needed to fill a position.

Your **job description** needs to define and discuss all the essential knowledge, skills, and abilities that are needed to fill the position. In addition, you will need to describe what kind of personality, experience, and education you believe a person who performs the job should have. To determine some of these attributes, sit down and do a job analysis covering the following areas:[20]

- The reason the job exists (including an explanation of job goals and how they relate to your position and other positions in the company).
- The mental or physical tasks involved (ranging from judging, planning, and managing to cleaning, lifting, and welding).
- How the job will be done (all of the methods and equipment to be used).
- The qualifications needed (what kind of training, knowledge, skills are necessary).

If some of these questions are difficult to answer, consider talking to other small business owners in your area. You may also discuss these issues with employees and supervisors at other noncompeting small businesses that offer similar positions.

To get started, write down the job title and whom that person will report to (define how the job relates to you or other positions in the small business). Next, develop a job statement or summary describing the position's major and minor duties. List any educational requirements, desired experience, and specialized skills or knowledge required. Include salary range and benefits (see "Compensation" later in this chapter). Finish by listing any physical or other special requirements associated with the job.

Figure 19.2 gives you an example of a job description for an internship in a growing small business. For a one-person business hiring its first employee, these guidelines may seem unnecessary. But remember, you are laying the foundation for your personnel policy, which will be essential as your small business grows. Keeping detailed records from the time you hire your first employee will make things a lot easier when you hire your tenth, twentieth, and so on.

Also, writing the job description will help you determine whether you need a part-time or full-time employee, whether the person should be permanent or temporary, and whether you could use an independent contractor to fill the position. The specifics for crafting a job description are given in Skill Module 19.1.

SKILL MODULE 19.1 Crafting a Job Description

In this skill module, you have the opportunity to write job descriptions for a student worker and for an instructor on your campus. Write a job description for the role of student worker, and ask one of your instructors about his or her job and write a description. In your instructor interview or when thinking about the student job, cover many of the areas and questions discussed to get a full view and perspective of the positions. Write a half-page job description using the following how-to steps:[21]

1. **Start with a Title:** Provide a job title for the position (two–three words). Beneath the title, you want to include important information related to the job such as the status (exempt vs. nonexempt) and to whom the employee reports.
   Example:
   Intern: A nonexempt summer position reporting to the CEO.
2. **Give a Job Overview (or Summary of the Job):** Be sure that this section is not more than three to four sentences long and that it explains the level and basic nature of this job position. You will be outlining details of the job in the following sections.
   Example:
   An entry-level job position providing administrative support to a technology business with three employees.
3. **Define the Duties and Responsibilities:** Write down all the tasks that the employee will be doing in this position. Be flexible in writing the duties and responsibilities to accommodate growth of the position. Be clear, concise, and complete.

Main duties include: scheduling appointments, giving information to callers, and generally relieving staff of clerical work and minor administrative and business detail.

4. **Knowledge, Skills, and Abilities:** These are basic qualities that the employee should possess. They could include:
   Knowledge of computer software, including: PowerPoint, Excel.
   Skilled at performing multiple tasks simultaneously.
   Ability to relate to people and make them feel comfortable.
5. **Credentials and Experience:** List the level of educational and professional experience the person should have (possibly allow for additional experience to make up for the lack of an educational degree).
   Minimum two years of college with coursework in business or related fields. Prior business experience desirable.
6. **Special Requirements:** Anything that may not have been covered up until this point should go here. For example:
   Frequent travel required to other universities and conferences.
   Job includes some evening and weekend hours.
   Ability to lift 15 lbs or more.

Then compare the descriptions with those of other students. You might also try to find the official job description for an instructor from your school. When comparing your description with the other ones, consider the following:

1. How difficult was it to define and narrow the many responsibilities of the position?
2. Were there differences between your description and the actual description?
3. How many similarities were there between your description and the actual description?
4. If there were discrepancies, where were the "gaps" between the two?
5. As a small business owner, what can you do to ensure there is a mutual understanding between you and the employee in describing the job/position as your business grows?
6. How can you get both formal and informal feedback from employees regarding the job on a continual basis?

Evaluating Job Prospects

Once you have a job description, you can use it to help you evaluate whether an individual would be the right match for the position and your small business. So what can you do to make sure you hire the right person for the job? This is probably one of the most difficult decisions you may be faced with making, especially since we are all not trained in the art and science of hiring employees. In making successful hiring decisions, rely on the information developed in your job description to identify the most important knowledge areas, skills, and abilities the ideal candidate should possess. Next, create the same specific questions that you will ask of all candidates that will clearly and behaviorally demonstrate to you that they have these critical factors. Do not simply accept the candidate's word that he or she possesses a certain skill or knowledge base. Ask that person to demonstrate the skill, solve a problem, or write or create something that clearly and concretely provides you with the proof you need to make an informed decision.

We recommend the behavioral-interviewing approach because it is one that entrepreneurs can do a good job on by themselves, and because the kinds of information it generates is something an entrepreneur can directly understand and relate to the applicant and the job in question.

You have heard of selection tests for jobs, and there are a variety of tests and simulations that can be used. However, these techniques usually require major up-front costs for training, validation, and the materials themselves. Work simulations hold many of the same issues, but are even more complex and costly. Either approach usually accounts for no more than 50 percent of the variation in performance among multiple candidates, and in real-world situations, often can account for only 10 percent of performance.[22] So we focus on using a behaviorally based interview (along with application forms and references) as the centerpiece of the selection process.

Interviewing can be a nervewracking experience for both interviewer and candidate. As an interviewer, be prepared as fully as possible, with specific questions to ask and a clear communication of job details. See Figure 19.3 to glean sample interview questions and start you thinking of additional questions you might want to ask in your own company setting.

Develop questions structured like those shown in Figure 19.3. These use slightly different techniques to obtain descriptions of situations the interviewee had encountered before. You will notice that the questions are designed so a "yes" or "no" answer is not applicable, and that most questions lend themselves to follow-up questions from you about the specifics of the experience. In the process, you are observing how the candidate analyzes situations, how rationally or logically the situation is presented, and whether or not, to the best of your judgment, the person is being truthful. Also notice what kinds of questions are not being asked—those about a person's race, religion, age, citizenship, marital status, disabilities, or arrest record—because such questions are illegal.

If at all possible, consider involving one or two other interviewers (if possible from within your small business) to look at a candidate who seems promising. This helps you be sure that you understand the individual as well as possible. In that way, you can all share your insights and impressions of the candidate. Furthermore, one interviewer can add an aspect to a question that another one (or even you as the owner) may have overlooked.

One of the temptations these days is to look up an applicant's profile on Facebook or LinkedIn. If you do this, keep a few key points in mind. First, if you do it for one person, you need to do it for everyone. Second, LinkedIn is generally a more relevant source than Facebook since people post their professional profiles on LinkedIn, while Facebook can be very personally focused and not necessarily job relevant. If you see a Facebook photo of a person with a cup of some drink, what do you actually *know* about the applicant? What was he or she drinking? Was the applicant drunk? Even if the person was, can you prove it would make him or her a bad employee? You can see the legal problems that diving into social media to supplement your decision making could create. So if you use it, be careful and consistent. Checking on this—and how best to do background checks—with your lawyer is a good idea.

Finally, make sure you know enough about a candidate before you hire that person, and never, ever hire even a moderately qualified person just because you need someone now. You want to be sure you haven't hired a problem. It can be long and painful to terminate someone and advertise, screen, interview and hire another person. Take your time to make sure you have the best person that best matches the position for your small business.

FIGURE 19.3

Typical Types of Behaviorally Based Interview Questions[23]

These help match the right person to the job based on questions tied to the demonstrated knowledge, skills, abilities, and experiences of the applicant.

1. *Tell me about a time when:*
   You worked effectively under pressure.
   You were creative in solving a problem.
   You had to deal with an irate customer.
   You were unable to complete a project on time.
2. *Describe:*
   One of your strengths and one of your weaknesses.
   Your three most important work-related values (and an example of where you demonstrated each value at work).
   A decision you made that was unpopular and how you implemented it.
   A time when you were tolerant of an opinion that was different than your own.
3. *Give an example of:*
   A goal you reached and tell me how you achieved it.
   An occasion when you used logic to solve a problem.
   A time when you anticipated potential problems and developed preventive measures.
   A time when you had to make an important decision with limited facts.
4. *The last time it happened, how did you:*
   Adapt to a difficult situation?
   Persuade team members to do things your way?
   Overcome a major obstacle at work?
   Preserve your integrity when it was put to the test at work?

Remember: (1) You can replace "work" with "school," "church," "club," or "dorm" depending on the experience you think the interviewee is likely to have. (2) Questions that ask what they have done give a better indication than questions asking what they would do.

Selecting the Right Person

Imagine you have crafted the job description, sought candidates from several sources, and interviewed the candidates using the same set of basic questions. If you are hiring your first employee, you probably learned a bit about yourself, your business, and your employee needs as you went through this process. You run a consulting business that helps local companies identify promising markets overseas. You split your time between your clients' offices, learning about their businesses, and your own office, where you work up prospects using the Internet and phone.

You started looking for someone to handle the office phone and e-mail when you were out, and to prepare reports for clients and sales catalogs for overseas customers from the templates you've developed. As you started talking to prospective employees, you realized that you could go any one of several ways: (1) Since you have an orderly process, you could hire someone relatively inexperienced (and inexpensive) and quickly get them up to speed doing the above tasks or (2) you could hire someone with more experience in international sales (and would need higher pay) who could actually handle finding overseas customers and negotiate pieces of deals while you are soliciting more business. You have a top candidate for either approach. How do you decide?

Recall the idea of fit introduced earlier. As the owner, you decide how the firm should be run and what will be important. Both people seem nice enough and you think you could get along well with either one. So look at something different. Do you like your current pace of business? If yes, the inexperienced person should help take off some of the stress you're facing now, and will cost you less in wages, so is less of a burden. You should be able to grow your business at your own rate, but you will also be responsible for training and checking up on this person until she or he gets experienced in the job and your approach to it.

If you want to grow the business more quickly, the experienced person can be of more help. The experienced person should be able to do more things upon starting and learn new ways more quickly because he or she understands the underlying ideas of your industry, but that person will require more money from you and may have ideas about the best way to do something that do not match your preferred way.

Notice that a lot of the decisions about hiring really involve the entrepreneurs' realization of what they want to see happen in the business. Sometimes this becomes apparent only by going through the hiring process. In fact, for first-time hiring situations, it can be a good thing to try someone in

SMALL BUSINESS INSIGHT

MAVENS & MOGULS, A MARKETING STRATEGY CONSULTING FIRM[24]

I feel like my role is to connect the dots . . . I'm a conductor of a world class orchestra.

—Paige Arnof-Fenn

Paige Arnof-Fenn, founder and CEO of Mavens & Moguls, launched her company in 2001. Paige had worked with companies at all stages that needed expert marketing advice, including projects for start-ups, authors, professional service firms, the Sundance Film Festival, Merrill Lynch, Sprint, and Delta Airlines. With Mavens & Moguls she has assembled a team of marketing all-stars, the best people that she has encountered in her career across all marketing disciplines. They are spread across the United States and as far away as Bangkok.

As the sole business owner of Mavens & Moguls, Paige relies on her virtual employees to knit together the network of experienced professionals who have actually "done it" for the top companies across a variety of industries. Working from their own offices, homes, or other private work spaces, they provide marketing strategy, planning, and execution. The real mavens and moguls specialize in promotion, PR, direct marketing, media, pricing strategy, positioning, customer acquisition, and new product launches. In many ways, all the areas of the marketing mix are covered that can be used to build a brand and grow a client's business.

the job part time in order to have a chance to refine what you want to see in the job description and in the business. In other situations, making use of the probationary period mentioned earlier can help define the job's potential end point, leaving you a graceful way out of having the wrong person in the job, or the wrong job described.

Training Your Employees

LO4 Describe employee training methods and resources.

Of course, it would be great if employees came to work fully prepared to meet your business needs. However, most employees (even the most ideal new hires) need training. The time and money you spend teaching employees how to do their jobs could turn out to be your small company's wisest investment.

To begin, you should first assess your small firm's training needs from the perspective of the business, the job itself (job description), and the needs of the employees. This assessment will provide answers to the following questions:

- *Where* is training needed? What key areas need the most attention?
- *What* specifically must an employee learn in order to be more productive?
- *Who* needs to be trained?

Once you have answered these questions, you can then design your training program. There are two different types of training: initial training and ongoing training. When employees first join your small business or start a new role, offering them the training they need to handle the position makes them feel valued, challenged, and rewarded.

Initial and Ongoing Training Methods

There are two broad types of training available to small businesses: on-the-job and off-the-job techniques. Individual circumstances and the where, what, and who of your training program determine which method to use.

on-the-job training
Delivered to employees while they perform their regular jobs; techniques include orientations, job instruction training, apprenticeships, internships and assistantships, job rotation, and coaching.

On-the-job training is delivered to employees while they perform their regular jobs. In this way, they do not lose time while they are learning. After a plan is developed for what should be taught, employees should be informed of the details. On-the-job techniques include orientations, job instruction training, apprenticeships, internships and assistantships, job rotation, and coaching.[25]

For on-the-job training in a small business, you need to stay abreast of all the jobs that need doing and define them so others can be trained in doing parts of the job. It is critical to design a job to make sure that nothing important is missed. To give you an idea on how to design on-the-job instruction that gives an employee a method to complete a certain task in a job, consider Skill Module 19.2, "Writing Instructions and Procedures."

SKILL MODULE 19.2 Writing Instructions and Procedures[26]

- Give the instruction/procedure a clear heading that summarizes the task.
- Show clearly who does what.
- Start each step or instruction with a verb that tells the reader to do something: "Open the valve . . ." "Press the emergency button . . . ." "Tell your supervisor . . . ."
- Use a numbered list when the order in which tasks are to be performed is important. Use a bulleted list (like this one) when the order is not important.
- Put notes, warnings, and prerequisite conditions at the start, or *before* the list item to which they refer.
- Don't mix instructions with conceptual information. Present any necessary background information before the instructions.
- Use a level of detail that is appropriate to your employees' skill level and will ensure they will be able to know how to complete the job task.

Along with on-the-job training techniques, off-the-job methods such as lectures, special study, videos, television conferences or discussions, case studies, role-playing, simulation, programmed instruction, and laboratory training are all possible. Most of these techniques can be used by small businesses, although some may be too costly.[27] Other affordable and ongoing training methods can be less formal. In fact, training can be as simple as encouraging employees to meet regularly to discuss issues and share new ideas and perspectives. If your firm is large enough, you can also assign mentors to junior employees. Mentors give less experienced employees the opportunity to learn from seasoned veterans. Employees will be more comfortable in the face of new challenges if they know where to go for help. Mentors can inspire employees to strive for greater levels of success, help them channel their ambitions, and teach them new ways of handling ongoing problems more effectively.

Three Guidelines for Training[28]

1. **Give your employees opportunities to use their new skills:** Many small business owners complain that it is sometimes useless to train employees. Owners may argue that employees will take the knowledge and leave for a higher-paying job at another firm. While this may happen, small business owners can help prevent it. Once your employees are trained, give them opportunities to use their new skills.
2. **Make training an ongoing process:** Good employees want to learn, and you should provide them with opportunities to do so. Give employees encouragement to talk to you when their learning curve goes flat and then find ways to provide them with challenges and the knowledge to meet them successfully.
3. **Think of training as an investment (as opposed to an expense):** Many small business owners hesitate to invest too much energy, time, or money in training employees. Feeling that the expense does not justify the end results, they choose instead to give new hires a crash course and then put them right to work. Results of that sink-or-swim approach include costly mistakes, unhappy workers, and low productivity.

Rewarding Employees

Congratulations! Your business is growing and you have hired your first employee(s), either full time, part time, or on a virtual basis. Most likely the hiring process was time consuming to ensure a perfect fit between your new employee and your company. So how are you going to retain your first employee and ensure you are meeting his or her needs? To retain productive employees and increase their job satisfaction, the simplest answer is to ask them what their needs are. Next, create an environment that appeals to them.

LO5 Recognize how to meetemployees' needs and expectations.

But when you do not have employees to ask, where do you start? Jill Kickul studied 23 owner promises, including everything from salary and health care to workload and opportunities for advancement, and distilled them down to five underlying factors, in order of most important to least important: autonomy and personal growth, rewards/opportunities, job security/responsibilities, benefits, and facilitating work.[29] The full list is given in Table 19.3.

Salary rewards, bonuses, and perks were not as important to employees as autonomy and personal growth; job security and responsibility were less important than benefits. But small business owners often implicitly or explicitly communicate conflicting terms when making **psychological contracts** with employees. To avoid this, denote strict limits on what you promise employees and how and when those promises will be delivered. Put what you agree to in writing to prevent problems when it comes time to evaluate whether you've delivered on the contract.

psychological contract
Refers to employees' beliefs about the promises between the employee and the firm. These beliefs are based on the perception that promises have been made (e.g., competitive wages, promotional opportunities, job training) in exchange for certain employee obligations such as giving of their energy, time, and technical skills.

Entrepreneurs need to make job offers and manage based on an **open-book policy**. If you work this way and your company hits a downturn and promises cannot be met, employees are less likely to react badly since they have a better understanding of the firm's situation. Five factors are most valuable to employees:

open-book policy
Concept that key employees should be able to see and understand a firm's financials, that they should have a part in moving the numbers in the right direction, and that they should have a direct stake in the strategy and success of the firm.

1. **Teamwork:** Fostering a sense of teamwork allows people to interact with one another on a professional level. Sharing ideas, working toward a common goal, analyzing one another's work, and communicating cross functionally help build stronger professional bonds which increase a sense of belonging and company fit.

TABLE 19.3 23 Rewards Offered Employees of Small Businesses

Factors	Psychological Contract Items
Autonomy and growth	Meaningful work Challenging and interesting work Participation in decision making Freedom to be creative Opportunity to develop new skills Increasing responsibilities A job that provides autonomy and control Recognition of accomplishments Career guidance and mentoring
Benefits	Health care benefits Vacation benefits Retirement benefits Tuition reimbursement
Rewards and opportunities	Opportunities for promotion and advancement Opportunities for personal growth Pay and bonuses tied to performance Job training Continual professional training
Job security and work responsibilities	Well-defined job responsibilities A reasonable workload Job security
Work facilitation	Adequate equipment to perform job Enough resources to do the job

Source: Jill Kickul, "Promises Made, Promises Broken: An Exploration of Employee Attraction and Retention Practices in Small Business," *Journal of Small Business Management* 39, no. 4 (October 2001), p. 325, based on factor scores. Reprinted with permission.

2. **Recognition:** Showing appreciation for a job well done or giving credit to an employee who introduced a great idea can go a long way in making your employee feel valued. Recognition can be given in person, by voice mail, through e-mail, or written in a memo or letter. You can also incorporate a reward system. Do you have star performers? Increase their motivation by recognizing their accomplishment with a certificate, plaque, or personal bonus such as a dinner or movie gift certificate. This will help them to feel valued for their hard work and dedication and encourage them to continue this behavior.[30]
3. **Training:** A common reason people leave a company is if they feel they are not developing professionally. Providing learning opportunities at every level of the organization through on-the-job training or professional training will increase your employees' capabilities, allow them to expand their job responsibility, and help to increase job satisfaction. Commitment to employees' development and growth is one way to ensure an employee is growing and will stay longer.[31]
4. **Empowerment:** This means letting employees make on-the-spot decisions for the companies' best interest. Making empowerment work requires giving employees permission to act, the knowledge to act, and the skill to act.[32] When empowerment works, it increases employees personal feelings of responsibility and increases their commitment to the company.
5. **Contribution:** Providing meaningful work for employees gives them the feeling or belief that the day's work was a valuable contribution to the company and that they made a difference.[33] Employees have to believe that the decisions they make and the work they perform have a direct impact on the product or service you provide.[34]

Although not included in the study, another key element on which the other factors depends is communication. Open communication is vital for new employees. Share your vision and the mission of the business. To be sure your employees feel valued, it is important to make time to talk about the direction of the company. Make sure *you* understand how they see what you have said and what they think you have promised.[35] To do this, you can have a casual conversation while working side by side. Or find time to schedule brief one-on-one meetings to make sure the conversation takes place and the message is understood. Employees want to know what the company is trying to do, where it is going, and what it stands for.[36] After you have communicated the goal of the position and your expectation of their performance during the hiring process, follow up with feedback on a consistent basis regarding their performance. And ask how they personally prefer to communicate and what they need in their work environment to maximize their productivity.

Increasingly, small entrepreneurial companies are implementing formal performance appraisals. Reviewing employees' performance is an ongoing process. Owners and managers need to communicate with employees and give year-round feedback to employees on the job regarding performance and company goals. Before conducting a formal review, it is important to understand that there are two parts to a review: (1) the performance review and (2) the pay review. These reviews should be held at different times of the year. The performance review typically occurs once a year to monitor your employees' job satisfaction, overall performance, and set career objectives. The goal of the performance review is to identify employee strengths, formally recognize performance, set goals to utilize the skills identified as strengths, and set direction for the upcoming year. It is also a time to identify areas of development and communicate with employees concerning how you will support them and the necessary steps they need to take to develop identified areas. It is a time to plan and set goals for the year ahead and to review work from the year past. The goal of the pay review is to reward your employees if they have performed all duties and met general requirements as discussed in initial job description conversations.

Small business owners with fewer than five employees may find formal performance reviews unnecessary or impersonal—taking away the strength of a small firm. But it is a good idea to conduct written reviews to track employee performance. This gives you an out if their performance becomes unsatisfactory after coaching or retraining. To successfully conduct an employee review, you should have a clear understanding of the position.[37] Next you should create a list of questions and issues that will be discussed in preparation for creating an evaluation sheet.[38] This list can include what the current responsibilities are, how well they are performing in the identified responsibilities, what needs to be improved or learned to be successful in position, and where employees are headed in their career. The evaluation sheet should include open-ended questions for the employees to fill out regarding job performance, strengths, areas of development, and what gets in the way of accomplishing the job.[39] For a sample appraisal and type of questions you may want to begin with, go to www.bizhelp24.com.

An appraisal form should be filled out and returned to you before the scheduled performance review so that you can learn the employees' goals, interests, and self-evaluation when you are crafting your comments.[40] Your comments during the review should address how the employee can grow, improve, and build on his or her current set of successes to contribute to the company, what you can do as a leader to provide resources, guidance, and opportunities, and what the individual needs to do on his or her own to continue to grow and succeed.[41]

Compensation, Benefits, and Perks

LO6 Develop a fair compensation and benefit plan.

One of the first steps in developing a compensation plan is to determine whether you are hiring someone for an hourly or salaried position. Most states have rules saying what kind of working situations justify one approach or another. Misclassifying a worker can lead to legal problem with the state and even the federal government. You can search online for *Part 551-Pay Administration under the Fair Labor Standards Act* to get the details.

The next step in figuring compensation is determining your organization's compensation philosophy. Do you believe in raising the level of base salaries in your organization or do you appreciate the flexibility of variable pay? A small business, with variable sales and income, may be better off controlling the levels of base salaries. When times are good, the business can tie bonus dollars to goals achieved.

The next step is to find comparison factors for salary. Research the salary range for similar positions and job descriptions. Determine whether you are competitive with organizations of similar size, sales, and markets. If you can find companies in the same industry, especially in your area or region, that is another good comparison source. You can check salary surveys and want ads, and scout out competitors to see if they are underpaying or overpaying their employees. You can get a start by searching Google for "salary comparison." Probably the best-known site for comparison information is Salary.com shown in Skill Module 19.3 and on the Online Learning Center. Paying too much is an unnecessary drain on your resources, but paying too little will make it difficult for you to find and keep the best people.[42]

SKILL MODULE 19.3 Finding Local Salaries and Benefits Information Online

There are two possible sources of online information on salaries and benefits specific to your locality. One is the state employment security office for your area. The best list of state offices is found at the Job-Hunt.org website, **(www.job-hunt.org/state_unemployment_offices.shtml)**. When looking at the state sites, the information you want is typically under "Employers." You will be looking for salary data. If it is not apparent, and the site has a search function, enter "salary data" in the search box to track it down.

Salary.com offers a wealth of information on salary and benefits, organized by type of job and locality. Over the years, more and more of its information has become available only for a fee, but basic information remains free and useful. Let's pick Provo/Mammoth, Utah (zip 84601) as our location and "retail cashier" as our position of interest.

The resulting page gives you several job positions. Choose the one which says "Retail Cashier—Full-Time." Below the description are many choices. As a potential employer, you want the report "For Employers: FREE Data." The resulting report has five panels. The first one gives you the range of the salary by percentile (a 90th percentile means 90 percent of people have lower numbers, and 10 percent have higher). To get the median (50 percent of people above, 50 percent of people below this level) salary for the position, look at the tab labeled "Benefits." Click on this and you will find the median salary as well as the median additional amount of money spent by the employer to provide the benefits typical in that zip code.

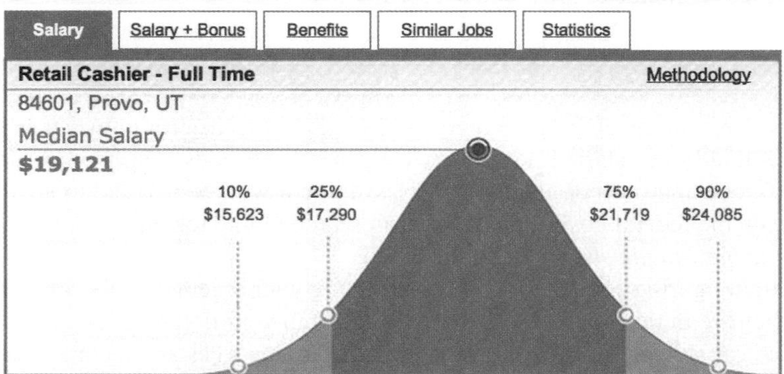

Core Compensation	Median	% of Total
Base Salary	$19,121	60.3%
Bonuses	$120	0.4%
Value of Benefits		
Social Security	$1,472	4.6%
401K/403B	$731	2.3%
Disability	$135	0.4%
Healthcare	$6,507	20.5%
Pension	$1,231	3.9%
Time Off	$2,368	7.5%
Total Compensation	**$31,685**	**100%**

As a potential employer, you need to keep both the base salary and the total salary in mind. Often potential employees screen jobs based on the base salary, so it is important to offer a competitive wage. But as an employer, that position can cost you as much as the total wage, which can be from 25 percent to even 50 percent higher than the base wage.

The last place to check online is the Living Wage Calculator at MIT **(http://livingwage.mit.edu/)**. A **living wage** is the amount needed for a person (or family of a particular size) to meet the basic necessities of life from a single job. In Provo, Utah, the 2012 living wage for one person was $16,783, so the median salary for a cashier given above does put the person about $195 a month above the poverty level. That is around $9.75 of spendable cash a working day over basic needs. For a person just starting out, with no family responsibilities, the median cashier's job may not be a bad one, for awhile.

living wage
The amount needed for a person (or family of a particular size) to meet the basic necessities of life from a single job.

When deciding on a wage, it is important to remember that some benefits are required, like Social Security and Disability, while others may be up to the entrepreneur's choice, like health care or retirement plans. If you expect the job you offer to be the employee's full-time job, it is important, and when you think about it, only fair, to make sure you cover their basic needs.

Typical Expenses

These figures show the individual expenses that went into the living wage estimate. Their values vary by family size, composition, and the current location.

	One Adult	One Adult, One Child	Two Adults	Two Adults, One Child	Two Adults, Two Children
Monthly Expenses:					
Food	$232	$378	$448	$594	$740
Child Care	$0	$572	$0	$572	$1,012
Medical	$76	$151	$152	$227	$302
Housing	$571	$667	$571	$667	$667
Transportation	$232	$397	$464	$629	$794
Other	$188	$369	$376	$557	$738
Monthly After-Tax Income That's Required	$1,299	$2,534	$2,011	$3,246	$4,253
Annual After-Tax Income That's Required	$15,588	$30,408	$24,132	$38,952	$51,041
Annual Taxes	$1,195	$2,158	$1,808	$2,839	$3,628
Annual Before-Tax Income That's Required	$16,783	$32,566	$25,940	$41,791	$54,669

Moreover, salary should be tied to a person's skills and experience. Subsequent increases need to be based on an employee's performance, value, and contribution to the small business. Use the information from the employee's performance appraisal form to help you determine the appropriate increase. You will also want to consider percentages of increase in salary in similar jobs in your local area.[43]

Bonuses and Long-Term Incentives[44]

Employee bonuses, usually paid in a single lump at the end of the year, are one way of providing performance incentives. Profit-sharing plans, stock options, or stock grants not only provide long-term incentives to employees, but they can also help retain valuable team members through your small business start-up phase. However, you also may want to consider these options once you are beyond the start-up phase and have stability in your business earnings overall.

Health Insurance[45]

Employer-sponsored health insurance is fairly standard among medium-sized companies, but not among small businesses. While an employer-sponsored plan saves employees money and gives them peace of mind in knowing that they won't be denied coverage, it is not always affordable to the small business owner. However, providing insurance to your employees sends the message that you care about their health and the health of their families. The Patient Protection and Affordable Care Act (popularly called Obamacare), does not require health insurance for small businesses with fewer than 30 employees, and in fact offers tax credits for firms with fewer than 25 employees. In addition, as health care exchanges come into operation, they will provide new options for lower-cost coverage for all small businesses. To minimize costs, consider having employees pick up part of the tab. Employees who have coverage through a spouse may want to opt out of a plan, particularly if there's a cost associated with it.

Retirement Plans[46]

401(k) plans have become popular because they are relatively easy to administer and are less expensive than traditional pension plans. Many employees like these plans because they maintain some control over the amount of their contribution and how the money is invested. Most small

THE THOUGHTFUL ENTREPRENEUR

LABOR UNIONS

Today a tiny percentage of small business employees are members of labor unions. A labor union is an organization of employees that usually work for the same employer at the same workplace. Labor unions try to get a "collective" contract for their members. The labor laws governing unions can be very complicated. If you are faced with a union organizing drive, you should contact a labor lawyer immediately to make sure that your response to the organizing drive is legal.

If your employees belong to a labor union, they probably already made a "union contract," which is also called a "collective bargaining agreement" with you. This agreement and contract covers wages, working conditions, and procedures for complaining about problems on the job.

Union contracts usually provide that employees cannot be fired, suspended, or disciplined without "good cause." This rule is usually found in a section of the contract titled "Grievance Procedure" or "Discipline." If an employee thinks you didn't have "good cause" to fire or discipline, he or she generally contacts the union. The union may decide to file a grievance for the worker against you. If the union files a grievance against you, you should see an attorney who specializes in labor law, who should help you decide how to defend against the grievance. If you have questions about labor unions, contact a business lawyer near you, or you can start some of the research yourself by contacting the U.S. Department of Labor, **www.dol.gov/compliance/**. Its main goal is to help employers and employees comply with Department of Labor laws and regulations as well as to give you additional information related to your state's laws and compliance issues specific to managing and operating your small business.

TABLE 19.4 Innovative Low-Cost and Free Perks for Your Employees[47]

- Time-off and flexible scheduling (esp. for families with children and elderly at home).
- Arrange discounts with local merchants for your employees.
- Offer free seminars onsite (your insurers, banks, and HMOs will often do this for free).
- Arrange pickups and deliveries at your location for your employees (like dry cleaning, auto cleaning, etc.).
- Offer supplemental services administered through payroll—but paid for by the employee (e.g., supplemental health insurance or retirement programs, prepaid legal services, etc.).
- Offer credit union memberships.
- Let employees buy excess inventory at a big discount.
- Special days (work from home days, family days, community service days, bring your dog days, pizza lunch day, etc.).
- Offer a group perk like two tickets to a movie that weekend.
- Free car washes in the lot (detailers will charge around $5 per car for external washes bought in bulk).
- Let employees expense work clothing bought for sales efforts.
- After-work party.
- Bring a continental breakfast for all.

companies try to put some kind of savings or 401(k) plan in place, even if they don't contribute money to them. Other incentives that you may want to consider include time off and flexible schedules such as holidays, vacations, sick days and personal days. An employer unable to offer competitive salaries may close part of the gap by offering more time off or flexible work hours. Some employers make no distinction between sick, vacation, and personal days and allow employees a set number of days off each year to be used at their discretion. This prevents employees from abusing sick days and keeps employees from feeling that they need to lie when a child is ill or a personal emergency arises.

Perks

Perks is short for perquisites, and refers to the privileges, services, or even tangible items given to employees as part of the overall compensation and benefits package. Perks is a great way to provide short-term boosts in motivation—in effect a psychological pick-me-up. Good perks do not have to cost a lot; in fact, some perks can be powerful, even if free. Consider the list of perk ideas given in Table 19.4.

The rule of thumb is that perks like these should take no more than 3 percent of the annual personnel budget. That said, a bagel and coffee breakfast for your staff may be a very inexpensive way to say you care about them, as well as being a great way to position them for a more productive day, and in the long term, that is what compensation and benefits are supposed to achieve.

Entrepreneurial Leadership

In most general management and business classes, when we talk about "leadership," what we really mean is administration. In fact, the two key factors in traditional leadership theories are task and person. If you are getting the job done, and you are keeping your people happy with each other and the firm, then you have achieved the primary goals of "leadership." Neither one of these key factors does much to explain what we commonly think of when we talk about leaders like Washington or Iacocca or Jobs. The disconnect is exactly the difference between everyday administration of your team and project, and that beyond the regular increment of energy that we imagine around people with entrepreneurial leadership.

Leadership is essential to the growth of any small business. If you intend to have employees, you need to be able to provide the skills of the entrepreneurial leader. In any year, about 75 percent of the businesses in the United States consist of only their owner. There are no employees. This remains true for most one-person businesses, and when larger small businesses are studied, we often find that businesses freeze their employee growth at particular levels. Some of this can be explained by a desire to avoid ever-increasing levels of federal and state laws, with their complexities and costs, but an even more powerful reason is that many entrepreneurs realize that there is an optimal size of firm for them to manage. It is central to your evaluating your potential for entrepreneurial leadership.

Entrepreneurial leadership looks at how you operate as the chief executive of your business. It has three key components over and above task and person—innovation, operation, and inspiration. Innovation is the idea that we look to the leader of a small business as its key visionary. The owner should be the person thinking about the future of the business, how to compete better, how to grow, what next new thing should be tried. Employees can contribute ideas, but in the end, the boss is the key to innovation. If you spend all your time worrying about today and spend no time thinking about tomorrow, eventually your business will lose.

Operation is often the scariest of the three components—although it is the one most closely related to the task and person elements of administrative leadership. Operation refers to the ability to manage the business as it grows. Some people have trouble delegating. Those people often feel out of control when they start to employ others, and the business suffers as a result. They may not know how to delegate, or even if they do, they want to rush in and take over when things "go bad" (i.e., "It was not done the way *I* would have done it."), and thus undermine the employees. Some bosses are just so personally disorganized that it can be difficult to explain or find or share with others the key information of the business, and so the business is locked inside their heads or on their piled-high desktop. If you have employees and they are unhappy, the most likely problem is one of operation.

Inspiration is the third component, and stems from the very reasonable expectation among employees and customers that the entrepreneur should be the business's biggest booster and champion. If you do not have 100 percent iron-clad belief in your business, its product and services, its people, and your ability to make it all work, how can anyone else? While the ability to deliver a stirring speech is an admirable inspirational skill, it is not necessary. Speaking quietly from the heart can work just as well, as long as it is apparent that it *is* from the heart, and it is backed by your own passion. Think of retired basketball coaches Phil Jackson and Bobby Knight. Both inspire, but one is quietly intense, and one is loudly bombastic.

How do you know if you have what it takes in terms of entrepreneurial leadership? Your past experience is the best indicator. If you have been a leader of teams, study groups, shifts at work, or church projects, and people seemed to get the job done and liked each other and you—you probably have what it takes to cover the operation. If you could keep them working when problems arose or times were tough, then you probably have what it takes in terms of inspiration.

If you have not had these sorts of opportunities, college is a great place to get them—in classes, in student organizations, and at work. If you have had these opportunities and they have not been positive, then you want to enroll in workshops and classes on leadership and supervision, and develop the behaviors you need to be successful. You can test out how well you are learning by volunteering to lead on and off campus. Innovation, the third component, is often easy for entrepreneurs because the process of creating and growing a business is a natural application of the innovative component of leadership.

Human Resource Issues in the Family Business

LO7 Explain the complexities of managing family within your business.

Family business is a catchall covering tens of millions of firms. In fact, some researchers estimate that 95 percent of all businesses are indeed family businesses.[48] From a one-person business with occasional infusions of free help from family members to larger family firms employing multiple generations of family members along with nonfamily employees, there are two key human resource management issues that continually surface in family businesses: striking a balance between nepotism and meritocracy as well as managing privilege. There are basic human resource management "best practices" that help whether the business is a family firm or a business with no family ties which get covered next, with a moment spent revisiting the issues of managing compensation and benefits within the family business and the family.

Nepotism, Meritocracy, and the Family Business

As a family business owner, you need to make a decision about how you feel about two ideas that at first do not fit easily together—nepotism and meritocracy. **Nepotism** is the management philosophy of selecting and promoting people based on family ties. Nepotism's advantages are involving people you know and hopefully trust in your business, being able to involve the person more completely (in terms of work time and family time) in the business, and having loyalty and support from your worker and their family in return. **Meritocracy** on the other hand is the management philosophy of selecting and promoting people based solely on their being the most capable person for the job.

nepotism
A management philosophy of selecting and promoting people based on family ties.

meritocracy
A management philosophy of selecting and promoting people based solely on their being the most capable person for the job.

When the family member is also the most capable person for the job, the two philosophies live in harmony. But what if you want to hire your son as manager and hopefully heir to the business, but there is a more capable person available to you? If you can afford to employ and use both, you may be able to eventually create a strong top management team using both people. If you can only afford to hire one person, this is when you have to make a hard decision as to which philosophy wins out.[49]

If you are extremely lucky, your family member might make life easy by saying that you hired the best person and that is the best for all in the long run. But it is just as likely that hiring meritocratically is seen as showing no loyalty to kin, and results in estranged relationships in the family. In a family business, if the family is stressed out, it almost always spills over into the business in negative and sometimes disastrous ways.

Sometimes it is important to recognize that "good enough" may well be just that. If the family member is good enough to do the job well (but perhaps not *as well* as the nonfamily candidate), hiring from the family may well make the most sense in the long run, to build the family and the family business. It is one situation where it might make sense to favor a slightly nepotistic philosophy over a strictly meritocratic one.

If you make that nepotistic decision, what you as the decision maker must do is avoid comparisons of the family member you hired to the "one that got away." It is your job to make every employee, including family members you hire, best able to contribute to the business. Part of being the boss is taking responsibility for your decisions, especially when that is difficult.[50]

The nepotism vs. meritocracy issues also comes up when the child of a family business owner considers coming into the family business. If this happens right after graduating, the nagging question for the owner, the potential heir, and the employees is whether the young person gets ahead because of his or her skill or family tie. The answer to this is simple and often highly beneficial to everyone—work somewhere else first.[51]

In particular, seek a job in a related industry, or with a customer, or even with a competitor with whom your family's business is friendly (e.g., a similar company operating in a different market). A job in one of these areas will give you insight into groups important to your business. It can expand your contacts in key areas like new customers or suppliers, and it can help you learn new ways of getting things done to bring back to the family business.

If you take a job elsewhere, and do a good job there, you return to the family business a proven winner in a more objective situation. You know you have done well, your new fellow employees know it, and your boss knows it. It helps by giving you a stronger basis for what you say, and what you say you are worth.

Managing Privilege

Nepotism has the potential to play a role in the everyday operations of your business and its human resources activities. In fact, many entrepreneurs purposely create a family business in order to give their family members jobs, a sense of purpose, incomes for now with the possibility of future ownership, *and* the privileges of flexibility. Part of the advantage they imagine for a family business is that it can accommodate family needs better than an impersonal, nonfamily business. So the boss's son, who works in the family business, needs time off to coach the grandson's hockey team. In a family business, a doting grandparent can give the time off. You can see how this could be great for the family, but come across as unfair to nonfamily employees.[52]

There is a way to handle this which is easy to say and hard to do—separate family and business. In those everyday occurrences at work, family members should be treated just like anyone else, with no special status or privileges. Making decisions based on what is best for the firm (a meritocratic philosophy) and what is fair to other employees (the basic idea of equality) is a great way to operate if you can do so without totally alienating your family.

Giving all employees similar privileges, or denying favorable treatment to your family are the options most likely to work overall. When looking at "similar privileges," realize that they do not have to be identical. Letting family and nonfamily members pick and choose from a set of privileges or benefits helps create a situation where people in the firm can opt for working (or not working) in a way that best fits with their needs.

Sometimes, the opposite can happen. Some owners hold expectations that their family should work longer and harder than anyone else, because, after all, it is the family's business.[53] If the family members are working harder without the promise of eventual ownership, they are unlikely to upset nonfamily members. If those family members are believed to be making a down payment of sweat equity for future ownership of the firm, there is a greater possibility of negative employee reaction, since the family members' harder work looks like it could have a large payout in the future. Realize that such situations reflect the creation of a type of career ladder—a sequence of increasingly responsible positions—for family members, with ownership at the top.

In the end, while employee ownership is a possibility (and is discussed as one of the options for firm endings in Chapter 20), it is a rare event. Family firms most often stay in the family. But to treat family and nonfamily as similarly as possible, it becomes especially important to create career ladders for nonfamily members. These may not lead to ownership, but can lead to increased skills, responsibilities, and income. Having career ladders for all employees is a way to help minimize the differences and show how important every employee's contribution is seen to be.

While talking about handling employees, let us jump from the best to the worst. Have you heard the phrase "With privilege comes responsibility"? Where that applies in a family business is when other family members want to saddle your firm with family members who are not a good fit to your business.[54]

When it is working well, having multiple generations together in a family business is a great experience. What sort of HR actions are most likely to minimize problems in a family business?

If you can find a place where their skills would be a good fit, then you may be able to sidestep a problem. There is another old saying that "For every pot, there is a lid," and that may be the best solution. If you end up saddled with this person, consider putting them to work where they can do the least harm to the business and to your employees. Also, since the family may have guilted you into hiring the person, don't be shy about reversing the process to guilt those same people into helping you make the new family employee toe the line. Obviously, if mentoring, coaching, or training can work to help them do well, those are great ways to resolve a tricky problem.

In the end, disciplining and even firing the relative may be necessary. "Sometimes people think just because they're family, they can take advantage of the rules," says Leon Eastmond, president of A. L. Eastmond & Sons Inc., a second-generation, family-run boiler/tank manufacturing and repair company in New York City. "But I won't tolerate such foolishness. Business is business, and I tell them that I don't dictate the terms of their behavior; the business does. If they don't act properly on the job, they'll be on a slippery banana with this company—even if they're members of the family."[55]

Good Human Resource Practices for All Businesses

As you have seen, there are times when a family business may need to reflect a bit of nepotism but that we recommend a general philosophy of meritocracy in handling employees, both family and nonfamily. This is true for most of the key elements of a good human resource (HR) approach. The professional way to craft a consistent HR process depends on a set of key elements:[56]

- Transparent procedures with consistent application: There should be procedures in place to handle the major human resource activities of a firm. They should be publicly known and they should be consistently and fairly applied.
- Job basics: The basics for every job should consist of the job description, which we talked about earlier in the chapter. The version of that job description used after the hire should also explain how this position relates to other jobs, so all people in the firm can be sure what is (and is not) the individual's responsibility.
- Job metrics: It should be possible to objectively evaluate how well someone is doing their job. It is ideal if the metric is clear enough for the employee to be certain that they did the job well or poorly. Note that metrics are not just for after the job. Knowing the metrics to be applied help employees know what is expected on the job.
- Task repair: People will make mistakes. That is true of everyone in business. When that happens, are there processes in place to help the mistake-maker learn what went wrong, and how to do a better job the next time? Knowing that learning (even trial-and-error learning) is a part of the job helps them feel less threatened and helps employees take the initiative when needed.
- Lines of communication: Even good employees can have a valid complaint about something in the firm and need an outlet to express their views. This can be as simple as a suggestion box (wooden or electronic), an open-door policy to hear complaints and suggestions, a special time set aside with your people to talk about their ideas and issues, or an ombudsperson or go-between who confidentially receives the complaints and suggestions and forwards them to the owner.
- Clear termination rules: Mistakes can happen, and will. Some will repeat, and if they do, it may be necessary to fire someone. Other mistakes will be so enormous that firing the person responsible may be the only way to save the firm. When firing is necessary, are the reasons for it clear to all? Are the rules and procedures used known to all, and applied the same way to all people, family and nonfamily alike? Firing is emotionally difficult for everyone, but having procedures that are known, known to be fair, and followed consistently help the process go more smoothly.
- Lines of appeal: Lines of appeal means having a way for the person who has failed to meet a metric, or made a mistake, or is facing firing to have their side of the story heard. In small businesses this can be tough since the owner might be the disciplinarian. In such cases, having a trusted employee (or even an entrepreneur outside the business who knows the business and people and is trusted by the owner) serve as the go-between can help.

Dividing Up Ownership and Dividends

Family businesses can also add complexity to compensation and benefit packages. This typically occurs when family members working in the business receive a compensation or benefits package which looks like it was modeled after the owners' packages instead of the other employees' packages. For example, owners of corporations often receive the base of their compensation as a salary as the CEO of the corporation. In addition, they receive a dividend from the corporation based on company profits and amount of stock owned.

Family members working in the business may also receive a similar package, which raises their annual salary above nonfamily employees in similar positions. The best ways to handle this are to create profit sharing plans or a bonus system for nonfamily employees based on performance.[57] These approaches help give everyone in the firm a stake in the outcome and a tangible benefit for good performance. There is often a temptation to declare salaries and dividends secret and assume you are done with the problem, but in reality few pay plans are secret, and HR-related secrets in most businesses are usually counterproductive.

The benefits problem is tougher to solve. Today, with health benefits so costly and so important to people, family businesses can end up with different levels of health care benefits for owners and employees. That type of difference is a bit easier to take than differences between family and nonfamily employees, since the health of the business directly depends on the health of the owner, not necessarily the other family members.

Obviously the best solution is treating family and nonfamily members the same. There are several possible ways to do this. Offering the higher level of benefits to all employees at a subsidized rate may make it easier for family members to get a superior benefits package without discriminating against other employees. Along these lines, the cost of these higher level of benefits can be paid for employees who are family members using money from the owner's or family's stock dividends.

You may notice that a recurring theme in this section is to treat people as close to the same as possible, and to be transparent and open in policies and communications in general.[58] That open, transparent, equal, and communicative approach is essential to a successful HR policy in the small business or family business. The natural human resource and competitive advantage of a small or family business is realized when the firm treats all of its people "like family." That usually reflects a personal touch, a focus on personal needs, and the flexibility to treat people equally well, even if that does not mean treating each person identically (which is how big businesses end up applying the idea of "equal treatment"). Small businesses and family businesses, especially in their early years, may not be able to afford the compensation and benefit packages of larger businesses, but they often have exceptionally loyal and hard-working employees. Why? Because that "like family" atmosphere in the small or family business makes a tremendous difference for good in a lot of employees. That atmosphere is driven more by open communication and personal concern than through other policies or payouts. That is why the key to successful human resource management in *every* type of small or family business rests with open communication.

CHAPTER SUMMARY

Evaluate the decision to hire full-time or part-time help.

- There are many additional expenses to having a full-time employee as opposed to a part-time employee. You need to consider the pros and cons and expand cautiously.
- The cost of adding an employee includes compensation, training time, employee taxes, and accounting costs.
- Whether you hire a part-time or full-time employee, it is important that the employee values your company's mission.

LO2 Understand how to recruit good employees on your budget.

- For the small business owner, there are inexpensive, alternative methods to consider in attracting and recruiting key employees.
- Networking, Internet recruiting, employee referrals, and company websites are several ways to look for talent for your small business. Also consider bartering and internships for part-time employees.
- Hire virtual employees that have experience with being self-motivated and disciplined, including former consultants and freelancers who are accustomed to dealing with deadlines and working independently.
- As you manage your virtual employees, make sure to spend time developing a system of task lists, schedules, and goals with varying time frames and clear deadlines.

LO3 Know how to match the right person to the job.

- The first step in hiring is writing a job description that discusses and reveals all the essential knowledge, skills, and abilities that are needed to fill the position.
- Use the job description to help you evaluate whether an individual would be the right match for the position and your small business.
- Use the information developed in the job description to identify the most important knowledge areas, skills, and abilities the ideal candidate should possess. Next, create specific questions that you will ask of all candidates that will clearly and behaviorally demonstrate to you that they have these critical factors.

LO4 Describe employee training methods and resources.

- To begin, you should first assess your small firm's training needs from the perspective of the business, the job itself (job description), and the needs of the employees.
- There are two different types of training: initial training and ongoing training.
- There are two broad types of training available to small businesses: on-the-job and off-the-job techniques. Individual circumstances and the where, what, and who of your training program determine which method to use.

LO5 Recognize how to meet employees' needs and expectations.

- Factors conducive to a positive and rewarding work environment include communication, teamwork, recognition, training, empowerment, and contribution.
- Increasingly, small entrepreneurial companies are implementing formal performance appraisals. Reviewing employees' performance is an ongoing process.
- The performance appraisal sheet should include open-ended questions for the employee to fill out regarding job performance, strengths, areas of development, and what gets in the way of accomplishing the job.

LO6 Develop a fair compensation and benefit plan.

- One of the first steps in developing a compensation plan is to determine your organization's salary philosophy. The next step is to find comparison factors for salary. Subsequent increases need to be based on employee performance, value, and contribution to the small business.
- Employee bonuses, usually paid in a single lump at the end of the year, are one way of providing performance incentives (consider also profit-sharing plans, stock options, or stock grants early or later on).
- While an employer-sponsored medical insurance plan saves employees money and gives them peace of mind in knowing that they won't be denied coverage, it may not always be affordable to the small business owner.

LO7 Explain the complexities of managing family within your business.

- Family business owners need to strike a balance between nepotism and meritocracy with which they can live.
- Treating everyone in the business the same is the best approach for minimizing the problems arising from favoring family members.
- Having open and transparent human resource policies and practices can help family and nonfamily businesses run more effectively.
- In all businesses, open communication is the key to effective human resource management.

KEY TERMS

employee fit, 624
probationary period, 625
Internet recruiting, 628
employee referral, 628
virtual employees, 630
job description, 632
on-the-job training, 636
psychological contract, 637
open-book policy, 637
living wage, 641
nepotism, 645
meritocracy, 645

DISCUSSION QUESTIONS

1. As a small business owner, you will most likely have the opportunity to hire either part-time or full-time employees. What do you need to consider in determining which one will be best for you and when to hire the first or another employee for your business?
2. Whether you hire a part-time or full-time employee, in what ways can you ensure that each type of employee knows and values your company's mission?
3. While a smaller firm can actually outperform large businesses in attracting high-quality employees, how can you communicate to the job market the multiple benefits of working within your firm? How can you get the word out about these advantages in a cost-effective manner?
4. What are the multiple benefits of hiring virtual employees for your small business? What are some of the ways to manage and foster productivity among your virtual employees? Are there any drawbacks to these methods?
5. What recommendations or suggestions would you give Paige Arnof-Fenn, founder and CEO of Mavens & Moguls, on how to manage and "orchestrate" her multiple virtual employees?
6. What are some of the different ways small business owners can write a job description for the first time? How can they ensure that they cover all the essential knowledge, skills, and abilities that are needed for the position? Why is this important?
7. As a new small business owner, what can you do to make sure you hire the right person for the job? This is probably one of the most difficult decisions you may be faced with making, especially since we all are not trained in the art and science of hiring employees.
8. What specific training guidelines would you incorporate into your business? What inexpensive techniques (on-the-job training) can you use after you make the first hire? Did the owner of the business where you are employed use any of these techniques with you? If so, how beneficial were they to your own development and learning?
9. What are creative ways that you can retain your first employee and ensure you are meeting his or her needs? Consider how you can meet or exceed the employee's "psychological contract."
10. Consider your previous employment position; did the firm have an open-book philosophy? How much information was shared regarding the strategy and financials of the business? What are the advantages and disadvantages of sharing too much or too little information with employees, particularly from a small business owner perspective?
11. Managing health care costs is one of the biggest concerns for small business owners; what are some creative ways that they can minimize some of these costs? In your own community, how have owners confronted these concerns and costs? Be specific with types and the size of the small firms you believe are being innovative in how they manage health care costs.
12. As mentioned by Dr. David Gage, clinical psychologist, "Families don't need written guidelines to operate, but family businesses do." What are some initial guidelines that should be defined in the family business?
13. As mentioned, one of the most common problems in a family business is the hiring of relatives who do not have talent to fulfill the necessary job responsibilities. What can you do if you are "stuck" with an unproductive family member to ensure that he or she does not disturb the work and interfere with the operations of the business?

EXPERIENTIAL EXERCISES

1. At ReCellular, Inc., a cellular phone remanufacturing company in Ann Arbor, Michigan, the small business owner put together a list of interview questions that immediately improved the hiring process. The owner first defined the qualities, characteristics, and basic aptitude he wanted to find in a potential remanufacturing employee. The owner wanted to find people who shared these characteristics:

   - Excellent attendance and dependability
   - Flexibility
   - Integrity and honesty
   - Motivated and dedicated
   - Detail-oriented
   - Team-oriented
   - Strong work ethic
   - Positive, polite, and approachable
   - Continuous improvement oriented
   - Good communication skills
   - Actual hands-on demonstration of capability to sort phones and identify cosmetic problems with phones

   The owner then worked with several online resources to structure questions that would indicate whether candidates had these characteristics. No list of questions is totally comprehensive; however, these questions are helping the interviewers find better candidates:

   - What made you decide to apply at ReCellular?
   - Tell me about yourself and your last/current job/class.
   - When we call your previous employer for references, what are they likely to tell us in regard to your dependability/attendance?
   - Tell me about a time when you demonstrated your trustworthiness or integrity in school or at work.

   This is, of course, a start—your job is to think of other questions that the small business owner may want to ask a potential employee (either for a full-time, part-time, or virtual assistant position).

2. You have just been asked by a small business owner to uncover U.S. and state laws that are relevant to managing people (in the future, when the small business owner is interested in hiring). Go to Businesslaw.gov and obtain three to four critical areas of information about specific laws within your state regarding: hiring issues, wage laws, taxes, health and safety, and termination.

3. Small business owner Jeff Birdsell opened Shauncey's Gourmet Ice Cream, Inc., in Battlefield Shopping Center in Springfield, Missouri. Like any small business owner, Jeff Birdsell realized that starting this venture would entail a tremendous commitment of time and energy. He had expected to work 60–80 hours a week indefinitely, and finds he works at least that. He estimates that he and his parents frequently tally up to 250 hours per week in the organization. Employee turnover at Shauncey's runs at 100 percent per year. What creative and innovative hiring and retention recommendations would you give Jeff as he manages both his family and part-time workers (especially with 100 percent employee turnover)?

MINI-CASE

VIVID SKY EMPLOYEE WAVE 3

It was 2006 and Vivid Sky's sole product, SkyBOX, had survived its pilot test. Designed as an in-stadium information service for fans, SkyBOX offered video feeds, statistics, infographics (like graphics of the last 10 pitches, last 10 hits, etc.), maps, live chats and voting, and in-seat ordering. All of this was delivered by wireless PDAs (think of a Palm Pilot) "hardened" to withstand dropping and spilled liquids.

SkyBOX got to this stage because of three different waves of employees. Founder Tim Hayden was tech savvy, but lacked the skills to write the code that would meld all of these different streams of data into one application. The first wave of programmers worked with Tim at his full-time employer. They shared Tim's love of sports and passion for using technology to revitalize the stadium experience. Together they created the overall design of the program and an interactive demo to show potential investors. These employees worked nights and weekends with no expectations. Since they couldn't put more time (and money) into the project, they decided to move on to other projects once Tim had a working model.

Tim used the local network he built as SkyBOX developed to recruit the next group of programmers. This group was even more skilled, and they were able to dedicate the time to build a "basic" application. For this, Tim was able to pay them a small amount as he continued to bootstrap the company. Unfortunately, they found that they lacked the time to take the SkyBOX to the level of refinement customers and investors were asking for. Lacking equity in the business, they left on their own when Tim asked them to.

The third wave of programmers had more time and wanted to take the "basic" SkyBOX to the next level. This group, recruited from across the country based on Tim's SkyBOX promotional trips, created a highly interactive application that was used for Vivid Sky's first stadium deployment. Because of their dedication, Tim decided to give the developers a bonus in the form of equity.

But the third wave of programmers faced two major challenges. Vivid Sky was receiving requests from numerous sports properties for national and international events, and the current development team couldn't keep up with the new opportunities. Also the current programmers were untested developers for the iPhone and iPod touch platform, which was the future of the company.

Tim faced the prospect of asking the third wave of programmers to leave Vivid Sky and give up their salaries and equity. He wasn't sure all of them would do this voluntarily, and he wasn't sure he could afford to share more of his own equity with a fourth wave of programmers. On the other hand, he knew his current programmers couldn't handle the conversion to the new platform. If he fires the programmers who don't go voluntarily, will it hamper efforts to recruit the fourth wave of programmers?

CASE DISCUSSION QUESTIONS

1. What were the differences in the sources of employees for Vivid Sky as it developed?
2. What are the benefits and problems of using equity to compensate employees? What about using pay?
3. How could Tim have managed the third wave of employees if he had hired them right off the bat?
4. Should Tim replace the third wave of programmers? If yes, how do you recommend he go about this doing this? Can you find a way for him to protect his share of the equity he has in the business?

SUGGESTED CASES AND ARTICLES

- Alaska Wildland Adventures, C-20

Available on McGraw-Hill Create™:

- Compensation at Carrington: The New Pay Plan

SUGGESTED VIDEOS

www.mhhe.com/katz4e

Video Case:

- For a written video case and corresponding clip, visit the OLC at www.mhhe.com/katz4e and select "Chapter 19".
- Unique Vacation Policy

SBTV.com Videos:

- Keeping the Employees Happy
- Should Your Small Business Hire Illegal Aliens?
- How to Fire a Problem Employee
- Help Wanted for the New First Time

STVP Videos:

- Take Care of Your Employees
- Defining Company Culture
- Attracting People in the Early Stages

CHAPTER

20 Achieving Success in the Small Business

● From tires to wholesale foods to sporting goods, Shoppers' Service evolved spinoffs, grew larger and smaller, and changed hands over the 42 years of its existence. By remaining flexible, creative, and committed, the owners enjoyed these changes—and made good profits, as well. How are you encouraged about small business ownership as a result of reading this story?

LEARNING OBJECTIVES

After you complete this chapter, you will be able to:

LO1 Recognize the stages of the small business life cycle.

LO2 Consider the impact of the product life cycle.

LO3 Understand the options for harvesting or closing the small business.

LO4 Know the firm-level critical success factors for small business.

LO5 Understand what success means with the quadruple bottom line.

Focus on Small Business: The Many Lives of Shoppers' Service Store

From 1962 to 2004, Shoppers' Service was an entrepreneurial company serving a variety of customer needs. Originally founded as a discount department store—sort of a mini-Walmart—in Memphis in 1962, its original owners, three European immigrants to Memphis—Morris, Sol, and Karl—combined their money, skills, and energy to start the business. Each had prior experience in small business ownership, and with their combined savings, contacts, and experience, Shoppers' grew to encompass the mini-discount store, a second store branch in the suburbs, a sporting goods wholesaling warehouse, a food wholesaling company, a tire store, and three pharmacies.

Along the way, the partners decided to go their separate ways. First Karl asked to leave, and he was given the pharmacies and tire store as his share of the assets. A few years later Sol left, taking with him the suburban branch discount store. Working solo, Morris sold off the warehouse and the original store, keeping the food wholesaling company going as his major source of income.

At each change in the business, the partners obtained expert assistance, working with attorneys, accountants, and industry consultants to make sure the valuations of the businesses were fairly determined. They also worked with the experts to minimize tax burdens on each of the soon-to-be separated firms and owners.

When Shoppers' closed with the death of Morris in 2004, the business had gone through three owners, five changes of its legal structure, over one dozen additions and deletions of subsidiary business entities, and forty-two years of profitable operations. Along the way it supported more than a dozen members of the three owners' families, and, at its peak, nearly twenty other employees. For all of that, the story of Shoppers' Service is like millions of other small businesses that start, grow, survive, and eventually succeed.

DISCUSSION QUESTIONS

1. How would you describe the stages in the life of Shoppers' Service Store?
2. How did Shoppers' Service make use of outside help?
3. How do you imagine long-term customers would describe Shoppers' Service over the years?
4. How successful would you say Shoppers' Service was as a business?

Small Business Life Cycle

LO1 Recognize the stages of the small business life cycle.

business life cycle
The sequence or pattern of developmental stages any business goes through during its life span.

Like every person, every small business is unique. But just as we all go through childhood and adolescence on the way to adulthood, as we saw with Shoppers' Service, so do small businesses. There is a lot of predictability in this growth process, and knowing the developmental stages of the **business life cycle** can help you better understand your business and your career as a small business owner. The small business life cycle is shown in Figure 20.1.

Several models exist for the life cycle of the small business firm.[1] Each divides the stages a bit differently. But all models have the same general ideas: (1) there are multiple stages, (2) the key issues, actions, and lessons at each stage are different from the other stages, and (3) the level of risk the business faces changes from stage to stage.

For most small businesses, though, the usual sequence of stages is emergence, existence, survival, success, and resource maturity. Let's look at each of these stages to see what they involve for the small business and the key issue you can expect to face in each. These stages and business growth patterns are shown in Figure 20.1.[2]

Emergence

Morris, Sol, and Karl were friends before they opened the business, and over several years they talked about a variety of business prospects before finally settling on Shoppers' Service. They were engaged in the stage called *emergence,* in which a person thinks about and takes actions toward starting a firm. Typically a lot more people think about starting a firm than actually take steps to do so. In 2011, 56 percent of youth aged 15–25 expressed an interest in owning their own firm. But in 2011, only 12.3 percent of the population was actually taking steps to start a firm.[3]

Getting from entrepreneurial thinking to entrepreneurial action is the challenge of the emergence stage.[4] Two techniques discussed earlier in the book can help you move from thought to action. One is using the BRIE behaviors from the Chapter 1 checklist to start on the road to creating a firm. The other is to get into business part time (as discussed in Chapter 5) as a way to lay a foundation for future entrepreneurial action.

Existence

When Shoppers' Service opened in 1962, the three partners had a lot of ideas, a fair amount of merchandise, an absolutely certain set of overhead costs, and no guarantee of sales. Sales did come, but it was a rocky first couple of years. This is typical of the *existence* stage, which is defined by having the business in operation, but not yet stable in terms of markets, operations, or finances. In 2012 according to the GEM studies, about 4.5 percent of Americans were involved with businesses in their existence stage. Existence is the second riskiest period after emergence. The reason risk is so

FIGURE 20.1

The Small Firm Life Cycle

Sources: Adapted from Churchill and Lewis (1983), Baumol (1968), Chandler and Hanks (1994), and Katz and Gartner (1988).

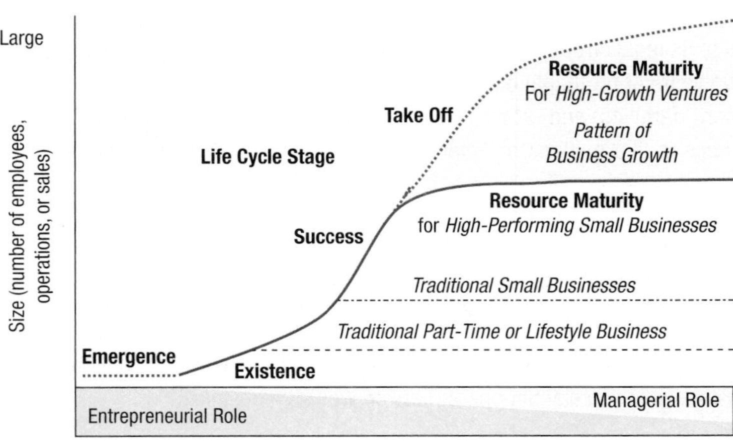

high is that many business owners lack the key information or experiences they need in marketing, production, and management.[5] The problems of mastering these three areas form what are called the **liabilities of newness** for small businesses in their existence stage.

liability of newness
The set of risks faced by firms early in their life cycles that comes from a lack of knowledge by the owners about the business they are in and by customers about the new business.

The solutions for liabilities of newness come from getting expertise as quickly as possible. For most owners of firms, personally getting more experience is risky because it takes too long. The safer way is to obtain help from others. As noted in Chapter 3, developing an extensive social network is essential for the success of any firm. Whether you use family, friends, industry contacts, or free or paid advisers, getting help helps you survive.

Success

Woody Allen once said that "Eighty percent of success is showing up,"[6] and it seems to be particularly true for small businesses transitioning from existence to success. The success stage occurs once the firm is established in its market. For Shoppers' Service, success came in the 1970s, when it was well known in the local market and started to have the profits for expansion. Success stage firms show consistently growing financial performance, usually with slowly rising sales.

Firms at this stage develop the information, skills, and most importantly the routines to grow the business's profits. Those profits aren't always taken in the form of money. Time off from work, a slower pace at work, or hiring additional personnel to take on more of the tasks of the owner are all ways that these profits can be used to make the owner's life easier. Used that way, the extra profits are called **slack resources** by economists, because they can be rechanneled into the business if needed. For most owners, though, these profits are called *flexibility*. All new businesses—from small businesses to high-growth firms—go through this stage. For most small business owners, this is a stage that lasts a long time. For the owners of high-growth businesses, this is only a chance to catch their breath and lay the groundwork for the period of takeoff.

slack resources
Profits that are available to be used to satisfy the preferences of the owner in how the business is run.

Resource Maturity

For most small businesses, resource maturity will follow the success stage. This stage is characterized by a stable level of sales and profits over several years. At this stage, the functional areas, the market, and the products or services are all being dealt with consistently and efficiently. The challenge of maturity is to avoid complacency. Shoppers' Service was able to sidestep that problem because of its changes in what would have been the maturity years, as the partners broke up and took pieces of the business with them, requiring adaptation. After years of consistency, customers and businesses can begin to take each other for granted. For your business, that can be deadly, because a competitor can come to your customer, show personal interest and competitive products or services or prices, and take your customer away. Since the rule of thumb is that getting a new customer costs five times as much as keeping an existing customer,[7] every lost customer is important. How do you avoid customer complacency?

Supersalesman Zig Ziglar says he learned from Australian psychologist Joseph Braysich the four key components for staving off customer complacency—recency, frequency, potency, and recommendation:[8]

- **Recency:** Be among the people your customers have seen in the past few days. Do this through magnetic business cards on their file cabinet, a phone call or e-mail to make sure they have everything they need, or a thank-you note saying that you appreciate their business.
- **Frequency:** You never know when your competitors will show up, so to make recency work, you have to stay in touch with customers on a frequent basis. This might be on a quarterly or monthly basis in cases where customers buy only a few times a year, but contacts can even be on a daily basis if that is how often customers buy from you. All forms of contact count here—visits, phone calls, e-mails, newsletters, business letters, and so on.
- **Potency:** Did you ever see a funny TV advertisement but a few days later could only recall the joke, but not the company being advertised? The problem was the potent part of the ad—the joke—was not related to the important part of the message—the business. When you contact customers, your message has to remind them that your firm values their business. A potent message is one that is remembered, and remembered for the right reasons.

- **Recommendation:** We all seek recommendations. It is a powerful way to get help and advice. Your customers hopefully see you and your firm as experts in certain areas of business. After all, you've been in business for years at this point. Making clear recommendations that can help your customers provides a memorable way to show that you think about, understand, and care about your customers and their business.

You'll will notice that these four characteristics are almost exactly the benefits of marketing via social media. Using the Internet to stay connected to your customers and to give them a way to share their opinions with you and one another is key to staving off complacency and keeping your customers involved with your business.

Takeoff

Although rare among small businesses, one possible complication is when the success stage leads into takeoff rather than resource maturity. Takeoff happens if a business embarks on a period of exceptional growth. For small businesses, it might come from landing an unexpectedly gigantic contract, expanding into multiple locations, or just being in the right place at the right time, as was the case for Sun-Hill Industries when it created the Stuff-a-Pumpkin.

The challenge Sun-Hill and other firms face in the possible takeoff stage is to understand the nature and demands of growth and get some control over it. Managing takeoff involves working extensively with potential sources of funding and other key resources, as well as working with markets outside and employees within the firm. It also often entails relearning the processes that led to this level of success, as a growth-oriented firm often needs to do things differently from one content with maintaining a stable state. One example of this is outsourcing or subcontracting for the growth-oriented firm to let the firm stay focused on its own key competencies. A growing nursery might subcontract out its bookkeeping and human resources functions so the managers at the nursery can focus on increasing sales and managing the expansion.

It is important to remember that most small businesses never go through the takeoff stage, and for those that do, the takeoff path often moves them into the high-growth firm model (discussed next) and away from small business. For firms that don't reach a possible takeoff stage situation, the jump is from the success stage to the resource maturity stage.

The lesson of the life cycle model of business is that much of your firm's development as a business is predictable within some broad terms. Knowing the stages of the life cycle and where your firm is among those stages can serve as a powerful reminder of the kinds of issues for which you

SMALL BUSINESS INSIGHT

SUCCESS = OPPORTUNITY + DANGER

Stuff-a-Pumpkins are the pumpkin-colored leaf bags you see on lawns around Halloween. You know the ones—they have a jack-o-lantern's face on them. They were the brainchild of Anita Dembiczak and Ben Zinbarg. Zinbarg's company, Sun-Hill Industries, had been operating consistently for 17 years in Stamford, Connecticut. When he came up with the idea, he spent his own money to get the first run of bags made. They sold out instantly at the discount stores where he tried them out. The stores clamored for more and demanded immediate delivery! But Dembiczak's, Zinbarg's, and Sun-Hill's finances were tapped out, and the discount stores were months away from paying for the bags they'd sold. Zinbarg went to his business banker, who refused to extend credit, even though Ben had contracts from big retailers. Twenty-three other banks also turned Ben down. He got the money needed to get out the next order by investing all his remaining personal money, securing a loan from a friend, and convincing suppliers and employees to delay receiving money owed them. He got the bags made and out to the retailers. But competitors meanwhile started to copy his bag, so he took the remaining money and started legal proceedings against these concept pirates.[9] Eventually he succeeded in getting the pirates on the run, but Zinbarg probably came to a new understanding of why the Chinese term for crisis consists of the symbols for opportunity and danger.[10]

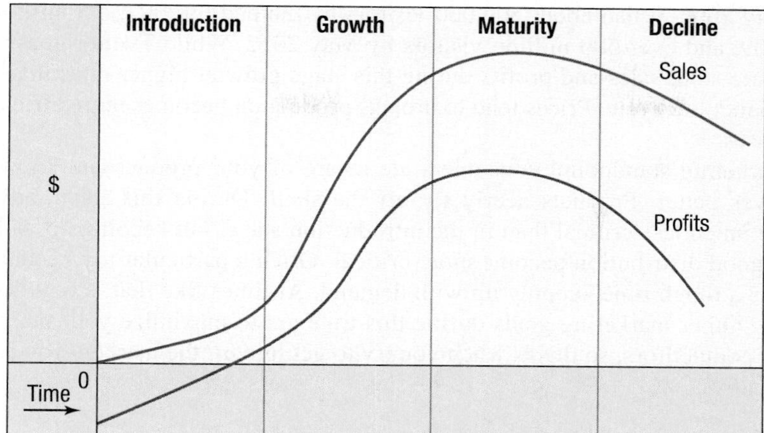

FIGURE 20.2

The Product Life Cycle

need to watch. Knowing the different possible life cycle paths for the resource maturity stage makes it possible to clearly choose when to grow, and what to expect if a higher-growth approach is in the cards for your firm.

Product Life Cycle[11]

LO2 Learn the product life cycle.

Just as firms go through life cycles, so do the products and services within them. Since the stages for products are very similar to those for firms, we will quickly review the four stages (Figure 20.2) in terms of their implications for managing your firm's growth.

Stage 1—Introduction

Most small businesses can only afford to launch a product on a small scale, so naturally the sales are low and profits not likely when a product emerges into the market. In fact many traditional marketing techniques described will depress profits at the start more than they will at later stages. For all the marketing money being spent, the risks from competition in the introduction stage are generally low since most competitors will wait to see if your product is a threat and has staying power before they act.

From a marketing standpoint, the more innovative the product, the slower the sales, because fewer customers are comfortable with such products. Me-too products have an easier time gaining customer acceptance. Either way, the best sales method is to focus on the *relative advantage* your product has over the competition. When possible show how easy the product is to use, and how easily or well it co-exists with the other products the customer owns. For people with taped music, moving to an MP3 player was a major hassle, and sales of the MP3 players didn't take off until download sites and tape to MP3 converters were cheap and easy. Providing samples or demonstration opportunities will also help seed the product during this phase.[12]

It should be noted that not all products survive the introduction phase of the product life cycle. Some products may take too long to begin making a profit because of high marketing expenses. Other products simply never catch on with consumers and never sell enough to cover their costs. And in reality many products in this stage get revised based on customer reactions and reasons behind lost sales. For online services, such revisions can be done on an almost daily basis, and very inexpensively. For products, the revision process can take weeks and cost thousands of dollars. Either way it gets done, products that are successful move on to the growth stage.

Stage 2—Growth

Like its firm counterparts of success and takeoff stages, during the growth stage acceptance of the product (whether innovative or imitative) increases rapidly. Think about Twitter. Although founded in July 2006, it had about 500,000 visitors by the end of 2007, 4.5 million visitors by December 2009, and over 500 million visitors by May 2012. While Twitter doesn't charge for products that are sold, sales and profits during this stage grow at higher rates than at any other part of the product life cycle. Prices tend to drop as production becomes more efficient and competition increases.

From a marketing standpoint, consumers are aware of your product and know how it will make their lives better. Products nearly fly off the shelf. During this stage, advertising and promotion are much less critical than in the introduction stage, but keeping up with production and ensuring good distribution become more critical. Often a particular toy becomes "hot" and production has a tough time keeping up with demand. At times like that, a $20 doll can go for $200 on eBay. Other marketing goals during this time are to maximize your market share and keep ahead of competitors, so this is when you try to get into *all* the markets you can nationally (or internationally).

iPod docking stations with speakers went through a fast 3-year sprint from introduction to maturity due to rapid adoption and rapid innovation.

Stage 3—Maturity

Once the rapid growth begins to slow down, the product enters the *maturity stage*.

During this stage sales will level off, and profits follow suit, but remember, both should be at fairly high levels. Keeping both at that fairly high level is the challenge the small business faces. Since there are few new users for the product, most gains in market share are made by stealing customers from competitors. So you'll focus on defending the market share you have. As weaker competitors start to leave the market, you'll have opportunities to take their "leftover" customers.

For example, think about docking/charging stations with expansion speakers for iPods. The first ones came out in 2007. By 2008, different ones were being proclaimed "hot products" by industry experts. The growth phase came then, and with the growing opportunities, so came competitors. Today in 2012 a quick check of Amazon.com shows over 1,300 products. There is probably no room for more competing products, and many of the 1,300 models—and their manufacturers—will drop out over the next year or two. This product is entering the maturity phase. The number of customers will probably remain flat for awhile, and the number of competitors will go down.

What can we expect for maturity-stage products? Price competition starts to rise, and manufacturers find ways to cut costs or introduce new features to keep or gain market share. Something as simple as coming out with new speakers in colors may spark customer interest and keep or gain market share. But the truly smart companies already realize it is critical to have new ideas in the pipeline now and to get them ready for commercialization. Later in this stage, you will see products available through outlets and outlet sites like Overstock.com. As of June 2012, Overstock.com had over 110 different iPod docks available for sale.

Techniques used to bolster sales during this period include:

- Advertisements become reminder ads or extol new uses for the product, for example, Chex cereal being promoted as a party mix, rather than as a breakfast food.
- Promotions (coupons, rebates, multipacks, etc.) flourish.
- Companies reposition brands to appeal to new markets, for example, Rembrandt toothpaste repositioned its product from being a smoker's toothpaste to a low-abrasion, whitening toothpaste for kids.[13]

A product can stay in the maturity stage for a long period of time. While the technology of the product may be older, the product is comfortable for the consumer. A quality product that inspires brand loyalty, such as Murphy's Oil Soap, can remain in the maturity stage for decades.

Stage 4—Decline

Once a product begins its permanent decline, this decline can be slow or fast, steady or unsteady. This decline may come from the introduction of a new technology such as MP3s replacing music CDs, and before that vinyl records, or digital televisions replacing analog ones. The decline may also be caused by a shift in consumer preferences, such as bell-bottom jeans going out of style.

Whatever the reason for the decline, the characteristics of the decline stage remain the same. Both sales and profits fall during this stage. Advertising and promotion expenses are usually nearly eliminated at this point. Companies pare back their product lines and don't market to less profitable segments in order to cut costs and squeeze as much profit out of the final stage as possible. Tab, a popular diet soda in the early 1980s, is now available in only certain locations with highly loyal consumers, such as Cincinnati, New York, Atlanta, Phoenix, and Houston.[14]

Some products' decline is permanent. For example, with the switch in the United States to digital television in 2009, the analog television is pretty much dead as a product. On the other hand, many products go into decline, only to be resurrected in the future as styles come back to old standards, or when a company finds a new way to revitalize the product, as in the case of high school band instruments and Yamaha discussed in Chapter 7. For example, in music the 45 record was popular in the 1940s and 1950s because its price fit what teens could afford. By the 1960s the 45 had declined. The growth of the MP3 player and the creation of new retailers like iTunes and Rhapsody willing to sell individual songs revitalized that type of music retailing. Similarly, hot rods were popular in the 1950s, but became very much a niche product, carried along by that generation. But for the manufacturers of car customization and performance equipment, video games like *Grand Theft Auto* and movies like *The Fast and the Furious* spurred a widespread renewal of their industry as "rice burners or "rice rockets" became the hot rods of the new millennium.

Service Life Cycle

While services do in fact go through the same four stages—introduction, growth, maturity, and decline—it can be somewhat easier to extend the life cycle and to virtually eliminate the decline stage of a service. Primarily, this is because services are often much easier to change "on the run." You can add and remove items from menus, change service levels, add additional services, revamp your website, and otherwise modify your service bundle more quickly than those who are manufacturing products. You can go with a low-carb menu to accommodate the Atkins and South Beach diet fad, just about as fast as you can have new menus printed or change your "daily specials" chalkboard. You can attend a seminar or course to learn about adding new skills and offer that service to your accounting or legal clients. Service changes can be done relatively quickly and, if they don't work out well, they can be removed just as quickly.

This process of on-the-run changes means that your service is starting new life cycles with each tweaking of its existing offering. The curves will look more like those in Figure 20.3, where curve 1 is the initial service bundle and curves 2–4 represent the incremental changes. While a major change (like from Italian food from Chinese) can bring a firm almost back to the starting point, in most other cases, the new service is on top of all existing services—has no impact on existing services—like adding a manicurist to your beauty salon.

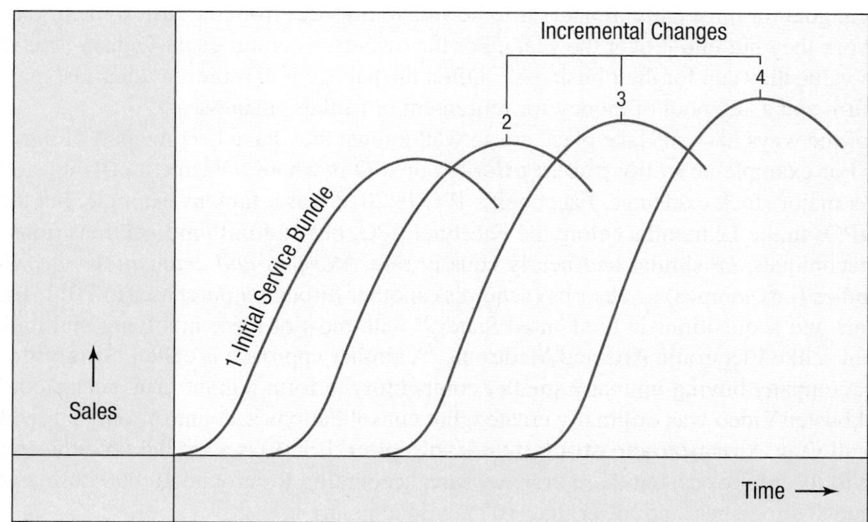

FIGURE 20.3
Service Life Cycle

Similar to products, new services will take a little time to attract customers, and initial advertising efforts will be to educate your clients as to the benefits of this service (or, perhaps, that you now offer this service). As sales seem to level off, continue to remind your customers that you offer the service and why it's better than that of your competition. Eventually, as sales drop off, eliminate the service totally or perform it only for those "old time" customers who ask for it.

Using the Product Life Cycle[15]

Many of the challenges in using the firm life cycle or the industry life cycle from Chapter 7 apply to using the product life cycle. It is hard to know exactly where in a cycle a particular product or service might be. Let's say Twitter's visit numbers grew by only 5 million from December 2011 to March 2012, but then dropped by over 4 million in April. Is Twitter reaching maturity or is it a minor slowdown in a meteoric rise? No one can tell for sure. A marketer must weigh many things before trying to decide what phase a product is in. Moreover, products often experience a "revival" as new generations discover them. Brands such as Oxydol, Fanta, Breck, and Ovaltine, after near extinction, are experiencing new popularity.[16] Tattoo shops, a service that was nearly extinct, have started a new life cycle as styles have changed.

At the other extreme, products like Murphy's Oil Soap mentioned earlier, or Morton Salt, or Coca-Cola—have lasted for decades and show no signs of stopping. The bottom line is that you must be aware of the product life cycle and consider where your product might be and what that means, but you should understand that the determination can be imperfect and somewhat unpredictable. You should keep trying to decipher the life cycle stage because using the product life cycle gives you, as the entrepreneur, a way to think about your product, customers, and competition. If you follow the advice given above, it can help identify many of the likely issues and offer advice on how to handle these challenges in marketing your product.

Closing the Small Business

LO3 Understand the options for harvesting or closing the small business.

As we note in Chapter 1, about 1 million businesses start each year, or about 1 million firms move into the existence stage of the life cycle each year. This sounds like a lot of activity, and it is important for our economy, but the really high levels of activity happen farther along in the life cycle. Every year, nearly 4 million firms go through changes in ownership or existence.

The type of exit is important not only for the entrepreneur, but also for the larger community. About half of all workers in the United States work in small firms, and when firms close down, small business employees lose jobs. There are also ripples throughout the community as other firms lose the business they got from the closing firm and its employees and as the larger community has one less source for goods or services. Entrepreneurial exits which transfer ownership have a greater chance of continuing the jobs, purchases, and product/service deliveries on which the community and its members depend.

harvest
Recover value through a sale of a firm or its assets.

initial public offering (IPO)
Transfer method describing the first-time public sale of a stock listed on a public stock exchange.

consolidation
A transfer method in which a small business is bought by a larger firm for the purpose of quickly growing the larger firm.

employee stock ownership plan
A formalized legal method to transfer some or all of the ownership of a business to its employees.

The ideal goal for most entrepreneurs is to be able to **harvest** from the firm some of the value of the hard work they put into it over the years. For the owners, a central goal of a harvest is to get the maximum value they can for their business.[17] Often the harvest will represent their last major return from the firm and a key pool of money for retirement or further businesses.

Some of the ways harvests take place are so well known they have become part of our everyday language. For example an **initial public offering** or IPO is where a business sells its stock to the public on a major stock exchange. Facebook's IPO in 2012 was a famous example, but there were only 121 IPOs in the 12 months before the Facebook IPO, out of 4 million firm transitions.

Other techniques are similar and nearly equally rare. *Mergers and acquisitions* are where one firm combines (i.e., merges) or absorbs (acquires) another through a purchase. In 2011, there were 460 mergers and acquisitions in the United States,[18] with most of these involving multibillion dollar companies like Electronic Arts and Medtronic. A similar approach is called **consolidation** and involves a company buying up many smaller competitors to form a giant firm, such as the case of how Blockbuster Video was originally created, but consolidations account for only a few thousand purchases all year. An **employee stock ownership plan** (ESOP) is a special tax-protected way to sell a firm to its employees, but these are very rare, accounting for around 10,000 businesses in the United States[19] altogether, and fewer than 100 are done in any year.[20]

FIGURE 20.4

The Hierarchy of Business Outcomes

So what does happen to the other 4 million businesses? There are two general possibilities for most small businesses. About half of the changes are **transfers**, which involve moving ownership from one legal entity, person, or group to another. Examples of transfers include selling a business in whole or in part, or arranging a succession of the business between family members, or giving the firm as a gift to someone who will keep the business a going concern. The other half are **terminations**, which refer to the methods for closing down a business, and include three major methods—walkaways, workouts, and bankruptcies.

transfer
An endgame strategy in which ownership is moved from one person or group to another.

termination
An endgame strategy in which the owner closes down a business.

As mentioned above, the goal of the owners is ideally to obtain value from the firm when they transfer or terminate it, but that goal sits at the top of a hierarchy of business outcomes that are a part of the way every owner thinks about their firm. The hierarchy is shown in Figure 20.4. The top of the hierarchy describes situations in which the owner leaves the firm with substantial funding, while the other extreme has situations of bankruptcy. Obviously owners would prefer to end up as high on the hierarchy as possible, and transfers are the technique that yield those results.

Transfers

There were, around 860,000 firms transferred within families, a process called *family business succession*. That year nearly 1 million *business sales* took place, where the business was transferred to people other than family. Successions and business sales generally occur only among the largest small businesses, such as high-performing small businesses and high-growth ventures, because only these firms generate the kinds of cash flows and profits that make paying the former owner possible.

Regardless of the method used for transferring or harvesting, the key issue remains the same—doing it well. All transfers are legally, financially, and operationally complex, but need to be done well. Because, between the federal and state taxes on transfers, on portions of larger estates, and on capital gains, a business can lose as much as half its value to the government.

There are three classes of strategies for managing transfers within a family.[21] One strategy is called **liquidity enhancement**, arranging (usually through a life insurance policy in your name held by your heirs) to generate cash to cover the estate taxes. A second strategy is called **tax management**, in which you structure your transfer to make tax payments as small and as manageable as possible. This includes selling small portions of your business to your heirs for cash or promissory notes (with the lowest legal interest rate possible). If done the right way (which requires a lawyer's help), this results in giving the heirs 14 years to pay for the shares with only interest payments necessary for the first five years. There are literally dozens of other tax management methods. The third strategy is called an **estate freeze** and depends on moving assets from the entrepreneur to the heirs when they are worth less. There are several methods for doing this including family limited partnerships and grantor retained annuity trusts (GRAT).

liquidity enhancement
An estate planning strategy which focuses on generating cash to cover likely estate taxes.

tax management
An estate planning strategy which focuses on minimizing estate tax payments.

estate freeze
An estate planning strategy which focuses on transferring assets to heirs when the asset costs are low.

Strategies can be combined as in the case of a charitable bailout where the entrepreneur puts the business into a tax management technique called a charitable remainder trust, getting income from the trust. After the entrepreneur dies, a life insurance policy on the entrepreneur held by the heirs—the classic liquidity enhancement approach—generates the cash to buy the business from the trust, with the purchase price going to a charity.

Current federal laws governing estate taxes on business transfers are changing on a yearly basis until 2013.[22] Meanwhile many states are decoupling their own estate tax laws from the federal approach.[23] In estate planning the best advice is to enlist the aid of lawyers and accountants with expertise in estate planning and in business buying and selling, and leave time to let the transfers take place in ways that minimize the tax burden on everyone.

For most part-time businesses and traditional small businesses, the firm cannot easily be sold because it does not generate enough profits to pay a current owner and a former owner. In such cases, the original owner must decide if it makes sense to close the business down and lose all invested value, or transfer the business in a way that lets some of the value be realized.

bankruptcy
An extreme form of business termination which uses a legal method for closing a business and paying off creditors when debts are substantially greater than assets.

walkaways
Business terminations in which the entrepreneur ends the business with its obligations met.

Bankruptcy is the most extreme business closing situation, which occurs when the business has such high debt that it cannot reasonably expect to earn back the funds required by its creditors. A lawyer's involvement can help owners protect as much of their personal assets as possible throughout the process and eventually recover their financial standing.

Several approaches are available. For small firms these include approaches such as a *pass off*, which happens when the owner realizes there is little chance of being able to sell the firm, but in the interest of keeping the firm going, or providing employees with a source of income, the owner gives the firm to someone as a gift, without compensation. In a 1998 survey of family business transfers, around 38 percent of firms used gifts as a major way to transfer ownership.[24] For pass offs, legal and accounting advice is necessary to make sure that the owner leaves all financial and tax obligations with the firm, permitting a clean exit.

Another typical form is the *sell off*. In this approach the assets of a firm—perhaps including the customer list, real estate, and even the inventory—are sold to another business, with the proceeds used to pay off the firm's remaining debts, and perhaps leaving the owner some small profit. Often the purchasing firm absorbs the assets, so the customers or real estate appear to move to another business. Transfers are estimated in the tens of thousands annually, but reliable statistics are hard to come by. The key to a successful sell off is finding customers for the assets and determining a price for the different assets. For assets that lead to revenue, such as customer lists or working real estate, it is typically possible to get an amount ranging from one-half year to two years profits from the asset, with more possible for negotiators with information on comparable deals.

Terminations

There are nearly as many terminations as transfers—around 1.8 million a year. Terminations are more likely for young firms, those four years old and less.[25] As noted, there are three types of terminations—walkaways, workouts, and bankruptcies. In a walkaway the entrepreneur ends the business with its obligations met. In a workout the firm's legal or financial obligations are not fully met at closing,[26] while **bankruptcy** refers to a legal method for closing a business and paying off creditors in extreme situations, and is quite rare with 47,806 in 2011.[27]

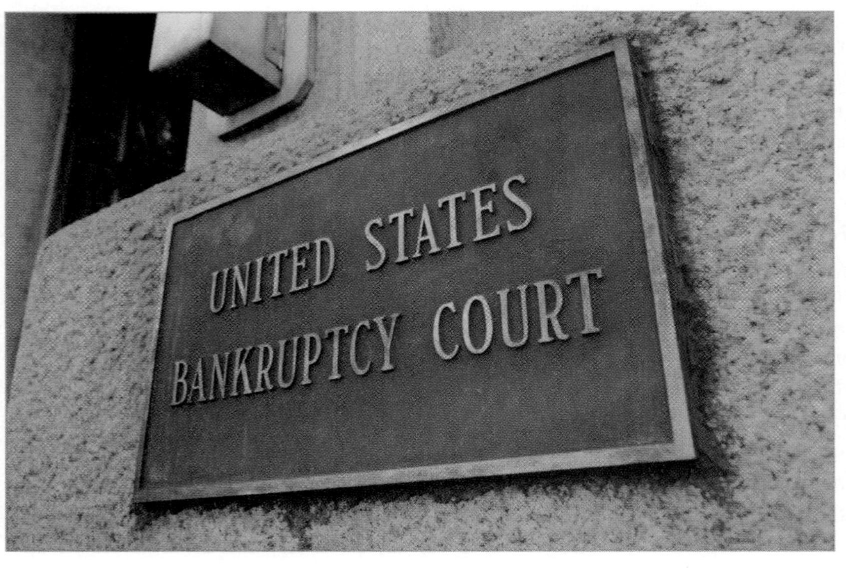

Walkaways

A **walkaway** describes the single most typical way businesses close down. Walkaways are businesses that close down with all debts paid. The entrepreneur might consider the business successful or unsuccessful at closing. About one-third of closing firms, around 600,000 a year, are considered by their owners to be successful, with the business ending voluntarily, often due to illness, old age, family moves, and choosing new opportunities.[28]

A successful walkaway depends on the owner having completed meeting all the firm's financial and organizational obligations. The goal in closing a business is "doing it right"—being able to walk away from the business with a sense of satisfaction.[29] The factors that lead to this include:

- All bills are paid off (or scheduled).
- All taxes are paid up, and the various levels of government are informed of the closure.
- Contracts, leases, and the like are fulfilled or formally terminated.
- Employees are let go as they find other jobs.
- Assets or inventory are depleted.
- No lawsuits consuming money and time.
- Customers placed so they get needed goods or services.
- If needed, insurance is continued to cover unexpected claims after the firm closes.

While signs like this signal the closing of a firm, it is hard to know from the sign if the firm is ending as a workout, a walkaway or a bankruptcy. Which approach is the most financially positive for the owner?

Workouts and Bankruptcy

In a **workout**, the entrepreneur feels that the business was less than successful, usually because of the result of poor use of the firm's human or financial assets, with an unsatisfying business experience (e.g., not enough leisure time, not enough time for family needs, too much conflict, not good at selling, etc.) the second most likely reason.[30] In a workout the entrepreneur arranges to pay off all debts, often doing this after the business is officially closed. This approach accounts for about one-half of all business closings, or roughly 1 million closings.

workout
A form of business termination in which the firm's legal or financial obligations are not fully met at closing.

In preparing the workout, the owner personally makes arrangements to pay off creditors. Often this involves asking for extended terms and smaller payments. The money for these payments might come from the sale or refinancing of a home, through selling business and personal assets, cashing out pensions or stocks, money from personal bank loans, or credit card advances. Most often, the funds come from a mixture of these efforts as well as from paychecks as the former owner becomes an employee for someone else.

In walkaways and workouts, a key goal for entrepreneurs is to maintain their goodwill and reputation in the business community, often as a means of maintaining trust for future entrepreneurial efforts. All small businesses face tough times, and entrepreneurs are often willing to extend terms to a former entrepreneur (and customer) who has fallen on hard times. As long as they feel confident they will get their money from the former owner and their own cash situation is not life-or-death tight, they are likely to accept extended terms.

When facing severe difficulties in arranging a payback, one worthwhile strategy is to enlist the aid of a consumer credit bureau. These agencies provide low-cost debt reduction advice and have experience in negotiating repayment schedules and making credit bureaus aware of debt remediation efforts. A good source for finding these bureaus in your area is to use the website of the National Foundation for Credit Counseling (www.nfcc.org/), which is the professional association for nonprofit credit counseling agencies. Your local Small Business Development Center can also refer you to local credit counseling agencies with small business experience.

In the more extreme cases of closing, entrepreneurs are so far in debt at the business's end that they have little or no chance to earn the money to pay back all the major debts. In such cases owners and firms need to declare bankruptcy. Because bankruptcy is a formal legal situation and one handled in the courts, it is important to involve a lawyer early in the process. The lawyer will not only help you work out the legal papers but will advise you on restructuring your debt and taking other actions to protect as much of your personal assets as possible.

Bankruptcy, you will recall from Chapters 13 and 14, is the legal form of insolvency, where liabilities are greater than assets. There are three forms of bankruptcy: Chapter 7, Chapter 11, and Chapter 13. Chapter 11 bankruptcy is the type you hear about big businesses declaring. It allows the firm to reorganize its operations and renegotiate with creditors to forgive some of the debt (desirable, but not legally required of the creditors) and lengthen payments for the remaining debt. Small firms can apply for Chapter 11, but the high costs of administering a Chapter 11 bankruptcy makes it rare in small businesses.

reorganization
The popular name for a Chapter 13 bankruptcy in which a bankrupt firm continues to operate while paying off debts identified by the bankruptcy trustee.

A more common variant for smaller firms is **reorganization** using a Chapter 13 bankruptcy. Like Chapter 11, the firm stays in business, and the remaining debt gets renegotiated so that a portion of it is forgiven if the remainder is paid off from your income over a set period of time. The bankruptcy court has to approve your filing Chapter 13 before you can, and there are several limits as to the amount and type of debt you face.

liquidation
The popular name for a Chapter 7 bankruptcy in which a bankrupt firm's assets are sold by the bankruptcy trustee and the proceeds used to pay the firm's debts.

If you don't qualify for Chapter 13, you will face a Chapter 7 bankruptcy. It is the well-known example of **liquidation** where all of your assets—business, cars, home—can be sold with the proceeds given to your creditors. You get to keep your clothes and household goods, but little else. That said, if your home or business does not get bought, it reverts back to you. The liquidation is in the hands of a bankruptcy trustee appointed by the court, and the trustee handles all issues. Once a Chapter 7 is completed, all remaining debts are declared discharged or wiped out by the court. In Chapter 11 and 13, you continue paying off debts for years as part of the agreement.

Simply put, if you think your firm is facing bankruptcy, it is important to find and work with a lawyer who specializes in bankruptcy. The area is too complex and specialized for do-it-yourself approaches to work. Also, a bankruptcy specialist can help with workarounds like a workout, which is often a reorganization done contractually without your declaring bankruptcy.

Why try to avoid bankruptcy? Going bankrupt will destroy your credit rating for anywhere from 6 to 10 years. It is public record, so everyone will know you declared bankruptcy, and in many communities it carries a negative social stigma. If you are at heart an entrepreneur, bankruptcy will make it hard for potential investors or creditors to trust you or your business. That said, realize that only a very small minority of all business closings are bankruptcies. That is good news for all of us because the low number of small business bankruptcies sends a message that most entrepreneurs do pay off their debts, which makes it easier for all of us to start businesses with other peoples' money on the line.

serial entrepreneurs
People who open multiple businesses throughout their career.

For entrepreneurs, the message of harvesting is an upbeat one. Of the 4 million firms that will change hands or close down this year, almost half will make the entrepreneurs richer, through sale and succession. Another quarter will have benefited from their businesses, and walk away ready to start their next firm. And start them they do. There is a special term for those owners who start multiple businesses in their careers—**serial entrepreneurs**. What do these entrepreneurs know? For those who are determined not only to survive but also to truly do well, the key is recognizing and building a firm along the lines of the critical success factors for small business.

The Not-So-Secret Secrets of Success

LO4 Know the firm-level critical success factors for small business.

Ask entrepreneurs what they hope to achieve and the universal answer is "success." But what is the measure of success for a business firm? One of the most famous models for success was offered by Daniel Katz and Robert Kahn. They suggest that the measure of success for any organization in the short term is profit, and in the long term is survival. In practice however, new businesses often face challenges in the reverse. In the short term their greatest need is to survive, even if there is no profit. For example, the typical mail order business will not show a profit for three to five years, according to John Schulte, chairman of the National Mail Order Association (NMOA).[31] The key for new firms is to do those things that will help them survive so that they get to the longer term, when to prove their legitimacy as a business, they need to show a profit.

Over the years the experience of small business consultants, experts, and researchers has converged on a set of critical success factors for small business.[32] Critical success factors (CSF) are processes, benchmarks, or components of the business that are essential for the business to be profitable and competitive in its market. They are by definition best practices for a given industry.

CSFs are important because they come from sources external to entrepreneurs, who are prone to biases in assessing the causes of success and failure in their businesses.[33] CSFs fall into two broad types—outside help and entrepreneurial experience. The CSFs below will seem familiar to you because they have been some of the major pieces of advice we have offered throughout the book. As we conclude our thinking about small business, it makes a lot of sense to bring together some of the most important CSFs that are under the control of the entrepreneur and give the firm the greatest possible chance of success.

EXHIBIT 20.1

How to Get Help

- Contact your local SBDC or SCORE or economic development office.
- Join the trade or professional association for your industry and get help or referrals from it.
- Ask successful entrepreneurs for advice and referrals.
- Talk to a lawyer or accountant or other for-profit expert.

To put it simply, help helps. People who get help from experts are far more likely to survive and achieve profitability than those who do not. Consider this. While the SBA has reported that 50 percent of owner-only firms fail in four years, 81.5 percent of clients of Small Business Development Centers are still going strong five years after starting.[34] As noted in the first chapter, 87 percent of incubator based start-ups are still going after five years.[35] See Exhibit 20.1 above for a listing of good sources for help. Time and time again similarly positive results are reported for students taking entrepreneurship and small business courses,[36] proving that small business education works.

The more you know, the better the chances for your firm to succeed. This can come from formal education past high school[37] (like this course) or from working in the industry or market. Anything that gives you the kinds of entrepreneurial or managerial competencies[38] (discussed in Chapter 3) or social[39] or networking[40] skills (discussed in Chapter 2) needed to start and run a business is useful.

But there is also a collection of other CSFs that have been repeatedly shown to be important. These CSFs help identify those businesses more likely to survive. These include:

- **Being incorporated:** Because incorporation usually involves a lawyer, who is likely to give small business owners advice and help them avoid some of the major pitfalls of a new firm.[41]
- **Employees:** Because employees are a way to get more done, to appeal to a larger market, a great source of expertise and feedback, as well as a larger responsibility, which usually means the owner has to make more sales to pay wages.[42]
- **Extreme start-up capital:** Businesses starting with no start-up capital and those starting with more than $50,000 are among those most likely to survive long term.[43] For those with the higher amounts, getting those funds implies prior hard work, and funds that size indicate a major investment, one an owner is more likely to work hard to protect. On the other hand, bootstrap entrepreneurs, who start with nothing, are likely to keep overhead low, live on a shoestring, and build their business over the long term, or change tracks quickly when new opportunities arise. The folks in the middle are those most likely to be undercapitalized for their industry and start-up situation.
- **Protectable intellectual property:** Such as patents or trademarks show preparation for the business, a potential asset, and implied expert assistance.[44]
- **Brand name affiliations or partners:** Having a major brand name shows that you have been checked out and found to be acceptable. It also increases the chances of favorable customer response.[45]
- **Optimal strategies:** Picking to start a business in a growing industry offers above average prospects of business growth.[46] Pursuing an imitator strategy shows a lower risk and greater learning from the mistakes of pioneers.[47]
- **Presales:** Perhaps the strongest benchmark is to have proven your idea through sales—in a pilot test, or through contracts, orders, or letters of intent from customers.[48]

Few businesses achieve all CSFs, but they provide a checklist for running your business in a way that increases its chances for survival. In addition, many of these CSFs are visible to customers, suppliers, and financiers, and convey the idea that you are running your business in a manner likely to lead to continued success.

Measuring Success with Four Bottom Lines

LO5 Understand what success means with the quadruple bottom line.

Originally, the *bottom line* referred to the profitability of a business, figured from the financial statements. For more than a hundred years in the thinking of economists, financiers, and accountants, it had been the ultimate and sovereign criterion of business success.

Today entrepreneurs and consultants realize that success can no longer be measured solely in terms of profits.[49] Financial success in business with a miserable family life or profits at the expense of public approval represent forms of "success" that leave a lot to be desired. There are four domains in which balanced entrepreneurs need to achieve success to be truly happy: the firm, the community, the family, and their own life.

But the bottom line concept, with its implication of some sort of adding up of pluses and minuses, still makes a lot of sense as a way for entrepreneurs to think about their business and life. In this section we talk about the four bottom lines of business—the firm, the community, the family, and the entrepreneur.

The Firm

Once started, it often seems that a firm takes on a life of its own. That is not surprising. Social systems researchers tell us that firms, as well as other types of groups, are living systems. Just as we think of a nation or culture as a living, growing entity, businesses are too.[50] As noted earlier, Daniel Katz and Robert Kahn suggest that the short-term measure of success for any organization is profit with survival the long-term measure, but in reality these are probably reversed for small businesses just starting out because new firms need to survive long enough to generate a profit. In effect, in order to succeed, you need to survive.

Entrepreneurs have the opportunity to define the level of profit that they seek. There are generally three levels: **supplemental profits** are intended as a secondary income for the entrepreneur, who has another job which provides his or her main income; **substitution profits** are intended to equal and replace the salary or wages the entrepreneur could draw working for someone else; **success profits** represent income levels higher than the person could make working for others.

supplemental profits
Returns above costs intended as a secondary income for entrepreneurs (where self-employment is secondary to their main job).

substitution profits
Returns intended to equal and replace the salary or wages the entrepreneur could draw working for someone else.

success profits
Returns at levels higher than the entrepreneur could make working for others.

The other measures of firm success can come from leadership of the industry. This can come through inventions and patents the business holds, which show its thought leadership, or from positions in professional and trade associations or in the marketplace, which make the firm distinctive in the eyes of customers and competitors.

For small businesses with employees, employee satisfaction and well being become a big part of the measure of success. Typically owners and employees in small businesses become a business family, with the owner taking on the parental role and responsibility. Making sure that the employees are taken care of becomes a key measure of success. In the opening vignette, at Shoppers' Service one of the key goals before closing down the firm was to first find a job for the one remaining employee.

Community

In the end, every small business is a part of its larger community, and one of the ways success gets measured is how the business relates to its community. Simply put, is the community better off for having the business present? In businesses operating for the long term, managing this bottom line is important to some extent. Few businesses operate to maximize the social bottom line over the profit one, but taking steps to be seen as a net benefit to the community is an expenditure worth making in the long run.

In small business, doing good takes many forms. In Chapter 2, we talk about five areas in which firms want to do good:

- Community impact, such as providing jobs to employees, business for other firms, and goods and services to customers.
- Building trust, such as through dependability and "doing the right thing."
- Promoting a positive culture, such as through promoting hard work, fair treatment, and developing the industry, market, and community.

- Enhancing flexibility by increasing the firm's and community's ability to respond to changes in the marketplace, economy, and environment.
- Fostering innovation, which is the basis for increasing profits, services, or goods offered, and competitive ability.

But many small business owners find themselves taking a more active role in the community, through charitable works, sponsoring others as they do good, and taking steps to ensure that the community remains a good place to be. This can range from picking up trash around the business to promoting professional standards and self-monitoring in the trade or industry association to taking a stand on issues important to the community.

Adopting a highway is one way a small business can show its community-mindedness. What other ways do you recall seeing locally?

Family

Time and time again, family has been shown to be the area that entrepreneurs worry about the most.[51] Running a business is time consuming, and often the demands of customers mean that the entrepreneur cannot control the schedule. Often that time comes out of family time. Making sure that you spend the time with your family and tackle the issues of communication and commitment that often underlie family problems is the key to success in this factor.

It is not easy. Reflecting on her years as founder and president of Tocquigny Advertising, Interactive and Marketing, in Austin, Texas, Yvonne Tocquigny observes, "I sometimes had a difficult time adjusting to the slower, gentler pace of home and was impatient and less nurturing than I should have been."[52]

Often the key is to leave personal time to make the transition from work to family—clearing your work list and your mind. It also helps to declare certain times as ones when you are unavailable, either letting others fill in, or letting voice mail take the messages.

Another key factor is keeping a portion of family time free of business issues, especially when other family members are involved in the business. Family time needs to be focused on the family, not the family business.[53]

Note that some entrepreneurs work best when combining family and work, while others work best when each is separate.[54] While you might quickly recognize which type you are, the measure of success is not based on your preference, but on that of your family. If your family complains that you do not seem to "be all here," then you are integrating too much and need to segregate business and family life more.

Yourself

So far, the domains discussed—the firm, the community, and the family—are external environments for the entrepreneur. You and your personal goals and desires count, too. They deserve the same chance for success that you strive for in the other settings. Part of what makes owning a small business rewarding to the entrepreneur is the possibility of personal returns—the fourth bottom line. Returns to the entrepreneur reflect the kinds of outcomes that the individual values. In Chapter 1, you learned about the rewards mentioned by most entrepreneurs—flexibility, income, and growth—as well as a collection of rewards that crop up occasionally, things like admiration, recognition, wealth, product creation, power, and family.[55]

The returns to the entrepreneur can include these and much more. Consider fun as an outcome. Sergey Brin and Larry Page of Google actually delayed growing their business to the IPO stage because they were afraid of having less fun when they became a public company.[56]

In the end, entrepreneurs go into business with a variety of expectations, dreams, and goals. A large reason for much of what we do—schooling, marrying, raising children, helping the community, and perhaps most of all, working—is to help us achieve those dreams. Entrepreneurship is one area in which, because you create the business and its goals, you have your best chance of capturing or creating your dream. Because of that, to be a successful entrepreneur, you need to be able to achieve those things in your life that are important to you.

Often the biggest risk to achieving that dream is getting caught up in the thousands of immediate demands on your time, attention, and life. Keeping track of your personal bottom line requires two key actions from yourself—keeping the dream alive and occasionally assessing yourself from the perspective of your dream.

Keeping the dream alive starts with giving a name to your dream and putting that name somewhere where you can remind yourself about your own personal ultimate goal. The other part is to schedule a meeting with yourself every once in a while—perhaps quarterly for a start—to assess how you are doing in achieving your dream and what you should do to help yourself.

Simply put, when you talk with entrepreneurs who consider themselves completely successful, you will find that they talk about what they were able to accomplish in their business, their community, their family, and their personal life. Knowing the four areas where success is critical, you can begin to think about how well you are achieving in each and begin the process for working up a plan to maximize your achievement of all forms of success. The procedure for doing this is discussed in Skill Module 20.1.

SKILL MODULE 20.1 Assessing the Four Bottom Lines

As discussed in this chapter, the four bottom lines of business refer to yourself, your family, your firm, and your society or community. In planning a business or evaluating it every once in a while (say once or twice a year), it makes sense to think about how well you and your business are doing at meeting the four bottom lines. Here is how to do it:

1. For yourself, pick the two or three personal goals you have for the business. Ask yourself what it is that you want to achieve through running your business or what you would miss the most if it were gone. List these.
2. For your family, ask what family members want from you personally (time with you, money to support their efforts and needs, etc.). List these.
3. For your firm, there are always three items of critical importance—profits, how well the firm does its job (making or selling products or services—this is based on customer and industry information), and how satisfied are the people involved in the business (owners and employees).
4. For your community, there are also clear indicators of outcome—economic contributions (profits, salaries, taxes), quality of life contributions (lack of pollution, providing needed products or services, supporting civic betterment), and industrial contributions (supporting the industry, operating responsibly, developing the industry through innovation and improvement).

In the matrix in Table 20.1 you can see that to evaluate these goals you need two pieces of information for each. The first is some sort of metric—a way to measure the degree of achievement. Despite the name, metrics do not have to be "hard" measures like dollars or customers. Opinions are acceptable, and behaviors are even better. With a metric in hand, you are ready to get the second piece of information, the achievement level. This is how you have scored on the metric. To really understand how well your firm is doing on all four bottom lines, you will want to ask others for their assessment on relevant goals. In the end, the evaluation of your business is your opinion, but checking your perceptions against those of knowledgeable others can help you identify areas for improvement and reinforce your recognition of areas of achievement.

TABLE 20.1 The Four Bottom Lines

Area	Goal	Metric	Achievement Level
Yourself	Feel in control of my life	Personal opinion	Achieved
Family	Have time for spouse and children	Their opinions	Spouse—Not Achieved Child (Ann)—Achieved Child (Roger)—Not Achieved
Firm	Profits or take outs	Practical income of $75,000 in cash or services a year	$71,000
Community	Satisfied employee Support local charities	Her opinion 5% of sales minimum	"Generally yes" 4.88%

Conclusion

The quadruple bottom line does a wonderful job of showing how starting and running your own small business can reward not only you, but your family, your firm, and your community. It is a means to gain control over the working portion of your life, and perhaps even all of it. It offers communities services and goods, employment, and innovations that make all our lives better. Doing a small business well is not easy. Even knowing the critical success factors for small firms does not mean that you can develop or achieve them. That means that in every small business effort there is always an element of risk.

But millions look at the prospects and decide to take those risks—nearly 40 million people in 2003, with 27 million already self-employed and another 13 million who have been, or are planning to be again. Why do so many do this? The answer is simple—because they want to and they can! Today, with the ready availability of help and the many ways to get into small business with less financial and personal risk than ever before, the chances for success in small business have never been higher.

And the returns from small business have never been greater. The opportunity to work your own way, with flexibility and support, increases as more different types of people, technologies, and businesses remake entrepreneurship for the twenty-first century. The chance for people to learn the right way to run businesses, whether part time or full time, local or global, has never been greater. Classes like the one you've taken and resources like the ones in this book are just the start. Having the right help can help, and now you know the kind of help available to you. You can do this. The time to do it is right now.

CHAPTER SUMMARY

LO1 Recognize the stages of the small business life cycle.

- Every firm goes through a similar sequence of developmental stages.
- Emergence comes before the firm starts, followed by existence.
- Survival happens to most firms, as does resource maturity.
- Some firms experience the takeoff stage, but most do not.
- Each stage poses a distinct challenge to the small business and owner.

LO2 Consider the impact of the product life cycle.

- Like the Industry Life Cycle, the stages of the Product Life Cycle include introduction, growth, maturity, and decline.
- From a marketing viewpoint, the different stages tell us about the competition and how to focus the individual elements of the marketing plan—product, price, promotion, and distribution.
- As services are usually more able to make incremental changes almost continually, the service life cycle is more typified by a series of mini-product life cycles.

LO3 Understand the options for harvesting or closing the small business.

- Harvests reflect an owner's efforts to take value out of a firm.
- Firms get transferred through sales or family succession.
- Terminations can be walkaways, workouts, or bankruptcies.
- The terminations that have legal repercussions, like bankruptcies, and almost any sort of transfers are complex enough that expert assistance is necessary.
- IPOs, ESOPs, mergers and acquisitions, and other specialized transfer techniques exist but are relatively rarely used.

LO4 Know the firm-level critical success factors for small business.

- Critical success factors are processes, benchmarks, or components of the business that are essential for the business to be profitable and competitive in its market.
- CSFs fall into two broad types—outside help and entrepreneurial experience.
- Specific experience factors that lead to success include being incorporated, having employees, having large or no start-up capital, protectable intellectual property, brand name affiliations, an optimal strategy, and preopening sales.

LO5 Understand what success means with the quadruple bottom line.

- Today entrepreneurs and consultants realize that success can no longer be measured solely in terms of profits.
- There are four domains in which balanced entrepreneurs need to achieve success to be truly happy: the firm, the community, the family, and their own life.
- Auditing the four bottom lines requires specifying the goal, the metric, and the achievement level.

KEY TERMS

business life cycle, 656
liability of newness, 657
slack resources, 657
harvest, 662
initial public offering (IPO), 662
consolidation, 662
employee stock ownership plan, 662
transfer, 663
termination, 663
liquidity enhancement, 663
tax management, 663
estate freeze, 663
bankruptcy, 664
walkaways, 664
workout, 665
reorganization, 665
liquidation, 666
serial entrepreneurs, 666
supplemental profits, 668
substitution profits, 668
success profits, 668

DISCUSSION QUESTIONS

1. What is the difference between a lifestyle business and a traditional small business?
2. What are some of the differences between a lifestyle business and a high-performing small business?
3. What are the stages of the small business life cycle? What stage do high-growth ventures go through that other forms of small business do not?
4. Pick one good and one service at each stage of the product life cycle. How did you conclude it was at that stage?
5. What is the difference between a transfer and a termination?
6. From the entrepreneur's perspective, what is the major reason for preferring a transfer of the business to a termination?
7. What are the key business characteristics needed for a successful walkaway?
8. Identify and compare three critical success factors for small businesses.
9. What are the four bottom lines of small business?
10. In assessing the four bottom lines, what is the difference between the goal and its metric? Why is each needed?

EXPERIENTIAL EXERCISES

1. Look up businesses for sale in an industry of your choice (or the industry assigned you by your professor), at a site such as **www.bizbuysell.com**. What kind of information does the website provide you? List three additional pieces of information you would most want to get. Can you think of other online or print resources you could use to find this information, such as online business databases your library has? Try and find at least one of these key pieces of information using these other resources.
2. Make your list of your personal goals for the "yourself" assessment in the quadruple bottom line exercise. Compare this list to the major reasons people give for going into business

(covered in Chapter 1). Which of your goals overlap the popular reasons and which are unique to yourself?

3. One of the most common ways to evaluate firm success is by profitability. Use a financial database such as the Risk Management Association's *Annual Statement Studies* to find out target profitability levels for your business.

MINI-CASE

TIM HAYDEN, VIVID SKY AND SKYBOX IN JULY 2009

It was the summer of 2009 and Tim had to make a decision. He had started with an idea of using advanced electronics to make any seat in the stadium "the best seat in the house." To do that he created SkyBOX, a program for displaying game videos, sports statistics, and interactive fan-focused social networking (like votes, chats, etc.) inside sports venues. In 2003 SkyBOX was imagined as a rental fleet of PDAs "hardened" against spills and drops and fed data through a Wi-Fi installation put into participating stadia. By 2009 the idea morphed into an application which could be run on 3G cell phones like the iPhone as well as personal computers equipped with cellular Wi-Fi.

SkyBOX was a darling of DEMO 2006, and could point to over 80 articles and news segments extolling the idea, the technology, and the charismatic founder behind it. *Inc.* magazine had profiled Vivid Sky in their 2006 valuation story. Pilot tests with the St. Louis Cardinals (Tim's hometown team), the Detroit Tigers, and the Detroit Redwings in 2007 and 2008 had been very successful. Since 2008 SkyBOX was on sale online at the iPhone Applications Store and had sold several hundred copies. In terms of buzz and media appreciation, SkyBOX was a winner.

The financial situation was the problem. Tim had sunk all his own money into Vivid Sky to bring it to market. He had advertisers lined up and ready to buy visibility on SkyBOX. He had access to the baseball, football, basketball, and hockey stadia, but he needed $1,000,000 to deploy the system. He had gotten half the funding from his family, local friends, and friends of friends, but the economic downturn meant he had been unable to get the remaining $500,000 investment from any of the Fortune 1000 firms looking at SkyBOX.

Tim had run out of money, again (he refused to use the $500,000 from family and friends unless he had the match). Tim pledged to keep looking for a way to get SkyBOX operational but, in the meantime, he found his four programmer employees jobs with firms he had dealt with along the way. One of those firms, a local sports conglomerate, called Tim with an offer—chief marketing officer of the conglomerate reporting to the CEO, and sporting a six-figure salary of his own. They needed an answer tomorrow.

Meanwhile, a group from the advanced technology team at one of the biggest media companies was asking Tim if he would be willing to sell them the SkyBOX technology so they can incorporate it into their cell phone offerings. No hard numbers have been given yet, but they are also interested in hiring back the four programmers and would be giving Tim ongoing consulting contracts. But try as he might, Tim couldn't get a go/no-go date from this group. He had just hung up on another one of those exhilarating and frustrating calls.

As he had so often in the six years shepherding SkyBOX to reality, Tim sat back and asked himself, "What's the entrepreneurial thing to do?"

CASE DISCUSSION QUESTIONS

1. Should Tim use the $500,000 raised to keep SkyBOX going until he can find other funding? Explain your reasoning.

2. In terms of the business outcomes shown in Figure 20.3, which outcomes is Tim's firm facing at this point?

3. Is there an entrepreneurial solution to dealing with both the chief marketing officer job offer and SkyBOX? Explain your reasoning.

SUGGESTED CASES AND ARTICLES

- Joseph Shaughnessy, BSI Constructors, St. Louis, C-21

Available on McGraw-Hill Create™:

- Dice, Inc.

SUGGESTED VIDEOS

www.mhhe.com/katz4e

Video Case:

- For a written video case and corresponding clip, visit the OLC at www.mhhe.com/katz4e and select "Chapter 20".
- Entrepreneurs and Failure

SBTV.com Videos:

- Dissolving a Corporation
- A Living Trust for the Small Business Owner
- Retirement Considerations Interview

STVP Videos:

- Exit Strategies Now and Then
- Difficult Negotiations
- Seeing Failure as Opportunity

Income Statements Years 1–3

YEAR 1
Income Statement
Accrual Basis

	January	February	March	April	May	June	July	August	September	October	November	December
REVENUES												
Cash sales	400	600	400	800	800	600	600	8,205	8,205	8,205	8,205	7,459
Charge sales	-	-	-	-	-	-	-	-	-	-	-	-
TOTAL SALES	400	600	400	800	800	600	600	8,205	8,205	8,205	8,205	7,459
COST OF GOODS SOLD	100	150	100	200	200	148	148	2,017	2,017	2,017	2,017	1,834
GROSS PROFIT	300	450	300	600	600	452	452	6,188	6,188	6,188	6,188	5,625
Direct Expenses												
Salaries & Wages	480	480	480	480	480	$480	$480	$4,141	$4,141	$4,141	$4,141	$4,141
Payroll taxes/benefits	42	42	42	42	42	42	42	358	358	358	358	358
Rent	$420	$280	$420	$490	$560	$560	$560	1,000	1,000	1,000	1,000	1,000
Spoilage	-	-	-	-				94	94	94	94	86
Telephone	310	110	110	110	110	110	110	110	110	110	110	110
Transportation						343	343	343	343	343	343	343
Insurance	167	167	167	167	167	167	167	167	167	167	167	167
Bad debt expense	-	-	-	-	-	-	-	-	-	-	-	-
TOTAL DIRECT EXPENSES	1,418	1,078	1,218	1,288	1,358	1,702	1,702	6,214	6,214	6,214	6,214	6,205
OPERATING MARGIN	(1,118)	(628)	(918)	(688)	(758)	(1,249)	(1,249)	(26)	(26)	(26)	(26)	(580)
General & Admin. Expenses												
Salaries	-	-	-	-	-	-	-	-	-	-	-	-
Payroll taxes/benefits	-	-	-	-	-	-	-	-	-	-	-	-
Rent	-	-	-	-	-	-	-	-	-	-	-	-
Utilities	-	-	-	-	-	-	-	-	-	-	-	-
Telephone	-	-	-	-	-	-	-	-	-	-	-	-
Transportation	-	-	-	-	-	-	-	-	-	-	-	-
Insurance	-	-	-	-	-	-	-	-	-	-	-	-
Legal & Accounting	2,703	35	35	35	35	35	35	35	35	35	35	35
	-	-	-	-	-	-	-	-	-	-	-	-
Marketing	2,135	64	25	64	25	25	25	275	25	75	102	25
Baking Equiptment Purchases	1,965	-	-	-	-	-	-	-	-	-	-	-
Equipment leases	-	-	-	-	-	-	-	-	-	-	-	-
Depreciation– Building	-	-	-	-	-	-	-	-	-	-	-	-
Depreciation– Equipment	7	19	19	27	214	214	214	214	214	214	214	214
TOTAL G&A	6,810	118	79	125	274	274	274	524	274	324	351	274
EBIT (Earnings Before Interest & Taxes)	(7,928)	(746)	(998)	(814)	(1,032)	(1,523)	(1,523)	(550)	(300)	(350)	(377)	(854)
Interest Expense	-	-	-	-	-	-	-	-	-	-	-	-
EARNINGS BEFORE TAXES	(7,928)	(746)	(998)	(814)	(1,032)	(1,523)	(1,523)	(550)	(300)	(350)	(377)	(854)

(Continued)

YEAR 2
Income Statement
Accrual Basis

	January	February	March	April	May	June	July	August	September	October	November	December	TOTAL
REVENUES													
Cash sales	7,459	7,459	9,696	9,696	9,696	12,307	12,307	12,307	10,666	10,666	10,666	9,025	121,951
Charge sales	-	-	-	-	-	-	-	-	-	-	-	-	-
TOTAL SALES	7,459	7,459	9,696	9,696	9,696	12,307	12,307	12,307	10,666	10,666	10,666	9,025	121,951
COST OF GOODS SOLD	1,834	1,834	2,384	2,384	2,384	3,026	3,026	3,026	2,622	2,622	2,622	2,219	29,980
GROSS PROFIT	5,625	5,625	7,313	7,313	7,313	9,281	9,281	9,281	8,044	8,044	8,044	6,806	91,970
Direct Expenses													
Salaries & Wages	$4,141	$4,141	$4,141	$4,141	$4,141	$4,141	$4,141	4,397	4,397	4,397	4,397	4,397	50,974
Payroll taxes/benefits	358	358	358	358	358	358	358	380	380	380	380	380	4,409
Rent	1,000	1,000	1,000	1,000	1,000	1,000	1,000	1,000	1,000	1,000	1,000	1,000	12,000
Spoilage	86	86	112	112	112	129	129	129	112	112	112	94	1,323
													-
Telephone	110	110	110	110	110	110	110	110	110	110	110	110	1,320
Transportation	343	343	343	343	343	343	343	343	343	343	343	343	4,120
Insurance	167	167	167	167	167	167	167	167	167	167	167	167	2,000
Bad debt expense	-	-	-	-	-	-	-	-	-	-	-	-	-
TOTAL DIRECT EXPENSES	6,205	6,205	6,231	6,231	6,231	6,248	6,248	6,526	6,509	6,509	6,509	6,492	76,146
OPERATING MARGIN	(580)	(580)	1,082	1,082	1,082	3,033	3,033	2,755	1,535	1,535	1,535	314	15,824
General & Admin. Expenses													
Salaries	-	-	-	-	-	-	-	-	-	-	-	-	504
Payroll taxes/benefits	-	-	-	-	-	-	-	-	-	-	-	-	-
Rent	-	-	-	-	-	-	-	-	-	-	-	-	-
Utilities	-	-	-	-	-	-	-	-	-	-	-	-	-
													-
Telephone	-	-	-	-	-	-	-	-	-	-	-	-	-
Transportation	-	-	-	-	-	-	-	-	-	-	-	-	-
Insurance	-	-	-	-	-	-	-	-	-	-	-	-	-
Legal & Accounting	35	35	35	35	35	35	35	35	35	35	35	35	420
	-	-	-	-	-	-	-	-	-	-	-	-	-
Marketing	25	64	25	64	25	25	25	25	25	75	102	25	504
Baking Equiptment Purchases	1,197	-	-	-	-	-	-	-	-	-	-	-	1,197
Equipment leases	-	-	-	-	-	-	-	-	-	-	-	-	-
Depreciation– Building	-	-	-	-	-	-	-	-	-	-	-	-	-
Depreciation– Equipment	214	214	214	214	214	214	214	214	214	214	214	214	2,564
TOTAL G&A	1,470	312	274	312	274	274	274	274	274	324	351	274	5,189
EBIT (Earnings Before Interest & Taxes)	(2,050)	(892)	808	769	808	2,760	2,760	2,481	1,261	1,211	1,184	41	10,635
Interest Expense	-	-	-	-	-	-	-	-	-	-	-	-	-
EARNINGS BEFORE TAXES	(2,050)	(892)	808	769	808	2,760	2,760	2,481	1,261	1,211	1,184	41	10,635

YEAR 3
Income Statement
Accrual Basis

	January	February	March	April	May	June	July	August	September	October	November	December	TOTAL
REVENUES													
Cash sales	9,025	9,025	13,948	13,948	13,948	14,440	14,440	14,440	12,635	12,635	12,635	11,733	152,852
Charge sales	-	-	-	-	-	-	-	-	-	-	-	-	-
TOTAL SALES	9,025	9,025	13,948	13,948	13,948	14,440	14,440	14,440	12,635	12,635	12,635	11,733	152,852
COST OF GOODS SOLD	2,219	2,219	3,429	3,429	3,429	3,550	3,550	3,550	3,106	3,106	3,106	2,884	37,577
GROSS PROFIT	6,806	6,806	10,519	10,519	10,519	10,890	10,890	10,890	9,529	9,529	9,529	8,848	115,275
Direct Expenses													
Salaries & Wages	4,397	4,397	4,397	4,397	4,397	4,397	4,397	8,307	8,307	8,307	8,307	8,307	72,317
Payroll taxes/benefits	380	380	380	380	380	380	380	719	719	719	719	719	6,255
Rent	1,000	1,000	1,000	1,000	1,000	1,000	1,000	1,150	1,150	1,150	1,150	1,150	12,750
Spoilage	94	94	146	146	146	137	137	137	120	120	120	112	1,512
													-
Telephone	110	110	110	110	110	110	110	110	110	110	110	110	1,320
Transportation	343	343	343	343	343	343	343	343	343	343	343	343	4,120
Insurance	167	167	167	167	167	167	167	167	167	167	167	167	2,000
Bad debt expense	-	-	-	-	-	-	-	-	-	-	-	-	-
TOTAL DIRECT EXPENSES	6,492	6,492	6,544	6,544	6,544	6,535	6,535	10,933	10,916	10,916	10,916	10,908	100,274
OPERATING MARGIN	314	314	3,975	3,975	3,975	4,355	4,355	(43)	(1,387)	(1,387)	(1,387)	(2,059)	15,001
General & Admin. Expenses													
Salaries	-	-	-	-	-	-	-	-	-	-	-	-	-
Payroll taxes/benefits	-	-	-	-	-	-	-	-	-	-	-	-	-
Rent	-	-	-	-	-	-	-	-	-	-	-	-	-
Utilities	-	-	-	-	-	-	-	-	-	-	-	-	-
													-
Telephone	-	-	-	-	-	-	-	-	-	-	-	-	-
Transportation	-	-	-	-	-	-	-	-	-	-	-	-	-
Insurance	-	-	-	-	-	-	-	-	-	-	-	-	-
Legal & Accounting	35	35	35	35	35	35	35	35	35	35	35	35	420
	-	-	-	-	-	-	-	-	-	-	-	-	-
Marketing	25	64	25	64	25	25	25	25	25	75	102	25	504
Baking Equiptment Purchases	1,197	-	-	-	-	-	-	-	-	-	-	-	1,197
Equipment leases	-	-	-	-	-	-	-	-	-	-	-	-	-
Depreciation– Building	-	-	-	-	-	-	-	-	-	-	-	-	-
Depreciation– Equipment	214	214	214	214	214	214	214	214	214	214	214	214	2,564
TOTAL G&A	1,470	312	274	312	274	274	274	274	274	324	351	274	4,685
EBIT (Earnings Before Interest & Taxes)	(1,156)	2	3,702	3,663	3,702	4,082	4,082	(317)	(1,661)	(1,711)	(1,738)	(2,333)	10,316
Interest Expense	-	-	-	-	-	-	-	-	-	-	-	-	-
EARNINGS BEFORE TAXES	(1,156)	2	3,702	3,663	3,702	4,082	4,082	(317)	(1,661)	(1,711)	(1,738)	(2,333)	10,316

Cash Flow Projections Years 1–3

CASH FLOW - Year 1	January	February	March	April	May	June	July	August	September	October	November	December
Cash flow from operations												
Receipts												
Cash sales	400	600	400	800	800	600	600	8,205	8,205	8,205	8,205	7,459
Accounts Receivable collections	-	-	-	-	-	-	-	-	-	-	-	-
Total receipts	400	600	400	800	800	600	600	8,205	8,205	8,205	8,205	7,459
Disbursements												
Prior month's inventory purchases	-	100	150	100	200	200	148	148	2,017	2,017	2,017	2,017
Direct expenses except bad debt	1,418	1,078	1,218	1,288	1,358	1,702	1,702	6,214	6,214	6,214	6,214	6,205
G&A except depreciation	6,803	99	60	99	60	60	60	310	60	110	137	60
Interest on long-term debt	-	-	-	-	-	-	-	-	-	-	-	-
Total disbursements	8,221	1,277	1,428	1,487	1,618	1,962	1,909	6,671	8,291	8,341	8,368	8,282
Net cash flow from operations	(7,821)	(677)	(1,028)	(687)	(818)	(1,362)	(1,309)	1,533	(86)	(136)	(163)	(824)
Cash flow from investing activities												
Purchase of Land	-	-	-	-	-	-	-	-	-	-	-	-
Purchase of Building	-	-	-	-	-	-	-	-	-	-	-	-
Purchase of Equipment	(1,086)	(1,739)	-	(1,086)	(28,700)	-	-	-	-	-	-	-
Net cash flow from investing activities	(1,086)	(1,739)	-	(1,086)	(28,700)	-	-	-	-	-	-	-
Cash flow from financing activities												
Investment by owners	50,000	-	-	-	-	-	-	-	-	-	-	-
Long-term loan additions(payments)	-	-	-	-	-	-	-	-	-	-	-	-
Net cash flow from long-term financing activities	50,000	-	-	-	-	-	-	-	-	-	-	-
Net cash increase(decrease)	41,093	(2,416)	(1,028)	(1,773)	(29,518)	(1,362)	(1,309)	1,533	(86)	(136)	(163)	(824)
Short-term Loan increase(decrease)	-	-	-	-	-	4	1,309	(1,313)	-	2	163	824
Beginning cash	-	41,093	38,677	37,649	35,876	6,358	5,000	5,000	5,220	5,134	5,000	5,000
Ending cash	41,093	38,677	37,649	35,876	6,358	5,000	5,000	5,220	5,134	5,000	5,000	5,000

CASH FLOW - Year 2	January	February	March	April	May	June	July	August	September	October	November	December	TOTAL
Cash flow from operations													
Receipts													
Cash sales	7,459	7,459	9,696	9,696	9,696	12,307	12,307	12,307	10,666	10,666	10,666	9,025	121,951
Accounts Receivable collections	-	-	-	-	-	-	-	-	-	-	-	-	-
Total receipts	7,459	7,459	9,696	9,696	9,696	12,307	12,307	12,307	10,666	10,666	10,666	9,025	121,951
Disbursements													
Prior month's inventory purchases	1,834	1,834	1,834	2,384	2,384	2,384	3,026	3,026	3,026	2,622	2,622	2,622	29,595
Direct expenses except bad debt	6,205	6,205	6,231	6,231	6,231	6,248	6,248	6,526	6,509	6,509	6,509	6,492	76,146
G&A except depreciation	1,257	99	60	99	60	60	60	60	60	110	137	60	2,121
Interest on long-term debt	-	-	-	-	-	-	-	-	-	-	-	-	-
Total disbursements	9,295	8,138	8,125	8,713	8,675	8,692	9,334	9,612	9,595	9,241	9,269	9,174	107,862
Net cash flow from operations	(1,837)	(679)	1,572	983	1,022	3,615	2,973	2,695	1,071	1,425	1,398	(149)	14,088
Cash flow from investing activities													
Purchase of Land	-	-	-	-	-	-	-	-	-	-	-	-	-
Purchase of Building	-	-	-	-	-	-	-	-	-	-	-	-	-
Purchase of Equipment	-	-	-	-	-	-	-	-	-	-	-	-	-
Net cash flow from investing activities	-	-	-	-	-	-	-	-	-	-	-	-	-
Cash flow from financing activities													
Investment by owners	-	-	-	-	-	-	-	-	-	-	-	-	-
Long-term loan additions(payments)	-	-	-	-	-	-	-	-	-	-	-	-	-
Net cash flow from long-term financing activities	-	-	-	-	-	-	-	-	-	-	-	-	-
Net cash increase(decrease)	(1,837)	(679)	1,572	983	1,022	3,615	2,973	2,695	1,071	1,425	1,398	(149)	14,088
Short-term Loan increase(decrease)	1,837	679	(1,572)	(983)	(950)	-	-	-	-	-	-	-	(989)
Beginning cash	5,000	5,000	5,000	5,000	5,000	5,071	8,686	11,659	14,355	15,426	16,851	18,248	5,000
Ending cash	5,000	5,000	5,000	5,000	5,071	8,686	11,659	14,355	15,426	16,851	18,248	18,099	18,099

(Continued)

CASH FLOW - Year 3	January	February	March	April	May	June	July	August	September	October	November	December	TOTAL
Cash flow from operations													
Receipts													
Cash sales	9,025	9,025	13,948	13,948	13,948	14,440	14,440	14,440	12,635	12,635	12,635	11,733	152,852
Accounts Receivable collections	-	-	-	-	-	-	-	-	-	-	-	-	-
Total receipts	9,025	9,025	13,948	13,948	13,948	14,440	14,440	14,440	12,635	12,635	12,635	11,733	152,852
Disbursements													
Prior month's inventory purchases	2,219	2,219	2,219	3,429	3,429	3,429	3,550	3,550	3,550	3,106	3,106	3,106	36,911
Direct expenses except bad debt	6,492	6,492	6,544	6,544	6,544	6,535	6,535	10,933	10,916	10,916	10,916	10,908	100,274
G&A except depreciation	1,257	99	60	99	60	60	60	60	60	110	137	60	2,121
Interest on long-term debt	-	-	-	-	-	-	-	-	-	-	-	-	-
Total disbursements	9,967	8,809	8,822	10,071	10,032	10,024	10,145	14,543	14,526	14,132	14,160	14,074	139,306
Net cash flow from operations	(942)	216	5,126	3,877	3,915	4,416	4,295	(103)	(1,891)	(1,497)	(1,524)	(2,341)	13,546
Cash flow from investing activities													
Purchase of Land	-	-	-	-	-	-	-	-	-	-	-	-	-
Purchase of Building	-	-	-	-	-	-	-	-	-	-	-	-	-
Purchase of Equipment	-	-	-	-	-	-	-	-	-	-	-	-	-
Net cash flow from investing activities	-	-	-	-	-	-	-	-	-	-	-	-	-
Cash flow from financing activities													
Investment by owners	-	-	-	-	-	-	-	-	-	-	-	-	-
Long-term loan additions(payments)	-	-	-	-	-	-	-	-	-	-	-	-	-
Net cash flow from long-term financing activities	-	-	-	-	-	-	-	-	-	-	-	-	-
Net cash increase(decrease)	(942)	216	5,126	3,877	3,915	4,416	4,295	(103)	(1,891)	(1,497)	(1,524)	(2,341)	13,546
Short-term Loan increase(decrease)	-	-	-	-	-	-	-	-	-	-	-	-	-
Beginning cash	18,099	17,157	17,373	22,498	26,375	30,290	34,707	39,002	38,899	37,008	35,510	33,986	18,099
Ending cash	17,157	17,373	22,498	26,375	30,290	34,707	39,002	38,899	37,008	35,510	33,986	31,645	31,645

Balance Sheet Years 1–3

BALANCE SHEET - Year 1	Balance	January	February	March	April	May	June	July	August	September	October	November	December
Cash	-	41,093	38,677	37,649	35,876	6,358	5,000	5,000	5,220	5,134	5,000	5,000	5,000
Accounts Receivable	-	-	-	-	-	-	-	-	-	-	-	-	-
Inventory	-												
Total Current Assets	-	41,093	38,677	37,649	35,876	6,358	5,000	5,000	5,220	5,134	5,000	5,000	5,000
Land	-	-	-	-	-	-	-	-	-	-	-	-	-
Building	-	-	-	-	-	-	-	-	-	-	-	-	-
Equipment	-	1,086	2,825	2,825	3,911	32,611	32,611	32,611	32,611	32,611	32,611	32,611	32,611
-LESS Accum. Depreciation	-	(7)	(27)	(46)	(73)	(287)	(500)	(714)	(928)	(1,141)	(1,355)	(1,569)	(1,782)
Net Fixed Assets	-	1,079	2,798	2,779	3,838	32,324	32,111	31,897	31,683	31,470	31,256	31,042	30,829
TOTAL ASSETS	-	42,172	41,475	40,428	39,714	38,682	37,111	36,897	36,903	36,603	36,256	36,042	35,829
LIABILITIES													
Accounts payable	-	100	150	100	200	200	148	148	2,017	2,017	2,017	2,017	1,834
Short-term loan inc. interest	-	-	-	-	-	-	4	1,313	-	-	2	166	989
Interest on long-term	-	-	-	-	-	-	-	-	-	-	-	-	-
TOTAL CURRENT	-	100	150	100	200	200	152	1,461	2,017	2,017	2,019	2,183	2,823
Long-term loans	-	-	-	-	-	-	-	-	-	-	-	-	-
Total liabilities	-	100	150	100	200	200	152	1,461	2,017	2,017	2,019	2,183	2,823
OWNERS' EQUITY													
Investment by owner	-	50,000	50,000	50,000	50,000	50,000	50,000	50,000	50,000	50,000	50,000	50,000	50,000
Retained earnings(loss)	-	(7,928)	(8,675)	(9,672)	(10,486)	(11,518)	(13,041)	(14,564)	(15,114)	(15,414)	(15,764)	(16,141)	(16,995)
Net equity	-	42,072	41,325	40,328	39,514	38,482	36,959	35,436	34,886	34,586	34,236	33,859	33,005
TOTAL LIAB AND OWNERS	-	42,172	41,475	40,428	39,714	38,682	37,111	36,897	36,903	36,603	36,256	36,042	35,829

(Continued)

BALANCE SHEET - Year 2	December	January	February	March	April	May	June	July	August	September	October	November	December
Cash	5,000	5,000	5,000	5,000	5,000	5,071	8,686	11,659	14,355	15,426	16,851	18,248	18,099
Accounts Receivable	-	-	-	-	-	-	-	-	-	-	-	-	-
Inventory													
Total Current Assets	5,000	5,000	5,000	5,000	5,000	5,071	8,686	11,659	14,355	15,426	16,851	18,248	18,099
Land	-	-	-	-	-	-	-	-	-	-	-	-	-
Building	-	-	-	-	-	-	-	-	-	-	-	-	-
Equipment	32,611	32,611	32,611	32,611	32,611	32,611	32,611	32,611	32,611	32,611	32,611	32,611	32,611
-LESS Accum. Depreciation	(1,782)	(1,996)	(2,210)	(2,423)	(2,637)	(2,851)	(3,064)	(3,278)	(3,492)	(3,705)	(3,919)	(4,133)	(4,347)
Net Fixed Assets	30,829	30,615	30,401	30,187	29,974	29,760	29,546	29,333	29,119	28,905	28,692	28,478	28,264
TOTAL ASSETS	35,829	35,615	35,401	35,187	34,974	34,831	38,233	40,992	43,474	44,331	45,542	46,726	46,363
LIABILITIES													
Accounts payable	1,834	1,834	1,834	2,384	2,384	2,384	3,026	3,026	3,026	2,622	2,622	2,622	2,219
Short-term loan inc. interest	989	2,826	3,505	1,933	950	-	-	-	-	-	-	-	-
Interest on long-term	-	-	-	-	-	-	-	-	-	-	-	-	-
TOTAL CURRENT	2,823	4,660	5,339	4,317	3,334	2,384	3,026	3,026	3,026	2,622	2,622	2,622	2,219
Long-term loans	-	-	-	-	-	-	-	-	-	-	-	-	-
Total liabilities	2,823	4,660	5,339	4,317	3,334	2,384	3,026	3,026	3,026	2,622	2,622	2,622	2,219
OWNERS' EQUITY													
Investment by owner	50,000	50,000	50,000	50,000	50,000	50,000	50,000	50,000	50,000	50,000	50,000	50,000	50,000
Retained earnings(loss)	(16,995)	(19,045)	(19,937)	(19,129)	(18,360)	(17,552)	(14,793)	(12,033)	(9,552)	(8,291)	(7,080)	(5,896)	(5,855)
Net equity	33,005	30,955	30,063	30,871	31,640	32,448	35,207	37,967	40,448	41,709	42,920	44,104	44,145
TOTAL LIAB AND OWNERS	35,829	35,615	35,401	35,187	34,974	34,831	38,233	40,992	43,474	44,331	45,542	46,726	46,363

BALANCE SHEET - Year 3	December	January	February	March	April	May	June	July	August	September	October	November	December
Cash	18,099	17,157	17,373	22,498	26,375	30,290	34,707	39,002	38,899	37,008	35,510	33,986	31,645
Accounts Receivable	-	-	-	-	-	-	-	-	-	-	-	-	-
Inventory													
Total Current Assets	18,099	17,157	17,373	22,498	26,375	30,290	34,707	39,002	38,899	37,008	35,510	33,986	31,645
Land	-	-	-	-	-	-	-	-	-	-	-	-	-
Building	-	-	-	-	-	-	-	-	-	-	-	-	-
Equipment	32,611	32,611	32,611	32,611	32,611	32,611	32,611	32,611	32,611	32,611	32,611	32,611	32,611
-LESS Accum. Depreciation	(4,347)	(4,560)	(4,774)	(4,988)	(5,201)	(5,415)	(5,629)	(5,842)	(6,056)	(6,270)	(6,483)	(6,697)	(6,911)
Net Fixed Assets	28,264	28,051	27,837	27,623	27,410	27,196	26,982	26,769	26,555	26,341	26,128	25,914	25,700
TOTAL ASSETS	46,363	45,207	45,210	50,121	53,785	57,486	61,689	65,770	65,454	63,349	61,638	59,900	57,345
LIABILITIES													
Accounts payable	2,219	2,219	2,219	3,429	3,429	3,429	3,550	3,550	3,550	3,106	3,106	3,106	2,884
Short-term loan inc. interest	-	-	-	-	-	-	-	-	-	-	-	-	-
Interest on long-term	-	-	-	-	-	-	-	-	-	-	-	-	-
TOTAL CURRENT	2,219	2,219	2,219	3,429	3,429	3,429	3,550	3,550	3,550	3,106	3,106	3,106	2,884
Long-term loans	-	-	-	-	-	-	-	-	-	-	-	-	-
Total liabilities	2,219	2,219	2,219	3,429	3,429	3,429	3,550	3,550	3,550	3,106	3,106	3,106	2,884
OWNERS' EQUITY													
Investment by owner	50,000	50,000	50,000	50,000	50,000	50,000	50,000	50,000	50,000	50,000	50,000	50,000	50,000
Retained earnings(loss)	(5,855)	(7,011)	(7,009)	(3,307)	356	4,057	8,139	12,220	11,904	10,243	8,532	6,794	4,461
Net equity	44,145	42,989	42,991	46,693	50,356	54,057	58,139	62,220	61,904	60,243	58,532	56,794	54,461
TOTAL LIAB AND OWNERS	46,363	45,207	45,210	50,121	53,785	57,486	61,689	65,770	65,454	63,349	61,638	59,900	57,345

CASE 1

BROTHERS GOING SEPARATE WAYS OR NOT?

Derrick and Kevin Petersen, twin brothers from a small town outside of Chicago, will soon graduate from a local business school. The boys have remained inseparable throughout their lives, including sports, hobbies, friends, and work. Decision time is now facing the young men in terms of career choices and tracks. While the brothers have always shared an interest in becoming business owners, their individual goals and newly acquired management training and vision may very well have them going separate ways after all these years.

The Petersen family owns and operates a very successful auto repair and towing business. Each of the five children in the family has worked for their parents throughout high school and during summers throughout college. The boys' parents took over the one-man business nearly 30 years ago. Since that time, they have purchased and now maintain a fleet of seven tow trucks and have expanded the garage to include four bays that provide a wide range of auto and truck repair services. The business generates about $4,000,000 in sales, a higher than industry average profit margin, and has provided the once poor family with a very good life.

The elder Petersens are approaching retirement and would love to see one of their kids continue the tradition. Kevin and his three other siblings have come and gone and made it very clear that they want no part of the business. Derrick remains as the lone ranger and is seriously considering the opportunity.

The elder Petersens are well known and respected for their quality work and service and for their active role in the community. They are set in their ways and have a hard time dealing with new ideas and with letting go. Derrick has many new ideas as to how he would grow the next generation of the business.

There is unused space above the garage that Derrick has talked about turning into a custom auto parts showroom. There is unused space on the property that Derrick would like to convert into self-service gas pumps and an automated car wash. Derrick has also commented on the great success that area competitors enjoy through the addition of a convenience store.

This has all resulted in a family-business conflict of sorts, as the parents want to work something out and get out, but continue to resist the changes that Derrick has offered. Derrick appreciates the knowledge, experience, and success that his parents have, but wants to be his own man and build his own empire if he is to stay on and make this his career. Derrick wants to take on his own new challenges and achieve his own personal rewards. A close friend of the family has recommended bringing in an objective outside consultant and attorney to work up a formal contract that everyone can live with.

Derrick's parents want the business to provide them with retirement income and would like the option of staying on as seasonal employees, as they plan to winter in the south and come home for the summer.

Derrick has many questions that need answering. He is unsure about the best legal form for the business to have. He is not sure how to best deal with his parents. He is not sure about the particulars for the best financial package, one that will reward his parents accordingly, and at the same time provide him with the best opportunity for continued success.

Brother Kevin has a very different mind-set. He wants to start up and own several businesses, but he does not want to be tied down or committed to any single one. He has $200,000 of seed money available to him through the family. He has taken the time to build a relationship with three of the bankers that the family has worked with for many years. He participated in an internship through the SBA while in school in order to familiarize himself with the programs and opportunities that the organization has to offer. He also spent a semester in London in order to learn more about the way business is conducted in Europe.

Kevin is interested in franchising. He envisions himself starting and perfecting a number of service businesses that he can eventually take national and international. He is interested in going public in order to raise large sums of capital and to expedite his expansion plans. Kevin is interested in e-commerce. He views that industry as being in the early growth stages of the product life cycle and feels that the time is right to enter that industry. There appears to be many opportunities to buy low and sell high to worldwide markets. Kevin is interested in real estate development. The family lives in the urban/suburban area of Chicago, which is the site of very active construction of new homes, condo units, and commercial developments. Kevin knows that there are many other such venues around the country and world with plenty of room for new developers.

Kevin is also interested in other parts of the world. He wants to live and work in China and South America and possibly eastern Europe. While he greatly enjoyed the people, activities, and surroundings of his childhood, he really does not want to go home. At the same time, graduation is just three months away, and Kevin does not have a job.

Derrick is encouraging Kevin to come home for a year and help him take over and grow the family business. Derrick feels that this will be an exciting and fun challenge and that it will give his brother time to put together a more specific plan for his own endeavors. That choice also comes with an immediate source of income and a free place to live.

QUESTIONS

1. Profile the brothers. Are they typical "small business" people or "entrepreneurs" or both? Is there really a difference?
2. Advise the brothers. Develop a strategic and tactical plan that best fits their goals and aspirations and that has the highest likelihood for success.
3. How would each brother make a contribution to the family, community, and economy if their efforts were successful?

CASE 2

REAL ESTATE MILLIONAIRES OF MEMPHIS

The one sure way to make money in Memphis, Tennessee, has always been through real estate, but the kinds of people who became millionaires this way defied a single, simple description. Consider five people who became millionaires within a few years of each other. All were in their early 30s when they struck it rich, but otherwise, they were a very varied group.

For example, Abe was the local "do it right" guy. He went to college, got his start in real estate working for a successful firm (he was one of the few African Americans in the local industry who specialized in commercial real estate), and built a nest egg. He left the firm after about five years to start his own, and he kept up his conscientious ways. He made a profit in his first year of operations through frugality and careful money management. He studied the market, the competition, and how and where the city was growing. He negotiated tirelessly but fairly to get the best price on land, and he developed it for the commercial market because that was where the money was.

Cal was the promoter. He was college-educated but seemed to have majored in partying. He was always talking up one big deal or another, developing major projects for tourists. More than anyone else in town, he sold visions of a future Memphis. He built his deals from the downtown out, looking for opportunities near the Mississippi River, which he saw as Memphis's key tourist attraction. He was always putting together consortia, but often forgot or failed to cover key details. His relationships with people were emotional roller coaster rides, and he likewise led a life of financial feast or famine, depending on where he and his latest project was. Just after his 30th birthday, one of his projects "came in," and he became a millionaire.

Lee went to college in engineering and joined her father's construction company right after graduation. She knew business as well as engineering and made the family firm a major force in home construction. She had a keen eye for where new subdivisions should go and was able to get the best work out of local architects and subcontractors. She was considered not only sharp, but kind to people and careful about the details of her homes and her firm. She prospered because her subdivisions were the best in town.

Dave ran a grocery on the outskirts of Memphis and said he "dabbled" in real estate. Self-educated, he largely limited his real estate dealings to when one came across the butcher shop refrigerated case in his grocery. All the locals knew him, and he knew every piece of property and its history from experience and listening to his customers. When someone needed to move or sell a deceased parent's farm, Dave was there with his checkbook, financed through the grocery. He did not prospect, and he resold land rather than developing it.

Frank also lived on the outskirts of town. Never graduating from high school, he apprenticed himself to a gas station owner as a teen. When the company needed to open a gas station just outside of Memphis, Frank agreed to do it, and the company financed his purchase of the gas station. At his gas station, Frank mostly sat outside in a rocking chair by the gas pump. He became a millionaire when gravel was discovered on his land and was mined by local gravel and building companies. Armed with serious money, Frank always said he was looking for his next deal, but he never found one.

QUESTIONS

1. In terms of the five types of entrepreneurial personalities mentioned in the chapter, do any of them fit the description of the Memphis real estate tycoons?
2. What role in their development as entrepreneurs would you think special conditions had—for example,

Abe being African American, Lee being a female in a male-dominated industry or working within a family business, or Frank or Dave going into serious business without a college education?

3. What kinds of competencies do you see these real estate entrepreneurs bringing to their business?
4. Are there any conclusions you can draw about there being an entrepreneurial personality type for the real estate business? What does it say about the kind of entrepreneur you can become with the personality you have?

CASE 3

G & R GARDEN CENTER: LAWN CARE SERVICES DIVISION

Rick and Gloria Ash started a new business in 1986 on the outskirts of Columbus, Ohio. Their original retail store with greenhouse attachment featured fresh-cut flowers, annuals, vegetables, and perennials. The building is on the grounds of Gloria's family farm, which enables the Ashes to grow some of their retail products from scratch. Gloria's parents gave the couple several acres of commercially zoned land as a wedding gift in 1982. The building and greenhouse construction were completed by Rick with a little help from his brothers. This combination of land acquisition and building construction resulted in a very low overhead situation that contributed to their start-up success.

An addition to the building was completed in 1991 and included several new and related product lines such as garden tools, soil and mulch products, gifts, seeds, and related accessories.

Gloria earned a horticulture degree at the local community college prior to the establishment of the business, and in 1997 she was able to fulfill a lifelong dream of starting a landscape design and installation service that became the company's next and newest product line. Gloria set up a small studio and office in the couple's nearby home and was able to acquire some new clients. Her timing was good, as the Columbus area experienced a housing boom during that period. New houses and new developments sprang up in every direction from the city. Their garden center was able to supply the plant materials that each new job required. Soon after, the Ashes expanded their product lines to include a new and wider variety of trees, shrubs, landscape terraces, patios, and walkways as a means to generate new sales and to complement Gloria's new service line.

The original start-up business and each expansion project (building addition, new products, design and installation service) have more than covered their costs but have only generated fair to moderate profit margins according to the Ashes. They attribute this mostly to the presence of their competition, which always seems to be growing. As a result, they have been reluctant to raise prices even though some product costs have risen.

One year later, the Ashes completed the final phase of their original long-range business plan with the addition of another new service—Big Rick, The Lawn & Garden Doctor. This new product line was added because of its very high profit projections coupled with the fact that the Ashes would (temporarily at least) have a monopoly on this market, as none of their competitors currently offer the service.

This new division specializes in the treatment and eradication of lawn and garden pests. There are many insects and diseases that affect plant life, some of which are fatal. In spite of the fact that the Ashes and other local garden centers offer high-quality plants to consumers, Mother Nature has a way of wreaking havoc on lawns, gardens, shrubs, and trees over time.

The start up of this division required a tremendous amount of time, effort, and expense as a result of the environmental and safety-related hazards of some of the products such as insecticides and fungicides.

The Ashes were required to train and license two of their employees as certified applications technicians. A custom built, high-security storage facility was required and built to house all hazardous materials. The building was secured with a locked, barbed-wire fence, an alarm system, and a hazardous material runoff-proof partition. A special liability insurance policy was purchased as well.

As expected, the new division turned out to be very profitable. Demand was strong, and the technicians' work was professional and effective. In fact, at the end of its first full year of existence, Big Rick, The Lawn & Garden Doctor turned a profit that almost matched that of all other divisions combined. At the company's monthly staff meeting, it therefore came as quite a surprise to everyone when Rick announced that he was seriously considering dropping the division entirely.

Rick Ash is a local native of the area. He has very strong family and community values and has always felt responsible for the welfare and happiness of his friends, neighbors, and especially his customers. He was always nervous and apprehensive that something bad would happen as a result of the pesticide or fungicide applications.

And then it happened. A customer's dog died as a result of eating some grass from a recently treated lawn. Big Rick's technician had taken every precaution. The area was properly treated, marked, and roped off, and the customer was instructed as to the after-care safety precautions which included a well-written handout and a signed liability waiver form. While the company was clearly not negligent, Rick was clearly upset.

Two months later, a lawsuit was filed against the company, claiming that the water runoff from the property of one of their customers had tainted a neighbor's well. The Ashes were forced to hire an attorney, and following a full and costly investigation were found to be not guilty of that charge. In fact, the case never even made it to court.

Gloria feels that Rick is overreacting. She points out that the company is in full compliance with every regulation and that Rick has gone out of his way to ensure the safety of all. Gloria also noted that no business can control the behavior or responsibility of its customers or of the population in general and that incidents beyond their control will naturally and always occur. In addition, the high profitability of the division will allow the Ashes to embark upon an aggressive advertising campaign aimed at improving the sales and profits of their other divisions.

Rick is losing sleep over all of this and is not sure what to do. He is worried about the image and reputation of his family and their business. He feels that the conditions surrounding the lawn and garden doctor business are in conflict with his values and conscience.

QUESTIONS

1. Present an argument in favor of retaining the new division that considers and incorporates the ethical and moral conflicts that Mr. Ash is experiencing.
2. Present an argument in favor of eliminating the new division, and make recommendations to improve overall company profits through means that will be socially and morally acceptable to Mr. Ash.
3. Aside from compliance with the law, just how much additional responsibility does a business owner have to his or her customer base, employees, suppliers, and the community at large? How do you feel about the old saying, "buyer beware"?

CASE 4

BIG BUSINESS IN A SMALL RURAL CITY

Bud Collier grew up "smack in the middle of a 100 mile-long hay field," as he puts it, near central Kansas. That part of the country features a lot of land, a lot of cattle, very large farms, agricultural processing centers, and relatively few people. The region has a number of very small farm towns, with populations of less than 1,000 located as much as 30 to 50 miles apart, and a much smaller number of small cities, with populations of 10,000 to 30,000 widely scattered throughout the state. There is an ongoing effort by state and federal agencies to support the development of commerce in those regions. Outside of farming and the few small retail shops that serve those small towns, there is not much happening in the way of new employment opportunities. The farm base continues to shrink, and natives of the area continue to move to other parts of the country after high school, college, or a hitch in the military.

Bud's small family farm is located near one of those small cities. He has earned a degree in marketing and graphic arts and now faces a dilemma and turning point in his life. He very much wants to go home and settle down in the community that he loves, wants to start a career related to his newly acquired skills and knowledge, but has no idea as to what or if that area has to offer him.

He developed a great interest in market research and data analysis while in school. Bud has studied national and international trends in business in an attempt to discover where the opportunities and connections lie between future product and service demand, his graphic arts and marketing skills, and his desired home base. He is trying hard to be creative and innovative and to "think outside the box" as he was often encouraged to do while in school. Bud is also trying to "make the data work for you" as his statistics professor often spoke about.

He has thought about and studied the data regarding food production and world hunger. His area of the country is capable of producing additional and abundant quantities of much needed agricultural products. The only thing standing in the way seems to be governments and politics. His area of the country is a national hub for the transportation and distribution of products from coast to coast and includes a number of major interstate highways. Bud has learned that health care and wellness and its many related industries are projected to become the number one source of jobs and opportunities to the new generation of college graduates. That industry offers options ranging from traditional forms of health care, to fitness, recreation and leisure, diet and nutrition, and nontraditional programs and practices. From a global perspective, Bud knows that China and the Pacific Rim and all of the so-called "Latino Nations" represent two gigantic and growing markets for virtually all consumer goods and services. His mind continues to race with thoughts and ideas as to how to connect these opportunities with his desired home base.

Bud also gained skills in the process and art of new product development while in school. He was often assigned to work with small groups of classmates to brainstorm ideas, to shrink the list to the best and most feasible, to conduct research and analysis, and to finally develop prototypes and test marketing strategies. Bud is now ready to do this for real; he also wants to incorporate his graphic arts skills into the mix. Bud has become very proficient in desktop publishing, computer animation, and video production. He is familiar with and proficient in current multimedia marketing software.

Soon after his return home, Bud learns that an old friend of the family is about to retire and sell his printing and stationery business. That business is located in the downtown of a nearby small city, population 26,000, near Bud's home and has provided a nice income and lifestyle for the proprietor. The shop sells greeting cards, office supplies, and other complementary paper products and includes a small warehouse and processing center where the owner is able to produce custom business cards, office stationery, and a limited line of brochures and flyers. Most of the equipment is old and labor-intensive with limited capabilities.

QUESTIONS

1. Use your imagination and creativity along with the information provided to identify a short list of the best opportunities for Bud to consider.
2. Should Bud consider purchasing the printing and stationery business, and if so, what do you see as his goal for the business, especially how could he expand production and sales given the limited opportunities that the location offers?
3. Business ideas are easy to come by. The more difficult task is determining the feasibility of business success. How would you go about doing that? What kind of information does Bud need in order to make an informed decision? What types and sources of data are available to assist you in determining your best opportunities?

CASE 5

THE AMBITIOUS COLLEGE KID WHO JUST CAN'T WAIT

Lyle Wong has been carrying a briefcase everywhere he goes since the age of 12 and has always been glad to let anyone and everyone know that he is an up and coming entrepreneur. At the age of 14, Lyle started and ran a flea market on weekends on a field next to his house. He rented space to vendors and sold his own merchandise on consignment for a commission. He then started and ran his own landscaping company during the following three summers. This required Lyle to first persuade his older brother to use his truck and become an employee, as Lyle was not yet old enough to drive. He then started and ran a DJ business during his last two years of high school. By the time Lyle graduated from high school, he had more than $75,000 in savings and mutual fund investments.

His parents had all they could do to keep him in high school. Although he earned straight A's, Lyle considered high school to be a waste of time and nothing but an obstacle to earning his first million. He was offered a full scholarship at a Michigan college. Thanks to some friendly and persistent convincing from his parents and from his already established business associates, Lyle agreed to give college a try as long as he could continue to conduct business.

Lyle is now a 19-year-old sophomore, majoring in computer science, with minors in business and international marketing, and lives in a dorm. He started a T-shirt business during his freshman year, which he says pacifies him for now, earns him spending money, and allows him to continue investing in his retirement portfolio.

He is ready to take it to the next level. Lyle has set a goal of accumulating $1,000,000 by the time he graduates from college. He is willing to do this "part time" since he is in school. Lyle has discovered that college takes up much less time than high school. He figures that he needs only about 30 hours a week to attend class, study, complete all assignments, and continue to earn straight As. He has decided to dedicate an additional 40 or 50 hours per week, his version of part time, to the next venture in order to earn him his first million.

Lyle is still undecided as to which direction to go with his next venture. He is thinking about setting up and running an entire operation from his dorm room. He views this as a location with free overhead. As a full-time student, Lyle also has access to many other on-campus resources. Those resources include an abundance of cheap help if needed, access to all computer technology, access to most on-campus buildings and facilities, free public transportation, and access to the student newspaper and radio station.

Lyle is thinking a lot about e-commerce. He knows that this gives him access to a worldwide customer base. Unlike his previous ventures, which were all very small and localized, Lyle is excited about the prospect of selling merchandise on a global basis. He has always liked the concept and role of the middleman, and is searching for product lines that he can buy low and sell high in volume. Lyle knows that the necessary infrastructure is already well established. There are an abundance of manufacturers, shippers, and consumers throughout the world. Lyle figures it is just a matter of putting together the right mix of those entities with him properly placed to reap the benefits.

Lyle's current and past ventures have given him a lot of good experience in key areas of business. Those include customer and employee relations, handling merchandise, and managing cash and the many details and tasks that arise from the normal day-to-day operations of most any business. He is now very computer literate, and in spite of his passion and drive for business success, Lyle has lots of friends, good social skills, and enjoys and participates in many hobbies, social events, and extracurricular activities.

QUESTIONS

1. Do you believe that Lyle can achieve his goal of earning $1,000,000 by graduation? Why or why not?
2. Help your colleague. You are familiar with the resources available to students on a typical college campus. Consider those resources and Lyle's goals, and develop a short list of the best products or services to consider. Include an outline and action plan to make it all happen.
3. Trying to start up a part-time business while being a full-time student in college could pose some problems for Lyle. What are the ones you think are most likely? How could he minimize their impact?
4. Do you see yourself taking a route similar to Lyle's? Could you do it? Will you do it?

CASE 6

THE GRANDE GENERAL STORE, EST. 1948—IT'S TIME TO SELL

Three generations of Grandes have dedicated their lives and careers to a small general store located on the outskirts of Denver, Colorado. Rocky and Anita Grande, the current owner-operators, have decided to sell the family business. They have declared themselves "tired, burned out, and ready to get out." Their two adult children have no interest in the business, and Rocky and Anita want to spend more time with their three young grandchildren.

They need help with setting a fair price for the business, with finding a qualified buyer, and with preparing a formal prospectus for use by investors, bankers, and others. The Grandes want the highest price possible and at the same time sincerely wish to see the business survive and prosper. It has been in the family for a long time, is a well-established part of the community, and has a dedicated workforce. Most of the employees have been with the company for more than 10 years. The Grandes will allow a buyer to continue to use the family/business name if desired.

What began as an old-fashioned general store (1940s–1960s) carrying everything from food and clothing, to tools, farm supplies, penny candy, and train tickets evolved into a traditional hardware store (1970s–present). The current 4,200 square feet of floor space is divided into four major departments: lawn and garden, paints, electrical and plumbing, and general hardware.

Sales and profits are divided equally between consumers and contractors. The store is located adjacent to a railroad siding with a storage building that allows for large shipments of merchandise to be received, stored, and sold. Building materials of all types (lumber, roofing, siding, Sheetrock, and so on) are picked up and delivered to local construction sites, which represent the mainstay of the contractor business.

The Grande family is well respected by all. Their honesty, loyalty, hard work, and community involvement have come back to bless them on many occasions. During tough economic times, suppliers often extend credit terms far beyond the norm. Customers and contractors are fiercely loyal to the Grande's business even with the presence of modern-day giant warehouse outlets that offer a wider variety of the same products for less money.

While the main buildings date back to 1948, the Grandes have upgraded their fleet of delivery trucks and forklifts. The inside of the store is a mix of the old and the new. State-of-the-art computers, paint processing equipment, and landscape machinery rentals are scattered around the old wooden building that still sports some original display fixtures and the wormy chestnut paneling that Rocky's grandfather Jeb installed during construction of the original building.

The principals have compiled the following summary financials for the past five years of operation:

Income (Profit and Loss) Statement Summary: 1998–2002 (in 000s)

	1998	1999	2000	2001	2002
Sales	$1,100	$1,215	$1,500	$1,800	$2,200
CGS—Cost of Goods Sold	550	600	732	822	995
GM—Gross Margin	550	615	768	978	1,205
Operating Expenses:	500	520	600	720	795
• Payroll					
• Mortgage/Debt					
• Insurance					
• Utilities					
• Supplies					
• Transportation					
• Depreciation					
Net Income before Taxes	$ 50	$ 95	$ 168	$ 258	$ 410
Taxes	15	29	50	77	123
Net Income	$ 35	$ 66	$ 118	$ 181	$ 287

Net Cash Flow from Operations: 1998–2002 (in 000s)

	1998	1999	2000	2001	2002
Cash In	$1,014	$1,098	$1,360	$1,617	$1,996
Cash Out	945	1,014	1,250	1,430	1,760
Net Cash Flow from Operations	$ 69	$ 84	$ 110	$ 187	$ 236

Balance Sheet Summary: January 1, 1998–2002 (in 000s)

	1998	1999	2000	2001	2002
Cash	$ 12	$ 19	$ 22	$ 23	$ 21
Inventory	41	47	59	65	80
Accounts Receivables	80	102	124	148	187
Land	$ 35	$ 35	$ 35	$ 35	$ 35
Buildings	612	567	505	459	414
Equipment	84	190	171	241	214
Accounts Payables	$ 36	$ 46	$ 51	$ 61	$ 71
Notes Payables	21	6	7	9	6
Long-Term Debt	$121	$225	$211	$278	$261
Owner's Equity/Net Worth	$686	$683	$647	$623	$613

Suburban Denver is considered a moderate- to high-growth region of the state and is projected to stay that way for years to come. New housing, new neighborhoods, new schools, new malls, and the like are under construction and in the planning stages throughout the area.

The Grande business sits on seven acres of land and includes room for growth, in terms of new buildings, increased parking, and other business options. The business was recently appraised by certified professionals. The assessed values are as follows:

• Land	$110,000
• Buildings	515,000
• Equipment	155,000
• Inventory	70,000
• Total Current Assessed Value	$850,000

The Grandes have compiled all their data into a prospectus and are about to formally put the business on the market. They have yet to settle on an asking price.

Two local area banks have indicated a willingness to offer a 15-year note to a qualified buyer for a maximum of $624,000 (which represents 80 percent of the assessed value of the land, buildings and equipment).

QUESTIONS

1. Use your entrepreneurial skills to evaluate this investment opportunity. Is this a business worth buying? If so, why? How much would you be willing to invest? Why?
2. Given the economic outlook in the Denver area, the land and physical plant, and the competition, what short- and long-term operational and growth strategies would you consider?

CASE 7

SCENTED CANDLES FOR MEN

It was such an obvious idea, a kid could think of it—and did. Imagine scented candles but with scents that would appeal to men? Instead of strawberries or roses or vanilla how about fresh-cut grass, or bourbon and coke, or a tailgate party?

It turns out that a 13-year-old Marysville, Ohio, boy named Hart Main came up with the idea in 2010 when the scented candles his sister was selling as a school fundraiser turned him off. He wondered why there weren't smells he liked. So with scents like cut grass and a new mitt, he got into the business. With a YouTube video and a website, he went live, and even a bit viral, in 2011.

A few hundred miles away, Johnson Bailey was in the second year of operating his company, The Original Man Candle. He came up with the idea while trying to think of an unusual present to give his dad. His first scent was Football, a leathery scent. A student at Oklahoma State, he built a business plan, won the campus competition, and even was a finalist on the TV program Shark Tank but didn't win an investment.

Unaware of each other, these student entrepreneurs were also unaware of the competition already out there. Mandles had already started in southeastern Michigan with scents like Bass Killer, inspired by freshwater and freshly caught fish, and The Slab, because everyone loves bacon, while California's ManScents has fragrances like Draft Style with a root beer smell or Smoke and Grill for that barbecue experience.

With all of these firms looking to grow their markets, the giant of the industry, Yankee Candle, watched and in 2012 nationally launched its first scent aimed at men: Man Town, which was inspired by a "man cave" with a mix of spices, woods, and musk. By this point, The Original Man Candle's website is offline, but the other competitors who created the industry are still in there pitching.

QUESTIONS

1. What kind of strategy would small businesses like these candlemakers choose when competing with a mass-market competitor like Yankee Candle? Why that approach?
2. How could Yankee Candle's getting into the business actually help the smaller competitors?
3. Is having an absolutely unique product essential to be successful in the market?
4. Hands-On: Go online and look at the websites and products for the firms mentioned in this case. What would be the competitive advantages of each of the firms? What makes each of them different?

CASE 8

THE EARLY STAGES OF PAINT CHECK SERVICES

Randy Bunge grew up in his grandfather's family business, inspecting paint jobs for a market mostly made up of businesses and government agencies who were having contractors paint their buildings and public works. He had some ideas about how to modernize the business, but his grandfather was content with the old ways of working. Still, his grandfather encouraged Randy to pursue his dream, so, with his father's support, Randy set out to create a new business called Paint Check Services (PCS).

In his entrepreneurship class, one of the first things Randy was required to do was create an elevator pitch for his business to help explain it to potential investors, suppliers, customers, and professional supports like accountants and lawyers. His first version of the pitch is given below.

Elevator Pitch—Paint Check Services

Mr. Customer, I know that you have recently decided to have your structure repainted. I would like to offer my third party inspection service to you. A third party inspector will ensure that the job is done correctly and eliminate a lot of headaches for you.

Hiring a painting firm on time and material gives them the incentive to drag the job out. So you are left with having to hire them on a contractual basis. The only problem is that this sets up an incentive to cut corners or use inferior materials. The most commonly cut corner in the painting industry is using PCS instead of the required thinner. In most cases the PCS will still allow the paint to go on nicely and everything will look nice when they are finished, but instead of getting a 10-year service life out of the coating, you will only get five to seven years. Having our inspectors on the job to watch the whole process will ensure you get the 10-year service life that you are expecting.

Our inspectors are highly qualified in the coatings field with several years of experience and NACE* training. The inspector we put on your job will watch every stage of the painting process to make sure it is being performed correctly and will report to you as often as you would like. Some customers want to see the inspector once a week to see how the job is going. Others like to see the inspector every morning for a progress report. The inspector will also create an electronic inspection report every day that will be e-mailed to you at the end of the day for you to keep in your records.

Bottom line, you can be confident that the job is being done correctly and that you will not have to spend any more time than you want to supervising the project.

* NACE is the professional organization for paint inspectors.

QUESTIONS

1. Using the description of the elevator pitch given in Chapter 8's "How to Write Your Elevator Pitch," evaluate this pitch. How does it do on the four parts of the pitch? How could it do better?
2. Would this pitch be equally effective with the four audiences mentioned (investors, suppliers, customers, and professional supports)? Did it "play favorites" with one or more audiences? What could be done to make it more universal in appeal?

CASE 9

THE HOUSE OF WINE—GRAND OPENING

CASE PERSPECTIVE

Fred and Larry Butts are excited and a bit nervous about their new wine and specialty store that is scheduled to celebrate its grand opening in about four months. Fred and Larry have spent the past year choosing a location for their new venture and completing a market research and business plan.

The couple purchased a lakeside parcel of property in the heart of the lakes region of upstate New York. Their newly built structure includes a 7,200-square-foot retail showroom (72 × 100) with a below-ground wine and inventory storage area of the same dimensions. The retail showroom is very elegant, featuring wood floors, a large number of beautiful windows, many of which overlook a scenic lake vista, bright stucco walls adorned with works of art and a high-end surround-sound system. The building is located on a busy road, and the parcel includes plenty of room for parking and possible building expansion.

Fred and Larry's market research indicates that the area is evenly divided between an upper-middle-class population of second home seasonal and year-round retirees, a white-collar population of insurance and banking people, and a blue-collar population of factory workers. The total population of the multitown region nearly doubles between Memorial Day and Labor Day each year (from 50,000 to 100,000+), as there are a large number of summer cottages and campgrounds that surround the many small lakes within their market radius. The region also enjoys a "leaf-peeping" tourist season in the fall and a pass-through and nearby ski market during the winter months.

Tourism is the area's major industry, followed closely by the manufacturing sector. There are no major cities nearby. The area consists of several small towns surrounded by beautiful hardwood forests, fresh water lakes and ponds, and several nearby small mountain ranges.

Fred and Larry's market research also revealed that there is currently very little direct competition in the area and that the fine wine and related products markets are growing steadily. Wine is currently available only in local convenience stores and supermarkets. Those establishments typically carry the lower-priced, lower-end, faster-moving selections. Fred and Larry are very optimistic about their chances for success, but are still faced with several important decisions to make prior to their grand opening.

Highlights of the financial section of Fred and Larry's business plan include the following:

- A budget of $150,000 for store fixtures, furniture, and other equipment.
- A budget of $250,000 for merchandise inventory.
- A beginning working capital balance of $100,000 (they expect this and their initial sales to support the net cash flow from operations for a period of six months, at which time the business is projected to support itself).
- A break-even sales volume of $650,000.
- All sales are for cash or credit.
- About half of their wine inventory must be paid for up front; the other half is purchased under 2/10/ net/30 terms.
- All complementary products (described below) are purchased under 2/10 net/30 and/or 2/10 net/45 terms.

Fred and Larry's major remaining unfinished business and related decisions revolve around their specific product mix, the specific layout of the store and warehouse, and their short-, medium-, and long-range marketing and promotion plan. Each is described below in more detail.

PRODUCT MIX

While wine is obviously Fred and Larry's major product line, there are a very wide range of products and prices to choose from. A single bottle of wine can sell from as little as $5 to as much as $10,000 or more. Wines are generally grouped into categories that sell from $5 to $8, $9 to $17, $18 to $30, $30 to $75, and $100+. There are red wines and white wines, small- to standard- to large-sized bottles, champagnes, after-dinner wines, and dessert wines. Wines can be sold by the case, as part of a gift set, on site and through the mail. The major producers of wine are found in France, Italy, Germany, South America, Australia, and California.

Fred and Larry need to select the "right" mix of complementary products. They already find themselves with vendors offering more products than they can possibly handle. Those products include but are not limited to assorted glassware; wine racks and storage units; corkscrews; cookbooks; party platters; serving utensils; coasters; dry, fresh, and frozen food products; tablecloths and napkins; newspapers and magazines; and so on.

Their goal is to operate an upscale, classy establishment and to make as much money as possible. They must pay attention to cash flow and store image. The cheaper wines move fast but generate a smaller profit per unit and portray a "lower-class image." The more expensive wines move more slowly, generate a much larger per unit profit, and portray an image of "upper-class elegance." They must also consider services as well as products. Those include but are not limited to delivery, catering, wine-tasting parties, wine classes, and so on.

STORE LAYOUT

With building construction nearly complete, Fred and Larry keep staring at their (now empty) 72 by 100 feet of retail/showroom space that they must soon fill with equipment, fixtures, products, and other accessories. The lower level must soon be filled with storage equipment, inventory, supplies, and other operational necessities. How should each level be laid out? What kind of display cases should they buy? How should they incorporate light, music, and other presentation aspects into their business? Where should the cash register be? What about an office? How should inventory be received, stored, and handled?

They must design their layout in a way that will maximize sales and profits; maximize their customer's buying experience; maximize the use of wall, floor, ceiling, and window space; minimize shoplifting; maximize safety; and minimize liability.

Outdoor presentation and layout decisions must be made as well. Those include but are not limited to road and building signage, lighting, parking lot design, trash and snow removal, landscaping, traffic flow, and safety.

SHORT-, MEDIUM-, AND LONG-RANGE MARKETING AND PROMOTION PLAN

Fred and Larry envision a three-phase marketing and promotion plan. In the short term (first six months), they want to maximize exposure by having as many people learn about and visit the store as possible. They want people to show up and have an experience that makes them want to come back soon and often. They want to generate enough sales to establish and sustain a positive cash flow within six months of their grand opening.

Their medium-range (six months to one year) goals call for the establishment of a never-ending positive cash flow from operations, a year-round local clientele to support that cash flow, and the beginning of a long era of word-of-mouth referrals.

Their long-range goals are focused on sales and profit stability and flexibility. Fred and Larry's first, second, and third year sales projections are $1,000,000, $1,500,000 and $2,000,000, respectively. At that point, their goal is to achieve an annual increase in sales of 5–10 percent. By the end of their fifth year, they want to be in the position of being able to sell the business for a substantial profit ($1,000,000 or more) or continue to run and grow the business if they are having fun.

QUESTIONS

1. Fred and Larry raised several issues regarding the product mix for their business. What product strategy do you think makes the most sense for The House of Wine? Why?
2. Given the market and product line options for this new business, what kind of pricing strategy do you think makes the most sense for the business?
3. Prepare a time line of strategies and actions that will help the principals achieve their short-, medium-, and long-term goals.

CASE 10

BUSINESS DEMISE

When you look at a page of a textbook chapter, you see a carefully organized grouping of body matter text lines, text boxes, photos with captions, and figures. For more than 200 years, the process of arranging material to be printed (called typesetting) was the same, with hundreds of small mom-and-pop businesses doing this type of work under contract for major publishers. Often, the shops were near the publisher's major installations, and the business relationships were based on personal contacts between publishers and typesetters. By the 1980s, Asian companies (primarily in India and China) came into the business, seeking work from the large American and British publishers.

Donald Sontag was a 32-year-old New Yorker who had been in the business and had the idea to buy a large number of the small mom-and-pop typesetting shops (called a rollup). He started by buying the 100-employee Carter Typesetting Company, an Iowa typesetter and one of the larger such companies, as a basis for the rollup. He had roughly 70 people employed in small shops in the Northeast. He also bought a 30-person Manila, Philippines typesetter to take advantage of the lower costs of Asian typesetting shops. His vision was on target. Carter soared to $10,000,000 in annual sales and profits of $1,000,000. His own bank account grew to over $2,000,000.

In the world economy of the 1990s, outsourcing from the United States to Asia was a growing phenomenon, and one from which Donald thought he was positioned to benefit. But even as he was taking the lead in this, and promoting this approach to his customers as a competitive advantage, his customers were themselves looking for Asian typesetters to forge direct business relations.

Ironically, the growth of the Internet made outsourcing easier for the large publishers. Originally, the graphic transfer machine needed for remote typesetting cost $45,000 and the slow data line cost $10,000 a year at least. Since typesetting was an industry composed of many small shops, it was uneconomical to try and equip all of them with the equipment. However, with the advent of digital typesetting programs and the growth of personal computers and the Internet, the graphic equipment dropped to a cost of $200, while a fast data line cost $1800 a year. Suddenly it was cost-effective for the major publishers and all typesetters to have the equipment and fast Internet hookups that made worldwide outsourcing feasible.

While the American typesetters like Carter originally had an edge on quality, the Asian shops were faster at adopting the new lower-cost technologies, which decreased their costs. As the Asian typesetters got more opportunities for business from the major publishers, they quickly improved their quality to keep these lucrative customers. Soon the American typesetting industry was losing market share to their Asian competitors.

At Carter, the employees were resisting the new technologies and were very protective of their good pay and perks. The workers (mostly women who were second breadwinners in their families) were more interested in protecting a lifestyle they valued than in meeting the economic and technological challenges of a newly competitive industry. In addition, they had trouble letting work go overseas, keeping it in Carter even when it made financial sense to send it overseas. The company's profitability was dropping quickly. Donald's partner Dan believed in "benevolent capitalism" (an idea about treating employees in as fair and considerate a way possible pioneered at IBM in the 1950s and 1960s) and was reluctant to press the employees for faster changes or cost-cutting activities.

Donald could see business moving overseas at an even faster rate. He could see the quality of the Asian typesetting improving dramatically and quickly. He saw the costs of the technology for outsourcing (and managing outsourced projects) improve in completeness and drop in cost at the same time. The all important question was, what should he do about this and what could he get the Carter Company to do?

QUESTIONS

1. How would you describe the problem the Carter Company is facing? What is causing it?
2. What strategy would you recommend Donald take to solve this business problem? Why?
3. How can Donald entice his customers at the big textbook publishers to use Carter instead of cutting their own deals with Asian typesetters?

CASE 11

THE STORY BEHIND SIGNS AND SIGNIFIERS

What happens when the distribution channel itself is falling apart? Up until the threshold of the new millennium, there were six major record labels that were the source of all hits: BMG, EMI, Polygram, Sony, Universal, and Warner. If one of them didn't pick up your band, you lived in poverty and obscurity. By 2011, the industry was in disarray. More music was being sold by more companies than ever before, because digital distribution of MP3s made obsolete a lot of the manufacturing requirements and expenditures of the big record labels.

So with the old giants in trouble and hundreds of small distributors being super-specialized by genre, like Reggaeinc.com for reggae, how does a new talent get recognized by the public?

That was the problem facing JD McPherson, who was an art teacher in the outskirts of Tulsa, Oklahoma, who had a long-time fascination with old rock-and-roll, rockabilly, and R&B. He dreamed of developing a record using the old styles and technologies of music combined with the best aspects of postmodern music like the Clash and the Pixies. He put together a couple of songs and connected with producer Jimmy Sutton via MySpace. Sutton liked what he heard and the two exchanged music and ideas for months via the Internet.

After about six months, Sutton finished his new Chicago home and all-analog studio—complete with old-fashioned microphones and a studio-grade tape recorder, and McPherson arrived with his ideas for an album. Bringing in Alex Hall, who handled the engineering and drums, the three banged out the album called *Signs and Signifiers* in a week in 2010, produced on Jimmy's own Hi-Style Records label. JD figured to get the MP3s out to the public and to take gigs to build his fan base—the usual distribution model for part-time musicians.

JD's general goal of growing his music changed gears when he was laid off from his teaching job. That motivated him to do whatever it took to make a success of his music. And that probably meant getting picked up by a record label, even a mid-sized one, to get a broader distribution through the multiple channels every record label cultivates full time. The key to the strategy was to make enough noise and visibility to get some label attention.

To accomplish this, JD and Jimmy approached building distribution like the record itself, involving the old and the new. Sutton made a limited run of actual records to send to key decision makers to grab attention. Meanwhile JD and Jimmy made a YouTube video (www.youtube.com/watch?v=aZGn4LncY0g) of the track of the album, "North Side Girl," and pushed it to their friends and followers. The video went a bit viral, getting 350,000 views within a few months, dovetailing with the attention the records received from key music gatekeepers including those at National Public Radio, who named JD an "artist you should know" in 2011 (www.npr.org/2011/12/07/143267601/5-must-hear-discoveries-of-2011-from-kexp), and continued to like him (www.npr.org/2012/05/18/153000478/jd-mcpherson-when-a-punk-goes-vintage). The question was, would this be enough to get the attention of a record label, and enough ahead of other musicians to get a distribution contract?

QUESTIONS

1. What is the model for distribution that JD and Jimmy are using for their original effort?
2. If they get a contract from a larger record label, what kind of distribution arrangement would be in place?
3. What are the financial trade-offs of the two approaches? What is the benefit of each approach?
4. With thousands of musicians distributing their music via YouTube and specialized music download websites, what other techniques should JD be using to support his efforts to get public and media attention?

Source: www.jdmcpherson.com/. K. Cole, "5 Artists You Should Know In 2011: NPR," NPR.org, December 12, 2011, www.npr.org/2011/12/07/143267601/5-must-hear-discoveries-of-2011-from-kexp (accessed July 16, 2012). NPR Staff, "JD McPherson: When A Punk Goes Vintage: NPR," NPR.org, May 18, 2012, www.npr.org/2012/05/18/153000478/jd-mcpherson-when-a-punk-goes-vintage (accessed July 16, 2012). E. R. Danton, "Album Stream: JD McPherson, 'Signs Signifiers'|Music News| Rolling Stone," Rollingstone.com, April 17, 2012, www.rollingstone.com/music/news/album-stream-jd-mcpherson-signs-signifiers-20120417 (accessed July 16, 2012). T. Lanham, "Former Middle-school Art Teacher Becomes Rockabilly Musician| Tom Lanham |Music| San Francisco Examiner," *San Francisco Examiner*, June 6, 2012, www.sfexaminer.com/entertainment/music/2012/06/former-middle-school-art-teacher-becomes-rockabilly-musician (accessed July 16, 2012).

CASE 12

THE WALLINGFORD BOWLING CENTER

A group of 12 lifelong friends put together $2 million of their own funds and built a $13 million, 48-lane bowling alley near Norfolk, Virginia. Two of the investors became employees of the corporation. Ned Flanders works full time as general manager, and James Ahmad, a licensed CPA, serves as controller.

The beautiful, modern-day facility features a multi-level spacious interior with three rows of 16 lanes on two separate levels of the building, a full-service bar, a small restaurant, a game room (pool, video games, pinball), and two locker rooms. The facility sits on a spacious lot with plenty of parking and room to grow.

The bowling center is located in the small blue-collar town of Wallingford. There is no direct competition within the town. The surrounding communities include a wide-ranging mix of ethnic groups, professionals, middle- to upper-middle-class private homes, and several apartment and condominium complexes ranging from singles to young married couples to senior citizen retirement units. Nearly 200,000 people live within 15 miles of Wallingford.

The bowling center is open 24 hours per day and has a staff of 27 part- and full-time employees. After four years of operation, the partners find themselves frustrated with the low-profit performance of the business. While sales are covering expenses, the partners are not happy with the end-of-year profit sharing pool. The most recent income statement follows:

Wallingford Bowling Center
Income Statement—2004

Sales		$3,844,000
Cost of Goods Sold		1,315,000
Gross Margin		$2,529,000
Operating Expenses:		$2,381,000
Mortgage	$960,000	
Depreciation	195,000	
Utilities	138,000	
Maintenance	125,000	
Payroll	700,000	
Supplies	127,000	
Insurance	136,000	
Taxable Income		148,000
Taxes		54,000
Net Income		$ 94,000

The bowling center operates at 100 percent capacity on Sunday through Thursday nights from 6:00 P.M. until midnight. Two sets of men's leagues come and go on each of those nights, occupying each lane with mostly five-person teams. Bowlers from each league consistently spend money at both the bar and restaurant. In fact, the men's leagues combine to generate about 60 percent of total current sales.

The bowling center operates at about 50 percent capacity on Friday and Saturday nights and on Saturday morning. The Friday and Saturday "open bowling" nights include mostly teenagers, young couples, and league members who come to practice in groups of two or three. The Saturday morning group is a kid's league, ages 10 through 14.

There are four women's leagues that bowl on Monday and Wednesday afternoons.

Business is extremely slow at the bowling center on Monday through Friday and Sunday mornings, and on the afternoons of Tuesday, Thursday, Friday, Saturday, and Sunday. It is not uncommon to have just three or four lanes in operation during those time periods.

The owners have taken a close look at the cost side of their business as a way to improve profitability. They concluded that while the total operating expense of $2,381,000 might appear to be high, there was in fact little room for expense cutting.

At a recent meeting of the partners, James Ahmad reported on the results of his three-month long investigation into the operating cost side of other bowling alleys and discovered that The Wallingford Bowling Center was very much in keeping with their industry. James went on to report that bowling alleys were considered to be "heavy to fixed cost operations" and that the key to success and profitability lies in maximizing capacity and sales dollars.

QUESTIONS

1. Develop a complete short marketing plan for this company. The goal of the plan is to increase capacity to as close to 100 percent as possible.
2. Given the particulars of this case, develop a list of the five best target market groups and the distinct features of the "4Ps" for each of those groups.

CASE 13

PARKER MOUNTAIN PRODUCTS, INC.

COMPANY HISTORY

The New England region of the United States includes a beautiful coastal stretch that extends from Maine to Rhode Island, through the states of New Hampshire, Massachusetts, and Connecticut. The area is famous for its summer tourism, which includes beaches, quaint villages and towns, restaurants, shops, historic sites and landmarks, and lobsters. Tens of thousands of people from around the world vacation in the area each year, especially during the summer season, which extends from Memorial Day to Labor Day.

Shortly after World War II, Ernest Parker returned to his hometown of Rochester, New Hampshire, and built a small factory that produces low-end glass and ceramic regional souvenirs. These products include wine glasses, general glassware, ceramic cups and bowls, and small platters. Each of these is decorated with a variety of painted images and words related to the specific coastal tourist towns and markets, that is, pictures of lobsters, seagulls, ocean waves, famous towns, and famous sites.

Ernest has provided steady employment for 35 production and support staff. The business has grown at a rate of about 5 percent per year (in sales). The most recent profit and loss statement is shown:

Parker Mountain Products, Inc.
Profit and Loss Statement—2001

Sales	$2,000,000
Cost of sales*	990,000
Gross profit	$1,010,000
Expenses	930,000
Net income	$ 80,000

*Includes direct materials only.

The entire production is sold through a small number of manufacturer's reps, wholesalers, and brokers. While the opportunity was always there to sell direct, Ernest chose to focus all his efforts on the production side of the business, allowing others to market, sell, and distribute the products to retail shops, hotels, and other vendors. The industry average or norm for profits is between 5 and 7 percent (net income to sales).

CURRENT SITUATION

Having now reached the age of 75, Ernest has decided to retire and turn the business over to his grandsons Chris and Ben, two young and ambitious entrepreneurs who recently graduated with honors from the renowned Applied Business Management program at the University of New Hampshire's Thompson School.

Chris and Ben are anxious to improve efficiency on the production side and to develop a variety of direct niche markets to complement their wholesale distribution on the marketing and sales side. The opportunity to add, drop, or shift the product mix, and to increase production and sales exists. In order to properly analyze and act on this, they have asked their bookkeeper to provide more specific production and cost data.

This information is presented below:

Product Line	No. of Units Produced	Selling Price per Unit	CGS per Unit	Total Variable Costs per Year
Platter	300,000	$2.00	$ .60	$240,000
Cups	200,000	2.50	1.50	160,000
Bowls	100,000	2.00	.20	80,000
General glassware	100,000	1.00	.70	80,000
Wine glasses	300,000	2.00	1.40	240,000

The total variable costs of $800,000 are assigned or charged to each product line based on the number of units produced. Total fixed costs for the factory are $80,000; selling and administrative costs for the total company are $50,000.

Chris and Ben have determined that the factory is now at 85 percent of capacity. They are certain that production can be increased without incurring any extra expense beyond direct materials.

They also know that the selling price could be increased by 15 percent as a result of a direct sales program. Their only uncertainty or fear is in disrupting the long-standing relationships that exist with the various manufacturers' reps, wholesalers, and brokers who have been able to sell all of the company's production for many years. They are afraid of "biting the hand that feeds them" by selling to an end user who currently buys from one of their own distributors.

QUESTIONS

1. As a first step, conduct a financial analysis of current operations by reformatting the income statement to include individual product lines as well as the total company. Analyze those data.
2. Use the information provided along with any assumptions you wish to make and construct a balance sheet and cash flow statement. Analyze those data.
3. What specific goals and standards of performance would you recommend for the new managers? What control process or audit system would you include for follow-up purposes?

CASE 14

NATE MOWER & SON, RESIDENTIAL PLUMBER(S)

Nate Mower has worked as a plumber in the Minneapolis area for 20 years. Nate has operated his business as a one-man show and has also had as many as six employees working on two or three jobs at a time.

During the winter months, Nate traditionally works alone, servicing local residents with routine plumbing repairs, furnace maintenance, and frozen pipes. During the summer months, Nate takes on a few new home construction plumbing and heating installations that call for the help of additional workers.

Nate has an excellent reputation for honesty and high-quality work. He has never had to advertise, as the work requests seem to be endlessly lined up and waiting. Nate works long hours, yet has managed to earn only a modest living for his wife Jessie and son Brett. In fact, Jessie has been heard to comment out loud to friends and family that Nate is "always busy and always broke." Several years back, Jessie had to take on a part-time cashier position at the local supermarket "just to put groceries on the table." The Mowers inherited Nate's grandparent's old farmhouse and have no mortgage. Nate drives around in his grandfather's old panel truck that he converted into the company work vehicle.

Nate is from the old school. He is a down-to-earth, hard-working country boy who loves to hunt and fish in his spare time. As Nate puts it, "I love my job and don't want to charge people too much for my work." Nate charges $25 per hour for his time (while onsite only) and provides all parts at cost. Nate believes that "it would be stealing" to mark up the price of parts that he buys from a nearby wholesale distribution center. Nate mails out bills when he gets around to it, usually late at night if he's not too tired.

Brett Mower has learned a lot about the trade from his father. He often went along with Nate on jobs when he was young, and worked for his father throughout high school, mostly during the summers. Brett has returned home from a tour of duty in the military and is thinking about becoming a partner in the family business. He has several serious concerns, however, and is not sure which way to turn.

Although Brett would never say so out loud, he acknowledges that his father does seem to be always busy and always broke. He wonders why his mother is forced to work to put groceries on the table and help pay the bills. The family has no mortgage and no car payments. His folks have never taken a vacation, rarely go out, and still don't own a personal computer.

Brett recalls many incidents of receiving angry letters from creditors and parts suppliers over past-due bills. There have also been a few bounced and delayed paychecks over the years. Nate is currently on "COD— only" status with his suppliers who also expect some payment toward outstanding payables.

Brett wonders whether the business could ever support two families. He is planning on marrying his childhood sweetheart within the next year and has dreams of a house, family, and career of his own.

And yet, business is booming. The phone never stops ringing, especially during the long winter months, and Nate has barely scratched the surface of the new home installation market. The Minneapolis area is booming with new home construction. There have been reports in the local papers that several jobs have been delayed because of a shortage of contractors, including plumbing and heating. The short- and long-term market outlook is excellent.

Brett has been anguishing over his next move. Nate is thrilled at the prospect of forming a partnership with his son. Brett wants to start a new life and career in his hometown but has serious concerns about the condition and future of his father's business. Jessie suggested that perhaps someone in the know should take a look at their books and point them in the right direction.

Nate's most recent IRS returns reveal the following:

Schedule C—Profit and Loss Statement—2007
Nathan Mower, Residential Plumber

Sales		$221,250
CGS		135,000
GM		$ 86,250
Expenses:		$ 49,500
Outside		
Labor	$39,500	
Truck	2,000	
Supplies	4,000	
Insurance	4,000	
Taxable income		$ 36,750

Balance Sheet Accounts—12/31/2007
Nathan Mower, Residential Plumber

Cash	$ 600	Accounts payable	$ 98,000
Accounts receivable	97,500	Notes payable	14,000
Inventory	143,400		
Land	0	Long-term debt	0
Buildings	0		
Equipment	36,000	Net worth	$165,500
	$277,500		$277,500

QUESTIONS

1. Using the above statements, provide specific recommendations that will alleviate Nate's cash flow problems.
2. Given the history of the company, is it possible for Brett to come on board, earn a living, and successfully grow the company? If so, how?

CASE 15

THE LANDLORDS: INVESTMENTS IN COMMERCIAL REAL ESTATE

Greg, Chris, and Nancy are midcareer high school teachers in the Pittsburgh area. They love their jobs, are very dedicated, and plan to stay on until they are eligible for retirement in about 15 or 20 years. The three teachers and friends have met on several occasions to brainstorm ideas for an outside business partnership. With kids about to enter college and a somewhat pessimistic outlook toward their retirement pensions, the three want to make some extra money.

Their financial goals are to supplement their annual incomes by $10,000 to $15,000 each for college tuition purposes and to build an equity base of about $300,000 each for retirement.

Following several meetings, some consultation with friends and advisers, and some local market research, they have settled on the business of commercial real estate investment, more specifically, multiunit rental properties.

The Pittsburgh and surrounding communities are currently experiencing and are projected to sustain above-average growth in both jobs and housing. In fact, there is a current shortage of both rental units and single-family housing in the area. As a result, rents have increased steadily during the past three to five years and currently average:

1-bedroom apartment	$750–$900 per month
2-bedroom apartment	$1,000–$1,200 per month
3-bedroom apartment	$1,200–$1,400 per month
4-bedroom apartment	$1,400–$1,800 per month

Tenants are responsible for heat, hot water, and electricity. Landlords provide parking and maintenance.

Interest rates are very low at this time and are therefore very attractive for borrowing and investing purposes. Greg has learned that local banks will finance commercial properties for up to 25 years at 6 percent interest. In addition, those banks will provide loans for up to 85 percent of assessed property values.

Multi-unit apartment buildings in the area range from $300,000 to $600,000 depending on size, condition, and neighborhood location. Most buildings include three to six separate units ranging from one to four bedrooms in size.

Greg, Chris, and Nancy want to locate and purchase enough buildings to meet their financial goals. Each building must therefore generate enough rental income to offset all costs and generate an after-tax profit. The buildings must also be carefully selected with regard to their expected growth in appreciation.

In addition to building and outside maintenance, the landlords are responsible for mortgage payments, city water and sewer bills, insurance, and local taxes. The IRS requires that depreciation be spread over a 28-year period.

The landlords each have $30,000 to invest for down payments on properties. One of their advisers urged them to set aside a portion of that amount for working capital depending on their cash flow outlook.

QUESTIONS

1. Greg, Chris, and Nancy could do their real estate rental business strictly self-financed or with bank loans. Which do you recommend and why? What are the monthly financial obligations under each approach?
2. Given their starting funds and loan opportunities, how large a real estate deal can they handle their first time out if they go the bank loan route?
3. One adviser mentioned putting aside a portion of their money for working capital. How much would you recommend they put aside? On what do you base your suggestion?
4. What are the typical cash flow problems that people in real estate rentals face? How can Greg, Chris, and Nancy prepare themselves to meet these?
5. Many real estate investments or projects are of a much greater magnitude than those in this case. How would you go about organizing and financing a project that required an investment of say $300 to $350 million?

CASE 16

RICHARD HARRIS AND HARRIS HOMES LLC

Many people who thought the devastation from 2005's Hurricane Katrina would be a golden opportunity for the Gulf Coast construction industry were sadly mistaken. Consider the situation of Richard Harris.

Harris had owned Harris Homes LLC about ten years when Katrina hit Ocean Springs, Mississippi. By 2004, his sales had grown to $3.5 million and his 2005 sales were on track for $5 million when the storm hit. Before the storm, he had $3 million in projects and $300,000 worth of vacant property. Before the storm, he was building 24 houses, and 12 of them were already under contract. When Katrina hit, those homes sustained damage, and even with insurance, Harris' out-of-pocket expenses to cover his deductible were around $100,000. The bad news was that paying those deductible expenses would eat up all of his working capital.

That money problem fed into another problem—people. Harris was employing 60 to 80 subcontracted workers, but now he couldn't make competitive offers to get the workers back. FEMA (the Federal Emergency Management Agency) was spending money for their Blue Roof emergency repair program, out-of-state contractors with fat bank accounts were hiring local workers at premium rates to help them start repairing and rebuilding, and the area's worker base was still depleted because of the people who evacuated the area and had not yet returned. Just as workers were scarce and going for premium prices, so were lumber and all building materials, as an entire region tried to rebuild at the same time.

Those 12 homes under contract were sold at pre-Katrina prices, in effect "locking-in" low prices the region will not see for months, perhaps years to come. Harris was obligated to finish those homes. However, the cabinetmaker, plumber, and electrician he had favored all had businesses underwater after Katrina, and may be out of business.

It is now about three weeks after Katrina (and the glancing blow from Hurricane Rita) hit. Looking at his immediate future, Harris knows he needs to get to work on the other nearly finished homes, which would get some new cash flowing into his business. He has applied for SBA disaster relief, but has been told it would be 90 days before any money became available—if he qualifies. He needs to move to get some of the potentially lucrative government contracts for rebuilding that are being offered. But even here, it is hard to know how to bid when prices are so unpredictable. For example, the cost of dumping debris from cleared land jumped from $1 a cubic yard to $4 after Katrina.

Harris had done several things right. He had insurance. He kept a set of records where they would be safe, making it easier to apply for government relief and insurance after the storm. He even had kept ready cash for expenses. Despite all of that, Katrina hit, and Richard Harris is looking at the possible loss of his business, right at the moment when the construction industry in his area appears about to enter a golden age of rebuilding.

QUESTIONS

1. What do you think are the two greatest risks facing Richard Harris's business? Why?
2. What actions can Richard take now to manage the risks you mentioned above?
3. From this experience, what recommendations would you make to Richard Harris to do an even better job of preparing for future hurricanes?

Source: Jackie Larson, "Gulf Coast Entrepreneurs Face Reality," Entrepreneur.com, September 22, 2005, www.entrepreneur.com/article/0,4621,323569,00.html.

CASE 17

THE HOUSE OF WINE (REVISITED)

Please refer back to Case 9. The focus now shifts to inventory management. The proprietors have a somewhat limited start-up budget for inventory and working capital. It is very important for them to buy the right quantity of the right products (part of asset management).

Inventory may be purchased with cash, through short-term loans from a bank (notes payable/line of credit), or through a credit arrangement with suppliers (accounts payable). There are also a variety of shipping and receiving programs and systems available.

QUESTIONS

1. Use the information from this case, Case 9, and your classroom discussions to create a detailed inventory management program for the proprietors.
2. How would you recommend they pay for the inventory?
3. What milestones in the House of Wine's operations do you think should occur in order to signal when a different approach to inventory might make sense?
4. When thinking about the House of Wine's inventory, will it make any difference that some inventory is time-limited (i.e., can spoil), other parts of it are seasonal, and some can be sold or held for long periods of time? If it is an issue, how do you propose to handle it?
5. Will the House of Wine face much in the way of accounts receivable problems? Why or why not?

CASE 18

THE DREADED LETTER

Tony Brown was an undergraduate student at the University of Missouri-Columbia. He had heard about a campus-wide competition for apps sponsored by the Donald W. Reynolds Journalism Institute. He had a brainstorm for an app that could help students find nearby available apartments. He enlisted three other students to help him prepare an app named NearBuy. In preparing for the competition, Tony and his team heard that the university had the potential to assert ownership over the resulting ideas. Some students dropped out rather than risk sharing their ownership, but Tony and his friends continued. They received the judges' choice award.

At the competition, University of Missouri System President Gary Forsee praised the team's efforts, pointing out that interdisciplinary student efforts like NearBuy's spur "economic development opportunities that benefit us all." The win also got them an all-expenses-paid trip to the 2009 Apple Worldwide Developers Conference to show off NearBuy on the new iPhone being introduced at that conference.

With attention like this, it is no wonder that it did well—passing 250,000 downloads in a few months. He also gained some visibility in the press in Columbia and the rest of the country.

Given the supportive words of System President Forsee, it came as a particular shock when they received the letter. It turned out that some of that visibility was perhaps not so good. One of the people who read the story of Tony's entrepreneurial good fortune was a lawyer with the University of Missouri. Reasoning that Tony developed the app for the student competition, the lawyer stated that the university should be entitled to a portion of the ownership of the app and the profits it had generated.

That was exactly what the letter Tony received stated. University of Missouri demanded a 25 percent ownership stake and two-thirds of the profits. As Tony said, "We were incredibly surprised, and intimidated at the same time." Here was their own university telling them in no-uncertain, legalistic terms, to hand over a major portion of their business. While the possibility of shared ownership was mentioned in the rules of the contest, the university made no move at that time to assert ownership. Tony and his team spent their own time, on their own laptops, and without much of any help from the university, to create the business. No professor or staffer helped them. How could it be fair that the university demanded ownership at this time?

Of greater importance, what should they do now?

QUESTIONS

1. What do Tony and his colleagues own—a product, a business, both or something else?
2. What would be their basis for claiming complete ownership of the NearBuy app or the firm behind it?
3. What would you recommend as a response by the NearBuy team?
4. Check out your own university's policy regarding ownership of ideas, products, or services developed by students. Is your entrepreneurial idea likely to be claimed by the university? If it is, what can you do to protect yourself?

Source: E. Smith, "New iPhone Application a Hit at Apple Global Conference," Donald W. Reynolds Journalism Institute, June 12, 2009, www.rjionline.org/news/new-iphone-application-hit-apple-global-conference (accessed July 15, 2012). "Student Inventors Prompt MU to Change Rules—Columbia Missourian," n.d., www.columbiamissourian.com/stories/2011/01/24/young-inventors-prompt-colleges-revamp-rules/ (accessed July 16, 2012). A. Scher Zagier, "University of Missouri Says Student Can Keep Full Ownership of App Created on Campus—NBCActionNews.com—Kansas City," *KSHB*, January 25, 2011, www.kshb.com//dpp/news/state/missouri/student-inventor-defends-self-created-app-against-school-lawyers-looking-for-a-cut (accessed July 16, 2012). "NearBuy—Real Estate for the iPhone," *NearBuy—Real Estate for the iPhone*, n.d., http://nearbuyclassifieds.wordpress.com/ (accessed July 16, 2012). T. Rae, "iPhone App Raises Questions About Who Owns Student Inventions," The Chronicle of Higher Education, *The Wired Campus*, January 31, 2011, http://chronicle.com/blogs/wiredcampus/iphone-app-raises-questions-about-who-owns-student-inventions/29265 (accessed July 16, 2012).

CASE 19

ALASKA WILDLAND ADVENTURES

Between August 10 and 11, 2003, a 500-acre fire raged across Alaska's Kenai Peninsula. Caught in the path of this blaze was a small lodge owned by Alaska Wildland Adventures, a Girdwood, Alaska-based ecotourism company. The facility was situated in a remote area inaccessible by car, and owner Kirk Hoessle feared firefighters would not reach it in time. What's more, it was the height of the company's peak season and the majority of his staff were occupied with running tours in other parts of the state, leaving him short on help. Hoessle assembled as many of his people as he could, but with the fire fast encroaching on the lodge, the situation was growing dire. It was at this point that help came from a most unexpected source: his former employees.

Dennis Weber, a former camp manager and owner of his own construction business, received word of Hoessle's emergency around midnight on August 10. He immediately packed up some equipment and made the three and a half hour trek from his home, about a mile north of Anchorage, to the Kenai Peninsula. He arrived in the early morning hours and joined a group of 15 people, about half of whom were former employees, in fighting the blaze. The group cleared trees and brush from the lodge's perimeter. "The firefighters didn't arrive until around evening," says Weber. "By that time we had the fire ring cut." With the help of Weber and other former employees as well as some assistance from Mother Nature—the winds shifted, diverting the fire—the lodge was spared.

The incident was a testament to the goodwill Hoessle has garnered over the years with his employees. "It was truly a beautiful thing," he says. "We would've struggled to keep the business intact had the fire gone through."

Hoessle attributes the loyalty of his former and current employees to creating a work environment grounded in trust and open communications. "I don't like to make decisions in a vacuum," he says. The majority of the company's workers are seasonal tour guides, and every year they are given an employee survey. Hoessle addresses his seasonal people's concerns and communicates all improvements at the beginning of each season. Hoessle also delegates a lot of decision making to employee committees. At times, these committees serve a strictly advisory function. On other issues, such as the company's holiday schedule, the employees are empowered to make the final decision. In order to avoid giving his people false expectations, Hoessle tells employees when their deliberations will be taken on a strictly advisory basis.

Not only does the company engage employees in the decision making process, but it practices open-book management. Alaska Wildland Adventures has a revenue sharing plan, and Hoessle believes that sharing the company's financial information helps to instill trust in the program. What's more, practicing open-book management has helped engage the employees. "Knowing the financials helps me understand the big picture," says sales manager Alicia Foster. "I know what we can afford and can make decisions from the perspective of my job."

Foster says that creating a good workplace has benefited the organization in a number of ways. For example, the company is involved in ecotourism, which entails providing an educational experience that does not disturb wildlife and other natural resources. It is a complex operation that requires heavy training for new guides. The company, however, has been able to keep its training expenditures at a reasonable level because many of its seasonal employees return year after year.

Sales representative Glenda Denny first heard of the company when she worked at a nearby hotel. There she had the opportunity to come in contact with its guides, and she says meeting them convinced her to join the company. "They were all so knowledgeable, and you could tell that they loved their jobs," she says. This stable and knowledgeable staff has helped to create a loyal clientele, as evidenced by the fact that about 40 percent of the company's business comes from referrals. What's more, it has fishing guests who have been returning for 15 years.

Most importantly, Alaska Wildland Adventures' inclusiveness and open-book management style has helped the company survive during tough economic times. The August 2003 fire wasn't the first time the company's viability was threatened. The travel industry has struggled since the terrorist attacks of September 11, 2001. And unlike its competitors who offer a more diversified catalog of vacation spots, Alaska Wildland Adventures is home grown and solely dependent on travel to the state.

The downturn in business has forced the company to make some difficult choices over the last couple of years. Faced with dwindling revenues, the organization needed to cut costs. Ultimately, Hoessle decided to reduce work schedules rather than lay people off. Everyone would take off 30 days without pay. Hoessle sought the insight of employees on how they would like to handle their schedules. Some chose to take their time off all at once; others chose to work four-day weeks. Hoessle extended loans to people who were struggling to get by on the new schedules.

Understanding the sacrifices his employees made, Hoessle found inexpensive ways to reward them. For example, the company has tried to give employees greater flexibility in their scheduling. Marketing coordinator Heather Dudick is a mother and she says that working a reduced, flexible schedule has made it easier to care for and spend quality time with her eight-year-old child. The company operates several lodges and encourages employees to make use of them during the off-season. The organization also owns a transferable ski pass, which staff members can use on their downtime.

It appears that Alaska Wildland Adventures has weathered the worst of the downturn. According to an Associated Press article the adventure travel industry was rebounding. Hoessle said that the company appeared poised for a good year. And the importance of his employees' loyalty, both past and current, in surviving the tough times is not lost on him. "People work here because they are attracted to our mission and environmental beliefs," he says. "They stay because they are treated well." The loyalty and the rebound paid off. Alaska Wildland was voted the world's top eco-tour operator by Condé Nast travel magazine in 2005.

QUESTIONS

1. How would you characterize Hoessle's open-book management style?
2. How do you think this style motivates and retains key staff and employees?
3. In what ways has Hoessle been able to reward employees despite slower growth and having to cut costs throughout the small business?
4. What additional recommendations would you make to Hoessle if he needed to bring in new employees, especially as the adventure travel industry begins to heat up?

Source: Reprinted from Todd Luchik, "Survival of the Fittest," Winningworkplaces.com, www.winningworkplaces.org/library/success/survival of the fittest.php. Used with permission.

CASE 20

JOSEPH SHAUGHNESSY, BSI CONSTRUCTORS, ST. LOUIS

To his family and friends, Joseph "Joe" Shaughnessy became a local TV star at age 68, appearing on screen with a new Fox TV sportscaster as honorary co-chair of the 2004 United Negro College Fund's Annual St. Louis Walkathon. How many construction company executives would be so well known that they would be used as a local charitable pitchman? Not many, and that speaks volumes about Joe Shaughnessy's career.

Joe's firm, BSI Constructors, shows the unexpected paths one entrepreneur's life can take. After graduating in Civil Engineering from Saint Louis University, Joe and friend Lorry Bannes went to work for St. Louis's Gamble Construction Company, where over 10 years they rose to executive positions. Wanting to get out on their own, they formed Bannes-Shaughnessy Incorporated in 1972 with carpenter and field supervisor Ed Clinard as the third owner, and a grand total of $27,500 in capital between them. Despite their prior experience, it took five years before they received their first million dollar contract. But once that milestone was passed, their firm grew. Clinard retired in 1980 and Bannes in 1988, so by 1989 Joe was the sole owner of the firm, now called BSI Constructors, Inc.

Throughout its life the firm was innovative, pioneering the building of the region's first earthquake proof building at the Missouri Botanical Garden. The company also had a reputation for high-quality building. Churches, hospitals, universities, and companies looking to build for the long term turned to Joe Shaughnessy's firm.

The firm was also compassionate. In 1975, it won the first national Build America award given by the Associated General Contractors of America for promoting minority subcontractor participation in the building industry. In 1989, Joe's firm would renovate a statue commemorating the first Jewish settlers in the New World on a no fee basis. In 1999, Joe (a devout Catholic) would give up weeks of his time and use of company facilities to organize the transportation for the St. Louis visit of Pope John Paul II.

Even when Joe solely owned BSI, he knew it was important to transition the ownership. He hoped to involve his children in the company and eventually pass it on to them. It was a close-knit family, and the company was like the eighth child for all seven. Many of the children worked in the company doing summer jobs, and helped on projects when needed. Eldest son Paul worked his way up through the ranks of the firm after working in mortgage banking for five years. Son Jim, who originally intended to pursue medicine, came back to the company after being successfully cured of leukemia and realizing he wanted to be productive immediately after graduating from Saint Louis University's Business School. Youngest son Dan, a Washington University Architecture School graduate, went into the business after six years with an international architecture firm. To set things straight, Joe started his transition process by writing a letter to all seven children explaining his view about the company and its need for clear management and control. Paul, with the most experience, would become president, with Jim and Dan continuing to work as executives of the company and being involved in business development and all company operations.

Today, Joe is the chairman of the board of BSI, and Paul is the president. The firm's revenues have reached $200 million a year and it continues to get many of the premier building contracts in the St. Louis region. Joe's involvement in civic activities makes him one of the best known entrepreneurs in St. Louis, and winner of the area's Ernst & Young Constructor Entrepreneur of the Year award in 1998.

QUESTIONS

1. How did Joe Shaughnessy seem to do in achieving the four bottom lines?
2. Did Joe balance with the four bottom lines at the same time, or did some come before others?
3. How did Joe use the business to promote beliefs he felt were important?
4. Some folks would say the solution to balancing the four bottom lines is to never sleep. How do you think Joe Shaughnessy would respond? Do you agree with that approach for yourself?

GLOSSARY

A

Accelerator An organization that supports start-up technology businesses by providing inexpensive office space, a variety of support services, and resources; most accelerators are associated with universities.

Access The opportunity to find and obtain opportunities offered to others.

Accounting equation The statement that assets equal liabilities plus owners' equity (assets = liabilities + owners' equity).

Accounts receivable Money owed to your business by customers who purchased your product on credit.

Accredited investors The SEC's term for individuals with a net worth greater than $1 million or a personal annual income of at least $200,000 in each of the two most recent years, who are therefore qualified to make private equity investments in businesses.

Acquisition cost The total cost of acquiring an asset, including such costs as purchase price, transportation, installation, testing, and calibrating in order to ready it for its first productive use.

Action The visible behavior a person takes.

Activity-based cost estimates An accounting method which assigns costs based on the different types of work a business does in order to sell a particular product or service.

Advertising Advertising is often used to support the corporate identity and value propositions that are established through public relations efforts. Part of conveying your message to your customers, advertising outlets include newspapers, magazines, billboards, television, and Internet banner ads, to name a few.

Age Discrimination in Employment Act An act of Congress that makes it illegal to discriminate against people who are older than 40 years of age.

Agent A middleman business which represents a manufacturer's product or service to other business-to-business middleman firms.

Aggrandizing Attempting to make your business or yourself seem more accomplished or grander than reality.

Americans with Disabilities Act of 1990 An act of Congress that requires that businesses make provisions for access by disabled people.

Arbitration A dispute resolution process held instead of court cases in which both sides present their case to a legal professional.

Arm's length transaction A business deal where the parties have a prior relation or affiliation, but where the business is conducted as if they were unrelated. This approach is done to help guard against potential conflicts of interest.

Articles of organization Document setting forth information about a limited liability company that is filed with the state to establish an LLC.

Articles of partnership Agreement between the partners of a firm on matters pertaining to the formation and operation of the partnership.

Articulate The concept that information flows from the income statement through the statements of retained earnings and owners' equity to the balance sheet.

Asset Something the business owns that is expected to have economic value in the future.

Assumed name filing or a fictitious name filing Filing made with a state(s) in which the business operates disclosing the trade name or assumed name of the business along with the owners of the business.

Auction A business setting in which products consigned from multiple sellers are available for bidding by customers.

Augmented product Core product plus features that tend to differentiate it from the competition.

B

B2B Business-to-business transactions.

B2C Business-to-consumer transactions.

Balance sheet A statement of what a business owns (assets), what it owes to others (liabilities), and how much value the owners have invested in it (equity).

Baldrige Award The Malcolm Baldrige National Quality Award is given by the U.S. government to businesses and nonprofit organizations that have been judged outstanding in seven measures of quality leadership; strategic planning; customer and market focus; measurement, analysis, and knowledge management; human resource focus; process management; and results (see www.quality.nist.gov).

Bank available balance The sum of money that has actually been received and paid out of a depositor's account.

Bank ledger balance The sum of deposits and withdrawals recorded in a bank's accounting records.

Bankrupt The financial state of having more debt than assets, such that net worth is negative.

Bankruptcy An extreme form of business termination which uses a legal method for closing a business and paying off creditors when debts are substantially greater than assets.

Bar coding Obtaining a Universal Product Code number and scan-ready visual tag, and printing it on the product or its packaging. Bar codes can then be scanned and recognized by others.

Barter The practice of trading goods and services without the use of money.

BATNA Best Alternative to a Negotiated Settlement is the strategy or action a person or firm would pursue if the current negotiation fails.

Bearer Any person or business entity who possesses a security.

Benefits Characteristics of a product or service that the target customer would consider worthwhile.

Best practices Activities identified by authoritative bodies as examples of optimal ways to get things done in a particular industry, profession, or trade.

Billboard principle An ethical model that asks whether someone would be comfortable having his or her decision and name advertised on a billboard for the public to see.

Blog A web page in which entries are posted in reverse chronological order (i.e., the most recent at the top of the page).

Blue ocean strategy A strategy based on creating a new product or service which has no competitors.

Book value The difference between the original acquisition cost and the amount of accumulated depreciation.

Boom A type of life cycle growth stage marked by a very rapid increase in sales in a relatively short time.

Bootstrapping Using low-cost or free techniques to minimize your cost of doing business.

Born international A new firm that opens a website immediately, thus being exposed to customers from around the world.

Bot A web-based program that uses artificial intelligence techniques to automate tasks such as searches.

Brainstorming A group discussion in which criticism is suspended in order to generate the maximum number of ideas.

Breakeven point The point at which total costs equal gross revenue.

Brochure A sales document, typically consisting of multiple panels (when folded) or multiple pages, describing your business or specific products or services.

Budget A financial plan for the future, based on a single level of operations; a quantitative expression of the use of resources necessary to achieve a business's strategic goals.

Bundling Combining two or more products in one unit and pricing it less than if the units were sold separately.

Business cards A 2- × 3½-inch cardboard card with your personal and company contact information; the key way of leaving information about yourself.

Business entity concept The concept that a business has an existence separate from that of its owners.

Business format franchising An agreement that provides a complete business format, including trade name, operational procedures, marketing, and products or services to sell.

Business life cycle The sequence or pattern of developmental stages any business goes through during its life span.

Business plan A document designed to detail the *major* characteristics of a firm—its product or service, its industry, its market, its manner of operating (production, marketing, management), and its financial outcomes on the firm's *present* and *future.*

Business risk The level of probability that the future economic state of the business will be worse than expected.

Business stationery A standard 8½- × 11-inch page of blank paper typically imprinted with your company's name and contact information.

Business-to-business (B2B) Business-to-business transactions. Sales of products or services that one firm sells to another firm.

Business-to-consumer (B2C) Business-to-consumer transactions. Sales of products or services directly to individuals.

Buyers People who purchase an existing business.

Buy-in The purchase of substantially less than 100 percent of a business.

Buyout The purchase of substantially all of an existing business.

Buyout insurance Insurance that provides money to owners of a business to buy the shares of any deceased owner from that owner's heirs.

C

Cannibalizing Taking business away from your employer.

Capital assets Assets that are expected to provide economic benefits for periods of time greater than one year.

Capital budgeting The process of deciding among various investment opportunities to create a specific spending plan.

Capital lease A lease in which at the end of the lease period the asset becomes the property of the lessee, possibly with an additional payment.

Captive pricing Setting the price for an item relatively low and then charging much higher prices for the expendables it uses.

Career A lifelong series of jobs or occupations.

Cash Money that is immediately available to be spent.

Cash budget A cash budget identifies when, how, and why cash is expected to come into the business, and when, how, and why it is expected to leave.

Cash disbursements budget A schedule of the amounts and timings of payments of cash out of a business.

Cash equivalents Assets that may be quickly converted to cash.

Cash flow The actual receipt and spending of cash by a business.

Cash flow statement A statement of the sources and uses of cash in a business for a specific period of time.

Cash receipts budget A schedule of the amounts and timings of the receipt of cash into a business.

Cash-to-cash cycle The time that is required for a business to acquire resources, convert them into product, sell the product, and receive cash from the sale.

Categorical questions Questions that are answered by selecting the proper category; for example, "What is your ethnicity? White, African American, Hispanic, Asian, American Indian, Other."

Caveat emptor Latin: let the buyer beware.

Certification An examination based acknowledgement that the firm is owned and operated as specified.

Channels People and firms who connect producers of goods and services with customers.

Charge back A reduction in the bank account of a merchant by a credit card company.

Check the box taxation A choice LLCs can make on their tax returns to be taxed as a corporation or a partnership.

Civil Rights Act of 1991 A series of acts by Congress that prohibit discrimination on the basis of race, color, religion, sex, or national origin.

Clearinghouse An entity that processes checks and electronic fund transfers for banks and other financial organizations.

Cognition A person's way of perceiving and thinking about their experience.

Cognitive dissonance Doubt that occurs after a purchase has been made. An inconsistency between experience and belief.

Co-insurance A contract stipulation that requires a policyholder to carry insurance in an amount equal to a stated minimum percentage of the market value of the property insured.

Collateral Something of value given or pledged as security for payment of a loan; collateral may consist of financial instruments, such as stocks, bonds, and negotiable paper, or of physical goods, such as trucks, machinery, land, or buildings.

Commercial paper Notes issued by creditworthy corporations.

Community development organization An organization authorized by the SBA to make insured loans to small businesses that are expected to increase economic activity within a specific geographic area.

Company book balance The sum of cash inflows and cash outflows recorded in the firm's accounting records.

Competencies Forms of business-related expertise.

Competition Any other business in the same industry as yours.

Competitive advantage The particular way a firm implements customer benefits that keeps the firm ahead of other firms in the industry or market.

Comprehensive budget Comprehensive budgets, also often referred to as *master budgets,* are sets of budgets that detail all projected receipts and spending for the budget period.

Comprehensive planners Entrepreneurs who develop long-range plans for all aspects of the business.

Concentrated strategy A marketing strategy in which a marketer selects one specific group of consumers and designs a marketing mix specifically for that group.

Conflict of interest A situation in which a person faces two or more competing standards or goals.

Consignment The practice of accepting goods for resale, without taking ownership of them and without being responsible to pay prior to their being sold.

Consignment shops Retail stores in which customers can come and buy products placed in the shops by a wide variety of sellers.

Consolidation A transfer method in which a small business is bought by a larger firm for the purpose of quickly growing the larger firm.

Consumer A private individual or household that is the end user of (the entity that "consumes") a product or service.

Contingency fee Fee paid by a client to an attorney for legal services that is dependent upon the outcome of a case.

Contract manufacturing An existing firm with the correct manufacturing capabilities makes your product for you.

Conversion franchising An agreement that provides an organization through which independent businesses may combine recourses.

Conversion rate The measure of how many visitors to your website (or people who click on your online advertisement) actually make a purchase from you.

Copyright Exclusive right given to the creator of a literary or artistic work to make use of that work.

Core competency The main work of a firm in a particular line of business.

Core product The very basic description of what a product is—a bar of soap, a house-cleaning service.

Corporate entrepreneurship The form of entrepreneurship which takes place in existing businesses around new products, services, or markets.

Corporation A legal "artificial" entity that is formed by filing specific documents with a state government.

Cost The value given up to obtain something that you want.

Cost of capital The percentage cost of obtaining future funds.

Cost of disposition Cost incurred in the activities necessary to get rid of an asset.

Cost of goods sold budget A schedule that shows the predicted cash of product actually sold during the accounting period.

Cost of operating The direct cost incurred in using an asset for the purpose for which it was intended.

Cost of owning Cost incurred in financing, insuring, taxing, or tracking an asset.

Cost strategy A generic strategy aimed at mass markets in which a firm offers a combination of cost benefits that appeals to the customer.

Cost to start-up The amount of money it takes to start a new business.

Cost-volume-profit analysis A managerial accounting technique which looks at the fixed and variable costs of a business to arrive at a number of unit sales (volume) to maximize profits.

Covenants The limitations imposed on an individual's property by their neighborhood group.

Cover letter A one-page document on business stationery (also called *letterhead*) that introduces the business plan and the business owner to the recipient and indicates why the recipient is being asked to read the plan.

Coverages Contractual provisions of insurance policies that specify what risks the insurance company is assuming.

Creation The entrepreneurial focus which looks at the making of new entities.

Creative destruction The way that newly created goods, services, or firms can hurt existing goods, services, or firms.

Creativity A process producing an idea or opportunity that is novel and useful, frequently derived from making connections among distinct ideas or opportunities.

Credit reporting agency A business that collects, collates, and reports information concerning an entity's use of debt.

Critical-point planners Entrepreneurs who develop plans focused on the most important aspect of the business first.

Crowdfunding Funding a business through the collective involvement of others to provide private donations, a loan, or investment.

Crowdsourcing Using a virtual group based on the Internet to obtain ideas or opinions.

CSI entrepreneurship The identification of three settings in which entrepreneurship can be pursued, corporate settings, social (charitable) settings, and independent settings.

Cultural resonance A concept in public interest which alludes to events with a broad appeal within the market or population.

Culture A set of shared norms, values, and orientations of a group of individuals, prescribing how people should think and behave in the organization.

Currency A concept in public importance which alludes to the degree to which the issue is immediate in its impact. (Ch. 10)

Currency The bills and coins printed by governments to represent money. (Ch. 14)

Current ratio The value of current assets divided by current liabilities.

Customer-focus The entrepreneurial focus which refers to being in tune with one's market.

Customer relationship management (CRM) The process of tracking the customer's different contacts with the firm, and using this data to help improve sales as well as the customer's experience.

Customer retention Techniques that focus on efforts to promote satisfaction with and interest in the firm.

Customer segment A group or subgroup of potential purchasers that can be approached in a coherent manner.

Customer vector A type of CRM report which segments by customer (or customer group) on purchases or dates of purchase.

D

Debt A legal obligation to pay money in the future.

Debt capital Money borrowed for the purposes of investment in a business.

Decline stage A life cycle stage in which sales and profits of the firm begin a falling trend.

Deductible An amount of loss that will not be paid by an insurance company.

Defendant Person or other entity being sued.

Degree of similarity The extent to which a product or service is like another.

Delegation The assignment of work to others over whom you have power.

Demand deposits Money held in checking and savings accounts.

Deposits and progress payments Cash payments received before product is completed or delivered.

Depreciation Regular and systematic reduction in income that transfers asset value to expense over time.

Design patent A 14-year patent for a new, original, and ornamental design for an article of manufacture.

Determination competencies Skills identified with the energy and focus needed to bring a business into existence.

Dichotomous questions Questions that have only two possible choices; for example, "Have you shopped here before?"

Differential advantage The characteristic that separates one company from another in product, price, promotion, and/or distribution.

Differentiated strategy A marketing strategy in which a marketer selects two or more distinct groups of consumers and designs specific marketing mixes to meet their needs. (Ch. 12)

Differentiation strategy A type of generic strategy aimed at clarifying how one product is unlike another in a mass market. (Ch. 7)

Direct competition Other companies that make a similar product or provide a similar service; for example, direct competition for Coca-Cola includes all other soft drink providers.

Direct exporting Exporting using no middlemen.

Direct mail A method of selling in which catalogs, brochures, letters, videos, and other pieces of marketing materials are mailed directly to customers from which they can mail, call, or e-mail an order. Direct faxing and direct e-mailing are more modern forms of direct mail.

Direct marketing Selling your goods or services to consumers without intermediaries, typically to select customer groups and typically with tracking of the results.

Direct response advertising Placing an advertisement in a magazine or newspaper, on television or radio, or in any other media. The ad contains an order blank with a phone number and e-mail or regular mail address with the intent of having the customer place an immediate order.

Direct sales Methods of going directly to your customer in order to sell your product. Vending machines, door-to-door salespeople, leasing space at a craft fair, farmer's markets, party sales, and most industrial sales are methods of direct selling.

Discounted cash flows Cash flows that have been reduced in value because they are to be received in the future.

Discounts for prompt payment A reduction in sales price provided to credit customers for paying outstanding amounts in a timely manner.

Disposal value The net amount realized after subtracting the costs of getting rid of an asset from its selling price.

Diversification A strategy whose goal is growth based on adding new products or services to the firm's existing collection of offerings.

Diversify To invest in multiple investments of differing risk profiles for the purpose of reducing overall investment risk.

Dividends Payments of profits to the owners of corporations.

Documentary draft A draft which can be exercised only when presented with specified shipping documents.

Domain name The specific name of an Internet site, consisting of a name followed by .com, .net, or a similar code.

Donations Monetary or other gifts to organizations or people who are in need.

Double taxation Earnings of the business are taxed twice with the business as well as its owners being subject to tax.

Due diligence The process of investigating a business to determine its value.

E

Early adopters A customer adoption segment that purchases after pioneers.

Early majority Customer adoption segment that purchases after early adopters, and whose demand creates a mass market.

Earnings multiple The ratio of the value of a firm to its annual earnings.

E-commerce The use of the Internet to conduct business transactions.

Economic development agency A government organization that works to increase economic activity in the form of job opportunities within a specific geographic area.

Economic order quantity (EOQ) A statistical technique that determines the quantity of inventory that a business must hold to minimize total inventory cost.

Economy of scale The idea that it is cheaper (per item) to make many of an item than few.

Effectuation An approach to entrepreneurial thinking that emphasizes creating opportunities by leveraging existing resources.

Efficiency The entrepreneurial focus which refers to doing the most work with the fewest resources. (Ch. 1)

Efficiency The comparison of productivity ratios to see the extent that an organization has generated more outputs with fewer inputs. (Ch. 16)

Efficiency-driven economies Nations with a largely industrialized economy.

Elastic product Product for which there are any number of substitutes and for which a change in price makes a difference in quantity purchased.

Elasticity A term from economics which describes the relationship between changes in two variables; for example, a small change in price (variable 1) resulting in a large change in sales (variable 2) would reflect high elasticity.

Electronic malls A group of companies—usually with a common target market—selling via the Internet through a specific site.

Elevator pitch A 30-second (100 words or less) action-oriented description of a business designed to sell the idea of the business to another.

Employee fit The match between the needs, expectations, and culture of the small business with the expectations and the skills of the individual employee.

Employee referral An underused, low-cost method for finding workers that rewards your employees for recommending potential candidates that would be a great employee fit.

Employee stock ownership plan A formalized legal method to transfer some or all of the ownership of a business to its employees.

Employee theft Misappropriation of business property by employees of that business.

Entrepreneur A person who owns or starts an organization, such as a business.

Entrepreneurial alertness A special set of observational and thinking skills that help entrepreneurs identify good opportunities; the ability to notice things that have been overlooked, without actually launching a formal search for opportunities, and the motivation to look for opportunities.

Entry wedge An opportunity that makes it possible for a new business to gain a foothold in a market.

Environment The sum of all of the forces outside of the firm or entrepreneur.

Equal Employment Opportunity Commission (EEOC) A commission established to enforce the provisions of the Equal Employment Opportunity Act.

Equipment Machinery, tools, or materials used in the performance of the work of the business.

Equity Ownership of a portion of a business.

Equity capital Money contributed to the businesses in return for part ownership of the business.

ESOP Employee stock option plan: a method for employees to purchase the business for which they work.

Estate freeze An estate planning strategy which focuses on transferring assets to heirs when the asset costs are low.

E-tailer An electronic retailer; a store that exists only on the Internet.

Ethical dilemma A situation that occurs when a person's values are in conflict, making it unclear whether a decision is the right thing to do.

Ethics A system of values that people consider in determining whether actions are right or wrong.

Ethics planning A process used to better consider issues of right and wrong.

Ethnographic research Data gathered by simple observation—seeing what consumers do, rather than asking them.

Exculpatory clause Part of a contract in which a party to the contract states that he or she will not be responsible for certain actions.

Executive summary A one- to two-page (250–500 words) overview of the business, its business model, market, expectations, and immediate goals. It is typically put at the start of a business plan and is the most popular summary form for a business plan.

Expense A decrease in owners' equity caused by consuming your product or service.

Expert business professionalization A situation that occurs when all the major functions of a firm are conducted according to the standard business practices of its industry.

External environment The entire world outside of the firm's boundary.

External (cost) factors Aspects of the world outside the business which could cause the business's costs to change.

External legitimacy The extent to which a small business is taken for granted, accepted, or treated as viable by organizations or people outside the small business or the owner's family.

External reference price An estimation of what a price should be based on information external to a consumer, such as advice, advertisements, or comparison shopping.

External relations The process of managing relations with the environment.

F

4 Ps of Marketing The four major components of a marketing effort—product, price, promotion, and placement.

Factor-driven economies Nations with little manufacturing and largely farming and raw material extracting industries.

Factoring Selling the rights to collect accounts receivable to an entity outside your business.

Factoring receivables Borrowing money secured by a firm's accounts receivable.

Fair Credit Reporting Act U.S. federal legislation specifying consumer's rights vis-à-vis credit reporting agencies.

Fair market value The price at which goods and services are bought and sold between willing sellers and buyers in an arm's-length transaction.

Family business A firm in which one family owns a majority stake and is involved in the daily management of the business.

Famous faces A concept in public recognition which alludes to connections of your event or firm to individuals the general public would recognize.

Favorable/unfavorable variance A label applied to variances to indicate their effect upon the income statement; favorable variances would result in profits being greater than budgeted, all other things being equal; unfavorable variances would result in profits being less than budgeted, all other things being equal.

Feasibility The extent to which an idea is viable and realistic and the extent to which you are aware of internal (to your business) and external (industry, market, and regulatory environment) forces that could affect your business.

Feedback The process of communicating within or to the organization about how the outputs worked or were received.

Fidelity bonds Bonds, also called *dishonesty bonds,* that repay employers for losses caused by dishonest or negligent employees.

Financial accounting A formal, rule-based set of accounting principles and procedures intended for use by outside owners, investors, banks, and regulators.

Financial flexibility A business's ability to manage cash flows in such a manner that the company can respond appropriately to unexpected opportunities and needs.

Financial leverage A measure of the amount of debt relative to total investment.

Financial management A set of theories and techniques used to optimize the receipt and use of capital assets.

Financial risk Uncertainty of returns; the probability of losing money.

Financial statements Formal summaries of the content of an accounting system's records of transactions.

Financial strength The ability of a business to survive adverse financial events.

Financing activities Activities through which cash is obtained from and paid to lenders, owners, and investors.

Firm An organization that sells to or trades with others.

Fixed costs Those costs that remain constant regardless of quantity of output, for example, rent.

Flat fees A method of billing for lawyers in which a fixed amount is paid for a certain task.

Flexibility rewards The ability of business owners to structure life in the way that suits their needs best.

Float Delays in the movement of money among depositors and banks.

Flyers A sales document to be posted or handed out, typically printed on a 81/2- × 11-inch sheet of colored paper (or printed in color on white stock to increase visibility).

Focus group A form of data gathering from a small group led by a moderator.

Focus strategy A generic strategy that targets a portion of the market, called a *segment* or *niche.*

Focuses of entrepreneurship The key directions the organization intends to pursue.

Forms of entrepreneurship The settings in which the entrepreneurial effort takes place.

Foundation An institution to which private wealth is contributed and from which private wealth is distributed for public purposes.

Founders People who create or start new businesses.

Franchise A prepackaged business bought, rented, or leased from a company called a *franchisor.* (Ch. 1)

Franchise A legal agreement that allows a business to be operated using the name and business procedures of another firm. (Ch. 6)

Free ink Mentions of your company or products in the media for which your firm did not pay.

Freight forwarders Firms specializing in arranging international shipments—packaging, transportation, and paperwork.

Fulfillment center A company that will warehouse your products and fill your customers' orders for you.

Full (or classic) business plan Contains a maximum of 25 single-spaced pages of text and 15 pages of financials and appendixes.

Full-time self-employment Working for yourself for more than 35 hours a week.

GAAP Generally Accepted Accounting Principles are the standardized rules for accounting procedures set out by the Financial Account Standards Board and used in all audits and submissions of accounting reports to the government.

Gain on investment The percentage amount that the payout of an investment differs from original cost: calculated as (payout – investment + dividends)/investment.

Gaming the payment process Using methods to appear to be paying bills on time, when in fact payment is being delayed or avoided.

General environment The major forces or sectors outside the firm which have impact on the lives of people, businesses, institutions, and nations.

Generic strategies Three widely applicable classic strategies for businesses of all types—differentiation, cost, and focus.

Gift Valuable assets or services donated to the business without any obligation to repay or give up any ownership interest.

Goal An intended outcome for your business.

Going concern concept The accounting concept that a business is expected to continue in existence for the foreseeable future.

Golden Rule An ethical model which suggests you treat others in the manner you wish to be treated.

Goods A physical product.

Goods or services The tangible things (goods) or intangible commodities (services) created for sale.

Good story A concept in public interest which alludes to an incident with good triumphing.

Grants Gifts of money made to a business for a specific purpose.

Green entrepreneurship Starting or running a firm in a manner which saves or improves the environment. (See *Sustainable entrepreneurship*.)

Gross profit Funds left over after deducting the cost of goods sold.

Growth rewards What people get from facing and beating challenges.

Growth stage An industry life cycle stage in which customer purchases increase at a dramatic rate.

Growth trap A financial crisis that is caused by a business growing faster than it can be financed.

Guerilla marketing The use of creative and relatively inexpensive ways to reach your customer. Examples include doorknob hangers, flyers under windshield wipers, T-shirts, balloons, and messages written on sidewalks.

H

Habit-driven planners Entrepreneurs who do not plan, preferring to let all actions be dictated by their routines.

Harvest Recover value through a sale of a firm or its assets.

Heir A person who becomes an owner through inheriting or being given a stake in a family business.

Heterogeneity A quality of a service in which each time it is provided it will be slightly different from the previous time.

Heuristic A commonsense rule, a rule-of-thumb.

High-growth venture A firm started with the intent of eventually going public, following the pattern of growth and operations of a big business.

High-performing small business A firm intended to provide the owner with a high income through sales or profits superior to those of the traditional small business.

Highly fragmented industries Collections of similar businesses in which virtually all firms have small market shares.

Hold harmless A type of waiver in which a party agrees not to hold another party responsible for certain events.

Home-based business A business that is operated from the owner's home.

Hourly fees A basis for legal charges in which the rate is based on a price per hour. Often lawyers will charge for fractions of an hour.

Human interest A concept in public interest which alludes to a character to whom the public can relate.

I

Identity The basic description of the firm, its "who, what, where, and why."

Imitative Characterized by being like or copying something that already exists.

Imitative strategy An overall strategic approach in which the entrepreneur does more or less what others are already doing.

Impression What it is called when someone notices a promotional effort.

Income rewards The money made by owning one's own business.

Income statement A statement that lists revenues and expenses and shows the amount of profit a business makes for a specified period of time.

Incremental innovation An overall strategic approach in which a firm patterns itself on other firms, with the exception of one or two key areas.

Incremental strategy Taking an idea and offering a way to do something slightly better than it is done presently.

Incubator A facility which offers subsidized space and business advice to companies in their earliest stages of operation.

Independent contractors Persons working to achieve a certain goal without being subjected to substantial controls by another.

Independent entrepreneurship The form of entrepreneurship in which a person or group own their own for-profit business.

Independent small business A business owned by an individual or small group.

Indirect competition Companies that provide alternatives that are dissimilar to your product/service that consumers might choose to meet a similar need; for example, indirect competition for Coca-Cola includes any other company providing items to quench thirst.

Indirect exporting Exporting using middlemen such as agents, export management companies, or export trading companies.

Industry The general name for the line of product or service being sold, or the firms in that line of business.

Industry analysis (IA) A research process that provides the entrepreneur with key information about the industry, such as its current situation and trends.

Industry dynamics Changes in competitors, sales, and profits in an industry over time.

Industry life cycle The stages an industry goes through from its birth to its ending. There are five stages: introduction, growth, maturity, decline, and death.

Industry specific knowledge Activities, knowledge, and skills specific to businesses in a particular industry.

Inelastic product Product for which there are few substitutes and for which a change in price makes very little difference in quantity purchased.

Informal capital Sources of funding from noninstitutional sources such as family, friends, and other individuals.

Informational plans Give potential customers or suppliers information about the company and its product or service.

Informational website An Internet site designed to introduce and explain a business to others.

Infringer Someone who uses intellectual property without the permission of the owner.

Initial public offering (IPO) Transfer method describing the first-time public sale of a stock listed on a public stock exchange.

Innovation The entreprenurial focus which looks at a new thing or a new way of doing things.

Innovation-driven economies Nations with high-value-added manufacturing and large service sectors.

Innovative strategy An overall strategic approach in which a firm seeks to do something that is very different from what others in the industry are doing.

Innovativeness The extent to which a product, service, or individual's thinking process is novel or an improvement over existing choices.

Inputs The materials, labor, and energy put into the production of a good or service.

Inseparability A quality of a service in which the service being done cannot be disconnected from the provider of the service.

Insurable value The amount of an asset for which a company will write an insurance policy.

Insurance A contract between two or more parties in which one party agrees, for a fee, to assume the risk of another.

Intangible assets Things of value that have no physical existence, for example, patents and trade secrets.

Intangible property Property that has no value of its own but that represents value, such as a stock certificate.

Integrative view An ethical overview which involves considering what is best for everyone involved in a situation.

Intellectual property Property coming from some sort of original thought, for example, patents, trade secrets, trademarks, and copyrights.

Interest A charge for the use of money, usually figured as a percentage of the principal.

Internal control A set of rules and procedures that work to limit the opportunity for employee theft or malfeasance.

Internal environment The people (owners, employees, and board members) inside the boundary of a firm.

Internal (cost) factors Aspects of or choices within the business which could cause the business's costs to change.

Internal reference price A consumer's mental image of what a product's price should be.

Internal understanding The extent to which employees, investors, and family members involved in the business know the business's purposes and operations.

Internet recruiting Method of recruiting that allows you to search a résumé database or post a job description to the web; a small business owner who knows exactly what he or she wants can use filters to search vast numbers of résumés with pinpoint accuracy.

Introduction stage The life cycle stage in which the product or service is being invented and initially developed.

Invention plan A business plan that provides information to potential licensees. Invention plans focus on the details of an invention, including intellectual property rights.

Inventory Products that are held for sale to customers.

Inventory valuation Determination of the amount of assets held by the firm for sale or production.

Investing activities The purchase and sale of land, buildings, equipment, and securities.

ISO Stands for the International Standards Organization, and refers to certification for having met a standard of quality that is consistently evaluated around the world (see www.iso.org).

Issue recognition A concept in public recognition which alludes to the extent to which the public is familiar with the issue or problem at hand.

J

Job description Defines and discusses all the essential knowledge, skills, and abilities that are needed to fill a position.

Joint venture An agreement between two or more entities to pool resources in order to complete a project.

Just-in-time inventory The practice of purchasing and accepting delivery of inventory only after it has been sold to the final customer.

K

Key business functions Activities common to all businesses such as sales, operations (also called *production*), accounting, finance, and human resources.

Key employee/partner plans Provides information on the company, product/service, market, and critical risks to prospective business or marketing partners or to prospective key employees.

Key employees Employees whose experience and skills are critical to the success of a business.

Keyword and description tags Terms included in the hidden portion of a web page (called the *document head*) which are used by search engines such as Yahoo! and Google to describe your website and evaluate its focus and category placement.

Keyword optimization The selection of words that describe a website ad that results in the site being displayed toward the beginning of a search engine's (e.g., Google, Yahoo!, etc.) listing for that term.

L

Laggard A customer adoption segment that holds off buying new products or services until either they are forced to or prices reach rock-bottom.

Late career entrepreneurs (also known as *second career entrepreneurs*) People who begin their businesses after having retired or resigned from work in corporations at age 50 or later.

Late majority A customer adoption segment describing people who wait until the technology has stabilized and the costs have begun to drop.

Law of supply and demand The economic theory that describes how the demand for products (or services) and the supply of them affect each other.

Legal entity A being, human or nonhuman, such as a corporation, that is recognized as having rights and duties, such as the right to own property.

Legitimacy The belief that a firm is worthy of consideration or doing business with because of the impressions or opinions of customers, suppliers, investors, or competitors.

Letter of credit A document issued by a bank that guarantees a buyer's payment for a specified period of time upon compliance with specified terms.

Liabilities Legal obligations to give up things of value in the future.

Liability of newness The set of risks faced by firms early in their life cycles that comes from a lack of knowledge by the owners about the business they are in and by customers about the new business.

License A legal agreement granting you rights to use a particular piece of intellectual property.

Licensee The person or firm which is obtaining the rights to use a particular piece of intellectual property.

Licensing Documented permission from the government to run your business.

Licensor The person or organization which is offering the rights to use a particular piece of intellectual property.

Lifestyle or part-time firm A small business primarily intended to provide partial or subsistence financial support for the existing lifestyle of the owner, most often through operations that fit the owner's schedule and way of working.

Limited liability company (LLC) A legal form of business organization that is created by filing required documentation with a state government. LLCs have a choice, under federal tax law, of being taxed as either corporations or partnerships.

Limited partnership A legal form of business organization that is created by filing required documentation with a state government; within a limited partnership, one or more partners may have no liability for the debts and actions of the partnership.

Liquidation A popular term for a Chapter 7 bankruptcy in which a bankrupt firm's assets are sold by the bankruptcy trustee and the proceeds used to pay the firm's debts.

Liquidity A measure of how quickly a company can raise money through internal sources by converting assets to cash.

Liquidity enhancement An estate planning method in which cash is generated (usually through a life insurance policy) to cover the estate taxes.

Litigation A formal dispute resolution method that operates using the court system, typically with a lawyer representing each party.

Living wage The amount needed for a person (or family of a particular size) to meet the basic necessities of life from a single job.

Lock box A locked receptacle for money, the keys to which are not available to those who physically handle the receptacle; a common example of a lock box is the coin receptacle for parking meters which cannot be opened by the workers who are responsible for collecting the deposited coins.

M

MACRS rate An Internal Revenue Service acronym for the Modified Accelerated Cost Recovery System. The MACRS approach lets taxpayers depreciate more of the cost earlier in the life of a capital expense.

Magic number The post-tax income the entrepreneur personally seeks from the business.

Mail order Sales made from ads in newspapers or magazines, with purchases taken online or by phone as well as by mail.

Main street businesses A popular term for small businesses reflecting the idea that these are the kinds of firms you would expect to find on the main street of a typical American city, and are the opposite of big business or "Wall Street" businesses.

Managerial accounting Accounting methods that are specifically intended to be used by managers for planning, directing, and controlling a business.

Manufacturer The entity which produces a product or service to be sold.

Manufacturers suggested retail price A target price set by a manufacturer for a product or service intended to provide profit for each intermediary in the distribution channel.

Margin The amount of profit, usually stated as a percentage of the total price.

Market The business term for the population of customers for your product or service.

Market expansion A strategy whose goal is growth, based on selling in areas or to groups previously not served by the business.

Market penetration A strategy whose goal is growth, based on selling more of the firm's product or service to the existing customer base.

Market research Research conducted to uncover market and customer needs and opportunities; it exists at two levels, primary and secondary.

Market segmentation The process of dividing the market into groups that have somewhat homogeneous needs for a product or service.

Marketable securities Stocks and bonds that are traded on an open market.

Marketing funnel The rule of thumb in marketing that it takes a large number of people to be made aware of your product in order to find a purchaser.

Marketing plan A systematic written plan of all phases of marketing for a business, including information on the product, price, distribution, and promotion strategy, as well as a clear identification of the target market and competition.

Marketing research Systematic collection and interpretation of data to support future marketing decisions.

Markup The amount an entrepreneur adds to costs to provide a profit.

Markup pricing A price-setting method where an amount is added to the cost of a product to set the retail price and provide a profit.

Mass market A customer group that involves large portions of the population.

Master budget A budget, also referred to as a *comprehensive budget*, which consists of sets of budgets that detail all projected receipts and spending for the budgeted period.

Mat release A news release that is typeset and thus may be photographically reproduced for inclusion in a newspaper.

Maturity stage The third life cycle stage, marked by a stabilization of demand, with firms in the industry moving to stabilize or improve profits through cost strategies.

Me-too products Products essentially similar to something already on the market.

Meritocracy A management philosophy of selecting and promoting people based solely on their being the most capable person for the job.

Microinventory The purchase of inventory only after a sale is made; very typical with Internet firms.

Mindshare The degree of attention your target market pays to your idea or organization.

Minimalized business professionalization A situation that occurs when the entrepreneur does nearly everything in the simplest way possible.

Mission statement A paragraph that describes the firm's goals and competitive advantages.

Money An accepted medium of exchange.

Moonlighting Working on your own part time after your regular job.

Multichannel marketing The use of several different channels to reach your customers, for example, a website, direct mail, and traditional retailing.

Multiple or bonus pack Combining more than one unit of the same product and pricing it lower than if each unit were sold separately.

Mutuality The action of each person helping another.

N

Necessity-driven entrepreneurship Creating a firm as an alternative to unemployment.

Nepotism A management philosophy of selecting and promoting people based on family ties.

Net profit The amount of money left after operating expenses are deducted from the business.

Net realizable value The amount for which an asset will sell, less the costs of selling.

Network marketing An approach to selling in which the salesperson recruits customers to become distributors of the product or service to others.

Networking Interacting with others in order to build relationships useful to a business.

New entrant business A firm whose product or service is established elsewhere, but is new to this market.

Newsworthy events To garner serious attention from the media and the public, a news story needs to deliver certain essentials that will hold their attention and keep your news in their thoughts. It should have public recognition, importance, and interest.

Niche market A narrowly defined segment of the population that is likely to share interests or concerns.

Noncash incentives Rewards that do not require payment of cash, such as stock options, compensating time off, or added vacation days.

Noncompete clause Part of a contract in which a person agrees not to open a certain type business or seek employment doing certain things in a particular area for a period of time.

Noncore projects Revenue-producing tasks and activities related to, but not part of, the primary strategy of a business.

Nonsufficient funds A situation that occurs when a check is returned to a depositor because the writer of the check did not have a bank available balance equal to or greater than the amount of the check.

Novelty Characterized by being different or new.

O

Occupation The type of activity a person does regularly for pay.

Occupational Safety and Health Administration (OSHA) A government agency created to enforce safety in the workplace.

Odd-even pricing Setting a price that ends in the number 5, 7, or 9.

Off-peak pricing Charging lower prices at certain times to encourage customers to come during slack periods.

On-the-job training Delivered to employees while they perform their regular jobs; techniques include orientations, job instruction training, apprenticeships, internships and assistantships, job rotation, and coaching.

Open-book policy Concept that key employees should be able to see and understand a firm's financials, that they should have a part in moving the numbers in the right direction, and that they should have a direct stake in the strategy and success of the firm.

Open-ended questions Questions that allow respondents to express themselves as they choose; for example, "What do you like about this book?"

Operating activities Activities involved in producing and selling goods and services.

Operating agreement A contract among LLC members outlining how the LLC will conduct itself.

Operating cycle See cash-to-cash cycle.

Operating lease A long-term rental in which ownership of the asset never passes to the person paying for the lease.

Operational plan Business plans designed to be used internally for management purposes.

Operations The process of transforming materials, labor, and energy into goods or services.

Opportunistic planners Entrepreneurs who start with a goal instead of a plan and look for opportunities to achieve it.

Opportunity competencies Skills necessary to identify and exploit elements of the business environment that can lead to a profitable and sustainable business.

Opportunity cost The value of an economic activity or event that is foregone in order to be able to undertake a different, specific activity or event.

Opportunity-driven entrepreneurship Creating a firm to improve's one's income or a product or service.

Opportunity recognition Searching and capturing new ideas that lead to business opportunities. This process often involves creative thinking that leads to discovery of new and useful ideas.

Optimum capital structure The ratio of debt to equity that provides the maximum level of profits.

Optimum price The highest price that will produce your desired level of sales in your intended market.

Optimum stocking level The amount of inventory that results in the minimum cost, when considering the cost of lost sales resulting from running out of stock, the number of units sold per day, and the number of days required to receive inventory.

Organizational culture A set of shared beliefs, basic assumptions, or common, accepted ways of dealing with problems and challenges within a company that demonstrate how things get done.

Outflow Funds being paid to others by the firm.

Outputs The service or product that is produced for sale.

Outside equity Money from selling part of your business to people who are not and will not be involved in the management of the business.

Outsourcing Contracting with people or companies outside your business to do work for your business.

Overall growth strategy One of four general ways to position a business based on the rate and level of growth entrepreneurs anticipate for their firm.

Overdraft A negative balance in a depositor's bank account.

Owner-managed firm A business run by the individual who owns it.

Owners' equity The difference between assets and liabilities of a business.

Parallel competition An imitative business that competes locally with others in the same industry.

Partitioned pricing Setting the price for a base item and then charging extra for each additional component.

Partnership Two or more people cooperating to conduct a business enterprise.

Part-time self-employment Working for yourself for 35 or fewer hours a week.

Pass through (taxation) Earnings of the business are distributed to the business owners and those owners (rather than the business) pay individual tax on the earnings.

Passion The intensely positive feeling entrepreneurs have for their business.

Patent A grant by the U.S. government to an inventor for an idea that is new, useful, and nonobvious, giving the inventor the exclusive right to make, use, or sell his or her idea.

Payables Amounts owed to vendors for merchandise or services purchased on credit (see *Receivables*).

Payback period The amount of time it takes a business to earn back the funds it paid out to obtain a capital asset.

Perceptual map A graphic display that positions products, services, brands, or companies according to their scores of important strategic dimensions.

Periodic inventory The process of physically counting business assets on a set schedule.

Periodic or random discounting Sales conducted at either predictable or nonpredictable intervals.

Perishability A service exhibits perishability in that if it is not used when offered, it cannot be saved for later use.

Permanance The impression of long-term continuity a business gives others.

Perpetual inventory A system of recording the receipt and sale of each item as it occurs.

Perseverance The ability to stick to activities over long periods, even in the face of setbacks.

Personal selling The process of selling your products and service; includes prospect and evaluate, prepare, present, close, and follow-up.

Physical inventory A count of all the inventory being held for sale at a specific point in time.

Piercing the veil The dissolution of a corporate form, making it back into a sole proprietorship or general partnership, if the court finds that the owner carelessly mixed up personal and business assets or finances.

Pilot test A preliminary run of a business, sales effort, program, or website with the goal of assessing how well the overall approach works and what problems it might have.

Pioneering business A firm whose product or service is new to the industry or is itself creating a new industry.

Plaintiff Person or other entity filing a lawsuit.

Planning style Ranging from comprehensive to habit-based, this shows about what and how much you ordinarily plan.

Plant A general term for the facilities of a business.

Plant patent A 20-year patent that covers new strains of living plant organisms, algae, or macro fungi.

Pledging receivables Giving a third party legal rights to debts owed your business in order to provide assurance that borrowed money will be repaid.

Point of indifference The price at which a buyer is indifferent about buying or not buying the business.

Point-of-sale system Hardware and software combinations that integrate inventory management directly into accounting software.

Poisoning the well Creating a negative impression among your employers' customers.

Potential for growth Refers to the potential market size.

Power A concept in public importance which alludes to potential shifts in control or influence.

Predetermined market segments Professionally compiled target audiences based on shared demographic, financial, shopping and psychographic characteristics.

Preselling Involves introducing your product to potential customers and taking orders for later delivery.

Press kit A type of sales kit sent to media outlets which is focused around a press release.

Press relations Activities used to establish and promote a favorable opinion by the media.

Press release A written announcement intended to draw news media attention to a specific event.

Prestige or premium pricing Setting a price above that of the competition so as to indicate a higher quality or that a product is a status symbol.

Prevention focus An entrepreneur's attention to minimizing losses, with a bias toward inaction or protective action to prevent loss.

Price gouging Charging an outrageously high price for something.

Price lining The practice of setting (usually) three price points: good quality, better quality, best quality.

Primary research Information collected to solve a problem at hand or answer current questions.

Private placement memorandum A specialized legal form of business plan crafted by lawyers for the purpose of soliciting formal investments.

Probationary period Trial period in which an employee has temporary status before a formal offer to work full time is presented.

Process of personal selling The process of selling your products and service; includes prospect and evaluate, prepare, present, and the close.

Product distribution franchising An agreement that provides specific brand name products which are resold by the franchisee in a specified territory.

Product expansion A strategy whose goal is growth, based on selling existing customers a product or service they have never bought before.

Productivity The ratio measure of how well a firm does in using its inputs to create outputs. Literally, productivity is outputs divided by inputs.

Professionalization The extent to which a firm meets or exceeds the standard business practices for its industry.

Profit, profitability The amount that revenues exceed expenses.

Profit before taxes The amount of profit earned by a business before calculating the amount of income tax owed.

Pro forma Latin for "in the form of" when used to describe financial statements, indicates estimated or hypothetical information.

Promotion focus An entrepreneur's attention to maximizing gains and pursuing opportunities likely to lead to gains.

Promotion/prevention focus The behaviors related to pursuing gains and preventing losses.

Promotional mix How much of each message conveyance you will use to sell your product as well as your objective in using each one.

Proof-of-concept website An Internet-based type of business plan providing information or demonstration of a product or service designed to solicit information on customer interest.

Property A general term for real estate, but it can also be applied as a legal term for anything owned or possessed.

Proprietary technology A product or service or an aspect of one that is kept as a trade secret or is protected legally using patent, copyright, trademark, or service mark.

Prospects Sales leads who actually make some sort of effort to learn more about the product, service, or business in anticipation of a possible purchase.

Protected classes States of being that are expressly prohibited from suffering discrimination: race, color, religion, sex, national origin, gender, age, or disability.

Proximity A concept in public recognition which alludes to the impact level of the issue being discussed.

Psychological contract Refers to employees' beliefs about the promises between the employee and the firm. These beliefs are based on the perception that promises have been made (e.g., competitive wages, promotional opportunities, job training) in exchange for certain employee obligations such as giving of their energy, time, and technical skills.

Public importance (1) Things that are considered important to large numbers of otherwise unrelated people, (2) things that are of civic importance, as opposed to private or corporate entities.

Public interest (1) Things that are generally considered to be beneficial to large numbers of people, (2) civic causes and benefits, as opposed to private and corporate benefits.

Public recognition Being recognized or acknowledged by large numbers of people, similar to "fame."

Public relations Activities used to establish and promote a favorable opinion by the public.

Publicity Information about your company and its activities that is disseminated to the public in order to gain their good opinion.

Pull-through system A term for just-in-time inventory systems in which product is ordered and placed into production only after a sale has been completed.

Pure innovation The process of creating new products or services, which results in a previously unseen product or service.

Q

Qualitative research Techniques for gathering information that rely on opinions expressed without a numerical basis ("real good" instead of "4 on a 5-point scale"). Popular techniques for qualitative research include interviews, small groups discussions, and observation.

Quantitative research Techniques that depend on categorizing responses into numbers, enabling statistical analysis of opinions. Examples include surveys and focus groups.

Quality A product's or service's fitness for use, measured as durability, reliability, serviceability, style, ease of use, and dependability.

R

Radical innovation strategy Rejecting existing ideas, and presenting a way to do things differently.

Reactive planners Entrepreneurs with a passive approach, who wait for cues from the environment to determine what actions to take.

Receivables Amounts that are owed to a business for merchandise that was sold on credit (see payables).

Reciprocal link A listed, live connection to a different website, which in turn displays a similar link to the first website.

Reconciling An accounting process that identifies the causes of all differences between book and bank balances.

Referral discount A discount given to a customer who refers a friend to the business.

Registration Information provided to the government concerning the existence of, name of, nature of, and contact information for your business.

Regulation of the workplace Laws and governmental rules that limit the freedom of business owners to manage their businesses as they please.

Rehabilitation Act of 1973 An act of Congress that provides training for workers who are injured on the job.

Reorganization The popular term for a Chapter 13 bankruptcy in which a bankrupt firm continues to operate while paying off debts identified by the bankruptcy trustee.

Replacement cost The total cost of replacing an asset with an essentially identical asset.

Replacement value The cost to acquire an essentially identical asset. (Ch. 6)

Replacement value The cost incurred to replace one asset with an identical asset. (Ch. 16)

Research and development (often abbreviated R&D) The part of a business (and a business plan) that is focused on creating new products or services and preparing new technologies, ideas, products, or services for the firm's market.

Reserve price A minimum acceptable selling price in an auction. If the bidding does not exceed the price, the sale will not go through.

Resource competencies The ability or skill of the entrepreneur at finding expendable components necessary to the operation of the business such as time, information, location, financing, raw materials, and expertise.

Retailer A middleman business which sells to consumers or end users of a product (typically in single or small quantities).

Retained earnings The sum of all profits and losses, less all dividends paid since the beginning of the business.

Retainer A fee paid by a client to an attorney to engage the attorney's services.

Retrenchment An organizational life cycle stage in which established firms must find new approaches to improve the business and its chances for survival.

Return on equity The ratio of profits to owner investment in a business.

Return on investment (ROI) A capital budgeting equation used to measure the relationship between initial investment and the profits that are expected to be received from making the investment.

Reverse auction An auction in which the low bid gets the business or wins.

Revolving credit A credit agreement that allows the borrower to pay all or part of the balance at any time; as the loan balance is paid off, it becomes available to be borrowed again.

Risk The level of probability that an investment will not produce expected gains.

Risks The parts of a business or business plan that expose the firm to any kind of loss—profits, sales, reputation, assets, customers, and so on.

Role conflict The kind of problem that arises when people have multiple responsibilities, such as parent and boss, and the different responsibilities make different demands on them.

Royalty A payment to a licensor based on the number or value of licensed items sold.

RSS feed An Internet messaging service that pushes (sends) whatever web material you specify to subscribers to that feed.

Safety stock An amount of inventory carried to ensure that you will not run out of inventory because of fluctuating levels of sales.

Sales leads People who receive a promotional impression and who give some thought to buying the product.

Sales promotion A form of communication that encourages the customer to act immediately, such as coupons, sales, or contests.

Sarbanes-Oxley Act A federal law describing the steps publicly traded businesses must take to protect and provide their key financial information.

Scalar questions Questions that are answered by some sort of scale; for example, "On a scale of 1 to 5, how do you like this book?"

Scale A characteristic of a market that describes the size of the market—a mass market or a niche market.

SCAMPER A creativity tool that provides cues to trigger breakthrough thinking. The letters stand for substitute, combine, adapt, modify, put to other uses, eliminate, and rearrange.

Scope A characteristic of a market that defines the geographic range covered by the market—from local to global.

Screening plan Also called a *mini-plan,* gives the basic overview of the firm and a detailed look at the financials.

Search engine optimization A general approach to website design intended to result in the site being displayed toward the beginning of a search engine's (e.g., Google, Yahoo!, etc.) listing for that term.

Secondary research Information already collected for some other purpose than the current problem or questions.

Segmentation The process of dividing the market into smaller portions of people who have common characteristics.

Self-efficacy A person's belief in his or her ability to achieve a goal.

Self-employed Working for yourself.

Separation of duties A type of internal control that separates the physical control of an asset from the person accounting for that asset.

Serial entrepreneurs People who open multiple businesses throughout their career.

Services A nonphysical product.

Set-asides Government contracting funds which are earmarked for particular kinds of firms, such as small businesses, minority-owned firms, women-owned firms, and the like.

Shake-out A type of life cycle stage following a boom in which there is a rapid decrease in the number of firms in an industry.

Sheltered workshop A nonprofit organization or institution that provides business services by using handicapped or rehabilitated workers.

Short-term debt Any debt that must be paid in less than one year from the date of the financial statement on which it is reported.

Single taxation Earnings of the business are taxed once with the owners paying the taxes.

Skimming Setting a price at the highest level the market will bear, usually because there is no competition at the time.

Slack resources Profits that are available to be used to satisfy the preferences of the owner in how the business is run.

Small and medium enterprise The international term for small businesses.

Small business Involves 1–50 people and has its owner managing the business on a day-to-day basis.

Small Business Administration A part of the United States government which provides support and advocacy for small businesses.

Small Business Development Center Offices co-sponsored by states and the Federal government that offer free or low-cost help to existing and potential small businesses.

Small business investment companies Private businesses that are authorized to make SBA insured loans to start-ups and small businesses.

Social capital Characteristics of a business, like trust, consistency, and networks, that represent potential social obligations which are an asset of the firm or entrepreneur.

Social entrepreneurship The form of entrepreneurship involving the creation of self-sustaining charitable and civic organizations, or for-profit organizations which invest significant profits in charitable activities.

Social network The entrepreneur's set of relationships and contacts with individuals and institutions.

Sole proprietorship A business owned by a single individual who is responsible for all debts and claims against the business.

Specialized business professionalization A situation that occurs when businesses have founders or owners who are passionate about one or two of the key business functions, such as sales, operations, accounting, finance, or human resources.

Spin-off A business that is created by separating part of an operating business into a separate entity.

Sponsored link A form of paid advertising that gets your company's website at the top of a search list.

Sponsorships Paying for a local organization's needs in exchange for recognition.

Standard business practice A business action that has been widely adopted within an industry or occupation.

Start-up A new business that is started from scratch.

Straight line for a useful life of 10 years Depreciation is computed using a straight line method over 10 years, so an asset would lose 10% of its value each year.

Strategic actions Competitive responses requiring a major commitment of resources.

Subcontract A contract by which a new party agrees to perform a duty that one of the original parties to a contract was already legally obligated to perform.

Substitution profits Returns intended to equal and replace the salary or wages the entrepreneur could draw working for someone else.

Success profits Returns at levels higher than the entrepreneur could make working for others.

Succession The process of intergenerational transfer of a business.

Succinct message Your key point in as few and as memorable words as possible.

Supplemental profits Returns above costs intended as a secondary income for entrepreneurs (where self-employment is secondary to their main job).

Suppy chain Like the value chain, the line of distribution of a product from its start as materials outside the target firm to its handling in the target firm to its handling by sellers into the hands of customers.

Surety bonds An agreement with an insurance or bonding company that will pay a specified amount in the event that the entity bonded fails to comply with specified contractual requirements.

Survey A data-collection method using a questionnaire—in person, on phone, on paper, or on the Internet.

Sustainable entrepreneurship Starting or running a firm in a manner which saves or improves the environment. (See *Green entrepreneurship*.)

Synergy A combination in which the whole is greater than the sum of its component parts.

T

Tactical actions Competitive responses with low resource requirements.

Tagline (also known as a slogan) Memorable catchphrase that captures the key idea of a business, its service, product, or customer.

Takeover Seizing of control of a business by purchasing its stock to be able to select the board of directors.

Tangibility An item's capability of being touched, seen, tasted, or felt.

Target market The group of people on which a marketer focuses promotion and sales efforts.

Task environment Those parts of the environment outside of the firm which directly and consistently touch on the firm.

Tax abatement A legal reduction in taxes by a government.

Tax accounting An accounting approach based on specific accounting requirements set by governmental taxing agencies.

Tax codes Laws and regulations that specify the requirements of taxation.

Tax credits Direct reductions in the amount of taxes that must be paid, dependent upon meeting some legal criteria.

Tax management An estate planning strategy which uses structured transfers of the business to make tax payments as small as possible.

Telemarketing Contact via telephone for the express purpose of selling a product or service. Telemarketing can either be inbound (customer calls company) or outbound (company calls customer).

Termination An endgame strategy in which the owner closes down a business.

Test marketing Selling your product or service in a limited area, for a limited time.

Time management The organizing process to help make the most efficient use of the day.

Time to start-up How long it takes to start a new business.

Timing purchases A method of controlling the timing of cash outflows that is invisible to suppliers and vendors.

Total product The entire bundle of products, services, and meanings of your offering; includes extras like service, warranty, or delivery, as well as what the product means to the customer.

Trade association (also known as *professional association*). A group of people in the same industry who band together to gather and share information and present and represent the industry to the public and government.

Trade discounts Percentage discounts from gross invoice amounts provided to encourage prompt payment.

Trade magazines The magazines that target specific industries and professions.

Trade name or assumed name or a doing business as (dba) The name under which a business is operated.

Trade name franchising An agreement that provides to the franchisee only the rights to use the franchisor's trade name and/ or trademarks.

Trade secret Confidential information within a company that gives that company a competitive advantage.

Trademark Distinctive word, slogan, or image that identifies a product and its origin.

Traditional small business A firm intended to provide a living income to the owner, and operating in a manner and on a schedule consistent with other firms in the industry and market.

Traffic generators Other businesses that bring customers (generate traffic) to the area.

Transfer An endgame strategy in which ownership is moved from one person or group to another.

Trendiness A concept in public recognition which alludes to the fit of the topic to current fashion or public interest.

Trust A feeling of fairness in all business transactions in which the firm engages, such as financial transactions, employee matters, regulatory compliance, and complaint resolution.

Tweet A 140-character or less message sent using the Twitter web service.

U

Undercapitalization Not having enough money available to the business to cover shortfalls in sales or profits.

Undifferentiated strategy A marketing strategy that uses no segmentation; assumes that all consumers have virtually identical needs and can be reached by the same marketing mix.

Universalism An ethical model that suggests that there is a code of right and wrong that everyone can see and follow.

Utilitarianism An ethical model that supports seeking the greatest good for the greatest number of people.

Utility patent A 20-year patent covering a process, machine, article of manufacture, composition of matter, or any new or useful improvement of an existing one.

V

Value proposition Small business owners' unique selling points that will be used to differentiate their products and/or services from those of the competition.

Variable costs Those costs that change with each unit produced, for example, raw materials.

Variance Permission from a government organization to act differently than the laws state. (Ch. 5)

Variance The difference between an actual and budgeted revenue or cost. (Ch. 13)

Variance analysis The process of determining the effect of price and quantity changes on revenues and expenses.

Viability The preliminary assessment of the potential for a business to be created or, once created, to survive.

Vicarious (indirect) liability Indirect liability or responsibility for the actions of another.

Viral marketing Any electronic equivalent of word-of-mouth advertising, in which the advertiser's message spreads quickly and widely via e-mail, website, blogs, and other online tools.

Virtual employees Independent contractors who provide specialized business services or support from a distance, through the Internet, telephone, fax, or another method of communication.

Virtual instant global entrepreneurship (VIGE) Deploying a business internationally using the e-commerce capabilities of the Internet.

Vision statement A very simple 5–10 word sentence or tagline that expresses the fundamental idea or goal of the firm.

Visuals A concept in public interest which alludes to the graphic interest held by an event.

Volatility The frequency of business starts and stops.

W

Waiver Part of a contract in which a party intentionally gives up legal rights or claims.

Walkaways Business terminations in which the entrepreneur ends the business with its obligations met.

Weighted average cost of capital (WAC) The expected average future cost of funds.

Whole of life costs The sum of all costs of capital assets, including acquisition, ownership, operation, and disposal.

Wholesaler A middleman business which buys (typically in large quantities) and sells (typically in smaller quantities) to businesses rather than consumers.

Word-of-mouth A means of spreading information about your business through the comments friends and customers make to other potential customers.

Workout A form of business termination in which the firm's legal or financial obligations are not fully met at closing.

Z

Zoning laws Government specifications for acceptable use of land and buildings in particular areas.

END NOTES

Chapter 1

1. This is based on a personal interview of Paul Scheiter by Jerome Katz, and also on A. Taranto, "American Entrepreneur | Paul Scheiter," *Ars Magna Studio—Photography Blog,* April 27, 2009, http://blog.arsmagnastudio.com/2009/04/27/american-entrepreneur-paul-scheiter/ and G. Lucas, "Paul Scheiter of Hedgehog Leatherworks," *Woods Monkey,* September 22, 2008, www.woodsmonkey.com/index.php?option=com_content&view=article&id=161:paul-scheiter-audio-interview&catid=73:inteviewsprofiles&Itemid=85, and M. Halverson, "Mind Games—The Graduate," *St. Louis Magazine,* February 2007, www.stlmag.com/St-Louis-Magazine/February-2007/Mind-Games-The-Graduate/#.
2. Self-efficacy has a long history in predicting entrepreneurial intention and action. The key work for many is N. Krueger and P. R Dickson, "How Believing in Ourselves Increases Risk Taking: Perceived Self-Efficacy and Opportunity Recognition," *Decision Sciences* 25, no. 3 (May 1, 1994), pp. 385–400. Other relevant works include C. C. Chen, P. G. Greene, and A. Crick, "Does Entrepreneurial Self-efficacy Distinguish Entrepreneurs from Managers?" *Journal of Business Venturing* 13, no. 4 (July 1998), pp. 295–316; C. P. Neck et al., "'I Think I Can; I Think I Can: A Self-leadership Perspective Toward Enhancing Entrepreneur Thought Patterns, Self-efficacy, and Performance," *Journal of Managerial Psychology* 14, no. 6 (January 11, 1999), pp. 477–501. F. Wilson, J. Kickul, and D. Marlino, "Gender, Entrepreneurial Self-Efficacy, and Entrepreneurial Career Intentions: Implications for Entrepreneurship Education," *Entrepreneurship Theory and Practice* 31, no. 3 (2007), pp. 387–406.
3. This link between planning and success has been shown worldwide in the works of Michael Frese and his colleagues in their studies of "action strategies." Their work shows that the intensity of the planning you do can make a difference between success and failure. M. Frese, M. van Gelderen, and M. Ombach, "How to Plan as a Small Scale Business Owner: Psychological Process Characteristics of Action Strategies and Success," *Journal of Small Business Management* 38, no. 2 (April 2000), pp. 1–18. J-L. Van Gelder et al., "Differences in Psychological Strategies of Failed and Operational Business Owners in the Fiji Islands," *Journal of Small Business Management* 45, no. 3 (May 26, 2007), pp. 388–400.
4. For help from experts, the key findings have come from James Chrisman and colleagues. In their latest study they reported that expert counseling improved performance whereas entrepreneurship classes increased the likelihood of venture creation. J. J. Chrisman et al., "Counseling Assistance, Entrepreneurship Education, and New Venture Performance," *Journal of Entrepreneurship and Public Policy* 1, no. 1 (April 20, 2012), pp. 63–83. The key study for education effects remains A. Charney and G. Libecap, *Impact of Entrepreneurship Education* (Kansas City, MO: Kauffman Center for Entrepreneurial Leadership, 2000), although there are now dozens of studies of individual programs.
5. B. Bucar, M. Glas, and R. D. Hisrich, "Ethics and Entrepreneurs: An International Comparative Study," *Journal of Business Venturing* 18, no. 2 (March 2003), pp. 261–281.
6. The 14.7 million estimate comes from Small Business Administration Office of Advocacy, "The Small Business Economy 2011," n.d., www.sba.gov/advocacy/849/6282, Table A.13. The 1 million new firms is a conservative estimate. The GEM studies of the United States show about a 4 percent entrepreneurial rate, and with 27.3 million firms, a 4 percent rate yields 1,092,000 firms. There were an estimated 552,600 new firms with employees in 2010 according to the SBA, Office of Advocacy, U.S. Small Business Administration, "SBA Frequently Asked Questions" (U.S. Small Business Administration, January 2011), www.sba.gov/sites/default/files/sbfaq.pdf, but this number does not include one-person firms, which usually outnumber employer firms by a 2-to-I margin.
7. These computations were based on the March 2012 Current Population Survey. The variables were analyzed using DataFerret. "Owner-managers" is a combination of the CPS occupations of "Managers, all other" and "Chief Executives," Construction combines "Construction Managers" and "Construction Laborers." All analyses were done by Jerome Katz.
8. Even among small business owners, calling someone an entrepreneur can be problematic. About one owner in eight was offended by the term in a 2001 poll, although "small business owner" was almost universally accepted. *NFIB—National Small Business Poll—Success, Satisfaction and Growth*) (Washington, DC: NFIB Research Foundation, 2001).
9. This fight among professors seems to have settled down to three competing camps—wealth creation, opportunity recognition, and firm creation. Wealth creation proponents usually define entrepreneurship as efforts to create wealth, especially through high-growth new ventures. Major centers for this approach are Harvard University and Babson College. The opportunity recognition approach is centered at the University of Chicago and University of Virginia. This approach sees entrepreneurship occurring when an individual finds and exploits some technological, economic, or market mismatch. The firm creation approach says that starting a business is where entrepreneurship occurs, and it is the favored model at Clemson University and Saint Louis University.
10. This number comes from estimates for 2010 included in Table A.1 from Small Business Administration Office of Advocacy, "The Small Business Economy 2011," n.d., www.sba.gov/advocacy/849/6282.
11. Also called "habitual entrepreneurs," see D. Ucbasaran, M. Wright, P. Westhead, and L. W. Busenitz, "The Impact of Entrepreneurial Experience on Opportunity Identification and Exploitation: Habitual and Novice Entrepreneurs" *Advances in Entrepreneurship, Firm Emergence and Growth,* no. 6 (December 9, 2003), pp. 231–263 and A. Amaral, R. Baptista, and F. Lima, "Serial Entrepreneurship: Impact of Human Capital on Time to Re-entry," *Small Business Economics* 37, no. 1 (2011), pp. 1–21.
12. M. Dell and C. Freedman, *Direct from Dell: Strategies That Revolutionized an Industry* (New York: Harper Business, 2000), www.amazon.com/exec/obidos/tg/detail//0756718775/102-2417352-1853726?v=glance&vi=excerpt.
13. Robert X. Cringley, *Accidental Empires: How the Boys of Silicon Valley Make Their Millions, Battle Foreign Competition, and Still Can't Get a Date* (New York: HarperInformation, 2000).
14. The "universally mentioned" rewards were those mentioned by 75 percent or more of potential or new small business owners—a much higher rate than working people in general mention. The "occasionally mentioned" rewards were those mentioned by less than 50 percent of potential or new small business owners, but were still mentioned more often than by working people. The "rarely mentioned" rewards were those in which entrepreneurs mention a reward significantly less often than working people do in general. The sample was 871 potential and new entrepreneurs, compared to a control group of 431 individuals. For details on the measures see Nancy M. Carter, William B. Gartner, and Kelly G. Shaver, "Career reasons." In William B. Gartner, Kelly G. Shaver, Nancy M. Carter, and Paul D. Reynolds (eds.), *Handbook of Entrepreneurial Dynamics: The Process of Business Creation* (Thousand Oaks, CA: Sage, 2004), pp. 142–152. The PSED analyses reported here were custom analyses performed by Dr. Jennifer Shaver.
15. Marc Fleury, "Doing It Wrong, Getting It Right," Entrepreneur's Byline, *BusinessweekOnline.* September 3, 2003, www.businessweek.com/smallbiz/content/sep2003/sb2003093_8638.htm.
16. Thomas J. Stanley, *The Millionaire Mind* (Kansas City, MO: Andrews McNeel, 2001). Thomas J. Stanley and William D. Danko, *The Millionaire Next Door* (New York: Pocket Books, 1996).
17. Devlin Smith, "Women of Substance—Experience: A Secret to Success," *Entrepreneur,* November 2003, www.entrepreneur.com/article/65012.
18. The 56 percent number comes from U.S. respondents aged 15–25 from InSites global survey, J. Van den Bergh, "Generation Y Around the World:

Global Youth Research by InSites," *Business & Management*, February 15, 2012, www.slideshare.net/joerivandenbergh/generation-y-around-the-world-by-insites-consulting. The 10 percent number (10.2 to be precise) reflects youth 18–24 and comes from A. Ali et al., *Global Entrepreneurship Monitor National Entrepreneurial Assessment for the United States of America: 2010 United States Report* (Babson Park, MA/New York, NY: Babson College/Baruch College, October 28, 2011), www.gemconsortium.org/docs/667/gem-usa-2010-report, Table 2.

19. W. C. Dunkelberg and H. Wade, *NFIB Small Business Economic Trends—June 2012, Small Business Economic Trends* (Washington DC: National Federation for Independent Business, June 2012), www.nfib.com/Portals/0/PDF/sbet/sbet201206.pdf.
20. Small Business Administration Office of Advocacy, "The Small Business Economy 2011," February 13, 2012, www.sba.gov/advocacy/849/6282.
21. J. Cornwall, *Bootstrapping* (Upper Saddle River, NJ: Prentice Hall, 2010). Center for Women's Business Research, *Bootstrapping—Financial Strategies* (McLean, VA: Center for Women's Business Research, February 2012), www.womensbusinessresearchcenter.org/Data/research/february2012survey/february_2012_short_survey.pdf.
22. Sarah Caron, "14 Big Businesses That Started in a Recession," inside-crm.com 24 May 2009, www.insidecrm.com/features/businesses-started-slump-111108/. Mandel, Michael, "Starting Successful New Companies in Recessions—BusinessWeek," Businessweek.com, May 3, 2009; May 24, 2009, www.businessweek.com/the_thread/economicsunbound/archives/2009/05/starting_succes.html. This list of airlines was based on Michael Masouras. "Companies founded after 2000—Freebase," Freebase.com. May 24, 2009, www.freebase.com/view/user/masouras/default_domain/views/companies_founded_after_2000, compared to operating airlines shown on "List of airlines—Planes," Plane.SpottingWorld.com, May 24, 2009, http://plane.spottingworld.com/List_of_airlines.
23. M. E. Biery, "The 20 Most-Profitable Industries," October 28, 2011, www3.cfo.com/article/2011/10/growth-strategies_most-profitable-industries-sageworks-private-companies. Sageworks, "The 20 Most Profitable Industries," *Sageworks, Inc.*, October 28, 2011, www.sageworksinc.com/pressroom.aspx?article=627&title=The-20-Most-Profitable-Industries&date=October-28-2011.
24. David Rottenberg, and Jeffrey Shuman, "Loser Chic—Entrepreneur.com," Entrepreneur.com, February 1999; May 24, 2009, www.entrepreneur.com/article/17228.
25. Mindy Carson, "Famous Mompreneurs and How They Made Their Fortunes—Associated Content," *Associated Content—Business & Finance*, April 21, 2009; www.associatedcontent.com/article/1662719/famous_mompreneurs_and_how_they_made.html. E.C., Hoffman III, "10 Famous Career Switchers," Businessweek.com June 28, 2007; images.businessweek.com/ss/07/06/0628_second_careers/index_01.htm.
26. The closure rates come from the Office of Advocacy, U.S. Small Business Administration, "SBA Frequently Asked Questions" (U.S. Small Business Administration, January 2011), www.sba.gov/sites/default/files/sbfaq.pdf. The analysis of closings come from B. Headd, "Redefining Business Success: Distinguishing Between Closure and Failure," *Small Business Economics* 21, no. 1 (2003), pp. 51–61.
27. Jerome Katz and William B. Gartner, "Properties of Emerging Organizations," *Academy of Management Review* 13, no. 3 (July 1988), pp. 429–441. Jerome A. Katz and Scott Safranski, "Standardization in the Midst of Innovation: Structural Implications of the Internet for SMEs," *Futures: The Journal of Policy, Planning and Future Studies* 35, no. 4 (May 2003), pp. 323–340. Sumit K. Kundu and Jerome A. Katz, "Born-International SMEs: Bi-Level Impacts of Resources and Intentions," *Small Business Economics* 20, no. 1 (February 2003), pp. 25–47. Jerome A. Katz and Susan Peters, "Understanding the Entrepreneur in the Growth Process of SMEs," *The International Journal of Entrepreneurship and Innovation Management* 1, no. 3/4 (2001), pp. 366–380. Nancy M. Carter, William B. Gartner, and Paul D. Reynolds, "Exploring Start-Up Sequences," *Journal of Business Venturing* 11, no. 3 (May 1996), pp. 151–166.
28. The theory was developed in the article: Jerome Katz and William B. Gartner, "Properties of Emerging Organizations," *Academy of Management Review* 13, no. 3 (July 1988), pp. 429–441. And extended in J. A. Katz and S. Peters, "Understanding the Entrepreneur in the Growth Process of SMEs," *The International Journal of Entrepreneurship and Innovation Management* 1, no. 3/4 (2001), pp. 366–380. Empirical work in the PSED study was reported in Nancy M. Carter, William B. Gartner, and Paul D. Reynolds, "Exploring Start-Up Sequences," *Journal of Business Venturing* 11, no. 3 (May 1996), pp. 151–166. An independent confirmation was reported in Sumit K. Kundu and Jerome A. Katz, "Born-International SMEs: Bi-Level Impacts of Resources and Intentions," *Small Business Economics* 20, no. 1 (February 2003), pp. 25–47. A shortened form of the scale they developed for the PSED remains in use in the Global Entrepreneurship Monitor.
29. Nancy M. Carter, William B. Gartner, and Paul D. Reynolds, "Exploring Start-Up Sequences," *Journal of Business Venturing* 11, no. 3 (May 1996), pp. 151–166.
30. Nancy M. Carter, William B. Gartner, and Paul D. Reynolds, "Exploring Start-Up Sequences," *Journal of Business Venturing* 11, no. 3 (May 1996), pp. 151–166 and Monica Diochon, Yvon Gasse, Teresa Menzies and Denis Garand, "From Conception to Inception: Initial Findings from the Canadian Study on Entrepreneurial Emergence (2001). ASAC 2001 Annual Meeting, www.sauder.ubc.ca/research/research_centres/era/arena5/papers/ASAC2001Revised%20Submission.pdf.
31. Jeffrey Pfeffer and Robert I. Sutton, *The Knowing-Doing Gap: How Smart Companies Turn Knowledge into Action* (Cambridge, MA: Harvard Business School Press, 1999), or see Alan M. Webber, "Why Can't We Get Anything Done?" *Fast Company*, June 2000, www.fastcompany.com/magazine/35/pfeffer.html.
32. U.S. Small Business Administration, Office of Advocacy, "SBA Frequently Asked Questions" (U.S. Small Business Administration, January 2011), www.sba.gov/sites/default/files/sbfaq.pdf.
33. SBA Office of Advocacy, *Small Business by the Numbers*, www.sba.gov/advo/stats/sbfaq.pdf and Z. J. Acs and C. Armington, "Endogenous Growth and Entrepreneurial Activity in Cities," Center for Economic Studies, U.S. Bureau of the Census, Working Paper #CES-WP-03-2, January 2003.
34. U.S. Small Business Administration, Office of Advocacy, "SBA Frequently Asked Questions" (U.S. Small Business Administration, January 2011), www.sba.gov/sites/default/files/sbfaq.pdf.
35. Joseph A. Schumpeter, *The Theory of Economic Development* (NewYork: Oxford, 1961) (1934).
36. Robert X. Cringley, *Accidental Empires: How the Boys of Silicon Valley Make Their Millions, Battle Foreign Competition, and Still Can't Get a Date*, (New York: HarperInformation, 1996).
37. Scott A. Shane, "Is the Independent Entrepreneur a Valuable Organizational Form?" *RISEbusiness*, www.riseb.org/shane.html.
38. See note 34.
39. History of Snowboarding Web site, www.sbhistory.de/.
40. Behind the Earmuff," *Kids World*, www.kidzworld.com/site/p880.htm. Mary Bellis, "Chester Greenwood, Earmuffs," *Inventors*, About.com, http://inventors.about.com/library/inventors/blgreenwood.htm. "Fascinating Facts about the Invention of Earmuffs by Chester Greenwood in 1873," *The Great Idea Finder*, www.ideafinder.com/history/inventions/story091.htm.
41. Krisztina Holly, "Visual Voice(TM) Telephony Software," *Thinkquest*, library.thinkquest.org/26451/contents/inventors/krisztinaholly.htm?tqskip1=1; Mary Bellis, About.com, Inventors "Krisztina Holly," inventors.about.com/library/inventors/blholly.htm.
42. Don Debelak, "A Novel Dilemma: To Reach Potential Customers with an Avant-Garde Product, You'll Need to Have a Few Tricks Up Your Sleeve," *Entrepreneur*, June 2003, www.entrepreneur.com/article/61972. And Drinksafe Technologies Web site, www.drinksafetech.com.

43. "Our Founders: Ed Lowe and Darlene Lowe," http://edwardlowe.org/index.peer?paqe=FDNfounders, July 9, 2005. Jenny Kee, "Author Mark Baven on Being Extreme: Do You Have What It Takes to Be an Extreme Entrepreneur? Let Mark Baven Show You the Ropes of Rule-Breaking, Risk-Taking Entrepreneurship," *Entrepreneur,* June 18, 2001, www.entrepreneur.com/article/41484.
44. This table was inspired by a table on small business innovation in the 1994 edition of *The State of Small Business.* [U.S. Small Business Administration, *The State of Small Business: A Report of the President, 1994* (Washington, DC: U.S. Government Printing Office, 1995), p. 114.] I tracked down the inventors of several of the small business innovations listed in the report and added several new ones, as well as all the student started innovations. I found the video laryngoscope in Melnie Reid, "How a Shop Assistant Saw the Light and Saved Lives." *The Times,* July 17, 2008, www.timesonline.co.uk/tol/news/uk/scotland/article 4354048-ece.
45. Small Business Administration, "The New American Revolution: The Role and Impact of Small Firms" (Washington, DC: U.S. Small Business Administration, Office of Economic Research, 1998).
46. Small Business Administration, *Rural and Urban Areas by Firm Size, 1990–1995* (Washington, DC: Office of Advocacy, 1999). www.sbaonline.sba.gov/advo/stats/urb_rur.pdf.
47. Economic development experts call these *central place theorems,* with the efforts to figure out how many stores a population can support called *demand-threshold studies.* Examples tend to be fairly localized and include: Thomas R. Harris and J. Scott Shonkwiler, "Interdependence of Retail Businesses," *Growth and Change* 28 no. 4 (Fall 1997), pp. 520–533. J. Scott Shonkwiler and Thomas R. Harris, "Rural Retail Thresholds and Interdependencies," *Journal of Regional Studies* 36 (1996), pp. 617–630. H. Gale, Jr., "Retail Sales Pull Factors in U.S. Counties," *The Review of Regional Studies* 26 (1996), pp. 177–196. David Darling and Stephen Tubene, "Determining the Population Thresholds of Minor Trade Centers: A Benchmark Study of Non-Metropolitan Cities in Kansas," *Review of Agricultural Economics* 18 no. 1, (January 1996), pp. 95–102. G. Ebai and T. Harris, "Factors Influencing Trade Area Activity in the Great Basin Area," *The Review of Regional Studies* 27 (1997), pp. 251–276.
48. The idea that living spaces are important to creativity (such as the kind we find in entrepreneurial and high-growth ventures) comes from Richard Florida, *The Rise of the Creative Class: And How It's Transforming Work, Leisure, Community and Everyday Life* (New York: Basic Books, 2004).
49. Robert Berner, "P&G: New and Improved: How A.G. Lafley Is Revolutionizing a Bastion of Corporate Conservatism," *BusinessWeek,* July 7, 2003, www.businessweek.com/magazine/content/03_27/b3840001_mz001.htm. You can find information about Trillium Health Care Products at www.brockville.com/newsdetails.cfm?IDIn=172_01.htm or at their corporate Web site www.trilliumhealth_care.com.
50. John E. Harmon, "On the Wings of a Buffalo or 'Mother Teressa's Wings'" *Atlas of Popular Culture in the Northeastern United States.* (Undated), www.geography.ccsu.edu/harmonj/atlas/buffwing.htm; Anchor Bar Web site, www.buffalowings.com/. Calvin Trillin, "An Attempt to Complile a Short History of the Buffalo Chicken Wing," *The New Yorker,* August 25, 1980, pp. 82–87 (Also reproduced in his book, *The Tummy Trilogy*) J. Ferrary, "Mother Teressa's Wings," *Travel-Holiday* 175, no. 5 (June 1992), p. 31.
51. D. J. Kelly, S. Singer, and M. Herrington, *Global Entrepreneurship Monitor: 2011 Global Report* (Babson Park USA/Santiago Chile/Kuala Lampur Malaysia: Babson College/Universidad del Desarrollo/Universiti Tun Abdul Razak, 2012), www.gemconsortium.org/docs/2201/gem-2011-global-report.
52. See note 51.
53. U.S. Government, International Trade Administration, "Small & Medium-Sized Exporting Companies: Statistical Overview, 2010," *Trade.Gov,* April 16, 2012, www.trade.gov/mas/ian/smeoutlook/index.asp.
54. Sumit K. Kundu and Jerome A. Katz, "Born-International SMEs: BI-Level Impacts of Resources and Intentions," *Small Business Economics* 20.1 (2003): 25.
55. Jerome A. Katz, Scott R. Safranski, and Omar Khan, "Virtual Instant Global Entrepreneurship," *Journal of International Entrepreneurship* 1.1 (2003): 43.
56. The ideas for independent businesses come from Jerome A. Katz and William B. Gartner, "Properties of Emerging Organizations," *Academy of Management Review,* 13(3) (July 1988), pp. 429–441, and William B. Gartner, "A Conceptual Framework for Describing the Phenomenon of New Venture Creation," *Academy of Management Review* 10, no. 4 (October 1985), pp. 696–706. The social entrepreneurship ideas are built from a number of sources including L. Gregory Dees and Beth Battle Anderson, "For-Profit Social Ventures," *International Journal of Entrepreneurship Education,* 2(1), (2002), www.senatehall.com/journals.php?journal=1; Douglas Henton, John Melville, and Kimberly Walesh, "The age of the civic entrepreneur: Restoring civil society and building economic community," *National Civic Review,* 6(2), (1997), pp. 149–156; Janna Mair and Ignasti Marti, "Social entrepreneurship research: A source of explanation, prediction, and delight," *Journal of World Business* 41, (2006), pp. 36–44; Julia Sass Rubin and Gregory M. Stankiewicz, "The Los Angeles Community Development Bank: The possible pitfalls of public-private partnerships," *Journal of Urban Affaris,* 23(2), (2001), pp. 133–153; and Sandra A. Waddock and James E. Post, "Social entrepreneurs and catalytic change," *Public Administration Review,* 51, (1991), pp. 393–401. The material on corporate entrepreneurs comes from Peter Drucker, "What business can learn from nonprofits," *Harvard Business Review,* 67(4), (1989), pp. 88–93; Steven Klepper, "Employee start-ups in high-tech industries," *Industrial and Corporate Change,* 10(2001), pp. 639–674; and Donald F. Kuratko, R. Duane Ireland, Jeffrey G. Covin, Jeffrey S. Hornsby, "A Model of Middle-Level Managers' Entrepreneurial Behavior," *Entrepreneurship Theory and Practice* 29 (6), (2005), pp. 699–716.
57. The ideas behind the focuses of entrepreneurship come from an analysis of works such as Katz and Gartner, *op.cit.,* Gartner, *op.cit.,* King and Roberts, *op.cit.,* and Kuratko, Ireland, Covin, Hornsby, *op.cit.* as well as David Bornstein, "Changing the world on a shoestring," *The Atlantic Monthly,* 281(1) (1998), pp. 34–39; Gregory G. Dess, and G. T. Lumpkin, "The role of entrepreneurial orientation in stimulating effective, corporate entrepreneurship," *Academy of Management Executive,* 19(2005), pp. 147–156; Gillian Mort, Jay Weerawardena, and Kashonia Carnegie, "Social entrepreneurship: Towards conceptualization." *International Journal of Nonprofit and Voluntary Sector Marketing,* 8(2003), pp. 76–88; Silvia Dorado, "Social Entrepreneurial Ventures: Different Values So Different Process of Creation, No?" *Journal of Developmental Entrepreneurship* (Dec 2006). FindArticles.com. 05 May. 2007. http://findarticles.com/p/articles/mi_qa3906/is_200612/ai_n17194471; Hans Westlund and Roger Bolton, "Local social capital and entrepreneurship," *Small Business Economics,* 21(2), (2003), pp. 77–113; and Fang Zhao, "Exploring the synergy between entrepreneurship and innovation," *International Journal of Entrepreneurial Behaviour & Research,* 11(1), (January 2005), pp. 25–41.
58. "Paul McCartney: Biography: Rolling Stone." rollingstone.com, May 25, 2009, www.rollingstone.com/artists/paulmccartney/biography; "Sir (James) Paul McCartney Biography—Biography.com." biography.com. May 25, 2009, www.biography.com/articles/Sir-(James)-Paul-McCartney-9390850. Steve. Shelokhonov. "Paul McCartney–Biography." *imdb—The Internet Movie Database,* May 25, 2009, www.imdb.com/name/nm0005200/bio.
59. Stuart Read, Saras Sarasvathy, Nick Dew, Robert Wiltbank, and Anne-Valérie Ohlsson, *Effectual Entrepreneurship* (London: Routledge, 2010).
60. Wrigley Company, "Juicy Fruit," *Wrigley: A Subsidiary of Mars, Incorporated,* n.d., www.wrigley.com/global/brands/juicy-fruit.aspx. Wrigley Company. "Heritage Timeline." *Wrigley: A Subsidiary of Mars, Incorporated,* n.d. www.wrigley.com/global/about-us/heritage-timeline.aspx.

61. John M. Mcguire, "Our Town 2000, They've Got the World on a Shelf," *St. Louis Post-Dispatch,* August 28, 2000, p. E1 (Everyday). Repps Hudson, "Small-Firm Owners Strive to Meet Their High Expectations," *St. Louis Post-Dispatch,* May 13, 2002, p. P. 22 (Business Plus). Janet Mcnichols, "Kirkwood City Council Honors Three Residents," *St. Louis Post-Dispatch,* January 1, 2001, p. P. 3 (West Post). John M. Mcguire, "Our Town 2000—Thai Dynamo Is a Reminder of How a Grocer Looks, Acts," *St. Louis Post-Dispatch,* August 28, 2000, p. E1 (Everyday). Dan Mihalopoulos, "Immigrant's Motto: "You Work Hard, You Can Make It," *St. Louis Post-Dispatch,* May 9, 1999, p. B 1 (Imagine St. Louis). Joan Little, "New Food Store Will Offer Exotic and Ethnic Variety: Opening of Global Food Market Set for March "99," *St. Louis Post-Dispatch,* November 26, 1998 p.P. 6 (West Post).

Chapter 2

1. Information about Laura Tidwell can be found at "*Girl Geek of the Week,*" January 2001, www.girlgeeks.org/innergeek/gkwk/gkwk_tidwell.shtml. Kathleen Williams, "Enginehouse Media's CEO Honored by Business Community," *PRWeb,* December 15, 2000, www.prweb.com/releases/2000/12/prweb21075.htm. [no author], "Laura Tidwell: An Internet Entrepreneur's Tips for Success," Women of.com [no date], www.womenof.com/Articles/cb121800.asp. The Ad Firm Web site, www.theadfirm.com. "Laura Tidwell," WITI: Empowering Women Through Technology, 2000, www.witi.com/wire/witiwomen/ltidwell/ltidwell_complete.shtml.
2. The description here looks at behavior in the founder (vs. inventor or developer) role and comes from Melissa Cardon, Joakim Wincent, Jagdip Singh, and Mateja Drnovsek, "The Nature and Experience of Entrepreneurial Passion," *The Academy of Management Review ARCHIVE* 34, no. 3 (July 1, 2009), pp. 511–532. The impacts of passion on employees comes from Melissa S. Cardon, "Is Passion Contagious? The Transference of Entrepreneurial Passion to Employees," *Human Resource Management Review* 18, no. 2 (June 2008), pp. 77–86, and Nicola Breugst, Anne Domurath, Holger Patzelt, and Anja Klaukien, "Perceptions of Entrepreneurial Passion and Employees' Commitment to Entrepreneurial Ventures," *Entrepreneurship: Theory and Practice* 36, no. 1 (January 2012), pp. 171–192, while the impact on investors comes from Xiao-Ping Chen, Xin Yao, and Suresh Kotha, "Entrepreneur Passion and Preparedness in Business Plan Presentations: A Persuasion Analysis of Venture Capitalists' Funding Decisions," *The Academy of Management Journal ARCHIVE* 52, no. 1 (February 1, 2009), pp. 199–214. However, while Chen *et al.* suggest that passion is important, planning can trump it.
3. This approach to perseverance as learned optimism (also known as resilience) comes from Daniel Seligman's thinking, specifically as applied by Norris F. Krueger Jr, "Entrepreneurial Resilience: Real and Perceived Barriers to Implementing Entrepreneurial Intentions," *SSRN eLibrary* (July 3, 2008), http://papers.ssrn.com/sol3/papers.cfm?abstract_id=1155269.
4. For example, in one group of entrepreneurs, the higher the perseverance scores, the higher their annual earnings. See Gideon D. Markman, Robert A. Baron, and David B. Balkin. "Are Perseverance and Self-efficacy Costless? Assessing Entrepreneurs' Regretful Thinking," *Journal of Organizational Behavior* 26, no. 1 (2005), pp. 1–19.
5. In addition to Kreuger's work, an effectuation-grounded approach can be seen in Mathew L. A. Hayward, William R. Forster, Saras D. Sarasvathy, and Barbara L. Fredrickson, "Beyond Hubris: How Highly Confident Entrepreneurs Rebound to Venture Again," *Journal of Business Venturing* 25, no. 6 (November 2010), pp. 569–578.
6. Joel Brockner, E. Tory Higgins, and Murray B. Low, "Regulatory Focus Theory and the Entrepreneurial Process," *Journal of Business Venturing* 19, no. 2 (March 2004), pp. 203–220.
7. Keith M. Hmieleski and Robert A. Baron, "Regulatory Focus and New Venture Performance: A Study of Entrepreneurial Opportunity Exploitation Under Conditions of Risk Versus Uncertainty," *Strategic Entrepreneurship Journal* 2, no. 4 (March 23, 2009), pp. 285–299. Jintong Tang, "Exploring the Constitution of Entrepreneurial Alertness: The Regulatory Focus View," *Journal of Small Business and Entrepreneurship* 22, no. 3 (2009), pp. 221–238.
8. Gideon D. Markman, Robert A. Baron, and David B. Balkin, "The Role of Regretful Thinking, Perseverance, and Self-efficacy in Venture Formation," *Advances in Entrepreneurship, Firm Emergence and Growth,* no. 6 (December 9, 2003), pp. 73–104. Gideon D. Markman, Robert A. Baron, and David B. Balkin, "Are Perseverance and Self-efficacy Costless? Assessing Entrepreneurs' Regretful Thinking," *Journal of Organizational Behavior* 26, no. 1 (2005), pp. 1–19.
9. These are inspired by the concept of Action Strategies from M. Frese, M. van Gelderen, and M. Ombach, "How to Plan as a Small Scale Business Owner: Psychological Process Characteristics of Action Strategies and Success," *Journal of Small Business Management* 38, no. 2 (April 2000), pp. 1–18. Frese and his colleagues do not have a survey to assess Action Strategies, so the concepts and the questions offered in the Skill Module reflect an application of their idea.
10. H. Chang, "Atiba is the Success of a Self-Taught Man," *The Tennessean, September* 10, 2003; "Enterprise Executive Profile: J. J. Rosen, Chief Executive Officer," *Nashville Business Journal,* March 2, 2001, http://nashville.bizjournals.com/nashville/stories/2001/03/05/smallb1.html; M. Capps, "Bootstrapping Atiba Software Adds C-level Exec," *Venture Nashville,* February 13, 2009, www.venturenashville.com/news.php?viewstory=238.
11. S. Escher et al., "The Moderator Effect of Cognitive Ability on the Relationship Between Planning Strategies and Business Success of Small Scale Business Owners in South Africa: A Longitudinal Study," *Journal of Developmental Entrepreneurship* 7, no. 3 (October 2002), pp. 305–318. A. M. F. Hiemstra, K. G. Van Der Kooy, and M. Frese, "Entrepreneurship in the Street Food Sector of Vietnam—Assessment of Psychological Success and Failure Factors," *Journal of Small Business Management* 44, no. 3 (June 15, 2006), pp. 474–481. J. Van Gelder et al., "Differences in Psychological Strategies of Failed and Operational Business Owners in the Fiji Islands," *Journal of Small Business Management* 45, no. 3 (May 26, 2007), pp. 388–400. M. von Gelderen, M. Frese, and R. Thurik, "Strategies, Uncertainty and Performance of Small Business Startups," *Small Business Economics* 15, no. 3 (2000), pp. 165–181.
12. J. Plazonja and A. Zildjian, *Avedis Zildjian The Father of Cymbals* (2003), www.zildjian.com/adaa/adaa_2003_legacy_6.asp. [No Author] Historical Timeline. Zildjian Company Web site, www.zildjian.com/EN-US/about/timeline.ad2 (July 10, 2005).
13. The self-efficacy questions are adapted from F. Wilson, J. Kickul, and D. Marlino, "Gender, Entrepreneurial Self-Efficacy, and Entrepreneurial Career Intentions: Implications for Entrepreneurship Education," *Entrepreneurship Theory and Practice* 31, no. 3 (2007), pp. 387–406. The passion questions are from N. Breugst, A. Domurath, H. Patzelt, and A. Klaukien, "Perceptions of Entrepreneurial Passion and Employees' Commitment to Entrepreneurial Ventures," *Entrepreneurship: Theory and Practice* 36, no. 1 (January 2012), pp. 171–192. The perseverance questions were the called "Entrepreneurial Intensity" in the Panel Study of Entrepreneurial Dynamics, from W. B. Gartner et al. (Eds.), *Handbook of Entrepreneurial Dynamics: The Process of Business Creation* (Thousand Oaks, CA: Sage Publications, 2004), pp. 186–195. The Promotion/Prevention focus comes from P. Lockwood, C. H. Jordan, and Z. Kunda, "Motivation by Positive or Negative Role Models: Regulatory Focus Determines Who Will Best Inspire Us," *Journal of Personality and Social Psychology* 83, no. 4 (October 2002), pp. 854–864, based on the suggestions of Keith Hmieleski and Robert Baron. The questions for planning style are inspired by the work on Action Styles by Michael Frese, while the questions on professionalization were inspired by the work on professionalization by Edgar Schein.
14. Scoring the Entrepreneurial Personality Overview is done is sections. Questions 1 through 4 measure self-efficacy from Chapter 1. Add up your score on these four items. The higher the score, the stronger your self-efficacy. Successful entrepreneurs tend to have above-average levels of

self-efficacy. Questions 5 through 9 measure your level of passion as a founder. Add up your score on these five items. The higher your score is, the stronger your level of passion. Successful entrepreneurs demonstrate high levels of passion for their business. Note that there are two other roles entrepreneurs find themselves in—as inventors and as business developers in established firms. There are different scales for measuring passion in those roles. Questions 10 through 13 measure your perseverance. Add up your score on these four items. The higher the score, the stronger your perseverance, and successful entrepreneurs have above-average perseverance levels. Questions 14 and 15 measure your promotion focus. Add up your score on these two items. The higher the score, the stronger your promotion focus. Questions 16 and 17 measure your prevention focus. Add up you score on these two items. The higher the score, the stronger your prevention focus. The best entrepreneurs show both promotion and prevention orientations. The ABCD ranking shows your planning style: "A" is a comprehensive planning style, "B" is a critical-point planning style, "C" is an opportunistic planning style, "D" is a reactive planning style, and "E" is a habitual planning style. Entrepreneurial success is greatest for comprehensive planners and decreases for each successive style. The FGH ranking shows your level of professionalization: "F" is the expert professionalization, "G" is specialized, and "H" is minimalized professionalization.

15. There are two major models of entrepreneurial competency—Mitchell *et al.* and Chandler/Hanks models. The Mitchell *et al.* model has been validated cross culturally, with very strong results, while the Chandler/Hanks model has seen wider use in U.S. studies. Although each model labels the competencies differently, the content of the competencies is very similar. The model presented here builds from the Mitchell *et al.* and Chandler/Hanks models, mapping their specific competencies to the BRIE model of Katz and Gartner introduced in Chapter 1. The key article on competencies is Ronald K. Mitchell, J. Brock Smith, Eric A. Morse, Kristie W. Seawright, Ana Maria Peredo, and Brian McKenzie, "Are Entrepreneurial Cognitions Universal? Assessing Entrepreneurial Cognitions across Cultures," *Entrepreneurship: Theory & Practice* 26, no. 4 (Summer 2002), pp. 9–32. Note that what are called *competencies* in this text are called *scripts* in the Mitchell works. The scripts are observed through their related cognitions. Gaylen N. Chandler and Steven H. Hanks, "Founder Competence, the Environment, and Venture Performance," *Entrepreneurship: Theory & Practice* 18, no. 3 (Spring 1994), pp. 77–89.
16. This skill is called *business ability competency* by Mitchell *et al.* and *managerial competency* by Chandler and Hanks.
17. This is called *organizational resources and capabilities* by Chandler and Hanks, while in the Mitchell *et al.* model resources are a part of arrangement competencies. The social competencies that make these easier or harder for the entrepreneur come from R. A. Baron and G. D. Markman, "Beyond Social Capital: The Role of Entrepreneurs' Social Competence in Their Financial Success," *Journal of Business Venturing* 18, no. 1 (January 2003), pp. 41–60.
18. In the Mitchell *et al.* model these are called *willingness competencies*, while in the Chandler/Hanks approach they make up a part of the entrepreneurial competence factor.
19. In the Chandler/Hanks model, this is called the *quality of the opportunity*, while opportunity factors make up much of the arrangements competency cluster.
20. See R. Mitchell and S. Chesteen, "Enhancing Entrepreneurial Expertise: Experiential Pedagogy and the Entrepreneurial Expert Script," *Simulation & Gaming* 26, no. 3 (September 1995), pp. 288–306.
21. William Gartner [W. B. Gartner, "A Conceptual Framework for Describing the Phenomenon of New Venture Creation," *Academy of Management Review* 10, no. 4 (October 1985), pp. 696–706] defined the entrepreneurial event as the interaction of the entrepreneur, the business itself, the process by which it is started, and the context or environment in which all this happens. Other works that have built on the Gartner idea include: L. Herron and H. J. Sapienza, "The Entrepreneur and the Initiation of New Venture Launch Activities," *Entrepreneurship: Theory & Practice* 17, no. 1 (Fall 1992), pp. 49–55; Douglas W. Naffziger, Jeffrey S. Hornsby, and Donald F. Kuratko, "A Proposed Research Model of Entrepreneurial Motivation," *Entrepreneurship: Theory & Practice* 18, no. 3 (Spring 1994), pp. 29–42; Carolyn Y. Woo, U. Daellenbach, and C. Nicholls-Nixon, "Theory Building in the Presence of 'Randomness': The Case of Venture Creation and Performance," *Journal of Management Studies* 31, no. 4 (July 1994), pp. 507–524; Richard C. Becherer and John G. Maurer, "The Proactive Personality Disposition and Entrepreneurial Behavior among Small Company Presidents," *Journal of Small Business Management* 37, no. 1 (January 1999), pp. 28–36. The term *entrepreneurial settings* follows the idea of environment in these studies. However, neither Gartner nor the subsequent researchers specified the exact nature of different types of settings. The settings described here are chosen because of their frequency.
22. Joseph Weber and Louis Lavelle, "Family, Inc." *BusinessWeek* online, November 10, 2003, www.businessweek.com:/print/magazine/content/03_45/b3857002.htm?mz.
23. R. Kurtz, "When Business Is in the Blood," *BusinessWeek* online, January 25, 2005, http://yahoo.businessweek.com/smallbiz/content/jan2005/sb20050125_3409.htm. D. Miller and I. Le Breton-Miller, *Managing for the Long Run: Lessons in Competitive Advantage from Great Family Businesses* (Boston: Harvard Business School Press, 2005).
24. Joseph Astrachan and Melissa C. Shanker, "Family Businesses' Contribution to the U.S. Economy: A Closer Look," *Family Business Review* 16, no. 3 (September 2003), pp. 211–219.
25. Joseph Weber and Louis Lavelle, "Family, Inc." *BusinessWeek* online, November 10, 2003, www.businessweek.com:/print/magazine/content/03_45/b3857002.htm?mz.
26. W. Gibb Dyer and Wendy Handler, "Entrepreneurship and Family Business: Exploring the Connections," *Entrepreneurship: Theory & Practice* 18, no. 1 (Fall 1994), pp. 71–83.
27. W. Gibb Dyer and Wendy Handler, "Entrepreneurship and Family Business: Exploring the Connections," *Entrepreneurship: Theory & Practice* 18, no. 1 (Fall 1994), pp. 71–83. Frank Hoy and Trudy Verser, "Emerging Business, Emerging Field: Entrepreneurship and the Family Firm," *Entrepreneurship: Theory & Practice* 18, no. 1 (Fall 1994), pp. 9–23.
28. David N. Laband and Bernard F. Lentz, "Like Father Like Son: Towards an Economic Theory of Occupational Following," *Southern Economic Journal* 50, no. 2 (October 1983), pp. 474–493. Bernard F. Lentz and David N. Laband, "Entrepreneurial Success and Occupational Inheritance among Proprietors," *Canadian Journal of Economics* 23, no. 3 (August 1990), pp. 563–579. Robert F. Scherer, James D. Bordzinski, and Frank A. Weibe, "Assessing Perception of Career Role-Model Performance: The Self-Employed Parent," *Perceptual and Motor Skills* 72, no. 2 (1991), pp. 555–560. Robert F. Scherer, James D. Brodzinski, and Frank A. Wiebe, "Entrepreneurship Career Selection And Gender: A Socialization Approach," *Journal of Small Business Management* 28, no. 2 (April 1990), pp. 37–44.
29. John L. Ward, *Perpetuating the Family Business: 50 Lessons Learned from Long Lasting, Successful Families in Business* (New York: Palgrave Macmillan, 2004).
30. A. P. Sherman, "Connect the Daughters: Sons Aren't the Only Off-spring Taking Over Family Businesses," *Entrepreneur* 30, no. 2 (December 2002), p. 36.
31. Charles R. Stoner, Richard I. Hartman, and Raj Arora, "Work-Home Role Conflict in Female Owners of Small Business: An Exploration Study," *Journal of Small Business Management* 28, no. 1 (January 1990), pp. 30–38.
32. E. H. Updike, "How to Avoid a Dysfunctional Family Business," *BusinessWeek,* March 2, 1998, p. 3. K. E. Gersick, J. A. Davis, M. McCollom Hampton, and I. Lansberg, *Generation to Generation: Life Cycles of the Family Business* (Boston: Harvard Business School Press, 1997).
33. Nancy J. Miller, Mary Winter, Margaret A. Fitzgerald, and Jennifo Paul, "Family Microenterprises: Strategies for Coping with Overlapping Family and Business Demands," *Journal of Developmental Entrepreneurship* 5, no. 2 (August 2000), pp. 87–114. Frank Hoy and Trody Verser, "Emerging Business, Emerging Field: Entrepreneurship and the Family Firm,"

Entrepreneurship: Theory & Practice 18, no. 1 (Fall 1994), pp. 9–23. Eric G. Flamholtz, *How to Make the Transition from an Entrepreneurship to a Professionally Managed Firm* (San Francisco: Jossey-Bass, 1986).

34. Paul Edwards and Sarah Edwards, "How to Manage Your Home-based Time," Entrepreneur.com, May 13, 2003, www.entrepreneur.com/homebasedbiz/worklifebalance/advicefrompaulandsarahedwards/article61974.html. Lisa Kanarek, "Keeping Time," Home-OfficeMag.com, January 2001, www.entrepreneur.com/worklife/worklifebalanceadvice/timemanagementandorganization/article35806.html. Rosalind Resnick, "Secrets to Staying Focused in Your Home Office," *Entrepreneur.com*, May 17, 2004, www.entrepreneur.com/homebasedbiz/worklifebalance/timemanagement/article70836.html. Sonja Treven and Vojko Potocan, "Training programmes for stress management in small businesses," *Education + Training,* 47, no. 8/9 (2005), pp. 640–652. Howard Van Auken and James Werbel, "Family Dynamic and Family Business Financial Performance: Spousal Commitment," *Family Business Review,* 19, no. 1 (2006), pp. 49–63.
35. Joseph Astrachan and Melissa C. Shanker, "Family Businesses' Contribution to the U.S. Economy: A Closer Look," *Family Business Review* 16, no. 3 (September 2003), pp. 211–219. Arthur Andersen Center for Family Business, *American Family Business Survey* (St. Charles, IL: Arthur Andersen Center for Family Business 1995). John Ward, *Keeping the Family Business Healthy: How to Plan for Continuing Growth, Profitability and Family Leadership* (San Francisco: Jossey-Bass, 1987). Ward suggested that around 88 percent of family firms fail by the third generation, with family infighting, rather than a lack of succession planning, taking a toll in later generations. Ward's sample was relatively small. A very large, multigenerational study of family firms in France suggested a much higher survival rate [see Dean Savage, *Founders, Heirs and Managers: French Industrial Leadership in Transition* (Beverly Hills: Sage, 1979)].
36. W. Gibb Dyer, Jr., *The Entrepreneurial Experience: Confronting Career Dilemmas of the Start-Up Executive* (San Francisco: Jossey-Bass, 1992), p.184.
37. Ernesto J. Poza, *Family Business* (Mason, OH: South-Western, 2004), pp. 28–29, 33.
38. Ibid., p. 33.
39. John Ward, *Keeping the Family Business Healthy: How to Plan for Continuing Growth, Profitability and Family Leadership* (San Francisco: Jossey-Bass, 1987). Ward suggested that around 88 percent of family firms fail by the third generation, with family infighting, rather than a lack of succession planning, taking a toll in later generations. Ward's sample was relatively small. A very large, multigenerational study of family firms in France suggested a much higher survival rate [see Dean Savage, *Founders, Heirs and Managers: French Industrial Leadership in Transition* (Beverly Hills: Sage, 1979)].
40. William G. Shuster, "Family Business in Crisis: Letting Go," *Jewelers Circular Keystone,* (March 2003), p. 84.
41. W. Gibb Dyer, Jr., *The Entrepreneurial Experience: Confronting Career Dilemmas of the Start-Up Executive* (San Francisco: Jossey-Bass, 1992), p. 184.
42. David Whitford, "Century-Old Companies Built to Last," *Fortune Small Business* 12, no. 5 (2002), pp. 28–34.
43. Eric G. Flamholtz and Yvonne Randle, *Growing Pains: Transitioning from an Entrepreneurship to a Professionally Managed Firm* (San Francisco: Jossey-Bass, 2000), pp. 64–65.
44. Joseph Weber and Louis Lavelle, "Family, Inc." *BusinessWeek* online, November 10, 2003, www.businessweek.com:/print/magazine/content/03_45/b3857002.html?mz.
45. W. Gibb Dyer, Jr., *The Entrepreneurial Experience: Confronting Career Dilemmas of the Start-Up Executive* (San Francisco: Jossey-Bass, 1992), p. 184.
46. Barnett Helzberg, Jr., "Sage Counsel for All Seasons," *BusinessWeek* online, August 13, 2003, www.businessweek.com:/print/smallbiz/content/aug2003/sb20030813_2077 htm?sb.
47. Ernesto J. Poza, Family Business (Mason, OH: South-Western, 2004), pp. 28–29, 33.
48. Ibid.
49. D. Bork, D. T. Jaffee, S. H. Lane, L. Dashew, and Q. G. Heisler, *Working with Family Businesses: A Guide for Professionals* (San Francisco: Jossey-Bass, 1996). N. C. Churchill and K. J. Hatten, "Non-Market Based Transfers of Wealth and Power: A Research Framework for Family Businesses," *American Journal of Small Business* 11, no. 3 (Spring 1987), p. 51. E. G. Flamholtz, *How to Make the Transition from an Entrepreneurship to a Professionally Managed Firm* (San Francisco: Jossey-Bass, 1986). R. Beckhard and W. G. Dyer, "Managing Continuity in the Family-Owned Business," *Organizational Dynamics* 12, no. 1 (Summer 1983), pp. 5–12.
50. S. Foley and G. N. Powell, "Reconceptualizing Work-Family Conflict for Business/Marriage Partners: A Theoretical Model," *Journal of Small Business Management* 35, no. 4 (October 1997), pp. 36–47.
51. Linda Moraski, "When a Partnership Turns Toxic," *BusinessWeek* online, December 17, 2003, www.businessweek.com:/print/smallbiz/content/dec2003/sb20031217_7845.htm?sb.
52. Robert D. Hisrich, *Small Business Solutions: How to Fix & Prevent the 13 Biggest Problems That Derail Business* (New York: McGraw-Hill, 2004), pp. 70–71. J. A. Cox, K. K. Moore, and P. M. Van Auken, "Working Couples in Small Business," *Journal of Small Business Management* 22, no. 4 (October 1984), pp. 24–30.
53. Howard E. Aldrich, Nancy M. Carter, and Martin Ruef, "Teams." In William B. Gartner, Kelly G. Shaver, Nancy M. Carter, and Paul D. Reynolds (eds.), *Handbook of Entrepreneurial Dynamics: the Process of Business Creation* (Thousand Oaks, CA: Sage, 2004), Table 27.1, page 307.
54. In Chapter 1, endnote 3, we explored the number of new firms annually. Applying the PSED findings from endnote 53 above, we have about 500,000 new firms started by teams.
55. The term *equity* comes from J. Stacy Adams motivational model called Equity Theory, which is often discussed in Introduction to Psychology courses. Two examples of applying it in partner situations include: Brian Tracy, "Is a Business Partnership Right for You?" Entrepreneur, February 21, 2005, www.entrepreneur.com/article/76362 and John A. Gromala and David F. Gage, "Mediating Personality Differences Behind Internal Business Disputes," *The CPA Journal,* 72, no. 3 (March 2002), pp. 68–69.
56. Paige Arnof-Fenn, "The Partner Track: How To Decide if You Should Fly Solo Or Not: The Second In A Two-Part Series On Business Partnerships," *Entrepreneur*, July 14, 2005, www.entrepreneur.com/author/978-2.
57. Robert D. Hisrich, *Small Business Solutions: How to Fix & Prevent the 13 Biggest Problems That Derail Business* (New York: McGraw-Hill, 2004), pp. 70–71. Joe A. Cox, Kris K. Moore, and Philip M. Van Auken, "Working Couples In Small Business," *Journal of Small Business Management*, 22, no. 4 (October 1984), pp. 24–30.
58. American Express OPEN, *The American Express OPEN State of Women-Owned Businesses Report—A Summary of Important Trends, 1997–2012* (New York: American Express OPEN, March 2012), http://media.nucleus.naprojects.com/pdf/State_of_Women-Owned_Businesses-Report_FINAL.pdf.
59. Ibid.
60. Ibid.
61. H. Pordeli and P. Wynkoop, *The Economic Impact of Women-Owned Businesses in the United States* (McLean, VA: Center for Women's Business Research, October 2009), www.womensbusinessresearchcenter.org/Data/research/economicimpactstud/econimpactreport-final.pdf.
62. These results were from the Kepler and Shane study, updated using the industries from the American Express OPEN 2012 report. E. Kepler and S. Shane, *Are Male and Female Entrepreneurs Really That Different,* Office of Advocacy Working Paper (Shaker Heights, OH: U.S. SBA Office of Advocacy, September 2007), http://archive.sba.gov/advo/research/rs309tot.pdf. American Express OPEN, *The American Express OPEN State of*

Women-Owned Businesses Report—A Summary of Important Trends, 1997–2012 (New York: American Express OPEN, March 2012), http://media.nucleus.naprojects.com/pdf/State_of_Women-Owned_Businesses-Report_FINAL.pdf.

63. All of these results about gender-driven entrepreneur differences are taken from E. Kepler and S. Shane, *Are Male and Female Entrepreneurs Really That Different,* Office of Advocacy Working Paper (Shaker Heights, OH: U.S. SBA Office of Advocacy, September 2007), http://archive.sba.gov/advo/research/rs309tot.pdf.
64. D.J. Kelly, C. G. Brush, P. C. Greene and Y. Litvosky, *Global Entrepreneurship Monitor 2010 Women's Report,* Global Entrepreneurship Monitor (Babson Park, MA: Babson College, 2011), www.babson.edu/Academics/centers/blank-center/global-research/gem/Documents/GEM%202010%20Womens%20Report%20V2.pdf.
65. American Express OPEN, *The American Express OPEN State of Women-Owned Businesses Report—A Summary of Important Trends, 1997–2012* (New York: American Express OPEN, March 2012), http://media.nucleus.naprojects.com/pdf/State_of_Women-Owned_Businesses-Report_FINAL.pdf.
66. Small Business Administration Office of Advocacy, "The Small Business Economy 2011," February 13, 2012, www.sba.gov/advocacy/849/6282, Table A.13.
67. Ibid.
68. Ibid.
69. Alicia M. Robb, "Entrepreneurial Performance by Women and Minorities: The Case of New Firms," *Journal of Developmental Entrepreneurship* 7, no. 4 (December 2002), pp. 383–397.
70. Karen E. Klein, "Women, the Loan Strangers," *BusinessWeek* online, May 28, 2004, www.businessweek.com/smallbiz/content/may2004/sb20040528_5382_sb010.htm. A. M. Robb, "Entrepreneurial Performance by Women and Minorities: The Case of New Firms," *Journal of Developmental Entrepreneurship* 7, no. 4 (December 2002), pp. 383–397.
71. Center for Women's Business Research, *Access to Markets: Perspectives from Large Corporations and Women's Business Enterprises* (Washington, DC: Center for Women's Business Research, 2003), www.womensbusinessresearch.org/pressreleases/2-4-2003/2-4-2003.htm.
72. K. S. Cavalluzzo and L. C. Cavalluzzo, "Market Structure and Discrimination: The Case of Small Business," *Journal of Money, Credit and Banking* 30, no. 4 (November 1998), pp. 771–792.
73. B. Weltman, "Government Contracting for Small and Minority-Owned Businesses," *American Express OPEN Forum,* February 7, 2012, www.openforum.com/articles/government-contracting-for-small-and-minority-owned-businesses.
74. National Minority Supply and Diversity Council, MBE—Certification NMSDC Web site (2005), www.nmsdc.org/MBEs/tool_kit_certification.html.
75. American Express Company, "Should You Consider Government Contracting?" Entrepreneur.com Web site (2002), www.entrepreneur.com/amex/article/0.5742,307414.00.html (July 10, 2005). J. B. Howroyd, "Minority Loan and Grant Programs: The Right Program Can Ease the Transition from Pre-Funding Planner to Full-Fledged Entrepreneur," Entrepreneur Biz Startups, May 20, 2002, www.entrepreneur.com/article/0,4621,299866,00.html.
76. Stephen Roper, "Entrepreneurial Characteristics, Strategic Choice and Small Business Performance," *Small Business Economics* 11, no. 1 (1998), pp. 11–24. Gangaram Singh and Alex DeNoble, "Early Retirees as the Next Generation of Entrepreneurs," *Entrepreneurship: Theory and Practice* 27, no. 3 (Spring 2003), pp. 207–226.
77. Joshua Kurlantzick, "About Face: The Face of Entrepreneurship Has Evolved Over the Years, and Today, It's Dramatically Different. But What Will the Entrepreneur of the Future Look Like?" *Entrepreneur,* January 2004, www.Entrepreneur.eom/article/0,4621,312260,00.html. David A. Baucus and Sherrie E. Human, "Second Career Entrepreneurs: A Multiple Case Study Analysis of Entrepreneurial Processes and Antecendent Variables," *Entrepreneurship: Theory and Practice* 18, no. 2 (Winter 1994), pp. 41–71. Wallace N. Davidson, Dan L. Worrell, and J. Fox, B. Jercary. "Early Retirement Programs and Firm Performance," *Academy of Management Journal* 39, no. 4 (August 1996), pp. 970–984.
78. Gangaram Singh and Anil Verma, "Is There Life after Career Employment? Labour Market Experience of Early Retires," in Victor W. Marshall, Walter R. Heinz, Helga Krueger, and Anil Verma (eds.), *Restructuring Work and the Life Course* (Toronto: University of Toronto Press, 2001).
79. Gangaram Singh and Alex DeNoble, "Early Retirees as the Next Generation of Entrepreneurs," *Entrepreneurship: Theory and Practice* 27, no. 3 (Spring 2003), pp. 207–226.
80. Andrea C. Poe, "Start a Business . . . Even After 50: Neither Shy nor Retiring, People over 50 Are Proving There's Life—and Profits—after Retirement as They Launch Second Careers as Entrepreneurs," *Entrepreneur* online Entrepreneur Extra, August 19, 2003, www.Entrepreneur.com/article/0,4621,310607,00.html. G. Singh and A. DeNoble, "Early Retirees as the Next Generation of Entrepreneurs," *Entepreneurship: Theory & Practice* 27, no. 3 (Spring 2003), pp. 207–226.
81. Andrea C. Poe, "Start a Business . . . Even After 50: Neither Shy nor Retiring, People over 50 Are Proving There's Life—and Profits—after Retirement as They Launch Second Careers as Entrepreneurs," *Entrepreneur* online Entrepreneur Extra, August 19, 2003, www.Entrepreneur.com/article/0,4621,310607,00,html.
82. Nichole L. Torres, "Late Bloomer: If You're Just Now Realizing You're an Entrepreneur at Heart, Not to Worry. Here's Why Starting a Business after 40 Could Be the Best Thing that Ever Happened to You," *Entrepreneur's Be Your Own Boss,* October 2003, www.entrepreneur.com/article/64674.
83. "America's First Businessman: George Washington's Business Acumen," *The Businessweek Video Library,* http://feedroom.businessweek.com/. Associated Press, "A Taste of George Washington's Whiskey—U.S. and Canada—msnbc.com," msnbc.com, April 9, 2007; www.msnbc.msn.com/id/18025413/. Lisa Brown, "Washington's Whiskey Hits the Barrel after 200 Year Hiatus—USA-TODAY.com," USATODAY.com, April 15, 2009; www.usatodav.com/travel/destinations/2009-04-15-mount-vernon-whiskey_N.htm. John Fund, "Moonshine Patriot: George Washington, Whiskey Entrepreneur," Leisure & Arts—WSJ.com, February 21, 2007; www.opinionjournal.com/la/?id=110009692. George Washington's Distillers, "Making George Washington's Whiskey," *Making George Washington's Whiskey,* http:\\makinggeorgewashingtonswhiskey.blogspot.com/. Thane Peterson, "BW Online, June 17, 2003, Washington Sipped Here," Businessweek.com, June 17, 2003; www.businessweek.com/bwdaily/dnflash/un2003/nf20030617_2197_db028.htm. Marta Roberts, "BW Online, May 22, 2001, George Washington Slept It Off Here," Businessweek.com, May 21, 2001; www.businessweek.com/bwdaily/dnflash/may2001/nf20010522_060.htm.

Chapter 3

1. Tim Hayden's story came from a 2003 classroom presentation in an Advanced Business Planning class Tim took with *ESB* co-author Jerome Katz at Saint Louis University.
2. The formal name for this overlap of entrepreneur and firm is called partial inclusion and was original to Daniel Katz and Robert L. Kahn, *The Social Psychology of Organizations,* 2nd ed. (New York: Wiley, 1978). A better-known approach for many comes from Karl E. Weick, *The Social Psychology of Organizing,* 2nd ed. (Reading, Mass: Addison-Wesley, 1979).
3. Definition is a paraphrase from Steve Robbins, *Essentials of Organizational Behavior,* 7th ed. (Upper Saddle River, New Jersey: Prentice-Hall, 2003), p. 231, and Edgar Schein, "The Role of the Founder in Creating Organizational Culture," *Organizational Dynamics,* Summer 1983, p. 14.

4. "Horizon-Chamber Collaboration Brings Wellness to Workplace." *The Business Monthly,* December 2007; http://209.116.252.254/12 2007/9.shtml. "Workplace Wellness Award," *The Horizon Foundation 2007,* www.thehorizonfoundation.org/ht/d/sp/i/1152/pid/1152. "Jolles Insurance," www.jollesinsurance.com/index.php. "WEPROMOTEHEALTH.COM," May 25, 2009, www.wepromotehealth.com/.

5. The profile is created from a series of interviews by *ESB* co-author Jerome Katz with Jim Allsup. The final version was approved by Mr. Allsup on May 30, 2009.

6. Kendra S. Albright, "Environmental Scanning: Radar for Success," Entrepreneur.com, (July 5, 2004), www.arma.org/bookstore/files/Albright.pdf. Donald L. Lester and John A. Parnell, "Firm Size and Environmental Scanning Pursuits across Organizational Life Cycle Stages," *Journal of Small Business and Enterprise Development* 15(3) (2008): 540–554.

7. Patricia Carr, "Revisiting the Protestant Ethic and the Spirit of Capitalism: Understanding the Relationship between Ethics and Enterprise," *Journal of Business Ethics* 47, no. 1 (September 2003), pp. 7–16. Jeffrey R. Cornwall and Michael J. Naughton, "Who Is the Good Entrepreneur? An Exploration within the Catholic Social Tradition," *Journal of Business Ethics* 44, no. 1 (April 2003), pp. 61–75.

8. This is the concept of cognitive legitimacy as discussed in: John Freeman, Glenn R. Carroll, and Michael T. Hannan (1983). "The liability of newness: Age dependence in organizational death rates," *American Sociological Review,* 48 (5), Oct, 692–710. Michael T. Hannan, and John Freeman (1984). "Structural inertia and organizational change," *American Sociological Review* 49 (2), April, pp. 149–164. Howard E. Aldrich & C. Marlene Fiol (1994). "Fools rush in? The institutional context of industry creation," *Academy of Management Review,* 19 (4), October, pp. 645–670.

9. Dean Shepherd and Andrew Zacharakis, "A New-Venture's Cognitive Legitimacy: An Assessment by Customers," *Journal of Small Business Management* 41, no. 2 (April 2003), pp. 148–167.

10. By the way, the fact that outsiders see entrepreneurs as a key source of legitimacy, while the entrepreneurs look outside themselves to their product as the legitimacy source, is a wonderful example of the classic psychological idea of causal attribution. People tend to see causes as being outside themselves, while outsiders are more likely to attribute cause to a person. For more on this in general, see Richard Nisbet, and Lee Ross, *Human Inference: Strategies and Shortcomings of Social Judgement* (Englewood Cliffs, NJ: Prentice Hall,1980). For an example in entrepreneurship, see Kelly G. Shaver, William B. Gartner, Elizabeth Crosby, Karolina Bakalarova, and Elizabeth J. Gatewood, "Attributions about Entrepreneurship: A Framework and Process for Analyzing Reasons for Starting a Business," *Entrepreneurship: Theory and Practice* 26, no. 2 (Winter 2001), pp. 5–32.

11. F. R. David, "An Empirical Study of Codes of Business Ethics: A Strategic Perspective," paper presented at the 48th Annual Academy of Management Conference, Anaheim, California, August 1988.

12. Kim T. Gordon, "Cross-Training: Join the Multichannel Marketing Revolution, and Get Ready to Pump Up Your Sales," *Entrepreneur,* July 2003. www.entrepreneur.com/article/62766.

13. Anat BarNir and Ken A. Smith, "Interfirm Alliances in the Small Business: The Role of Social Networks," *Journal of Small Business Management* 40, no. 3 (July 2002), pp. 219–232. T. A. Ostgaard and S. Birley "Personal Networks and Firm Competitive Strategy—A Strategic or Coincidental Match?" *Journal of Business Venturing* 9, no. 4 (July 1994), pp. 281–305. Herminia Ibarra, "Personal Networks of Women and Minorities in Management: A Conceptual Framework," *Academy of Management Review* 18, no. 1 (January 1993), pp. 56–87. Sue Birley,. "The Role of Networks in the Entrepreneurial Process," *Journal of Business Venturing* 1, no. 1 (Winter 1985), pp. 107–117.

14. Heidi M. Neck, G. Dale Meyer, Boyd Cohen, and Andrew C. Corbett, "An Entrepreneurial System View of New Venture Creation," *Journal of Small Business Management* 42, no. 2 (April 2004), pp. 190–209. Danny Mackinnon, Keith Chapman, and Andrew Cumbers, "Networking, Trust and Embeddedness amongst SMEs in the Aberdeen Oil Complex," *Entrepreneurship and Regional Development* 16, no. 2 (March 2004), pp. 87–106. Robert A. Baron and Gideon D. Markman, "Beyond Social Capital: The Role of Entrepreneurs' Social Competence in Their Financial Success," *Journal of Business Venturing* 18, no. 1 (January 2003), pp. 41–60. Sarah D. Dodd, "Social Network Membership and Activity Rates: Some Comparative Data," *International Small Business Journal* 15, no. 4 (July/September 1997), pp. 80–87. Eric L. Hansen, "Entrepreneurial Networks and New Organization Growth," *Entrepreneurship Theory and Practice* 19, no. 4 (Summer 1995), pp. 7–20. Tone A. Ostgaard and Sue Birley, "Personal Networks and Firm Competitive Strategy—A Strategic or Coincidental Match?" *Journal of Business Venturing* 9, no. 4 (July 1994), pp. 281–306. Howard E. Aldrich and Carlos Zimmer, "Entrepreneurship through Social Networks," in Donald L. Sexton and Ray W. Smilor (eds.), *The Art and Science of Entrepreneurship* (Cambridge, MA: Ballinger, 1986), pp. 3–24. Sue Birley, "The Role of Networks in the Entrepreneurial Process," *Journal of Business Venturing* 1, no. 1 (Winter 1985), pp. 107–117.

15. David A. Whetten and Alison Mackey, "A Social Actor Conception of Organizational Identity and Its Implications for the Study of Organizational Reputation," *Business & Society* 41, no. 4 (December 2002), pp. 393–414. Concept taken from p. 394.

16. Howard E. Aldrich and Nancy M. Carter (2004), "Social Networks," In William B. Gartner, Kelly G. Shaver, Nancy M. Carter, and Paul D. Reynolds (Eds.), *Handbook of Entrepreneurial Dynamics: The Process of Business Creation* (Thousand Oaks, CA: Sage, 2004).

17. Paula Caproni, *The Practical Coach: Management Skills for Everyday Life* (Upper Saddle River, NJ, Prentice Hall, 2000). Other articles that use similar approaches and show positive effects include: Jeff Gold, Dave Devins, and Alistair Johnson, "What Is the Value of Mentoring in a Small Business? Using Narrative Evaluation to Find Out," *British Journal of Guidance & Counselling* 31, no. 1 (February 2003), pp. 51–62. Tony Kent, Charles Dennis, and Sue Tanton, "An Evaluation of Mentoring for SME Retailers," *International Journal of Retail & Distribution Management* 31, no. 8/9 (2003), pp. 440–465. R. Sullivan, "Entrepreneurial Learning and Mentoring," *International Journal of Entrepreneurial Behaviour & Research* 6, no. 3 (2000), pp. 160–175.

18. Ivan Misner, "Start by Learning How to Tailor Your Networking Approach for Different Occasions," *Entrepreneur—Sales & Marketing,* March 22, 2004, www.entrepreneur.com/article/0,4621,314878,00.html. Kim T. Gordon, "Attracting Customers: Use Your Business's Assets to Bring in More Clients, *Entrepreneur,* August 07, 2000, www.entrepreneur.com/article/31152. Dorothy P. Moore, *Careerpreneurs-Lessons from Leading Women Entrepreneurs on Building a Career Without Boundaries* (Palo Alto, CA: Davies-Black Publishing, 2001). Cynthia E. Griffin, "Gender Blender: Boys Don't Have Cooties, So Don't Be Afraid to Mingle at Mixed-Gender Functions," *Entrepreneur* (October 2001), www.entrepreneur.com/article/44294. Erin Chambers, "A Warm Reception for Female Execs," *BusinessWeek* online, December 9, 2004, www.businessweek.com/smallbiz/content/dec2004/sb2004129-3272-sb013.htm. Sherry Alpert, "Making a Network Connection," *BusinessWeek* online, September 18, 2003, www.businessweek.com/smallbiz/content/sep2003/sb20030918 4557.htm.

19. Amanda C. Kooser, "Crowd Control: Having Trouble Finding the Ideal System for Managing Your Customer Relationships? We've Got Advice to Get You Moving in the Right Direction," *Entrepreneur,* August 2003, www.entrepreneur.com/article/63248 Kimberly L. McCall, "Contact Solution: Face It, Post-its and Spiral Notebooks Won't Cut It When It Comes to Contact Management. Go High-Tech and Save Yourself the Headache," *Entrepreneur,* June 2002, www.entrepreneur.com/article/51904 Kim T. Gordon. "Managing Your Contacts: Our Homebased Expert Tells You Why You Can't Live without a Good Contact Management Program," HomeOfficeMag.com, December 2000, www.entrepreneur.com/article/34818.

20. Tad Hogg and Lada Adamic. "Enhancing Reputation Mechanisms via Online Social Networks," *Proceedings of the 5th ACM conference on*

Electronic Commerce. New York, NY, USA, 2004, http://protal.acm.org/citation.cfm?id=988772.988811. Catherine Holahan, "Social Networking Goes Niche: MySpace and Friendster's Runaway Popularity and Exposure Have Helped Spawn an Array of Targeted Networking Sites," *BusinessWeek* online, March 14, 2007, www.businessweek.com/print/technology/content/mar2007/tc20070314_884996.htm. Marko A. Rodriguez, Daniel J. Steinbock, Jennifer H. Watkins, Carlos Gershenson, Johan Bollen, Victor Grey, and Brad deGraf, "Smartocracy: Social Networks For Collective Decisionmaking," Hawaii International Conference On Systems Science (HICSS). IEEE Computer Society, 2007, www.cse.ucsc.edu/~okram/papers/smartocracy-hicss2007.pdf.

21. *BusinessWeek* online, Undated. "A Guide to Social Networking: Tip Sheet (CEO Guide To Technology: Tip Sheet)," www.businessweek.com/technology/ceo_tipsheet/2006_5.htm. Pat Thomas and Susan Moisey, "Women Entrepreneurs: Informal Learning and the Internet," *Journal of Small Business & Entrepreneurship* 19, no. 2 (2006) pp. 183–201. Lena L. West, "Becoming More Social," Entrepreneur.com Online, April 9, 2007, www.entrepreneur.com/article/176798.
22. Ian I. Mitroff and Murat C. Alpaslan, "Preparing for Evil," *Harvard Business Review,* 81, no. 4 (April 2003), p. 109. Ian I. Mitroff, *Crisis Leadership: Preparing for the Unthinkable* (New York: Wiley, 2003). D. Creelman, "Interview: Ian Mitroff on crisis leadership," 2004, HR.com, http://hradmin1.hr.com/HRcom/index.cfm/WeeklyMag/9A954EE7-B500-4AC4-A13DF077B83214E2?ost=wmFeature.
23. Norman R. Augustine, "Managing the Crisis You Tried to Prevent," *Harvard Business Review,* 73, no. 6 (November/December 1995), pp. 147–158.
24. Dan Millar, "ICM Crisis Report: News Coverage of Business Crises during 2002" 12 no. 1 (May 2003). The Institute for Crisis Management www.crisisexperts.com/02creport.htm. Theresa Forsman, "Contemplating the Unthinkable: An Entrepreneur Who Lacks a Plan for Coping with Catastrophe Is a Victim in the Making, Says Crisis-Management Expert Debra Traverso," *BusinessWeek,* October 2, 2001, www.businessweek.com/smallbiz/content/oct2001/sb20011003_514.htm. Michael Seid and Kay Marie Ainsley, "Managing Your Reputation: Follow These Tips to Save Your Brand during a Crisis," *Entrepreneur,* October 22, 2001, www.entrepreneur.com/article/45572. Christopher D. Lancette, "Critical Thinking: A Crisis Has Hit. Now What?" *Entrepreneur,* June 1999, www.entrepreneur.com/article/17788.
25. Daniel Tynan, "In Case of Emergency: A Smoke Alarm or a Life Preserver May Save Your Life, But They Won't Save Your Business. You Need a Real Disaster Plan Now. Your Business's Survival Depends on It," *Entrepreneur,* April 2003, www.Entrepreneur.com/article/0,4621,307161,00.html. Institute for Crisis Management, "Crisis Management and Crisis Communications" (Louisville, KY: The Institute for Crisis Management, 2000), www.crisisexperts.com/management.htm. Michael Seid and Kay Marie Ainsley, "Managing Your Reputation: Follow These Tips to Save Your Brand during a Crisis," *Entrepreneur,* October 22, 2001, www.entrepreneur.com/article/45572. Christopher D. Lancette, "Critical Thinking: A Crisis Has Hit. Now What?" *Entrepreneur* June 1999, www.entrepreneur.com/article/17788.
26. Scott J. Vitell, Erin B. Dickerson, and Troy A. Festervand, "Ethical Problems, Conflicts and Beliefs of Small Business Professionals," *Journal of Business Ethics* 28, no. 1 (November 2000), pp. 15–24. Ruth Clark and John Aram, "Universal Values, Behavioral Ethics and Entrepreneurship," *Journal of Business Ethics* 16, no. 5 (April 1997), pp. 561–572.
27. LaRue T. Hosmer, *The Ethics of Management,* 6th ed. (Boston: McGraw-Hill/Irwin, 2008.)
28. This example came from an interview conducted by Prof. Kathy Lund, Dean of Idaho State University-Pocatello, in May 2004. At the request of the entrepreneur, his name, his town, and his business's name are disguised.
29. Nichole L. Torres, "Ethically Speaking," *Entrepreneur,* December 2005, www.entrepreneur.com/magazine/entrepreneur/2005/december/81076.html.
30. Kimberly Blanton, "Dark Side of Subprime Loans—*The Boston Globe,*" boston.com, August 3, 2005; www.boston.com/business/personalfinance/articles/2005/08/03/dark_side_of_subprime_loans/. Steve Christ, "IMF Warns Toxic Debt May Exceed $4 Trillion," WealthDaily.com, April 9, 2009, www.wealthdaily.com/articles/imf-toxic-debt/1771. "Foreclosed: The Failure to Regulate Abusive Lending Practices: An Interview with Debbie Goldstein," *Multinational Monitor,* March 1, 2009, www.multinationalmonitor.org/mm2009/012009/interview-goldstein.html.
31. Lawrence M. Salinger, and Geis, Gilbert. "Caveat Emptor," *Encyclopedia of White-Collar & Corporate Crime.* (Thousand oaks CA. Sage, 2004). pp. 145–146; May 27, 2009 http://books.google.com/books?id=0f7yTNb_V3QC&pg=PA146&lpg=PA146&dq=%22caveat+emptor%22,+corporate&source=bl&ots=0eLuQT8JSV&sig=a6Wp4JC30KZrd77RDJQHdnopL6o&hl=en&ei=7JlcSqDHDoryMr_NsZIP&sa=X&oi=book_result&ct=result&resnum=6#PPA146,M1.
32. The negotiation approaches used here are adapted from Roger Fisher, William Ury, and Bruce Patton, *Getting to Yes: Negotiating Agreement without Giving in*, 2nd ed. (New York: Houghton Mifflin Harcourt, 1991).
33. Lisa Miller, "Ethics: It Isn't Just the Big Guys," *BusinessWeek* online, July 25, 2003, www.businessweek.com/smallbiz/content/10/2003/sb20030725_3531.htm.
34. M. H. Morris, M. Schindehutte, J. Walton, and J. Allen, "The Ethical Context of Entrepreneurship: Proposing and Testing a Developmental Framework," *Journal of Business Ethics* 40, no. 4 (November 2002), pp. 331–361. Hai Y. Teoh and Siang L. Foo, "Moderating Effects of Tolerance of Ambiguity and Risk Taking Propensity on the Role Conflict-Perceived Performance Relationship: Evidence from Singaporean Entrepreneurs," *Journal of Business Venturing* 12, no. I (January 1997), pp. 67–81.
35. For state government initiatives, see Amy Tsao, "A Primer on Drug 'Reimporting,'" *BusinessWeek* online, April 21, 2004. http://businessweek.com/bwdaily/dnflash/apr2004/nf20040421_1767_db_080.htm. For more about Rx Depot see Associated Press, "Judge Hears Testimony in Canada Drug Case." *St. Louis Post-Dispatch,* October 10, 2003, p C2. Also see Theresa Agovino, "Entrepreneur Fills an Order for Trouble," *St. Louis Post-Dispatch,* October 8, 2003, p. E1. For information on online pharmacies and some of the issues lawmakers are wrestling with, see Amy Tsao, "An Iffy Prognosis for Online Pharmacies," *BusinessWeek* online, November 25, 2003. www.businessweek.com/technology/content/nov2003/ tc20031125_2272_tc136.htm.
36. Melissa S. Baucus and Caryn L. Beck-Dudley. "Designing Ethical Organizations: Avoiding the Long-Term Negative Effects of Rewards and Punishments." *Journal of Business Ethics* 56 (2005), pp. 355–370. BusinessWeek.com. SMALL BIZ—FEATURES, Online Extra: How to play with the Big Guys. September 10, 2001. www.businessweek.com/magazine/content/01_37/b3748628.htm; Brenda Joyner, E. Dinah Payne, and Cecily A. Raiborn, "Building values, business ethics and corporate social responsibility into the developing organization." *Journal of Developmental Enterpreneurship* 7, no. 1 (Apr. 2002), pp. 113–131. *Robert J. McGarvey,* "Lords Of Discipline: 'Gimme 10!' Is not the way to change your employees' behavior." *Entrepreneur,* January 2000. www.entrepreneur.com/magazine/entrepreneur/2000/January/18856.html.
37. Johnson, "The Gift," *Annual Advances 1990* (New York: McGraw-Hill, 1990), pp. 300–301.

Chapter 4

1. This case is based on J. Samuelson, "Aaaaa-choo" *Forbes* 157 no. 5 (March 11, 1996), pp. 82–86; R. Lieber, *Upstart Start-Ups* (New York: Broadway Books, 1998); and information from the corporate Website of Magnetic Poetry, www.magneticpoetry.com.
2. R. Lieber, *Upstart Start-ups* (New York: Broadway Books, 1998).
3. "Poetry Makes a Fashion Statement," press release, July 10, 2001, www.magneticpoetry.com.
4. C. M. Gaglio, "Opportunity Identification: Review, Critique and Suggested Research Directions," in J. A. Katz (ed.), *Advances in Entrepreneurship, Firm*

Emergence and Growth, vol. 3 (Greenwich, CT: JAI Press, 1997), pp. 139–202. S. Venkataraman, "The Distinctive Domain of Entrepreneurship Research," in J. A. Katz (ed.), *Advances in Entrepreneurship, Firm Emergence and Growth*, vol. 3 (Greenwich, CT: JAI Press, 1997), pp. 119–138. I. Kirzner, *Perception, Opportunity, and Profit* (Chicago: University of Chicago Press, 1979). H. H. Stevenson and J. C. Jarillo, "A Paradigm of Entrepreneurship: Entrepreneurial Management," *Strategic Management Journal* 11, Summer 1990, pp. 17–27.

5. I. Kirzner, *Competition and Entrepreneurship* (Chicago: University of Chicago Press, 1973). I. Kirzner, *Perception, Opportunity, and Profit* (Chicago: University of Chicago Press, 1979). I. Kirzner, *Discovery and the Capitalist Process* (Chicago: University of Chicago Press, 1985).
6. C. M. Gaglio and J. A. Katz, "The Psychological Basis of Opportunity Identification: Entrepreneurial Alertness," *Small Business Economics* 16, no. 2, 2001, pp. 95–111.
7. G. E. Hills and R. P. Singh, "Opportunity Recognition." In *Handbook of Entrepreneurial Dynamics: The Process of Business Creation*, eds. W. B. Gartner, K. G. Shaver, N. M. Carter, and P. D. Reynolds. (Thousand Oaks, CA: Sage, 2004), Table 24.1, page 266.
8. Dame Anita Roddick, "Our history and values: a message from Dame Anita Roddick, The Body Shop founder" *The Body Shop* (corporate Web site), 2004, www.thebodyshop.com/bodyshop/company/index.jsp.
9. R. Lieber, *Upstart Start-ups* (New York: Broadway Books, 1998).
10. Geoff Williams, "Innovative Model: Joey Reiman has thought up stuff you've only dreamed about—and now he's going to share his secrets of innovation with you," *Entrepreneur*, September 2002, www.entrepreneur.com/article/54604.
11. URL for this article www.entrepreneur.com/article/61066.
12. Information comes from the corporate Web site of The Fat Hat Company, www.fathat.com.
13. G. E. Hills and R. P. Singh, "Opportunity Recognition," in *Handbook of Entrepreneurial Dynamics: the process of business creation*, ed. W. B. Gartner, K. G. Shaver, N. M. Carter, and P. D. Reynolds (Thousand Oaks, CA: Sage, 2004), Table 24.4, page 268.
14. M. Michalko, *Thinkertoys* (Berkeley, CA: Ten Speed Press, 1991).
15. G. Wallas, *The Art of Thought* (New York: Franklin Watts, 1926).
16. S. G. Isaksen, K. B. Dorval, and D. J. Treffinger, *Creative Approaches to Problem Solving* (New York: Kendall-Hunt Publishing Co., 2000).
17. L. K. Gundry and M. LaMantia, *Breakthrough Teams for Breakneck Times: Unlocking the Genius of Creative Collaboration* (New York: Dearborn Books, 2001).
18. Ibid.
19. C. W. Prather and L. K. Gundry, *Blueprints for Innovation* (New York: American Management Association, 1995).
20. Dean A. Shepherd and Mark Shanley, *New Venture Strategy* (Thousand Oaks, CA: Sage Publications, 1998).
21. Connie M. Gaglio and Jerome A. Katz, "The Psychological Basis of Opportunity Identification: Entrepreneurial Alertness," *Small Business Economics* 16 no. 2 (2001), pp. 95–111.
22. These results come from a custom analysis of the Panel Study of Entrepreneurial Dynamics (PSED) done by Dr. Jennifer L. D. Shaver. Additional information on the PSED can be found in *Handbook of Entrepreneurial Dynamics: The Process of Business Creation*, eds. W. B. Gartner, K. G. Shaver, N. M. Carter, and P. D. Reynolds (Thousand Oaks, CA: Sage, 2004).
23. This outline is adapted from, Ewing Marion Kauffman Foundation, *The Business Mentor CD-ROM*, Kansas City, MO: Ewing Marion Kauffman Foundation, 2001.
24. Michael V. Copeland and Om Malik, "How to Build a Bulletproof Startup," *Business 2.0 Magazine*, May 24, 2006 (June 2006 issue), http://i.cnn.net/money/magazines/business2/startups/bulletproof.pdf. Janelle Elms, "Bring in eBay Customers with Your Site," *Entrepreneur*, August 2006, www.entrepreneur.com/article/159936. Mike Fitzgerald, "Lesson 5: Use Cheap Web Tools," *Inc. Magazine*, July 2006, www.inc.com/magazine/20060701/bootstrapping-15.html. Gwen Moran, "If You Build It," Entrepreneur.com, April 01, 2007, www.entrepreneur.com/ebusiness/ebaycenter/boostingyoursales/article176310.html. Jerome A. Katz, Scott R. Safranski, and Omar Khan, "Virtual Instant Global Entrepreneurship: Cybermediation for Born International Service Firms," *Journal of International Entrepreneurship* 1, no. 1, March 2003, pp. 43–57.
25. "News and Updates: Core77 Design Awards Spotlights TikTok+LunaTik," LunaTik.com, September 20, 2011, http://updates.lunatik.com/?page=3. "TikTok+LunaTik Multi-Touch Watch Kits," www.kickstarter.com, December 16, 2010, www.kickstarter.com/projects/1104350651/tiktok-lunatik-multi-touch-watch-kits.
26. A. Daniels, "Generating Great Ideas from Employees," *Entrepreneur* (September 18, 2000).
27. The example of AltiTunes came from R. Lieber, *Upstart Start-ups* (New York: Broadway Books, 1998), and from the corporate Web site of AltiTunes, www.altitunes.com.

Chapter 4 Appendix

1. This feasibility study was developed by Laurel Ofstein, a student at DePaul University in May 2005, under the direction of Professor Lisa Gundry of DePaul University.
2. www.newmansownorganics.com/pet/home/index.php.
3. www.naturapet.com.
4. www.onlynaturalpet.com.
5. www.omhpet.com.
6. www.threedog.com.
7. www.flintriver.com.
8. www.howlinghound.com.
9. www.happydogtoys.com.
10. www.kongcompany.com.
11. www.fatcats.com.
12. www.woofonline.com.
13. www.dogztogz.com.
14. www.ruffruffandmeow.com.
15. www.sba.gov/starting/regulations.html.
16. www.illinoisbiz.biz/bus/step_by_step.html.
17. Mike Troy, "Knows No Bounds for Love of Fido," *DSN Retailing Today* 41, no. 23 (December 16, 2002), pp. 40–41.
18. Rebecca Gardyn, "Animal Magnetism," *American Demographics* 24, no. 5 (May 2002), pp. 30–37.
19. April Y. Pennington, "Hot Stuff: Want to Know What's Hot for 2004? We've Got the Businesses, Markets and Trends You Shouldn't Miss Out On," *Entrepreneur* (December 2003), www.entrepreneur.com/article/0,4621,311833,00.html. Steve Cooper, "Fever Pitch," *Entrepreneur* (December 2004), www.entrepreneur.com/article/0,4621,318038,00.html.
20. Alicia Suman, "Pet Owners," *Target Marketing* 26, no. 8 (August 2003), pp. 61–62.
21. Steve Cooper, "Fever Pitch."
22. "Organic Pet Food Gets Paws Up: Niche Grows Fast, Despite High Prices," *USA Today,* July 14, 2004, www.usatoday.com/money/industries/food/2004-07-13-organicx.htm.
23. American Pet Products Manufacturers Association, Inc., "Fact Sheet: Industry Statistics & Trends." *American Pet Products Manufacturers Association, Inc.* (corporate website), http://site05.fuzweb2.fuzint.com/press_industrytrends.asp.
24. Alicia Suman, "Pet Owners" (citing Mediamark Research).
25. Alicia Suman, "Pet Owners" (citing U.S. Census Bureau).
26. Alicia Suman, "Pet Owners" (citing Mediamark Research and Third Wave Research Group analysis of BLS 1999 Consumer Expenditure Survey data).
27. http://site05.fuzweb2.fuzint.com/press_industrytrends.asp.
28. April Y. Pennington, "Hot Stuff."

29. June Campbell, "Mark Your Territory in the Pet Industry," *Entrepreneurnewz* (September 8, 2003), (www.entrepreneurnewz.com/entrepreneurnewz-19-20030908MarkYourTerritoryinthePetIndustry.html).
30. www.bccresearch.com/food.
31. Rebecca Gardyn, "Animal Magnetism" (citing pet industry analyst Julia Dvorko of Business Communications Co.).
32. http://site05.fuzweb2.fuzint.com/press_industrytrends.asp.
33. See endnote 32.
34. Joseph Tarnowski, "Pet Project: Giant Eagle Mixes Creative Merchandising, Special Events, and Just Plain Love to Create a Pet Program that Caters to Owners as Much as Animals," *Progressive Grocer* 83, no. 13 (September 15, 2004), p. 68.
35. http://egov.cityofchicago.org/webportal/COCWebPortal/COC_EDITORIAL/RetailChicago_2004_North_2.pdf.
36. www.petco.com.
37. www.petsmart.com.
38. www.omahasteaks.com.
39. www.oldnavy.com; www.harley_davidson.com.
40. www.samandwillys.com.
41. See endnote 35.
42. http://factfinder.census.gov/servlet/QT_Table?_bm=y&-geo_id=86000US60657&-qr_name=DEC_2000_SF3_U_DP3&-ds_name=DEC_2000_SF3_U&-_lang=en&-redoLog=false&-_sse=on.
43. www.salary.com.

Chapter 5

1. Jerome Katz's interview with Kathryn Otoshi, Chicago, IL, March 2, 2007; Doug Chiang Studio, "Web Site Production Credits", 2006, www.dchiang.com/dchiang/webcredits.html#kathryn; Kathryn Otoshi, "KO Kid's Books-By Kathryn Otoshi" (Web site), 2007, www.kokidsbooks.com; LucasArts, "Lucas Company Greetings", December 08, 2003, www.starwars.com/community/news/holiday/news20031208.html.
2. PSED, question 331a asks people starting a business if they work for someone else more or less than 35 hours a week. 74.4 percent reported working for others full time, i.e., more than 35 hours a week.
3. Office of Advocacy, U.S. Small Business Administration, "Frequently Asked Questions," September, 2008, www.sba.gov/advo/stats/sbfaq.pdf.
4. Fairlie, Robert W., Kauffman Index of Entrepreneurial Activity, 1996–2011 (March 2012). Available at SSRN: http://ssrn.com/abstract=2027008 or http://dx.doi.org/10.2139/ssrn.2027008.
5. Sources include: Joseph J. Fucini and Suzy Fucini, *Entrepreneurs: The Men and Women behind Famous Brand Names and How They Made It* (Boston: G. K. Hall, 1985). Brendan Howard, "Making Time: Not Ready for the Burden of a Full-Time Business? How Do Your Evenings and Weekends Look?" *Entrepreneur,* June 2000, www.entrepreneur.com/article/28442. Adam Cohen, *The Perfect Store: Inside eBay* (Boston: Back Bay Books, 2003), www.businessknowhow.com/manage/perfectstore2.htm.
6. David Gumpert in *Burn Your Business Plan* (Needham, MA: Lauson Publishing, 2002) suggests 100 hours, but the range is given as rules of thumb in government (http://bellzinc.sympatico.ca/en/content/503613?skin=sli) and commercial (e.g., www.capital-connection.com/bpconsulting.html) sites.
7. U.S. Census Bureau, "2007 Economic Census, Release Date: 3/17/2009, Sector 00: EC0700CADV1: All sectors: Core Business Statistics Series: Advance Summary Statistics for the United States (2007 NAICS Basis): 2007," *Detailed Statistics—American FactFinder,* March 17, 2009; June 4, 2009, http://factfinder.census.gov/servlet/IBQTable?_bm=y&-geo_id=&-ds_name=EC0700CADV1&-_lang=en.
8. Computed from numbers provided in Office of Advocacy, U.S. Small Business Administration, "Frequently Asked Questions," September 2008, www.sba.gov/advo/stats/sbfaq.pdf.
9. The material in this section is based on the following articles: Broderick Perkins, "Create the Ideal Space For Business at Home," 2001, www.startupjournal.com/howto/workhome/20011012-perkins.html; Meredith Gould, "Space Quest," *Entrepreneur,* 2000, www.Entrepreneur.com/article/0,4621,280012,00.html; Broderick Perkins, "Realize the Dream of a Home-Based Business," 2001, www.startupjournal.com/howto/workhome/20011026-perkins.html; Cliff Ennico, "The Reality of Working from Home," *Entrepreneur,* 2002, www.entrepreneur.com/article/53186; Paul Edwards and Sarah Edwards, "Handling Houseguests in Your Home Office," *Entrepreneur,* August 2003, www.entrepreneur.com/article/63922; Owen Thomas "You, Incorporated," *Business 2.0,* December 2002/January 2003.
10. An old listing can be found at www.cyburbia.org/directory/index.php?t=sub_pages&cat=217, but it is no longer being updated. A good listing of practical zoning help can be found at the Realtors' site at www.realtor.org/library/library/fg803.
11. Cliff Ennico, "Avoiding the Zoning Trap," Entrepreneur.com, August 15, 2005, www.entrepreneur.com/article/79464.
12. Paul and Sarah Edwards, "Dealing With Zoning Restrictions," Home OfficeMag.com, December 2001, www.entrepreneur.com/article/46816; Paul and Sarah Edwards, "Bad Zoning Laws? Get 'Em Changed!" HomeOfficeMag.com, June 01, 2003, www.entrepreneur.com/article/62418; Entrepreneur.com, 2007, "Zoning: Home Is Where the Business Is, And It's Also Where a Lot of Regulations Are," Entrepreneur.com; www.entrepreneur.com/article/38884; Karen E. Spaeder, "Is Your Home Zoned for Business?" Entrepreneur.com, January 26, 2004, www.entrepreneur.com/article/68844.
13. Paul and Sarah Edwards, "Bad Zoning Laws? Get 'Em Changed!" HomeOfficeMag.com, June 01, 2003, www.entrepreneur.com/article/62418; Karen E. Spaeder, "Is Your Home Zoned for Business?" Entrepreneur.com, January 26, 2004, www.entrepreneur.com/article/38884.
14. Personal story, used with permission.
15. Meredith Gould, "Space Quest," *Entrepreneur,* October 2000, www.entrepreneur.com/article/32992. Reprinted with permission of Entrepreneur.com.
16. Azreila Jaffe, "When Is It Time to Move the Office Out of the Home?" www.jbsa.com/content/suites/hb_teleworking/time_to_move.shtml.
17. For more information regarding the impact of the Internet on small and medium businesses see Hee Dae Kim, In Lee, & Choong Kwon Lee, "Building Web 2.0 enterprises: A study of small and medium enterprises in the United States," *International Small Business Journal,* 29 (4) August 2011. Available from http://isb.sagepub.com/content/early/2011/08/12/0266242611409785.abstract last visited June 5, 2012. Also see Judith Jeffcote, Caroline Chappel, and Sylvia Feindt, "Best Practice in SME Adoption of e-Commerce," *Benchmarking,* 9, no. 2 (2002), pp. 122–132; S. McCue, "Small Firms and the Internet: Force or Farce?" *International Business Trade Forum,* 1999; B. Kleindl, "Competitive Dynamics and New Business Models for SMEs in the Virtual Marketplace," *Journal of Developmental Entrepreneurship* 5, no. 1 (2000), pp. 73–85; C. Chappel and S. Feindt, "Analysis of E-Commerce Practice in SMEs," 1999, http://kite/tsa/de, P. Haynes, R. Becherer, and M. L. Helms, "Small and Mid-Sized Businesses and Internet Use: Unrealized Potential?" *Internet Research: Electronic Networking Applications and Policy* 8, no. 3 (1990); Dick Anderson, "Marketplace: Creating and Nurturing a Premier E-business," *Journal of Interactive Marketing* 14, no. 3 (2000), pp. 67–78.
18. John, Horrigan, "The Internet and Consumer Choice," *Pew Internet & American Life Project,* May 18, 2008; June 7, 2009, www.pewinternet.org/Reports/2008/The-Internet-and-Consumer-Choice.aspx.
19. U.S. Census Bureau. "E-Stats/Historical Data." www.census.gov/econ/estats/archives.html.
20. Conversation with David W. Peters, vice president of Letrah, used with permission, June 20, 2005.
21. Mary Kathleen Flynn, "No. 1 Tweeter about Twitter Is MKFlynn, says Klout (Dealscape—Technology)," TheDeal.com, May 19, 2009;

www.thedeal.com/dealscape/2009/05/mkflynn tweets the most about.php. Mark Hefflinger, "StockTwits Gets $800K to Follow Investor Chatter on Twitter I Digital Media Wire," dmwmedia.com, May 19, 2009; www.dmwmedia.com/news/2009/05/19/stocktwits-gets-$800k-follow-investor-chatter-twitter. Peter, Kafka, "Twitter App Investors Still Writing Checks: StockTwits Raises a Round," *BetaWorks; MediaMemo,* May 18, 2009, http://mediamemo.allthingsd.com/tag/betaworks/.

22. Don Debelak, "Working the Web," *Entrepreneur,* 1998, www.entrepreneur.com/article/16130.
23. Gerry Grant, "Search Optimization Campaigns Build Brand," *Marketing News,* September 29, 2003; Yong Seck Sohn, Hangun Houn, and Dae Ryon Chang, "A Model of Consumer Information Search and Online Network Externality," *Journal of Interactive Marketing* 16, no. 4 (2002), pp. 2–14.
24. Nancy Einhart, "How to Get Them Buzzing to Your Site," *Business 2.0,* October 2003.
25. This pie chart was built from comScore, Inc. data. The data were reported as percentages, from www.comscore.com/Press Events/Press Releases/2012/3/comScore Releases February 2012 U.S. Search Engine Rankings.
26. Philippa Gamse, "Are Search Engines Worth It Any More?" (2003), www.jbsba.com/cgi-bin/articlesbybtsub.cgi?art=441.
27. Figure 5.4 measures the number of SSL certificates issued to Web sites. SSL (secure socket layer) is a protocol for encrypting communications between a website and a user of the website. It is one of the key components of transaction security on the Internet, so the count of certificates gives a good approximatation of the number of e-commerce websites. Paul Mutton, "One Million SSL Sites on the Web—Netcraft," Netcraft.com, February 1, 2009; http://news.netcraft.com/archives/2009/02/01/one million ssl sites on the web.html.
28. U.S. Census Bureau, "U.S. Census Bureau E-Stats: 2010 E-Commerce Multi-Sector Report," *E-Stats Main Page,* May 28, 2009; www.census.gov/econ/estats/2010/2010reportfinal.pdf. Released May 2012.
29. The number of sellers on eBay is reported to be about 4 million, with roughly 500,000 who get their primary income from eBay or already have a full-time business and use eBay for a secondary sales outlet. These numbers come from Leslie Walker, "EBay Sellers Fell into Careers That Fill Their Lives," washingtonpost.com, June 20, 2005, www.washingtonpost.com/wp-dyn/content/article/2005/06/29/AR2005062902935 pf.html. The listing fees on eBay came from a search of eBay on June 7, 2009.
30. Miniwatts Marketing Group, "World Internet Usage and Population Statistics," *Internet World Stats: Usage and Population Statistics,* www.internetworldstats.com/stats.htm.
31. Melissa Campanelli, "Anti-Fraud Measures for Your Site," *Entrepreneur,* September 2006, www.entrepreneur.com/ebusiness/operations/article166010.html. Amanda C. Kooser, "Card Tricks," *Entrepreneur,* February 2002, www.entrepreneur.com/magazine/entrepreneur/2002/february/48322.html. Tim Miller, "Chargebacks: A Huge Price to Pay," *Entrepreneur,* June 25, 2001, www.entrepreneur.com/money/paymentsandcollections/acceptingpayments/article41670.html.
32. Sandy D. Jap, "An Exploratory Study of the Introduction of Online Reverse Auctions," *Journal of Marketing* 67 (July 2003) pp. 96–107.
33. Melissa Campanelli, "Help Wanted," *Entrepreneur,* 2003, www.entrepreneur.com/article/63816.
34. Cliff Ennico, "Selling Your Specialty Merchandise Online," *Entrepreneur,* 2003.
35. Jacquelyn Lynn, "Let the Bidding Begin," *Entrepreneur,* 2003, www.entrepreneur.com/article/0,4621,310583,00.html.
36. Tim W. Knox, "The Secret to eBay Success," *Entrepreneur,* 2003, www.entrepreneur.com/article/71112.
37. Compiled from information from Tim W. Knox, "The Secret to eBay Success," *Entrepreneur,* 2003, www.entrepreneur.com/article/71112; Marsha Collier, "eBay For Dummies, 7th Edition. New York: Wiley, 2011.
38. Jacquelyn Lynn, Op. cit.
39. Michael Krauss, "EBay 'Bids' on Small-biz Firms to Sustain Growth," *Marketing News,* December 8, 2003.
40. Devlin Smith, "Parties Victorian: Build a Business around Tea Time . . . and Victorian Times," *HomeOfficeMag.com,* July 2001, www.entrepreneur.com/article/41818.
41. Michael L. Sheffield, "Closing the Sale as a Network Marketer: How to Get a Commitment Out of Prospective Customers," *Entrepreneur* online, April 21, 2003, www.entrepreneur.com/article/61244.
42. Multilevel marketing resources are also available at *Entrepreneur magazine,* www.entrepreneur.com/businessopportunities/networkmarketing/archive114792.html.
43. Chris Penttila, "Retailiatory Strike: Don't Let the Big Boxes Win without a Fight. There's Plenty of Room for Start-ups to Make Their Mark in Retail," *Entrepreneur,* December 2002, www.Entrepreneur.com/article/0,4621,304515,00.html.
44. Jan Kingaard, "How to Select a Shopping Center Location: Your Plan for Retail Success Requires a Shopping Center or Mall Location," *Entrepreneur* online, Management Section. February 10, 2005, www.entrepreneur.com/article/0,4621,319969,00.html.
45. Jan Kingaard, "How to Select a Shopping Center Location: Your Plan for Retail Success Requires a Shopping Center or Mall Location," *Entrepreneur* online, Management Section. February 10, 2005, www.entrepreneur.com/article/0,4621,319969,00.html.
46. Paul Edwards and Sarah Edwards, "Treasure Hunt: Hit the Mark When You're Hunting for Products to Sell," *Entrepreneur,* December 2003, www.entrepreneur.com/article/65678.
47. Mike, Hogan, "Make Your Car an Office on Wheels—Entrepreneur.com," Entrepreneur.com, February 2006; June 8, 2009, www.entrepreneur.com/technology/newsandtrends/article82968.html.
48. Lisa, Druxman, "Mama Needs to Get out of the Home Office—Entrepreneur.com," Entrepreneur.com, August 21, 2008; June 8, 2009, www.entrepreneur.com/startingabusiness/mompreneur/mompreneurcolumnistlisadruxman/article196600.html.
49. J. A. Katz and W. B. Gartner. "Properties of emerging organizations." *Academy of Management Review* 13, no. 3 (July, 1988), pp. 429–441.
50. See endnote 2.
51. Mark Henricks, "Just To-Do It: Having Trouble Getting Organized?" *Entrepreneur,* August 2004, www.entrepreneur.com/article/71810.
52. Nichole L. Torres, "Juggling Multiple Tasks: How to Find the Time to Do All You Need to Do—and Then Some," *Entrepreneur,* July 6, 2004, www.entrepreneur.com/article/71688.
53. Another useful site is maintained by the U.S. Small Business Administration at www.sba.gov/hotlist/license.html.
54. American Express—The Open Network. "Learning to Delegate," *Entrepreneur,* December 09, 2002, www.entrepreneur.com/article/0.4621.305082.00.html, M. A. Johnston, "Delegation and Organizational Structure in Small Businesses: Influence of Managers Attachment Patterns," *Group & Organization Management* 25, no. 1 (March 1, 2000), pp. 4–22. Robert McGarvey, "To the Rescue: Always Stepping in to Save the Day?" *Entrepreneur,* March 2000, www.entrepreneur.com/article/17326. Alexander Ardichvili, Brian Harmon, Richard N. Cardozo, Paul D. Reynolds, and Mary L. Williams, "The New Venture Growth: Functional Differentiation and the Need for Human Resource Development Interventions," *Human Resource Development Quarterly* 9, no. 1 (Spring 1998), pp. 55–70. Robert Mc-Garvey, "Ready, Set, Delegate! Handing Out Tasks Is the Key to Growing Your Business" *Entrepreneur,* July 1998, www.entrepreneur.com/article/16046. Glenn H. Matthews, "Run Your Business or Build an Organization?" *Harvard Business Review* 62, no. 2 (March/April 1984), pp. 34–39.
55. Dun & Bradstreet, D&B 21st Annual Small Business Survey Summary Report/Full Report, 2002, http://sbs.dnb.com/survey/2002survey.pdf.

The sample was 543 firms with 1–25 employees, although only about half that number reported on the Web site and computer functions.

56. R. N. Lussier, "A Nonfinancial Business Success versus Failure Prediction Model for Young Firms," *Journal of Small Business Management* 33, no. 1 (January 1995), pp. 8–20. R. N. Lussier, and S. Pfeifer. "A Crossnational Prediction Model for Business Success," *Journal of Small Business Management* 39, no. 3 (July 2001), pp. 228–239.
57. Chris Penttila, "Close the Loop: If You're Outsourcing Projects Right and Left, Make Sure the Information You Need Is Rolling Back to You," *Entrepreneur,* October 2003, www.entrepreneur.com/article/64532. P. Jacobs, "So You Want to Be a Mountain Climber—Changing Careers One New Experience at a Time," *Global Career Coaching* (corporate Web site), www.gccoach.com/documents/SoYouWanttoBeAMountain ClimberOct03 000.pdf, Additional information was also obtained from the Gourmet Gatherings corporate website. www.gourmetgatherings.com.
58. www.sba.gov/content/5-steps-registering-your-business.
59. Lynn Neeley, "Bootstrap Finance," Coleman Foundation White Paper, 2002, www.colemanchairs.org/files/documents/4/Neeley.pdf. Verne Harnish, "Finding Money You Didn't Know You Had," *Fortune Small Business* 12, no. 5 (June 2002), pp. 67–68. Mary Kay Sullivan, "Small Business Familiarity with Sources of Financing: Impact of Location and Size," U.S. Association for Small Business and Entrepreneurship, annual meeting, 2000, www.usasbe.org/knowledge/proceedings/2000/sullivan.pdf. Bob Weinstein, "Walk This Way: Lessons in the Fine Art of Bootstrapping," *Entrepreneur,* October 1998, www.Entrepreneur.com/article/0,4621,229429,00.html. Howard E. Van Auken and Lynn Neeley, "Evidence of Bootstrap Financing among Small Start-Up Firms," *Journal of Entrepreneurial and Small Business Finance* 5, no. 3 (1996), pp. 235–249.
60. Stephanie Clifford, "How to Start a Business for (Almost) Nothing," *Inc.*, July 2006, www.inc.com/magazine/20060701/bootstrapping-intro.html. Michael Fitzgerald, "CRM Made Simple," *Inc.* January 2007. www.inc.com/magazine/20070101/technology-tools.html. Mike Fitzgerald, "Something for Nothing," *Inc.* November 2006, www.inc.com/magazine/20061101/handson-technology.html. Derek Gehl, "12 Free Tools for Online Businesses," *Entrepreneur.com,* June 27, 2005, www.entrepreneur.com/ebusiness/ebusinesscolumnist/article78504.html. *Inc.* Magazine Staff, "The Open-Source Advantage," *Inc.*, January 2007. www.inc.com/magazine/20070101/technology-software-adv.html. Gwen Moran, "If You Build It," Entrepreneur.com, April 01, 2007. www.entrepreneur.com/ebusiness/ebaycenter/boostingyoursales/article176310.html.
61. Michael McMyne and Nicole Amare, *Student Entrepreneurs: 14 Undergraduate All-Stars Tell Their Stories* (St. Louis, MO: Premium Press America, 2003), pp. 42–50.
62. J. Finegan, "Bootstrapping: Great Companies Started with Less than a Thousand Dollars: CEOs from 11 different companies share tips and suggestions on how to fund a start-up with under $1,000," *Inc.*, August 1995, www.inc.com/magazine/19950801/2363.html. Jerry Useem, "Should You Lie? Permissible or Not, Lying Has a Hallowed Place in the World of Business," *Fortune Small Business,* October 14, 1999, www.fortune.com/fortune/smallbusiness/managing/articles/0,15114,360720,00.html. MSGI Security Solutions Inc., "Board of Directors," MSGI Security Solutions, Inc. (corporate website), www.mediaservices.com/about/board.cfm.
63. Carla Goodman, "The Big Time: You've Tested the Part-Time Waters; Now Take the Full-Time Plunge," *Business Start-Ups,* August 1998, www.entrepreneur.com/article/16124.
64. K. Petrova, "Part-Time Entrepreneurship and Wealth Effects: New Evidence from the Panel Study of Entrepreneurial Dynamics," Working Paper, Boston College Department of Economics, September 2004, www..bc.edu/~petrovak/html/research/jmp.pdf.

Chapter 6

1. This example comes from a personal interview with T. Caldbeck, TLC Remodeling LLC, May 5, 2012.
2. Lyrics and tune by Paul Simon.
3. Ronald S. Burt and Holly Raider, "Creating careers: Women's paths to entrepreneurship." Unpublished manuscript (2002), University of Chicago, Chicago, IL, www.sfu.ca/~insna/SunbeltAbstracts/Abstracts/Burt_&_Riader.html. Arnold C. Cooper and William Dunkelberg, "Entrepreneurship and paths to business ownership," *Strategic Management Journal* (1986) 7, pp. 53–68. Calin Gurau, "Bio-Entrepreneurship in Different Economic Systems: A Comparative Analysis of Bio-Entrepreneurs' Profile in UK, France, and Germany," *International Journal of Biotechnology* (2006), 8, no. 3–4, pp. 169–186. Mary C. Mattis, "Women entrepreneurs: out from under the glass ceiling," *Women in Management Review* (April 2004), 19, no. 3, pp. 154–163.
4. B. Headd, "Redefining Business Success: Distinguishing between Closure and Failure," *Small Business Economics* 21, no. 1 (August 2003), pp. 51–61.
5. D. A. Veasley, "Incubators Build Economies, Benefit communities," *Birmingham Business Journal*, August 15, 2003; July 2005, http://birmingham.bizjournals.com/birmingham/stories/2003/08/11/focus6.html.
6. For example, see Oregon SBDC Network , *ASBDC Accreditation Self-Study* (Eugene, OR: Oregon, SBDC Network, November 2002). www.bizcenter.org/networkselfstudy/2002OregonSelf-Study.pdf; p. 25. J. J. Chrisman, "The Influence of Outsider-Generated Knowledge Resources on Venture Creation," *Journal of Small Business Management* 37, no. 4 (1999), pp. 42–58. J. J. Chrisman and W. E. McMullan, "A Preliminary Assessment of Outsider Assistance as a Knowledge Resource: The Longer-Term Impact of New Venture Counseling," *Entrepreneurship Theory and Practice* 24, no. 3 (2000), pp. 37–53. James J. Chrisman and W. Ed McMullan, "Outsider Assistance as a Knowledge Resource for New Venture Survival," *Journal of Small Business Management* 42, no. 3 (2004), pp. 229–244. A. Charney and G. Libecap, *Impact of Entrepreneurship Education* (Kansas City, MO: Kauffman Center for Entrepreneurial Leadership, 2000). L. Kolvereid and O. Moen, "Entrepreneurship among Business Graduates: Does a Major in Entrepreneurship Make a Difference?" *Journal of European Industrial Training* 21, no. 4 (1997), pp. 154–160. W. E. McMullan and L. M. Gillin, "Entrepreneurship Education: Developing Technological Start-Up Entrepreneurs. A Case Study of a Graduate Entrepreneurship Programme at Swinburne University," *Technovation* 18, no. 4, (1998), pp. 275–286. T. V. Menzies, and J. C. Paradi, "Encouraging Technology-Based Ventures: Entrepreneurship Education and Engineering Graduates," *New England Journal of Entrepreneurship* 5, no. 2 (2002), pp. 57–64. T. V. Menzies and J. C. Paradi, "Entrepreneurship Education and Engineering Students: Career Path and Business Performance," *International Journal of Entrepreneurship and Innovation* 6, no. 2 (2003), pp. 85–96. N. B. Upton, D. L. Sexton, and C. Moore, "Have We Made a Difference? An Examination of Career Activity of Entrepreneurship Majors since 1981" (abstract), *Frontiers of Entrepreneurship Research,*1995 edition, pp. 727–728.
7. Brian Headd, "Redefining Business Success: Distinguishing between Closure and Failure," *Small Business Economics* 21, no. 1 (2003) pp. 51–61.
8. Recorded interview with Josh Fraser February 13, 2010. www.onlineaspect.com/2010/02/15/mixergy-interview/.
9. "Failed Startups The other side to entrepreneurship." EventVue. http://failedstartups.wordpress.com/page/2/.
10. Blog written by Rob Johnson Friday, February 5, 2010. http://blog.eventvue.com/post/372936164/post-mortem.
11. Ibid.
12. These statistics come from the Panel Study of Entrepreneurial Dynamics. William B. Gartner, Kelly G. Shaver, Nancy M. Carter, and Paul D. Reynolds

(eds.), *Handbook of Entrepreneurial Dynamics: The Process of Business Creation* (Thousand Oaks, CA: Sage, 2004).
13. E. Ries, *The Lean Startup* (New York: Crown Business, 2011).
14. B. Horovitz, "KFC Tries to Revive the Colonel's Prestige," *USA Today,* reprinted in *Money* (September 9, 2010), p. 3b.
15. "Colonel Sanders," *I've Got A Secret* (April 6, 1964), rebroadcast by GSN (March 30, 2008).
16. Ozersky, "KFC's Colonel Sanders: He Was Real, Not Just an Icon," *Time* (September 15, 2010), www.time.com/time/nation/article/0,8599,2019218,00.html.
17. Wikipedia contributors, "Colonel Sanders," http://en.wikipedia.org/w/index.php?title=Colonel_Sanders&oldid=495450840.
18. R. Green, and J. J. Carroll, *Investigating Entrepreneurial Opportunities* (Thousand Oaks, CA: Sage 2000).
19. Professional Association of Innkeepers International (PAII), *Eighth Biennial Industry Study of Bed-and-Breakfast & Country Inns* (Santa Barbara, CA, 2003).
20. L. Marx and G. Shaler, "Bargaining Power in Sequential Contracting," Duke/UNC Micro-Theory Working Paper 3, 2002.
21. Financial Accounting Standards Board, "Statement of Financial Accounting Standards No. 142," *Goodwill and Other Intangible Assets* (2001).
22. McDonald's Corporation, *Annual Report,* 2002, p. 10.
23. Sarah E. Lockyer, "One Year Later: Ground Round Sizzles under Franchisee Co-op," *Nation's Restaurant News,* February 28, 2005. Carlye Adler, "The Ground Round Rebound: Stunned by a Sudden Bankruptcy, Stubborn Franchisees Step in to Buy Their Parent Company," *Fortune Small Business Magazine,* February 2005. Michael Peña, "Richmond's Job Center Gets Downsized," *East Bay Business Times,* April 2004.
24. Sandra King, "Organizational Performance and Conceptual Capability: The Relationship between Organizational Performance and Successors' Capability in a Family-Owned Firm," *Family Business Review* 16, no. 3 (September 2003), pp. 173–182. Patricia Schiff Estess, "Class Acts: Family Business Forums Are a One-Stop Education Resource," *Entrepreneur* December 1996, www.entrepreneur.com/article/13568. A. Ibrahim and W. Ellis, *Family Business Management: Concepts and Practices* (Dubuque, IA: Kendall/Hunt Publishing, 1994).
25. Rod P. Burkert, "A Good Deal Depends on Preparation," *Journal of Accountancy,* 196, no. 5 (November 2003), pp. 47–52.
26. Stephen Weinstein, "Add a New Owner to Your Firm," *Journal of Accountancy* 196, no. 2 (August 2003), pp. 43–48.
27. The ideas here are derived from Chris Kelleher, "Preventing Feuds in the Family Business: Handling Delicate Topics—Like Succession Planning—with Care Is Key to Keeping the Peace in Any Family Business," *Entrepreneur,* June 14, 2004, www.entrepreneur.com/article/71132. Nichole L. Torres, "Family Affair When Business and Family Mix, the Key to Success is Communication," *Entrepreneur's Be Your Own Boss,* September 2004, www.entrepreneur.com/article/72314. Patricia Schiff Estess, "Class Acts: Family Business Forums Are a One-Stop Education Resource," *Entrepreneur,* December 1996, www.entrepreneur.com/article/13568.
28. Dominique Besson and Slimane Haddadj, "Dysfunctions in Owner-Manager Succession Process in Family Firms and How a SEAM Intervener-Researcher Can Address Them," *Journal of Organizational Change Management* 16, no. 1 (2003), pp. 83–89.
29. Isabelle Le Breton-Miller, Danny Miller, and Lloyd P. Steier, "Toward an Integrative Model of Effective FOB Succession," *Entrepreneurship: Theory & Practice* 28, no. 4 (Summer 2004), pp. 305–328. William S. White, Timothy D. Krinke, and David L. Geller, "Family Business Succession Planning: Devising an Overall Strategy," *Journal of Financial Service Professionals* 58, no. 3 (May 2004), pp. 67–86.
30. Scott Bernard Nelson, "Leave It to Them: Make Sure Your Family Gets What It Needs by Including a Disclaimer Provision in Your Estate Plan," *Entrepreneur,* August 2004, www.entrepreneur.com/article/71782. Paul DeCeglie, "State of the Estate: What Is Estate Planning and Why Should You Be Doing It Now?" Entrepreneur's Start-Ups, January 2001, www.entrepreneur.com/article/77778.

Chapter 7

1. This case is based on Nick Tostenrude, "Turning 25¢ into $1: The Unique Advantages and Disadvantages of Being Young Entrepreneurs," in Michael McMyne and Nicole Amare, *Student Entrepreneurs: 14 Undergraduate All-Stars Tell Their Stories* (Nashville: Premium Press, 2003).
2. G. E. Hills and R. P. Singh, "Opportunity Recognition," in *Handbook of Entrepreneurial Dynamics: The Process of Business Creation,* eds. W. B. Gartner, K. G. Shaver, N. M. Carter, and P. D. Reynolds (Thousands Oaks, CA: Sage, 2004), Table 24.1, p. 266.
3. SIC codes are slowly being replaced by the North American Industry Classification System (NAICS). NAICS uses a six-digit code and offers original categories reflecting newer industries, such as those related to the Internet. For NAICS information, check out the NAICS page at the Census Bureau, www.census.gov/epcd/naics02/.
4. Thomas J. Stanley and William D. Danko, *The Millionaire Next Door* (New York: Pocket Books, 1996).
5. Anita Campbell, "Top 30 Most Profitable Small Businesses during 2008," *Small Business Trends* 2 (February 2009), June 11, 2009, http://smallbiztrends.com/2009/02/top-30-most-profitable-small-businesses-2008.html. Anita Campbell, "What Are the Most profitable Small Businesses in a Recession?" *Small Business Trends,* January 27, 2009; http://smallbiztrends.com/2009/01/profitable-small-businesses-recession.html. Maureen Farrell, "The Most and Least Profitable Businesses to Start—Forbes.com," forbes.com, January 18, 2008, www.forbes.com/2008/01/18/citigroup-sageworks-nyu-ent-fin=cx_mf_0118mostprofitable.html. Scott Shane, "Are There Recession-Proof Industries for Small Businesses?" *Small Business Trends,* December 1, 2008, http://smallbiztrends.com/2008/12/recession-proof-small-businesses.html. Mindy Woolen, "Industry Trends >> Blog Archive >> Most Profitable Industries of 2008," Sageworks.com, January 28, 2009; www.sageworksinc.com/industrytrends/index.php/mostprofitable-industries-of-2008/.
6. Sarah Caron, "14 Big Businesses that Started in a Recession," insidecrm.com, May 24, 2009, www.insidecrm.com/features/businesses started-slump-111108/. Michael Mandel, "Starting Successful New Companies in Recessions—BusinessWeek," Businessweek.com, May 3, 2009; May 24, 2009, www.businessweek.com/the_thread/economicsunbound/archives/2009/05/starting_succes.html. This list of airlines was based on Michael Masouras, "Companies Founded after 2000—Freebase," Freebase.com, May 24, 2009, www.freebase.com/view/user/masouras/default_domain/views/companies_founded_after_2000, compared to operating airlines shown on "List of Airlines—Planes," Plane Spotting World, May 24, 2009, http://plane. spottingworld.com/List_of_airlines.
7. Stanley and Danko, op. cit.
8. PSED Q327, "If someone asked you which kind of person you are, would you say that you preferred doing things better or doing things differently?" Of respondents, 63.3 percent said doing things better, while 32.4 percent said doing things differently.
9. The ideas in this section build on three works. Michael Porter talked about the topic in general in his 1980 masterpiece *Competitive Strategy* (Free Press). Karl Vesper really gave the first detailed workup of imitation-innovation strategies in his 1990 book *New Venture Strategy* (Prentice Hall). The most advanced thinking on the topic can be found in Dean Shepherd and Mark Shanley's 1998 book *New Venture Strategy* (Sage).

10. Sheila Himmel, "Feeling Welcome at Satay House," *The Mercury News*, May 3, 2002, www.bayarea.com/mld/mercurynews/entertainment/eye/3189323.htm.
11. [No author], "CONSUMER WEB SERVICES DVD Movie Rental Plot Pits Tiny Netflix Vs. Blockbuster," *Investor's Business Daily*, 1061–2890, March 21, 2001, p. A08. [No author], "DVD Renter Netflix Crafts New Plot Line; Molding Itself After HBO; The distribution company foresees its subscribers getting a host of content," *Investor's Business Daily*, 1061–2890, Nov 26, 2003, p. A04. [No author], "Blockbuster battles Netflix," *Variety*, 0042–2738, v395 i13 (August 16, 2004), p. 2. Tara Lemmey, "Push the Positive for Customers; Any Revenue Model That Takes Advantage of Human Frailty Is Vulnerable. Case in Point: Blockbuster. Opportunist: Netflix," *BusinessWeek* Online, Sept 13, 2005.
12. Michael V. Copeland, "Start Last, Finish First," *Business 2.0*, February 2, 2006, http://money.cnn.com/magazines/business2/business2_archive/2006/01/01/8368119/index.htm. Mauro F. Guillén, "Structural Inertia, Imitation, and Foreign Expansion: South Korean Firms and Business Groups in China, 1987–95," *Academy of Management Journal*, 45, (2002) pp. 509–525. Henrik Barth, "Fit among Competitive Strategy, Administrative Mechanisms, and Performance: A Comparative Study of Small Firms in Mature and New Industries," *Journal of Small Business Management* 41, No. 2 (April 2003), pp. 133–147. David Newton, "To Spark Business Growth, Follow the Leader in Your Industry," *Entrepreneur*, October 2003, www.entrepreneur.com/magazine/entrepreneur/2003/october/64478.html.
13. Nichole L. Torres, "Designing Women—A 'by Women, for Women, about Women' Attitude Is Making this Greeting Card Company a Success," *Entrepreneur*, July 2001, www.entrepreneur.com/article/41436.
14. This is question Q291 in the PSED, "Within the first three to four years, what percentage of your customers do you expect to be ... located within x miles?" Because the numbers are averages of percentages reported, they don't necessarily add up to 100 percent.
15. Adapted from discussion of the drivers of value and costs in Gordon Walker, *Modern Competitive Strategy* (Boston: McGraw-Hill, 2004) and in Michael Porter, *Competitive Strategy: Techniques for Analyzing Industries and Competitors* (New York: Free Press, 1980).
16. The model for life cycle comes from strategy texts like Gordon Walker, *Modern Competitive Strategy* (Boston: McGraw-Hill, 2004) and Gregory G. Dess and G. T. Lumpkin, *Strategic Management: Creating Competitive Advantage* (Boston: McGraw-Hill/Irwin, 2003). The discussion of the auto industry's growth comes from Renato Bertodo, "The Strategic Alliance: Automotive Paradigm of the 1990s." *International Journal of Technology Management*, 5, no. 4 (1990), pp. 375–388, Edward K. Miller, *Century on Wheels: The Story of the American Automotive Industry* (Houston, TX: Pioneer Publications, 1987), and H. Eugene Weiss, *Chrysler, Ford, Durant, and Sloan: Founding Giants of the American Automotive Industry* (Jefferson, NC: McFarland, 2003).
17. These generic strategies for business come from Michael E. Porter, *Competitive Strategy: Techniques for Analyzing Industries and Competitors* (New York: Free Press, 1980).
18. This list adapts and labels Shepherd and Shanley (p. 59) with two exceptions. One of their categories, "Products with special features appealing to specific niches" is treated here as a variant of customization. Second, the comprehensiveness supra-strategy (p. 61) is provided.
19. James Carpenter, "Little Guy Is No. 1 Volume Car Dealer," *The Salt Lake Tribune and Deseret Morning News*, www.utahbusinessandindustry.com/2003article/menlove2.asp.
20. Gary Nabham, "Food for Thought: Eating In—the Benefits of Locally Grown Food," *Sierra Magazine*, November/December 2002, www.sierraclub.org/sierra/200211/food.asp.
21. Karl Vesper, *New Venture Strategy* (Prentice Hall, 1990).
22. Tax Resources, Inc., www.taxaudit.com.
23. The latest news can be found at the SBA's Regulatory Flexibility Act Enforcement Page, www.sba.gov/advo/laws/law_lib.html.
24. Initiative for a Competitive Inner City, Inner city 100 Winners 2003 SLR contracting, www.icic.org/vsh/oin/smRenderfs.php?phpsessid=b5238b7a7e0007c805caf97833ab6fda&cerror Fred O. Williams, Inner-City Success Story, *Buffalo News*, April 26, 2003, www. buffaloniagara.org/news.asp?ID=25&ARCHIVED=1.
25. Michael Porter, *Competitive Strategy: Techniques for Analyzing Industries and Competitors* (New York: Free Press, 1980).

Chapter 8

1. Lisa K. Gundry and Aaron A. Buchko, *Field Casework: Methods for Consulting to Small and Startup Businesses* (Thousand Oaks, CA: Sage Publications, 1996). B. Honig, "Who Gets the Goodies? An Examination of Microenterprise Credit in Jamaica," *Entrepreneurship and Regional Development* 10 (1998), pp. 313–334.
2. The ideas in this table come from David Gumpert, *How to Really Create a Successful Business Plan: Step-by-Step Guide* (4th ed.) (Needham, MA: Lauson Publishing, 2003), chap. 10. D. A. Shepherd and A. L. Zacharakis, "A New Venture's Cognitive Legitimacy: An Assessment by Customers," *Journal of Small Business Management* 41, no. 2 (April 2003), pp. 148–167. D. A. Shepherd and A. L. Zacharakis, "Venture Capitalists' Expertise: A Call for Research into Decision Aids and Cognitive Feedback," *Journal of Business Venturing* 17, no. 1 (January 2002), pp. 1–20. Dean Shepherd and Evan Douglas, *Attracting Equity Investors* (Thousand Oaks, CA: Sage, 1999). J. Hall and C. W. Hofer, "Venture Capitalists' Decision Criteria in New Venture Evaluation," *Journal of Business Venturing*, 8, no. 1 (January 1993), pp. 25–42. Robert Ronstadt, *Entrepreneurial Finance* (Gilmanton, NH, Lord Publishing, 1988), chap. 10.
3. John L. Nesheim, *High Tech Start-Up* (revised and updated ed.) (New York: Free Press, 2000).
4. Twenty-eight percent of owners wrote a formal plan while 26 percent had an informal or partial plan. Sarah Bartlett, "Seat of the Pants," *Inc.*, October 2002, www.inc.com/magazine/20021015/24772.html.
5. F. Delmar and S. Shane, "Does Business Planning Facilitate the Development of New Ventures?" *Strategic Management Journal* 24, no. 12 (December 2003), p. 1165. Nancy Upton, Elisabeth J. Teal, and Joe T. Felan, "Strategic and Business Planning Practices of Fast Growth Family Firms," *Journal of Small Business Management* 39, no. 1 (January 2001), pp. 60–72. Brian Gibson and Gavin Cassar, "Planning Behavior Variables in Small Firms," *Journal of Small Business Management* 40, no. 3 (July 2002), p. 171 (16 pgs).
6. F. Delmar and S. Shane, "Does Business Planning Facilitate the Development of New Ventures?" *Strategic Management Journal* 24, no. 12 (December 2003), p. 1165. B. Honig and T. Karlsson, "Institutional Forces and the Written Business Plan," *Journal of Management* 30, no. 1 (2004), pp. 29–48. B. J. Orser, S. Hogarth-Scott, and A. L. Riding, "Performance, Firm Size, and Management Problem Solving," *Journal of Small Business Management* 38, no. 4 (October 2000), pp. 42–58. Stephen C. Perry, "The Relationship between Written Business Plans and the Failure of Small Businesses in the U.S.," *Journal of Small Business Management* 39, no. 3 (July 2001), pp. 201–209.
7. B. Honig and T. Karlsson, "Institutional Forces and the Written Business Plan," *Journal of Management* 30, no. 1 (2004), pp. 29–48.
8. John L. Nesheim, *High Tech Start-Up* (rev. and updated ed.) (New York: Free Press, 2000).
9. Question 114 in the PSED: What is the current form of your business plan: unwritten or in your head, informally written, formally prepared, or something else?
10. Sources include: Cliff Ennico, "The 30-Second Business Plan: Want to Impress a Potential Investor Quickly? Here's Exactly What to Say," *Entrepreneur*, January 20, 2003, www.entrepreneur.com/article/58946. Ben Casnocha, "Perfecting the Elevator Pitch: Learn to Rattle Off a Spiel Quickly about Your Company, and Soon You'll Have More Contacts Than You'll Know

What to Do With," TeenStartUps.com, February 2003, www.entrepreneur.com/article/59274. Stan Mandel, "The Elevator Pitch: Engage People, Move to Action . . . in 2 Minutes," Wake Forest University, 2003.

11. A. L. Zacharakis, "Writing a Business Plan," in W. Bygrave and A. Zacharakis (eds.), *The Portable MBA in Entrepreneurship*, 3rd ed. (New York: Wiley, 2003).
12. Gregory G. Dess and G. T. Lumpkin, *Strategic Management: Creating Competitive Advantage* (Boston: McGraw-Hill/Irwin, 2003), pp. 27–29. Gordon Walker, *Modern Competitive Strategy* (Burr Ridge, IL: McGraw-Hill/Irwin, 2003), pp. 263–264. Guy Kawasaki, *The Art of the Start* (New York: Penguin Group, 2004).
13. Gregory G. Dess and G. T. Lumpkin, *Strategic Management: Creating Competitive Advantage* (Boston: McGraw-Hill/Irwin, 2003), p. 27.
14. Robert X. *Cringley, Accidental Empires* (New York: HarperBusiness, 1996).
15. Mark Henricks, "Words to Live By," *Entrepreneur*, September 1998, www.entrepreneur.com/article/16392.
16. Excalibur Seasoning, Mission Statement (Pekin, IL: Excalibur Seasoning), www.excaliburseasoning.com/About.htm.
17. Gregory G. Dess and G. T. Lumpkin, *Strategic Management: Creating Competitive Advantage* (Boston: McGraw-Hill/Irwin, 2003), pp. 28–29. Gordon Walker, *Modern Competitive Strategy* (Burr Ridge, IL: McGraw-Hill/Irwin, 2004) pp. 263–264.
18. Fantastic Gift Baskets, Inc., "Why We're Different." Raleigh, NC, www.fantasticbaskets.com/Different.html.
19. There is no standard time for elevator pitches. For example, the Wake Forest Elevator Pitch Competition allows two minutes for the pitch, but that is one of the longest times. For the MIT Enterprise Forums, the pitch is limited to one minute. Outside of these formal settings, communications experts tell us that listeners lose interest after 30 seconds. That in large part explains why 30 seconds is the length of the typical television commercial.
20. These come from AdSlogans.com, www.adslogans.com/samples/index.html.
21. Jim Horan, *The One Page Business Plan for the Creative Entrepreneur* (Berkeley, CA: One Page Business Plan Company, 2004).The version in this chapter is an adaptation of his approach and is included with his permission.
22. This outline for the full business plan was developed specifically for small businesses, but its roots are in a number of works on business planning. These include Jeffry Timmons and Stephen Spinelli, *New Venture Creation: Entrepreneurship for the 21st Century* (Boston: McGraw-Hill/Irwin, 2003); David Gumpert, *How to Really Create a Successful Business Plan: Step-By-Step Guide* (4th ed.) (Needham, MA: Lauson Publishing, 2003); Edward G. Rogoff, *Bankable Business Plans* (Thompson/Texere, 2004); Kauffman Foundation, *New Business Mentor* (Kansas City, MO: Kauffman Foundation, 2002); and J. D. Ryan and Gail Hyduke, *Small Business: An Entrepreneur's Plan* (Cincinnati, OH: Southwestern, 2003).
23. These numbers are fairly standard in a number of settings. For example, Linda Pinson and Jerry Jinnett gave these numbers in their SBA how-to guide, "How To Write A Business Plan" (Managing and Planning Series, MP-32, 1993), www.sba.gov/library/pubs/mp-32.txt or www.sba.gov/library/pubs/mp-32.pdf, and the same numbers are consistently used in the major business plan competitions.
24. Edward G. Rogoff, *Bankable Business Plans* (Mason OH: Thompson/Texere, 2004). David Gumpert, *How to Really Create a Successful Business Plan: Step-By-Step Guide*, 4th ed. (Needham, MA: Lauson Publishing, 2003). David Gumpert, *Burn Your Business Plan* (Needham, MA: Lauson Publishing, 2002).
25. Dean Shepherd and Mark Shanley, *New Venture Strategy* (Thousand Oaks, CA: Sage, 1998).
26. There is a tremendous range of models for different types of plans. Examples include: Edward G. Rogoff, *Bankable Business Plans* (Mason, OH: Thompson/Texere, 2004); A. L. Zacharakis, "Writing a Business Plan," in W. Bygrave and A. Zacharakis (eds.) *The Portable MBA in Entrepreneurship*, 3rd ed. (New York: Wiley, 2003); David Gumpert, *How to Really Create a Successful Business Plan: Step-By-Step Guide,* 4th ed. (Needham, MA: Lauson Publishing, 2003); Jill E. Kapron, *BizPlan Builder* (Mountain View, CA: JIAN/Southwestern, 1999); the ICVE model developed through R. K. Mitchell, J. B. Smith, K. W. Seawright, and E. A. Morse, "Cross-Cultural Cognitions and the Venture Creation Decision," *Academy of Management Journal,* 43 no. 5 (October 2000) pp. 974–993; and Dean Shepherd and Evan Douglas, *Attracting Equity Investors* (Thousand Oaks, CA: Sage, 1999).
27. Michael McMyne and Nicole Amare, *Student Entrepreneurs: 14 Undergraduate All Stars Tell Their Stories* (St. Louis: St. Louis University/Premium Press, 2003).
28. The approach here is inspired by three sources on the critical analysis of business plans: Robert C. Ronstadt, *Entrepreneurial Finance: Taking Control of Your Financial Decision Making* (Gilmanton NH: Lord Publishing, 1988); David Gumpert, *Burn Your Business Plan* (Needham, MA: Lauson Publishing, 2002); and most of all Dean Shepherd and Evan Douglas, *Attracting Equity Investors* (Thousand Oaks, CA: Sage, 1999).
29. R. K. Mitchell, J. B. Smith, K. W. Seawright, and E. A. Morse, "Cross-Cultural Cognitions and the Venture Creation Decision," *Academy of Management Journal* 43, no. 5 (October 2000), pp. 974–993. G. N. Chandler and S. H. Hanks, "Founder Competence, the Environment, and Venture Performance," *Entrepreneurship Theory and Practice* 19 (1999), pp. 77–89. G. N. Chandler, and E. Jansen, "The Founder's Self-Assessed Competence and Venture Performance," *Journal of Business Venturing* 7 (1992), pp. 223–236.
30. Margaret Fletcher and Simon Harris, "Seven Aspects of Strategy Formation," *International Small Business Journal* 20, no. 3 (August 2002), p. 297 (16 pgs).
31. C. L. Nicholls-Nixon, A. C. Cooper, and C. Y. Woo, "Strategic Experimentation: Understanding Change and Performance in New Ventures," *Journal of Business Venturing* 15, no. 5–6 (September–November 2000), pp. 493–521.
32. Adapted from "Michael Cain," in Michael McMyne, and Nicole Amare, *Student Entrepreneurs: 14 Undergraduate All Stars Tell Their Stories* (St. Louis: St. Louis University/Premium Press, 2003), pp. 59–67.
33. www.slu.edu/services/cc/jobsearch/chronologicalresume.pdf. Used with permission.

Chapter 9

1. www.beyondfleece.com/about_us/bio/
2. Susan Fournier, "Consumers and Their Brands: Developing Relationship Theory in Consumer Research," *Journal of Consumer Research*, March 1998, pp. 343–373.
3. Chiranjeev Kohli and Douglas W. LaBahn, "Creating Effective Brand Names: A Study of the Naming Process," *Journal of Advertising Research*, January/February 1997, pp. 67–75. See also Leonard L. Berry, Edwin F. Lefkowith and Terry Clark, "In Services, What's in a Name?" *Harvard Business Review*, September/October 1998, pp. 28–30.
4. Tomima Edmark, "On Your Mark . . .," *Entrepreneur*, April 1999, www.entrepreneur.com/article/0,4621,230153,00.html.
5. Robert G. Cooper and Elko J. Kleinschmidt, "Benchmarking the Firm's Critical Success Factors in New Business Development," *The Journal of Product Innovation Management* 12 (1995), pp. 374–391.
6. Laura Tiffany, "Got a Lemon?" *Entrepreneur*, May 1999, www.entrepreneur.com/article/17646. Tim W. Know, "Evaluating Your e-Business Idea," Entrepreneur, May 26, 2003, www.entrepreneur.com/article/184990.
7. Albert H. Rubenstein, "At the Front End of the R&D/Innovation Process: Idea Development and Entrepreneurship," *International Journal of Technology* 9, nos. 5, 6, 7 (1994), pp. 652–678.
8. Don Debelak, "Inspired Minds Want to Know," *Entrepreneur*, January 1999, www.entrepreneur.com/article/17050.

9. Don Debelak, "Where's the Big Idea?" *Entrepreneur*, March 1998, www.entrepreneur.com/article/75660.
10. Don Debelak, "Testing the Waters," *Entrepreneur*, February 1998, www.entrepreneur.com/article/0,4621,228009,00.html.
11. D. Taylor, "How Do I Create a Private, Closed Facebook Group?" AskDaveTaylor.com, January 2010, www.askdavetaylor.com/how_to_create_private_closed_facebook_group.html.
12. Greg A. Stevens and James Burley, "Piloting the Rocket of Radical Innovation," *Research Technology Management* 46, no. 2 (Mar/Apr 2003), pp. 16–26. See also Greg A. Stevens and James Burley, "3000 Raw Ideas, 1 Commercial Success!" *Research Technology Management* 40, no. 3 (May/June 1997), pp. 16–27.
13. Phillip Kotler and Gary Armstrong, *Principles of Marketing*, 9th ed. (New York: Prentice Hall, 2000).
14. Don Debelak, "I Needed That," *Entrepreneur*, May 2002, www.entrepreneur.com/article/51140.
15. Robert McMath and Thom Forbes, "Look Before You Leap," *Entrepreneur*, April 1998, www.entrepreneur.com/article/15414.
16. Teresa McUsic, "Differentiate Those Differences to Stay Competitive," *St. Louis Post Dispatch*, April 17, 2000, p. BP17.
17. www.kyptonitelock.com and www.kryptonitelock.com/inetisscripts/abtinetis.exe/templateform@psublic?tn=aboout_media.
18. S.N. Lewis, "The Chateau Mouton Lockdown," *The Wall Street Journal Weekend Journal* (2007), pp. W1 and W8.
19. O.C. Ferrell and M.D. Hartline, *Marketing Strategy* (Mason, OH: Thompson–Southwestern, 2005), p.193.
20. Robert McGarvey and Babs S. Harrison, "Name Your Price," *Entrepreneur*, July 2000, www.entrepreneur.com/article/29222. Beverly Williams, "The Price Is Right," *Entrepreneur*, October 3, 2000. www.entrepreneur.com/article/0,4621,280990,00.html. Ian Benoliel, "Pricing Your Product," *Entrepreneur*, July 22, 2002, www.entrepreneur.com/article/0,4621,301698,00.html. Rosalind Resnick, "Setting the Right Price," *Entrepreneur*, November 10, 2003, www.entrepreneur.com/article/65484. Tim W. Knox, "Secrets to Setting Your Price," *Entrepreneur*, April 2, 2004, www.entrepreneur.com/article/70174. Lipe, op. cit. Small Business Administration, "Pricing Your Product." Telephone communication with Screaming Eagle Winery staff, June 22, 2012.
21. S. Seget, *Pharmaceutical Pricing Strategies* (London: Reuters Business Insight Healthcare, 2005).
22. European Telework Online, op. cit.
23. Darrell Zahorsky, "Super Charge Your Business with Profit Pricing Strategies," 2004, http://sbinformation.about.com/cs/marketresearch/a/pricing_p.htm.
24. "Inventing Success," *Business 2.0*, April 2003, p. 105.
25. Marty Nemko, "Perfecting Your Pricing Strategies," *Entrepreneur*, March 2000, www.entrepreneur.com/article/23350. Michel A. Habib and Alexander P. Ljungqvist, "Underpricing and Entrepreneurial Wealth Losses in IPOs: Theory and Evidence," *The Review of Financial Studies* 14, no. 2 (Summer 2001), pp. 433–458.
26. Cliff Ennico, "Set the Right Price for Your Product or Service," *Entrepreneur*, June 1, 2003, www.entrepreneur.com/article/62382.
27. J. R. Baum, E. A. Locke, and K. G. Smith, "A Multidimensional Model of Venture Growth," *Academy of Management Journal* 44, no. 2 (2001), pp. 292–303; see also, Elisabeth J. Teal, Nancy Upton, and Samuel L. Seaman, "A Comparative Analysis of Strategic Marketing Practices of High-Growth U.S. Family and Nonfamily Firms," *Journal of Developmental Entrepreneurship* 8, no. 2 (August 2003), p. 177.
28. Timothy Matanovich, Gary L. Lillien, and Arvind Rangaswamy, "Engineering the Price-Value Relationship," *Marketing Management*, Spring 1999, pp. 48–53.
29. J. Monahan, op. cit.
30. Ennico; and Knox, op. cit.
31. Gordon; Weinstein; and Monahan, op. cit.
32. Don Debelak, "Look What I Found!" *Entrepreneur*, July 2002, www.entrepreneur.com/article/0,4621,300831,00.html.
33. K. Carroll and D. Coates, "Teaching Price Discrimination: Some Clarifications," *Southern Economic Journal* 66 (1999), pp. 466–480.
34. Mark Hendricks, "The Art of (Price) War," *Entrepreneur*, April 2002, www.entrepreneur.com/article/0,4621,297992,00.html.
35. Kim T. Gordon, "How to Price Your Product," *Entrepreneur*, March 5, 2001, www.entrepreneur.com/article/0,4621,287402,00.html.
36. Roberta Maynard, "Take the Guesswork Out of Pricing," *Nation's Business*, December 1997, pp. 27–30.
37. Bob Weinstein, "What Price Success," *Entrepreneur*, March 1999, www.entrepreneur.com/article/17366.
38. Jacquelyn Lynn, "The Middle of the Road," *Business Start-Ups*, December 1996, p. 33.
39. Julie Monahan, "Name Your Price," *Entrepreneur*, December 1999, www.entrepreneur.com/article/0,4621,231863,00.htm.
40. Small Business Administration, op. cit.
41. Eric Anderson and Duncan Simester, "Mind Your Pricing Cues," *Harvard Business Review* 81, no. 9 (September 2003), p. 96.
42. Joel Dean, "Pricing Policies for New Products," *Harvard Business Review* (November/December 1976), p. 141–153.
43. Jean-Noel Kapferer, "Managing Luxury Brands," *Journal of Brand Management*, July 1999, pp. 251–260.
44. Weinstein, op. cit.
45. Robert M. Schindler and Thomas Kilbarian, "Increased Consumer Sales Response through Use of 99-Ending Prices," *Journal of Retailing*, Summer 1996, pp. 187–199. See also Robert M. Schindler, "Patterns of Rightmost Digits Used in Advertising Prices: Implications for Nine-Ending Effects," *Journal of Consumer Research*, September 1997, pp. 192–201.
46. www.makersmarkcollector.com/home.shtml.
47. "When the Price is Right," *Entrepreneur*, www.entrepreneur.com/article/54994.
48. Barbara Kiviat, "Sneaky Pricing," *Time Magazine*, September 19, 2003.
49. Priya Raghubir and Kim Corfman, "When Do Price Promotions Affect Pretrial Brand Evaluations?" *Journal of Marketing Research* 36 (1999), pp. 211–222.
50. Kiviat, op. cit.
51. Thea Singer, "Upstarts: Children's Hair Salons," *Inc.*, July 2001, http://pf.inc.com/magazine/20010701/22874.html.
52. Corliss L. Green, "Media Exposure's Impact on Perceived Availability and Redemption of Coupons by Ethnic Customers," *Journal of Advertising Research*, 25, no. 2 (March–April 1995), pp. 55–64.
53. Kapil Bawa and Srini S. Srinivasan, "Coupon Attractiveness and Coupon Proneness: A Framework for Modeling Coupon Redemption," *Journal of Marketing Research* 14, no. 4 (November 1997), pp. 517–525.
54. Peter Tat, William A. Cunningham III, and Emin Babakus, "Consumer Perceptions of Rebates," *Journal of Advertising Research* 28, no. 40 (August/September 1994), pp. 45–50.
55. John Burtzloff, "Keep Customers Coming Back for More," *Entrepreneur*, June 10, 2002, www.entrepreneur.com/article/52780.
56. HOW Staff, "Designers' Hourly Rates: Are You Charging Enough?" HOWdesign. com, February 12, 2008, www.howdesign.com/design-business/pricing/hourly-rates/.
57. Ellen Rohr, "Keep Your Business from Closing," *Entrepreneur*, July 3, 2000, www.entrepreneur.com/article/29980.
58. Gwen Moran, "Flash!" *Entrepreneur*, June 2000, www.entrepreneur.com/article/29646.
59. Ennico, op. cit. also Tony Parinello, "Should You Offer Extra Services or Lower Prices?" *Entrepreneur*, July 1, 2002, www.entrepreneur.com/article/53310.
60. See G. Bruce Friesen, "Dynamic Pricing: Teaching Your Clients to Dance," *Consulting to Management* 14, no. 1 (March 2003), pp. 33–38. Also Ellen Garbarino and Olivia F. Lee, "Dynamic Pricing in Internet Retail: Effects on Consumer Trust," *Psychology & Marketing* 20, no. 6 (June 2003), pp. 495–513.

61. Personal interviews with Dongzhou Gongbu and from a business plan for the Aba Sichuan Dairy Company written by Dr. Susan D. Peters, July 2002.

Chapter 10

1. This vignette was developed using material taken from an interview with Addie Swartz, conducted by Jill Kickul in April 2004, as well as excerpted from the Beacon Street Girls press release, "Introducing The Beacon Street Girls, Entrepreneur/Mother of Two Creates Fun, Values-oriented Books and Accessories for Girls Who Are, Between Toys and Boys'," written by Ellen Miller and Alan Ryan.
2. Sherri Dorfman "Value Proposition" *Marketing News*, 54; (March 1, 2006), John Williams (February 6, 2006) "Building a Money-Making Brand," www.entrepreneur.com/marketing/branding/ imageandbrandingcolumnistjohnwilliams/article83258.html, Dodo Zu Knyphausen-Aufsess, "Corporate Venture Capital: Who Adds Value?" *Venture Capital: An International Journal of Entrepreneurial Finance*, 7, no. 1 (January–March 2005), pp. 23–49.
3. R. Cooper, "Marketing From the Inside Out: Analyzing Your Market," *Entrepreneur*, May 28, 2002, www.entrepreneur.com/article/52104.
4. See for example, William O. Bearden, Thomas N. Ingram, and Raymond W. LaForge, *Marketing: Principles & Perspectives*, 4th ed., (Boston: McGraw-Hill, 2004), pp. 147–176.
5. Laura Clampitt Douglas "Designing Your Promotion Materials," *Entrepreneur*, (August 21, 2000), www.entrepreuner.com/homebasedbiz/homebasedbasics/marketing/article31668.html.
6. Lance E. Brouthers and George Nakos, "The Role of Systematic International Market Selection on Small Firms Export Performance," *Journal of Small Business Management* 43, no. 4 (2005), pp. 363–381. Laura Clampitt Douglas "Designing Your Promotion Materials," *Entrepreneur*, (August 21, 2000), www.entrepreneur.com/homebasedbiz/homebasedbasics/marketing/article31668.html.
7. Jean Brandau and Andrea Young, "Competitive Intelligence in Entrepreneurial and Start-Up Businesses," *Competitive Intelligence Review* 11, no. 1 (2000), pp. 74–84. Kathy J. Kobliski (2007), "Finding Ad Inspiration," www.entrepreneur.com/advertising/howtoguides/article44226.html.
8. Kim T. Gordon "Total Recall", *Entrepreneur*, (November 2003) www.entrepreneur.com/article/65130..
9. Ibid.
10. Jim Emerson, "*Market Overview*—Kid Power" (Special Report: Marketing to Children), *Direct Magazine* (Jul 26, 2005), http://directmag.com/exclusive/specialreports/2004_may_12_direct_listline_0/.
11. Lance E. Brouthers and George Nakos, "The Role of Systematic International Market Selection on Small Firms Export Performance," *Journal of Small Business Management* 43, no. 4 (2005), pp. 363–381. Roy Williams (April 11, 2005), "Target Your Market with Appropriate Ad Copy," *Entrepreneur*, www.entrepreneur.com/advertising/adcolumnistroyhwilliams/article76978.html.
12. Roy Williams "Cheap and Effective Advertising Techniques," *Entrepreneur*, (January 5, 2004), www.entrepreneur.com/advertising/columnistroyhwilliams/article66236.html.
13. Anonymous "SCORE's Top Marketing and Public Relations Tips," *Entrepreneur*, (December 6, 2006), www.entrepreneur.com/grow/score/index.html#market.
14. Michael Myser "Marketing Made Easy," *Business 2.0*, (June 2006), pp. 43–45.
15. NielsenWire, "Buzz in the Blogosphere: Millions More Bloggers and Blog Readers," *NeilsenWire*, March 8, 2012, http://blog.nielsen.com/nielsenwire/online_mobile/buzz-in-the-blogosphere-millions-more-bloggers-and-blog-readers/.
16. A. Hoeksema, "Want Free Publicity? Try These Websites," *Reuters Blogs - Entrepreneurial*, n.d., http://blogs.reuters.com/small-business/2011/01/24/want-free-publicity-try-these-websites/
17. K. Bodnar, "10 Simple Strategies for Business Blog Content," *HubSpot Blog*, June 1, 2010, http://blog.hubspot.com/blog/tabid/6307/bid/6023/10-Simple-Strategies-for-Business-Blog-Content.aspx?utm_source=feedburner
18. Michael V. Copeland and Andrew Tilin "The New Instant Companies," Business 2.0, (June 2005), pp. 82–94.
19. L. Story, "Anywhere the Eye Can See, It's Likely to See an Ad," *The New York Times*, January 15, 2007, sec. Business/Media & Advertising, www.nytimes.com/2007/01/15/business/media/15everywhere.html.
20. Michael Warshaw,"A Web Strategy Runs Through It", *Inc.*, November 1, 2001, www.inc.com/internet/articles/200111/23622.html.
21. Anonymous "SCORE's Top Marketing and Public Relations Tips," *Entrepreneur*, (December 6, 2006), www.entreperneur.com/article/0,4621,324728,00.html.
22. Terri Lammers Prior (Ed.), *301 Great Ideas for Selling Smarter.* (Boston: Inc. Publishing, 1998).
23. Anonymous "SCORE's Top Marketing and Public Relations Tips," *Entrepreneur* (December 6, 2006), www.entrepreneur.com/grow/score/index.html#market.
24. Michael C. Copeland and Om Malik (June 2006), "How to Build a Bulletproof Start-up," *Business 2.0*, pp. 76–92.
25. Nichole L. Torres "Almost Famous," *Entrepreneur*, (June 2003), www.entrepreneur.com/magazine/entreperneursstartupsmagazine/2003/june/62194.html. Anonymous "60-Second Guide to Generating Publicity for Your Business," *Entrepreneur*, (2007), www.entrepreneur.com/growyourbusiness/scoreresources/60secondguides/article81348.html.
26. Margie Fisher "7 Ways to Milk Your Media Coverage," *Entrepreneur*, (April 6, 2006), www.entrepreneur.com/marketing/publicrelations/article159500.html; Al Lautenslager "Getting the Most from a Press Release," *Entrepreneur*, (September 16, 2002), www.entrepreneur.com/marketing/publicrelations/gettingpress/article55540.html.
27. Based on information from the following: Al Lautenslager "A Press Release Primer," *Entrepreneur*, (2007), www.entrepreneur.com/marketing/publicrelations/gettingpress/article62050.html. Randall Hansen, "A Barebones Guide to Writing Successful Press Releases" (Deland FL: Stetson Marketing Department, 2005), www.stetson.edu/~rhansen/prhowto.html.
28. This is an actual title of a case study by Richard P. Green II and Susan D. Peters.
29. Catherine Seda "Make a Great First Impression," *Entrepreneur*, (October 2006), www.entrepreneur.com/ebusiness/gettingtraffic/article167634.html.
30. Anonymous (undated), "Components of a Press Release," http://prntoolkit.prnewswire.com/entrepreneur/home1.shtml.
31. Excerpted from Randall Hansen, "A Barebones Guide to Writing Successful Press Releases" (Deland, FL: Stetson University Marketing Department, 2005), www.stetson.edu/~Rhansen/prhowto.html. Used with permission.
32. Al Lautenslager "The Ingredients of a Press Kit," *Entrepreneur*, (2007), www.entrepreneur.com/marketing/publicrelations/prbasics/article57260.html.
33. Charlotte Ryan, *Prime Time Activism* (Boston: South End Press, 1991), p. 35.
34. Based on information from the following: Al Lautenslager "Implementing a PR Strategy in 7 Days," *Entrepreneur*, (March 15, 2004), www.entrepreneur.com/marketing/publicrelations/prbasics/article69924.html; Margie Fisher "The Making of a PR Story," *Entrepreneur*, (March 6, 2006), www.entrepreneur.com/marketing/publicrelations/article83772.html. Al Lautenslager (April 19, 2004), "Who Should Receive Your Press Release?" *Entrepreneur*, www.entrepreneur.com/marketing/publicrelations/gettingpress/article70496.html. Mark Nowlan "8 Ways to Get the Media Buzzing," *Entrepreneur*, (July 10, 2006), www.entrepreneur.com/marketing/publicrelations/prcolumnist/article159508.html. Anonymous "SCORE's Top Marketing and Public Relations Tips," *Entrepreneur*, (December 6, 2006), www.entrepreneur.com/article/0,4621,324728,00.html.
35. Sean M. Lyden "How to Generate Publicity," *Entrepreneur*, (July 22, 2002), www.entrepreneur.com/article/53788.

36. Jane Applegate "How to Generate Publicity for Your Business," *Entrepreneur*, (2007), www.entrepreneur.com/marketing/publicrelations/article42738.html.
37. Al Lautenslager "Using Publicity to Your Advantage," *Entrepreneur*, (July 15, 2002), www.entrepreneur.com/article/53644.
38. For all her tips and more details, see: Margie Fisher "10 Creative Ways to Get PR," *Entrepreneur*, (February 6, 2006), www.entrepreneur.com/marketing/publicrelations/article83268.html.
39. Anonymous "SCORE's Top Marketing and Public Relations Tips," *Entrepreneur*, (December 6, 2006), www.entrepreneur.com/article/0,4621,324728,00.html.
40. Deborah L. Vence "Cookie Dough," *Marketing News*, (October 27, 2003), p. 10.
41. Excerpted from Kirk Hallahan, "A Publicity Primer," in Hallahan Course Resources (website), 1996, Fort Collins, CO: Colorado State University. http://lamar.colostate.edu/Hallahan/hpubty.htm. Used with permission.
42. Based on the following: Jack Ferrari "Selling 101," *Entrepreneur*, (November 1, 2005), www.entrepreneur.com/sales/aslestechniques/article80782.html; Tom Duncan, *Principles of Advertising & IMC* (2nd ed.), (Boston, MA: McGraw-Hill, 2005), pp. 523–527. Barry Farber "On the Horizon" *Entrepreneur*, (January 2001), p. 119. Brian Caulfield "How to Land the Deal" *Business 2.0*, (April 2004), p. 85.
43. Alan J. Zell "Business Etiquette—The Rule for Business Survival," (undated), http://sellingselling.com/articles/bizetq.html.
44. Cord Cooper, "The Art of Closing a Deal," *Investor's Business Daily*, March 2, 2003. Cord Cooper, "Deal with People Effectively—Stressing Value over Cost," *Investor's Business Daily*, January 27, 2005, p. A3. Cord Cooper, "Deal with People Effectively—Sidestep Sales Slip-Ups," *Investor's Business Daily*, February 24, 2005, p. A3. Cord Cooper, "Deal and Communicate Effectively—Hit Your Mark Each Time," *Investor's Business Daily*, July 14, 2005, p. A4. Cord Cooper, "Take Action—Art of a Successful Deal," *Investor's Business Daily*, November 23, 2005, p. A4. Cord Cooper, "Deal with People Effectively—How to Clinch the Deal," *Investors Business Daily*, September 7, 2006, p. A3. Cord Cooper, "Cut New Deals, and Win," *Investor's Business Daily*, March 27, 2007, p. A3.
45. For more information on the steps of personal selling, visit www.udel.edu/alex/chapt20.html and Sales & Marketing Top Secrets at www.entrepreneur.com.
46. William O. Bearden, Thomas N. Ingram, and Raymond W. LaForge, *Marketing*, 4th ed. (Boston, MA McGraw-Hill, 2004). Frederick F. Reichheld and W. Earl Sasser, Jr., 1990. "Zero Defections: Quality Comes to Services," *Harvard Business Review* 5, pp. 105–111. Rafi A. Mohammed, Robert J. Fisher, Bernard J. Jaworski, and Gordon J. Paddison, *Internet Marketing: Building Advantage in a Networked Economy*, 2nd ed. (Boston, MA: McGraw-Hill/Irwin-MarketSpaceU, 2004).
47. William O. Bearden, Thomas N. Ingram, and Raymond W. LaForge, *Marketing*, 4th ed. (Boston MA: McGraw-Hill, 2004). Robert L. Desatnick, *Managing to Keep the Customer: How to Achieve and Maintain Superior Customer Service Throughout the Organization* (San Francisco, CA: Jossey-Bass,1988). Rafi A. Mohammed, Robert J. Fisher, Bernard J. Jaworski, and Gordon J. Paddison, *Internet Marketing: Building Advantage in a Networked Economy*, 2nd ed. (Boston: McGraw-Hill/Irwin-MarketSpaceU, 2004).
48. Charles M. Futrell, *Fundamentals of Selling: Customers for Life through Service* (Boston, MA: McGraw-Hill/Irwin, 2006).
49. William O. Bearden, Thomas N. Ingram, and Raymond W. LaForge, *Marketing*, 4th ed., Boston: McGraw-Hill, 2004). Charles M. Futrell, *Fundamentals of Selling: Customers for Life through Service* (Boston: McGraw-Hill/Irwin, 2006). Vince Pesce, *A Complete Manual of Professional Selling* (New York: Prentice Hall, 1989).
50. Peter Alexander, "Tech Solutions That Help Keep Customers Satisfied," *Entrepreneur*, October 05, 2006, www.entrepreneur.com/technology/techtrendscolumnistpeteralexander/article168528.html. Ramon Ray, "Free Software You Should Consider," *Entrepreneur*, April 30, 2007, www.entrepreneur.com/technology/techbasicscolumnist/article177710.html.
51. Adapted from Rafi A. Mohammed, Robert J. Fisher, Bernard J. Jaworski, and Gordon J. Paddison, *Internet Marketing: Building Advantage in a Networked Economy*, 2nd ed., (Boston, MA: McGraw-Hill/Irwin-MarketSpaceU, 2004), p. 664.
52. Orabrush, "Orabrush.com STORY OF ORABRUSH," Orabrush.com, www.orabrush.com/story. Wasserman, T. "Orabrush Parlays YouTube Success Into Walmart Deal [EXCLUSIVE]." *Mashable*, September 20, 2011. http://mashable.com/2011/09/20/orabrush-walmar/. Shackleton, L. "The Orabrush Story: How a Utah Man Used YouTube to Build a Multi-million Dollar Business," *Google | Official Blog*, November 15, 2011. http://googleblog.blogspot.com/2011/11/orabrush-story-how-utah-man-used.html. J. Neff, "How Orabrush Got National Walmart Deal with YouTube Videos | News—Advertising Age," *Advertising Age*, September 20, 2011, http://adage.com/article/news/orabrush-national-walmart-deal-youtube-videos/229914/.

Chapter 11

1. Don Debelak, "Rookie Rules," *Entrepreneur*, September 1999, www.entrepreneur.com/article/18240.
2. Gary L. Frazier, "Organizing and Managing Channels of Distribution," *Journal of the Academy of Marketing Science* 27, no. 2 (1999), pp. 226–240.
3. E. Rosen, *The Anatomy of Buzz: How to Create Word of Mouth Marketing* (New York: Doubleday, 2000).
4. David Stokes, "Entrepreneurial Marketing: A Conceptualisation from Qualitative Research," *Qualitative Market Research* 3, no. 1 (2000), pp. 47–54.
5. Lissan Levin and Jacob Zhavi, "The Economics of Selection of Mail Orders," *Journal of Interactive Marketing* 15, no. 3 (2001), pp. 53–71. Füsan F. Gonul and Byung-Do Kim, "Mailing Smarter to Catalog Customers," *Journal of Interactive Marketing* 14, no. 2 (2000), pp. 2–16.
6. Sean M. Lyden, "Make Newspaper Ads Work for You," *Entrepreneur*, May 27, 2002, www.entrepreneur.com/article/52098. Reprinted with permission of Entrepreneur.com.
7. Kristin Zhivago "You and CAN-SPAM" January 23, 2004 www.marketing-technology.com/MT/canspam.cfm.
8. M. Trusov, R. E. Bucklin, and K. Pauwels, "Effects of Word-of-Mouth Versus Traditional Marketing: Findings from an Internet Social Networking Site," *Journal of Marketing* 73, no. 5 (September 2009), pp. 90–102.
9. Don Debelak, "Lights, Camera, Action," *Entrepreneur*, April 2003, www.entrepreneur.com/article/72148.
10. Michael H. Morris, Minet Schindehutte, and Raymond W. LaForge, "Entrepreneurial Marketing: A Construct for Integrating Emerging Entrepreneurship and Marketing Perspectives," *Journal of Marketing Theory and Practice* 10, no. 4 (2002), pp. 1–19; K. J. Clancy and P. C. Krieg, *Counter-intuitive Marketing: Achieve Great Results Using Uncommon Sense* (New York: Free Press, 2000).
11. Michael McMyne, *Student Entrepreneurs* (St. Louis: Premium Press America, 2003).
12. Personal story, used with permission.
13. Kim T. Gordon, "Cross-Training," *Entrepreneur*, July 2003, www.entrepreneur.com/article/62766.
14. Melissa Campanelli, "Fulfilling Orders," *Entrepreneur*, 2000, www.entrepreneur.com/article/27696.
15. Art Avery, "Order Fulfillment for Your Small E-business: Should You Beg, Borrow or Buy?" (2000), www.etailersdigest.com/resources/Specials/BegBorrow.htm.
16. George Matyjewicz, 'Doc' Don Avery, Kris Campbell, and Dave Campbell, "Online Logistics and Order Fulfillment Solutions for E-Tailers" (1999). www.etailersdigest.com/resources/Specials/Logistics.htm.
17. Andy Gibbs, "How to Sell Your Product," IPFrontline.com, November 17, 2000, www.ipfrontline.com/depts/article.aspx?id=256&deptid=2.

18. *MBA CASE STUDY: How Orabrush Got into Walmart*, 2011, www.youtube.com/watch?v=4oKYeWf3dPA&feature=youtube_gdata_player J. Neff, "How Orabrush Got National Walmart Deal with YouTube Videos | News—Advertising Age," *Advertising Age*, September 20, 2011, http://adage.com/article/news/orabrush-national-walmart-deal-youtube-videos/229914/ T. Wasserman, "Orabrush Parlays YouTube Success Into Walmart Deal [EXCLUSIVE]." *Mashable*, September 20, 2011. http://mashable.com/2011/09/20/orabrush-walmar/. You can also see a video from Orabrush about this episode at www.youtube.com/watch?v=4oKYeWf3dPA&feature=player_embedded.
19. Paul Edwards and Sarah Edwards, "It's in the Mail," *Entrepreneur*, 2003, www.entrepreneur.com/article/60430.
20. For academic studies on e-tailers, see Heiko de B. Wijnolds and Michael W. Little, "Regulatory Issues for Global E-Tailers: Marketing Implications," *Academy of Marketing Science Review*, 2001, pp. 1–17; Gary J. Stockport, George Kunnarth, and Rashida Sedik, "Boo.com, the Path to Failure," *Journal of Interactive Marketing* 15, no. 4 (2001), pp. 56–70.
21. Don Debelak, "Who Needs 'Em?" *Entrepreneur*, 2000, www.entrepreneur.com/article/29558.
22. U.S. Department of Commerce, International Trade Administration, "Exporting is good for your bottom line," n.d., www.trade.gov/cs/factsheet.asp.
23. Oystein Moen, "The Relationship between Firm Size, Competitive Advantages, and Export Performance Revisited," *International Small Business Journal* 18, no. 1 (1999), pp. 53–72.
24. Ibid.
25. Benjamin M. Oviatt and Patricia Phillips McDougall, "Towards a Theory of International New Ventures," *Journal of International Business Studies* 25, no.1 (1994), pp. 45–65. S. K. Kundu and J. A. Katz, "Born-International SMEs: Bi-level Impacts of Resources and Intentions," *Small Business Economics* 20, no. 1 (2003), pp. 25–47.
26. For more about SMEs and exporting, see Pierre-Andre Julien and Charles Ramagalahy, "Competitive Strategy and Performance of Exporting SMEs: An Empirical Investigation of the Impact of Their Export Information Search and Competency," *Entrepreneurship Theory and Practice* 27, no. 3 (2003), pp. 227–246; Neil A. Morgan, Anna Kaleka, and Constantine S. Katsikeas, "Antecedents of Export Venture Performance: A Theoretical Model and Empirical Assessment," *Journal of Marketing* 68 (January 2004), pp. 90–108.
27. Carla Goodman, "Going Global," *Entrepreneur*, 1996, www.entrepreneur.com/article/13480.
28. Jerome A. Katz, Scott R. Safranski, and Omar Khan, "Virtual Instant Global Entrepreneurship: Cybermediation for Born International Service Firms," *Journal of International Entrepreneurship* 1 (2003), pp. 43–57.
29. S. K. Kundu and J. A. Katz, "Born-International SMEs: Bi-level Impacts of Resources and Intentions," *Small Business Economics* 20, no. 1 (2003), pp. 25–47.
30. "How to Take Your Country Global" *Entrepreneur*, 2003, www.entrepreneur.com/article/0,4621,312297,00.html.
31. George Matyjewicz, et al., op. cit.
32. Laura Tiffany, op. cit.
33. Carla Goodman, op. cit.
34. Beverley Williams, "Zoning Information and Resources," www.jbsja.com/content/suites/hb_teleworking/zoning.shtml.
35. Virginia Baldwin Gilbert, "Start-ups Are Poised to Fly Away from Incubator Nest," *St. Louis Post-Dispatch*, February 2, 2002, www.niduscenter.com/m_arts_html/post_02-25-02a.html.
36. Michael H. Seid and Kay Marie Ainsley, "What Makes a Location Great?" *Entrepreneur*, March 2001, www.entrepreneur.com/article/0,4621,287982,00.html.
37. Julie Bennett, "Location Is Everything to Franchise Hopefuls," http://startupjournal.com/columnist/franchiseinsight/20020814-bennett.html
38. Michael H. Seid and Kay Marie Ainsley, "Finding a Great Location," *Entrepreneur*, April 2001, www.entrepreneur.com/article/0,4621,288851,00.html.
39. Rieva Lesonsky, "Cart Blanche," *Entrepreneur*, 2003, www.entrepreneur.com/article/63244.
40. Michael H. Seid and Kay Marie Ainsley, "Finding a Great Location," *Entrepreneur*, April 2001, www.entrepreneur.com/article/39848.
41. Julie Bennett, op. cit.
42. Peter Carbonara and Maggie Overfelt, "The Dot-Com Factories," *Fortune*, 2000, www.fortune.com/fortune/print/0,15935,360353,00.html.
43. Michael H. Seid and Kay Marie Ainsley, "Finding a Great Location," *Entrepreneur*, April 2001, www.entrepreneur.com/article/39848.
44. Michael H. Seid and Kay Marie Ainsley, "What Makes a Location Great?" *Entrepreneur*, March 2001, www.entrepreneur.com/article/0,4621,287982,00.html.
45. Cliff Ennico, "Franchise Business—Finding Space for Your Franchised Business," *Entrepreneur*, April 26, 2004, June 26, 2009, www.entrepreneur.com/management/operations/location/article70514.html.
46. The advice in the bullet points in this section come from Cliff Ennico, "Franchise Business—Finding Space for Your Franchised Business," *Entrepreneur*, April 26, 2004, www.entreperenuer.com/management/operations/location/article70514.html. Cliff Ennico, "Retail Business—Negotiating Your Shopping Center Lease," *Entrepreneur*, October 17, 2005, www.entrepreneur.com/management/operations/location/article80604.html. Rieva Lesonsky, "Commercial Leases," *Entrepreneur*, 1998, June 26, 2009, www.entrepreneur.com/management/operations/location/article21886.html. Jeffrey Steinberger, "How to Get out of a Commercial Lease," *Entrepreneur*, January 24, 2007, June 26, 2009, www.entrepreneur.com/management/legalcenter/legalissuescolumnistjeffreysteinberger/article173568.html. Nichole L. Torres, "Small Business—Lease Lessons," *Entrepreneur*, December 2004, www.entrepreneur.com/startingabusiness/startupbasics/location//article73744.html.
47. Rieva Lesonsky, "Commercial Leases." *Entrepreneur*, 1998, www.entrepreneur.com/management/operations/location/article21886.html.
48. Julie Baker, A. Parasuraman, Dhruv Grewal, and Glenn B. Voss, "The Influence of Multiple Store Environment Cues of Perceived Merchandise Value and Patronage Intentions," *Journal of Marketing* 66 (April 2002), pp. 120–140.
49. "Release Me?" *Entrepreneur*, 1998, www.entrepreneur.com/article/22564.
50. Information from this case comes from Chris Taylor, "E-Commerce," *Fortune*, 2004, www.fortune.com/fortune/print/0,15935,575869,00.html; and Lisa Baertlein, "eBay Gets Boost as Middlemen Make Comeback" *Los Angeles Times*, (January 20, 2004). I. Steiner, "eBay Drop-off Store Auction Drop Closes Stores, Lays Off Staff," *eCommerce Bytes*, January 10, 2005, www.auctionbytes.com/cab/abn/y05/m01/i10/s00. There are videos of Randy explaining the original model for the business in a series of videos from 2004 at www.academicearth.org/lectures/the-current-state-of-auctiondrop.

Chapter 12

1. Personal and Internet interviews with Mingkit "Jerry" Lai conducted spring 2004 by Professor Susan Peters.
2. See Tim Mazzavol, "Do Formal Business Plans Really Matter?—A Survey of Small Business Owners in Australia," paper presented at the International Council for Small Business Conference, 2000. Available online at www.scbaer.acu.edu. See also R. Brooksbank, "The Basic Marketing Planning Process: A Practical Framework for the Smaller Business," *Marketing Intelligence and Planning*, 14, no. 1 (1996). G. Lancaster, and I. Waddelow, "An Empirical Investigation into the Process of Strategic Marketing Planning in SMEs: Its Attendant Problems and Proposals

Towards a New Practical Paradigm," *Journal of Marketing Management* 14 (1998), pp. 853–878.

3. Ann Dugan, "The Value of Research" *Entrepreneur,* October 22, 2001, www.entrepreneur.com/article/0,4621,293951,00.html. Karen E. Spaeder, "Define Your Target Audience to Grow Sales," *Entrepreneur,* June 1, 2003, www.entrepreneur.com/article/0, 4621,309165,00.html.
4. Don Debelek, "Want Some of This?" *Entrepreneur,* June 2002, www.entrepreneur.com/article/0,4621,299768,00.html.
5. "Seems the Only Problem with New Products Is That They're New," *Brandweek,* August 22, 1994, pp. 36–40.
6. See, for example, G. Dean Kortge and Patrick A. Okonkwo, "Simultaneous New Product Development: Reducing the New Product Failure Rate," *Industrial Marketing Management,* 18, no. 4 (1989), pp. 301–306; Sharad Sarin and Gour M. Kapur, "Lessons From New Product Failure: Five Case Studies," *Industrial Marketing Management* 19, no. 4 (1990), pp. 301–314; Peter L. Link, "Keys to New Product Success and Failure," *Industrial Marketing Management* 16, no. 2 (1987), pp. 109–118. Gwen Moran, "23 Hours to a Great Marketing Plan," *Entrepreneur,* June 1, 2006, www.entrepreneur.com/article/159816.
7. Laura Tiffany, "Researching Your Market," *Entrepreneur,* August 7, 2001, www.entrepreneur.com/article/43024.
8. S. Hogarth-Scott, K. Watson, and N. Wilson, "Do Small Businesses Have to Practice Marketing to Survive and Grow?" *Marketing Intelligence and Planning* 14, no. 1 (1996).
9. Data for this table were extracted from www.Websurveyor.com.
10. See Gerald Zaltman, "Rethinking Market Research: Putting People Back In" *Journal of Marketing Research,* November 1997, pp. 424–437; Stephen Groves, and Raymond P. Fisk, "Observational Data Collection Methods for Services Marketing: An Overview," *Journal of the Academy of Marketing Science,* Summer 1992, pp. 216–224; Rebecca Piirto, "Socks, Ties, Videotapes," *American Demographics,* September 1991.
11. Stever Robbins, "Down and Dirty Market Research," *Entrepreneur,* August 12, 2002, www.entrepreneur.com/article/54550.
12. Judith Langer, "15 Myths of Qualitative Research: It's Conventional, But Is It Wisdom?" *Marketing News,* March 1, 1999, pp. 13–14.
13. See Janet Ilieva, Steve Baron, and Nigel M. Healey, "Online Surveys in Marketing Research: Pros and Cons," *International Journal of Marketing Research* 44, no. 3 (2002), pp. 361–376. Michael P. Cronin, "On-the-Cheap Market Research," *Inc.* June 1992, p. 108. Robert Hayes, "Internet-Based Surveys Provide Fast Results," *Marketing News,* April 13, 1998, p. 13; Phil Levine, Bill Ahlauser, Dale Kulp, and Rick Hunter, "Internet Interviewing," *Marketing Research,* Summer 1999, pp. 33–36.
14. Paul E. Green, Yoram Wind, Abba M. Krieger, and Paul Saatsoglou, "Applying Qualitative Data," *Marketing Research,* Spring 2000, pp. 17–25.
15. Don Debelek, "Want Some of This?" *Entrepreneur,* June 2002, www.entrepreneur.com/article/51926.
16. Phaedra Hise, "Grandma Got Run Over by Bad Research," *Inc.,* January 1998, www.inc.com/magazine/19980101/851.html
17. See, for example, David M. Georgoff and Robert G. Murdock, "Manager's Guide to Forecasting," *Harvard Business Review,* January–February 1986, pp. 110–120. Angelo Guadagno, "Mastering the 'Magic' of Sales Forecasting," *American Salesman,* November 1, 1995; Carlo D. Smith, "An Integrated Model of Factors Affecting Sales Forecasting Management," *Academy of Marketing Science* 90, 1999; Donald McBane, "Benchmarking Sales Forecasting Performance Measures," *Journal of Personal Selling and Sales Management,* 2001.
18. Stever Robbins, "Down and Dirty Market Research," *Entrepreneur,* August 12, 2002, www.entrepreneur.com/article/0,4621, 302407,00.html.
19. Steven K. Baker, "Forecasting Your Sales Revenue," *Entrepreneur,* May 7, 2001, www.entrepreneur.com/article/0,4621,389242,00.html.
20. David Carson and Audrey Gilmore, "Marketing at the Interface: Not 'What' But 'How,' *Journal of Marketing Theory and Practice* 8, no. 2 (Spring 2000), pp. 1–8. Kenneth J. Cook, "Why You Are in Trouble if You Think Marketing Is Just Sales," *Small Business Forum* 14, no. 3 (Winter 1996–1997), pp. 43–49.
21. Rebecca Cooper, "Marketing from the Inside Out: A Coach's Perspective," *Entrepreneur,* May 20, 2002, www.entrepreneur.com/article/52006.
22. G. David Doran, "Upper Crust," *Entrepreneur,* June 1999, www.entrepreneur.com/article/17844 Ruth's Chris Steak House Website www.ruthchris.com.
23. Carol Tice, "Seven Ways to Avoid Competing on Price, *Entrepreneur,* September 30, 2011, www.entrepreneur.com/blog/220406.
24. Personal and Internet interviews with Mingkit "Jerry" Lai conducted spring 2004 by Professor Susan Peters.
25. Laura Tiffany, "The Ingredients of a Marketing Plan," *Entrepreneur,* August 7, 2001, www.entrepreneur.com/article/43026.
26. Cook, op. cit.
27. Sumit K. Kundu and Jerome A. Katz, "Born-International SMEs: Bi-level Impacts of Resources and Intentions," *Small Business Economics,* 20, no. 1 (2003), pp. 25–47.
28. www.backbonemedia.net/clientBite.html.
29. Laura Clampitt Douglas, "Landing Customers," Entrepreneur, March 2, 2002, www.entrepreneur.com/article/49568.
30. Karen E. Spaeder, "Who Is Your Market—and What Do They Want?" *Entrepreneur,* March 18, 2002, www.entrepreneur.com/article/50024.
31. Cliff Ennico, "Expanding Your Target Market," *Entrepreneur,* October 28, 2002, www.entrepreneur.com/article/56528.
32. Based on www.entrepreneur.com/formnet/downloads/mkt03.doc.
33. Kathy Ellis, "Today's Marketing Plan," *The American Salesman* 49, no. 3 (March 2004), pp. 21–25.
34. Kim T. Gordon, "The Structure of a Marketing Plan," *Entrepreneur,* November 2000, www.entrepreneur.com/article/33900.
35. Donald Lehmann and Russell Winer, *Analysis for Market Planning,* 6th ed., (Burr Ridge, IL: McGraw-Hill, 2005). Also see virtually any marketing textbook for similar layouts.
36. Laura Tiffany, "How to Create a Marketing Plan," *Entrepreneur,* August 7, 2001, www.entrepreneur.com/article/0,4621,291706,00.html.
37. Larry Chiagouris and Brant Wansley "Start-Up Marketing," *Marketing Management* 12, no. 5 (September/October 2003), p. 39.
38. Lehman and Winer, op. cit.
39. Gwen Moran, op. cit.
40. Ibid.
41. Mark Henricks, "Change of Face," *Entrepreneur,* April 2000, www.entrepreneur.com/article/24840.
42. This marketing plan was originally written by Shannon Shehee of California State Polytechnic University—Pomona, under the direction of Prof. Susan Peters.

Chapter 13

1. "Welcome to the Curious Sofa," n.d., http://curioussofa.com/.
2. E. Gorey, *The Curious Sofa* (New York: Harcourt Brace & Co., 1997).
3. D. Dusenberry, "Curious Sofa Diaries: Nine Years Today," n.d., http://curioussofa.blogspot.com/2009/09/nineyears-today.html.
4. J. Goltz, "Stress Test: Is It Time to Shut Down Your Business?" *NYTimes.com/CNNMoney,* n.d., http://money.cnn.com/2009/04/01/smallbusiness/stress_test.fsb/index.htm.
5. J. Goltz, "The Dusenberry Diary: Living the Dream? Or Just Living?" *NYTimes.com/CNNMoney,* n.d., http://boss.blogs.nytimes.com/2009/11/10/the-dusenberry-diary-living-the-dream-or-just-living/.
6. "The Dusenberry Diary: When Passion Meets Math," *NYTimes.com/CNNMoney,* n.d., http://boss.blogs.nytimes.com/2009/06/23/the-dusenberry-diary-when-passion-meets-math/.
7. This is a loose interpretation of the bases for accounting. The definitive explanation is found in the FASB's Statements of Financial Accounting

Concepts, numbers 4 through 8. Available in pdf format at www.fasb.org/jsp/FASB/Page/SectionPage&cid=1176156317989.

8. P. Danner, "'Bad Accounting' or Illegal?" *San Antonio Express-News*," n.d., www.mysanantonio.com/business/article/Bad-accounting-or-illegal-1334193.php.
9. P. Danner, "'Bad Accounting' or Illegal?" *San Antonio Express-News.*
10. J. Davenport, "12-Year Sentence for Developer" *San Antonio Express-News*, n.d., www.mysanantonio.com/default/article/12-year-sentence-for-developer-1337478.php.
11. A complete description of the quality of financial accounting information is presented in Concepts Statement No. 6, "Elements of Financial Statements." Available in pdf format at www.fasb.org/jsp/FASB/Page/SectionPage&cid=1176156317989.
12. It is common for these statements to be presented as only three separate documents by combining the statements of retained earnings and owners' equity into the equity section of the balance sheet. Regardless of whether they are combined or presented as separate statements, they contain the same information and follow the same general format.
13. An economist defines *income* as a change in wealth. This implies, for example, that if a business purchased a plot of land some time ago for $100,000, and today, because of the development of adjacent property, several potential buyers each offered to pay $200,000 to purchase the land, then the business has income equal to the $100,000 increase in the value of the real estate. Accounting does not, however, recognize as income the increase in wealth caused by the increase in value of the land. If, and only if, the land is sold to an outside party will the increase in value be recognized as income in the accounting statements. For accounting purposes, income, gains, expenses, and losses are recognized only when a transaction takes place between nonrelated entities.
14. An economist would say that it is converted without facing any discount from the true economic value of the asset.
15. C. Koornhof, "Accounting Information on Flexibility," Dissertation, University of Pretoria, 1997.
16. Technically, owners are insiders. However, absentee owners often have little, if any, access to the financial records of small businesses. Thus they are listed as outside investors for the purposes of using financial accounting statements for disclosure.
17. S. Holmes and D. Nicholls, "An Analysis of the Use of Accounting Information by Australian Small Business," *Journal of Small Business Management*, April 1988, pp. 57–68.
18. Airlines use "revenue passenger miles" as the measure of output. A revenue passenger mile is one paying passenger being flown one mile. Thus, a 100-seat commuter plane that flies 600 miles will produce 60,000 revenue passenger miles if full, but zero revenue passenger miles if empty.
19. R. C. Cressy, "Small Business Failure: Failure to Fund or Failure to Learn?" in Z. Acs, B. Karlsson, and C. Karlsson (eds.), *Entrepreneurship, Small and Medium Sized Enterprises and the Macro Economy* (Cambridge: Cambridge University Press, 1999), pp. 161–185.
20. C. Bianchi, "Commercial and Financial Policies in Family Firms: The Small Business Growth Management Flight Simulator," *Simulation & Gaming* 31, no. 2 (2000), pp. 197–230.
21. M. J. Peel and J. Bridge, "Planning Business Objectives and Capital Budgeting in Japanese, German and Domestic SMEs: Some Evidence from the UK Manufacturing Sector," *Journal of Small Business and Enterprise Development* 6, no. 4 (2000), pp. 350–365.
22. Dorothy A. Davis, "Internal Controls for the Small Owner-Operated Business," Small Business Institute Directors Association National Meeting, www.Sbaer.Uca.Edu/Research/Sbida/1991/Pdf/03.Pdf.
23. R. N. Lussier and S. Pfeifer, "A Cross-National Prediction Model for Business Success," *Journal of Small Business Management* 39, no. 3 (2001), pp. 228–239.
24. M. J. Peel, "Timeliness of Private Company Accounts and Predicting Corporate Failure," *The Investment Analyst: The Journal of the Society of Investment Analysts*, no. 83, pp. 23–27.
25. This definition is deliberately simple. The analysis as presented overstates both the price variance and the efficiency variance by ignoring the common variance. In practice this analysis is sufficient for all but the most sophisticated cost analysis systems.
26. H. A. Simon, "Rational Decision Making in Business Organizations," in L. Green and J. H. Kagel (eds.), *Advances in Behavioral Economics*, vol. 1 (Norwood, NJ: Ablex, 1987), pp. 18–47.
27. In practice, an outsourcing decision should not be made based solely on a financial analysis. Multiple factors, especially the effect upon the strategy of the business should be considered. See J. Bowles, "Outsourcing for Competitive Advantage," *Forbes*, June 7, 2004, p. 101.

Chapter 14

1. The Focus on Small Business feature is based on information from the following: "On Front Lines of Debt Crisis, Luggage Maker Fights for Life," *WSJ.com*, n.d., http://online.wsj.com/article/SB123145502270765963.html?KEYWORDS=cash+flow+killed+small+business#project%3DRIPPLE0901%26articleTabs%3Darticle; J. Jargon, "Restitching J. W. Hulme, a Firm That Nearly Unraveled," *WSJ.com*, n.d., http://online.wsj.com/article/SB10001424052748704532204575397292080990632.html; "Recovery's in Bag for Luxury Luggage Maker," *StarTribune.com*, n.d., www.startribune.com/business/103013544.html; C. Newmarker, "Journal Article, New Investor Save 104-year-old Bag Maker," *Minneapolis/St. Paul Business Journal*, n.d., www.bizjournals.com/twincities/stories/2009/10/12/story6.html?page=all.
2. NFIB Educational Foundation, *National Small Business Poll: The Cash Flow Problem*, Washington, DC, 2001.
3. NFIB Education Foundation, "Business Starts and Stops" (Washington, DC: NFIB Education Foundation, 1999).
4. Evan Smith, "John Mackey," *Texas Monthly* 33, no. 3 (2005), pp. 122–132.
5. Federal Reserve Bank of Dallas, *Money, Banking and Monetary Policy*, 1995, p. 1.
6. In case the term is new to you, it comes from Joseph Heller's 1961 classic book (and 1970 movie) of the same name. It means that the situation is hopeless no matter what you do.
7. If you're interested, look at the 1998 Survey of Small Business Finance, which is conducted every five years. See "Financing Patterns of Small Firms: Findings from the 1998 Survey of Small Business Finance," done by the Federal Reserve and stored by the SBA at: www.sba.gov/advo/stats/ssbf_98.pdf. A particularly interesting look at financing (especially self-financing) comes from Charles Ou and George W. Haynes, "Uses of Equity Capital by Small Firms—Findings from the Surveys of Small Business Finances (for 1993 & 1998)," Paper presented at the Academy of Entrepreneurial Finance 14th International Conference, April 30–May 2, 2003, Chicago, Illinois.
8. www.startupjournal.com/financing/credit/20011005-clark.html; www.babyeinstein.com/B2C/about_founder_F32.shtml; www.usatoday.com/life/2002/2002-06-25-baby-genius.htm.
9. http://business.uschamber.com/P14/P14_1105.asp.
10. Paul Deceglie, "Fun with Funding: If You Left Your Creativity Somewhere with Your Coloring Books, You're Not Ready to Find Financing in the Post-Dot-com Era," *Entrepreneur*, BizOpp Zone, September 14, 2001, www.entrepreneur.com/article/44428. John F. Dalrymple, *International Business Profile Benchmarking for the SME Sector-Does it Work?* (RMIT University, Centre for Quality Management Research, 2001), www.cmqr.rmit.edu.au/publications/jdimprov.pdf. S. Mian and C. Smith, "Accounts Receivable Management Policy: Theory and Evidence," *Journal of Finance* 47 (1992), pp. 169–200.

11. Jonathan A. Scott and Morris G. Danielson, "Bank Loan Availability and Trade Credit Demand," *The Financial Review* 39 (2004), pp. 579–600, www.blackwell-synergy.com/links/doi/10.1111/j.07328516.2004.00089.x/pdf. A. N. Berger and G. F. Udell, "Small Business Credit Availability and Relationship Lending: The Importance of Bank Organizational Structure," *Economic Journal* 112 (2002), pp. 32–53.
12. Judy Gedge, "Does Your Collections System Need a Checkup?" *Entrepreneur, March 29, 2004,* www.entrepreneur.com/article/70086. Paul DeCeglie, "Gimme My Money: Steps You Can Take to Collect on Past Due Accounts Receivable," *Business Start-Ups*, August 2000, www.entrepreneur.com/article/30200. W. Lim and M. Rashid, "An Operational Theory Integrating Cash Discount and Product Pricing Policies," *Journal of American Academy of Business* 2(2002), pp. 282–288. W. Beranek, "Behavioral Relations, Operating Factors and the Optimal Cash Dis-count," the 7th International Symposium on Cash, Treasury and Working Capital Management, Chicago, October 1991.
13. See G. Udell, *Asset-Based Finance* (New York: The Commercial Finance Association, 2004); A. N. Berger and G. F. Udell, "Small Business and Debt Finance," in Zoltan J. Acs and David B. Audretsch (eds.), *Handbook of Entrepreneurship* (Norwell, MA: Kluwer Academic Publishing, 2003); M. R. Bakker, L. Klapper, and G. F. Udell, "The Role of Factoring in Commercial Finance: The Case of Eastern Europe," Working Paper, 2004.
14. See Mie-Yun Lee, "Factor Your Receivables for More Cash: Need a Quick Cash Infusion? A Factoring Service Can Help You Out," *Entrepreneur*, June 03, 2002, www.entrepreneur.com/article/52344 Jan Norman, "How to Factor: Get Money to Grow!" *Business Start-Ups*, November 1998, www.entrepreneur.com/article/16636.
15. One other approach is called *activity-based costing* (or ABC), which looks at which services, products, or internal operations add to your profits or add to your costs. It is used most often for companies with several different types of products, services, or markets and can help you pare down to those things that can truly make a positive difference in your bottom line. For an introduction, see Mark Henricks, "Beneath The Surface: Suspicious Not All Areas of Your Company Are Bringing in a Profit? Break It Down with Activity-Based Costing," *Entrepreneur*, October 1999, www.entrepreneur.com/article/18388.
16. For some other ideas, look at Jan Norman, "How to Manage Your Cash Flow: You're Making Sales, But Are You Making Money?" *Business Start-Ups*, June 1998, www.entrepreneur.com/article/15728.
17. Nancy R. Lockwood, "Work-Life Balance: Challenges and Solutions," Society for Human Resource Management, *2003 SHRM Research Quarterly*, 2003, www.ispi.org/pdf/suggestedReading/11_Lockwood_WorkLifeBalance.pdf. Aubrey C. Daniels, "Choosing an Employee Incentive Program: With So Many Choices Out There, How Do You Pick the Best One for Your Business?" *Entrepreneur*, September 02, 2002, www.entrepreneur.com/article/54952. G. A. Marken, "Ten Low-Cost Steps to Keep Employees from Job Hunting," *Water Quality Products* 7, no. 4 (April 2002), www.wwdmag.com/wwd/index.cfm/powergrid/rfah=%7Ccfap=/CFID/2522697/CFTKEN/34858572/fuseaction/showArticle/articleID/3032. Marvin Collins, *The Human Use of Human Resources* (New York: McGraw Hill, 1981).
18. Mark Henricks, "Trading Up: No Cash? No Problem," *Entrepreneur's Be Your Own Boss*, February 2005, www.entrepreneur.com/article/76128. Kirk Whisler and Nichole Torres, "Barter to the Cause: Does Cutting Costs Sound Like a Good Start-Up Idea?" *Entrepreneur*, October 2002, www.entrepreneur.com/article/55484. Kurt J. Samson, "Better Business? Think Barter Business Why Trading for Products and Services Makes Great Financial Sense," *Home Office*, August 1999, www.entrepreneur.com/article/25704.
19. "On Front Lines of Debt Crisis, Luggage Maker Fights for Life," *WSJ.com*, n.d., http://online.wsj.com/article/SB123145502270765963.html?KEYWORDS=cash+flow+killed+small+business#project%3DRIPPLE0901%26articleTabs%3Darticle.
20. "C. Newmarker, "New Investor Saves 104-year-old Bag Maker," *Minneapolis/St. Paul Business Journal*," n.d., www.bizjournals.com/twincities/stories/2009/10/12/story6.html?page=all.
21. "Restitching a Luggage Firm," *ProQuest*, n.d., http://search.proquest.com.tamusa.idm.oclc.org/docview/734669029/137D20325E817C5BAEA/1?accountid=130967#.
22. D. Youngblood, "Recovery's in Bag for Luxury Luggage Maker," *StarTribune.com*, n.d., www.startribune.com/business/103013544.html.
23. See C. O'Gorman. "The Sustainability of Growth in Small- and Medium-Sized Enterprises," *International Journal of Entrepreneurial Behaviour and Research* 7, no. 2 (February 2001), pp. 60–75. Kevin Mole, "Business Advice to Fast Growth Small Firms" (Telford: University of Wolverhampton, 1999), http://mubs.mdx.ac.uk/research/Discussion_Papers/Business_and_Management/dpapmsno_4.pdf.

Chapter 15

1. Certainly, these investment vehicles are not truly risk-free. At the minimum, they have term risk. A full discussion of the elements of investment is far beyond the scope of this text.
2. The actual annual effective interest rate is 22.47 percent.
   $r = \left[\frac{fv}{c}\right]^{\frac{1}{n}} - 1 \quad r = (150{,}000/100{,}000)^{1/2} - 1 \quad r = 0.224745$
3. Bootstrapping comes from an old saying that a person started poor and became successful through diligence and hard work had "pulled himself up by his bootstraps."

4. P. D. Reynolds, "Informal and Early Formal Financial Support in the Business Creation Process: Exploration with PSED II Data Set.", n.d., http://web.ebscohost.com.tamusa.idm.oclc.org/ehost/pdfviewer/pdfviewer?sid=be77b594-7bc9-4230-bdea-9617eb8c482b%40sessionmgr11&vid=1&hid=10.
5. J. Cornwall, *Bootstrapping* (Upper Saddle River, NJ: Prentice Hall, 2010); J. Ebben and A. Johnson, "Bootstrapping in Small Firms: An Empirical Analysis of Change over Time," *Journal of Business Venturing* 21, no. 6 (November 2006), pp. 851–865; J. Winborg and H. Landstrom, "Financial Bootstrapping in Small Businesses: Examining Small Business Managers' Resource Acquisition Behaviors," *Journal of Business Venturing* 16, no. 3 (May 2001), pp. 235–255.
6. Cornwall, *Bootstrapping*, p. 2.
7. "A Literature Review and Research Agenda for Crowdfunding of Social Ventures by Othmar Lehner :: SSRN," n.d., http://papers.ssrn.com/sol3/papers.cfm?abstract_id=2102525.
8. "38738_wps3405.pdf," n.d., www.ksri.org/bbs/files/research02/38738_wps3405.pdf A Survey of Securities Laws and Enforcement (working paper).
9. H. R. Huhman, "JOBS Act to Jumpstart the Job Market—Forbes," n.d., www.forbes.com/sites/work-inprogress/2012/04/05/jobs-act-to-jumpstart-the-job-market/.
10. "Entrepreneurship and the U.S. Economy," *U.S. Dept. of Labor: Bureau of Labor Statistics*, n.d., www.bls.gov/bdm/entrepreneurship/entrepreneurship.htm/.
11. "Business Enterprise—The 2012 Statistical Abstract—U.S. Census Bureau," n.d., www.census.gov/compendia/statab/cats/business_enterprise.html.
12. P. D. Reynolds, "Informal and Early Formal Financial Support in the Business Creation Process: Exploration with PSED II Data Set," n.d., http://web.ebscohost.com.tamusa.idm.oclc.org/ehost/pdfviewer/pdfviewer?sid=be77b594-7bc9-4230-bdea-9617eb8c482b%40sessionmgr11&vid=1&hid=10.
13. M. Hudson, "Important Things for Entrepreneurs to Know About Angel Investors," n.d., www.angelresourceinstitute.org/data/Documents/Resources/AngelCapitalEducation/What_Ents_Should_Know_About_Angels.pdf.

14. R. Wiltbank and W. Boeker, *Returns to Angel Investors in Groups*, Angel Capital Education Foundation (Kansas City, MO: Kauffman Foundation of Entrepreneurship, November 2007), www.angelresourceinstitute.org/data/Documents/Resources/AngelCapitalEducation/RSCH_-_ACEF_-_Returns_to_Angel_Investor_in_Groups.pdf.
15. Rendering is the process of converting dead animals into usable fats and protein.
16. J. A. Katz, "Modelling Entrepreneurial Career Progressions: Concepts and Considerations," *Entrepreneurship: Theory and Practice.* 19, no. 2 (Winter 1994), pp. 23–40. J. A. Katz, "A Psychosocial Cognitive Model of Employment Status Choice," *Entrepreneurship: Theory and Practice* 17, no. 1 (1992), pp. 29–37. J. A. Katz, "Secondary Analysis in Entrepreneurship: An Introduction to Data Bases and Data Management," *Journal of Small Business Management* 30, no. 20 (1992), pp. 74–86.
17. Crystal Detamore-Rodman, "The Search Is On: Entrepreneurs and Experts All Agree: If You're Willing to Hunt Around, You Can Score Financing to Get Your Homebased Business Off the Ground," *Entrepreneur's Be Your Own Boss,* June 2003, www.entrepreneur.com/article/62238. Cliff Ennico, "Accepting Money from Friends & Family: 4 Ways to Get Your Cash without Wreaking Havoc on Your Personal Relationships," Entrepreneur.com—*Money & Finance,* May 06, 2002, www.entrepreneur.com/article/51542 Stever Robbins, "Asking Friends and Family for Financing: Heed our Warnings before You Play This Dangerous Game," *Entrepreneur,* October 1, 2001, www.entrepreneur.com/article/44612.
18. Actually, Freud most likely never made this statement; however, it has entered popular folklore and is usually attributed to him.
19. R. Cialdini, *Influence: The Psychology of Persuasion* (New York: William Morrow and Company, 1993).
20. A. Komter and W. Vollebergh, "Gift-Giving and the Emotional Significance of Family and Friends," *Journal of Marriage and the Family* 59, no. 3 (August 1997), pp. 747–757.
21. C. Ou and G. W. Haynes, "Uses of Equity Capital by Small Firms—Findings from the Surveys of Small Business Finances (for 1993 & 1998)," presented at the 14th Annual Conference on Entrepreneurial Finance and Business Ventures at the De Paul University Chicago, Illinois, on April 30–May 2, 2003, www.sba.gov/advo/stats/wkp03co.pdf.
22. R. Pettit and R. Singer, "Small Business Finance: A Research Agenda," *Financial Management,* Autumn 1985, pp. 47–60.

Chapter 16

1. B. Cummings, "They Even Stole a Backhoe in Broad Daylight," *The New York Times,* January 6, 2005.
2. C. D. Bader, "Construction Equipment Theft: A Billion-Dollar Problem," *Grading & Excavation Contractor,* November/December 2004.
3. Cummings, op. cit.
4. www.pprhealthcare.com/index.shtml.
5. REL's Annual Working Capital surveys, 2004, www.relconsult.com/website/website.nsf/Articles/.
6. Ellyn Spragins, "Get Paid First!" *Fortune Small Business* 15, no. 1 (February 2005), p. 85.
7. Rieva Lesonsky, "Inventory Control: When It Comes to Inventory, the Key Is Striking a Balance between Too Little and Too Much," *Entrepreneur,* 2006. www.entrepreneur.com/article/21842.
8. Gwen Moran, "Cover Your Bases: If You Thought Database Marketing Was Just Wasting Your Time with Fliers and Mailing Lists, Take Another Look—at the Net," *Entrepreneur,* February 2000, www.entrepreneur.com/article/18988.
9. "Dell Does What Others Have Given Up," *Forbes World Media Digest,* 2005, http://Forbes.com/technology.
10. Mike Hogan, "The Outer Limits: With Larger PC-Makers Struggling, Why Is Alienware Doing So Well?" *Entrepreneur,* March 2005, www.entrepreneur.com/article/76244. "Cutting the Edge Hardware," interview with Alex Aguila, www.ownt.com/hardware/interviews/2003/alienware/alienware.shtm. Ed Duggan, "Alienware, a Miami Computer Maker, Could Top Sales of $50 million," *South Florida Business Journal,* August 16, 2002, www.bizjournals.com/southflorida/stories/2002/08/19/smallb1.html?t5printable.
11. Jerome A. Katz, Scott R. Safranski, and Omar Khan, "Virtual Instant Global Entrepreneurship: Cybermediation for Born International Service Firms," *Journal of International Entrepreneurship* 1, no. 1 (March 2003), pp. 43–57.
12. Stephen Barlas, "Industrial Cleanser: The EPA Is Targeting Small Business for Pollution Cleanup," *Entrepreneur,* January 2000, www.Entrepreneur.com/article/0,4621,232505,00.html.
13. Amanda C. Kooser, "Who's Paying for Computer Recycling: The Newest Standard for Modems," *Entrepreneur*, August 2, 2002, www.entrepreneur.com/article/53730.
14. Because depreciation is a noncash expense, it causes net operating profit to be an amount less than net cash inflows, all other things being equal. (Refer to Chapter 13 "Accounting for Small Business" for a more complete discussion of depreciation.)
15. David A. Kirby and Stefan Kaiser, "Joint Ventures as an Internationalisation Strategy for SMEs," *Small Business Economics* 21, no. 3 (Spring 2003), pp. 229–242. Marc J. Dollinger, Peggy A. Golden, and Todd Saxton, "The Effect of Reputation on the Decision to Joint Venture," *Strategic Management Journal* 18, no. 2 (1997), pp. 127–140.
16. I. Groves, "Vermont Sock Maker Looking for Experienced Workers Cabot, Company, Socks, Top News," *Burlington Times News,* n.d., www.thetimesnews.com/news/cabot-10499-company-socks.html.
17. Ibid.
18. R. Graham, "Business People—Vermont: Cabot Hosiery Mills," n.d., www.vermontguides.com/2006/11-nov/cobot_mills.html.
19. "Darn Tough Vermont Reports Q1 2012 Results Best in Company's History," *Outdoor USA Magazine,* n.d., www.odrmag.com/financialreports/1467-darn-tough-vermont-reports-q1-2012-results-bestin-companyshistory.html.
20. There is a caveat if you use Excel, however. The built-in net present value function of Excel does not provide for time period 0. Therefore, you must calculate the present value of the cash flows of periods 1, 2, 3, . . . , *n* and then add the initial negative investment cash flow to the number provided by the Excel function.
21. Stever Robbins, "How Much Is This Business Worth? If You're Interested in Purchasing an Existing Business, Here Are a Few Ways to Gauge Its Value," *Entrepreneur,* January 12, 2004, www.entrepreneur.com/article/66442.

Chapter 17

1. K. Kline, "No More Brush-Offs for This Crew," *BusinessWeek,* October 29, 2003.
2. Financial risk is discussed in detail in Chapter 15, "Small Business Finance."
3. Doris A. Christopher, "Small Business Pilfering: The "trusted" Employee(s)," *Business Ethics: A European Review* 12, no 3 (2003), pp. 284–297. Note that there is a lot of disagreement on how much theft there is. In an SBA-sponsored survey, only 2 percent of small businesses reported employee theft in the prior year, but it is better to be safe than sorry. The SBA study was Bonnie Fisher, "Small Businesses, Big Burdens: The Nature and Incidence of Crime within and against Small Business and Its Customers and Employees, Their Causes, Their Effects, and Their Prevention," Washington: U.S. Small Business Administration, Office of

Advocacy Research Report no 176. March 1997, www.sba.gov/advo/research/rs176.pdf.

4. Anita Dennis, "The Downside of Good Times," *Journal of Accountancy* 190, no. 5 (2002), pp. 53–55. Neil H. Snyder, O. Whitfield Broome, and Karen Zimmerman, "Using Internal Controls to Reduce Employee Theft in Small Businesses," *Journal of Small Business Management* 27, no. 3 (July 1989), pp. 48–55.
5. Thomas M. Sullivan, "Closing the Tax Gap and the Impact on Small Business," Testimony of the Chief Counsel for Advocacy to the U.S. House of Representatives, Committee on Small Business, April 27, 2005, www.sba.gov/advo/laws/test05_0427.html. W. M. Crain and T. D. Hopkins, "The Impact of Regulatory Costs on Small Firms," U.S. Small Business Administration, Office of Advocacy (SBAHQ-00-R-0027), October 2001, www.sba.gov/advo/research/rs207tot.pdf.
6. 42 USC Pub. L. 88-352, Title VII, Sec. 701 (b).
7. Except industries in SIC codes 55–69, 71–74, and 81–89.
8. J. VandeHei, "Clint Eastwood Saddles Up for Disability-Act Showdown," *The Wall Street Journal* May 9, 2000.
9. "Americans with Disabilities Act of 1990, as Amended," n.d., www.ada.gov/pubs/ada.htm.
10. "Jury Makes Eastwood's Day," ABC News, n.d., http://abcnews.go.com/Entertainment/story?id=115096&page=1#.UAxGAvWwXmV.
11. W. Olsen, "Grace Period for ADA Modifications Proposed in Congress," blog, Overlawyered, March 25, 2011, www.lexisnexis.com/hottopics/lnacademic.
12. General Aviation Revitalization Act (GARA), 1994.
13. "Afterthestorm_missouri_27scommitmenttojoplin.pdf", n.d., http://209.59.145.158/downloads/Presentations_2012/afterthestorm_missouri_27scommitmenttojoplin.pdf.
14. M. Shelton, "Businesses In Joplin, MO, Find Economic Opportunity", n.d., www.wbez.org/story/2011-09-13/businesses-joplin-mo-find-economic-opportunity-91935; "Joplin Business Listing | Joplin Business Directory | Joplin Open Business | Relocated Businesses," n.d., http://joplintornado.info/joplin_open_for_business/joplin_open_for_business.htm.
15. Separation of duties is discussed more fully in Chapter 16, "Assets: Inventory and Operations Management."
16. Gene Gable (ed.), "Heavy Metal Madness: Put on a Happy Face!" *Creativepro.com,* April 22, 2004, www.creativepro.com/story/feature/21223.html. See also Yahoo's answer at http://ask.yahoo.com/ask/20011213.html, and the international angle on the "smiley face" story at www.goodbyemag.com/apr01/ball.html.
17. R. Hollinger, "National Retail Security Survey Final Report," University of Florida, 2001.
18. J. Wells, "2004 Report to the Nation on Occupational Fraud and Abuse," Association of Certified Fraud Examiners, Austin, TX, 2004, www.cfenet.com.
19. Thomas M. Sullivan, "Closing the Tax Gap and the Impact on Small Business," Testimony of the Chief Counsel for Advocacy to the U.S. House of Representatives, Committee on Small Business, April 27, 2005, www.sba.gov/advo/laws/test05_0427.html.
20. Leo Standora, "Heidi Has a Leg Up—$2m Insurance!" *New York Daily News,* September 7, 2004, p. 3.
21. Ibid.
22. Ibid.
23. U.S. Consumer Product Safety Commission, "Amusement Ride-Related Injuries and Deaths in the United States: 1987–2000," Bethesda, MD, 2001.
24. The Outdoor Amusement Association Web Site, November 27, 2004, www.oaba.org/facts2.htm/.
25. M. Holmer, "The Value of Social Security Disability Insurance," Public Policy Institute of AARP, Washington, DC, 2001.
26. T. Zayatz, "Social Security Disability Insurance Program Worker Experience: Actuarial Study No. 114," Social Security Administration, Washington, DC, 1999.

Chapter 18

1. This article is based on: Randall Roberts, "B-Money in the Bank: St. Louis Native B-Money Is Hanging with Rap's Heavy Hitters," *Riverfront Times,* December 6 2006 (St. Louis), www.riverfronttimes.com/2006-12-06/music/b-money-in-the-bank/. All quotes come from this article and are used with permission. Kevin C. Johnson, "St. Louisan Wins Grammy for Work with Beyonce," St. Louis *Post-Dispatch*, 02/22/2007, www.stltoday.com/stltoday/entertainment/columnists.nsf/kevinjohnson/story/6E9B89B710A94682862572880082B63D?OpenDocument. Randall Roberts, "STLOG: B-Money's Beat Kicks Off the New Jay-Z," Nov. 21, 2006 at 12:01:04 PM, http://blogs.riverfronttimes.com/stlog/2006/11/bmoneys_beat_kicks_off_the_new.php.
2. Robert A. Kagan, "On Surveying the Whole Legal Forest," *Law and Social Inquiry,* vol. 28, 2003, pp. 833-872, www.journals.uchicago.edu/cgi-bin/resolve?id=doi:10.1086/380082&erFrom= 445040558813465220Guest. Christian Wollschlager, "Exploring the Global Landscapes of Litigation Rates," in Jürgen Brand and Dieter Stempel (eds.), Soziologie des Rechts: Fetschrift fur Erhard Blankenburg zum 60, Geburtstag. (Baden-Baden, Germany: Nomos Berlagsgesellschaft, 1998), pp. 587–88.
3. Pamela Rohland, "Follow Suit: What to Do when You Get Sued," *Entrepreneur-Business Start-Ups,* April 2000, www.entrepreneur.com/article/25032.
4. Cliff Ennico, "How to Hire an Attorney: Hiring a Good Lawyer Is Crucial to Any Successful Business," *Entrepreneur,* January 20, 2003, www.entrepreneur.com/article/58326.
5. Karen E. Spaeder, "Is Your Home Zoned for Business? How to Research, Comply with and Change Local Zoning Laws in Your Home-Based Business's Favor," *Entrepreneur—Home Office,* January 26, 2004, www.Entrepreneur.com/article/0,4621,313950,00.html.
6. Christopher L. Hansen, "Special Report: Home-Based Zoning: What Issues Are at Stake for Homebased Businesses Fighting Zoning Ordinances?" *Entrepreneur—Home Office,* January 1, 2001. Laura Tiffany, "Zoning: Home Is Where the Business Is, and It's Also Where a Lot of Regulations Are," *Entrepreneur—Home Office,* March 21, 2001.
7. "The Basics of Sole Proprietorships: Chances Are, You're Already Running a Sole Proprietorship," *Entrepreneur,* May 12, 2005, www.entrepreneur.com/article/77798.
8. These tips are adapted from Asheesh Advani, "Negotiation Tips for Start-Ups: Follow These Suggestions for Negotiating with Employees, Investors and Suppliers When Your Business Has No Revenue," *Entrepreneur,* April 4, 2005, www.entrepreneur.com/article/76894. Max H. Bazerman, "Creating Value, Weighing Values," *Negotiation,* April 2005, pp. 3–5. Tony Parinello, "Dealmaking Basics: Tips for Negotiating Your Way to a Smooth Sale," *Entrepreneur,* May 12, 2003, www.entrepreneur.com/node/sales/212-17. Sean Silverthorne, "Five Questions for Max Bazerman," *HBS Working Knowledge,* September 4, 2001, http://hbswk.hbs.edu/item.jhtml?id=2472&t=negotiation&noseek=one. Max H. Bazerman and James J. Gillespie, "Betting on the Future: The Virtues of Contingent Contracts," *Harvard Business Review* 77, no. 5 (September/October 1999), pp. 155–160.
9. This is a variation of the idea of "tit for tat," where two parties immediately achieve balance.
10. Robert Axelrod, *The Evolution of Cooperation* (New York: Basic Books, 1984). See also the Evolution of Cooperation Web site at http://pscs.physics.lsa.umich.edu/Software/CC/ECHome.html. For a business-oriented approach, consider looking at John Stewart, *Evolution's Arrow: The Direction of Evolution and the Future of Humanity* (Steamboat

Springs, CO: Chapman Press, 2000). The entire text is available for a free download at http://users.tpg.com.au/users/jes999/index.htm.

11. The key books on negotiating come from the Program on Negotiating at Harvard Law School (www.pon.harvard.edu/main/home/index.php3). They are R. Fisher, W. Ury, and B. Patton, *Getting to Yes: Negotiating without Giving In* (New York: Penguin Books, 1991): and W. Ury, *Getting Past No: Negotiating Your Way from Confrontation to Cooperation* (New York: Bantam Books, 1993). Another book you might find useful for working with very problematic types is R. M. Bramson, *Coping with Difficult People* (New York: Dell, 1981).
12. Internal Revenue Service, "Independent Contractor (Self-Employed) or Employee?" Internal Revenue Service, June 15, 2009, July 17, 2009, www.irs.gov/businesses/small/article/0,,id=99921,00.html.
13. Steven C. Bahls and Jane Easter Bahls, "RA-A-A-ID! Creepy Competitors Raiding Your Work Force? The Law Can Be the Perfect Bug Spray," *Entrepreneur,* September 2000, www.entrepreneur.com/article/31548.
14. David Rountree, "Head Over Heels: Former Auburn Gymnast and Husband Turn Her Talent into Success," *Birmingham Business Journal,* June 6, 2005, http://birmingham.bizjournals.com/birmingham/stories/2005/06/06/smallb1.html.
15. Chris Kelleher, "5 Litigation Secrets: These Tips May Keep Your Business Out of Court—or Possibly Help You Win if You Get There," *Entrepreneur,* July 12, 2004, www.entrepreneur.com/article/71770.
16. W. Michael Hoffman, Laura P. Hartman, and Mark Rowe, "You've Got Mail . . . and the Boss Knows: A Survey by the Center for Business Ethics of Companies' Email and Internet Monitoring," *Business and Society Review* 108, no. 3 (2003), pp. 285-307. American Marketing Association with the ePolicy Institute and Clearswift, *2003 E-Mail Rules, Policies and Practices Survey* (New York: American Marketing Association, 2003), www.amanet.org/research/pdfs/Email_Policies_Practices.pdf. Robert McGarvey, "Watch and Learn . . . or Watch and Feel Like a Slimy Interloper," *Entrepreneur,* December 2000, www.entrepreneur.com/article/45374.
17. Chris Kelleher, "How to Protect Your Business's Trade Secrets: These Five Rules Will Help Safeguard Some of Your Company's Most Important Assets," *Entrepreneur,* May 1, 2005, www.entrepreneur.com/article/77680.
18. Jane Easter Bahls, "The Name Game: You Can Shield Your Trade Name from Being Ripped Off by a Larger Company—If It's Distinctive Enough," *Entrepreneur,* January 2005, www.entrepreneur.com/article/77322. "The Source of the Nile(s):Trademark Law's Personal Name Rule Shows Flexibility," *Ideas on Intellectual Property Law* (Manchester, NH: McLane Intellectual Property Practice Group, October/November 2004), pp. 2–3. Eugene R. Quinn, Jr., *Beanie Babies Trademark Infringement?* (Albany NY: Hiscock & Barclay, LLP, 2004), www.hiscockbarclay.com/pdf/IPnewsletter_hb_0504.pdf.

Chapter 19

1. Talicia A. Flint, "Employees vs. Contractors Who Are the Best Players for Your Team?" HomeOfficeMag.com, May 2001, www.entrepreneur.com/article/40224.
2. These numbers come from estimates for 2010 included in Table A.1 from Small Business Administration Office of Advocacy, "The Small Business Economy 2011," n.d., www.sba.gov/advocacy/849/6282.
3. B. A. Kirchhoff, *Entrepreneurship and Dynamic Capitalism* (Westport, CT: Quorum Books, 1994). B. Phillips and B. A. Kirchhoff, "Formation, Growth and Survival Small Firm Dynamics in the U.S. Economy," *Small Business Economics* 1 (1989), pp. 65–74. D. Birch, *Job Creation in America* (New York: Free Press, 1987).
4. Joanna L. Krotz, "5 Tips for Hiring Your First Employee," Microsoft Small Business Center (2005). www.microsoft.com/smallbusiness/issues/management/recruiting_Staffing/5_tips_for_hiring_your_first_employee.mspx.
5. Ibid.
6. Gideon D. Markman and Robert A. Baron, "Individual Differences and the Pursuit of New Ventures: A Model of Person-Entrepreneurship Fit," in Jerome A. Katz and Theresa M. Welbourne (eds.), *Advances in Entrepreneurship, Firm Emergence and Growth,* vol. 5 (Oxford: JAI/Elsevier, 2002), pp. 23–54.
7. Allbusiness.com, "Is Employee Probation a Good Idea?" Allbusiness.com (2005), www.allbusiness.com/articles/EmploymentHR/749-33-1817.html. Wayne F. Cascio and Herman Aguinis, "Chapter 3: Staffing Twenty-First–Century Organizations," *Academy of Management Annals* 2, no. 1 (2008), pp. 133–165.
8. Krotz. "5 Tips for Hiring Your First Employee," op. cit.
9. Joanna L. Krotz, "Are You a Control Freak? 5 Ways to Stop," Microsoft Small Business Center (2005). www.microsoft.com/smallbusiness/issues/management/leadership_training/are_you_a_control_freak_5_ways_to_stop.mspx.
10. Ian O. Williamson, Daniel M. Cable, and Howard E. Aldrich, "Smaller but Not Necessarily Weaker: How Small Businesses Can Overcome Barriers to Recruitment. Managing People in Entrepreneurial Organizations," *Advances in the Study of Entrepreneurship Firm Emergence and Growth,* vol. 5 (Greenwich, CT: JAI Press, 2002), pp. 83–106.
11. Jeff Taylor, "A Monster Success," *The Economist* 307, no. 8368 (March 27, 2004), p. 66.
12. Chris Penttila, "How Embarrassing! Highly Publicized Dry Spells Are Poor Recruiting Tools," *Entrepreneur,* August 2002, p. 66.
13. Dale Duncan and Peter Hausdorf, "Firm Size and Internet Recruiting in Canada," *Journal of Small Business Management* 42, no. 3 (July 2004), p. 325.
14. Businesstown.com, "Hiring Top Performers," Businesstown.com (undated), www.businesstown.com/hiring/hiring-top.asp, adapted from Bob Adams and Peter Veruki, *Adams Streetwise Hiring Top Performers: 600 Ready-to-Ask Interview Questions and Everything Else You Need to Hire Right* (Cincinnati: Adams Media Corporation, 1997).
15. Joanna L. Krotz, "Tips for Outsourcing Your Small-Business Needs," Microsoft Small Business Center (2005). www.microsoft.com/smallbusiness/resources/management/recruiting_staffing/tips_for outsourcing_your_small_business_needs.mspx.
16. Jerome A. Katz, Scott R. Safranski, and Omar Khan, "Virtual Instant Global Entrepreneurship: Cybermediation for Born International Service Firms," *Journal of International Entrepreneurship* 1 (2003), pp. 43–57. Robyn Greenspan, "Managing Virtual Employees," ecommerce-guide.com, February 28, 2002, //e-commerceguide.com/news/news/article.php/983281.
17. Gisda M. Pedroza, "Hiring Telecommuters, Before You Set Up Employees in Their Own Home Offices, Make Sure You Can Handle the Costs," *Entrepreneur,* January 2002, www.entrepreneur.com/article/47760.
18. Katz, Safranski, and Khan, op. cit. Greenspan, op. cit.
19. The ideas in the following section are from No-Cost Staffing Options on www.toolkit.cch.com.
20. Entrepreneur.com, "How to Write a Job Analysis and Description," *Entrepreneur.com,* October 23, 2002, www.entrepreneur.com/article/0,4621,304062,00.html.
21. Chris Kelleher, "Writing Great Job Descriptions," *Entrepreneur,* May 10, 2004, www.entrepreneur.com/article/0,4621, 315429,00.html.
22. Wayne F. Cascio and Herman Aguinis, "Chapter 3: Staffing Twenty-First–Century Organizations," *Academy of Management Annals* 2, no. 1 (2008), pp. 133–165. Cascio and Aguinis argue that most studies of selection device effectiveness using actual (vs. adjusted) statistics show results indicating a statistically significant but very small (low-power) improvement in predictive power. Meanwhile, using adjusted results has not been shown to work in real-world selection situations. They contend using *in situ* approaches such as internships and contingent work is the

best way to sample. Cascio in earlier works (as well as Schmitt) have pointed out that behavioral interviewing is the next best approach.

23. Alison Doyle, "Behavioral Interview—Behavioral-Based Interviewing." About.com, July 20, 2009, http://jobsearch.about.com/cs/interviews/a/behavioral.htm. Susan M. Heathfield, "Behavioral Interviews: Use Behavioral Interviewing to Select the Best." About.com, July 20, 2009, http://humanresources.about.com/od/interviewing/a/behavior_interv_2.htm. Elaine D. Pulakos and Neal Schmitt, "Experience-Based and Situational Interview Questions: Studies of Validity," *Personnel Psychology* 48, no. 2 (1995), pp. 289–308. U.K. Work Ministry, "Work Ministry—The Interview," Work Ministry, 2004, July 20, 2009, www.workministry.com/resources/Interview3.shtml.
24. Adapted from the Mavens and Mogul Web site, www.mavensandmoguls.com/, and from Inc Magazine, "Entrepreneur of the Year: The Accidental Entrepreneur—Paige Arnof-Fenn," www.inc.com/entrepreneur/profile/index.php? arnof-fenn52.
25. The ideas here are excerpted and adapted from Gary Roberts, Gary Seldon and Carlotta Roberts, "Human Resources Management" Emerging Business Series, Monograph EB-4. (Washington DC: U.S. Small Business Administration, undated), www.sba.gov/library/pubs/eb-4.txt.
26. Adapted from "TechScribe Writing," *How to Write Instructions* (Sheffield, South Yorkshire, 2004), www.techscribe.co.uk/ta/ how_to_write_instructions.htm.
27. Excerpted from Gary Roberts, Gary Seldon and Carlotta Roberts, "Human Resources Management" Emerging Business Series, Monograph EB-4. (Washington DC: U.S. Small Business Administration, undated), www.sba.gov/library/pubs/eb-4.txt.
28. Allbusiness.com, "Secrets of Effective Employee Training." Allbusiness.com (2005). www.allbusiness.com/articles/EmploymentHR/1465-33-1817.html.
29. Jill Kickul, "Promises Made, Promises Broken: Employee Attraction and Retention in Small Businesses," *Journal of Small Business Management* 39, no. 4 (2001), pp. 320–335.
30. Adapted from Commerce Clearing House, "Building Employee Involvement," *Business Owners Toolkit* (Riverwoods, IL: Commerce Clearing House, 2005), www.toolkit.cch.com/text/P05_7200.asp.
31. Elcha Shain Buckman, "Motivating and Retaining Non-Family Employees in a Family-Owned Business." *The UMASS Family Business Center Online Newsletter* (Hadley, MA: The UMASS Family Business Center, 1998), www.umass.edu/fambiz/motivate_key_employees.htm.
32. This well-put concept was contributed by an anonymous user and reviewer of *Entrepreneurial Small Business.*
33. Buckman, op. cit.
34. Building Employees' Involvement, on www.toolkit.cch.com.
35. David Newton, "Of One Mind: Keep Employees by Getting on the Same Page from the Get-Go," *Entrepreneur,* August 2003, p. 23. www.entrepreneur.com/article/63276.
36. Alison Stein Wellner, "What Makes Employees Want to Stick Around?" *BusinessWeek,* March 2000, 3.20.00. www.businessweek.com/smallbiz/content/mar2000/sb000320a.htm.
37. Peter L. Allen, "Performance Appraisal Question and Answer Book," *Harvard Management Communication Letter* 6, no. 3 (March 2003), p. 3.
38. BizHelp23.com, "Employee Appraisal." BizHelp23.com (Sheffield, UK: BizHelp24.com, 2005), www.bizhelp24.com/personaldevelopment/employee_appraisal.shtml.
39. Gina Imperato, "How to Give Good Feedback," *Fast Company,* September 17, 1998, p. 144.
40. Allbusiness.com, "Making Performance Appraisals Work," Allbusiness.com (2005), www.allbusiness.com/articles/content/1383-33-1817.html.
41. David G. Javitch, "Establishing an Employee Review System," Entrepreneur.com, April 05, 2004, www.entrepreneur.com/article/70172.
42. This section is excerpted from an outstanding description of practical compensation management in small businesses which came from Allbusiness.com, "Key Compensation Components," Allbusiness.com, undated, www.allbusiness.com/articles/EmploymentHR/794-33-1773.html.
43. Staff of *Family Business,* "The Power of Base Pay," Inc., October 1999, www.inc.com/articles/1999/10/19037.html.
44. Allbusiness.com, "Key Compensation Components," op. cit.
45. Ibid. The Henry J. Kaiser Family Foundation, "Implementation Timeline," Health Reform Source, 2013, http://healthreform.kff.org/timeline.aspx
46. Ibid.
47. Rich Mintzer. "20 Low-Cost Employee Perks," Entrepreneur.com, December 08, 2006, www.entrepreneur.com/humanresources/compensationandbenefits/article171630.html. Entrepreneur.com, "Low-Cost Benefits That'll Make Your Employees Happy," October 23, 2002, www.entrepreneur.com/humanresources/compensationandbenefits/article 56492. html. Aliza Pilar Sherman, "How Women Business Owners Reward Their Staff," Entrepreneur, September 2005, www.entrepreneur.com/humanresources/managingemployees/motivationandretention/article79320.html.
48. Catherine M. Daily and Marc J. Dollinger, *Alternative Methodologies for Identifying Family—versus Nonfamily-Managed Businesses* (Columbus, Ohio: Max M. Fisher College of Business, Ohio State University, 1994). John Ward and Christina Dolan, "Defining and Describing Family Business Ownership Configurations," *Family Business Review,* 11 (1998), pp. 305–310.
49. Eric Flamholtz and Yvonne Randle, *Growing Pains: How to Make the Transition from an Entrepreneurship to a Professionally Managed Firm* (San Francisco: Jossey-Bass, 2007).
50. Barbara Blouin, Katherine Gibson, and Margaret Kiersted, *The Legacy of Inherited Wealth: Interviews with Heirs* (Halifax, N.S.: Trio Press, 1995). Paul C. Rosenblatt, Leni de Mik, Roxanne arie Anderson, and Patricia A. Johnson, *The Family in Business* (San Francisco: Jossey-Bass Publishers, 1985).
51. Dennis T. Jaffe, *Working with the Ones You Love: Conflict Resolution & Problem Solving Strategies for a Successful Family Business* (Berkeley, CA: Conari Press, 1990). David Javitch, "David Javitch: Employee Management—How to Earn Employees' Respect," Entrepreneur.com, June 02, 2003, www.entrepreneur.com/humanresources/employ-eemanagementcolumnistdavidjavitch/article62284.html.
52. Flamholtz and Randle, 2007.
53. Rosenblatt et al., 1985.
54. David Bork, *Family Business, Risky Business: How to Make It Work* (New York, NY: AMACOM, American Management Association, 1986). Gideon Maas and Andre Diederichs, *Manage Family in Your Family Business* (Northcliff, South Africa: Frontrunner, 2007). U.S. Small Business Administration, *Challenges in Managing a Family Business,* Management and Planning Series, Monograph MP-3 (Washington DC: U.S. Small Business Administration, undated), www.sba.gov/library/pubs/mp-3.txt. Jeff Wuorio, "How to Fire a Family Member," Microsoft Small Business Center (2005), www.microsoft.com/smallbusiness/issues/management/employee_relations/how_to_fire_a_family_member.mspx.
55. Patricia Schiff Estess, "Don't Get Personal: Taking the Personal out of Personnel Isn't Easy When You're Talking about Family," *Entrepreneur,* January 2000 www.entrepreneur.com/article/18852.
56. Craig E. Aronoff and John L. Ward, *From Siblings to Cousins: Prospering in the Third Generation and Beyond,* Family Business Leadership *Series,* no. 22 (Marietta, GA: Family Enterprise Publishers, 2007). David Bork, *Family Business, Risky Business: How to Make It Work* (New York, NY: AMACOM, American Management Association, 1986). Eric Flamholtz and Yvonne Randle, *Growing Pains: How to Make the Transition from an Entrepreneurship to a Professionally Managed Firm* (San Francisco: Jossey-Bass, 2007). David G. Javitch, "By Setting Clear Standards and Involving Employees in the Review Process, Your Entire Company Can Benefit from Formal Appraisals," Entrepreneur.com, April 05, 2004, www.entrepreneur.com/article/0,4621,314968,00.html. Sandra W. King, George T. Solomon, and Lloyd W. Fernald Jr., "Issues in Growing a Family Business: A Strategic Human Resource Model," *Journal of Small Business Management* 39, no. 1 (January 2001), pp. 3–13. Paul C. Rosenblatt, Leni de Mik,

Roxanne arie Anderson, and Patricia A. Johnson, *The Family in Business* (San Francisco: Jossey-Bass Publishers, 1985).

57. Patricia Schiff Estess, "Theory of Un-Relativity: How to Keep Nonfamily Managers Happy in Order to Grow Your Business," *Entrepreneur,* March 1999, www.entrepreneur.com/magazine/entrepreneur/1999/march/17328.html. Patricia Schiff Estess, "Attracting Non-Family Employees: As Appealing as the Cozy Atmosphere of a Family Business May Be, You Can't Beat Incentives for Hooking Good Managers," *Entrepreneur,* December 1999, www.entrepreneur.com/magazine/entrepreneur/1999/december/18656.html. Eric Flamholtz and Yvonne Randle, *Growing Pains: How to Make the Transition from an Entrepreneurship to a Professionally Managed Firm* (San Francisco: Jossey-Bass, 2007).
58. Craig E. Aronoff and John L. Ward, *From Siblings to Cousins: Prospering in the Third Generation and Beyond,* Family Business Leadership Series, no. 22 (Marietta, GA: Family Enterprise Publishers, 2007). Dennis T. Jaffe, *Working with the Ones You Love: Conflict Resolution & Problem Solving Strategies for a Successful Family Business* (Berkeley, CA: Conari Press, 1990). Nichole L. Torres, "Family Affair: When Business and Family Mix, the Key to Success Is Communication," *Entrepreneur's Start-Ups,* September 2004, www.entrepreneur.com/magazine/entrepreneursstartupsmagazine/2004/september/72314.html. Paul C. Rosenblatt, Leni de Mik, Roxanne arie Anderson, and Patricia A. Johnson, *The Family in Business* (San Francisco: Jossey-Bass Publishers, 1985).

Chapter 20

1. Look at Mark Hendricks, "Stage Right: Make Smarter Management Decisions by Knowing What Stage Your Company's In," *Entrepreneur,* April 1997, www.entrepreneur.com/article/14090. The most famous model comes from Larry Greiner "Evolution and Revolution as Organizations Grow," *Harvard Business Review* 76, no. 3 (May 1998); pp. 55–68, a revisiting of Greiner's 1972 *HBR* article of the same name. Neil C. Churchill and Virginia L. Lewis adapted Greiner's model in "The Five Stages of Small Business Growth," *Harvard Business Review,* May–June 1983. A three-stage simplification follows the ideas expressed by Kelin E. Gersick, Ivan Lansberg, Michele Desjardins, and Barbara Dunn, "Stages and Transitions: Managing Change in the Family Business" *Family Business Review* XII no. 4 (1999), pp. 287–297, www.lgassoc.com/library/articles/112-Stages&Transitions.pdf; and in their book, Kelin Gersick, John Davis, Marion McCollum Hampton, and Ivan Lansberg, *Generation to Generation: Life Cycles of the Family Business* (Cambridge: Harvard University Press, 1997).
2. The model is derived from four major works on small business life stages: William J. Baumol, "Entrepreneurship in Economic Theory," *American Economic Review,* LVIII, no. 2 (May 1968), pp. 64–71; Gaylen Chandler & Steven H. Hanks, "Market Attractiveness, Resource-Based Capabilities; Venture Strategies and Venture Performance," *Journal of Business Venturing.* 9 no. 4 (1994), pp. 331–349; Neil C. Churchill and Virginia L. Lewis, "The five stages of small business growth," *Harvard Business Review* 61 (June 1983), pp. 30–40; and Jerome Katz and William B. Gartner "Properties of Emerging Organizations," *The Academy of Management Review* 13, no. 3 (July 1988), pp. 429–441.
3. The 12.3 percent rate comes from D. J. Kelly, S. Singer, and M. Herrington, *Global Entrepreneurship Monitor: 2011 Global Report* (Babson Park USA/ Santiago Chile / Kuala Lampur Malaysia: Babson College/Universidad del Desarrollo/ Universiti Tun Abdul Razak, 2012), www.gemconsortium.org/docs/2201/gem-2011-global-report. The 56% rate among 15–25 year olds comes from Joeri Van den Bergh, "Generation Y Around the World: Global Youth Research by InSites Con . . . ", February 15, 2012, www.slideshare.net/joerivandenbergh/generation-y-around-the-world-by-insites-consulting.
4. Rieva Lesonsky, "It's Never Too Late," *Entrepreneur,* November 2003, www.entrepreneur.com/article/65024. Jacquelyn Lynn, "Don't Be Afraid: Are You a Big Scaredy-Cat? Here's How to Turn Terror into Super-Confidence," *Entrepreneur,* June 2000, www.entrepreneur.com/article/28316. Rieva Lesonsky, "What's the Big Idea? Start-Up Ideas Are All Around . . . Once You Know Where to Look," *Business Start-Ups,* November 1998, www.entrepreneur.com/author/311-3. J. Katz, "Longitudinal Analysis of Entrepreneurial Follow-Through," *Journal of Entrepreneurship and Regional Development* 2, no. 1 (1990), pp. 15–25.
5. D. A. Shepherd and M. Shanley, *New Venture Strategy* (Newbury Park, CA: Sage, 1998). D. A. Shepherd, E. J. Douglas, and M. Shanley, "New Venture Survival: Ignorance, External Shocks, and Risk Reduction Strategies," *Journal of Business Venturing* 15 (2000), pp. 393–410. H. Robert Dodge, Sam Fullerton, and John E. Robbins, "Stage of the Organizational Life Cycle and Competition as Mediators of Problem Perception for Small Businesses," *Strategic Management Journal* 15, no. 2 (February 1994), pp. 121–135.
6. *Simpson's Contemporary Quotations,* compiled by James B. Simpson, 1988. Quoted by Thomas J. Peters and Robert H. Waterman, *In Search of Excellence* (New York: Harper & Row, 1982), www.bartleby.com/63/54/2254.html.
7. Mark Henricks, "Staying Power: Zero Defections Strategy Keeps Customers Coming Back," *Entrepreneur,* July 1997, www.entrepreneur.com/article/15786. Frederick F. Reichheld, *The Loyalty Effect, The Hidden Force Behind Growth, Profits, and Lasting Value* (Cambridge: Harvard Business School Press, 1996). Robert C. Blattberg, Gary Getz, and Jacquelyn S. Thomas, *Customer Equity: Building and Managing Relationships as Valuable Assets* (Boston: Harvard Business School Press, 2001). Roland T. Rust and R. L. Oliver, "Should We Delight the Customer," *Journal of The Academy of Marketing Sciences* 28, no.1 (2000), pp. 86–94. Sandy D. Jap, Control Mechanisms and the Relationship Life Cycle: Implications for Safeguarding Specific Investments and Developing Commitment," *Journal of Marketing Research* 37, no. 2 (May 2000), p. 227. F. F. Reichheld and W. E. Sasser, "Zero Defections: Quality Comes to Services," *Harvard Business Review,* 1990, pp. 105–111. R. T. Rust, A. J. Zahorik, and T. L. Keiningham, "Return on Quality (ROQ): Making Service Quality Financially Accountable," *Journal of Marketing* 59 (1995), pp. 58–70. Valarie A. Zeithaml, "Service Quality, Profitability, and The Economic Worth of Customers: What We Know and What We Need to Learn," *Academy of Marketing Science Journal* 28, no. 1 (2000), p. 67.
8. Zig Ziglar, *Zig Ziglar's Secrets of Closing the Sale* (Berkeley Pub Group, 1985). The ideas came from the long out-of-print Australian series, "10 Sales Cassettes by Dr. Joseph Braysich." Other good sources for this approach include: Kim T. Gordon, "Building Customer Relationships: Increase Your Sales through Better Relationships with Your Existing Customers," *Entrepreneur,* January 01, 2001, www.entrepreneur.com/article/35876. Nichole L. Torres, "Marketing Buzz 09/02: Sell Better by Understanding the Six Different Customer Types; How to Respond to Bad Press," *Entrepreneur,* September 2002, www.entrepreneur.com/article/54530.
9. D. Guithues-Amrhein and J. A. Katz, "Assessing the Mortality Risk of a Business," *Journal of Enterprising Culture* 7, no. 3 (1999) or www.sbaer.uca.edu/Research/1998/ICSB/n004.htm. Joan Stableford, "Business Notes: It's Here: the Great Pumpkin," *Time* 136, no. 21 (November 12, 1990), p. 64. Joan Stableford, "For Sun Hill Industries, Success Last Year Was in the Bag," *Fairfield County Business Journal* 22, no 19 (May 27, 1991), p. 10. The pirate pursuit resulted in a legal battle, which was decided in Zinbarg's favor in 1999; see United States Court of Appeals for the Federal Circuit, 98-1498 (Serial No. 08/427,732), in Re Anita Dembiczak and Benson Zinbarg, www.law.emory.edu/fedcircuit/apr99/98-1498.wp.html.
10. mereChina, "Fun Chinese Lessons—9: Danger and Opportunity: The Chinese Expression for Crisis," www.merechina.com/language/chineselesson9.shtml.
11. Kim T. Gordon, "Pros and Cons of Expanding Your Product Line, "Entrepreneur, June 7, 2004, www.entrepreneur.com/article/71094.

12. Rosabeth Moss Kantor, "The 15-Minute Competitive Advantage" *Business 2.0*, February 2002, p. 87.
13. R. McMath, "Inventions, Profitability—Look Before You Leap," *Entrepreneur*, April 1, 1998, www.entrepreneur.com/article/15414.
14. Arundhati Parmar, "Where Are They Now?" *Marketing News*, April 14, 2003, pp. 1, 13, 14.
15. Adam Barak and Geoffrey Wilson, "Pricing Policies to Handle Patent Loss or Expiry," *International Journal of Medical Marketing* 3, no. 3, June 2003, p. 245.
16. Ibid.
17. Rod P. Burkert, "A Good Deal Depends on Preparation," *Journal of Accountancy* 196, no. 5 (November 2003), pp. 47–52.
18. B. F. Roizen, "M&A Activity Drops, but Prices Paid Spikes 77% in 2011," *VatorNews*, January 3, 2012, http://vator.tv/news/2012-01-03-m-a-activity-drops-but-prices-paid-spikes-77-in-2011.
19. The ESOP Association, "ESOP Facts and Figures Statistics," 2012, www.esopassociation.org/media/media_statistics.asp. C. Tawney and J. Levitsky, "Small Enterprise Development as a Strategy for Reducing the Social Cost of Restructuring and the Privatization Process: Public and Private Initiatives," Interdepartmental Action Programme on Privatization, Restructuring and Economic Democracy, Working Paper IPPRED-6, 2000, International Labour Organization (ILO), www.ilo.org/public/english/employment/ent/papers/ippred6.htm. G. B. Hansen, "ESOPs in the USA", presentation to the ILO seminar "The Economies in Transition and the Employment Problem: The Role of Cooperatives and Associations," Kiev, Ukraine, 1993.
20. The ESOP Association, "ESOP Statistics, Facts and Figures," 2012, www.esopassociation.org/media/media_statistics.asp.
21. The strategies come from the following overlapping sources: Kenneth J. Klassen and Richard C. Sansin, "A Model of Dynamic Tax Planning with an Application to Estate Freezes," *Journal of the American Taxation Association* 28, no. 1 (2006), pp. 1–24. Isabelle Le Breton-Miller, Danny Miller, and Lloyd P. Steier, "Toward an Integrative Model of Effective FOB Succession," *Entrepreneurship: Theory & Practice* 28, no. 4 (Summer 2004), pp. 305–328. C. J. Prince, "Death and Taxes—Entrepreneur.com." Entrepreneur.com, May 2006. July 21, 2009, www.entrepreneur.com/magazine/entrepreneur/2006/may/159926.html. William S. White, Timothy D. Krinke, and David L. Geller, "Family Business Succession Planning: Devising an Overall Strategy," *Journal of Financial Service Professionals* 58, no. 3 (May 2004), pp. 67–86. Remember that we strongly recommend finding a qualified estate planning attorney to make sure these strategies are done correctly.
22. Scott Bernard Nelson, "Leave It to Them: Make Sure Your Family Gets What It Needs by Including a Disclaimer Provision in Your Estate Plan," *Entrepreneur,* August 2004, www.entrepreneur.com/article/71782.
23. Paul DeCeglie, "State of the Estate: What Is Estate Planning and Why Should You Be Doing It Now?" *Entrepreneur Start-Ups,* January 2001, www.entrepreneur.com/article/35164.
24. N. Upton and B. Petty, "Funding Options for Transferring the Family-Held Firm: A Comparative Analysis," presented at the 18th annual meeting of the Babson Research Conference, Ghent, Belgium, April 1998. N. Upton and B. Petty, "Venture Capital Funding of Family Business Transition: An Exploratory Analysis," *Proceedings of the United States Association of Small Business and Entrepreneurship,* 1998, pp. 94–101. Neil C. Churchill and Kenneth J. Hatten, "Non-Market-Based Transfers of Wealth and Power: A Research Framework for Family Businesses," *American Journal of Small Business* 12, no. 2 (Fall 1987), pp. 53–66.
25. Brian Headd, "Redefining Business Success: Distinguishing between Closure and Failure," *Small Business Economics* 21, no. 1 (2003), pp. 51–61. Timothy Bates and Alfred Nucci, "An Analysis of Small Business Size and Rate of Discontinuance," *Journal of Small Business Management* 27, no. 4 (1989), pp. 1–8. Small Business Administration, U.S. "Small Business Economic Indicators for 2003" (Washington DC: Small Business Administration, August 2004).
26. This approach follows the practical concept pioneered by Dun & Bradstreet in its *Business Failure Reports.* What we call a walkaway was what D&B called a "business discontinuance" and referred to a business that closed having not left any creditors or legal actions pending. A "business failure" in D&B's language was a firm that closed with unpaid creditors or pending legal actions. These are called *failures* here. The source is Dun & Bradstreet, "Business Failure Record" (Murray Hill, NJ: Dun & Bradstreet, 1998), www.dnb.com/newsview/bfr96-97.pdf.
27. U.S. Courts Administrative Office, "Table F2. U.S. Bankruptcy Courts—Business and Nonbusiness Cases Commenced, by Chapter of the Bankruptcy Code, During the 12 Month Period Ending December 31, 2011," www.uscourts.gov/uscourts/Statistics/BankruptcyStatistics/BankruptcyFilings/2011/1211_f2.pdf.
28. Brian Headd, "Redefining Business Success: Distinguishing between Closure and Failure," *Small Business Economics* 21, no. 1 (2003), pp. 51–61.
29. P. Jennings and G. Beaver, "The Performance and Competitive Advantage of Small Firms: A Management Perspective," *International Small Business Journal* 15 (1997), pp. 63–75. Brian Headd, "Redefining Business Success: Distinguishing between Closure and Failure," *Small Business Economics* 21, no. 1 (2003), pp. 51–61. J. Watson and J. Everett, "Do Small Businesses Have High Failure Rates?" *Journal of Small Business Management* 34, no. 4 (1996), pp. 45–62. J. Watson and J. Everett, "Defining Small Business Failure," *International Small Business Journal* 11, no. 3 (1993), pp. 35–48.
30. Stephen C. Perry, "A Comparison of Failed and Non-Failed Small Businesses in the United States: Do Men and Women Use Different Planning and Decision Making Strategies?" *Journal of Developmental Entrepreneurship* 7, no. 4 (December 2002), pp. 415–428. R. M. Hodgetts and D. F. Kuratko, *Effective Small Business Management* (New York: Wiley, 2002). L. Waghorne, "The Cold Hard Facts," *Chartered Accountants Journal of New Zealand* 79, no. 7 (2000).
31. Laura Tiffany, "Mail Order: Want to Go Retail but Don't Want to Deal with the Hassles of a Storefront? Follow the Paths Forged by Wards and Sears by Starting a Mail-Order Company," *Entrepreneur,* February 22, 2001, www.entrepreneur.com/ article/0,4621,287061-5,00.html.
32. Experts in management information systems have put in the most work applying CSF approaches to small businesses. For example, see Riyad Eid, Myfanwy Trueman, and Abdel Moneim Ahmed, "A Cross-Industry Review of B2B Critical Success Factors," *Internet Research: Electronic Networking Applications and Policy* 12, no. 2 (2002), pp. 110–123. T. Butler and B. Fitzgerald, "Unpacking the Systems Development Process: An Empirical Application of the CSF Concept in a Research Context," *The Journal of Strategic Information Systems* 8, no. 4 (1999), pp. 351–371. G. K. Kanji and A. M. Tambi, "Total Quality Management in UK Higher Education Institutions," *Total Quality Management* 10, no. 1 (1999), pp. 129–153.
33. Edward G. Rogoff, Myung-Soo Lee, and Dong-Churl Suh, "Who Done It?" Attributions by Entrepreneurs and Experts of the Factors That Cause and Impede Small Business Success. *Journal of Small Business Management* 42, no. 4 (October 2004), pp. 364–376. E. J. Gatewood, K. G. Shaver, J. B. Powers, and W. B. Gartner, "Entrepreneurial Expectancy, Task Effort, and Performance," *Entrepreneurship: Theory & Practice* 27, no. 2 (2002), pp. 187–206. K. G. Shaver, W. B. Gartner, E. Crosby, K. Bakalarova, and E. J. Gatewood, "Attributions about Entrepreneurship: A Framework and Process for Analyzing Reasons for Starting a Business," *Entrepreneurship: Theory & Practice* 26, no. 2 (2001), pp. 5–32.
34. J. J. Chrisman, "The Influence of Outsider-Generated Knowledge Resources on Venture Creation," *Journal of Small Business Management* 37, no. 4 (1999), pp. 42–58. James J. Chrisman and W. Ed McMullan, "A Preliminary Assessment of Outsider Assistance as a Knowledge Resource: The Longer-Term Impact of New Venture Counseling," *Entrepreneurship: Theory & Practice* 24, no. 3 (2000), pp. 37–53. James J. Chrisman and W. Ed McMullan, "Outsider Assistance as a Knowledge Resource for New Venture Survival," *Journal of Small Business Management* 42, no. 3 (2004), pp. 229–244.

35. Devron A. Veasley, "In Depth: Small Business Resource Guide—Business Incubation. Incubators Build Economies, Benefit Communities," *Birmingham Business Journal,* November 8, 2003, http://birmingham.bizjournals.com/birmingham/stories/2003/08/11/focus6.html.
36. A. Charney and G. Libecap, *Impact of Entrepreneurship Education* (Kansas City, MO: Kauffman Center for Entrepreneurial Leadership, 2000). L. Kolvereid, and O. Moen, "Entrepreneurship among Business Graduates: Does a Major in Entrepreneurship Make a Difference?" *Journal of European Industrial Training* 21, no. 4 (1997), pp. 154–160. W. E. McMullan, and L. M. Gillin, "Entrepreneurship Education: Developing Technological Start-Up Entrepreneurs. A Case Study of a Graduate Entrepreneurship Programme at Swinburne University," *Technovation* 18, no. 4 (1998), pp. 275–286. T.V. Menzies, and J. C. Paradi, "Encouraging Technology-Based Ventures: Entrepreneurship Education and Engineering Graduates," *New England Journal of Entrepreneurship* 5, no. 2 (2002), pp. 57–64. T. V. Menzies, and J. C. Paradi, "Entrepreneurship Education and Engineering Students: Career Path and Business Performance," *International Journal of Entrepreneurship and Innovation* 6, no. 2 (2003), pp. 85–96. N. B. Upton, D. L. Sexton, and C. Moore, "Have We Made a Difference? An Examination of Career Activity of Entrepreneurship Majors since 1981" (abstract), *Frontiers of Entrepreneurship Research* 1995 edition (Wellesley, MA: Babson College, 1995), pp. 727–728.
37. Brian Headd, "Redefining Business Success: Distinguishing between Closure and Failure," *Small Business Economics* 21, no. 1 (2003), pp. 51–61. J. Katz, "A Psychosocial Cognitive Model of Employment Status Choice," *Entrepreneurship: Theory & Practice* 16, no. 1 (1992), pp. 29–37.
38. G. N. Chandler and S. H. Hanks, "Founder Competence, the Environment, and Venture Performance," *Entrepreneurship: Theory & Practice* 18, no. 3 (1994), pp. 77–89. R. K. Mitchell, B. Smith, K. W. Seawright, and E. A. Morse, "Cross-Cultural Cognitions and the Venture Creation Decision," *Academy of Management Journal* 43 (2000), pp. 974–993.
39. Robert A. Baron and Gideon D. Markman, "Beyond Social Capital: The Role of Entrepreneurs' Social Competence in Their Financial Success," *Journal of Business Venturing* 18, no. 1 (2003), pp. 41–60.
40. Gerard George, D. Robley Wood Jr., and Raihan Kahn, "Networking Strategy of Boards: Implications for Small and Medium-Sized Enterprises," *Entrepreneurship and Regional Development* 13, no. 3 (2001), pp. 269–285.
41. This is one of the oldest findings in small business research, starting with K. B. Mayer and S. Goldstein, "The First Two Years: Problems of Small Firm Growth and Survival," Washington: Small Business Administration; and continuing through Brian Headd, "Redefining Business Success: Distinguishing between Closure and Failure," *Small Business Economics* 21, no. 1 (2003), pp. 51–61.
42. Brian Headd, "Redefining Business Success: Distinguishing between Closure and Failure," *Small Business Economics* 21, no. 1 (2003), pp. 51–61.
43. Ibid.
44. D. A. Shepherd and M. Shanley, *New Venture Strategy* (Newbury Park, CA: Sage, 1998). D. A. Shepherd, E. J. Douglas, and M. Shanley, "New Venture Survival: Ignorance, External Shocks, and Risk Reduction Strategies," *Journal of Business Venturing* 15 (2000), pp. 393–410.
45. Susan A. Sherer and Bill Adams, "Collaborative Commerce: The Role of Intermediaries in e-Collaboration," *Journal of Electronic Commerce Research* 2, no. 2 (2001), pp. 66–77.
46. G. T. Lumpkin and G. G. Dess, "Clarifying the Entrepreneurial Orientation Construct and Linking It to Performance," *Academy of Management Review* 21, no. 1 (1996), pp. 135–172. G. T. Lumpkin and G. G. Dess, "Linking Two Dimensions of Entrepreneurial Orientation to Firm Performance: The Moderating Role of Environment and Industry Life Cycle," *Journal of Business Venturing* 16, no. 5 (2001), pp. 429–451. D. A. Shepherd and M. Shanley, *New Venture Strategy* (Newbury Park, CA: Sage, 1998).
47. D. A. Shepherd and M. Shanley, *New Venture Strategy* (Newbury Park, CA: Sage, 1998). D. A. Shepherd, E. J. Douglas, and M. Shanley, "New Venture Survival: Ignorance, External Shocks, and Risk Reduction Strategies," *Journal of Business Venturing* 15 (2000), pp. 393–410.
48. Dean A. Shepherd and Evan J. Douglas, *Attracting Equity Investors: Positioning, Preparing and Presenting the Business Plan* (Newbury Park, CA: Sage, 1999.)
49. W. Gibb Dyer, *The Entrepreneurial Experience: Confronting the Career Dilemmas of the Start-Up Executive* (San Francisco: Jossey-Bass, 1992) or Dorothy Perrin Moore, *Careerpreneurs: Lesson from Leading Women Entrepreneurs on Building a Career without Boundaries* (Palo Alto, CA: Davies Black, 2000).
50. This approach is called *open-systems theory* or *living systems theory* in the social sciences. Some of the most famous models for studying organizations are rooted in this approach such as Daniel Katz and Robert L. Kahn, *The Social Psychology of Organizations* (New York: Wiley, 1978), or William B. Gartner, "A Conceptual Framework for Describing the Phenomenon of New Venture Creation," *Academy of Management Review* 10 (1985), pp. 696–706.
51. The latest list comes from home-business gurus Paul Edwards and Sarah Edwards, "The Dark Side, Prepare Yourself for Being Home Based by Understanding the Downside," *Entrepreneur's Be Your Own Boss,* June 2003, www.entrepreneur.com/article/62208.
52. Aliza Pilar Sherman, "Teaching by Example," *Entrepreneur,* December 2003, www.entrepreneur.com/article/65554.
53. Patricia Schiff Estess, "Gag Order," *Entrepreneur,* September 2000, www.entrepreneur.com/article/31546. Quentin Fleming, *Keep the Family Baggage out of the Family Business* (New York: Fireside, 2000). Patricia Schiff Estess, "Close Encounters," *Entrepreneur,* July 1998, www.entrepreneur.com/article/16030.
54. Paul Edwards and Sarah Edwards, "The Dark Side: Prepare Yourself for Being Home Based by Understanding the Downside," *Entrepreneur's Be Your Own Boss,* June 2003, www.entrepreneur.com/article/62208. Paul Edwards and Sara Edwards, *Working from Home* (Los Angeles: Tarcher, 1999).
55. Not surprisingly, there is a lot of disagreement on what exactly constitutes the triple bottom line. For example, for big businesses, the conventional thinking is economic, social, and environmental returns. See European Business Forum/PriceWaterhouseCoopers, "EBF on . . . Sustainable Development" (London: European Business Forum, 2003), www.pwc.com/pl/eng/inssol/publ/2003/corp_efb_rap.pdf, or Knowledge @ Wharton, "The Triple Bottom Line: Student Activists Demand More from B-Schools," Wharton School Public Policy and Management Web site, May 13, 2003. http://knowledge.wharton.upenn.edu/index. cfm?fa=viewfeature&id=773; or John Elkington, *Cannibals with Forks: The Triple Bottom Line of the 21st Century Business* (Gabriola Island, BC, Canada: New Society Publishers, 1998). In small businesses, the idea of firm, community, and personal returns is better established through works such as W. Gibb Dyer, *The Entrepreneurial Experience: Confronting the Career Dilemmas of the Start-Up Executive* (San Francisco: Jossey-Bass, 1992); or Dorothy Perrin Moore, *Careerpreneurs: Lesson from Leading Women Entrepreneurs on Building a Career without Boundaries* (Palo Alto, CA: Davies Black, 2000). A very good article on how the triple bottom line operates in family businesses can be found in Robyn Eversole, "Balancing Act: Business and Household in a Small Bolivian City," *Development in Practice* 12, no. 5 (2002), pp. 589–601.
56. Google, Inc., "Amendment No. 9 to Form S-1: Registration Statement, under the Securities Act of 1933" (Washington, DC: US Securities and Exchange Commission (2004) http://sec.gov/Archives/edgar/data/1288776/000119312504142742/ds1a.htm. Warren Bennis, "Warren Bennis: Google's Growth Engine," *CIO Insight,* June 1, 2004, www.cioinsight.com/article2/0,1397,1609425,00.asp. Mary Anne Ostrom and Matt Marshall, "Inside Google: Internet Search Engine's Founders Keep Ideas Rolling and Profits Pouring In," *Mercury News,* May 4, 2003, www.madville.com/link.php?id=39525&t=23.

PHOTO CREDITS

Chapter 1

Opener Courtesy of Paul Scheiter/ Hedgehog Leatherworks.

p. 6 (clockwise from top left) ColorBlind Images/Blend Images LLC, Jupiterimages/ Comstock Premium/Alamy, DKP/Stockbyte/ Getty Images, Ariel Skelley/Blend Images LLC.

p. 7 Justin Sullivan/ Getty Images.

p. 12 Cathrin Mueller/ Bongarts/Getty Images.

p. 16 DB Apple/dpa/ Corbis.

p. 18 Anchor Bar & Restaurant.

p. 21 (top left) Robert Whitaker/ Getty Images.

p. 21 (bottom left) Michael Ochs Archives/Getty Images.

p. 21 (right) Shahar Azran/ WireImage.

p. 22 Library of Congress, Prints and Photographs Division [LC-USZ62 -110811].

Chapter 2

Opener The Ad Firm.

p. 31 © Steve Hix/ Somos Images/ Corbis.

p. 36 Courtesy Common Dog.

p. 38 Purestock/ SuperStock.

p. 43 Digital Vision/ Getty Images.

p. 44 Realistic Reflections.

Chapter 3

Opener Courtesy Jerome Katz.

p. 55 David Perez Shadi/Getty Images.

p. 65 The McGraw-Hill Companies/ Denise McCullough, photographer.

p. 69 Courtesy Ronald Reagan Library.

p. 73 AP Photo/Richard Patterson.

Chapter 4

Opener Used with permission, Magnetic Poetry.

p. 84 Traction Experts, Inc.

Table 4.1 Courtesy of Google.

p. 90 Bonnie-Kamin/ PhotoEdit.

Chapter 5

Opener Courtesy of Kathryn Otoshi.

p. 125 Brand X/ Jupiterimages/ Getty Images.

p. 126 rbfoto/Brand X Pictures/ Jupiterimages.

p. 127 BananaStock Ltd.

p. 133 The McGraw-Hill Companies, Inc./ John Flournoy, photographer.

p. 139 The McGraw-Hill Companies, Inc./ Lars A Niki, photographer.

p. 140 Comstock/ PictureQuest.

p. 142 Courtesy Courtney Hennessy Hopson.

Chapter 6

Opener Courtesy of Thomas Caldbeck.

p. 160 Courtesy of New Product-Works/ www.newproductworks.com.

Table 6.1 Bernardo De Niz/ Bloomberg via Getty Images.

p. 173 The McGraw-Hill Companies, Inc./ Andrew Resek, photographer.

Chapter 7

Opener Courtesy EnableMart/ www.enablemart.com.

p. 191 Photo by Jon Perimutter.

p. 195 The McGraw-Hill Companies, Inc./ Mark Dierker, photographer.

Chapter 8

Opener BananaStock/ PunchStock.

p. 220 Wake Forest University.

p. 239 Daniel J. Watkins Photography.

p. 240 ColorBlind Images/ Blend Images LLC.

p. 248 Courtesy of Christina Jett and Natalie Gamez, Red Jett Sweets.

p. 256–260 Courtesy of Google Maps.

Chapter 9

Opener © 2006 Brent Rubey–Beyond-Clothing.com.

p. 275 (top) Courtesy of zipcar.com.

p. 275 (bottom) ASSOCIATED PRESS RF.

p. 278 Photo reproduced by permission of Dyson Limited.

p. 282 3D Systems Corporation.

p. 284 Photo by Kryptonite, a registered trademark of Schlage Lock Company.

p. 287 © 2012 Screaming Eagle, Oakville, CA, All rights reserved.

p. 288 Mark Wilson/ Getty Images.

p. 290 Courtesy Ultra-Pet.

p. 294 © 2012 Procter & Gamble.

p. 297 Realimage/ Alamy.

Chapter 10

Opener Courtesy B*tween Productions, Inc.

p. 311 The McGraw-Hill Companies, Inc./ Andrew Resek, photographer.

p. 312 © 2012 Entravision Communications Corporation, All rights reserved.

p. 313 © The Nielsen Company.

p. 315 © Dave's Gourmet, Inc.

p. 320 1999 © IMS Communications Ltd./Capstone Design, All rights reserved.
p. 322 Getty images/Digital Vision.
p. 324 Corbis, All rights reserved.
p. 325 Courtesy Legacy Ink/www.legacyinkdesign.com.
p. 328 Realistic Reflections.
p. 331 Vermont Teddy Bear Company ®/www.vermontteddybear.com.
p. 332 Steve Cole/Getty Images.
p. 335 Jack Hollingsworth/Blend Images LLC.

Chapter 11

Opener © Bloomimage/Corbis RF.
p. 349 1154 LILL STUDIO/photo by Bob Hughes.
p. 354 Photo courtesy the Michael Alan Group.
p. 357 Ingram Publishing.
p. 358 © 2010–2012 Orabrush, Inc. All rights reserved.
p. 361 Royalty-Free/Corbis RF.
p. 365 © Kelly-Mooney Photography/Corbis.
p. 369 Dennis Light/Light Photographic.
p. 371 Jim Zuckerman/Corbis.

Chapter 12

Opener ZOU QING/AFP/Getty Images.
p. 386 Purestock/SuperStock.
p. 387 Steve Cole/Getty Images.
p. 392 Courtesy of Ruth's Chris Restaurant Group.
p. 394 (top) © Tom & Dee Ann McCarthy/Corbis, © Courtesy of The Advertising Archives.

Chapter 13

Opener–409 Courtesy Debbie Dusenberry/www.curioussofa.com.
p. 411 JOHN DAVENPORT/jdavenport@express-news.net.

Chapter 14

Opener © Dick Youngblood/Star Tribune n.d.
p. 451 Courtesy of J.W. Hulme Factory.
p. 454 AP Photo/Suzanne Plunkett.
p. 459 The Baby Einstein Company.

Chapter 15

Opener Courtesy INCELL Corporation, LLC.
p. 503 Courtesy http://business.usa.gov.
p. 507 © Bob Jacobson/Corbis RF.

Chapter 16

Opener Jennifer Adleman, U.S. Geological.
p. 521 Courtesy Dwight Cooper.
p. 525 Photo Courtesy Alienware Corporation.
p. 527 http://barcodes.gs1us.org.
p. 529 Dennis MacDonald/PhotoEdit.
p. 536 © 2005–2011 Cabot Hosiery Mills Inc, All rights reserved.

Chapter 17

Opener © Rolf Schulten/imagebroker/Corbis.
p. 561 © Reuters/Corbis.
p. 564 Courtesy of David and Sherree Starrett, owners.
p. 567 Photo provided courtesy of World Smile Corp. All rights reserved.
p. 570 AP Photo/Danny Johnston.
p. 577 Fred Duval/FilmMagic.
p. 578 Franck Prevel/Reuters/Corbis.

Chapter 18

Opener Chuck Savage/Corbis.
p. 594 Screenshot courtesy of SBA.gov.
p. 595 © James Leyne/Corbis.
p. 597 Panera, LLC.
p. 606 Courtesy Litigation Fairness.gov.
p. 615 Courtesy of Paul Scheiter.

Chapter 19

Opener PerkettPR, Inc.
p. 628–634 © Royalty Free/Corbis.
p. 646 Ariel Skelley/Blend Images LLC.

Chapter 20

Opener © Kayte Keioma/PhotoEdit.
p. 660 McGraw-Hill Companies, Inc./Jill Braaten, photographer.
p. 664 © Jack Hollingsworth/Corbis RF.

NAME AND ORGANIZATION INDEX

A

B

C

G

H

I

J

M

N

X

Y

Z

SUBJECT INDEX

A

B

C

F

G

H

I

J

N

O

T

U

V

W

Y

Z